caring connections

How Parents Can Facilitate Infants' and Toddlers' Language Development

Linguist Naomi Baron (1992) in *Growing Up with Language*, and more recently Ellen Galinsky (2010) in *Mind in the Making*, provided ideas to help parents facilitate their infants' and toddlers' language development. Their suggestions are summarized below:

- **Be an active conversational partner.** Talk to your baby from the time it is born. Initiate conversation with the baby. If the baby is in a day-long child-care program, ensure that the baby receives adequate language stimulation from adults.
- **Talk in a slowed-down pace and don't worry about how you sound to other adults when you talk to your baby.** Talking in a slowed-down pace will help your baby detect words in the sea of sounds they experience. Babies enjoy and attend to the high-pitched sound of child-directed speech.
- **Use parent-look and parent-gesture, and name what you are looking at.** When you want your child to pay attention to something, look at it and point to it. Then name it, for example, saying "Look, Alex, there's an airplane."
- **When you talk with infants and toddlers, be simple, concrete, and repetitive.** Don't try to talk to them in abstract, high-level ways or think you have to say something new or different all of the time. Using familiar words often will help them remember the words.

It is a good idea for parents to begin talking to their babies at the start. The best language teaching occurs when the talking is begun before infants become capable of their first intelligible speech. *What are some other guidelines for parents to follow in helping their infants and toddlers develop their language skills?*

- **Play games.** Use word games like peek-a-boo and pat-a-cake to help infants learn words.
- **Remember to listen.** Since toddlers' speech is often slow and laborious, parents are often tempted to supply words and thoughts for them. Be patient and let toddlers express themselves, no matter how painstaking the process is or how great a hurry you are in.
- **Expand and elaborate language abilities and horizons with infants and toddlers.** Ask questions that encourage answers other than "Yes" and "No." Actively repeat, expand, and recast the utterances. Your toddler might say, "Dada." You could follow with, "Where's Dada?", and then you might continue, "Let's go find him."
- **Adjust to your child's idiosyncrasies instead of working against them.** Many toddlers have difficulty pronouncing words and making themselves understood. Whenever possible, make toddlers feel that they are being understood.
- **Resist making normative comparisons.** Be aware of the ages at which your child reaches specific milestones (such as the first word, first 50 words), but do not measure this development rigidly against that of other children. Such comparisons can bring about unnecessary anxiety.

---

connecting with careers

Rodney Hammond, Health Psychologist

In describing his college experiences, Rodney Hammond said, "When I started as an undergraduate at the University of Illinois, Champaign-Urbana, I hadn't decided on my major. But to help finance my education, I took a part-time job in a child development research program sponsored by the psychology department. There, I observed inner-city children in settings designed to enhance their learning. I saw firsthand the contribution psychology can make, and I knew I wanted to be a psychologist" (American Psychological Association, 2003, p. 26).

Rodney Hammond went on to obtain a doctorate in school and community psychology with a focus on children's development. For a number of years, he trained clinical psychologists at Wright State University in Ohio and directed a program to reduce violence in ethnic minority youth. Hammond and his associates taught at-risk youth how to use social skills to effectively manage conflict and how to recognize situations that could lead to violence. Today, Hammond is director of Violence Prevention at the Centers for Disease Control and Prevention in Atlanta. Hammond says that if you are interested in people and problem solving, psychology is a wonderful way to put these together. (Source: American Psychological Association, 2003, pp. 26–27)

Rodney Hammond counseling an adolescent girl about the risks of adolescence and how to effectively cope with them.

64% of developmental psychology instructors state that fostering critical thinking is a top goal of their course.

Reflect *Your Own Personal Journey of Life*
- If you were the parent of a 4-year-old child, would you try to train the child to develop conservation skills? Explain.

> *Children* helps students develop understandings of the applications of developmental psychology through examples in the text, *Caring Connections,* and *Connecting with Careers.* They are also prompted to think about how psychology applies to their own lives through *Reflect: Your Own Personal Journey of Life* questions.

CHILDREN

Twelfth Edition

JOHN W. SANTROCK
University of Texas at Dallas

McGraw Hill

Connect
Learn
Succeed™

1 2 3 4 5 6 7 8 9 0 DOW/DOW 0 9 8 7 6 5 4 3 2

ISBN: 978-0-07-803512-8
MHID: 0-07-803512-0

Vice President Editorial: *Michael Ryan*
Sponsoring Editor: *Allison McNamara*
Marketing Manager: *Julia Flohr Larkin*
Developmental Editor: *Elisa Adams*
Editorial Coordinator: *Sarah Kiefer*
Project Manager: *Jane Mohr*
Production Service: *Melanie Field/Strawberry Field Publishing*
Manuscript Editor: *Janet Tilden*
Text and Cover Designer: *Preston Thomas*
Art Editor: *Janet Robbins*
Illustrator: *Judy Waller*
Photo Research: *Jennifer Blankenship*
Buyer: *Carol A. Bielski*
Media Project Manager: *Jennifer Barrick*
Digital Product Manager: *Jay Gubernick*
Composition: *9.5/12 Meridien Roman by Aptara®, Inc.*
Printer: *RR Donnelley*

Credits: The credits section for this book begins on page C-1 and is considered an extension of the copyright page.

Library of Congress Cataloging-in-Publication Data

Santrock, John W.
  Children / John Santrock. — 12th ed.
      p. cm.
  Includes bibliographical references and index.
  ISBN 978-0-07-803512-8 (alk. paper) — ISBN 0-07-803512-0 (alk. paper)
1. Child development. 2. Adolescence. I. Title.
  HQ767.9.S268 2012
  305.23—dc23

                            2011051321

With special appreciation to my grandchildren: Jordan, Alex, and Luke

Jordan Bowles

Alex and Luke, the Bellucci Brothers

about the author

John W. Santrock

John Santrock received his Ph.D. from the University of Minnesota in 1973. He taught at the University of Charleston and the University of Georgia before joining the program in psychology in the School of Behavioral and Brain Sciences at the University of Texas at Dallas, where he currently teaches a number of undergraduate courses and recently was given the university's Effective Teaching Award.

John Santrock, teaching an undergraduate class

John has been a member of the editorial boards of *Child Development* and *Developmental Psychology*. His research on father custody is widely cited and used in expert witness testimony to promote flexibility and alternative considerations in custody disputes. John also has authored the following exceptional McGraw-Hill texts: *Adolescence* (14th ed.), *Life-Span Development* (13th ed.), *A Topical Approach to Life-Span Development* (6th ed.), and *Educational Psychology* (5th ed.).

For many years, John was involved in tennis as a player, teaching professional, and coach of professional tennis players. At the University of Miami (Florida), the tennis team on which he played still holds the NCAA Division I record for most consecutive wins (137) in any sport. His wife, Mary Jo, has a Master's degree in special education and has worked as a teacher and Realtor. John and Mary Jo have two daughters—Tracy, who also is a Realtor, and Jennifer, who is a medical sales specialist. They have one granddaughter, Jordan, 20, and two grandsons, Alex, 7, and Luke, 6. Tracy recently completed the Boston and New York Marathons, and Jennifer was in the top 100 ranked players on the Women's Professional Tennis Tour. In the last decade, John also has spent time painting expressionist art.

brief contents

contents

SECTION 1   THE NATURE OF CHILDREN'S DEVELOPMENT 4

SECTION 2   BEGINNINGS 52

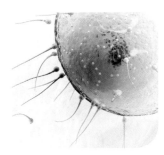

SECTION 3   # INFANCY 132

SECTION 5 **MIDDLE AND LATE CHILDHOOD 322**

expert consultants

Children's development has become an enormous, complex field, and no single author, or even several authors, could possibly keep up with all of the rapidly changing content in the many different areas in this field. To solve this problem, author John Santrock has sought the input of leading experts about content in a number of areas of children's development beginning with the fifth edition of this text. The experts provide detailed evaluations and recommendations in their area(s) of expertise.

Among the expert consultants for earlier editions of Children were Urie Bronfenbrenner, Diana Baumrind, Tiffany Field, Nel Noddings, Ross Thompson, Sandra Graham, James Marcia, Florence Denmark, Rosalind Charlesworth, David Sadker, Mary Lou Hyson, Algea Harrison, Campbell Leaper, Janet DiPietro, Allan Wigfield, Barbara Pan, and Peter Scales.

The biographies and photographs of the expert consultants for the twelfth edition of this text, who (like the expert consultants for the fifth through eleventh editions) literally represent a Who's Who in the field of children's development, follow.

Martha Ann Bell

Dr. Bell is a leading expert in developmental cognitive neuroscience. She currently is a professor of psychology at Virginia Tech University. Dr. Bell obtained her Ph.D. in human development from the University of Maryland. Her research specialization is developmental cognitive neuroscience. She examines developmental change in frontal lobe functioning using both behavioral and electrophysiological methods. Dr. Bell's current work, funded by the National Institutes of Health (National Institute of Child Health and Human Development) focuses on individual differences in the development of executive function and emotion regulation across infancy and early childhood. She is a fellow of American Psychological Association Division 7 (Developmental Psychology) and is the editor of the journal *Infancy*. She also recently co-edited (with Susan D. Calkins)

Child Development at the Intersection of Emotion and Cognition. Her research has been published in journals such as *Developmental Psychobiology*, *Developmental Neuropsychology*, *Child Development*, and *Brain and Cognition*.

"I have always been very impressed with Professor Santrock's textbooks. For Children, *the content in each chapter is truly outstanding, succinct, and clearly written. The "extras," such as the human interest stories that begin each chapter, pull the reader into wanting to know more about the content of the chapter. . . . It is clear that Professor Santrock takes great care in writing his textbooks because the work discussed is the most current in the field and the references are top-notch and very appropriate for this undergraduate text. He highlights the research of the top people in the field. I am most impressed with the number of 2010 and 2011 citations/references in the sections that I read."*
—**Martha Ann Bell**

John E. Bates

Dr. John Bates is one of the world's leading experts on infant temperament and socioemotional development. He currently is a professor in psychological and brain sciences at Indiana University. Dr. Bates received his undergraduate degree in psychology at the University of Washington and his Ph.D. in clinical psychology at UCLA, with minors in developmental and social psychology. A major focus of his research is the development of behavior problems versus positive adjustment. Dr. Bates has especially been interested in the role of children's temperament characteristics, in combination with experiences such as parenting. Most of his research has been longitudinal in nature, including one study from age 6 months

to 17 years, another study from age 5 to age 25 (which includes analyses of temperament-environment interactions, and also gene-environment interactions), and yet another study from age 30 months to 42 months.

"These chapters were a pleasure to read. . . . It is impressive how the chapters integrate the new research with more classic findings, theoretical principles, and common sense. I was also impressed, especially in the first half of Chapter 13 (Socioemotional Development in Middle and Late Childhood) with how a wide variety of research topics can be discussed, one after another, while maintaining a good level of coherence, a sense of a unified perspective on development. One gets a real sense of development in all of its complexity. There is a positive embrace of complexity in the research. . . . Kudos!" —**John E. Bates**

Scott P. Johnson

Dr. Johnson is one of the world's leading experts on perceptual and cognitive development in infancy. He is currently a Professor of Psychology and Professor of Psychiatry and Biobehavioral Sciences at UCLA. Dr. Johnson obtained his Ph.D. from Arizona State University and then did postdoctoral work in the Center for Visual Science at the University of Rochester. His research interests center on mechanisms of perceptual, cognitive, motor, social, and cortical development, and relations among different developmental processes. Current research topics include object perception, face perception, intermodal perception, visual attention, early language development, and learning mechanisms in typical and at-risk populations. In studying infants, Dr. Johnson uses a combination of methods, including preferential looking, eye movements, electroencephalography, and connectionist modeling. He is currently associate editor of the journal *Cognition* and has served on the editorial boards of *Infancy, Infant Behavior & Development, Developmental Psychology,* the *British Journal of Developmental Psychology,* and *Frontiers in Neuroscience.*

> *"I think Chapter 5 (Physical Development in Infancy) is terrific. . . . I am impressed also with Chapter 6 (Cognitive Development in Infancy) and likewise I was especially impressed with the section on language acquisition, within which an author can get completely mired in details. John Santrock has hit the highlights but doesn't dwell on any one of them. Lots of information, presented clearly, and easily digestible."*
> **—Scott P. Johnson**

Jennifer Connolly

Dr. Connolly is a leading expert on socioemotional development in adolescence. She currently holds the position of Professor of Clinical-Developmental Psychology at York University where she also is Director of the Larmarsh Center for Research on Violence and Conflict Resolution. Dr. Connolly obtained her Ph.D. at Concordia University. Her research focuses on the development of romantic relationships in adolescence and their impact on adjustment. Dr. Connolly's current research examines romantic relationships among mainstream and high-risk youth. In studying these relationships, Dr. Connolly's research helps to clarify when and why these relationships lead to positive outcomes or, conversely, maladaptive outcomes, especially dating aggression.

> *"Within each domain, John Santrock provides a summary of the central issues, backed up with current research evidence. The material is accurate and timely and it is summarized in an accessible manner that will be well understood by undergraduate students. In addition to its accessible writing style, the book will appeal to students and instructors because of its use of explicit teaching aids that allow students to monitor their acquisition of the material. These include the use of illustrations and quotes that highlight particular points in the text, questions in the text that direct attention to applied issues. . . . I find the material to be accurate and up to date. The references rely quite heavily on recent review chapters, which has the advantage of giving the student reader some good reference directions to pursue if there is particular interest in a topic."* **—Jennifer Connolly**

Natasha Cabrera

Dr. Cabrera is an expert on parent-child relationships and children's socioemotional development. She obtained her Ph.D. at the University of Denver and is currently a professor at the University of Maryland. Prior to coming to the University of Maryland, Dr. Cabrera held the position of Expert in Child Development with the Demographic and Behavioral Sciences Branch of the National Institute of Child Health and Human Development. Her current research focuses on father involvement; children's developmental trajectories in low-income and minority families; ethnic and cultural differences in fathering and mothering; family processes and children's outcomes; and the mechanisms that link early experience to children's later development. Dr. Cabrera's research has been published in journals on policy, methodology, theory, and the implications of father involvement on children's development. She also is the author of several books, including *Handbook of Father Involvement: Multidisciplinary Perspectives* (second edition forthcoming), and two co-edited volumes titled *Latina/o Child Psychology and Mental Health.*

> *"The book has many strengths, including the integration of recent research findings on various domains of development, the focus on diversity, the Connecting with Research sections, the appeal to contemporary issues, the integration of theoretical perspectives into the chapters, and the layout of the book. These aspects make the book not only accessible to students, but also a good learning tool."* **—Natasha Cabrera**

Beverly Goldfield

Dr. Beverly Goldfield is an expert on children's language development. She obtained her Ph.D. in the Graduate School of Education at Harvard University where she also was a postdoctoral fellow in the psychology department. Dr. Goldfield currently holds the position of Professor of Psychology at Rhode Island College in Providence, Rhode Island, where she is Director of the Psychology Honors Program. Dr. Goldfield is a developmental psychologist who examines cognitive and social factors related to early language development.

Her research focuses on individual differences, the onset of the vocabulary spurt, the noun bias in early word learning, and the link between word comprehension and word production. She is currently a principal investigator in the Rhode Island Idea Network of Biomedical Research Excellence (INBRE), which supports talented undergraduates who are committed to pursuing a career in research.

"The book is informative and engaging. The text is clearly written, with illustrations, tables, and figures that provide additional incentives to learning."—**Beverly Goldfield**

Larry Nelson

Dr. Larry Nelson is an expert on children's and adolescents' socioemotional development. He obtained his Ph.D. at the University of Maryland at College Park. Dr. Nelson currently is a professor in the School of Family Life at Brigham Young University. His research focuses on two major areas: (1) social developmental factors such as parenting, culture, and self-perception involved in young children's shy and withdrawn behavior; (2) socioemotional aspects of emerging adulthood such as identity, social competence, shyness, culture/religion, and parent-child relationships. Dr. Nelson has published numerous

articles in leading national and international journals, as well as chapters in edited books. He also has received several awards for distinguished contributions as a teacher-scholar.

"I believe the chapters I reviewed include some of the most interesting research and much important research in the field . . . while not overwhelming the reader and providing an easy to read and engaging writing style. I believe the information is straightforward and presented without a strong political bias that permeates far too many textbooks on the market today. I think the coverage of potentially controversial topics is extremely fair."—**Larry Nelson**

Making Connections . . . From My Classroom to *Children* to You

Having taught two or more undergraduate courses in developmental psychology—child development, adolescence, and life-span development—every year across four decades, I'm always looking for ways to improve my course and *Children.* Just as McGraw-Hill looks to those who teach the child development course for input, each year I ask the students in my undergraduate developmental courses to tell me what they like about the course and the text, and what they think could be improved. What have my students told me lately about my course and text? Students said that highlighting connections among the different aspects of children's development would help them to better understand the concepts. As I thought about this, it became clear that a connections theme would provide a systematic, integrative approach to the course material. I used this theme to shape my current goals for my course, which in turn influence the main goals of this text, as follows:

1. **Connecting with today's students** to help students learn about children's development more effectively;

2. **Connecting with research on children's development** to provide students with the best and most recent *theory and research* in the world today about each of the periods of children's development;

3. **Connecting development processes** to guide students in making *developmental connections* across different points in children's development;

4. **Connecting development to real life** to help students understand ways to *apply* content about child development to the real world and improve children's lives, and to motivate students to think deeply about *their own personal journey through life* and better understand who they were as children and how their experiences and development have influenced who they are today.

Connecting with Today's Students

My students often report that development courses are challenging because so much material is covered. To help today's students focus on the key ideas, the Learning Goals System I developed for *Children* provides extensive learning connections throughout the chapters. The learning system connects the chapter-opening outline, learning goals for the chapter, mini-chapter maps that open each main section of the chapter, **Review, Connect, Reflect** questions at the end of each main section, and the chapter summary at the end of each chapter.

The learning system keeps the key ideas in front of the student from the beginning to the end of the chapter. The main headings of each chapter correspond to the learning goals, which are presented in the chapter-opening spread. Mini-chapter maps that link up with the learning goals are presented at the beginning of each major section in the chapter.

Then, at the end of each main section of a chapter, the learning goal is repeated in **Review, Connect, Reflect,** which prompts students to review the key topics in the section, to connect these topics to existing knowledge, and to relate what they have learned to their own personal journey through life. **Reach Your Learning Goals,** at the end of each chapter, guides students through the bulleted chapter review, connecting with the chapter outline/learning goals at the beginning of the chapter and the **Review, Connect, Reflect** material at the end of major chapter sections.

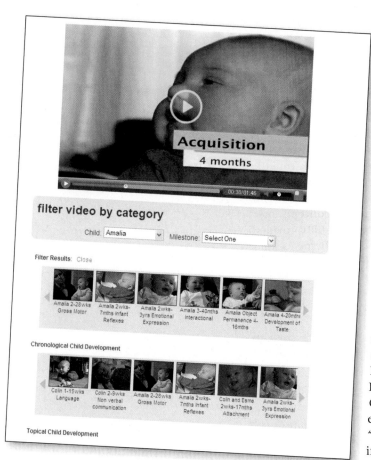

Milestones Video Program

To supplement the text, *Milestones* is a video program that shows students what developmental concepts look like by letting them watch actual humans develop. Students are able to track several individuals starting from infancy and watch them achieve major developmental milestones, both physically and cognitively.

Connecting with Research on Children's Development

Over the years, I have made every effort to include the most up-to-date research available. I continue this tradition in this edition by looking closely at specific areas of research, involving experts in related fields, and updating research throughout. *Connecting with Research*, formerly called *Research in Child Development*, describes a study or program to illustrate how research in child development is conducted and how it influences our understanding of the discipline. Topics range from "How Can the Newborn's Perception Be Studied?" (Chapter 5), to "What Are Some Important Findings in the National Longitudinal Study of Child Care in the United States?" (Chapter 7), to "Can Parents Suggest False Events to Children?" (Chapter 9), to "Evaluation of a Family Program Designed to Reduce Drinking and Smoking in Young Adolescents" (Chapter 14).

The tradition of obtaining detailed, extensive input from a number of leading experts in different areas of child development also continues in this edition. Biographies and photographs of the leading experts in the field of child development appear on pages xiii to xv, and the chapter-by-chapter highlights of new research content will be described shortly. Finally, the research discussions have been updated for each developmental period and topic. I expended every effort to make this edition of *Children* as contemporary and up-to-date as possible. To that end, there are more than 1,200 citations from 2009, 2010, and 2011 in the text.

Connecting Development Processes

Too often we forget or fail to notice the many connections from one point in child development to another. I have substantially increased attention to these connections in the text narrative. I also created two new features to help students connect topics across the stages of child development. *Developmental Connection*, which appears multiple times in each chapter, points readers to places where the topic is discussed in a previous, current, or subsequent chapter. This feature highlights links across topics of development *and* connections among biological, cognitive, and socioemotional processes. The key developmental processes are typically discussed in isolation from each other, so students often fail to see the connections among them. Included in *Developmental Connection* is a brief description of the backward or forward connection. For example, the developmental connection to the left appears in the margin next to the discussion of working memory in middle and late childhood (Chapter 12).

developmental **connection**

Cognitive Processes. In early childhood, executive functioning especially involves advances in cognitive inhibition, cognitive flexibility, and goal setting. Chapter 9, p. 271

Furthermore, a new *Connect* question has been added to the self-reviews at the end of each section—***Review, Connect, Reflect***—so students can practice making connections among topics. For example, in Chapter 11, a Connect item is:

- In Chapters 6 and 9, you read about the development of attention in infancy and early childhood. How might ADHD be linked to earlier attention difficulties?

Connecting Development to Real Life

In addition to helping students make research and developmental connections, *Children* shows the important real-life connections to the concepts discussed in the text. In recent years, students in my development course have increasingly told me that they want more of this type of information. In this edition, real-life connections are explicitly made in the chapter-opening vignette as well as in ***Caring Connections, Connecting with Diversity, Connecting with Careers, How Would You . . . ?*** questions that pertain to five career areas, and ***Reflect: Your Own Personal Journey of Life.***

Each chapter begins with a story designed to spark students' interest and motivate them to read the chapter. Among the chapter-opening stories are those involving the journey of pregnancy and the birth of "Mr. Littles" (Chapter 3), Reggio Emilia's children and their early childhood education program (Chapter 9), children living in the South Bronx (Chapter 13), and Jewel Cash and her amazing contributions to her community (Chapter 16)

Caring Connections provides applied information about parenting, education, or health and well-being related to topics ranging from "From Waterbirth to Music Therapy" (Chapter 4), to "Parents, Coaches, and Children's Sports" (Chapter 11), to "Strategies for Increasing Children's Creative Thinking" (Chapter 12).

Children puts a strong emphasis on diversity. For a number of editions, this text has benefited from having one or more leading experts on diversity to ensure that it provides students with current, accurate, sensitive information related to diversity in children's development. The diversity expert for this edition of *Children* is Natasha Cabrera, a professor at the University of Maryland.

Diversity is discussed in every chapter. **Connecting with Diversity** interludes also appear in every chapter, focusing on a diversity topic related to the material at that point in the chapter. Topics range from "The Increased Diversity of Adopted Children and Adoptive Parents" (Chapter 2) to "Cultural Variations in Guiding Infants' Motor Development" (Chapter 5) to "Bilingual Education" (Chapter 12), to "Cross-Cultural Comparisons of Secondary Schools" (Chapter 15).

Connecting with Careers, formerly called *Careers in Child Development,* profiles careers ranging from genetic counselor (Chapter 2) to toy designer (Chapter 9) to supervisor of gifted and talented education (Chapter 12), all of which require a knowledge of children's development. The careers highlighted extend from the Careers Appendix immediately following Chapter 1, which provides a comprehensive overview of careers to show students where knowledge of children's development could lead them.

How Would You . . . ? These questions in the margins of each chapter highlight issues involving five main career areas of children's development: psychology, human development and family studies, education, health professions (such as nursing and pediatrics), and social work. The ***How Would You . . . ?*** questions ensure that this book orients students to concepts that are important to their understanding of children's development. I have asked instructors specializing in these fields to contribute ***How Would You . . . ?*** questions for each chapter. Strategically placed in the margin next to the relevant chapter content, these questions highlight essential ideas for students to take away from chapter content.

Finally, part of applying knowledge of children's development to the real world is understanding how it affects oneself. Accordingly, one of the goals of my child development course and this text is to motivate students to think deeply about their own journey of life. In reflecting about ways to encourage students to make personal connections to content in the text, I added a ***Reflect: Your Own Personal Journey of Life*** prompt in the end-of-section review. This question asks students to reflect on some aspect of the discussion in the section they have just read and connect it to their own life. For example, in Chapter 1, related to a discussion of the early-later experience issue in development in the section, students are asked,

- Can you identify an early experience that you believe contributed in important ways to your development? Can you identify a recent or current (later) experience that you think had (is having) a strong influence on your development?

Chapter-by-Chapter Changes

Following are the main chapter-by-chapter changes that were made in this new edition of *Children*.

Chapter 1: Introduction

- Expanded discussion of poverty and children, including updated statistics on the percentage of U.S. children under 18 years of age living in poverty (U.S. Census Bureau, 2012)

- Expanded coverage of Bronfenbrenner's contributions (Gauvain & Parke, 2010; Parke & Clarke-Stewart, 2011)

- New section on cohort effects (Schaie, 2011; Schaie & Willis, 2012)

- New material on cohort effects involving Millennial children, adolescents, and their parents, and how their experiences differ from those of their counterparts in earlier generations

- New Figure 1.14 showing neuroimages of the brains of two adolescents (one a non-drinker, the other a heavy drinker) while they are engaging in a memory task

- Inclusion of recent research and commentary on Millennials involving ethnic diversity and technology, based on a recent national survey by the Pew Research Center (2010)

Chapter 2: Biological Beginnings

- Inclusion of changes based on leading expert Kirby Deater-Deckard's recommendations

- Expanded discussion of criticisms of evolutionary psychology to include it being on a time scale that does not permit empirical study

- New introductory material connecting the discussion of evolution and genetics

- Updated coverage of susceptibility (Paquette & others, 2010) and longevity genes (Bauer & others, 2010)

- Description of a recent study that found exposure to radiation changes the rate of DNA synthesis (Lee & others, 2011)

- Expanded and updated material on modifications in DNA expression as a result of stress, radiation, and temperature (Georgakilas, 2011)

- Updated and expanded coverage of gene-gene interaction to include recent studies of immune system functioning (Reijmerink & others, 2011), asthma (Gu & Zhao, 2011), cancer (Bapat & others, 2010), and arthritis (Liu, Ackerman, & Carulli, 2011)

- Updated material on noninvasive prenatal diagnosis (NIPD) (Deng & others, 2011; Du & others, 2011)

- New information about the time at which fetal sex determination can be made and by which procedures (Miura & others, 2011)

- Discussion of a recent meta-analysis indicating that a baby's sex can be determined as early as 7 weeks into pregnancy (Devaney & others, 2011)

- Coverage of recent reviews regarding child and adolescent outcomes for individuals conceived by new reproductive technologies (Golombok, 2011a, b; Golombok & Tasker, 2010)

- New description of research on the age at which children are adopted and whether they engage in juvenile delinquency (Laubjerg & Petersson, 2011)

- Coverage of a recent within-family design of families with a biological child and an adopted child indicating only a slight trend in externalizing problems for adopted children (Glover & others, 2010)

- Discussion of a recent study of improved cognitive development in children who were adopted after they had lived in foster homes and institutions (van den Dries & others, 2010)

- Updated coverage of the concept of G × E, which involves the interaction of a specific measured variation in the DNA sequence and a specific measured aspect of the environment (Caspi & others, 2011; Lahey & others, 2011; Rutter & Dodge, 2011)

- Description of recent research indicating that variations in dopamine-related genes interact with supportive or unsupportive environments to influence children's development (Bakermans-Kranenburg & van IJzendoorn, 2011)

- Update on Judith Harris' (2009) view that parents matter far less than most people think in influencing children's development

Chapter 3: Prenatal Development

- Expanded and updated commentary about transport of drugs across the placenta (Eshkoli & others, 2011; Menezes, Malek, & Keelan, 2011)

- Description of a recent study that found cigarette smoke increased oxidative stress, weakening the fetal membranes from which the placenta develops (Menon & others, 2011)

- Discussion of a recent study that found exposure to passive tobacco smoke was linked to neural tube defects (Suarez & others, 2011)

- New coverage of a link between maternal diabetes and obesity and the development of neural tube defects (Yazdy & others, 2010)

- New discussion of how much weight gain during pregnancy is best for obese women, as well as the importance of their losing weight and increasing exercise prior to becoming pregnant (Simmons, 2011)

- Coverage of a recent study indicating that the risk of exercise-related injury during pregnancy was low (Vladutiu, Evenson, & Marshall, 2010)

- Description of a recent experimental study that found a three-month aerobic exercise program improved pregnant women's health-related quality of life (Montoya Arizabaleta & others, 2010)
- Inclusion of recent research indicating that exercise during pregnancy improved mothers' perception of their health (Barkat & others, 2011)
- Coverage of a recent experimental study of the effects of a CenteringPregnancy Plus program on high-stress pregnant women (Ickovics & others, 2011)
- Discussion of a recent research review of prenatal home visits that showed a link to improved prenatal care use but less evidence for their influence on newborns' birth weights (Issel & others, 2011)
- Inclusion of information from a recent research review indicating that high levels of caffeine consumption by pregnant women do not increase the risk of miscarriage, congenital malformations, or growth retardation (Brent, Christian, & Diener, 2011)
- Discussion of a recent meta-analysis linking maternal smoking during pregnancy to a modest increase in risk for childhood non-Hodgkin lymphoma (Antonopoulos & others, 2011)
- Description of recent research on the negative effects of cocaine exposure prenatally on children's attention and externalizing problems (Minnes & others, 2010; Richardson & others, 2011)
- New information from research on a link between prenatal cocaine exposure and elevated blood pressure at 9 years of age (Shankaran & others, 2011)
- Discussion of prenatal methamphetamine exposure and decreased brain activation, especially in the frontal lobes, in 7- to 15-year-olds (Roussotte & others, 2011)
- Updated guidelines for eating certain types of fish during pregnancy (American Pregnancy Association, 2011; Mayo Clinic, 2011)
- Updated coverage of health outcomes among the offspring of diabetic mothers (Huda & others, 2010)
- Description of a recent research study linking failure to take folic acid supplements in the first trimester of pregnancy with toddlers' behavioral problems (Roza & others, 2010)
- Discussion of two recent studies indicating fertility problems in women exposed to PCBs (Cohn & others, 2011; Meeker & others, 2011)
- Inclusion of recent research that found 16-month-olds exposed to PCBs prenatally had lower scores on the Bayley Scales (Park & others, 2010)
- Description of recent research on more than 30,000 offspring that identified the stage of prenatal development when maternal exposure to stress was most likely to increase the risk of preterm birth (Class & others, 2011)
- Coverage of a recent research review that linked maternal depression to preterm birth (Dunkel Schetter, 2011)

Chapter 4: Birth

- New material on the recent increase in home births to non-Latino White women (MacDorman, Declercq, & Menacker, 2011)
- Discussion of a recent study that found waterbirth was linked with a shorter second stage of labor (Cortes, Basra, & Kelleher, 2011)
- Updated coverage of the increased evidence that acupuncture can have positive effects on labor and delivery (Citkovitz, Schnyer, & Hoskins, 2011)
- Coverage of a research study indicating that massage therapy was effective in reducing pain in pregnant women and alleviating prenatal depression (Field & others, 2008)
- Update on the dramatic increase in cesarean deliveries in the United States suggesting that if the current rate of increase continues, more than 50 percent of U.S. babies will be cesarean deliveries (Solheim & others, 2011)
- Discussion of a recent study indicating that low Apgar scores are linked with development of ADHD in childhood (Li & others, 2011)
- Updated coverage of the percentage of infants born preterm in the U.S., including the overall rate and ethnic variations in 2009 (National Center for Health Statistics, 2011)
- Expanded and updated material on progestin and preterm birth, including multiple births (Lucovnik & others, 2011)
- Description of a recent research review that concluded kangaroo care reduced the risk of mortality in low birth weight infants (Conde-Agudelo, Belizan, & Diaz-Rossello, 2011)
- Coverage of a recent study that revealed the mechanisms responsible for weight gain in massaged preterm infants (Field, Diego, & Hernandez-Reif, 2011)
- Updated coverage of fathers' adjustment during the postpartum period (Dietz & others, 2009; Smith & Howard, 2008)
- Coverage of a recent research review of the interaction difficulties of depressed mothers and their infants (Field, 2010)
- Two new books recommended in the end-of-chapter feature, Making a Difference: *YOU: Having a Baby* (2011) and *Be Prepared: A Practical Handbook for New Dads* (2004)

Chapter 5: Physical Development in Infancy

- Changes in coverage of the development of the brain based on comments from expert consultant Martha Ann Bell
- New commentary about the successful use of the electroencephalogram (EEG) in learning about the development of the brain in infancy (Diaz & Bell, 2011; Cuevas & Bell, 2011)

- Recognition of John Richards and his colleagues (2009, 2010; Richards, Reynolds, & Courage, 2010; Sanchez, Richards, & Almli, 2011) for their important research on the development of the brain in infancy

- Update on the role of myelination in providing energy for neurons (Campbell & Mahad, 2011)

- New section, "The Neuroconstructivist View," that describes an increasingly popular perspective on the development of the brain (Diamond, Casey, & Munakata, 2011; Johnson & de Haan, 2011; Westerman, Thomas, & Karmiloff-Smith, 2011)

- New material on the most common sleep problem in infancy (The Hospital for Sick Children & others, 2010)

- Coverage of a recent study linking maternal emotional availability with fewer infant sleep problems (Teti & others, 2010)

- Discussion of a recent study indicating that paternal involvement in infant care was related to fewer infant sleep problems (Tikotzky, Sadeh, & Glickman-Gavrieli, 2010)

- Description of recent research on early-life risk factors that are linked to infant sleep duration (Nevarez & others, 2010)

- Updated information about infant-parent bed sharing and an increasing trend of recommending that this not occur until the infant is at least six months old (McIntosh, Tonkin, & Gunn, 2010)

- Coverage of a recent study indicating that infant-parent bed sharing was linked with more infant sleep problems, such as disordered breathing (Kelmanson, 2010)

- Description of a recent meta-analysis linking breastfeeding to a lower incidence of SIDS (Hauck & others, 2011)

- Updated discussion of the WIC program, including recent research, in the Caring Connections interlude (WIC New York, 2011)

- New coverage of a recent literacy intervention program with Spanish-speaking families in the Los Angeles WIC program that increased literacy resources and activities in homes, which in turn led to a higher level of school readiness in children (Whaley & others, 2011)

- Updated and expanded coverage of SIDS, including the role of brain stem functioning and the neurotransmitter serotonin (Duncan & others, 2010; Kinney & others, 2009)

- Changes in the material on motor development based on feedback from leading expert Karen Adolph

- Changes in the discussion of perceptual development based on leading expert Scott Johnson's evaluation

- Updated discussion of infant reflexes arguing that reflexes are not exclusively inborn, genetic mechanisms but instead are movements that infants can deliberately control (Adolph & Robinson, 2011)

- New coverage of recent research indicating that alternating leg movements occur during the fetal period and at birth (Adolph & Robinson, 2011)

- Revised information about the percentage of infants who do not crawl in some cultures with information that about one-fourth of infants in Jamaica don't crawl (Hopkins, 1991)

- Revised and updated information about cultural variations in promoting or restricting motor development and outcomes of these practices (Adolph, Karasik, & Tamis-LeMonda, 2010)

- Inclusion of recent research indicating that training infants to use sticky mittens resulted in advances in their reaching behavior (Libertus & Needham, 2010)

- Inclusion of recent information about the development of sophisticated eye-tracking equipment to study infant perception, including a new photo of an infant in a study using eye-tracking equipment (Franchak & others, 2010)

- Deletion of older figure on eye tracking (Banks & Salapatek, 1983) because it was done a number of years ago with rudimentary equipment and does not accurately portray newborns' eye movements

- Coverage of a recent study indicating that young infants looked longest at reddish hues and shortest at greenish hues (Franklin & others, 2010)

- New commentary about critics of the visual cliff concluding that it likely is a better test of social referencing and fear of heights than depth perception

- Updated information about how various tastes are experienced prenatally through the amniotic fluid (Mennella, 2009)

- Added commentary suggesting that most perception is intermodal (Bahrick, 2010)

- New entry in end-of-chapter Resources section referencing *The Baby Food Bible* by Eileen Behan (2008)

Chapter 6: Cognitive Development in Infancy

- Description of a recent study indicating that joint attention enhanced the long-term memory of 9-month-old infants (Kopp & Lindenberger, 2011)

- Discussion of a recent study that revealed a region of the prefrontal cortex was activated when 5-month-old infants engaged in joint attention with another person (Grossmann & Johnson, 2010)

- New figure that summarizes age-related changes in the length of time over which memory occurs in infancy (Bower, 2009)

- Updated coverage of concept formation, including a revised definition of concepts

- Addition of recent commentary about learning by infant researcher Alison Gopnik (2010) on the importance of putting things into the right categories

- Coverage of a recent longitudinal study on the stability of intelligence from 12 months to 4 years of age (Blaga & others, 2009)

- Modifications and updates of the discussion of language development based on comments by leading expert Catherine McBride-Chang

- Discussion of recent research on differences in early gesture as explanations for SES disparities in child vocabulary at school entry (Rowe & Goldin-Meadow, 2009)
- New material on cross-linguistic differences in early word learning (Lieven & Stoll, 2010)
- Expanded material on why children in low-income families may have difficulty with language development
- Expanded and updated material on how parents can facilitate their infants' and toddlers' language development based on recent recommendations by Ellen Galinsky (2010)
- New discussion of cultural variations in language support (Ochs & Schieffelin, 2008; Schieffelin, 2005)
- Important new entry in Resources section on Ellen Galinsky's (2010) wonderful book, *Mind in the Making*, which includes a number of strategies for improving infants' attention, cognitive skills, communication, and learning

Chapter 7: Socioemotional Development in Infancy

- Added commentary about the importance of the communication aspect of emotion, especially in infancy (Witherington & others, 2010)
- Expanded coverage of the onset of emotions in infancy, including Jerome Kagan's (2010) conclusion that emotions such as guilt, pride, despair, shame, and jealousy, which require thought, cannot be experienced in the first year because of the structural immaturity of the infant's brain
- New material on the importance of smiling in infancy as a means of developing a new social skill and serving as a key social signal (Campos, 2009)
- Coverage of a recent study linking behavioral inhibition at 3 years of age with shyness four years later (Volbrecht & Goldsmith, 2010)
- Added commentary about the importance of locomotion for the development of independence in the infant and toddler years (Campos, 2009)
- Discussion of a recent longitudinal study linking shyness/inhibition in infancy/childhood to social anxiety at 21 years of age (Bohlin & Hagekull, 2009)
- Added information about research indicating that decreases in infants' negative emotionality are related to higher levels of parents' sensitivity, involvement, and responsivity (Wachs & Bates, 2010)
- Inclusion of recent research on the early appearance of infants' conscious awareness of their bodies, which emerges during the second year (Brownell & others, 2009)
- Description of a recent study linking security of attachment at 24 and 36 months to the child's social problem-solving skills at 54 months (Raike & Thompson, 2009)
- Discussion of a recent study of maternal sensitive parenting and infant attachment security (Finger & others, 2009)

- Coverage of a recent meta-analysis linking Type D insecure attachment to externalizing problems (Fearon & others, 2010)
- Added information about the link of maternal sensitivity to secure infant attachment not being especially strong (Campos, 2009)
- Expanded discussion of fathers and mothers as caregivers
- Description of a recent study of multiple child-care arrangements and young children's behavioral outcomes (Morrissey, 2009)
- New Connecting with Careers box on Wanda Mitchell, Child-Care Director
- Coverage of recent research linking early higher quality of child care with higher cognitive-academic achievement and lower externalizing behavior at 15 years of age (Vandell & others, 2010)
- Inclusion of the following important point about the NICHD SECCYD research: findings consistently show that family factors are considerably stronger and more consistent predictors of a wide variety of child outcomes than are child-care experiences (quality, quantity, type)
- Description of a recent study using the NICHD SECCYD data indicating that the worst socioemotional outcomes for children occurred when both home and child-care settings conferred risk (Watamura & others, 2011)

Chapter 8: Physical Development in Early Childhood

- Description of a recent fMRI study indicating brain locations that were linked to 9- and 10-year-olds' conservation success in comparison with non-conserving 5- and 6-year-olds (Houde & others, 2011)
- Coverage of a recent study indicating that growth hormone treatment of very short children was effective in partially reducing the height deficit in adulthood (Deodati & Cianfarani, 2011)
- Inclusion of recent research indicating that growth hormone treatment of very short children was linked with increased height as well as improvements in self-esteem and mood (Chaplin & others, 2011)
- Description of a recent study linking sleep problems in early childhood with subsequent attention problems that in some cases persist into early adolescence (O'Callaghan & others, 2010)
- Coverage of a recent study indicating that having trouble sleeping in childhood was related to alcohol use problems in adolescence and early adulthood (Wong & others, 2010)
- Coverage of a recent analysis indicating that chronic child sleep disorders that deprive children of adequate sleep may lead to impaired brain development (Jan & others, 2010)
- Description of a recent study that found the vegetable most frequently consumed by 2- and 3-year olds-was French fries or other fried potatoes (Fox & others, 2010)

- Discussion of a recent study indicating that preschool children who were overweight had a significant risk of being overweight/obese at 11 years of age (Shankaran & others, 2011)
- New coverage of a recent study of child health and nutrition programs in Haiti that helped to reduce the impact of economic hardship on children's growth (Donegan & others, 2010)
- New main section on exercise, including recent research
- Description of a recent study that found parental smoking was a risk factor for higher blood pressure in children (Simonetti & others, 2011)
- New entry in Resources section on *The State of the World's Children 2011* by UNICEF

Chapter 9: Cognitive Development in Early Childhood

- Coverage of a recent research study linking television watching and video game playing to children's attention problems (Swing & others, 2010)
- New material on using computer exercises to improve children's attention, including information regarding a Web site (www.teach-the-brain.org/learn/attention/index.htm) that explains how to use the games with children (Jaeggi, Berman, & Jonides, 2009; Steiner & others, 2011; Tang & Posner, 2009)
- New discussion indicating that memory strategies develop more rapidly in middle and late childhood than in early childhood (Schneider, 2011)
- New discussion of the increasing interest in executive functioning, including the importance of its early development in the preschool years (Zelazo & Muller, 2011)
- Inclusion of recent research by Stephanie Carlson (2010, 2011) on developmental changes in children's executive functioning, including descriptions and photographs of the tasks used in her research
- Transfer of material on strategies and movement to their discussion to Chapter 12, "Cognitive Development in Middle and Late Childhood"
- Updated and revised description of the Connecting with Careers profile on Helen Hadani (formerly Helen Schwe) and her new work
- New discussion of variations in early literacy across countries, including comparisons of children learning English and Chinese (McBride & others, 2008)
- Expanded and updated discussion of the characteristics and goals of developmentally appropriate education (Barbarin & Miller, 2009; Bredekamp, 2011)
- New coverage of recent studies of the influence of Project Head Start on children's cognitive, language, and math skills and achievement (Hindman & others, 2010; Puma & others, 2010)
- New material on strategies for using books with preschoolers (Galinsky, 2010)

- New entry in the Resources section describing Ellen Galinsky's (2010) superb book, *Mind in the Making,* which provides numerous strategies parents and teachers can use to positively guide children's cognitive development

Chapter 10: Socioemotional Development in Early Childhood

- New coverage of perspective taking in understanding others, including the role of executive functioning in perspective taking
- Description of recent research on young children's understanding of joint commitments (Grafenhain & others, 2009)
- New commentary about how current research on theory of mind and young children's social understanding disagrees with Piaget's egocentrism concept
- Discussion of a recent study linking young children's emotional understanding with their prosocial behavior (Ensor, Spencer, & Hughes, 2010)
- Coverage of a recent study that found fathers' emotion coaching was related to children's social competence (Backer, Fenning, & Crnic, 2011)
- Discussion of research indicating that mothers' knowledge about what distresses and comforts their children predicts children's coping, empathy, and prosocial behavior (Vinik, Almas, & Grusec, 2011)
- New commentary about recent research on Asian American parents and Confucian goals (Russell, Crockett, & Chao, 2010)
- Description of a recent study in six countries linking physical punishment to high rates of aggression in children (Gershoff, 2010)
- Updated coverage of parental use of moderate versus severe punishment (Grusec, 2011)
- Description of a recent study of father involvement and coparenting (Jia & Schoppe-Sullivan, 2011)
- Updated statistics on child maltreatment (U.S. Department of Health and Human Services, 2010)
- Discussion of a recent study linking child maltreatment with financial and employment-related difficulties in adulthood (Zielinski, 2009)
- New discussion of E. Mark Cummings and his colleagues' (Cummings & Davies, 2010; Cummings, El-Sheikh, & Kouros, 2009; Cummings & Merrilees, 2009; Koss & others, 2011) emotional security theory and its focus on the type of marital conflict that is negative for children's development
- Expanded and updated coverage of the impact of the relationship between divorced parents on children's socioemotional development and visitations by the noncustodial parent (Fabricus & others, 2010)
- Coverage of a recent study indicating that an intervention aimed at improving the mother-child relationship was linked to improvements in the coping skills of children in divorced families (Velez & others, 2011)

- Additional commentary about father involvement dropping off more than mother involvement following a divorce, especially among fathers of girls

- Inclusion of information about joint custody working best for children when the divorced parents can get along with each other (Parke & Clarke-Stewart, 2011)

- Additional commentary about parental work's effect on children indicating that it is not only a maternal employment issue but often involves the father as well (Parke & Clarke-Stewart, 2011)

- Coverage of recent information about child and adolescent outcomes among individuals conceived by new reproductive technologies, which are increasingly used by gay and lesbian adults (Golombok, 2011a, b; Golombok & Tasker, 2010)

- New Connecting with Diversity interlude with expanded and updated material on immigrant families and their bicultural orientation, including recent research by Ross Parke and his colleagues (2011) on immigrant Mexican American families

- New discussion of the role of immigrant adolescents as cultural brokers for their parents (Villanueva & Buriel, 2010)

- Discussion of a recent study linking early and persistent poverty to lower cognitive functioning in 5-year-old children (Schoon & others, 2011)

- Coverage of a recent study linking 3- to 5-year-olds' sleep problems to (1) watching TV after 7 p.m. and (2) watching violent TV shows (Garrison & others, 2011)

Chapter 11: Physical Development in Middle and Late Childhood

- Inclusion of recent research on 9-year-olds that focused on the connection between physical activity level and risk for metabolic disease (Parrett & others, 2011)

- Description of recent research showing links between aerobic exercise and cognitive skills in children and adolescents (Best, 2011; Davis & others, 2011)

- Discussion of a recent study on parents' roles in limiting children's sedentary activity (Edwardson & Gorley, 2010)

- Inclusion of recent research that found both peers and family members teased overweight children more than normal-weight children (McCormack & others, 2011)

- Coverage of a recent study on the effectiveness of a school-based program for increasing children's physical activity (Kreimler & others, 2010)

- Coverage of a recent study linking sports participation to a lower incidence of being overweight or obese (Antonogeorgos & others, 2011)

- Description of a recent study that found having two overweight/obese parents significantly increased the likelihood that children would be overweight/obese (Xu & others, 2011)

- Inclusion of information about a recent successful behavior modification program that increased overweight and obese children's exercise and reduced their TV viewing time (Goldfield, 2011)

- Updated discussion of parenting interventions to help overweight and obese children lose weight (Collins & others, 2011; Robertson & others, 2011)

- Updated discussion of childhood cancer, including improvement in survival rates for some childhood cancers (National Cancer Institute, 2011; Wayne, 2010)

- New commentary about the recent increase in childhood diabetes in the United States and other countries (Harron & others, 2011; National Center for Health Statistics, 2011)

- Updated statistics on the percentage of children who have asthma (National Center for Health Statistics, 2009)

- Updated statistics on the percentage of students with various disabilities who receive special education services in U.S. schools (National Center for Education Statistics, 2010)

- Coverage of a recent study indicating delayed development in the frontal lobes of children with ADHD, likely due to delayed or decreased myelination (Nagel & others, 2011)

- Description of a recent study that linked cigarette smoking during pregnancy to ADHD in 6- to 7-year-old children (Sciberras, Ukoumunne, & Efron, 2011)

- Updated discussion of the role of neurotransmitters in ADHD to include dopamine (Beaulieu & Gainetdinov, 2011; Mahmoudi-Gharaei & others, 2011)

- New coverage of executive functioning deficits in children with ADHD (Jacobson & others, 2011; Rinsky & Henshaw, 2011)

- New material on deficits in theory of mind in children with ADHD (Buhler & others, 2011; Shauai, Chan, & Wang, 2011)

- New discussion of the role that connectivity between different brain regions might play in the development of autism (Mostofsky & Ewen, 2011; Muller & others, 2011)

- New Figure 11.7, a scene from the DVD animations used in research by Baron-Simon and others (2007)

Chapter 12: Cognitive Development in Middle and Late Childhood

- New figure illustrating Baddeley's working memory model

- New coverage of three recent studies of working memory that illustrate the wide-ranging impact of working memory capacity on children's cognitive development and achievement (Andersson, 2010; Asian, Zellner, & Bauml, 2010; Welsh & others, 2010)

- New section on improving children's memory

- Expanded coverage of strategies for improving children's memory skills, including memory development expert

Patricia Bauer's (2009) emphasis on consolidation and reconsolidation in memory through variation on an instructional theme and repeated linking

- New material on Peter Ornstein and his colleagues' view (Ornstein, Coffman, & Grammar, 2009; Ornstein & others, 2010) that it is important for instructors to embed memory-relevant language in their teaching
- Expanded discussion of children's creative thinking, including recent research indicating a decline in creative thinking by U.S. schoolchildren and increased interest in teaching creative thinking in Chinese schools (Kim, 2010; Plucker, 2010)
- Description of a recent research review that concluded more than 1,000 genes may influence an individual's intelligence (Davies & others, 2011)
- Discussion of a recent study that revealed an accelerated Flynn effect for children whose mothers have more education and for children from higher-income families (Ang, Rodgers, & Wanstrom, 2010)
- Expanded coverage of reading, including the importance of fluency and metacognitive strategies in becoming a good reader (Gorsuch & Taguchi, 2010; Snowling & Gobel, 2011)
- Inclusion of information about a recent study that indicated a computer-based program emphasizing phonics improved first-grade students' reading skills (Savage & others, 2009)
- Coverage of recent research indicating that bilingual children have a smaller vocabulary in each language than monolingual children do (Bialystok, 2011)
- New coverage of Carol Dweck's recent research and ideas about improving students' growth mindset by teaching them about the brain's plasticity and explaining how the brain changes when you put considerable effort into learning (Blackwell & others, 2007; Dweck & Masters, 2009)
- New material about Carol Dweck's recent development of computer modules, called "Brainology," that explain how the brain works and how through work and effort students can make their brains work better (Blackwell & Dweck, 2008; Dweck & Master, 2009)
- Description of recent research indicating that a number of aspects of children's development are influenced by their parents' self-efficacy (Steca & others, 2011)
- Coverage of a recent large-scale longitudinal study that focused on the importance of access to academic resources at home, especially in African American or low-SES students' achievement (Xia, 2010)

Chapter 13: Socioemotional Development in Middle and Late Childhood

- Discussion of a recent study that focused on the positive aspects of perspective-taking skills in children who are emotionally reactive (Bengtsson & Arvidsson, 2011)

- New descriptions of three recent studies on how various aspects of disasters and traumatic events affect children (Catani & others, 2010; Chemtob & others, 2010; Peek & Slough, 2010)
- New material on dose/response effects in the study of how disasters and traumatic events affect children's adjustment and adaptation (Masten & Osofsky, 2010; Obradovic, Shaffer, & Masten, 2011)
- Coverage of a recent study on the developmental increase in self-control in middle and late childhood and its links to lower levels of deviant behavior and to heightened warmth and positive affect in parenting (Vazsonyi & Huang, 2010)
- Inclusion of a recent study of self-regulation in children from low-income families (Buckner, Mezzacappa, & Beardslee, 2009)
- Much expanded, revised, and updated material on the domain theory of moral development and social conventional reasoning (Helwig & Turiel, 2011; Nucci & Gingo, 2011; Smetana, 2011a, b)
- Coverage of a recent study that revealed links between a higher level of multicultural experience and increased open mindedness, a growth mindset, and higher moral judgment (Narváez & Hill, 2010)
- Coverage of a recent gender stereotyping study of 6- to 10-year-olds who indicated that math is for boys (Cvencek, Meltzoff, & Greenwald, 2011)
- Description of a recent research review focused on girls' negative attitudes about math and the negative expectations that parents and teachers have for girls' math competence (Gunderson, 2011)
- Discussion of a recent meta-analysis that found no gender difference in math aptitude in adolescents (Lindberg & others, 2010)
- Description of a recent research review indicating that girls engage in more relational aggression than boys in adolescence but not in childhood (Smith, Rose, & Schwartz-Mette, 2010)
- Updated and expanded discussion of gender differences in emotion (Hertenstein & Keltner, 2011)
- Description of three recent suicides by young people in middle and late childhood and early adolescence that likely were influenced by bullying (Meyers, 2010)
- New emphasis on the importance of considering contexts in the study of bullying (Salmivalli & others, 2009; Schwartz & others, 2010)
- Coverage of two recent studies of bullies' popularity in the peer group (Veenstra & others, 2010; Witvliet & others, 2010)
- Description of a recent study on peer victimization and its link to lower academic achievement (Nakamoto & Schwartz, 2010)
- Inclusion of recent research on links between children's cyber aggression and negative peer relations outcomes (Schoffstall & Cohen, 2011)

- Description of a recent study linking bullying and moral disengagement (Obermann, 2011)
- Discussion of recent research on outcomes of 9- to 19-year-old African American boys who experienced the New Hope antipoverty program (McLoyd & others, 2011)

Chapter 14: Physical Development in Adolescence

- New discussion of how social policy regarding adolescents needs to be changed
- New material on the work of Peter Benson and his colleagues (2010; Benson & Scales, 2011; Scales, Benson, & Roehlkepartain, 2011)
- Description of a recent survey that found only 20 percent of U.S. 15-year-olds reported having had meaningful relationships outside their family that have helped them to succeed in life (Search Institute, 2010)
- New discussion of genetic and environmental contributions to puberty (He & others, 2010; Belsky & others, 2010)
- Inclusion of recent information on a longitudinal study of the sequence of pubertal events in boys and girls (Susman & others, 2010)
- Discussion of a recent study of gender differences in the aesthetic aspects of adolescents' body image (Abbott & Barber, 2010)
- Inclusion of information about a recent study of adolescents linking positive body images to health-enhancing behavior, especially regular exercise (Frisen & Holmqvist, 2010)
- Coverage of a recent study that found a link between early maturation and substance abuse as well as early sexual intercourse (Gaudineau & others, 2010)
- Description of a recent study linking pubertal timing with subsequent engagement in delinquency (Negriff, Susman, & Trickett, 2011)
- Revised and updated data (Figure 14.5) on the percentage of adolescents who reported having had sexual intercourse, including a recent gender reversal for twelfth-graders in which a higher percentage of twelfth-grade girls than twelfth-grade boys reported having had sex (Eaton & others, 2010)
- Updated statistics on the percentage of U.S. adolescents reporting that they are currently sexually active (Eaton & others, 2010)
- Revised and updated data on the percentage of non-Latino White, African American, and Latino adolescents who report having had sexual intercourse (Eaton & others, 2010)
- Reorganized, updated, and expanded material on risk factors in adolescent sexuality
- Discussion of a recent study that revealed a link between neighborhood poverty concentration and 15- to 17-year-old boys' and girls' sexual initiation (Cubbin & others, 2010)

- Description of the results from a recent research review of a number of aspects of connectedness, such as family connectedness and parent-adolescent communication about sexuality, linking such connections to adolescent sexuality outcomes (Markham & others, 2010)
- Description of recent research linking deviant peer relations in early adolescence with an increased incidence of multiple sexual partners at age 16 (Lansford & others, 2010)
- Updated information about trends in the percentage of sexually active adolescents who reported having used a condom the last time they had sexual intercourse (Eaton & others, 2010)
- Coverage of the recent decline in births to adolescent girls to a record low in 2009, including a new figure illustrating the decline (Ventura & Hamilton, 2011)
- Inclusion of information about some sex education programs that are not abstinence-plus sexuality, in which programs promote abstinence as well as contraceptive use (Realini & others, 2010)
- New description of the leveling off in the occurrence of overweight in adolescence in the last half of the first decade of the twenty-first century, not just in the United States but in other countries as well (Rokholm, Baker, & Sorensen, 2010)
- Inclusion of recent research linking obesity in adolescence with the development of severe obesity in emerging adulthood (The & others, 2010)
- Discussion of a recent longitudinal study of overweight and obesity from 14 years of age to 24 years of age (Patton & others, 2011)
- Description of recent research linking a higher level of exercise in adolescence with a lower level of alcohol, cigarette, and marijuana use (Terry-McElrath, O'Malley, & Johnston, 2011)
- New discussion of links between screen-based activity and physical exercise in adolescents, including recent research indicating that adolescents who combine low physical activity and high screen-based activity are nearly twice as likely to be overweight (Sisson & others, 2010)
- Description of a recent study on delaying school start time for ninth- to twelfth-grade students and their improved sleep, alertness, mood, and health (Owens, Belon, & Moss, 2010)
- New content on a comparison of U.S. and Asian adolescents' sleep patterns (Gradisar, Gardner, & Dohnt, 2011)
- New coverage of sleep in emerging adulthood (Galambos, Howard, & Maggs, 2011)
- Discussion of a recent study of emerging adults' sleep patterns and indications that first-year college students have bedtimes and risetimes that are later than those of seniors in high school but that bedtimes and risetimes begin getting earlier by the third and fourth year of college (Lund & others, 2010)

- Discussion of recent research on the role of attachment insecurity, body dissatisfaction, and need for approval in the development of anorexia nervosa and bulimia nervosa (Abbate-Daga & others, 2010)
- Updated coverage of the Monitoring the Future study's assessment of drug use by secondary school students (Johnston & others, 2011)
- Coverage of recent research that found parental monitoring was linked to lower substance abuse in adolescence (Tobler & Komro, 2010)
- Description of a recent research review that indicated adolescents who more frequently ate dinner with their families were less likely to have substance abuse problems (Sen, 2010)
- Discussion of recent research on positive and negative aspects of adolescents' interaction and relationships with parents and adolescent drinking and smoking (Guttman & others, 2011)
- Description of a recent study indicating that a key factor related to depression in overweight adolescents was body dissatisfaction (Mond & others, 2011)
- Coverage of recent research on a link between attachment insecurity and eating disorders in adolescence (Abbate-Daga & others, 2010)

Chapter 15: Cognitive Development in Adolescence

- Description of a recent research study indicating that adolescents envision that they are vulnerable to experiencing a premature death (Fischhoff & others, 2010)
- Expanded and updated coverage of the importance of perspective taking and ego development in explaining the imaginary audience and personal fable (Lapsley & Hill, 2010)
- Inclusion of recent research on the importance of distinguishing between two types of invulnerability (danger and psychological), which have different outcomes (Lapsley & Hill, 2010)
- Expanded and updated content on executive functioning in adolescence
- New section on the importance of controlling attention and reducing interfering thoughts in adolescence
- New section on metacognition
- Discussion of a recent study that found young adolescents increasingly use metacognitive skills from 12 to 14 years of age, and use them more effectively in math and history classes than in other subjects (van der Stel & Veenman, 2010)
- Inclusion of information about a recent study of the important role of metacognition in adolescents' ability to effectively generate hypotheses (Kim & Pedersen, 2010)
- Description of a recent study with college students indicating that metacognition is a key factor in the ability to engage effectively in critical thinking (Magno, 2010)

- New coverage of Darcia Narváez's (2010a) recent emphasis on the importance of sustaining classroom and school climates in the hidden curriculum
- Description of a recent study linking college students' personality traits with their likelihood of engaging in academic cheating (Williams, Nathanson, & Paulhus, 2010)
- New discussion of the history and current efforts of the U.S. government to engage students in service to the community and nation
- Updated material on the percent of college freshmen who estimate that there is a very good chance they will participate in volunteer or community work (Pryor & others, 2010)
- Update of college freshmen's religious activities and preferences (Pryor & others, 2009)
- New coverage of distinctions between religion, religiousness, and spirituality based on a recent analysis by Pamela King and her colleagues (2011)
- Coverage of a recent study linking religious attendance with a lower level of substance abuse in adolescents (Good & Willoughby, 2010)
- Discussion of recent research on church engagement and a lower level of depression in adolescents (Kang & Romo, 2010)
- Inclusion of recent research that found spirituality was related to a number of positive adolescent sexual outcomes (House & others, 2010)
- Description of recent research linking parents' religiosity with adolescents' lower levels of risky sexual behavior (Landor & others, 2010)
- Updated coverage of school dropout rates, including new Figure 15.4 that shows dropout rates by gender and ethnicity, as well as a significant decrease of Latino dropouts in the first decade of the twenty-first century (National Center for Education Statistics, 2010)
- New discussion of the controversy in determining school dropout rates

Chapter 16: Socioemotional Development in Adolescence

- Coverage of a recent study indicating that individuals from 12 to 20 years of age increasingly pursue in-depth exploration of their identity (Klimstra & others, 2010)
- Coverage of a recent meta-analysis of 124 studies focused on developmental changes in Marcia's identity statuses (Kroger, Martinussen, & Marcia, 2010)
- New section, "Parental Monitoring," that especially provides recent information about the increasing interest in studying adolescents' management of their parents' access to information (Laird & Marrero, 2010; Smetana, 2011)
- Description of a recent analysis that concluded the most consistent outcomes of secure attachment in adolescence involve positive peer relations and the development of emotion regulation capacities (Allen & Miga, 2010)

- Description of a recent study of developmental changes in adolescents and emerging adults' attachments to important people in their lives and links to behavioral problems (Rosenthal & Kobak, 2010)
- Discussion of a recent study of young adolescents' friendships and depression (Brendgen & others, 2010)
- Description of recent research on the negative outcomes of adolescent girls having an older romantic partner (Haydon & Halpern, 2011)
- Expanded and updated material on immigrant families and their bicultural orientation, including recent research by Ross Parke and his colleagues (2011)
- New discussion of the role of immigrant adolescents as cultural brokers for their parents (Villanueva & Buriel, 2010)
- Substantial updating of trends in media use by adolescents, based on the 2009 national survey of more than 2,000 U.S. adolescents as well as comparisons with earlier national surveys (Rideout, Foehr, & Roberts, 2010)
- Coverage of a recent national survey of trends in adolescents' use of social media, including dramatic increases in social networking and text messaging, and declines in tweeting and blogging (Lenhart & others, 2010)
- New commentary about text messaging now being the main way that adolescents prefer connecting with their friends (Lenhart & others, 2010)
- Inclusion of information that Facebook replaced Google as the most frequently visited Internet site in 2010
- Description of a recent study of parenting predictors of adolescent media use (Padilla-Walker & Coyne, 2011)
- Inclusion of recent research linking problematic mother-child relationships in early adolescence with negative peer relations on the Internet in emerging adulthood (Szwedo, Mikami, & Allen, 2011)
- Discussion of recent research on the role of parental monitoring and support during adolescence in reducing criminal behavior in emerging adulthood (Johnson & others, 2011)
- Inclusion of recent research on the role of engaged parenting and mothers' social network support in

- reducing delinquency in low-income families (Ghazarian & Roche, 2010)
- Description of a recent study that found repeated poverty was an important risk factor for delinquency (Najman & others, 2010)
- Coverage of a recent study that revealed male Chinese adolescents and emerging adults experience more depression than their female counterparts do (Sun & others, 2010)
- Inclusion of recent research indicating that mother-daughter co-rumination was linked to increased anxiety and depression in adolescent daughters (Waller & Rose, 2010)
- Coverage of research indicating that exposure to maternal depression prior to age 12 predicted risk processes during development (difficulties in family relationships, for example), which set the course for the development of the adolescent's depression (Garber & Cole, 2010)
- Discussion of recent research indicating that four types of bullying were linked to adolescents' depression (Wang, Nansel, & Ianotti, 2011)
- Inclusion of recent research indicating that weight-related concerns increase adolescent girls' depressive symptoms (Vaughan & Halpern, 2010)
- Description of recent research from the National Longitudinal Study of Adolescent Health indicating that parental loss predicted an increase in suicide attempts 1 year later but not 7 years later (Thompson & Light, 2011)
- Inclusion of recent research on suicide attempts by young Latinas (Zayas & others, 2010)
- Discussion of a recent study linking sexual victimization to suicide attempts in adolescence (Plener, Singer, & Goldbeck, 2011)
- Updated coverage of outcomes for the Fast Track delinquency intervention study through age 19 that found the program was successful in reducing juvenile arrest rates (Conduct Problems Prevention Research Group, 2010a)
- Two new entries in the end-of-chapter Resources list: Sheryl Feinstein's (2010) *101 Insights and Strategies for Parenting Teenagers* and Laurence Steinberg's (2011) *You and Your Adolescent*

ACKNOWLEDGMENTS

I very much appreciate the support and guidance provided to me by many people at McGraw-Hill. Mike Sugarman, Publisher, has brought a wealth of publishing knowledge and vision to bear on improving my texts. Allison McNamara, Sponsoring Editor, deserves special mention for the superb work she has done on this book. Cara Labell, Senior Development Editor, has contributed extensively to many aspects of reviewing, editing, and production for this new edition. Sarah Kiefer, Editorial Coordinator, also has helped a great deal in the editorial process. Julia Flohr Larkin, Marketing Manager, has contributed in numerous positive ways to this book. Janet Tilden did an outstanding job as the book's copy editor, and Melanie Field was terrific in coordinating the book's production.

Thanks go to my wife, Mary Jo, for her unwavering support of my writing and books over a number of decades. And special thanks to our children, Tracy and Jennifer, and more recently our granddaughter, Jordan, and grandsons, Alex and Luke, for providing many special moments that have helped to shape my thinking about how children and adolescents develop.

REVIEWERS

Expert Consultants

Children's development has become an enormous, complex field, and no single author can possibly be an expert in all aspects of the field. To solve this problem, beginning with the fifth edition, I have sought the input of leading experts in many different areas of children's development. This tradition continues in the twelfth edition of *Children*. The experts have provided me with detailed recommendations of new research to include in every period of children's development. The panel of experts is literally a *Who's Who* in the field of children's development. The experts' photographs and biographies appear on pp. xiii–xv.

General Text Reviewers

I also owe a great deal of thanks to the instructors who teach child development and who have provided feedback about the book. I am also indebted to the individuals who reviewed previous editions and whose recommendations have been carried forward into the present edition.

John A. Addleman, *Messiah College*

Linda Anderson, *Northwestern Michigan College*

Christine Anthis, *Southern Connecticut State University*

Harry H. Avis, *Sierra College*

Diana Baumrind, *University of California–Berkeley*

Lori A. Beasley, *University of Central Oklahoma*

Patricia J. Bence, *Tompkins Cortland Community College*

Michael Bergmire, *Jefferson College*

Belinda Blevins-Knabe, *University of Arkansas–Little Rock*

Albert Bramante, *Union County College*

Ruth Brinkman, *St. Louis Community College, Florissant Valley*

Eileen Donahue Brittain, *City College of Harry S Truman*

Urie Bronfenbrenner, *Cornell University*

Phyllis Bronstein, *University of Vermont*

Dan W. Brunworth, *Kishwaukee College*

Carole Burke-Braxton, *Austin Community College*

Jo Ann Burnside, *Richard J. Daley College*

Victoria Candelora, *Brevard Community College*

Alison S. Carson, *Hofstra University*

Rosalind Charlesworth, *Weber State University*

Nancy Coghill, *University of Southwest Louisiana*

Malinda Jo Colwell, *Texas Tech University*

Jennifer Cousins, *University of Houston*

Dixie R. Crase, *Memphis State University*

Kathleen Crowley-Long, *The College of Saint Rose*

Florence Denmark, *Pace University*

Sheridan DeWolf, *Grossmont Community College*

Swen H. Digranes, *Northeastern State University*

Ruth Doyle, *Casper College*

Laura Duvall, *Heartland Community College*

Celina V. Echols, *Southeastern Louisiana State University*

Beverly Edmondson, *Buena Vista University*

Timothy P. Eicher, *Dixie Community College*

Sarah Erikson, *University of New Mexico*

Jennifer Fager, *Western Michigan University*

Karen Falcone, *San Joaquin Delta College*

JoAnn Farver, *Oklahoma State University*

Greta Fein, *University of Maryland*

Tiffany Field, *University of Miami (FL)*

Johanna Filp, *Sonoma State University*

Kate Fogarty, *University of Florida at Gainesville*

Cheryl Fortner-Wood, *Winthrop College*

Dale Fryxell, *Chaminade University*

Janet Fuller, *Mansfield University*

Thomas Gerry, *Columbia Greene Community College*

Sam Givhan, *Minnesota State University*

Art Gonchar, *University of La Verne*

Sandra Graham, *UCLA*

Susan Hale, *Holyoke Community College*

Barbara Springer Hammons, *Palomar College*

Cory Anne Hansen, *Arizona State University*

Barbara H. Harkness, *San Bernardino Valley College*

Algea Harrison, *Oakland University*

Susan Heidrich, *University of Wisconsin*

Ashleigh Hillier, *Ohio University*

Alice S. Hoenig, *Syracuse University*

Sally Hoppstetter, *Palo Alto College*

Robert J. Ivy, *George Mason University*

Diane Carlson Jones, *Texas A&M University*

Ellen Junn, *Indiana University*

Marcia Karwas, *California State University–Monterey*

Melvyn B. King, *State College of New York at Cortland*

Kathleen Kleissler, *Kutztown University*

Dene G. Klinzing, *University of Delaware*

Claire B. Kopp, *UCLA*

Cally Beth Kostakis, *Rockland Community College*

Tara L. Kuther, *Western Connecticut State University*

Linda Lavine, *State University of New York–Cortland*

Sara Lawrence, *California State University–Northridge*

Hsin-Hui Lin, *University of Houston at Victoria*

Gloria Lopez, *Sacramento City College*

James E. Marcia, *Simon Fraser University*

Deborah N. Margolis, *Boston College*

Julie Ann McIntyre, *Russell Sage College*

Mary Ann McLaughlin, *Clarion University*

Chloe Merrill, *Weber State College*

Karla Miley, *Black Hawk College*

Jody Miller, *Los Angeles Pierce College*

Carrie L. Mori, *Boise State University*

Joyce Munsch, *California State University at Northridge*

Barbara J. Myers, *Virginia Commonwealth University*

Jeffrey Nagelbush, *Ferris State University*

Sonia Nieves, *Broward Community College*

Caroline Olko, *Nassau Community College*

Sandy Osborne, *Montana State University*

William H. Overman, *University of North Carolina at Wilmington*

Michelle Paludi, *Michelle Paludi & Affiliates*

Susan Peet, *Bowling Green State University*

Pete Peterson, *Johnson County Community College*

Joe Price, *San Diego State University*

Charles L. Reid, *Essex County College*

Barbara Reynolds, *College of the Sequoias*

Cynthia Rickert, *Dominican College*

Richard Riggle, *Coe College*

Lynne Rompelman, *Concordia University–Wisconsin*

James A. Rysberg, *California State University, Chico*

Marcia Rysztak, *Lansing Community College*

David Sadker, *The American University, Washington DC*

Peter C. Scales, *Search Institute*

Pamela Schuetze-Pizarro, *Buffalo State College*

Pamela A. Schulze, *University of Akron*

Diane Scott-Jones, *University of Illinois*

Clyde Shepherd, *Keene State College*

Carol S. Soule, *Appalachian State University*

Dorothy D. Sweeney, *Bristol Community College*

Anita Thomas, *Northeastern Illinois University*

Ross A. Thompson, *University of Nebraska at Lincoln*

Kourtney Vaillancourt, *New Mexico State University*

Naomi Wagner, *San Jose State University*

Richard L. Wagner, *Mount Senario College*

Patricia J. Wall, *Northern Arizona University*

Dorothy A. Wedge, *Fairmont State College*

Carla Graham Wells, *Odessa College*

Teion Wells, *Florida State University–Tallahassee*

Becky G. West, *Coahoma Community College*

Alida Westman, *Eastern Michigan University*

Allan Wigfield, *University of Maryland, College Park*
Marilyn E. Willis, *Indiana University of Pennsylvania*
Mary E. Wilson, *Northern Essex Community College*
Susan D. Witt, *University of Akron*
Bonnie Wright, *Gardner Webb University*
Sarah Young, *Longwood College*
William H. Zachry, *University of Tennessee, Martin*

SUPPLEMENTS

For the Instructor

The instructor side of the Online Learning Center at http://www.mhhe.com/ santrockc12e contains the Instructor's Manual, Test Bank files, PowerPoint slides, Image Gallery, and other valuable material to help you design and enhance your course. Ask your local McGraw-Hill representative for your password.

Instructor's Manual   Each chapter of the *Instructor's Manual* is introduced by a Total Teaching Package Outline. This fully integrated tool helps instructors more easily locate and choose among the many resources available for the course by linking each element of the Instructor's Manual to a particular teaching topic within the chapter. These elements include chapter outlines, suggested lecture topics, classroom activities and demonstrations, suggested student research projects, essay questions, critical thinking questions, and implications for guidance.

Test Bank and Computerized Test Bank   This comprehensive Test Bank includes more than 1,500 multiple-choice and approximately 75 essay questions. Organized by chapter, the questions are designed to test factual, applied, and conceptual understanding. All test questions are compatible with EZ Test, McGraw-Hill's Computerized Test Bank program.

PowerPoint Slides   These presentations cover the key points of each chapter and include charts and graphs from the text. They can be used as is, or you may modify them to meet your specific needs.

McGraw-Hill's Visual Assets Database for Lifespan Development ("VAD")
McGraw-Hill's Visual Assets Database for Lifespan Development (VAD 2.0) www. mhhe.com/vad is an online database of videos for use in the developmental psychology classroom, created specifically for instructors. You can customize classroom presentations by downloading the videos to your computer and showing the videos on their own or insert them into your course cartridge or PowerPoint presentations. All of the videos are available with or without captions. Ask your McGraw-Hill representative for access information.

For the Student

Online Learning Center (OLC)   This companion Web site, at www.mhhe.com/ santrockc12e, offers a wide variety of student resources. **Multiple Choice, True/ False,** and **Matching Tests** for each chapter reinforce key principles, terms, and ideas and cover all the major concepts discussed throughout the text. Entirely different from the test items in the Test Bank, the questions have been written to quiz students but also to help them learn. Key terms from the text are reproduced in a **Glossary of Key Terms** where they can be accessed in alphabetical order for easy reference and review. **Decision Making Scenarios** present students with the opportunity to apply the information in the chapter to realistic situations and to see the effects of their decisions.

CHILDREN

Twelfth Edition

If I had my child to raise over again

If I had my child to raise over again,

I'd finger paint more, and point the finger less.

I'd do less correcting, and more connecting.

I'd take my eyes off my watch, and watch with my eyes.

I would care to know less, and know to care more.

I'd take more hikes and fly more kites.

I'd stop playing serious, and seriously play.

I would run through more fields, and gaze at more stars.

I'd do more hugging, and less tugging.

I would be firm less often, and affirm much more.

I'd build self-esteem first, and the house later.

I'd teach less about the love of power,

And more about the power of love.

—Diane Loomans

In every child who is born, under no matter what circumstances, and of no matter what parents, the potentiality of the human race is born again.

—JAMES AGEE
American Writer, 20th Century

The Nature of Children's Development

Examining the shape of childhood allows us to understand it better. Every childhood is distinct, the first chapter of a new biography in the world. This book is about children's development, its universal features, its individual variations, its nature at the beginning of the twenty-first century. *Children* is about the rhythm and meaning of children's lives, about turning mystery into understanding, and about weaving together a portrait of who each of us was, is, and will be. In Section 1 you will read "Introduction" (Chapter 1).

chapter 1 INTRODUCTION

Ted Kaczynski sprinted through high school, not bothering with his junior year and making only passing efforts at social contact. Off to Harvard at age 16, Kaczynski was a loner during his college years. One of his roommates at Harvard said that he avoided people by quickly shuffling by them and slamming the door behind him. After obtaining his Ph.D. in mathematics at the University of Michigan, Kaczynski became a professor at the University of California at Berkeley. His colleagues there remember him as hiding from social circumstances—no friends, no allies, no networking.

After several years at Berkeley, Kaczynski resigned and moved to a rural area of Montana where he lived as a hermit in a crude shack for 25 years. Town residents described him as a bearded eccentric. Kaczynski traced his own difficulties to growing up as a genius in a kid's body and sticking out like a sore thumb in his surroundings as a child. In 1996, he was arrested and charged as the notorious Unabomber, America's most wanted killer. Over the course of 17 years, Kaczynski had sent 16 mail bombs that left 23 people wounded or maimed and 3 people dead. In 1998, he pleaded guilty to the offenses and was sentenced to life in prison.

A decade before Kaczynski mailed his first bomb, Alice Walker spent her days battling racism in Mississippi. She had recently won her first writing fellowship, but rather than use the money to follow her dream of moving to Senegal, Africa, she put herself into the heart and heat of the civil rights movement. Walker had grown up knowing the brutal effects of poverty and racism. Born in 1944, she was the eighth child of Georgia sharecroppers who earned $300 a year. When Walker was 8, her brother accidentally shot her in the left eye with a BB gun. Because her parents had no car, it took them a week to get her to a hospital. By the time she received medical care, she was blind in that eye, and it had developed a disfiguring layer of scar tissue. Despite the counts against her, Walker overcame pain and anger and went on to win a Pulitzer Prize for her book *The Color Purple*. She became not only a novelist but also an essayist, a poet, a short-story writer, and a social activist.

What leads one individual, so full of promise, to commit brutal acts of violence and another to turn poverty and trauma into a rich literary harvest? If you have ever wondered why people turn out the way they do, you have asked yourself the central question we will explore in this book.

Ted Kaczynski, the convicted Unabomber, traced his difficulties to growing up as a genius in a kid's body and not fitting in when he was a child.

Ted Kaczynski, about age 14.

What might be some reasons Alice Walker was able to overcome trauma in her childhood and develop in impressive ways?

Alice Walker, about age 8.

preview

Why study children? Perhaps you are, or will be, a parent or teacher, and responsibility for children is, or will be, a part of your everyday life. The more you learn about children, the better you can guide them. Perhaps you hope to gain an understanding of your own history—as an infant, as a child, and as an adolescent. Perhaps you accidentally came across the course description and found it intriguing. Whatever your reasons, you will discover that the study of child development is provocative, intriguing, and informative. In this first chapter, we explore why caring for children is so important, describe historical changes in the study of children's development, examine the nature of development, and outline how science helps us to understand it.

Why Is Caring for Children Important?

 LG1 Explain why it is important to study children's development, and identify five areas in which children's lives need to be improved.

The Importance of Studying Children's Development

Improving the Lives of Children

Caring for children is an important theme of this text. To think about why caring for children is such an important theme, we will explore why it is beneficial to study children's development and identify some areas in which children's lives need to be improved. Just what do we mean when we speak of an individual's development? **Development** is the pattern of change that begins at conception and continues through the life span. Most development involves growth, although it also includes decline.

THE IMPORTANCE OF STUDYING CHILDREN'S DEVELOPMENT

How might you benefit from examining children's development? Perhaps you are, or will be, a parent or teacher and you want to learn about children so that you can become a better parent or educator. Perhaps you hope to gain some insight about how your childhood experiences have shaped the person you are today. Or perhaps you think that the study of children's development might raise some provocative issues. Whatever your reasons for reading this book, you will discover that the study of children's development is intriguing and filled with information about who we are and how we came to be this way.

As we indicated earlier, most human development involves growth, but it also includes decline. For example, think about how your ability to speak and write your native language has grown since you were a young child. But your ability to achieve a high level of competence in learning to speak a new language has probably declined (Thomas & Johnson, 2008). In this book, we examine children's development from the point of conception through adolescence. You will see yourself as an infant, as a child, and as an adolescent—and be stimulated to think about how those years influenced you.

> We reach backward to our parents and forward to our children and through their children to a future we will never see, but about which we need to care.
>
> —CARL JUNG
> *Swiss Psychoanalytic Theorist, 20th Century*

IMPROVING THE LIVES OF CHILDREN

If you were to pick up a newspaper or magazine in any U.S. town or city, you might see headlines like these: "Political Leanings May Be Written in the Genes," "Mother Accused of Tossing Children into Bay," "Gender Gap Widens," and "FDA Warns About ADHD Drug." Researchers are examining these and many other topics of contemporary concern. The roles that health and well-being, parenting, education, and sociocultural contexts play in children's development, as well as how social policy is related to these issues, are a special focus of this textbook.

development The pattern of movement or change that begins at conception and continues through the human life span.

Luis Vargas, Clinical Child Psychologist

Luis Vargas is the director of the Clinical Child Psychology Internship Program and a professor in child and adolescent psychiatry at the University of New Mexico School of Medicine. Vargas obtained an undergraduate degree in psychology from Trinity University in Texas and a Ph.D. in clinical psychology at the University of Nebraska–Lincoln.

Vargas' work includes assessing and treating children, adolescents, and their families, especially when a child or adolescent has a serious mental disorder. He also trains mental health professionals to provide culturally responsive and developmentally appropriate mental health services. In addition, he is interested in cultural and assessment issues involving children, adolescents, and their families. He co-authored (with Joan Koss-Chiono, a medical anthropologist) *Working with Latino Youth: Culture, Context, and Development* (1999).

Vargas' clinical work is heavily influenced by contextual and ecological theories of development (which we discuss later in this chapter). His first undergraduate course in human development, and subsequent courses in development, contributed to his decision to pursue a career in clinical child psychology.

Luis Vargas conducting a child therapy session.

For more information about the work of clinical child psychologists, see the Careers in Child Development appendix that follows Chapter 1 (pp. 46–50).

Health and Well-Being   Does a pregnant woman endanger her fetus if she has a few beers a week? How does a poor diet affect a child's ability to learn? Are children exercising less today than in the past? What roles do parents and peers play in whether adolescents abuse drugs? Throughout this text we discuss many questions like these regarding health and well-being. Investigating these questions, and exploring possible answers, is an important goal for just about everyone.

Health professionals today recognize the power of lifestyles and psychological states in health and well-being (Insel & Roth, 2012; Hahn, Payne, & Lucas, 2011). In every chapter of this book, issues of health and well-being are integrated into our discussion.

Clinical psychologists are among the health professionals who help people improve their well-being. In this chapter's *Connecting with Careers* profile, you can read about clinical psychologist Luis Vargas, who helps adolescents with problems. A Careers Appendix that follows Chapter 1 describes the education and training required to become a clinical psychologist and to pursue other careers in child development.

Parenting   Can two gay men raise a healthy family? Are children harmed if both parents work outside the home? Do adopted children fare as well as children raised by their biological parents? How damaging is divorce to children's development? We hear many questions like these related to pressures on the contemporary family (Parke & Clarke-Stewart, 2011; Powell, 2012). We examine these questions and others that provide a context for understanding factors that influence parents' lives and how effectively they rear their children. How parents, as well as other adults, can make a positive difference in children's lives is a major theme of this book.

Children learn to love when they are loved

You might be a parent someday or might already be one. You should take seriously the importance of rearing your children, because they are the future of our society. Good parenting takes considerable time. If you plan to become a parent, commit yourself day after day, week after week, month after month, and year after year to providing your children with a warm, supportive, safe, and stimulating environment that will make them feel secure and allow them to reach their full potential as human beings. The poster shown on page 9, which states "Children learn to love when they are loved," reflects this theme.

developmental **connection**

Parenting. Which parenting style is most often linked with positive child outcomes? Chapter 10, p. 300

Understanding the nature of children's development can help you become a better parent (Grusec, 2011). Many parents learn parenting practices from their parents. Unfortunately, when parenting practices and child-care strategies are passed from one generation to the next, both desirable and undesirable ones are usually perpetuated. This book and your instructor's lectures in this course can help you become more knowledgeable about children's development and sort through which practices in your own upbringing you should continue with your own children and which you should abandon.

Education   There is widespread agreement that something needs to be done to improve the education of our nation's children (Cunningham & Allington, 2011; Taylor & Fratto, 2012). A number of questions are involved in improving schools. For example, are they failing to teach children how to read and write and calculate adequately? Should there be more accountability in schools, with effectiveness of student learning and teaching assessed by formal tests? Have schools become too soft and watered down? Should they make more demands on, and have higher expectations of, children? Should schooling involve less memorization and more attention to the development of children's ability to process information efficiently? Should schools focus only on developing the child's knowledge and cognitive skills, or should they pay more attention to the whole child and consider the child's socioemotional and physical development as well? For example, should schools be dramatically changed so that they serve as a locus for a wide range of services, such as primary health care, child care, preschool education, parent education, recreation, and family counseling, as well as the traditional educational activities such as learning in the classroom? Are U.S. schools teaching children to be immoral? In this text, we examine such questions about the state of education in the United States and consider recent research on solutions to educational problems.

Sociocultural Contexts and Diversity   Health and well-being, parenting, and education—like development itself—are all shaped by their sociocultural context (Bennett, 2011; Shiraev, 2011). The term **context** refers to the settings in which development occurs. These settings are influenced by historical, economic, social, and cultural factors (Chen, Howard, & Brooks-Gunn, 2011). Four contexts to which we pay special attention in this text are culture, ethnicity, socioeconomic status, and gender.

Culture encompasses the behavior patterns, beliefs, and all other products of a specific group of people that are passed on from generation to generation. Culture results from the interaction of people over many years (Kitayama, 2011). A cultural group can be as large as the United States or as small as an isolated Appalachian town. Whatever its size, the group's culture influences the behavior of its members (Matsumoto & Juang, 2012). **Cross-cultural studies** compare aspects of two or more cultures. The comparison provides information about the degree to which development is similar, or universal, across cultures, or is instead culture-specific (Fung, 2011; Zhang & Sternberg, 2011).

Ethnicity (the word *ethnic* comes from the Greek word for "nation") is rooted in cultural heritage, nationality, race, religion, and language. African Americans,

How Would You...?
If you were a **psychologist,** how would you explain the importance of examining sociocultural factors in developmental research?

context The settings, influenced by historical, economic, social, and cultural factors, in which development occurs.

culture The behavior patterns, beliefs, and all other products of a group that are passed on from generation to generation.

cross-cultural studies Comparisons of one culture with one or more other cultures. These comparisons provide information about the degree to which children's development is similar, or universal, across cultures, and the degree to which it is culture-specific.

ethnicity A characteristic based on cultural heritage, nationality, race, religion, and language.

Latinos, Asian Americans, Native Americans, Polish Americans, and Italian Americans are a few examples of ethnic groups. Diversity exists within each ethnic group (Koppelman & Goodhart, 2011; Marks, Patton, & Garcia Coll, 2011). Contrary to stereotypes, not all African Americans live in low-income circumstances; not all Latinos are Catholics; not all Asian Americans are high school math whizzes.

Socioeconomic status (SES) refers to a person's position within society based on occupational, educational, and economic characteristics. Socioeconomic status implies certain inequalities. Generally, members of a society have (1) occupations that vary in prestige, with some individuals having more access than others to higher-status occupations; (2) different levels of educational attainment, with some individuals having more access than others to better education; (3) different economic resources; and (4) different levels of power to influence a community's institutions. These differences in people's ability to control resources and to participate in society's rewards produce unequal opportunities (Cheah & Leung, 2011; McLoyd & others, 2011).

Gender   Gender is another key dimension of children's development. **Gender** refers to the characteristics of people as males and females. Few aspects of our development are more central to our identity and social relationships than gender (Best, 2010; Matlin, 2012). How you view yourself, your relationships with other people, your life, and your goals are shaped to a great extent by whether you are male or female and how your culture defines the proper roles of males and females (Eagly & Wood, 2011).

These two Korean-born children on the day they became U.S. citizens represent the dramatic increase in the percentage of ethnic minority children in the United States.

Each of these dimensions of the sociocultural context—culture, ethnicity, SES, and gender—helps to mold how an individual develops through life, as discussions in later chapters demonstrate. We explore, for example, questions such as the following:

developmental connection

Peers. Peers especially play an important role in gender development during childhood. Chapter 10, p. 298

- Do infants around the world form attachments with their parents in the same way, or do these attachments differ from one culture to another?

- Does poverty influence the likelihood that young children will be provided with fewer educational opportunities than children growing up in more affluent families?

- Is there a parenting style that is universally effective, or does the effectiveness of different types of parenting depend on the ethnic group or culture?

- If adolescents from minority groups identify with their ethnic culture, is that likely to help or hinder their socioemotional development?

In the United States, the sociocultural context has become increasingly diverse in recent years (Wright & others, 2012). The population includes an increasing percentage of children from ethnic minority families, especially Latino and Asian American, who recently have immigrated to the United States. This changing demographic tapestry promises not only the richness that diversity produces but also difficult challenges in extending the American dream to all individuals (Chao & Otsuki-Clutter, 2011; Murry & others, 2011).

We discuss sociocultural contexts and diversity in each chapter. In addition, a *Connecting with Diversity* interlude appears in every chapter. The first Diversity interlude, which focuses on gender, families, and children's development around the world, follows.

Resilience, Social Policy, and Children's Development   Some children develop confidence in their abilities despite negative stereotypes about their gender or their ethnic group. And some children triumph over poverty or other adversities. They show *resilience*. Think back to the chapter-opening story about Alice Walker. In spite of

socioeconomic status (SES) An individual's position within society based on occupational, educational, and economic characteristics.

gender The characteristics of people as females or males.

connecting with diversity

Gender, Families, and Children's Development

Around the world, the experiences of male and female children and adolescents continue to be quite different (Brown & Larson, 2002; UNICEF, 2012). Except in a few areas, such as Japan, the Philippines, and Western countries, males have far greater access to educational opportunities than females. In many countries, adolescent females have less freedom to pursue a variety of careers and engage in various leisure acts than males. Gender differences in sexual expression are widespread, especially in India, Southeast Asia, Latin America, and Arab countries—where there are far more restrictions on the sexual activity of adolescent females than of males. In certain areas around the world, these gender differences do appear to be narrowing over time. In some countries, educational and career opportunities for women are expanding, and in some parts of the world control over adolescent girls' romantic and sexual relationships is weakening. However, in many countries females still experience considerable discrimination, and much work is needed to bridge the gap between the rights of males and females.

In certain parts of the world, children grow up in closely knit families with extended-kin networks "that provide a web of connections and reinforce a traditional way of life" (Brown & Larson, 2002, p. 6). For example, in Arab countries, adolescents are required to adopt strict codes of conduct and loyalty. However, in Western countries such as the United States, children and adolescents are growing up in much larger numbers in divorced families and stepfamilies. Parenting in Western countries has become less authoritarian than it was in the past.

Doly Akter, age 17, lives in a slum in Dhaka, Bangladesh, where sewers overflow, garbage rots in the streets, and children are undernourished. Nearly two-thirds of young women in Bangladesh get married before they are 18. Doly recently organized a club supported by UNICEF in which girls go door-to-door to monitor the hygiene habits of households in their neighborhood. The monitoring has led to improved hygiene and health in the families. Also, her group has managed to stop several child marriages by meeting with parents and convincing them that it is not in their daughter's best interests. When talking with parents in their neighborhoods, the girls in the club emphasize the importance of staying in school and how this will improve their daughter's future. Doly says that the girls in her UNICEF group are far more aware of their rights than their mothers ever were (UNICEF, 2007).

Some of the trends that are occurring in many countries around the world "include greater family mobility, migration to urban areas, family members working in distant cities or countries, smaller families, fewer extended-family households, and increases in mothers' employment" (Brown & Larson, 2002, p. 7). Unfortunately, many of these changes may reduce the ability of families to provide time and resources for children and adolescents.

Source	Characteristic
Individual	Good intellectual functioning
	Appealing, sociable, easygoing disposition
	Self-confidence, high self-esteem
	Talents
	Faith
Family	Close relationship to caring parent figure
	Authoritative parenting: warmth, structure, high expectations
	Socioeconomic advantages
	Connections to extended supportive family networks
Extrafamilial Context	Bonds to caring adults outside the family
	Connections to positive organizations
	Attending effective schools

FIGURE 1.1

CHARACTERISTICS OF RESILIENT CHILDREN AND THEIR CONTEXTS

racism, poverty, her low socioeconomic status, and a disfiguring eye injury, she went on to become a successful author and champion for equality.

Are there certain characteristics that cause children like Alice Walker to be resilient? Are there other characteristics that influence children to behave like Ted Kaczynski, who despite his intelligence and education became a killer? After analyzing research on this topic, Ann Masten (2001, 2006, 2007, 2009, 2011, 2012) concludes that a number of individual factors, such as good intellectual functioning, influence resiliency. In addition, as Figure 1.1 shows, the families and extrafamilial contexts of resilient children tend to show certain features. For example, resilient children are likely to have a close relationship to a caring parent figure and bonds to caring adults outside the family.

Should governments take action to improve the contexts of children's development and aid their resilience? **Social policy** is a government's course of action designed to promote the welfare of its citizens. The shape and scope of social policy related to children are tied to the political system. The values held by citizens and elected officials, the nation's economic strengths and weaknesses, and partisan politics all influence the policy agenda.

When concern about broad social issues is widespread, comprehensive social policies often result. Child labor laws were established in the early twentieth century not only to protect children but also to provide jobs for adults; federal child-care funding during World War II was justified by the need for women laborers in factories; and Head Start and other War on Poverty programs in the 1960s were implemented to decrease intergenerational poverty.

Out of concern that policy makers are doing too little to protect the well-being of children, researchers increasingly are undertaking studies that they hope will lead to wise and effective decision making about social policy (Benson & Scales, 2011). Children who grow up in poverty represent a special concern (McLoyd & others, 2011). In 2009, 20.1 percent (an increase from 18.5 in 2008 and the highest since 1995) of U.S. children were living in families that had incomes below the poverty line (U.S. Census Bureau, 2012). As indicated in Figure 1.2, one study found that a higher percentage of U.S. children in poor families than in middle-income families were exposed to family turmoil, separation from a parent, violence, crowding, excessive noise, and poor housing (Evans & English, 2002). One study also revealed that the more years children spent living in poverty, the higher their physiological indices of stress (Evans & Kim, 2007).

The U.S. figure of 20.1 percent of children living in poverty is much higher than the rates in other industrialized nations. For example, Canada has a child poverty rate of 9 percent and Sweden has a rate of 2 percent.

In the United States, the national government, state governments, and city governments all play a role in influencing the well-being of children. When families fail or seriously endanger a child's well-being, governments often step in to help. At the national and state levels, policy makers have debated for decades whether helping poor parents ends up helping their children as well. Researchers are providing some answers by examining the effects of specific policies (Larson & Angus, 2011; Scales, Benson, & Roehlkepartain, 2011).

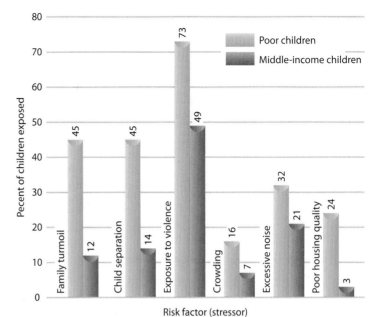

FIGURE **1.2**

EXPOSURE TO SIX STRESSORS AMONG POOR AND MIDDLE-INCOME CHILDREN. One study analyzed the exposure to six stressors among poor children and middle-income children (Evans & English, 2002). Poor children were much more likely to face each of these stressors.

Marian Wright Edelman, president of the Children's Defense Fun (shown here interacting with young children), has been a tireless advocate of children's rights and has been instrumental in calling attention to the needs of children. *What are some of these needs?*

social policy A government's course of action designed to promote the welfare of its citizens.

developmental **connection**

Socioeconomic Status. Growing up in poverty is linked to negative outcomes for children's language skills. Chapter 6, p. 195

For example, the Minnesota Family Investment Program (MFIP) was designed in the 1990s primarily to influence the behavior of adults—specifically, to move adults off the welfare rolls and into paid employment. A key element of the program was its guarantee that adults participating in the program would receive more income if they worked than if they did not. When the adults' income rose, how did that affect their children? A study of the effects of MFIP found that increases in the incomes of working poor parents were linked with benefits for their children (Gennetian & Miller, 2002). The children's achievement in school improved, and their behavior problems decreased. A current MFIP study is examining the influence of specific services on low-income families at risk for child maltreatment and other negative outcomes for children (Minnesota Family Investment Program, 2011).

Developmental psychologists and other researchers have examined the effects of many other government policies. They are seeking ways to help families living in poverty improve their well-being, and they have offered many suggestions for improving government policies (McLoyd & others, 2011; Phillips & Lowenstein, 2011).

Children are the legacy we leave for the time we will not live to see.

—Aristotle
Greek Philosopher, 4th Century B.C.

Review Connect Reflect

 LG1 Explain why it is important to study children's development, and identify five areas in which children's lives need to be improved.

Review

- Why is it important to study children's development?
- What are five aspects of children's development that need to be improved?

Connect

- How is the concept of resilience related to the story about Ted Kaczynski and Alice Walker at the beginning of the chapter?

Reflect *Your Own Personal Journey of Life*

- Imagine what your development as a child would have been like in a culture that offered fewer or distinctively different choices than your own. How might your development have been different if your family had been significantly richer or poorer than it was?

What Characterizes Development?

 LG2 Discuss processes, periods, cohort effects, and issues in development.

Biological, Cognitive, and Socioemotional Processes

Periods of Development

Age and Cohort Effects

Issues in Development

Ah! What would the world be to us
If the children were no more?
We should dread the desert behind us
Worse than the dark before.

—Henry Wadsworth Longfellow
American Poet, 19th Century

Each of us develops in certain ways like all other individuals, like some other individuals, and like no other individuals. Most of the time, our attention is directed to a person's uniqueness, but psychologists who study development are drawn to our shared characteristics as well as what makes us unique. As humans, we all have traveled some common paths. Each of us—Leonardo da Vinci, Joan of Arc, George Washington, Martin Luther King, Jr., and you—walked at about the age of 1, engaged in fantasy play as a young child, and became more independent as a youth. What shapes this common path of human development, and what are its milestones?

BIOLOGICAL, COGNITIVE, AND SOCIOEMOTIONAL PROCESSES

The pattern of human development is created by the interplay of several processes—biological, cognitive, and socioemotional. **Biological processes** produce changes in an individual's body. Genes inherited from parents, the development of the brain, height and weight gains, motor skills, and the hormonal changes of puberty all reflect the role of biological processes in development.

Cognitive processes refer to changes in an individual's thought, intelligence, and language. The tasks of watching a mobile swinging above a crib, putting together a two-word sentence, memorizing a poem, solving a math problem, and imagining what it would be like to be a movie star all involve cognitive processes.

Socioemotional processes involve changes in an individual's relationships with other people, changes in emotions, and changes in personality. An infant's smile in response to her mother's touch, a child's attack on a playmate, another's development of assertiveness, and an adolescent's joy at the senior prom all reflect socioemotional development.

Biological, cognitive, and socioemotional processes are inextricably intertwined (Diamond, Casey, & Munakata, 2011). Consider a baby smiling in response to a parent's touch. This response depends on biological processes (the physical nature of touch and responsiveness to it), cognitive processes (the ability to understand intentional acts), and socioemotional processes (the act of smiling often reflects a positive emotional feeling, and smiling helps to connect us in positive ways with other human beings). Nowhere is the connection across biological, cognitive, and socioemotional processes more obvious than in two rapidly emerging fields:

- *Developmental cognitive neuroscience,* which explores links between development, cognitive processes, and the brain (Johnson & de Haan, 2012)

- *Developmental social neuroscience,* which examines connections between socioemotional processes, development, and the brain (Bell, Greene, & Wolfe, 2010)

In many instances, biological, cognitive, and socioemotional processes are bidirectional. For example, biological processes can influence cognitive processes and vice versa. Thus, although usually we will study the different processes of development (biological, cognitive, and socioemotional) in separate locations, keep in mind that we are talking about the development of an integrated human child with a mind and body that are interdependent (see Figure 1.3). In many places throughout the book we will call attention to these connections.

PERIODS OF DEVELOPMENT

For the purposes of organization and understanding, a child's development is commonly described in terms of periods, which are given approximate age ranges. The most widely used classification of developmental periods describes a child's

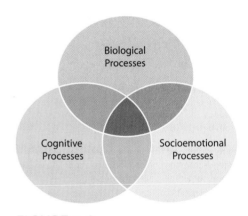

FIGURE **1.3**

CHANGES IN DEVELOPMENT ARE THE RESULT OF BIOLOGICAL, COGNITIVE, AND SOCIOEMOTIONAL PROCESSES. The processes interact as individuals develop.

biological processes Changes in an individual's body.

cognitive processes Changes in an individual's thought, intelligence, and language.

socioemotional processes Changes in an individual's relationships with other people, changes in emotions, and changes in personality.

"This is the path to adulthood. You're here."

© Robert Weber/The New Yorker Collection/
www.cartoonbank.com

development in terms of the following sequence: the prenatal period, infancy, early childhood, middle and late childhood, and adolescence.

The **prenatal period** is the time from conception to birth, roughly a nine-month period. During this amazing time, a single cell grows into an organism with a brain and behavioral capabilities.

Infancy is the developmental period that extends from birth to about 18 to 24 months of age. Infancy is a time of extreme dependence on adults. Many psychological activities are just beginning—the ability to speak, to coordinate sensations and physical actions, to think with symbols, and to imitate and learn from others.

Early childhood is the developmental period that extends from the end of infancy to about 5 or 6 years of age; sometimes this period is called the preschool years. During this time, young children learn to become more self-sufficient and to care for themselves; they develop school readiness skills (following instructions, identifying letters), and they spend many hours in play and with peers. First grade typically marks the end of this period.

Middle and late childhood is the developmental period that extends from about 6 to 11 years of age; sometimes this period is referred to as the elementary school years. Children master the fundamental skills of reading, writing, and arithmetic, and they are formally exposed to the larger world and its culture. Achievement becomes a more central theme of the child's world, and self-control increases.

Adolescence is the developmental period of transition from childhood to early adulthood, entered at approximately 10 to 12 years of age and ending at 18 to 22 years of age. Adolescence begins with rapid physical changes—dramatic gains in height and weight; changes in body contour; and the development of sexual characteristics such as enlargement of the breasts, development of pubic and facial hair, and deepening of the voice. The pursuit of independence and an identity are prominent features of this period of development. More and more time is spent outside the family. Thought becomes more abstract, idealistic, and logical.

Today, developmentalists do not suggest that change ends with adolescence (Schaie, 2011; Schaie & Willis, 2012). Instead, they describe development as a life-long process. However, the purpose of this text is to describe the changes in development that take place from conception through adolescence. All of these periods of development are produced by the interplay of biological, cognitive, and socio-emotional processes (see Figure 1.4).

AGE AND COHORT EFFECTS

A *cohort* is a group of people who are born at a similar point in history and share similar experiences as a result, such as living through the Vietnam War or growing up in the same city around the same time. These shared experiences may produce a range of differences among cohorts. For example, children and their parents who grew up during the Great Depression and World War II are likely to differ from their counterparts during the booming 1990s in their educational opportunities and economic status, in how they were raised, their attitudes and experiences related to gender, and their exposure to technology. In research on development, **cohort effects** are due to a person's time of birth, era, or generation but not to actual age.

In recent years, generations have been given labels by the popular culture. The most recent label is **Millennials,** the generation born after 1980 that is the first to come of age and enter emerging adulthood in the new millennium. Thus, today's children and most of their parents are Millennials. Two characteristics of Millennials stand out: (1) their ethnic diversity, and (2) their connection to technology (Pew Research Center, 2010).

As their ethnic diversity has increased in comparison with prior generations, many Millennial adolescents and emerging adults are more tolerant and open-minded

prenatal period The time from conception to birth.

infancy The developmental period that extends from birth to 18 to 24 months of age.

early childhood The developmental period that extends from the end of infancy to about 5 to 6 years of age; sometimes called the preschool years.

middle and late childhood The developmental period that extends from about 6 to 11 years of age; sometimes called the elementary school years.

adolescence The developmental period of transition from childhood to early adulthood, entered at approximately 10 to 12 years of age and ending at 18 to 22 years of age.

cohort effects Effects due to a person's time of birth, era, or generation but not to actual age.

Millennials The generation born after 1980, which is the first generation to come of age and enter emerging adulthood in the new millennium; members of this generation are characterized by their ethnic diversity and their connection to technology.

Periods of Development

Prenatal period   Infancy   Early childhood   Middle and late childhood   Adolescence

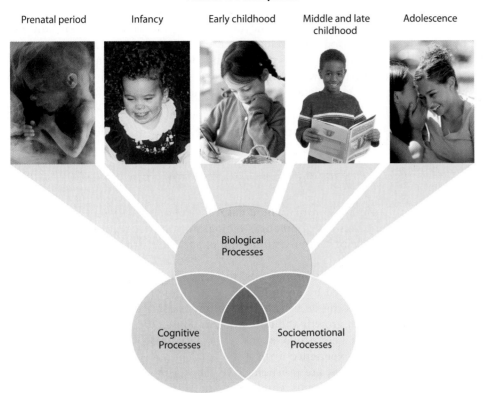

Processes of Development

FIGURE **1.4**

PROCESSES AND PERIODS OF DEVELOPMENT. Development moves through the prenatal, infancy, early childhood, middle and late childhood, and adolescent periods. These periods of development are the result of biological, cognitive, and socioemotional processes.

than their counterparts in older cohorts. One survey indicated that 60 percent of today's adolescents say their friends include someone from a different ethnic group (Teenage Research Unlimited, 2004).

Another major cohort change involving Millennials is the dramatic increase in their use of media and technology (Brown & Bobkowski, 2011; Rideout, Foehr, & Roberts, 2010). According to one analysis,

> They are history's first "always connected" generation. Steeped in digital technology and social media, they treat their multi-tasking hand-held gadgets almost like a body part—for better or worse. More than 8-in-10 say they sleep with a cell phone glowing by the bed, poised to disgorge texts, phone calls, e-mails, songs, news, videos, games, and wake-up jingles. But sometimes convenience yields to temptation. Nearly two-thirds admit to texting while driving. (Pew Research Center, 2010, p. 1)

We will have much more to say about technology in childhood and adolescence in Chapter 10, "Socioemotional Development in Early Childhood," and Chapter 16, "Socioemotional Development in Adolescence."

ISSUES IN DEVELOPMENT

Many questions about children's development remain unanswered. For example, what exactly drives the biological, cognitive, and socioemotional processes of development, and how do experiences during infancy influence middle childhood

developmental **connection**

Biological Processes. Can specific genes be linked to specific environmental experiences in influencing the child's development? Chapter 2, p. 60

How Would You...?

If you were an **educator,** how would you apply your understanding of the developmental influences of nature and nurture to create appropriate classroom strategies for students who display learning or behavioral problems?

Continuity

Discontinuity

FIGURE **1.5**

CONTINUITY AND DISCONTINUITY IN DEVELOPMENT. *Is our development like that of a seedling gradually growing into a giant oak? Or is it more like that of a caterpillar suddenly becoming a butterfly?*

or adolescence? Despite all of the knowledge that researchers have acquired, debate continues about the relative importance of factors that influence the developmental processes and about how the periods of development are related. The most important issues in the study of children's development include nature and nurture, continuity and discontinuity, and early and later experience.

Nature and Nurture The **nature-nurture issue** involves the debate about whether development is primarily influenced by nature or by nurture. Nature refers to an organism's biological inheritance, nurture to its environmental experiences. Almost no one today argues that development can be explained by nature alone or by nurture alone. But some ("nature" proponents) claim that the more important influence on development is biological inheritance, and others ("nurture" proponents) claim that environmental experiences are the more important influence.

According to the nature proponents, just as a sunflower grows in an orderly way—unless it is defeated by an unfriendly environment—so does a person. The range of environments can be vast, but evolutionary and genetic foundations produce commonalities in growth and development (Buss, 2012). We walk before we talk, speak one word before two words, grow rapidly in infancy and less so in early childhood, and experience a rush of sexual hormones in puberty. Extreme environments—those that are psychologically barren or hostile—can stunt development, but nature proponents emphasize the influence of tendencies that are genetically wired into humans (Mader, 2012).

By contrast, other psychologists emphasize the importance of nurture, or environmental experiences, to development (Russell, 2011). Experiences run the gamut from the individual's biological environment (nutrition, medical care, drugs, and physical accidents) to the social environment (family, peers, schools, community, media, and culture). For example, a child's diet can affect how tall the child grows and even how effectively the child can think and solve problems. Despite their genetic wiring, a child born and raised in a poor village in Bangladesh and a child in the suburbs of Denver are likely to have different skills, different ways of thinking about the world, and different ways of relating to people.

Continuity and Discontinuity Think about your own development for a moment. Did you become the person you are gradually, like the seedling that slowly, cumulatively grows into a giant oak? Or did you experience sudden, distinct changes, like the caterpillar that changes into a butterfly (see Figure 1.5)?

The **continuity-discontinuity issue** focuses on the extent to which development involves gradual, cumulative change (continuity) or distinct stages (discontinuity). For the most part, developmentalists who emphasize nurture usually describe development as a gradual, continuous process, like the seedling's growth into an oak. Those who emphasize nature often describe development as a series of distinct stages, like the change from caterpillar to butterfly.

Consider continuity first. As the oak grows from seedling to giant oak, it becomes more oak—its development is continuous. Similarly, a child's first word, though seemingly an abrupt, discontinuous event, is actually the result of weeks and months of growth and practice. Puberty, another seemingly abrupt, discontinuous occurrence, is actually a gradual process occurring over several years.

Viewed in terms of discontinuity, each person is described as passing through a sequence of stages in which change is qualitatively rather than quantitatively different. As the caterpillar changes to a butterfly, it is not more caterpillar but an altogether different kind of organism—its development is discontinuous. Similarly, at some point a child moves from not being able to think abstractly about the world to being able to do so. This change is a qualitative, discontinuous change in development, not a quantitative, continuous change.

Early and Later Experience The **early-later experience issue** focuses on the degree to which early experiences (especially in infancy) or later experiences are the key determinants of the child's development. That is, if infants experience harmful circumstances, can those experiences be overcome by later, positive ones? Or are the early experiences so critical—possibly because they are the infant's first, prototypical experiences—that their influence cannot be overridden by a later, better environment? To those who emphasize early experiences, life is an unbroken trail on which a psychological quality can be traced back to its origin (Kagan, 1992, 2000). In contrast, to those who emphasize later experiences, development is like a river, continually ebbing and flowing.

What is the nature of the early and later experience issue?

The early-later experience issue has a long history and continues to be hotly debated among developmentalists (Kagan, 2010; Thompson, 2011a; Schaie, 2011). The ancient Greek philosopher Plato was sure that infants who were rocked frequently become better athletes. Nineteenth-century New England ministers told parents in Sunday afternoon sermons that the way they handled their infants would determine their children's later character. Some developmentalists argue that, unless infants experience warm, nurturing care during the first year or so of life, their development will never quite be optimal (Cassidy & others, 2011).

In contrast, later-experience advocates argue that children are malleable throughout development and that later sensitive caregiving is just as important as earlier sensitive caregiving (Fingerman & Birditt, 2011). A number of experts on life-span development stress that too little attention has been given to later experiences in development (Park & Bischof, 2011; Schaie & Willis, 2012). They accept that early experiences are important contributors to development but hold them to be no more important than later experiences. Jerome Kagan (2000, 2010) points out that even children who show the qualities of an inhibited temperament, which is linked to heredity, have the capacity to change their behavior. In his research, almost one-third of a group of children who had an inhibited temperament at 2 years of age were not unusually shy or fearful when they were 4 years of age (Kagan & Snidman, 1991).

People in Western cultures, especially those influenced by Freudian theory, have tended to support the idea that early experiences are more important than later experiences (Lamb & Sternberg, 1992). The majority of people in the world do not share this belief. For example, people in many Asian countries believe that experiences occurring after about 6 to 7 years of age are more important to development than are earlier experiences. This stance stems from the long-standing belief in Eastern cultures that children's reasoning skills begin to develop in important ways during middle childhood.

Evaluating the Developmental Issues Most developmentalists recognize that it is unwise to take an extreme position on the issues of nature and nurture, continuity and discontinuity, and early and later experiences. Development is not all nature or all nurture, not all continuity or all discontinuity, and not all early or later experiences. Nature and nurture, continuity and discontinuity, and early and later experiences all play a part in development through the human life span. Along with this consensus, there is still spirited debate about how strongly development is influenced by each of these factors (Posada & Kaloustian, 2010; Schaie & Willis, 2012). Are girls less likely to do well in math mostly because of inherited characteristics or because of society's expectations and because of how girls are raised? Can enriched experiences during adolescence remove deficits resulting from poverty, neglect, and poor schooling during childhood? The answers also have a bearing on social policy decisions about children and adolescents—and consequently on each of our lives.

nature-nurture issue The issue regarding whether development is primarily influenced by nature or nurture. The "nature" proponents claim that biological inheritance is the more important influence on development; the "nurture" proponents assert that environmental experiences are more important.

continuity-discontinuity issue The issue regarding whether development involves gradual, cumulative change (continuity) or distinct stages (discontinuity).

early-later experience issue The issue of the degree to which early experiences (especially infancy) or later experiences are the key determinants of the child's development.

How Is Child Development a Science?

LG3 Summarize why research is important in child development, the main theories of child development, and research methods, designs, and challenges.

- The Importance of Research
- Theories of Child Development
- Research Methods for Collecting Data
- Research Designs
- Research Challenges

This section introduces the theories and methods that are the foundation of the science of child development. We consider why research is important in understanding children's development and examine the main theories of children's development, as well as the main methods and research designs that researchers use. At the end of the section, we explore some of the ethical challenges researchers face and the biases they must guard against to protect the integrity of their results and respect the rights of the participants in their studies.

Science refines everyday thinking.

—ALBERT EINSTEIN
German-born American Physicist, 20th Century

THE IMPORTANCE OF RESEARCH

Some individuals have difficulty thinking of child development as a science like physics, chemistry, and biology. Can a discipline that studies how parents nurture children, how peers interact, what are the developmental changes in children's thinking, and whether watching TV hour after hour is linked with being overweight be equated with disciplines that study the molecular structure of a compound and how gravity works? Is child development really a science? The answer is yes. Science is defined not by what it investigates, but by how it investigates. Whether you're studying photosynthesis, butterflies, Saturn's moons, or children's development, it is the way you study that makes the approach scientific or not.

Scientific research is objective, systematic, and testable. It reduces the likelihood that information will be based on personal beliefs, opinions, and feelings (Jackson, 2011; Stangor, 2011). Scientific research is based on the **scientific method,** an approach that can be used to discover accurate information. It includes these steps: conceptualize the problem, collect data, draw conclusions, and revise research conclusions and theory.

The first step, *conceptualizing a problem*, involves identifying the problem. At a general level, this may not seem like a difficult task. However, researchers must go beyond a general description of the problem by isolating, analyzing, narrowing, and

scientific method An approach that can be used to obtain accurate information. It includes these steps: (1) conceptualize the problem, (2) collect data, (3) draw conclusions, and (4) revise research conclusions and theory.

focusing more specifically on what they want to study. For example, a team of researchers decides to study ways to improve the achievement of children from impoverished backgrounds. Perhaps they choose to examine whether mentoring that involves sustained support, guidance, and concrete assistance can improve the children's academic performance. At this point, even more narrowing and focusing takes place. For instance, what specific strategies should the mentors use? How often will they see the children? How long will the mentoring program last? What aspects of the children's achievement will be assessed?

As part of the first step in formulating a problem to study, researchers often *draw on theories and develop a hypothesis*. A **theory** is an interrelated, coherent set of ideas that helps to explain and to make predictions. For example, a theory on mentoring might attempt to explain and predict why sustained support, guidance, and concrete experience make a difference in the lives of children from impoverished backgrounds. The theory might focus on children's opportunities to model the behavior and strategies of mentors, or it might focus on the effects of individual attention, which might be missing in the children's lives. A hypothesis is a specific testable assumption or prediction. A **hypothesis** is often written as an if-then statement. In our example, a sample hypothesis might be: If children from impoverished backgrounds are given individual attention by mentors, the children will spend more time studying and make higher grades. Testing a hypothesis can inform researchers whether or not a theory may be accurate.

The second step in the scientific method is to *collect information (data)*. In the study of mentoring, the researchers might decide to conduct the mentoring program for six months. Their data might consist of classroom observations, teachers' ratings, and achievement tests given to the mentored children before the mentoring began and at the end of six months of mentoring.

Once data have been collected, child development researchers use *statistical procedures* to understand the meaning of the data (Spatz, 2012). Then they try to *draw conclusions*. In this third step, statistics help to determine whether or not the researchers' observations are due to chance.

After data have been collected and analyzed, researchers compare their findings with those of other researchers on the same topic. The final step in the scientific method is *revising research conclusions and theory*.

THEORIES OF CHILD DEVELOPMENT

A wide range of theories makes understanding children's development a challenging undertaking. Just when you think one theory has the most helpful explanation of children's development, another theory crops up and makes you rethink your earlier conclusion. To keep from getting frustrated, remember that child development is a complex, multifaceted topic. No single theory has been able to account for all aspects of child development. Each theory contributes an important piece to the child development puzzle. Although the theories sometimes disagree, much of their information is complementary rather than contradictory. Together they let us see the total landscape of development in all its richness.

We briefly explore five major theoretical perspectives on development: psychoanalytic, cognitive, behavioral and social cognitive, ethological, and ecological. As you will see, these theoretical approaches examine in varying degrees the three major processes involved in children's development: biological, cognitive, and socioemotional.

Psychoanalytic Theories **Psychoanalytic theories** describe development as primarily unconscious (beyond awareness) and heavily colored by emotion. Psychoanalytic theorists emphasize that behavior is merely a surface characteristic and that a true understanding of development requires analyzing the symbolic meanings of behavior and the deep inner workings of the mind. Psychoanalytic theorists also stress that early experiences with parents extensively shape development. These characteristics are highlighted in the psychoanalytic theory of Sigmund Freud (1856–1939).

How Would You...?
If you were a **health-care professional,** how would you apply the scientific method to examine developmental concerns such as adolescent pregnancy?

theory An interrelated, coherent set of ideas that helps to explain and make predictions.

hypothesis A specific assumption or prediction that can be tested to determine its accuracy.

psychoanalytic theories Describe development as primarily unconscious and heavily colored by emotion. Behavior is merely a surface characteristic, and the symbolic workings of the mind have to be analyzed to understand behavior. Early experiences with parents are emphasized.

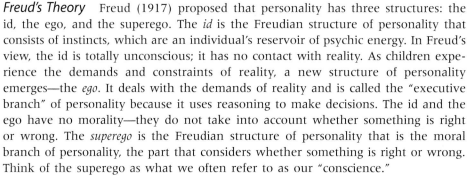

Oral Stage	Anal Stage	Phallic Stage	Latency Stage	Genital Stage
Infant's pleasure centers on the mouth.	Child's pleasure focuses on the anus.	Child's pleasure focuses on the genitals.	Child represses sexual interest and develops social and intellectual skills.	A time of sexual reawakening; source of sexual pleasure becomes someone outside the family.
Birth to 1½ Years	**1½ to 3 Years**	**3 to 6 Years**	**6 Years to Puberty**	**Puberty Onward**

FIGURE **1.6**
FREUDIAN STAGES

Sigmund Freud, the pioneering architect of psychoanalytic theory. *What are some characteristics of Freud's theory?*

Freud's Theory   Freud (1917) proposed that personality has three structures: the id, the ego, and the superego. The *id* is the Freudian structure of personality that consists of instincts, which are an individual's reservoir of psychic energy. In Freud's view, the id is totally unconscious; it has no contact with reality. As children experience the demands and constraints of reality, a new structure of personality emerges—the *ego*. It deals with the demands of reality and is called the "executive branch" of personality because it uses reasoning to make decisions. The id and the ego have no morality—they do not take into account whether something is right or wrong. The *superego* is the Freudian structure of personality that is the moral branch of personality, the part that considers whether something is right or wrong. Think of the superego as what we often refer to as our "conscience."

As Freud listened to, probed, and analyzed his patients, he became convinced that their problems were the result of experiences early in life. He thought that as children grow up, their focus of pleasure and sexual impulses shifts from the mouth to the anus and eventually to the genitals. As a result, we go through five stages of psychosexual development: oral, anal, phallic, latency, and genital (see Figure 1.6). Our adult personality, Freud claimed, is determined by the way we resolve conflicts between sources of pleasure at each stage and the demands of reality.

Freud's theory has been significantly revised by a number of psychoanalytic theorists. Many contemporary psychoanalytic theorists maintain that Freud overemphasized sexual instincts; they place more emphasis on cultural experiences as determinants of an individual's development. Unconscious thought remains a central theme, but most contemporary psychoanalysts stress that conscious thought plays a greater role than Freud envisioned. Next, we outline the ideas of an important revisionist of Freud's ideas—Erik Erikson.

Erik Erikson with his wife, Joan, an artist. Erikson generated one of the most important developmental theories of the twentieth century. *Which stage of Erikson's theory are you in? Does Erikson's description of this stage characterize you?*

Erikson's Psychosocial Theory   Erik Erikson (1902–1994) recognized Freud's contributions but argued that Freud misjudged some important dimensions of human development. For one thing, Erikson (1950, 1968) said we develop in psychosocial stages rather than in psychosexual stages, as Freud maintained. According to Freud, the primary motivation for human behavior is sexual in nature; according to Erikson, it is social and reflects a desire to affiliate with other people. According to Freud, our basic personality is shaped in the first five years of life; according to Erikson, developmental change occurs throughout the life span. Thus, in terms of the early versus later experience issue described earlier in this chapter, Freud argued that early experience is far more important than later experiences, whereas Erikson emphasized the importance of both early and later experiences.

In **Erikson's theory,** eight stages of development unfold as we go through life (see Figure 1.7). At each stage, a unique developmental task confronts individuals with a crisis that must be resolved. According to Erikson, this crisis is not a catastrophe but a turning point marked by both increased vulnerability and enhanced potential. The more successfully an individual resolves the crises, the healthier his or her development will be.

Trust versus mistrust is Erikson's first psychosocial stage, which is experienced in the first year of life. Trust in infancy sets the stage for a lifelong expectation that the world will be a good and pleasant place to live.

After gaining trust in their caregivers, infants begin to discover that their behavior is their own. They start to assert their sense of independence, or autonomy. If infants are restrained too much or punished too harshly, they are likely to develop a sense of shame and doubt. This is Erikson's second stage of development, *autonomy versus shame and doubt*, which occurs in late infancy and toddlerhood (1 to 3 years of age).

Initiative versus guilt, Erikson's third stage of development, occurs during the preschool years. As preschool children encounter a widening social world, they face new challenges that require active, purposeful behavior. Children are asked to assume responsibility for their bodies, their behavior, their toys, and their pets—and they take initiative. Feelings of guilt may arise, though, if the child is irresponsible and is made to feel too anxious.

Industry versus inferiority is Erikson's fourth developmental stage, occurring approximately in the elementary school years. Children's initiative brings them in contact with a wealth of new experiences. As they move into middle and late childhood, they direct their energy toward mastering knowledge and intellectual skills. At no other time is the child more enthusiastic about learning than at the end of early childhood's period of expansive imagination. The danger is that the child can develop a sense of inferiority—feeling incompetent and unproductive.

During the adolescent years, individuals are faced with finding out who they are, what they are all about, and where they are going in life. This is Erikson's fifth developmental stage, *identity versus identity confusion*. Adolescents are confronted with many new roles and adult statuses—vocational and romantic, for example. If they explore roles in a healthy manner and arrive at a positive path to follow in life, then they achieve a positive identity. If parents push an identity on adolescents, and if adolescents do not adequately explore many roles and define a positive future path, then identity confusion reigns.

Intimacy versus isolation is Erikson's sixth developmental stage, which individuals experience during the early adulthood years. At this time, individuals face the developmental task of forming intimate relationships. Erikson describes intimacy as finding oneself yet losing oneself in another. If the young adult forms healthy friendships and an intimate relationship with another, intimacy will be achieved; if not, isolation will result.

Generativity versus stagnation, Erikson's seventh developmental stage, occurs during middle adulthood. By generativity Erikson means primarily a concern for helping the younger generation to develop and lead useful lives. The feeling of having done nothing to help the next generation is stagnation.

Integrity versus despair is Erikson's eighth and final stage of development, which individuals experience in late adulthood. During this stage, a person reflects on the past. Through many different routes, the person may have developed a positive outlook in most or all of the previous stages of development. If so, the person's review of his or her life will reveal a life well spent, and the person will feel a sense of satisfaction—integrity will be achieved. If the person had resolved many of the earlier stages negatively, the retrospective glances likely will yield doubt or gloom—the despair Erikson described.

Each of Erikson's stages has a "positive" pole, such as trust, and a "negative" pole, such as mistrust. In the healthy solution to the crisis of each stage, the positive pole dominates, but Erikson maintained that some exposure or commitment to the negative side is sometimes inevitable. For example, learning to trust is an important outcome of Erikson's first stage, but you cannot trust all people under all circumstances and survive. We discuss Erikson's theory again in the chapters on socioemotional development. In the *Caring Connections* interlude, you can read about some effective strategies for improving the lives of children based on Erikson's view.

Erikson's Stages	Developmental Period
Integrity versus despair	Late adulthood (60s onward)
Generativity versus stagnation	Middle adulthood (40s, 50s)
Intimacy versus isolation	Early adulthood (20s, 30s)
Identity versus identity confusion	Adolescence (10 to 20 years)
Industry versus inferiority	Middle and late childhood (elementary school years, 6 years to puberty)
Initiative versus guilt	Early childhood (preschool years, 3 to 5 years)
Autonomy versus shame and doubt	Infancy (1 to 3 years)
Trust versus mistrust	Infancy (first year)

FIGURE **1.7**
ERIKSON'S EIGHT LIFE-SPAN STAGES

Erikson's theory Includes eight stages of human development. Each stage consists of a unique developmental task that confronts individuals with a crisis that must be resolved.

Strategies for Parenting, Educating, and Interacting with Children Based on Erikson's Theory

Parents, child-care specialists, teachers, counselors, youth workers, and other adults can adopt positive strategies for interacting with children based on Erikson's theory. These strategies are described below.

1. ***Nurture infants and develop their trust, then encourage and monitor toddlers' autonomy.*** Because infants depend on others to meet their needs, it is critical for caregivers to consistently provide positive, attentive care for infants. Infants who experience consistently positive care feel safe and secure, sensing that people are reliable and loving, which leads them to develop trust in the world. Caregivers who neglect or abuse infants are likely to have infants who develop a sense of mistrust in their world. Now that they have developed a sense of trust in their world, as infants move into the toddler years it is important that they are given the freedom to explore it. Toddlers whose caregivers are too restrictive or harsh are likely to develop shame and doubt, sensing that they can't adequately do things on their own. As toddlers gain more independence, caregivers need to monitor their exploration and curiosity because there are many things that can harm them, such as running into the street and touching a hot stove.

2. ***Encourage initiative in young children.*** Children should be given a great deal of freedom to explore their world. They should be allowed to choose some of the activities they engage in. If their requests for doing certain activities are reasonable, the requests should be honored. Children need to be provided exciting materials that will stimulate their imagination. Young children at this stage love to play. It not only benefits their socioemotional development but also is an important medium for their cognitive growth. Criticism should be kept to a minimum so that children will not develop high levels of guilt and anxiety. Young children are going to make lots of mistakes and have lots of spills. They need good models far more than harsh critics. Structure their activities and environment for success rather than failure by giving them developmentally appropriate tasks. For example, young children get frustrated when they have to sit for long periods of time and do academic paper-and-pencil tasks.

3. ***Promote industry in elementary school children.*** It was Erikson's hope that teachers could provide an atmosphere in which children would become passionate about learning. In Erikson's words, teachers should mildly but firmly coerce children into the adventure of finding out that they can learn to accomplish things that they themselves would never have thought they could do. In elementary school, children thirst to know. Most arrive at elementary school steeped in curiosity and a motivation to master tasks. In Erikson's view, it is important for teachers to nourish this motivation for mastery and curiosity. Teachers need to challenge students but not overwhelm them; be firm in requiring students to be productive without being overly critical; and especially be tolerant of honest mistakes and make sure that every student has opportunities for many successes.

4. ***Stimulate identity exploration in adolescence.*** It is important to recognize that the adolescent's identity is multidimensional. Aspects include vocational goals; intellectual achievement; and interests in hobbies, sports, music, and other areas. Adolescents can be asked to write essays about such dimensions, exploring who they are and what they want to do with their lives. They should be encouraged to think independently and to freely express their views, which stimulates their self-exploration. Adolescents can also be encouraged to listen to debates on political and ideological issues, which stimulates them to examine different perspectives. Another good strategy is to encourage adolescents to talk with a school counselor about career options as well as other aspects of their identity. Teachers can have people from different careers come and talk about their work with students regardless of grade level.

What are some applications of Erikson's theory for effective parenting?

Evaluating the Psychoanalytic Theories   The contributions of psychoanalytic theories include these ideas: (1) early experiences play an important part in development; (2) family relationships are a central aspect of development; (3) personality can be better understood if it is examined developmentally; (4) activities of the mind are not entirely conscious—unconscious aspects need to be considered; and (5) in Erikson's theory, changes take place in adulthood as well as in childhood.

Sensorimotor Stage	**Preoperational Stage**	**Concrete Operational Stage**	**Formal Operational Stage**
The infant constructs an understanding of the world by coordinating sensory experiences with physical actions. An infant progresses from reflexive, instinctual action at birth to the beginning of symbolic thought toward the end of the stage.	The child begins to represent the world with words and images. These words and images reflect increased symbolic thinking and go beyond the connection of sensory information and physical action.	The child can now reason logically about concrete events and classify objects into different sets.	The adolescent reasons in more abstract, idealistic, and logical ways.
Birth to 2 Years of Age	**2 to 7 Years of Age**	**7 to 11 Years of Age**	**11 Years of Age Through Adulthood**

FIGURE **1.8**
PIAGET'S FOUR STAGES OF COGNITIVE DEVELOPMENT

Psychoanalytic theories have been criticized for several reasons. First, the main concepts of psychoanalytic theories are difficult to test scientifically. Second, much of the data used to support psychoanalytic theories come from individuals' reconstruction of the past, often the distant past, and are of unknown accuracy. Third, the sexual underpinnings of development are given too much importance (especially in Freud's theory), and the unconscious mind is given too much credit for influencing development. In addition, psychoanalytic theories (especially in Freud's theory) present an image of humans that is too negative and are culture- and gender-biased, treating Western culture and males as the measure for evaluating everyone.

Cognitive Theories   Whereas psychoanalytic theories stress the importance of the unconscious, cognitive theories emphasize conscious thoughts. Three important cognitive theories are Piaget's cognitive developmental theory, Vygotsky's sociocultural cognitive theory, and information-processing theory.

Piaget's Cognitive Developmental Theory   **Piaget's theory** states that children actively construct their understanding of the world and go through four stages of cognitive development. Two processes underlie the four stages of development in Piaget's theory: organization and adaptation. To make sense of our world, we organize our experiences. For example, we separate important ideas from less important ideas, and we connect one idea to another. In addition to organizing our observations and experiences, we *adapt*, adjusting to new environmental demands (Miller, 2011).

Piaget (1896–1980) also proposed that we go through four stages in understanding the world (see Figure 1.8). Each stage is age-related and consists of a distinct way of thinking, a different way of understanding the world. Thus, according to Piaget (1954), the child's cognition is qualitatively different in one stage compared with another. What are Piaget's four stages of cognitive development like?

The *sensorimotor stage*, which lasts from birth to about 2 years of age, is the first Piagetian stage. In this stage, infants construct an understanding of the world by

How Would You...?
If you were a **human development and family studies professional,** how would you apply psychoanalytic theory to advise the foster family of a newly placed child who reports no history of abuse yet shows considerable violent behavior?

Piaget's theory States that children actively construct their understanding of the world and go through four stages of cognitive development.

coordinating sensory experiences (such as seeing and hearing) with physical, motoric actions—hence the term *sensorimotor*.

The *preoperational stage*, which lasts from approximately 2 to 7 years of age, is Piaget's second stage. In this stage, children begin to go beyond simply connecting sensory information with physical action and represent the world with words, images, and drawings. However, according to Piaget, preschool children still lack the ability to perform what he calls operations, which are internalized mental actions that allow children to do mentally what they previously could only do physically. For example, if you imagine putting two sticks together to see whether they would be as long as another stick, without actually moving the sticks, you are performing a concrete operation.

The *concrete operational stage*, which lasts from approximately 7 to 11 years of age, is the third Piagetian stage. In this stage, children can perform operations that involve objects, and they can reason logically as long as reasoning can be applied to specific or concrete examples. For example, concrete operational thinkers understand that two rows of four nickels have the same number of nickels regardless of how far apart the nickels in the row are spaced. However, concrete operational thinkers cannot imagine the steps necessary to complete an algebraic equation, which is too abstract for thinking at this stage of development.

The *formal operational stage*, which appears between the ages of 11 and 15 and continues through adulthood, is Piaget's fourth and final stage. In this stage, individuals move beyond concrete experiences and think in abstract and more logical terms. As part of thinking more abstractly, adolescents develop images of ideal circumstances. They might think about what an ideal parent is like and compare their parents to this ideal standard. They begin to entertain possibilities for the future and are fascinated with what they can be. In solving problems, they become more systematic, developing hypotheses about why something is happening the way it is and then testing these hypotheses.

In sum, this brief introduction to Piaget's theory that children's cognitive development goes through four stages is provided here, along with other theories, to give you a broad understanding. Later in the text, when we study cognitive development in infancy, early childhood, middle and late childhood, and adolescence, we return to Piaget and examine his theory in more depth.

Vygotsky's Sociocultural Cognitive Theory   Like Piaget, the Russian developmentalist Lev Vygotsky (1896–1934) said that children actively construct their knowledge. Unlike Piaget, Vygotsky (1962) did not propose that cognitive development occurs in stages, and he gave social interaction and culture far more important roles in cognitive development than Piaget did. **Vygotsky's theory** is a sociocultural cognitive theory that emphasizes how culture and social interaction guide cognitive development.

Vygotsky portrayed the child's development as inseparable from social and cultural activities (Daniels, 2011). He argued that development of memory, attention, and reasoning involves learning to use the inventions of society, such as language, mathematical systems, and memory strategies. Thus in one culture, children might learn to count with the help of a computer; in another, they might learn by using beads. According to Vygotsky, children's social interaction with more-skilled adults and peers is indispensable to their cognitive development. Through this interaction, they learn to use the tools that will help them adapt and be successful in their culture. For example, if you regularly help a child learn how to read, you not only advance a child's reading skills but also communicate to the child that reading is an important activity in his or her culture.

Vygotsky's theory has stimulated considerable interest in the view that knowledge is situated and collaborative (Parke & Clarke-Stewart, 2011). In this view,

Jean Piaget, the famous Swiss developmental psychologist, changed the way we think about the development of children's minds. *What are some key ideas in Piaget's theory?*

developmental **connection**

Cognitive Theory. We owe to Piaget the entire field of children's cognitive development, but a number of criticisms of his theory have been made. Chapter 12, p. 355

Vygotsky's theory A sociocultural cognitive theory that emphasizes how culture and social interaction guide cognitive development.

knowledge is not generated from within the individual but rather is constructed through interaction with other people and objects in the culture, such as books. This suggests that knowledge can best be advanced through interaction with others in cooperative activities.

Vygotsky's theory, like Piaget's, remained virtually unknown to American psychologists until the 1960s, but eventually both became influential among educators as well as psychologists. We examine ideas about learning and teaching that are based on Vygotsky's theory when we study cognitive development in early childhood.

The Information-Processing Theory Early computers may be the best candidates for the title of "founding fathers" of information-processing theory. Although many factors stimulated the growth of this theory, none was more important than the computer. Psychologists began to wonder if the logical operations carried out by computers might tell us something about how the human mind works. They drew analogies between a computer's hardware and the brain and between computer software and cognition.

This line of thinking helped to generate **information-processing theory,** which emphasizes that individuals manipulate information, monitor it, and strategize about it. Unlike Piaget's theory, but like Vygotsky's theory, information-processing theory does not describe development as stage-like. Instead, according to this theory, individuals develop a gradually increasing capacity for processing information, which allows them to acquire increasingly complex knowledge and skills (Bjorklund, 2012; Halford & Andrews, 2011; Sternberg & Sternberg, 2012).

Robert Siegler (2006, 2007, 2011a, b), a leading expert on children's information processing, states that thinking is information processing. In other words, when individuals perceive, encode, represent, store, and retrieve information, they are thinking. Siegler emphasizes that an important aspect of development is learning good strategies for processing information. For example, becoming a better reader might involve learning to monitor the key themes of the material being read.

Evaluating the Cognitive Theories The primary contributions of cognitive theories are that (1) they present a positive view of development, emphasizing conscious thinking; (2) they emphasize the individual's active construction of understanding (especially Piaget's and Vygotsky's theories); (3) Piaget's and Vygotsky's theories underscore the importance of examining developmental changes in children's thinking; and (4) information-processing theory offers detailed descriptions of cognitive processes.

There are several criticisms of cognitive theories. First, Piaget's stages are not as uniform as he theorized. Piaget also underestimated the cognitive skills of infants and overestimated the cognitive skills of adolescents. Second, the cognitive theories do not give adequate attention to individual variations in cognitive development. Third, information-processing theory does not provide an adequate description of developmental changes in cognition. In addition, psychoanalytic theorists argue that the cognitive theories do not give enough credit to unconscious thought.

Behavioral and Social Cognitive Theories In the early twentieth century, as Freud was interpreting patients' unconscious minds through their early childhood experiences, Ivan Pavlov and John B. Watson were conducting detailed observations of behavior in controlled laboratory settings. Their work provided the foundations of *behaviorism,* which essentially holds that we can study scientifically only what can be directly observed and measured. Out of the behavioral tradition grew the belief that development is observable behavior that can be learned through experience with the environment (Miltenberger, 2012). In terms of the continuity-discontinuity issue discussed earlier in this chapter, the behavioral and social cognitive theories emphasize continuity in development and argue that development does not occur in stage-like fashion. The three versions of the behavioral and social cognitive theories that we explore are Pavlov's classical conditioning, Skinner's operant conditioning, and Bandura's social cognitive theory.

There is considerable interest today in Lev Vygotsky's sociocultural cognitive theory of child development. *What were Vygotsky's basic ideas about children's development?*

information-processing theory Emphasizes that individuals manipulate information, monitor it, and strategize about it. Central to this theory are the processes of memory and thinking.

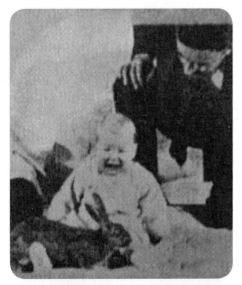

In 1920, Watson and Rayner conditioned 11-month-old Albert to fear a white rat by pairing the rat with a loud noise. When little Albert was subsequently presented with other stimuli similar to the white rat, such as the rabbit shown here with little Albert, he was afraid of them, too. This illustrates the principle of stimulus generalization in classical conditioning.

B. F. Skinner was a tinkerer who liked to make new gadgets. The younger of his two daughters, Deborah, was raised in Skinner's enclosed Air-Crib, which he invented because he wanted to control her environment completely. The Air-Crib was sound-proofed and temperature-controlled. Debbie, shown here as a child with her parents, is currently a successful artist, is married, and lives in London. *What do you think about Skinner's Air-Crib?*

social cognitive theory The view of psychologists who emphasize behavior, environment, and cognition as the key factors in development.

Pavlov's Classical Conditioning   In the early 1900s, the Russian physiologist Ivan Pavlov (1927) knew that dogs innately salivate when they taste food. He became curious when he observed that dogs salivate to various sights and sounds before eating their food. For example, when an individual paired the ringing of a bell with the food, the bell ringing subsequently elicited salivation from the dogs when it was presented by itself. With this experiment, Pavlov discovered the principle of *classical conditioning*, in which a neutral stimulus (in our example, ringing a bell) acquires the ability to produce a response originally produced by another stimulus (in our example, food).

In the early twentieth century, John Watson demonstrated that classical conditioning occurs in humans. He showed an infant named Albert a white rat to see if he was afraid of it. He was not. As Albert played with the rat, a loud noise was sounded behind his head. As you might imagine, the noise caused little Albert to cry. After several pairings of the loud noise and the white rat, Albert began to cry at the sight of the rat even when the noise was not sounded (Watson & Rayner, 1920). Albert had been classically conditioned to fear the rat. Similarly, many of our fears may result from classical conditioning: Fear of the dentist may be learned from a painful experience, fear of driving from being in an automobile accident, fear of heights from falling off a high chair when we were infants, and fear of dogs from being bitten.

Skinner's Operant Conditioning   Classical conditioning may explain how we develop many involuntary responses such as fears, but B. F. Skinner argued that a second type of conditioning accounts for the development of other types of behavior. According to Skinner (1938), through *operant conditioning* the consequences of a behavior produce changes in the probability of the behavior's occurrence. A behavior followed by a rewarding stimulus is more likely to recur, whereas a behavior followed by a punishing stimulus is less likely to recur. For example, when a person smiles at a child after the child has done something, the child is more likely to engage in the activity than if the person gives the child a nasty look.

According to Skinner, such rewards and punishments shape development. For example, Skinner's approach argues that shy people learned to be shy as a result of experiences they had while growing up. It follows that modifications in an environment can help a shy person become more socially oriented. Also, for Skinner the key aspect of development is behavior, not thoughts and feelings. He emphasized that development consists of the pattern of behavioral changes that are brought about by rewards and punishments.

Bandura's Social Cognitive Theory   Some psychologists agree with the behaviorists' notion that development is learned and is influenced strongly by environmental interactions. However, unlike Skinner, they argue that cognition is also important in understanding development. **Social cognitive theory** holds that behavior, environment, and cognition are the key factors in development.

American psychologist Albert Bandura (1925–) is the leading architect of social cognitive theory. Bandura (2001, 2007, 2010a, b) emphasizes that cognitive processes have important links with the environment and behavior. His early research program focused heavily on *observational learning* (also called *imitation*, or *modeling*), which is learning that occurs through observing what others do. For example, a young boy might observe his father yelling in anger and treating other people with hostility; with his peers, the young boy later acts very aggressively, showing the same characteristics as his father's behavior. A girl might adopt the dominant and sarcastic style of her teacher, saying to her younger brother, "You are so slow. How can you do this work so slowly?" Social cognitive theorists stress that people acquire a wide range of behaviors, thoughts, and feelings through observing others' behavior and that these observations play important roles in children's development.

What is cognitive about observational learning, in Bandura's view? He proposes that people cognitively represent the behavior of others and then sometimes adopt this behavior themselves.

Bandura's (2001, 2007, 2010a, b) most recent model of learning and development includes three elements: behavior, the person/cognition, and the environment. An individual's confidence that he or she can control his or her success is an example of a person factor; strategies are an example of a cognitive factor. As shown in Figure 1.9, behavior, person/cognitive, and environmental factors operate interactively. Behavior can influence person factors and vice versa. Cognitive activities can influence the environment, the environment can change the person's cognition, and so on.

Evaluating the Behavioral and Social Cognitive Theories Contributions of the behavioral and social cognitive theories include (1) their emphasis on the importance of scientific research; (2) their focus on environmental determinants of behavior; (3) the identification and explanation of observational learning (by Bandura); and (4) the inclusion of person/cognitive factors (in social cognitive theory).

Criticisms of the behavioral and social cognitive theories include the objections that they give (1) too little emphasis to cognition (in Pavlov's and Skinner's theories); (2) too much emphasis to environmental determinants; (3) inadequate attention to developmental changes; and (4) inadequate recognition to human spontaneity and creativity.

Behavioral and social cognitive theories emphasize the importance of environmental experiences in human development. Next we turn our attention to a theory that underscores the importance of the biological foundations of development—ethological theory.

Albert Bandura has been one of the leading architects of social cognitive theory. *What is the nature of his theory?*

Ethological Theory American developmental psychologists began to pay attention to the biological bases of development thanks to the work of European zoologists who pioneered the field of ethology. **Ethology** stresses that behavior is strongly influenced by biology, is tied to evolution, and is characterized by critical or sensitive periods. These are specific time frames during which, according to ethologists, the presence or absence of certain experiences has a long-lasting influence on individuals.

European zoologist Konrad Lorenz (1903–1989) helped bring ethology to prominence. In his best-known experiment, Lorenz (1965) studied the behavior of greylag geese, which will follow their mother as soon as they hatch.

In a remarkable set of experiments, Lorenz separated the eggs laid by one goose into two groups. One group he returned to the goose to be hatched by her. The other group was hatched in an incubator. The goslings in the first group performed as predicted. They followed their mother as soon as they hatched. However, those in the second group, which saw Lorenz when they first hatched, followed him everywhere, as though he were their mother. Lorenz marked the goslings and then placed both groups under a box. Mother goose and "mother" Lorenz stood aside as the box lifted. Each group of goslings went directly to its "mother." Lorenz called this process *imprinting*, the rapid, innate learning within a limited critical period of time that involves attachment to the first moving object seen.

Ethological research and theory at first had little or nothing to say about the nature of social relationships across the human life span, and the theory stimulated few studies with humans. Ethologists' view that normal development requires that certain behaviors emerge during a critical period, a fixed time period very early in development, seemed to be overdrawn.

developmental **connection**

Achievement. Bandura emphasizes that self-efficacy is a key person/cognitive factor in children's achievement. Chapter 12, p. 379

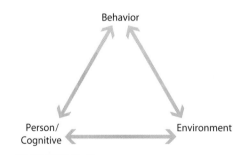

FIGURE **1.9**

BANDURA'S SOCIAL COGNITIVE MODEL. The arrows illustrate how relations between behavior, person/cognition, and environment are reciprocal rather than unidirectional.

ethology Stresses that behavior is strongly influenced by biology, is tied to evolution, and is characterized by critical or sensitive periods.

Konrad Lorenz, a pioneering student of animal behavior, is followed through the water by three imprinted greylag geese. Describe Lorenz's experiment with the geese. *Do you think his experiment would have the same results with human babies? Explain.*

developmental connection

Attachment. Human babies go through a series of phases in developing an attachment to a caregiver. Chapter 7, p. 217

How Would You…?

If you were an **educator,** how might you explain a student's chronic failure to complete homework from the mesosystem level? From the exosystem level?

Bronfenbrenner's ecological theory An environmental systems theory that focuses on five environmental systems: microsystem, mesosystem, exosystem, macrosystem, and chronosystem.

eclectic theoretical orientation An orientation that does not follow any one theoretical approach but rather selects from each theory whatever is considered the best in it.

However, John Bowlby (1969, 1989) illustrated an important application of ethological theory to human development. Bowlby argued that attachment to a caregiver over the first year of life has important consequences throughout the life span. In his view, if this attachment is positive and secure, the individual will likely develop positively in childhood and adulthood. If the attachment is negative and insecure, life-span development will likely not be optimal. Thus, in this view the first year of life is a sensitive period for the development of social relationships. In Chapter 7, "Socioemotional Development in Infancy," we explore the concept of infant attachment in much greater detail.

Contributions of ethological theory include (1) an increased focus on the biological and evolutionary basis of development; (2) use of careful observations in naturalistic settings; and (3) an emphasis on sensitive periods of development.

Criticisms of ethological theory include the following: (1) the concepts of critical and sensitive periods are perhaps too rigid; (2) the emphasis on biological foundations is too strong; (3) cognition receives inadequate attention; and (4) the theory is better at generating research with animals than with humans.

Another theory that emphasizes the biological aspects of human development—evolutionary psychology—is presented in Chapter 2, "Biological Beginnings," along with views on the role of heredity in development.

Ecological Theory   Ethological theory stresses biological factors, whereas ecological theory emphasizes environmental factors. One ecological theory that has important implications for understanding children's development was created by Urie Bronfenbrenner (1917–2005).

Bronfenbrenner's ecological theory (1986, 2000; Bronfenbrenner & Morris, 2006) holds that development reflects the influence of several environmental systems. The theory identifies five environmental systems (see Figure 1.10):

- *Microsystem*—the setting in which the individual lives. These contexts include the person's family, peers, school, neighborhood, and work. It is in the microsystem that the most direct interactions with social agents take place—with parents, peers, and teachers, for example.

- *Mesosystem*—relations between microsystems or connections between contexts. Examples are the relation of family experiences to school experiences, school experiences to church experiences, and family experiences to peer experiences. For example, children whose parents have rejected them may have difficulty developing positive relations with teachers.

- *Exosystem*—links between a social setting in which the individual does not have an active role and the individual's immediate context. For example, a husband's or child's experience at home may be influenced by a mother's experiences at work. The mother might receive a promotion that requires more travel, which might increase conflict with the husband and change patterns of interaction with the child.

- *Macrosystem*—the culture in which individuals live. Remember from earlier in this chapter that *culture* refers to the behavior patterns, beliefs, and all other products of a group of people that are passed on from generation to generation. Remember also that cross-cultural studies—comparisons of one culture with one or more other cultures—provide information about the generality of development (Fung, 2011).

- *Chronosystem*—the patterning of environmental events and transitions over the life course, as well as sociohistorical circumstances (Schaie, 2011). For example, divorce is one transition. Researchers have found that the negative effects of divorce on children often peak in the first year after the divorce (Hetherington, 2006). By two years after the divorce, family interaction is less chaotic and more stable. As an example of sociohistorical circumstances, consider how the opportunities for women to pursue a career have increased during the last 30 years.

Bronfenbrenner (2000; Bronfenbrenner & Morris, 2006) has added biological influences to his theory and now describes it as a *bioecological* theory. Nonetheless, ecological, environmental contexts still predominate in Bronfenbrenner's theory.

Contributions of the theory include a systematic examination of macro and micro dimensions of environmental systems, and attention to connections between environmental systems. A further contribution of Bronfenbrenner's theory is an emphasis on a range of social contexts beyond the family, such as neighborhood, religious, school, and workplace, as influential in children's development (Gauvain & Parke, 2010; Parke & Clarke-Stewart, 2011). Criticisms include giving inadequate attention to biological factors and placing too little emphasis on cognitive factors.

An Eclectic Theoretical Orientation The theories that we have discussed were developed at different points in the twentieth century, as Figure 1.11 shows. No single theory described in this chapter can explain entirely the rich complexity of children's development, but each has contributed to our understanding of development. Psychoanalytic theory best explains the unconscious mind. Erikson's theory best describes the changes that occur in adult development. Piaget's, Vygotsky's, and the information-processing views provide the most complete description of cognitive development. The behavioral and social cognitive and ecological theories have been the most adept at examining the environmental determinants of development. The ethological theories have highlighted biology's role and the importance of sensitive periods in development.

In short, although theories are helpful guides, relying on a single theory to explain development is probably a mistake. This book instead takes an **eclectic theoretical orientation,** which does not follow any one theoretical approach but rather selects from each theory whatever is considered its best features. In this way, you can view the study of development as it actually exists—with different theorists

Urie Bronfenbrenner developed ecological theory, a perspective that is receiving increased attention. *What is the nature of ecological theory?*

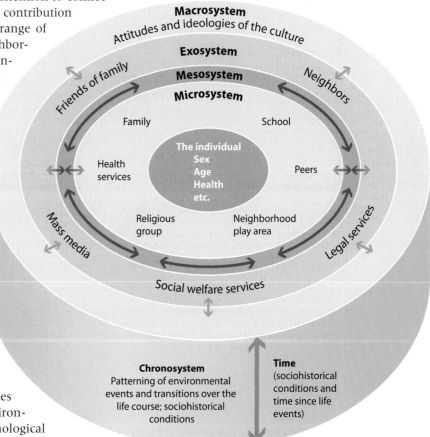

FIGURE **1.10**

BRONFENBRENNER'S ECOLOGICAL THEORY OF DEVELOPMENT. Bronfenbrenner's ecological theory consists of five environmental systems: microsystem, mesosytem, exosystem, macrosystem, and chronosystem.

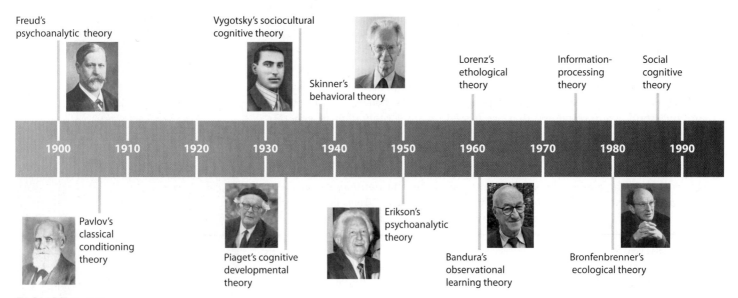

FIGURE **1.11**

TIME LINE FOR MAJOR DEVELOPMENTAL THEORIES

making different assumptions, stressing different empirical problems, and using different strategies to discover information. Figure 1.12 compares the main theoretical perspectives in terms of how they view important developmental issues in children's development.

RESEARCH METHODS FOR COLLECTING DATA

If they follow an eclectic orientation, how do scholars and researchers determine that one feature of a theory is somehow better than another? The scientific method discussed earlier in this chapter provides the guide. Recall that the steps in the scientific method involve conceptualizing the problem, collecting data, drawing conclusions,

THEORY	ISSUES		
	Nature and nurture	**Early and later experience**	**Continuity and discontinuity**
Psychoanalytic	Freud's biological determinism interacting with early family experiences; Erikson's more balanced biological/cultural interaction perspective	Early experiences in the family very important influences	Emphasis on discontinuity between stages
Cognitive	Piaget's emphasis on interaction and adaptation; environment provides the setting for cognitive structures to develop. Vygotsky's theory involves interaction of nature and nurture with strong emphasis on culture. The information-processing approach has not addressed this issue extensively; mainly emphasizes biological/environment interaction.	Childhood experiences important influences	Discontinuity between stages in Piaget's theory; no stages in Vygotsky's theory or the information-processing approach
Behavioral and Social Cognitive	Environment viewed as the main influence on development	Experiences important at all points in development	Continuity with no stages
Ethological	Strong biological view	Early experience very important, which can contribute to change early in development; after early critical or sensitive period has passed, stability likely to occur	Discontinuity because of early critical or sensitive period; no stages
Ecological	Strong environmental view	Experiences involving the five environmental systems important at all points in development	No stages but little attention to the issue

FIGURE **1.12**

A COMPARISON OF THEORIES AND ISSUES IN CHILD DEVELOPMENT

What are some important strategies in conducting observational research with children?

and revising research conclusions and theories. Through scientific research, the features of theories can be tested and refined.

Whether we are interested in studying attachment in infants, the cognitive skills of children, or the peer relations of adolescents, we can choose from several ways of collecting data. Here we outline the measures most often used, including their advantages and disadvantages, beginning with observation.

Observation   Scientific observation requires an important set of skills (Gravetter & Forazano, 2012). Unless we are trained observers and practice our skills regularly, we might not know what to look for, we might not remember what we saw, we might not realize that what we are looking for is changing from one moment to the next, and we might not communicate our observations effectively.

For observations to be effective, they have to be systematic. We need to have some idea of what we are looking for. We have to know whom we are observing, when and where we will observe, how the observations will be made, and how they will be recorded.

Where should we make our observations? We have two choices: the laboratory and the everyday world.

When we observe scientifically, we often need to control certain factors that determine behavior but are not the focus of our inquiry (Jackson, 2011). For this reason, some research in children's development is conducted in a **laboratory,** a controlled setting with many of the complex factors of the "real world" removed. For example, suppose you want to observe how children react when they see other people act aggressively. If you observe children in their homes or schools, you have no control over how much aggression the children observe, what kind of aggression they see, which people they see acting aggressively, or how other people treat the children. In contrast, if you observe the children in a laboratory, you can control these and other factors and therefore have more confidence about how to interpret your observations.

Laboratory research does have some drawbacks, however. First, it is almost impossible to conduct research without the participants' knowing they are being studied. Second, the laboratory setting is unnatural and therefore can cause the participants to behave unnaturally. Third, people who are willing to come to a university laboratory may not fairly represent groups from diverse cultural backgrounds. Fourth, people who are unfamiliar with university settings and with the idea of "helping science" may be intimidated by the laboratory setting. In addition, some aspects of children's development are difficult, if not impossible, to examine in the laboratory. Last, laboratory studies of certain types of stress may even be unethical.

Naturalistic observation provides insights that we sometimes cannot achieve in the laboratory (Langston, 2011). **Naturalistic observation** means observing behavior in real-world settings, making no effort to manipulate or control the situation.

laboratory A controlled setting in which many of the complex factors of the "real world" are removed.

naturalistic observation Observing behavior in real-world settings.

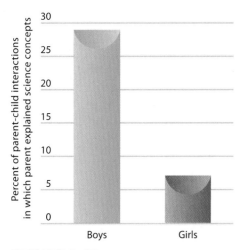

FIGURE **1.13**

PARENTS' EXPLANATIONS OF SCIENCE TO SONS AND DAUGHTERS AT A SCIENCE MUSEUM. In a naturalistic observation study at a children's science museum, parents were more than three times more likely to explain science to boys than to girls (Crowley & others, 2001). The gender difference occurred regardless of whether the father, the mother, or both parents were with the child, although the gender difference was greatest for fathers' science explanations to sons and daughters.

standardized test A test with uniform procedures for administration and scoring. Many standardized tests allow a person's performance to be compared with the performance of other individuals.

case study An in-depth look at a single individual.

Life-span researchers conduct naturalistic observations at sporting events, child-care centers, work settings, malls, and other places people live in and frequent.

Naturalistic observation was used in one study that focused on conversations in a children's science museum (Crowley & others, 2001). Parents were more than three times more likely to engage boys than girls in explanatory talk while visiting exhibits at the science museum, suggesting a gender bias that encourages boys more than girls to be interested in science (see Figure 1.13). In another study, Mexican American parents who had completed high school used more explanations with their children when visiting a science museum than Mexican American parents who had not completed high school (Tenenbaum & others, 2002).

Survey and Interview   Sometimes the best and quickest way to get information about people is to ask them for it. One technique is to *interview* them directly. A related method is the *survey* (sometimes referred to as a questionnaire), which is especially useful when information from many people is needed (Babble, 2011). A standard set of questions is used to obtain people's self-reported attitudes or beliefs about a specific topic. In a good survey, the questions are clear and unbiased, allowing respondents to answer unambiguously.

Surveys and interviews can be used to study a wide variety of topics ranging from religious beliefs to sexual habits to attitudes about gun control to beliefs about how to improve schools. Surveys and interviews today are conducted in person, over the telephone, and over the Internet.

One problem with surveys and interviews is the tendency of participants to answer questions in a way that they think is socially acceptable or desirable rather than telling what they truly think or feel (Leedy & Ormrod, 2010). For example, on a survey or in an interview some individuals might say that they do not take drugs even though they do.

Standardized Test   A **standardized test** has uniform procedures for administration and scoring. Many standardized tests allow a person's performance to be compared with the performance of other individuals—thus they provide information about individual differences among people (Gregory, 2011). One example is the Stanford-Binet intelligence test, which is described in Chapter 12, "Cognitive Development in Middle and Late Childhood." Your score on the Stanford-Binet test tells you how your performance compares with that of thousands of other people who have taken the test (Drummond & Jones, 2010).

Standardized tests also have three key weaknesses. First, they do not always predict behavior in nontest situations. Second, standardized tests are based on the belief that a person's behavior is consistent and stable, yet personality and intelligence—two primary targets of standardized testing—can vary with the situation. For example, individuals may perform poorly on a standardized intelligence test in an office setting but score much higher at home where they are less anxious. This criticism is especially relevant for members of minority groups, some of whom have been inaccurately classified as mentally retarded on the basis of their scores on intelligence tests. A third weakness of standardized tests is that many psychological tests developed in Western cultures might not be appropriate in other cultures (Shiraev & Levy, 2010). The experiences of people in differing cultures may lead them to interpret and respond to questions differently.

Case Study   A **case study** is an in-depth look at a single individual. Case studies are performed mainly by mental health professionals, when—for either practical or ethical reasons—the unique aspects of an individual's life cannot be duplicated and tested in other individuals. A case study provides information about one person's fears, hopes, fantasies, traumatic experiences, upbringing, family relationships, health, or anything that helps the psychologist understand the person's mind and behavior. In later chapters, we discuss vivid case studies, such as studies of Michael

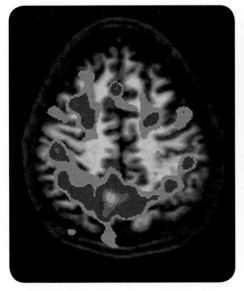
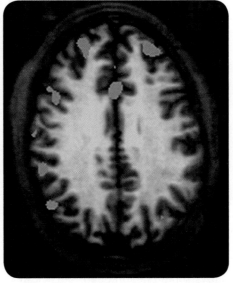

FIGURE **1.14**
BRAIN IMAGING OF 15-YEAR-OLD ADOLESCENTS. The two brain images indicate how alcohol can influence the functioning of an adolescent's brain. Notice the pink and red coloring (which indicates effective brain functioning involving memory) in the brain of the 15-year-old non-drinker (*left*) while engaging in a memory task and the lack of those colors in the brain of the 15-year-old under the influence of alcohol (*right*).

Rehbein, who had much of the left side of his brain removed at 7 years of age to end severe epileptic seizures.

Case histories provide dramatic, in-depth portrayals of people's lives, but we must be cautious about generalizing from this information (Babble, 2011). The subject of a case study is unique, with a genetic makeup and personal history that no one else shares. In addition, case studies involve judgments of unknown reliability. Psychologists who conduct case studies rarely check to see if other psychologists agree with their observations.

Physiological Measures   Researchers are increasingly using *physiological measures* when they study children's development (Nelson, 2011). For example, as puberty unfolds, the blood levels of certain hormones increase. To determine the nature of these hormonal changes, researchers take blood samples from willing adolescents (Dorn & Biro, 2011).

Another physiological measure that is increasingly being used is neuroimaging, especially *functional magnetic resonance imaging (fMRI)*, in which electromagnetic waves are used to construct images of a person's brain tissue and biochemical activity. Figure 1.14 compares the brain images of two adolescents—one a non-drinker and the other a heavy drinker—while engaged in a memory task. We will have much more to say about neuroimaging and other physiological measures at various points in this book.

Mahatma Gandhi was the spiritual leader of India in the middle of the twentieth century. Erik Erikson conducted an extensive case study of Gandhi's life to determine what contributed to his identity development. *What are some limitations of the case study approach?*

RESEARCH DESIGNS

Suppose you want to find out whether the children of permissive parents are more likely than other children to be rude and unruly. The data-collection method that researchers choose often depends on the goal of their research. The goal may be to describe a phenomenon, to describe relationships between phenomena, or to determine the causes or effects of a phenomenon.

Perhaps you decide that you need to observe both permissive and strict parents with their children and compare them. How would you do that? In addition to choosing a method for collecting data, you would need a research design. There are three main types of research design: descriptive, correlational, and experimental.

Descriptive Research   All of the data-collection methods that we have discussed can be used in **descriptive research,** which aims to observe and record behavior.

descriptive research A research design that has the purpose of observing and recording behavior.

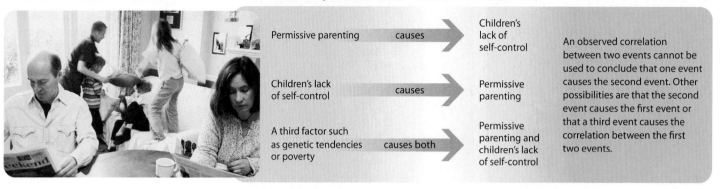

Observed Correlation: As permissive parenting increases, children's self-control decreases.

Possible explanations for this observed correlation

Permissive parenting → causes → Children's lack of self-control

Children's lack of self-control → causes → Permissive parenting

A third factor such as genetic tendencies or poverty → causes both → Permissive parenting and children's lack of self-control

An observed correlation between two events cannot be used to conclude that one event causes the second event. Other possibilities are that the second event causes the first event or that a third event causes the correlation between the first two events.

FIGURE **1.15**

POSSIBLE EXPLANATIONS OF CORRELATIONAL DATA

For example, a researcher might observe the extent to which people are altruistic or aggressive toward each other. By itself, descriptive research cannot prove what causes some phenomenon, but it can reveal important information about people's behavior (Babble, 2011).

Correlational Research Correlational research goes beyond describing phenomena to provide information that will help us to predict how people will behave. In **correlational research,** the goal is to describe the strength of the relationship between two or more events or characteristics. The more strongly the two events are correlated (or related or associated), the more effectively we can predict one event from the other (Heiman, 2012).

For example, to study whether children of permissive parents have less self-control than other children, you would need to carefully record observations of parents' permissiveness and their children's self-control. The data could then be analyzed statistically to yield a numerical measure, called a **correlation coefficient,** a number based on a statistical analysis that is used to describe the degree of association between two variables. The correlation coefficient ranges from −1.00 to +1.00. A negative number means an inverse relation. For example, researchers often find a negative correlation between permissive parenting and children's self-control. By contrast, they often find a positive correlation between parental monitoring of children and children's self-control.

The higher the correlation coefficient (whether positive or negative), the stronger the association between the two variables. A correlation of 0 means that there is no association between the variables. A correlation of −.40 is stronger than a correlation of +.20 because we disregard whether the correlation is positive or negative in determining the strength of the correlation.

A caution is in order, however. Correlation does not equal causation (Spatz, 2012). The correlational finding just mentioned does not mean that permissive parenting necessarily causes low self-control in children. It could mean that, but it also could mean that a child's lack of self-control caused the parents to simply throw up their arms in despair and give up trying to control the child. It also could mean that other factors, such as heredity or poverty, caused the correlation between permissive parenting and low self-control in children. Figure 1.15 illustrates these possible interpretations of correlational data.

Throughout this book, you will read about numerous correlational research studies. Keep in mind how easy it is to assume causality when two events or characteristics merely are correlated.

Experimental Research To study causality, researchers turn to experimental research. An **experiment** is a carefully regulated procedure in which one or more factors believed to influence the behavior being studied are manipulated, while all other factors are held constant. If the behavior under study changes when a factor

correlational research A research design whose goal is to describe the strength of the relationship between two or more events or characteristics.

correlation coefficient A number based on statistical analysis that is used to describe the degree of association between two variables.

experiment A carefully regulated procedure in which one or more of the factors believed to influence the behavior being studied are manipulated, while all other factors are held constant.

is manipulated, we say that the manipulated factor has caused the behavior to change. In other words, the experiment has demonstrated cause and effect. The cause is the factor that was manipulated. The effect is the behavior that changed because of the manipulation. Nonexperimental research methods (descriptive and correlational research) cannot establish cause and effect because they do not involve manipulating factors in a controlled way (Stangor, 2011).

Independent and Dependent Variables   Experiments include two types of change-able factors, or variables: independent and dependent. An *independent variable* is a manipulated, influential, experimental factor. It is a potential cause. The label *independent* is used because this variable can be manipulated independently of other factors to determine its effect. One experiment may include several independent variables.

A *dependent variable* is a factor that can change in an experiment, in response to changes in the independent variable. As researchers manipulate the independent variable, they measure the dependent variable for any resulting effect.

For example, suppose that you conducted a study to determine whether aerobic exercise by pregnant women changes the breathing and sleeping patterns of newborn babies. You might require one group of pregnant women to engage in a certain amount of exercise each week while another group of pregnant women does not exercise; thus, the amount of exercise is the independent variable. When the infants are born, you would observe and measure their breathing and sleeping patterns. These patterns are the dependent variable, the factor that changes as the result of your manipulation.

Experimental and Control Groups   Experiments can involve one or more experimental groups and one or more control groups. An *experimental group* is a group whose experience is manipulated. A *control group* is a comparison group that is as much like the experimental group as possible and that is treated in every way like the experimental group except for the manipulated factor (independent variable). The control group serves as a baseline against which the effects of the manipulated condition can be compared.

Random assignment is an important principle for deciding whether each participant will be placed in the experimental group or in the control group. Random assignment means that researchers assign participants to experimental and control groups by chance. It reduces the likelihood that the experiment's results will be due to any preexisting differences between groups (Gravetter & Forzano, 2012). In the example of the effects of aerobic exercise by pregnant women on the breathing and sleeping patterns of their newborns, you would randomly assign half of the pregnant women to engage in aerobic exercise over a period of weeks (the experimental group) and the other half to not exercise over the same number of weeks (the control group). Figure 1.16 illustrates the nature of experimental research.

Time Span of Research   Researchers in child development have a special concern with studies that focus on the relation of age to some other variable. To do this, they can study different individuals of various ages and compare them, or they can study the same individuals as they age over time.

Cross-Sectional Approach   The **cross-sectional approach** is a research strategy in which individuals of different ages are compared at one time. A typical cross-sectional study might include a group of 5-year-olds, 8-year-olds, and 11-year-olds. The groups can be compared with respect to a variety of dependent variables: IQ, memory, peer relations, attachment to parents, hormonal changes, and so on. All of these comparisons can be accomplished in a short time. In some studies, data are collected in a single day. Even in large-scale cross-sectional studies with hundreds of participants, data collection does not usually take longer than several months to complete.

The main advantage of the cross-sectional study is that researchers don't have to wait for children to grow older. Despite its efficiency, the cross-sectional approach

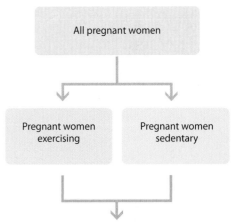

Independent variable

Dependent variable

Newborns' breathing and sleeping patterns

FIGURE **1.16**

PRINCIPLES OF EXPERIMENTAL RESEARCH. Imagine that you decide to conduct an experimental study of the effects of aerobic exercise by pregnant women on their newborns' breathing and sleeping patterns. You would randomly assign pregnant women to experimental and control groups. The experimental-group women would engage in aerobic exercise over a specified number of sessions and weeks. The control group would not. Then, when the infants are born, you would assess their breathing and sleeping patterns. If the breathing and sleeping patterns of newborns whose mothers were in the experimental group are different from those of the control group, you would conclude that aerobic exercise caused these effects.

cross-sectional approach A research strategy in which individuals of different ages are compared at one time.

has its drawbacks. It gives no information about how individual children change or about the stability of their characteristics. It can obscure the increases and decreases of development—the hills and valleys of growth and development.

Longitudinal Approach   The **longitudinal approach** is a research strategy in which the same individuals are studied over a period of time, usually several years or more. For example, if a study of self-esteem were conducted longitudinally, the same children might be assessed three times—at 5, 8, and 11 years of age. Some longitudinal studies take place over shorter time frames, even just a year or so.

Longitudinal studies provide a wealth of information about important issues such as stability and change in development and the influence of early experience on later development, but they are not without their problems (Gibbons, Hedeker, & DuToit, 2010; Sliwinski, 2011). They are expensive and time-consuming. Also, the longer the study lasts, the more participants drop out. For example, children's families may move, get sick, lose interest, and so forth. Those who remain in the study may be dissimilar to those who drop out, biasing the results. Those individuals who remain in a longitudinal study over a number of years may be more compulsive and conformity-oriented or they might have more stable lives.

Earlier in the chapter we described *cohort effects,* which are effects due to a person's time of birth, era, or generation, but not to actual age. Cohort effects are important in research on children, adolescents, and their parents because they can powerfully affect the dependent measures in a study ostensibly concerned with age (Schaie, 2011; Schaie & Willis, 2012). Cross-sectional studies can show how different cohorts respond, but they can confuse age changes and cohort effects. Longitudinal studies are effective in studying age changes but only within one cohort.

So far we have discussed many aspects of scientific research in child development. In the *Connecting with Research* interlude, you can read about the research journals in which the findings of research studies are published.

RESEARCH CHALLENGES

The scientific foundation of research in child development helps to minimize the effect of research bias and maximize the objectivity of the results. Still, subtle challenges remain for each researcher to resolve. One is to ensure that research is conducted in an ethical way; another is to recognize, and try to overcome, deeply buried personal biases related to gender and ethnicity.

Conducting Ethical Research   The explosion in technology has forced society to grapple with looming ethical questions that were unimaginable only a few decades ago. The same line of research that enables previously sterile couples to have children might someday let prospective parents "call up and order" the characteristics they prefer in their children or tip the balance of males and females in the world. For example, should embryos left over from procedures for increasing fertility be saved or discarded? Should people with inheritable fatal diseases (such as Huntington disease) be discouraged from having children?

Researchers also face ethical questions both new and old. They have a responsibility to anticipate the personal problems their research might cause and to at least inform the participants of the possible fallout. Safeguarding the rights of research participants is a challenge because the potential harm is not always obvious (Jackson, 2011).

Ethics in research may affect you personally if you ever serve as a participant in a study. In that event, you need to know your rights as a participant and the responsibilities of researchers to ensure that these rights are safeguarded.

If you ever become a researcher in child development yourself, you will need an even deeper understanding of ethics. Even if you only carry out experimental projects in psychology courses, you must consider the rights of the participants in those projects.

Today, proposed research at colleges and universities must pass the scrutiny of a research ethics committee before the research can be initiated. In addition, the

longitudinal approach A research strategy in which the same individuals are studied over a period of time, usually several years or more.

Why Are Research Journals Important in the Field of Child Development?

Regardless of whether you pursue a career in child development, psychology, or some related scientific field, you can benefit by learning about the journal process. As a student you might be required to look up original research in journals. As a parent, teacher, or nurse you might want to consult journals to obtain information that will help you understand and work more effectively with people. And as an inquiring person, you might look up information in journals after you have heard or read something that piqued your curiosity.

A journal publishes scholarly and academic information, usually in a specific domain—like physics, math, sociology, or our current interest, child development. Scholars in these fields publish most of their research in journals, which are the source of core information in virtually every academic discipline.

An increasing number of journals publish information about child development. Among the leading journals in child development are *Developmental Psychology, Child Development, Developmental Psychopathology, Pediatrics, Pediatric Nursing, Infant Behavior and Development, Journal of Research on Adolescence, Human Development,* and many others. Also, a number of journals that do not focus solely on development publish articles on various aspects of human development. These journals include *Journal of Educational Psychology, Sex Roles, Journal of Cross-Cultural Research, Journal of Marriage and the Family, Exceptional Children,* and *Journal of Consulting and Clinical Psychology.*

Every journal has a board of experts who evaluate articles submitted for publication. Each submitted paper is accepted or rejected on the basis of factors such as its contribution to the field, methodological excellence, and clarity of writing. Some of the most prestigious journals reject as many as 80 to 90 percent of the articles submitted.

Research journals are the core of information in virtually every academic discipline. Those shown here are among the increasing number of research journals that publish information about child development. *What are the main parts of a research article that presents findings from original research?*

Journal articles are usually written for other professionals in the specialized field of the journal's focus—therefore, they often contain technical language and terms specific to the discipline that are difficult for nonprofessionals to understand. Their organization often takes this course: abstract, introduction, method, results, discussion, and references.

The *abstract* is a brief summary that appears at the beginning of the article. The abstract lets readers quickly determine whether the article is relevant to their interests. The *introduction* introduces the problem or issue that is being studied. It includes a concise review of research relevant to the topic, theoretical ties, and one or more hypotheses to be tested. The *method* section consists of a clear description of the subjects evaluated in the study, the measures used, and the procedures that were followed. The method section should be sufficiently clear and detailed so that by reading it another researcher could repeat or replicate the study. The *results* section reports the analysis of the data collected. In most cases, the results section includes statistical analyses that are difficult for nonprofessionals to understand. The *discussion* section describes the author's conclusions, inferences, and interpretation of what was found. Statements are usually made about whether the hypotheses presented in the introduction were supported, limitations of the study, and suggestions for future research. The last part of the journal article, called *references*, includes bibliographic information for each source cited in the article. The references section is often a good resource for finding other articles relevant to the topic that interests you.

Where do you find journals such as those we have described? Your college or university library likely has some of them, and some public libraries also carry journals. Online resources such as PsycINFO, which can facilitate the search for journal articles, are available to students on many campuses.

American Psychological Association (APA) has developed ethics guidelines for its members. The code of ethics instructs psychologists to protect their participants from mental and physical harm. The participants' best interests need to be kept foremost in the researcher's mind (Wiersman & Jurs, 2009). APA's guidelines address four important issues: informed consent, confidentiality, debriefing, and deception.

- *Informed consent.* All participants must know what their participation will involve and what risks might develop. For example, participants in a study on dating should be told beforehand that a questionnaire might stimulate thoughts about issues in their relationship that they have not considered. Participants also should be informed that in some instances a discussion of the issues might improve their relationship, but in others might worsen the relationship and even end it. Even after informed consent is given, participants must retain the right to withdraw from the study at any time and for any reason.

- *Confidentiality.* Researchers are responsible for keeping all of the data they gather on individuals completely confidential and, when possible, completely anonymous.

- *Debriefing.* After the study has been completed, participants should be informed of its purpose and the methods that were used. In most cases, the experimenter also can inform participants in a general manner beforehand about the purpose of the research without leading participants to behave in a way they think that the experimenter is expecting. When preliminary information about the study is likely to affect the results, participants can at least be debriefed after the study has been completed.

- *Deception.* This is an ethical issue that researchers debate extensively. In some circumstances, telling the participants beforehand what the research study is about substantially alters the participants' behavior and invalidates the researcher's data. In all cases, however, the psychologist must ensure that the deception will not harm the participants and that the participants will be told the complete nature of the study (debriefed) as soon as possible after the study is completed.

Minimizing Bias Studies of children's development are most useful when they are conducted without bias or prejudice toward any specific group of people. Of special concern is bias based on gender and bias based on culture or ethnicity.

Gender Bias For most of its existence, our society has had a strong gender bias, a preconceived notion about the abilities of males and females that prevented individuals from pursuing their own interests and achieving their potential (Matlin, 2012). Gender bias also has had a less obvious effect within the field of child development. For example, it is not unusual for conclusions to be drawn about females' attitudes and behaviors from research conducted with males as the only participants.

developmental **connection**

Gender. Gender stereotyping continues to be extensive. Recent research indicates that girls and older children use a higher percentage of gender stereotypes than younger children and boys. Chapter 13, p. 401

Furthermore, when researchers find gender differences, their reports sometimes magnify those differences (Denmark & others, 1988). For example, a researcher might report that 74 percent of the boys in a study had high achievement expectations versus only 67 percent of the girls and go on to talk about the differences in some detail. In reality, this might be a rather small difference. It also might disappear if the study were repeated, or the study might have methodological problems that don't allow such strong interpretations.

Pam Reid is a leading researcher who studies gender and ethnic bias in development. To read about Pam's interests, see the *Connecting with Careers* profile.

Cultural and Ethnic Bias In recent years, there has been a growing realization that research on children's development needs to include more children from diverse ethnic groups (Brady-Smith & others, 2011). Historically, children from ethnic

connecting with careers

Pam Reid, Educational and Developmental Psychologist

When she was a child, Pam Reid liked to play with chemistry sets. Reid majored in chemistry during college and wanted to become a doctor. However, when some of her friends signed up for a psychology class as an elective, she also decided to take the course. She was intrigued by learning about how people think, behave, and develop—so much so that she changed her major to psychology. Reid went on to obtain her Ph.D. in psychology (American Psychological Association, 2003, p. 16).

For a number of years Reid was a professor of education and psychology at the University of Michigan, where she also was a research scientist at the Institute for Research on Women and Gender. Her main focus has been on how children and adolescents develop social skills, with a special interest in the development of African American girls (Reid & Zalk, 2001). In 2004, Reid became provost and executive vice-

Pam Reid (*center*) with students at Saint Joseph College in Hartford, Connecticut, where she is the president of the college.

president at Roosevelt University in Chicago. In January 2008 she was appointed president of Saint Joseph College in Hartford, Connecticut.

For more information about what professors, researchers, and educational psychologists do, see pages 46–47 in the Careers in Children's Development appendix that follows this chapter.

minority groups (African American, Latino, Asian American, and Native American) were excluded from most research in the United States and simply thought of as variations from the norm or average. If minority children were included in samples and their scores didn't fit the norm, they were viewed as confounds or "noise" in data and discounted. Given the fact that children from diverse ethnic groups were excluded from research on child development for so long, we might reasonably conclude that children's real lives are perhaps more varied than research data have indicated in the past.

Researchers also have tended to overgeneralize about ethnic groups (Wright & others, 2012). **Ethnic gloss** is the use of an ethnic label such as African American or Latino in a superficial way that portrays an ethnic group as being more homogeneous than it really is (Trimble, 1988). For example, a researcher might describe a research sample like this: "The participants were 60 Latinos." A more complete

ethnic gloss The use of an ethnic label such as African American or Latino in a superficial way that portrays an ethnic group as being more homogeneous than it really is.

Look at these two photographs, one (*left*) of all non-Latino White boys, the other (*right*) of boys and girls from diverse ethnic backgrounds. Consider a topic in child development such as independence seeking, cultural values, parenting education, or health care. *If you were conducting research on this topic, might the results of the study be different depending on whether the participants in your study were the children in the photo on the left or the photo on the right?*

description of the Latino group might be something like this: "The 60 Latino participants were Mexican Americans from low-income neighborhoods in the southwestern area of Los Angeles. Thirty-six were from homes in which Spanish is the dominant language spoken, 24 from homes in which English is the main language spoken. Thirty were born in the United States, 30 in Mexico. Twenty-eight described themselves as Mexican American, 14 as Mexican, 9 as American, 6 as Chicano, and 3 as Latino." Ethnic gloss can cause researchers to obtain samples of ethnic groups that are not representative of the group's diversity, which can lead to overgeneralization and stereotyping.

Research on ethnic minority children and their families has not been given adequate attention, especially in light of their significant rate of growth (Cheah & Leung, 2011; Fung, 2011). Until recently, ethnic minority families were combined in the category "minority," which masks important differences among ethnic groups as well as diversity within an ethnic group. At present and in the foreseeable future, the growth of minority families in the United States will be mainly due to the immigration of Latino and Asian families. Researchers need to take into account their acculturation level and the generational status of parents and children, and to explore how these factors influence family processes and child outcomes (Chao & Otsuki-Clutter, 2011). More attention also needs to be given to biculturalism because the complexity of diversity means that some children of color identify with two or more ethnic groups (Marks, Patton, & Garcia Coll, 2011).

Review Connect Reflect

LG3 Summarize why research is important in child development, the main theories of child development, and research methods, designs, and challenges.

Review

- Why is research on child development important?
- What are the main theories of child development?
- What are the main research methods for collecting data about children's development?
- What types of research designs do child development researchers use?
- What are some research challenges in studying children's development?

Connect

- Which of the research methods for collecting data would be appropriate or inappropriate for studying Erikson's stage of trust versus mistrust? Why?

Reflect *Your Own Personal Journey of Life*

- Imagine that you are conducting a research study on the sexual attitudes and behaviors of adolescents. What ethical safeguards should you use in conducting the study?

topical connections

In the next chapter, you'll continue to learn about theory and research as you explore the biological underpinnings of children's development. You will read about the evolutionary perspective and the genetic foundations of development. Challenges and choices people encounter when deciding to reproduce are covered, including the new reproductive choices made possible by advancing technology. Many aspects of adopting children also are examined. These topics set the stage for an introduction to the complex interaction of heredity and environment in children's development.

looking forward

Why Is Caring for Children Important?

 LG1 Explain why it is important to study children's development, and identify five areas in which children's lives need to be improved.

> The Importance of Studying Children's Development

> Improving the Lives of Children

- Studying children's development is important because it will help you to better understand your own childhood and provide you with strategies for being a competent parent or educator.

- Health and well-being are important areas in which children's lives can be improved. Today, many children in the United States and around the world need improved health care. We now recognize the importance of lifestyles and psychological states in promoting health and well-being. Parenting is an important influence on children's development. One-parent families, working parents, and child care are among the family issues that influence children's well-being. Education can also contribute to children's health and well-being. There is widespread concern that the education of children needs to be more effective, and there are many views in contemporary education about ways to improve schools. Sociocultural contexts are important influences on children's development. Culture, ethnicity, socioeconomic status, and gender are four key aspects of sociocultural contexts. Social policy is a national government's course of action designed to influence the welfare of its citizens. Researchers increasingly are conducting studies that are related to social policy.

What Characterizes Development?

 LG2 Discuss processes, periods, cohort effects, and issues in development.

> Biological, Cognitive, and Socioemotional Processes

> Periods of Development

> Age and Cohort Effects

> Issues in Development

- Three key processes of development are biological, cognitive, and socioemotional. Biological processes (such as genetic inheritance) involve changes in an individual's physical nature. Cognitive processes (such as thinking) consist of changes in an individual's thought, intelligence, and language. Socioemotional processes (such as smiling) include changes in an individual's relationships with others, in emotions, and in personality.

- Childhood's five main developmental periods are (1) prenatal—conception to birth, (2) infancy—birth to 18 to 24 months, (3) early childhood—end of infancy to about 5 to 6 years of age, (4) middle and late childhood—about 6 to 11 years of age, and (5) adolescence—begins at about 10 to 12 and ends at about 18 to 22 years of age.

- Cohort effects are due to a person's time of birth, era, or generation but not to actual age. Two characteristics of today's children and most of their parents—the generation labeled Millennials—that stand out are (1) their ethnic diversity and (2) their connection to technology.

- The nature-nurture issue focuses on the extent to which development is mainly influenced by nature (biological inheritance) or nurture (environmental experience). Some developmentalists describe development as continuous (gradual, cumulative change), while others describe it as discontinuous (a sequence of abrupt stages). The early-later experience issue focuses on whether early experiences (especially in infancy) are more important in development than later experiences. Most developmentalists recognize that extreme positions on the nature-nurture, continuity-discontinuity, and early-later experience issues are not supported by research. Despite this consensus, they continue to debate the degree to which each position influences children's development.

How Is Child Development a Science?

LG3 Summarize why research is important in child development, the main theories of child development, and research methods, designs, and challenges.

The Importance of Research

- When we base information on personal experience, we aren't always objective. Research provides a vehicle for evaluating the accuracy of information. Scientific research is objective, systematic, and testable. Scientific research is based on the scientific method, which includes these steps: conceptualize the problem, collect data, draw conclusions, and revise research conclusions and theory.

Theories of Child Development

- Psychoanalytic theories describe development as primarily unconscious and as heavily colored by emotion. The two main psychoanalytic theories in developmental psychology are Freud's and Erikson's. Freud proposed that individuals go through five psychosexual stages—oral, anal, phallic, latency, and genital. Erikson's theory emphasizes eight psychosocial stages of development. The three main cognitive theories are Piaget's cognitive developmental theory, Vygotsky's sociocultural cognitive theory, and information-processing theory. Cognitive theories emphasize conscious thoughts. In Piaget's theory, children go through four cognitive stages: sensorimotor, preoperational, concrete operational, and formal operational. Vygotsky's sociocultural cognitive theory emphasizes how culture and social interaction guide cognitive development. The information-processing theory emphasizes that individuals manipulate information, monitor it, and strategize about it. Three versions of the behavioral and social cognitive approach are Pavlov's classical conditioning, Skinner's operant conditioning, and Bandura's social cognitive theory. Ethology stresses that behavior is strongly influenced by biology, is tied to evolution, and is characterized by critical or sensitive periods. Ecological theory is Bronfenbrenner's environmental systems view of development. It consists of five environmental systems: microsystem, mesosystem, exosystem, macrosystem, and chronosystem. An eclectic theoretical orientation does not follow any one theoretical approach but rather selects from each theory whatever is considered the best aspects of it.

Research Methods for Collecting Data

- Research methods for collecting data about child development include observation (in a laboratory or a naturalistic setting), survey (questionnaire) or interview, standardized test, case study, and physiological measures.

Research Designs

- Descriptive research aims to observe and record behavior. In correlational research, the goal is to describe the strength of the relationship between two or more events or characteristics. Experimental research involves conducting an experiment, which can determine cause and effect. An independent variable is the manipulated, influential, experimental factor. A dependent variable is a factor that can change in an experiment, in response to changes in the independent variable. Experiments can involve one or more experimental groups and control groups. In random assignment, researchers assign participants to experimental and control groups by chance. When researchers decide about the time span of their research, they can conduct cross-sectional or longitudinal studies.

Research Challenges

- Researchers' ethical responsibilities include seeking participants' informed consent, ensuring their confidentiality, debriefing them about the purpose and potential personal consequences of participating, and avoiding unnecessary deception of participants. Researchers need to guard against gender, cultural, and ethnic bias in research. Every effort should be made to make research equitable for both females and males. Individuals from varied ethnic backgrounds need to be included as participants in child research, and overgeneralization about diverse members within a group must be avoided.

key terms

development 8
context 10
culture 10
cross-cultural studies 10
ethnicity 10
socioeconomic status (SES) 11
gender 11
social policy 12
biological processes 15
cognitive processes 15
socioemotional processes 15

prenatal period 16
infancy 16
early childhood 16
middle and late childhood 16
adolescence 16
cohort effects 16
Millennials 16
nature-nurture issue 18
continuity-discontinuity issue 18
early-later experience issue 19

scientific method 20
theory 21
hypothesis 21
psychoanalytic theories 21
Erikson's theory 22
Piaget's theory 25
Vygotsky's theory 26
information-processing theory 27
social cognitive theory 28
ethology 29
Bronfenbrenner's ecological theory 30

eclectic theoretical orientation 31
laboratory 33
naturalistic observation 33
standardized test 34
case study 34
descriptive research 35
correlational research 36
correlation coefficient 36
experiment 36
cross-sectional approach 37
longitudinal approach 38
ethnic gloss 41

key people

Ann Masten 12
Sigmund Freud 22
Erik Erikson 22

Jean Piaget 25
Lev Vygotsky 26
Robert Siegler 27

Ivan Pavlov 28
B. F. Skinner 28
Albert Bandura 28

Konrad Lorenz 29
John Bowlby 30
Urie Bronfenbrenner 30

connecting with improving the lives of children

MAKING A DIFFERENCE

Lessons for Life

Marian Wright Edelman is one of America's foremost crusaders in the quest for improving the lives of children. Here are some of the main strategies she advocates for improving not only children's lives but our own as well (Edelman, 1992, pp. xxi, 42, 60):

- *"Don't feel as if you are entitled to anything that you don't sweat and struggle for."* Take the initiative to create opportunities. Don't wait around for people to give you favors. A door never has to stay closed. Push on it until it opens.
- *"Don't be afraid of taking risks or of being criticized."* We all make mistakes. It is only through making mistakes that we learn how to do things right. "It doesn't matter how many times you fall down. What matters is how many times we get up." We need "more courageous shepherds and fewer sheep."
- *"Don't ever stop learning and improving your mind or you're going to get left behind."* College is a great investment, but don't think you can park your mind there and everything you need to know will somehow be magically poured into it. Be an active learner. Be curious and ask questions. Explore new horizons.
- *"Stand up for children."* According to Edelman, this is the most important mission in the world. Parenting and nurturing the next generation of children are our society's most important functions, and we need to take them more seriously than we have in the past.

RESOURCES

Children's Defense Fund
25 E Street
Washington, DC 20001
800–424–9602
www.childrensdefense.org
The Children's Defense Fund provides a strong and effective voice for children and adolescents who cannot vote, lobby, or speak for themselves. The Children's Defense Fund is especially interested in the needs of poor, minority, and handicapped children and adolescents. The fund provides information, technical assistance, and support to a network of state and local child and youth advocates. The Children's Defense Fund publishes a number of excellent books and pamphlets related to children's needs.

Handbook of Child Psychology
Edited by William Damon and Richard Lerner (6th ed., Vols. 1–4, 2006)
New York: John Wiley
The *Handbook of Child Psychology* is the standard reference work for overviews of theory and research in this field. It has in-depth discussions of many topics that we explore in this book.

appendix

Careers in Children's Development

Each of us wants to find a rewarding career and enjoy the work we do. The field of child development offers an amazing breadth of career options that can provide extremely satisfying work.

If you decide to pursue a career in child development, what career options are available to you? There are many. Professors in colleges and universities teach courses in areas of child development, education, family development, nursing, and medicine. Teachers impart knowledge, understanding, and skills to children and adolescents. Counselors, clinical psychologists, nurses, and physicians help parents and children of different ages to cope more effectively with their lives and maintain their well-being. Various professionals work with families to improve the quality of family functioning.

Although an advanced degree is not absolutely necessary in some areas of child development, you usually can expand your opportunities (and income) considerably by obtaining a graduate degree. Many careers in child development pay reasonably well. For example, psychologists earn well above the median salary in the United States. Also, by working in the field of child development you can guide people in improving their lives, understand yourself and others better, possibly advance the state of knowledge in the field, and have an enjoyable time while you are doing these things.

If you are considering a career in child development, would you prefer to work with infants? Children? Adolescents? Parents? As you go through this term, try to spend some time with children of different ages. Observe their behavior. Talk with them about their lives. Think about whether you would like to work with children of this age in your life's work.

Another important aspect of exploring careers is to talk with people who work in various jobs. For example, if you have some interest in becoming a school counselor, call a school, ask to speak with a counselor, and set up an appointment to discuss the counselor's career and work.

Something else that should benefit you is to work in one or more jobs related to your career interests while you are in college. Many colleges and universities have internships or work experiences for students who major in such fields as child development. In some instances, these jobs earn course credit or pay; in others, they are strictly on a volunteer basis. Take advantage of these opportunities. They can provide you with valuable experiences to help you decide if this is the right career for you—and they can help you get into graduate school, if you decide you want to go.

In the upcoming sections, we profile careers in four areas: education and research; clinical and counseling; medical, nursing, and physical development; and families and relationships. These are not the only career options in child development, but they should provide you with an idea of the range of opportunities available and information about some of the main career avenues you might pursue. In profiling these careers, we address the amount of education required, the nature of the training, and a description of the work.

Education and Research

Numerous career opportunities in child development involve education or research. These range from college professor to child-care director to school psychologist.

College/University Professor

Courses in child development are taught in many programs and schools in colleges and universities, including psychology, education, nursing, child and family studies, social work, and medicine. The work that college professors do includes teaching courses at either the undergraduate or graduate level (or both), conducting research in a specific area, advising students and/or directing their research, and serving on college or university committees. Some college instructors do not conduct research as part of their jobs but instead focus mainly on teaching. Research is most likely to be part of the job description at universities with master's and Ph.D. programs. A Ph.D. or master's degree almost always is required to teach in some area of child development in a college or university. Obtaining a doctoral degree usually takes four to six years of graduate work. A master's degree requires approximately two years of graduate work. The training involves taking graduate courses, learning to conduct research, and attending and presenting papers at professional meetings. Many graduate students work as teaching or research assistants for professors in an apprenticeship relationship that helps them to become competent teachers and researchers.

If you are interested in becoming a college or university professor, you might want to make an appointment with your instructor in this class on child development to learn more about his or her profession and work. To read about the work of one college professor, see the *Connecting with Careers* profile.

Researcher

Some individuals in the field of child development work in research positions. In most instances, they have either a master's or Ph.D. in some area of child development. The researchers might work at a university, in some cases in a university professor's research program, in government at such agencies as the National Institute of Mental Health, or in private industry. Individuals who have full-time research positions in child development generate innovative research ideas, plan studies, and carry out the research by collecting data, analyzing the data, and then interpreting it. Then they will usually attempt to publish the research in a scientific journal. A researcher often works in a collaborative manner with other researchers on a project and may present the research at scientific meetings. One researcher might spend much of his or her time in laboratory; another researcher might work out in the field, such as in schools, hospitals, and so on.

Elementary School Teacher

The work of an elementary or secondary school teacher involves teaching in one or more subject areas, preparing the curriculum, giving tests, assigning grades, monitoring students' progress, conducting parent-teacher conferences, and attending in-service workshops. Becoming an elementary or secondary school teacher requires a minimum of an undergraduate degree. The training involves taking a wide range of courses with a major or concentration in education, as well as completing a supervised practice-teaching internship.

Valerie Pang, Professor of Teacher Education

Valerie Pang is a professor of teacher education at San Diego State University and formerly was an elementary school teacher. Like Dr. Pang, many professors of teacher education hold a doctoral degree and have experience in teaching at the elementary or secondary school level.

Pang earned a doctorate at the University of Washington. She has received a Multicultural Educator Award from the National Association of Multicultural Education for her work on culture and equity. She also was given the Distinguished Scholar Award by the American Educational Research Association's Committee on the Role and Status of Minorities in Education.

Pang (2005) believes that competent teachers need to:

- Recognize the power and complexity of cultural influences on students.
- Be sensitive to whether their expectations for students are culturally biased.
- Evaluate whether they are doing a good job of seeing life from the perspective of students who come from different cultures.

Valerie Pang is a professor in the School of Education of San Diego State University and formerly was an elementary school teacher. Valerie believes it is important for teachers to create a caring classroom that affirms all students.

Exceptional Children (Special Education) Teacher

A teacher of exceptional children spends concentrated time with individual children who have a disability or are gifted. Among the children a teacher of exceptional children might work with are children with learning disabilities, ADHD (attention deficit hyperactivity disorder), mental retardation, or a physical disability such as cerebral palsy. Some of this work will usually be done outside of the student's regular classroom, and some of it will be carried out when the student is in the regular classroom. A teacher of exceptional children works closely with the student's regular classroom teacher and parents to create the best educational program for the student. Becoming a teacher of exceptional children requires a minimum of an undergraduate degree. The training consists of taking a wide range of courses in education and a concentration of courses in educating children with disabilities or children who are gifted. Teachers of exceptional children often continue their education after obtaining their undergraduate degree and attain a master's degree.

To read about the work of one teacher of exceptional children, see the Connecting with Careers interlude on page 371 in Chapter 12.

Early Childhood Educator

Early childhood educators work on college faculties and have a minimum of a master's degree in their field. In graduate school, they take courses in early childhood education and receive supervisory training in child-care or early childhood programs. Early childhood educators usually teach in community colleges that award an associate's degree in early childhood education.

Preschool/Kindergarten Teacher

Preschool teachers teach mainly 4-year-old children, and kindergarten teachers primarily teach 5-year-old children. They usually have an undergraduate degree in education, specializing in early childhood education. State certification to become a preschool or kindergarten teacher usually is required.

Family and Consumer Science Educator

Family and consumer science educators may specialize in early childhood education or instruct middle and high school students about such matters as nutrition, interpersonal relationships, human sexuality, parenting, and human development. Hundreds of colleges and universities throughout the United States offer two- and four-year degree programs in family and consumer science. These programs usually include an internship requirement. Additional education courses may be needed to obtain a teaching certificate. Some family and consumer educators go on to graduate school for further training, which provides a background for possible jobs in college teaching or research.

To read about the work of one family and consumer science educator, see the Connecting with Careers interlude on page 440 in Chapter 14.

Educational Psychologist

An educational psychologist most often teaches in a college or university and conducts research in such areas of educational psychology as learning, motivation, classroom management, and assessment. Most educational psychologists have a doctorate in education, which takes four to six years of graduate work. They help to train students who will take various positions in education, including educational psychologist, school psychologist, and teacher.

To read about the work of one educational psychologist, see the Connecting with Careers interlude on page 41 in Chapter 1.

School Psychologist

School psychologists focus on improving the psychological and intellectual well-being of elementary and secondary school students. They may work in a centralized office in a school district or in one or more schools. They give psychological tests, interview students and their parents, consult with teachers, and may provide counseling to students and their families.

School psychologists usually have a master's or doctoral degree in school psychology. In graduate school, they take courses in counseling, assessment, learning, and other areas of education and psychology.

Clinical and Counseling

There are a wide variety of clinical and counseling jobs that are linked with child development. These range from child clinical psychologist to adolescent drug counselor.

Clinical Psychologist

Clinical psychologists seek to help people with psychological problems. They work in a variety of settings, including colleges and universities, clinics, medical schools, and private practice. Some clinical psychologists only conduct psychotherapy; others do psychological assessment and psychotherapy; and some also do research. Clinical psychologists may specialize in a particular age group, such as children (child clinical psychologist).

Clinical psychologists have either a Ph.D. (which involves clinical and research training) or a Psy.D. degree (which involves only clinical training). This graduate training usually takes five to seven years and includes courses in clinical psychology and a one-year supervised internship in an accredited setting toward the end of the training. In most cases, they must pass a test to become licensed in a state and to call themselves clinical psychologists.

To read about the work of one clinical psychologist, see the Connecting with Careers interlude on page 9 in Chapter 1.

Psychiatrist

Like clinical psychologists, psychiatrists might specialize in working with children (child psychiatry) or adolescents (adolescent psychiatry). Psychiatrists might work in medical schools in teaching and research roles, in a medical clinic, or in private practice. In addition to administering drugs to help improve the lives of people with psychological problems, psychiatrists also may conduct psychotherapy. Psychiatrists obtain a medical degree and then do a residency in psychiatry. Medical school takes approximately four years, and the psychiatry residency another three to four years. Unlike psychologists (who do not go to medical school) in most states, psychiatrists can administer drugs to clients.

To read about the work of one child psychiatrist, see the Connecting with Careers interlude on page 417 in Chapter 13.

Counseling Psychologist

Counseling psychologists work in the same settings as clinical psychologists and may do psychotherapy, teach, or conduct research. In many instances, however, counseling psychologists do not work with individuals who have a severe mental disorder. A counseling psychologist might specialize in working with children, adolescents, and/or families.

Counseling psychologists go through much of the same training as clinical psychologists, although in a graduate program in counseling rather than clinical psychology. Counseling psychologists have either a master's degree or a doctoral degree. They also must go through a licensing procedure. One type of master's degree in counseling leads to the designation of licensed professional counselor.

School Counselor

School counselors help to identify students' abilities and interests, guide students in developing academic plans, and explore career options with students. They may help students cope with adjustment problems. They may work with students individually, in small groups, or even in a classroom. They often consult with parents, teachers, and school administrators when trying to help students with their problems.

High school counselors advise students on choosing a major, fulfilling admissions requirements for college, taking entrance exams, applying for financial aid, and enrolling in appropriate vocational and technical training. Elementary school counselors are mainly involved in counseling students about social and personal problems. They may observe children in the classroom and at play as part of their work. School counselors usually have a master's degree in counseling.

To read about the work of one high school counselor, see the Connecting with Careers interlude on page 477 in Chapter 15.

Career Counselor

Career counselors help individuals to identify their best career options and guide them in applying for jobs. They may work in private industry or at a college or university. They usually interview individuals and give them vocational or psychological tests to target careers that fit their interests and abilities. Sometimes they help individuals to create résumés or conduct mock interviews to help them feel comfortable in a job interview. They may create and promote job fairs or other recruiting events to help individuals obtain jobs.

Social Worker

Social workers often are involved in helping people with social or economic problems. They may investigate, evaluate, and attempt to rectify reported cases of abuse, neglect, endangerment, or domestic disputes. They can intervene in families if necessary and provide counseling and referral services to individuals and families.

Social workers have a minimum of an undergraduate degree from a school of social work that includes course work in various areas of sociology and psychology. Some social workers also have a master's or doctoral degree. They often work for publicly funded agencies at the city, state, or national level, although increasingly they work in the private sector in areas such as drug rehabilitation and family counseling.

In some cases, social workers specialize in a certain area, as is true of a medical social worker who has a master's degree in social work (MSW). This involves graduate course work and supervised clinical experiences in medical settings. A medical social worker might coordinate a variety of support services provided to people with a severe or long-term disability. Family-care social workers often work with families who need support services.

Drug Counselor

Drug counselors provide counseling to individuals with drug abuse problems. They may work on an individual basis with a substance abuser or conduct group therapy sessions. They may work in private practice, with a state or federal government agency, with a company, or in a hospital setting. Some drug counselors specialize in working with adolescents or families. Most states provide a certification procedure for obtaining a license to practice drug counseling.

At a minimum, drug counselors go through an associate's or certificate program. Many have an undergraduate degree in substance-abuse counseling, and some have master's and doctoral degrees.

Medical, Nursing, and Physical Development

Careers in child development include a wide range of occupations in the medical and nursing areas, as well as jobs pertaining to improving some aspect of the child's physical development.

Obstetrician/Gynecologist

An obstetrician/gynecologist prescribes prenatal and postnatal care and performs deliveries in

connecting with careers

Katherine Duchen Smith, Nurse and Child-Care Health Consultant

Katherine Duchen Smith has a master's degree in nursing and works as a child-care health consultant. She lives in Fort Collins, Colorado, and in 2004 was appointed as the public relations chair of the National Association of Pediatric Nurse Practitioners (NAPNAP), which has more than 6,000 members.

Smith provides health consultation and educational services to child-care centers, private schools, and hospitals. She also teaches in the Regis University Family Nurse Practitioner Program. Smith developed an interest in outreach and public-relations activities during her five-year term as a board member for the Fort Collins Poudre Valley Hospital System. Later, she became the organization's outreach consultant.

As child-care health consultants, nurses might provide telephone consultation and link children, families, or staff with primary care providers. In underserved areas, they might also be asked to administer immunizations, help chronically ill children access specialty care, or develop a comprehensive health promotion or injury prevention program for caregivers and families.

Katherine Duchen Smith (*left*), nurse and child-care health consultant, at a child-care center where she is a consultant.

maternity cases. The individual also treats diseases and injuries of the female reproductive system. Obstetricians may work in private practice, in a medical clinic, in a hospital, or in a medical school. Becoming an obstetrician/gynecologist requires a medical degree plus three to five years of residency in obstetrics/gynecology.

Pediatrician

A pediatrician monitors infants' and children's health, works to prevent disease or injury, helps children attain optimal health, and treats children with health problems. Pediatricians may work in private practice, in a medical clinic, in a hospital, or in a medical school. As medical doctors, they can administer drugs to children and may counsel parents and children on ways to improve the children's health. Many pediatricians on the faculty of medical schools also teach and conduct research on children's health and diseases. Pediatricians have attained a medical degree and completed a three- to five-year residency in pediatrics.

Neonatal Nurse

A neonatal nurse is involved in the delivery and care of the newborn infant. The neonatal nurse may work to improve the health and well-being of infants born under normal cir-

cumstances or be involved in the delivery of care to premature and critically ill neonates.

A minimum of an undergraduate degree in nursing with a specialization in the newborn is required. This training involves course work in nursing and the biological sciences, as well as supervisory clinical experiences.

Nurse-Midwife

A nurse-midwife formulates and provides comprehensive care to selected maternity patients, cares for the expectant mother as she prepares to give birth and guides her through the birth process, and cares for the postpartum patient. The nurse-midwife also may provide care to the newborn, counsel parents on the infant's development and parenting, and provide guidance about health practices. Becoming a nurse-midwife generally requires an undergraduate degree from a school of nursing. A nurse-midwife most often works in a hospital setting.

Pediatric Nurse

Pediatric nurses have a degree in nursing that takes from two to five years to complete. Some also may obtain a master's or doctoral degree in pediatric nursing. Pediatric nurses take courses in biological sciences, nursing care, and pediatrics, usually in a school of

nursing. They also undergo supervised clinical experiences in medical settings. They monitor infants' and children's health, work to prevent disease or injury, and help children attain optimal health. They may work in hospitals, schools of nursing, or with pediatricians in private practice or at a medical clinic.

To read about the work of one pediatric nurse practitioner, see the Connecting with Careers Development interlude above and the Connecting with Careers interlude on page 253 in Chapter 8.

Audiologist

An audiologist has a minimum of an undergraduate degree in hearing science. This includes courses and supervisory training. Audiologists assess and identify the presence and severity of hearing loss, as well as problems in balance. Some audiologists also go on to obtain a master's and/or doctoral degree. They may work in a medical clinic, with a physician in private practice, in a hospital, or in a medical school.

Speech Therapist

Speech therapists are health-care professionals who are trained to identify, assess, and treat speech and language problems. They may work with physicians, psychologists, social workers, and other health-care professionals as a team to help individuals with physical or psychological problems that include speech and language disorders. Speech pathologists have a minimum of an undergraduate degree in the speech and hearing science or communications disorders area. They may work in private practice, in hospitals and medical schools, and in government agencies with individuals of any age. Some specialize in working with children or with a particular type of speech disorder.

To read about the work of one speech therapist, see the Connecting with Careers interlude on page 342 in Chapter 11.

Genetic Counselor

Genetic counselors work as members of a health-care team, providing information and support to families who have members with birth defects or genetic disorders and to families who may be at risk for a variety of inherited conditions. They identify families at risk and provide supportive counseling. They serve as educators and resource people for other health-care professionals and the public. Almost half work in university medical centers, and another one-fourth work in private hospital settings.

Most genetic counselors enter the field after majoring in undergraduate disciplines such as biology, genetics, psychology, nursing, public health, and social work. They have specialized graduate degrees and experience in medical genetics and counseling.

Families and Relationships

A number of careers are available for working with families and relationship problems. These range from being a child welfare worker to marriage and family therapist.

Child Welfare Worker

A child welfare worker is employed by the child protective services unit of each state. The child welfare worker protects the child's rights, evaluates any maltreatment the child might experience, and may have the child removed from the home if necessary. A child social worker has a minimum of an undergraduate degree in social work.

Child Life Specialist

Child life specialists work with children and their families when the child needs to be hospitalized. They monitor the child patient's activities, seek to reduce the child's stress, help the child cope effectively, and assist the child in enjoying the hospital experience as much as possible. Child life specialists may provide parent education and develop individualized treatment plans based on an assessment of the child's development, temperament, medical plan, and available social supports.

Child life specialists have an undergraduate degree. As undergraduates, they take courses in child development and education and usually take additional courses in a child life program.

To read about the work of one child life specialist, see the Connecting with Careers interlude on page 336 in Chapter 11.

Marriage and Family Therapist

Marriage and family therapists work on the principle that many individuals who have psychological problems benefit when psychotherapy is provided in the context of a marital or family relationship. Marriage and family therapists may provide marital therapy, couples therapy to individuals in a relationship who are not married, and family therapy to two or more members of a family.

Marriage and family therapists have a master's or doctoral degree. They go through a training program in graduate school similar to that of a clinical psychologist but with a focus on marital and family relationships. To practice marital and family therapy in most states, it is necessary to go through a licensing procedure.

To read about the work of one marriage and family specialist, see the Connecting with Careers interlude on page 303 in Chapter 10.

There are one hundred and ninety-three living species of monkeys and apes. One hundred and ninety-two of them are covered with hair. The exception is the naked ape, self-named Homo sapiens.

—DESMOND MORRIS
British Zoologist, 20th Century

Beginnings

The rhythm and meaning of life involve beginnings. Questions are raised about how, from so simple a beginning, endless forms develop, grow, and mature. What was this organism, what is this organism, and what will this organism be? In Section 2, you will read three chapters: "Biological Beginnings" (Chapter 2), "Prenatal Development" (Chapter 3), and "Birth" (Chapter 4).

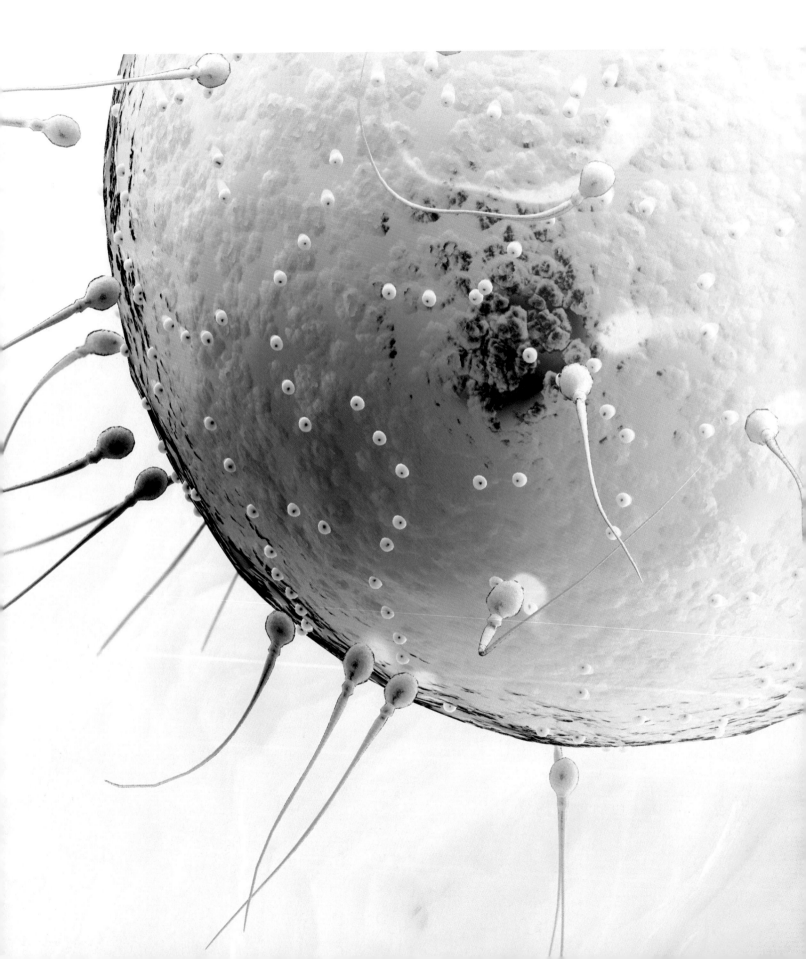

chapter 2 BIOLOGICAL BEGINNINGS

Jim Springer and Jim Lewis are identical twins. They were separated at 4 weeks of age and did not see each other again until they were 39 years old. Both worked as part-time deputy sheriffs, vacationed in Florida, drove Chevrolets, had dogs named Toy, and married and divorced women named Betty. One twin named his son James Allan, and the other named his son James Alan. Both liked math but not spelling, enjoyed carpentry and mechanical drawing, chewed their fingernails down to the nubs, had almost identical drinking and smoking habits, had hemorrhoids, put on 10 pounds at about the same point in development, first suffered headaches at the age of 18, and had similar sleep patterns.

Jim and Jim do have some differences. One wears his hair over his forehead, the other slicks it back and has sideburns. One expresses himself best orally; the other is more proficient in writing. But, for the most part, their profiles are remarkably similar.

Jim Lewis (*left*) and Jim Springer (*right*).

Jim and Jim were part of the Minnesota Study of Twins Reared Apart, directed by Thomas Bouchard and his colleagues (Bouchard, 1995, 2008; Johnson & others, 2007). The study brings identical twins (identical genetically because they come from the same fertilized egg) and fraternal twins (who come from different fertilized eggs) from all over the world to Minneapolis to investigate their lives. There the twins complete personality and intelligence tests, and they provide detailed medical histories, including information about diet and smoking, exercise habits, chest X-rays, heart stress tests, and electroencephalograms (EEGs). The twins are asked more than 15,000 questions about their family and childhood, personal interests, vocational orientation, values, and aesthetic judgments.

Another pair of identical twins in the Minnesota study, Daphne and Barbara, are called the "giggle sisters" because, after being reunited, they were always making each other laugh. A thorough search of their adoptive families' histories revealed no gigglers. The giggle sisters ignored stress, avoided conflict and controversy whenever possible, and showed no interest in politics.

Two other identical twin sisters were separated at 6 weeks and reunited in their fifties. Both described hauntingly similar nightmares in which they had doorknobs and fishhooks in their mouths as they smothered to death. The nightmares began during early adolescence and stopped within the past 10 to 12 years. Both women were bed wetters until about 12 or 13 years of age, and their educational and marital histories are remarkably similar.

When genetically identical twins who were separated as infants show such striking similarities in their tastes and habits and choices, can we conclude that their genes must have caused the development of those tastes and habits and choices? Other possible causes need to be considered. The twins shared not only the same genes but also some experiences. Some of the separated twins lived together for several months prior to their adoption; some of the twins had been reunited prior to testing (in some cases, many years earlier); adoption agencies often place twins in similar homes; and even strangers who spend several hours together and start comparing their lives are likely to come up with some coincidental similarities (Joseph, 2006). The Minnesota study of identical twins points to both the importance of the genetic basis of human development and the need for further research on genetic and environmental factors.

topical connections

In Chapter 1 you learned about the historical background of child development, its growing importance as a field of study, and the way its researchers conduct their work. You studied the key processes and periods in child development and identified ways in which the science of child development can improve the lives of children. The forthcoming discussion of genetics and the previous coverage of theories (psychoanalytic, cognitive, behavioral and social cognitive, ethological, and ecological) in Chapter 1 provide a knowledge basis to examine one of development's major issues and debates—how strongly development is influenced by heredity (nature) and environment (nurture).

◀ ▬ *looking back* ▬ ▬ ▬ ▬

preview

The examples of Jim and Jim, the giggle sisters, and the identical twins who had the same nightmares stimulate us to think about our genetic heritage and the biological foundations of our existence. Organisms are not like billiard balls, moved by simple, external forces to predictable positions on life's pool table. Environmental experiences and biological foundations work together to make us who we are. Our exploration of life's biological beginnings focuses on evolution, genetic foundations, challenges and choices regarding reproduction, and the interaction of heredity and environment.

What Is the Evolutionary Perspective?

 LG1 Discuss the evolutionary perspective on development.

Natural Selection and Adaptive Behavior   Evolutionary Psychology

As our earliest ancestors left the forest to feed in the savannahs, and then to form hunting societies on the open plains, their minds and behaviors changed, and they eventually established humans as the dominant species on Earth. How did this evolution come about?

> What endless questions vex the thought, of whence and whither, when and how.
>
> —SIR RICHARD BURTON
> *British Explorer, 19th Century*

NATURAL SELECTION AND ADAPTIVE BEHAVIOR

Natural selection is the evolutionary process by which those individuals of a species that are best adapted are the ones that survive and reproduce. To understand what this means, let's return to the middle of the nineteenth century, when the British naturalist Charles Darwin was traveling around the world, observing many different species of animals in their natural surroundings. Darwin, who published his observations and thoughts in *On the Origin of Species* (1859), noted that most organisms reproduce at rates that would cause enormous increases in the population of most species and yet populations remain nearly constant. He reasoned that an intense, constant struggle for food, water, and resources must occur among the many young born in each generation, because many of the young do not survive. Those that do survive, and reproduce, pass on their characteristics to the next generation. Darwin observed that these survivors are better *adapted* to their world than are the nonsurvivors (Brooker, 2011). The best-adapted individuals survive to leave the most offspring. Over the course of many generations, organisms with the characteristics needed for survival make up an increased percentage of the population. Over many, many generations, this could produce a gradual modification of the whole population. If environmental conditions change, however, other characteristics might become favored by natural selection, moving the species in a different direction (Mader, 2012).

All organisms must adapt to particular places, climates, food sources, and ways of life. An eagle's claws are a physical adaptation that facilitates predation. *Adaptive behavior* is behavior that promotes an organism's survival in the natural habitat (Johnson, 2012; Pluess & Belsky, 2011). For example, attachment between a caregiver and a baby ensures the infant's closeness to a caregiver for feeding and protection from danger, thus increasing the infant's chances of survival. Or consider pregnancy sickness, which is a tendency for women to become nauseated during pregnancy and avoid certain foods (Schmitt & Pilcher, 2004). Women with pregnancy sickness tend to avoid foods such as coffee that are higher in toxins that could harm the fetus. Thus, pregnancy sickness may be an evolution-based adaptation that enhances the offspring's ability to survive.

How does the attachment of this Vietnamese baby to its mother reflect the evolutionary process of adaptive behavior?

EVOLUTIONARY PSYCHOLOGY

Although Darwin introduced the theory of evolution by natural selection in 1859, his ideas only recently have become a popular framework for explaining behavior. Psychology's newest approach, **evolutionary psychology,** emphasizes the importance of adaptation, reproduction, and "survival of the fittest" in shaping behavior. "Fit" in this sense refers to the ability to bear offspring that survive long enough to bear offspring of their own. In this view, natural selection favors behaviors that increase reproductive success: the ability to pass your genes to the next generation (Bjorklund, 2007, 2012; Bjorklund & Pellegrini, 2011).

David Buss (1995, 2008, 2012) has been especially influential in stimulating new interest in how evolution can explain human behavior. He argues that just as evolution shapes our physical features, such as body shape and height, it also pervasively influences our decision making, our degree of aggression, our fears, and our mating patterns. For example, assume that our ancestors were hunters and gatherers on the plains and that men did most of the hunting and women stayed close to home, gathering seeds and plants for food. If you have to travel some distance from your home in an effort to find and slay a fleeing animal, you need not only certain physical traits but also the ability to use certain types of spatial thinking. Men born with these traits would be more likely than men without them to survive, to bring home lots of food, and to be considered attractive mates—and thus to reproduce and pass on these characteristics to their children. In other words, these traits would provide a reproductive advantage for males and, over many generations, men with good spatial thinking skills might become more numerous in the population. Critics point out that this scenario might or might not have actually happened.

Evolutionary Developmental Psychology   Recently, interest has grown in using the concepts of evolutionary psychology to understand human development

evolutionary psychology Branch of psychology that emphasizes the importance of adaptation, reproduction, and "survival of the fittest" in shaping behavior.

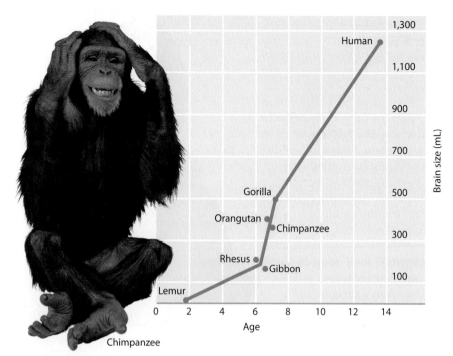

FIGURE **2.1**

THE BRAIN SIZES OF VARIOUS PRIMATES AND HUMANS IN RELATION TO THE LENGTH OF THE CHILDHOOD PERIOD. Compared with other primates, humans have both a larger brain and a longer childhood period. *What conclusions can you draw from the relationship indicated by this graph?*

Children in all cultures are interested in the tools that adults in their cultures use. For example, this 11-month-old boy from the Efe culture in the Democratic Republic of the Congo in Africa is trying to cut a papaya with an apopau (a smaller version of a machete). *Might the infant's behavior be evolutionary-based or be due to both biological and environmental conditions?*

(Bjorklund, 2007, 2012; Bjorklund & Pellegrini, 2011). Following are some ideas proposed by evolutionary developmental psychologists (Bjorklund & Pellegrini, 2002).

An extended childhood period evolved because humans require time to develop a large brain and learn the complexity of human societies. Humans take longer to become reproductively mature than any other mammal (see Figure 2.1). During this extended childhood period, they develop a large brain and the experiences needed to become competent adults in a complex society.

Many evolved psychological mechanisms are domain-specific. That is, the mechanisms apply only to a specific aspect of a person's makeup. According to evolutionary psychology, information processing is one example. In this view, the mind is not a general-purpose device that can be applied equally to a vast array of problems. Instead, as our ancestors dealt with certain recurring problems such as hunting and finding shelter, specialized modules evolved that processed information related to those problems—for example, a module for physical knowledge for tracking animals, a module for mathematical knowledge for trading, and a module for language.

Evolved mechanisms are not always adaptive in contemporary society. Some behaviors that were adaptive for our prehistoric ancestors may not serve us well today. For example, the food-scarce environment of our ancestors likely led to humans' propensity to gorge when food is available and to crave high-caloric foods, a trait that might lead to an epidemic of obesity when food is plentiful.

Evaluating Evolutionary Psychology   Although evolutionary psychology is getting increased attention, it remains just one theoretical approach among many. Like the theories described in Chapter 1, it has limitations, weaknesses, and critics. Albert Bandura (1998), whose social cognitive theory was described in Chapter 1, acknowledges the important influence of evolution on human adaptation. However, he rejects what he calls "one-sided evolutionism," which sees social behavior as the product of evolved biology. An alternative is a *bidirectional view*, in which environmental and biological conditions influence each other. In this view, evolutionary pressures created changes in biological structures that allowed the use of tools, which enabled our ancestors to manipulate the environment, constructing new environmental conditions. In turn, environmental innovations produced new selection pressures that led to the evolution of specialized biological systems for consciousness, thought, and language.

In other words, evolution gave us bodily structures and biological potentialities; it does not dictate behavior. People have used their biological capacities to produce diverse cultures—aggressive and pacific, egalitarian and autocratic. As American scientist Stephen Jay Gould (1981) concluded, in most domains of human functioning, biology allows a broad range of cultural possibilities.

The "big picture" idea of natural selection leading to the development of human traits and behaviors is difficult to refute or test because it is on a time scale that does not lend itself to empirical study. Thus, studying specific genes in humans and other species—and their links to traits and behaviors—may be the best approach for testing ideas that emerge from the evolutionary psychology perspective.

Review *Connect* Reflect

LG1 Discuss the evolutionary perspective on development.

Review

- How can natural selection and adaptive behavior be defined?
- What is evolutionary psychology? What are some basic ideas about human development proposed by evolutionary developmental psychologists? How can evolutionary psychology be evaluated?

Connect

- In Chapter 1, you learned about how different developmental processes interact. How was that principle reinforced by the information in this section?

Reflect *Your Own Personal Journey of Life*

- Which is more persuasive to you: the views of evolutionary psychologists or those of their critics? Why?

What Are the Genetic Foundations of Development?

LG2 Describe what genes are and how they influence human development.

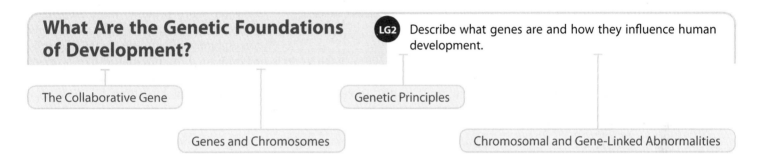

The Collaborative Gene

Genes and Chromosomes

Genetic Principles

Chromosomal and Gene-Linked Abnormalities

Genetic influences on behavior evolved over time and across many species. Our many traits and characteristics that are genetically influenced have a long evolutionary history that is retained in our DNA. In other words, our DNA is not just inherited from our parents; it's also what we've inherited as a species from the species that came before us.

Let's take a closer look at DNA and its role in human development. How are characteristics that suit a species for survival transmitted from one generation to the next? Darwin did not know because genes and the principles of genetics had not yet been discovered. Each of us carries a "genetic code" that we inherited from our parents. Because a fertilized egg carries this human code, a fertilized human egg cannot grow into an egret, eagle, or elephant.

THE COLLABORATIVE GENE

Each of us began life as a single cell weighing about one twenty-millionth of an ounce! This tiny piece of matter housed our entire genetic code—instructions that orchestrated growth from that single cell to a person made of trillions of cells, each containing a replica of the original code. That code is carried by our genes (Raven, 2011). What are genes and what do they do? For the answer, we need to look into our cells.

The nucleus of each human cell contains **chromosomes,** which are threadlike structures made up of deoxyribonucleic acid, or DNA. **DNA** is a complex molecule that has a double helix shape, like a spiral staircase, and contains genetic information. **Genes,** the units of hereditary information, are short segments of DNA, as you can see in Figure 2.2. They direct cells to reproduce themselves and to assemble proteins. Proteins, in turn, are the building blocks of cells as well as the regulators that direct the body's processes (Mader, 2012).

Each gene has its own location, its own designated place on a particular chromosome. Today, there is a great deal of enthusiasm about efforts to discover the

chromosomes Threadlike structures made up of deoxyribonucleic acid, or DNA.

DNA A complex molecule with a double helix shape; contains genetic information.

genes Units of hereditary information composed of DNA. Genes direct cells to reproduce themselves and manufacture the proteins that maintain life.

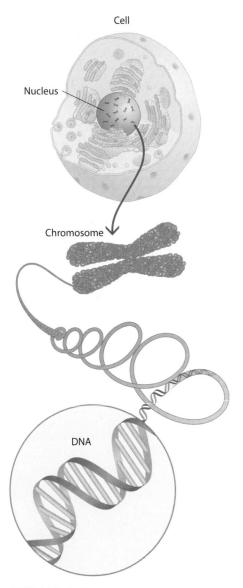

Cell

Nucleus

Chromosome

DNA

FIGURE 2.2

CELLS, CHROMOSOMES, DNA, AND GENES.
(*Top*) The body contains trillions of cells. Each cell contains a central structure, the nucleus. (*Middle*) Chromosomes are threadlike structures located in the nucleus of the cell. Chromosomes are composed of DNA. (*Bottom*) DNA has the structure of a spiral staircase. A gene is a segment of DNA.

How Would You...?
If you were a **psychologist,** how would you explain to an enthusiast of the Human Genome Project that genes don't provide an exact blueprint for how children's development will unfold?

mitosis Cellular reproduction in which the cell's nucleus duplicates itself with two new cells being formed, each containing the same DNA as the parent cell, arranged in the same 23 pairs of chromosomes.

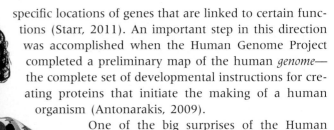

A positive result from the Human Genome Project. Shortly after Andrew Gobea was born, his cells were genetically altered to prevent his immune system from failing.

specific locations of genes that are linked to certain functions (Starr, 2011). An important step in this direction was accomplished when the Human Genome Project completed a preliminary map of the human *genome*— the complete set of developmental instructions for creating proteins that initiate the making of a human organism (Antonarakis, 2009).

One of the big surprises of the Human Genome Project was a report indicating that humans have only about 30,000 genes (U.S. Department of Energy, 2001). More recently, the number of human genes has been revised further downward to approximately 20,500 (Ensembl Human, 2008). Scientists had thought that humans had as many as 100,000 or more genes. They had also believed that each gene programmed just one protein. In fact, humans appear to have far more proteins than they have genes, so there cannot be a one-to-one correspondence between genes and proteins (Commoner, 2002). Each gene is not translated, in automaton-like fashion, into one and only one protein. A gene does not act independently, as developmental psychologist David Moore (2001) emphasized by titling his book *The Dependent Gene.*

Rather than being a group of independent genes, the human genome consists of many genes that collaborate with each other and with nongenetic factors inside and outside the body. The collaboration operates at many points. For example, the cellular machinery mixes, matches, and links small pieces of DNA to reproduce the genes, and that machinery is influenced by what is going on around it.

Whether a gene is turned "on"—that is, working to assemble proteins—is also a matter of collaboration. The activity of genes (*genetic expression*) is affected by their environment (Gottlieb, 2007). For example, hormones that circulate in the blood make their way into the cell where they can turn genes "on" and "off." And the flow of hormones can be affected by environmental conditions, such as light, day length, nutrition, and behavior. Numerous studies have shown that external events outside the original cell and the person, as well as events inside the cell, can excite or inhibit gene expression (Gottlieb, 2007). Recent research has documented that factors such as stress, radiation, and temperature can influence gene expression (Georgakilas, 2011). For example, one study revealed that an increase in the concentration of stress hormones such as cortisol produced a fivefold increase in DNA damage (Flint & others, 2007). A recent study also found that exposure to radiation changed the rate of DNA synthesis in cells (Lee & others, 2011).

GENES AND CHROMOSOMES

Genes are not only collaborative, they are enduring. How do the genes manage to get passed from generation to generation and end up in all of the trillion cells in the body? Three processes explain the heart of the story: mitosis, meiosis, and fertilization.

Mitosis, Meiosis, and Fertilization   All of the cells in your body, except the sperm and egg, have 46 chromosomes arranged in 23 pairs. These cells reproduce by a process called mitosis. During **mitosis,** the cell's nucleus—including the chromosomes—duplicates itself and the cell divides. Two new cells are formed, each containing the same DNA as the original cell, arranged in the same 23 pairs of chromosomes.

Calvin and Hobbes

by Bill Watterson

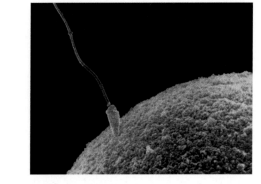

FIGURE 2.3

A SINGLE SPERM PENETRATING AN EGG AT THE POINT OF FERTILIZATION

However, a different type of cell division—**meiosis**—forms eggs and sperm (or gametes). During meiosis, a cell of the testes (in men) or ovaries (in women) duplicates its chromosomes but then divides *twice*, thus forming four cells, each of which has only half of the genetic material of the parent cell (Johnson, 2012). By the end of meiosis, each egg or sperm has 23 *unpaired* chromosomes.

During **fertilization,** an egg and a sperm fuse to create a single cell, called a **zygote** (see Figure 2.3). In the zygote, the 23 unpaired chromosomes from the egg and the 23 unpaired chromosomes from the sperm combine to form one set of 23 paired chromosomes—one chromosome of each pair from the mother's egg and the other from the father's sperm. In this manner, each parent contributes half of the offspring's genetic material.

Figure 2.4 shows 23 paired chromosomes of a male and a female. The members of each pair of chromosomes are both similar and different: Each chromosome in the pair contains varying forms of the same genes, at the same location on the chromosome. A gene for hair color, for example, is located on both members of one pair of chromosomes, in the same location on each. However, one of those chromosomes might carry the gene for blond hair; the other chromosome in the pair might carry the gene for brown hair.

Do you notice any obvious differences between the chromosomes of the male and the chromosomes of the female in Figure 2.4? The difference lies in the 23rd pair. Ordinarily, in females this pair consists of two chromosomes called *X chromosomes;* in males the 23rd pair consists of an X and a *Y chromosome.* The presence of a Y chromosome is what makes an individual male.

Sources of Variability

Combining the genes of two parents in offspring increases genetic variability in the population, which is valuable for a species because it provides more characteristics for natural selection to operate on (Raven, 2011). In fact, the human genetic process creates several important sources of variability.

meiosis A specialized form of cell division that occurs to form eggs and sperm (or gametes).

fertilization A stage in reproduction whereby an egg and a sperm fuse to create a single cell, called a zygote.

zygote A single cell formed through fertilization.

FIGURE 2.4

THE GENETIC DIFFERENCE BETWEEN MALES AND FEMALES. Set (*a*) shows the chromosome structure of a male, and set (*b*) shows the chromosome structure of a female. The last pair of 23 pairs of chromosomes is in the bottom right box of each set. Notice that the Y chromosome of the male is smaller than the X chromosome of the female. To obtain this kind of chromosomal picture, a cell is removed from a person's body, usually from the inside of the mouth. The chromosomes are stained by chemical treatment, magnified extensively, and then photographed.

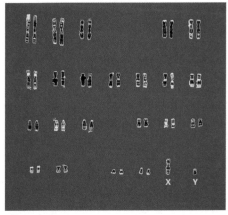

(a)

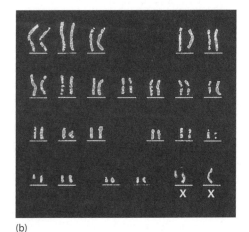

(b)

First, the chromosomes in the zygote are not exact copies of those in the mother's ovaries and the father's testes. During the formation of the sperm and egg in meiosis, the members of each pair of chromosomes are separated, but which chromosome in the pair goes to the gamete is a matter of chance. In addition, before the pairs separate, pieces of the two chromosomes in each pair are exchanged, creating a new combination of genes on each chromosome. Thus, when chromosomes from the mother's egg and the father's sperm are brought together in the zygote, the result is a truly unique combination of genes (Goodenough & McGuire, 2012).

If each zygote is unique, how do identical twins like those discussed in the opening of the chapter exist? Identical twins (also called monozygotic twins) develop from a single zygote that splits into two genetically identical replicas, each of which becomes a person. *Fraternal twins* (called dizygotic twins) develop from separate eggs and separate sperm, making them genetically no more similar than ordinary siblings.

Another source of variability comes from DNA (Lewis, 2010). Chance, a mistake by cellular machinery, or damage from an environmental agent such as radiation may produce a *mutated gene*, which is a permanently altered segment of DNA (Mader, 2012).

Even when their genes are identical, however, people vary. The difference between genotypes and phenotypes helps us to understand this source of variability. All of a person's genetic material makes up his or her **genotype.** However, not all of the genetic material is apparent in our observed and measurable characteristics. A **phenotype** consists of observable characteristics. Phenotypes include physical characteristics (such as height, weight, and hair color) and psychological characteristics (such as personality and intelligence).

For each genotype, a range of phenotypes can be expressed, providing another source of variability (Gottlieb, 2007). An individual can inherit the genetic potential to grow very large, for example, but good nutrition, among other things, will be essential to achieving that potential. The giggle sisters introduced in the chapter opening might have inherited the same genetic potential to be very tall, but if Daphne had grown up malnourished, she might have ended up noticeably shorter than Barbara. This principle is so widely applicable it has a name: heredity-environment interaction (or gene-environment interaction).

GENETIC PRINCIPLES

What determines how a genotype is expressed to create a particular phenotype? Much is unknown about the answer to this question (Starr, 2011). However, a number of genetic principles have been discovered, among them those of dominant-recessive genes, sex-linked genes, genetic imprinting, and polygenically determined characteristics.

Dominant-Recessive Genes Principle   In some cases, one gene of a pair always exerts its effects; it is *dominant*, overriding the potential influence of the other gene, called the *recessive* gene. This is the *dominant-recessive genes principle*. A recessive gene exerts its influence only if the two genes of a pair are both recessive. If you inherit a recessive gene for a trait from each of your parents, you will show the trait. If you inherit a recessive gene from only one parent, you may never know you carry the gene. Brown hair, farsightedness, and dimples rule over blond hair, nearsightedness, and freckles in the world of dominant-recessive genes.

Can two brown-haired parents have a blond-haired child? Yes, they can. Suppose that each parent has a dominant gene for brown hair and a recessive gene for blond hair. Because dominant genes override recessive genes, the parents have brown hair, but both are carriers of blondness and pass on their recessive genes for blond hair. With no dominant gene to override them, the recessive genes can make the child's hair blond (see Figure 2.5).

Sex-Linked Genes   Most mutated genes are recessive. When a mutated gene is carried on the X chromosome, the result is called *X-linked inheritance*. The implications for males may be very different from those for females (Bermejo-Alvarez &

genotype A person's genetic heritage; the actual genetic material.

phenotype The way an individual's genotype is expressed in observed and measurable characteristics.

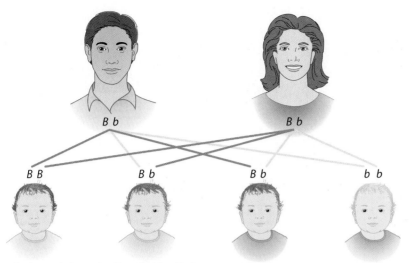

B = Gene for brown hair   *b* = Gene for blond hair

others, 2011; Davies, 2010). Remember that males have only one X chromosome. Thus, if there is an altered, disease-creating gene on the X chromosome, males have no "backup" copy to counter the harmful gene and therefore may carry an X-linked disease. However, females have a second X chromosome, which is likely to be unchanged. As a result, they are not likely to have the X-linked disease. Thus, most individuals who have X-linked diseases are males. Females who have one changed copy of the X gene are known as "carriers," and they usually do not show any signs of the X-linked disease. Hemophilia and fragile X syndrome, which we discuss later in the chapter, are examples of X-linked inherited diseases (Borjas & others, 2010).

Genetic Imprinting   *Genetic imprinting* occurs when genes have differing effects depending on whether they are inherited from the mother or the father. A chemical process "silences" one member of the gene pair. For example, as a result of imprinting, only the maternally derived copy of a gene might be active, while the paternally derived copy of the same gene is silenced—or vice versa. Only a small percentage of human genes appears to undergo imprinting, but it is a normal and important aspect of development (Wakeling, 2011). When imprinting goes awry, development is disturbed, as in the case of Beckwith-Wiedemann syndrome, a growth disorder, and Wilms tumor, a type of cancer (Barber & others, 2011; Choufani, Shuman, & Weksberg, 2010).

Polygenic Inheritance   Genetic transmission is usually more complex than the simple examples we have examined thus far (Engler & Marillonnet, 2011; Walker & Gore, 2011). Few characteristics reflect the influence of only a single gene or pair of genes. Most are determined by the interaction of many different genes; they are said to be *polygenically determined* (Barnett & others, 2011). Even simple characteristics such as height, for example, reflect the interaction of many genes, as well as the influence of the environment.

The term *gene-gene interaction* is increasingly used to describe studies that focus on the interdependence of two or more genes in influencing characteristics, behavior, diseases, and development (Baye & others, 2011). For example, recent studies have documented gene-gene interaction in children's immune system functioning (Reijmerink & others, 2011), asthma (Gu & Zhao, 2011), cancer (O'Mara & others, 2011), cardiovascular disease (Jylhava & others, 2009), and arthritis (Liu, Ackerman, & Carulli, 2011).

CHROMOSOMAL AND GENE-LINKED ABNORMALITIES

Sometimes abnormalities characterize the genetic process. Some of these abnormalities involve whole chromosomes that do not separate properly during meiosis. Other abnormalities are produced by harmful genes.

Name	Description	Treatment	Incidence
Down syndrome	An extra chromosome causes mild to severe retardation and physical abnormalities.	Surgery, early intervention, infant stimulation, and special learning programs	1 in 1,900 births at age 20 1 in 300 births at age 35 1 in 30 births at age 45
Klinefelter syndrome (XXY)	An extra X chromosome causes physical abnormalities.	Hormone therapy can be effective	1 in 1,000 male births
Fragile X syndrome	An abnormality in the X chromosome can cause mental retardation, learning disabilities, or short attention span.	Special education, speech and language therapy	More common in males than in females
Turner syndrome (XO)	A missing X chromosome in females can cause mental retardation and sexual underdevelopment.	Hormone therapy in childhood and puberty	1 in 2,500 female births
XYY syndrome	An extra Y chromosome can cause above-average height.	No special treatment required	1 in 1,000 male births

FIGURE **2.6**

SOME CHROMOSOMAL ABNORMALITIES. The treatments for these abnormalities do not necessarily erase the problem but may improve the individual's adaptive behavior and quality of life.

These athletes, several of whom have Down syndrome, are participating in a Special Olympics competition. Notice the distinctive facial features of the individuals with Down syndrome, such as a round face and a flattened skull. *What causes Down syndrome?*

Chromosomal Abnormalities Occasionally when a gamete is formed, the sperm and ovum do not have their normal set of 23 chromosomes. The most notable examples involve Down syndrome and abnormalities of the sex chromosomes (see Figure 2.6).

Down Syndrome An individual with **Down syndrome** has a round face, a flattened skull, an extra fold of skin over the eyelids, a protruding tongue, short limbs, and retardation of motor and mental abilities. The syndrome is caused by the presence of an extra copy of chromosome 21 (Peters & Petrill, 2011). It is not known why the extra chromosome is present, but the health of the male sperm or female ovum may be involved.

Down syndrome appears approximately once in every 700 live births. Women between the ages of 16 and 34 are less likely to give birth to a child with Down syndrome than are younger or older women. African American children are rarely born with Down syndrome.

Sex-Linked Chromosomal Abnormalities Recall that a newborn normally has either an X and a Y chromosome, or two X chromosomes. Human embryos must possess at least one X chromosome to be viable. The most common sex-linked chromosomal abnormalities involve the presence of an extra chromosome (either an X or Y) or the absence of one X chromosome in females.

Klinefelter syndrome is a genetic disorder in which males have an extra X chromosome, making them XXY instead of XY (Ryan, 2010). Males with this disorder have undeveloped testes, and they usually have enlarged breasts and become tall (Aksglaede & others, 2011). One study revealed significant impairment in language, academic, attentional, and motor abilities in boys with the syndrome (Ross & others, 2008). Klinefelter syndrome occurs approximately once in every 1,000 live male births.

Fragile X syndrome is a genetic disorder that results from an abnormality in the X chromosome, which becomes constricted

developmental **connection**

Conditions, Diseases, and Disorders. *Mental retardation* can be classified in several ways. Chapter 12, p. 370

and often breaks (Heulins & Kooy, 2011). The physical appearance of children with fragile X syndrome often appears normal, although these children typically have prominent ears, a long face, a high-arched palate, and soft skin. Mental deficiency often is an outcome, but it may take the form of mental retardation, a learning disability, or a short attention span. One study revealed that boys with fragile X syndrome were characterized by cognitive deficits in inhibition, memory, and planning (Hooper & others, 2008). This disorder occurs more frequently in males than in females, possibly because the second X chromosome in females negates the effects of the abnormal X chromosome (Kuehn, 2011).

Turner syndrome is a chromosomal disorder in females in which either an X chromosome is missing, making the person XO instead of XX, or part of one X chromosome is deleted. Females with Turner syndrome are short in stature and have a webbed neck (Ranke & Lindberg, 2011). They might be infertile and have difficulty in mathematics, but their verbal ability often is quite good (Murphy & Mazzocco, 2008). Turner syndrome occurs in approximately 1 of every 2,500 live female births (Kim & others, 2011).

The **XYY syndrome** is a chromosomal disorder in which the male has an extra Y chromosome (Bishop & others, 2011; Boyd & others, 2011). Early interest in this syndrome focused on the belief that the extra Y chromosome found in some males contributed to aggression and violence. However, researchers subsequently found that XYY males are no more likely to commit crimes than are XY males.

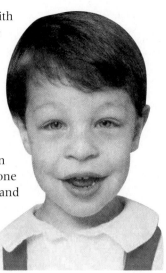
A boy with fragile X syndrome.

Gene-Linked Abnormalities Abnormalities can be produced not only by an uneven number of chromosomes but also by harmful genes (Johnson, 2012). More than 7,000 such genetic disorders have been identified, although most of them are rare.

Phenylketonuria (PKU) is a genetic disorder in which the individual cannot properly metabolize phenylalanine, an amino acid. It results from a recessive gene and occurs about once in every 10,000 to 20,000 live births. Today, phenylketonuria is easily detected, and it is treated by a diet that prevents an excess accumulation of phenylalanine (Cotugno & others, 2011). If phenylketonuria is left untreated, however, excess phenylalanine builds up in the child, producing mental retardation and hyperactivity. Phenylketonuria accounts for approximately 1 percent of institutionalized individuals who are mentally retarded, and it occurs primarily in non-Latino Whites.

The story of phenylketonuria has important implications for the nature-nurture issue. Although phenylketonuria is a genetic disorder (nature), how or whether a gene's influence in phenylketonuria is played out depends on environmental influences because the disorder can be treated (nurture) (Cotugno & others, 2011). That is, the presence of a genetic defect *does not* inevitably lead to the development of the disorder *if* the individual develops in the right environment (one free of phenylalanine). This is one example of the important principle of heredity-environment interaction. Under one environmental condition (phenylalanine in the diet), mental retardation results, but when other nutrients replace phenylalanine, intelligence develops in the normal range. The same genotype has different outcomes depending on the environment (in this case, the nutritional environment).

Sickle-cell anemia, which occurs most often in African Americans, is a genetic disorder that impairs the body's red blood cells. Red blood cells carry oxygen to the body's cells and are usually disk-shaped. In sickle-cell anemia, a recessive gene causes the red blood cell to become a hook-shaped "sickle" that cannot carry oxygen properly and dies quickly. As a result, the body's cells do not receive adequate oxygen, causing anemia and early death (Dworkis & others, 2011; Eckman & Embury, 2011). About 1 in 400 African American babies is affected by sickle-cell anemia. One in 10 African Americans is a carrier, as is 1 in 20 Latin Americans. A National Institutes of Health (2008) panel concluded that the only FDA-approved drug (hydroxyurea) to treat sickle-cell anemia in adolescents and adults is not widely

Down syndrome A chromosomally transmitted form of mental retardation, caused by the presence of an extra copy of chromosome 21.

Klinefelter syndrome A genetic disorder in which males have an extra X chromosome, making them XXY instead of XY.

fragile X syndrome A genetic disorder involving an abnormality in the X chromosome, which becomes constricted and often breaks.

Turner syndrome A chromosomal disorder in females in which either an X chromosome is missing, making the person XO instead of XX, or the second X chromosome is partially deleted.

XYY syndrome A chromosomal disorder in which males have an extra Y chromosome.

phenylketonuria (PKU) A genetic disorder in which the individual cannot properly metabolize phenylalanine, an amino acid. PKU is now easily detected—but if left untreated, results in mental retardation and hyperactivity.

sickle-cell anemia A genetic disorder that affects the red blood cells and occurs most often in people of African descent.

Name	Description	Treatment	Incidence
Cystic fibrosis	Glandular dysfunction that interferes with mucus production; breathing and digestion are hampered, resulting in a shortened life span.	Physical and oxygen therapy, synthetic enzymes, and antibiotics; most individuals live to middle age.	1 in 2,000 births
Diabetes	Body does not produce enough insulin, which causes abnormal metabolism of sugar.	Early onset can be fatal unless treated with insulin.	1 in 2,500 births
Hemophilia	Delayed blood clotting causes internal and external bleeding.	Blood transfusions/injections can reduce or prevent damage due to internal bleeding.	1 in 10,000 males
Huntington's disease	Central nervous system deteriorates, producing problems in muscle coordination and mental deterioration.	Does not usually appear until age 35 or older; death likely 10 to 20 years after symptoms appear.	1 in 20,000 births
Phenylketonuria (PKU)	Metabolic disorder that, left untreated, causes mental retardation.	Special diet can result in average intelligence and normal life span.	1 in 10,000 to 1 in 20,000 births
Sickle-cell anemia	Blood disorder that limits the body's oxygen supply; it can cause joint swelling, as well as heart and kidney failure.	Penicillin, medication for pain, antibiotics, and blood transfusions.	1 in 400 African American children (lower among other groups)
Spina bifida	Neural tube disorder that causes brain and spine abnormalities.	Corrective surgery at birth, orthopedic devices, and physical/medical therapy.	2 in 1,000 births
Tay-Sachs disease	Deceleration of mental and physical development caused by an accumulation of lipids in the nervous system.	Medication and special diet are used, but death is likely by 5 years of age.	1 in 30 American Jews is a carrier.

FIGURE 2.7
SOME GENE-LINKED ABNORMALITIES

used. Research is currently being conducted in a study named Baby HUG to determine if the drug works with babies.

Other diseases that result from genetic abnormalities include cystic fibrosis, diabetes, hemophilia, spina bifida, and Tay-Sachs disease (Bell & others, 2011; Geborek & Hjelte, 2011). Figure 2.7 provides further information about these diseases. Someday scientists may identify why these and other genetic abnormalities occur and discover how to cure them.

Dealing with Genetic Abnormalities Every individual carries DNA variations that might predispose the person to serious physical diseases or mental disorders. But not all individuals who carry a genetic disorder display the disorder. Other genes or developmental events sometimes compensate for genetic abnormalities (Gottlieb, 2007). For instance, recall the example of phenylketonuria from the previous section: Even though individuals might carry the genetic disorder of phenylketonuria, it is not expressed when phenylalanine is replaced by other nutrients in their diet.

Thus, genes are not destiny, but genes that are missing, nonfunctional, or mutated can be associated with disorders (Hensen & others, 2011; Jentarra & others, 2011). Identifying such genetic flaws could enable doctors to predict an individual's risks, recommend healthy practices, and prescribe the safest and most effective drugs (McDermott, Downing, & Stratton, 2011). A decade or two from now, parents of a newborn baby may be able to leave the hospital with a full genome analysis of their offspring that reveals disease risks.

However, this knowledge might bring important costs as well as benefits (Tarini, 2012). Who would have access to a person's genetic profile? An individual's ability to land and hold jobs or obtain insurance might be threatened if it is known that a person is considered at risk

During a physical examination for a college football tryout, Jerry Hubbard, 32, learned that he carried the gene for sickle-cell anemia. Daughter Sara is healthy but daughter Avery (in the print dress) has sickle-cell anemia. *If you were a genetic counselor, would you recommend that this family have more children? Explain.*

Holly Ishmael, Genetic Counselor

Holly Ishmael is a genetic counselor at Children's Mercy Hospital in Kansas City. She obtained an undergraduate degree in psychology and then a master's degree in genetic counseling from Sarah Lawrence College.

Genetic counselors, like Ishmael, work as members of a health-care team, providing information and support to families with birth defects or genetic disorders. They identify families at risk by analyzing inheritance patterns and explore options with the family. Some genetic counselors, like Ishmael, become specialists in prenatal and pediatric genetics; others might specialize in cancer genetics or psychiatric genetic disorders.

Ishmael says, "Genetic counseling is a perfect combination for people who want to do something science-oriented, but need human contact and don't want to spend all of their time in a lab or have their nose in a book" (Rizzo, 1999, p. 3).

Genetic counselors have specialized graduate degrees in the areas of medical genetics and counseling. They enter graduate school with undergraduate backgrounds from a variety of disciplines, including biology, genetics, psychology, public health, and social work. There are

Holly Ishmael (*left*) in a genetic counseling session.

approximately thirty graduate genetic counseling programs in the United States. If you are interested in this profession, you can obtain further information from the National Society of Genetic Counselors at www.nsgc.org.

for some disease. For example, should an airline pilot or a neurosurgeon who is predisposed to develop a disorder that makes one's hands shake be required to leave that job early?

Genetic counselors, usually physicians or biologists who are well versed in the field of medical genetics, understand the kinds of problems just described, the odds of encountering them, and helpful strategies for offsetting some of their effects (Clarke & Thirlaway, 2011; Vos & others, 2011). A research review found that many individuals who receive genetic counseling find it difficult to quantify risk and tend to overestimate risk (Sivell & others, 2008). To read about the career and work of a genetic counselor, see the *Connecting with Careers* profile.

Review *Connect* Reflect

 Describe what genes are and how they influence human development.

Review

- What are genes?
- How are genes passed on from one generation to another?
- What basic principles describe how genes interact?
- What are some chromosomal and gene-linked abnormalities?

Connect

- Explain how environment interacts with genes in gene-linked abnormalities.

Reflect *Your Own Personal Journey of Life*

- Would you want to be able to access a full genome analysis of yourself or your offspring? Why or why not?

Prenatal Diagnostic Tests   Infertility and Reproductive Technology   Adoption

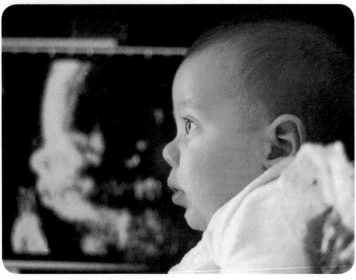

A 6-month-old infant poses with the ultrasound sonography record taken four months into the baby's prenatal development. *What is ultrasound sonography?*

The facts and principles we have discussed regarding meiosis, genetics, and genetic abnormalities are a small part of the recent explosion of knowledge about human biology. This knowledge not only helps us understand human development but also opens up many new choices to prospective parents, choices that can also raise ethical questions.

PRENATAL DIAGNOSTIC TESTS

One choice open to prospective mothers is the extent to which they should undergo prenatal testing. A number of tests can indicate whether a fetus is developing normally; these include ultrasound sonography, fetal MRI, chorionic villus sampling, amniocentesis, maternal blood screening, and noninvasive prenatal diagnosis (NIPD). There has been a dramatic increase in research on the use of less invasive techniques, such as fetal MRI and NIPD, which pose lower risks to the fetus than more invasive techniques such as chorionic villus sampling and amniocentesis (Du & others, 2011; Nemec & others, 2011).

Ultrasound Sonography   An ultrasound test is often conducted seven weeks into a pregnancy and at various times later in pregnancy. Ultrasound sonography is a prenatal medical procedure in which high-frequency sound waves are directed into the pregnant woman's abdomen. The echo from the sounds is transformed into a visual representation of the fetus's inner structures. This technique can detect many structural abnormalities in the fetus, including microencephaly, a form of mental retardation involving an abnormally small brain; it can also determine the number of fetuses and give clues to the baby's sex (Masselli & others, 2011). This test poses virtually no risk to the woman or the fetus.

Fetal MRI   The development of brain-imaging techniques has led to increasing use of *fetal MRI* to diagnose fetal malformations (Schmid & others, 2011) (see Figure 2.8). MRI stands for magnetic resonance imaging, which uses a powerful magnet and radio images to generate detailed images of the body's organs and structure. Currently, ultrasound is still the first choice in fetal screening, but fetal MRI can provide more detailed images than ultrasound. In many instances, ultrasound will indicate a possible abnormality, and then fetal MRI will be used to obtain a clearer, more detailed image (Mangione & others, 2011). Among the fetal malformations that fetal MRI may be able to detect better than ultrasound sonography are certain abnormalities of the central nervous system, chest, gastrointestinal tract, genital/urinary system, and placenta (Nemec & others, 2011; Triulzi, Manganaro, & Volpe, 2011; Wikstrom, Ahlstrom, & Axelsson, 2011).

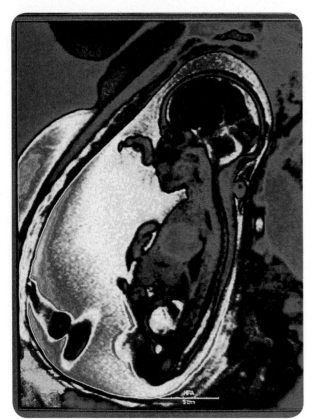

FIGURE **2.8**

A FETAL MRI, WHICH IS INCREASINGLY BEING USED IN PRENATAL DIAGNOSIS OF FETAL MALFORMATIONS

Chorionic Villus Sampling   At some point between 9.5 and 12.5 weeks of pregnancy, chorionic villus sampling may be used to detect genetic defects and chromosomal abnormalities such as the ones discussed in the previous section (Basaran, Basaran, & Topatan, 2011). Diagnosis takes approximately 10 days. *Chorionic villus sampling (CVS)* is a prenatal medical procedure in which a small sample of the placenta (the vascular organ that links the fetus to the mother's uterus) is removed (Akolekar & others, 2011). There is a small risk of limb deformity when CVS is used.

developmental connection

Biological Processes. Discover what the development of the fetus is like at the times when chorionic villus sampling and amniocentesis can be used. Chapter 3, p. 87

Amniocentesis   Between the 14th and 20th weeks of pregnancy, amniocentesis may be performed. *Amniocentesis is a prenatal medical procedure in which a sample of amniotic fluid is withdrawn by syringe and tested for chromosomal or metabolic disorders* (Athanasiadis & others, 2011). The amniotic fluid is found within the amnion, a thin sac in which the embryo is suspended. Ultrasound sonography is often used during amniocentesis so that the syringe can be placed precisely. The later amniocentesis is performed, the better its diagnostic potential. The earlier it is performed, the more useful it is in deciding how to handle a pregnancy. It may take two weeks for enough cells to grow and amniocentesis test results to be obtained. Amniocentesis brings a small risk of miscarriage—about 1 woman in every 200 to 300 miscarries after amniocentesis.

Both amniocentesis and chorionic villus sampling provide valuable information about the presence of birth defects, but they also raise difficult issues for parents about whether an abortion should be obtained if birth defects are present (Zhang & others, 2010). Chorionic villus sampling allows a decision to be made sooner, at a time when abortion is safer and less traumatic. Although earlier reports indicated that chorionic villus sampling brings a slightly higher risk of pregnancy loss than amniocentesis, a recent U.S. study of more than 40,000 pregnancies found that loss rates for CVS decreased from 1998 to 2003 and that there is no longer a difference in pregnancy loss risk between CVS and amniocentesis (Caughey, Hopkins, & Norton, 2006).

Maternal Blood Screening   During the 16th to 18th weeks of pregnancy, maternal blood screening may be performed. *Maternal blood screening* identifies pregnancies that have an elevated risk for birth defects such as spina bifida (a defect in the spinal cord) and Down syndrome (Ballard, 2011). The current blood test is called the *triple screen* because it measures three substances in the mother's blood. After an abnormal triple screen result, the next step is usually an ultrasound examination. If an ultrasound does not explain the abnormal triple screen results, amniocentesis is typically used.

How Would You…?

If you were a **health-care professional,** how would you discuss the benefits and risks of having prenatal diagnostic tests with a woman who has just found out that she is pregnant?

Noninvasive Prenatal Diagnosis (NIPD)   *Noninvasive prenatal diagnosis (NIPD)* is increasingly being explored as an alternative to procedures such as chorionic villus sampling and amniocentesis (Jackson & Pyeritz, 2011; Tsui, Chiu, & Lo, 2011). At this point, NIPD has mainly focused on the isolation and examination of fetal cells circulating in the mother's blood and analysis of cell-free fetal DNA in maternal plasma. Researchers already have used NIPD to successfully test for genes inherited from a father that cause cystic fibrosis and Huntington disease. They also are exploring the potential for using NIPD to diagnose Down syndrome and to identify a baby's sex as early as five weeks after conception (Deng & others, 2011; Du & others, 2011). Being able to detect an offspring's sex and to identify various diseases and defects so early raises ethical concerns about couples' motivation to terminate a pregnancy (Benn & Chapman, 2010).

Technical challenges still characterize the use of NIPD, but its benefit in reducing risk makes it an attractive diagnostic candidate (Tsui & others, 2011). The main technical challenge is to efficiently separate out the fetal cells, which comprise only about one of every million cells in a mother's blood.

A technician using a micro-needle to inject human sperm into a human egg cell as part of an in vitro fertilization procedure. The injected sperm fertilizes the egg, and the resulting zygote is then grown in the laboratory until it reaches an early stage of embryonic development. Then it is implanted in the uterus.

Fetal Sex Determination Chorionic villus sampling has often been used to determine the sex of the fetus at some point between 11 and 13 weeks of gestation. Recently, however, some noninvasive techniques have been able to determine the sex of the fetus at an earlier point by assessing cell-free DNA in maternal plasma (Hill & others, 2011; Miura & others, 2011). A recent meta-analysis concluded that the baby's sex can be determined as early as seven weeks into pregnancy (Devaney & others, 2011).

INFERTILITY AND REPRODUCTIVE TECHNOLOGY

Recent advances in biological knowledge have also opened up many choices for infertile people. Approximately 10 to 15 percent of couples in the United States experience infertility, which is defined as the inability to conceive a child after 12 months of regular intercourse without contraception. The cause of infertility can rest with the woman or the man. The woman may not be ovulating (releasing eggs to be fertilized), she may be producing abnormal ova, her fallopian tubes by which ova normally reach the womb may be blocked, or she may have a disease that prevents implantation of the embryo into the uterus. The man may produce too few sperm, the sperm may lack motility (the ability to move adequately), or he may have a blocked passageway (Hesmet & Lo, 2006).

In the United States, more than 2 million couples seek help for infertility every year. In some cases of infertility, surgery may correct the cause; in others, hormone-based drugs may improve the probability of having a child. Of the 2 million couples who seek help for infertility every year, about 40,000 try high-tech assisted reproduction. By far the most common technique used is *in vitro fertilization (IVF)*, in which eggs and sperm are combined in a laboratory dish. If any eggs are successfully fertilized, one or more of the resulting eggs are transferred into the woman's uterus. A national U.S. study in 2004 by the Centers for Disease Control and Prevention found the success rate of IVF depends on the mother's age (see Figure 2.9).

The creation of families by means of the new reproductive technologies raises important questions about the physical and psychological consequences for children (Gurgan & Demirol, 2007; Wagenaar & others, 2008a). One result of fertility treatments is an increase in multiple births (Jones, 2007; Reddy & others, 2007). Twenty-five to 30 percent of pregnancies achieved by fertility treatments—including in vitro fertilization—now result in multiple births. A recent research review concluded that the two main risk factors associated with assisted reproductive techniques are multiple pregnancies and low birth weight (Basatemur & Sutcliffe, 2008). Any multiple birth increases the likelihood that the babies will have life-threatening and costly problems, such as extremely low birth weight (Cheung, 2006).

Not nearly as many studies have examined the psychological outcomes of IVF as the physical outcomes. To read about a study that addresses these consequences, see the *Connecting with Research* interlude that follows.

ADOPTION

Although surgery and fertility drugs can sometimes resolve infertility problems, another choice is to adopt a child (Scott, Roberts, & Glennen, 2011). Adoption is the social and legal process by which a parent-child relationship is established between persons unrelated at birth. As we see

FIGURE **2.9**

SUCCESS RATES OF IN VITRO FERTILIZATION VARY ACCORDING TO THE WOMAN'S AGE

Are There Developmental Outcomes in Adolescence of In Vitro Fertilization?

A longitudinal study examined 34 in vitro fertilization families, 49 adoptive families, and 38 families with a naturally conceived child (Golombok, MacCallum, & Goodman, 2001). Each type of family included a similar portion of boys and girls. Also, the age of the young adolescents did not differ according to family type (mean age of 11 years, 11 months).

Children's socioemotional development was assessed by (1) interviewing the mother and obtaining detailed descriptions of any problems the child might have; (2) administering a Strengths and Difficulties questionnaire to the child's mother and teacher; and (3) administering the Social Adjustment Inventory for Children and Adolescents, which examines functioning in school, peer relationships, and self-esteem.

No significant differences between the children from the in vitro fertilization, adoptive, and naturally conceiving families were found. The results from the Social Adjustment Inventory for Children and Adolescents are shown in Figure 2.10. Recent reviews by leading researchers conclude that the children and adolescents conceived through new reproductive technologies—such as in vitro fertilization—are as well adjusted as their counterparts conceived by natural means (Golombok, 2011a, b; Golombok & Tasker, 2010).

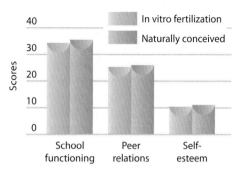

FIGURE **2.10**

SOCIOEMOTIONAL FUNCTIONING OF CHILDREN CONCEIVED THROUGH IN VITRO FERTILIZATION OR NATURALLY CONCEIVED. This graph shows the results of a study that compared the socioemotional functioning of young adolescents who had either been conceived through in vitro fertilization (IVF) or naturally conceived (Golombok, MacCallum, & Goodman, 2001). For each type of family, the study included a similar portion of boys and girls and children of similar age (mean age of 11 years, 11 months). Although the means for the naturally conceived group were slightly higher, this is likely due to chance: There were no significant differences between the groups.

What additional types of studies do you think researchers might conduct to study possible developmental effects of new reproductive technologies? How long do you think the children in such studies should be followed, for instance?

next in the *Connecting with Diversity* interlude, an increase in diversity has characterized the adoption of children in the United States in recent years.

The changes in adoption practices over the last several decades make it difficult to generalize about the average adopted child or average adoptive parent. As we see next, though, some researchers have provided useful comparisons between adopted children and nonadopted children and their families.

How do adopted children fare after they are adopted? Children who are adopted very early in their lives are more likely to have positive outcomes than children adopted later in life (Bernard & Dozier, 2008). In one study, the later adoption occurred, the more problems the adoptees had. Infant adoptees had the fewest adjustment difficulties; those adopted after they were 10 years of age had the most problems (Sharma, McGue, & Benson, 1996). A recent Danish study indicated that being adopted was not a risk for juvenile delinquency if the individual was adopted at 12 months of age or earlier (Laubjerg & Petersson, 2011). However, those adopted after 12 months of age had 3 to 4 times higher risk of becoming a juvenile delinquent than their nonadopted counterparts.

A majority of adopted children and adolescents (including those adopted at older ages, transracially, and across national borders) adjust effectively, and their parents report considerable satisfaction with their decision to adopt (Brodzinsky & Pinderhughes, 2002; Castle & others, 2010). A research review of 88 studies also revealed no difference in the self-esteem of adopted and nonadopted children and

The Increased Diversity of Adopted Children and Adoptive Parents

A number of changes have characterized adoptive children and adoptive parents in the last three to four decades (Brodzinsky & Pinderhughes, 2002). In the first half of the twentieth century, most children adopted in the United States were healthy, non-Latino White infants who were adopted at birth or soon after; however, in recent decades as abortion became legal and the use of contraception increased, fewer of these infants became available for adoption. Increasingly, U.S. couples adopted a much wider diversity of children—from other countries, from other ethnic groups, children with physical and/or mental problems, and children who had been neglected or abused.

Changes also have characterized adoptive parents in the last three to four decades (Brodzinsky & Pinderhughes, 2002). In the first half of the twentieth century, most adoptive parents were from non-Latino White middle or upper socioeconomic status backgrounds who were married and did not have any type of disability. However, in recent decades, increased diversity has characterized adoptive parents. Many adoption agencies today have no income requirements for adoptive parents and now allow adults from a wide range of backgrounds to adopt children, including single adults, gay and lesbian adults, and older adults.

Do these changes in adoption practices matter? They open opportunities for many children and many couples, but possible effects of changes in the characteristics of parents on the outcomes for children are still unknown. For example, in one study, adopted adolescents were more likely to have problems if the adoptive parents had low levels of education (Miller & others, 2000). In another study, international adoptees showed fewer behavior problems and were less likely to be using mental health services than domestic adoptees

An increasing number of Hollywood celebrities are adopting children from developing countries. Actress Angelina Jolie (*above*) with her adopted children, carrying adopted daughter Zahara with adopted sons Maddox and Pax alongside them.

(Juffer & van IJzendoorn, 2005). More research is needed before definitive conclusions can be reached about the changing demographic characteristics of adoption.

adolescents, as well as no differences between transracial and same-race adoptees (Juffer & van IJzendoorn, 2007).

Most studies of adopted and nonadopted children compare different families (adoptive and nonadoptive). A recent study used a different strategy: studying families who had a biological child of their own and an adopted child (Glover & others, 2010). Findings similar to studies of between-family comparisons occurred with only a slight (but nonsignificant) trend for adopted children to show more internalized (depression, for example) and externalized (antisocial behavior, for example) problems.

In other comparisons, adopted children and adolescents fare much better than children and adolescents in long-term foster care or in an institutional environment (Bernard & Dozier, 2008). A recent study of infants in China revealed that their cognitive development improved 2 to 6 months following their adoption from foster homes and institutions (van den Dries & others, 2010). To read more about adoption, see the *Caring Connections* interlude in which we discuss effective parenting strategies with adopted children.

Parenting Adopted Children

Many of the keys to effectively parenting adopted children are no different from those for effectively parenting biological children: Be supportive and caring, be involved and monitor the child's behavior and whereabouts, be a good communicator, and help the child learn to develop self-control. However, parents of adopted children face some unique circumstances (Fontenot, 2007; Von Korff & Grotevant, 2011). They need to recognize the differences involved in adoptive family life, communicate about these differences, show respect for the birth family, and support the child's search for self and identity.

Following are some of the problems parents face when their adopted children are at different points in development and some recommendations for how to handle these problems (Brodzinsky & Pinderhughes, 2002, pp. 288–292):

- **Infancy.** Researchers have found few differences in the attachment that adopted and nonadopted infants form with their parents. However, attachment can become problematic if parents have unresolved fertility issues or the child does not meet the parents' expectations. Counselors can help prospective adoptive parents develop realistic expectations.

- **Early childhood.** Because many children begin to ask where they came from when they are about 4 to 6 years old, this is a natural time to begin to talk in simple ways to children about their adoption status (Warshak, 2008). Some parents (although not as many as in the past) decide not to tell their children about the adoption. This secrecy may create psychological risks for the child if he or she later finds out about the adoption.

What are some strategies for parenting adopted children at different points in their development?

- **Middle and late childhood.** During the elementary school years, children begin to show more interest in their origins and may ask questions related to where they came from, what their birth parents looked like, and why their birth parents chose not to raise them.

    As they grow older, children may develop mixed feelings about being adopted and question their adoptive parents' explanations. It is important for adoptive parents to recognize that this ambivalence is normal. Also, problems may arise from the desire of adoptive parents to make life too perfect for the adoptive child and to present a perfect image of themselves to the child. The result too often is that adopted children feel that they cannot release any angry feelings or openly discuss problems.

- **Adolescence.** Adolescents are likely to develop more abstract and logical thinking, to focus their attention on their bodies, and to search for an identity. These characteristics provide the foundation for adopted adolescents to reflect on their adoption status in more complex ways, such as focusing on looking different from their adoptive parents. As they explore their identity, adopted adolescents may have difficulty incorporating their adoptive status into their identity in positive ways. It is important for adoptive parents to understand the complexity of the adopted adolescent's identity exploration and be patient with the adolescent's lengthy identity search.

Review *Connect* Reflect

LG3 Identify some important reproductive challenges and choices.

Review

- What are some common prenatal diagnostic tests?
- What are some techniques that help infertile people to have children?
- How does adoption affect children's development?

Connect

- In Chapter 1, you learned about the different methods for collecting data.

How would you characterize the methods used in prenatal diagnostic testing?

Reflect *Your Own Personal Journey of Life*

- If you were an adult who could not have children, would you want to adopt a child? Why or why not?

How Do Heredity and Environment Interact? The Nature-Nurture Debate

LG4 Characterize some of the ways that heredity and environment interact to produce individual differences in development.

- Behavior Genetics
- Shared and Nonshared Environmental Experiences
- Conclusions About Heredity-Environment Interaction
- Heredity-Environment Correlations
- The Epigenetic View and Gene × Environment (G × E) Interaction

In each section of this chapter so far, we have examined parts of the nature-nurture debate. We have seen how the environment exerts selective pressures on the characteristics of species over generations, examined how genes are passed from parents to children, and discussed how reproductive technologies and adoption influence the course of children's lives. But in all of these situations, heredity and environment interact to produce development. After all, Jim and Jim (and each of the other pairs of identical twins discussed in the opening of the chapter) have the same genotype, but they are not the same person; each is unique. What made them different? Whether we are studying how genes produce proteins, their influence on how tall a person is, or how PKU might affect an individual, we end up discussing heredity-environment interactions.

Is it possible to untangle the influence of heredity from that of environment and discover the role of each in producing individual differences in development? When heredity and environment interact, how does heredity influence the environment, and vice versa?

BEHAVIOR GENETICS

Behavior genetics is the field that seeks to discover the influence of heredity and environment on individual differences in human traits and development (Gregory, Ball, & Button, 2011; Silberg, Maes, & Eaves, 2010). Note that behavior genetics does not determine the extent to which genetics or the environment affects an individual's traits. Instead, what behavior geneticists try to do is to figure out what is responsible for the differences among people—that is, to what extent do people differ because of differences in genes, environment, or a combination of these? To study the influence of heredity on behavior, behavior geneticists often use either twins or adoption situations.

In the most common **twin study,** the behavioral similarity of identical twins (who are genetically identical) is compared with the behavioral similarity of fraternal twins. Recall that although fraternal twins share the same womb, they are no more genetically alike than siblings who do not share the same birthday. Thus, by comparing groups of identical and fraternal twins, behavior geneticists capitalize on the basic knowledge that identical twins are more similar genetically than are fraternal twins (Isen & others, 2009). For example, one study revealed that conduct problems were more prevalent in identical twins than fraternal twins; the researchers concluded that the study demonstrated an important role for heredity in conduct problems (Scourfield & others, 2004).

However, several issues complicate interpretation of twin studies. For example, perhaps the environments of identical twins are more similar than the environments of fraternal twins. Adults might stress the similarities of identical twins more than those of fraternal twins, and identical twins might perceive themselves as a "set" and play together more than fraternal twins do. If so, the influence of the environment on the observed similarities between identical and fraternal twins might be very significant.

Twin studies compare identical twins with fraternal twins. Identical twins develop from a single fertilized egg that splits into two genetically identical organisms. Fraternal twins develop from separate eggs, making them genetically no more similar than nontwin siblings. *What is the nature of the twin study method?*

behavior genetics The field that seeks to discover the influence of heredity and environment on individual differences in human traits and development.

twin study A study in which the behavioral similarity of identical twins is compared with the behavioral similarity of fraternal twins.

Heredity-Environment Correlation	Description	Examples
Passive	Children inherit genetic tendencies from their parents, and parents also provide an environment that matches their own genetic tendencies.	Musically inclined parents usually have musically inclined children and they are likely to provide an environment rich in music for their children.
Evocative	The child's genetic tendencies elicit stimulation from the environment that supports a particular trait. Thus genes evoke environmental support.	A happy, outgoing child elicits smiles and friendly responses from others.
Active (niche-picking)	Children actively seek out "niches" in their environment that reflect their own interests and talents and are thus in accord with their genotype.	Libraries, sports fields, and a store with musical instruments are examples of environmental niches children might seek out if they have intellectual interests in books, talent in sports, or musical talents, respectively.

FIGURE **2.11**
EXPLORING HEREDITY-ENVIRONMENT CORRELATIONS

In an **adoption study,** investigators seek to discover whether the behavior and psychological characteristics of adopted children are more like those of their adoptive parents, who have provided a home environment, or more like those of their biological parents, who have contributed their heredity (Burt & others, 2011; Gregory, Ball, & Button, 2011). Another form of the adoption study compares adopted and biological siblings.

HEREDITY-ENVIRONMENT CORRELATIONS

The difficulties that researchers encounter when they interpret the results of twin studies and adoption studies reflect the complexities of heredity-environment interaction. Some of these interactions are *heredity-environment correlations,* which means that individuals' genes may influence the types of environments to which they are exposed. In a sense, individuals "inherit" environments that may be related or linked to genetic "propensities" (Loehlin, 2010). Behavior geneticist Sandra Scarr (1993) described three ways that heredity and environment are correlated (see Figure 2.11):

- **Passive genotype-environment correlations** occur because biological parents, who are genetically related to the child, provide a rearing environment for the child. For example, the parents might have a genetic predisposition to be intelligent and read skillfully. Because they read well and enjoy reading, they provide their children with books to read. The likely outcome is that their children, given their own inherited predispositions from their parents and their book-filled environment, will become skilled readers.

- **Evocative genotype-environment correlations** occur because a child's characteristics elicit certain types of environments. For example, active, smiling children receive more social stimulation than passive, quiet children do. Cooperative, attentive children evoke more pleasant and instructional responses from the adults around them than uncooperative, distractible children do.

- **Active (niche-picking) genotype-environment correlations** occur when children seek out environments that they find compatible and stimulating. *Niche-picking* refers to finding a setting that is suited to one's abilities. Children select from their surrounding environment some aspect that they respond to, learn about, or ignore. Their active selections of environments are related to

adoption study A study in which investigators seek to discover whether, in behavior and psychological characteristics, adopted children are more like their adoptive parents, who provided a home environment, or more like their biological parents, who contributed their heredity. Another form of the adoption study compares adopted and biological siblings.

passive genotype-environment correlations Correlations that exist when the biological parents, who are genetically related to the child, provide a rearing environment for the child.

evocative genotype-environment correlations Correlations that exist when the child's characteristics elicit certain types of physical and social environments.

active (niche-picking) genotype-environment correlations Correlations that exist when children seek out environments they find compatible and stimulating.

How Would You...?

If you were a **health-care professional,** how would you explain heredity-environment interaction to new parents who are upset about discovering that their child has a treatable genetic defect?

their particular genotype. For example, outgoing children tend to seek out social contexts in which to interact with people, whereas shy children don't. Children who are musically inclined are likely to select musical environments in which they can successfully perform their skills. How these "tendencies" come about will be discussed later in this chapter under the topic of the epigenetic view.

Scarr argues that the relative importance of the three genotype-environment correlations changes as children develop from infancy through adolescence. In infancy, much of the environment that children experience is provided by adults. Thus, passive genotype-environment correlations are more common in the lives of infants and young children than they are for older children and adolescents who can extend their experiences beyond the family's influence and create their environments to a greater degree.

Notice that this analysis gives the preeminent role in development to heredity—the analysis describes how heredity may influence the types of environments that children experience. Critics argue that the concept of heredity-environment correlation gives heredity too much of a one-sided influence in determining development because it does not consider the role of prior environmental influences in shaping the correlation itself (Gottlieb, Wahlsten, & Lickliter, 2006). Before considering this criticism and a different view of the heredity-environment linkage, let's take a closer look at how behavior geneticists analyze the environments involved in heredity.

SHARED AND NONSHARED ENVIRONMENTAL EXPERIENCES

Behavior geneticists have argued that to understand the environment's role in differences between people, we should distinguish between shared and nonshared environments. That is, we should consider experiences that children share in common with other children living in the same home, and experiences that are not shared (Burt, McGue, & Iacono, 2010; Klahr & others, 2011).

Shared environmental experiences are siblings' common experiences, such as their parents' personalities or intellectual orientation, the family's socioeconomic status, and the neighborhood in which they live. By contrast, **nonshared environmental experiences** are a child's unique experiences, both within the family and outside the family, that are not shared with a sibling. Even experiences occurring within the family can be part of the "nonshared environment." For example, parents often interact differently with each sibling, and siblings interact differently with parents (Hetherington, Reiss, & Plomin, 1994; Plomin & Daniels, 2011). Siblings often have different peer groups, different friends, and different teachers at school.

Tennis stars Venus and Serena Williams. *What might be some shared and nonshared environmental experiences they had while they were growing up that contributed to their tennis stardom?*

shared environmental experiences Siblings' common experiences, such as their parents' personalities and intellectual orientation, the family's socioeconomic status, and the neighborhood in which they live.

nonshared environmental experiences The child's own unique experiences, both within the family and outside the family, that are not shared by another sibling. Thus, experiences occurring within the family can be part of the "nonshared environment."

Behavior geneticist Robert Plomin (2004, 2011) has found that shared environment accounts for little of the variation in children's personality or interests. In other words, even though two children live under the same roof with the same parents, their personalities are often very different. Further, Plomin (2004, 2011) argues that heredity influences the nonshared environments of siblings through the heredity-environment correlations we described earlier. For example, a child who has inherited a genetic tendency to be athletic is likely to spend more time in environments related to sports; a child who has inherited a tendency to be musically inclined is more likely to spend time in environments related to music.

What are the implications of Plomin's interpretation of the roles of shared and nonshared environments in development? In the *Nurture Assumption*, Judith Harris (1998) argued that what parents do does not make a difference in their children's and adolescents' behavior. Yell at them. Hug them. Read to them. Ignore them. Harris says it won't influence how they turn out. She argues that genes and peers are far more important than parents in shaping children's and adolescents' development.

Genes and peers do matter, but Harris' descriptions of peer influences do not take into account the complexity of peer contexts and developmental trajectories (Hartup, 2009). In addition, Harris is wrong in saying that parents don't matter. For example, in the early child years parents play an important role in selecting children's peers and indirectly influencing children's development. Volumes of parenting literature with many research studies document the importance of parents in children's development (Grusec, 2011; Parke & Clarke-Stewart, 2011; Russell, 2011).

Despite the strong criticism of her views, Harris (2009) published a revised and updated edition of her earlier book, restating her claim that parents matter far less than most people think. We discuss parents' important roles throughout this book.

Heredity-Environment Correlation View

Heredity ⟶ Environment

Epigenetic View

Heredity ⟷ Environment

FIGURE 2.12

COMPARISON OF THE HEREDITY-ENVIRONMENT CORRELATION AND EPIGENETIC VIEWS

THE EPIGENETIC VIEW AND GENE × ENVIRONMENT (G × E) INTERACTION

Critics argue that the concept of heredity-environment correlation gives heredity too much of a one-sided influence in determining development because it does not consider the role of prior environmental influences in shaping the correlation itself (Gottlieb, 2007). However, earlier in the chapter we discussed how genes are collaborative, not determining an individual's traits in an independent manner but rather in an interactive manner with the environment.

The Epigenetic View In line with the concept of a collaborative gene, Gilbert Gottlieb (2007) emphasizes the **epigenetic view,** which states that development is the result of an ongoing, bidirectional interchange between heredity and the environment. Figure 2.12 compares the heredity-environment correlation and epigenetic views of development.

Let's look at an example that reflects the epigenetic view. A baby inherits genes from both parents at conception. During prenatal development, toxins, nutrition, and stress can influence some genes to stop functioning while others become stronger or weaker (Pluess & others, 2011). During infancy, environmental experiences such as toxins, nutrition, stress, learning, and encouragement continue to modify the genetic activity and the activity of the nervous system that directly underlie behavior (Gottlieb, 2007). Heredity and environment operate together—or collaborate—to produce a person's intelligence, temperament, height, weight, ability to pitch a baseball, ability to read, and so on (Dodge & Rutter, 2011; Gregory, Ball, & Button, 2011).

Gene × Environment (G × E) Interaction An increasing number of studies are exploring how the interaction between heredity and environment influences development, including interactions that involve specific DNA sequences (Caspi & others, 2011; Goldman & others, 2010; Rutter & Dodge, 2011). One study found that individuals who have a short version of a genotype labeled 5-HTTLPR (a gene involving the neurotransmitter serotonin) have an elevated risk of developing depression only if they *also* have stressful lives (Caspi & others, 2003). Thus, the specific gene did not link directly to the development of depression, but rather interacted with environmental exposure to stress to predict whether individuals

How Would You...?
If you were a **human development and family studies professional,** how would you apply the epigenetic view to explain why one identical twin can develop alcoholism while the other twin does not?

epigenetic view Emphasizes that development is the result of an ongoing, bidirectional interchange between heredity and environment.

would develop depression; however, some studies have not replicated this finding (Risch & others, 2009). In a recent study, adults who experienced parental loss as young children were more likely to have unresolved attachment as adults only when they had the short version of the 5-HTTLPR gene (Caspers & others, 2009). The long version of the serotonin transporter gene apparently provided some protection and ability to cope better with parental loss. Other recent research has found that variations in dopamine-related genes interact with supportive or unsupportive rearing environments to influence children's development (Bakermans-Kranenburg & van IJzendoorn, 2011). The type of research just described is referred to as **gene × environment (G × E) interaction**—the interaction of a specific measured variation in DNA and a specific measured aspect of the environment (Dodge & Rutter, 2011; Knafo, Israel, & Ebstein, 2011; Lahey & others, 2011).

developmental **connection**

Nature and Nurture. The nature and nurture interaction is one of the main issues in the study of children's development. Chapter 1, p. 18

CONCLUSIONS ABOUT HEREDITY-ENVIRONMENT INTERACTION

If a strong, fast, athletic girl wins a championship tennis match in her high school, is her success due to heredity or to environment? Of course, the answer is both.

> The interaction of heredity and environment is so extensive that to ask which is more important, nature or nurture, is like asking which is more important to a rectangle, height or width.
>
> —WILLIAM GREENOUGH
> *Contemporary Developmental Psychologist,*
> *University of Illinois at Urbana*

The relative contributions of heredity and environment are not additive. That is, we can't say that such-and-such a percentage of nature and such-and-such a percentage of experience make us who we are. Nor is it accurate to say that full genetic expression happens once, around conception or birth, after which we carry our genetic legacy into the world to see how far it takes us. Genes produce proteins throughout the life span, in many different environments. Or they don't produce these proteins, depending in part on how harsh or nourishing those environments are.

The emerging view is that complex behaviors have some *genetic loading* that gives people a propensity for a particular developmental trajectory. However, the actual development requires more: an environment. And that environment is complex, just like the mixture of genes we inherit (Grusec, 2011; Thompson, 2011a). Environmental influences range from the things we lump together under "nurture" (such as parenting, family dynamics, schooling, and neighborhood quality) to biological encounters (such as viruses, birth complications, and even biological events in cells).

Consider for a moment the cluster of genes associated with diabetes. The child who carries this genetic mixture might experience a world of loving parents, nutritious meals, and regular medical intervention. Or the child's world might include parental neglect, a diet high in sugar, and little help from competent physicians. In which of these environments are the child's genes likely to result in diabetes?

If heredity and environment interact to determine the course of development, is that all there is to answering the question of what causes development? Are children completely at the mercy of their genes and environment as they develop? Children's genetic heritage and environmental experiences are pervasive influences on their development (Gregory, Ball, & Button, 2011). But children's development is not only the outcome of their heredity and the environment they experience. Children also can author a unique developmental path by changing the environment. As one psychologist recently concluded:

> In reality, we are both the creatures and creators of our worlds. We are . . . the products of our genes and environments. Nevertheless, . . . the stream of causation that shapes the future runs through our present choices. . . . Mind matters. . . . Our hopes, goals, and expectations influence our future. (Myers, 2010, p. 168)

To what extent are this young girl's piano skills likely due to heredity, environment, or both? Explain.

gene × environment (G × E) interaction The interaction of a specific measured variation in the DNA and a specific measured aspect of the environment.

Review *Connect* Reflect

 LG4 Characterize some of the ways that heredity and environment interact to produce individual differences in development.

Review

- What is behavior genetics?
- What are three types of heredity-environment correlations?
- What is meant by the concepts of shared and nonshared environmental experiences?
- What is the epigenetic view of development? What characterizes gene × environment (G × E) interaction?
- What conclusions can be reached about heredity-environment interaction?

Connect

- Of passive, evocative, and active genotype-environment correlations, which is the best explanation for the similarities discovered between the twins (Jim and Jim, for example) discussed in the story that opened the chapter?

Reflect *Your Own Personal Journey of Life*

- Someone tells you that she has analyzed her genetic background and environmental experiences and reached the conclusion that environment definitely has had little influence on her intelligence. What would you say to this person about her ability to make this self-diagnosis?

topical **connections** ----

In the remaining chapters of this text you will continue to read about biological influences on development, especially in the chapters on prenatal development (Chapter 3), birth (Chapter 4), and the chapters on physical development in infancy (Chapter 5), early childhood (Chapter 8), middle and late childhood (Chapter 11), and adolescence (Chapter 14), but also in the chapters on cognitive and socioemotional development. In the next chapter, you learn about the amazing developmental journey from conception to birth, including how expectant mothers can best promote their offspring's health and well-being during pregnancy.

looking forward -- ->

reach your **learning goals**

What Is the Evolutionary Perspective? **LG1** Discuss the evolutionary perspective on development.

Natural Selection and Adaptive Behavior

- Natural selection is the process by which those individuals of a species that are best adapted survive and reproduce. Darwin proposed that natural selection fuels evolution. In evolutionary theory, adaptive behavior is behavior that promotes the organism's survival in a natural habitat.

Evolutionary Psychology

- Evolutionary psychology holds that adaptation, reproduction, and "survival of the fittest" are important in shaping behavior. Ideas proposed by evolutionary developmental psychology include the view that we humans need an extended juvenile period to develop a large brain and learn the complexity of human social communities. Many evolved psychological mechanisms are domain-specific. Like other theoretical approaches to development, evolutionary psychology has limitations. Bandura rejects "one-sided evolutionism" and argues for a bidirectional link between biology and environment. Biology allows for a broad range of cultural possibilities.

What Are the Genetic Foundations of Development?

 LG2 Describe what genes are and how they influence human development.

The Collaborative Gene

- Short segments of DNA constitute genes, the units of hereditary information that direct cells to reproduce and manufacture proteins. Except in the sperm and egg, the nucleus of each human cell contains 46 chromosomes (arranged in 23 pairs), which are composed of DNA. Genes act collaboratively, not independently.

Genes and Chromosomes

- Genes are passed on to new cells when chromosomes are duplicated during the processes of mitosis and meiosis, which are two ways in which new cells are formed. When an egg and a sperm unite in the fertilization process, the resulting zygote contains the genes from the chromosomes in the father's sperm and the mother's egg. Despite this transmission of genes from generation to generation, variability is created in several ways, including the exchange of chromosomal segments during meiosis, mutations, and the distinction between a genotype and a phenotype.

Genetic Principles

- Genetic principles that describe how genes interact include those involving dominant-recessive genes, sex-linked genes, genetic imprinting, and polygenic inheritance.

Chromosomal and Gene-Linked Abnormalities

- Chromosomal abnormalities produce Down syndrome, which is caused by the presence of an extra copy of chromosome 21, as well as sex-linked chromosomal abnormalities such as Klinefelter syndrome, fragile X syndrome, Turner syndrome, and XYY syndrome. Gene-linked abnormalities involve harmful genes. Gene-linked disorders include phenylketonuria (PKU) and sickle-cell anemia. Genetic counseling offers couples information about their risk of having a child with inherited abnormalities.

What Are Some Reproductive Challenges and Choices?

 LG3 Identify some important reproductive challenges and choices.

Prenatal Diagnostic Tests

- Amniocentesis, ultrasound sonography, fetal MRI, chorionic villus sampling, maternal blood screening, and noninvasive prenatal diagnosis (NIPD) are used to determine whether a fetus is developing normally. There has been a dramatic increase in research on less invasive diagnosis, such as fetal MRI and NIPD.

Infertility and Reproductive Technology

- Approximately 10 to 15 percent of U.S. couples have infertility problems, some of which can be corrected through surgery or fertility drugs. An additional option includes in vitro fertilization.

Adoption

- Although adopted children and adolescents have more problems than their nonadopted counterparts, the vast majority of adopted children adapt effectively. When adoption occurs very early in development, the outcomes for the child are improved. Because of the dramatic changes that have occurred in adoption in recent decades, it is difficult to generalize about the average adopted child or average adoptive family.

How Do Heredity and Environment Interact? The Nature-Nurture Debate

 LG4 Characterize some of the ways that heredity and environment interact to produce individual differences in development.

Behavior Genetics

- Behavior genetics seeks to discover the influence of heredity and environment on individual differences in the traits and development of humans. Methods used by behavior geneticists include twin studies and adoption studies.

Heredity-Environment Correlations

- In Scarr's heredity-environment correlations view, heredity directs the types of environments that children experience. She describes three genotype-environment correlations: passive, evocative, and active (niche-picking). Scarr maintains that the relative importance of these three genotype-environment correlations changes as children develop.

Shared and Nonshared Environmental Experiences

- Shared environmental experiences refer to siblings' common experiences, such as their parents' personalities and intellectual orientation, the family's socioeconomic status, and the neighborhood in which they live. Nonshared environmental experiences involve the child's unique experiences, both within the family and outside the family, that are not shared with a sibling. Many behavior geneticists argue that differences in the development of siblings are due to nonshared environmental experiences (and heredity) rather than shared environmental experiences.

The Epigenetic View and Gene × Environment (G × E) Interaction

- The epigenetic view emphasizes that development is the result of an ongoing, bidirectional interchange between heredity and environment. Gene × environment interaction involves the interaction of a specific measured variation in the DNA and a specific measured aspect of the environment. An increasing number of G × E studies are being conducted.

Conclusions About Heredity-Environment Interaction

- Complex behaviors have some genetic loading that gives people a propensity for a particular developmental trajectory. However, actual development also requires an environment, and that environment is complex. The interaction of heredity and environment is extensive. Much remains to be discovered about the specific ways that heredity and environment interact to influence development.

---

key terms

evolutionary
  psychology 57
chromosomes 59
DNA 59
genes 59
mitosis 60
meiosis 61
fertilization 61
zygote 61
genotype 62

phenotype 62
Down syndrome 64
Klinefelter syndrome 64
fragile X syndrome 64
Turner syndrome 65
XYY syndrome 65
phenylketonuria (PKU) 65
sickle-cell anemia 65
behavior genetics 74
twin study 74

adoption study 75
passive genotype-
  environment
  correlations 75
evocative genotype-
  environment
  correlations 75
active (niche-picking)
  genotype-environment
  correlations 75

shared environmental
  experiences 76
nonshared environmental
  experiences 76
epigenetic view 77
gene × environment (G × E)
  interaction 77

key people

Thomas Bouchard 55
Charles Darwin 56
David Buss 57

Albert Bandura 58
Stephen Jay Gould 58
David Moore 60

Sandra Scarr 75
Robert Plomin 76
Judith Harris 77

Gilbert Gottlieb 77

connecting with improving the lives of children

MAKING A DIFFERENCE

Some Prepregnancy Strategies

Even before a woman becomes pregnant, she can adopt some strategies that may make a difference in how healthy the pregnancy is and its developmental outcomes:

- *Become knowledgeable about prepregnancy planning and health-care providers.* The kinds of health-care providers who are qualified to provide care for pregnant women include an obstetrician/gynecologist, a family practitioner, a nurse practitioner, and a certified nurse-midwife.

- *Meet with a health professional before conception.* A good strategy is for both potential parents to meet with a health professional prior to conception to assess their health and review personal and family histories. During this meeting, the health professional will discuss nutrition and other aspects of health that might affect the baby.

- *Find a health-care provider who is competent.* The health-care provider should (1) take time to do a thorough family history; (2) not be patronizing; (3) be knowledgeable and stay current on prenatal testing; (4) be honest about risks, benefits, and side effects of any tests or treatments; and (5) inspire trust.

RESOURCES

American Fertility Association
www.theafa.org
The American Fertility Association provides information about infertility and possible solutions to it.

How Healthy Is Your Family Tree?
by Carol Krause (1995)
New York: Simon & Schuster
In this book, you will learn how to create a family medical tree. Once you put together a family medical tree, a specialist or genetic counselor can help you understand it.

National Down Syndrome Society
www.ndss.org
The National Down Syndrome Society (NDSS) provides resources and advocacy for individuals with Down syndrome and their families.

National Organization for Rare Disorders (NORD)
www.rarediseases.org
NORD supports awareness and education about rare birth defects and genetic disorders.

The Twins Foundation
www.twinsfoundation.com
For information about twins and multiple births, contact The Twins Foundation.

chapter 3 PRENATAL DEVELOPMENT

chapter outline

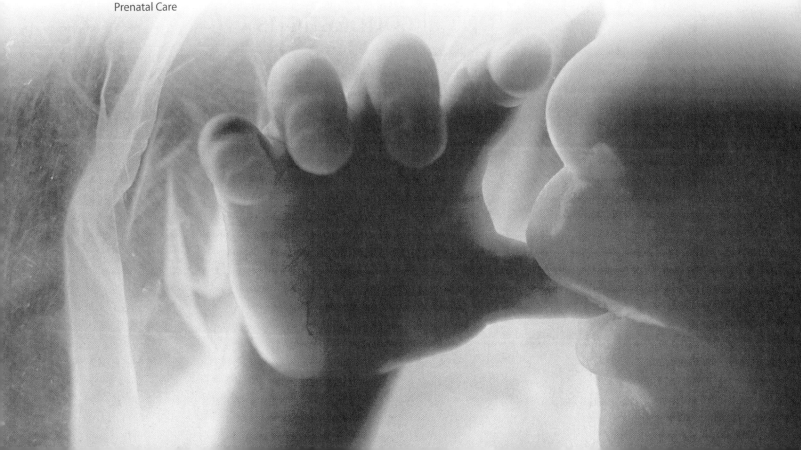

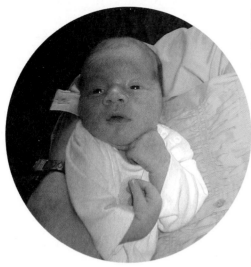

Alex, also known as "Mr. Littles."

Diana and Roger married when he was 38 and she was 34. Both worked full-time and were excited when Diana became pregnant. Two months later, Diana began to have some unusual pains and bleeding. Just two months into her pregnancy she had lost the baby. Diana thought deeply about why she was unable to carry the baby to full term. It was about the time she became pregnant that the federal government began to warn that eating certain types of fish with a high mercury content on a regular basis during pregnancy can cause a miscarriage. Although most early miscarriages are the result of embryonic defects, she eliminated these fish from her diet.

Six months later, Diana became pregnant again. She and Roger read about pregnancy, prenatal development, and birth, and signed up for birth preparation classes. Each Friday night for eight weeks they practiced simulated contractions. They talked about what kind of parents they wanted to be and discussed what changes in their lives the baby would make. When they found out that their offspring was going to be a boy, they gave him a nickname: "Mr. Littles."

This time, Diana's pregnancy went well, and Alex, also known as Mr. Littles, was born. During the birth, however, Diana's heart rate dropped precipitously and she was given a stimulant to raise it. Apparently the stimulant also increased Alex's heart rate and breathing to a dangerous point, and he had to be placed in a neonatal intensive care unit (NICU).

Several times a day, Diana and Roger visited Alex in the NICU. A number of babies in the NICU who had a very low birth weight had been in intensive care for weeks, and some of these babies were not doing well. Fortunately, Alex was in better health. After several days in the NICU, his parents were permitted to take home a very healthy Alex.

topical **connections**

In the last chapter you learned about the evolutionary perspective, genetic foundations of development, the reproductive challenges and choices parents today may face, and the nature-nurture debate. This chapter explores the remarkable course of prenatal development, including the phenomenal growth of the brain. Potential hazards to the offspring's and the mother's health also are covered.

◀ - *looking back*

preview

This chapter chronicles the truly amazing changes that take place from conception to birth. Imagine . . . at one time you were suspended in a sea of fluid in your mother's womb. In this chapter, you will explore the course of prenatal development, expectant parents' experiences, and some potential hazards to prenatal development.

What Is the Course of Prenatal Development? **LG1** Discuss the three periods of prenatal development.

The Germinal Period   The Embryonic Period   The Fetal Period   The Brain

Imagine how Alex ("Mr. Littles") came to be. Out of thousands of eggs and millions of sperm, one egg and one sperm united to produce him. Had the union of sperm and egg come a day or even an hour earlier or later, he would have been very different—maybe even of the opposite sex. Conception occurs when a single sperm cell from the male unites with an ovum (egg) in the female's fallopian tube in a process called fertilization. Over the next few months, the genetic code, discussed in Chapter 2, "Biological Beginnings," directs a series of changes in the fertilized egg, but many events and hazards will influence how that egg develops and becomes tiny Alex.

Typical prenatal development begins with fertilization and ends with birth, lasting 266 days (38 weeks) from conception. It can be divided into three periods: germinal, embryonic, and fetal.

> The history of man for nine months preceding his birth would probably be far more interesting and contain events of greater moment than all three score and ten years that follow it.
>
> —**SAMUEL TAYLOR COLERIDGE**
> *English Poet and Essayist, 19th Century*

THE GERMINAL PERIOD

The **germinal period** is the period of prenatal development that takes place in the first two weeks after conception. It includes the creation of the fertilized egg, called a *zygote*, cell division, and the attachment of the zygote to the uterine wall.

Rapid cell division by the zygote continues throughout the germinal period. (Recall from Chapter 2, "Biological Beginnings," that this cell division occurs through a process called *mitosis*.) By approximately one week after conception, the differentiation of these cells—their specialization for different tasks—has already begun. At this stage, the group of cells, now called the **blastocyst,** consists of an inner mass of cells that will eventually develop into the embryo and the **trophoblast,** an outer layer of cells that later provides nutrition and support for the embryo. *Implantation*, the attachment of the zygote to the uterine wall, takes place about 10 to 14 days after conception. Figure 3.1 illustrates some of the most significant developments during the germinal period.

THE EMBRYONIC PERIOD

The **embryonic period** is the period of prenatal development that occurs from two to eight weeks after conception. During the embryonic period, the rate of cell differentiation intensifies, support systems for cells form, and organs appear.

This period begins as the blastocyst attaches to the uterine wall. The mass of cells is now called an *embryo*, and three layers of cells form. The embryo's **endoderm** is the inner layer of cells, which will develop into the digestive and respiratory systems. The **mesoderm** is the middle layer, which will become the circulatory system, bones, muscles, excretory system, and reproductive system. The **ectoderm** is the outermost layer, which will become the nervous system and brain, sensory receptors (ears, nose, and eyes, for example), and skin parts (hair and nails, for example). Every body part eventually develops from these three layers. The endoderm primarily produces internal

germinal period The period of prenatal development that takes place in the first two weeks after conception. It includes the creation of the zygote, continued cell division, and the attachment of the zygote to the uterine wall.

blastocyst The inner mass of cells that develops during the germinal period. These cells later develop into the embryo.

trophoblast The outer layer of cells that develops in the germinal period. These cells later provide nutrition and support for the embryo.

embryonic period The period of prenatal development that occurs two to eight weeks after conception. During the embryonic period, the rate of cell differentiation intensifies, support systems for the cells form, and organs appear.

endoderm The inner layer of cells, which develops into digestive and respiratory systems.

mesoderm The middle layer of cells, which becomes the circulatory system, bones, muscles, excretory system, and reproductive system.

ectoderm The outermost layer of cells, which becomes the nervous system and brain, sensory receptors (ears, nose, and eyes, for example), and skin parts (hair and nails, for example).

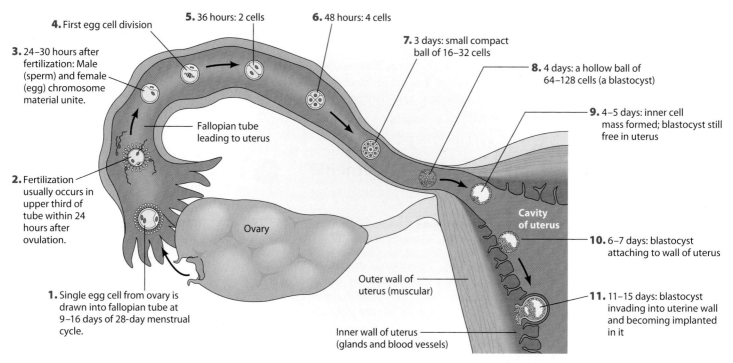

4. First egg cell division

5. 36 hours: 2 cells

6. 48 hours: 4 cells

7. 3 days: small compact ball of 16–32 cells

3. 24–30 hours after fertilization: Male (sperm) and female (egg) chromosome material unite.

8. 4 days: a hollow ball of 64–128 cells (a blastocyst)

9. 4–5 days: inner cell mass formed; blastocyst still free in uterus

Fallopian tube leading to uterus

2. Fertilization usually occurs in upper third of tube within 24 hours after ovulation.

Ovary

Cavity of uterus

10. 6–7 days: blastocyst attaching to wall of uterus

1. Single egg cell from ovary is drawn into fallopian tube at 9–16 days of 28-day menstrual cycle.

Outer wall of uterus (muscular)

11. 11–15 days: blastocyst invading into uterine wall and becoming implanted in it

Inner wall of uterus (glands and blood vessels)

FIGURE **3.1**

SIGNIFICANT DEVELOPMENTS IN THE GERMINAL PERIOD. Just one week after conception, cells of the blastocyst have already begun specializing. The germination period ends when the blastocyst attaches to the uterine wall. *Which of the steps shown in the drawing occur in the laboratory when IVF (described in Chapter 2) is used?*

amnion The life-support system that is a thin bag or envelope that contains a clear fluid in which the developing embryo floats.

umbilical cord Contains two arteries and one vein, and connects the baby to the placenta.

placenta A disk-shaped group of tissues in which small blood vessels from the mother and the offspring intertwine but don't join.

organogenesis Process of organ formation that takes place during the first two months of prenatal development.

body parts, the mesoderm primarily produces parts that surround the internal areas, and the ectoderm primarily produces surface parts.

As the embryo's three layers form, life-support systems for the embryo develop rapidly. These life-support systems include the amnion, the umbilical cord (both of which develop from the fertilized egg, not the mother's body), and the placenta. The **amnion** is like a bag or an envelope and contains a clear fluid in which the developing embryo floats. The amniotic fluid provides an environment that is temperature and humidity controlled, as well as shockproof. The **umbilical cord** contains two arteries and one vein that connect the baby to the placenta. The **placenta** consists of a disk-shaped group of tissues in which small blood vessels from the mother and the offspring intertwine but do not join.

Figure 3.2 illustrates the placenta, the umbilical cord, and the blood flow in the expectant mother and developing organism. Very small molecules—oxygen, water, salt, food from the mother's blood, as well as carbon dioxide and digestive wastes from the offspring's blood—pass back and forth between the mother and embryo or fetus (Woolett, 2011). Virtually any drug or chemical substance the pregnant woman ingests can cross the placenta to some degree, unless it is metabolized or altered during passage, or is too large (Eshkoll & others, 2011; Menezes, Malek, & Keelan, 2011). A recent study revealed that cigarette smoke weakened and increased the oxidative stress of fetal membranes, from which the placenta develops (Menon & others, 2011). Large molecules that cannot pass through the placental wall include red blood cells and harmful substances, such as most bacteria, maternal wastes, and hormones. The complex mechanisms that govern the transfer of substances across the placental barrier are still not entirely understood (Meschia, 2011; Nelson & Burton, 2011).

By the time most women find out that they are pregnant, the major organs have begun to form. **Organogenesis** is the name given to the process of organ formation during the first two months of prenatal development. While the organs

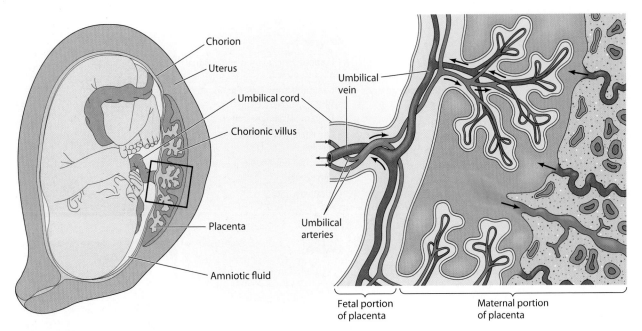

FIGURE 3.2

THE PLACENTA AND THE UMBILICAL CORD. The area bound by the square in the right half of the illustration is enlarged. Arrows indicate uterine veins to the maternal circulation. The exchange of materials takes place across the layer separating the maternal and fetal blood supplies, so the bloods never come into contact. *What is known about how the placental barrier works and its importance?*

are being formed, they are especially vulnerable to environmental changes (Hashimoto-Toril & others, 2011). In the third week after conception, the neural tube that eventually becomes the spinal cord forms. At about 21 days, eyes begin to appear, and at 24 days the cells for the heart begin to differentiate. During the fourth week, the urogenital system becomes apparent, and arm and leg buds emerge. Four chambers of the heart take shape, and blood vessels appear. From the fifth to the eighth week, arms and legs differentiate further; at this time, the face starts to form but still is not very recognizable. The intestinal tract develops and the facial structures fuse. At eight weeks, the developing organism weighs about 1/30 ounce and is just over 1 inch long.

THE FETAL PERIOD

The **fetal period,** lasting about seven months, is the prenatal period between two months after conception and birth in typical pregnancies. Growth and development continue their dramatic course during this time.

Three months after conception, the fetus is about 3 inches long and weighs about 3 ounces. It has become active, moving its arms and legs, opening and closing its mouth, and moving its head. The face, forehead, eyelids, nose, and chin are distinguishable, as are the upper arms, lower arms, hands, and lower limbs. In most cases, the genitals can be identified as male or female. By the end of the fourth month of pregnancy, the fetus has grown to 6 inches in length and weighs 4 to 7 ounces. At this time, a growth spurt occurs in the body's lower parts. For the first time, the mother can feel arm and leg movements.

By the end of the fifth month, the fetus is about 12 inches long and weighs close to a pound. Structures of the skin have formed—toenails and fingernails, for example. The fetus is more active, showing a preference for a particular position in the womb. By the end of the sixth month, the fetus is about 14 inches long and has gained another half pound to a pound. The eyes and eyelids are completely formed, and a fine layer of hair covers the head. A grasping reflex is present and irregular breathing movements occur.

fetal period The prenatal period of development that begins two months after conception and lasts for seven months on average.

First trimester (first 3 months)

Conception to 4 weeks

- Is less than 1/10 inch long
- Beginning development of spinal cord, nervous system, gastrointestinal system, heart, and lungs
- Amniotic sac envelops the preliminary tissues of entire body
- Is called a "zygote"

8 weeks

- Is just over 1 inch long
- Face is forming with rudimentary eyes, ears, mouth, and tooth buds
- Arms and legs are moving
- Brain is forming
- Fetal heartbeat is detectable with ultrasound
- Is called an "embryo"

12 weeks

- Is about 3 inches long and weighs about 1 ounce
- Can move arms, legs, fingers, and toes
- Fingerprints are present
- Can smile, frown, suck, and swallow
- Sex is distinguishable
- Can urinate
- Is called a "fetus"

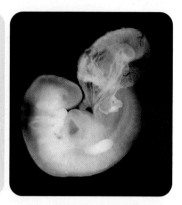

Second trimester (middle 3 months)

16 weeks

- Is about 6 inches long and weighs about 4 to 7 ounces
- Heartbeat is strong
- Skin is thin, transparent
- Downy hair (lanugo) covers body
- Fingernails and toenails are forming
- Has coordinated movements; is able to roll over in amniotic fluid

20 weeks

- Is about 12 inches long and weighs close to 1 pound
- Heartbeat is audible with ordinary stethoscope
- Sucks thumb
- Hiccups
- Hair, eyelashes, eyebrows are present

24 weeks

- Is about 14 inches long and weighs 1 to 1 1/2 pounds
- Skin is wrinkled and covered with protective coating (vernix caseosa)
- Eyes are open
- Waste matter is collected in bowel
- Has strong grip

Third trimester (last 3 months)

28 weeks

- Is about 16 inches long and weighs about 3 pounds
- Is adding body fat
- Is very active
- Rudimentary breathing movements are present

32 weeks

- Is 16 1/2 to 18 inches long and weighs 4 to 5 pounds
- Has periods of sleep and wakefulness
- Responds to sounds
- May assume the birth position
- Bones of head are soft and flexible
- Iron is being stored in liver

36 to 38 weeks

- Is 19 to 20 inches long and weighs 6 to 7 1/2 pounds
- Skin is less wrinkled
- Vernix caseosa is thick
- Lanugo is mostly gone
- Is less active
- Is gaining immunities from mother

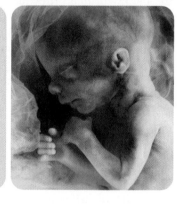

FIGURE **3.3**

THE THREE TRIMESTERS OF PRENATAL DEVELOPMENT. Both the germinal and embryonic periods occur during the first trimester. The end of the first trimester as well as the second and third trimesters are part of the fetal period.

How Would You...?

If you were a **human development and family studies professional,** how would you characterize the greatest risks at each period of prenatal development?

neurons The term for nerve cells, which handle information processing at the cellular level.

neurogenesis The formation of new neurons.

As early as six months of pregnancy (about 24 to 25 weeks after conception), the fetus for the first time has a chance of surviving outside the womb—that is, it is *viable.* Infants born between 24 and 37 weeks of pregnancy usually need help breathing because their lungs are not yet fully mature. By the end of the seventh month, the fetus is about 16 inches long and weighs about 3 pounds.

During the last two months of prenatal development, fatty tissues develop, and the functioning of various organ systems—heart and kidneys, for example—steps up. During the eighth and ninth months, the fetus grows longer and gains substantial weight—about another 4 pounds. At birth, the average American baby weighs 7½ pounds and is about 20 inches long.

Figure 3.3 gives an overview of the main events during prenatal development. Notice that instead of describing development in terms of germinal, embryonic, and fetal periods, Figure 3.3 divides prenatal development into equal periods of three months, called *trimesters*. Remember that the three trimesters are not the same as the three prenatal periods we have discussed. The germinal and embryonic periods occur in the first trimester. The fetal period begins toward the end of the first trimester and continues through the second and third trimesters. Viability (the chances of surviving outside the womb) occurs at the very end of the second trimester.

developmental **connection**

Brain Development. At birth, infants' brains weigh approximately 25 percent of what they will when adulthood is reached. Chapter 5, p. 137

THE BRAIN

One of the most remarkable aspects of the prenatal period is the development of the brain (Nelson, 2011). By the time babies are born, they have approximately 100 billion **neurons,** or nerve cells, which handle information processing at the cellular level in the brain. During prenatal development, neurons spend time moving to the right locations and are starting to become connected. The basic architecture of the human brain is assembled during the first two trimesters of prenatal development. In typical development, the third trimester of prenatal development and the first two years of postnatal life are characterized by increasing connectivity and functioning of neurons (Nelson, 2011).

As the human embryo develops inside its mother's womb, the nervous system begins forming as a long, hollow tube located on the embryo's back. This pear-shaped *neural tube*, which forms about 18 to 24 days after conception, develops out of the ectoderm. The tube closes at the top and bottom about 24 days after conception. Figure 3.4 shows that the nervous system still has a tubular appearance six weeks after conception.

Two birth defects related to a failure of the neural tube to close are anencephaly and spina bifida. When *anencephaly* occurs (that is, when the head end of the neural tube fails to close), the highest regions of the brain fail to develop and the fetus dies in the womb, during childbirth, or shortly after birth (Stoll & others, 2011). *Spina bifida*, an incomplete development of the spinal cord, results in varying degrees of paralysis of the lower limbs. Individuals with spina bifida usually need assistive devices such as crutches, braces, or wheelchairs. A strategy that can help to prevent neural tube defects is for pregnant women to take adequate amounts of the B vitamin folic acid, a topic we will discuss further later in this chapter (Collins & others, 2011; Rasmussen & Clemmensen, 2010). And both maternal diabetes and obesity place the fetus at risk for developing neural tube defects (Yazdy & others, 2010). Also, a recent study found that maternal exposure to passive tobacco smoke was linked to neural tube defects (Suarez & others, 2011).

In a normal pregnancy, once the neural tube has closed, a massive proliferation of new immature neurons begins to take place at about the fifth prenatal week and continues throughout the remainder of the prenatal period. The generation of new neurons is called **neurogenesis.** At the peak of neurogenesis, it is estimated that as many as 200,000 neurons are being generated every minute.

At approximately 6 to 24 weeks after conception, *neuronal migration* occurs (Zeisel, 2011). This involves cells moving outward from their point of origin to their appropriate locations and creating the different levels, structures, and regions of the brain (Liu, 2011). Once a cell has migrated to its target destination, it must mature and develop a more complex structure (Higginbotham, Yokota, & Anton, 2011).

At about 23 prenatal weeks, connections between neurons begin to occur, a process that continues postnatally (Kostovic, Judas, & Sedmark, 2011). We will have much more to consider about the structure of neurons, their connectivity, and the development of the infant brain in Chapter 5, "Physical Development in Infancy."

FIGURE **3.4**

EARLY FORMATION OF THE NERVOUS SYSTEM. The photograph shows the primitive, tubular appearance of the nervous system at six weeks in the human embryo.

Yelyi Nordone, 12, of New York City, recently cast her line out into the pond during Camp Spifida at Camp Victory, near Millville, Pennsylvania. Camp Spifida is a week-long residential camp for children with spina bifida.

What Are Some Important Strategies That Enhance the Expectant Mother's Health and Prenatal Care?

 LG2 Summarize how nutrition, exercise, and prenatal care are important aspects of the expectant mother's pregnancy.

The Expectant Mother's Nutrition and Weight Gain   Exercise   Prenatal Care

What can an expectant mother do to stay healthy and to improve her baby's chances of being born healthy? Among the most important strategies she can adopt involve nutrition, exercise, and prenatal care.

THE EXPECTANT MOTHER'S NUTRITION AND WEIGHT GAIN

The mother's nutrition can have a strong influence on the development of the fetus. Here we discuss the mother's nutritional needs and optimal nutrition during pregnancy.

The best assurance of an adequate caloric intake during pregnancy is a satisfactory weight gain over time (Phelan & others, 2011). The optimal weight gain depends on the expectant mother's height, bone structure, and prepregnant nutritional state. However, maternal weight gains that average from 25 to 35 pounds are associated with the best reproductive outcomes.

An increasing number of pregnant women gain more than this recommended amount (Innis, 2011). Maternal obesity adversely affects pregnancy outcomes through increased rates of hypertension, diabetes, respiratory complications, and infections in the mother (Poston & others, 2011; Roman & others, 2011). Also, pregnancies in obese women are characterized by a higher incidence of neural tube defects, preterm deliveries, and late fetal deaths (McKnight & others, 2011). Management of obesity including weight loss and increased exercise prior to pregnancy is likely to benefit the mother and the baby (Simmons, 2011). Limiting gestational weight gain to 11 to 20 pounds among pregnant women is likely to improve outcomes for the mother and the child (Simmons, 2011). We further discuss obesity as a potential hazard to prenatal development later in the chapter.

The pattern of weight gain is also important. The ideal pattern of weight gain during pregnancy is 2 to 4.4 pounds during the first trimester, followed by an

How much do you know about prenatal development and maintaining a healthy pregnancy? How much weight gain on average should occur during pregnancy?

average gain of 1 pound per week during the last two trimesters. In the second trimester, most of the weight gain is due to increased blood volume; the enlargement of breasts, uterus, and associated tissue and fluid; and the deposit of maternal fat. In the third trimester, weight gain mainly involves the fetus, placenta, and amniotic fluid. A 25-pound weight gain during pregnancy is generally distributed in this way: 11 pounds: fetus, placenta, and amniotic fluid; 5 pounds: maternal stores; 4 pounds: increased blood volume; 3 pounds: tissue fluid; and 2 pounds: uterus and breasts.

During the second and third trimesters, inadequate gains of less than 2.2 pounds per month or excessive gains of more than 6.6 pounds per month should be evaluated and the need for nutritional counseling considered. Inadequate weight gain has been associated with low birth weight infants. Sudden sharp increases in weight of 3 to 5 pounds in a week may result from fluid retention and may require evaluation.

The recommended daily allowance (RDA) for all nutrients increases during pregnancy (Barger, 2010). The expectant mother should eat three meals a day, with nutritious snacks of fruits, cheese, milk, or other foods between meals if desired. More frequent, smaller meals also are recommended. Water is an essential nutrient. Four to six 8-ounce glasses of water and a total of 8 to 10 cups (64 to 80 ounces) of total fluid should be consumed daily. The need for protein, iron, vitamin D, folacin, calcium, phosphorus, and magnesium increases by 50 percent or more. Recommended increases for other nutrients range from 15 to 40 percent (see Figure 3.5). Researchers have found that women who take a multivitamin prior to pregnancy may be at a reduced risk for delivering a preterm infant (Vahratian & others, 2004).

What are some guidelines for expectant mothers' eating patterns?

EXERCISE

How much and what type of exercise is best during pregnancy depend to some degree on the course of the pregnancy, the expectant mother's fitness, and her customary activity level. Normal participation in exercise can continue throughout an uncomplicated pregnancy (Lovelady, 2011; Phelan & others, 2011). In general, the skilled sportswoman is no longer discouraged from participating in sports she participated in prior to her pregnancy. However, pregnancy is not the appropriate time to begin strenuous activity.

Because of the increased emphasis on physical fitness in our society, more women routinely jog as part of a physical fitness program prior to pregnancy. There are few concerns about continuing to jog during the early part of pregnancy, but in the latter part of pregnancy there is some concern about the jarring effect of jogging on the breasts and abdomen. As pregnancy progresses, low-impact activities such as walking, swimming, water aerobics, and bicycling are safer and provide fitness as well as greater comfort, eliminating the bouncing associated with jogging (Cavalcante & others, 2009). A recent study of almost 1,500 pregnant women found that the incidence of exercise-related injuries was low (Vladutiu, Evenson, & Marshall, 2010).

Exercise during pregnancy helps prevent constipation, conditions the body, and is associated with a more positive mental state (Rafla, Nair, & Kumar, 2008; Streuling & others, 2011). A recent experimental study found that pregnant women who completed a three-month supervised aerobic exercise program showed improved health-related quality of life, including better physical functioning and reduced bodily pain, than their counterparts who did not participate in the program (Montoya Arizabaleta & others, 2010).

Another recent study revealed that exercise during pregnancy improved mothers' perception of their health (Barakat & others, 2011).

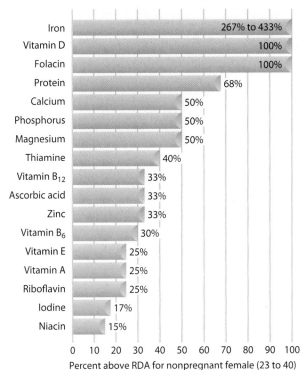

Nutrient	Percent above RDA
Iron	267% to 433%
Vitamin D	100%
Folacin	100%
Protein	68%
Calcium	50%
Phosphorus	50%
Magnesium	50%
Thiamine	40%
Vitamin B₁₂	33%
Ascorbic acid	33%
Zinc	33%
Vitamin B₆	30%
Vitamin E	25%
Vitamin A	25%
Riboflavin	25%
Iodine	17%
Niacin	15%

Percent above RDA for nonpregnant female (23 to 40)

FIGURE 3.5

RECOMMENDED NUTRIENT INCREASES FOR EXPECTANT MOTHERS

How might a woman's exercise in pregnancy benefit her and her offspring?

However, it is important to remember not to overdo it. Pregnant women should always consult their physician before starting any exercise program (Olson & others, 2009).

Might the mother's exercise during pregnancy be related to the development of the fetus and the birth of the child? Few studies have been conducted on this topic, but several studies indicate that moderate exercise three to four times a week was linked to healthy weight gain in the fetus and a normal birth weight, whereas the risk of low birth weight increased for women who exercised intensely most days of the week and for women who exercised less than twice a week or not at all (Campbell & Mottols, 2001). Two recent studies confirmed that physical exercise during pregnancy is not linked to an increase in preterm birth (Hegaard & others, 2008; Juhl & others, 2008). In one of the studies, compared with sedentary pregnant women, women who engaged in light leisure-time physical activity had a 24 percent reduced likelihood of preterm delivery, and those who participated in moderate to heavy leisure-time physical activity had a 66 percent reduced risk of preterm delivery (Hegaard & others, 2008).

To read about some guidelines for exercise during pregnancy, see the *Caring Connections* interlude.

PRENATAL CARE

Although prenatal care varies enormously, it usually involves a defined schedule of visits for medical care, which typically includes screening for manageable conditions and treatable diseases that can affect the baby or the mother (London & others, 2011). In addition to medical care, prenatal programs often include comprehensive educational, social, and nutritional services (Ickovics & others, 2011).

The education provided in prenatal care varies during the course of pregnancy. Those in the early stages of pregnancy as well as couples who are anticipating a pregnancy may participate in early prenatal classes (Davidson & others, 2011). In addition to providing information on dangers to the fetus, early prenatal classes often discuss the development of the embryo and the fetus; sexuality during pregnancy; choices about the birth setting and care providers; nutrition, rest, and exercise; common discomforts of pregnancy and relief measures; psychological changes in the expectant mother and her partner; and factors that increase the risk of preterm labor and possible symptoms of preterm labor. Early classes also may include information about the advantages and disadvantages of breast feeding and bottle feeding. (Fifty to eighty percent of expectant mothers decide how they will feed their infant prior to the sixth month of pregnancy.) During the second or third trimester of pregnancy, prenatal classes focus on preparing for the birth, infant care and feeding, choices about birth, and postpartum self-care.

Does prenatal care matter? Information about pregnancy, labor, delivery, and caring for the newborn can be especially valuable for first-time mothers (Lowdermilk, Perry, & Cashion, 2011; Murray & McKinley, 2010). Prenatal care is also very important for women in poverty because it links them with other social services (Mattson & Smith, 2011). The legacy of prenatal care continues after the birth because women who experience this type of care are more likely to get preventive care for their infants.

Research contrasting the experiences of mothers who had prenatal care and those who did not supports the importance of prenatal care (Bhutta & others, 2011; McFarlin, 2009). One study found that U.S. women who had no prenatal care were far more likely than their counterparts who received prenatal care to

Partners or friends take classes with prospective mothers in many prenatal care programs. *What characterizes the content of prenatal care programs?*

How Would You...?
If you were a **human development and family studies professional,** how would you justify the need for prenatal education classes for couples expecting a child?

Exercise Guidelines for Expectant Mothers

Exercise during pregnancy is just as important during pregnancy as it is before or after pregnancy. The following guidelines for exercise are recommended for expectant mothers by the American College of Obstetricians and Gynecologists (2008, pp. 1–4):

- ***Adapting to changes in the woman's body.*** Some of the changes in the woman's body during pregnancy require adaptations in exercise. Joints and ligaments become more mobile during pregnancy. Avoiding jerky, bouncy, or high-impact motions can reduce the risk of injuring joints and ligaments. During pregnancy women carry

What are some recommended guidelines for exercise during pregnancy?

extra weight, and the pregnant woman's center of gravity shifts, placing stress on joints and muscles, especially in the pelvis and lower back. Thus, maintaining balance while exercising during pregnancy is sometimes difficult and requires attention. The extra weight pregnant women carry makes their bodies work harder, so it is important not to exercise too strenuously.

- ***Getting started.*** Before starting an exercise program, pregnant women should talk with their doctor to ensure that they don't have an obstetric or health condition that might limit their activity. Women with the following conditions will be advised by their doctor not to exercise during pregnancy: risk factors for preterm labor, vaginal bleeding, and premature rupture of membranes.

- ***Choosing safe exercises.*** Most types of exercise are safe during pregnancy, but some types involve positions and movements that may be uncomfortable, tiring, or harmful. For example, after the first trimester of pregnancy, women should not do exercises that require

them to lie flat on their backs. Some sports are safe during pregnancy, even for beginners. Walking is a good exercise for anyone, swimming is excellent because it works so many muscles, cycling provides a good aerobic workout (because balance is affected by pregnancy, a stationary bicycle is recommended in later pregnancy); aerobic exercise is effective in keeping the heart and lungs strong; and strength training can tone muscles and help prevent some common aches and pains during pregnancy. Women who were runners or played racquet sports before becoming pregnant should talk with their doctor about taking certain precautions if they plan to continue these activities during pregnancy. The following activities should be avoided during pregnancy: downhill snow skiing, contact sports, and scuba diving.

- ***Establishing a routine.*** Exercise is most practical during the first 24 weeks of pregnancy; during the last three months many exercises that were easy earlier in pregnancy are often difficult. It is important to begin each exercise session with a 5- to 10-minute warm-up and end each session with a 5- to 10-minute cool-down. During the warm-up and cool-down periods, stretching exercises should be done. Pregnant women should not exercise to the point of exhaustion. If pregnant women experience any of the following problems, they should stop exercising and call their doctor: vaginal bleeding, dizziness or feeling faint, increased shortness of breath, chest pain, headache, muscle weakness, calf pain or swelling, uterine contractions, decreased fetal movement, or fluid leaking from the vagina.

have infants who had low birth weight, increased mortality, and a number of other physical problems (Herbst & others, 2003). In other studies, low birth weight and preterm deliveries were common among U.S. mothers who received no prenatal care, and the absence of prenatal care increased the risk for preterm birth almost threefold in both non-Latino White and African American women (Stringer & others, 2005).

Inadequate prenatal care may help explain a disturbing fact: Rates of infant mortality and low birth weight indicate that many other nations have healthier babies than the United States (Goldenberg & Culhane, 2007). In many countries

Rachel Thompson, Obstetrician/Gynecologist

Rachel Thompson is the senior member of Houston Women's Care Associates, which specializes in health care for women. She has one of Houston's most popular obstetrics/gynecology (OB/GYN) practices. Thompson's medical degree is from Baylor College of Medicine, where she also completed her internship and residency.

In addition to her clinical practice, Thompson is a clinical instructor in the Department of Obstetrics and Gynecology at Baylor College of Medicine. Thompson says that one of the unique features of their health-care group is that the staff comprises only women who are full-time practitioners.

Rachel Thompson (*right*), talking with one of her patients at Houston Women's Care Associates.

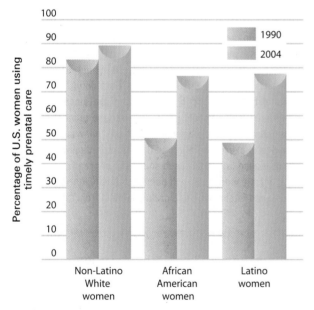

FIGURE **3.6**

PERCENTAGE OF U.S. WOMEN USING TIMELY PRENATAL CARE: 1990 TO 2004. From 1990 to 2004, the use of timely prenatal care increased by 7 percent (to 89.1) for non-Latino White women, by 25 percent (to 76.5) for African American women, and by 28 percent (to 77.4) for Latino women in the United States.

that have a lower percentage of low birth weight infants than the United States, mothers receive either free or very low cost prenatal and postnatal care, and can receive paid maternity leave from work that ranges from 9 to 40 weeks. In Norway and the Netherlands, prenatal care is coordinated with a general practitioner, an obstetrician, and a midwife. To read about the work and career of a U.S. obstetrician/gynecologist, see the *Connecting with Careers* profile.

Why do some U.S. women receive inadequate prenatal care? Sometimes the reasons are tied to the health-care system, to provider practices, and to their own individual and social characteristics (Handler & others, 2011; Magriples & others, 2008). Women who do not want to be pregnant, who have negative attitudes about being pregnant, or who unintentionally become pregnant are more likely to delay prenatal care or to miss appointments. As we noted earlier, adolescent girls are less likely than adult women to obtain prenatal care. Within the United States, there are differences among ethnic groups both in the health of babies and in prenatal care (Wasserman, Bender, & Lee, 2007). During the 1980s, more than one-fifth of all non-Latino White mothers and one-third of all African American mothers did not receive prenatal care in the first trimester of their pregnancy, and 5 percent of White mothers and 10 percent of African American mothers received no prenatal care at all (Wegman, 1987).

The situation has been improving. From 1990 to 2004, the use of timely prenatal care increased among women from a variety of ethnic backgrounds in the United States, although non-Latino White women were still more likely to obtain prenatal care than African American and Latino women (Martin & others, 2005) (see Figure 3.6). The United States needs more comprehensive medical and educational services to improve the quality of prenatal care and to reduce the number of low birth weight and preterm infants (Burger, 2010).

An innovative program that is rapidly expanding in the United States and other countries is CenteringPregnancy (Ickovics & others, 2011; Massey, Rising, & Ickovics, 2006; Teate & others, 2009). This relationship-centered program provides complete prenatal care in a group setting. CenteringPregnancy replaces traditional 15-minute physician visits with 90-minute peer group support sessions and self-examination led by a physician or certified nurse-midwife. Groups of up to 10 women (and often their partners) meet regularly beginning at 12 to 16 weeks of pregnancy. The sessions emphasize empowering women to play an active role in experiencing a positive pregnancy. A recent study revealed that CenteringPregnancy groups made more prenatal visits, had higher breast feeding rates, and were more satisfied with their prenatal care than women in individual care (Klima & others, 2009). In another recent study, high-stress women were randomly assigned to a CenteringPregnancy Plus group, group prenatal care, or standard individual care from 18 weeks gestation to birth (Ickovics & others, 2011). The most stressed women in the Centering-Pregnancy Plus group showed increased self-esteem and decreased stress and social conflict in their third trimester of pregnancy; their social conflict and depression also were lower at one year postpartum.

Some prenatal programs for parents focus on home visitation (Lee & others, 2009). A recent research review concluded that prenatal home visits were linked to improved use of prenatal care, although there was less evidence that they improve newborns' birth weight (Issel & others, 2011). Research evaluations indicate that the most successful home visitation program is the Nurse-Family Partnership created by David Olds and his colleagues (2004, 2007; Zielinski, Eckenrode, & Olds, 2009). The Nurse-Family Partnership involves home visits by trained nurses beginning in the second or third trimester of prenatal development. The extensive program consists of approximately 50 home visits from the prenatal period through 2 years of age. The home visits focus on the mother's health, access to health care, parenting, and improvement of the mother's life by providing her with guidance in education, work, and relationships. Research revealed that the Nurse-Family Partnership has numerous positive outcomes including fewer pregnancies, better work circumstances, and stability in relationship partners for the mother and improved academic success and social development for the child (Olds & others, 2004, 2007).

In another home visitation program, high-risk pregnant women and adolescents, many living in poverty conditions, were provided biweekly home visitation services that encouraged healthy prenatal behavior, offered social support, and provided links to medical and other community services (Lee & others, 2009). Compared with a control group of pregnant women and adolescents who did not receive the home visits, the home visitation group gave birth to fewer low birth weight infants.

Cultures around the world have differing views of pregnancy. In the *Connecting with Diversity* interlude, we explore some of these beliefs.

Some cultures treat pregnancy simply as a natural occurrence; others see it as a medical condition (Walsh, 2006). How expectant mothers behave during pregnancy may depend in part on the prevalence of traditional home-care remedies and folk beliefs, the importance of indigenous healers, and the influence of health-care professionals in their culture. In various cultures women may consult herbalists and/or faith healers during pregnancy (Mbonye, Neema, & Magnussen, 2006).

Health-care workers should assess whether a woman's beliefs or practices pose a threat to her or the fetus. If they do, health-care professionals should consider a culturally sensitive way to handle the problem (Kenner, Sugrue, & Finkelman, 2007).

A CenteringPregnancy program. This increasingly popular program alters routine prenatal care by bringing women out of exam rooms and into relationship-oriented groups.

Cultural Beliefs About Pregnancy

All cultures have beliefs and practices that surround life's major events, and one such event is pregnancy. When a woman who immigrated to the United States becomes pregnant, the beliefs and practices of her native culture may be as important as, or more important than, those of the mainstream U.S. culture that now surrounds her. The conflict between cultural traditions and Western medicine may pose a risk for the pregnancy and a challenge for the health-care professional who wishes to give proper care while respecting the woman's values.

The American Public Health Association (2006) has identified a variety of cultural beliefs and practices that are observed among various immigrant groups, such as the following:

- *Food cravings.* Latin American, Asian, and some African cultures believe that it is important for a pregnant woman's food cravings to be satisfied because they are thought to be the cravings of the baby. If cravings are left unsatisfied, the baby might take on certain unpleasant personality and/or physical traits, perhaps characteristic of the food (Taylor, Ko, & Pan, 1999). As an example, in African cultures women often eat soil, chalk, or clay during pregnancy; this is believed to satisfy the baby's hunger as well as affirming soil as a symbol of female fertility (American Public Health Association, 2006).

- *"Hot-cold" theory of illness.* Many cultures in Latin America, Asia, and Africa characterize foods, medications, and illnesses as "hot" or "cold"; this has nothing to do with temperature or spiciness, but with traditional definitions and categories. Most of these cultures view pregnancy as a "hot" condition, although the Chinese view it as "cold" (Taylor, Ko, & Pan, 1999). As a result, a woman may resist taking a prescribed medication because of concern that it could create too much "heat" and cause a miscarriage; in Indian culture, iron-rich foods are also considered unacceptably "hot" for pregnant women (DeSantis, 1998).

- *Extended family.* In many immigrant cultures, the extended family is a vital support system, and health-care decisions are made that prioritize

In India, a midwife checks on the size, position, and heartbeat of a fetus. Midwives deliver babies in many cultures around the world. *What are some cultural variations in prenatal care?*

the needs of the family over those of the individual. Western health-care providers need to be sensitive to this dynamic, which runs counter to today's practices of protecting patient confidentiality and autonomy.

- *Stoicism.* In many Asian cultures, stoicism is valued, as suffering is seen as part of life (Uba, 1992). Physicians are also viewed with great respect. As a result, a pregnant Asian woman may behave submissively and avoid voicing complaints to her health-care provider, but may privately fail to follow the provider's advice (Assanand & others, 1990).

Review *Connect* Reflect

 LG2 Summarize how nutrition, exercise, and prenatal care are important aspects of the expectant mother's pregnancy.

Review

- What are some recommendations for the expectant mother's nutrition and weight gain?
- What role does exercise play in the mother's health during pregnancy?
- What are some important aspects of prenatal care?

Connect

- How would nutrition and exercise be incorporated into an ideal prenatal care program?

Reflect *Your Own Personal Journey of Life*

- What are some beliefs about pregnancy and prenatal development in your culture?

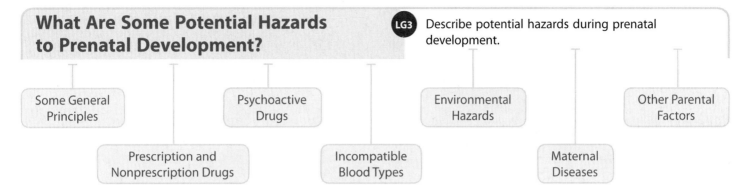

What Are Some Potential Hazards to Prenatal Development?

LG3 Describe potential hazards during prenatal development.

- Some General Principles
- Prescription and Nonprescription Drugs
- Psychoactive Drugs
- Incompatible Blood Types
- Environmental Hazards
- Maternal Diseases
- Other Parental Factors

For Alex, the baby discussed at the opening of this chapter, the course of prenatal development went smoothly. His mother's womb protected him as he developed. Despite this protection, however, the environment can affect the embryo or fetus in many well-documented ways.

SOME GENERAL PRINCIPLES

A **teratogen** is any agent that can potentially cause a physical birth defect. (The word comes from the Greek word *tera* meaning "monster.") The field of study that investigates the causes of birth defects is called *teratology* (Bajai & Gross, 2011; Holmes & Westgate, 2011). Some exposures to teratogens do not cause physical birth defects but can alter the developing brain and influence cognitive and behavioral functioning, in which case the field of study is called *behavioral teratology.*

Teratogens include drugs, incompatible blood types, environmental pollutants, infectious diseases, nutritional deficiencies, maternal stress, advanced maternal and paternal age, and environmental pollutants. In fact, thousands of babies are born deformed or mentally retarded every year as a result of events that occurred in the mother's life as early as one or two months before conception. As we further discuss teratogens, you will see that factors related to the father also can influence prenatal development.

So many teratogens exist that practically every fetus is exposed to at least some of them. For this reason, it is difficult to determine which teratogen causes which problem. In addition, it may take a long time for the effects of a teratogen to show up. Only about half of all potential effects appear at birth.

The time of exposure, dose, and genetic susceptibility to a particular teratogen influence both the severity of the damage to an embryo or fetus and the type of defect:

- *Time of Exposure.* Teratogens do more damage when they occur at some points in development than at others (Holmes & Westgate, 2011). Damage during the germinal period may even prevent implantation. In general, the embryonic period is more vulnerable than the fetal period (Ortigosa Gomez & others, 2011).

- *Dose.* The dose effect is rather obvious—the greater the dose of an agent, such as a drug, the greater the effect.

- *Genetic Susceptibility.* The type or severity of abnormalities caused by a teratogen is linked to the genotype of the pregnant woman and the genotype of the embryo or fetus (Erickson, 2010; Schachter & Kohane, 2011). For example, how a mother metabolizes a particular drug can influence the degree to which the drug effects are transmitted to the embryo or fetus. Differences in placental membranes and placental transport also affect exposure. The extent to which an embryo or fetus is vulnerable to a teratogen may also depend on its genotype (Dufour-Rainfray & others, 2011; Marinucci & others, 2009). Also, for unknown reasons, male fetuses are far more likely to be affected by teratogens than are female fetuses (DiPietro, 2008).

teratogen Any agent that can potentially cause a physical birth defect. The field of study that investigates the causes of birth defects is called *teratology.*

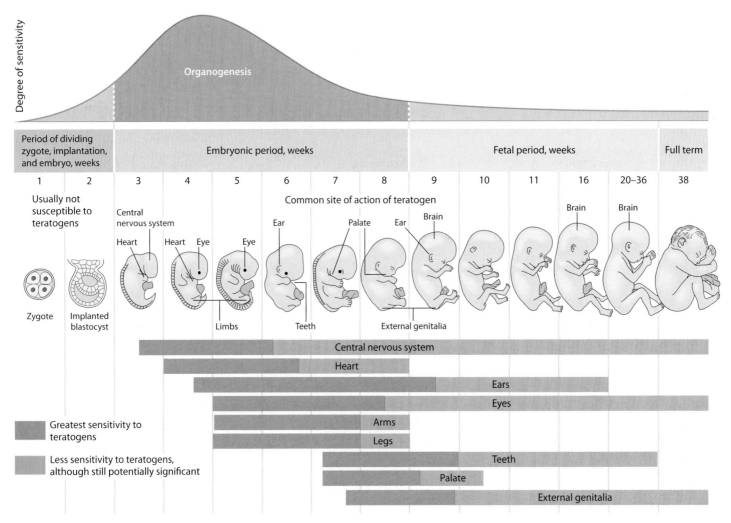

FIGURE 3.7

TERATOGENS AND THE TIMING OF THEIR EFFECTS ON PRENATAL DEVELOPMENT. The danger of structural defects caused by teratogens is greatest early in embryonic development. The period of organogenesis (red color) lasts for about six weeks. Later assaults by teratogens (blue-green color) mainly occur in the fetal period and instead of causing structural damage are more likely to stunt growth or cause problems with organ function.

Figure 3.7 summarizes additional information about the effects of time of exposure to a teratogen. The probability of a structural defect is greatest early in the embryonic period, when organs are being formed (Holmes, 2011). Each body structure has its own critical period of formation. Recall from Chapter 1 that a *critical period* is a fixed time period very early in development during which certain experiences or events can have a long-lasting effect on development. The critical period for the nervous system (week 3) is earlier than that for arms and legs (weeks 4 and 5).

After organogenesis is complete, teratogens can no longer cause anatomical defects. Instead, exposure during the fetal period is more likely to stunt growth or to create problems in the way organs function. To examine some key teratogens and their effects, let's begin with drugs.

PRESCRIPTION AND NONPRESCRIPTION DRUGS

Many U.S. women are given prescriptions for drugs while they are pregnant—especially antibiotics, analgesics, and asthma medications. Prescription as well as nonprescription drugs, however, may have effects on the embryo or fetus that the women never imagined (Holmes, 2011).

The damage that drugs can do was tragically highlighted in 1961, when many pregnant women took a popular sedative, thalidomide, to alleviate their morning sickness. In adults, the effects of thalidomide are typically not damaging; in embryos, however, they are devastating. Not all infants were affected in the same way. If the mother took thalidomide on day 26 (probably before she knew she was pregnant), an arm might not grow. If she took the drug two days later, the arm might not grow past the elbow. The thalidomide tragedy shocked the medical community and parents and taught a valuable lesson: Taking the wrong drug at the wrong time is enough to physically handicap the offspring for life (Holmes, 2011).

Prescription drugs that can function as teratogens include antibiotics, such as streptomycin and tetracycline; some antidepressants; certain hormones such as progestin and synthetic estrogen; and Accutane (isotretinoin), which often is prescribed for acne (Kraft & Freiman, 2011; Patel, Beste, & Blackwell, 2011).

Nonprescription drugs that can be harmful include diet pills and aspirin (Wojtowicz & others, 2011). Recent research revealed that low doses of aspirin pose no harm for the fetus but that high doses can contribute to maternal and fetal bleeding (James, Brancazio, & Price, 2008; Marret & others, 2010).

PSYCHOACTIVE DRUGS

Psychoactive drugs are drugs that act on the nervous system to alter states of consciousness, modify perceptions, and change moods. Examples include caffeine, alcohol, and nicotine, as well as illicit drugs such as cocaine, methamphetamine, marijuana, and heroin.

Caffeine People often consume caffeine when they drink coffee, tea, or cola, or when they eat chocolate. A recent research review found that high amounts of caffeine consumption by pregnant women do not increase the risk of miscarriage, congenital malformations, or growth retardation (Brent, Christian, & Diener, 2011). However, an earlier review of studies on caffeine consumption during pregnancy concluded that a small increase in the risks for spontaneous abortion and low birth weight occurs for pregnant women who consume more than 150 milligrams of caffeine daily (approximately two cups of brewed coffee or two to three 12-ounce cans of cola) (Fernandez & others, 1998). (Low birth weight is linked to a variety of health and developmental problems that we will discuss later in the chapter.) One study revealed that pregnant women who consumed 200 or more milligrams of caffeine a day had an increased risk of miscarriage (Weng, Odouli, & Li, 2008). Thus, the extent to which caffeine consumption by pregnant women has negative effects on offspring continues to be debated (Maslova & others, 2010). However, the U.S. Food and Drug Administration recommends that pregnant women either not consume caffeine or consume it only sparingly.

Alcohol Heavy drinking by pregnant women can be devastating to their offspring (Brocardo, Gil-Mohapel, & Christie, 2011; Frost, Gist, & Adriano, 2011). **Fetal alcohol spectrum disorders (FASD)** are a cluster of abnormalities and problems that appear in the offspring of mothers who drink alcohol heavily during pregnancy (Klingenberg & others, 2010). The abnormalities include facial deformities and defects of the limbs, face, and heart. Some children with FASD have these bodily malformations, but others don't. Most children with FASD are characterized by learning problems, and many are below average in intelligence with some being mentally retarded (Dalen & others, 2009). Although women who drink heavily during pregnancy are at a higher risk of having a child with FASD, not all pregnant heavy drinkers have children with FASD.

Drinking alcohol during pregnancy, however, can have serious effects on offspring even when they are not afflicted with FASD (Cheng & others, 2011). Serious malformations, such as those produced by FASD, are not found in infants born to mothers who are moderate drinkers, but even moderate drinking can have a negative effect on the offspring.

What are some guidelines for alcohol use during pregnancy? The U.S. Surgeon General recommends that no alcohol be consumed during pregnancy. And research suggests that it may not be wise to consume alcohol at the time of conception. One study revealed that intakes of alcohol by both men and women during the week of conception increased the risk of early pregnancy loss (Henriksen & others, 2004).

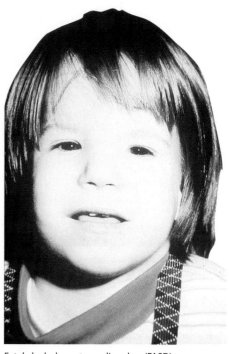

Fetal alcohol spectrum disorders (FASD) are characterized by a number of physical abnormalities and learning problems. Notice the wide-set eyes, flat cheekbones, and thin upper lip in this child with FASD.

How Would You...?

If you were a **social worker,** how would you counsel a woman who continues to drink alcohol in the early weeks of pregnancy because she believes alcohol can't harm the baby until it has developed further?

fetal alcohol spectrum disorders (FASD) A cluster of abnormalities and problems that appears in the offspring of mothers who drink alcohol heavily during pregnancy.

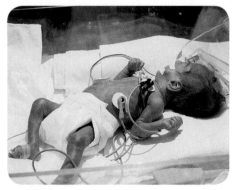

Nicotine Cigarette smoking by pregnant women can also adversely influence prenatal development, birth, and postnatal development. Preterm births and low birth weights, fetal and neonatal deaths, and respiratory problems and sudden infant death syndrome (SIDS, also known as crib death) are more common among the offspring of mothers who smoked during pregnancy (Beyerlein & others, 2011; Civelek & others, 2011). A recent review concluded that tobacco (active maternal smoking and environmental smoke) is a key contributor to intrauterine (within the womb) growth retardation (Romo, Carceller, & Tobajas, 2009). One study also linked heavy smoking during pregnancy to nicotine withdrawal symptoms in newborns (Godding & others, 2004).

Maternal smoking during pregnancy has been identified as a risk factor for the development of attention deficit hyperactivity disorder in offspring (Knopik, 2009). A research review indicated that environmental tobacco smoke was linked to an increased risk of low birth weight in offspring (Leonardi-Bee & others, 2008). And a recent meta-analysis indicated that maternal smoking during pregnancy was linked to a modest increase in risk for childhood non-Hodgkin lymphoma (Antonopoulos & others, 2011).

Intervention programs designed to help pregnant women stop smoking can reduce some of smoking's negative effects, especially by raising birth weights (Murin, Rafii, & Bilello, 2011). One study revealed that women who quit smoking during pregnancy had offspring with higher birth weights than their counterparts who continued smoking (Jaddoe & others, 2008). To read further about the negative outcomes of smoking during pregnancy, see the *Connecting with Research* interlude.

Cocaine Does cocaine use during pregnancy harm the developing embryo and fetus? The most consistent finding is that cocaine exposure during prenatal development is associated with reduced birth weight, length, and head circumference (Gouin & others, 2011). Also, in other studies, prenatal cocaine exposure has been linked to lower arousal, less effective self-regulation, higher excitability, and lower quality of reflexes at 1 month of age (Ackerman, Riggins, & Black, 2010; Lester & others, 2002); to impaired motor development in the second year of life (Richardson, Goldschmidt, Leech, & Willford, 2011); to slower growth rate through 10 years of age (Richardson, Goldschmidt, & Larkby, 2008); to elevated blood pressure at 9 years of age (Shankaran & others, 2010); to impaired language development and information processing (Beeghly & others, 2006; Lewis & others, 2007), including attention deficits (especially impulsivity) (Accornero & others, 2007; Richardson & others, 2011); to learning disabilities at age 7 (Morrow & others, 2006); to increased likelihood of being in a special education program that involves support services (Levine & others, 2008); and to increased behavioral problems, especially externalizing problems such as high rates of aggression and delinquency (Minnes & others, 2010; Richardson & others, 2011).

Some researchers argue that these findings should be interpreted cautiously. Why? Because other factors in the lives of pregnant women who use cocaine (such as poverty, malnutrition, and other substance abuse) often cannot be ruled out as possible contributors to the problems found in their children (Hurt & others, 2005; Messiah & others, 2011). For example, cocaine users are more likely than nonusers to smoke cigarettes, use marijuana, drink alcohol, and take amphetamines.

Despite these cautions, the weight of research evidence indicates that children born to mothers who use cocaine are likely to have neurological and cognitive deficits (Field, 2007; Mayer & Zhang, 2009; Richardson & others, 2011). Cocaine should never be used by pregnant women.

Methamphetamine Methamphetamine, like cocaine, speeds up an individual's nervous system. Babies born to mothers who use methamphetamine, or "meth," during pregnancy are at risk for a number of problems, including high infant mortality, low birth weight, and developmental and behavioral problems (Forrester &

What are some links between expectant mothers' drinking and cigarette smoking and outcomes for their offspring?

This baby was exposed to cocaine prenatally. *What are some of the possible effects on development of being exposed to cocaine prenatally?*

Is Expectant Mothers' Cigarette Smoking Related to Cigarette Smoking by Their Adolescent Offspring?

Nicotine and other substances in cigarette smoke cross the placental barrier and pass from the expectant mother to the fetus, stimulating the fetal brain as early as the first trimester of pregnancy (Menon & others, 2011). Researchers are exploring the possibility that this prenatal exposure of the brain to cigarette smoke may predispose individuals to be more vulnerable to addiction in adolescence.

One study explored whether expectant mothers' cigarette smoking and marijuana use were linked to an increased risk for substance use in adolescence by their offspring (Porath & Fried, 2005). One hundred fifty-two 16- to 21-year-olds were asked to complete a drug history questionnaire that included their past and current cigarette smoking. A urine sample was also obtained from the participants and analyzed for the presence of drugs. The adolescent participants' mothers had been asked about the extent of their cigarette smoking during their pregnancy several decades earlier as part of the Ottawa Prenatal Prospective Study.

The results indicated that adolescent offspring of mothers who reported having smoked cigarettes during pregnancy were more than twice as likely to have initiated smoking during adolescence than their counterparts whose mothers reported not smoking during their pregnancy. These findings indicate that cigarette smoking by expectant mothers is a risk factor for later cigarette smoking by their adolescent offspring. Such results add to the strength of the evidence that supports drug use prevention and cessation among expectant mothers.

How do you think health-care professionals might use this type of evidence to counsel expectant mothers about cigarette smoking during pregnancy? Should the government include this evidence as part of its antismoking campaign?

Merz, 2007; Piper & others, 2011). One study revealed that meth exposure during prenatal development was linked to decreased arousal, increased stress, and poor movement quality in newborns (Smith & others, 2008). Another study found that prenatal exposure to meth was linked to less brain activation in a number of areas, especially the frontal lobes, in 7- to 15-year-olds (Roussotte & others, 2011).

Meth use during pregnancy is increasing, and some experts conclude that meth use during pregnancy has become a greater problem in the United States than cocaine use (Elliott, 2004). One survey revealed that 5 percent of U.S. women used methamphetamine during their pregnancy (Arria & others, 2006).

Marijuana An increasing number of studies find that marijuana use by pregnant women also has negative outcomes for their offspring (Huizink & Mulder, 2006; Williams & Ross, 2007). A research review concluded that marijuana use by pregnant women is related to deficits in memory and information processing in their offspring (Kalant, 2004). For example, in a longitudinal study, prenatal marijuana exposure was related to learning and memory difficulties at age 11 (Richardson & others, 2002). Other studies have linked prenatal marijuana exposure to lower intelligence in children (Goldschmidt & others, 2008) and to depressive symptoms at 10 years of age (Gray & others, 2005). Further, research results have found connections between prenatal exposure to marijuana and marijuana use at 14 years of age (Day, Goldschmidt, & Thomas, 2006). In sum, marijuana use is not recommended for pregnant women.

Heroin It is well documented that infants whose mothers are addicted to heroin show several behavioral difficulties at birth (Ortigosa Gomez & others, 2011). These difficulties include withdrawal symptoms such as tremors, irritability, abnormal crying, disturbed sleep, and impaired motor control. Many infants still show behavioral problems at their first birthday, and attention deficits may appear later in development. The most common treatment for heroin addiction, methadone, is associated with very severe withdrawal symptoms in newborns (Blandthorn, Forster, & Love, 2011). One study revealed that in comparison with late methadone treatment (less than six months prior to birth), continuous methadone treatment during pregnancy was linked to improved neonatal outcomes (Burns & others, 2007).

INCOMPATIBLE BLOOD TYPES

Incompatibility between the mother's and father's blood types poses another risk to prenatal development. Blood types are created by differences in the surface structure of red blood cells. One type of difference in the surface of red blood cells creates the familiar blood groups—A, B, O, and AB. A second difference creates what is called Rh-positive and Rh-negative blood. If a surface marker, called the Rh factor, is present in an individual's red blood cells, the person is said to be Rh-positive; if the Rh marker is not present, the person is said to be Rh-negative. If a pregnant woman is Rh-negative and her partner is Rh-positive, the fetus may be Rh-positive. If the fetus' blood is Rh-positive and the mother's is Rh-negative, the mother's immune system may produce antibodies that will attack the fetus. Such an assault can result in any number of problems, including miscarriage or stillbirth, anemia, jaundice, heart defects, brain damage, or death soon after birth (Li & others, 2010).

Generally, the first Rh-positive baby of an Rh-negative mother is not at risk, but with each subsequent pregnancy the risk increases. A vaccine (RhoGAM) may be given to the mother within three days of the first child's birth to prevent her body from making antibodies that will attack any future Rh-positive fetuses in subsequent pregnancies. Also, babies affected by Rh incompatibility can be given blood transfusions before or immediately after birth (Goodnough & others, 2011).

ENVIRONMENTAL HAZARDS

Many aspects of our modern industrial world can endanger the embryo or fetus. Some specific hazards to the embryo or fetus that are worth a closer look include radiation, toxic wastes, and other chemical pollutants (Raabe & Muller, 2008; Wiesel & others, 2011).

Radiation can cause a gene mutation (an abrupt, permanent change in DNA). Chromosomal abnormalities are elevated among the offspring of fathers exposed to high levels of radiation in their occupations (Schrag & Dixon, 1985). X-ray radiation also can affect the developing embryo or fetus, especially during the first several weeks after conception when women do not yet know they are pregnant. Possible effects include microencephaly (an abnormally small brain), mental retardation, and leukemia. Women and their physicians should weigh the risk of an X-ray when an actual or potential pregnancy is involved (Menias & others, 2007; Rajaraman & others, 2011). However, a routine diagnostic X-ray of a body area other than the abdomen, with the woman's abdomen protected by a lead apron, is generally considered safe (Brent, 2009, 2011).

Environmental pollutants and toxic wastes are also sources of danger to unborn children. Among the dangerous pollutants are carbon monoxide, mercury, and lead, as well as certain fertilizers and pesticides. Exposure to lead can come from lead-based paint that flakes off the walls of a home or from leaded gasoline emitted by cars on a nearby busy highway. Early exposure to lead can affect children's mental development (Canfield & Jusko, 2008). For example, a study revealed that a moderately high maternal lead level in the first trimester of pregnancy was linked to lower scores on an index of mental development in infancy (Hu & others, 2007).

MATERNAL DISEASES

Maternal diseases and infections can produce defects in offspring by crossing the placental barrier, or they can cause damage during birth. Rubella (German measles) is one disease that can cause prenatal defects. The greatest damage occurs if a mother contracts rubella in the third or fourth week of pregnancy, although

An explosion at the Chernobyl nuclear power plant in the Ukraine produced radioactive contamination that spread to surrounding areas. Thousands of infants were born with health problems and deformities as a result of the nuclear contamination, including this boy whose arm did not form. *Other than radioactive contamination, what are some types of environmental hazards to prenatal development?*

infection during the second month is also damaging (Kobayashi & others, 2005). A rubella outbreak in 1964–1965 resulted in 30,000 prenatal and neonatal (newborn) deaths, and more than 20,000 affected infants were born with malformations, including mental retardation, blindness, deafness, and heart problems. Elaborate preventive efforts ensure that rubella will never again have such disastrous effects. A vaccine that prevents German measles is now routinely administered to children, and women who plan to have children should have a blood test before they become pregnant to determine whether they are immune to the disease (Reef & others, 2011).

Syphilis (a sexually transmitted infection) is more damaging later in prenatal development—four months or more after conception. Rather than affecting organogenesis, as rubella does, syphilis damages organs after they have formed. Damage includes eye lesions, which can cause blindness, and skin lesions (Caddy & others, 2011; Ishaque & others, 2011). When syphilis is present at birth, problems can develop in the central nervous system and gastrointestinal tract (Yakoob & others, 2010). Most states require that pregnant women be given a blood test to detect the presence of syphilis.

Another infection that has received widespread attention recently is genital herpes. Newborns contract this virus when they are delivered through the birth canal of a mother with genital herpes (Li & others, 2011; Nigro & others, 2011). About one-third of babies delivered through an infected birth canal die; another one-fourth become brain damaged. If an active case of genital herpes is detected in a pregnant woman close to her delivery date, a cesarean section can be performed (delivery of the infant through an incision in the mother's abdomen) to keep the virus from infecting the newborn (Patel & others, 2011).

AIDS is a sexually transmitted infection that is caused by the human immunodeficiency virus (HIV), which destroys the body's immune system. A mother can infect her offspring with HIV/AIDS in three ways: (1) during gestation across the placenta, (2) during delivery through contact with maternal blood or fluids, and (3) postpartum (after birth) through breast feeding. The transmission of AIDS through breast feeding is especially a problem in many developing countries (UNICEF, 2011). Babies born to HIV-infected mothers can be (1) infected and symptomatic (show HIV symptoms), (2) infected but asymptomatic (not show HIV symptoms), or (3) not infected at all. An infant who is infected and asymptomatic may still develop HIV symptoms until 15 months of age.

In the early 1990s, before preventive treatments were available, 1,000 to 2,000 infants were born with HIV infection each year in the United States. Since then, transmission of HIV from mothers to fetuses has been reduced dramatically (Anderson & Cu-Uvin, 2009). Only about one-third as many cases of newborns with HIV appear today as in the early 1990s. This decline is due to the increase in counseling and voluntary testing of pregnant women for HIV and to the use of zidovudine (AZT) by infected women during pregnancy and by the infant after birth. In many poor countries, however, treatment with AZT is limited, and HIV infection of infants remains a major problem (Guidozzi & Black, 2009).

The more widespread disease of diabetes, characterized by high levels of sugar in the blood, also affects offspring (Heude & others, 2011; Ovesen, Rasmussen, & Kesmodel, 2011). A research review indicated that newborns with physical defects are more likely to have diabetic mothers than newborns without such defects (Eriksson, 2009). Moreover, women who have gestational diabetes (a condition in which women without previously diagnosed diabetes develop high blood glucose levels during pregnancy) may deliver very large infants (weighing 10 pounds or more), and the infants themselves are at risk for diabetes (Gluck & others, 2009).

developmental **connection**

Conditions, Diseases, and Disorders. The greatest incidence of HIV/AIDS is in sub-Saharan Africa, where as many as 30 percent of mothers have HIV; many are unaware that they are infected with the virus. Chapter 5, p. 135; Chapter 8, p. 254; Chapter 14, p. 437

OTHER PARENTAL FACTORS

So far we have discussed drugs, environmental hazards, maternal diseases, and incompatible blood types that can harm the embryo or fetus. Here we explore other characteristics of the mother and father that can affect prenatal and child development, including nutrition, age, and emotional states and stress.

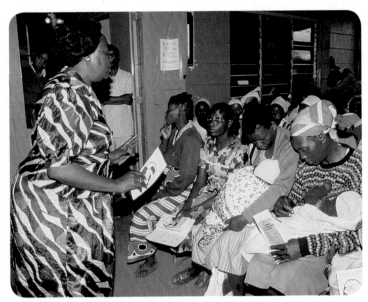

Because the fetus depends entirely on its mother for nutrition, it is important for the pregnant woman to have good nutritional habits. In Kenya, this government clinic provides pregnant women with information about how their diet can influence the health of their fetus and offspring. *What might the information about diet be like?*

Maternal Diet and Nutrition   A developing embryo or fetus depends completely on its mother for nutrition, which comes from the mother's blood (Lowdermilk & Perry, 2012). The nutritional status of the embryo or fetus is determined by the mother's total caloric intake and by her intake of proteins, vitamins, and minerals. Children born to malnourished mothers are more likely than other children to be malformed.

Women who are overweight before and during pregnancy can also put their offspring at risk, and an increasing number of pregnant women in the United States are overweight (Poston & others, 2011; Rasmussen & others, 2010). Researchers have found that obese women have a significant risk of fetal death (McKnight & others, 2011). Studies indicate that prepregnancy maternal obesity doubles the risk of stillbirth and neonatal death and is linked with defects in the central nervous system of offspring (Anderson & others, 2005; Frederick & others, 2008). Further, one analysis proposed that overnutrition in fetal life (due to overeating on the part of the pregnant woman) results in a series of neuroendocrine changes that in turn program the development of fat cells and disrupt the appetite regulation system (McMillen & others, 2008). In this analysis, it was predicted that such early fetal programming is likely linked to being overweight in childhood and adolescence.

One aspect of maternal nutrition that is important for normal prenatal development is folic acid, a B-complex vitamin (Talaulikar & Arulkumaran, 2011). As we indicated earlier in the chapter, a lack of folic acid is linked with neural tube defects in offspring, such as spina bifida (Collins & others, 2011). A study of more than 34,000 pregnant women revealed that taking folic acid either alone or as part of a multivitamin for at least one year prior to conceiving was linked with a 70 percent lower risk of delivering between 20 to 28 weeks and a 50 percent lower risk of delivering between 28 and 32 weeks (Bukowski & others, 2008). A recent study revealed that toddlers of mothers who had not taken folic acid supplements during the first trimester of pregnancy had more behavioral problems (Roza & others, 2010). The U.S. Public Health Service recommends that pregnant women consume a minimum of 400 micrograms of folic acid per day (about twice the amount the average woman gets in one day). Orange juice and spinach are examples of foods rich in folic acid.

Eating fish is often recommended as part of a healthy diet, but pollution has made many fish a risky choice for pregnant women. Some fish contain high levels of mercury, which is released into the air both naturally and by industrial pollution (Wells & others, 2011). When mercury falls into the water, it can become toxic and accumulate in large fish, such as shark, swordfish, king mackerel, and some species of large tuna. Mercury is easily transferred across the placenta, and the embryo's developing brain and nervous system are highly sensitive to the metal (Bose-O'Reilly & others, 2010). Researchers have found that high levels of prenatal mercury exposure are linked to adverse outcomes,

developmental **connection**

Conditions, Diseases, and Disorders. What are some key factors that influence whether individuals will become overweight or obese? Chapter 8, p. 247; Chapter 11, p. 332; Chapter 14, p. 442

including miscarriage, preterm birth, and lower intelligence (Axelrad & others, 2007; Xue & others, 2007). The U.S. Food and Drug Administration (2004) gave the following recommendations for women of childbearing age and young children: Don't eat shark, swordfish, king mackerel, or tilefish; eat up to 12 ounces (two average meals) a week of fish and shellfish that are lower in mercury, such as shrimp, canned light tuna, salmon, pollock, and catfish. Such precautions also have been voiced by the Mayo Clinic (2011) and the American Pregnancy Association (2011).

PCB-polluted fish also pose a risk to fertility and prenatal development. PCBs (polychlorinated biphenyls) are chemicals that were used in manufacturing until they were banned in the 1970s in the United States, but they are still present in landfills, sediments, and wildlife. Recent studies found that PCB exposure in women was linked to a higher rate of infertility and a higher probability of in vitro fertilization implantation failure (Cohn & others, 2011; Meeker & others, 2011).

One study that kept track of the extent to which pregnant women ate PCB-polluted fish from Lake Michigan examined their children as newborns, young children, and at 11 years of age (Jacobson & others, 1984; Jacobson & Jacobson, 2002, 2003). The women who had eaten more PCB-polluted fish were more likely to have smaller, preterm infants who were more apt to react slowly to stimuli. Among preschool children, greater prenatal exposure to PCBs was linked with less effective short-term memory, and 11-year-olds showed lower verbal intelligence and reading comprehension. A recent study also revealed that 16-month-old infants who had been exposed to PCBs prenatally had lower scores on the widely used assessment of infant development, the Bayley Scales (Park & others, 2010).

developmental **connection**

Parenting. Adolescent pregnancy creates negative developmental trajectories for both mothers and their offspring. Chapter 14, p. 438

Maternal Age When possible harmful effects on the fetus and infant are considered, two maternal ages are of special interest: adolescence and 35 and older (Malizia, Hacker, & Penzias, 2009; Rudang & others, 2011). One study revealed that the rate of stillbirth was elevated for adolescent girls and for women 35 years and older (Bateman & Simpson, 2006).

The mortality rate of infants born to adolescent mothers is double that of infants born to mothers in their twenties. Although this high rate probably reflects the immaturity of the mother's reproductive system, other factors such as poor nutrition, lack of prenatal care, and low socioeconomic status may also play a role (Smithbattle, 2007). Adequate prenatal care decreases the probability that a child born to an adolescent girl will have physical problems. However, adolescents are the least likely of women in all age groups to obtain prenatal assistance from clinics and health services.

Maternal age is also linked to the risk that a child will have Down syndrome (Ghosh & others, 2010). As discussed in Chapter 2, "Biological Beginnings," an individual with *Down syndrome* has distinctive facial characteristics, short limbs, and retardation of motor and mental abilities. Advanced maternal age confers a much greater risk of having a baby with Down syndrome. When the mother reaches 40 years of age, the probability is slightly more than 1 in 100 that a baby born to her will have Down syndrome, and by age 50 it is almost 1 in 10.

When mothers are 35 years and older, risks also increase for low birth weight, for preterm delivery, and for fetal death (Fretts, Zera, & Heffner, 2008; Mbugua Gitau & others, 2009). One study found that low birth weight delivery increased by 11 percent and preterm delivery increased by 14 percent in women 35 years and older (Tough & others, 2002). In another study, fetal death was low for women 30 to 34 years of age but increased progressively for women 35 to 44 years of age (Canterino & others, 2004).

What are some of the risks for infants born to adolescent mothers?

How Would You...?

If you were a **health-care professional,** how would you advise a couple in their late thirties or early forties who are considering having a baby?

How do pregnant women's emotional states and stress affect prenatal development and birth?

How Would You...?

If you were a **health-care professional,** how would you advise an expectant mother who is experiencing extreme psychological stress?

We still have much to learn about the role of the mother's age in pregnancy and childbirth (Montana, 2007). As women remain active, exercise regularly, and are careful about their nutrition, their reproductive systems may remain healthier at older ages than was thought possible in the past. For example, in one study, two-thirds of the pregnancies of women 45 years and older in Australia were free of complications (Callaway, Lust, & McIntyre, 2005).

Emotional States and Stress   When a pregnant woman experiences intense fears, anxieties, and other emotions or negative mood states, physiological changes occur that may affect her fetus (Breedlove & Fryzelka, 2011; Brunton & Russell, 2011; Leung & others, 2010). A mother's stress may also influence the fetus indirectly by increasing the likelihood that the mother will engage in unhealthy behaviors such as taking drugs and receiving poor prenatal care.

High maternal anxiety and stress during pregnancy can have long-term consequences for the offspring (Dunkel Schetter, 2011; Monk, Fitelson, & Werner, 2011). A research review indicated that pregnant women with high levels of stress are at increased risk for having a child with emotional or cognitive problems, attention deficit hyperactivity disorder (ADHD), and language delay (Taige & others, 2007). A recent study of more than 30,000 offspring revealed that across the nine months of pregnancy, their risk of being born preterm was highest when maternal exposure to stress occurred during the fifth and sixth months of pregnancy (Class & others, 2011).

Might maternal depression also have an adverse effect on birth outcomes? A recent research review concluded that maternal depression during pregnancy is linked to preterm birth (Dunkel Schetter, 2011). Another recent study found that depressed African American pregnant women had elevated levels of anxiety, anger, daily hassles, sleep disturbance, and cortisol (Field & others, 2009). This combination of negative maternal factors may contribute to the higher rate of preterm and low birth weight African American newborns.

Positive emotional states also appear to make a difference to the fetus. Pregnant women who are optimistic thinkers have less adverse outcomes than pregnant women who are pessimistic thinkers (Loebel & Yali, 1999). Optimists are more likely to believe that they have control over the outcomes of their pregnancies.

Paternal Factors   So far, we have discussed how characteristics of the mother—such as drug use, disease, diet and nutrition, age, and emotional states—can influence prenatal development and the development of the child. Might there also be some paternal risk factors? Indeed, there are several. Men's exposure to lead, radiation, certain pesticides, and petrochemicals may cause abnormalities in sperm that lead to miscarriage or diseases, such as childhood cancer (Cordier, 2008; Fear & others, 2007; Monge & others, 2007). When fathers have a diet low in vitamin C, their offspring have a higher risk of birth defects and cancer (Fraga & others, 1991). Also, it has been speculated that, when fathers take cocaine, it may attach itself to sperm and cause birth defects, but the evidence for this effect is not yet strong. In one study, long-term use of cocaine by men was related to low sperm count, low motility, and a higher number of abnormally formed sperm (Bracken & others, 1990). Cocaine-related infertility appears to be reversible if users stop taking the drug for at least one year.

The father's smoking during the mother's pregnancy also can cause problems for the offspring. In one investigation, the newborns of fathers who smoked around their wives during the pregnancy were 4 ounces lighter at birth for each pack of cigarettes smoked per day than were the newborns whose fathers had not smoked while their wives were pregnant (Rubin & others, 1986). In a study in China, the longer the fathers smoked, the higher the risk that their children would develop cancer (Ji & others, 1997). In yet another study, heavy paternal smoking was associated with the risk of early pregnancy loss (Venners & others, 2004). All of these negative effects may be related to maternal exposure to secondhand smoke.

The father's age also makes a difference (Maconochie & others, 2007; Yang & others, 2007). About 5 percent of children with Down syndrome have older fathers. The offspring of older fathers also face increased risk for other birth defects, including dwarfism and Marfan syndrome, which involves head and limb deformities.

There are also risks to offspring when both the mother and father are older (Dunson, Baird, & Colombo, 2004). In one study, the risk of an adverse pregnancy outcome, such as miscarriage, rose considerably when the woman was 35 years or older and the man was 40 years of age or older (de la Rocheborchard & Thonneau, 2002).

Much of our discussion so far in this chapter has focused on what can go wrong with prenatal development. Prospective parents should take steps to avoid the hazards to fetal development that we have described. But it is important to keep in mind that most of the time, prenatal development does not go awry and development occurs along the positive path that we described at the beginning of the chapter.

In one study, in China, the longer fathers smoked the greater the risk that their children would develop cancer (Ji & others, 1997). *What are some other paternal factors that can influence the development of the fetus and the child?*

Review Connect Reflect

LG3 Describe potential hazards during prenatal development.

Review

- What is teratology? What are some general principles regarding teratogens?
- Which prescription and nonprescription drugs can influence prenatal development?
- How do different psychoactive drugs affect prenatal development?
- How do incompatible blood types influence prenatal development?
- What are some environmental hazards that can influence prenatal development?
- Which maternal diseases can affect prenatal development?
- What other parental factors can affect prenatal development?

Connect

- In Chapter 2, you read about chromosomal and gene-linked

abnormalities that can affect prenatal development. How are the symptoms of the related conditions or risks similar to or different from those caused by teratogens or other hazards?

Reflect *Your Own Personal Journey of Life*

- If you are a woman, imagine that you have just found out you are pregnant. What health-enhancing strategies will you follow during the prenatal period? If you are a man, imagine you are the partner of a woman who has just learned that she is pregnant. What can you do to increase the likelihood that the prenatal period will go smoothly?

topical connections

The next chapter takes us to the moment of birth. You will learn about the birth process and the transition from fetus to newborn, see how the newborn's health and responsiveness are assessed, read about low birth weight and preterm babies, find out about special ways to nurture them, and examine what happens during the postpartum period.

looking forward

What Is the Course of Prenatal Development?

 Discuss the three periods of prenatal development.

The Germinal Period

The Embryonic Period

The Fetal Period

The Brain

- The germinal period lasts from conception until about two weeks later. It includes the creation of a fertilized egg, which is called a zygote, and cell division. The period ends when the zygote attaches to the uterine wall in a process called implantation.

- The embryonic period lasts from about two to eight weeks after conception. The embryo differentiates into three layers of cells (endoderm, mesoderm, and ectoderm), life-support systems develop, and organ systems form (organogenesis).

- The fetal period lasts from about two months after conception until nine months, or when the infant is born. Growth and development continue their dramatic course, and organ systems mature to the point at which life can be sustained outside the womb.

- The growth of the brain during prenatal development is nothing short of remarkable. By the time babies are born, they have approximately 100 billion neurons, or nerve cells. Neurogenesis is the term that means the formation of new neurons. The nervous system begins with the formation of a neural tube at 18 to 24 days after conception. Proliferation and neuronal migration are two processes that characterize brain development in the prenatal period. The basic architecture of the brain is formed in the first two trimesters of prenatal development.

What Are Some Important Strategies That Enhance the Expectant Mother's Health and Prenatal Care?

 Summarize how nutrition, exercise, and prenatal care are important aspects of the expectant mother's pregnancy.

The Expectant Mother's Nutrition and Weight Gain

Exercise

Prenatal Care

- The best assurance of adequate caloric intake during pregnancy is a satisfactory weight gain over time. Maternal weight gain that averages 25 to 35 pounds is often linked with the best reproductive outcomes. The RDA for all nutrients increases during pregnancy, and the need for such nutrients as vitamin D, folacin, and iron increases by more than 50 percent.

- If the expectant mother's health allows, exercise can benefit her well-being during pregnancy and may reduce the risk of a preterm birth. How much and what type of exercise are appropriate depends to some extent on the course of pregnancy, the expectant mother's fitness, and her customary activity level.

- Prenatal care varies extensively but usually involves medical care services with a defined schedule of visits and often includes educational, social, and nutritional services. Much needs to be done to improve prenatal care in the United States, especially for low-income families.

What Are Some Potential Hazards to Prenatal Development?

 Describe potential hazards during prenatal development.

Some General Principles

- Teratology is the field that investigates the causes of birth defects. Any agent that can potentially cause birth defects is called a teratogen. The time of exposure, dose, and genetic susceptibility influence the severity of the damage to an unborn child and the type of defect that occurs.

Prescription and Nonprescription Drugs

Psychoactive Drugs

Incompatible Blood Types

Environmental Hazards

Maternal Diseases

Other Parental Factors

- Prescription drugs that can be harmful include antibiotics, some antidepressants, and certain hormones. Nonprescription drugs that can be harmful include diet pills and aspirin.

- Legal psychoactive drugs that are potentially harmful to prenatal development include alcohol, nicotine, and caffeine. Fetal alcohol spectrum disorders (FASD) consist of a cluster of abnormalities that appear in offspring of mothers who drink heavily during pregnancy. Even when pregnant women drink moderately, negative effects on their offspring have been found. Cigarette smoking by pregnant women can have serious adverse effects on prenatal and child development (such as low birth weight and SIDS). Illegal psychoactive drugs that are potentially harmful to offspring include methamphetamine, which can produce high infant mortality, low birth weight, and developmental problems; marijuana, which can result in a child's impaired information processing; cocaine, which is associated with reduced birth weight, length, and head circumference; and heroin, which produces behavioral problems at birth and may result in attention deficits later in development.

- Incompatibility of the mother's and the father's blood types can also be harmful to the fetus. A woman is at risk when she has a negative Rh factor and her partner has a positive Rh factor. If the fetus is Rh-positive and the mother is Rh-negative, the mother's immune system may attack the fetus, resulting in problems such as miscarriage or brain damage.

- Environmental hazards include radiation, environmental pollutants, and toxic wastes.

- Syphilis, rubella (German measles), genital herpes, and AIDS are infectious diseases that can harm the fetus.

- Other parental factors include maternal diet and nutrition, age, emotional states and stress, and paternal factors. A developing fetus depends entirely on its mother for nutrition. One nutrient that is especially important very early in development is folic acid. A potential hazard to prenatal development occurs when the mother consumes fish with a high mercury content. Maternal age can negatively affect the offspring's development if the mother is an adolescent or over 35. High stress in the mother is linked with less than optimal prenatal and birth outcomes. Paternal factors that can adversely affect prenatal development include exposure to lead, radiation, certain pesticides, and petrochemicals, as well as smoking.

key terms

germinal period 85
blastocyst 85
trophoblast 85
embryonic period 85
endoderm 85

mesoderm 85
ectoderm 85
amnion 86
umbilical cord 86
placenta 86

organogenesis 86
fetal period 87
neurons 89
neurogenesis 89
teratogen 97

fetal alcohol spectrum
   disorders (FASD) 99

key people

David Olds 95

connecting with improving the lives of children

MAKING A DIFFERENCE

Maximizing Positive Prenatal Outcomes

What are some strategies during pregnancy that are likely to maximize positive outcomes for prenatal development?

- *Eat nutritiously and monitor weight gain.* The recommended daily allowances for all nutrients increase during pregnancy. A pregnant woman should eat three balanced meals a day and nutritious snacks between meals if desired. Weight gains that average 25 to 35 pounds are associated with the best reproductive outcomes.

- *Engage in safe exercise.* How much and what type of exercise is best during pregnancy depends to some degree on the course of the pregnancy, the expectant mother's fitness, and her customary activity level. Normal participation in exercise can continue throughout an uncomplicated pregnancy. It is important to remember not to overdo exercise. Exercising for shorter intervals and decreasing the intensity of exercise as pregnancy proceeds are good strategies. Pregnant women should always consult a physician before starting an exercise program.

- *Don't drink alcohol or take other potentially harmful drugs.* An important strategy for pregnancy is to totally abstain from alcohol and other drugs such as nicotine and cocaine. In this chapter, we considered the harmful effects that these drugs can have on the developing fetus. Fathers also need to be aware of potentially harmful effects of their behavior on prenatal development.

- *Have a support system of family and friends.* The pregnant woman benefits from a support system of family members and friends. A positive relationship with a spouse helps keep stress levels down, as does a close relationship with one or more friends.

- *Reduce stress and stay calm.* Try to maintain an even, calm emotional state during pregnancy. High stress levels can harm the fetus. Pregnant women who are feeling a lot of anxiety can reduce their anxiety level through a relaxation or stress management program.

- *Stay away from environmental hazards.* We saw in this chapter that some environmental hazards, such as pollutants and toxic wastes, can harm prenatal development. Be aware of these hazards and stay away from them.

- *Get excellent prenatal care.* The quality of prenatal care varies extensively. The education the mother receives about pregnancy, labor and delivery, and care of the newborn can be valuable, especially for first-time mothers.

- *Read a good book for expectant mothers.* An excellent one is *What to Expect When You're Expecting,* which is described below.

RESOURCES

March of Dimes
www.marchofdimes.com
A major emphasis on the part of the March of Dimes is to promote healthy pregnancy. Their Web site includes extensive information about many aspects of pregnancy and prenatal development.

National Center for Education in Maternal and Child Health (NCEMCH)
www.ncemch.org
NCEMCH answers questions about pregnancy and childbirth, high-risk infants, and maternal and child health programs. It also publishes free maternal and child health publications.

Pregnancy.org
www.pregnancy.org
This extensive Web site provides up-to-date information about pregnancy and prenatal development.

What to Expect When You're Expecting
by Heidi Murkoff, Arlene Eisenberg, and Sandee Hathaway
(4th ed., 2008)
New York: Workman

This highly popular book on pregnancy and prenatal development provides detailed month-by-month descriptions of pregnancy and prenatal growth.

Prenatal Care Tips
Pregnant women can call this toll-free number provided by the federal government for prenatal care advice and referral to local health-care providers: 800–311–2229.

chapter 4 BIRTH

Tanner Roberts was born in a suite at St. Joseph's Medical Center in Burbank, California (Warrick, 1992). Let's examine what took place in the hours leading up to his birth. It is day 266 of his mother Cindy's pregnancy. She is in the frozen-food aisle of a convenience store and feels a sharp pain, starting in the small of her back and reaching around her middle, which causes her to gasp. For weeks, painless Braxton Hicks spasms (named for the gynecologist who discovered them) have been flexing her uterine muscles. But these practice contractions were not nearly as intense and painful as the one she just experienced. After six hours of irregular spasms, her uterus settles into a more predictable rhythm.

At 3 a.m., Cindy and her husband Tom are wide awake. They time Cindy's contractions with a stopwatch. The contractions are now only six minutes apart. It's time to call the hospital. A short time later, Tom and Cindy arrive at the hospital's labor-delivery suite. A nurse puts a webbed belt and fetal monitor around Cindy's middle to measure her labor. The monitor picks up the fetal heart rate. With each contraction of the uterine wall, Tanner's heartbeat jumps from its resting state of about 140 beats to 160 to 170 beats per minute. When the cervix is dilated to more than 4 centimeters, or almost half open, Cindy receives her first medication. As Demerol begins to drip into her veins, the pain of her contractions is less intense. Tanner's heart rate dips to 130 and then 120.

Contractions are now coming every three to four minutes, each one lasting about 25 seconds. The Demerol does not completely obliterate Cindy's pain. She hugs her husband as the nurse urges her to "Relax those muscles. Breathe deep. Relax. You're almost there."

Each contraction briefly cuts off Tanner's source of oxygen, his mother's blood. However, in the minutes of rest between contractions, Cindy's deep breathing helps rush fresh blood to the baby's heart and brain.

At 8 a.m., Cindy's cervix is almost completely dilated and the obstetrician arrives. Using a tool made for the purpose, he reaches into the birth canal and tears the membranes of the amniotic sac, and about half a liter of clear fluid flows out. Contractions are now coming every two minutes, and each one is lasting a full minute.

By 9 a.m., the labor suite has been transformed into a delivery room. Tanner's body is compressed by his mother's contractions and pushes. As he nears his entrance into the world, the compressions help press the fluid from his lungs in preparation for his first breath. Squeezed tightly in the birth canal, the top of Tanner's head emerges. His face is puffy and scrunched. Although fiercely squinting because of the sudden light, Tanner's eyes are open. Tiny bubbles of clear mucus are on his lips. Before any more of his body emerges, the nurse cradles Tanner's head and suctions his nose and mouth. Tanner takes his first breath, a large gasp followed by whimpering, and then a loud cry. Tanner's body is wet but only slightly bloody as the doctor lifts him onto his mother's abdomen. The umbilical cord, still connecting Tanner with his mother, slows and stops pulsating. The obstetrician cuts it, severing Tanner's connection to his mother's womb. Now Tanner's blood flows not to his mother's body for nourishment—but to his own lungs, intestines, and other organs.

topical **connections** — — — — — — — — — — — —

The last chapter outlined the course of prenatal development and the strategies expectant mothers can use to enhance their health and their offspring's health. You also learned about some of the potential hazards that can occur during prenatal development. And you read about the remarkable prenatal development of the brain, which contains approximately 100 billion neurons at the time birth is reached. This chapter takes you through the birth process and its immediate aftermath—the postpartum period.

◀ — *looking back* — — — — — — — — — — — — — — — — — —

preview

As the story of Tanner Roberts' birth reveals, many changes take place during the birth of a baby. In this chapter, we explore what happens during the birth process, describe measures of neonatal health and responsiveness, discuss the development of preterm and low birth weight infants, and identify characteristics of the postpartum period.

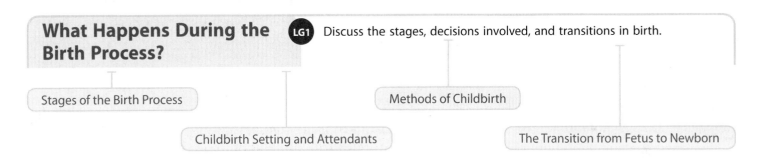

What Happens During the Birth Process? **LG1** Discuss the stages, decisions involved, and transitions in birth.

Stages of the Birth Process

Childbirth Setting and Attendants

Methods of Childbirth

The Transition from Fetus to Newborn

Nature writes the basic script for how birth occurs, but parents make important choices about conditions surrounding birth. What is the sequence of physical steps when a child is born?

STAGES OF THE BIRTH PROCESS

The birth process occurs in three stages. The first stage is the longest of the three. Uterine contractions are 15 to 20 minutes apart at the beginning and last up to a minute apiece. These contractions cause the woman's cervix to stretch and open. As the first stage progresses, the contractions come closer together, appearing every two to five minutes. Their intensity increases. By the end of the first birth stage, contractions dilate the cervix to an opening of about 4 inches, so that the baby can move from the uterus to the birth canal. For a woman having her first child, the first stage lasts an average of 12 to 14 hours; for subsequent children, this stage may be shorter.

The second birth stage begins when the baby's head starts to move through the cervix and the birth canal. It terminates when the baby completely emerges from the mother's body. With each contraction, the mother bears down hard to push the baby out of her body. By the time the baby's head is out of the mother's body, the contractions come almost every minute and last for about a minute. This stage typically lasts approximately 45 minutes to an hour.

> There was a star danced, and under that I was born.
>
> —**WILLIAM SHAKESPEARE**
> *English Playwright, 17th Century*

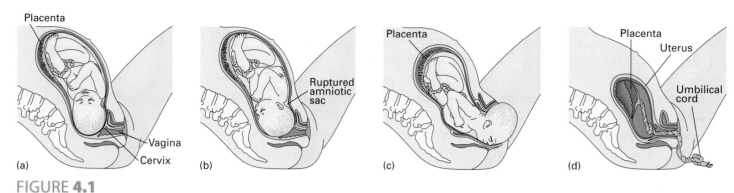

FIGURE **4.1**

THE STAGES OF BIRTH. (*a*) First stage: cervix is dilating; (*b*) late first stage (transition stage): cervix is fully dilated and the amniotic sac has ruptured, releasing amniotic fluid; (*c*) second stage: birth of the infant; (*d*) third stage: delivery of the placenta (afterbirth).

Afterbirth is the third stage, at which time the placenta, umbilical cord, and other membranes are detached and expelled. This final stage is the shortest of the three birth stages, lasting only minutes (see Figure 4.1).

CHILDBIRTH SETTING AND ATTENDANTS

In the United States, 99 percent of births take place in hospitals (Martin & others, 2005). However, a 5 percent increase in home births occurred in 2005 and 2006 (MacDorman, Declercq, & Menacker, 2011). This increase in home births occurred mainly for non-Latino White women, especially those who were older and married. For non-Latino White women, two-thirds of home births were attended by a midwife.

Some women with good medical histories and low risk for problems may choose a delivery at home or in a freestanding birth center, which is usually staffed by nurse-midwives. Births at home are far more common in many other countries—for example, in Holland 35 percent of the babies are born at home. Some critics worry that the U.S. tendency to view birth through a medical lens may lead to unnecessary medical procedures (Hausman, 2005).

The people who assist a mother during birth vary across cultures. In U.S. hospitals, it has become the norm for fathers or birth coaches to remain with the mother throughout labor and delivery. In the East African Nigoni culture, men are completely excluded from the childbirth process. When a woman is ready to give birth, female relatives move into the woman's hut and the husband leaves, taking his belongings (clothes, tools, weapons, and so on) with him. He is not permitted to return until after the baby is born. In some cultures, childbirth is an open, community affair. For example, in the Pukapukan culture in the Pacific Islands, women give birth in a shelter that is open for villagers to observe.

Midwives   Midwifery is the norm throughout most of the world (Byrom & Simon, 2011; Kitzinger, 2011). In Holland, more than 40 percent of babies are delivered by midwives rather than doctors. But in 2003, 91 percent of U.S. births were attended by physicians, and only 8 percent of women who delivered a baby were attended by a midwife (Martin & others, 2005). However, the 8 percent figure in 2003 represents a substantial increase from less than 1 percent of U.S. women attended by a midwife in 1975 (Martin & others, 2005). Ninety-five percent of the midwives who delivered babies in the United States in 2003 were certified nurse-midwives. Compared with physicians, certified nurse-midwives generally spend more time with patients during prenatal visits, place more emphasis on patient counseling and education, provide more emotional support, and are more likely to stay with the patient during the entire labor and delivery process, which may explain the higher rate of positive outcomes for babies delivered by certified nurse-midwives than for those delivered by doctors (Davis, 2005).

A woman in the African !Kung culture giving birth in a sitting position. Notice the help and support being given by another woman. *What are some cultural variations in childbirth?*

afterbirth The third stage of birth, when the placenta, umbilical cord, and other membranes are detached and expelled.

Doulas In many countries, a doula attends a childbearing woman. *Doula* is a Greek word that means "a woman who helps." A **doula** is a caregiver who provides continuous physical, emotional, and educational support for the mother before, during, and after childbirth. Doulas remain with the mother throughout labor, assessing and responding to her needs. Researchers have found positive effects when a doula is present at the birth of a child (Akhavan & Lundgren, 2011; Dahlen, Jackson, & Stevens, 2011). In one study, low-income pregnant women who were given doula support spent a shorter time in labor and their newborns had a higher health rating at one and five minutes after birth than their low-income counterparts who did not receive doula support (Campbell & others, 2006). And a recent study revealed that doula care was linked to improved childbirth outcomes such as shorter labor and to a higher rate of breast feeding (Nommsen-Rivers & others, 2009).

In the United States, most doulas work as independent providers hired by the expectant mother. Doulas typically function as part of a "birthing team," serving as an adjunct to the midwife or the hospital's obstetric staff (Dundek, 2006). Managed care organizations are increasingly offering doula support as a part of regular obstetric care.

METHODS OF CHILDBIRTH

U.S. hospitals often allow the mother and her obstetrician to choose from a range of options available for delivering a baby. Key choices involve the use of medication, whether to use any of a number of nonmedicated techniques to reduce pain, and when to resort to a cesarean delivery (Moleti, 2009).

A doula assisting a birth. *What types of support do doulas provide?*

Medication Three basic kinds of drugs are used for labor: analgesics, anesthesia, and oxytocics. Analgesics are used to relieve pain. **Analgesics** include tranquilizers, barbiturates, and narcotics (such as Demerol).

Anesthesia is used in late first-stage labor and during expulsion of the baby to block sensation in an area of the body or to block consciousness. There is a trend toward not using general anesthesia, which blocks consciousness, in normal births because general anesthesia can be transmitted through the placenta to the fetus (Pennell & others, 2011). An *epidural block* is regional anesthesia that numbs the woman's body from the waist down. Even this drug, thought to be relatively safe, has come under recent criticism because it is associated with fever, extended labor, and increased risk for cesarean delivery (Birnbach & Ranasinghe, 2008).

Oxytocin is a synthetic hormone that is used to stimulate contractions; pitocin is the most widely used oxytocin (Ratcliffe, 2008). The benefits and risks of using oxytocin as part of childbirth continue to be debated (Mendelson, 2009).

Predicting how a drug will affect an individual woman and her fetus is difficult (Lowdermilk, Perry, & Cashion, 2011). A particular drug might have only a minimal effect on one fetus yet have a much stronger effect on another. The drug's dosage also is a factor (Davidson & others, 2012). Stronger doses of tranquilizers and narcotics given to decrease the mother's pain potentially have a more negative effect on the fetus than mild doses. It is important for the mother to assess her level of pain and have a voice in deciding whether she should receive medication.

Natural and Prepared Childbirth For a brief time not long ago, the idea of avoiding all medication during childbirth gained favor in the United States. Instead, many women chose to reduce the pain of childbirth through techniques known as natural childbirth, and a method called prepared childbirth became popular. Today, at least some medication is used in the typical childbirth, but elements of natural childbirth and prepared childbirth remain popular (Hogan & others, 2007; Hotelling, 2009).

Natural childbirth is the method that aims to reduce the mother's pain by decreasing her fear through education about childbirth and by teaching her to use

doula A caregiver who provides continuous physical, emotional, and educational support to the mother before, during, and after childbirth.

analgesics Drugs used to alleviate pain, such as tranquilizers, barbiturates, and narcotics.

anesthesia Drugs used in late first-stage labor and during expulsion of the baby to block sensation in an area of the body or to block consciousness.

oxytocin A synthetic hormone that is used to stimulate contractions.

natural childbirth Method developed in 1914 by English obstetrician Grantly Dick-Read that attempts to reduce the mother's pain by decreasing her fear through education about childbirth and breathing methods and relaxation techniques during delivery.

Linda Pugh, Perinatal Nurse

Perinatal nurses work with childbearing women to support health and growth during the childbearing experience. Linda Pugh (Ph.D., R.N.C.) is a perinatal nurse on the faculty at the Johns Hopkins University School of Nursing. She is certified as an inpatient obstetric nurse and specializes in the care of women during labor and delivery. Pugh teaches nursing to both undergraduate and graduate students. In addition to educating professional nurses and conducting research, Pugh consults with hospitals and organizations about women's health issues.

Pugh's research interests include nursing interventions with low-income breast feeding women, ways to prevent and ameliorate fatigue during childbearing, and the effectiveness of breathing exercises during labor.

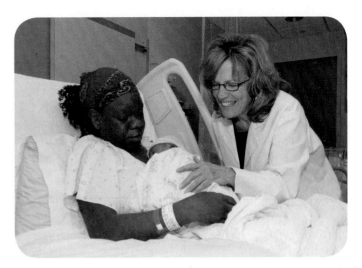

Linda Pugh (*right*) with a new mother and baby.

An instructor conducting a Lamaze class. *What characterizes the Lamaze method?*

> We must respect this instant of birth, this fragile moment. The baby is between two worlds, on a threshold.
>
> —**FREDERICK LEBOYER**
> *French Obstetrician, 20th Century*

breathing methods and relaxation techniques during delivery (Romano & Lothian, 2008). This approach was developed in 1914 by English obstetrician Grantly Dick-Read. Dick-Read believed that the doctor's relationship with the mother plays an important role in reducing her perception of pain and that the doctor should be present, providing reassurance, during her active labor prior to delivery.

French obstetrician Ferdinand Lamaze developed a method similar to natural childbirth that is known as **prepared childbirth,** or the Lamaze method. It includes a special breathing technique to control pushing in the final stages of labor, as well as more detailed education about anatomy and physiology than Dick-Read's approach provides. The Lamaze method has become very popular in the United States. The pregnant woman's partner usually serves as a coach who attends childbirth classes with her and encourages her to use specific breathing and relaxation techniques during delivery.

Many other prepared childbirth techniques have been developed (Davidson & others, 2012). They usually include elements of Dick-Read's natural childbirth or Lamaze's method, plus one or more other components. For instance, the Bradley method emphasizes the father's role as a labor coach. Virtually all of the prepared childbirth methods emphasize education, relaxation and breathing exercises, and support.

In sum, proponents of current prepared childbirth methods believe that when information and support are provided, women know *how* to give birth. To read about one nurse whose research focuses on fatigue during childbearing and breathing exercises during labor, see the *Connecting with Careers* profile. And to read about the increased variety of techniques now being used to reduce stress and control pain during labor, see the *Caring Connections* interlude.

Cesarean Delivery Normally, the baby's head comes through the vagina first. But if the baby is in a **breech position,** the baby's buttocks are the first part to emerge from the vagina. In 1 of every 25 deliveries, the baby's head is

From Waterbirth to Music Therapy

The effort to reduce stress and control pain during labor has recently led to an increase in the use of some older and some newer nonmedicated techniques (Kalder & others, 2011; Simkin & Bolding, 2004). These include waterbirth, massage, acupuncture, hypnosis, and music therapy.

Waterbirth

Waterbirth involves giving birth in a tub of warm water. Some women go through labor in the water and get out for delivery, while others remain in the water during the delivery. The rationale for waterbirth is that the baby has been in an amniotic sac for many months and that delivery in a similar environment is likely to be less stressful for the baby and the mother (Meyer, Weible, & Woeber, 2010). Mothers get into the warm water when contractions become closer together and more intense. Getting into the water too soon can cause labor to slow or stop. Reviews of research have indicated mixed results for waterbirths (Cluett & Burns, 2009; Field, 2007). A recent study did find that waterbirth was linked with a shorter second stage of labor (Cortes, Basra, & Kelleher, 2011). Waterbirth has been practiced more often in European countries such as Switzerland and Sweden in recent decades than in the United States but is increasingly being included in U.S. birth plans.

What characterizes the use of waterbirth in delivering a baby?

Massage

Massage is increasingly used to assist mothers prior to and during delivery (Stager, 2009–2010). Researchers have found that massage can reduce pain and anxiety during labor (Chang, Chen, & Huang, 2006). One study revealed that massage therapy reduced pain in pregnant women and alleviated prenatal depression in both parents and improved their relationship (Field & others, 2008).

Acupuncture

Acupuncture, the insertion of very fine needles into specific locations in the body, is used as a standard procedure to reduce the pain of childbirth in China,

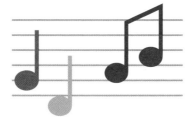

although only recently has it been used in the United States for this purpose. Recent research indicates that acupuncture can have positive effects on labor and delivery (Borup & others, 2009; Citkovitz, Schnyer, & Hoskins, 2011; Smith & others, 2011).

Hypnosis

Hypnosis, the induction of a psychological state of altered attention and awareness in which the individual is unusually responsive to suggestions, is increasingly being used during childbirth (Wilcox, 2010). Some studies have indicated positive effects of hypnosis for reducing pain during childbirth (Abbasi & others, 2011).

Music Therapy

Music therapy during childbirth, in which music is played to reduce stress and manage pain, is increasingly used (Hunter, 2009; Liu, Chang, & Chen, 2010). Few research studies have been conducted to determine its effectiveness.

---

still in the uterus when the rest of the body is out. Breech births can cause respiratory problems. As a result, if the baby is in a breech position, a surgical procedure known as a cesarean section, or a cesarean delivery, is usually performed. In a **cesarean delivery,** the baby is removed from the mother's uterus through an incision made in her abdomen. Cesarean deliveries also are performed if the baby is lying crosswise in the uterus, if the baby's head is too large to pass through the mother's pelvis, if the baby develops complications, or if the mother is bleeding vaginally.

Because of increased rates of respiratory complications, elective cesarean delivery is not recommended prior to 39 weeks of gestation unless there is an indication of fetal lung maturity (Greene, 2009). The benefits and risks of cesarean sections continue to be debated (Bangdiwala & others, 2010; Minguez-Milio & others, 2011). Some critics believe that too many babies are delivered by cesarean section in the

prepared childbirth Developed by French obstetrician Ferdinand Lamaze; this childbirth method is similar to natural childbirth but teaches a special breathing technique to control pushing in the final stages of labor and also provides a more detailed anatomy and physiology course.

breech position Position of the baby within the uterus that causes the buttocks to be the first part to emerge from the vagina.

cesarean delivery Delivery in which the baby is removed from the mother's uterus through an incision made in her abdomen. This also is sometimes referred to as a cesarean section.

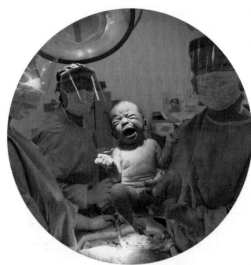

What characterizes the transition from fetus to newborn?

United States (Blakey, 2011). More cesarean sections are performed in the United States than in any other country in the world. In 2009, 33 percent of babies in the United States were born by cesarean deliveries (Solheim & others, 2011).

THE TRANSITION FROM FETUS TO NEWBORN

Much of our discussion of birth so far has focused on the mother. Being born also involves considerable stress for the baby. During each contraction, when the placenta and umbilical cord are compressed as the uterine muscles draw together, the supply of oxygen to the fetus decreases. If the delivery takes too long, the baby can develop *anoxia*, a condition in which the fetus or newborn receives an insufficient supply of oxygen. Anoxia can cause brain damage (Davidson & others, 2012).

The baby has considerable capacity to withstand the stress of birth. Large quantities of adrenaline and noradrenaline, hormones that protect the fetus in the event of oxygen deficiency, are secreted in stressful circumstances. These hormones increase the heart's pumping activity, speed up heart rate, channel blood flow to the brain, and raise the blood-sugar level. Never again in life will such large amounts of these hormones be secreted. This circumstance underscores how stressful it is to be born and also how well prepared and adapted the fetus is for birth (Van Beveren, 2011).

At the time of birth, the baby is covered with a protective skin grease called *vernix caseosa*. This vernix, which consists of fatty secretions and dead cells, is thought to help protect the baby's skin against heat loss before and during birth.

Immediately after birth, the umbilical cord is cut and the baby is on its own. Before birth, oxygen came from the mother via the umbilical cord, but now the baby is self-sufficient and can breathe on its own. Now 25 million little air sacs in the lungs must be filled with air. These first breaths may be the hardest ones an individual takes.

Review Connect Reflect

LG1 Discuss the stages, decisions involved, and transitions in birth.

Review

- What are the three stages involved in the birth process?
- What characterizes the childbirth setting and attendants?
- What are the main methods of childbirth?
- What is the fetus/newborn transition like?

Connect

- How might prenatal care (described in Chapter 3) be linked to the difficulty of the birth process?

Reflect *Your Own Personal Journey of Life*

- If you are a female who would like to have a baby, which birth strategy would you prefer? Why? If you are male, how involved would you want to be in helping your partner through the birth of your baby? Explain.

What Are Some Measures of Neonatal Health and Responsiveness?

LG2 Describe three measures of neonatal health and responsiveness.

Apgar Scale A widely used method to assess the health of newborns at one and five minutes after birth. The Apgar Scale evaluates infants' heart rate, respiratory effort, muscle tone, body color, and reflex irritability.

Almost immediately after birth, after the baby and mother have been introduced, a newborn is taken to be weighed, cleaned up, and tested for signs of developmental problems that might require urgent attention (Therrell & others, 2010). The **Apgar Scale** is widely used to assess the health of newborns at one and five minutes after birth. The Apgar Scale evaluates infants' heart rate, respiratory effort, muscle tone,

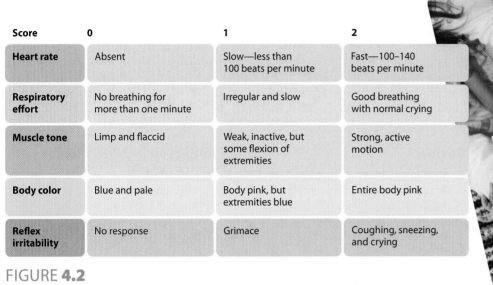

Score	0	1	2
Heart rate	Absent	Slow—less than 100 beats per minute	Fast—100–140 beats per minute
Respiratory effort	No breathing for more than one minute	Irregular and slow	Good breathing with normal crying
Muscle tone	Limp and flaccid	Weak, inactive, but some flexion of extremities	Strong, active motion
Body color	Blue and pale	Body pink, but extremities blue	Entire body pink
Reflex irritability	No response	Grimace	Coughing, sneezing, and crying

FIGURE 4.2

THE APGAR SCALE. A newborn's score on the Apgar Scale indicates whether the baby has urgent medical problems. *What are some trends in the Apgar scores of U.S. babies?*

body color, and reflex irritability. An obstetrician or a nurse does the evaluation and gives the newborn a score, or reading, of 0, 1, or 2 on each of these five health signs (see Figure 4.2). A total score of 7 to 10 indicates that the newborn's condition is good. A score of 5 indicates there may be developmental difficulties. A score of 3 or below signals an emergency and indicates that the baby might not survive.

The Apgar Scale is especially good at assessing the newborn's ability to respond to the stress of delivery and the demands of a new environment (Reynolds, 2010; Shehata & others, 2011). It also identifies high-risk infants who need resuscitation. A recent study revealed that in comparison with children who have high Apgar scores (9 to 10), the risk of developing attention deficit hyperactivity disorder (ADHD) in childhood was 75 percent higher for newborns with low Apgar scores (1 to 4) and 63 percent higher for those with Apgar scores of 5 or 6 (Li & others, 2011). For a more thorough assessment of the newborn, however, the Brazelton Neonatal Behavioral Assessment Scale or the Neonatal Intensive Care Unit Network Neurobehavioral Scale may be used.

The **Brazelton Neonatal Behavioral Assessment Scale (NBAS)** is typically performed within 24 to 36 hours after birth. It is also used as a sensitive index of neurological competence up to one month after birth for typical infants and in many studies as a measure of infant development (Costa & Figueiredo, 2011; Hernandez-Martinez & others, 2011). The NBAS assesses the newborn's neurological development, reflexes, and reactions to people and objects. Sixteen reflexes, such as sneezing, blinking, and rooting, are assessed, along with reactions to circumstances, such as the infant's reaction to a rattle.

A very low NBAS score can indicate brain damage, or stress to the brain that may heal in time. If an infant merely seems sluggish, parents are encouraged to give the infant attention and become more sensitive to the infant's needs. Parents are shown how the newborn can respond to people and how to stimulate such responses. These communications with parents can improve their interaction skills with both high-risk infants and healthy, responsive infants (Girling, 2006).

developmental **connection**

Physical Development. What are some individual differences in the reflex of sucking in young infants? Chapter 5, p. 152

Brazelton Neonatal Behavioral Assessment Scale (NBAS) A test performed within 24 to 36 hours after birth to assess newborns' neurological development, reflexes, and reactions to people.

An "offspring" of the NBAS, the **Neonatal Intensive Care Unit Network Neurobehavioral Scale (NNNS)** provides a more comprehensive analysis of the newborn's behavior, neurological and stress responses, and regulatory capacities (Lester, Tronick, & Brazelton, 2004; Lester & others, 2011). Whereas the NBAS was developed to assess normal, healthy, full-term infants, the NNNS was developed by T. Berry Brazelton, along with Barry Lester and Edward Tronick, to assess the "at-risk" infant. It is especially useful for evaluating preterm infants (although it may not be appropriate for those younger than 30 weeks' gestational age) and substance-exposed infants (Lester & others, 2011).

Review *Connect* Reflect

LG2 Describe three measures of neonatal health and responsiveness.

Review

- How can the Apgar Scale, the Brazelton Neonatal Behavioral Assessment Scale, and the Neonatal Intensive Care Unit Network Neurobehavioral Scale be characterized?

Connect

- What tests are used to assess individual differences in older infants (see Chapter 6, "Cognitive Development")?

Reflect *Your Own Personal Journey of Life*

- Imagine you are the parent of a newborn. Why might you want your offspring assessed by the NBAS or the NNNS in addition to the Apgar scale?

How Do Low Birth Weight and Preterm Infants Develop?

 LG3 Characterize the development of low birth weight and preterm infants.

Preterm and Small for Date Infants

Nurturing Preterm Infants

Consequences of Preterm Birth and Low Birth Weight

Various conditions that pose threats for newborns have been given different labels. We next examine these conditions and discuss interventions for improving outcomes of preterm infants.

PRETERM AND SMALL FOR DATE INFANTS

Three related conditions pose threats to many newborns: having a low birth weight, being preterm, and being small for date. **Low birth weight infants** weigh less than 5½ pounds at birth. *Very low birth weight* newborns weigh less than 3½ pounds, and *extremely low birth weight* newborns weigh less than 2 pounds. **Preterm infants** are those born three weeks or more before the pregnancy has reached its full term—in other words, before the completion of 37 weeks of gestation (the time between fertilization and birth). **Small for date (small for gestational age) infants** are those whose birth weight is below normal when the length of the pregnancy is considered. They weigh less than 90 percent of what all babies of the same gestational age weigh. Small for date infants may be preterm or full term. One study found that small for date infants had more than a fourfold risk of death (Regev & others, 2003).

In 2009, 12.2 percent of U.S. infants were born preterm—a 35 percent increase since the 1980s and a decrease of 0.6 percent since 2006 (National Center for Health

Neonatal Intensive Care Unit Network Neurobehavioral Scale (NNNS) An "offspring" of the NBAS, the NNNS provides a more comprehensive analysis of the newborn's behavior, neurological and stress responses, and regulatory capacities.

low birth weight infants Babies that weigh less than 5½ pounds at birth.

preterm infants Babies born three weeks or more before the pregnancy has reached its full term.

small for date (small for gestational age) infants Babies whose birth weight is below normal when the length of pregnancy is considered.

connecting with diversity

Incidence and Causes of Low Birth Weight Around the World

Most, but not all, preterm babies are also low birth weight babies. The incidence of low birth weight varies considerably from country to country. In some countries, such as India and Sudan, where poverty is rampant and the health and nutrition of mothers are poor, the percentage of low birth weight babies reaches as high as 31 percent (see Figure 4.3). In the United States, there has been an increase in low birth weight infants in the last two decades. The U.S. low birth weight rate of 8.2 percent in 2007 is considerably higher than that of many other developed countries (Hamilton & others, 2009). For example, only 4 percent of the infants born in Sweden, Finland, Norway, and Korea are low birth weight, and only 5 percent of those born in New Zealand, Australia, and France are low birth weight.

The causes of low birth weight also vary (Mortensen & others, 2009). In the developing world, low birth weight stems mainly from the mother's poor health and nutrition (Christian, 2009). For example, diarrhea and malaria, which are common in developing countries, can impair fetal growth if the mother becomes affected while she is pregnant. In developed countries, cigarette smoking during pregnancy is the leading cause of low birth weight (Fertig, 2010). In both developed and developing countries, adolescents who give birth when their bodies have not fully matured are at risk for having low birth weight babies (Malamitsi-Puchner & Boutsikou, 2006). In the United States, the increase in the number of low birth weight infants is due to such factors as the use of drugs, poor nutrition, multiple

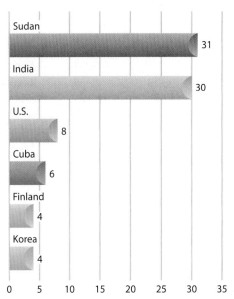

FIGURE **4.3**

PERCENTAGE OF INFANTS BORN WITH LOW BIRTH WEIGHT IN SELECTED COUNTRIES

births, reproductive technologies, and improved technology and prenatal care, resulting in a higher survival rate of high-risk babies (Chen & others, 2007). Nonetheless, poverty still is a major factor in preterm birth in the United States (Simmons & others, 2011). Women living in poverty are more likely to be obese, have diabetes and hypertension, smoke cigarettes and use illicit drugs, and they are less likely to have regular prenatal care (Nagahawatte & Goldenberg, 2008).

Statistics, 2011). The increase in preterm birth is likely due to such factors as the increasing number of births to women 35 years of age or older, increasing rates of multiple births, increased management of maternal and fetal conditions (for example, inducing labor preterm if medical technology indicates that it will increase the likelihood of survival), increased maternal substance abuse (tobacco, alcohol), and increased stress (Goldenberg & Culhane, 2007). Ethnic variations characterize preterm birth (Lhila & Long, 2011). For example, in 2009, the likelihood of being born preterm was 12.2 percent for all U.S. infants and 10.9 percent for non-Latino White infants, but the rate was 17.5 percent for African American infants (National Center for Health Statistics, 2011).

Recently, there has been considerable interest in the role that progestin might play in reducing preterm births (Lucovnik & others, 2011). Recent research reviews indicate that progestin is most effective in reducing preterm births when it is administered to women with a history of a previous spontaneous birth at less than 37 weeks (da Fonseca & others, 2009), to women who have a short cervical length of 15 millimeters or less (da Fonseca & others, 2009), and to women with a singleton rather than multiple offspring (Lucovnik & others, 2011).

See the *Connecting with Diversity* interlude to learn about how the incidence and causes of low birth weight vary across countries.

developmental **connection**

Nutrition. A recent study revealed that taking folic acid either alone or as part of a multivitamin for one year prior to conceiving was linked to a substantial reduction in preterm birth (Bukowski & others, 2008). Chapter 3, p. 104

How Would You...?

If you were a **social worker,** how would you advise couples living in poverty who are considering having a child about reducing the risk of having a low birth weight child?

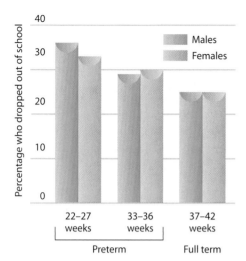

FIGURE **4.4**

PERCENTAGE OF PRETERM AND FULL-TERM BIRTH INFANTS WHO DROPPED OUT OF SCHOOL

developmental **connection**

At-Risk Conditions. A home visitation program for high-risk pregnant women and adolescents that encouraged healthy prenatal behavior, provided social support, and linked them to medical and other community services, decreased their risk of delivering a low birth weight baby (Lee & others, 2009). Chapter 3, p. 95

How Would You…?

If you were a **health-care professional,** how would you advise hospital administrators about implementing kangaroo care or massage therapy in the neonatal intensive care unit?

CONSEQUENCES OF PRETERM BIRTH AND LOW BIRTH WEIGHT

Although most preterm and low birth weight infants are healthy, as a group they have more health and developmental problems than normal birth weight infants (Morse & others, 2009). For preterm birth, the terms *extremely preterm* and *very preterm* are increasingly used (London & others, 2011). *Extremely preterm infants* are those born at less than 28 weeks gestation, and *very preterm infants* are those born at less than 33 weeks of gestation. Figure 4.4 shows the results of a Norwegian study indicating that the earlier preterm infants are born, the more likely they will drop out of school (Swamy, Ostbye, & Skjaerven, 2008). A research review also revealed that very preterm infants had lower IQ scores, had less effective information-processing skills, and were more at risk for behavioral problems than full-term infants (Johnson, 2007).

The number and severity of these problems increase when infants are born very early and as their birth weight decreases (Baron & others, 2011; Duncan & others, 2011; Ni, Huang, & Guo, 2011). Survival rates for infants who are born very early and very small have risen, but with this improved survival rate have come increased rates of severe brain damage. The earlier the birth and the lower the birth weight, the greater the likelihood of brain injury. Approximately 7 percent of moderately low birth weight infants (3 pounds 5 ounces to 5 pounds 8 ounces) have brain injuries. This figure increases to 20 percent for the smallest newborns (1 pound 2 ounces to 3 pounds 5 ounces).

At school age, children who were born low in birth weight are more likely than their normal birth weight counterparts to have a learning disability, attention deficit hyperactivity disorder, or breathing problems such as asthma (Anderson & others, 2011; Santo, Portuguez, & Nunes, 2009). A recent study found that extremely low birth weight children at 8 years of age had more symptoms of anxiety, attention deficit hyperactivity disorder, and autistic syndrome disorders than their normal weight counterparts (Hack & others, 2009). One study revealed that 17-year-olds who were born with low birth weight were 50 percent more likely than normal birth weight individuals to have reading and mathematics deficits (Breslau, Paneth, & Lucia, 2004). Approximately 50 percent of all low birth weight children are enrolled in special education programs.

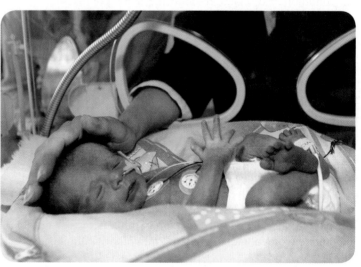

A "kilogram kid," weighing less than 2.3 pounds at birth. *What are some long-term outcomes for weighing so little at birth?*

NURTURING PRETERM INFANTS

An important strategy when considering how to treat low birth weight and preterm births is to reduce the risk of low birth weight before it occurs. Some effects of being born low in birth weight can be reduced or even reversed. Intensive enrichment programs that provide medical and educational services for both the parents and children can improve short-term outcomes for low birth weight children (Massaro & others, 2009; Nearing & others, 2011).

At present, federal laws mandate that services for school-aged children must be expanded to include family-based care for infants born with severe disabilities. The availability of services for moderately low birth weight children who do not have severe physical problems varies, but most states do not provide these services.

Two increasingly used interventions in the Neonatal Intensive Care Unit (NICU) are kangaroo care and massage therapy. **Kangaroo care** involves skin-to-skin contact, in which the baby, wearing only a diaper, is held upright against the parent's bare chest, much as a baby kangaroo is carried by its mother. Kangaroo care is typically practiced for two to three hours per day, skin-to-skin over an extended time in early infancy (Ahmed & others, 2011; Arora, 2009).

Why use kangaroo care with preterm infants? Preterm infants often have difficulty coordinating their breathing and heart rate, and the close physical contact with the parent provided by kangaroo care can help to stabilize the preterm infant's heartbeat, temperature, and breathing (Cong, Ludington-Hoe, & Walsh, 2011). Preterm infants who experience kangaroo care also gain more weight than their counterparts who are not given this care (Gathwala, Singh, & Singh, 2010). And a recent research review concluded that kangaroo care decreased the risk of mortality in low birth weight infants (Conde-Agudelo, Belizan, & Diaz-Rossello, 2011). Kangaroo care increasingly is being recommended for full-term infants as well (Ferber & Makhoul, 2008).

Many preterm infants experience less touch than full-term infants because they are isolated in temperature-controlled incubators. The research of Tiffany Field has led to a surge of interest in the role that massage might play in improving the developmental outcomes for preterm infants. To read about her research, see the *Connecting with Research* interlude.

A new mother practicing kangaroo care. *What is kangaroo care?*

developmental **connection**

Attachment. A classic study of infant monkey with cloth and wire surrogate mothers demonstrated the important role that touch plays in infant attachment. Chapter 7, p. 216

kangaroo care A way of holding a preterm infant so that there is skin-to-skin contact.

connecting with research

How Does Massage Therapy Benefit the Health and Well-Being of Babies?

Throughout history and in many cultures, caregivers have massaged infants. In Africa and Asia, infants are routinely massaged by parents or other family members for several months after birth. In the United States, interest in using touch and massage to improve the growth, health, and well-being of infants has been stimulated by the research of Tiffany Field (2001, 2007; Diego, Field, & Hernandez-Reif, 2008; Field, Diego, & Hernandez-Reif, 2008, 2010), director of the Touch Research Institute at the University of Miami School of Medicine.

In one study, preterm infants in a neonatal intensive care unit (NICU) were randomly assigned to a massage therapy group or a control group. For five consecutive days, the preterm infants in the massage group

were given three 15-minute moderate-pressure massages (Hernandez-Reif, Diego, & Field, 2007). Behavioral observations of the following stress behaviors were made on the first and last days of the study: crying, grimacing, yawning, sneezing, jerky arm and leg movements, startles, and finger flaring. The various stress behaviors were summarized in a composite stress behavior index. As indicated in Figure 4.5, massage had a stress-reducing effect on the preterm infants, which is especially important because they encounter numerous stressors while they are hospitalized.

In another study, Field and her colleagues (2004) tested a more cost-effective massage strategy. They taught mothers how to massage

(continued)

(continued)

their full-term infants rather than having health-care professionals do the massage. Beginning from day one of the newborn's life to the end of the first month, once a day before bedtime the mothers massaged the babies using either light or moderate pressure. Infants who were massaged with moderate pressure gained more weight, performed better on the orientation scale of the Brazelton, were less excitable and less depressed, and were less agitated during sleep.

Field has demonstrated the benefits of massage therapy for infants who face a variety of problems. For example, preterm infants exposed to cocaine in utero who received massage therapy gained weight and improved their scores on developmental tests (Wheeden & others, 1993). Another study investigated 1- to 3-month-old infants born to depressed adolescent mothers (Field & others, 1996). The infants of depressed mothers who received massage therapy had lower stress—as well as improved emotionality, sociability, and soothability—compared with the nonmassaged infants of depressed mothers.

In a research review of massage therapy with preterm infants, Field and her colleagues (2004) concluded that the most consistent findings involve two positive results: (1) increased weight gain, and (2) discharge from the hospital three to six days earlier. A recent study revealed that

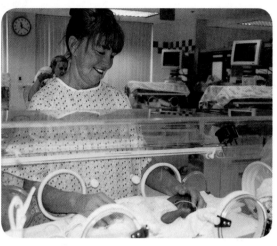

Shown here is Tiffany Field massaging a newborn infant. *What types of infants has massage therapy been shown to help?*

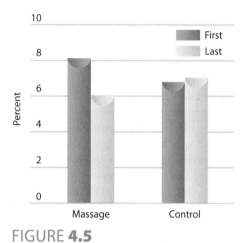

FIGURE 4.5

PRETERM INFANTS SHOW REDUCED STRESS BEHAVIORS AND ACTIVITY AFTER FIVE DAYS OF MASSAGE THERAPY (HERNANDEZ-REIF, DIEGO, & FIELD, 2007)

the mechanisms responsible for increased weight gain as a result of massage therapy were stimulation of the vagus nerve (one of 12 cranial nerves leading to the brain) and in turn the release of insulin (a food absorption hormone) (Field, Diego, & Hernandez-Reif, 2011).

In light of Field's findings, do you think expectant parents should routinely be taught how to massage their infants, even when prenatal development and birth have gone smoothly? Why or why not?

Review Connect Reflect

LG3 Characterize the development of low birth weight and preterm infants.

Review

- What is a low birth weight infant? How can preterm and small for date infants be distinguished?
- What are the long-term outcomes for low birth weight infants?
- What is known about the roles of kangaroo care and massage therapy with preterm infants?

Connect

- What are some different types of learning disabilities (Chapter 11, "Physical Development in Middle and Late Childhood")?

Reflect *Your Own Personal Journey of Life*

- Imagine that you are the parent of a newborn. Would you rather have your newborn experience kangaroo care or massage therapy?

LG4 Explain the physical and psychological aspects of the postpartum period.

Physical Adjustments

Emotional and Psychological Adjustments

Bonding

The weeks after childbirth present challenges for many new parents and their off-spring. This is the **postpartum period,** the period after childbirth or delivery that lasts for about six weeks or until the mother's body has completed its adjustment and has returned to a nearly prepregnant state. It is a time when the woman adjusts, both physically and psychologically, to the process of childbearing.

The postpartum period involves a great deal of adjustment and adaptation. The baby has to be cared for. The mother has to recover from childbirth, to learn how to take care of the baby, and to learn to feel good about herself as a mother. The father needs to learn how to take care of his recovering partner, to learn how to take care of the baby, and to learn how to feel good about himself as a father. Many health professionals believe that the best way to meet these challenges is with a family-centered approach that uses the family's resources to support an early and smooth adjustment to the newborn by all family members. The adjustments needed are physical, emotional, and psychological.

PHYSICAL ADJUSTMENTS

A woman's body makes numerous physical adjustments in the first days and weeks after childbirth (Mattson & Smith, 2011). She may have a great deal of energy or feel exhausted and let down. Most new mothers feel tired and need rest. Though these changes are normal, the fatigue can undermine the new mother's sense of well-being and confidence in her ability to cope with a new baby and a new family life.

A concern is the loss of sleep that the primary caregiver experiences in the postpartum period (Hunter, Rychnovsky, & Yount, 2009; Montgomery-Downs & others, 2010). One analysis indicated that the primary caregiver loses as much as 700 hours of sleep in the first year following the baby's birth (Maas, 2008). In the 2007 Sleep in America Survey, a substantial percentage of women reported loss of sleep during pregnancy and in the postpartum period (National Sleep Foundation, 2007) (see Figure 4.6). The loss of sleep can contribute to stress, relationship conflict, and impaired decision making (Meerlo, Sgoifo, & Suchecki, 2008).

After delivery, a mother's body undergoes sudden and dramatic changes in hormone production. When the placenta is delivered, estrogen and progesterone levels drop steeply and remain low until the ovaries start producing hormones again.

Involution is the process by which the uterus returns to its prepregnant size five or six weeks after birth. Immediately following birth, the uterus weighs 2 to 3 pounds. By the end of five or six weeks, the uterus weighs 2 to 3½ ounces. Nursing the baby helps contract the uterus at a rapid rate.

If a woman has regularly engaged in conditioning exercises during pregnancy, exercise will help her recover her former body contour and strength. With a caregiver's approval, the new mother can begin some exercises as soon as one hour after delivery. One study found that women who maintained or increased their exercise from prepregnancy to postpartum had better maternal well-being than women who engaged in no exercise or decreased their exercise from prepregnancy to postpartum (Blum, Beaudoin, & Caton-Lemos, 2005).

Relaxation techniques are also helpful during the postpartum period. Five minutes of slow breathing on a stressful day in the postpartum period can relax and refresh the new mother, and this will indirectly benefit the new baby.

postpartum period The period after childbirth when the mother adjusts, both physically and psychologically, to the process of childbearing. This period lasts for about six weeks, or until her body has completed its adjustment and has returned to a near-prepregnant state.

involution The process by which the uterus returns to its prepregnant size.

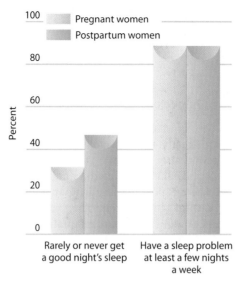

FIGURE **4.6**

SLEEP DEPRIVATION IN PREGNANT AND POSTPARTUM WOMEN

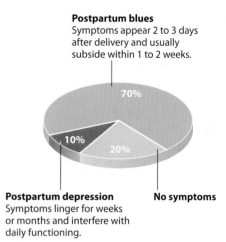

Postpartum blues Symptoms appear 2 to 3 days after delivery and usually subside within 1 to 2 weeks.

Postpartum depression Symptoms linger for weeks or months and interfere with daily functioning.

No symptoms

FIGURE **4.7**

POSTPARTUM BLUES AND POSTPARTUM DEPRESSION AMONG U.S. WOMEN. Some health professionals refer to the postpartum period as the "fourth trimester." Though the time span of the postpartum period does not necessarily cover three months, the term "fourth trimester" suggests continuity and the importance of the first several months after birth for the mother.

EMOTIONAL AND PSYCHOLOGICAL ADJUSTMENTS

How Would You...?
If you were a human **development and family studies professional,** how would you talk with mothers and fathers about vulnerabilities in mental health and relationships in the postpartum period?

Emotional fluctuations are common for mothers in the postpartum period. For some women, emotional fluctuations decrease within several weeks after the delivery, but other women experience more long-lasting emotional swings.

As shown in Figure 4.7, about 70 percent of new mothers in the United States have what are called "baby blues." About two to three days after birth, they begin to feel depressed, anxious, and upset. These feelings may come and go for several weeks after the birth, often peaking about three to five days after birth.

Postpartum depression involves a major depressive episode that typically occurs about four weeks after delivery. In other words, women with postpartum depression have such strong feelings of sadness, anxiety, or despair that for at least a two-week period they have trouble coping with their daily tasks. Without treatment, postpartum depression may become worse and last for many months (Nolen-Hoeksema, 2011). And many women with postpartum treatment don't seek help. For example, one recent study found that 15 percent of the women reported postpartum depression symptoms but less than half sought help (McGarry & others, 2009). Estimates indicate that 10 to 14 percent of new mothers experience postpartum depression.

Several antidepressant drugs are effective in treating postpartum depression and appear to be safe for breast feeding women (Logsdon, Wisner, & Hanusa, 2009). Psychotherapy, especially cognitive therapy, is an effective treatment of postpartum depression for many women (Miller & Larusso, 2011; Pearlstein & others, 2009). In addition, engaging in regular exercise may help reduce postpartum depression (Daley, Macarthur, & Winter, 2007).

Can a mother's postpartum depression affect the way she interacts with her infant? A recent research review concluded that the interaction difficulties of depressed mothers and their infants occur across cultures and socioeconomic status groups, and encompass less sensitivity of the mothers and less responsiveness on the part of infants (Field, 2010). Several caregiving activities also are compromised including feeding, sleep routines, and safety practices.

postpartum depression Involves a major depressive episode characterized by strong feelings of sadness, anxiety, or despair in new mothers, making it difficult for them to carry out daily tasks.

bonding A close connection, especially a physical bond between parents and their newborn in the period shortly after birth.

Diane Sanford, Clinical Psychologist and Postpartum Expert

Diane Sanford has a doctorate in clinical psychology, and for many years she had a private practice that focused on marital and family relationships. But after she began collaborating with a psychiatrist whose clients included women with postpartum depression, Dr. Sanford, along with a women's health nurse, founded Women's Healthcare Partnership in St. Louis, Missouri, which specializes in women's adjustment during the postpartum period. Subsequently, they added a marriage and family relationships counselor and a social worker to their staff, and then later hired nurse educators, a dietician, and a fitness expert as consultants (Source: Clay, 2001).

Diane Sanford holding an infant of one of the mothers who comes to her for help in coping with postpartum issues.

To read about an individual who specializes in helping women adjust during the postpartum period, see the *Connecting with Careers* profile.

Fathers also undergo considerable adjustment in the postpartum period, even when they work away from home all day. Many fathers feel that the baby comes first and gets all of the mother's attention; some feel that they have been replaced by the baby.

The father's support and caring can play a role in whether the mother develops postpartum depression (Dietz & others, 2009; Persson & others, 2011). A recent study revealed that higher support by fathers was related to lower incidence of postpartum depression in women (Smith & Howard, 2008).

Some fathers develop postpartum depression, and it can be detrimental to the child's development (Schumacher, Zubaran, & White, 2008). A recent study revealed that paternal postpartum depression (independent of maternal postpartum depression) was linked to psychological disorders in their children seven years later (Ramchandani & others, 2008).

To help the father adjust, parents should set aside some special time to spend together. The father's postpartum reaction also likely will be improved if he has taken childbirth classes with the mother and is an active participant in caring for the baby.

The postpartum period is a time of considerable adjustment and adaptation for both the mother and the father. Fathers can provide an important support system for mothers, especially in helping mothers care for young infants. What kinds of tasks might the father of a newborn do to support the mother?

BONDING

A special component of the parent-infant relationship is **bonding,** the formation of a connection, especially a physical bond involving touch between parents and the newborn in the period shortly after birth. Sometimes hospitals seem determined to deter bonding. Drugs given to the mother to make her delivery less painful can make the mother drowsy, interfering with her ability to respond to and stimulate the newborn. Mothers and newborns are often separated shortly after delivery, and preterm infants are isolated from their mothers even more than are full-term infants.

Do these practices do any harm? Some physicians believe that during the period shortly after birth, the parents and newborn need to form an emotional attachment as a foundation for

developmental **connection**

Theories. Lorenz demonstrated the importance of bonding in greylag geese, but the first few days of life are unlikely to be a critical period for bonding in human infants. Chapter 1, p. 29

A mother bonds with her infant moments after it is born. *How critical is bonding for the development of social competence later in childhood?*

optimal development in years to come (Kennell, 2006). Is there evidence that close contact between mothers in the first several days after birth is critical for optimal development later in life? Although some research supports this bonding hypothesis (Klaus & Kennell, 1976), a body of research challenges the significance of the first few days of life as a critical period (Bakeman & Brown, 1980; Rode & others, 1981). Indeed, the extreme form of the bonding hypothesis—that the newborn must have close contact with the mother in the first few days of life to develop optimally—simply is not true.

Nonetheless, the weakness of the bonding hypothesis should not be used as an excuse to keep motivated mothers from interacting with their newborns. Such contact brings pleasure to many mothers. In some mother-infant pairs—including preterm infants, adolescent mothers, and mothers from disadvantaged circumstances—early close contact may establish a climate for improved interaction after the mother and infant leave the hospital.

Many hospitals now offer a rooming-in arrangement, in which the baby remains in the mother's room most of the time during its hospital stay. However, if parents choose not to use this rooming-in arrangement, the weight of the research suggests that this decision will not harm the infant emotionally (Lamb, 1994).

Review *Connect* Reflect

 Explain the physical and psychological aspects of the postpartum period.

Review

- What does the postpartum period involve? What physical adjustments does the woman's body make in this period?
- What emotional and psychological adjustments characterize the postpartum period?
- Is bonding critical for optimal development?

Connect

- How can exercise help pregnant women before delivery and women with postpartum depression (Chapter 3, "Prenatal Development")?

Reflect *Your Own Personal Journey of Life*

- If you are a female who plans to have children, what can you do to adjust effectively in the postpartum period? If you were the partner of a new mother, what could you do to help during the postpartum period?

·topical **connections**

In the next three chapters that compose Section 3 of this text, you will explore the physical, cognitive, and socioemotional development of infants, including key theoretical, research, and applied aspects of the first 18 to 24 months of life. You will learn about the remarkable and complex physical development of infants' motor skills, such as learning to sit and walk (Chapter 5); read about the early development of infants' cognitive skills, such as the ability to form concepts (Chapter 6); and examine infants' surprisingly sophisticated socioemotional development, as reflected in their motivation to share and perceive others' actions as intentionally motivated (Chapter 7).

In the next chapter, you will follow the dramatic physical development of the infant through the first months of life, tracing how motor skills are acquired and how perception and the senses develop during a period of remarkable physical growth and change.

looking forward

What Happens During the Birth Process?

 LG1 Discuss the stages, decisions involved, and transitions in birth.

Stages of the Birth Process

Childbirth Setting and Attendants

Methods of Childbirth

The Transition from Fetus to Newborn

- The first stage of birth is the longest and lasts about 12 to 14 hours for a woman having her first child. During it, the cervical opening dilates to about 4 inches in diameter. The second stage begins when the baby's head starts to move through the cervix and ends with the baby's complete emergence. The third stage is delivery of the afterbirth.

- In the United States, the vast majority of births occur in hospitals and are attended by physicians. Many hospitals now have birthing centers. Some women who have good medical histories and who are at low risk for problem deliveries have babies at home. In many countries, such as Holland, much higher percentages of babies are born at home. Some births are attended by a midwife, and in many countries a doula attends.

- Among the methods of delivery are medicated, natural and prepared, and cesarean. The three basic kinds of drugs used in delivering a baby are analgesics, anesthesia, and oxytocics. Predicting how a particular drug will affect an individual pregnant woman and the fetus is difficult. Today the trend is toward using some medication during childbirth but keeping it to a minimum, if possible. Some believe that the U.S. cesarean rate is too high. The Lamaze method of prepared childbirth is widely used in the United States.

- In some cases, if the delivery takes too long, anoxia can occur. Anoxia involves an insufficient supply of oxygen during the fetus/newborn transition. Being born involves considerable stress, but the baby is well prepared and adapted to handle the stress. Large quantities of stress-related hormones (adrenaline and noradrenaline) are secreted during the fetus/newborn transition.

What Are Some Measures of Neonatal Health and Responsiveness?

 LG2 Describe three measures of neonatal health and responsiveness.

- For many years, the Apgar Scale has been used to assess the newborn's health. It is used one and five minutes after birth and assesses heart rate, respiratory effort, muscle tone, body color, and reflex irritability. The Brazelton Neonatal Behavioral Assessment Scale (NBAS) is performed within 24 to 36 hours after birth to evaluate the newborn's neurological development, reflexes, and reactions to people. Recently, the Neonatal Intensive Care Unit Network Neurobehavioral Scale (NNNS) was constructed; it provides a more comprehensive analysis of the newborn's behavior, neurological and stress responses, and regulatory capacities.

How Do Low Birth Weight and Preterm Infants Develop?

 LG3 Characterize the development of low birth weight and preterm infants.

Preterm and Small for Date Infants

- Low birth weight infants weigh less than 5½ pounds at birth. Low birth weight babies may be preterm (born three weeks or more before the pregnancy has reached full term) or small for date (also called small for gestational age, which refers to infants whose birth weight is below normal when the length of pregnancy is considered). Small for date infants may be preterm or full term.

- Although most low birth weight babies are normal and healthy, as a group they have more health and developmental problems than full-term babies do. The number and severity of the problems increase when infants are born very early and at very low birth weight.

- Kangaroo care, a way of holding a preterm infant so that there is skin-to-skin contact, has positive effects on preterm infants. Massage therapy is increasingly being used with preterm infants and has positive outcomes.

What Happens During the Postpartum Period? Explain the physical and psychological aspects of the postpartum period.

- The postpartum period is the period after childbirth or delivery. It is a time when the woman adjusts, both physically and psychologically, to the process of childbearing. It lasts for about six weeks, or until the body has completed its adjustment. Physical adjustments include fatigue, involution, hormonal changes that include a dramatic drop in estrogen and progesterone, and exercises to recover former body contour and strength.

- Emotional fluctuations are common among mothers during the postpartum period. These fluctuations may be due to hormonal changes, fatigue, inexperience or lack of confidence in caring for a newborn, or the extensive demands involved in caring for a newborn. For some, these emotional fluctuations are minimal and disappear within a few weeks, but for others they can be more long-lasting. Postpartum depression involves such strong feelings of sadness, anxiety, or despair that new mothers have difficulty carrying out daily tasks. Postpartum depression affects approximately 10 percent of new mothers. The father also goes through a postpartum adjustment. He may feel that the baby now receives all of his wife's attention. Being an active participant in caring for the baby helps ease the father's postpartum reaction. Both parents need to set aside special time to spend together.

- Bonding refers to the formation of a connection between parents and the newborn shortly after birth. Bonding has not been found to be critical in the development of a competent infant or child, although it may stimulate positive interaction in some mother-infant pairs.

key terms

key people

connecting with improving the lives of children

MAKING A DIFFERENCE

Effective Birth Strategies

Here are some birth strategies that may benefit the baby and the mother:

- *Take a childbirth class.* These classes provide information about the childbirth experience.
- *Become knowledgeable about different childbirth techniques.* We considered a number of different childbirth techniques in this chapter, including Lamaze and use of doulas. Obtain more detailed information about such techniques by reading a good book, such as *YOU: Having a Baby* by Michael Rosen and Mehmet Oz (New York: Free Press, 2011), and *Be Prepared: A Practical Handbook for New Dads* by Gary Greenberg and Jeannie Hayden (New York: Simon & Schuster, 2004).
- *Use positive intervention with at-risk infants.* Massage can improve the developmental outcome of at-risk infants. Intensive enrichment programs that include medical, educational, psychological, occupational, and physical domains can benefit low birth weight infants. Intervention with low birth weight infants should involve an individualized plan.
- *Involve the family in the birth process.* If they are motivated to participate, the husband, partner, and siblings can benefit from being involved in the birth process. A mother, sister, or friend can also provide support.
- *Know about the adaptation required in the postpartum period.* The postpartum period involves considerable adaptation and adjustment by the mother and the father. The mother's adjustment is both physical and emotional. Exercise and relaxation techniques can benefit mothers during the postpartum period. So can an understanding, supportive husband.

RESOURCES

Lamaze International
www.lamaze.com
Lamaze provides information about the Lamaze method and taking or teaching Lamaze classes.

The Doula Book
by Marshall Klaus, John Kennell, and Phyllis Klaus (2002)
New York: Perseus Books
Learn more about how valuable a doula can be in the childbirth process.

Birth: Issues in Perinatal Care
This multidisciplinary journal on perinatal care is written for health professionals and contains articles on research and clinical practice, review articles, and commentary.

International Cesarean Awareness Network
www.icanon-line.org
This organization provides extensive information and advice about cesarean birth.

Postpartum Support International (PSI)
www.postpartum.net
PSI provides information about postpartum depression.

Babies are such a nice way to start people.

—DON HEROLD
American Writer, 20th Century

Infancy

As newborns, we were not empty-headed organisms. We had some basic reflexes, among them crying, kicking, and coughing. We slept a lot, and occasionally we smiled, although the meaning of our first smiles was not entirely clear. We ate and we grew. We crawled and then we walked, a journey of a thousand miles beginning with a single step. Sometimes we conformed; sometimes others conformed to us. Our development was a continuous creation of more complex forms. Our helpless kind demanded meeting the eyes of love. We juggled the necessity of curbing our will with becoming what we could will freely. Section 3 contains three chapters: "Physical Development in Infancy" (Chapter 5), "Cognitive Development in Infancy" (Chapter 6), and "Socioemotional Development in Infancy" (Chapter 7).

chapter 5

PHYSICAL DEVELOPMENT IN INFANCY

Latonya is a newborn baby in Ghana. During her first days of life, she has been kept apart from her mother and bottle fed. Manufacturers of infant formula provide the hospital where she was born with free or subsidized milk powder. Her mother has been persuaded to bottle feed rather than breast feed her. When her mother bottle feeds Latonya, she overdilutes the milk formula with unclean water. Latonya's feeding bottles have not been sterilized. Latonya becomes very sick. She dies before her first birthday.

Ramona was born in Nigeria with a "baby-friendly" program. In this program, babies are not separated from their mothers when they are born, and the mothers are encouraged to breast feed them. The mothers are told of the perils that bottle feeding can bring because of unsafe water and unsterilized bottles. They also are informed about the advantages of breast milk, which include its nutritious and hygienic qualities, its ability to immunize babies against common illnesses, and its role in reducing the mother's risk of breast and ovarian cancer. Ramona's mother is breast feeding her. At 1 year of age, Ramona is very healthy.

For many years, maternity units in hospitals favored bottle feeding and did not give mothers adequate information about the benefits of breast feeding. In recent years, the World Health Organization and UNICEF have tried to reverse the trend toward bottle feeding of infants in many impoverished countries. They instituted the baby-friendly program in many of these countries. They also persuaded the International Association of Infant Formula Manufacturers to stop marketing their baby formulas to hospitals in countries where the government supports the baby-friendly initiatives. For the hospitals themselves, costs actually were reduced as infant formula, feeding bottles, and separate nurseries became unnecessary. For example, baby-friendly Jose Fabella Memorial Hospital in the Philippines reported saving 8 percent of its annual budget. Still, there are many places in the world where the baby-friendly initiatives have not been implemented (UNICEF, 2004).

The advantages of breast feeding in impoverished countries are substantial (Mwiru & others, 2011; UNICEF, 2012). However, these advantages must be balanced against the risk of passing HIV to the baby through breast milk if the mother has the virus; the majority of mothers don't know their HIV status (Mepham & others, 2011). In some areas of Africa, more than 30 percent of mothers have the HIV virus.

(Top) An HIV-infected mother breast feeding her baby in Nairobi, Africa. (Bottom) A Rwandan mother bottle feeding her baby. *What are some concerns about breast versus bottle feeding in impoverished countries?*

topical connections

In the last chapter, you read about the transformation from fetus to newborn, and the baby's remarkable capacity to withstand the stress of the birth process. You learned how preterm and low birth weight babies can be nurtured in their first days and weeks of life, and how new mothers adjust—physically and psychologically—during the postpartum period. In this chapter, you will read about many aspects of the infant's physical development, including breathtaking advances in the development of the brain, motor skills, and perception.

◄ *looking back*

preview

It is very important for infants to get a healthy start. When they do, their first two years of life are likely to be a time of amazing development. In this chapter, we focus on the biological domain and the infant's physical development, exploring physical growth, motor development, and sensory and perceptual development.

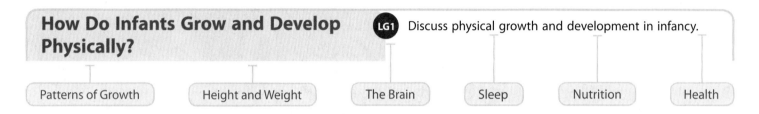

How Do Infants Grow and Develop Physically?

LG1 Discuss physical growth and development in infancy.

Patterns of Growth · Height and Weight · The Brain · Sleep · Nutrition · Health

PATTERNS OF GROWTH

An extraordinary proportion of the total body is occupied by the head during pre-natal development and early infancy (see Figure 5.1). The **cephalocaudal pattern** is the sequence in which the earliest growth always occurs at the top—the head—with physical growth and differentiation of features gradually working their way down from top to bottom (for example, shoulders, middle trunk, and so on) (Pedroso, 2008). This same pattern occurs in the head area, because the top parts of the head—the eyes and brain—grow faster than the lower parts, such as the jaw.

Sensory and motor development generally proceed according to the cephalo-caudal principle. For example, infants see objects before they can control their torso, and they can use their hands long before they can crawl or walk. However, development does not follow a rigid blueprint. One study found that infants reached for toys with their feet prior to reaching with their hands (Galloway & Thelen, 2004). On average, infants first touched the toy with their feet when they were 12 weeks old and with their hands when they were 16 weeks old.

> A baby is the most complicated object made by unskilled labor.
>
> —ANONYMOUS

cephalocaudal pattern The sequence in which the earliest growth always occurs at the top—the head—with physical growth and feature differentiation gradually working from top to bottom.

proximodistal pattern The sequence in which growth starts at the center of the body and moves toward the extremities.

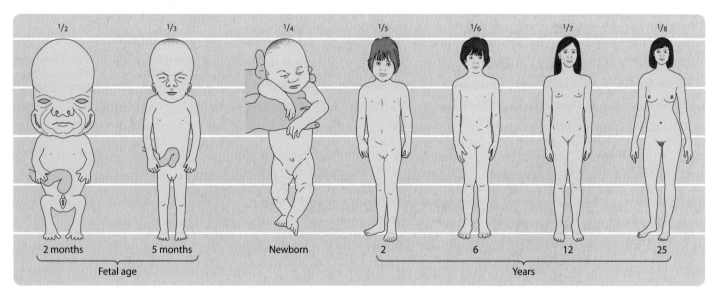

FIGURE **5.1**

CHANGES IN PROPORTIONS OF THE HUMAN BODY DURING GROWTH. As individuals develop from infancy through adulthood, one of the most noticeable physical changes is that the head becomes smaller in relation to the rest of the body. The fractions listed refer to head size as a proportion of total body length at different ages.

Growth also follows the **proximodistal pattern,** the sequence in which growth starts at the center of the body and moves toward the extremities. For example, infants control the muscles of their trunk and arms before they control their hands and fingers, and they use their whole hands before they can control several fingers.

HEIGHT AND WEIGHT

The average North American newborn is 20 inches long and weighs 7½ pounds. Ninety-five percent of full-term newborns are 18 to 22 inches long and weigh between 5½ and 10 pounds.

In the first several days of life, most newborns lose 5 to 7 percent of their body weight before they adjust to feeding by sucking, swallowing, and digesting. Then they grow rapidly, gaining an average of 5 to 6 ounces per week during the first month. They have doubled their birth weight by the age of 4 months and have nearly tripled it by their first birthday. Infants grow about 1 inch per month during the first year, reaching approximately 1½ times their birth length by their first birthday.

Growth slows considerably in the second year of life (Hockenberry & Wilson, 2011). By 2 years of age, infants weigh approximately 26 to 32 pounds, having gained a quarter to half a pound per month during the second year; now they have reached about one-fifth of their adult weight. At 2 years of age, the average infant is 32 to 35 inches in height, which is nearly half of their adult height.

THE BRAIN

We described the amazing growth of the brain from conception to birth in Chapter 3, "Prenatal Development." By the time it is born, the infant that began as a single cell is estimated to have a brain that contains approximately 100 billion nerve cells, or neurons. Extensive brain development continues after birth, through infancy and later (Bell, 2011; Nelson, 2011). Because the brain is still developing so rapidly in infancy, the infant's head should be protected from falls or other injuries and the baby should never be shaken. *Shaken baby syndrome,* which includes brain swelling and hemorrhaging, affects hundreds of babies in the United States each year (Squier, 2011). A recent analysis found that fathers most often were the perpetrators of shaken baby syndrome, followed by child-care providers and boyfriends of the victims' mothers (National Center on Shaken Baby Syndrome, 2011).

Studying the brain's development in infancy is not as easy as it might seem. Even the latest brain-imaging technologies cannot make out fine details in adult brains and cannot be used with babies. Positron emission tomography (PET) scans pose a radiation risk to babies, and infants often wiggle too much to allow technicians to capture accurate images using magnetic resonance imaging (MRI). However, researchers have been successful in using the electroencephalogram (EEG), a measure of the brain's electrical activity, to learn about the brain's development in infancy (Bell & Diaz, 2011; Cuevas & Bell, 2011). Among the researchers who are making strides in finding out more about the brain's development in infancy are Charles Nelson and his colleagues and John Richards and his colleagues (Nelson, 2007, 2011; Moulson & Nelson, 2008; Richards, 2009, 2010; Richards, Reynolds, & Courage, 2010; Sanchez, Richards, & Almi, 2011) (see Figure 5.2).

The Brain's Development   At birth, the newborn's brain is about 25 percent of its adult weight. By the second birthday, the brain is about 75 percent of its adult weight. However, the brain's areas do not mature uniformly.

How Would You...?
If you were a **health-care professional,** how would you talk with parents about shaken baby syndrome?

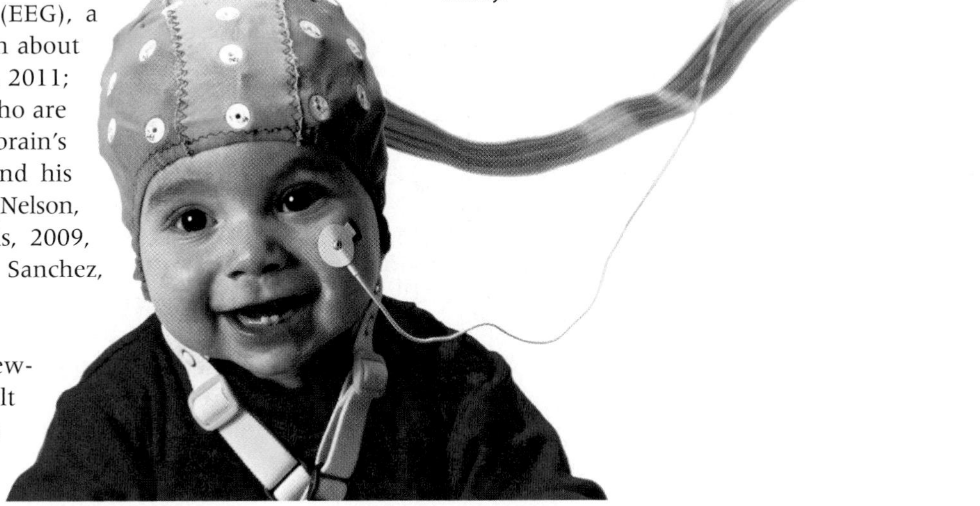

FIGURE **5.2**

MEASURING THE ACTIVITY OF AN INFANT'S BRAIN. By attaching up to 128 electrodes to a baby's scalp to measure the brain's activity, Charles Nelson and his colleagues (2006) have found that even newborns produce distinctive brain waves that reveal they can distinguish their mother's voice from another woman's, even while they are asleep. *Why is it so difficult to measure infants' brain activity?*

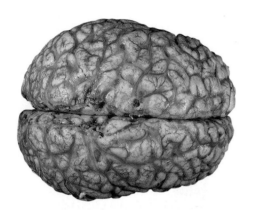

developmental **connection**

Brain Development. How does the brain change from conception to birth? Chapter 3, p. 89

Mapping the Brain   Scientists analyze and categorize areas of the brain in numerous ways (Nelson, 2011; Zelazo & Lee, 2010). We are most concerned with the portion farthest from the spinal cord, known as the **forebrain,** which includes the cerebral cortex and several structures beneath it. The **cerebral cortex** covers the forebrain like a wrinkled cap. It has two halves, or hemispheres (see Figure 5.3). Based on ridges and valleys in the cortex, scientists distinguish four main areas, called lobes, in each hemisphere. Although the lobes usually work together, each has a somewhat different primary function (see Figure 5.4):

- *Frontal lobes* are involved in voluntary movement, thinking, personality, emotion, memory, sustained attention, and intentionality or purpose.

- *Occipital lobes* function in vision.

- *Temporal lobes* have an active role in hearing, language processing, and memory.

- *Parietal lobes* play important roles in registering spatial location, maintaining attention, and administering motor control.

To some extent, the type of information handled by neurons depends on whether they are in the left or right hemisphere of the cortex (Van der Haegen & others, 2011). Speech and grammar, for example, depend on activity in the left hemisphere in most people; humor and the use of metaphors depend on activity in the right hemisphere (Diaz, Barrett, & Hogstrom, 2011; Pang & others, 2011). This specialization of function in one hemisphere of the cerebral cortex or the other is called **lateralization.** However, most neuroscientists agree that complex functions such as reading or performing music involve both hemispheres. Labeling people as "left-brained" because they are logical thinkers and "right-brained" because they are creative thinkers does not correspond to the way the brain's hemispheres work (Stroobant, Buijus, & Vingerhoets, 2009). Complex thinking in normal people is the outcome of communication between both hemispheres of the brain (Diaz & Hogstrom, 2011; van Ettinger-Veenstra & others, 2010).

At birth, the hemispheres of the cerebral cortex already have started to specialize: Newborns show greater electrical brain activity in the left hemisphere than the right hemisphere when they are listening to speech sounds (Hahn, 1987). How are the areas of the brain different in the newborn and the infant from those in an adult, and why do the differences matter? Important differences have been documented at both cellular and structural levels.

FIGURE **5.3**

THE HUMAN BRAIN'S HEMISPHERES. The two hemispheres of the human brain are clearly seen in this photograph. It is a myth that the left hemisphere is the exclusive location of language and logical thinking or that the right hemisphere is the exclusive location of emotion and creative thinking.

Changes in Neurons   Within the brain, the type of nerve cells called neurons send electrical and chemical signals, communicating with each other. As we discussed in Chapter 3, "Prenatal Development," a *neuron* is a nerve cell that handles information processing (see Figure 5.5). Extending from the neuron's cell body are two types of fibers known as axons and dendrites. Generally, the axon carries signals away from the cell body and dendrites carry signals toward it. A *myelin sheath,* which is a layer of fat cells, encases many axons (see Figure 5.5). The myelin sheath insulates axons and helps electrical signals travel faster down the axon. Myelination also is involved in providing energy to neurons and in facilitating communication (Campbell & Mahad, 2011). At the end of the axon are terminal buttons, which release chemicals called *neurotransmitters* into synapses, tiny gaps between neurons' fibers. Chemical interactions in synapses connect axons and dendrites, allowing information to pass from neuron to neuron. Think of the synapse as a river that blocks a road. A grocery truck arrives at one bank of the river, crosses by ferry, and continues its journey to market. Similarly, a message in the brain is "ferried" across the synapse by a

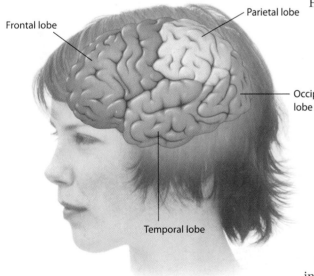

Frontal lobe

Parietal lobe

Occipital lobe

Temporal lobe

FIGURE **5.4**

THE BRAIN'S FOUR LOBES. Shown here are the locations of the brain's four lobes: frontal, occipital, temporal, and parietal.

neurotransmitter, which pours out information contained in chemicals when it reaches the other side of the river.

Neurons change in two very significant ways during the first years of life. First, *myelination,* the process of encasing axons with fat cells, begins prenatally and continues after birth, even into adolescence (Diamond, Casey, & Munakata, 2011). Second, connectivity among neurons increases, creating new neural pathways, as Figure 5.6 illustrates. New dendrites grow, connections among dendrites increase, and synaptic connections between axons and dendrites proliferate. Whereas myelination speeds up neural transmissions, the expansion of dendritic connections facilitates the spreading of neural pathways in infant development.

Researchers have discovered an intriguing aspect of synaptic connections: Nearly twice as many of these connections are made as will ever be used (Huttenlocher & Dabholkar, 1997). The connections that are used grow stronger and survive, while the unused ones are replaced by other pathways or disappear (Turrigiano, 2010). In the language of neuroscience, these connections are "pruned." For example, the more a baby engages in physical activity or uses language, the more those pathways will be strengthened.

Changes in Regions of the Brain   Figure 5.7 vividly illustrates the dramatic growth and later pruning of synapses in the visual, auditory, and prefrontal cortex (Huttenlocher & Dabholkar, 1997). Notice that "blooming and pruning" vary considerably by brain region. For example, the peak of synaptic overproduction in the visual cortex occurs at about the fourth postnatal month, followed by a gradual retraction until the middle to end of the preschool years (Huttenlocher & Dabholkar, 1997). In areas of the brain involved in hearing and language, a similar, though somewhat later, course is detected. However, in the *prefrontal cortex,* the area of the brain where higher-level thinking and self-regulation occur, the peak of overproduction occurs at just over 3 years of age; it is not until middle to late adolescence that the adult density of synapses is achieved. Both heredity and environment are thought to influence the timing and course of synaptic overproduction and subsequent retraction.

Meanwhile, the pace of myelination also varies in different areas of the brain (Gogtay & Thompson, 2010). Myelination for visual pathways occurs rapidly after birth and is completed in the first six months. Auditory myelination is not completed until 4 or 5 years of age.

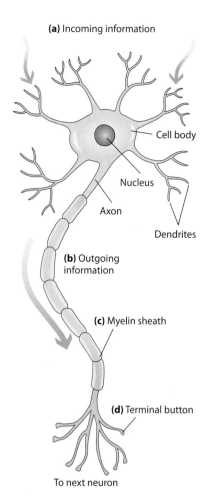

FIGURE **5.5**

THE NEURON. (*a*) The dendrites of the cell body receive information from other neurons, muscles, or glands through the axon. (*b*) Axons transmit information away from the cell body. (*c*) A myelin sheath covers most axons and speeds information transmission. (*d*) As the axon ends, it branches out into terminal buttons.

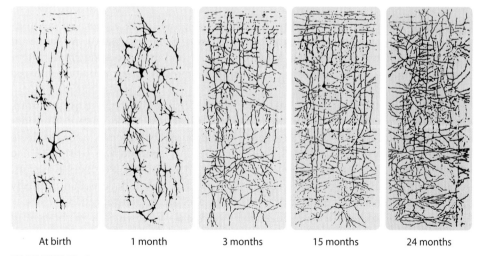

| At birth | 1 month | 3 months | 15 months | 24 months |

FIGURE **5.6**

THE DEVELOPMENT OF DENDRITIC SPREADING. Note the increase in connectedness between neurons over the course of the first two years of life.

Reprinted by permission of the publisher from *The Postnatal Development of the Human Cerebral Cortex, Vols. I–VIII* by Jesse LeRoy Conel, Cambridge, Mass.: Harvard University Press. Copyright © 1939, 1941, 1947, 1951, 1955, 1959, 1963, 1967 by the President and Fellows of Harvard College. Copyright © renewed 1967, 1969, 1975, 1979, 1983, 1987, 1991.

forebrain The region of the brain that is farthest from the spinal cord and includes the cerebral cortex and several structures beneath it.

cerebral cortex Tissue that covers the forebrain like a wrinkled cap and includes two halves, or hemispheres.

lateralization Specialization of function in one hemisphere of the cerebral cortex or the other.

FIGURE 5.7

SYNAPTIC DENSITY IN THE HUMAN BRAIN FROM INFANCY TO ADULTHOOD. The graph shows the dramatic increase and then pruning in synaptic density for three regions of the brain: visual cortex, auditory cortex, and prefrontal cortex. Synaptic density is believed to be an important indication of the extent of connectivity between neurons.

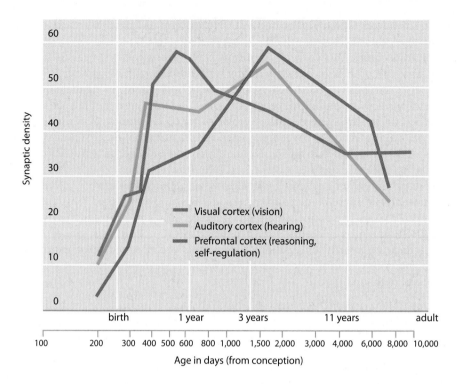

developmental connection

Brain Development. Changes in the prefrontal cortex in adolescents have important implications for their development. Chapter 14, p. 433

In general, some areas of the brain, such as the primary motor areas, develop earlier than others, such as the primary sensory areas. The frontal lobes are immature in the newborn. However, as neurons in the frontal lobes become myelinated and interconnected during the first year of life, infants develop an ability to regulate their physiological states, such as sleep, and gain more control over their reflexes. Cognitive skills that require deliberate thinking do not emerge until later in the first year (Bell, 2011; Bell & Fox, 1992; Cuevas & Bell, 2010). Indeed, the prefrontal region of the frontal lobe has the most prolonged development of any brain region, with changes detectable at least into emerging adulthood (Blakemore & others, 2011; Steinberg, 2011).

Early Experience and the Brain   Children who grow up in a deprived environment may have depressed brain activity (Fox, Levitt, & Nelson, 2010). As shown in Figure 5.8, a child who grew up in the unresponsive and unstimulating environment of a Romanian orphanage showed considerably depressed brain activity compared with a normal child.

Are the effects of deprived environments irreversible? There is reason to think the answer is no. The brain demonstrates both flexibility and resilience. Consider 14-year-old Michael Rehbein. At age 7, he began to experience uncontrollable seizures—as many as 400 a day. Doctors said the only solution was to remove the left hemisphere of his brain where the seizures were occurring. Recovery was slow, but his right hemisphere began to reorganize and take over functions that normally occur in the brain's left hemisphere, including speech (see Figure 5.9).

Neuroscientists believe that what wires the brain—or rewires it, in the case of Michael Rehbein—is repeated experience. Each time a baby tries to touch an attractive object or gazes intently at a face, tiny bursts of electricity shoot through the brain, knitting together neurons into circuits. The results are some of the behavioral milestones we discuss in this chapter.

The Neuroconstructivist View   Not long ago, scientists thought that our genes determined how our brains were "wired" and that the brain cells responsible for

neuroconstructivist view In this view, biological processes and environmental conditions influence the brain's development; the brain has plasticity and is context dependent; and brain development is closely linked with cognitive development.

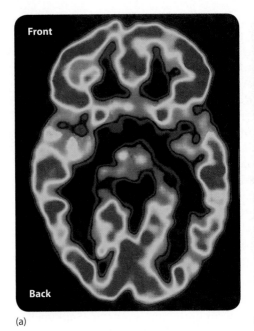

Front

Back

(a)

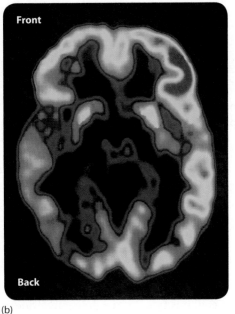

Front

Back

(b)

(a)

FIGURE **5.8**

EARLY DEPRIVATION AND BRAIN ACTIVITY. These two photographs are PET (positron emission tomography) scans—which use radioactive tracers to image and analyze blood flow and metabolic activity in the body's organs. These scans show the brains of (*a*) a normal child and (*b*) an institutionalized Romanian orphan who experienced substantial deprivation since birth. In PET scans, the highest to lowest brain activity is reflected in the colors of red, yellow, green, blue, and black, respectively. As can be seen, red and yellow show up to a much greater degree in the PET scan of the normal child than in that of the deprived Romanian orphan.

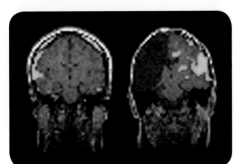

(b)

FIGURE **5.9**

PLASTICITY IN THE BRAIN'S HEMISPHERES.
(*a*) Michael Rehbein at 14 years of age. (*b*) Michael's right hemisphere (*left*) has reorganized to take over the language functions normally carried out by corresponding areas in the left hemisphere of an intact brain (*right*). However, the right hemisphere is not as efficient as the left, and more areas of the brain are recruited to process speech.

processing information just maturationally unfolded with little or no input from environmental experiences. Whatever brain your heredity dealt you, you were essentially stuck with. This view, however, turned out to be wrong. Instead, it has become clear that the brain has plasticity and its development depends on context (Diamond, Casey, & Munakata, 2011; Nelson, 2011).

The infant's brain depends on experiences to determine how connections are made (Johnson, 2011). Before birth, it appears that genes mainly direct basic wiring patterns. Neurons grow and travel to distant places awaiting further instructions (Nelson, 2011). After birth, the inflowing stream of sights, sounds, smells, touches, language, and eye contact help shape the brain's neural connections.

In the increasingly popular **neuroconstructivist view,** (a) biological processes (genes, for example) and environmental experiences (enriched or impoverished, for example) influence the brain's development; (b) the brain has plasticity and is influenced by contexts; and (c) development of the brain is closely linked with the child's cognitive development. These factors constrain or advance the construction of cognitive skills (Johnson & de Haan, 2011; Westerman, Thomas, & Karmiloff-Smith, 2011). The neuroconstructivist view emphasizes the importance of interactions between experience and gene expression in the brain's development, in much the same way that the epigenetic view proposes.

SLEEP

A recent research review concluded that infants 0 to 2 years of age slept an average of 12.8 hours a day, with a range of 9.7 to 15.9 hours (Galland & others, 2011). The most common infant sleep-related problem reported by parents is nighttime waking (The Hospital for Sick Children & others, 2010). Surveys

developmental **connection**

Nature and Nurture. In the epigenetic view, development is an ongoing, bidirectional interchange between heredity and environment. Chapter 2, p. 77

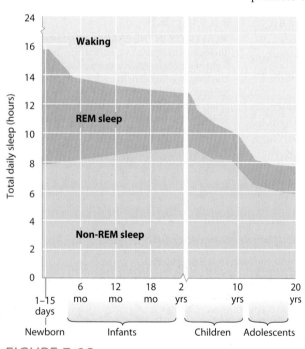

→ developmental **connection**

Sleep. What are some sleep problems that can develop in childhood and adolescence? Chapter 8, p. 245; Chapter 14, p. 444

indicate that 20 to 30 percent of infants have difficulty going to sleep at night and staying asleep throughout the night (Sadeh, 2008). A recent study revealed that the mother's emotional availability at bedtime was linked to fewer infant sleep problems, supporting the premise that parents' emotional availability to infants in sleep contexts increases feelings of safety and security, and consequently better-regulated infant sleep (Teti & others, 2010). And a recent study found that a higher involvement of fathers in overall infant care was related to fewer infant sleep problems (Tikotzky, Sadeh, & Glickman-Gavrieli, 2010). However, infant nighttime waking problems have consistently been linked to excessive parental involvement in sleep-related interactions with their infant (Sadeh, 2008). And a recent study revealed that maternal depression during pregnancy, early introduction of solid foods, infant TV viewing, and child-care attendance were related to shorter duration of infant sleep (Nevarez & others, 2010).

REM Sleep   In REM sleep, the eyes flutter beneath closed lids; in non-REM sleep, this type of eye movement does not occur and sleep is quieter (Sankupellay & others, 2011). Figure 5.10 shows developmental changes in the average number of total hours spent in REM and non-REM sleep. By the time they reach adulthood, individuals spend about one-fifth of their night in REM sleep, and REM sleep usually appears about one hour after non-REM sleep. However, about half of an infant's sleep is REM sleep, and infants often begin their sleep cycle with REM sleep rather than non-REM sleep (Sadeh, 2008). A much greater amount of time is taken up by REM sleep in infancy than at any other point in the life span. By the time infants reach 3 months of age, the percentage of time they spend in REM sleep falls to about 40 percent, and REM sleep no longer begins their sleep cycle.

Why do infants spend so much time in REM sleep? Researchers are not certain. The large amount of REM sleep may provide infants with added self-stimulation, since they spend less time awake than do older children. REM sleep also might promote the brain's development in infancy (Graven, 2006).

When adults are awakened during REM sleep, they frequently report that they have been dreaming, but when they are awakened during non-REM sleep they are much less likely to report they have been dreaming (Cartwright & others, 2006). Since infants spend more time than adults in REM sleep, can we conclude that they dream a lot? We don't know whether infants dream or not, because they don't have any way of reporting dreams.

Shared Sleeping   Some child experts stress that there are benefits to shared sleeping (as when an infant sleeps in the same bed with its mother). They state that it can promote breast feeding, lets the mother respond more quickly to the baby's cries, and allows her to detect breathing pauses in the baby that might be dangerous (Pelayo & others, 2006). Sharing a bed with a mother is common practice in many countries, such as Guatemala and China, whereas in others, such as the United States and Great Britain, most newborns sleep in a crib, either in the same room as the parents or in a separate room.

Shared sleeping remains a controversial issue, with some experts recommending it and others arguing against it, although recently the recommendation trend in the United States has been to avoid infant-parent bed sharing, especially until the infant is at least 6 months of age (McIntosh, Tonkin, & Gunn, 2010; Norton & Grellner, 2011). The American Academy of Pediatrics Task Force on Infant Positioning and

FIGURE 5.10
DEVELOPMENTAL CHANGES IN REM AND NON-REM SLEEP

SIDS (AAPTFIPS) (2000) recommends against shared sleeping. Its members argue that in some instances bed sharing might lead to sudden infant death syndrome (SIDS), as could be the case if a sleeping mother rolls over on her baby. Recent studies have found that bed sharing is linked with a greater incidence of SIDS, especially when parents smoke (Bajanowski & others, 2007; Senter & others, 2010). And a recent study of 2-month-old infants revealed that they had more sleep problems such as disordered breathing when they shared a bed with parents (Kelmanson, 2010).

SIDS **Sudden infant death syndrome (SIDS)** is a condition that occurs when infants stop breathing, usually during the night, and die suddenly without an apparent cause. SIDS remains the highest cause of infant death in the United States, with nearly 3,000 infant deaths attributed to it annually (Montagna & Chokroverty, 2011). Risk of SIDS is highest at 2 to 4 months of age (Centers for Disease Control and Prevention, 2011).

Since 1992, the American Academy of Pediatrics (AAP) has recommended that infants be placed to sleep on their backs to reduce the risk of SIDS, and the frequency of prone sleeping (on their stomachs) among U.S. infants has dropped dramatically (AAPTFIPS, 2000). Researchers have found that SIDS does indeed decrease when infants sleep on their backs rather than their stomachs or sides (Senter & others, 2010; Yiallourou & others, 2011). Among the reasons given for prone sleeping being a high-risk factor for SIDS are that it impairs the infant's arousal from sleep and restricts the infant's ability to swallow effectively (Franco & others, 2010; Mitchell, 2009).

In addition to sleeping in a prone position, researchers have found that the following are risk factors for SIDS:

- SIDS is more likely to occur in infants who do not use a pacifier when they go to sleep than in those who do use a pacifier (Jenik & Vain, 2010; Moon & others, 2011).

- A recent meta-analysis concluded that breast feeding is linked to a lower incidence of SIDS (Hauck & others, 2011).

- Low birth weight infants are 5 to 10 times more likely to die of SIDS than are their normal-weight counterparts (Horne & others, 2002).

- Infants whose siblings have died of SIDS are two to four times as likely to die of it (Lenoir, Mallet, & Calenda, 2000).

- Six percent of infants with sleep apnea, a temporary cessation of breathing in which the airway is completely blocked, usually for 10 seconds or longer, die of SIDS (Ednick & others, 2010; McNamara & Sullivan, 2000).

- African American and Eskimo infants are four to six times as likely as all others to die of SIDS (Ige & Shelton, 2004; Kitsantas & Gaffney, 2010).

- SIDS is more common in lower socioeconomic groups (Mitchell & others, 2000).

- SIDS is more common in infants who are passively exposed to cigarette smoke (Dietz & others, 2010).

- SIDS is more common when infants and parents share the same bed (Senter & others, 2010).

- SIDS is more common if infants sleep in soft bedding (McGarvey & others, 2006).

- SIDS is less common when infants sleep in a bedroom with a fan. A recent study revealed that sleeping in a bedroom with a fan lowers the risk of SIDS by 70 percent (Coleman-Phox, Odouli, & Li, 2008).

- SIDS occurs more often in infants with abnormal brain stem functioning involving the neurotransmitter serotonin (Duncan & others, 2010).

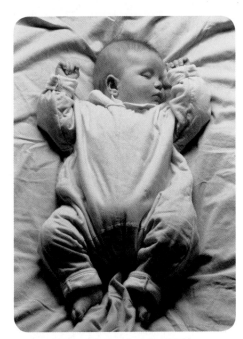

Is this a good sleep position for infants? Why or why not?

How Would You...?
If you were a **health-care professional,** how would you advise parents about preventing SIDS?

sudden infant death syndrome (SIDS) A condition that occurs when an infant stops breathing, usually during the night, and suddenly dies without an apparent cause.

NUTRITION

From birth to 1 year of age, human infants nearly triple their weight and increase their length by 50 percent. What do they need to sustain this growth, and what characterizes their eating behavior?

Nutritional Needs and Eating Behavior   Individual differences among infants in terms of their nutrient reserves, body composition, growth rates, and activity patterns make defining actual nutrient needs difficult (Schiff, 2011; Wardlaw & Smith, 2011). However, because parents need guidelines, nutritionists recommend that infants consume approximately 50 calories per day for each pound they weigh—more than twice an adult's requirement per pound.

A number of developmental changes involving eating characterize the infant's first year (Black & Hurley, 2007). As infants' motor skills improve, they change from using suck-and-swallow movements with breast milk or formula to chew-and-swallow movements with semisolid and then more complex foods. As their fine motor control improves in the first year, they transition from being fed by others toward self-feeding. "By the end of the first year of life, children can sit independently, can chew and swallow a range of textures, are learning to feed themselves, and are making the transition to the family diet and meal patterns" (Black & Hurley, 2007, p. 1). At this point, infants need to have a diet that includes a variety of foods—especially fruits and vegetables.

developmental connection

Nutrition. Children's eating behavior is strongly influenced by their caregivers' behavior. Chapter 8, p. 246

Caregivers play very important roles in infants' early development of eating patterns (Black & others, 2009). Caregivers who are not sensitive to developmental changes in infants' nutritional needs, neglectful caregivers, and conditions of poverty can contribute to the development of eating problems in infants (Black & Lozoff, 2008).

A national study of more than 3,000 randomly selected 4- to 24-month-olds documented that many U.S. parents aren't feeding their babies enough fruits and vegetables but are feeding them too much junk food (Fox & others, 2004). Up to one-third of the babies ate no vegetables and fruit but frequently ate French fries, and almost half of the 7- to 8-month-old babies were fed desserts, sweets, or sweetened drinks. By 15 months, French fries were the most common vegetable the babies ate.

Such poor dietary patterns early in development can result in more infants being overweight. One analysis revealed that in 1980, 3.4 percent of U.S. babies less than 6 months old were overweight, a percentage that increased to 5.9 percent in 2001 (Kim & others, 2006). As shown in Figure 5.11, as younger infants become older infants, an even greater percentage are overweight. Also in this study, in addition to the 5.9 percent of infants less than 6 months old who were overweight in 2001, another 11 percent were categorized as at risk for being overweight. In this study, infants were categorized as overweight if they were above the 95th percentile for their age and gender on a weight-for-height index; they were labeled at risk for being overweight if they were between the 85th and 95th percentile.

Breast Versus Bottle Feeding   For the first four to six months of life, human milk or an alternative formula is the baby's source of nutrients and energy. For years, debate has focused on whether breast feeding is better for the infant than bottle feeding. The

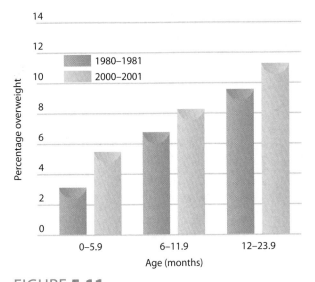

FIGURE **5.11**

PERCENTAGE OF OVERWEIGHT U.S. INFANTS IN 1980–1981 AND 2000–2001. Note: Infants above the 95th percentile for their age and gender on a weight-for-height index were categorized as overweight.

FIGURE **5.12**

TRENDS IN BREAST FEEDING IN THE UNITED STATES: 1970–2004

growing consensus is that breast feeding is better for the baby's health (Dykes, 2011; Monica & du Plessis, 2011; Silfverdal, 2011). Since the 1970s, breast feeding by U.S. mothers has soared (see Figure 5.12). In 2004, more than two-thirds of U.S. mothers breast fed their newborns, and more than a third breast fed their 6-month-olds. The American Academy of Pediatrics (AAP) and the American Dietetic Association strongly endorse breast feeding throughout the infant's first year (AAP Work Group on Breastfeeding, 1997; James & Dobson, 2005).

What are some of the benefits of breast feeding? The following conclusions have been reached based on the current state of research.

EVALUATION OF BENEFITS FOR THE CHILD

- *Gastrointestinal infections.* Breast fed infants have fewer gastrointestinal infections (Garofalo, 2010).

- *Lower respiratory tract infections.* Breast fed infants have fewer lower respiratory tract infections (Ip & others, 2009).

- *Allergies.* A recent research review by the American Academy of Pediatrics indicated that there is no evidence that breast feeding reduces the risk of allergies in children (Greer & others, 2008).

- *Asthma.* The recent research review by the American Academy of Pediatrics concluded that exclusive breast feeding for three months protects against wheezing in babies, but whether it prevents asthma in older children is unclear (Greer & others, 2008).

- *Otitis media.* Breast fed infants are less likely to develop this middle ear infection (Pelton & Leibovitz, 2009).

- *Overweight and obesity.* Consistent evidence indicates that breast fed infants are less likely to become overweight or obese in childhood, adolescence, and adulthood.

- *Diabetes.* Breast fed infants are less likely to develop type 1 diabetes in childhood (Ping & Hagopian, 2006) and type 2 diabetes in adulthood (Villegas & others, 2008).

Human milk or an alternative formula is a baby's source of nutrients for the first four to six months. The growing consensus is that breast feeding is better for the baby's health, although controversy still swirls about the issue of breast feeding versus bottle feeding. *Why is breast feeding strongly recommended by pediatricians?*

How Would You...?

If you were a **health-care professional**, how would you advise mothers about whether to breast feed or bottle feed their infants?

- *SIDS.* Breast fed infants are less likely to experience SIDS (Stuebe & Schwarz, 2010).

- *Cognitive development and cardiovascular health.* In a large-scale research review, no conclusive evidence for benefits of breast feeding was found for children's cognitive development and cardiovascular system (Agency for Healthcare Research and Quality, 2007).

EVALUATION OF BENEFITS FOR THE MOTHER

- *Breast cancer.* Consistent evidence indicates a lower incidence of breast cancer in women who breast feed their infants (Akbari & others, 2011).

- *Ovarian cancer.* Evidence also reveals a reduction in ovarian cancer in women who breast feed their infants (Stuebe & Schwarz, 2010).

- *Type 2 diabetes.* Some evidence suggests a small reduction in type 2 diabetes in women who breast feed their infants (Stuebe & Schwarz, 2010).

- *Weight loss, bone health, and mental health.* In a large-scale research review, no conclusive evidence could be found for maternal benefits of breast feeding on return to prepregnancy weight, osteoporosis, and postpartum depression (Agency for Healthcare Research and Quality, 2007; Ip & others, 2009).

developmental connection

Research Methods. How does a correlational study differ from an experimental study? Chapter 1, p. 36

Which women are least likely to breast feed? They include mothers who work full-time outside the home, mothers under age 25, mothers without a high school education, African American mothers, and mothers in low-income circumstances (Merewood & others, 2007). In one study of low-income mothers in Georgia, interventions (such as counseling focused on the benefits of breast feeding and the free loan of a breast pump) increased the incidence of breast feeding (Ahluwalia & others, 2000). Increasingly, mothers who return to work in the infant's first year of life use a breast pump to extract breast milk that can be stored for later feeding of the infant when the mother is not present.

The AAP Work Group on Breastfeeding (AAPWGB) strongly endorses breast feeding throughout the first year of life (AAPWGB, 1997). Are there circumstances when mothers should not breast feed? Yes. A mother should not breast feed (1) when the mother is infected with HIV or some other infectious disease that can be transmitted through her milk, (2) if she has active tuberculosis, or (3) if she is taking any drug that may not be safe for the infant (Mepham & others, 2011).

Some women cannot breast feed their infants because of physical difficulties; others feel guilty if they terminate breast feeding early (Walshaw & Owens, 2006). Mothers may also worry that they are depriving their infants of important emotional and psychological benefits if they bottle feed rather than breast feed. Some researchers have found, however, that there are no psychological differences between breast fed and bottle fed infants (Ferguson, Harwood, & Shannon, 1987; Young, 1990).

A further issue in interpreting the benefits of breast feeding was underscored in a recent large-scale research review (Ip & others, 2009). While highlighting a number of breast feeding benefits for children and mothers, the report issued a caution about breast feeding research: None of the findings imply causality. Breast versus bottle feeding studies are correlational, not experimental, and women who breast feed are wealthier, older, more educated, and likely more health-conscious than their bottle-feeding counterparts—characteristics that could explain why breast fed children are healthier.

Malnutrition in Infancy Many infants around the world are malnourished (UNICEF, 2012). Early weaning of infants from breast milk to inadequate sources of nutrients, such as unsuitable and unsanitary cow's milk formula, can cause protein deficiency and malnutrition in infants. However, as we saw in the chapter-opening story, a concern in developing countries is the increasing number of women who are HIV-positive

This Honduran child has kwashiorkor. Notice the telltale sign of kwashiorkor—a greatly expanded abdomen. *What are some other characteristics of kwashiorkor?*

and the fear that they will transmit this virus to their offspring (Mepham & others, 2011). Breast feeding is more optimal for mothers and infants in developing countries, except for mothers who have or are suspected of having HIV/AIDS.

Two life-threatening conditions that can result from malnutrition are marasmus and kwashiorkor. **Marasmus** is caused by a severe protein-calorie deficiency and results in a wasting away of body tissues in the infant's first year. The infant becomes grossly underweight and his or her muscles atrophy. **Kwashiorkor,** caused by severe protein deficiency, usually appears between 1 and 3 years of age. Children with kwashiorkor sometimes appear to be well fed even though they are not because the disease can cause the child's abdomen and feet to swell with water (Ahrens & others, 2008). Kwashiorkor causes a child's vital organs to collect the nutrients that are present and deprive other parts of the body of them. The child's hair becomes thin, brittle, and colorless, and the child's behavior often becomes listless.

Even if not fatal, severe and lengthy malnutrition is detrimental to physical, cognitive, and social development (Bentley, Wasser, & Creed-Kanashiro, 2011; Laus & others, 2011). In a longitudinal study spanning two decades in rural Guatemala, Ernesto Pollitt and his colleagues (1993) found that early nutritional supplements in the form of protein and increased calories can have positive long-term effects on cognitive development. The researchers also found that the relation of nutrition to cognitive performance is moderated both by the time period during which the supplement is given and by socioeconomic status. Although there still was a positive nutritional influence when supplementation began after 2 years of age, the effect on cognitive development was less powerful. Also, the children in the lowest socioeconomic groups benefited more than did the children in higher socioeconomic groups.

Another study linked the diets of rural Guatemalan infants with their social development at the time they entered elementary school (Barrett, Radke-Yarrow, & Klein, 1982). Children whose mothers had been given nutritional supplements during pregnancy, and who had received more nutritious, high-calorie foods in their first two years of life, were more active, more involved, more helpful with their peers, less anxious, and happier than their counterparts who had not been given nutritional supplements. To read further about providing nutritional supplements to improve infants' and young children's nutrition, see the *Caring Connections* interlude.

Adequate early nutrition is an important aspect of healthy development (Schiff, 2011). In addition to sound nutrition, children need a nurturing, supportive environment (Ventura, Gromis, & Lohse, 2010). One individual who has stood out as an advocate of caring for children is T. Berry Brazelton, who is featured in the *Connecting with Careers* profile.

HEALTH

Among the important aspects of infant health are immunization and accident prevention. Immunization has greatly improved children's health.

Immunization   One of the most dramatic advances in infant health has been the decline of infectious disease over the last four decades because of widespread immunization for preventable diseases. Although many available immunizations can be given at any age, the recommended schedule is to begin in infancy (Hammer & others, 2010). The recommended age for various immunizations is presented in Figure 5.13.

Accident Prevention   Accidents are a major cause of death in infancy, especially from 6 to 12 months of age (Erkal, 2010). Infants need to be closely monitored as their locomotor and manipulative skills develop along with a strong desire to explore their environment (Davidson & others, 2012). Aspiration of foreign objects, suffocation, falls, poisoning, burns, and motor vehicle accidents are among the most common accidents in infancy (Burns & others, 2009). All infants, newborns included, should be secured in special infant car seats in the backseat of a car rather than being held on an adult's lap or placed in the seat of the car.

How Would You...?

If you were **a social worker,** how would you counsel parents living in poverty about the importance of healthy nutrition for their infant?

Age	Immunization
Birth	Hepatitis B
2 months	Diphtheria, tetanus, pertussis Polio Influenza Pneumococcal
4 months	Hepatitis B Diphtheria, tetanus, pertussis Polio Influenza Pneumococcal
6 months	Diphtheria, tetanus, pertussis Influenza Pneumococcal
1 year	Influenza Pneumococcal
15 months	Measles, mumps, rubella Influenza Varicella
18 months	Hepatitis B Diphtheria, tetanus, pertussis Polio
4 to 6 years	Diphtheria, tetanus, pertussis Polio Measles, mumps, rubella
11 to 12 years	Measles, mumps, rubella
14 to 16 years	Tetanus, diphtheria

FIGURE **5.13**

RECOMMENDED IMMUNIZATION SCHEDULE OF INFANTS AND CHILDREN

How Would You...?

If you were a **human development and family studies professional,** how would you discuss infant safety concerns with parents?

marasmus A wasting away of body tissues in the infant's first year, caused by severe protein-calorie deficiency.

kwashiorkor A condition caused by a severe deficiency in protein in which the child's abdomen and feet become swollen with water; usually appears between 1 and 3 years of age.

Improving the Nutrition of Infants and Young Children Living in Low-Income Families

Poor nutrition also is a special concern in the lives of infants in low-income families in the United States. To address this problem, the WIC (Women, Infants, and Children) program provides federal grants to states for healthy supplemental foods, health-care referrals, and nutrition education for women from low-income families beginning in pregnancy, and to infants and young children up to 5 years of age who are at nutritional risk (Food & Nutrition Service, 2009; WIC New York, 2011). WIC serves approximately 7,500,000 participants in the United States.

Positive influences on infants' and young children's nutrition and health have been found for participants in WIC (Davis, Lazariu, & Sekhobo, 2010; Sekhobo & others, 2010). A recent study revealed that a WIC program that introduced peer counseling services for pregnant women increased breast feeding initiation by 27 percent (Olson & others, 2010). Another recent study found that entry in the first trimester of pregnancy to the WIC program in Rhode Island reduced maternal cigarette smoking (Brodsky, Viner-Brown, & Handler, 2009).

Participants in the WIC program. *What are some of the changes that were implemented in the WIC program recently?*

T. Berry Brazelton, Pediatrician

T. Berry Brazelton is America's best-known pediatrician as a result of his numerous books, television appearances, and newspaper and magazine articles about parenting and children's health. He takes a family-centered approach to child development issues and communicates with parents in easy-to-understand ways.

Dr. Brazelton founded the Child Development Unit at Boston Children's Hospital and created the Brazelton Neonatal Behavioral Assessment Scale, a widely used measure of the newborn's health and well-being (which you read about in Chapter 4, "Birth"). He also has conducted a number of research studies on infants and children and has been president of the Society for Research in Child Development, a leading research organization.

T. Berry Brazelton, pediatrician, with a young child.

How Do Infants Develop Motor Skills?

LG2 Describe infants' motor development.

The Dynamic Systems View   Reflexes   Gross Motor Skills   Fine Motor Skills

As a newborn, Ramona, whom we met in the chapter-opening story, could suck, fling her arms wide, and tightly grip a finger placed in her tiny hand. Within just two years, she would be toddling around on her own, opening doors and jars as she explored her little world. Are her accomplishments inevitable? How do infants develop their motor skills, and which skills do they develop at various ages?

THE DYNAMIC SYSTEMS VIEW

Developmentalist Arnold Gesell (1934) thought his painstaking observations had revealed how people develop their motor skills. He had discovered that infants and children develop rolling, sitting, standing, and other motor skills in a fixed order and within specific time frames. These observations, said Gesell, show that motor development comes about through the unfolding of a genetic plan, or maturation.

Later studies, however, demonstrated that the sequence of developmental milestones is not as fixed as Gesell indicated and not due as much to heredity as Gesell argued (Adolph & Robinson, 2012; Adolph, Karasik, & Tamis-LeMonda, 2010). In the last two decades, the study of motor development experienced a renaissance as psychologists acquired new insights about how motor skills develop (Spencer, 2009; Thelen & Smith, 1998, 2006). One increasingly influential viewpoint is dynamic systems theory, proposed by Esther Thelen.

According to **dynamic systems theory,** infants assemble motor skills for perceiving and acting (Thelen & Smith, 2006). To develop motor skills, infants must perceive something in the environment that motivates them to act and use their perceptions to fine-tune their movements. Motor skills represent solutions to the infant's goals (Keen, 2011).

How is a motor skill developed, according to this theory? When infants are motivated to do something, they might create a new motor behavior. The new behavior is the result of many converging factors: the development of the nervous system, the body's physical properties and its possibilities for movement, the goal the child

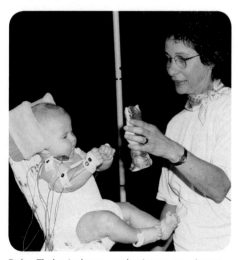

Esther Thelen is shown conducting an experiment to discover how infants learn to control their arms to reach and grasp for objects. A computer device is used to monitor the infant's arm movements and to track muscle patterns. Thelen's research is conducted from a dynamic systems perspective. *What is the nature of this perspective?*

dynamic systems theory The perspective on motor development that seeks to explain how motor skills are assembled for perceiving and acting.

How might dynamic systems theory explain the development of this infant's walking skills?

is motivated to reach, and the environmental support for the skill (Corbetta, 2009; von Hofsten, 2008). For example, babies learn to walk only when maturation of the nervous system allows them to control certain leg muscles, when their legs have grown enough to support their weight, and when they want to move.

Mastering a motor skill requires the infant's active efforts to coordinate several components of the skill. Infants explore and select possible solutions to the demands of a new task; they assemble adaptive patterns by modifying their current movement patterns. The first step occurs when the infant is motivated by a new challenge—such as the desire to cross a room—and gets into the "ball-park" of the task demands by taking a couple of stumbling steps. Then, the infant "tunes" these movements to make them smoother and more effective. The tuning is achieved through repeated cycles of action and perception of the consequences of that action. According to the dynamic systems view, even universal milestones, such as crawling, reaching, and walking, are learned through this process of adaptation: Infants modulate their movement patterns to fit a new task by exploring and selecting possible configurations (Adolph & Robinson, 2012).

To see how dynamic systems theory explains motor behavior, imagine that you offer a new toy to a baby named Gabriel (Thelen & others, 1993). There is no exact program that can tell Gabriel ahead of time how to move his arm and hand and fingers to grasp the toy. Gabriel must adapt to his goal—grasping the toy—and the context. From his sitting position, he must make split-second adjustments to extend his arm, holding his body steady so that his arm and torso don't plow into the toy. Muscles in his arm and shoulder contract and stretch in a host of combinations, exerting a variety of forces. He improvises a way to reach out with one arm and wrap his fingers around the toy.

Thus, according to dynamic systems theory, motor development is not a passive process in which genes dictate the unfolding of a sequence of skills over time (Spencer, 2009). Rather, the infant actively puts together a skill to achieve a goal within the constraints set by the infant's body and environment. Nature and nurture, the infant and the environment, are all working together as part of an ever-changing system.

As we examine the course of motor development, we will see how dynamic systems theory applies to some specific skills. First, though, let's examine how motor development begins with reflexes.

> The experiences of the first three years of life are almost entirely lost to us, and when we attempt to enter into a small child's world, we come as foreigners who have forgotten the landscape and no longer speak the native tongue.
>
> —SELMA FRAIBERG
> *Developmentalist and Child Advocate, 20th Century*

REFLEXES

Newborns are not completely helpless. Among other things, they have some basic reflexes (Pedroso, 2008). For example, newborns hold their breath and contract their throat to keep water out. **Reflexes** allow infants to respond adaptively to their environment before they have had the opportunity to learn.

The rooting and sucking reflexes are important examples. Both have survival value for newborn mammals, who must find a mother's breast to obtain nourishment. The **rooting reflex** occurs when the infant's cheek is stroked or the side of the mouth is touched. In response, the infant turns its head toward the side that was touched in an apparent effort to find something to suck. The **sucking reflex** occurs when newborns suck an object placed in their mouth. This reflex enables newborns to get nourishment before they have associated a nipple with food; it also serves as a self-soothing or self-regulating mechanism.

Another example is the **Moro reflex,** which occurs in response to a sudden, intense noise or movement (see Figure 5.14). When startled, newborns will arch their back, throw back their head, and fling out their arms and legs. Then they rapidly close their arms and legs. The Moro reflex is believed to be a way of

reflexes Built-in reactions to stimuli that govern the newborn's movements, which are automatic and beyond the newborn's control.

rooting reflex A newborn's built-in reaction that occurs when the infant's cheek is stroked or the side of the mouth is touched. In response, the infant turns its head toward the side that was touched in an apparent effort to find something to suck.

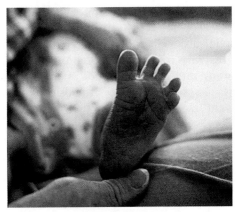

Babinski reflex

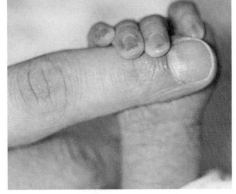

Grasping reflex

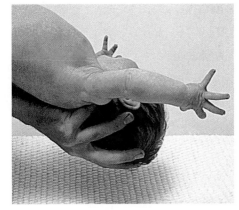

Moro reflex

Reflex	Stimulation	Infant's Response	Developmental Pattern
Blinking	Flash of light, puff of air	Closes both eyes	Permanent
Babinski	Sole of foot stroked	Fans out toes, twists foot in	Disappears after 9 months to 1 year
Grasping	Palms touched	Grasps tightly	Weakens after 3 months, disappears after 1 year
Moro (startle)	Sudden stimulation, such as hearing loud noise or being dropped	Startles, arches back, throws head back, flings out arms and legs and then rapidly closes them to center of body	Disappears after 3 to 4 months
Rooting	Cheek stroked or side of mouth touched	Turns head, opens mouth, begins sucking	Disappears after 3 to 4 months
Stepping	Infant held above surface and feet lowered to touch surface	Moves feet as if to walk	Disappears after 3 to 4 months
Sucking	Object touching mouth	Sucks automatically	Disappears after 3 to 4 months
Swimming	Infant put face down in water	Makes coordinated swimming movements	Disappears after 6 to 7 months
Tonic neck	Infant placed on back	Forms fists with both hands and usually turns head to the right (sometimes called the "fencer's pose" because the infant looks like it is assuming a fencer's position)	Disappears after 2 months

FIGURE 5.14

INFANT REFLEXES. This chart describes some of the infant's reflexes.

grabbing for support while falling; it would have had survival value for our primate ancestors.

Some reflexes—coughing, sneezing, blinking, shivering, and yawning, for example—persist throughout life. They are as important for the adult as they are for the infant. Other reflexes, though, disappear several months following birth, as the infant's brain matures and voluntary control over many behaviors develops. The rooting and Moro reflexes, for example, tend to disappear when the infant is 3 to 4 months old.

The movements involved in some reflexes eventually become incorporated into more complex, voluntary actions. One important example is the **grasping reflex,** which occurs when something touches the infant's palms (see Figure 5.14). The infant responds by grasping tightly. By the end of the third month, the grasping reflex diminishes, and the infant shows a more voluntary grasp. As its motor

sucking reflex A newborn's built-in reaction to automatically suck an object placed in the mouth. The sucking reflex enables the infant to get nourishment before he or she has associated a nipple with food and also serves as a self-soothing or self-regulating mechanism.

Moro reflex A neonatal startle response that occurs in reaction to a sudden, intense noise or movement. When startled, newborns arch their back, throw their head back, and fling out their arms and legs. Then they rapidly close their arms and legs, bringing them close to the center of the body.

grasping reflex A neonatal reflex that occurs when something touches the infant's palms. The infant responds by grasping tightly.

development becomes smoother, the infant will grasp objects, carefully manipulate them, and explore their qualities.

Individual differences in reflexive behavior are soon apparent after birth. For example, the sucking capabilities of newborns vary considerably. Some newborns are efficient at forcefully sucking and obtaining milk; others are not as adept and get tired before they are full. Most infants take several weeks to establish a sucking style that is coordinated with the way the mother is holding the infant, the way milk is coming out of the bottle or breast, and the infant's temperament (Blass, 2008).

The old view of reflexes was that they were exclusively genetic, built-in mechanisms that governed the infant's movements. The new perspective on infant reflexes says that they are not entirely automatic or completely beyond the infant's control. For example, infants can control such movements as alternating their legs to make a mobile jiggle or changing their sucking rate to listen to a recording (Adolph & Robinson, 2012).

GROSS MOTOR SKILLS

Ask any parents about their baby, and sooner or later you are likely to hear about one or more advances in motor skills, such as "Cassandra just learned to crawl," "Jesse is finally sitting alone," or "Angela took her first step last week." Parents proudly announce such milestones as their children transform themselves from babies unable to lift their heads to toddlers who grab things off the grocery store shelf, chase a cat, and participate actively in the family's social life (Thelen, 2000). These milestones are examples of **gross motor skills,** skills that involve large-muscle activities, such as moving one's arms and walking.

What are some developmental changes in posture during infancy?

The Development of Posture How do gross motor skills develop? As a foundation, these skills require postural control (Adolph & Joh, 2009). For example, to track moving objects, you must be able to control your head in order to stabilize your gaze; before you can walk, you must be able to balance on one leg.

Posture is more than just holding still and straight. Posture is a dynamic process that is linked with sensory information in the skin, joints, and muscles, which tell us where we are in space; in vestibular organs in the inner ear that regulate balance and equilibrium; and in vision and hearing (Thelen & Smith, 2006).

Newborn infants cannot voluntarily control their posture. Within a few weeks, though, they can hold their heads erect, and soon they can lift their heads while prone. By 2 months of age, babies can sit while supported on a lap or an infant seat, but they cannot sit independently until they are 6 or 7 months of age. Standing also develops gradually during the first year of life. By about 8 to 9 months of age, infants usually learn to pull themselves up and hold onto a chair, and they often can stand alone by about 10 to 12 months of age.

Learning to Walk Locomotion and postural control are closely linked, especially in walking upright (Adolph & Berger, 2011; Adolph & Robinson, 2012). To walk upright, the baby must be able both to balance on one leg as the other is swung forward and to shift weight from one leg to the other.

Even young infants can make the alternating leg movements that are needed for walking. The neural pathways that control leg alternation are in place from a very early age, even at birth or before. Indeed, researchers have found that alternating leg movements occur during the fetal period and at birth (Adolph & Robinson, 2012).

If infants can produce forward stepping movements so early, why does it take them so long to learn to walk? The key skills in learning to walk appear to be stabilizing balance on one leg long enough to swing the other forward and shifting the

gross motor skills Motor skills that involve large-muscle activities, such as walking.

weight without falling. This is a difficult biomechanical problem to solve, and it takes infants about a year to do it.

In learning to locomote, infants discover what kinds of places and surfaces are safe for locomotion (Snapp-Childs & Corbetta, 2009). Karen Adolph (1997) investigated how experienced and inexperienced crawling infants and walking infants go down steep slopes (see Figure 5.15). Newly crawling infants, who averaged about 8½ months in age, rather indiscriminately went down the steep slopes, often falling in the process (with an experimenter next to the slope to catch them). After weeks of practice, the crawling babies became more adept at judging which slopes were too steep to crawl down and which ones they could navigate safely. New walkers also could not judge the safety of the slopes, but experienced walkers accurately matched their skills with the steepness of the slopes. They rarely fell downhill, either refusing to go down the steep slopes or going down backward in a cautious manner. Experienced walkers perceptually assessed the situation—looking, swaying, touching, and thinking before they moved down the slope. With experience, both the crawlers and the walkers learned to avoid the risky slopes where they would fall, integrating perceptual information with the development of a new motor behavior. In this research, we again see the importance of perceptual-motor coupling in the development of motor skills. Thus, practice is very important in the development of new motor skills (Adolph & Robinson, 2012).

The First Year: Motor Development Milestones and Variations

Figure 5.16 summarizes important accomplishments in gross motor skills during the first year, culminating in the ability to walk easily. The timing of these milestones, especially the later ones, may vary by as much as two to four months, and experiences can modify the onset of these accomplishments. For example, in the early 1990s, pediatricians began recommending that parents place their babies on their backs when they sleep. Following that instruction, babies who back-sleep began crawling later, typically several weeks later than babies who sleep prone (Davis & others, 1998). Also, some infants do not follow the standard sequence of motor accomplishments (Eaton, 2008). For example, many American infants never crawl on their belly or on their hands and knees. They may discover an idiosyncratic form of locomotion before walking, such as rolling, or they might never locomote until they get upright (Adolph & Robinson, 2012). In Jamaica, approximately one-fourth of babies skip crawling (Hopkins, 1991).

According to Karen Adolph and Sarah Berger (2005), the early view that growth and motor development simply reflect the age-related output of maturation is, at best, incomplete. Rather, infants develop new skills with the guidance of their caregivers in a real-world environment of objects, surfaces, and planes.

Development in the Second Year

The motor accomplishments of the first year bring increasing independence, allowing infants to explore their environment more extensively and to initiate interaction with others more readily. In the second year of life, toddlers become more motorically skilled and mobile. Motor activity during the second year is vital to the child's competent development and few restrictions, except for safety, should be placed on their adventures.

By 13 to 18 months, toddlers can pull a toy attached to a string and use their hands and legs to climb up a number of steps. By 18 to 24 months, toddlers can walk quickly or run stiffly for a short distance, balance on their feet in a squatting position while playing with objects on the floor, walk backward without losing their balance, stand and kick a ball without falling, stand and throw a ball, and jump in place.

Can parents give their babies a head start on becoming physically fit and physically talented through structured exercise classes? Most infancy experts recommend against structured exercise classes for babies. But there are other ways of guiding infants' motor development. Caregivers in some cultures do handle babies vigorously,

Newly crawling infant

Experienced walker

FIGURE 5.15

THE ROLE OF EXPERIENCE IN CRAWLING AND WALKING INFANTS' JUDGMENTS OF WHETHER TO GO DOWN A SLOPE. Karen Adolph (1997) found that locomotor experience rather than age was the primary predictor of adaptive responding on slopes of varying steepness. Newly crawling and walking infants could not judge the safety of the various slopes. With experience, they learned to avoid slopes where they would fall. When expert crawlers began to walk, they again made mistakes and fell, even though they had judged the same slope accurately when crawling. Adolph referred to this as the *specificity of learning* because it does not transfer across crawling and walking.

How Would You...?
If you were a **psychologist,** how would you advise parents who are concerned that their infant is one or two months behind the average gross motor milestones?

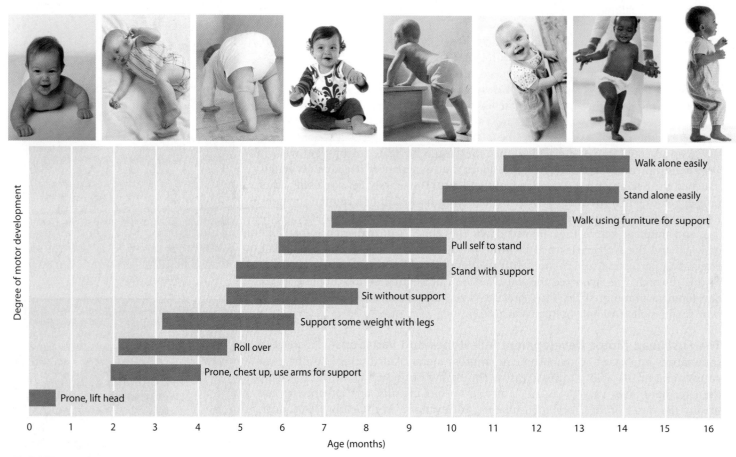

FIGURE **5.16**

MILESTONES IN GROSS MOTOR DEVELOPMENT. The horizontal red bars indicate the range in which most infants reach various milestones in gross motor development.

Reprinted from *Journal of Pediatrics*, Vol. 71, W. K. Frankenburg & J. B. Dodds, "The Denver Developmental Screening Test," pp. 181–191. Copyright 1967, with permission from Elsevier. http://www.sciencedirect.com/science/journal/00223476

A baby is an angel whose wings decrease as his legs increase.

—FRENCH PROVERB

and this practice might advance motor development, as we discuss in the *Connecting with Diversity* interlude.

FINE MOTOR SKILLS

Whereas gross motor skills involve large muscle activity, **fine motor skills** involve finely tuned movements. Grasping a toy, using a spoon, buttoning a shirt, or accomplishing anything that requires finger dexterity demonstrates fine motor skills. Infants have hardly any control over fine motor skills at birth, but newborns do have many components of what will become finely coordinated arm, hand, and finger movements.

The onset of reaching and grasping marks a significant achievement in infants' ability to interact with their surroundings. During the first two years of life, infants refine how they reach and grasp (Keen, 2011). Initially, infants reach by moving their shoulders and elbows crudely, swinging toward an object. Later, when infants reach for an object they move their wrists, rotate their hands, and coordinate their thumb and forefinger. Infants do not have to see their own hands in order to reach for an object (Clifton & others, 1993). Cues from muscles, tendons, and joints, not sight of the limb, guide reaching by 4-month-old infants.

Infants refine their ability to grasp objects by developing two types of grasps. Initially, infants grip with the whole hand, which is called the *palmer grasp*. Later, toward the end of the first year, infants also grasp small objects with their thumb

fine motor skills Motor skills that involve finely tuned movements, such as finger dexterity.

connecting with diversity

Cultural Variations in Guiding Infants' Motor Development

Mothers in developing countries tend to stimulate their infants' motor skills more than mothers in more developed countries (Hopkins, 1991). In many African, Indian, and Caribbean cultures, mothers massage and stretch their infants during daily baths (Adolph, Karasik, & Tamis-LeMonda, 2010). Mothers in the Gusii culture of Kenya also encourage vigorous movement in their babies.

Do these cultural variations make a difference in the infant's motor development? When caregivers provide babies with physical guidance by physically handling them in special ways (such as stroking, massaging, or stretching) or by giving them opportunities for exercise, the infants often reach motor milestones earlier than infants whose caregivers have not provided these

(*Left*) In the Algonquin culture in Quebec, Canada, babies are strapped to a cradle board for much of their infancy. (*Right*) In Jamaica, mothers massage and stretch their infants' arms and legs. *To what extent do cultural variations in the activity infants engage in influence the time at which they reach motor milestones?*

activities (Adolph, Karasik, & Tamis-LeMonda, 2010). For example, Jamaican mothers expect their infants to sit and walk alone two to three months earlier than English mothers do (Hopkins & Westra, 1990). And in sub-Saharan Africa, traditional practices in many villages involve mothers and siblings engaging babies in exercises, such as frequent exercise for trunk and pelvic muscles (Super & Harkness, 2010).

Many forms of restricted movement—such as Chinese sandbags, orphanage restrictions, and failure of caregivers to encourage movement

in Budapest—have been found to produce substantial delays in motor development (Adolph, Karasik, & Tamis-LeMonda, 2010). In some rural Chinese provinces, babies are placed in a bag of fine sand, which acts as a diaper and is changed once a day. The baby is left alone, face up, and is visited only when being fed by the mother (Xie & Young, 1999). Some studies of swaddling show small effects on creating delays in motor development, but other studies show no delays. Cultures that do swaddle infants usually do so early in the infant's development when the infant is not yet mobile; when the infant becomes more mobile, swaddling decreases.

and forefinger, which is called the *pincer grip*. Their grasping system is very flexible. They vary their grip on an object depending on its size, shape, and texture, as well as the size of their own hands relative to the object's size. Infants grip small objects with their thumb and forefinger (and sometimes their middle finger too), whereas they grip large objects with all of the fingers of one hand or both hands.

Perceptual-motor coupling is necessary for the infant to coordinate grasping (Keen, 2005). Which perceptual system the infant is most likely to use in coordinating grasping varies with age. Four-month-old infants rely greatly on touch to determine how they will grip an object; 8-month-olds are more likely to use vision as a guide (Newell & others, 1989). This developmental change is efficient because vision lets infants preshape their hands as they reach for an object.

Experience plays a role in reaching and grasping (Smitsman & Corbetta, 2010). In one study, 3-month-old infants participated in play sessions wearing "sticky mittens"—"mittens with palms that stuck to the edges of toys and allowed the infants to pick up the toys" (Needham, Barrett, & Peterman, 2002, p. 279) (see Figure 5.17). Infants who participated in sessions with the mittens grasped and manipulated objects earlier in their development than a control group of infants who did not receive the "mitten" experience. The experienced infants

A young girl using a pincer grip to pick up puzzle pieces.

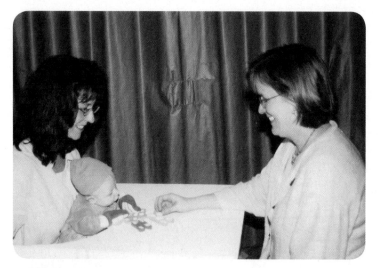

FIGURE **5.17**

INFANTS' USE OF "STICKY MITTENS" TO EXPLORE OBJECTS. Amy Needham and her colleagues (2002) found that "Sticky Mittens" enhanced young infants' object exploration skills.

looked at the objects longer, swatted at them more during visual contact, and were more likely to mouth the objects. In a recent study, 5-month-old infants whose parents trained them to use the sticky mittens for 10 minutes a day over a two-week period showed advances in their reaching behavior at the end of the two weeks (Libertus & Needham, 2010).

Just as infants need to exercise their gross motor skills, they also need to exercise their fine motor skills (Keen, 2011; Needham, 2009). Especially when they can manage a pincer grip, infants delight in picking up small objects. Many develop the pincer grip and begin to crawl at about the same time, and infants at this time pick up virtually everything in sight, especially on the floor, and put the objects in their mouth. Thus, parents need to be vigilant in regularly monitoring what objects are within the infant's reach (Keen, 2005).

Review *Connect* Reflect

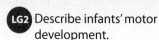 Describe infants' motor development.

Review

- What is dynamic systems theory?
- What are some reflexes that infants have?
- How do gross motor skills develop in infancy?
- How do fine motor skills develop in infancy?

Connect

- What are the differences between the grasping reflex present at birth and the fine motor grasping skills an infant develops between 4 and 12 months of age?

Reflect *Your Own Personal Journey of Life*

- Think of a motor skill that you perform. How would dynamic systems theory explain your motor skill performance?

How Can Infants' Sensory and Perceptual Development Be Characterized?

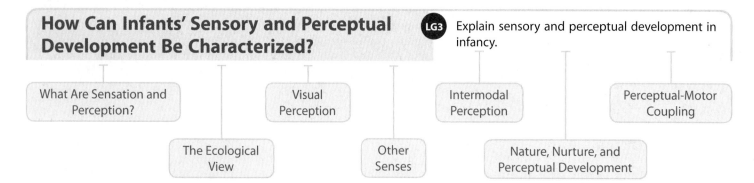

LG3 Explain sensory and perceptual development in infancy.

How do sensations and perceptions develop? Can newborns see? If so, what can they perceive? What about the other senses—hearing, smell, taste, and touch? What are they like in newborns, and how do they develop? Can infants put together information from two modalities, such as sight and sound? These are among the intriguing questions that we will explore in this section.

WHAT ARE SENSATION AND PERCEPTION?

How does a newborn know that her mother's skin is soft rather than rough? How does a 5-year-old know what color his hair is? How does a 10-year-old know that a firecracker is louder than a cat's meow? Infants and children "know" these things because of information that comes through the senses. Without vision, hearing, touch, taste, smell, and other senses, we would be isolated from the world; we would live in dark silence, a tasteless, colorless, feelingless void.

Sensation occurs when information interacts with sensory *receptors*—the eyes, ears, tongue, nostrils, and skin. The sensation of hearing occurs when waves of pulsating air are collected by the outer ear and conducted through the bones of the inner ear and the *cochlea*, where mechanical vibrations are converted into electrical impulses. Then the electrical impulses move to the *auditory nerve*, which transmits them to the brain. The sensation of vision occurs as rays of light contact the eyes and become focused on the *retina*, where light is converted into electrical impulses. Then the electrical impulses are transmitted by the *optic nerve* to the visual centers of the brain.

Perception is the interpretation of what is sensed. The air waves that contact the ears might be interpreted as noise or as musical sounds, for example. The physical energy transmitted to the retina of the eye might be interpreted as a particular color, pattern, or shape, depending on how it is perceived.

THE ECOLOGICAL VIEW

In recent decades, much of the research on perceptual development in infancy has been guided by the ecological view of Eleanor and James J. Gibson (E. Gibson, 1969, 1989, 2001; J. Gibson, 1966, 1979). They argue that we do not have to take bits and pieces of data from sensations and build up representations of the world in our minds. Instead, our perceptual system can select from the rich information that the environment itself provides.

According to the Gibsons' **ecological view,** we directly perceive information that exists in the world around us. Perception brings us into contact with the environment in order to interact with and adapt to it. Perception is designed for action. Perception gives people such information as when to duck, when to turn their bodies through a narrow passageway, and when to put up their hands to catch something.

In the Gibsons' view, all objects and surfaces have **affordances,** which are opportunities for interaction offered by objects that fit within our capabilities to perform activities. A pot may afford you something to cook with, and it may afford a toddler something to bang. Adults immediately know when a chair is appropriate for sitting, when a surface is safe for walking, or when an object is within reach. We directly and accurately perceive these affordances by sensing information from the environment—the light or sound reflecting from the surfaces of the world—and from our own bodies through muscle receptors, joint receptors, and skin receptors.

An important developmental question is "What affordances can infants or children detect and use?" In one study, for example, when babies who could walk were faced with a squishy waterbed, they stopped and explored it, then chose to crawl rather than walk across it (Gibson & others, 1987). They combined perception and action to adapt to the demands of the task.

Studying the infant's perception has not been an easy task. What do you think some of the research challenges might be? The *Connecting with Research* interlude describes some of the ingenious ways researchers study the infant's perception.

VISUAL PERCEPTION

What do newborns see? How does visual perception develop in infancy?

How would you use the Gibsons' ecological theory of perception and the concept of affordance to explain the role that perception is playing in this baby's activity?

sensation The product of the interaction between information and the sensory receptors—the eyes, ears, tongue, nostrils, and skin.

perception The interpretation of what is sensed.

ecological view The view that perception functions to bring organisms in contact with the environment and to increase adaptation.

affordances Opportunities for interaction offered by objects that fit within our capabilities to perform functional activities.

connecting with research

How Can the Newborn's Perception Be Studied?

After years of work, scientists have developed research methods and tools sophisticated enough to examine the subtle abilities of infants and to interpret their complex actions (Bendersky & Sullivan, 2007).

Visual Preference Method

Robert Fantz (1963) was a pioneer in this effort. Fantz made an important discovery that advanced the ability of researchers to investigate infants' visual perception: Infants look at different things for different lengths of time. Fantz placed infants in a "looking chamber," which had two visual displays on the ceiling above the infant's head. An experimenter viewed the infant's eyes by looking through a peephole. If the infant was fixating on one of the displays, the experimenter could see the display's reflection in the infant's eyes. This arrangement allowed the experimenter to determine how long the infant looked at each display. Fantz (1963) found that infants only 2 days old look longer at patterned stimuli, such as faces and concentric circles, than at red, white, or yellow discs. Infants 2 to 3 weeks old preferred to look at patterns—a face, a piece of printed matter, or a bull's-eye—longer than at red, yellow, or white discs (see Figure 5.18). Fantz's research method—studying whether infants can distinguish one stimulus from another by measuring the length of time they attend to different stimuli—is referred to as the **visual preference method.**

Habituation and Dishabituation

Another way that researchers have studied infant perception is to present a stimulus (such as a sight or a sound) a number of times. If there is a decrease in the infant's response to the stimulus after several presentations, it indicates that the infant is no longer interested in looking at the stimulus. If the researcher now presents a new stimulus, the infant's response will recover—indicating the infant could discriminate between the old and new stimulus (Snyder & Torrence, 2008).

Habituation is the name given to decreased responsiveness to a stimulus after repeated presentations of the stimulus. **Dishabituation** is the recovery of a habituated response after a change in stimulation. Newborn infants can habituate to repeated sights, sounds, smells, or touches (Rovee-Collier, 2004). Among the measures researchers use in habituation studies are sucking behavior (sucking stops when the young infant attends to a novel object), heart and respiration rates, and the length of time the infant looks at an object. Figure 5.19 shows the results of one study of habituation and dishabituation with newborns (Slater, Morison, & Somers, 1988).

High-Amplitude Sucking

To assess an infant's attention to sound, researchers often use a method called *high-amplitude sucking.* In this method, infants are given a nonnutritive nipple to suck, and the nipple is connected to "a sound generating system. Each suck causes a noise to be generated and the infant learns quickly that sucking brings about this noise. At first, babies suck frequently, so the noise occurs often. Then, gradually, they lose interest in hearing repetitions of the same noise and begin to suck less frequently. At this point, the experimenter changes the sound that is being

FIGURE **5.18**

FANTZ'S EXPERIMENT ON INFANTS' VISUAL PERCEPTION. (*a*) Infants 2 to 3 weeks old preferred to look at some stimuli more than others. In Fantz's experiment, infants preferred to look at patterns rather than at color or brightness. For example, they looked longer at a face, a piece of printed matter, or a bull's-eye than at red, yellow, or white discs. (*b*) Fantz used a "looking chamber" to study infants' perception of stimuli.

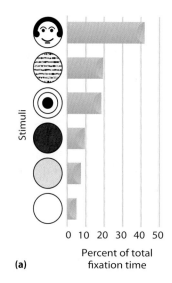

Stimuli

Percent of total fixation time

(a)

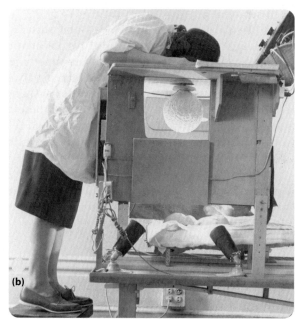

(b)

Habituation

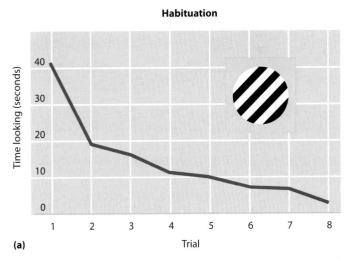

(a)

Dishabituation

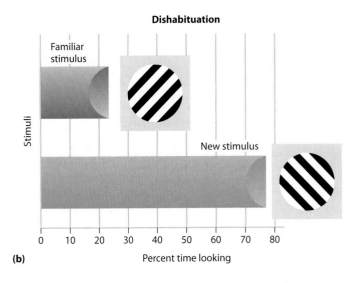

(b)

FIGURE **5.19**

HABITUATION AND DISHABITUATION. In the first part of one study (*a*), 7-hour-old newborns were shown a stimulus. As indicated, the newborns looked at it an average of 41 seconds when it was first presented to them (Slater, Morison, & Somers, 1988). Over seven more presentations of the stimulus, they looked at it less and less. In the second part of the study (*b*), infants were presented with both the familiar stimulus to which they had just become habituated and a new stimulus (which was rotated 90 degrees). The newborns looked at the new stimulus three times as much as the familiar stimulus.

generated. If the babies renew vigorous sucking, we infer that they have discriminated the sound change and are sucking more because they want to hear the interesting new sound" (Menn & Stoel-Gammon, 2009, p. 67).

The Orienting Response and Tracking

A technique that can be used to determine whether an infant can see or hear is the *orienting response,* which involves turning one's head toward a sight or sound. Another technique, *tracking,* consists of eye movements that follow (*track*) a moving object and can be used to evaluate an infant's early visual ability or to determine an infant's reaction to a noise (Bendersky & Sullivan, 2007). Eye-tracking equipment that assesses the infant's eye movements as the infant tracks an object is increasingly being used in infant perception research (Gredeback, Johnson, & von Hofsten, 2010). Figure 5.20 shows an infant wearing an eye-tracking headgear in a

FIGURE **5.20**

AN INFANT WEARING EYE-TRACKING HEADGEAR.
Photo from Karen Adolph's laboratory at New York University.

recent study on visually guided motor behavior and social interaction (Franchak & others, 2011).

Equipment

Technology can facilitate the use of most methods for investigating the infant's perceptual abilities. Videotape equipment allows researchers to investigate elusive behaviors. High-speed computers make it possible to perform complex data analysis in minutes. Other equipment records respiration, heart rate, body movement, visual fixation, and sucking behavior, which provide clues to what the infant is perceiving.

What other applications of computer technology, such as motion-capture or three-dimensional modeling, do you think might someday be useful in studying children's perception?

FIGURE **5.21**

VISUAL ACUITY DURING THE FIRST MONTHS OF LIFE. The four photographs represent a computer estimation of what a picture of a face looks like to a 1-month-old, 2-month-old, 3-month-old, and 1-year-old (which approximates that of an adult).

developmental connection

Socioemotional Development. The focused social interaction of face-to-face play early in infant development is part of many mothers' motivation to create a positive emotional state in their infants. Chapter 7, p. 215

visual preference method A method used to determine whether infants can distinguish one stimulus from another by measuring the length of time they attend to different stimuli.

habituation Decreased responsiveness to a stimulus after repeated presentations of the stimulus.

dishabituation Recovery of a habituated response after a change in stimulation.

Visual Acuity and Human Faces   Psychologist William James (1890/1950) called the newborn's perceptual world a "blooming, buzzing confusion." More than a century later, we can safely say that he was wrong. Even the newborn perceives a world with some order. That world, however, is far different from the one perceived by the toddler or the adult.

Just how well can infants see? At birth, the nerves and muscles and lens of the eye are still developing. As a result, newborns cannot see small things that are far away. Estimates of the newborn's visual acuity varies from 20/240 to 20/640 on the well-known Snellen chart used for eye examinations, which means that a newborn can see at 20 feet what a normal adult can see at 240 to 640 feet. In other words, an object 20 feet away is only as clear to the newborn as it would be if it were 640 feet away from an adult with normal vision (20/20). By 6 months of age, though, *on average* vision is 20/40 (Aslin & Lathrop, 2008).

Infants show an interest in human faces soon after birth (Lee & others, 2011). Figure 5.21 shows a computer estimation of what a picture of a face looks like to an infant at different ages from a distance of about 6 inches. Infants spend more time looking at their mother's face than a stranger's face as early as 12 hours after being born (Bushnell, 2003). By 3 months of age, infants match voices to faces, distinguish between male and female faces, and discriminate between faces of their own ethnic group and those of other ethnic groups (Kelly & others, 2007, 2009; Liu & others, 2011).

Also, as we discussed in the *Connecting with Research* interlude, young infants can perceive certain patterns. With the help of his "looking chamber," Robert Fantz (1963) revealed that even 2- to 3-week-old infants prefer to look at patterned displays rather than nonpatterned displays. For example, they prefer to look at a normal human face rather than one with scrambled features, and prefer to look at a bull's-eye target or black and white stripes rather than a plain circle.

Color Vision   The infant's color vision also improves (Aslin & Lathrop, 2008). By 8 weeks, and possibly as early as 4 weeks, infants can discriminate some colors (Kelly, Borchert, & Teller, 1997). By 4 months of age, they have color preferences that mirror those of adults in some cases, preferring saturated colors such as royal blue over pale blue, for example (Bornstein, 1975). A recent study involving viewing of blue, yellow, red, and green hues by 4- to 5-month-old infants revealed that they looked longest at reddish hues and shortest at greenish hues (Franklin & others, 2010). In part, the changes in vision described here reflect maturation. Experience, however, is also necessary for color vision to develop normally (Sugita, 2004).

Perceptual Constancy   Some perceptual accomplishments are especially intriguing because they indicate that the infant's perception goes beyond the information provided by the senses (Johnson, 2012b; Slater & others, 2011). This is the case in *perceptual constancy*, in which sensory stimulation is changing but perception of the physical world remains constant. If infants did not develop perceptual constancy, each time they saw an object at a different distance or in a different orientation, they would perceive it as a different object. Thus, the development of perceptual constancy allows infants to perceive their world as stable. Two types of perceptual constancy are size constancy and shape constancy.

Size constancy is the recognition that an object remains the same even though the retinal image of the object changes as you move toward or away from the object. The farther away from us an object is, the smaller its image is on our eyes. Thus, the size of an object on the retina is not sufficient to tell us its actual size. For example, you perceive a bicycle standing right in front of you as smaller than the car parked across the street, even though the bicycle casts a larger image on your eyes than the car does. When you move away from the bicycle, you do not perceive it to be shrinking even though its image on your retinas shrinks; you perceive its size to be constant.

But what about babies? Do they have size constancy? Researchers have found that babies as young as 3 months of age show size constancy (Bower, 1966; Day & McKenzie, 1973). However, at 3 months of age, a baby's ability is not full-blown. It continues to develop until 10 or 11 years of age (Kellman & Banks, 1998).

Shape constancy is the recognition that an object remains the same shape even though its orientation to us changes. Look around the room you are in right now. You likely see objects of varying shapes, such as tables and chairs. If you get up and walk around the room, you will see these objects from different sides and angles. Even though your retinal image of the objects changes as you walk and look, you will still perceive the objects as the same shape.

Do babies have shape constancy? As with size constancy, researchers have found that babies as young as 3 months of age have shape constancy (Bower, 1966; Day & McKenzie, 1973). Three-month-old infants, however, do not have shape constancy for irregularly shaped objects such as tilted planes (Cook & Birch, 1984).

Perception of Occluded Objects
Look around the context where you are now. You likely see that some objects are partly occluded by other objects that are in front of them—possibly a desk behind a chair, some books behind a computer, or a car parked behind a tree. Do infants perceive an object as complete when it is partly occluded by an object in front of it?

In the first two months of postnatal development, infants don't perceive occluded objects as complete, instead perceiving only what is visible (Johnson, 2011, 2012a, b). Beginning at about 2 months of age, infants develop the ability to perceive occluded objects as whole (Slater, Field, & Hernandez-Reif, 2007). How does perceptual completion develop? In Scott Johnson's (2010, 2011, 2012a, b) research, learning, experience, and self-directed exploration via eye movements play key roles in the development of perceptual completion in young infants.

Many of the objects in the world that are occluded appear and disappear behind closer objects, as when you are walking down the street and see cars appear and disappear behind buildings as they move or you move. Can infants predictively track briefly occluded moving objects? They develop the ability to track briefly occluded moving objects at about 3 to 5 months of age (Bertenthal, 2008). A study explored 5- to 9-month-old infants' ability to track moving objects that disappeared gradually behind an occluded partition, disappeared abruptly, or imploded (shrank quickly in size) (see Figure 5.22) (Bertenthal, Longo, & Kenny, 2007). In this study, the infants were more likely to accurately predict the moving object when it disappeared gradually rather than disappearing abruptly or imploding.

Depth Perception
Might infants even perceive depth? To investigate this question, Eleanor Gibson and Richard Walk (1960) constructed a miniature cliff with a drop-off covered by glass in their laboratory. They placed infants on the edge of this

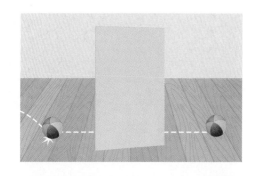

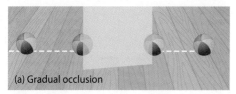
(a) Gradual occlusion

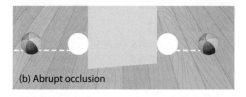

(b) Abrupt occlusion

(c) Implosion

FIGURE **5.22**

INFANTS' PREDICTIVE TRACKING OF A BRIEFLY OCCLUDED MOVING BALL. The top panel shows the visual scene that infants experienced. At the beginning of each event, a multicolored ball bounced up and down with an accompanying bounding sound, and then rolled across the floor until it disappeared behind the partition. Parts a, b, and c show the three stimulus events that the 5- to 9-month-old infants experienced: (a) Gradual occlusion—the ball gradually disappears behind the right side of the occluding partition located in the center of the display. (b) Abrupt occlusion—the ball abruptly disappears when it reaches the location of the white circle and then abruptly reappears 2 seconds later at the location of the second white circle on the other side of the occluding partition. (c) Implosion—the rolling ball quickly decreases in size as it approaches the occluding partition and rapidly increases in size as it reappears on the other side of the occluding partition.

size constancy The recognition that an object remains the same even though the retinal image of the object changes as you move toward or away from the object.

shape constancy The recognition that an object's shape remains the same even though its orientation to us changes.

FIGURE **5.23**

EXAMINING INFANTS' DEPTH PERCEPTION ON THE VISUAL CLIFF. Eleanor Gibson and Richard Walk (1960) found that most infants would not crawl out on the glass, which, according to Gibson and Walk, indicated that they had depth perception. However, critics point out that the visual cliff is a better indication of the infant's social referencing and fear of heights than of the infant's perception of depth.

visual cliff and had their mothers coax them to crawl onto the glass (see Figure 5.23). Most infants would not crawl out on the glass, choosing instead to remain on the opaque side, an indication that they could perceive depth. However, critics point out that the visual cliff likely is a better test of social referencing and fear of heights than depth perception.

The 6- to 12-month-old infants in the visual cliff experiment had extensive visual experience. Do younger infants without this experience still perceive depth? Since younger infants do not crawl, this question is difficult to answer. Two- to four-month-old infants show differences in heart rate when they are placed directly on the transparent side of the visual cliff instead of on the opaque side (Campos, Langer, & Krowitz, 1970). However, these differences might mean that young infants respond to differences in some visual characteristics of the transparent and opaque sides of the visual cliff, with no actual knowledge of depth. Although researchers do not know exactly how early in life infants can perceive depth, we do know that infants develop the ability to use binocular cues to depth by about 3 to 4 months of age.

OTHER SENSES

Other sensory systems besides vision also develop during infancy. We explore development in hearing, touch and pain, smell, and taste.

Hearing During the last two months of pregnancy, as the fetus nestles in its mother's womb, it can hear sounds such as the mother's voice, music, and so on (Kisilevsky & others, 2009). Two psychologists wanted to find out if a fetus that heard Dr. Seuss' classic story *The Cat in the Hat* while still in the mother's womb would prefer hearing the story after birth (DeCasper & Spence, 1986). During the last months of pregnancy, 16 women read *The Cat in the Hat* to their fetuses. Then, shortly after the infants were born, the mothers read either *The Cat in the Hat* or a story with a different rhyme and pace, *The King, the Mice and the Cheese* (which had not been read aloud during prenatal development). The infants sucked on a nipple in a different way when the mothers read the two stories, suggesting that the infants recognized the pattern and tone of *The Cat in the Hat* (see Figure 5.24). This study

FIGURE **5.24**

HEARING IN THE WOMB. (*a*) Pregnant mothers read *The Cat in the Hat* to their fetuses during the last few months of pregnancy. (*b*) When they were born, the babies preferred listening to a recording of their mothers reading *The Cat in the Hat*, as evidenced by their sucking on a nipple that produced this recording, rather than another story, *The King, the Mice and the Cheese*.

(a)

(b)

illustrates not only that a fetus can hear but also that it has a remarkable ability to learn even before birth.

What kind of changes in hearing take place during infancy? They involve perception of a sound's loudness, pitch, and localization:

- *Loudness.* Immediately after birth, infants cannot hear soft sounds quite as well as adults can; a stimulus must be louder to be heard by a newborn than by an adult (Trehub & others, 1991). For example, an adult can hear a whisper from about 4 to 5 feet away, but a newborn requires that sounds be closer to a normal conversational level to be heard at that distance.

- *Pitch.* Infants are also less sensitive to the pitch of a sound than adults are. Pitch is the perception of the frequency of a sound. A soprano voice sounds high-pitched, a bass voice low-pitched. Infants are less sensitive to low-pitched sounds and are more likely to hear high-pitched sounds (Aslin, Jusczyk, & Pisoni, 1998). By 2 years of age, infants have considerably improved their ability to distinguish sounds with different pitches.

- *Localization.* Even newborns can determine the general location from which a sound is coming—but by 6 months of age, they are more proficient at localizing sounds or detecting their origins. Their ability to localize sounds continues to improve in the second year (Burnham & Mattock, 2010).

Touch and Pain Do newborns respond to touch? Can they feel pain?

Newborns do respond to touch. A touch to the cheek produces a turning of the head; a touch to the lips produces sucking movements.

Newborns can also feel pain (Field & Hernandez-Reif, 2008). If and when you have a son and consider whether he should be circumcised, the issue of an infant's pain perception probably will become important to you. If circumcision is performed, it is usually done about the third day after birth. Will your young son experience pain if he is circumcised when he is 3 days old? An investigation by Megan Gunnar and her colleagues (1987) found that newborn infant males cried intensely during circumcision. The circumcised infants also display amazing resiliency. Within several minutes after the surgery, they can nurse and interact in a normal manner with their mothers. And, if allowed to, the newly circumcised newborn drifts into a deep sleep, which seems to serve as a coping mechanism.

For many years, doctors performed operations on newborns without anesthesia. This practice was accepted because of the dangers of anesthesia and because of the supposition that newborns do not feel pain. As researchers demonstrated that newborns can feel pain, the practice of operating on newborns without anesthesia is being challenged. Anesthesia now is used in some circumcisions (Taddio, 2008).

Smell Newborns can differentiate odors (Doty & Shah, 2008). The expressions on their faces seem to indicate that they like the way vanilla and strawberry smell but do not like the way rotten eggs and fish smell (Steiner, 1979). In one investigation, 6-day-old infants who were breast fed showed a clear preference for smelling their mother's used breast pad rather than a clean breast pad (MacFarlane, 1975) (see Figure 5.25). However, when they were 2 days old, they did not show this preference, an indication that they require several days of experience to recognize this odor.

Taste Sensitivity to taste is present even before birth (Doty & Shah, 2008). Human newborns learn tastes prenatally through the amniotic fluid and in breast milk after birth (Beauchamp & Mennella, 2009; Mennella, 2009). In one study, even at only 2 hours of age, babies made different facial expressions when they tasted sweet, sour, and bitter solutions (Rosenstein & Oster, 1988) (see Figure 5.26). At about 4 months of age, infants begin to prefer salty tastes, which as newborns they had found to be aversive (Doty & Shah, 2008).

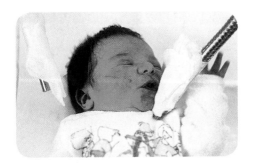

FIGURE **5.25**

NEWBORNS' PREFERENCE FOR THE SMELL OF THEIR MOTHER'S BREAST PAD. In the experiment by MacFarlane (1975), 6-day-old infants preferred to smell their mother's breast pad rather than a clean one that had never been used, but 2-day-old infants did not show the preference, indicating that this odor preference requires several days of experience to develop.

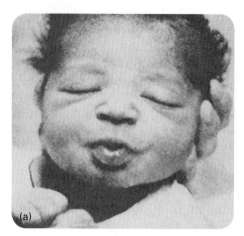

(a)

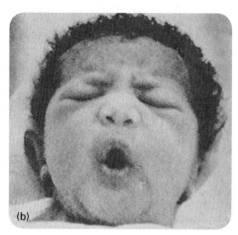

(b)

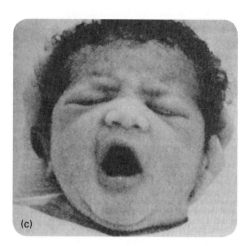

(c)

FIGURE **5.26**

NEWBORNS' FACIAL RESPONSES TO BASIC TASTES. Facial expressions elicited by (*a*) a sweet solution, (*b*) a sour solution, and (*c*) a bitter solution.

What is intermodal perception? Which two senses is this infant using to integrate information about the blocks?

intermodal perception The ability to relate and integrate information from two or more sensory modalities, such as vision and hearing.

INTERMODAL PERCEPTION

Imagine yourself playing basketball or tennis. You are experiencing many visual inputs: the ball coming and going, other players moving around, and so on. However, you are experiencing many auditory inputs as well: the sound of the ball bouncing or being hit, the grunts and groans of the players, and so on. There is good correspondence between much of the visual and auditory information: When you see the ball bounce, you hear a bouncing sound; when a player stretches to hit a ball, you hear a groan. When you look at and listen to what is going on, you do not experience just the sounds or just the sights; you put all these things together. You experience a unitary episode. This is **intermodal perception,** which involves integrating information from two or more sensory modalities, such as vision and hearing (Bremner & others, 2011). Most perception is intermodal (Bahrick, 2010).

Early, exploratory forms of intermodal perception exist even in newborns (Bahrick & Hollich, 2008; Sann & Streri, 2007). For example, newborns turn their eyes and their head toward the sound of a voice or rattle when the sound is maintained for several seconds (Clifton & others, 1981), but the newborn can localize a sound and look at an object only in a crude way (Bechtold, Bushnell, & Salapatek, 1979). These early forms of intermodal perception become sharpened with experience during the first year of life (Hollich, Newman, & Jusczyk, 2005). In one study, infants as young as 3½ months old looked more at their mother when they also heard her voice and longer at their father when they also heard his voice (Spelke & Owsley, 1979). Thus, even young infants can coordinate visual-auditory information involving people.

Can young infants put vision and sound together as precisely as adults do? In the first six months, infants have difficulty connecting sensory input from different modes, but in the second half of the first year they show an increased ability to make this connection mentally.

Thus, babies are born into the world with some innate abilities to perceive relations among sensory modalities, but their intermodal abilities improve considerably through experience (Bahrick, 2010). As with all aspects of development, in perceptual development, nature and nurture interact and cooperate (Johnson, 2011, 2012a, b; Slater & others, 2011).

NATURE, NURTURE, AND PERCEPTUAL DEVELOPMENT

Now that we have discussed many aspects of perceptual development, let's explore one of developmental psychology's key issues as it relates to perceptual development: the nature-nurture issue. There has been a long-standing interest in how strongly infants' perception is influenced by nature or nurture (Aslin, 2009; Johnson, 2011, 2012a, b; Slater & others, 2011). In the field of perceptual development, nature proponents are referred to as *nativists* and those who emphasize learning and experience are called *empiricists*.

In the nativist view, the ability to perceive the world in a competent, organized way is inborn or innate. At the beginning of our discussion of perceptual development, we examined the ecological view of the Gibsons because it has played such a pivotal role in guiding research in perceptual development. In some quarters, the Gibsons' ecological view has been described as leaning toward a nativist explanation of perceptual development because it holds that perception is direct and evolved over time to allow the detection of size and shape constancy, a three-dimensional world, intermodal perception, and so on early in infancy. However, the Gibsons' view is not entirely nativist because they emphasized that perceptual development involves distinctive features that are detected at different ages (Slater & others, 2011). Further, the Gibsons argued that a key question in infant perception is what information is available in the environment and how infants learn to generate, differentiate, and discriminate the information—certainly not a nativist view.

The Gibsons' ecological view is quite different from Piaget's constructivist view (discussed in Chapter 1), which reflects an empiricist approach to explaining perceptual development. According to Piaget, much of perceptual development in infancy must await the development of a sequence of cognitive stages for infants to construct more complex perceptual tasks. Thus, in Piaget's view, the ability to perceive size and shape constancy, a three-dimensional world, intermodal perception, and so on develops later in infancy than the Gibsons envision.

Today, it is clear that an extreme empiricist position on perceptual development is unwarranted. Much of early perception develops from innate (nature) foundations, and the basic foundation of many perceptual abilities can be detected in newborns, whereas others unfold maturationally (Arterberry, 2008). However, as infants develop, environmental experiences (nurture) refine or calibrate many perceptual functions, and they may be the driving force behind some functions. The accumulation of experience with and knowledge about their perceptual world contributes to infants' ability to perceive coherent perceptions of people and things (Johnson, 2012b; Slater & others, 2011).

Thus, a full portrait of perceptual development includes the influence of nature, nurture, and a developing sensitivity to information (Arterberry, 2008).

What roles do nature and nurture play in the infant's perceptual development?

developmental **connection**

Theories. Piaget's theory states that children construct their understanding of the world through four stages of cognitive development. Chapter 1, p. 25

PERCEPTUAL-MOTOR COUPLING

As we come to the end of this chapter, we return to the important theme of perceptual-motor coupling. The distinction between perceiving and doing has been a time-honored tradition in psychology. However, a number of experts on perceptual and motor development question whether this distinction makes sense (Adolph & Robinson, 2012; Slater & others, 2010, 2011; Thelen & Smith, 2006). The main thrust of research in Esther Thelen's dynamic systems approach is to explore how people assemble motor behaviors for perceiving and acting. The main theme of the ecological approach of Eleanor and James J. Gibson is to discover how perception guides action. Action can guide perception, and perception can guide action. Only by moving one's eyes, head, hands, and arms and by moving from one location to another can an individual fully experience his or her environment and learn how to adapt to it. Perception and action are coupled.

Babies, for example, continually coordinate their movements with perceptual information to learn how to maintain balance, reach for objects in space, and move across various surfaces and terrains (Adolph & Robinson, 2012; Slater & others,

> The infant is by no means as helpless as it looks and is quite capable of some very complex and important actions.
>
> —HERB PICK
> *Contemporary Developmental Psychologist, University of Minnesota*

How are perception and action coupled in infants' development?

2010, 2011; Thelen & Smith, 2006). They are motivated to move by what they perceive. Consider the sight of an attractive toy across the room. In this situation, infants must perceive the current state of their bodies and learn how to use their limbs to reach the toy. Although their movements at first are awkward and uncoordinated, babies soon learn to select patterns that are appropriate for reaching their goals.

Equally important is the other part of the perception-action coupling. That is, action educates perception (Adolph & Joh, 2009; Adolph & Robinson, 2012). For example, watching an object while exploring it manually helps infants to discriminate its texture, size, and hardness. Locomoting in the environment teaches babies about how objects and people look from different perspectives, or whether surfaces will support their weight. Individuals perceive in order to move and move in order to perceive. Perceptual and motor development do not occur in isolation from each other but instead are coupled.

How do infants develop new perceptual-motor couplings? Recall from our discussion earlier in this chapter that in the traditional view of Gesell, infants' perceptual-motor development is prescribed by a genetic plan to follow a fixed and sequential progression of stages in development. The genetic determination view has been replaced by the dynamic systems view that infants learn new perceptual-motor couplings by assembling skills for perceiving and acting. New perceptual-motor coupling is not passively accomplished; rather, the infant actively develops a skill to achieve a goal within the constraints set by the infant's body and the environment (Adolph & Robinson, 2012).

Review Connect Reflect

 LG3 Explain sensory and perceptual development in infancy.

Review

- What are sensation and perception?
- What is the ecological view of perception?
- How does visual perception develop in infancy?
- How do hearing, touch and pain, smell, and taste develop in infancy?
- What is intermodal perception?
- What is the nativist view of perception? What is the empiricist view?
- How is perceptual-motor development coupled?

Connect

- How might the development of vision and hearing contribute to infants' gross motor development?

Reflect *Your Own Personal Journey of Life*

- How much sensory stimulation would you provide for your baby? A little? A lot? Could you overstimulate your baby? Explain.

topical connections

In the next chapter, you will read about the remarkable cognitive changes that characterize infant development and how early infants process information about their world. Advances in infants' cognitive development—together with the development of the brain and perceptual-motor advances that were discussed in this chapter—allow infants to adapt more effectively to their world.

looking forward

How Do Infants Grow and Develop Physically?

 Discuss physical growth and development in infancy.

> Patterns of Growth

> Height and Weight

> The Brain

> Sleep

> Nutrition

> Health

- The cephalocaudal pattern is the sequence in which growth proceeds from top to bottom. The proximodistal pattern is the sequence in which growth starts at the center of the body and moves toward the extremities.

- The average North American newborn is 20 inches long and weighs 7½ pounds. Infants grow about 1 inch per month in the first year and nearly triple their weight by their first birthday. The rate of growth slows in the second year.

- One of the most dramatic changes in the brain in the first two years of life is dendritic spreading, which increases the connections between neurons. Myelination, which speeds the conduction of nerve impulses, continues through infancy and even into adolescence. The cerebral cortex has two hemispheres (left and right). Lateralization refers to specialization of function in one hemisphere or the other. Early experiences play an important role in brain development. Neural connections are formed early in an infant's life. The neuroconstructivist view is an increasingly popular view of the brain's development. Before birth, genes mainly direct neurons to different locations. After birth, the inflowing stream of sights, sounds, smells, touches, language, and eye contact helps shape the brain's neural connections, as does stimulation from caregivers and others.

- Newborns usually sleep about 18 hours a day. By 6 months of age, many American infants approach adultlike sleeping patterns. REM sleep—during which dreaming occurs—is present more in early infancy than in childhood and adulthood. Sleeping arrangements for infants vary across cultures. In America, infants are more likely to sleep alone than in many other cultures. Some experts believe shared sleeping can lead to sudden infant death syndrome (SIDS), a condition that occurs when a sleeping infant suddenly stops breathing and dies without an apparent cause.

- A number of developmental changes characterize infants' nutritional needs and eating behavior in infancy. Caregivers play important roles in infants' development of healthy eating patterns. The growing consensus is that in most instances breast feeding is superior to bottle feeding for both the infant and the mother, although the correlational nature of studies must be considered. Severe infant malnutrition is still prevalent in many parts of the world. A special concern in impoverished countries is early weaning from breast milk and the misuse and hygiene problems associated with bottle feeding in these countries.

- Widespread immunization of infants has led to a significant decline in infectious diseases. Accidents are a major cause of death in infancy. These accidents include the aspiration of foreign objects, suffocation, falls, and automobile accidents.

How Do Infants Develop Motor Skills?

 Describe infants' motor development.

> The Dynamic Systems View

- Thelen's dynamic systems theory seeks to explain how motor skills are assembled for perceiving and acting. Perception and action are coupled. According to this theory, motor skills are the result of many converging factors, such as the development of the nervous system, the body's physical properties and its movement possibilities, the goal the child is motivated to reach, and environmental support for the skill. In the dynamic systems view, motor development is far more complex than the result of a genetic blueprint.

Reflexes	• Reflexes—built-in reactions to stimuli—govern the newborn's behavior. They include the sucking, rooting, and Moro reflexes. The rooting and Moro reflexes disappear after three to four months. Permanent reflexes include coughing and blinking. For infants, sucking is an especially important reflex because it provides a means of obtaining nutrition.
Gross Motor Skills	• Gross motor skills involve large-muscle activities. Key skills developed during infancy include control of posture and walking. Although infants usually learn to walk by their first birthday, the neural pathways that allow walking begin to form earlier. The time at which infants reach milestones in the development of gross motor skills may vary by as much as two to four months, especially for milestones in late infancy.
Fine Motor Skills	• Fine motor skills involve finely tuned movements. The onset of reaching and grasping marks a significant accomplishment, and this becomes more refined during the first two years of life.

How Can Infants' Sensory and Perceptual Development Be Characterized?

 Explain sensory and perceptual development in infancy.

What Are Sensation and Perception?	• Sensation occurs when information interacts with sensory receptors. Perception is the interpretation of sensation.
The Ecological View	• Created by the Gibsons, the ecological view states that we directly perceive information that exists in the world around us. Perception brings people in contact with the environment to interact with and adapt to it. Affordances provide opportunities for interaction offered by objects that fit within our capabilities to perform activities.
Visual Perception	• Researchers have developed a number of methods to assess the infant's perception, including the visual preference method (which Fantz used to determine young infants' interest in looking at patterned over nonpatterned displays), habituation and dishabituation, and tracking. The infant's visual acuity increases dramatically in the first year of life. Infants' color vision improves as they develop. Young infants systematically scan human faces. By 3 months of age, infants show size and shape constancy. At approximately 2 months of age, infants develop the ability to perceive occluded objects as complete. In Gibson and Walk's classic study, infants as young as 6 months of age had depth perception.
Other Senses	• The fetus can hear several weeks prior to birth. Immediately after birth, newborns can hear, but their sensory threshold is higher than that of adults. Developmental changes in the perception of loudness, pitch, and localization of sound occur during infancy. Newborns can respond to touch and feel pain. Newborns can differentiate odors, and sensitivity to taste may be present before birth.
Intermodal Perception	• Early, exploratory forms of intermodal perception—the ability to relate and integrate information from two or more sensory modalities—are present in newborns and become sharper over the first year of life.
Nature, Nurture, and Perceptual Development	• In perception, nature advocates are referred to as nativists and nurture proponents are called empiricists. The Gibsons' ecological view that has guided much of perceptual development research leans toward a nativist approach but still allows for developmental changes in distinctive features. Piaget's constructivist view leans toward an empiricist approach emphasizing that many perceptual accomplishments must await the development of cognitive stages in infancy. A strong empiricist approach is unwarranted. A full account of perceptual development includes the roles of nature, nurture, and the developing sensitivity to information.
Perceptual-Motor Coupling	• Perception and action are often not isolated but rather are coupled. Individuals perceive in order to move and move in order to perceive.

key terms

cephalocaudal pattern 136	marasmus 147	gross motor skills 152	habituation 158
proximodistal pattern 137	kwashiorkor 147	fine motor skills 154	dishabituation 158
forebrain 138	dynamic systems theory 149	sensation 157	size constancy 161
cerebral cortex 138	reflexes 150	perception 157	shape constancy 161
lateralization 138	rooting reflex 150	ecological view 157	intermodal perception 164
neuroconstructivist view 141	sucking reflex 150	affordances 157	
sudden infant death	Moro reflex 150	visual preference	
syndrome (SIDS) 143	grasping reflex 151	method 158	

key people

Charles Nelson 137	T. Berry Brazelton 148	Eleanor and James J.	William James 160
John Richards 137	Esther Thelen 149	Gibson 157	Richard Walk 161
Ernesto Pollitt 147	Karen Adolph 153	Robert Fantz 158	

connecting with **improving the lives of children**

MAKING A DIFFERENCE

Supporting the Infant's Physical Development

What are some good strategies for helping the infant develop in physically competent ways?

- *Be flexible about the infant's sleep patterns.* Don't try to put the infant on a rigid sleep schedule. By about 4 months of age, most infants have moved closer to adultlike sleep patterns.
- *Provide the infant with good nutrition.* Make sure the infant has adequate energy and nutrient intake. Provide this in a loving and supportive environment. Don't put an infant on a diet. Weaning should be gradual, not abrupt.
- *Breast feed the infant, if possible.* Breast feeding provides more ideal nutrition than bottle feeding. If work prevents the mother from breast feeding the infant while she is away from home, she should consider "pumping."
- *Give the infant extensive opportunities to explore safe environments.* Infants don't need exercise classes, but they should be provided with many opportunities to actively explore safe environments. Infants should not be constricted to small, confined environments for any length of time.
- *Don't push the infant's physical development or get uptight about physical norms.* In American culture, we tend to want our child to grow faster than other children. Remember that there is wide individual variation in normal physical development. Just because an infant is not at the top of a physical chart doesn't mean parents should start pushing the infant's physical skills. Infants develop at different paces. Respect and nurture the infant's individuality.

RESOURCES

The Amazing Infant
by Tiffany Field (2007)
Malden, MA: Blackwell
The Amazing Infant is an outstanding book on infant development, written by one of the world's leading researchers on infant development. The book accurately captures the flavor of the young infant as an active learner and one far more competent than once was believed.

Solve Your Child's Sleep Problems
by Richard Ferber (2006)
New York: Simon & Schuster
Solve Your Child's Sleep Problems helps parents recognize when their infant or child has a sleep problem and tells them what to do about it.

The Baby Food Bible
by Eileen Behan (2008)
New York: Ballantine
A guide for parents that provides extensive information about encouraging an early foundation for developing healthy eating habits, with special attention given to foods based on guidelines of the American Academy of Pediatrics.

chapter 6

COGNITIVE DEVELOPMENT IN INFANCY

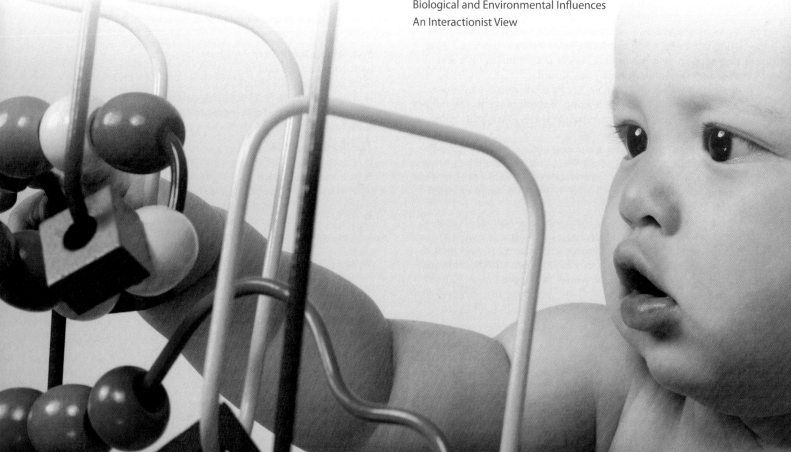

Jean Piaget, the famous Swiss psychologist, was a meticulous observer of his three children: Laurent, Lucienne, and Jacqueline. His books on cognitive development are filled with these observations. Here are a few of Piaget's observations of his children in infancy (Piaget, 1952):

- At 21 days of age, "Laurent found his thumb after three attempts: prolonged sucking begins each time. But, once he has been placed on his back, he does not know how to coordinate the movement of the arms with that of the mouth and his hands draw back even when his lips are seeking them" (p. 27).

- "During the third month, thumb sucking becomes less important to Laurent because of new visual and auditory interests. But, when he cries, his thumb goes to the rescue."

- Toward the end of Lucienne's fourth month, while she is lying in her crib, Piaget hangs a doll above her feet. Lucienne thrusts her feet at the doll and makes it move. "Afterward, she looks at her motionless foot for a second, then recommences. There is no visual control of her foot, for the movements are the same when Lucienne only looks at the doll or when I place the doll over her head. On the other hand, the tactile control of the foot is apparent: after the first shakes, Lucienne makes slow foot movements as though to grasp and explore" (p. 159).

- At 11 months, "Jacqueline is seated and shakes a little bell. She then pauses abruptly in order to delicately place the bell in front of her right foot; then she kicks hard. Unable to recapture it, she grasps a ball which she then places at the same spot in order to give it another kick" (p. 225).

- At 1 year, 2 months, "Jacqueline holds in her hands an object which is new to her: a round, flat box which she turns all over, shakes, [and] rubs against the bassinet. . . . She lets it go and tries to pick it up. But she only succeeds in touching it with her index finger, without grasping it. She nevertheless makes

topical connections

In Chapter 5, you learned that impressive advances occur in the development of the brain during infancy. Engaging in various physical, cognitive, and socioemotional activities strengthens the baby's neural connections. Motor and perceptual development also are key aspects of the infant's development. An important part of this development is the coupling of perceptions and actions. The nature-nurture issue continues to be debated with regard to the infant's perceptual development. In this chapter, you will build on your understanding of the infant's brain, motor, and perceptual development by further examining how infants develop their competencies, focusing on how advances in their cognitive development help them adapt to their world, and how the nature-nurture issue is an important aspect of the infant's cognitive and language development.

◄ — *looking back*

an attempt and presses on the edge. The box then tilts up and falls again"
(p. 273). Jacqueline shows an interest in this result and studies the fallen box.

- At 1 year, 8 months, "Jacqueline arrives at a closed door with a blade of grass in each hand. She stretches out her right hand toward the [door] knob but sees that she cannot turn it without letting go of the grass. She puts the grass on the floor, opens the door, picks up the grass again, and enters. But when she wants to leave the room, things become complicated. She puts the grass on the floor and grasps the doorknob. But then she perceives that in pulling the door toward her she will simultaneously chase away the grass which she placed between the door and the threshold. She therefore picks it up in order to put it outside the door's zone of movement" (p. 339).

For Piaget, these observations reflect important changes in the infant's cognitive development. Piaget believed that infants go through six substages as they progress in less than two short years from Laurent's thumb sucking to Jacqueline's problem solving.

preview

Piaget's descriptions of infants are just the starting point for our exploration of cognitive development. Excitement and enthusiasm about the study of infant cognition have been fueled by an interest in what newborns and infants know, by continued fascination about innate and learned factors in the infant's cognitive development, and by controversies about whether infants construct their knowledge (Piaget's view) or know their world more directly. In this chapter, you will study not only Piaget's theory of infant development but also learning, remembering, and conceptualizing by infants; individual differences; and language development.

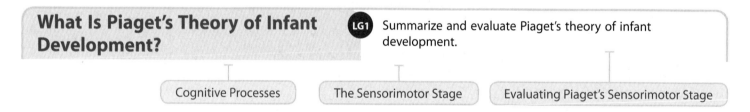

What Is Piaget's Theory of Infant Development?

LG1 Summarize and evaluate Piaget's theory of infant development.

Cognitive Processes | The Sensorimotor Stage | Evaluating Piaget's Sensorimotor Stage

Poet Nora Perry once asked, "Who knows the thoughts of a child?" As much as anyone, Piaget knew. Through careful observations of his own three children—Laurent, Lucienne, and Jacqueline—and observations of and interviews with other children, Piaget changed perceptions of the way children think about the world.

We are born capable of learning.

—JEAN-JACQUES ROUSSEAU
Swiss-Born French Philosopher, 18th Century

Piaget's theory is a general, unifying story of how biology and experience sculpt cognitive development. Piaget thought that just as our physical bodies have structures that enable us to adapt to the world, we build mental structures that help us to adapt to the world. *Adaptation* involves adjusting to new environmental demands. Piaget stressed that children actively construct their own cognitive worlds; information is not just poured into their minds from the environment. He sought to discover how children at different points in their development think about the world and how systematic changes in their thinking occur.

schemes In Piaget's theory, actions or mental representations that organize knowledge.

assimilation Piagetian concept involving incorporation of new information into existing schemes.

accommodation Piagetian concept of adjusting schemes to fit new information and experiences.

COGNITIVE PROCESSES

What processes do children use as they construct their knowledge of the world? Piaget developed several concepts to answer this question; especially important are schemes, assimilation, accommodation, organization, equilibrium, and equilibration.

Schemes   As the infant or child seeks to construct an understanding of the world, said Piaget (1954), the developing brain creates **schemes.** These are actions or mental representations that organize knowledge. In Piaget's theory, behavioral schemes (physical activities) characterize infancy and mental schemes (cognitive activities) develop in childhood (Lamb, Bornstein, & Teti, 2002). A baby's schemes are structured by simple actions that can be performed on objects, such as sucking, looking, and grasping. Older children have schemes that include strategies and plans for solving problems. For example, in the descriptions at the opening of this chapter, Laurent displayed a scheme for sucking; Jacqueline displayed a problem-solving scheme when she was able to open the door without losing her blade of grass. By the time we have reached adulthood, we have constructed an enormous number of diverse schemes, ranging from knowing how to drive a car to balancing a budget to understanding the concept of fairness.

In Piaget's view, what is a scheme? What schemes might this young infant be displaying?

Assimilation and Accommodation   To explain how children use and adapt their schemes, Piaget offered two concepts: assimilation and accommodation. **Assimilation** occurs when children use their existing schemes to deal with new information or experiences. **Accommodation** occurs when children adjust their schemes to take new information and experiences into account.

Think about a toddler who has learned the word *car* to identify the family's car. The toddler might call all moving vehicles on roads "cars," including motorcycles and trucks; the child has assimilated these objects to his or her existing scheme. But the child soon learns that motorcycles and trucks are not cars and fine-tunes the category to exclude motorcycles and trucks, thus accommodating the scheme.

Assimilation and accommodation operate even in very young infants. Newborns reflexively suck everything that touches their lips; they assimilate all sorts of objects into their sucking scheme. By sucking different objects, they learn about their taste, texture, shape, and so on. After several months of experience, though, they construct their understanding of the world differently. Some objects, such as fingers and the mother's breast, can be sucked, and others, such as fuzzy blankets, should not be sucked. In other words, they accommodate their sucking scheme.

How might assimilation and accommodation be involved in infants' sucking?

Organization   To make sense out of their world, said Piaget, children cognitively organize their experiences. **Organization** in Piaget's theory is the grouping of isolated behaviors and thoughts into a higher-order system. Continual refinement of this organization is an inherent part of development. A boy who has only a vague idea about how to use a hammer may also have a vague idea about how to use other tools. After learning how to use each one, he relates these uses, organizing his knowledge.

Equilibration and Stages of Development   Assimilation and accommodation always take the child to a higher ground, according to Piaget. In trying to understand the world, the child inevitably experiences cognitive conflict, or *disequilibrium*. That is, the child is constantly faced with counterexamples to his or her existing schemes and with inconsistencies. For example, if a child believes that pouring water from a short and wide container into a tall and narrow container changes the amount of water, then the child might be puzzled by where the "extra" water came from and whether there is actually more water to drink. The puzzle creates disequilibrium; for Piaget, an internal search for equilibrium creates motivation for change. The child assimilates and accommodates, adjusting old schemes, developing new schemes, and organizing and reorganizing the old and new schemes. Eventually, the organization is fundamentally different from the old organization; it is a new way of thinking.

In short, according to Piaget, children constantly assimilate and accommodate as they seek *equilibrium*. There is considerable movement between states of cognitive equilibrium and disequilibrium as assimilation and accommodation work in concert to produce cognitive change. **Equilibration** is the name Piaget gave to this mechanism by which children shift from one stage of thought to the next.

developmental **connection**

Cognitive Theory. Recall the main characteristics of Piaget's four stages of cognitive development. Chapter 1, p. 25

organization Piaget's concept of grouping isolated behaviors and thoughts into a higher-order system, a more smoothly functioning cognitive system.

equilibration A mechanism that Piaget proposed to explain how children shift from one stage of thought to the next.

Substage	Age	Description	Example
1 Simple reflexes	Birth to 1 month	Coordination of sensation and action through reflexive behaviors.	Rooting, sucking, and grasping reflexes; newborns suck reflexively when their lips are touched.
2 First habits and primary circular reactions	1 to 4 months	Coordination of sensation and two types of schemes: habits (reflex) and primary circular reactions (reproduction of an event that initially occurred by chance). Main focus is still on the infant's body.	Repeating a body sensation first experienced by chance (sucking thumb, for example); then infants might accommodate actions by sucking their thumb differently from how they suck on a nipple.
3 Secondary circular reactions	4 to 8 months	Infants become more object-oriented, moving beyond self-preoccupation; repeat actions that bring interesting or pleasurable results.	An infant coos to make a person stay near; as the person starts to leave, the infant coos again.
4 Coordination of secondary circular reactions	8 to 12 months	Coordination of vision and touch—hand-eye coordination; coordination of schemes and intentionality.	Infant manipulates a stick in order to bring an attractive toy within reach.
5 Tertiary circular reactions, novelty, and curiosity	12 to 18 months	Infants become intrigued by the many properties of objects and by the many things they can make happen to objects; they experiment with new behavior.	A block can be made to fall, spin, hit another object, and slide across the ground.
6 Internalization of schemes	18 to 24 months	Infants develop the ability to use primitive symbols and form enduring mental representations.	An infant who has never thrown a temper tantrum before sees a playmate throw a tantrum; the infant retains a memory of the event, then throws one himself the next day.

FIGURE **6.1**

PIAGET'S SIX SUBSTAGES OF SENSORIMOTOR DEVELOPMENT

sensorimotor stage The first of Piaget's stages, which lasts from birth to about 2 years of age, in which infants construct an understanding of the world by coordinating sensory experiences with motoric actions.

simple reflexes Piaget's first sensorimotor substage, which corresponds to the first month after birth. In this substage, sensation and action are coordinated primarily through reflexive behaviors.

first habits and primary circular reactions Piaget's second sensorimotor substage, which develops between 1 and 4 months of age. In this substage, the infant coordinates sensation and two types of schemes: habits and primary circular reactions.

primary circular reaction A scheme based on the attempt to reproduce an event that initially occurred by chance.

secondary circular reactions Piaget's third sensorimotor substage, which develops between 4 and 8 months of age. In this substage, the infant becomes more object-oriented, moving beyond preoccupation with the self.

coordination of secondary circular reactions Piaget's fourth sensorimotor substage, which develops between 8 and 12 months of age. Actions become more outwardly directed, and infants coordinate schemes and act with intentionality.

tertiary circular reactions, novelty, and curiosity Piaget's fifth sensorimotor substage, which develops between 12 and 18 months of age. In this substage, infants become intrigued by the many properties of objects and by the many things that they can make happen to objects.

internalization of schemes Piaget's sixth and final sensorimotor substage, which develops between 18 and 24 months of age. In this substage, the infant develops the ability to use primitive symbols.

The result of these processes, according to Piaget, is that individuals go through four stages of development. A different way of understanding the world makes each stage more advanced than the one before it. Cognition is *qualitatively* different in one stage compared with another. In other words, the way children reason at one stage is different from the way they reason at another stage. In this chapter, our focus is on Piaget's stage of infant cognitive development. In later chapters, when we study cognitive development in early, middle, and late childhood, and in adolescence, we explore the last three Piagetian stages.

THE SENSORIMOTOR STAGE

The **sensorimotor stage** lasts from birth to about 2 years of age. In this stage, infants construct an understanding of the world by coordinating sensory experiences (such as seeing and hearing) with physical, motoric actions—hence the term "sensorimotor." At the beginning of this stage, newborns have little more than reflexes with which to work. At the end of the sensorimotor stage, 2-year-olds can produce complex sensorimotor patterns and use primitive symbols. We first summarize Piaget's descriptions of how infants develop. Later we consider criticisms of his view.

Substages Piaget divided the sensorimotor stage into six substages: (1) simple reflexes; (2) first habits and primary circular reactions; (3) secondary circular reactions; (4) coordination of secondary circular reactions; (5) tertiary circular reactions, novelty, and curiosity; and (6) internalization of schemes (see Figure 6.1).

Simple reflexes, the first sensorimotor substage, corresponds to the first month after birth. In this substage, sensation and action are coordinated primarily through reflexive behaviors, such as rooting and sucking. Soon the infant produces behaviors that resemble reflexes in the absence of the usual stimulus for the reflex. For example, a newborn will suck a nipple or bottle only when it is placed directly in the baby's mouth or touched to the lips. Even in the first month of life, the infant is initiating action and actively structuring experiences.

First habits and primary circular reactions is the second sensorimotor substage, which develops between 1 and 4 months of age. In this substage, the infant coordinates sensation and two types of schemes: habits and primary circular reactions. A habit is a scheme based on a reflex that has become completely separated from its eliciting stimulus. For example, infants in substage 1 suck when bottles are put to their lips or when they see a bottle. Infants in substage 2 might suck even when no bottle is present. A circular reaction is a repetitive action.

A **primary circular reaction** is a scheme based on the attempt to reproduce an event that initially occurred by chance. For example, suppose an infant accidentally sucks his fingers when they are placed near his mouth. Later, he searches for his fingers to suck them again, but the fingers do not cooperate because the infant cannot coordinate visual and manual actions.

Habits and circular reactions are stereotyped—that is, the infant repeats them the same way each time. During this substage, the infant's own body remains the infant's center of attention. There is no outward pull by environmental events.

Secondary circular reactions is the third sensorimotor substage, which develops between 4 and 8 months of age. In this substage, the infant becomes more object-oriented, moving beyond preoccupation with the self. The infant's schemes are not intentional or goal-directed, but they are repeated because of their consequences. By chance, an infant might shake a rattle. The infant repeats this action for the sake of its fascination. This is a *secondary circular reaction:* an action repeated because of its consequences. The infant also imitates some simple actions, such as the baby talk or burbling of adults, and some physical gestures. However, the baby imitates only actions that he or she is already able to produce.

Coordination of secondary circular reactions is Piaget's fourth sensorimotor substage, which develops between 8 and 12 months of age. To progress into this substage, the infant must coordinate vision and touch, hand and eye. Actions become more outwardly directed. Significant changes during this substage involve the coordination of schemes and intentionality. Infants readily combine and recombine previously learned schemes in a coordinated way. They might look at an object and grasp it simultaneously, or they might visually inspect a toy, such as a rattle, and finger it simultaneously, exploring it tactilely. Actions are even more outwardly directed than before. Related to this coordination is the second achievement—the presence of intentionality. For example, infants might manipulate a stick in order to bring a desired toy within reach or they might knock over one block to reach and play with another one. Similarly, when 11-month-old Jacqueline, as described in the chapter opening, placed the ball in front of her and kicked it, she was demonstrating intentionality.

Tertiary circular reactions, novelty, and curiosity is Piaget's fifth sensorimotor substage, which develops between 12 and 18 months of age. In this substage, infants become intrigued by the many properties of objects and by the many things that they can make happen to objects. A block can be made to fall, spin, hit another object, and slide across the ground. *Tertiary circular reactions* are schemes in which the infant purposely explores new possibilities with objects, continually doing new things to them and exploring the results. Piaget says that this stage marks the starting point for human curiosity and interest in novelty.

Internalization of schemes is Piaget's sixth and final sensorimotor substage, which develops between 18 and 24 months of age. In this substage, the infant develops the ability to use primitive symbols. For Piaget, a symbol is an internalized sensory image or word that represents an event. Primitive symbols permit the infant to think about concrete events without directly acting them out or perceiving them. Moreover, symbols allow the infant to manipulate and transform the represented events in simple ways. In a favorite Piagetian example, Piaget's young daughter saw a matchbox being opened and closed. Later, she mimicked the event by opening and closing her mouth. This was an obvious expression of her image of the event.

This 7-month-old is in Piaget's substage of secondary circular reactions. *What might the infant do to suggest he is in this substage?*

This 17-month-old is in Piaget's stage of tertiary circular reactions. *What might the infant do to suggest that she is in this stage?*

developmental **connection**

Cognitive Processes. What are some changes in symbolic thought in young children? Chapter 9, p. 260

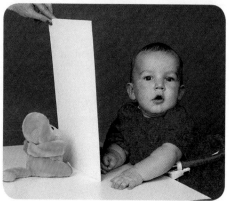

FIGURE 6.2

OBJECT PERMANENCE. Piaget argued that object permanence is one of infancy's landmark cognitive accomplishments. For this 5-month-old boy, "out-of-sight" is literally out of mind. The infant looks at the toy monkey (*top*), but, when his view of the toy is blocked (*bottom*), he does not search for it. Several months later, he will search for the hidden toy monkey, an action reflecting the presence of object permanence.

Object Permanence   Imagine how chaotic and unpredictable your life would be if you could not distinguish between yourself and your world. This is what the life of a newborn must be like, according to Piaget. There is no differentiation between the self and world; objects have no separate, permanent existence.

By the end of the sensorimotor period, objects are both separate from the self and permanent. **Object permanence** is the understanding that objects continue to exist even when they cannot be seen, heard, or touched. Acquiring the sense of object permanence is one of the infant's most important accomplishments, according to Piaget.

How could anyone know whether an infant had developed a sense of object permanence? The principal way that object permanence is studied is by watching an infant's reaction when an interesting object disappears (see Figure 6.2). If infants search for the object, it is assumed that they believe it continues to exist.

Object permanence is just one of the basic concepts about the physical world developed by babies. To Piaget, children, even infants, are much like little scientists, examining the world to see how it works. How do adult scientists try to discover what these "baby scientists" are finding out about the world? The *Connecting with Research* interlude that follows describes some of the ways.

EVALUATING PIAGET'S SENSORIMOTOR STAGE

Piaget opened up a new way of looking at infants with his view that their main task is to coordinate their sensory impressions with their motor activity. However, the infant's cognitive world is not as neatly packaged as Piaget portrayed it, and some of Piaget's explanations for the cause of change are debated. In the past several decades, sophisticated experimental techniques have been devised to study infants, and there have been a large number of research studies on infant development. Much of the new research suggests that Piaget's view of sensorimotor development needs to be modified (Baillargeon & others, 2011; Johnson, 2012a, b; Quinn, 2011).

The A-not-B Error   One modification concerns Piaget's claim that certain processes are crucial in transitions from one stage to the next. The data do not always support his explanations. For example, in Piaget's theory, an important feature in the progression into substage 4, *coordination of secondary circular reactions*, is an infant's inclination to search for a hidden object in a familiar location rather than to look for the object in a new location. Thus, if a toy is hidden twice, initially at location A and subsequently at location B, 8- to 12-month-old infants search correctly at location A initially. But when the toy is subsequently hidden at location B, they make the mistake of continuing to search for it at location A. **A-not-B error** is the term used to describe this common mistake. Older infants are less likely to make the A-not-B error because their concept of object permanence is more complete.

Researchers have found, however, that the A-not-B error does not show up consistently (Sophian, 1985). The evidence indicates that A-not-B errors are sensitive to the delay between hiding the object at B and the infant's attempt to find it (Diamond, 1985). Thus, the A-not-B error might be due to a failure in memory. Another explanation is that infants tend to repeat a previous motor behavior (Clearfield & others, 2006; Smith, 1999).

developmental **connection**

Perception. Eleanor Gibson was a pioneer in crafting the ecological perception view of development. Chapter 5, p. 157

Perceptual Development and Expectation   A number of theorists, such as Eleanor Gibson (2001) and Elizabeth Spelke (1991), maintain that infants' perceptual abilities are highly developed very early in life. Spelke argues that young infants interpret the world as having predictable occurrences. For example, in Chapter 5, "Physical Development in Infancy," we discussed research that demonstrated the presence of intermodal perception—the ability to coordinate information from two or more sensory modalities, such as vision and hearing—by 3½ months of age, much earlier than Piaget would have predicted (Spelke & Owsley, 1979).

object permanence Piagetian term for understanding that objects continue to exist, even when they cannot directly be seen, heard, or touched.

A-not-B error This occurs when infants make the mistake of selecting the familiar hiding place (A) rather than the new hiding place (B) as they progress into substage 4 in Piaget's sensorimotor stage.

How Do Researchers Study Infants' Understanding of Object Permanence and Causality?

Two accomplishments of infants that Piaget examined were the development of object permanence and the child's understanding of causality. Let's examine two research studies that address these topics.

In both studies, Renée Baillargeon and her colleagues used a research method that involves *violation of expectations.* In this method, infants see an event happen as it normally would. Then, the event is changed, often in a way that creates a physically impossible event. Infants look longer at the changed event, indicating that they are surprised by it. In other words, the infant's reaction is interpreted to indicate that the infant had certain expectations about the world that were violated.

In one study focused on object permanence, researchers showed infants a toy car that moved down an inclined track, disappeared behind a screen, and then reemerged at the other end, still on the track (Baillargeon & DeVos, 1991) (see Figure 6.3a). After this sequence was repeated several times, something different occurred: A toy mouse was placed *behind* the tracks but was hidden by the screen while the car rolled by (see Figure 6.3b). This was the "possible" event. Then, the researchers created an "impossible event": The toy mouse was placed on the tracks but was secretly removed after the screen was lowered so that the car seemed to go through the mouse (see Figure 6.3c). In this study, infants as young as 3½ months of age looked longer at the impossible event than at the possible event, an indication that they were surprised by it. Their surprise suggested that they remembered not only the existence of the toy mouse (object permanence) but also its location.

Another study focused on the infant's understanding of causality (Kotovsky & Baillargeon, 1994). In this research, a cylinder rolls down a ramp and hits a toy bug at the bottom of the ramp. By 5½ and 6½ months of age, after infants have seen how far the bug will be pushed by a medium-sized cylinder, their reactions indicate that they understand that the bug will roll farther if it is hit by a large cylinder than if it is hit by a small cylinder. Thus, by the middle of the first year of life, these infants understand that the size of a moving object determines how far it will move a stationary object that it collides with.

In Baillargeon's (2008; Baillargeon & others, 2011; Luo & Baillargeon, 2011) view, infants have a preadapted, innate bias called the *principle of persistence* that explains their assumption that objects don't change their properties—including how solid they are, their location, their color, and their form—unless some external factor (a person who moves the object, for example) obviously intervenes. Shortly, we revisit the extent to which nature and nurture are at work in the changes that take place in the infant's cognitive development.

The research findings discussed in this interlude and other research indicate that infants develop object permanence and causal reasoning much earlier than Piaget proposed (Baillargeon & others, 2011). Indeed, as you will see in the next section, a major theme of infant cognitive development today is that infants are more cognitively competent than Piaget envisioned.

How does the discovery of infants' early cognitive competence affect our understanding of Piaget's research on infant development?

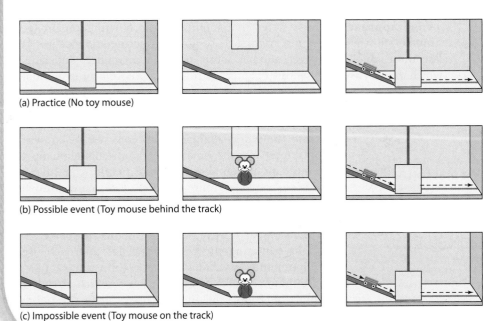

(a) Practice (No toy mouse)

(b) Possible event (Toy mouse behind the track)

(c) Impossible event (Toy mouse on the track)

FIGURE **6.3**

USING THE VIOLATION OF EXPECTATIONS METHOD TO STUDY OBJECT PERMANENCE IN INFANTS. If infants looked longer at (*c*) than at (*b*), researchers reasoned that the impossible event in (*c*) violated the infants' expectations and that they remembered that the toy mouse existed.

A 4-month-old in Elizabeth Spelke's infant perception laboratory is tested to determine whether she knows that an object in motion will not stop in midair. Spelke concluded that at 4 months babies don't expect objects like these balls to obey gravitational constraints, but they do expect objects to be solid and continuous. Research by Spelke, Renée Baillargeon, and others suggests that infants develop an ability to understand how the world works earlier than Piaget envisioned. However, critics such as Andrew Meltzoff fault their research and conclude there is still controversy about how early some infant cognitive accomplishments occur.

Research also suggests that infants develop the ability to understand how the world works at a very early age (Baillargeon & others, 2011; Quinn, 2011). What kinds of expectations do infants form? Are we born expecting the world to obey basic physical laws, such as gravity, or when do we learn about how the world works? Experiments by Elizabeth Spelke (1991, 2000; Spelke & Hespos, 2001) have addressed these questions. She placed babies before a puppet stage and showed them a series of actions that are unexpected if you know how the physical world works—for example, one ball seemed to roll through a solid barrier, another seemed to leap between two platforms, and a third appeared to hang in midair (Spelke, 1979). Spelke measured and compared the babies' looking times for unexpected and expected actions. She concluded that, by 4 months of age, even though infants do not yet have the ability to talk about objects, move around objects, manipulate objects, or even see objects with high resolution, they expect objects to be solid and continuous. However, at 4 months of age, infants do not expect an object to obey gravitational constraints (Spelke & others, 1992). Similarly, research by Renée Baillargeon (1995, 2004) documents that infants as young as 3 to 4 months expect objects to be *substantial* (in the sense that other objects cannot move through them) and *permanent* (in the sense that objects continue to exist when they are hidden).

In sum, researchers such as Baillargeon and Spelke conclude that infants see objects as bounded, unitary, solid, and separate from their background, possibly at birth or shortly thereafter, but definitely by 3 to 4 months of age, much earlier than Piaget envisioned. Young infants still have much to learn about objects, but the world appears both stable and orderly to them.

By 6 to 8 months, infants have learned to perceive gravity and support—that an object hanging on the end of a table should fall, that ball bearings will travel farther when rolled down a longer rather than a shorter ramp, and that cup handles will not fall when attached to a cup (Slater, Field, & Hernandez-Reif, 2007). As infants develop, their experiences and actions on objects help them to understand physical laws (Bremner, 2010).

The Nature-Nurture Issue   In considering the big issue of whether nature or nurture plays the more important role in infant development, Elizabeth Spelke (Kinzler, Dupoux, & Spelke, 2011; Spelke, 2000; Spelke & Kinzler, 2007) comes down clearly on the side of nature. Spelke endorses a **core knowledge approach,** which states that infants are born with domain-specific innate knowledge systems. Among these domain-specific knowledge systems are those involving space, number sense, object permanence, and language (which we discuss later in this chapter). Strongly influenced by evolution, the core knowledge domains are theorized to be prewired to allow infants to make sense of their world. After all, Spelke concludes, how could infants possibly grasp the complex world in which they live if they didn't come into the world equipped with core sets of knowledge? In this approach, the innate core knowledge domains form a foundation around which more mature cognitive functioning and learning develop. The core knowledge approach argues that Piaget greatly underestimated the cognitive abilities of infants, especially young infants (Hyde & Spelke, 2011; Kinzler, Dupoux, & Spelke, 2011).

In criticizing the core knowledge approach, British developmental psychologist Mark Johnston (2008) says that the infants Spelke assesses in her research already have accumulated hundreds, and in some cases even thousands, of hours of experience in grasping what the world is about, which gives considerable room for the environment's role in the development of infant cognition (Highfield, 2008). According to Johnston (2008), infants likely come into the

> Infants know that objects are substantial and permanent at an earlier age than Piaget envisioned.
>
> —Renée Baillargeon
> *Contemporary Psychologist, University of Illinois*

developmental **connection**

Nature and Nurture. The nature-nurture issue is also important in understanding perceptual development. Chapter 5, p. 164

core knowledge approach View that infants are born with domain-specific innate knowledge systems.

world with "soft biases to perceive and attend to different aspects of the environment, and to learn about the world in particular ways." Although debate about the cause and course of infant cognitive development continues, most developmentalists today agree that Piaget underestimated the early cognitive accomplishments of infants and that both nature and nurture are involved in infants' cognitive development.

Conclusions   In sum, many researchers conclude that Piaget wasn't specific enough about how infants learn about their world and that infants, especially young infants, are more competent than Piaget thought (Baillargeon & others, 2011; Diamond, Casey, & Munakata, 2011; Johnson, 2012a, b; Kinzler, Dupoux, & Spelke, 2011; Meltzoff, 2011). As researchers have examined the specific ways that infants learn, the field of infant cognition has become very specialized. There are many researchers working on different questions, with no general theory emerging that can connect all of the different findings (Nelson, 1999). Their theories often are local theories, focused on specific research questions, rather than grand theories like Piaget's (Kuhn, 1998). If there is a unifying theme, it is that investigators in infant development seek to understand more precisely how developmental changes in cognition take place and to consider the big issue of nature and nurture (Aslin, 2009). As they seek to answer more precisely the contributions of nature and nurture to infant development, researchers face the difficult task of determining whether the course of acquiring information, which is very rapid in some domains, is best accounted for by an innate set of biases (that is, core knowledge), or by the extensive input of environmental experiences to which the infant is exposed (Aslin, 2009).

What revisions in Piaget's theory of sensorimotor development do contemporary researchers conclude need to be made? What characterizes the nature-nurture controversy in infant cognitive development?

Review Connect Reflect

LG1 Summarize and evaluate Piaget's theory of infant development.

Review

- What cognitive processes are important in Piaget's theory?
- What are some characteristics of Piaget's stage of sensorimotor development?
- What are some contributions and criticisms of Piaget's sensorimotor stage?

Connect

- You just read that by the age of 6 to 8 months infants have learned to perceive gravity and support. What physical development occurring around this same time period (discussed in Chapter 5) might contribute to the infant's understanding of these concepts?

Reflect *Your Own Personal Journey of Life*

- What are some implications of Piaget's theory of infant development for parenting?

How Do Infants Learn, Remember, and Conceptualize?

LG2 Describe how infants learn, remember, and conceptualize.

| Conditioning | Attention | Memory | Imitation | Concept Formation |

When Piaget hung a doll above 4-month-old Lucienne's feet, as described at the beginning of the chapter, would she remember the doll? If Piaget had rewarded her for moving the doll with her foot, would the reward have affected Lucienne's behavior? If he had showed her how to shake the doll's hand, could she have imitated him? If he had showed her a different doll, could she have formed the concept of a "doll"?

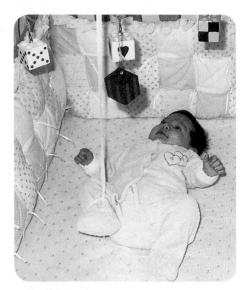

FIGURE **6.4**

CONDITIONING AND MEMORY IN INFANTS.
In Rovee-Collier's experiment, operant conditioning was used to demonstrate that infants as young as 2½ months of age can retain information from the experience of being conditioned. *What did infants recall in Rovee-Collier's experiment?*

developmental connection

Theories. The behavioral and social cognitive approaches emphasize continuity rather than discontinuity in development. Chapter 1, p. 18

developmental connection

Attention. In early childhood, children make significant advances in sustained attention. Chapter 8, p. 239

attention The focusing of mental resources on select information.

Questions like these might be examined by researchers taking the behavioral and social cognitive or information processing approaches introduced in Chapter 1. In contrast to Piaget's theory, these approaches do not describe infant development in terms of stages. Instead, they document gradual changes in the infant's ability to understand and process information about the world. In this section, we explore what researchers using these approaches can tell us about how infants learn, remember, and conceptualize.

CONDITIONING

In Chapter 1, we described Pavlov's classical conditioning (in which, as a result of pairing, a new stimulus comes to elicit a response previously given to another stimulus) and Skinner's operant conditioning (in which the consequences of a behavior produce changes in the probability of the behavior's occurrence). Infants can learn through both types of conditioning. For example, if an infant's behavior is followed by a rewarding stimulus, the behavior is likely to recur.

Operant conditioning has been especially helpful to researchers in their efforts to determine what infants perceive (Rovee-Collier & Barr, 2010; Rovee-Collier & Cuevas, 2009). For example, infants will suck faster on a nipple when the sucking behavior is followed by a visual display, music, or a human voice (Rovee-Collier, 2008).

Carolyn Rovee-Collier (1987) also demonstrated how infants can retain information from the experience of being conditioned. She placed a 2½-month-old baby in a crib under an elaborate mobile (see Figure 6.4). She then tied one end of a ribbon to the baby's ankle and the other end to the mobile. Subsequently, she observed that the baby kicked and made the mobile move. The movement of the mobile was the reinforcing stimulus (which increased the baby's kicking behavior) in this experiment. Weeks later, the baby was returned to the crib, but its foot was not tied to the mobile. The baby kicked, which suggests it had retained the information that if it kicked a leg, the mobile would move.

ATTENTION

Attention, the focusing of mental resources on select information, improves cognitive processing on many tasks. Even newborns can detect a contour and fix their attention on it. Older infants scan patterns more thoroughly. By 4 months, infants can selectively attend to an object.

Attention in the first year of life is dominated by an *orienting/investigative process* (Rothbart, 2011). This process involves directing attention to potentially important locations in the environment (that is, *where*) and recognizing objects and their features (such as color and form) (that is, *what*) (Courage & Richards, 2008). Orienting attention to an object or event involves the parietal lobes in the cerebral cortex (Posner, 2003; Rothbart, 2011). (Figure 5.4 on page 138 illustrates the location of the parietal lobes in the brain.)

From 3 to 9 months of age, infants can deploy their attention more flexibly and quickly. Another important type of attention is *sustained attention,* also referred to as *focused attention* (Richards, 2010). New stimuli typically elicit an orienting response followed by sustained attention. It is sustained attention that allows infants to learn about and remember characteristics of a stimulus as it becomes familiar. Researchers have found that infants as young as 3 months of age engage in 5 to 10 seconds of sustained attention. From this age through the second year, the length of sustained attention increases (Courage & Richards, 2008).

Habituation and Dishabituation   Closely linked with attention are the processes of habituation and dishabituation, which we discussed in Chapter 5, "Physical

Development in Infancy" (Colombo, Kapa, & Curtendale, 2011). If you say the same word or show the same toy to a baby several times in a row, the baby usually pays less attention to it each time. This is *habituation*—decreased responsiveness to a stimulus after repeated presentations of the stimulus. *Dishabituation* is the increase in responsiveness after a change in stimulation. Chapter 5 described some of the measures that researchers use to study whether habituation is occurring, such as sucking behavior (sucking stops when an infant attends to a novel object), heart rates, and the length of time the infant looks at an object.

Infants' attention is strongly governed by novelty and habituation (Snyder & Torrence, 2008). When an object becomes familiar, attention becomes shorter, making infants more vulnerable to distraction. One study found that 10-month-olds were more distractible than 26-month-olds (Ruff & Capozzoli, 2003).

Researchers study habituation to determine the extent to which infants can see, hear, smell, taste, and experience touch (Colombo & Mitchell, 2009). Studies of habituation can also indicate whether infants recognize something they have previously experienced. Habituation provides a measure of an infant's maturity and well-being. Infants who have brain damage do not habituate well.

This young infant's attention is riveted on the blue toy frog that has just been placed in front of him. His attention to the toy frog will be strongly regulated by the processes of habituation and dishabituation. *What characterizes these processes?*

Knowing about habituation and dishabituation can help parents interact effectively with infants. Infants respond to changes in stimulation. Wise parents sense when an infant shows an interest and realize that they may have to repeat something many times for the infant to process information. But if the stimulation is repeated often, the infant stops responding to the parent. In parent-infant interaction, it is important for parents to do novel things and to repeat them often until the infant stops responding. The parent stops or changes behaviors when the infant redirects his or her attention (Rosenblith, 1992).

Joint Attention Another aspect of attention that is an important part of infant development is **joint attention,** in which individuals focus on the same object or event. Joint attention requires (1) an ability to track another's behavior, such as following someone's gaze; (2) one person directing another's attention; and (3) reciprocal interaction (Butterworth, 2004). Early in infancy, joint attention usually involves a caregiver pointing or using words to direct an infant's attention. Emerging forms of joint attention occur at about 7 to 8 months, but it is not until toward the end of the first year that joint attention skills are frequently observed (Heimann & others, 2006). In a study conducted by Rechele Brooks and Andrew Meltzoff (2005), at 10 to 11 months of age infants first began engaging in "gaze following," looking where another person has just looked (see Figure 6.5). And by their first birthday, infants have begun to direct adults' attention to objects that capture their interest (Heimann & others, 2006).

Joint attention plays important roles in many aspects of infant development and considerably increases infants' ability to learn from other people (Carpenter, 2011; Meltzoff, 2011). Nowhere is this more apparent than in observations of interchanges between caregivers and infants as infants are learning language (Tomasello, 2011). When caregivers and infants frequently engage in joint attention, infants say their first word earlier and develop a larger vocabulary (Carpenter, Nagell, & Tomasello, 1998; Flom & Pick, 2003; Hirotani & others, 2009). Later in the chapter in our discussion of language, we further discuss joint attention as an early predictor of language development in older infants and toddlers (Tomasello, 2011). A recent study also revealed that the extent to which 9-month-old infants engaged in joint attention was linked to their long-term memory (a one-week delay), possibly because joint attention enhances the relevance of attended items (Kopp & Lindenberger, 2011). Another recent study of 5-month-old

How Would You...?
If you were a **human development and family studies professional**, what strategies would you recommend to help parents improve an infant's development of attention?

A mother and her infant daughter engaging in joint attention. *What about this photograph tells you that joint attention is occurring? Why is joint attention an important aspect of infant development?*

joint attention Occurs when individuals focus on the same object or event and are able to track each other's behavior; one individual directs another's attention, and reciprocal interaction is present.

FIGURE 6.5

GAZE FOLLOWING IN INFANCY. Researcher Rechele Brooks shifts her eyes from the infant to a toy in the foreground (*a*). The infant then follows her eye movement to the toy (*b*). Brooks and colleague Andrew Meltzoff (2005) found that infants begin to engage in this kind of behavior called "gaze following" at 10 to 11 months of age. *Why might gaze following be an important accomplishment for an infant?*

(a) (b)

Age Group	Length of Delay
6-month-olds	24 hours
9-month-olds	1 month
10–11-month-olds	3 months
13–14-month-olds	4–6 months
20-month-olds	12 months

FIGURE 6.6

AGE-RELATED CHANGES IN THE LENGTH OF TIME OVER WHICH MEMORY OCCURS
From *Learning and the Infant Mind* edited by Amanda Woodward and Amy Needham (2008), p. 12, Table 1. © 2005 by Amanda Woodward and Amy Needham. By permission of Oxford University Press, Inc.

memory A central feature of cognitive development, involving the retention of information over time.

implicit memory Memory without conscious recollection; involves skills and routine procedures that are automatically performed.

explicit memory Conscious memory of facts and experiences.

infants found that a region of the prefrontal cortex was activated when they engaged in joint attention with another person (Grossmann & Johnson, 2010).

MEMORY

Memory involves the retention of information over time. Attention plays an important role in memory as part of a process called *encoding,* which is the process by which information gets into memory. What can infants remember, when?

Some researchers such as Rovee-Collier (2008) have concluded that infants as young as 2 to 6 months of age can remember some experiences through 1½ to 2 years of age. However, critics such as Jean Mandler (2004), a leading expert on infant cognition, argue that the infants in Rovee-Collier's experiments are displaying only implicit memory. **Implicit memory** refers to memory without conscious recollection—memories of skills and routine procedures that are performed automatically. In contrast, **explicit memory** refers to the conscious memory of facts and experiences.

When people think about memory, they are usually referring to explicit memory. Most researchers find that babies do not show explicit memory until the second half of the first year (Bauer, Larkina, & Deocampo, 2011; Bauer & others, 2003; Mandler & McDonough, 1993). Then, explicit memory improves substantially during the second year of life (Bauer, Larkina, & Deocampo, 2011; Carver & Bauer, 2001). In a longitudinal study, infants were assessed several times during their second year (Bauer & others, 2000). Older infants showed more accurate memory and required fewer prompts to demonstrate their memory than younger infants. Figure 6.6 summarizes how long infants of different ages can remember information (Bauer, 2009). As indicated in Figure 6.6, researchers have documented that 6-month-olds can remember information for 24 hours, but by 20 months of age infants can remember information they encountered 12 months earlier (Bauer, Larkina, & Deocampo, 2011).

What changes in the brain are linked to infants' memory development? From about 6 to 12 months of age, the maturation of the hippocampus and the surrounding cerebral cortex, especially the frontal lobes, makes the emergence of explicit memory possible (Morasch & Bell, 2009; Nelson, 2011) (see Figure 6.7). Explicit memory continues to improve in the second year as these brain structures further mature and connections between them increase. Less is known about the areas of the brain involved in implicit memory in infancy.

Let's examine another aspect of memory. Do you remember your third birthday party? Probably not. Most adults can remember little if anything from the first three years of their life. This is called *infantile,* or *childhood, amnesia.* The few reported adult memories of life at age 2 or 3 are at best very sketchy (Newcombe, 2008). Elementary school children also do not remember much of their early childhood years (Lie & Newcombe, 1999).

What is the cause of infantile amnesia? One reason older children and adults have difficulty recalling events from their infant and early childhood years is that during these early years the prefrontal lobes of the brain are immature; this area of the brain is believed to play an important role in storing memories of events (Boyer & Diamond, 1992).

In sum, most of young infants' conscious memories appear to be rather fragile and short-lived, although their implicit memory of perceptual-motor actions can be substantial (Bauer, Larkina, & Deocampo, 2011; Mandler, 2004). By the end of the second year, long-term memory is more substantial and reliable (Bauer, Larkina, & Deocampo, 2011).

IMITATION

Can infants imitate someone else's emotional expressions? If an adult smiles, will the baby follow with a smile? If an adult protrudes her lower lip, wrinkles her forehead, and frowns, will the baby show a sad face?

Infant development researcher Andrew Meltzoff (2004, 2007, 2011; Meltzoff & Moore, 1999; Meltzoff & Williamson, 2010) has conducted numerous studies of infants' imitative abilities. He sees infants' imitative abilities as biologically based, because infants can imitate a facial expression within the first few days after birth. He also emphasizes that the infant's imitative abilities do not resemble a hardwired response but rather involve flexibility and adaptability. In Meltzoff's observations of infants across the first 72 hours of life, the infants gradually displayed more complete imitation of an adult's facial expression, such as protruding the tongue or opening the mouth wide (see Figure 6.8).

Meltzoff (2007, 2011; Meltzoff & Williamson, 2010) concludes that infants don't blindly imitate everything they see and often make creative errors. He also argues that beginning at birth there is an interplay between learning by observing and learning by doing (Piaget emphasized learning by doing).

Not all experts on infant development accept Meltzoff's conclusions that newborns are capable of imitation. Some say that these babies were engaging in little more than automatic responses to a stimulus.

Meltzoff (2005, 2011) also has studied **deferred imitation,** which occurs after a time delay of hours or days. Piaget held that deferred imitation doesn't occur until about 18 months of age. Meltzoff's research suggested that it occurs much earlier. In one study, Meltzoff (1988) demonstrated that 9-month-old infants could imitate actions—such as pushing a recessed button in a box, which produced a beeping sound—that they had seen performed 24 hours earlier. Also, in a recent study, engagement in deferred imitation at 9 months of age was a strong predictor of more extensive production of communicative gestures at 14 months of age (Heimann & others, 2006). Two of the most common infant gestures are (1) extending the arm to show the caregiver something the infant is holding, and (2) pointing with the arm and index finger extended at some interesting object or event.

CONCEPT FORMATION

Along with attention, memory, and imitation, concepts are key aspects of infants' cognitive development (Quinn, 2011). **Concepts** are cognitive groupings of similar objects, events, people, or ideas. Without concepts, you would see each object and event as unique; you would not be able to make any generalizations.

Do infants have concepts? Yes, they do, although we do not know just how early concept formation begins (Mandler, 2009; Quinn, 2011). Using habituation experiments like those described earlier in the chapter, some researchers have found that infants as young as 3 to 4 months of age can group together objects with similar appearances, such as animals (Quinn, 2011). This research capitalizes on the knowledge that infants are more likely to look at a novel object than a familiar object.

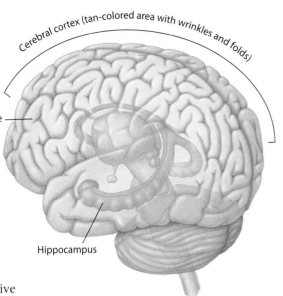

FIGURE **6.7**

KEY BRAIN STRUCTURES INVOLVED IN EXPLICIT MEMORY DEVELOPMENT IN INFANCY

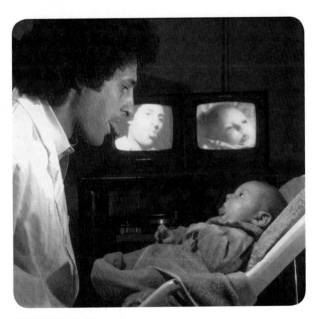

FIGURE **6.8**

INFANT IMITATION. Infant development researcher Andrew Meltzoff protrudes his tongue in an attempt to get the infant to imitate his behavior. *How do Meltzoff's findings about imitation compare with Piaget's descriptions of infants' abilities?*

deferred imitation Imitation that occurs after a delay of hours or days.

concepts Cognitive groupings of similar objects, events, people, or ideas.

FIGURE **6.9**

CATEGORIZATION IN 9- TO 11- MONTH-OLDS. These are the stimuli used in the study that indicated 9- to 11-month-old infants categorize perceptually similar objects as different (birds and planes) (Mandler & McDonough, 1993).

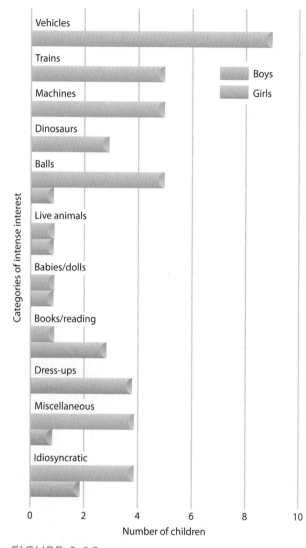

FIGURE **6.10**

CATEGORIZATION OF BOYS' AND GIRLS' INTENSE INTERESTS

> Infants are creating concepts and organizing their world into conceptual domains that will form the backbone of their thought throughout life.
>
> —JEAN MANDLER
>
> *Contemporary Psychologist,*
> *University of California–San Diego*

Jean Mandler (2004, 2009) argues that these early categorizations are best described as *perceptual categorization*. That is, the categorizations are based on similar perceptual features of objects, such as size, color, and movement, as well as parts of objects, such as legs for animals. Mandler (2004) concludes that it is not until about 7 to 9 months of age that infants form *conceptual* categories rather than just making perceptual discriminations between different categories. In one study of 9- to 11-month-olds, infants classified birds as animals and airplanes as vehicles even though the objects were perceptually similar—airplanes and birds with their wings spread (Mandler & McDonough, 1993) (see Figure 6.9).

Further advances in categorization occur in the second year of life (Booth, 2006). Many infants' "first concepts are broad and global in nature, such as 'animal' or 'indoor thing.' Gradually, over the first two years these broad concepts become more differentiated into concepts such as 'land animal,' then 'dog,' or to 'furniture,' then 'chair'" (Mandler, 2009, p. 1). Also in the second year, infants often categorize objects on the basis of their shape (Landau, Smith, & Jones, 1998).

Learning to put things into the correct categories—what makes something one kind of thing rather than another kind of thing, such as what makes a bird a bird, or a fish a fish—is an important aspect of cognitive development. As infant development researcher Alison Gopnik (2010, p. 159) recently pointed out, "If you can sort the world into the right categories—put things in the right boxes—then you've got a big advance on understanding the world."

Do some very young children develop an intense, passionate interest in a particular category of objects or activities? A study of 11-month-old to 6-year-old children confirmed that they do (DeLoache, Simcock, & Macari, 2007). A striking finding was the large gender difference in categories, with an intense interest in particular categories stronger among boys than among girls. Categorization of boys' intense interests focused on vehicles, trains, machines, dinosaurs, and balls; girls' intense interests were more likely to involve dress-ups and books/reading (see Figure 6.10). When your author's grandson Alex was 18 to 24 months old, he already had developed an intense, passionate interest in the category of vehicles. He categorized vehicles into such subcategories as cars, trucks, earthmoving equipment, and buses. In addition to common classifications of cars into police cars, jeeps, taxis, and such, and trucks into fire trucks, dump trucks, and the like, his categorical knowledge of earthmoving equipment included bulldozers and excavators, and he categorized buses into school buses, London buses, and funky Malta buses (retro buses on the island of Malta). Later, at 2 to 3 years of age,

Alex developed an intense, passionate interest in categorizing dinosaurs.

In sum, the infant's advances in processing information—through attention, memory, imitation, and concept formation—is much richer, more gradual, and less stage-like and occurs earlier than was envisioned by earlier theorists, such as Piaget (Bauer, Larkina, & Deocampo, 2011; Diamond, Casey, & Munakata, 2011; Johnson, 2011a, b; Quinn, 2011). As leading infant researcher Jean Mandler (2004) concluded, "The human infant shows a remarkable degree of learning power and complexity in what is being learned and in the way it is represented" (p. 304).

The author's grandson Alex at 2 years of age showing his intense, passionate interest in the category of vehicles while playing with a London taxi and a funky Malta bus.

How Would You...?

If you were an **educator,** how would you talk with parents about the importance of their infant developing concepts?

Review *Connect* Reflect

LG2 Describe how infants learn, remember, and conceptualize.

Review

- How do infants learn through conditioning?
- What is attention? What characterizes attention in infants?
- What is memory?
- To what extent can infants remember?
- How is imitation involved in infant learning?
- When do infants develop concepts, and how does concept formation change during infancy?

Connect

- In this section, you learned that explicit memory develops in the second year as the hippocampus and frontal lobes mature and connections between them increase. What did you learn in the text associated with Figure 5.6 in the previous chapter that might also contribute to improvements in a cognitive process like memory during this same time frame?

Reflect *Your Own Personal Journey of Life*

- If a friend told you that she remembers being abused by her parents when she was 2 years old, would you believe her? Explain your answer.

How Are Individual Differences in Infancy Assessed, and Do These Assessments Predict Intelligence?

LG3 Discuss infant assessment measures and the prediction of intelligence.

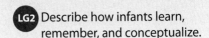

Measures of Infant Development   Predicting Intelligence

So far in this chapter, we have discussed how the cognitive development of infants generally progresses. We have emphasized what is typical of the largest number of infants or the average infant, but the results obtained for *most* infants do not apply to all infants. It is advantageous to know whether an infant is developing at a slow, normal, or advanced pace during the course of infancy. If an infant advances at an especially slow rate, then some form of enrichment may be necessary. If an infant develops at an advanced pace, parents may be advised to provide toys that stimulate cognitive growth in slightly older infants. How is an infant's cognitive development assessed?

Toosje Thyssen Van Beveren, Infant Assessment Specialist

Toosje Thyssen Van Beveren is a developmental psychologist at the University of Texas Medical Center in Dallas and a senior lecturer at the University of Texas at Dallas. She has a master's degree in child clinical psychology and a Ph.D. in human development. Recently, Van Beveren has been involved in a 12-week program called New Connections, a comprehensive intervention for young children who were affected by substance abuse prenatally and for their caregivers.

In the New Connections program, Van Beveren assesses infants' developmental status and progress. She might refer the infants to a speech, physical, or occupational therapist and monitor the infants' services and progress. Van Beveren trains the program staff and encourages them to use the exercises she recommends. She also discusses the child's problems with the primary caregivers, suggests activities, and assists them in enrolling infants in appropriate programs.

During her graduate work at the University of Texas at Dallas, Van Beveren was author John Santrock's teaching assistant in his undergraduate course on life-span development for four years. As a teaching assistant, she attended classes, graded exams, counseled students, and

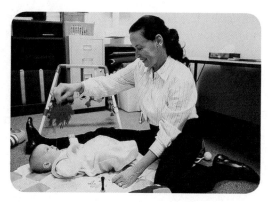

Toosje Thyssen Van Beveren conducting an infant assessment.

occasionally gave lectures. Currently, Van Beveren is a senior lecturer in the psychology department at UT–Dallas, teaching an undergraduate course in child development and a graduate course in infant development. In Van Beveren's words, "My days are busy and full. My work with infants is often challenging. There are some disappointments, but mostly the work is enormously gratifying."

MEASURES OF INFANT DEVELOPMENT

Individual differences in infant cognitive development have been studied primarily through the use of developmental scales or infant intelligence tests. For example, in Chapter 4, "Birth," we discussed the Brazelton Neonatal Behavioral Assessment Scale (NBAS) and the Neonatal Intensive Care Unit Network Neurobehavioral Scale (NNNS), which are used to evaluate newborns. To read about the work of one infant assessment specialist, see the *Connecting with Careers* profile.

The most important early contributor to the testing of infants was Arnold Gesell (1934). He developed a measure that helped to sort out potentially normal babies from abnormal ones. This was especially useful to adoption agencies, which had large numbers of babies awaiting placement. Gesell's examination was used widely for many years and still is frequently employed by pediatricians to distinguish between normal and abnormal infants. The current version of the Gesell test has four categories of behavior: motor, language, adaptive, and personal-social. The **developmental quotient (DQ)** combines subscores in these categories to provide an overall score.

The widely used **Bayley Scales of Infant Development** were developed by Nancy Bayley (1969) in order to assess infant behavior and predict later development. The current version, the Bayley Scales of Infant and Toddler Development— Third Edition (Bayley-III), has five scales: cognitive, language, motor, socio-emotional, and adaptive (Bayley, 2005). The first three scales are administered directly to the infant, the latter two are questionnaires given to the caregiver. The Bayley-III also is more appropriate for use in clinical settings than the two previous editions (Lennon & others, 2008).

How should a 6-month-old perform on the Bayley cognitive scale? The 6-month-old infant should be able to vocalize pleasure and displeasure, persistently search

developmental quotient (DQ) An overall score that combines subscores in motor, language, adaptive, and personal-social domains in the Gesell assessment of infants.

Bayley Scales of Infant Development Scales developed by Nancy Bayley that are widely used in assessing infant development. The current version, the Bayley Scales of Infant and Toddler Development—Third Edition (Bayley-III), has five components: a cognitive scale, a language scale, a motor scale, a socio-emotional scale, and an adaptive scale.

for objects that are just out of immediate reach, and approach a mirror that is placed in front of the infant by the examiner. By 12 months of age, the infant should be able to inhibit behavior when commanded to do so, imitate words the examiner says (such as *Mama*), and respond to simple requests (such as "Take a drink").

The explosion of interest in infant development has produced many new measures, especially tasks that evaluate the ways infants process information (Rose, Feldman, & Wallace, 1992). The Fagan Test of Infant Intelligence is increasingly being used (Fagan, 1992). This test focuses on the infant's ability to process information in such ways as encoding the attributes of objects, detecting similarities and differences between objects, forming mental representations, and retrieving these representations. For example, it uses the amount of time babies look at a new object compared with the amount of time they spend looking at a familiar object to estimate their intelligence.

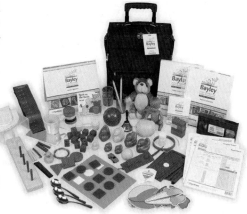

Items in the Bayley-III Scales of Infant Development.

PREDICTING INTELLIGENCE

The infant-testing movement grew out of the tradition of IQ testing. However, IQ tests of older children pay more attention to verbal ability. Tests for infants contain far more items related to perceptual-motor development and include measures of social interaction.

A recent longitudinal study examined the intelligence of 200 children from 12 months (using the Bayley scales) to 4 years (using the Stanford-Binet test) of age (Blaga & others, 2009). The results indicated considerable stability from late infancy through the preschool years. However, overall scores on tests such as the Gesell and the Bayley scales in infancy do not correlate highly with IQ scores obtained later in childhood. This is not surprising, because the components tested in infancy are not the same as the components assessed by IQ tests later in childhood.

Unlike the Gesell and Bayley scales, the Fagan test is correlated with measures of intelligence in older children. In fact, evidence is accumulating that measures of habituation and dishabituation are linked to intelligence in childhood and adolescence (Fagan, Holland, & Wheeler, 2007; Kavsek, 2004). One recent study revealed that habituation at 3 or 6 months of age was linked to verbal skills and intelligence assessed at 32 months of age (Domsch, Lohaus, & Thomas, 2009). It is important, however, not to go too far and think that connections between cognitive development in early infancy and later cognitive development are so strong that no discontinuity takes place. Some important changes in cognitive development occur after infancy, changes that we describe in later chapters.

developmental **connection**

Intelligence. The two most widely used tests of intelligence in older children, adolescents, and adults are the Stanford-Binet tests and the Wechsler scales. Chapter 12, p. 364

Review Connect Reflect

LG3 Discuss infant assessment measures and the prediction of intelligence.

Review

- What are some measures of individual differences in infancy?
- Do tests of infants predict intelligence later in life?

Connect

- In this section, you learned that measures of habituation and dishabituation are linked to intelligence. In the second section of this chapter, what advice was given to parents regarding habituation and dishabituation?

Reflect *Your Own Personal Journey of Life*

- Parents have their 1-year-old infant assessed with a developmental scale, and the infant does very well on it. How confident should they be that the infant is going to be a genius when he or she grows up?

What Is the Nature of Language, and How Does It Develop in Infancy?

LG4 Describe the nature of language and how it develops in infancy.

Defining Language

How Language Develops

An Interactionist View

Language's Rule Systems

Biological and Environmental Influences

In 1799, a nude boy was observed running through the woods in France. The boy was captured when he was 11 years old. He was called the Wild Boy of Aveyron and was believed to have lived in the woods alone for six years (Lane, 1976). When found, he made no effort to communicate. He never learned to communicate effectively. A modern-day wild child named Genie was discovered in Los Angeles in 1970. Sadly, despite intensive intervention, Genie has never acquired more than a primitive form of language. Both cases—the Wild Boy of Aveyron and Genie—raise questions about the biological and environmental determinants of language, topics that we also examine later in the chapter. First, though, we need to define language.

DEFINING LANGUAGE

Language is a form of communication—whether spoken, written, or signed—that is based on a system of symbols. Language consists of the words used by a community and the rules for varying and combining them.

Think how important language is in our everyday lives. We need language to speak with others, listen to others, read, and write. Our language enables us to describe past events in detail and to plan for the future. Language lets us pass down information from one generation to the next and create a rich cultural heritage.

Language allows us to communicate with others. *What are some important characteristics of language?*

All human languages have some common characteristics (Berko Gleason, 2009). These include infinite generativity and organizational rules. **Infinite generativity** is the ability to produce an endless number of meaningful sentences using a finite set of words and rules. Rules describe the way language works. Let's explore what these rules involve.

LANGUAGE'S RULE SYSTEMS

When nineteenth-century American writer Ralph Waldo Emerson said, "The world was built in order and the atoms march in tune," he must have had language in mind. Language is highly ordered and organized (MacWhinney, 2010). The organization involves five systems of rules: phonology, morphology, syntax, semantics, and pragmatics.

Phonology   Every language is made up of basic sounds. **Phonology** is the sound system of the language, including the sounds that are used and how they may be combined (Kuhl & Damasio, 2011; Stoel-Gammon & Sosa, 2010). For example, English has the initial consonant cluster *spr* as in *spring*, but no words begin with the cluster *rsp*.

Phonology provides a basis for constructing a large and expandable set of words out of two or three dozen phonemes. A phoneme is the basic unit of sound in a language; it is the smallest unit of sound that affects meaning. For example, in English the sound represented by the letter p, as in the words *pot* and *spot*, is a phoneme. The /p/ sound is slightly different in the two words, but this variation is not distinguished in English, and therefore the /p/ sound is a single phoneme. In some languages, such as Hindi, the variations of the /p/ sound represent separate phonemes.

language A form of communication, whether spoken, written, or signed, that is based on a system of symbols.

infinite generativity The ability to produce an endless number of meaningful sentences using a finite set of words and rules.

phonology The sound system of the language, including the sounds that are used and how they may be combined.

FRANK & ERNEST. © Thaves. Reprinted with permission.

Morphology **Morphology** refers to the units of meaning involved in word formation. A *morpheme* is a minimal unit of meaning; it is a word or a part of a word that cannot be broken into smaller meaningful parts. Every word in the English language is made up of one or more morphemes. Some words consist of a single morpheme (for example, *help*), whereas others are made up of more than one morpheme (for example, *helper* has two morphemes, *help + er,* with the morpheme *-er* meaning "one who," in this case "one who helps"). Thus, not all morphemes are words by themselves; for example, *pre-, -tion,* and *-ing* are morphemes.

Just as the rules that govern phonology describe the sound sequences that can occur in a language, the rules of morphology describe the way meaningful units (morphemes) can be combined in words (Tager-Flusberg & Zukowski, 2009). Morphemes have many jobs in grammar, such as marking tense (for example, *she walks* versus *she walked*) and number (*she walks* versus *they walk*).

Syntax **Syntax** involves the way words are combined to form acceptable phrases and sentences (Tager-Flusberg & Zukowski, 2009). If someone says to you, "Bob slugged Tom" or "Bob was slugged by Tom," you know who did the slugging and who was slugged in each case because you have a syntactic understanding of these sentence structures. You also understand that the sentence "You didn't stay, did you?" is a grammatical sentence but that "You didn't stay, didn't you?" is unacceptable and ambiguous.

If you learn another language, English syntax will not get you very far. For example, in English an adjective usually precedes a noun (as in *blue sky*), whereas in Spanish the adjective usually follows the noun (*cielo azul*). Despite the differences in their syntactic structures, however, syntactic systems in all of the world's languages have some common ground (MacWhinney, 2010). For example, no language we know of permits sentences like the following one:

The mouse the cat the farmer chased killed ate the cheese.

It appears that language users cannot process subjects and objects arranged in too complex a fashion in a sentence.

Semantics **Semantics** refers to the meaning of words and sentences (Li, 2009). Every word has a set of semantic features, which are required attributes related to meaning. *Girl* and *women,* for example, share many semantic features but differ semantically in regard to age.

Words have semantic restrictions on how they can be used in sentences (Pan & Uccelli, 2009). The sentence *The bicycle talked the boy into buying a candy bar* is syntactically correct but semantically incorrect. The sentence violates our semantic knowledge that bicycles don't talk.

Pragmatics A final set of language rules involves **pragmatics,** the appropriate use of language in different contexts. Pragmatics covers a lot of territory (Bryant, 2009). When you take turns speaking in a discussion or use a question to convey a command ("Why is it so noisy in here?" "What is this, Grand Central Station?"), you are demonstrating knowledge of pragmatics. You also apply the pragmatics of

morphology Units of meaning involved in word formation.

syntax The ways words are combined to form acceptable phrases and sentences.

semantics The meaning of words and sentences.

pragmatics The appropriate use of language in different contexts.

Rule System	Description	Examples
Phonology	The sound system of a language. A phoneme is the smallest sound unit in a language.	The word *chat* has three phonemes or sounds: /ch/ /ā/ /t/. An example of phonological rule in the English language is that while the phoneme /r/ can follow the phonemes /t/ or /d/ in an English consonant cluster (such as *track* or *drab*), the phoneme /l/ cannot follow these letters.
Morphology	The system of meaningful units involved in word formation.	The smallest sound units that have a meaning are called morphemes, or meaning units. The word *girl* is one morpheme, or meaning unit; it cannot be broken down any further and still have meaning. When the suffix *s* is added, the word becomes *girls* and has two morphemes because the *s* changed the meaning of the word, indicating that there is more than one girl.
Syntax	The system that involves the way words are combined to form acceptable phrases and sentences.	Word order is very important in determining meaning in the English language. For example, the sentence "Sebastian pushed the bike" has a different meaning than "The bike pushed Sebastian."
Semantics	The system that involves the meaning of words and sentences.	Vocabulary involves knowing the meaning of individual words. For example, semantics includes knowing the meaning of such words as *orange*, *transportation*, and *intelligent*.
Pragmatics	The system of using appropriate conversation and knowledge of how to effectively use language in context.	An example is using polite language in appropriate situations, such as being mannerly when talking with one's teacher. Taking turns in a conversation involves pragmatics.

FIGURE **6.11**

THE RULE SYSTEMS OF LANGUAGE

FIGURE **6.12**

FROM UNIVERSAL LINGUIST TO LANGUAGE-SPECIFIC LISTENER. In Patricia Kuhl's research laboratory, babies listen to tape-recorded voices that repeat syllables. When the sounds of the syllables change, the babies quickly learn to look at the bear. Using this technique, Kuhl has demonstrated that babies are universal linguists until about 6 months of age, but in the next six months become language-specific listeners. *Does Kuhl's research give support to the view that either "nature" or "nurture" is the source of language acquisition?*

English when you use polite language in appropriate situations (for example, when talking to your teacher) or tell stories that are interesting, jokes that are funny, and lies that convince. In each of these cases, you are demonstrating that you understand the rules of your culture for adjusting language to suit the context.

At this point, we have discussed five important rule systems involved in language. An overview of these rule systems is presented in Figure 6.11.

HOW LANGUAGE DEVELOPS

According to an ancient historian, in the thirteenth century Emperor Frederick II of Germany had a cruel idea. He wanted to know what language children would speak if no one talked to them. He selected several newborns and threatened their caregivers with death if they ever talked to the infants. Frederick never found out what language the children spoke because they all died. Today, we are still curious about infants' development of language, although our experiments and observations are, to say the least, far more humane than the evil Frederick's.

Whatever language they learn, infants all over the world follow a similar path in language development. What are some key milestones in this development?

Recognizing Language Sounds Long before they begin to learn words, infants can make fine distinctions among the sounds of the language. In Patricia Kuhl's (1993, 2000, 2007, 2009, 2011) research, phonemes from languages all over the world are piped through a speaker for infants to hear (see Figure 6.12). A box with a toy bear in it is placed where the infant can see it. A string of identical syllables is played, and then the syllables are changed (for example, ba ba ba ba, and then pa pa pa pa). If the infant turns its head when the syllables change, the box lights up and the bear dances and drums, and the infant is rewarded for noticing the change.

Kuhl's (2007, 2009, 2011) research has demonstrated that from birth up to about 6 months of age, infants are "citizens of the world": they recognize when sounds change most of the time, no matter what language the syllables come from. But over the next six months, infants get even better at perceiving the changes in sounds from their "own" language, the one their parents speak, and they gradually lose the ability to recognize differences that are not important in their own language.

Babbling and Other Vocalizations Long before infants speak recognizable words, they produce a number of vocalizations (Sachs, 2009). The functions of these early vocalizations are to practice making sounds, to communicate, and to attract attention (Lock & Zukow-Goldring, 2010). Babies' sounds go through this sequence during the first year:

- *Crying.* Babies cry even at birth. Crying can signal distress, but as we will discuss in Chapter 7, "Socioemotional Development in Infancy," different types of cries signal different things.

- *Cooing.* Babies first coo at about 1 to 2 months. These gurgling sounds are made in the back of the throat and usually express pleasure during interaction with the caregiver.

- *Babbling.* In the middle of the first year babies babble— that is, they produce strings of consonant-vowel combinations, such as "ba, ba, ba, ba."

Long before infants speak recognizable words, they communicate by producing a number of vocalizations and gestures. *At approximately what ages do infants begin to produce different types of vocalizations and gestures?*

Gestures   Infants start using gestures, such as showing and pointing, at about 8 to 12 months of age. They may wave bye-bye, nod to mean "yes," show an empty cup to ask for more milk, and point to a dog to draw attention to it. Some early gestures are symbolic, as when an infant smacks her lips to indicate food/drink. Pointing is considered by language experts to be an important index of the social aspects of language, and it follows a developmental sequence from pointing without checking on adult gaze to pointing while looking back and forth between an object and the adult (Goldin-Meadow & Iverson, 2010). Lack of pointing is a significant indicator of problems in the infant's communication system (Lock & Zukow-Goldring, 2010). For example, failure to engage in pointing characterizes many autistic children. The ability to use the pointing gesture effectively improves in the second year of life as advances in other aspects of language communication occur (Colonnesi & others, 2011).

A recent study found that in families of high socioeconomic status (SES), parents were more likely to use gestures when communicating with their 14-month-old infants (Rowe & Goldin-Meadow, 2009). Further, the infants' use of gestures at 14 months of age in high-SES families was linked to a larger vocabulary at 54 months of age.

First Words   Babies understand their first words earlier than they speak them. As early as 5 months of age, infants recognize their name when someone says it. And as early as 6 months, they recognize "Mommy" and "Daddy." On the average, infants understand about 50 words at about 13 months, but they can't say this many words until about 18 months (Menyuk, Liebergott, & Schultz, 1995). Thus, in infancy *receptive vocabulary* (words the child understands) considerably exceeds *spoken vocabulary* (words the child uses).

A child's first words include those that name important people (*dada*), familiar animals (*kitty*), vehicles (*car*), toys (*ball*), food (*milk*), body parts (*eye*), clothes (*hat*), household items (*clock*), and greeting terms (*bye*). These were the first words of babies 50 years ago. They are the first words of babies today. Children often express various intentions with their single words, so that "cookie" might mean, "That's a cookie" or "I want a cookie."

The infant's spoken vocabulary rapidly increases once the first word is spoken (Fenson & others, 2007). The average 18-month-old can speak about 50 words, but the average 2-year-old can speak about 200 words. This rapid increase in vocabulary that begins at approximately 18 months is called the *vocabulary spurt* (Bloom, Lifter, & Broughton, 1985).

Like the timing of a child's first word, the timing of the vocabulary spurt varies (Lieven, 2008). Figure 6.13 shows the range for these two language milestones in 14 children. On average, these children said their first word at 13 months and had a vocabulary spurt at 19 months. However, the ages for the first word of individual children varied from 10 to 17 months and for their vocabulary spurt from 13 to 25 months.

What characterizes the infant's early word learning?

How Would You...?
If you were a **psychologist,** how would you advise parents whose 18-month-old has not yet spoken his or her first word?

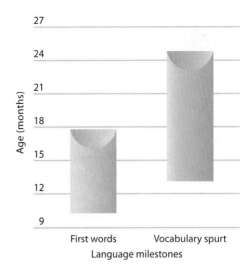

FIGURE **6.13**

VARIATION IN LANGUAGE MILESTONES. *What are some possible explanations for variations in the timing of these milestones?*

Around the world, most young children learn to speak in two-word utterances at about 18 to 24 months of age. *What are some examples of these two-word utterances?*

telegraphic speech The use of content words without grammatical markers such as articles, auxiliary verbs, and other connectives.

Cross-linguistic differences occur in word learning (Lieven & Stoll, 2010). Children learning Mandarin Chinese, Korean, and Japanese acquire more verbs earlier in their development than do children learning English. This cross-linguistic difference reflects the greater use of verbs in the language input to children in these Asian languages.

Children sometimes overextend or underextend the meanings of the words they use (Pan & Uccelli, 2009; Woodward & Markman, 1998). *Overextension* is the tendency to apply a word to objects that are inappropriate for the word's meaning. For example, children at first may say "*dada*" not only for "father" but also for other men, strangers, or boys. With time, overextensions decrease and eventually disappear. *Underextension* is the tendency to apply a word too narrowly; it occurs when children fail to use a word to name a relevant event or object. For example, a child might use the word *boy* to describe a 5-year-old neighbor but not apply the word to a male infant or to a 9-year-old male.

Two-Word Utterances   By the time children are 18 to 24 months of age, most of their communication consists of two-word utterances (Tomasello, 2011). To convey meaning with just two words, the child relies heavily on gesture, tone, and context. The wealth of meaning children can communicate with a two-word utterance includes the following (Slobin, 1972):

- Identification: "See doggie."
- Location: "Book there."
- Repetition: "More milk."
- Negation: "Not wolf."
- Possession: "My candy."
- Attribution: "Big car."
- Agent-action: "Mama walk."
- Action-direct object: "Hit you."
- Action-indirect object: "Give Papa."
- Action-instrument: "Cut knife."
- Question: "Where ball?"

These examples are from children whose first language is English, German, Russian, Finnish, Turkish, or Samoan.

Notice that the two-word utterances omit many parts of speech and are remarkably succinct. In fact, in every language, a child's first combinations of words have this economical quality; they are telegraphic. **Telegraphic speech** is the use of content words without grammatical markers such as articles, auxiliary verbs, and other connectives. Telegraphic speech is not limited to two words. "Mommy give ice cream" and "Mommy give Tommy ice cream" also are examples of telegraphic speech.

BIOLOGICAL AND ENVIRONMENTAL INFLUENCES

We have discussed a number of language milestones in infancy; Figure 6.14 summarizes the approximate time at which infants typically reach these milestones. But what makes this amazing development possible? Everyone who uses language in some way "knows" its rules and has the ability to create an infinite number of words and sentences. Where does this knowledge come from? Is it the product of biology? Is language learned and influenced by experiences?

Biological Influences   The ability to speak and understand language requires a certain vocal apparatus as well as a nervous system with certain capabilities. The nervous system and vocal apparatus of humanity's predecessors changed over

In the wild, chimps communicate through calls, gestures, and expressions, which evolutionary psychologists believe might be the roots of true language. *How strong is biology's role in language?*

Typical Age	Language Milestones
Birth	Crying
2 to 4 months	Cooing begins
5 months	Understands first word
6 months	Babbling begins
7 to 11 months	Change from universal linguist to language-specific listener
8 to 12 months	Uses gestures, such as showing and pointing / Comprehension of words appears
13 months	First word spoken
18 months	Vocabulary spurt starts
18 to 24 months	Uses two-word utterances / Rapid expansion of understanding of words

FIGURE 6.14

SOME LANGUAGE MILESTONES IN INFANCY.
Despite great variations in the language input received by infants, around the world they follow a similar path in learning to speak.

hundreds of thousands or millions of years. With advances in the nervous system and vocal structures, *Homo sapiens* went beyond the grunting and shrieking of other animals to develop speech. Although estimates vary, many experts believe that humans acquired language about 100,000 years ago, which in evolutionary time, represents a very recent acquisition. It gave humans an enormous edge over other animals and increased the chances of human survival.

Some language scholars view the remarkable similarities in how children acquire language all over the world as strong evidence that language has a biological basis. There is evidence that particular regions of the brain are predisposed to be used for language. Two regions involved in language were first discovered in studies of brain-damaged individuals: **Broca's area,** an area in the left frontal lobe of the brain involved in producing words, and **Wernicke's area,** a region of the brain's left hemisphere involved in language comprehension (see Figure 6.15). Damage to either of these areas produces types of **aphasia,** which is a loss or impairment of language processing. Individuals with damage to Broca's area have difficulty producing words correctly; individuals with damage to Wernicke's area have poor comprehension and often produce incomprehensible speech.

Linguist Noam Chomsky (1957) proposed that humans are biologically prewired to learn language at a certain time and in a certain way. He said that children are born into the world with a **language acquisition device (LAD),** a biological endowment that enables the child to detect certain features and rules of language, including phonology, syntax, and semantics. Children are prepared by nature with the ability to detect the sounds of language, for example, and to follow rules such as how to form plurals and ask questions.

Chomsky's LAD is a theoretical construct, not a physical part of the brain. Is there evidence for the existence of a LAD? Supporters of the LAD concept cite the uniformity of language milestones across languages and cultures, evidence that children create language even in the absence of well-formed input, and biological substrates of language. But, as we will see, critics argue that even if infants have something like a LAD, it cannot explain the whole story of language acquisition.

developmental connection

Brain Development. Much of language is processed in the brain's left hemisphere, although the right hemisphere is involved in some aspects of language. Chapter 5, p. 138

Broca's area An area in the brain's left frontal lobe involved in speech production.

Wernicke's area An area of the brain's left hemisphere that is involved in language comprehension.

aphasia A loss or impairment of language processing caused by brain damage in Broca's area or Wernicke's area.

language acquisition device (LAD) Chomsky's term that describes a biological endowment that enables the child to detect the features and rules of language, including phonology, syntax, and semantics.

Environmental Influences   Decades ago, behaviorists opposed Chomsky's hypothesis and argued that language represents nothing more than chains of responses acquired through reinforcement (Skinner, 1957). A baby happens to babble "Ma-ma"; Mama rewards the baby with hugs and smiles; the baby says "Mama" more and more. Bit by bit, said the behaviorists, the baby's language is built up. According to behaviorists, language is a complex learned skill, much like playing the piano or dancing.

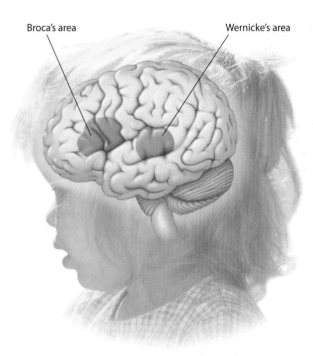

Broca's area   Wernicke's area

FIGURE **6.15**

BROCA'S AREA AND WERNICKE'S AREA. Broca's area is located in the frontal lobe of the brain's left hemisphere, and it is involved in the control of speech. Wernicke's area is a portion of the left hemisphere's temporal lobe that is involved in understanding language. *How does the role of these areas of the brain relate to lateralization, which was discussed in Chapter 5?*

FIGURE **6.16**

SOCIAL INTERACTION AND BABBLING. One study focused on two groups of mothers and their 8-month-old infants (Goldstein, King, & West, 2003). One group of mothers was instructed to smile and touch their infants immediately after the babies cooed and babbled; the other group was also told to smile and touch their infants but in a random manner, unconnected to sounds the infants made. The infants whose mothers immediately responded in positive ways to their babbling subsequently made more complex, speechlike sounds, such as "da" and "gu." The research setting for this study, which underscores how important caregivers are in the early development of language, is shown here.

There are several problems with the behaviorist view of language learning. First, it does not explain how people create novel sentences—sentences that people have never heard or spoken before. Second, children learn the syntax of their native language even if they are not reinforced for doing so. Social psychologist and psycholinguist Roger Brown (1973) spent long hours observing parents and their young children. He found that parents did not directly or explicitly reward or correct the syntax of most children's utterances. That is, parents did not say "good," "correct," "right," "wrong," and so on. Also, parents did not offer direct corrections such as "You should say two shoes, not two shoe." However, as we will see shortly, many parents do expand on their young children's grammatically incorrect utterances and recast many of those that have grammatical errors.

The behavioral view is no longer considered a viable explanation of how children acquire language. But a great deal of research describes ways in which children's environmental experiences influence their language skills (Goldstein & Schwade, 2008). Many language experts argue that a child's experiences, the particular language to be learned, and the context in which learning takes place can strongly influence language acquisition (Berko Gleason, 2009; Goldfield & Snow, 2009).

Language is not learned in a social vacuum. Most children are bathed in language from a very early age (Kuhl, 2009, 2011). The Wild Boy of Aveyron who never learned to communicate effectively had lived in social isolation for years. The support and involvement of caregivers and teachers greatly facilitate a child's language learning (Snow & Kang, 2006). For example, one study found that when mothers immediately smiled and touched their 8-month-old infants after they babbled, the infants subsequently made more complex speechlike sounds than when mothers responded to their infants in a random manner (Goldstein, King, & West, 2003) (see Figure 6.16).

Michael Tomasello (2003, 2006, 2011) stresses that young children are intensely interested in their social world and that early in their development they can understand the intentions of other people. His interaction view of language emphasizes that children learn language in specific contexts. For example, when a toddler and a father are jointly focused on a book, the father might say, "See the birdie." In this case, even a toddler understands that the father intends to name something and knows to look in the direction of the pointing. Through this kind of joint attention, early in their development children are able to use their social skills to acquire language (Carpenter, 2011; Tomasello, 2011). For example, one study revealed that joint visual attention behavior at 10 to 11 months of age (before children spoke their first words) was linked to vocabulary growth at 14, 18, and 24 months of age (Brooks & Meltzoff, 2008). Another study revealed that joint attention at 12 and 18 months predicted language skills at 24 months of age (Mundy & others, 2007).

In particular, researchers have found that the child's vocabulary development is linked to the family's socioeconomic status and the type of talk that parents direct to their children (Pan & Uccelli, 2009). To read about these links, see the *Connecting with Diversity* interlude that follows.

One intriguing component of the young child's linguistic environment is **child-directed speech,** language spoken in a higher pitch than normal with simple words and sentences (Bohannon & Bonvillian, 2009; Clark, 2009). It is hard to use child-directed speech when not in the presence of a baby. As soon as we start talking to a baby, though, most of us shift into child-directed speech. Much of this is automatic and something most parents are not aware they are doing. Even 4-year-olds speak in simpler ways to 2-year-olds than to their 4-year-old friends. Child-directed speech has the important function of capturing the infant's attention and maintaining communication (Jaswal & Fernald, 2007).

connecting with diversity

Language Environment, Poverty, and Language Development

What characteristics of a family make a difference to a child's language development? Socioeconomic status has been linked with how much parents talk to their children and with young children's vocabulary (Pan & Uccelli, 2009; Raizada & others, 2008). Betty Hart and Todd Risley (1995) observed the language environments of children whose parents were professionals and children whose parents were on welfare. Compared with the professional parents, the parents on welfare talked much less to their young children, talked less about past events, and provided less elaboration. As indicated in Figure 6.17, the children of the professional parents had a much larger vocabulary at 36 months of age than the children of the welfare parents.

Other research has linked how much mothers speak to their infants and the infants' vocabularies. For example, in one study by Janellen Huttenlocher and her colleagues (1991), infants whose mothers spoke more often to them had markedly higher vocabularies. By the second birthday, vocabulary differences were substantial.

However, a study of 1- to 3-year-old children living in low-income families found that the sheer amount of maternal talk was not the best predictor of a child's vocabulary growth (Pan & others, 2005). Rather, it was maternal language and literacy skills, and mothers' use of diverse vocabulary, that best predicted children's vocabulary development. Also, mothers who frequently used pointing gestures had children with a greater vocabulary. Pointing usually occurs in concert with speech and it may enhance the meaning of mothers' verbal input to their children.

A recent study revealed that maternal sensitivity (responds warmly to the child's bids and anticipates her child's emotional needs, for example), regardless of socioeconomic status and ethnicity, was positively linked with growth in young children's receptive and expressive language development from 18 to 36 months of age (Pungello & others, 2009). In this study, negative intrusive parenting (physically restraining the child or dominating interaction with the child with unnecessary verbal direction, for example) was related to a slower rate of growth of receptive language.

These research studies and others (NICHD Early Child Care Research Network, 2005) demonstrate the important effect that early speech input and poverty can have on the development of a child's language skills. Children in low-income families are more likely to have less educated parents, have inadequate nutrition, live in low-income communities, and attend substandard schools than children in middle- and high-income families (Snow, Burns, & Griffin, 1998). However, living in a low-income family should not be used as the sole identifier in predicting whether children will have difficulties in language development, such as a low vocabulary and reading problems. If children growing up in low-income families experience effective instruction and support, they can develop effective language skills (Barbarin & Aikens, 2009; Wasik & Newman, 2009).

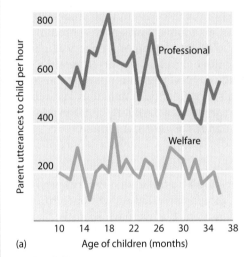

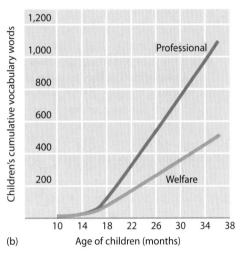

(a) Age of children (months)

(b) Age of children (months)

FIGURE **6.17**

LANGUAGE INPUT IN PROFESSIONAL AND WELFARE FAMILIES AND YOUNG CHILDREN'S VOCABULARY DEVELOPMENT. (*a*) In this study (Hart & Risley, 1995), parents from professional families talked with their young children more than parents from welfare families. (*b*) All of the children learned to talk, but children from professional families developed vocabularies that were twice as large as those from welfare families. Thus, by the time children go to preschool, they already have experienced considerable differences in language input in their families and developed different levels of vocabulary that are linked to their socioeconomic context. *Does this study indicate that poverty caused deficiencies in vocabulary development?* From Betty Hart and Todd R. Risley, *Meaningful Differences in the Everyday Experiences of Young American Children*, pp. 47, 60. © 1995 by Paul H. Brookes Publishing Co., Inc., Baltimore. Reprinted by permission of the publisher and author.

Adults often use strategies other than child-directed speech to enhance the child's acquisition of language, including recasting, expanding, and labeling:

- *Recasting* is rephrasing something the child has said, perhaps turning it into a question or restating the child's immature utterance in the form of a fully grammatical sentence. For example, if the child says, "The dog was barking,"

child-directed speech Language spoken in a higher pitch than normal, with simple words and sentences.

> The linguistics problems children have to solve are always embedded in personal and interpersonal contexts.
>
> —LOIS BLOOM
> *Contemporary Psychologist, Columbia University*

What is shared reading and how might it benefit infants and toddlers?

How Would You...?

If you were a **human development and family studies professional**, how would you encourage parents to talk with their infants and toddlers?

the adult can respond by asking, "When was the dog barking?" Effective recasting lets the child indicate an interest and then elaborates on that interest.

- *Expanding* is restating, in a linguistically sophisticated form, what a child has said. For example, a child says, "Doggie eat," and the parent replies, "Yes, the doggie is eating."
- *Labeling* is identifying the names of objects. Young children are forever being asked to identify the names of objects. Roger Brown (1958) called this "the original word game" and claimed that much of a child's early vocabulary is motivated by this adult pressure to identify the words associated with objects.

Parents use these strategies naturally and in meaningful conversations. Parents do not need to use a particular method to teach their children to talk, even for children who are slow in learning language. Children usually benefit when parents follow the child's lead, talking about things the child is interested in at the moment, and when parents provide information in ways that children can process effectively (Pan, 2008). If children are not ready to take in some information, they are likely to tell you (perhaps by turning away). Thus, giving the child more information is not always better.

Infants, toddlers, and young children benefit when adults read books to and with them (shared reading) (DeLoache & Ganea, 2009; Khandekar & others, 2011). In one study, a majority of U.S. mothers in low-income families reported that they were reading to their infants and toddlers with some regularity (Raikes & others, 2006). In this study, non-Latino White, more highly educated mothers who were parenting a firstborn child were more likely to read books to their infants and toddlers than were African American and Latino mothers who were parenting later-born children. Reading daily to children at 14 to 24 months of age was positively related to the children's language and cognitive development at 36 months of age.

Remember, the encouragement of language development, not drill and practice, is the key. Language development is not a simple matter of imitation and reinforcement. To read further about ways that parents can facilitate children's language development, see the applications in the *Caring Connections* interlude.

AN INTERACTIONIST VIEW

If language acquisition depended only on biology, then the Wild Boy of Aveyron and Genie (discussed earlier in the chapter) should have talked without difficulty. A child's experiences influence language acquisition. But we have seen that language does have strong biological foundations. No matter how much you converse with a dog, it won't learn to talk. In contrast, children are biologically prepared to learn language. Children all over the world acquire language milestones at about the same time and in about the same order. However, there are cultural variations in the type of support given to children's language development. For example, caregivers in the Kaluli culture prompt young children to use a loud voice and particular morphemes that direct the speech act performed (calling out) and to refer to names, kinship relations, and places where there has been a shared past experience that indicates a closeness to the person being addressed (Ochs & Schieffelin, 2008; Schieffelin, 2005).

Environmental influences are also very important in developing competence in language (Goldfield & Snow, 2009). Children whose parents provide them with a rich verbal environment show many positive benefits (Beatty & Pratt, 2011). Parents who pay attention to what their children are trying to say, expand their children's utterances, read to them, and label things in the environment, are providing valuable benefits for them (Berko Gleason, 2009).

An interactionist view emphasizes that both biology and experience contribute to language development. How much of the language is biologically determined and how much depends on interaction with others is a subject of debate among linguists and psychologists (Beatty & Pratt, 2011; Lieven & Stoll, 2010). However, all agree that both biological capacity and relevant experience are necessary (Berko Gleason, 2009; Howard & others, 2011).

How Parents Can Facilitate Infants' and Toddlers' Language Development

Linguist Naomi Baron (1992) in *Growing Up with Language,* and more recently Ellen Galinsky (2010) in *Mind in the Making,* provided ideas to help parents facilitate their infants' and toddlers' language development. Their suggestions are summarized below:

- *Be an active conversational partner.* Talk to your baby from the time it is born. Initiate conversation with the baby. If the baby is in a day-long child-care program, ensure that the baby receives adequate language stimulation from adults.
- *Talk in a slowed-down pace and don't worry about how you sound to other adults when you talk to your baby.* Talking in a slowed-down pace will help your baby detect words in the sea of sounds they experience. Babies enjoy and attend to the high-pitched sound of child-directed speech.
- *Use parent-look and parent-gesture, and name what you are looking at.* When you want your child to pay attention to something, look at it and point to it. Then name it, for example, saying "Look, Alex, there's an airplane."
- *When you talk with infants and toddlers, be simple, concrete, and repetitive.* Don't try to talk to them in abstract, high-level ways or think you have to say something new or different all of the time. Using familiar words often will help them remember the words.

It is a good idea for parents to begin talking to their babies at the start. The best language teaching occurs when the talking is begun before infants become capable of their first intelligible speech. *What are some other guidelines for parents to follow in helping their infants and toddlers develop their language skills?*

- *Play games.* Use word games like peek-a-boo and pat-a-cake to help infants learn words.
- *Remember to listen.* Since toddlers' speech is often slow and laborious, parents are often tempted to supply words and thoughts for them. Be patient and let toddlers express themselves, no matter how painstaking the process is or how great a hurry you are in.
- *Expand and elaborate language abilities and horizons with infants and toddlers.* Ask questions that encourage answers other than "Yes" and "No." Actively repeat, expand, and recast the utterances. Your toddler might say, "Dada." You could follow with, "Where's Dada?", and then you might continue, "Let's go find him."
- *Adjust to your child's idiosyncrasies instead of working against them.* Many toddlers have difficulty pronouncing words and making themselves understood. Whenever possible, make toddlers feel that they are being understood.
- *Resist making normative comparisons.* Be aware of the ages at which your child reaches specific milestones (such as the first word, first 50 words), but do not measure this development rigidly against that of other children. Such comparisons can bring about unnecessary anxiety.

Review *Connect* Reflect

 Describe the nature of language and how it develops in infancy.

Review

- What is language?
- What are language's rule systems?
- How does language develop in infancy?
- What are some biological and environmental influences on language?
- To what extent do biological and environmental influences interact to produce language development?

Connect

- In Chapter 1, you learned that the more years children spend living in poverty, the more their physiological indices of stress are elevated. In this chapter, you learned about the role of SES in children's language acquisition and vocabulary building. How might these factors influence children's performance when they go to school?

Reflect *Your Own Personal Journey of Life*

- Would it be a good idea for you as a parent to hold large flash cards of words in front of your baby for several hours each day to help the baby learn language and improve the baby's intelligence? Why or why not? What do you think Piaget would say about this activity?

Advances in infants' cognitive development are linked to their socioemotional development. For example, in Chapter 7 you will learn about the infant's developing social orientation and understanding, which involve perceiving people as engaging in intentional and goal-directed behavior, joint attention, and cooperation. Also in Chapter 7, you will study many aspects of the infant's emotional development, temperament, attachment, and child care. And in Chapter 9, you will read about two major theorists—Piaget and Vygotsky—and how they propose that young children's thinking advances. You will see how young children become more capable of sustaining their attention; learn about the astonishing rate at which preschool children's vocabulary expands; and explore variations in early childhood education.

looking forward – – →

reach your **learning goals**

What Is Piaget's Theory of Infant Development?

 LG1 Summarize and evaluate Piaget's theory of infant development.

Cognitive Processes

- In Piaget's theory, children construct their own cognitive worlds, building mental structures to adapt to their world. Schemes are actions or mental representations that organize knowledge. Behavioral schemes (physical activities) characterize infancy, whereas mental schemes (cognitive activities) develop in childhood. Assimilation occurs when children incorporate new information into existing schemes; accommodation refers to children's adjustment of their schemes in the face of new information. Through organization, children group isolated behaviors into a higher-order, more smoothly functioning cognitive system. Equilibration is a mechanism Piaget proposed to explain how children shift from one stage of thought to the next. As children experience cognitive conflict in trying to understand the world, they use assimilation and accommodation to obtain equilibrium. The result is a new stage of thought. According to Piaget, there are four qualitatively different stages of thought.

The Sensorimotor Stage

- In sensorimotor thought, the first of Piaget's four stages, the infant organizes and coordinates sensory experiences with physical movements. The stage lasts from birth to about 2 years of age. The sensorimotor stage has six substages: simple reflexes; first habits and primary circular reactions; secondary circular reactions; coordination of secondary circular reactions; tertiary circular reactions, novelty, and curiosity; and internalization of schemes. One key accomplishment of this stage is object permanence, the ability to understand that objects continue to exist even though the infant is no longer observing them. Another aspect involves infants' understanding of cause and effect.

Evaluating Piaget's Sensorimotor Stage

- Piaget opened up a whole new way of looking at infant development in terms of coordinating sensory input with motoric actions. In the past decades, revisions of Piaget's view have been proposed based on research. For example, researchers have found that a stable and differentiated perceptual world is established earlier than Piaget envisioned, and infants begin to develop concepts as well. The nature-nurture issue in regard to infant cognitive development continues to be debated. Spelke endorses a core knowledge approach, which states that infants are born with domain-specific innate knowledge systems. Critics argue that Spelke has not given adequate attention to early experiences that infants have.

How Do Infants Learn, Remember, and Conceptualize?

 Describe how infants learn, remember, and conceptualize.

Conditioning

- Both classical and operant conditioning occur in infants. Operant conditioning techniques have especially been useful to researchers in demonstrating infants' perception and retention of information about perceptual-motor actions.

Attention

- Attention is the focusing of mental resources on select information, and in infancy attention is closely linked with habituation. In the first year, much of attention is of the orienting/investigative type, but sustained attention also becomes important. Habituation is the repeated presentation of the same stimulus, causing reduced attention to the stimulus. If a different stimulus is presented and the infant pays increased attention to it, dishabituation is occurring. Joint attention plays an important role in infant development, especially in the infant's acquisition of language.

Memory

- Memory is the retention of information over time. Infants as young as 2 to 6 months of age can retain information about some experiences. However, many experts argue that what we commonly think of as memory (consciously remembering the past, or explicit memory) does not occur until the second half of the first year of life. By the end of the second year, explicit memory continues to improve. The hippocampus and frontal lobes of the brain are involved in development of explicit memory in infancy. The phenomenon of not being able to remember events that occurred before the age of 2 or 3—known as infantile, or childhood, amnesia—may be due to the immaturity of the prefrontal lobes of the brain at that age.

Imitation

- Meltzoff has shown that newborns can match their behaviors (such as protruding their tongue) to a model. His research also shows that deferred imitation occurs as early as 9 months of age.

Concept Formation

- Concepts are cognitive groupings of similar objects, events, people, or ideas. Mandler argues that it is not until about 7 to 9 months of age that infants form conceptual categories, although we do not know precisely when concept formation begins. Infants' first concepts are broad. Over the first two years of life, these broad concepts gradually become more differentiated. Many infants and young children develop an intense interest in a particular category (or categories).

How Are Individual Differences in Infancy Assessed, and Do These Assessments Predict Intelligence?

 Discuss infant assessment measures and the prediction of intelligence.

Measures of Infant Development

- Developmental scales for infants grew out of the tradition of IQ testing of older children. These scales are less verbal than IQ tests. Gesell's test is still widely used by pediatricians to distinguish normal and abnormal infants; it provides a developmental quotient (DQ). The Bayley scales, developed by Nancy Bayley, continue to be widely used today to assess infant development. The current version, the Bayley-III, consists of cognitive, language, motor, socioemotional, and adaptive scales. Increasingly used, the Fagan Test of Infant Intelligence assesses how effectively the infant processes information.

Predicting Intelligence

- Global scores on the Gesell and Bayley scales are not good predictors of childhood intelligence. However, measures of information processing such as speed of habituation and degree of dishabituation do correlate with intelligence later in childhood. There is both continuity and discontinuity between infant cognitive development and cognitive development later in childhood.

What Is the Nature of Language, and How Does It Develop in Infancy?

 LG4 Describe the nature of language and how it develops in infancy.

- Defining Language

- Language's Rule Systems

- How Language Develops

- Biological and Environmental Influences

- An Interactionist View

- Language is a form of communication, whether spoken, written, or signed, that is based on a system of symbols. Language consists of all the words used by a community and the rules for varying and combining them. It is marked by infinite generativity.

- Phonology is the sound system of the language, including the sounds that are used and how they may be combined. Morphology refers to the units of meaning involved in word formation. Syntax is the way words are combined to form acceptable phrases and sentences. Semantics involves the meaning of words and sentences. Pragmatics is the appropriate use of language in different contexts.

- Among the milestones in infant language development are crying (birth), cooing (1 to 2 months), babbling (6 months), making the transition from universal linguist to language-specific listener (7 to 11 months), using gestures (8 to 12 months), comprehension of words (8 to 12 months), first word spoken (13 months), vocabulary spurt (18 months), rapid expansion of understanding words (18 to 24 months), and two-word utterances (18 to 24 months).

- In evolution, language clearly gave humans an enormous advantage over other animals and increased their chance of survival. Broca's area and Wernicke's area are important locations for language processing in the brain's left hemisphere. Chomsky argues that children are born with the ability to detect basic features and rules of language. In other words, they are biologically prepared to learn language with a prewired language acquisition device (LAD). The behavioral view—that children acquire language as a result of reinforcement—has not been supported. Adults help children acquire language through child-directed speech, recasting, expanding, and labeling. Environmental influences are demonstrated by differences in the language development of children as a consequence of being exposed to different language environments in the home. Parents should talk extensively with an infant, especially about what the baby is attending to.

- Today, most language researchers believe that children everywhere arrive in the world with special social and linguistic capacities that make language acquisition possible. How much of the language is biologically determined and how much depends on interaction with others is a subject of debate among linguists and psychologists. However, all agree that both biological capacity and relevant experience are necessary.

key terms

key people

connecting with improving the lives of children

MAKING A DIFFERENCE

Nourishing the Infant's Cognitive Development

What are some good strategies for helping infants develop in cognitively competent ways?

- *Provide the infant with many play opportunities in a rich and varied environment.* Give the infant extensive opportunities to experience objects of different sizes, shapes, textures, and colors. Recognize that play with objects stimulates the infant's cognitive development.
- *Actively communicate with the infant.* Don't let the infant spend long bouts of waking hours in social isolation. Infants need caregivers who actively communicate with them. This active communication with adults is necessary for the infant's competent cognitive development.
- *Don't try to overaccelerate the infant's cognitive development.* Most experts stress that infants cognitively benefit when they learn concepts naturally. The experts emphasize that restricting infants to a passive role and showing them flash cards to accelerate their cognitive development are not good strategies.

RESOURCES

Mind in the Making
by Ellen Galinsky (2010)
New York: HarperCollins
A must-read book for parents of infants and young children. Galinsky interviewed a number of leading experts in children's

development and distilled their thoughts in easy-to-read fashion. The book provides abundant examples of how to improve infants' attention, communication, cognitive skills, and learning.

Growing Up with Language
by Naomi Baron (1992)
Reading, MA: Addison-Wesley
Baron focuses on three representative children and their families. She explores how children put their first words together, struggle to understand meaning, and use language as a creative tool. She shows parents how they play a key role in their child's language development.

How Babies Talk
by Roberta Golinkoff and Kathy Hirsh-Pasek (2000)
New York: Plume
Targeted for parents, this book by leading experts details the fascinating world of infant language. Included are activities parents can use with their infants and indicators of delayed language that can alert parents to possible language problems.

The Development of Language
by Jean Berko Gleason and Nan Ratner (7th ed., 2009)
Boston: Allyn & Bacon
A number of leading experts provide up-to-date discussion of many aspects of language development, including the development of language, language rule systems, and communication in infancy.

An increasing number of fathers are staying home to care for their children (Lamb, 2010). Consider 17-month-old Darius. On weekdays, Darius' father, a writer, cares for him during the day while his mother works full-time as a landscape architect. Darius' father is doing a great job of caring for him. He keeps Darius nearby while he is writing and spends lots of time talking to him and playing with him. From their interactions, it is clear that they genuinely enjoy each other.

Last month, Darius began spending one day a week at a child-care center. His parents carefully selected the center after observing a number of centers and interviewing teachers and center directors. His parents placed him in the center one day a week because they wanted Darius to get some experience with peers and his father to have time out from caregiving.

Darius' father looks to the future and imagines the Little League games Darius will play in and the many other activities he can enjoy with Darius. Remembering how little time his own father spent with him, he is dedicated to making sure that Darius has an involved, nurturing experience with his father.

When Darius' mother comes home in the evening, she spends considerable time with him. Darius shows a positive attachment to both his mother and his father.

Many fathers are spending more time with their infants today than in the past.

topical connections

Chapter 6 described the development of cognitive abilities in infancy, including the ability to learn, remember, and conceptualize, as well as to understand and acquire language. Until now, what you have read about socioemotional development has mainly focused on such topics as the social situations and emotions of parents before and after the arrival of their infants, including parents' feelings of joy, anticipation, anxiety, and stress during pregnancy; how a mother's optimism may lead to less adverse outcomes for her fetus; and parents' emotional and psychological adjustments during the postpartum period. In this chapter, you will study many intriguing aspects of infants' socioemotional development.

looking back

preview

In Chapters 5 and 6, you read about how the infant perceives, learns, and remembers. Infants also are socioemotional beings, capable of displaying emotions and initiating social interaction with people close to them. The main topics that we will explore are emotional understanding and attachment, and the social contexts of the family and child care.

How Do Emotions and Personality Develop in Infancy?

LG1 Discuss emotional and personality development in infancy.

Emotional Development   Temperament   Personality Development

Anyone who has been around infants for even a brief time detects that they are emotional beings. Not only do infants express emotions, but they also vary in their temperament. Some are shy and others are outgoing, for example. In this section, we explore these and other aspects of emotional and personality development in infants.

EMOTIONAL DEVELOPMENT

Imagine your life without emotion. Emotion is the color and music of life, as well as the tie that binds people together. How do psychologists define and classify emotions, and why are they important to development? How do emotions develop during the first two years of life?

Blossoms are scattered by the wind
And the wind cares nothing, but
The blossoms of the heart,
No wind can touch.

—**Yoshida Kenko**
Buddhist Monk, 14th Century

What Are Emotions?   For our purposes, we will define **emotion** as feeling, or affect, that occurs when a person is in a state or an interaction that is important to him or her, especially to his or her well-being. Psychologists classify the broad range of emotions in many ways, but almost all classifications designate an emotion as either positive or negative (Izard, 2009).

Positive emotions include enthusiasm, joy, and love. Negative emotions include anxiety, anger, guilt, and sadness. Although emotion consists of more than communication, in infancy the communication aspect is at the forefront of emotion (Witherington & others, 2010).

developmental connection

Brain Development. The maturation of the amygdala and prefrontal cortex may be linked to adolescent risk taking. Chapter 14, p. 433

Biological and Environmental Influences   Biology's importance to emotion also is apparent in the changes in a baby's emotional capacities (Bell, Greene, & Wolfe, 2010; Rothbart, 2011). Certain regions of the brain that develop early in life (such as the brain stem, hippocampus, and amygdala) play a role in distress, excitement, and rage, and even infants display these emotions (Kagan, 2010). But, as we discuss later in the chapter, infants only gradually develop the ability to regulate their emotions, and this ability seems to be tied to the gradual maturation of frontal regions of the cerebral cortex that can exert control over other areas of the brain (Zelazo, Qu, & Kesek, 2010).

Social relationships, in turn, provide the setting for the development of a rich variety of emotions (Denham & others, 2011; Thompson, 2011a, b). When toddlers hear their parents quarreling, they often react with distress and inhibit their play. Well-functioning families make each other laugh and may develop a light mood to defuse conflicts. Biological evolution has endowed human beings to be *emotional*, but embeddedness in relationships and culture with others provides diversity in emotional experiences. For example, researchers have found that East Asian infants display less frequent and less positive and negative emotions than non-Latino White

emotion Feeling, or affect, that occurs when a person is in a state or interaction that is important to him or her. Emotion can be characterized as positive (enthusiasm, joy, love, for example) or negative (anxiety, guilt, or sadness, for example).

primary emotions Emotions that are present in humans and other animals, and emerge early in life; examples are joy, anger, sadness, fear, and disgust.

infants (Cole & Tan, 2007). Throughout childhood, East Asian parents encourage their children to show emotional reserve rather than to be emotionally expressive (Cole & Tan, 2007). Further, Japanese parents try to prevent children from experiencing negative emotions, whereas non-Latino White mothers more frequently respond after their children become distressed and then help them cope (Rothbaum & Trommsdorff, 2007). In sum, biological evolution has endowed human beings to be emotional, but culture and relationships with others provide diversity in emotional experiences (Eisenberg, 2010; Super & Harkness, 2010; Thompson, 2011b).

Early Emotions A leading expert on infant emotional development, Michael Lewis (2007, 2008, 2010) distinguishes between primary emotions and self-conscious emotions. **Primary emotions** are emotions that are present in humans and other animals; these emotions appear in the first six months of the human infant's development. Primary emotions include surprise, interest, joy, anger, sadness, fear, and disgust (see Figure 7.1 for infants' facial expressions of some of these early emotions). In Lewis' classification, **self-conscious emotions** require self-awareness that involves consciousness and a sense of "me." Self-conscious emotions include jealousy, empathy, embarrassment, pride, shame, and guilt—most of these occurring for the first time at some point in the second half of the first year through the second year.

Researchers such as Joseph Campos (2005) and Michael Lewis (2007, 2010) debate about how early in the infant and toddler years various emotions first appear and in what sequence. As an indication of the controversy regarding when certain emotions first are displayed by infants, consider jealousy. Some researchers argue that jealousy does not emerge until approximately 18 months of age (Lewis, 2007), whereas others emphasize that it is displayed much earlier (Draghi-Lorenz, 2007). Some research studies suggest that the appearance of jealousy might occur as early as 6 months of age (Hart & others, 2004). In one study, 6-month-old infants observed their mothers giving attention either to a lifelike baby doll (hugging or gently rocking it, for example) or to a book. When mothers directed their attention to the doll, the infants were more likely to display negative emotions, such as anger and sadness, which may have indicated their jealousy (Hart & Carrington, 2002) (see Figure 7.2). On the other hand, their expressions of anger and sadness simply may have reflected frustration in not being able to have the novel doll to play with.

Debate about the onset of an emotion such as jealousy illustrates the complexity and difficulty of indexing early emotions. That said, some experts on infant socioemotional development, such as Jerome Kagan (2010), conclude that the structural immaturity of the infant brain make it unlikely that emotions which require thought—such as guilt, pride, despair, shame, empathy, and jealousy—can be experienced in the first year. Thus, both Kagan (2010) and Campos (2009) argue that so-called "self-conscious" emotions don't occur until after the first year, which increasingly reflects the view of most developmental psychologists. Thus, in regard to the photograph in Figure 7.2, it is unlikely that the 6-month-old infant is experiencing jealousy.

Emotional Expression and Social Relationships Emotional expressions are involved in infants' first relationships. The ability of infants to communicate emotions permits coordinated interactions with their caregivers and the beginning of an emotional bond between them (Thompson, 2010, 2011a, b, 2012). Not only do parents change their emotional expressions in response to infants' emotional expressions, but infants also modify their emotional expressions in response to their parents' emotional expressions. In other words, these

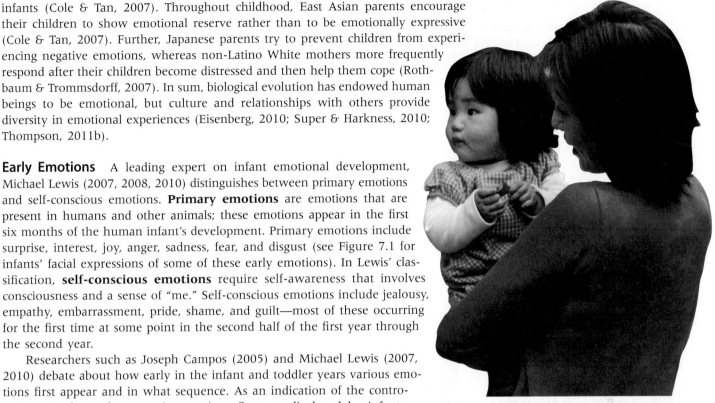

How do Japanese mothers handle their infants' and children's emotional development differently from non-Latino White mothers?

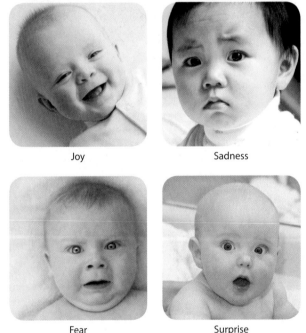

Joy   Sadness

Fear   Surprise

FIGURE **7.1**

EXPRESSION OF DIFFERENT EMOTIONS IN INFANTS

self-conscious emotions Emotions that require self-awareness, especially consciousness and a sense of "me"; examples include jealousy, empathy, and embarrassment.

FIGURE **7.2**

IS THIS THE EARLY EXPRESSION OF JEALOUSY? In the study by Hart and Carrington (2002), the researchers concluded that the 6-month-old infants who observed their mothers giving attention to a baby doll displayed negative emotions—such as anger and sadness—which may indicate the early appearance of jealousy. However, experts on emotional development, such as Joseph Campos (2009) and Jerome Kagan (2010), argue that it is unlikely emotions such as jealousy appear in the first year. *Why do they conclude that it is unlikely jealousy occurs in the first year?*

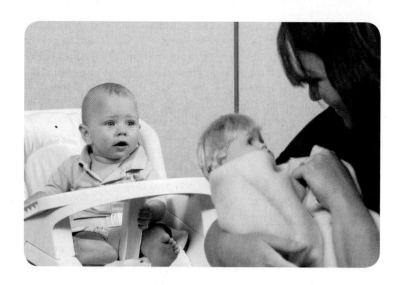

What are some different types of cries?

How Would You...?

If you were a **human development and family studies professional,** how would you respond to the parents of a 13-month-old baby who are concerned because their son has suddenly started crying every morning when they drop him off at child care—despite the fact that he has been going to the same child-care center for over six months?

basic cry A rhythmic pattern usually consisting of a cry, a briefer silence, a shorter inspiratory whistle that is higher pitched than the main cry, and then a brief rest before the next cry.

anger cry A cry similar to the basic cry, with more excess air forced through the vocal cords.

pain cry A sudden appearance of a long, initial loud cry without preliminary moaning, followed by breath holding.

interactions are mutually regulated. Because of this coordination, the interactions are described as reciprocal, or synchronous, when all is going well. Sensitive, responsive parents help their infants grow emotionally, whether the infants respond in distressed or happy ways (Thompson & Waters, 2011).

Cries and smiles are two emotional expressions that infants display when interacting with parents. These are babies' first forms of emotional communication.

Crying   Crying is the most important mechanism newborns have for communicating with their world. The first cry verifies that the baby's lungs have filled with air. Cries also may provide information about the health of the newborn's central nervous system. Newborns even tend to respond with cries and negative facial expressions when they hear other newborns cry (Dondi, Simion, & Caltran, 1999).

Babies have at least three types of cries:

- **Basic cry.** A rhythmic pattern that usually consists of a cry, followed by a briefer silence, then a shorter inspiratory whistle that is somewhat higher in pitch than the main cry, then another brief rest before the next cry. Some infancy experts stress that hunger is one of the conditions that incite the basic cry.

- **Anger cry.** A variation of the basic cry in which more excess air is forced through the vocal cords.

- **Pain cry.** A sudden long, initial loud cry followed by breath holding; no preliminary moaning is present. The pain cry is triggered by a high-intensity stimulus.

Most adults can determine whether an infant's cries signify anger or pain (Zeskind, 2007). Parents can distinguish the cries of their own baby better than those of another baby.

Smiling   Smiling is critical as a means of developing a new social skill and is a key social signal (Witherington & others, 2010). Two types of smiling can be distinguished in infants:

- **Reflexive smile.** A smile that does not occur in response to external stimuli and appears during the first month after birth, usually during sleep.

- **Social smile.** A smile that occurs in response to an external stimulus, typically a face in the case of the young infant. Social smiling occurs as early as 4 to 6 weeks of age in response to a caregiver's voice.

The infant's social smile can have a powerful impact on caregivers (Witherington & others, 2010). Following weeks of endless demands, fatigue, and little reinforcement, an infant starts smiling at them and all of the caregivers' efforts are rewarded.

Fear One of a baby's earliest emotions is fear, which typically first appears at about 6 months of age and peaks at about 18 months. However, abused and neglected infants can show fear as early as 3 months (Witherington & others, 2010). Researchers have found that infant fear is linked to guilt, empathy, and low aggression at 6 to 7 years of age (Rothbart, 2011).

The most frequent expression of an infant's fear involves **stranger anxiety,** in which an infant shows a fear and wariness of strangers. Stranger anxiety usually emerges gradually. It first appears at about 6 months of age in the form of wary reactions. By age 9 months, the fear of strangers is often more intense, reaching a peak toward the end of the first year of life (Scher & Harel, 2008).

Not all infants show distress when they encounter a stranger. Besides individual variations, whether an infant shows stranger anxiety also depends on the social context and the characteristics of the stranger (Kagan, 2008).

Infants show less stranger anxiety when they are in familiar settings. It appears that, when infants feel secure, they are less likely to show stranger anxiety.

In addition to stranger anxiety, infants experience fear of being separated from their caregivers. The result is **separation protest**—crying when the caregiver leaves. Separation protest is initially displayed by infants at approximately 7 to 8 months and peaks at about 15 months (Kagan, 2008). One study revealed that separation protest peaked at about 13 to 15 months in four different cultures (Kagan, Kearsley, & Zelazo, 1978). As indicated in Figure 7.3, the percentage of infants who engaged in separation protest varied across cultures, but the infants reached a peak of protest at about the same age—just before the middle of the second year of life.

Emotional Regulation and Coping During the first year of life, the infant gradually develops an ability to inhibit, or minimize, the intensity and duration of emotional reactions (Calkins & Markovitch, 2010). From early in infancy, babies put their thumbs in their mouths to soothe themselves. But at first, infants mainly depend on caregivers to help them soothe their emotions, as when a caregiver rocks an infant to sleep, sings lullabies to the infant, gently strokes the infant, and so on.

Later in infancy, when they become aroused, infants sometimes redirect their attention or distract themselves in order to reduce their arousal. By 2 years of age, toddlers can use language to define their feeling states and the context that is upsetting them (Kopp, 2008). A toddler might say, "Feel bad. Dog scare." This type of communication may allow caregivers to help the child in regulating emotion.

Contexts can influence emotional regulation (Thompson, 2010, 2011a, b). Infants are often affected by fatigue, hunger, time of day, which people are around them, and where they are. Infants must learn to adapt to different contexts that require emotional regulation. Further, new demands appear as the infant becomes older and parents modify their expectations. For example, a parent may take it in stride if a 6-month-old infant screams in a grocery store but may react very differently if a 2-year-old starts screaming.

To soothe or not to soothe—should a crying baby be given attention and soothed, or does this attention spoil the infant? Many years ago, the behaviorist John Watson (1928) argued that parents spend too much time responding to infant crying. As a consequence, he said, parents reward crying and increase its incidence. Some researchers, such as Jacob Gewirtz, have found that a caregiver's quick, soothing

He who binds to himself a joy.
Does the winged life destroy;
But he who kisses the joy as it flies
Lives in eternity's sun rise.

—**WILLIAM BLAKE**
English Poet, 19th Century

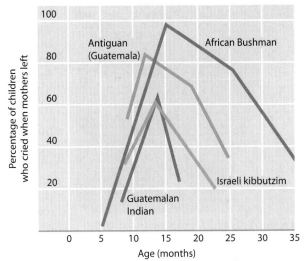

FIGURE **7.3**

SEPARATION PROTEST IN FOUR CULTURES. Note that separation protest peaked at about the same time in all four cultures in this study (13 to 15 months of age) (Kagan, Kearsley, & Zelazo, 1978). However, a higher percentage (100 percent) of infants in an African Bushman culture engaged in separation protest compared to only about 60 percent of infants in Guatemalan Indian and Israeli kibbutzim cultures. *What might explain the fact that separation protest peaks at about the same time in these cultures?*
Reprinted by permission of the publisher from *Infancy: It's Place in Human Development* by J. Kagan, R. B. Kearsley, and P. R. Zelazo, p. 107, Harvard University Press, © 1978 by the President and Fellows of Harvard College.

How Would You…?

If you were a **social worker,** how would you advise a parent who is frustrated with her 18-month-old child because she tends to whine and cry excessively compared to her 3-year-old sibling?

reflexive smile A smile that does not occur in response to external stimuli. It happens during the month after birth, usually during sleep.

social smile A smile in response to an external stimulus, which, early in development, typically is a face.

stranger anxiety An infant's fear and wariness of strangers; it tends to appear in the second half of the first year of life.

separation protest An infant's distressed reaction when the caregiver leaves.

response to crying increased crying (Gewirtz, 1977). However, infancy experts Mary Ainsworth (1979) and John Bowlby (1989) stress that you can't respond too much to infant crying in the first year of life. They argue that a quick, comforting response to the infant's cries is an important ingredient in the development of a strong bond between the infant and caregiver. In one of Ainsworth's studies, infants whose mothers responded quickly when they cried at 3 months of age cried less later in the first year of life (Bell & Ainsworth, 1972).

Controversy still characterizes the question of whether or how parents should respond to an infant's cries. Some developmentalists argue that an infant cannot be spoiled in the first year of life, a view suggesting that parents should soothe a crying infant. This reaction should help infants develop a sense of trust and secure attachment to the caregiver. A recent study revealed that mothers' emotional reactions (anger and anxiety) to crying increased the risk of subsequent attachment insecurity (Leerkes, Parade, & Gudmundson, 2011).

TEMPERAMENT

Do you get upset a lot? Does it take much to get you angry, or to make you laugh? Even at birth, babies seem to have different emotional styles. One infant is cheerful and happy much of the time; another baby seems to cry constantly. These tendencies reflect **temperament,** which involves individual differences in behavioral styles, emotions, and characteristic ways of responding. With regard to its link to emotion, temperament refers to individual differences in how quickly the emotion is shown, how strong it is, how long it lasts, and how quickly it fades away (Campos, 2009).

Describing and Classifying Temperament   How would you describe your temperament or the temperament of a friend? Researchers have described and classified the temperament of individuals in different ways. Here we examine three of those ways.

Chess and Thomas' Classification   Psychiatrists Alexander Chess and Stella Thomas (Chess & Thomas, 1977; Thomas & Chess, 1991) identified three basic types, or clusters, of temperament:

- An **easy child** is generally in a positive mood, quickly establishes regular routines in infancy, and adapts easily to new experiences.
- A **difficult child** reacts negatively and cries frequently, engages in irregular daily routines, and is slow to accept change.
- A **slow-to-warm-up child** has a low activity level, is somewhat negative, and displays a low intensity of mood.

Should a crying baby be given attention and soothed, or does this spoil the infant? Should the infant's age, the type of cry, and the circumstances be considered?

"Oh, he's cute, all right, but he's got the temperament of a car alarm."
© Barbara Smaller/The New Yorker Collection/ www.cartoonbank.com

temperament An individual's behavioral style and characteristic way of emotionally responding.

easy child A child who is generally in a positive mood, who quickly establishes regular routines in infancy, and who adapts easily to new experiences.

difficult child A child who tends to react negatively and cry frequently, who engages in irregular daily routines, and who is slow to accept new experiences.

slow-to-warm-up child A child who has a low activity level, is somewhat negative, and displays a low intensity of mood.

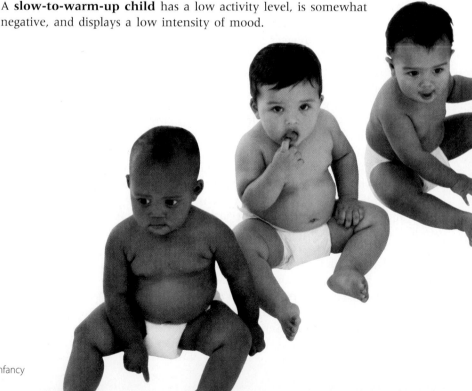

In their longitudinal investigation, Chess and Thomas found that 40 percent of the children they studied could be classified as easy, 10 percent as difficult, and 15 percent as slow to warm up. Notice that 35 percent did not fit any of the three patterns. Researchers have found that these three basic clusters of temperament are moderately stable across the childhood years. A recent study revealed that young children with a difficult temperament showed more problems when they experienced low-quality child care and fewer problems when they experienced high-quality child care than did young children with an easy temperament (Pluess & Belsky, 2009).

Kagan's Behavioral Inhibition   Another way of classifying temperament focuses on the differences between a shy, subdued, timid child and a sociable, extraverted, bold child (Asendorph, 2008). Jerome Kagan (2002, 2008, 2010) regards shyness with strangers (peers or adults) as one feature of a broad temperament category called *inhibition to the unfamiliar.* Beginning about 7 to 9 months, inhibited children react to many aspects of unfamiliarity with initial avoidance, distress, or subdued affect. In Kagan's research, inhibition shows some continuity from infancy through early childhood, although a substantial number of infants who are classified as inhibited become less so by 7 years of age.

Rothbart and Bates' Classification   New classifications of temperament continue to be forged. Mary Rothbart and John Bates (2006) argue that three broad dimensions best represent what researchers have found to characterize the structure of

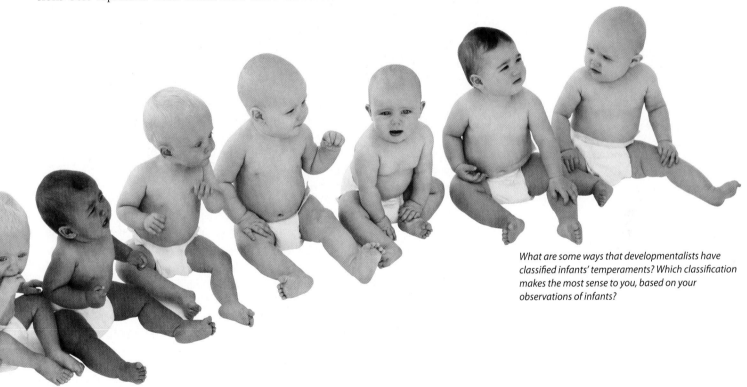

What are some ways that developmentalists have classified infants' temperaments? Which classification makes the most sense to you, based on your observations of infants?

temperament: extraversion/surgency, negative affectivity, and effortful control (self-regulation):

- *Extraversion/surgency* includes "positive anticipation, impulsivity, activity level, and sensation seeking" (Rothbart, 2004, p. 495). Kagan's uninhibited children fit into this category.

- *Negative affectivity* includes "fear, frustration, sadness, and discomfort" (Rothbart, 2004, p. 495). These children are easily distressed; they may fret and cry often. Kagan's inhibited children fit this category.

- *Effortful control* (self-regulation) includes "attentional focusing and shifting, inhibitory control, perceptual sensitivity, and low-intensity pleasure" (Rothbart, 2004, p. 495). Infants who are high on effortful control show an ability to keep their arousal from getting too high and have strategies for soothing themselves. By contrast, children low on effortful control are often unable to control their arousal; they become easily agitated and intensely emotional.

The description of temperament categories so far reflects the development of normative capabilities of children, not individual differences in children. The development of these capabilities, such as effortful control, allows individual differences to emerge (Bates, 2008; Bates, Schermerhorn, & Goodnight, 2010). For example, although maturation of the brain's prefrontal lobes must occur for any child's attention to improve and the child to achieve effortful control, some children develop effortful control but others do not. And it is these individual differences in children that are at the heart of what temperament is (Bates, 2008; Bates, Schermerhorn, & Goodnight, 2010).

Biological Foundations and Experience   How does a child acquire a certain temperament? Kagan (2002, 2008, 2010) argues that children inherit a physiology that biases them to have a particular type of temperament. However, through experience they may learn to modify their temperament to some degree (Thompson, Winer, & Goodvin, 2010). For example, children may inherit a physiology that biases them to be fearful and inhibited, but they learn to reduce their fear and inhibition to some degree.

Physiological characteristics have been linked with different temperaments. In particular, an inhibited temperament is associated with a unique physiological pattern that includes high and stable heart rate, high level of the hormone cortisol, and high activity in the right frontal lobe of the brain (Kagan, 2008). This pattern may be tied to the excitability of the amygdala, a structure of the brain that plays an important role in fear and inhibition. And the development of effortful control is linked to advances in the brain's frontal lobes (Bates, 2008).

developmental **connection**

Nature and Nurture. Twin and adoption studies have been used in the effort to sort out hereditary and environmental influences on development. Chapter 2, p. 74

What is heredity's role in the biological foundations of temperament? Twin and adoption studies suggest that heredity has a moderate influence on differences in temperament within a group of people (Buss & Goldsmith, 2007).

Developmental Links   Is temperament in childhood linked with adjustment in adulthood? In one study, children who had an easy temperament at 3 to 5 years of age were likely to be well adjusted as young adults (Chess & Thomas, 1977). In contrast, many children who had a difficult temperament at 3 to 5 years of age were not well adjusted as young adults. Also, other researchers have found that boys with a difficult temperament in childhood are less likely as adults to continue their formal education, whereas girls with a difficult temperament in childhood are more likely to experience marital conflict as adults (Wachs, 2000).

Inhibition is another temperament characteristic that has been studied extensively (Kagan, 2008, 2010). A recent study revealed that behavioral inhibition at 3 years of age was linked to shyness four years later (Volbrecht & Goldsmith, 2010). Also, research indicates that individuals with an inhibited temperament in childhood are less likely as adults to be assertive or to experience social support, and more likely to delay entering a stable job track (Asendorph, 2008). In the Uppsala (Sweden) Longitudinal Study, shyness/inhibition in infancy/childhood was linked to social anxiety at 21 years of age (Bohlin & Hagekull, 2009).

In sum, these studies reveal some continuity between certain aspects of temperament in childhood and adjustment in early adulthood (Rothbart, 2011; Wachs

& Bates, 2010). However, keep in mind that these connections between childhood temperament and adult adjustment are based on only a small number of studies; more research is needed to verify these linkages.

Developmental Contexts   What accounts for the continuities and discontinuities between a child's temperament and an adult's personality? Physiological and heredity factors likely are involved in continuity. Links between temperament in childhood and personality in adulthood also might vary, depending on the contexts in individuals' experience (Bates, Schermerhorn, & Goodnight, 2010; Wachs & Bates, 2010).

The reaction to an infant's temperament may depend, in part, on culture (Chen & others, 2011; Fung, 2011; Super & Harkness, 2010). For example, behavioral inhibition is more highly valued in China than in North America, and researchers have found that Chinese infants are more inhibited than Canadian infants (Chen & others, 1998). The cultural differences in temperament were linked to parental attitudes and behaviors. Canadian mothers of inhibited 2-year-olds were less accepting of their infants' inhibited temperament, whereas Chinese mothers were more accepting.

In short, many aspects of a child's environment can encourage or discourage the persistence of temperament characteristics (Rothbart, 2011; Rothbart & Bates, 2006; Wachs & Bates, 2010). One useful way of thinking about these relationships applies the concept of goodness of fit, which we examine next.

Goodness of Fit and Parenting   **Goodness of fit** refers to the match between a child's temperament and the environmental demands the child must cope with. Some temperament characteristics pose greater parenting challenges than others, at least in modern Western societies (Bates, Schermerhorn, & Goodnight, 2010; Rothbart, 2011). When children are prone to distress, as exhibited by frequent crying and irritability, their parents may eventually respond by ignoring the child's distress or trying to force the child to "behave." In one research study, though, extra support and training for mothers of distress-prone infants improved the quality of mother-infant interaction (van den Boom, 1989).

To read further about some positive strategies for parenting that take into account the child's temperament, see the *Caring Connections* interlude.

PERSONALITY DEVELOPMENT

Emotions and temperament form key aspects of personality—the enduring personal characteristics of individuals. Let's now examine characteristics that often are thought of as central to personality development during infancy: trust and the development of self and independence.

Trust   According to Erik Erikson (1968), the first year of life is characterized by the trust versus mistrust stage of development. Following a life of regularity, warmth, and protection in the mother's womb, the infant faces a world that is less secure. Erikson proposed that infants learn trust when they are cared for in a consistent, warm manner. If the infant is not well fed and kept warm on a consistent basis, a sense of mistrust is likely to develop.

Trust versus mistrust is not resolved once and for all in the first year of life. It arises again at each successive stage of development, a pathway that can have positive or negative outcomes. For example, children who leave infancy with a sense of trust can still have their sense of mistrust activated at a

An infant's temperament can vary across cultures. *What do parents need to know about a child's temperament?*

developmental **connection**

Culture. Cross-cultural studies seek to determine culture-universal and culture-specific aspects of development. Chapter 1, p. 10

How Would You...?

If you were a **social worker,** how would you apply information about an infant's temperament to maximize the goodness of fit in a clinical setting?

developmental **connection**

Personality. Erikson proposed that individuals go through eight stages in the course of human development. Chapter 1, p. 22

goodness of fit Refers to the match between a child's temperament and the environmental demands with which the child must cope.

Parenting and the Child's Temperament

What are the implications of temperamental variations for parenting? Although answers to this question necessarily are speculative, the following conclusions regarding the best parenting strategies to use in relation to children's temperament were reached by temperament experts Ann Sanson and Mary Rothbart (1995):

- *Attention to and respect for individuality.* One implication is that it is difficult to generate general prescriptions for "good" parenting. A goal might be accomplished in one way with one child and in another way with another child, depending on the child's temperament. Parents need to be sensitive and flexible to the infant's signals and needs. Researchers have found that decreases in infant negative emotionality are related to higher levels of parents' sensitivity, involvement, and responsiveness (Wachs & Bates, 2010).

- *Structuring the child's environment.* Crowded, noisy environments can pose greater problems for some children (such as "difficult" children) than others (such as "easygoing" children). We might also expect that a fearful, withdrawing child would benefit from slower entry into new contexts.

- *The "difficult child" and packaged parenting programs.* Programs for parents often focus on dealing with children who have "difficult" temperaments. In some cases, "difficult child" refers to Thomas and Chess' description of a child who reacts negatively, cries frequently, engages in irregular daily routines, and is slow to accept change. In others, the concept might be used to describe a child who is irritable, displays anger frequently, does not follow directions well, or shows some other negative characteristic. Acknowledging that some children are harder than others to parent is often helpful, and advice on how to handle specific difficult characteristics can be useful. However, whether a specific characteristic is difficult depends on its fit with the environment. To label a child "difficult" has the danger of becoming a self-fulfilling prophecy. If a child is identified as "difficult," people may treat the child in a way that actually elicits "difficult" behavior.

Too often, we pigeonhole children into categories without examining the context (Rothbart, 2011; Rothbart & Bates, 2006). Nonetheless, caregivers need to take children's temperament into account. Research does not yet allow for many highly specific recommendations, but, in general, caregivers should (1) be sensitive to the individual characteristics of the child, (2) be flexible in responding to these characteristics, and (3) avoid applying negative labels to the child.

What are some good strategies for parents to adopt when responding to their infant's temperament?

later stage, perhaps if their parents are separated or divorced under conflictual circumstances.

The Developing Sense of Self Real or imagined, the sense of self is a strong motivating force in life. When does the individual begin to sense a separate existence from others?

Studying the self in infancy is difficult mainly because infants cannot tell us how they experience themselves. Infants cannot verbally express their views of the self. They also cannot understand complex instructions from researchers.

One ingenious strategy to test infants' visual self-recognition is the use of a mirror technique, in which an infant's mother first puts a dot of rouge on the infant's nose. Then an observer watches to see how often the infant touches its nose. Next, the infant is placed in front of a mirror, and observers detect whether nose touching increases. Why does this matter? The idea is that increased nose touching indicates that the infant recognizes the self in the mirror and is trying to touch or rub off the rouge because the rouge violates the infant's view of the self. Increased touching indicates that the infant realizes that it is the self in the

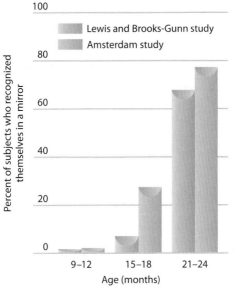

FIGURE **7.4**

THE DEVELOPMENT OF SELF-RECOGNITION IN INFANCY. The graph shows the findings of two studies in which infants less than 1 year of age did not recognize themselves in the mirror. A slight increase in the percentage of infant self-recognition occurred around 15 to 18 months of age. By 2 years of age, a majority of children recognized themselves. *Why do researchers study whether infants recognize themselves in a mirror?*

mirror but that something is not right since the real self does not have a dot of rouge on it.

Figure 7.4 displays the results of two investigations that used the mirror technique. The researchers found that before they were 1 year old, infants did not recognize themselves in the mirror (Amsterdam, 1968; Lewis & Brooks-Gunn, 1979). Signs of self-recognition began to appear among some infants when they were 15 to 18 months old. By the time they were 2 years old, most children recognized themselves in the mirror. In sum, infants begin to develop a self-understanding called self-recognition at approximately 18 months of age (Hart & Karmel, 1996; Lewis, 2005).

Late in the second year and early in the third year, toddlers show other emerging forms of self-awareness that reflect a sense of "me" (Thompson, Winer, & Goodvin, 2011). For example, they refer to themselves by saying "Me big"; they label internal experiences such as emotions; they monitor themselves as when a toddler says, "Do it myself"; and they say that things are theirs (Bullock & Lutkenhaus, 1990; Fasig, 2000). A recent study revealed that it is not until the second year that infants develop a conscious awareness of their own bodies (Brownell & others, 2009). This developmental change in body awareness marks the beginning of children's representation of their own three-dimensional body shape and appearance, providing an early step in the development of their self-image and identity (Brownell, 2011).

How Would You...?
If you were a **human development and family studies professional,** how would you work with a parent who shows signs of being overly protective or critical to the point of impairing the toddler's independence?

Independence   Not only does the infant develop a sense of self in the second year of life, but independence also becomes a more central theme in the infant's life (Mangelsdorf & Wong, 2008). The theories of Margaret Mahler and Erik Erikson have important implications for both self-development and independence. Mahler (1979) argues that the child goes through a separation and then an individuation process. *Separation* involves the infant's movement away from the mother. *Individuation* involves the development of self.

Erikson (1968), like Mahler, stressed that independence is an important issue in the second year of life. Erikson describes the second stage of development as the stage of autonomy versus shame and doubt. Autonomy builds as the infant's mental and motor abilities develop. At this point in development, not only can infants walk, but they can also climb, open and close, drop, push and pull, and hold and let go. Infants feel pride in these new accomplishments and want to do everything themselves, whether the activity is flushing a toilet, pulling the wrapping off a package,

Erikson argued that autonomy versus shame and doubt is the key developmental theme of the toddler years. *What are some good strategies for parents to use with their toddlers?*

or deciding what to eat. It is important for parents to recognize the motivation of toddlers to do what they are capable of doing at their own pace. Then they can learn to control their muscles and their impulses themselves. But when caregivers are impatient and do for toddlers what they are capable of doing themselves, shame and doubt develop. Every parent has rushed a child from time to time. It is only when parents consistently overprotect toddlers or criticize accidents (wetting, soiling, spilling, or breaking, for example) that children develop an excessive sense of shame and doubt about their ability to control themselves and their world. As we discuss in later chapters, Erikson argued that the stage of autonomy versus shame and doubt has important implications for the individual's future development.

developmental **connection**

Personality. Two key points in development when there is a strong push for independence are the second year of life and early adolescence. Chapter 16, p. 149

Review *Connect* Reflect

LG1 Discuss emotional and personality development in infancy.

Review

- What is the nature of an infant's emotions, and how do they change?
- What is temperament, and how does it develop in infancy?
- What are some important aspects of personality in infancy, and how do they develop?

Connect

- Earlier in this section, you read that the early development of the hippocampus in infants plays a role in their emotions. In Chapter 5, you also learned that the hippocampus is also connected to another key cognitive process. What is that process?

Reflect *Your Own Personal Journey of Life*

- How would you describe your temperament? Does it fit one of Chess and Thomas' three styles—easy, slow to warm up, or difficult? If you have siblings, is your temperament similar to or different from theirs?

How Do Social Orientation/Understanding and Attachment Develop in Infancy?

LG2 Describe the development of social orientation/understanding and attachment in infancy.

Social Orientation/Understanding

Attachment and Its Development

Individual Differences in Attachment

Developmental Social Neuroscience and Attachment

So far, we have discussed how emotions and emotional competence change as children develop. We have also examined the role of emotional style; in effect, we have seen how emotions set the tone of our experiences in life. But emotions also write the lyrics because they are at the core of our relationships with others.

SOCIAL ORIENTATION/UNDERSTANDING

In Ross Thompson's view (2006, 2011a, b, 2012) of socioemotional beings, infants show a strong interest in the social world and are motivated to orient to it and understand it. In earlier chapters, we described many of the biological and cognitive foundations that contribute to the infant's development of social orientation and understanding. We call attention to relevant biological and cognitive factors as we explore social orientation; locomotion; intention, goal-directed behavior, and cooperation; and social referencing.

Social Orientation From early in their development, infants are captivated by the social world. As we discussed in our coverage of infant perception in Chapter 5, "Physical Development in Infancy," young infants stare intently at faces and are attuned to the sounds of human voices, especially those of their caregivers (Ramsey-Rennels & Langlois, 2007). Later, they become adept at interpreting the meaning of facial expressions.

Face-to-face play often begins to characterize caregiver-infant interactions when the infant is about 2 to 3 months of age. The focused social interaction of face-to-face play may include vocalizations, touch, and gestures (Leppanen & others, 2007). Such play is part of many mothers' motivation to create a positive emotional state in their infants (Thompson, 2010).

In part because of such positive social interchanges between caregivers and infants, by 2 to 3 months of age infants respond to people differently from the way they do to objects, showing more positive emotion toward people than inanimate objects such as puppets (Legerstee, 1997). At this age, most infants expect people to react positively when the infants initiate a behavior, such as a smile or a vocalization. This finding has been discovered by use of a method called the *still-face paradigm*, in which the caregiver alternates between engaging in face-to-face interaction with the infant and remaining still and unresponsive (Conradt & Ablow, 2010). As early as 2 to 3 months of age, infants show more withdrawal, negative emotions, and self-directed behavior when their caregivers are still and unresponsive (Adamson & Frick, 2003). The frequency of face-to-face play decreases after 7 months of age as infants become more mobile (Thompson, 2006).

Infants also learn about the social world through contexts other than face-to-face play with a caregiver. Even though infants as young as 6 months of age show an interest in each other, their interaction with peers increases considerably in the last half of the second year. As increasing numbers of U.S. infants experience child care outside the home, they are spending more time in social play with peers. Later in the chapter, we further discuss child care.

Locomotion Recall from earlier in the chapter how important independence is for infants, especially in the second year of life. As infants develop the ability to crawl, walk, and run, they are able to explore and expand their social world. These newly developed self-produced locomotor skills allow the infant to independently initiate social interchanges on a more frequent basis (Laible & Thompson, 2007). Remember from Chapter 5, "Physical Development in Infancy," that the development of these gross motor skills is the result of a number of factors, including the development of the nervous system, the goal the infant is motivated to reach, and environmental support for the skill (Adolph & Robinson, 2011).

The infant's and toddler's push for independence also is likely paced by the development of locomotion skills (Campos, 2009). Locomotion is also important for its motivational implications. Once infants have the ability to move in goal-directed pursuits, the reward from these pursuits leads to further efforts to explore and develop skills.

Intention, Goal-Directed Behavior, and Cooperation

Perceiving people as engaging in intentional and goal-directed behavior is an important social cognitive accomplishment, and this initially occurs toward the end of the first year (Thompson, 2010). Joint attention and gaze following help the infant to understand that other people have intentions (Carpenter, 2011; Meltzoff, 2011). Recall from Chapter 6, "Cognitive Development in Infancy," that *joint attention* occurs when the caregiver

developmental **connection**

Biological, Cognitive, and Socioemotional Processes.
Discussing biological, cognitive, and socioemotional processes together reminds us of an important aspect of development: These processes are intricately intertwined (Diamond, Casey, & Munakata, 2011). Chapter 1, p. 15

A mother and her baby engaging in face-to-face play. *At what age does face-to-face play usually begin, and when does it typically start decreasing in frequency?*

developmental **connection**

Theories. The dynamic systems view is increasingly used to explain how infants develop. Chapter 5, p. 149

FIGURE **7.5**

THE COOPERATION TASK. The cooperation task consisted of two handles on a box, atop which was an animated musical toy, surreptitiously activated by remote control when both handles were pulled. The handles were placed far enough apart that one child could not pull both handles. The experimenter demonstrated the task, saying, "Watch! If you pull the handles, the doggie will sing" (Brownell, Ramani, & Zerwas, 2006).

What is social referencing? What are some developmental changes in social referencing?

social referencing "Reading" emotional cues in others to help determine how to act in a particular situation.

attachment A close emotional bond between two people.

and infant focus on the same object or event. By their first birthday, infants have begun to direct the caregiver's attention to objects that capture their interest (Heimann & others, 2006).

One study involved presenting 1- and 2-year-olds with a simple cooperative task that consisted of pulling a lever to get an attractive toy (Brownell, Ramani, & Zerwas, 2006) (see Figure 7.5). Any coordinated actions of the 1-year-olds appeared to be more coincidental rather than cooperative, whereas the 2-year-olds' behavior was characterized as more active cooperation to reach a goal. In this study, the infants also were assessed with two social understanding tasks, observation of children's behavior in a joint attention task, and the parents' perceptions of the language the children use about the self and others (Brownell, Ramani, & Zerwas, 2006). Those with more advanced social understanding were more likely to cooperate. To cooperate, the children had to connect their own intentions with the peer's intentions and put this understanding to use in interacting with the peer to reach a goal.

Social Referencing   Another important social cognitive accomplishment in infancy is developing the ability to "read" the emotions of other people. **Social referencing** is the term used to describe "reading" emotional cues in others to help determine how to act in a specific situation. The development of social referencing helps infants to interpret ambiguous situations more accurately, as when they encounter a stranger and need to know whether or not to fear the person (Kim, Walden, & Knieps, 2010). By the end of the first year, a mother's facial expression—either smiling or fearful—influences whether an infant will explore an unfamiliar environment.

Infants become better at social referencing in the second year of life (Witherington & others, 2010). At this age, they tend to "check" with their mother before they act; they look at her to see if she is happy, angry, or fearful.

Infants' Social Sophistication and Insight   In sum, researchers are discovering that infants are more socially sophisticated and insightful at younger ages than was previously envisioned (Thompson, 2011a, b). Such sophistication and insight are reflected in infants' perceptions of others' actions as intentionally motivated and goal-directed and their motivation to share and participate in that intentionality by their first birthday (Carpenter, 2011). More advanced social cognitive skills of infants could be expected to influence their understanding and awareness of **attachment** to a caregiver.

ATTACHMENT AND ITS DEVELOPMENT

There is no shortage of theories about why infants become attached to a caregiver. Three theorists discussed in Chapter 1—Freud, Erikson, and Bowlby—proposed influential views.

Freud noted that infants become attached to the person or object that provides oral satisfaction. For most infants, this is the mother, since she is most likely to feed the infant. Is feeding as important as Freud thought? A classic study by Harry Harlow (1958) revealed that the answer is no (see Figure 7.6).

Harlow removed infant monkeys from their mothers at birth; for six months they were reared by surrogate (substitute) "mothers." One surrogate mother was made of wire, the other of cloth. Half of the infant monkeys were fed by the wire mother, half by the cloth mother. Periodically, the amount of time the infant monkeys spent with either the wire or the cloth mother was computed. Regardless of which mother fed them, the infant monkeys spent far more time with the cloth mother. Even if the wire mother but not the cloth mother provided nourishment, the infant monkeys spent more time with the cloth mother. And when Harlow

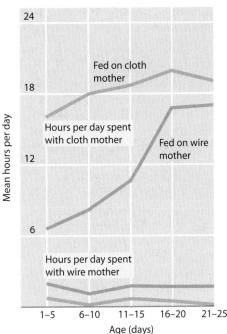

24

18

Fed on cloth mother

Hours per day spent with cloth mother

12

Fed on wire mother

6

Hours per day spent with wire mother

Mean hours per day

1–5   6–10   11–15   16–20   21–25

Age (days)

FIGURE **7.6**

CONTACT TIME WITH WIRE AND CLOTH SURROGATE MOTHERS. *Regardless of whether the infant monkeys were fed by a wire or a cloth mother, they overwhelmingly preferred to spend contact time with the cloth mother.* How do these results compare with what Freud's theory and Erikson's theory would predict about human infants?

frightened the monkeys, those "raised" by the cloth mother ran to the mother and clung to it; those raised by the wire mother did not. Whether the mother provided comfort seemed to determine whether the monkeys associated the mother with security. This study clearly demonstrated that feeding is not the crucial element in the attachment process and that contact comfort is important.

Physical comfort also plays a role in Erik Erikson's (1968) view of the infant's development. Recall Erikson's proposal that the first year of life represents the stage of trust versus mistrust. Physical comfort and sensitive care, according to Erikson (1968), are key to establishing a basic trust in infants. The infant's sense of trust, in turn, is the foundation for attachment and sets the stage for a lifelong expectation that the world will be a good and pleasant place to be.

The ethological perspective of British psychiatrist John Bowlby (1969, 1989) also stresses the importance of attachment in the first year of life and the responsiveness of the caregiver. Bowlby stresses both infants and their primary caregivers are biologically predisposed to form attachments. He argues that the newborn is biologically equipped to elicit attachment behavior. The baby cries, clings, coos, and smiles. Later, the infant crawls, walks, and follows the mother. The immediate result is to keep the primary caregiver nearby; the long-term effect is to increase the infant's chances of survival.

Attachment does not emerge suddenly but rather develops in a series of phases, moving from a baby's general preference for human beings to a partnership with primary caregivers. Following are four such phases based on Bowlby's conceptualization of attachment (Schaffer, 1996):

- *Phase 1: From birth to 2 months.* Infants instinctively direct their attachment to human figures. Strangers, siblings, and parents are equally likely to elicit smiling or crying from the infant.

- *Phase 2: From 2 to 7 months.* Attachment becomes focused on one figure, usually the primary caregiver, as the baby gradually learns to distinguish familiar from unfamiliar people.

- *Phase 3: From 7 to 24 months.* Specific attachments develop. With increased locomotor skills, babies actively seek contact with regular caregivers, such as the mother or father.

In Bowlby's model, what are four phases of attachment?

- *Phase 4: From 24 months on.* Children become aware of others' feelings, goals, and plans and begin to take these into account in forming their own actions.

Researchers' recent findings that infants are more socially sophisticated and insightful than was previously envisioned suggests that some of the characteristics of Bowlby's phase 4, such as understanding the goals and intentions of the attachment figure, appear to be developing in phase 3 as attachment security is taking shape.

Bowlby argued that infants develop an *internal working model* of attachment, a simple mental model of the caregiver, their relationship, and the self as deserving of nurturant care. The infant's internal working model of attachment with the caregiver influences the infant's and later, the child's, subsequent responses to other people (Posada & Kaloustian, 2010). The internal model of attachment also has played a pivotal role in the discovery of links between attachment and subsequent emotional understanding and self-perception.

In sum, attachment emerges from the social cognitive advances that allow infants to develop expectations for the caregiver's behavior and to determine the affective quality of their relationship (Thompson, 2010, 2011a). These social cognitive advances include recognizing the caregiver's face, voice, and other features, as well as developing an internal working model of expecting the caregiver to provide pleasure in social interaction and relief from distress.

INDIVIDUAL DIFFERENCES IN ATTACHMENT

Although attachment to a caregiver intensifies midway through the first year, isn't it likely that the quality of babies' attachment experiences varies? Mary Ainsworth (1979) thought so. Ainsworth created the **Strange Situation,** an observational measure of infant attachment in which the infant experiences a series of introductions, separations, and reunions with the caregiver and an adult stranger in a prescribed order. In using the Strange Situation, researchers hope that their observations will provide information about the infant's motivation to be near the caregiver and the degree to which the caregiver's presence provides the infant with security and confidence.

Based on how babies respond in the Strange Situation, they are described as being securely attached or insecurely attached (in one of three ways) to the caregiver:

- **Securely attached babies** use the caregiver as a secure base from which to explore the environment. When in the presence of their caregiver, securely attached infants explore the room and examine toys that have been placed in it. When the caregiver departs, securely attached infants might protest mildly, and when the caregiver returns these infants reestablish positive interaction with her, perhaps by smiling or climbing on her lap. Subsequently, they often resume playing with the toys in the room.

- **Insecure avoidant babies** show insecurity by avoiding the mother. In the Strange Situation, these babies engage in little interaction with the caregiver, are not distressed when she leaves the room, usually do not reestablish contact on her return, and may even turn their back on her. If contact is established, the infant usually leans away or looks away.

- **Insecure resistant babies** often cling to the caregiver and then resist her by fighting against the closeness, perhaps by kicking or pushing away. In the Strange Situation, these babies often cling anxiously to the caregiver and don't explore the playroom. When the caregiver leaves, they often cry loudly and push away if she tries to comfort them on her return.

- **Insecure disorganized babies** are disorganized and disoriented. In the Strange Situation, these babies might appear dazed, confused, and fearful. To be classified as disorganized, babies must show strong patterns of avoidance and resistance or display certain specified behaviors, such as extreme fearfulness around the caregiver.

How Would You...?

If you were a **psychologist,** how would you identify an insecurely attached infant? How would you encourage a parent to strengthen the attachment bond?

Strange Situation An observational measure of infant attachment that requires the infant to move through a series of introductions, separations, and reunions with the caregiver and an adult stranger in a prescribed order.

securely attached babies Babies that use the caregiver as a secure base from which to explore their environment.

insecure avoidant babies Babies that show insecurity by avoiding the caregiver.

insecure resistant babies Babies that often cling to the caregiver, then resist her by fighting against the closeness, perhaps by kicking or pushing away.

insecure disorganized babies Babies that show insecurity by being disorganized and disoriented.

Evaluating the Strange Situation Does the Strange Situation capture important differences among infants? As a measure of attachment, it may be culturally biased. For example, German and Japanese babies often show different patterns of attachment from those of American infants. As illustrated in Figure 7.7, German infants are more likely to show an avoidant attachment pattern and Japanese infants are less likely to display this pattern than U.S. infants (van IJzendoorn & Kroonenberg, 1988). The avoidant pattern in German babies likely occurs because their caregivers encourage them to be independent (Grossmann & others, 1985). Also as shown in Figure 7.7, Japanese babies are more likely than American babies to be categorized as resistant. This may have more to do with the Strange Situation as a measure of attachment than with attachment insecurity itself. Japanese mothers rarely let anyone unfamiliar with their babies care for them. Thus, the Strange Situation might create considerably more stress for Japanese infants than for American infants, who are more accustomed to separation from their mothers (Miyake, Chen, & Campos, 1985). Even though there are cultural variations in attachment classification, the most frequent classification in every culture studied so far is secure attachment (van IJzendoorn & Kroonenberg, 1988).

Some critics stress that behavior in the Strange Situation—like other laboratory assessments—might not indicate what infants do in a natural environment. But researchers have found that infants' behaviors in the Strange Situation are closely related to how they behave at home in response to separation and reunion with their mothers (Pederson & Moran, 1996). Thus, many infant researchers stress that the Strange Situation continues to show merit as a measure of infant attachment.

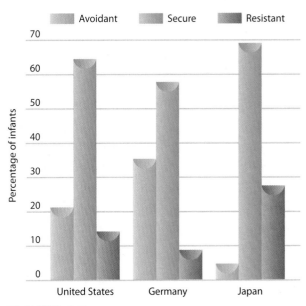

FIGURE 7.7

CROSS-CULTURAL COMPARISON OF ATTACHMENT. In one study, infant attachment in three countries—the United States, Germany, and Japan—was measured in the Ainsworth Strange Situation (van IJzendoorn & Kroonenberg, 1988). The dominant attachment pattern in all three countries was secure attachment. However, German infants were more avoidant and Japanese infants were less avoidant and more resistant than U.S. infants. *What are some explanations for differences in how German, Japanese, and American infants respond to the Strange Situation?*

Caregiving Styles and Attachment Is the style of caregiving linked with the quality of the infant's attachment? Securely attached babies have caregivers who are sensitive to their signals and are consistently available to respond to their infants' needs (Bigelow & others, 2010). These caregivers often let their babies have an active part in determining the onset and pacing of interaction in the first year of life. A recent study revealed that maternal sensitivity in responding was linked to infant attachment security (Finger & others, 2009). Another study found that maternal sensitivity in parenting was linked with secure attachment in infants in two different cultures: the United States and Colombia (Posada & others, 2002). Although maternal sensitivity is linked to the development of secure attachment in infancy, it is important to note that the connection is not especially strong (Campos, 2009).

How do the caregivers of insecurely attached babies interact with them? Caregivers of avoidant babies tend to be unavailable or rejecting (Posada & Kaloustian, 2010). They often don't respond to their babies' signals and have little physical contact with them. When they do interact with their babies, they may behave in an angry and irritable way. Caregivers of resistant babies tend to be inconsistent; sometimes they respond to their babies' needs, and sometimes they don't. In general, they tend not to be very affectionate with their babies and show little synchrony when interacting with them. Caregivers of disorganized babies often neglect or physically abuse them (Cicchetti, 2010; Connell-Carrick, 2011). In some cases, these caregivers are depressed. In sum, caregivers' interactions with infants influence whether infants are securely or insecurely attached to the caregivers (Sroufe, Coffino, & Carlson, 2010).

What is the nature of secure and insecure attachment? How are caregiving styles related to attachment classification?

Interpreting Differences in Attachment Do individual differences in attachment matter? Ainsworth notes that secure attachment in the first year of life provides an important foundation for psychological development later in life. The securely attached infant moves freely away from the mother but keeps track of

How Would You...?

If you were a **health-care professional,** how would you use an infant's attachment style and/or a parent's caregiving style to determine whether an infant may be at risk for neglect or abuse?

where she is through periodic glances. The securely attached infant responds positively to being picked up by others and, when put back down, freely moves away to play. An insecurely attached infant, by contrast, avoids the mother or is ambivalent toward her, fears strangers, and is upset by minor, everyday separations.

If early attachment to a caregiver is important, it should relate to a child's social behavior later in development. For some children, early attachments seem to foreshadow later functioning (Fearon & others, 2010; Posada & Kaloustian, 2010). In the extensive longitudinal study conducted by Alan Sroufe and his colleagues (2005; Sroufe, Coffino, & Carlson, 2010), early secure attachment (assessed by the Strange Situation at 12 and 18 months) was linked with positive emotional health, high self-esteem, self-confidence, and socially competent interaction with peers, teachers, camp counselors, and romantic partners through adolescence. Another study found that attachment security at 24 and 36 months was linked to the child's enhanced social problem-solving at 54 months (Raikes & Thompson, 2009). And a recent meta-analysis revealed that disorganized attachment was more strongly linked to externalizing problems (aggression and hostility, for example) than were avoidant and resistant attachment (Fearon & others, 2010).

developmental **connection**

Nature and Nurture. What is involved in gene-environment (G × E) interaction? Chapter 2, p. 77

For some children, though, there is little continuity. Not all research reveals the power of infant attachment to predict subsequent development (Roisman & Groh, 2011; Thompson, 2012). In one longitudinal study, attachment classification in infancy did not predict attachment classification at 18 years of age (Lewis, 1997). In this study, the best predictor of an insecure attachment classification at 18 was the occurrence of parental divorce in the intervening years.

Consistently positive caregiving over a number of years is likely an important factor in connecting early attachment and the child's functioning later in development. Indeed, researchers have found that early secure attachment and subsequent experiences, especially maternal care and life stresses, are linked with children's later behavior and adjustment (Thompson, 2011a).

Some developmentalists note that too much emphasis has been placed on the attachment bond in infancy. Jerome Kagan (2000), for example, emphasizes that infants are highly resilient and adaptive; he argues that they are evolutionarily equipped to stay on a positive developmental course, even in the face of wide variations in parenting. Kagan and others stress that genetic characteristics and temperament play more important roles in a child's social competence than the attachment theorists, such as Bowlby and Ainsworth, are willing to acknowledge (Bakermans-Kranenburg & others, 2007). For example, if some infants inherit a low tolerance for stress, this characteristic, rather than an insecure attachment bond, may be responsible for an inability to get along with peers. A recent study found links between disorganized attachment in infancy, a specific gene, and level of maternal responsiveness. In this study, a disorganized attachment style developed in infancy only when infants had the short version of the serotonin transporter gene—5-*HTTLPR* (Spangler & others, 2009). Infants were not characterized by this attachment style when they had the long version of the gene (Spangler & others 2009). Further, this gene-environment interaction occurred only when mothers showed a low level of responsiveness toward their infants.

Another criticism of attachment theory is that it ignores the diversity of socializing agents and contexts that exists in an infant's world. A culture's value system can influence the nature of attachment (van IJzendoorn & Sagi-Schwartz, 2009). Mothers' expectations for infants to be independent are high in northern Germany, whereas Japanese mothers are more strongly motivated to keep their infants close to them (Grossmann & others, 1985; Rothbaum & others, 2000). Not surprisingly, northern German infants tend to show less distress than Japanese infants when separated from their mother. Also, in some cultures, infants show attachments to many people. Among the Hausa (who live in Nigeria), both grandmothers and

In the Hausa culture, siblings and grandmothers provide a significant amount of care for infants. *How might these variations in care affect attachment?*

siblings provide a significant amount of care for infants (Harkness & Super, 1995). Infants in agricultural societies tend to form attachments to older siblings, who are assigned a major responsibility for younger siblings' care. Researchers recognize the importance of competent, nurturant caregivers in an infant's development (Parke & Clarke-Stewart, 2011). At issue, though, is whether or not secure attachment, especially to a single caregiver, is critical (Lamb, 2010; Thompson, 2012).

Despite such criticisms, there is ample evidence that security of attachment is important to development (Lamb, 2010; Thompson, 2012). Secure attachment in infancy is important because it reflects a positive parent-infant relationship and provides the foundation that supports healthy socioemotional development in the years that follow.

DEVELOPMENTAL SOCIAL NEUROSCIENCE AND ATTACHMENT

In Chapter 1 you read about the emerging field of *developmental social neuroscience*, which examines connections between socioemotional processes, development, and the brain. Attachment is one of the main areas in which theory and research on developmental social neuroscience has focused (Beauchamp & Anderson, 2010; Parsons & others, 2010). These connections of attachment and the brain involve the neuroanatomy of the brain, neurotransmitters, and hormones.

developmental connection

Brain Development. Connections are increasingly being made between brain development and socioemotional processes. Chapter 1, p. 15; Chapter 14, p. 434

Theory and research on the role of the brain's regions in mother-infant attachment is just emerging (de Haan & Gunnar, 2009). A recent theoretical view proposed that the prefrontal cortex likely has an important role in maternal attachment behavior, as do the subcortical (areas of the brain lower than the cortex) regions of the amygdala (which is strongly involved in emotion) and the hypothalamus (Gonzalez, Atkinson, & Fleming, 2009). An ongoing fMRI longitudinal study is exploring the possibility that different attachment patterns can be distinguished by different patterns of brain activity (Strathearn, 2007).

Research on the role of hormones and neurotransmitters in attachment has emphasized the importance of two neuropeptide hormones—oxytocin and vasopressin—in the formation of the maternal-infant bond (Bales & Carter, 2009). Oxytocin, a mammalian hormone that also acts as a neurotransmitter in the brain, is released during breast feeding and by contact and warmth (Campbell, 2010). Oxytocin is especially thought to be a likely candidate in the formation of infant-mother attachment (Bales & Carter, 2009).

The influence of these neuropeptides on the neurotransmitter dopamine in the nucleus accumbens (a collection of neurons in the forebrain that are involved in pleasure) likely is important in motivating approach to the attachment object (de Haan & Gunnar, 2009). Figure 7.8 shows the regions of the brain we have described that are likely to be important in infant-mother attachment.

In sum, it is likely that a number of brain regions, neurotransmitters, and hormones are involved in the development of infant-mother attachment. Key candidates for influencing this attachment are connections between the prefrontal cortex, amygdala, and hypothalamus; the neuropeptides oxytocin and vasopressin; and the activity of the neurotransmitter dopamine in the nucleus accumbens.

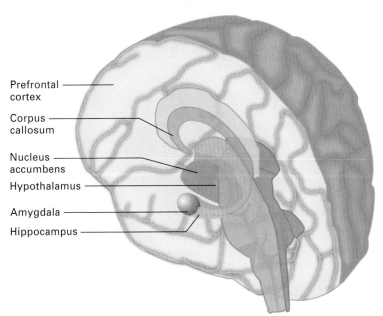

Prefrontal cortex

Corpus callosum

Nucleus accumbens

Hypothalamus

Amygdala

Hippocampus

FIGURE **7.8**

REGIONS OF THE BRAIN PROPOSED AS LIKELY IMPORTANT IN INFANT-MOTHER ATTACHMENT. *Note:* This illustration shows the brain's left hemisphere. The corpus callosum is the large bundle of axons that connect the brain's two hemispheres.

Review *Connect* Reflect

LG2 Describe the development of social orientation/ understanding and attachment in infancy.

Review

- How do social orientation/understanding develop in infancy?
- What is attachment, and how is it conceptualized?
- What are some individual variations in attachment? How are caregiving styles related to attachment? What are some criticisms of attachment theory?
- What characterizes the study of developmental social neuroscience and attachment?

Connect

- How might the infant's temperament be related to the way in which attachment is

classified? Look at the temperament categories we described in the first main section of this chapter and reflect on how these might be more likely to show up in infants in some attachment categories than others.

Reflect *Your Own Personal Journey of Life*

- Imagine that you are the parent of an infant. What could you do to improve the likelihood that your baby will have a secure attachment with you?

How Do Social Contexts Influence Socioemotional Development in Infancy?

 LG3 Explain how social contexts influence the infant's development.

The Family   Child Care

Now that we have explored the infant's emotional and personality development and attachment, let's examine the social contexts in which these occur. We begin by studying a number of aspects of the family and then turn to a social context in which infants increasingly spend time—child care.

THE FAMILY

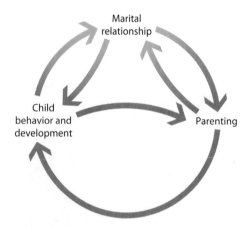

FIGURE 7.9

INTERACTION BETWEEN CHILDREN AND THEIR PARENTS: DIRECT AND INDIRECT EFFECTS

The family can be thought of as a constellation of subsystems—a complex whole made up of interrelated, interacting parts—defined in terms of generation, gender, and role. Each family member participates in several subsystems (Parke & Clarke-Stewart, 2011). The father and child represent one subsystem, the mother and father another, the mother-father-child represent yet another, and so on.

These subsystems have reciprocal influences on each other (Russell, 2011). For example, Jay Belsky (1981) emphasizes that marital relations, parenting, and infant behavior and development can have both direct and indirect effects on each other (see Figure 7.9). An example of a direct effect is the influence of the parents' behavior on the child. An indirect effect is how the relationship between the spouses mediates the way a parent acts toward the child (Hsu, 2004). For example, marital conflict might reduce the efficiency of parenting, in which case marital conflict would indirectly affect the child's behavior. The simple fact that two people are becoming parents may have profound effects on their relationship.

The Transition to Parenthood   When people become parents through pregnancy, adoption, or stepparenting, they face disequilibrium and must adapt. Parents want to develop a strong attachment with their infant, but they still want to maintain strong attachments to their spouse and friends, and possibly continue their careers. Parents ask themselves how this new being will change their lives. A baby places new restrictions on partners; no longer will they be able to rush out to a movie on

reciprocal socialization Socialization that is bidirectional; children socialize parents, just as parents socialize children.

scaffolding Adjusting the level of guidance to fit the child's performance.

a moment's notice, and money may not be readily available for vacations and other luxuries. Dual-career parents ask, "Will it harm the baby to place her in child care? Will we be able to find responsible baby-sitters?"

In a longitudinal investigation of couples from late pregnancy until 3½ years after the baby was born, couples enjoyed more positive marital relations before the baby was born than after (Cowan & Cowan, 2000; Cowan & others, 2005). Still, almost one-third showed an increase in marital satisfaction. Some couples said that the baby had both brought them closer together and moved them farther apart; being parents enhanced their sense of themselves and gave them a new, more stable identity as a couple. Babies opened men up to a concern with intimate relationships, and the demands of juggling work and family roles stimulated women to manage family tasks more efficiently and pay attention to their own personal growth.

The Bringing Home Baby project is a workshop for new parents that emphasizes strengthening the couples' relationship, understanding and becoming acquainted with the baby, resolving conflict, and developing parenting skills. Evaluations of the project revealed that parents who participated improved their ability to work together as parents, fathers were more involved with their baby and sensitive to the baby's behavior, mothers had a lower incidence of postpartum depression symptoms, and their babies showed better overall development than participants in a control group (Gottman, Shapiro, & Parthemer, 2004; Shapiro & Gottman, 2005).

What kinds of adaptations do new parents need to make?

Reciprocal Socialization   Socialization between parents and children is not a one-way process. Parents do socialize children, but socialization in families is reciprocal (Gauvain & Parke, 2010; Parke & Clarke-Stewart, 2011). **Reciprocal socialization** is socialization that is bidirectional; children socialize parents just as parents socialize children. These reciprocal interchanges and mutual influence processes are sometimes referred to as *transactional* (Sameroff, 2009).

> We never know the love of our parents until we have become parents.
>
> —HENRY WARD BEECHER
> *American Writer, 19th Century*

For example, the interaction of mothers and their infants is sometimes symbolized as a dance in which successive actions of the partners are closely coordinated. This coordinated dance can assume the form of synchrony—that is, each person's behavior depends on the partner's previous behavior. Or the interaction can be reciprocal in a precise sense—in which the actions of the partners can be matched, as when one partner imitates the other or when there is mutual smiling.

An important example of early synchronized interaction is mutual gaze or eye contact. In one study, the mother and infant engaged in a variety of behaviors while they looked at each other; by contrast, when they looked away from each other, the rate of such behaviors dropped considerably (Stern & others, 1977). In another study, synchrony in parent-child relationships was positively related to children's social competence (Harrist, 1993).

Another example of synchronization occurs in **scaffolding,** which means adjusting the level of guidance to fit the child's performance (Bibok, Carpendale, & Muller, 2009). The parent responds to

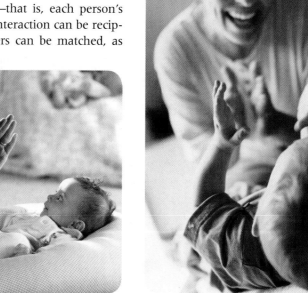

Caregivers often play games such as peek-a-boo and pat-a-cake. *How is scaffolding involved in these games?*

the child's behavior with scaffolding, which in turn affects the child's behavior. For example, in the game peek-a-boo, parents initially cover their babies, then remove the covering, and finally register "surprise" at the babies' reappearance. As infants become more skilled at peek-a-boo, infants gradually do some of the covering and uncovering. Parents try to time their actions in such a way that the infant takes turns with the parent. In addition to peek-a-boo, pat-a-cake and "so-big" are other caregiver games that exemplify scaffolding and turn-taking sequences.

How Would You...?

If you were an **educator,** how would you explain the value of games and the role of scaffolding in the development of infants and toddlers?

FIGURE **7.10**

PARENTS' METHODS FOR MANAGING AND CORRECTING INFANTS' UNDESIRABLE BEHAVIORS. Shown here are the percentages of parents who had used various corrective methods by the time infants were 12 and 24 months old. Source: Based on data presented in Vittrup, Holden, & Buck (2006).

Method	12 Months	24 Months
Spank with hand	14	45
Slap infant's hand	21	31
Yell in anger	36	81
Threaten	19	63
Withdraw privileges	18	52
Time-out	12	60
Reason	85	100
Divert attention	100	100
Negotiate	50	90
Ignore	64	90

Scaffolding can be used to support children's efforts at any age. A recent study of Hmong families living in the United States revealed that maternal scaffolding, especially in the form of cognitive support, of young children's problem solving the summer before kindergarten predicted the children's reasoning skills in kindergarten (Stright, Herr, & Neitzel, 2009).

Managing and Guiding Infants' Behavior In addition to sensitive parenting that involves warmth and caring and can result in secure attachment to parents, other important aspects of parenting infants involve managing and guiding their behavior in an attempt to reduce or eliminate undesirable behaviors (Holden, Vittrup, & Rosen, 2011). This management process includes (1) being proactive and childproofing the environment so infants won't encounter potentially dangerous objects or situations, and (2) engaging in corrective methods when infants engage in undesirable behaviors, such as excessive fussing and crying, throwing objects, and so on.

One study assessed discipline and corrective methods that parents had used by the time infants were 12 and 24 months old (Vittrup, Holden, & Buck, 2006) (see Figure 7.10). Notice in Figure 7.10 that the main method parents used by the time infants were 12 months old was diverting the infants' attention, followed by reasoning, ignoring, and negotiating. Also note in Figure 7.10 that more than one-third of parents had yelled at their infant, about one-fifth had slapped the infant's hands or threatened the infant, and approximately one-sixth had spanked the infant by their first birthday.

As infants move into the second year of life and become more mobile and capable of exploring a wider range of environments, parental management of the toddler's behavior often triggers even more corrective feedback and discipline (Holden, Vittrup, & Rosen, 2011). As indicated in Figure 7.10, in the study just described, parental yelling increased from 36 percent at 1 year of age to 81 percent at 2 years of age, slapping the infant's hands increased from 21 percent at 1 year to 31 percent at age 2, and spanking increased from 14 percent at 1 year to 45 percent at age 2 (Vittrup, Holden, & Buck, 2006).

A special concern is that such corrective disciplinary tactics not become abusive. Too often what starts out as mild to moderately intense discipline on the part of parents can move into highly intense anger. In Chapter 10, you will read more extensively about the use of punishment with children and child abuse.

Mothers and Fathers as Caregivers An increasing number of U.S. fathers stay home full-time with their children (Cohen, 2009; Lamb, 2010). As indicated in Figure 7.11, there was a 300-plus

developmental **connection**

Cognitive Theory. A version of scaffolding is an important aspect of Lev Vygotsky's sociocultural cognitive theory. Chapter 9, p. 264

developmental **connection**

Parenting. Psychologists give a number of reasons why harsh physical punishment can be harmful to children's development. Chapter 10, p. 302

percent increase in stay-at-home fathers in the United States from 1996 to 2006. A large portion of the full-time fathers have career-focused wives who provide the main family income. One study revealed that the stay-at-home fathers were as satisfied with their marriage as traditional parents, although they indicated that they missed their daily life in the workplace (Rochlen & others, 2008). In this study, the stay-at-home fathers reported that they tended to be ostracized when they took their children to playgrounds and often were excluded from parent groups.

Can fathers take care of infants as competently as mothers can? Observations of fathers and their infants suggest that fathers have the ability to act as sensitively and responsively as mothers with their infants (Parke & Clarke-Stewart, 2011). Consider the Aka pygmy culture in Africa where fathers spend as much time interacting with their infants as do their mothers (Hewlett, 2000; Hewlett & Mac-Farlan, 2010). Remember, however, that although fathers can be active, nurturant, involved caregivers with their infants as Aka pygmy fathers do, in many cultures men have not chosen to follow this pattern (Parke & Clarke-Stewart, 2011).

Do fathers behave differently toward infants than mothers do? Maternal interactions usually center on child-care activities—feeding, changing diapers, bathing. Paternal interactions are more likely to include play (Parke & Clarke-Stewart, 2011). Fathers engage in more rough-and-tumble play. They bounce infants, throw them up in the air, tickle them, and so on (Lamb, 2010). Mothers do play with infants, but their play is less physical and arousing than that of fathers.

An Aka pygmy father with his infant son. In the Aka culture, fathers were observed to be holding or nearby their infants 47 percent of the time.

FIGURE 7.11

THE INCREASE IN THE NUMBER OF U.S. FATHERS STAYING AT HOME FULL-TIME WITH THEIR CHILDREN

(Graph: y-axis labeled "Number of U.S. fathers at home full-time with their children (thousands)" with values 40, 80, 120, 160; x-axis labeled "Year" with values 1996, 2001, 2006; line rises from about 40 in 1996 to about 150 in 2006.)

CHILD CARE

Many U.S. children today experience multiple caregivers. Most do not have a parent staying home to care for them; instead, the children have some type of care provided by others—"child care." Many parents worry that child care will reduce their infants' emotional attachment to them, retard the infants' cognitive development, fail to teach them how to control anger, and allow them to be unduly influenced by their peers. How extensive is child care? Are the worries of these parents justified?

Parental Leave Today far more young children are in child care than at any other time in history. About 2 million children in the United States currently receive formal, licensed child care, and uncounted millions of children are cared for by unlicensed baby-sitters. To read about child-care policies in different countries, see the *Connecting with Diversity* interlude.

Variations in Child Care Because the United States does not have a policy of paid leave for child care, child care in the United States has become a major national concern (Belsky, 2009). Many factors influence the effects of child care, including the age of the child, the type of child care, and the quality of the program.

The type of child care varies extensively (Friedman, Melhuish, & Hill, 2010; Phillips & Lowenstein, 2011). Child care is provided in large centers with elaborate facilities and in private homes. Some child-care centers are commercial operations; others are nonprofit centers run by churches, civic groups, and employers.

How do most fathers and mothers interact differently with infants?

> We have all the knowledge necessary to provide absolutely first-rate child care in the United States. What is missing is the commitment and the will.
>
> —EDWARD ZIGLER
>
> *Contemporary Developmental Psychologist, Yale University*

Child-Care Policies Around the World

Child-care policies around the world vary in eligibility criteria, leave duration, benefit level, and the extent to which parents take advantage of the policies (Tolani & Brooks-Gunn, 2008). Europe has led the way in creating new standards of parental leave: The European Union (EU) mandated a paid 14-week maternity leave in 1992. In most European countries today, working parents on leave receive from 70 to 100 percent of the worker's prior wage and paid leave averages about 16 weeks (Tolani & Brooks-Gunn, 2008). The United States currently allows workers up to 12 weeks of unpaid leave to care for a newborn.

Most countries restrict eligible benefits to women employed for a minimum time prior to childbirth (Tolani & Brooks-Gunn, 2008). In Denmark, even unemployed mothers are eligible for extended parental leave related to childbirth. In Sweden, parents can take an 18-month job-protected parental leave with benefits allowed to be shared by parents and applied to full-time or part-time work.

How are child-care policies in many European countries, such as Sweden, different from those in the United States?

Some child-care providers are professionals; others are mothers who want to earn extra money. Figure 7.12 presents the primary care arrangement for children under 5 years of age with employed mothers (Clarke-Stewart & Miner, 2008).

In the United States, approximately 15 percent of children 5 years of age and younger attend more than one child-care arrangement. A recent study of 2- and 3-year-olds revealed that an increase in the number of child-care arrangements the children experienced was linked to an increase in behavioral problems and a decrease in prosocial behavior (Morrissey, 2009).

What constitutes a high-quality child-care program for infants? In high-quality child care (Clarke-Stewart & Miner, 2008, p. 273):

> . . . caregivers encourage the children to be actively engaged in a variety of activities, have frequent, positive interactions that include smiling, touching, holding, and speaking at the child's eye level, respond properly to the child's questions or requests, and encourage children to talk about their experiences, feelings, and ideas.

High-quality child care also involves providing children with a safe environment, access to age-appropriate toys and participation in age-appropriate activities, and a low caregiver–child ratio that allows caregivers to spend considerable time with children on an individual basis. To read about one individual who provides quality child care to individuals from impoverished backgrounds, see the *Connecting with Careers* profile. What do U.S. studies of child care tell us about its outcomes? In the *Connecting with Research* interlude, you can find out about one ongoing research project.

What are some strategies parents can follow in regard to child care? Child-care expert Kathleen McCartney (2003, p. 4) offered this advice:

- *Recognize that the quality of your parenting is a key factor in your child's development.*
- *Make decisions that will improve the likelihood you will be good parents.* "For some this will mean working full-time"—for personal fulfillment, income, or both. "For others, this will mean working part-time or not working outside the home."

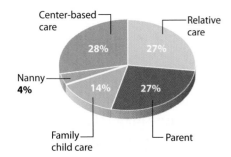

FIGURE 7.12

PRIMARY CARE ARRANGEMENTS IN THE UNITED STATES FOR CHILDREN UNDER 5 YEARS OF AGE WITH EMPLOYED MOTHERS

Wanda Mitchell, Child-Care Director

Wanda Mitchell is the Center Director of the Hattie Daniels Day Care Center in Wilson, North Carolina. Her responsibilities include directing the operation of the center, which involves creating and maintaining an environment in which young children can learn effectively, and ensuring that the center meets state licensing requirements. Wanda obtained her undergraduate degree from North Carolina A & T University, majoring in child development. Prior to her current position, she had been an education coordinator for Project Head Start and an instructor at Wilson Technical Community College. Describing her work, Wanda says, "I really enjoy working in my field. This is my passion. After graduating from college, my goal was to advance in my field."

Wanda Mitchell, child-care director, working with some of the children at her center.

- *Monitor your child's development.* "Parents should observe for themselves whether their children seem to be having behavior problems." They need to talk with their child-care providers and their pediatrician about their child's behavior
- *Take some time to find the best child care.* Observe different child-care facilities and be certain that you like what you see. "Quality child care costs money, and not all parents can afford the child care they want. However, state subsidies, and other programs like Head Start, are available for families in need."

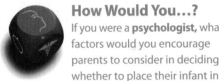

How Would You...?
If you were a **psychologist,** what factors would you encourage parents to consider in deciding whether to place their infant in child care so that both parents can return to work?

What Are Some Important Findings in the National Longitudinal Study of Child Care in the United States?

A longitudinal study of U.S. child care was initiated by the National Institute of Child Health and Human Development (NICHD) in 1991. Data were collected on a diverse sample of almost 1,400 children and their families at ten locations across the United States over a period of seven years. Researchers used multiple methods (trained observers, interviews, questionnaires, and testing), and measured many facets of children's development, including physical health, cognitive development, and socioemotional development. Following are some of the results of what is now referred to as the NICHD Study of Early Child Care and Youth Development, or NICHD SECCYD (NICHD Early Child Care Network, 2001, 2002, 2003, 2004, 2005, 2006).

- ***Patterns of use.*** Many families placed their infants in child care very soon after the child's birth, and there was considerable instability in the child-care arrangements. By 4 months of age, nearly three-fourths of the infants had entered some form of nonmaternal child care. Almost half of the infants were cared for by a relative when they first entered care; only 12 percent were enrolled in child-care centers. Low-income families were more likely than more affluent families to use child care, but infants from low-income families who were in child care averaged as many hours as other income groups. In the preschool years, mothers who were single, those with more education, and families with higher incomes used more hours of center-based care than other families did. Minority families and mothers with less education used more hours of care by relatives.

- ***Quality of care.*** Evaluations of quality of care were based on such characteristics as group size, child–adult ratio, physical environment, caregiver characteristics (such as formal education, specialized training, and child-care experience), and caregiver behavior (such as sensitivity to children). An alarming conclusion is that a majority of the child care

(continued)

(continued)

in the first three years of life was of unacceptably low quality. Positive caregiving by non-parents in child-care settings was infrequent—only 12 percent of the children studied experienced positive nonparental child care (such as positive talk and language stimulation)! Further, infants from low-income families experienced lower quality of child care than infants from higher-income families. When quality of caregivers' care was high, children performed better on cognitive and language tasks, were more cooperative with their mothers during play, showed more positive and skilled interaction with peers, and had fewer behavior problems. Caregiver training and good child–staff ratios were linked with higher cognitive and social competence when children were 54 months of age. A recent study revealed that higher-quality child care from birth to 4½ years of age was linked to higher cognitive-academic achievement at 15 years of age (Vandell & others, 2010). In this study, early higher-quality care also was related to youth reports of less externalizing behavior (lower rates of delinquency, for example).

- **Amount of child care.** In general, when children spent 30 hours or more per week in child care, their development was less than optimal (Ramey, 2005). In a recent study, more hours of early nonrelative child care was related to higher levels of risk taking and impulsivity at 15 years of age (Vandell & others, 2010).
- **Family and parenting influences.** The influence of families and parenting was not weakened by extensive child care. Parents played a significant role in helping children to regulate their emotions. Especially important parenting influences were being sensitive to children's needs, being involved with children, and cognitively stimulating them. Indeed, parental sensitivity has been the most consistent predictor of a secure attachment, with child-care experiences being relevant in many cases only when mothers engage in insensitive parenting (Friedman, Melhuish, & Hill, 2010). An important point about the extensive NICHD research is that findings show that family factors are considerably stronger and more consistent predictors of a

What are some important findings from the national longitudinal study of child care conducted by the National Institute of Child Health and Human Development?

wide variety of child outcomes than are child-care experiences (such as quality, quantity, type). The worst outcomes for children occur when both home and child-care settings are of poor quality. For example, a recent study involving the NICHD SECCYD data revealed that worse socioemotional outcomes (more problem behavior, low level of prosocial behavior) for children occurred when they experienced both home and child-care environments that conferred risk (Watamura & others, 2011).

What do these research finding suggest about what the U.S. child-care system is doing well? What could be improved about the system? If you were a researcher involved in this study, what other questions would you want to explore?

Review **Connect** Reflect

LG3 Explain how social contexts influence the infant's development.

Review

- What are some important family processes in infant development?
- How does child care influence infant development?

Connect

- In Chapter 5, you learned about a fine motor skills experiment involving 3-month-olds and grasping. What concept in the last section of this chapter relates to the use of "sticky mittens" in the experiment in Chapter 5?

Reflect *Your Own Personal Journey of Life*

- Imagine that a friend of yours is getting ready to put her baby in child care. What advice would you give to her? Do you think she should stay home with the baby? Why or why not? What type of child care would you recommend?

In Chapter 10, you will study socioemotional development in early childhood. Babies no more, young children make considerable progress in the development of their self, their emotions, and their social interactions. In early childhood, they show increased self-understanding and understanding of others, as well as ability to regulate their emotions. In early childhood, relationships and interactions with parents and peers expand children's knowledge of and connections with the social world. Additionally, play becomes not only something they enjoy doing on a daily basis but also a wonderful context for advancing both their socioemotional and cognitive development. Many of the advances in young children's socioemotional development become possible because of the remarkable changes in their brain and cognitive development, which you will read about in Chapters 8 and 9.

looking forward

reach your **learning goals**

How Do Emotions and Personality Develop in Infancy?

 LG1 Discuss emotional and personality development in infancy.

Emotional Development

- Emotion is feeling, or affect, that occurs when people are in a state or an interaction that is important to them. Emotion can be classified as either positive (for example, joy) or negative (for example, anger). Psychologists hold that emotions, especially facial expressions of emotions, have a biological foundation. Biological evolution endowed humans to be emotional, but embeddedness in culture and relationships provides diversity in emotional experiences. Emotions play key roles in parent-child relationships. Infants display a number of emotions early in their development, although researchers debate the onset and sequence of these emotions. Lewis distinguishes between primary emotions and self-conscious emotions. Crying is the most important mechanism newborns have for communicating with their world. Babies have at least three types of cries—basic, anger, and pain cries. Controversy swirls about whether babies should be soothed when they cry, although increasingly experts recommend immediately responding in a caring way in the first year. Social smiling occurs as early as 2 months of age and then increases considerably from 2 to 6 months. Two fears that infants develop are stranger anxiety and separation from a caregiver (which is reflected in separation protest). As infants develop, it is important for them to engage in emotional regulation.

Temperament

- Temperament is an individual's behavioral style and characteristic way of emotionally responding. Chess and Thomas classified infants as (1) easy, (2) difficult, or (3) slow to warm up. Kagan proposed that inhibition to the unfamiliar is an important temperament category. Rothbart and Bates' view of temperament emphasizes this classification: (1) extraversion/surgency, (2) negative affectivity, and (3) effortful control (self-regulation). Physiological characteristics are associated with different temperaments. Children inherit a physiology that biases them to have a particular type of temperament, but through experience they learn to modify their temperament style to some degree. Goodness of fit refers to the match between a child's temperament and the environmental demands the child must cope with. Goodness of fit can be an important aspect of a child's adjustment.

Although research evidence is sketchy at this point in time, some general recommendations are that caregivers should (1) be sensitive to the individual characteristics of the child, (2) be flexible in responding to these characteristics, and (3) avoid negative labeling of the child.

Personality Development

- Erikson argued that an infant's first year is characterized by the stage of trust versus mistrust. Some infants develop signs of self-recognition at about 15 to 18 months of age. Independence becomes a central theme in the second year of life. Mahler argues that the infant separates himself or herself from the mother and then develops individuation. Erikson stressed that the second year of life is characterized by the stage of autonomy versus shame and doubt.

How Do Social Orientation/Understanding and Attachment Develop in Infancy?

 Describe the development of social orientation/ understanding and attachment in infancy.

Social Orientation/ Understanding

- Infants show a strong interest in the social world and are motivated to understand it. Infants orient to the social world early in their development. Face-to-face play with a caregiver begins to occur at 2 to 3 months of age. Newly developed self-produced locomotion skills significantly expand the infant's ability to initiate social interchanges and explore their social world more independently. Perceiving people as engaging in intentional and goal-directed behavior is an important social cognitive accomplishment, and this initially occurs toward the end of the first year. Social referencing increases in the second year of life.

Attachment and Its Development

- Attachment is a close emotional bond between two people. In infancy, contact comfort and trust are important in the development of attachment. Bowlby's ethological theory stresses that the caregiver and the infant are biologically predisposed to form an attachment. Attachment develops in four phases during infancy.

Individual Differences in Attachment

- Securely attached babies use the caregiver, usually the mother, as a secure base from which to explore the environment. Three types of insecure attachment are avoidant, resistant, and disorganized. Ainsworth created the Strange Situation, an observational measure of attachment. Ainsworth argues that secure attachment in the first year of life provides an important foundation for psychological development later in life. Caregivers of secure babies are sensitive to the babies' signals and are consistently available to meet their needs. Caregivers of avoidant babies tend to be unavailable or rejecting. Caregivers of resistant babies tend to be inconsistently available to their babies and usually are not very affectionate. Caregivers of disorganized babies often neglect or physically abuse their babies. The strength of the link between early attachment and later development has varied somewhat across studies. Some critics argue that attachment theorists have not given adequate attention to genetics and temperament. Other critics stress that they have not adequately taken into account the diversity of social agents and contexts. Cultural variations in attachment have been found, but in all cultures studied to date, secure attachment is the most common classification.

Developmental Social Neuroscience and Attachment

- Increased interest is being directed toward the role of the brain in the development of attachment. The hormone oxytocin is a key candidate for influencing the development of maternal-infant attachment.

How Do Social Contexts Influence Socioemotional Development in Infancy?

 Explain how social contexts influence the infant's development.

The Family

- The transition to parenthood requires considerable adaptation and adjustment on the part of parents. Children socialize parents, just as parents socialize children. Mutual regulation and scaffolding are important aspects of reciprocal socialization. Belsky's model describes direct and indirect effects. An important parental task involves managing and correcting infants' undesirable behaviors. The mother's primary role when interacting with the infant is caregiving; the father's is playful interaction.

Child Care

- More U.S. children are in child care now than at any earlier point in history. The quality of child care is uneven, and child care remains a controversial topic. Quality child care can be achieved and seems to have few adverse effects on children. In the NICHD child-care study, infants from low-income families were more likely to receive the lowest quality of care. Also, higher quality of child care was linked with fewer child problems.

key terms

emotion 204	social smile 206	goodness of fit 211	insecure resistant
primary emotions 205	stranger anxiety 207	social referencing 216	babies 218
self-conscious emotions 205	separation protest 207	attachment 216	insecure disorganized
basic cry 206	temperament 208	Strange Situation 218	babies 218
anger cry 206	easy child 208	securely attached babies 218	reciprocal socialization 223
pain cry 206	difficult child 208	insecure avoidant	scaffolding 223
reflexive smile 206	slow-to-warm-up child 208	babies 218	

key people

Michael Lewis 205	John Bowlby 208	John Bates 209	Jay Belsky 222
Joseph Campos 205	Alexander Chess 208	Erik Erikson 211	Kathleen McCartney 226
John Watson 207	Stella Thomas 208	Margaret Mahler 213	
Jacob Gewirtz 207	Jerome Kagan 209	Ross Thompson 214	
Mary Ainsworth 208	Mary Rothbart 209	Harry Harlow 216	

connecting with improving the lives of children

MAKING A DIFFERENCE

Nurturing the Infant's Socioemotional Development

What are the best ways to help the infant develop socioemotional competencies?

- *Develop a secure attachment with the infant.* Infants need the warmth and support of one or more caregivers. The caregiver(s) should be sensitive to the infant's signals and respond in a nurturing way.
- *Be sure that both the mother and the father nurture the infant.* Infants develop best when both the mother and the father provide warm, nurturant support. Fathers need to seriously evaluate their responsibility in rearing a competent infant.
- *Select competent child care.* If the infant will be placed in child care, spend time evaluating different options. Be sure the infant–caregiver ratio is low. Also assess whether the adults enjoy and are knowledgeable about interacting with infants. Confirm that the facility is safe and provides stimulating activities.
- *Understand and respect the infant's temperament.* Be sensitive to the characteristics of each child. It may be necessary to provide extra support for distress-prone infants, for example. Avoid negative labeling of the infant.
- *Adapt to developmental changes in the infant.* An 18-month-old toddler is very different from a 6-month-old infant. Be knowl-

edgeable about how infants develop, and adapt to the changing infant. Let toddlers explore a wider but safe environment.
- *Be physically and mentally healthy.* Infants' socioemotional development benefits when their caregivers are physically and mentally healthy. For example, a depressed parent may not sensitively respond to the infant's signals.
- *Read a good book on infant development.* Any of T. Berry Brazelton's books is a good start. One is *Touchpoints.* Two other good books by other authors are *Infancy* by Tiffany Field and *Baby Steps* by Claire Kopp.

RESOURCES

The Happiest Baby on the Block
by Harvey Karp (2002)
New York: Bantam
An outstanding book on ways to calm a crying baby.

Touchpoints: Birth to Three
by T. Berry Brazelton and Joshua Sparrow (2006)
Cambridge, MA: Da Capo Press
Covering the period from birth through age 3, Brazelton and Sparrow focus on the concerns and questions parents have about the child's feelings, behavior, and development.

You are troubled at seeing him spend his early years doing nothing. What! Is it nothing to be happy? Is it nothing to skip, to play, to run about all day long? Never in his life will he be so busy as now.

—JEAN-JACQUES ROUSSEAU
Swiss-Born French Philosopher, 18th Century

Early Childhood

In early childhood, our greatest untold poem was being only 4 years old. We skipped and ran and played all the sun long, never in our lives so busy, busy being something we had not quite grasped yet. Who knew our thoughts, which we worked up into small mythologies all our own? Our thoughts and images and drawings took wings. The blossoms of our heart, no wind could touch. Our small world widened as we discovered new refuges and new people. When we said, "I," we meant something totally unique, not to be confused with any other. Section 4 consists of three chapters: "Physical Development in Early Childhood" (Chapter 8), "Cognitive Development in Early Childhood" (Chapter 9), and "Socioemotional Development in Early Childhood" (Chapter 10).

PHYSICAL DEVELOPMENT IN EARLY CHILDHOOD

Teresa Amabile remembers that, when she was in kindergarten, she rushed in every day, excited and enthusiastic about getting to the easel and painting with bright colors and big brushes. Children in Teresa's class had free access to a clay table with all kinds of art materials on it. Teresa remembers going home every day and telling her mother she wanted to draw and paint. Teresa's kindergarten experience, unfortunately, was the high point of her enthusiasm for art classes in school.

A description of Teresa's further childhood experiences with art and creativity follows (Goleman, Kaufman, & Ray, 1993, p. 60):

> The next year she entered a strict, traditional school, and things began to change. As she tells it, "Instead of having free access to art materials every day, art became just another subject, something you had for an hour and a half every Friday afternoon." Week after week, all through elementary school, it was the same art class. And a very restricted, even demoralizing one at that.

The children were not given any help in developing their skills. Also, the teacher graded the children on the art they produced, adding evaluation pressure to the situation. Teresa was aware at that time that her motivation for doing artwork was being completely destroyed. In her words, "I no longer wanted to go home at the end of the day and take out my art materials and draw or paint."

In spite of the negative instruction imposed upon her in art classes, Teresa Amabile continued her education and eventually obtained a Ph.D. in psychology. In part because of her positive experiences in kindergarten, she became one of the leading researchers on creativity. Her hope is that more elementary schools will not crush children's enthusiasm for creativity, the way hers did. So many young children, like Teresa, are excited about exploring and creating, but by the time they reach the third or fourth grade, many don't like school, let alone have any sense of pleasure in their own creativity.

topical connections

Physical growth in infancy is dramatic. Even though physical growth in early childhood slows, it is not difficult to distinguish young children from infants when you look at them. Most young children lose their "baby fat," and their legs and trunks become longer. In addition to what you can see with the naked eye, much development also continues below the surface in the brain. In infancy, myelination of axons in the brain paved the way for development of such functions as full visual capacity. Continued myelination in early childhood provides children with much better hand-eye coordination.

looking back

preview

As twentieth-century Welsh poet Dylan Thomas artfully observed, young children do "run all the sun long." And as their physical development advances, young children's small worlds widen. We begin this chapter by examining how young children's bodies grow and change. Then we discuss the development of young children's motor skills and conclude by exploring important aspects of their health.

How Does a Young Child's Body and Brain Grow and Change?

 LG1 Discuss growth and change in the young child's body and brain.

```
Height and Weight          The Brain
```

The greatest person ever known
Is one all poets have outgrown;
The poetry, innate and untold,
Of being only four years old.

—**Christopher Morley**
American Novelist, 20th Century

The bodies of 5-year-olds and 2-year-olds are different. Notice that the 5-year-old not only is taller and weighs more, but also has a longer trunk and legs than the 2-year-old. *Can you think of some other physical differences between 2- and 5-year-olds?*

In this section, we examine the height and weight changes for boys and girls in early childhood along with individual growth patterns. In addition, we look at how the brain and nervous system continue to develop, and how young children's cognitive abilities expand.

HEIGHT AND WEIGHT

Remember from Chapter 5, "Physical Development in Infancy," that the infant's growth in the first year is rapid. During the infant's second year, the growth rate begins to slow down, and the growth rate continues to slow in early childhood. Otherwise, we would be a species of giants. The average child grows 2½ inches in height and gains between 5 and 7 pounds a year during early childhood. As the preschool child grows older, the percentage of increase in height and weight decreases with each additional year (McMahon & Stryjewski, 2012). Figure 8.1 shows the average height and weight of children as they age from 2 to 6 years (Centers for Disease Control and Prevention, 2000). Girls are only slightly smaller and lighter than boys during these years, a difference that continues until puberty. During the preschool years, both boys and girls slim down as the trunks of their bodies lengthen. Although their heads are still somewhat large for their bodies, by the end of the preschool years most children have lost their top-heavy look. Body fat also shows a slow, steady decline during the preschool years. The chubby baby often looks much leaner by the end of early childhood. Girls have more fatty tissue than boys, and boys have more muscle tissue.

Growth patterns vary individually (Florin & Ludwig, 2011). Think back to your elementary school years. This was probably the first time you noticed that some children were taller than you, some shorter; some were stronger, some weaker. Much of the variation is due to heredity, but environmental experiences are involved to some extent. A review of the height and weight of children around the world concluded that the two most important contributors to height differences are ethnic origin and nutrition (Meredith, 1978). The urban, middle-socioeconomic-status, and firstborn children were taller than rural, lower-socioeconomic status, and later-born children. The children whose mothers smoked during pregnancy were half an inch shorter than the children whose mothers did not smoke during pregnancy. In the United States, African American children are taller than non-Latino White children.

Why are some children unusually short? The primary contributing influences are congenital factors (genetic or prenatal problems), growth hormone deficiency, a physical problem that develops in childhood, maternal smoking during pregnancy, or an emotional difficulty (Albertsson-Wikland, 2011; Wit, Kiess, & Mullis, 2011).

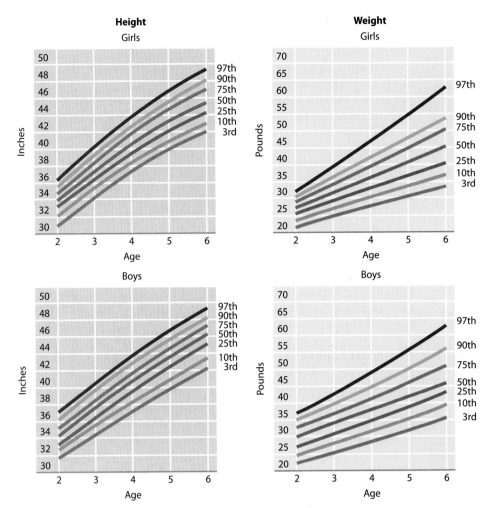

FIGURE **8.1**

HEIGHT AND WEIGHT CHANGES FROM 2 THROUGH 6 YEARS OF AGE. These graphs show the percentiles of height and weight for boys and girls from 2 through 6 years of age in the United States.

Chronically sick children are shorter than their rarely sick counterparts. Children who have been physically abused or neglected may not secrete adequate growth hormone, the lack of which can restrict their physical growth. **Growth hormone deficiency** is the absence or deficiency of growth hormone produced by the pituitary gland to stimulate the body to grow. Growth hormone deficiency may occur during infancy or later in childhood (Marcdante, Kliegman, & Behran, 2011). As many as 10,000 to 15,000 U.S. children may have growth hormone deficiency (Stanford University Medical Center, 2012). Without treatment, most children with growth hormone deficiency will not reach a height of five feet. Treatment involves regular injections of growth hormone and usually lasts several years (Rosenfeld & Bakker, 2008). Some children receive injections daily, others several times a week. Twice as many boys as girls are treated with growth hormone (Lee & Howell, 2006). A recent research review concluded that growth hormone therapy with children of short stature was partially effective in reducing the deficit in height as adults (Deodati & Cianfarani, 2011).

There has been a significant increase in treating very short children with growth hormone therapy (Albertsson-Wiland, 2011; Collett-Solberg, 2011). Some medical experts have expressed concern that many young children who are being treated with growth hormone therapy are merely short but don't have a growth hormone deficiency. In such cases, parents often perceive that there is a handicap in being short, especially in boys.

Few studies have been conducted on the psychological and social outcomes of having very short stature in childhood. A recent study did reveal that growth hormone treatment of children very short in stature was linked to an increase in height as well as improvements in self-esteem and mood (Chaplin & others, 2011).

growth hormone deficiency The absence or deficiency of growth hormone produced by the pituitary gland to stimulate the body to grow.

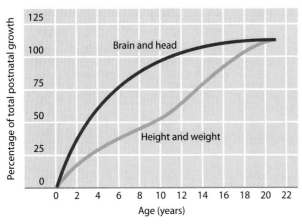

FIGURE 8.2

GROWTH CURVES FOR THE HEAD AND BRAIN AND FOR HEIGHT AND WEIGHT. The more rapid growth of the brain and head can easily be seen. Height and weight advance more gradually over the first two decades of life.

From Human Biology and Ecology by Albert Damon. Figure 10.6, copyright © 1977 by W. W. Norton & Company, Inc. Used with permission of W. W. Norton & Company, Inc. This selection may not be reproduced, stored in a retrieval system, or transmitted in any form or by any means without the prior written permission of the publisher.

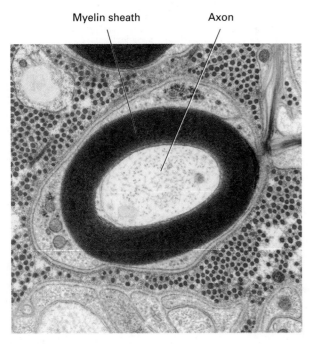

FIGURE 8.3

A MYELINATED NERVE FIBER. The myelin sheath, shown in brown, encases the axon (white). This image was produced by an electron microscope that magnified the nerve fiber 12,000 times. *What role does myelination play in the brain's development and children's cognition?*

myelination The process in which the nerve cells are covered and insulated with a layer of fat cells, which increases the speed at which information travels through the nervous system.

THE BRAIN

One of the most important physical developments during early childhood is the continuing development of the brain and nervous system (Nelson, 2011). Although the brain continues to grow in early childhood, it does not grow as rapidly as in infancy. By the time children reach 3 years of age, the brain is three-quarters of its adult size. By age 6, the brain has reached about 95 percent of its adult volume (Lenroot & Giedd, 2006). Thus, the brain of a 5-year-old is nearly the size it will be when the child reaches adulthood, but as we see in later chapters, the development that occurs inside the brain continues through the remaining childhood and adolescent years (Casey, Jones, & Somerville, 2011).

The brain and the head grow more rapidly than any other part of the body. The top parts of the head, the eyes, and the brain grow faster than the lower portions, such as the jaw. Figure 8.2 reveals how the growth curve for the head and brain advances more rapidly than the growth curve for height and weight. At 5 years of age, when the brain has attained approximately 90 percent of its adult weight, the 5-year-old's total body weight is only about one-third of what it will be when the child reaches adulthood.

Neuronal Changes In Chapter 3, "Prenatal Development," and Chapter 5, "Physical Development in Infancy," we discussed the brain's development during the prenatal and infancy periods. Changes in neurons in early childhood involve connections between neurons and myelination, just as they did in infancy (Johnson & de Haan, 2011). Communication in the brain is characterized by the transmission of information between neurons, or nerve cells. Some of the brain's increase in size during early childhood is due to the increase in the number and size of nerve endings and receptors, which allows more effective communication to occur.

Neurons communicate with each other through *neurotransmitters* (chemical substances) that carry information across gaps (called *synapses*) between the neurons. One neurotransmitter that has been shown to increase substantially in the 3-to-6-year age period is *dopamine* (Diamond, 2001). We return to a discussion of dopamine later in this section.

Some of the brain's increase in size also is due to the increase in **myelination,** in which nerve cells are covered and insulated with a layer of fat cells (see Figure 8.3). This has the effect of increasing the speed and efficiency of information traveling through the nervous system. Myelination is important in the development of a number of children's abilities (Diamond, Casey, & Munakata, 2011). For example, myelination in the areas of the brain related to hand-eye coordination is not complete until about 4 years of age. One fMRI study of children (mean age: 4 years) found that children with developmental delay of motor and cognitive milestones had significantly reduced levels of myelination (Pujol & others, 2004). Myelination in the areas of the brain related to focusing attention is not complete until the end of the middle childhood years or later.

Structural Changes Until recently, scientists lacked adequate technology to detect sensitive changes and view detailed maps of the developing human brain. However, sophisticated brain-scanning techniques, such as magnetic resonance imaging (MRI), now allow us to better detect these changes (Gogtay & Thompson, 2010). With high-resolution MRI, scientists have evolved spatially complex, four-dimensional growth pattern maps of the developing brain, allowing the brain to be monitored with greater sensitivity than ever before. Using these techniques, scientists have discovered that children's brains undergo dramatic anatomical changes between the ages of 3 and 15 (Thompson & others, 2000). By repeatedly obtaining brain scans of the same children for up to four years, they found that the children's brains experience rapid, distinct spurts of growth. The amount of brain material in some areas can nearly double within as little as a year, followed by a drastic loss of tissue as unneeded cells are purged and the brain continues to reorganize itself. The scientists found that the overall size of the brain did not show dramatic growth in the 3-to-15-year age range. However, what did dramatically change were local patterns within the brain.

Researchers have found that in children from 3 to 6 years of age, the most rapid growth takes place in the frontal lobe areas involved in planning and organizing new actions, and in maintaining attention to tasks. They have discovered that from age 6 through puberty, the most rapid growth takes place in the temporal and parietal lobes, especially areas that play major roles in language and spatial relations.

developmental **connection**

Brain Development. In middle and late childhood, cortical thickening occurs in the frontal lobes, which may be linked to improvements in language abilities such as reading. Chapter 11, p. 327

The Brain and Cognitive Development The substantial increases in memory and rapid learning that characterize infants and young children are related to cell loss, synaptic growth, and myelination. Somewhat amazingly, neuroscientists have found that the density of synapses peaks at 4 years of age (Moulson & Nelson, 2008). Some leading cognitive scientists argue that the true episodic memory (memory for the when and where of life's happenings, such as remembering what one had for breakfast this morning) and self-awareness do not develop until about this time (4 years of age) (Craik, 2006). However, recall from Chapter 6, "Cognitive Development in Infancy," and Chapter 7, "Socioemotional Development in Infancy," that some infant development researchers conclude that episodic memory and self-awareness emerge in infancy (Bauer, Larkina, & Deocampo, 2011).

These aspects of the brain's maturation, combined with opportunities to experience a widening world, contribute to children's emerging cognitive abilities. Consider a child who is learning to read and is asked by a teacher to read aloud to the class. Input from the child's eyes is transmitted to the child's brain, then passed through many brain systems, which translate (process) the patterns of black and white into codes for letters, words, and associations. The output occurs in the form of messages to the child's lips and tongue. The child's own gift of speech is possible because brain systems are organized in ways that permit language processing.

The brain is organized according to many neural circuits, which are neural networks composed of many neurons with certain functions (Westerman, Thomas, & Karmiloff-Smith, 2011). One neural circuit is thought to have an important function in the development of attention and working memory (a type of short-term memory that is like a mental workbench in performing many cognitive tasks) (Krimer & Goldman-Rakic, 2001). This neural circuit involves the *prefrontal cortex*, and the neurotransmitter dopamine may be a key aspect of information transmission in the prefrontal cortex and this neural circuit (Diamond, 2001) (see Figure 8.4). The maturation of the prefrontal cortex is important in the development of a number of cognitive and socioemotional skills, including attention, memory, and self-regulation (Diamond, Casey, & Munakata, 2011).

In sum, scientists are beginning to chart connections between children's cognitive development in areas such as attention and memory, brain regions such as the prefrontal cortex, and the transmission of information at the level of the neuron such as the neurotransmitter dopamine (Johnson & de Haan, 2011). As advancements in technology allow scientists to "look inside" the brain to observe its activity, we will likely see an increased precision in our understanding of the brain's functioning in various aspects of cognitive development (Diamond, Casey, & Munakata, 2011).

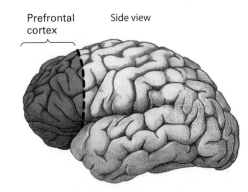

Prefrontal cortex   Side view

Frontal view

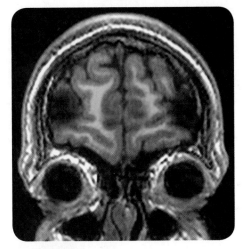

FIGURE 8.4

THE PREFRONTAL CORTEX. The prefrontal cortex, the highest level in the brain, shows extensive development from 3 to 6 years of age and, as will be seen in later chapters, continues to grow through the remainder of childhood and adolescence. The prefrontal cortex plays important roles in attention, memory, and self-regulation. The image on the top shows a side view of the location of the prefrontal cortex. The image on the bottom (frontal view) is a composite of more than 100 fMRI images of the prefrontal cortex that were taken to assess individuals' speed of processing information under different conditions.

How Do Young Children's Motor Skills Develop?

LG2 Describe changes in motor development in early childhood.

Gross and Fine Motor Skills

Young Children's Artistic Drawings

Running as fast as you can, falling down, getting right back up and running just as fast as you can . . . building towers with blocks . . . scribbling, scribbling, and scribbling some more . . . cutting paper with scissors . . . During your preschool years, you probably developed the ability to perform all of these activities.

GROSS AND FINE MOTOR SKILLS

Considerable progress is made in both gross and fine motor skills during early childhood. Young children develop a sense of mastery through increased proficiency in gross motor skills such as walking and running. Improvement in fine motor skills—such as being able to turn the pages of a book, one at a time—also contributes to the child's sense of mastery in the second year. First, let's explore changes in gross motor skills.

Gross Motor Skills The preschool child no longer has to make an effort simply to stay upright and to move around. As children move their legs with more confidence and carry themselves more purposefully, moving around in the environment becomes more automatic.

At 3 years of age, children enjoy simple movements, such as hopping, jumping, and running back and forth, just for the sheer delight of performing these activities. They take considerable pride in showing how they can run across a room and jump all of 6 inches. The run-and-jump will win no Olympic gold medals, but for the 3-year-old the activity is a source of considerable pride and accomplishment.

At 4 years of age, children are still enjoying the same kinds of activities, but they have become more adventurous. They scramble over low jungle gyms as they display their athletic prowess. Although they have been able to climb stairs with one foot on each step for some time, they are just beginning to be able to come down the same way. They still often revert to putting two feet on each step.

At 5 years of age, children are even more adventuresome than when they were at 4. It is not unusual for self-assured 5-year-olds to perform hair-raising stunts on practically any climbing object. Five-year-olds run hard and enjoy races with each other and their parents. A summary of development in gross motor skills during early childhood is shown in Figure 8.5.

37 to 48 Months	49 to 60 Months	61 to 72 Months
Throws ball underhanded (4 feet)	Bounces and catches ball	Throws ball (44 feet, boys; 25 feet, girls)
Pedals tricycle 10 feet	Runs 10 feet and stops	Carries a 16-pound object
Catches large ball	Pushes/pulls a wagon/doll buggy	Kicks rolling ball
Completes forward somersault (aided)	Kicks 10-inch ball toward target	Skips alternating feet
Jumps to floor from 12 inches	Carries 12-pound object	Roller skates
Hops three hops with both feet	Catches ball	Skips rope
Steps on footprint pattern	Bounces ball under control	Rolls ball to hit object
Catches bounced ball	Hops on one foot four hops	Rides bike with training wheels

FIGURE 8.5

THE DEVELOPMENT OF GROSS MOTOR SKILLS IN EARLY CHILDHOOD. *Note:* The skills are listed in the approximate order of difficulty within each age period.

You probably have arrived at one important conclusion about preschool children: They are very, very active. Indeed, 3-year-old children have the highest activity level of any age in the entire human life span. They fidget when they watch television. They fidget when they sit at the dinner table. Even when they sleep, they move around quite a bit.

Designing and implementing a developmentally appropriate movement curriculum (one that's appropriate for the child's age and the child individually) facilitates the development of children's gross motor skills. To read further about supporting young children's motor development, see the *Caring Connections* interlude.

There can be long-term negative effects for children who fail to develop basic motor skills. These children will not be as able to join in group games or participate

caring connections

Supporting Young Children's Motor Development

If you observe young children, you will see that they spend a great deal of time engaging in motor activities such as running, jumping, throwing, and catching. These activities can form the basis of advanced, sports-related skills. For children to progress to effective, coordinated, and controlled motor performance, interaction with and instruction from supportive adults can be beneficial.

How can early childhood educators support young children's motor development? When planning physical instruction for young children, it is important to keep in mind that their attention span is rather short, so instruction should be brief and to the point. Young children need to practice skills in order to learn them, so instruction should be followed with ample time for practice (Thompson, 2006).

Fitness is an important dimension of people's lives, and it is beneficial to de-

What are some effective strategies for supporting young children's motor development?

velop a positive attitude toward exercise early in life. Preschoolers need vigorous activities for short periods of time. They can be encouraged to rest or change to a quieter activity as needed.

Movement, even within the classroom, can improve a child's stamina. Such movement activities might be as basic as practicing locomotor skills or as complex as navigating an obstacle course. A number of locomotor skills (such as walking, running, jumping, sliding, skipping, and leaping) can be practiced forward and backward. And it is important to keep practice fun, allowing children to enjoy movement for the sheer pleasure of it (Sutterby & Frost, 2006).

37 to 48 Months	49 to 60 Months	61 to 72 Months
Approximates a circle in drawing	Strings and laces shoelace	Folds paper into halves and quarters
Cuts paper	Cuts following a line	Traces around hand
Pastes using pointer finger	Strings 10 beads	Draws rectangle, circle, square, and triangle
Builds three-block bridge	Copies figure X	Cuts interior piece from paper
Builds eight-block tower	Opens and places clothespins (one-handed)	Uses crayons appropriately
Draws 0 and +	Builds a five-block bridge	Makes clay object with two small parts
Dresses and undresses doll	Pours from various containers	Reproduces letters
Pours from pitcher without spilling	Prints first name	Copies two short words

FIGURE 8.6

THE DEVELOPMENT OF FINE MOTOR SKILLS IN EARLY CHILDHOOD. *Note:* The skills are listed in the approximate order of difficulty within each age period.

developmental **connection**

Physical Development. Participation in sports can have positive or negative outcomes for children. Chapter 11, p. 330

Denver Developmental Screening Test II A test used to diagnose developmental delay in children from birth to 6 years of age; includes separate assessments of gross and fine motor skills, language, and personal-social ability.

placement stage Kellogg's term for 2- to 3-year-olds' drawings that are drawn on a page in placement patterns.

shape stage Kellogg's term for 3-year-olds' drawings consisting of diagrams in different shapes.

design stage Kellogg's term for 3- to 4-year-olds' drawings that mix two basic shapes into more complex designs.

in sports during their school years and in adulthood. However, the positive development of motor skills has benefits besides participation in games and sports. Engaging in motor skills fulfills young children's needs and desires for movement, and exercise builds muscles, strengthens the heart, and enhances aerobic capacity.

Fine Motor Skills   At 3 years of age, children show a more mature ability to place and handle things than they did when they were infants. Although for some time they have had the ability to pick up the tiniest objects between their thumb and forefinger, they are still somewhat clumsy at it. Three-year-olds can build surprisingly high block towers, each block placed with intense concentration but often not in a completely straight line. When 3-year-olds play with a simple jigsaw puzzle, they are rather rough in placing the pieces. Even when they recognize the location a piece fits into, they are not very precise in positioning the piece. They often try to force the piece in the location or pat it vigorously.

By 4 years of age, children's fine motor coordination has improved substantially and is more precise. Sometimes 4-year-old children have trouble building high towers with blocks because in their efforts to place each of the blocks perfectly, they may upset those already stacked. By age 5, children's fine motor coordination has improved. Hand, arm, and body all move together under better command of the eye. Mere towers no longer interest the 5-year-old, who now wants to build a house or a church, complete with steeple, although adults may still need to be told what each finished project is meant to be. A summary of the development of fine motor skills in early childhood is shown in Figure 8.6.

How do developmentalists measure children's motor development? The **Denver Developmental Screening Test II** is a simple, inexpensive, fast method of diagnosing developmental delay in children from birth through 6 years of age. The test is individually administered and includes separate assessments of gross and fine motor skills, as well as language and personal-social ability (Thompson & others, 2010). Among the gross motor skills this test measures are the child's ability to sit, walk, long jump, pedal a tricycle, throw a ball overhand, catch a bounced ball, hop on one foot, and balance on one foot. Fine motor skills measured by the test include the child's ability to stack cubes, reach for objects, and draw a person.

YOUNG CHILDREN'S ARTISTIC DRAWINGS

In the story that opened the chapter, you read about Teresa Amabile's artistic skills and interest during kindergarten. The story revealed how these skills were restricted once she went to elementary school. Indeed, many young children show a special interest in drawing, just as Teresa did.

The unintended irregularities of children's drawings suggest spontaneity, freedom, and directness (Golomb, 2008). They may use lavish colors that come close, but perhaps won't match the reality of their subjects. Form and clarity give way to bold lines flowing freely on the page. It is not the end product that matters so much, but the joy of creating, the fun of mixing colors, experimenting with different mediums, and getting messy in the process.

Young children often use the same formula for drawing different things. Though modified in small ways, one basic form can cover a range of objects. When children begin to draw animals, they portray them in the same way they portray humans: standing upright with a smiling face, legs, and arms. Pointed ears may be a clue to adults about the

"You moved."
© Lee Lorenz/The New Yorker Collection/ www.cartoonbank.com

nature of the particular beast. As children become more sophisticated, their drawing of a cat will look more catlike to an adult. It may be resting on all four paws, tail in the air, and fur gleaming.

Not all children embrace art with equal enthusiasm, and the same child may want to draw one day but have no interest in it the next day. For most children, however, art is an important vehicle for conveying feelings and ideas that are not easily expressed in words (Thompson, 2006). Drawing and constructing also provide children with a hands-on opportunity to use their problem-solving skills to develop creative ways to represent scale, space, and motion (Yarrow, 2010). Parents can provide a context for artistic exploration by giving children a work space where they are not overly concerned about messiness or damage. They can make supplies available, have a bulletin board display space for the child's art, and support and encourage the child's art activity. When viewing children's art, many parents take special delight in hearing about the creative process. Questions such as "Can you tell me about this?" and "What were you thinking about when you made this?" encourage children and help parents to see the world through their children's eyes.

Developmental Changes and Stages   The development of fine motor skills in the preschool years allows children to become budding artists. There are dramatic changes in how children depict what they see. Art provides unique insights into children's perceptual worlds—what they are attending to, how space and distance are viewed, how they experience patterns and forms (Dorn, Madeja, & Sabol, 2004). Rhoda Kellogg is a creative teacher of preschool children who has observed and guided young children's artistic efforts for many decades. She has assembled an impressive array of tens of thousands of drawings produced by more than 2,000 preschool children. Adults who are unfamiliar with young children's art often view the productions of this age group as meaningless scribbles. However, Kellogg (1970) documented that young children's artistic productions are orderly, meaningful, and structured.

By their second birthday, children can scribble. Scribbles represent the earliest form of drawing. Every form of graphic art, no matter how complex, contains the lines found in children's artwork, which Kellogg calls the 20 basic scribbles. These include vertical, horizontal, diagonal, circular, curving, waving or zigzag lines and dots. As young children progress from scribbling to picture making, they go through four distinguishable stages: placement, shape, design, and pictorial (see Figure 8.7).

Following young children's scribbles is the **placement stage,** Kellogg's term for 2- to 3-year-olds' drawings, drawn on a page in placement patterns. One example of these patterns is the spaced border pattern shown in Figure 8.7*b.* The **shape stage** is Kellogg's term for 3-year-olds' drawings consisting of diagrams in different shapes (see Figure 8.7*c*). Young children draw six basic shapes: circles, squares or rectangles, triangles, crosses, Xs, and forms. The **design stage** is Kellogg's term for 3- to 4-year-olds' drawings in which young children mix two basic shapes into a more complex design (see Figure 8.7*d*). This stage occurs rather quickly after the

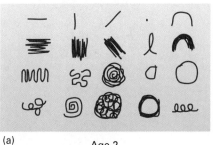

(a)   Age 2
20 basic scribbles

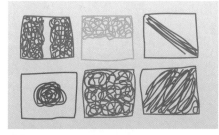

(b)   Age 2 to 3
Placement stage

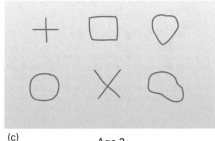

(c)   Age 3
Shape stage

(d)   Age 3 to 4
Design stage

(e)   Age 4 to 5
Pictorial stage

FIGURE **8.7**

THE STAGES OF YOUNG CHILDREN'S ARTISTIC DRAWINGS

At which of Kellogg's stages of children's art is this young girl's drawing?

shape stage. The **pictorial stage** is Kellogg's term for 4- to 5-year-olds' drawings that consist of objects that adults can recognize (see Figure 8.7e).

Child Art in Context   Claire Golomb (2002, 2008) has studied and conducted research on children's art for a number of decades. Golomb especially criticizes views of young children's art that describe it as primitive and a reflection of conceptual immaturity. She argues that children, like all novices, tend to use forms economically, and their comments indicate that their simplified version works. Rather than reflecting conceptual immaturity, Golomb views children's art as inventive problem solving.

Golomb maintains that developmental changes in the way children draw are not strictly age-related but also depend on talent, motivation, familial support, and cultural values. Thus, her view contrasts with Kellogg's universal stage approach in which all children go through the same sequence in developing art skills, which we just discussed. In Golomb's view, child art flourishes in sociocultural contexts where tools are made available and where this activity is valued. In Chapter 9, "Cognitive Development in Early Childhood," we look further at young children's art, paying special attention to the role of cognitive development in their art.

Review Connect Reflect

 LG2 Describe changes in motor development in early childhood.

Review

- How do gross and fine motor skills change in early childhood?
- How can young children's artistic drawings be characterized?

Connect

- Would you characterize the development of gross motor skills as occurring more rapidly in infancy or in early childhood?

Reflect *Your Own Personal Journey of Life*

- Assume that you are the director of a preschool program, and the parents ask you to develop a program to teach the children how to participate in sports. Think through how you would explain to parents why most 3-year-olds are not ready for participation in sports programs. Include in your answer information about 3-year-olds' limited motor skills, as well as the importance of helping children learn basic motor skills first rather than having unrealistic expectations for young children's development of sports skills.

What Are Some Important Aspects of Young Children's Health?

 LG3 Characterize the health of young children.

| Sleep and Sleep Problems | Nutrition | Exercise | Health, Safety, and Illness |

So far, we have discussed young children's body growth and change, as well as their development of motor skills. In this section, we explore another aspect of young children's physical development—health. To learn more about young children's health, we focus on how it is affected by sleep, nutrition, exercise, safety practices, and illnesses.

developmental **connection**

Sleep. What sleep disorder in infancy leads to the most infant deaths, and at what age is the infant most at risk for this disorder? Chapter 5, p. 143

SLEEP AND SLEEP PROBLEMS

Experts recommend that young children get 11 to 13 hours of sleep each night (National Sleep Foundation, 2011). Most young children sleep through the night and have one daytime nap. Not only is the amount of sleep children get important, but so is uninterrupted sleep (Owens & Mindell, 2011). Also, it sometimes is difficult to get young children to go to sleep as they drag out their bedtime routine (Hoban, 2004). One study found that bedtime resistance was associated with conduct problems or hyperactivity in children (Carvalho Bos & others, 2009).

Helping the child slow down before bedtime often contributes to less resistance in going to bed. Reading the child a story, playing quietly with the child in the bath, and letting the child sit on the caregiver's lap while listening to music are quieting activities.

How Would You...?
If you were a **human development and family studies professional,** how would you advise parents of a young child who is resisting going to bed at night?

Sleep Problems   Children can experience a number of sleep problems (Owens & Mindell, 2011). One estimate indicates that more than 40 percent of children experience a sleep problem at some point in their development (Boyle & Cropley, 2004). The following research studies indicate links between children's sleep problems and negative developmental outcomes:

- Children who had trouble sleeping in childhood were more likely to have alcohol use problems in adolescence and early adulthood (Wong & others, 2010).

- Sleep problems in early childhood were a subsequent indicator of attention problems that in some cases persisted into early adolescence (O'Callaghan & others, 2010).

- A recent analysis concluded that chronic sleep disorders that deprive children of adequate sleep may result in impaired brain development (Jan & others, 2010).

- Preschool children who did not get adequate sleep were more likely to experience injuries that required medical attention (Koulouglioti, Cole, & Kitzman, 2008).

- A short sleep duration in young children was linked with being overweight (Hart, Cairns, & Jelalian, 2011).

Let's now explore four specific sleep problems in children: nightmares, night terrors, sleepwalking, and sleep talking. **Nightmares** are frightening dreams that awaken the sleeper, more often toward the morning than just after the child has gone to bed at night. Caregivers should not worry about young children having occasional nightmares because almost every child has them. If children have nightmares persistently, it may indicate that they are feeling too much stress during their waking hours (Owens & Mindell, 2011).

Night terrors are characterized by a sudden arousal from sleep and an intense fear, usually accompanied by a number of physiological reactions, such as rapid heart rate and breathing, loud screams, heavy perspiration, and physical movement (Bruni & others, 2008). In most instances, the child has little or no memory of what happened during the night terror. Night terrors are less common than nightmares and occur more often in deep sleep than do nightmares. Many children who experience night terrors return to sleep rather quickly after the night terror. Children usually outgrow night terrors.

Somnambulism (sleepwalking) occurs during the deepest stage of sleep. Approximately 15 percent of children sleepwalk at least once, and from 1 to 5 percent do it regularly. Most children outgrow the problem without professional intervention.

Sleep talkers are soundly asleep as they speak, although occasionally they make fairly coherent statements for a brief period of time. Most of the time, though, you can't understand what children are saying during sleep talking. There is nothing abnormal about sleep talking, and there is no reason to try to stop it from occurring.

What characterizes young children's sleep? What are some sleep problems in childhood?

NUTRITION

Four-year-old Bobby is on a steady diet of double cheeseburgers, French fries, and chocolate milk shakes. Between meals, he gobbles up candy bars and marshmallows. He hates green vegetables. Bobby, a preschooler, already has developed poor nutritional habits. What are a preschool child's energy needs? What is a preschooler's eating behavior like?

pictorial stage Kellogg's term for 4- to 5-year-olds' drawings depicting objects that adults can recognize.

nightmares Frightening dreams that awaken the sleeper.

night terrors Incidents characterized by sudden arousal from sleep, intense fear, and usually physiological reactions such as rapid heart rate and breathing, loud screams, heavy perspiration, and physical movement.

somnambulism Sleep walking; occurs in the deepest stage of sleep.

FIGURE **8.8**

RECOMMENDED ENERGY INTAKES FOR CHILDREN AGES 1 THROUGH 10

Age	Weight (kg)	Height (cm)	Energy needs (calories)	Calorie ranges
1 to 3	13	90	1,300	900 to 1,800
4 to 6	20	112	1,700	1,300 to 2,300
7 to 10	28	132	2,400	1,650 to 3,300

Energy Needs Feeding and eating habits are important aspects of development during early childhood (Wardlaw & Smith, 2012). What children eat affects their skeletal growth, body shape, and susceptibility to disease. The preschool child requires up to 1,800 calories per day. Figure 8.8 shows the increasing energy needs of children as they move from infancy through the childhood years. Energy needs of individual children of the same age, sex, and size vary. However, an increasing number of children have an energy intake that exceeds what they need (Schiff, 2011). A recommendation by the World Health Organization is that on average for children 7 years of age and younger, boys should have an 18 percent, and girls a 20 percent, reduction in energy intake (Butte, 2006).

Diet, Eating Behavior, and Parental Feeding Styles A national study found that from the late 1970s through the late 1990s, key dietary shifts took place in U.S. children: greater away-from-home consumption; large increases in total energy from salty snacks, soft drinks, and pizza; and large decreases in energy from low- and medium-fat milk and medium- and high-fat beef and pork (Nielsen, Siega-Riz, & Popkin, 2002). These dietary changes occurred for children as young as 2 years of age through the adult years.

What are some positive strategies parents can adopt regarding their young children's eating behavior?

A national study revealed that 45 percent of children's meals exceed recommendations for saturated and trans fat, which can raise cholesterol levels and increase the risk of heart disease (Center for Science in the Public Interest, 2008). In addition, this study found that one-third of children's daily caloric intake comes from restaurants, twice the percentage consumed away from home in the 1980s. Nearly all of the available children's meals at KFC, Taco Bell, Sonic, Jack in the Box, and Chick-fil-A were too high in calories. A recent study of 2- and 3-year-olds found that French fries and other fried potatoes were the vegetable they were most likely to consume (Fox & others, 2010).

Young children's eating behavior is strongly influenced by their caregivers' behavior (Black & Hurley, 2007; Ostbye & others, 2011). Young children's eating behavior improves when caregivers eat with children on a predictable schedule, model eating healthy food, make mealtimes pleasant occasions, and engage in certain feeding styles. Distractions from television, family arguments, and competing activities should be minimized so children can focus on eating. A sensitive/responsive caregiver feeding style, in which the caregiver is nurturant, provides clear information about what is expected, and appropriately responds to children's cues, is recommended (Black & Hurley, 2007). Forceful and restrictive caregiver behaviors are not recommended. For example, a restrictive feeding style is linked to children being overweight (Black & Lozoff, 2008).

Another problem is that many parents do not recognize that their children are overweight. One recent study of parents with 2- to 17-year-old children found that few parents of overweight children perceived their children to be too heavy or were worried about their children's weight (Eckstein & others, 2006).

How Would You...?

If you were a **health-care professional,** how would you work with parents to increase the nutritional value of meals and snacks they provide to their young children?

Fat and Sugar Consumption   Although some health-conscious parents may be providing too little fat in their infants' and children's diets, other parents are raising their children on diets in which the percentage of fat is far too high (Schiff, 2011). In a national survey, 4- to 18-year-olds often consumed the high-fat varieties of milk, yogurt, cheese, ice cream, and dairy-based toppings (Kranz, Lin, & Wagstaff, 2007).

Our changing lifestyles, in which we often eat on the run and pick up fast-food meals, contribute to the increased fat levels in children's diets. Most fast-food meals are high in protein, especially meat and dairy products. But the average American child does not need to be concerned about getting enough protein. What must be of concern is the vast number of young children who are being weaned on fast foods that are not only high in protein but also high in fat. Eating habits become ingrained very early in life; unfortunately, it is during the preschool years that many people get their first taste of fast food. The American Heart Association recommends that the daily limit for calories from fat should be approximately 35 percent.

The concern surrounding food choices not only involves excessive fat in children's diets but also excessive sugar (Harris & others, 2011). Consider Robert, age 3, who loves chocolate. His mother lets him have three chocolate candy bars a day. He also drinks an average of four cans of caffeinated cola a day, and he eats sugar-coated cereal each morning at breakfast. The average American child consumes almost 2 pounds of sugar per week (Riddle & Prinz, 1984). One study found that children from low-income families were likely to consume more sugar than their counterparts from higher-income families (Kranz & Siega-Riz, 2002).

How does sugar consumption influence the health and behavior of young children? The association of sugar consumption with children's health problems—dental cavities and obesity, for example—has been widely documented (Li, 2011).

In sum, although there is individual variation in appropriate nutrition for children, their diets should be well balanced and should include fats, carbohydrates, protein, vitamins, and minerals (Wardlaw & Smith, 2012). An occasional candy bar does not hurt, but a steady diet of hamburgers, French fries, milk shakes, and candy bars should be avoided.

> Spinach: Divide into little piles. Rearrange again into new piles. After five or six maneuvers, sit back and say you are full.
>
> —**Delia Ephron**
> *American Writer and Humorist, 20th Century*

> This would be a better world for children if parents had to eat the spinach.
>
> —**Groucho Marx**
> *American Comedian, 20th Century*

"Fussy Eaters," Sweets, and Snacks   Many young children get labeled as "fussy" or "difficult eaters" when they are only trying to exercise the same rights to personal taste and appetite that adults take for granted (Dovey & others, 2008). Caregivers should allow for the child's developing tastes in food. However, when young children eat too many sweets—candy bars, cola, and sweetened cereals, for example—they can spoil their appetite and then not want to eat more nutritious foods at mealtime. Thus, caregivers need to be firm in limiting the amount of sweets young children eat.

Overweight Young Children   Being overweight has become a serious health problem in early childhood (Blake, 2011; Marcdante, Kleigman, & Behrman, 2011; Schiff, 2011). The Centers for Disease Control and Prevention (2011) has established categories for obesity, overweight, and at risk for being overweight. These categories are determined by body mass index (BMI), which is computed by a formula that takes into account height and weight. Children and adolescents whose BMI is at or above the 97th percentile are classified as obese; those whose BMI is at or above the 95th percentile are overweight; and those whose BMI is at or above the 85th percentile are at risk of becoming overweight.

The percentages of young children who are overweight or at risk of becoming overweight in the United States have increased dramatically in recent decades, and these percentages are likely to grow unless changes occur in children's lifestyles (Sorte, Daeschel, & Amador, 2011). A study revealed that in 2003–2006, 11 percent

What are some trends in the eating habits and weight of young children?

of U.S. 2- to 19-year-olds were obese, 16 percent were overweight, and 38 percent were at risk of becoming overweight (Ogden, Carroll, & Flegal, 2008). The good news from this large-scale study is that the percentages in these categories have started to level off rather than increase as they had done in the last several decades. However, a comparison of 34 countries revealed that the United States had the second highest rate of child obesity (Janssen & others, 2005).

The risk that overweight children will continue to be overweight when they are older was documented in a study in which 80 percent of the children who were at risk for being overweight at age 3 were also at risk for being overweight or were overweight at age 12 (Nader & others, 2006). A recent study revealed that preschool children who were overweight were at significant risk for being overweight/obese at age 12 (Shankaran & others, 2011).

Being overweight also is linked to young children's psychological makeup. In one study, the relation between weight status and self-esteem in 5-year-old girls was examined (Davison & Birth, 2001). The girls who were overweight had lower body self-esteem than those who were not overweight. Thus, as early as 5 years of age, being overweight is linked with lower self-esteem.

Prevention of obesity in children includes helping children and parents see food as a way to satisfy hunger and nutritional needs, not as proof of love or as a reward for good behavior (Nowicka & Flodmark, 2008). Snack foods should be low in fat, in simple sugars, and in salt, as well as high in fiber. Routine physical activity should be a daily occurrence (Wuest & Fisette, 2012).

developmental **connection**

Nutrition. A number of intervention programs have been conducted in an effort to help overweight and obese children to lose weight. Chapter 11, p. 333

Malnutrition in Young Children from Low-Income Families

Malnutrition continues to be a major threat to millions during the childhood years (Schiff, 2011). Malnutrition and starvation are a daily fact of life for children in many developing countries that have high rates of poverty (UNICEF, 2011). A recent study revealed that two food-assisted maternal and child health programs (both emphasized food provision, communication about behavior change, and preventive health services) helped to reduce the impact of economic hardship on stunting of children's growth in Haiti (Donnegan & others, 2010).

A common nutritional problem in early childhood is iron deficiency anemia, which results in chronic fatigue (Bartle, 2007). This problem results from the failure to eat adequate amounts of quality meats and dark green vegetables. Young children from low-income families are most likely to develop iron deficiency anemia (Lonnerdal & Kelleher, 2007).

Some researchers argue that malnutrition is directly linked to cognitive deficits because of negative effects on brain development (Liu & others, 2003). However, an increasing number of researchers conclude that the links between child undernutrition, physical growth, and cognitive development are more complex (Marcon, 2003). For example, nutritional influences can be viewed in the context of socioemotional factors that often coincide with undernutrition. Thus, children who vary considerably from the norm in physical growth also differ on other biological and socioemotional factors that might influence cognitive development. For example, children who are underfed often are also less supervised, less stimulated, and less educated than children who are well nourished. As we discussed earlier, poverty is an especially strong risk factor that interacts with children's nutritional status to affect physical and cognitive development (Black & others, 2008).

Malnutrition may be linked to other aspects of development in addition to cognitive deficits. One longitudinal study found that U.S. children who were malnourished at 3 years of age showed more aggressive and hyper-active behavior at age 8, had more externalizing problems at age 11, and evidenced more excessive motor behavior at age 17 (Liu & others, 2004).

EXERCISE

Because of their activity level and the development of large muscles, especially in the arms and legs, preschool children need daily exercise (Jago & others, 2010; Wuest & Fisette, 2012). Guidelines recommend that preschool children engage in two hours of physical activity per day, divided into one hour of structured activity and one hour of unstructured free play (National Association for Sport and Physical Education, 2002).

The following three studies address the importance of physical activity in young children:

- Observations of 3- to 5-year-old children during outdoor play at preschools revealed that the preschool children were mainly sedentary even when participating in outdoor play (Brown & others, 2009). In this study, throughout the day the preschoolers were sedentary 89 percent of the time, engaged in light activity 8 percent of the time, and participated in moderate to vigorous physical activity only 3 percent of the time.

- Preschool children's physical activity was enhanced by family members' engaging in sports together and by parents' perception that it was safe for their children to play outside (Beets & Foley, 2008).

- Preschool children's physical activity varied greatly across different child-care centers (Bower & others, 2008). Opportunities to be active, presence of fixed and portable play equipment, and physical activity training were linked to preschool children's higher levels of physical activity in the centers.

In sum, the child's life should be centered around activities, not meals (Lumpkin, 2011). Just how important are these activities in young children's lives? See the *Connecting with Research* interlude for insight from one research study.

HEALTH, SAFETY, AND ILLNESS

In the effort to make a child's world safer, one of the main strategies is to prevent childhood injuries. And in considering young children's health, it important to examine contexts in which they live.

developmental **connection**

Health. As boys and girls reach and progress through adolescence, they exercise less. Chapter 14, p. 443

How Would You...?

If you were a **health-care professional,** how would you advise parents who want to get their talented 4-year-old child in a soccer league for preschool children?

How much physical activity should preschool children engage in per day?

connecting with research

Physical Activity in Young Children Attending Preschools

One study examined the activity levels of 281 3- to 5-year-olds in nine preschools (Pate & others, 2004). The preschool children wore accelerometers, a small activity monitor, for four to five hours a day. Height and weight assessments of the children were made to calculate their BMI.

Guidelines recommend that preschool children engage in two hours of physical activity per day, divided into one hour of structured activity and one hour of unstructured free play (National Association for Sport and Physical Education, 2002). In this study, the young children participated in an average of 7.7 minutes per hour of moderate to vigorous activity, usually in a block of time when they were outside. Over the course of eight hours of a preschool day, these children would get approximately one hour of moderate and vigorous physical activity—only about 50 percent of the amount recommended. The researchers concluded that young children are unlikely to engage in another hour per day of moderate and vigorous physical activity outside their eight hours spent in preschool and thus are not getting adequate opportunities for physical activity.

Gender and age differences characterized the preschool children's physical activity. Boys were more likely to engage in moderate or vigorous physical activity than girls were. Four- and 5-year-old children were more likely to be sedentary than 3-year-old children.

The young children's physical activity levels also varied according to the particular preschool they attended. The extent to which they participated in moderate and vigorous physical activity ranged from

What are some guidelines for preschool children's exercise?

4.4 to 10.2 minutes per hour across the nine preschools. Thus, the policies and practices of particular preschools influence the extent to which children engage in physical activity. The researchers concluded that young children need more vigorous play and organized activities.

Can you think of any other ways in which researchers could test and confirm the findings of this study?

Preventing Childhood Injuries   Young children's active and exploratory nature, coupled with unawareness of danger in many instances, often puts them in situations in which they are at risk for injuries. Most of young children's cuts, bumps, and bruises are minor, but some accidental injuries can produce serious injuries or even death.

In the United States, motor vehicle accidents are the leading cause of death in young children, followed by cancer and cardiovascular disease (National Vital Statistics Reports, 2004) (see Figure 8.9). In addition to motor vehicle accidents, other accidental deaths in children involve drowning, falls, burns, and poisoning (Duke & others, 2011).

Notice in Figure 8.9 that the seventh leading cause of death in young children in the United States involves firearms. In one cross-cultural comparison, the rate of firearm-related death among children under 15 years of age in 26 industrialized countries was the highest in the United States (American Academy of Pediatrics, 2001). Among those industrialized countries with no firearm-related deaths in children were Japan, Singapore, and the Netherlands.

Many of young children's injuries can be prevented (Snowdon & others, 2008). Among the preventive measures are regularly restraining children in automobiles, reducing access to firearms, and making homes and playgrounds safer (Durbin, 2011).

Influences on children's safety include the acquisition and practice of individual skills and safety behaviors, family and home influences, school and peer influences, and the community's actions. Notice that these influences reflect Bronfenbrenner's ecological model of development that we described in Chapter 1. Figure 8.10 shows how these ecological contexts can influence children's safety, security, and injury prevention (Sleet & Mercy, 2003). We will have more to say about contextual influences on young children's health shortly.

Reducing access to firearms is a wise strategy (Fraga & others, 2010). In 12 states that passed laws requiring that firearms be made inaccessible to children, unintentional shooting deaths of children fell by almost 25 percent. In one study, many parents in homes with firearms reported that their children never handled the firearms, but interviews with their children contradicted the parents' perceptions (Baxley & Miller, 2006).

Deaths of young children due to automobile accidents have declined considerably in the United States since the invention of the seat belt. All U.S. states and the District of Columbia have laws that require young children to be restrained in the back seats of cars, either in specially designed seats or by seat belts. In many instances, when young children are killed today in automobile accidents, they are unrestrained. Although many parents today use car seats or "booster seats" for their children, most don't install the seats properly. If the seat is not installed correctly, children are at risk for serious injury or death in automobile accidents (Cease, King, & Monroe, 2011). Nearly all local police departments will assist parents in installing their children's car seats safely. This service is provided free of charge.

Most fatal non-vehicle-related deaths in young children occur in or around the home. Young children have drowned in bathtubs and swimming pools, been burned in fires and explosions, experienced falls from heights, and drunk or eaten poisonous substances.

Playgrounds also can be a source of children's injuries (Macpherson & others, 2010). One of the major problems is that playground equipment is often not constructed over impact-absorbing surfaces such as wood chips or sand.

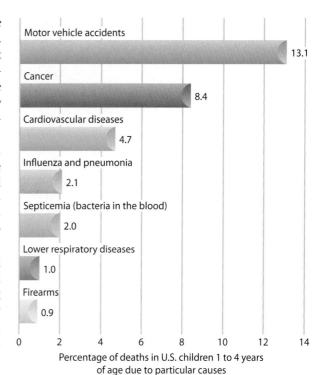

Percentage of deaths in U.S. children 1 to 4 years of age due to particular causes

FIGURE **8.9**

MAIN CAUSES OF DEATH IN CHILDREN 1 THROUGH 4 YEARS OF AGE. These figures show the percentages of deaths in U.S. children 1 to 4 years of age due to particular causes in 2002 (National Vital Statistics Reports, 2004).

Individual
Development of social skills and ability to regulate emotions
Impulse control (such as not darting out into a street to retrieve a ball)
Frequent use of personal protection (such as bike helmets and safety seats)

Family/Home
High awareness and knowledge of child management and parenting skills
Frequent parent protective behaviors (such as use of child safety seats)
Presence of home safety equipment (such as smoke alarms and cabinet locks)

School/Peers
Promotion of home/school partnerships
Absence of playground hazards
Injury prevention and safety promotion policies and programs

Community
Availability of positive activities for children and their parents
Active surveillance of environmental hazards
Effective prevention policies in place (such as pool fencing)

FIGURE **8.10**

CHARACTERISTICS THAT ENHANCE YOUNG CHILDREN'S SAFETY. In each context of a child's life, steps can be taken to create conditions that enhance the child's safety and reduce the likelihood of injury. *How are the contexts listed in the figure related to Bronfenbrenner's theory (described in Chapter 1)?*

Contexts of Young Children's Health Among the contexts affecting young children's health are poverty and ethnicity, home and child care, environmental tobacco smoke, and exposure to lead. In addition to discussing these issues, we will discuss the state of illness and health in the world's children.

Poverty and Ethnicity Low income is linked with poor health in young children (Hernandez, Montana, & Clark, 2010). Many health problems of young children in poverty begin before birth when their mothers receive little or no health care, which can produce a low birth weight child and other complications that may continue to affect the child years later (Miller, Sadegh-Nobari, & Lillie-Blanton, 2011). Children living in poverty may experience unsanitary conditions, live in crowded housing, and be inadequately supervised (Neumann, Gewa, & Bwibo, 2004). Children in poverty are more likely to be exposed to lead poisoning than children growing up in higher socioeconomic conditions (Morrissey-Ross, 2000). The families of many children in poverty do not have adequate medical insurance, and thus the children often receive less adequate medical care than do children living in higher socioeconomic conditions (Cousineau, Stevens, & Farias, 2011).

Ethnicity is also linked to children's health (Carlo & others, 2011). For example, one study found that even when socioeconomic status was controlled, Latino, African American, and Asian American children were less likely to have had a usual health-care source, health professional, doctor visit, and dental visit in the past year (Shi & Stevens, 2005). Another study revealed that children whose parents had limited English proficiency were three times more likely to have fair or poor health status than their English-proficient counterparts (Flores, Abreu, & Tomany-Korman, 2005).

How Would You...?
If you were a **health-care professional,** how would you advise parents of young children to improve the safety of their home?

Safety at Home and in Child Care Caregivers—whether they are parents at home or teachers and supervisors in child care—play an important role in protecting the health of young children (Schnitzer, Covington, & Kruse, 2011). For example, by controlling the speed of the vehicles they drive, by decreasing or eliminating their drinking—especially before driving—and by not smoking around children, caregivers enhance the likelihood that children will be healthy (Tinsley, 2003).

Young children may lack the intellectual skills—including reading ability—to discriminate between safe and unsafe household substances. And they may lack the impulse control to keep from running out into a busy street while chasing a ball. In these and many other situations, competent adult supervision and monitoring of young children are important to prevent injuries. In communicating with young children, caregivers need to make sure that the information they give to children is cognitively simple. And an important strategy is that parents guide children in learning how to control and regulate their own health behavior.

Parents also should invest effort in finding a competent health-care provider for their children (Hickson & Clayton, 2002, p. 456). This "includes consulting sources of information and asking questions likely to provide useful information about practice characteristics that may affect the parent-doctor relationship. Parents, for example, might seek information concerning a physician's willingness to answer questions and involve parents in decision making or at least to outline options. Parents might also inquire about the physician's style of practice and philosophies about treatment, behavior management, nutrition, and other general health maintenance practices." To read about Barbara Deloin, a pediatric nurse who promotes positive parent-child experiences and positive links of families to the health-care system, see the *Connecting with Careers* profile that follows.

Environmental Tobacco Smoke Estimates indicate that approximately 22 percent of children and adolescents in the United States are exposed to tobacco smoke in the home. An increasing number of studies reach the conclusion that

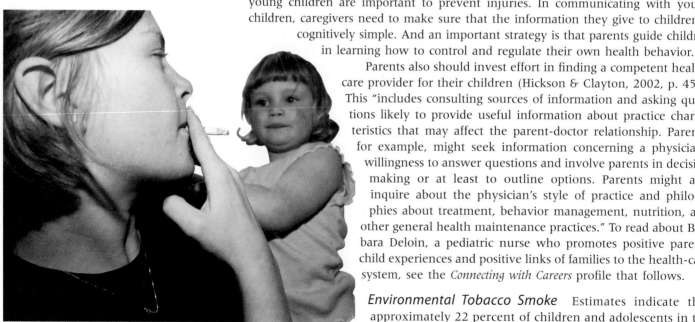

What are some negative outcomes for children when they experience environmental tobacco smoke?

Barbara Deloin, Pediatric Nurse

Barbara Deloin is a pediatric nurse in Denver, Colorado. She practices nursing in the Pediatric Oral Feeding Clinic and is involved in research as part of an irritable infant study for the Children's Hospital in Denver. She is on the faculty of nursing at the Colorado Health Sciences Center. Deloin previously worked in San Diego where she was coordinator of the Child Health Program for the County of San Diego.

Deloin's research interests focus on children with special health-care needs, especially high-risk infants and children, and promoting positive parent-child experiences. She is a former president of the National Association of Pediatric Nurse Associates and Practitioners.

For more information about what pediatric nurses do, see page 49 in the Careers in Children's Development appendix.

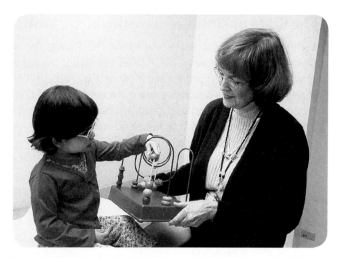

Barbara Deloin, conducting a pediatric evaluation.

children are at risk for health problems when they live in homes in which a parent smokes (Bhatt & Smyth, 2011; Constant & others, 2011; Oberg & others, 2011). If the mother smoked, her children were twice as likely to develop respiratory problems (Etzel, 1988). In one study, young children whose fathers smoked at home were more likely to have upper respiratory tract infections than those whose fathers did not smoke at home (Shiva & others, 2004). Children exposed to tobacco smoke in the home are more likely to develop wheezing symptoms and asthma than children in nonsmoking homes (Chang, 2009). A recent study found that parental smoking was a risk factor for higher blood pressure in children (Simonetti & others, 2011). And another recent study revealed that exposure to secondhand smoke was related to young children's sleep problems, including sleep-disordered breathing (Yolton & others, 2010).

How Would You...?
If you were a **health-care professional,** how would you talk with parents about the impact of secondhand smoke on children's health in order to encourage parents to stop smoking?

Exposure to Lead   There are special concerns about lead poisoning in young children (Burke & Miller, 2011; Soto-Jimenez & Flegal, 2011). Approximately 3 million children under 6 years of age are estimated to be at risk for lead poisoning, which might harm their development (Ahamed & others, 2005). As we mentioned earlier, children in poverty are at greater risk for lead poisoning than children living in higher socioeconomic conditions (Kersey, Chi, & Cutts, 2011). Lead can get into children's bloodstreams through food or water that is contaminated by lead, from putting lead-contaminated fingers in their mouths, or from inhaling dust from lead-based paint. The negative effects of high lead levels in children's blood include lower intelligence, lower achievement, attention deficit hyperactivity disorder, and elevated blood pressure (Abelsohn & Sanborn, 2010; Bellinger, 2008). One study found that 5-year-old children exposed to lead performed more poorly on tests of memory and problem solving (Canfield, Gendle, & Cory-Slechta, 2004). Because of such negative outcomes, the Centers for Disease Control and Prevention recommends that children be screened for the presence of lead contamination in their blood.

To read further about children's illness and health, see the *Connecting with Diversity* interlude.

The State of Illness and Health in the World's Children

Each year UNICEF produces a report titled *The State of the World's Children*. In a recent report, UNICEF (2008) emphasized the importance of information about the under-5 mortality rate of a nation. UNICEF concluded that the under-5 mortality rate is the result of a wide range of factors, including the nutritional health and health knowledge of mothers, the level of immunization, dehydration, availability of maternal and child health services, income and food availability in the family, availability of clean water and safe sanitation, and the overall safety of the child's environment.

UNICEF periodically reports rankings of nations' under-5 mortality rates. In 2006, 38 nations had a lower under-5 mortality rate than the United States, with Singapore, Sweden, Iceland, San Marino, and Liechtenstein having the lowest rates of all nations (UNICEF, 2008). The relatively high under-5 mortality rate of the United States compared with other developed nations is due to such factors as poverty and inadequate health care. The devastating effects on the health of young children occur in countries where poverty rates are high (UNICEF, 2009). The poor are the majority in nearly one of every five nations in the world. They often experience lives of hunger, malnutrition, illness, inadequate access to health care, unsafe water, and a lack of protection from harm (Imdad, Sadig, & Bhutta, 2011; UNICEF, 2011).

A leading cause of childhood death in impoverished countries is dehydration caused by diarrhea. In 1980, diarrhea was responsible for over 4.6 million childhood deaths. Oral rehydration therapy (ORT) was introduced in 1979 and quickly became the foundation for controlling diarrheal diseases. ORT now is given to the majority of children in impoverished countries suffering with diarrhea, which has decreased the number of deaths due to dehydration caused by diarrhea.

Acute respiratory infections, such as pneumonia, also have killed many children under the age of 5. Many of these children's lives could have been saved with antibiotics administered by a community health worker. Undernutrition also is a contributing factor to many deaths of children under the age of 5 in impoverished countries (Amuna & Zotor, 2008).

In the last decade, there has been a dramatic increase in the number of young children who have died because of HIV/AIDS transmitted to them by their parents (UNICEF, 2008). Deaths in young children due to HIV/AIDS especially occur in countries with high rates of poverty and low levels of education (Boeving & Forsyth, 2008). For example, the uneducated are four times more likely to believe that there is no way to avoid AIDS and three times more likely to be unaware that the virus can be transmitted from mother to child (UNICEF, 2008).

Many of the deaths of young children around the world can be prevented by a reduction in poverty and improvements in nutrition, sanitation, education, and health services (Imdad, Sadig, & Bhutta, 2011; UNICEF, 2011).

Many children in impoverished countries die before reaching the age of 5 from dehydration and malnutrition brought about by diarrhea. *What are some of the other main causes of death in young children around the world?*

Review

- What is the nature of sleep and sleep problems in young children?
- What are young children's energy needs? What characterizes young children's eating behavior?
- What are some important aspects of exercise in the lives of young children?
- How can the nature of children's injuries be summarized? How do contexts influence children's health?

Connect

- In this section, you learned that experts recommend that young children get 11 to 13 hours of sleep a night during early childhood. How does that compare with what you learned about sleep requirements in infancy?

Reflect *Your Own Personal Journey of Life*

- If you become a parent of a young child, what precautions will you take to improve your child's health?

topical connections

In Chapter 9 you will explore the fascinating world of young children's cognitive development, their remarkable advances in language development, and the role of education in their development. In Chapter 11, you will read about the continuing changes in children's physical development in middle and late childhood. Their motor skills become smoother and more coordinated during the elementary school years. And the development of their brain—especially in the prefrontal cortex—provides the foundation for a number of cognitive and language advances, including the use of strategies and reading skills.

looking forward ---- →

reach your learning goals

How Does a Young Child's Body and Brain Grow and Change?

LG1 Discuss growth and change in the young child's body and brain.

- Height and Weight
- The Brain

- The average child grows 2½ inches in height and gains between 5 and 7 pounds a year during early childhood. Growth patterns vary individually, though. Some children are unusually short because of congenital factors, growth hormone deficiency, a physical problem that develops during childhood, maternal smoking during pregnancy, or an emotional difficulty.

- By age 6, the brain has reached about 95 percent of its adult volume. Some of the brain's growth is due to increases in the number and size of nerve endings and receptors. One neurotransmitter that increases in concentration from 3 to 6 years of age is dopamine. Researchers have found that changes in local patterns in the brain occur from 3 to 15 years of age. From 3 to 6 years of age, the most rapid growth occurs in the frontal lobes. From age 6 through puberty, the most substantial growth takes place in the temporal and parietal lobes. Increasing brain maturation contributes to changes in cognitive abilities. One link involves the prefrontal cortex, dopamine, and improved attention and working memory.

How Do Young Children's Motor Skills Develop?

 Describe changes in motor development in early childhood.

Gross and Fine Motor Skills

- Gross motor skills increase dramatically in early childhood. Children become increasingly adventuresome as their gross motor skills improve. It is important for early childhood educators to design and implement developmentally appropriate activities for young children's gross motor skills. Three types of these activities are fundamental movement, daily fitness, and perceptual-motor. Fine motor skills also improve substantially during early childhood. The Denver Developmental Screening Test II is a simple, inexpensive method of diagnosing developmental delay and includes separate assessments of gross and fine motor skills.

Young Children's Artistic Drawings

- The development of fine motor skills allows young children to become budding artists. Scribbling begins at 2 years of age, followed by four stages of drawing, culminating in the pictorial stage at 4 to 5 years of age. Golomb argues that it is important to explore the sociocultural contexts of children's art and that factors such as talent, motivation, familial support, and cultural values influence the development of children's art.

What Are Some Important Aspects of Young Children's Health?

 Characterize the health of young children.

Sleep and Sleep Problems

- Young children should get 11 to 13 hours of sleep each night. Most young children sleep through the night and have one daytime nap. Helping the young child slow down before bedtime often leads to less resistance in going to bed. Among the sleep problems that can develop in young children are nightmares, night terrors, somnambulism (sleepwalking), and sleep talking.

Nutrition

- Energy needs increase as children go through the early childhood years. The preschool child requires up to 1,800 calories daily. National assessments indicate that a large majority of young children in the United States do not have a healthy diet and that their eating habits have worsened over the last two decades. Too many parents are rearing young children on diets that are high in fat and sugar. Children's diets should contain well-balanced proportions of fats, carbohydrates, protein, vitamins, and minerals. A special concern is malnutrition in young children from low-income families.

Exercise

- Exercise should be a daily occurrence for young children. Guidelines recommend that they get two hours of exercise per day. The young child's life should be centered around activities rather than meals.

Health, Safety, and Illness

- In the United States, motor vehicle accidents are the leading cause of deaths among young children. Firearm deaths are especially high among young children in the United States in comparison with other countries. Among the strategies for preventing childhood injuries are restraining children in automobiles, preventing access to firearms, and making the home and playground safer. Among the contexts involved in children's health are poverty and ethnicity, home and child care, environmental tobacco smoke, and exposure to lead. The most devastating effects on the health of young children occur in countries with high poverty rates. Among the problems that low-income families face in these countries are hunger, malnutrition, illness, inadequate access to health care, unsafe water, and a lack of protection from harm. In recent decades, the trend in children's illness and health has been toward prevention as vaccines have been developed to reduce the occurrence of diseases in children. Parents play an important role in protecting young children's health. They influence their children's health by the way they behave in regard to children's illness symptoms. Parents can use a number of positive strategies in coping with the stress of having a chronically ill child. Parents need to invest effort in selecting a competent health-care provider for their children.

key terms

key people

connecting with improving the lives of children

MAKING A DIFFERENCE

Supporting Young Children's Physical Development

What are some good strategies for supporting young children's physical development?

- *Give young children plenty of opportunities to be active and explore their world.* Young children are extremely active and should not be constrained for long periods of time. Competent teachers plan daily fitness activities for young children. Preschool-aged children are too young for organized sports.

- *Make sure that young children's motor activities are fun and appropriate for their age.* Young children should enjoy the motor activities they participate in. Also, don't try to push young children into activities more appropriate for older children. For example, don't try to train a 3-year-old to ride a bicycle or have a 4-year-old take tennis lessons.

- *Give young children ample opportunities to engage in art.* Don't constrain young children's drawing. Let them freely create their artwork.

- *Provide young children with good nutrition.* Know how many calories preschool children need to meet their energy needs, which are greater than in infancy. Too many young children are raised on fast foods. Monitor the amount of fat and sugar in young children's diets. Nutritious midmorning and midafternoon snacks are recommended, in addition to breakfast, lunch, and dinner. Make sure that young children get adequate iron, vitamins, and protein.

- *Make sure that young children have regular medical checkups.* These are especially important for children living in impoverished conditions, who are less likely to get such checkups.

- *Be a positive health role model for young children.* When you have young children as passengers, control the speed of the vehicle when you are driving. Don't smoke in their presence. Eat healthy foods. Just by being in your presence, young children will imitate many of your behaviors.

- *Make sure children play in safe places.* Walk through the areas where children play and check for any potential hazards.

RESOURCES

Child Art in Context
by Claire Golomb (2002)
Washington, DC: American Psychological Association

One of the world's leading experts on children's art reviews the latest research and presents her contextual theory of children's art. Includes many children's drawings to illustrate points related to the theory.

American Academy of Pediatrics
www.aap.org

This Web site provides extensive information about strategies for improving children's health.

How Children Learn to Be Healthy
by Barbara Tinsley (2003)
New York: Cambridge University Press

A leading expert explores the ways in which health behavior develops in children, especially focusing on the roles of parents, schools, and the media in influencing children's health.

The State of the World's Children 2011
by UNICEF
Geneva, SWIT: UNICEF

Each year, UNICEF publishes *The State of the World's Children*, which has a special focus on children's health. Enter the title of the book on a search engine and you will be able to access the entire book free.

chapter 9

COGNITIVE DEVELOPMENT IN EARLY CHILDHOOD

chapter outline

The Reggio Emilia approach is an educational program for young children that was developed in the northern Italian city of Reggio Emilia. Children of single parents and children with disabilities have priority in admission; other children are admitted according to a scale of needs. Parents pay on a sliding scale based on income.

The children are encouraged to learn by investigating and exploring topics that interest them. A wide range of stimulating media and materials is available for children to use as they learn music, movement, drawing, painting, sculpting, collages, puppets and disguises, and photography, for example (Schroeder-Yu, 2008).

In this program, children often explore topics in a group, which fosters a sense of community, respect for diversity, and a collaborative approach to problem solving (Hyson, Copple, & Jones, 2006). Two co-teachers are present to serve as guides for children. The Reggio Emilia teachers consider a project to be an adventure, which can start from an adult's suggestion, from a child's idea, or from an event,

A Reggio Emilia classroom in which young children explore topics that interest them.

such as a snowfall or another unexpected happening. Every project is based on what the children say and do. The teachers allow children enough time to think and craft a project.

At the core of the Reggio Emilia approach is the image of children who are competent and have rights, especially the right to outstanding care and education. Parent participation is considered essential, and cooperation is a major theme in the schools. Many early childhood education experts believe the Reggio Emilia approach provides a supportive, stimulating context in which children are motivated to explore their world in a competent and confident manner (Inan, Trundle, & Kantor, 2010; Linder, 2010).

topical connections

In Chapter 8, you learned how a young child's body and brain grow and change. In Chapter 6, a special emphasis was the increasing consensus that infants' cognitive development is more advanced than Piaget envisioned. You learned that infants make amazing progress in their attentional, memory, concept formation, and language skills. In this chapter, you will discover that these information-processing skills continue to show remarkable advances in early childhood.

◀ *looking back*

preview

Children make a number of significant cognitive advances in early childhood. In the opening section, we explore the cognitive changes described by three major theories of cognitive development. Then we examine the dramatic changes in young children's language, and conclude by discussing a wide range of topics involving early childhood education.

What Are Three Views of the Cognitive Changes That Occur in Early Childhood?

 LG1 Describe three views of the cognitive changes that occur in early childhood.

- Piaget's Preoperational Stage
- Vygotsky's Theory
- Information Processing

The cognitive world of the preschool child is creative, free, and fanciful. Preschool children's imaginations work overtime, and their mental grasp of the world improves. Our coverage of cognitive development in early childhood focuses on three theories: Piaget's, Vygotsky's, and information processing.

developmental **connection**

Cognitive Development. Object permanence is an important accomplishment during the sensorimotor stage. Chapter 6, p. 176

PIAGET'S PREOPERATIONAL STAGE

Remember from Chapter 6, "Cognitive Development in Infancy," that during Jean Piaget's first stage of development, the sensorimotor stage, the infant progresses in the ability to organize and coordinate sensations and perceptions with physical movements and actions. The **preoperational stage,** which lasts from approximately 2 to 7 years of age, is the second Piagetian stage. In this stage, children begin to represent the world with words, images, and drawings. They form stable concepts and begin to reason. At the same time, the young child's cognitive world is dominated by egocentrism and magical beliefs.

Because Piaget called this stage "preoperational," it might sound like an unimportant waiting period. Not so. However, the label *preoperational* emphasizes that the child does not yet perform **operations,** which are reversible mental actions that allow children to do mentally what before they could do only physically. Mentally adding and subtracting numbers are examples of operations. *Preoperational thought* is the beginning of the ability to reconstruct in thought what has been established in behavior. It can be divided into two substages: the symbolic function substage and the intuitive thought substage.

The Symbolic Function Substage   The **symbolic function substage** is the first substage of preoperational thought, occurring roughly between the ages of 2 and 4. In this substage, the young child gains the ability to mentally represent an object that is not present. This ability vastly expands the child's mental world (Carlson & Zelazo, 2008; DeLoache, 2011). Young children use scribble designs to represent people, houses, cars, clouds, and so on; they begin to use language and engage in pretend play. However, although young children make distinct progress during this substage, their thought still has important limitations, two of which are egocentrism and animism.

Egocentrism is the inability to distinguish between one's own perspective and someone else's perspective. Piaget and Barbel Inhelder (1969) initially studied young children's egocentrism by devising the three mountains task (see Figure 9.1). The

---

preoperational stage Piaget's second stage, lasting from 2 to 7 years of age, during which time children begin to represent the world with words, images, and drawings. In this stage, they also form stable concepts and begin to reason. At the same time, their cognitive world is dominated by egocentrism and magical beliefs.

operations In Piaget's theory, reversible mental actions that allow children to do mentally what they formerly did physically.

symbolic function substage Piaget's first substage of preoperational thought, in which the child gains the ability to mentally represent an object that is not present (occurs roughly between 2 and 4 years of age).

egocentrism Piaget's concept that describes the inability to distinguish between one's own perspective and someone else's perspective.

animism The belief that inanimate objects have lifelike qualities and are capable of action.

intuitive thought substage Piaget's second substage of preoperational thought, in which children begin to use primitive reasoning and want to know the answers to all sorts of questions (occurs between about 4 and 7 years of age).

Model of Mountains

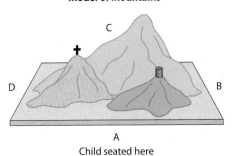

Child seated here

Photo 1
(View from A)

Photo 2
(View from B)

Photo 3
(View from C)

Photo 4
(View from D)

FIGURE **9.1**

THE THREE MOUNTAINS TASK. The mountain model on the far left shows the child's perspective from view A, where he or she is sitting. The four squares represent photos showing the mountains from four different viewpoints of the model—A, B, C, and D. The experimenter asks the child to identify the photo in which the mountains look as they would from position B. To identify the photo correctly, the child has to take the perspective of a person sitting at spot B. Invariably, a child who thinks in a preoperational way cannot perform this task. When asked what a view of the mountains looks like from position B, the child selects Photo 1, taken from location A (the child's own view at the time) instead of Photo 2, the correct view.

child walks around the model of the mountains and becomes familiar with what the mountains look like from different perspectives and can see that there are different objects on the mountains. The child is then seated on one side of the table on which the mountains are placed. The experimenter moves a doll to different locations around the table, at each location asking the child to select from a series of photos the one photo that most accurately reflects the view that the doll is seeing. Children in the preoperational stage often pick their own view rather than the doll's view. Preschool children frequently show the ability to take another's perspective on some tasks but not others.

Animism, another limitation of preoperational thought, is the belief that inanimate objects have lifelike qualities and are capable of action. A young child might show animism by saying, "That tree pushed the leaf off, and it fell down" or "The sidewalk made me mad; it made me fall down." A young child who uses animism fails to distinguish the appropriate occasions for using human and nonhuman perspectives (Opfer & Gelman, 2011).

Possibly because young children are not very concerned about reality, their drawings are fanciful and inventive. Suns are blue, skies are yellow, and cars float on clouds in their symbolic, imaginative world. One 3½-year-old looked at a scribble he had just drawn and described it as a pelican kissing a seal (see Figure 9.2a). The symbolism is simple but strong, like abstractions found in some modern art. Twentieth-century Spanish artist Pablo Picasso commented, "I used to draw like Raphael but it has taken me a lifetime to draw like young children." During the elementary school years, a child's drawings become more realistic, neat, and precise (see Figure 9.2b). Suns are yellow, skies are blue, and cars travel on roads (Winner, 1986).

The Intuitive Thought Substage

The **intuitive thought substage** is the second substage of preoperational thought, occurring between approximately 4 and 7 years of age. During this substage, children begin to use primitive reasoning and want to know the answers to all sorts of questions. Consider 4-year-old Tommy, who is at the beginning of the intuitive thought substage. Although he is starting to develop his own ideas about the world he lives in, his ideas are still simple, and he is not very good at thinking things out. He has difficulty understanding events that he knows are taking place but that he cannot see. His fantasized thoughts bear little resemblance to reality. He cannot yet answer the question "What if?" in any reliable way. For example, he has only a vague idea of what would happen if a car were to hit him. He also has difficulty negotiating traffic because he cannot do the mental calculations necessary to estimate whether an approaching car will hit him when he crosses the road.

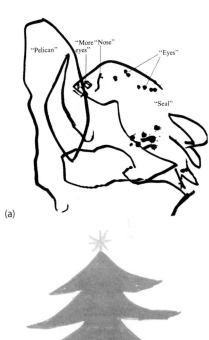

(a)

(b)

FIGURE **9.2**

THE SYMBOLIC DRAWING OF YOUNG CHILDREN. (a) A 3½-year-old's symbolic drawing. Halfway into his drawing, the 3½-year-old artist said it was a "pelican kissing a seal." (b) This 11-year-old's drawing is neater and more realistic but also less inventive.

FIGURE **9.3**

PIAGET'S CONSERVATION TASK. The beaker task is a well-known Piagetian task to determine whether a child can think operationally—that is, can mentally reverse actions and show conservation of the substance. (*a*) Two identical beakers are presented to the child. Then the experimenter pours the liquid from B into C, which is taller and thinner than A or B. (*b*) The child is asked if these beakers (A and C) have the same amount of liquid. The preoperational child says "no." When asked to point to the beaker that has more liquid, the preoperational child points to the tall, thin beaker.

(a)   A   B   C

(b)   A   B   C

By the age of 5, children have just about exhausted the adults around them with "why" questions. The child's questions signal the emergence of interest in reasoning and in figuring out why things are the way they are. Following are some samples of the questions children ask during the questioning period of 4 to 6 years of age (Elkind, 1976):

What makes you grow up?

Who was the mother when everybody was a baby?

Why do leaves fall?

Why does the sun shine?

Piaget called this substage *intuitive* because young children seem so sure about their knowledge and understanding yet are unaware of how they know what they know. That is, they know something but know it without the use of rational thinking.

Centration and the Limits of Preoperational Thought

One limitation of preoperational thought is **centration**, a centering of attention on one characteristic to the exclusion of all others. Centration is most clearly evidenced in young children's lack of **conservation,** the awareness that altering an object's or a substance's appearance does not change its basic properties. For example, to adults, it is obvious that a certain amount of liquid stays the same, regardless of a container's shape. But this is not at all obvious to young children. Instead, they are struck by the height of the liquid in the container; they focus on that characteristic to the exclusion of others.

The situation that Piaget devised to study conservation is his most famous task. In the conservation task, children are presented with two identical beakers, each filled to the same level with liquid (see Figure 9.3). They are asked if these beakers have the same amount of liquid, and they usually say yes. Next, the liquid from one beaker is poured into a third beaker, which is taller and thinner than the first two. Then, the children are asked if the amount of liquid in the tall, thin beaker is equal to that which remains in one of the original beakers. Children who are less than 7 or 8 years old usually say no and justify their answers in terms of the differing height or width of the beakers. Older children usually answer yes and justify their answers appropriately ("If you poured the water back, the amount would still be the same").

In Piaget's theory, failing the conservation-of-liquid task is a sign that children are at the preoperational stage of cognitive development. The failure demonstrates not only centration but also an inability to mentally reverse actions. For example,

"I still don't have all the answers, but I'm beginning to ask the right questions."
© Lee Lorenz/The New Yorker Collection/
www.cartoonbank.com

centration The focusing of attention on one characteristic to the exclusion of all others.

conservation The concept that an object's or substance's basic properties stay the same even though its appearance has been altered.

Type of Conservation	Initial Presentation	Manipulation	Preoperational Child's Answer
Number	Two identical rows of objects are shown to the child, who agrees they have the same number.	One row is lengthened and the child is asked whether one row now has more objects.	Yes, the longer row.
Matter	Two identical balls of clay are shown to the child. The child agrees that they are equal.	The experimenter changes the shape of one of the balls and asks the child whether they still contain equal amounts of clay.	No, the longer one has more.
Length	Two sticks are aligned in front of the child. The child agrees that they are the same length.	The experimenter moves one stick to the right, then asks the child if they are equal in length.	No, the one on the top is longer.

FIGURE 9.4

SOME DIMENSIONS OF CONSERVATION: NUMBER, MATTER, AND LENGTH. *What characteristics of preoperational thought do children demonstrate when they fail these conservation tasks?*

in the conservation-of-matter example shown in Figure 9.4, preoperational children say that the longer shape has more clay because they assume that "longer is more." Preoperational children cannot mentally reverse the clay-rolling process to see that the amount of clay is the same in both the shorter ball shape and the longer stick shape. A recent fMRI brain imaging study of conservation of number revealed that advances in a network in the parietal and frontal lobes were linked to 9- and 10-year-olds' conservation success when compared to non-conserving 5- and 6-year-olds (Houde & others, 2011).

Some developmentalists disagree with Piaget's estimate of when children's conservation skills emerge (Byrnes, 2008). For example, Rochel Gelman (1969) showed that when the child's attention to relevant aspects of the conservation task is improved, the child is more likely to conserve. Gelman has also demonstrated that attentional training on one dimension, such as number, improves the preschool child's performance on another dimension, such as mass. Thus, Gelman argues that conservation appears earlier than Piaget thought and that attention is especially important in explaining conservation.

VYGOTSKY'S THEORY

Piaget's theory is a major developmental theory. Another developmental theory that focuses on children's cognition is Lev Vygotsky's theory. Like Piaget, Vygotsky (1896–1934) emphasized that children actively construct their knowledge and understanding. In Piaget's theory, children develop ways of thinking and understanding by their actions and interactions with the physical world. In Vygotsky's theory, children are more often described as social creatures than in Piaget's theory. They develop their ways of thinking and understanding primarily through social interaction (Gauvain & Parke, 2010; Goncu & Gauvain, 2011). Their cognitive development depends on the tools provided by society, and their minds are shaped by the cultural context in which they live (Daniels, 2011).

We briefly considered Vygotsky's theory in Chapter 1. Here we take a closer look at his ideas about how children learn and his view of the role of language in cognitive development.

The Zone of Proximal Development Vygotsky's (1962) belief in the importance of social influences, especially instruction, on children's cognitive development is reflected in his concept of the zone of proximal development. **Zone of proximal development (ZPD)** is Vygotsky's term for the range of tasks that are too difficult for the child to master alone but that can be learned with guidance and assistance of

How Would You...?

If you were an **educator,** how would you apply Vygotsky's concept of the zone of proximal development and the concept of scaffolding to help a young child complete a puzzle?

zone of proximal development (ZPD) Vygotsky's term for the range of tasks that are too difficult for children to achieve alone but can be achieved with the guidance and assistance of adults or more-skilled children.

adults or more-skilled children. Thus, the lower limit of the ZPD is the level of skill reached by the child working independently. The upper limit is the level of additional responsibility the child can accept with the assistance of an able instructor (see Figure 9.5). The ZPD captures the child's cognitive skills that are in the process of maturing and can be accomplished only with the assistance of a more-skilled person (Daniels, 2011). Vygotsky (1962) called these the "buds" or "flowers" of development, to distinguish them from the "fruits" of development, which the child already can accomplish independently.

developmental **connection**

Parenting. Scaffolding also is an important strategy for parents to adopt in interacting with their infants. Chapter 7, p. 223

Scaffolding   Closely linked to the idea of the ZPD is the concept of scaffolding. **Scaffolding** means changing the level of support. Over the course of a teaching session, a more-skilled person (a teacher or an advanced peer) adjusts the amount of guidance to fit the child's current performance (Daniels, 2011). When the student is learning a new task, the more-skilled person may use direct instruction. As the student's competence increases, the person gives less guidance.

Language and Thought   According to Vygotsky, children use speech not only for social communication but also to help in solving problems. Vygotsky (1962) further argued that young children use language to plan, guide, and monitor their behavior. This use of language for self-regulation is called *private speech.* For Piaget, private speech is egocentric and immature—but for Vygotsky, it is an important tool of thought during the early childhood years (Wertsch, 2008).

Vygotsky said that language and thought initially develop independently of each other and then merge. He emphasized that all mental functions have external, or social, origins. Children must use language to communicate with others before they can focus inward on their own thoughts. Children also must communicate externally and use language for a long period of time before they can make the transition from external to internal speech. This transition period occurs between 3 and 7 years of age and involves talking to oneself. After a while, the self-talk becomes second nature to children, and they can act without verbalizing. At this point, children have internalized their egocentric speech in the form of *inner speech,* which becomes their thoughts.

Vygotsky maintained that children who use a lot of private speech are more socially competent than those who don't. He argued that private speech represents an early transition in becoming more socially communicative. For Vygotsky, when young children talk to themselves, they are using language to govern their behavior and guide themselves. For example, a child working on a puzzle might say to herself, "Which pieces should I put together first? I'll try those green ones first. Now I need some blue ones. No, that blue one doesn't fit there. I'll try it over here."

Researchers have found support for Vygotsky's view that private speech plays a positive role in children's development (Winsler, Carlton, & Barry, 2000). Researchers have found that children use private speech more when tasks are difficult, after they have made an error, and when they are not sure how to proceed (Berk, 1994). They also have discovered that children who use private speech are more attentive and improve their performance more than children who do not use private speech (Berk & Spuhl, 1995).

Teaching Strategies   Vygotsky's theory has been embraced by many teachers and has been successfully applied to education (Daniels, 2011; Goncu & Gauvain, 2011). Here are some ways Vygotsky's theory can be incorporated in classrooms:

- *Assess the child's ZPD.* Like Piaget, Vygotsky did not hold that formal, standardized tests are the best way to assess children's learning. Rather, Vygotsky argued that assessment should focus on determining the child's zone of proximal development. The skilled helper presents the child with tasks of varying difficulty to determine the best level at which to begin instruction.

Upper limit

Level of additional responsibility child can accept with assistance of an able instructor

Zone of proximal development (ZPD)

Lower limit

Level of problem solving reached on these tasks by child working alone

FIGURE 9.5

VYGOTSKY'S ZONE OF PROXIMAL DEVELOPMENT. Vygotsky's zone of proximal development has a lower limit and an upper limit. Tasks in the ZPD are too difficult for the child to perform alone. They require assistance from an adult or a more-skilled child. As children experience the verbal instruction or demonstration, they organize the information in their existing mental structures, so they can eventually perform the skill or task alone.

scaffolding In regard to cognitive development, Vygotsky used this term to describe the changing level of support over the course of a teaching session, with the more-skilled person adjusting guidance to fit the child's current performance level.

- *Use the child's ZPD in teaching.* Teaching should begin toward the zone's upper limit, so that the child can reach the goal with help and move to a higher level of skill and knowledge. Offer just enough assistance. You might ask, "What can I do to help you?" Or simply observe the child's intentions and attempts and provide support when needed. When the child hesitates, offer encouragement. And encourage the child to practice the skill. You may watch and appreciate the child's practice or offer support when the child forgets what to do.

- *Use more-skilled peers as teachers.* Remember that it is not just adults who are important in helping children learn. Children also benefit from the support and guidance of more-skilled children (John-Steiner, 2007).

- *Monitor and encourage children's use of private speech.* Be aware of the developmental change from externally talking to oneself when solving a problem during the preschool years to privately talking to oneself in the early elementary school years. In the elementary school years, encourage children to internalize and self-regulate their talk to themselves.

- *Place instruction in a meaningful context.* Educators today are moving away from abstract presentations of material and, instead, provide students with opportunities to experience learning in real-world settings. For example, instead of just memorizing math formulas, students work on math problems with real-world implications.

- *Transform the classroom with Vygotskian ideas.* What does a Vygotskian classroom look like? The Kamehameha Elementary Education Program (KEEP) is based on Vygotsky's theory (Tharp, 1994). The ZPD is the key element of instruction in this program. Children might read a story and then interpret its meaning. Many of the learning activities take place in small groups. All children spend at least 20 minutes each morning in a setting called "Center One." In this context, scaffolding is used to improve children's literacy skills. The instructor asks questions, responds to students' queries, and builds on the ideas that students generate. Thousands of children from low-income families have attended KEEP public schools—in Hawaii, on an Arizona Navajo reservation, and in Los Angeles. Compared with a control group of non-KEEP children, the KEEP children participated more actively in classroom discussion, were more attentive in class, and had higher reading achievement (Tharp & Gallimore, 1988).

The *Caring Connections* interlude further explores the implications of Vygotsky's theory for children's education.

Lev Vygotsky (1896–1934), shown here with his daughter, reasoned that children's cognitive development is advanced through social interaction with more-skilled individuals embedded in a sociocultural backdrop. *How is Vygotsky's theory different from Piaget's?*

How can Vygotsky's ideas be applied to educating children?

Evaluating Vygotsky's Theory Even though their theories were proposed at about the same time, most of the world learned about Vygotsky's theory later than they learned about Piaget's theory, so Vygotsky's theory has not yet been evaluated as thoroughly. Vygotsky's view of the importance of sociocultural influences on children's development fits with the current belief that it is important to evaluate the contextual factors in learning (Goncu & Gauvain, 2011).

We already have compared certain aspects of Vygotsky's and Piaget's theories, such as Vygotsky's emphasis on the importance of inner speech in development and Piaget's view that such speech is immature. Although both theories are constructivist, Vygotsky's is a **social constructivist approach,** which emphasizes the social contexts of learning and the construction of knowledge through social interaction (O'Donnell, 2011).

In moving from Piaget to Vygotsky, the conceptual shift is from the individual to collaboration, social interaction, and sociocultural activity (Halford, 2008). The endpoint of cognitive development for Piaget is formal operational thought. For Vygotsky, the endpoint can differ depending on which skills are considered to be the most important in a particular culture. For Piaget, children construct knowledge by

social constructivist approach An approach that emphasizes the social contexts of learning and the fact that knowledge is mutually built and constructed; Vygotsky's theory is a social constructivist approach.

caring connections

Tools of the Mind

Tools of the Mind is an early childhood education curriculum that emphasizes children's development of self-regulation and the cognitive foundations of literacy (Hyson, Copple, & Jones, 2006). The curriculum was created by Elena Bodrova and Deborah Leong (2007) and has been implemented in more than 200 classrooms. Most of the children in the Tools of the Mind programs are at risk because of their living circumstances, which in many instances involve poverty and other difficult conditions such as being homeless and having parents with drug problems.

Tools of the Mind is grounded in Vygotsky's (1962) theory with special attention given to cultural tools and developing self-regulation, the zone of proximal development, scaffolding, private speech, shared activity, and the importance of play. In a Tools of the Mind classroom, dramatic play has a central role. Teachers guide children in creating themes that are based on the children's interests, such as treasure hunt, store, hospital, and restaurant. Teachers also incorporate field trips, visitor presentations, videos, and books in the development of children's play. They help children develop a play plan, which increases

the maturity of their play. Play plans describe what the children expect to do in the play period, including the imaginary context, roles, and props to be used. The play plans increase the quality of their play and self-regulation.

Scaffolding writing is another important theme in the Tools of the Mind classroom. Teachers guide children in planning their own message by drawing a line to stand for each word the child says. Children then repeat the message, pointing to each line as they say the word. Then, the child writes on the lines, trying to represent each word with some letters or symbols. Figure 9.6 shows how the scaffolding writing process improved a 5-year-old child's writing over the course of two months.

Research assessments of children's writing in Tools of the Mind classrooms revealed that they have more advanced writing skills than children in other early childhood programs (Bodrova & Leong, 2007) (see Figure 9.6). For example, they write more complex messages, use more words, spell more accurately, show better letter recognition, and have a better understanding of the concept of a sentence.

(a) Five-year-old Aaron's independent journal writing prior to using the scaffolding writing technique.

(b) Aaron's journal two months after using the scaffolding writing technique.

FIGURE 9.6

WRITING PROGRESS OF A 5-YEAR-OLD BOY OVER TWO MONTHS USING THE SCAFFOLDING WRITING PROCESS IN TOOLS OF THE MIND

	Vygotsky	**Piaget**
Sociocultural Context	Strong emphasis	Little emphasis
Constructivism	Social constructivist	Cognitive constructivist
Stages	No general stages of development proposed	Strong emphasis on stages (sensorimotor, preoperational, concrete operational, and formal operational)
Key Processes	Zone of proximal development, language, dialogue, tools of the culture	Schema, assimilation, accommodation, operations, conservation, classification
Role of Language	A major role; language plays a powerful role in shaping thought	Language has a minimal role; cognition primarily directs language
View on Education	Education plays a central role, helping children learn the tools of the culture	Education merely refines the child's cognitive skills that have already emerged
Teaching Implications	Teacher is a facilitator and guide, not a director; establish many opportunities for children to learn with the teacher and more-skilled peers	Also views teacher as a facilitator and guide, not a director; provide support for children to explore their world and discover knowledge

FIGURE 9.7

COMPARISON OF VYGOTSKY'S AND PIAGET'S THEORIES

transforming, organizing, and reorganizing previous knowledge. For Vygotsky, children construct knowledge through social interaction (Daniels, 2011). The implication of Piaget's theory for teaching is that children need support to explore their world and discover knowledge. The main implication of Vygotsky's theory for teaching is that students need many opportunities to learn with the teacher and more-skilled peers. In both Piaget's and Vygotsky's theories, teachers serve as facilitators and guides, rather than as directors and molders of learning. Figure 9.7 compares Vygotsky's and Piaget's theories.

Criticisms of Vygotsky's theory also have surfaced (Karpov, 2006). Some critics point out that Vygotsky was not specific enough about age-related changes (Goncu & Gauvain, 2011). Another criticism claims that Vygotsky did not adequately describe how changes in socioemotional capabilities contribute to cognitive development (Gauvain, 2008). Yet another criticism is that he overemphasized the role of language in thinking. Also, his emphasis on collaboration and guidance has potential pitfalls. Might facilitators be too helpful in some cases, as when a parent becomes too overbearing and controlling? Further, some children might become lazy and expect help when they could have done something on their own.

INFORMATION PROCESSING

Piaget's and Vygotsky's theories provided important ideas about how young children think and how their thinking changes. More recently, the information-processing approach has generated research that illuminates how children process information during the preschool years. What are the limitations and advances in the young child's ability to pay attention to the environment, to remember, to develop strategies and solve problems, and to understand their own mental processes and those of others?

Attention Recall from Chapter 6, "Cognitive Development in Infancy," that *attention* was defined as the focusing of mental resources on select information. The child's ability to pay attention improves significantly during the preschool years (Rothbart, 2011). Toddlers wander around, shift attention from one activity

What are some advances in children's attention in early childhood?

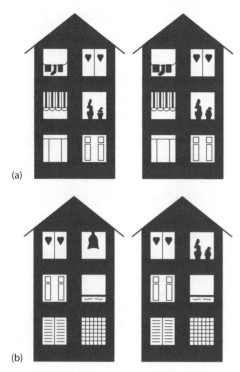

(a)

(b)

FIGURE **9.8**

THE PLANFULNESS OF ATTENTION. In one study, children were given pairs of houses to examine, like the ones shown here (Vurpillot, 1968). For three pairs of houses, what was in the windows was identical (*a*). For the other three pairs, the windows had different items in them (*b*). By filming the reflection in the children's eyes, it could be determined what they were looking at, how long they looked, and the sequence of their eye movements. Children under 6 examined only a fragmentary portion of each display and made their judgment on the basis of insufficient information. By contrast, older children scanned the windows in more detailed ways and were more accurate in their judgments of which were identical.

Reprinted from *Journal of Experimental Child Psychology,* 6(4), E. Vurpillot, "The Development of Scanning Strategies and Their Relation to Visual Differentiation," pp. 632–650. Copyright 1968, with permission from Elsevier. http://www.sciencedirect.com/science/journal/00220965

executive attention Involves action planning, allocating attention to goals, error detection and compensation, monitoring progress on tasks, and dealing with novel or difficult circumstances.

sustained attention Focused and extended engagement with an object, task, event, or other aspect of the environment.

to another, and seem to spend little time focused on any one object or event. By comparison, the preschool child might be observed watching television for a half hour. One study videotaped young children in their homes (Anderson & others, 1985). In 99 families who were observed for 4,672 hours, visual attention to television dramatically increased during the preschool years. However, a recent research study revealed that television watching and video game playing were both linked to attention problems in children (Swing & others, 2010).

Young children especially make advances in two aspects of attention—executive attention and sustained attention (Rothbart & Gartstein, 2008). **Executive attention** involves action planning, allocating attention to goals, error detection and compensation, monitoring progress on tasks, and dealing with novel or difficult circumstances. **Sustained attention** is focused and extended engagement with an object, task, event, or other aspect of the environment.

Mary Rothbart and Maria Gartstein (2008, p. 332) recently described why advances in executive and sustained attention are so important in early childhood:

> The development of the . . . executive attention system supports the rapid increases in effortful control in the toddler and preschool years. Increases in attention are due, in part, to advances in comprehension and language development. As children are better able to understand their environment, this increased appreciation of their surroundings helps them to sustain attention for longer periods of time.

In at least two ways, however, the preschool child's control of attention is still deficient:

- *Salient versus relevant dimensions.* Preschool children are likely to pay attention to stimuli that stand out, or are *salient,* even when those stimuli are not relevant to solving a problem or performing a task. For example, if a flashy, attractive clown presents the directions for solving a problem, preschool children are likely to pay more attention to the clown than to the directions. After the age of 6 or 7, children attend more efficiently to the dimensions of the task that are relevant, such as the directions for solving a problem. This change reflects a shift to cognitive control of attention, so that children act less impulsively and reflect more.

- *Planfulness.* Although in general young children's planning improves as part of advances in executive attention, when experimenters ask children to judge whether two complex pictures are the same, preschool children tend to use a haphazard comparison strategy, not examining all of the details before making a judgment. By comparison, elementary-school-age children are more likely to systematically compare the details across the pictures, one detail at a time (Vurpillot, 1968) (see Figure 9.8).

In Central European countries, such as Hungary, kindergarten children participate in exercises designed to improve their attention (Mills & Mills, 2000; Posner & Rothbart, 2007). For example, in one eye-contact exercise, the teacher sits in the center of a circle of children, and each child is required to catch the teacher's eye before being permitted to leave the group. In other exercises created to improve attention, teachers have children participate in stop-go activities during which they have to listen for a specific signal, such as a drumbeat or an exact number of rhythmic beats, before stopping the activity. Computer exercises also recently have been developed to improve children's attention (Jaeggi, Berman, & Jonides, 2009; Steiner & others, 2011; Tang & Posner, 2009). For example, one study revealed that five days of computer exercises that involved learning how to use a joystick, working memory, and the resolution of conflict improved the attention of 4- to 6-year-old children (Rueda, Posner, & Rothbart, 2005). In one of the computer games, young children have to move a joystick to keep a cat on the grass and out of the mud, and in another they help a cat find a duck in a pond. Although not commercially available, further information about computer exercises for improving children's attention can be found at www.teach-the-brain.org/learn/attention/index.

Preschool children's ability to control and sustain their attention is related to school readiness (Rothbart, 2011). For example, a study of more than 1,000 children revealed that their ability to sustain their attention at 54 months of age was linked to their school readiness (which included achievement and language skills) (NICHD Early Child Care Research Network, 2005). And in a recent study, children whose parents and teachers rated them higher on a scale of having attention problems at 54 months of age had a lower level of social skills in peer relations in the first and third grades than did their counterparts who were rated lower on the attention problems scale at 54 months of age (NICHD Early Child Care Research Network, 2009).

Memory   *Memory*—the retention of information over time—is a central process in children's cognitive development. In Chapter 6, "Cognitive Development in Infancy," we saw that many of an infant's memories are fragile and, for the most part, short-lived—except for the memory of perceptual-motor actions, which can be substantial (Mandler, 2004). Thus, we saw that to understand the infant's capacity to remember, we need to distinguish *implicit memory* from *explicit memory*. Explicit memory itself, however, comes in many forms. One distinction occurs between relatively permanent retention, or *long-term memory,* and *short-term memory.*

Short-Term Memory   In **short-term memory,** individuals retain information for up to 30 seconds if there is no rehearsal of the information. Using rehearsal (repeating information after it has been presented), we can keep information in short-term memory for a much longer period. One method of assessing short-term memory is the memory-span task. You hear a short list of stimuli—usually digits—presented at a rapid pace (one per second, for example). Then you are asked to repeat the digits.

Research with the memory-span task suggests that short-term memory increases during early childhood (Schneider, 2011). For example, in one investigation, memory span increased from about 2 digits in 2- to 3-year-old children to about 5 digits in 7-year-old children, yet between 7 and 13 years of age memory span increased only by 1½ digits (Dempster, 1981) (see Figure 9.9). Keep in mind, though, that memory span varies from one individual to another.

Why does memory span change with age? Rehearsal of information is important; older children rehearse the digits more than younger children. Speed and efficiency of processing information are important, too, especially the speed with which memory items can be identified (Schneider, 2011).

The speed-of-processing explanation highlights a key point in the information-processing perspective: The speed with which a child processes information is an important aspect of the child's cognitive abilities, and there is abundant evidence that the speed with which many cognitive tasks are completed improves dramatically across the childhood years (Kail, 2007).

How Accurate Are Young Children's Long-Term Memories?   Sometimes the long-term memories of preschoolers seem to be erratic, but young children can remember a great deal of information if they are given appropriate cues and prompts. One area in which children's long-term memory is being examined extensively relates to whether young children should be allowed to testify in court (Bruck & Ceci, 2011; Ceci & others, 2010). Increasingly, young children are being allowed to testify, especially if they are the only witnesses to abuse, a crime, and so forth. Several factors influence the accuracy of a young child's memory (Bruck & Ceci, 1999):

- *There are age differences in children's susceptibility to suggestion.* Preschoolers are the most suggestible age group in comparison with older children and adults (Ceci, Papierno, & Kulkofsky, 2007). For example, preschool children are more susceptible to misleading or incorrect post-event information (Ghetti & Alexander, 2004). Despite these age differences, there is still concern about older children when they are subjected to suggestive interviews (Bruck & Ceci, 2011).

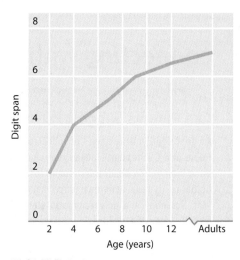

FIGURE **9.9**

DEVELOPMENTAL CHANGES IN MEMORY SPAN. In one study, from 2 years of age to 7 years of age children's memory span increased about 3 digits to 5 digits (Dempster, 1981). By 12 years of age, memory span had increased on average only another 1½ digits, to 7 digits. *What factors might contribute to the increase in memory span during childhood?*

"Can we hurry up and get to the test? My short-term memory is better than my long-term memory." Copyright © 1999. Reprinted courtesy of Bunny Hoest and Parade.

short-term memory The memory component in which individuals retain information for up to 30 seconds, assuming there is no rehearsal.

Can Parents Suggest False Events to Children?

As described in Bruck and Ceci (1999, pp. 429–430), a study by Deborah Poole and D. Stephen Lindsay revealed how parents can subtly influence their young children's memory for events. Preschool children participated in four activities (such as lifting cans with pulleys) with "Mr. Science" in a university laboratory (Poole & Lindsay, 1995). Four months later, the children's parents were mailed a storybook with a description of their child's visit to see Mr. Science. The storybook described two of the activities in which the child had participated, but it also described two in which the child had not participated. Each description ended with this fabrication of what happened when it was time to leave the laboratory: "Mr. Science wiped (child's name) hands and face with a wet-wipe. The cloth got close to (child's name) mouth and tasted real yucky."

Parents read the descriptions to their children three times. Later, the children told the experimenter that they had participated in the activities that actually had only been mentioned in the descriptions read by their parents. For example, when asked whether Mr. Science had put

anything yucky in their mouth, more than half of the young children said that he had. Subsequently, when asked whether Mr. Science put something in their mouth or their parent just read this to them in a story, 71 percent of the young children said that it really happened.

This study shows how subtle suggestions can influence children's inaccurate reporting of nonevents. If such inaccurate reports are pursued in follow-up questioning by an interviewer who suspected that something sexual occurred, the result could be a sexual interpretation. This study also revealed the difficulty preschool children have in identifying the source of a suggestion (called *source-monitoring errors*). Children in this study confused their parent's reading the suggestion to them with their experience of the suggestion.

How might researchers expand on this study to test the influence of other adults on children's memories? Do you think any ethical issues would arise in such research?

Four-year-old Jennifer Royal was the only eyewitness to one of her playmates' being shot to death. She was allowed to testify in open court, and the clarity of her statements helped to convict the gunman. *What are some issues involved in whether young children should be allowed to testify in court?*

- *There are individual differences in susceptibility.* Some preschoolers are highly resistant to interviewers' suggestions, whereas others immediately succumb to the slightest suggestion (Ceci & others, 2010). A research review concluded that suggestibility is linked to low self-concept, low support from parents, and mothers' insecure attachment in romantic relationships (Bruck & Melnyk, 2004).

- *Interviewing techniques can produce substantial distortions in children's reports about highly salient events.* Children are suggestible not just regarding peripheral details but also about the central aspects of an event (Bruck & Ceci, 2011). Nonetheless, young children are capable of recalling much that is relevant about an event (Goodman, Batterman-Faunce, & Kenney, 1992). When children do accurately recall an event, the interviewer often has a neutral tone, there is limited use of misleading questions, and there is an absence of any motivation for the child to make a false report (Bruck & Ceci, 2011).

Can false memories be induced in children? See the *Connecting with Research* interlude to read about a study that addresses this question.

In sum, whether a young child's eyewitness testimony is accurate or not may depend on a number of factors such as the type, number, and intensity of the suggestive techniques the child has experienced (Bruck & Ceci, 2011; Schneider, 2011). It appears that the reliability of young children's reports has as much to do with the skills and motivation of the interviewer as with any natural limitations on young children's memory (Ceci & others, 2007).

executive functioning An umbrella-like concept that consists of a number of higher-level cognitive processes linked to the development of the brain's prefrontal cortex. Executive functioning involves managing one's thoughts to engage in goal-directed behavior and self-control.

Executive Function Recently, increasing interest has been directed toward the development of children's **executive functioning,** an umbrella-like concept that consists of a number of higher-level cognitive processes linked to the development of the brain's prefrontal cortex. Executive functioning involves managing one's thoughts to engage in goal-directed behavior and exercise self-control. Earlier in this chapter, we described the recent interest in *executive attention*, which comes under the umbrella of executive functioning.

In early childhood, executive functioning especially involves developmental advances in cognitive inhibition (such as inhibiting a strong tendency that is incorrect), cognitive flexibility (such as shifting attention to another item or topic), and goal-setting (such as sharing a toy or mastering a skill like catching a ball) (Beck & others, 2011; Carlson, 2010; Zelazo & Muller, 2011). During early childhood, the relatively stimulus-driven toddler is transformed into a child capable of flexible, goal-directed problem solving that characterizes executive functioning (Zelazo & Muller, 2011).

Stephanie Carlson (2010) has conducted a number of research studies on young children's executive functioning. In one study, Carlson and her colleagues (2005) gave young children a task called Less Is More, in which they are shown two trays of candy—one with five pieces, the other with two—and told that the tray they pick will be given to a stuffed animal seated at the table. Three-year-olds consistently selected the tray with the five pieces of candy, thus giving away more candy than they kept for themselves. However, 4-year-olds were far more likely to choose the tray with only two pieces of candy, keeping five pieces for themselves, and thus inhibiting their impulsiveness far better than the 3-year-olds did. In another study, young children were read either *Planet Opposite*—a fantasy book in which everything is turned upside down—or *Fun Town*—a reality-oriented fiction book (Carlson & White, 2011). After being read one of the books, the young children completed the Less Is More task. Sixty percent of the 3-year-olds who heard the *Planet Opposite* story chose the five pieces of candy compared to only 20 percent of their counterparts who heard the more straightforward story. The results indicated that learning about a topsy-turvy imaginary world likely helped the young children become more flexible in their thinking.

Researchers have found that advances in executive functioning in the preschool years are linked with school readiness (Bierman & others, 2008). Significant advances in the development of executive functioning occur in middle and late childhood (Diamond, Casey, & Munakata, 2011). Adult-level executive functioning emerges in early adolescence on many tasks, but on some tasks executive functioning continues to improve during the adult years (Zelazo & Muller, 2011).

Some developmental psychologists use their training in areas such as cognitive development to pursue careers in applied areas. To read about the work of Helen Hadani, an individual who followed this path, see the *Connecting with Careers* profile.

Researcher Stephanie Carlson administers the Less Is More task to a 4-year-old boy. *What were the results of Carlson's research?*

The Child's Theory of Mind   Even young children are curious about the nature of the human mind (Wellman, 2011). They have a **theory of mind,** which refers to awareness of one's own mental processes and the mental processes of others. Studies of theory of mind view the child as "a thinker who is trying to explain, predict, and understand people's thoughts, feelings, and utterances" (Harris, 2006, p. 847). Researchers are increasingly discovering that children's theory of mind is linked to cognitive processes (Wellman, 2011). For example, one study found that theory of mind competence at age 3 is related to a higher level of metamemory at age 5 (Lockl & Schneider, 2007).

Developmental Changes   Children's theory of mind changes as they develop through childhood (Gelman, 2009; Wellman, 2011). Some changes occur quite early in development, as we see next.

From 18 months to 3 years of age, children begin to understand three mental states:

- *Perceptions.* By 2 years of age, children recognize that another person will see what's in front of her own eyes instead of what's in front of the child's eyes (Lempers, Flavell, & Flavell, 1977), and by 3 years of age, they realize

theory of mind A concept that refers to awareness of one's own mental processes and the mental processes of others.

Helen Hadani, Developmental Psychologist, Toy Designer, and LANGO Regional Director

Helen Hadani obtained a Ph.D. from Stanford University in developmental psychology. As a graduate student at Stanford, she worked part-time for Hasbro Toys testing its children's software on preschoolers. Her first job after graduate school was with Zowie Entertainment, which was subsequently bought by LEGO. In her work as a toy designer there, Helen conducted experiments and focus groups at different stages of a toy's development, in addition to studying the age-effectiveness of the toy. In Helen's words, "Even in a toy's most primitive stage of development . . . you see children's creativity in responding to challenges, their satisfaction when a problem is solved or simply their delight in having fun" (Schlegel, 2000, p. 50).

More recently, she began working for LANGO, a company established on the premise that every American child should learn a foreign language. LANGO uses music, games, and art to help children learn a second language. Helen is currently a regional director for LANGO.

Helen Hadani, a developmental psychologist, with some of the toys and materials for guiding children in learning a second language.

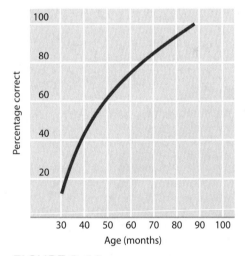

FIGURE **9.10**

DEVELOPMENTAL CHANGES IN FALSE-BELIEF PERFORMANCE. False-belief performance—the child's understanding that a person has a false belief that contradicts reality—dramatically increases from 2½ years of age through the middle of the elementary school years. In a summary of the results of many studies, 2½-year-olds gave incorrect responses about 80 percent of the time (Wellman, Cross, & Watson, 2001). At 3 years, 8 months, they were correct about 50 percent of the time, and after that, gave increasingly correct responses.

that looking leads to knowing what's inside a container (Pratt & Bryant, 1990).

- *Emotions.* The child can distinguish between positive (for example, happy) and negative (sad, for example) emotions. A child might say, "Tommy feels bad."

- *Desires.* All humans have some sort of desires. But when do children begin to recognize that someone else's desires may be different from their own? Toddlers recognize that if people want something, they will try to get it. For instance, a child might say, "I want my mommy."

Two- to three-year-olds understand the way that desires are related to actions and to simple emotions. For example, they understand that people will search for what they want and that if they obtain it, they are likely to feel happy, but if they don't they will keep searching for it and are likely to feel sad or angry (Wellman & Woolley, 1990). Children also refer to desires earlier and more frequently than they refer to cognitive states such as thinking and knowing (Bartsch & Wellman, 1995).

One of the landmark developments in understanding others' desires is recognizing that someone else may have desires that differ from one's own (Wellman, 2011). Eighteen-month-olds understand that their own food preferences may not match the preferences of others—they will give an adult the food to which she says "Yummy!" even if the food is something that the infants detest (Repacholi & Gopnik, 1997). As they get older, they can verbalize that they themselves do not like something but an adult might (Flavell & others, 1992).

Between the ages of 3 and 5, children come to understand that the mind can represent objects and events accurately or inaccurately. The realization that people can have *false beliefs*—beliefs that are not true—develops in a majority of children by the time they are 5 years old (Wellman, Cross, & Watson, 2001) (see Figure 9.10).

This point is often described as a pivotal one in understanding the mind—recognizing that beliefs are not just mapped directly into the mind from the surrounding world, but also that different people can have different, and sometimes incorrect, beliefs (Liu & others, 2008). In a classic false-belief task, young children were shown a Band-Aids box and asked what was inside (Jenkins & Astington, 1996). To the children's surprise, the box actually contained pencils. When asked what a child who had never seen the box would think was inside, 3-year-olds typically responded, "Pencils." However, the 4- and 5-year-olds, grinning at the anticipation of the false beliefs of other children who had not seen what was inside the box, were more likely to say "Band-Aids."

In a similar task, children are told a story about Sally and Anne: Sally places a toy in a basket and then leaves the room (see Figure 9.11). In her absence, Anne takes the toy from the basket and places it in a box. Children are asked where Sally will look for the toy when she returns. The major finding is that 3-year-olds tend to fail false-belief tasks, saying that Sally will look in the box (even though Sally could not know that the toy has moved to this new location). Four-year-olds and older children tend to pass the task, correctly saying that Sally will have a "false belief"—she will think the object is in the basket, even though that belief is now false. The conclusion from these studies is that children younger than 4 years old do not understand that it is possible to have a false belief.

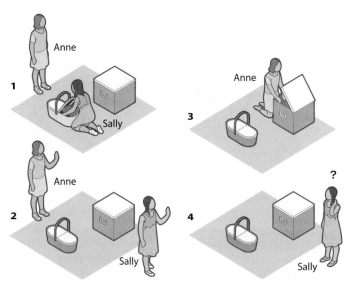

FIGURE **9.11**

THE SALLY AND ANNE FALSE-BELIEF TASK. In the false-belief task, the skit above in which Sally has a basket and Anne has a box is shown to children. Sally places a toy in her basket and then leaves. While Sally is gone and can't watch, Anne removes the toy from Sally's basket and places it in her box. Sally then comes back and the children are asked where they think Sally will look for her toy. Children are said to "pass" the false-belief task if they understand that Sally looks in her basket first before realizing the toy isn't there.

However, there are reasons to question the focus on this one supposedly pivotal moment in the development of a theory of mind. For example, the false-belief task is a complicated one that involves a number of factors such as the characters in the story and all of their individual actions (Bloom & German, 2000). Children also have to disregard their own knowledge in making predictions about what others would think, which is difficult for young children (Birch & Bloom, 2003). Another important issue is that there is more to understanding the minds of others than this false-belief task would indicate.

One example of a limitation in 3- to 5-year-olds' understanding the mind is how they think about thinking. Preschoolers often underestimate when mental activity is likely occurring. For example, they sometimes think that a person who is sitting quietly or reading is not actually thinking very much (Flavell, Green, & Flavell, 1995). Their understanding of their own thinking is also limited. One study revealed that even 5-year-olds have difficulty reporting their thoughts (Flavell, Green, & Flavell, 1995). Children were asked to think quietly about the room in their home where they kept their toothbrushes. Shortly after this direction, many children denied they had been thinking at all and failed to mention either a toothbrush or a bathroom. In another study, when 5-year-olds were asked to try to have no thoughts at all for about 20 seconds, they reported that they were successful at doing this (Flavell, Green, & Flavell, 2000). By contrast, most of the 8-year-olds said they engaged in mental activity during the 20 seconds and reported specific thoughts.

It is only beyond the preschool years—at approximately 5 to 7 years of age—that children have a deepening appreciation of the mind itself rather than just an understanding of mental states. For example, they begin to recognize that people's behaviors do not necessarily reflect their thoughts and feelings (Flavell, Green, & Flavell, 1993). Not until middle and late childhood do children see the mind as an active constructor of knowledge or a processing center (Flavell, Green, & Flavell, 1998) and move from understanding that beliefs can be false to realizing that the same event can be open to multiple interpretations (Carpendale & Chandler, 1996). For

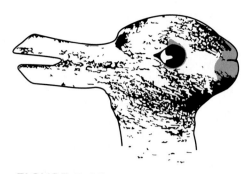

FIGURE 9.12
AMBIGUOUS LINE DRAWING

A young boy with autism. *What are some characteristics of autistic children? What are some deficits in autistic children's theory of mind?*

developmental connection

Disorders. The current consensus is that autism is a brain dysfunction with abnormalities in brain structure and neurotransmitters, and that genetic factors play an important role in its occurrence. Chapter 11, p. 344

developmental connection

Disorders. Boys are four times more likely to be autistic than girls are. Chapter 11, p. 344

example, in one study, children saw an ambiguous line drawing (for example, a drawing that could be seen as either a duck or a rabbit); one puppet told the child she believed the drawing was a duck while another puppet told the child he believed the drawing was a rabbit (see Figure 9.12). Before the age of 7, children said that there was one right answer, and it was not okay for both puppets to have different opinions.

Although most research on children's theory of mind focuses on children around or before their preschool years, at 7 years of age and beyond there are important developments in the ability to understand the beliefs and thoughts of others. While it is important to understand that people may have different interpretations of the same thing, it is also important to recognize that some interpretations and beliefs may still be evaluated on the basis of the merits of arguments and evidence (Kuhn, Cheney, & Weinstock, 2000). In early adolescence, children begin to understand that people can have ambivalent feelings (Harter, 2006). They start to recognize that the same person can feel both happy and sad about the same event. They also engage in more recursive thinking: thinking about what other people are thinking about.

Individual Differences   As in other developmental research, there are individual differences in the ages when children reach certain milestones in their theory of mind (Wellman, 2011). For example, preschoolers who have more siblings perform better on theory of mind tasks than preschoolers with fewer siblings, especially if they have older siblings (McAlister & Peterson, 2007). Children who talk with their parents about feelings frequently as 2-year-olds show better performance on theory of mind tasks (Ruffman, Slade, & Crowe, 2002), as do children who frequently engage in pretend play (Harris, 2000).

Executive function, which describes several functions discussed earlier in this chapter, such as planning and inhibition, that are important for flexible, future-oriented behavior, also may be connected to theory of mind development (Doherty, 2008). For example, in one executive function task, children are asked to say the word *night* when they see a picture of a sun, and the word *day* when they see a picture of a moon and stars. Children who perform better at executive function tasks seem also to have a better understanding of theory of mind (Sabbagh & others, 2006).

Theory of Mind and Autism   Another individual difference in understanding the mind involves autism (Wellman, 2011). Approximately 1 in 150 children are estimated to have some type of autism (National Autism Association, 2010). Autism can usually be diagnosed by the age of 3 years, and sometimes earlier. Children with autism show a number of behaviors different from those exhibited by other children their age, including deficits in social interaction and communication as well as repetitive behaviors or interests.

Children and adults with autism have difficulty in social interactions, often described as huge deficits in theory of mind (Adler & others, 2010). These deficits are generally greater than deficits in children the same mental age with mental retardation (Baron-Cohen, 2009, 2011). Researchers have found that autistic children have difficulty in developing a theory of mind, especially in understanding others' beliefs and emotions (Williams & Happe, 2011). Although children with autism tend to do poorly in reasoning on false-belief tasks, they can perform much better on reasoning tasks requiring an understanding of physical causality (Peterson, 2005).

Review Connect Reflect

LG1 Describe three views of the cognitive changes that occur in early childhood.

Review

- What characterizes Piaget's stage of preoperational thought?
- What does Vygotsky's theory suggest about how preschool children construct knowledge?
- What are some important ways in which information processing changes during early childhood? What characterizes children's theory of mind?

Connect

- What are some differences between the attention of young children and the attention of infants (see Chapter 6, "Cognitive Development in Infancy")?

Reflect *Your Own Personal Journey of Life*

- If you were the parent of a 4-year-old child, would you try to train the child to develop conservation skills? Explain.

How Do Young Children Develop Language? **LG2** Summarize how language develops in early childhood.

- Understanding Phonology and Morphology
- Changes in Syntax and Semantics
- Advances in Pragmatics
- Young Children's Literacy

Toddlers move rather quickly from producing two-word utterances to creating three-, four-, and five-word combinations. Between 2 and 3 years of age, they begin the transition from saying simple sentences that express a single proposition to saying complex sentences.

As young children learn the special features of their own language, there are extensive regularities in how they acquire that particular language (Berko Gleason, 2009). For example, all children learn the prepositions *on* and *in* before other prepositions. Children learning other languages, such as Russian or Chinese, also acquire the particular features of those languages in a consistent order.

UNDERSTANDING PHONOLOGY AND MORPHOLOGY

During the preschool years, most children gradually become more sensitive to the sounds of spoken words and become increasingly capable of producing all the sounds of their language. By the time children are 3 years of age, they can produce all the vowel sounds and most of the consonant sounds (Stoel-Gammon & Sosa, 2010).

Young children can even produce complex consonant clusters such as *str-* and *mpt-*. They notice rhymes, enjoy poems, make up silly names for things by substituting one sound for another (such as *bubblegum, bubblebum, bubbleyum*), and clap along with each syllable in a phrase.

By the time children move beyond two-word utterances, they demonstrate a knowledge of morphology rules (Tager Flusberg & Zukowski, 2009). Children begin using the plural and possessive forms of nouns (such as *dogs* and *dog's*). They put appropriate endings on verbs (such as *-s* when the subject is third-person singular and *-ed* for the past tense). They use prepositions (such as *in* and *on*), articles (such as *a* and *the*), and various forms of the verb *to be* (such as "I *was* going to the store"). Some of the best evidence for changes in children's use of morphological rules occurs in their overgeneralization of the rules, as when a preschool child say "foots" instead of "feet," or "goed" instead of "went."

In a classic experiment that was designed to study children's knowledge of morphological rules, such as how to make a plural, Jean Berko (1958) presented preschool children and first-grade children with cards such as the one shown in Figure 9.13.

This is a wug.

Now there is another one. There are two of them. There are two _____.

FIGURE **9.13**

STIMULI IN BERKO'S STUDY OF YOUNG CHILDREN'S UNDERSTANDING OF MORPHOLOGICAL RULES. In Jean Berko's (1958) study, young children were presented cards, such as this one with a "wug" on it. Then the children were asked to supply the missing word; in supplying the missing word, they had to say it correctly, too. "Wugs" is the correct response here.

Children were asked to look at the card while the experimenter read aloud the words on the card. Then the children were asked to supply the missing word. This task might sound easy, but Berko was interested in the children's ability to apply the appropriate morphological rule—in this case, to say "wugs" with the z sound that indicates the plural.

Although the children's answers were not perfect, they were much better than chance. What makes Berko's study impressive is that most of the words were made up for the experiment. Thus, the children could not base their responses on remembering past instances of hearing the words. That they could make the plurals or past tenses of words they had never heard before was proof that they knew the morphological rules.

CHANGES IN SYNTAX AND SEMANTICS

Preschool children also learn and apply rules of syntax (Lieven, 2008; Tager Flusberg & Zukowski, 2009). They show a growing mastery of complex rules for how words should be ordered.

Consider *wh-* questions, such as "Where is Daddy going?" or "What is that boy doing?" To ask these questions properly, the child must know two important differences between *wh-* questions and affirmative statements (for instance, "Daddy is going to work" and "That boy is waiting on the school bus"). First, a *wh-* word must be added at the beginning of the sentence. Second, the auxiliary verb must be inverted—that is, exchanged with the subject of the sentence. Young children learn quite early where to put the *wh-* word, but they take much longer to learn the auxiliary-inversion rule. Thus, preschool children might ask, "Where Daddy is going?" and "What that boy is doing?"

Gains in semantics also characterize early childhood. Vocabulary development is dramatic (Pan & Uccelli, 2009). Some experts have concluded that between 18 months and 6 years of age, young children learn approximately one new word every waking hour (Gelman & Kalish, 2006)! By the time they enter first grade, it is estimated that children know about 14,000 words (Clark, 1993).

developmental **connection**

Language Development. The average 2-year-old can speak about 200 words. Chapter 6, p. 191

ADVANCES IN PRAGMATICS

Changes in pragmatics also characterize young children's language development (Aktar & Herold, 2008; Bryant, 2009). A 6-year-old is simply a much better conversationalist than a 2-year-old is (Lieven, 2008). What are some of the improvements in pragmatics during the preschool years?

Young children begin to engage in extended discourse (Aktar & Herold, 2008). For example, they learn culturally specific rules of conversation and politeness, and become sensitive to the need to adapt their speech in different settings. Their developing linguistic skills and increasing ability to take the perspective of others contribute to their generation of more competent narratives.

As children get older, they become increasingly able to talk about things that are not here (Grandma's house, for example) and not now (what happened to them yesterday or might happen tomorrow, for example). A preschool child can tell you what she wants for lunch tomorrow, something that would not have been possible at the two-word stage of language development.

Around 4 to 5 years of age, children learn to change their speech style to suit the situation. For example, even 4-year-old children speak to a 2-year-old differently from the way they would talk to a same-aged peer; they use shorter sentences with the 2-year-old. They also speak to

What are some advances in pragmatics that characterize children's cognitive development in early childhood?

an adult differently from a same-aged peer, using more polite and formal language with the adult (Shatz & Gelman, 1973).

Peers also can play an important role in aspects of language other than pragmatics. A recent study of more than 1,800 4-year-olds revealed that peers' expressive language abilities (transmitting language to others) were positively linked with young children's expressive and receptive (what a child hears and reads) language development (Mashburn & others, 2009).

YOUNG CHILDREN'S LITERACY

The concern about the ability of U.S. children to read and write has led to a careful examination of preschool and kindergarten children's experiences, with the hope that a positive orientation toward reading and writing can be developed early in life (Jalongo, 2011; Otto, 2010). Parents and teachers need to provide young children with a supportive environment in which to develop literacy skills (Beatty & Pratt, 2011). Children should be active participants and be immersed in a wide range of interesting listening, talking, writing, and reading experiences. One study revealed that children whose mothers had more education had more advanced emergent literacy skills than children whose mothers had less education (Korat, 2009). Another recent study found that literacy experiences (such as how often the child was read to), the quality of the mother's engagement with her child (such as attempts to cognitively stimulate the child), and provision of learning materials (such as age-appropriate learning materials and books) were important home literacy experiences in low-income families that were linked to the children's language development in positive ways (Rodriguez & others, 2009).

So far, our discussion of early literacy has focused on U.S. children. Researchers have found that the extent to which phonological awareness is linked to learning to read effectively varies across language to some extent (McBride-Chang, 2004). For example, one study of second-grade students from Beijing, Hong Kong, Korea, and the United States revealed that phonological awareness may be more important for early reading development in English and Korean than in Chinese (McBride-Chang & others, 2005). Further, rates of dyslexia (severe reading disability) differ across countries and are linked with the spelling and phonetic rules that characterize the language (McBride-Chang & others, 2008). English is one of the more difficult languages because of its irregular spellings and pronunciations. In countries where English is spoken, the rate of dyslexia is higher than in countries where the alphabet script is more phonetically pronounced.

What are some strategies for using books effectively with preschool children? Ellen Galinsky (2010) recently emphasized these strategies:

- *Use books to initiate conversation with young children.* Ask them to put themselves in the book characters' places and imagine what they might be thinking or feeling.

- *Use what and why questions.* Ask young children what they think is going to happen next in a story and then to see if it occurs.

- *Encourage children to ask questions about stories.*

- *Choose some books that play with language.* Creative books on the alphabet, including those with rhymes, often interest young children.

The advances in language that take place in early childhood lay the foundation for later development during the elementary school years, as we will see in Chapter 13, "Socio-emotional Development in Middle and Late Childhood."

What are some strategies for increasing young children's literacy?

Review

- How do phonology and morphology change during early childhood?
- What characterizes young children's understanding of syntax and semantics in early childhood?
- What advances in pragmatics occur in early childhood?
- What are some effective ways to guide young children's literacy?

Connect

- In this section, you learned that children can sometimes overgeneralize the rules

for morphology. How is this different from or similar to the concept of overextension as it relates to infants' speech (discussed in Chapter 6)?

Reflect *Your Own Personal Journey of Life*

- As a parent, what would you do to improve the likelihood that your child would enter first grade with excellent literacy skills?

What Are Some Important Features of Young Children's Education?

 LG3 Evaluate different approaches to early childhood education.

Variations in Early Childhood Education

Controversies in Early Childhood Education

Educating Young Children Who Are Disadvantaged

To the teachers at a Reggio Emilia program (described in the chapter opening), preschool children are active learners, exploring the world with their peers, constructing their knowledge of the world in collaboration with their community, aided but not directed by the teachers. In many ways, the Reggio Emilia approach applies ideas consistent with the views of Piaget and Vygotsky discussed in this chapter. Do educators' beliefs make a difference to the children they teach? How do other early education programs treat children, and how do the children fare? Our exploration of early childhood education focuses on variations in programs, education for children who are disadvantaged, and some controversies in early childhood education.

VARIATIONS IN EARLY CHILDHOOD EDUCATION

Attending preschool is rapidly becoming the norm for U.S. children (Follari, 2011). Thirty-eight states have publicly funded preschool programs for 3- and 4-year-old children (King & Kepner, 2008). Many other 3- and 4-year-old children attend private preschool programs.

There are many variations in the ways young children are educated (Morrison, 2011). The foundation of early childhood education has been the child-centered kindergarten.

The Child-Centered Kindergarten Nurturing is a key aspect of the **child-centered kindergarten,** which emphasizes the education of the whole child and concern for his or her physical, cognitive, and socioemotional development (Marion, 2010). Instruction is organized around the child's needs, interests, and learning styles. Emphasis is on the process of learning, rather than what is learned (Hendrick & Weissman, 2010). The child-centered kindergarten honors three principles: Each child follows a unique developmental pattern; young children learn best through

child-centered kindergarten Education that involves the whole child by considering the child's physical, cognitive, and socioemotional development and addressing the child's needs, interests, and learning styles.

What are some characteristics of the child-centered kindergarten?

firsthand experiences with people and materials; and play is extremely important to the child's total development. *Experimenting, exploring, discovering, trying out, restructuring, speaking,* and *listening* are frequent activities in excellent kindergarten programs. Such programs are closely attuned to the developmental status of 4- and 5-year-old children.

The Montessori Approach   Montessori schools are patterned after the educational philosophy of Maria Montessori (1870–1952), an Italian physician-turned-educator who crafted a revolutionary approach to young children's education at the beginning of the twentieth century. Her work began in Rome with a group of children who were mentally retarded. She was successful in teaching them to read, write, and pass examinations designed for normal children. Some time later, she turned her attention to poor children from the slums of Rome and had similar success in teaching them. Her approach has since been adopted extensively in private nursery schools in the United States.

The **Montessori approach** is a philosophy of education in which children are given considerable freedom and spontaneity in choosing activities. They are allowed to move from one activity to another as they desire. The teacher acts as a facilitator rather than a director. The teacher shows the child how to perform intellectual activities, demonstrates interesting ways to explore curriculum materials, and offers help when the child requests it (Murray, 2011). Montessori teachers encourage children to make decisions from an early age, which helps them to engage in self-regulated problem solving and manage their time effectively (Hyson, Copple, & Jones, 2006; Rambusch, 2010). The number of Montessori schools in the United States has expanded dramatically in recent years, from one school in 1959 to 355 schools in 1970 to approximately 4,000 in 2005 (Whitescarver, 2006).

Larry Page and Sergey Brin, founders of the highly successful Internet search engine, Google, said that their early years at Montessori schools were a major factor in their success (International Montessori Council, 2006). During an interview with Barbara Walters, they said they learned how to be self-directed and self-starters at Montessori (ABC News, 2005). They commented that Montessori experiences encouraged them to think for themselves and allowed them the freedom to develop their own interests.

Some developmentalists favor the Montessori approach, but others believe that it neglects children's social development (Chattin-McNichols, 1992). For example, while Montessori fosters independence and the development of cognitive skills, it

Montessori approach An educational philosophy in which children are given considerable freedom and spontaneity in choosing activities and specially designed curriculum materials.

deemphasizes verbal interaction between the teacher and child and peer interaction. Montessori's critics also argue that it restricts imaginative play and that its heavy reliance on self-corrective materials may not adequately allow for creativity and for a variety of learning styles (Goffin & Wilson, 2001).

What are some differences in developmentally appropriate and inappropriate practice?

How Would You...?

If you were an **educator,** how would you design a developmentally appropriate lesson to teach kindergarten children the concept of gravity?

developmentally appropriate practice (DAP) Education that focuses on the typical developmental patterns of children (age appropriateness) as well as the uniqueness of each child (individual appropriateness). Such practice contrasts with *developmentally inappropriate practice,* which ignores the concrete, hands-on approach to learning. For example, direct teaching largely through abstract paper-and-pencil activities presented to large groups of young children is believed to be developmentally inappropriate.

Project Head Start Compensatory education designed to provide children from low-income families the opportunity to acquire skills and experiences that are important for school success.

Developmentally Appropriate and Inappropriate Education

Many educators and psychologists conclude that preschool and young elementary school children learn best through active, hands-on teaching methods such as games and dramatic play. They know that children develop at varying rates and that schools need to allow for these individual differences. They also argue that schools should focus on facilitating children's socioemotional development as well as their cognitive development. Educators refer to this type of schooling as **developmentally appropriate practice (DAP),** which is based on knowledge of the typical development of children within a particular age span (age appropriateness), as well as on the uniqueness of the individual child (individual appropriateness). DAP emphasizes the importance of creating settings that encourage children to be active learners and reflect children's interests and capabilities (Bredekamp, 2011; Kostelnik, Soderman, & Whiren, 2011). Desired outcomes for DAP include thinking critically, working cooperatively, solving problems, developing self-regulatory skills, and enjoying learning. The emphasis in DAP is on the process of learning rather than on its content (Barbarin & Miller, 2009; Bredekamp, 2011). Figure 9.14 provides examples of the National Association for the Education of Young Children's (NAEYC) guidelines for developmentally appropriate practices (NAEYC, 2009).

Do developmentally appropriate educational practices improve young children's development? Some researchers have found that young children in developmentally appropriate classrooms are likely to feel less stress, be more motivated, be more socially skilled, have better work habits, be more creative, have better language skills, and demonstrate better math skills than children in developmentally inappropriate classrooms (Hart & others, 2003). However, not all studies find DAP to have significant positive effects (Hyson, Copple, & Jones, 2006). Among the reasons that it is difficult to generalize from the research findings on developmentally appropriate education is that individual programs often vary, and developmentally appropriate education is an evolving concept. Recent changes in the concept have given more attention to how strongly academic skills should be emphasized and how they should be taught.

EDUCATING YOUNG CHILDREN WHO ARE DISADVANTAGED

For many years, U.S. children from low-income families did not receive any education before they entered the first grade. Often, they began first grade already several steps behind their classmates in their readiness to learn. In the summer of 1965, the federal government began an effort to break the cycle of poverty and poor education for young children in the United States through **Project Head Start.** It is a compensatory program designed to provide children from low-income families the opportunity to acquire the skills and experiences important for success in school. After almost half a century, Head Start continues to be the largest federally funded program for U.S. children, with almost 1 million U.S. children enrolled annually (Zigler & Styfco, 2010). In 2007, 3 percent of Head Start children were 5 years old, 51 percent were 4 years old, 36 percent were 3 years old, and 10 percent were under 3 years of age (Administration for Children and Families, 2008).

Early Head Start was established in 1995 to serve children from birth to 3 years of age. In 2007, half of all new funds appropriated for Head Start programs were used for the expansion of Early Head Start. Researchers have found positive effects

Core Considerations in Developmentally Appropriate Practice

1 Knowledge to Consider in Making Decisions

In all aspects of working with children, early childhood practitioners need to consider these three areas of knowledge: (1) What is known about child development and learning, especially age-related characteristics; (2) What is known about each child as an individual; and (3) What is known about the social and cultural contexts in which children live.

2 Challenging and Achievable Goals

Keeping in mind desired goals and what is known about the children as a group and individually, teachers plan experiences to promote children's learning and development.

Principles of Child Development and Learning That Inform Practice

1 All the domains of development and learning—physical, cognitive, and social—are important, and they are linked.

2 Many aspects of children's learning and development follow well-documented sequences, with later abilities, skills, and knowledge building on those already acquired.

3 Development and learning proceed at varying rates from child to child, and at uneven rates across different areas of a child's individual functioning.

4 Development and learning result from the interaction of biology and experience.

5 Early experiences have strong effects—both cumulative and delayed—on children's development and learning; optimal periods exist for certain types of development and learning.

6 Development proceeds toward greater complexity, self-regulation, and symbolic or representational capacities.

7 Children develop best when they have secure, consistent relationships with responsive adults and opportunities for positive peer relations.

8 Development and learning occur in and are influenced by multiple social and cultural contexts.

9 Always mentally active in seeking to understand the world around them, children learn in a variety of ways; a wide range of teaching strategies can be effective in guiding children's learning.

10 Play is an important context for developing self-regulation and for promoting language, cognition, and competence.

11 Development and learning advance when children are challenged to achieve at a level just beyond their current mastery and when they are given opportunities to practice newly acquired skills.

12 Children's experiences shape their motivation and approaches to learning, such as persistence, initiative, and flexibility; in turn, these characteristics influence their learning and development.

Guidelines for Developmentally Appropriate Practice

1 Creating a Caring Community of Learners

Each member of the community should be valued by the others; relationships are an important context through which children learn; practitioners ensure that members of the community feel psychologically safe.

2 Teaching to Enhance Development and Learning

The teacher takes responsibility for stimulating, directing, and supporting children's learning by providing the experiences that each child needs.

3 Planning Curriculum to Achieve Important Goals

The curriculum is planned to help children achieve goals that are developmentally appropriate and educationally significant.

4 Assessing Children's Development and Learning

In developmentally appropriate practice, assessments are linked to the program's goals for children.

5 Establishing Reciprocal Relationships with Families

A positive partnership between teachers and families benefits children's learning and development.

FIGURE **9.14**

RECOMMENDATIONS BY NAEYC FOR DEVELOPMENTALLY APPROPRIATE PRACTICE IN EARLY CHILDHOOD PROGRAMS SERVING CHILDREN FROM BIRTH THROUGH AGE 8. Source: NAEYC (2009). Developmentally appropriate practice in early childhood programs serving children from birth through age 8. Washington, DC: NAEYC.

for Early Head Start (Hoffman & Ewen, 2007). A recent study revealed that Early Head Start had a protective effect on risks young children might experience in relation to parenting stress, language development, and self-control (Ayoub, Vallotton, & Mastergeorge, 2011).

Head Start programs are not all created equal. One estimate is that 40 percent of the 1,400 Head Start programs are of questionable quality (Zigler & Styfco, 1994). More attention needs to be given to developing Head Start programs that are of consistently high quality. One individual who is strongly motivated to make Head Start a valuable learning experience for young children from disadvantaged backgrounds is Yolanda Garcia. To read about her work, see the *Connecting with Careers* profile.

Evaluations support the positive influence of quality early childhood programs on both the cognitive and social worlds of disadvantaged young children (Phillips

How Would You...?

If you were a **health-care professional,** how would you explain the importance of including health services as part of an effective Head Start program?

Yolanda Garcia, Director of Children's Services/Head Start

Yolanda Garcia has worked in the field of early childhood education and family support for three decades. She has been the director of the Children's Services Department for the Santa Clara, California, County Office of Education since 1980. As director, she is responsible for managing child development programs for 2,500 3- to 5-year-old children in 127 classrooms. Her training includes two master's degrees, one in public policy and child welfare from the University of Chicago and another in educational administration from San Jose State University.

Garcia has served on many national advisory committees that have resulted in improvements in the staffing of Head Start programs. Most notably, she served on the Head Start Quality Committee that recommended the development of Early Head Start and revised performance

Yolanda Garcia, director of Children's Services/Head Start, working with a Head Start child in Santa Clara, California.

standards for Head Start programs. Garcia currently is a member of the American Academy of Science Committee on the Integration of Science and Early Childhood Education.

& Lowenstein, 2011). A recent national evaluation of Head Start revealed that the program had a positive influence on the language and cognitive development of 3- and 4-year-olds (Puma & others, 2010). However, by the end of the first grade, there were few lasting outcomes. One exception was a larger vocabulary for those who went to Head Start as 4-year-olds and better oral comprehension for those who went to Head Start as 3-year-olds. Another recent study found that when young children initially began Head Start, they were well below their more academically advantaged peers in literacy and math (Hindman & others, 2010). However, by the end of the first grade, the Head Start children were on par with national averages in literacy and math.

One high-quality early childhood education program (although not a Head Start program) is the Perry Preschool program in Ypsilanti, Michigan, a two-year preschool program that includes weekly home visits from program personnel. In analyses of the long-term effects of the program, adults who had been in the Perry Preschool program were compared with a control group of adults from the same background who had not received the enriched early childhood education (Schweinhart & others, 2005; Weikart, 1993). Those who had been in the Perry Preschool program had fewer teen pregnancies and better high school graduation rates, and at age 40 more were in the workforce, owned their own homes, had a savings account, and had fewer arrests.

CONTROVERSIES IN EARLY CHILDHOOD EDUCATION

Three controversies in early childhood education involve (1) the curriculum, (2) universal preschool education, and (3) school readiness.

What Should the Curriculum Emphasize in Early Childhood Education? Regarding the curriculum controversy, on one side are those who advocate a child-centered, constructivist

What is the curriculum controversy in early childhood education?

approach much like that emphasized by the NAEYC along the lines of developmentally appropriate practice (Bredekamp, 2011). On the other side are those who advocate an academic, direct instruction approach.

In practice, many high-quality early childhood education programs include both academic and constructivist approaches. Many education experts like Lilian Katz (1999), though, worry about academic approaches that place too much pressure on young children to achieve and don't provide any opportunities to actively construct knowledge. Competent early childhood programs also should focus on both cognitive development and socioemotional development, not exclusively on cognitive development (NAEYC, 2002).

How Would You...?
If you were a **psychologist,** how would you advise preschool teachers to balance the development of young children's skills for academic achievement with opportunities for healthy social interaction?

Should All Children Be Provided with Preschool Education?   Another early childhood education controversy focuses on whether preschool education should be instituted for all U.S. 4-year-old children. Edward Zigler and his colleagues (2006) argued that the United States should have universal preschool education. They emphasize that quality preschools prepare children for school readiness and academic success. Zigler and his colleagues (2006) cite research that shows quality preschool programs increase the likelihood that once children go to elementary and secondary school they will be less likely to be retained in a grade or drop out of school. They also point to analyses indicating that universal preschool would bring cost savings on the order of billions of dollars because of a diminished need for remedial services (Karoly & Bigelow, 2005).

Critics of universal preschool education argue that the gains attributed to preschool and kindergarten education are often overstated. They especially stress that research has not proven that nondisadvantaged children improve as a result of attending a preschool. Thus, the critics say it is more important to improve preschool education for young children who are disadvantaged than to fund preschool education for all 4-year-old children. Some critics, especially homeschooling advocates, emphasize that young children should be educated by their parents, not by schools. Thus, controversy continues to characterize whether universal preschool education should be implemented.

What Is Required for School Readiness?   Educational reform has prompted considerable concern about children's readiness to enter kindergarten and first grade (Morrison & Hindman, 2008). National studies suggest that 40 percent of children who finish kindergarten are not ready for first grade (Kauffman, Early Education Exchange, 2002).

Craig and Sharon Ramey (1999, 2004) reviewed scientific research on school readiness and concluded that the following six caregiver activities are necessary in the infant and early childhood years to ensure that children will be ready for elementary school (Ramey & Ramey, 1999, p. 145):

1. Encourage exploration.
2. Mentor in basic skills.
3. Celebrate developmental advances.
4. Research and extend new skills.
5. Protect from inappropriate disapproval, teasing, and punishment.
6. Guide and limit behavior.

A child's attention is an important aspect of school-entry readiness.

A longitudinal study using six data sets examined various factors that might be linked to school readiness and the extent they predicted later achievement in reading and math (Duncan & others, 2007). Across all six data sets, the strongest predictors of later achievement were school-entry-level math, reading, and attention skills. However, school-entry-level socioemotional behaviors, such as internalizing and

Early Childhood Education in Japan and Developing Countries

As in the United States, there is diversity in Japanese early childhood education. Some Japanese kindergartens have specific aims, such as providing early musical training or practicing Montessori strategies. In large cities, some kindergartens are attached to universities that have elementary and secondary schools. In most Japanese preschools, however, little emphasis is put on academic instruction.

In one study, 300 Japanese and 210 American preschool teachers, child development specialists, and parents were asked about various aspects of early childhood education

What characterizes early childhood education in Japan?

A kindergarten class in Kingston, Jamaica. *What characterizes kindergarten in many developing countries like Jamaica?*

(Tobin, Wu, & Davidson, 1989). Only 2 percent of the Japanese respondents listed "to give children a good start academically" as one of their top three reasons for a society to have preschools. In contrast, over half the American respondents chose this as one of their top three choices. Japanese preschools do not teach reading, writing, and mathematics but rather skills like persistence, concentration, and the ability to function as a member of a group. The vast majority of young Japanese children are taught to read at home by their parents.

In the comparison of Japanese and American parents, more than 60 percent of the Japanese parents said that the purpose of preschool is to give children experience at being a member of the group, compared with only 20 percent of the U.S. parents (Tobin, Wu, & Davidson, 1989) (see Figure 9.15). Lessons in living and

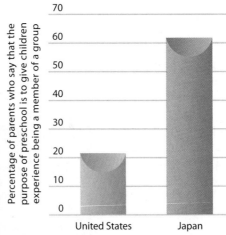

FIGURE 9.15

COMPARISON OF JAPANESE AND U.S. PARENTS' VIEWS ON THE PURPOSE OF PRESCHOOL

working together grow naturally out of the Japanese culture. In many Japanese kindergartens, children wear the same uniforms, including caps, in specific colors to indicate the classrooms to which they belong. They have identical sets of equipment, kept in identical drawers and shelves. This system is not intended to turn the young children into robots, as some Americans have surmised, but to impress on them that other people, just like themselves, have needs and desires that are equally important (Hendry, 1995).

Japan is a highly advanced industrialized country. What about developing countries—how do they compare to the United States in educating young children? The wide range of programs and emphasis on the education of the whole child—physically, cognitively, and socioemotionally—that characterizes U.S. early childhood education does not exist in many developing countries (Roopnarine & Metingdogan, 2006). Economic pressures and parents' belief that education should be academically rigorous have produced teacher-centered rather than child-centered early childhood education programs in most developing countries. Among the countries in which this type of early childhood education has been observed are Jamaica, China, Thailand, Kenya, and Turkey. In these countries, young children are usually given few choices and are educated in highly structured settings. Emphasis is on learning academic skills through rote memorization and recitation (Lin, Johnson, & Johnson, 2003). Programs in Mexico, Singapore, Korea, and Hong Kong have been observed to be closer to those in the United States in their emphasis on curriculum flexibility and play-based methods (Cisneros-Cohernour, Moreno, & Cisneros, 2000).

externalizing problems, and social skills showed little connection to later academic achievement.

In some developed countries, such as Japan, as well as in many developing countries, the goals of early childhood education are quite different from those of American programs. To read about the differences, see the *Connecting with Diversity* interlude.

Review

- What are some variations in early childhood education?
- What are the main efforts to educate young children who are disadvantaged?
- What are four controversies about early childhood education?

Connect

- Earlier in the chapter, you read about Piaget's and Vygotsky's cognitive theories.

Which side of the curriculum controversy in early childhood education—child-centered, constructivist, or direct instruction—would be supported by Piaget's and Vygotsky's theories? Why?

Reflect *Your Own Personal Journey of Life*

- What type of early childhood education program would you want your child to attend?

---

topical **connections**

In the next chapter, you will read about the many advances in the socioemotional development of young children. The cognitive advances we discussed in this chapter, combined with the socioemotional experiences young children have in interacting with others, pave the way for social cognitive advances in understanding the self and others. In Chapters 11 and 12, you will read about the continuing changes in children's physical and cognitive development in middle and late childhood. In terms of physical development, the development of the brain—especially in the prefrontal cortex—provides the foundation for the development of a number of cognitive advances, including strategies and reading skills.

looking forward - - →

---

reach your **learning goals**

What Are Three Views of the Cognitive Changes That Occur in Early Childhood?

LG1 Describe three views of the cognitive changes that occur in early childhood.

Piaget's Preoperational Stage

- According to Piaget, in the preoperational stage, which lasts from about 2 to 7 years of age, children cannot yet perform operations, which are reversible mental actions, but they begin to represent the world with words, images, and drawings, to form stable concepts, and to reason. During the symbolic function substage, which occurs between 2 and 4 years of age, children begin to mentally represent an object that is not present; their thought is limited by egocentrism and animism. During the intuitive thought substage, which stretches from about 4 to 7 years of age, children begin to reason and to bombard adults with questions. Thought at this substage is called intuitive because children seem so sure about their knowledge yet are unaware of how they know what they know. Centration and a lack of conservation also characterize the preoperational stage.

Vygotsky's Theory

- Vygotsky's theory represents a social constructivist approach to development. According to Vygotsky, children construct knowledge through social interaction, and they use language not only to communicate with others but also to plan, guide, and monitor their own behavior and to help them solve problems. His theory suggests that adults should access and use the child's zone of proximal development (ZPD), which is the range of tasks that are too difficult for children to master alone but that can be learned with the guidance and assistance of adults or more-skilled children. The theory also suggests that adults and peers should teach through scaffolding, which involves changing the level of support over the course of a teaching session, with the more-skilled person adjusting guidance to fit the student's current performance level.

Information Processing

- The child's ability to attend to stimuli dramatically improves during early childhood. Advances in executive attention and sustained attention are especially important in early childhood, but the young child still attends to the salient rather than the relevant features of a task. Significant improvement in short-term memory occurs during early childhood. With good prompts, young children's long-term memories can be accurate, although young children can be led into developing false memories. Advances in executive functioning, an umbrella-like concept that consists of a number of higher-level cognitive processes linked to the development of the prefrontal cortex, occur in early childhood. Executive functioning involves managing one's thoughts to engage in goal-directed behavior and to exercise self-control. Theory of mind is the awareness of one's own mental processes and the mental processes of others. Children begin to understand mental states involving perceptions, desires, and emotions from 18 months to 3 years of age; by 5 years of age a majority realize that people can have false beliefs. It is only beyond the preschool years that children have a deepening appreciation of the mind itself rather than just understanding mental states. Autistic children have difficulty developing a theory of mind.

How Do Young Children Develop Language? Summarize how language develops in early childhood.

Understanding Phonology and Morphology

- Young children increase their grasp of language's rule systems. In terms of phonology, most young children become more sensitive to the sounds of spoken language. Berko's classic experiment demonstrated that young children understand morphological rules.

Changes in Syntax and Semantics

- Preschool children learn and apply rules of syntax involving how words should be ordered. In terms of semantics, vocabulary development increases dramatically during early childhood.

Advances in Pragmatics

- Young children's conversational skills improve, they increase their sensitivity to the needs of others in conversation, and they learn to change their speech style to suit the situation.

Young Children's Literacy

- There has been increased interest in young children's literacy. Young children need to develop positive images of reading and writing skills through a supportive environment. Children should be active participants in their education and be immersed in a wide range of interesting and enjoyable listening, talking, writing, and reading experiences.

What Are Some Important Features of Young Children's Education? LG3 Evaluate different approaches to early childhood education.

Variations in Early Childhood Education

- The child-centered kindergarten emphasizes the education of the whole child, with particular attention to individual variation, the process of learning, and the importance of play in development. The Montessori approach allows children to choose from a range of activities while teachers serve as facilitators. Developmentally appropriate practice focuses on the typical patterns of children (age appropriateness) and the uniqueness of each child (individual appropriateness). Such practice contrasts with developmentally inappropriate practice, which ignores the concrete, hands-on approach to learning.

Educating Young Children Who Are Disadvantaged

- The U.S. government has tried to break the poverty cycle with programs such as Head Start. Model programs have been shown to have positive effects on children who live in poverty.

- Controversy characterizes early childhood education curricula. On the one side are the child-centered, constructivist advocates; on the other are those who advocate a direct instruction, academic approach. Another controversy involves whether universal preschool education should be provided for all U.S. 4-year-olds. A third controversy focuses on school readiness, in which skills in math, reading, and attention are especially important in predicting later academic achievement.

key terms

preoperational stage 260	intuitive thought substage 261	social constructivist approach 265	child-centered kindergarten 278
operations 260	centration 262	executive attention 268	Montessori approach 279
symbolic function substage 260	conservation 262	sustained attention 268	developmentally appropriate practice
egocentrism 260	zone of proximal development (ZPD) 263	short-term memory 269	(DAP) 280
animism 261	scaffolding 264	executive functioning 270	Project Head Start 280
		theory of mind 271	

key people

Jean Piaget 260	Lev Vygotsky 263	Mary Rothbart 268	Jean Berko 275
Barbel Inhelder 260	Elena Bodrova 266	Maria Gartstein 268	Maria Montessori 279
Rochel Gelman 263	Deborah Leong 266	Stephanie Carlson 271	

connecting with improving the lives of children

MAKING A DIFFERENCE

Nourish the Young Child's Cognitive Development

What are some good strategies for helping young children develop their cognitive competencies?

- *Provide opportunities for the young child's development of symbolic thought.* Give the child ample opportunities to scribble and draw. Provide the child with opportunities to engage in make-believe play. Don't criticize the young child's art and play. Let the child's imagination flourish.

- *Encourage exploration.* Let the child select many of the activities he or she wants to explore. Don't have the child do rigid paper-and-pencil exercises that involve rote learning. The young child should not be spending lots of time passively sitting, watching, and listening.

- *Be an active language partner with the young child.* Encourage the young child to speak in entire sentences instead of using single words. Be a good listener. Ask the child lots of questions. Don't spend time correcting the child's grammar; simply model correct grammar yourself when you talk with the child. Don't correct the young child's writing. Spend time selecting age-appropriate books for the young child. Read books with the young child.

- *Become sensitive to the child's zone of proximal development.* Monitor the child's level of cognitive functioning. Know what tasks the child can competently perform alone and those that are too difficult, even with your help. Guide and assist the child in the proper performance of skills and use of tools in the child's zone of proximal development. Warmly support the young child's practice of these skills.

- *Evaluate the quality of the child's early childhood education program.* Make sure the early childhood program the child attends involves developmentally appropriate education. The program should be age appropriate and individual appropriate for the child. It should not be a high-intensity, academic-at-all-costs program. Don't pressure the child to achieve at this age.

RESOURCES

National Association for the Education of Young Children (NAEYC)
800–424–2460
www.naeyc.com
NAEYC is an important professional organization that advocates for young children and has developed guidelines for a number of dimensions of early childhood education. It publishes the excellent journal *Young Children.*

Mind in the Making
by Ellen Galinsky (2010)
New York: HarperCollins
An excellent book for parents who want to guide their children's cognitive development in a positive direction. Drawing upon interviews with leading experts in children's cognitive development, Galinsky describes seven essential skills that children need.

chapter 10

SOCIOEMOTIONAL DEVELOPMENT IN EARLY CHILDHOOD

In his memoir *Burning Fence: A Western Memoir of Fatherhood,* award-winning novelist Craig Lesley describes one memory from his early childhood:

Lifting me high above his head, my father placed me in the crotch of the Bing cherry tree growing beside my mother's parents' house in The Dalles. A little frightened at the dizzying height, I pressed my palms into the tree's rough, peeling bark. My father stood close, reassuring. I could see his olive skin, dazzling smile, and sharp-creased army uniform.

"Rudell, don't let him fall." My mother watched, her arms held out halfway, as if to catch me. . . .

"That's enough. Bring him down now." My mother's arms reached out farther.

Laughing, my father grabbed me under the arms, twirled me around, and plunked me into the grass. I wobbled a little. Imprinted on my palms was the pattern of the tree bark, and I brushed off the little bark pieces on my dungarees. . . .

This first childhood memory of my father remains etched in my mind. . . . When I grew older, I realized that my father had never lifted me into the cherry tree. After Rudell left, I never saw him until I was fifteen. My grandfather had put me in the tree. Still, the memory of my father lifting me into the tree persists. . . . Apparently, my mind has cross-wired the photographs of my handsome father in his army uniform with the logical reality that my grandfather set me in the crotch of the tree.

Why can I remember the event so vividly? I guess because I wanted so much for my father to be there. I have no easy answers. (Lesley, 2005, pp. 8–10)

Like millions of other children, Lesley experienced a family torn by divorce; he would also experience abuse by a stepfather. When his father left, Lesley was an infant, but even as a preschooler, he felt his father's absence. Once he planned to win a gift for his father so that his grandmother "could take it to him and then he'd come to see me" (Lesley, 2005, p. 16). In just a few years, the infant had become a child with a complicated emotional and social life.

topical connections

In Chapter 7, you learned that as infants, children's socioemotional development reflects considerable progress as their caregivers (especially their parents) socialize them, and they develop more sophisticated ways of initiating social interactions with others. Development of a secure attachment is a key aspect of infancy, and the development of autonomy in the second year of life also signals an important accomplishment. As children move through infancy, it is important for caregivers to guide them in regulating their emotions. Temperament also is a central characteristic of the infant's profile, and some temperament styles are more adaptive than others. The use of child-care providers has become increasingly common in recent years, and the quality of this care varies considerably. Parents continue to play key roles in children's development in the early childhood period, but peers begin to play more important roles as well.

◀ — *looking back*

preview

In early childhood, children's emotional lives and personalities develop in significant ways as their small worlds widen. In addition to the continuing influence of family relationships, peers take on a more significant role in children's development and play fills the days of many young children's lives.

What Characterizes Young Children's Emotional and Personality Development?

LG1 Discuss emotional and personality development in early childhood.

The Self   Emotional Development   Moral Development   Gender

Many changes characterize young children's socioemotional development in early childhood. Their developing minds and social experiences produce remarkable advances in the development of their self, emotional maturity, moral understanding, and gender awareness.

THE SELF

We learned in Chapter 7, "Socioemotional Development in Infancy," that during the second year of life children make considerable progress in self-recognition. In the early childhood years, young children develop in many ways that enable them to enhance their self-understanding.

Initiative Versus Guilt In Chapter 1, you read about Erik Erikson's (1968) eight developmental stages that are encountered during certain time periods in the human life span. As you learned in the chapter, Erikson's first stage, trust versus mistrust, describes what he considers to be the main developmental task of infancy. Erikson's psychosocial stage associated with early childhood is *initiative versus guilt.* By now, children have become convinced that they are persons of their own; during early childhood, they begin to discover what kind of person they will become. They identify intensely with their parents, who most of the time appear to them to be powerful and beautiful, although often unreasonable, disagreeable, and sometimes even dangerous. During early childhood, children use their perceptual, motor, cognitive, and language skills to make things happen. They have a surplus of energy that permits them to forget failures quickly and to approach new areas that seem desirable—even if dangerous—with undiminished zest and some increased sense of direction. On their own *initiative,* then, children at this stage exuberantly move out into a wider social world.

The great governor of initiative is *guilt.* Young children's initiative and enthusiasm may bring them not only rewards but also guilt, which lowers self-esteem.

> When I say "I," I mean something absolutely unique and not to be confused with any other.
>
> —UGO BETTI
> *Italian Playwright, 20th Century*

Self-Understanding and Understanding Others Recent research studies have revealed that young children are more psychologically aware—of themselves and others—than used to be thought (Lewis & Carpendale, 2011; Thompson, Winer, & Goodvin, 2011). This increased psychological awareness reflects young children's expanding psychological sophistication.

Self-Understanding In Erikson's portrait of early childhood, the young child clearly has begun to develop **self-understanding,** which is the representation of self, the substance and content of self-conceptions (Harter, 2006). Though not the whole of personal identity, self-understanding provides its rational underpinnings.

self-understanding The child's cognitive representation of self, the substance and content of the child's self-conceptions.

As we saw in Chapter 7, "Socioemotional Development in Infancy," early self-understanding involves self-recognition. In early childhood, young children think that the self can be described by many material characteristics, such as size, shape, and color. They distinguish themselves from others through many physical and material attributes. Says 4-year-old Sandra, "I'm different from Jennifer because I have brown hair and she has blond hair." Says 4-year-old Ralph, "I am different from Hank because I am taller and I am different from my sister because I have a bicycle." Physical activities are also a central component of the self in early childhood (Keller, Ford, & Meacham, 1978). For example, pre-school children often describe themselves in terms of activities such as play. In sum, in early childhood, children often provide self-descriptions that involve body attributes, material possessions, and physical activities.

Although young children mainly describe themselves in terms of concrete, observable features and action tendencies, at about 4 to 5 years of age, as they hear others use psychological trait and emotion terms, they begin to include these in their own self-descriptions (Thompson, 2006). Thus, in a self-description, a 4-year-old might say, "I'm not scared. I'm always happy."

Young children's self-descriptions are typically unrealistically positive, as reflected in the comment of the 4-year-old above who says he is always happy, which he is not (Harter, 2006). This optimism occurs because they don't yet distinguish between their desired competence and their actual competence, tend to confuse ability and effort (thinking that differences in ability can be changed as easily as can differences in effort), don't engage in spontaneous social comparison of their abilities with those of others, and tend to compare their present abilities with what they could do at an earlier age (by which they usually look quite good). Perhaps as adults we should all be so optimistic about our abilities!

Understanding Others   Children also make advances in their understanding of others in early childhood (Lewis & Carpendale, 2011; Schneider & others, 2011). As we saw in Chapter 9, "Cognitive Development in Early Childhood," young children's theory of mind includes understanding that other people have emotions and desires (Wellman, 2011). And, at about 4 to 5 years of age, children not only start describing themselves in terms of psychological traits but they also begin to perceive others in terms of psychological traits. Thus, a 4-year-old might say, "My teacher is nice."

To understand others, it is necessary to take their perspective. **Perspective taking** is the social cognitive process involved in assuming the perspective of others and understanding their thoughts and feelings. Executive functioning, discussed in Chapter 9, "Cognitive Development in Early Childhood," is at work in perspective taking (Galinsky, 2010). Among the executive functions called on when young children engage in perspective taking are cognition inhibition (controlling one's own thoughts to consider the perspective of others) and cognitive flexibility (seeing situations in different ways).

Something important for children to develop is an understanding that people don't always give accurate reports of their beliefs (Mills, Elashi, & Archacki, 2011). Researchers have found that even 4-year-olds understand that people may make statements that aren't true to obtain what they want or to avoid trouble (Lee & others, 2002). For example, one study revealed that 4- and 5-year-olds were increasingly skeptical of another child's claim to be sick when the children were informed that the child was motivated to avoid having to go to camp (Gee & Heyman, 2007).

Another important aspect of understanding others involves understanding joint commitments. A recent study revealed that 3-year-olds, but not 2-year-olds, recognized

What characterizes young children's self-understanding?

Young children are more psychologically aware of themselves and others than used to be thought. Some children are better than others at understanding people's feelings and desires—and, to some degree, these individual differences are influenced by conversations caregivers have with young children about feelings and desires.

perspective taking The social cognitive process involved in assuming the perspective of others and understanding their thoughts and feelings.

developmental **connection**

Cognitive Theory. In Piaget's view, young children are egocentric in that they don't distinguish between their perspective and someone else's. Chapter 9, p. 261

when an adult is committed and when they themselves are committed to joint activity that involves obligation to a partner (Grafenhain & others, 2009).

Individual differences characterize young children's social understanding (Lewis & Carpendale, 2011; Thompson & Virmani, 2011). Some young children are better than others at understanding what people are feeling and what they desire, for example. To some degree, these individual differences are linked to conversations caregivers have with young children about other people's feelings and desires, and children's opportunities to observe others talking about people's feelings and desires. For example, a mother might say to a 3-year-old, "Next time, you should think about Raphael's feelings before you hit him."

Both the extensive theory of mind research (discussed in Chapter 9) and the recent research on young children's social understanding underscore that young children are not as *egocentric* as Piaget envisioned (Sokol & others, 2010).

EMOTIONAL DEVELOPMENT

The young child's growing awareness of self is linked to the ability to feel an expanding range of emotions. Young children, like adults, experience many emotions during the course of a day. Their emotional development in early childhood allows them to try to make sense of other people's emotional reactions and to begin to control their own emotions.

Expressing Emotions   Recall from Chapter 7, "Socioemotional Development in Infancy," that even young infants experience emotions such as joy and fear, but to experience *self-conscious emotions,* children must be able to refer to themselves and be aware of themselves as distinct from others (Lewis, 2010). Pride, shame, embarrassment, and guilt are examples of self-conscious emotions. Self-conscious emotions do not appear to develop until self-awareness appears around 18 months of age.

During the early childhood years, emotions such as pride and guilt become more common. They are especially influenced by parents' responses to children's behavior. For example, a young child may experience shame when a parent says, "You should feel bad about biting your sister."

A young child expressing the emotion of shame, which occurs when a child evaluates his or her actions as not living up to standards. A child experiencing shame wishes to hide or disappear. *Why is shame called a self-conscious emotion?*

Understanding Emotions   Among the most important changes in emotional development in early childhood is an increased understanding of emotion (Denham & others, 2011). During early childhood, young children increasingly understand that certain situations are likely to evoke particular emotions, facial expressions indicate specific emotions, emotions affect behavior, and emotions can be used to influence others' emotions (Cole & others, 2009). In a recent study, young children's emotion understanding was linked to how extensively they engaged in prosocial behavior (Ensor, Spencer, & Hughes, 2010).

Between 2 and 4 years of age, children considerably increase the number of terms they use to describe emotions. During this time, they are also learning about the causes and consequences of feelings (Denham & others, 2011).

When they are 4 to 5 years of age, children show an increased ability to reflect on emotions. They also begin to understand that the same event can elicit different feelings in different people. Moreover, they show a growing awareness that they need to manage their emotions to meet social standards.

Regulating Emotions   As we saw in Chapter 7, "Socioemotional Development in Infancy," emotion regulation is an important aspect of development. Emotion regulation especially plays a key role in children's ability to manage the demands and conflicts they face in interacting with others (Thompson, 2011c).

Emotion-Coaching and Emotion-Dismissing Parents Parents can play an important role in helping young children regulate their emotions. Depending on how they talk with their children about emotion, parents can be described as taking an *emotion-coaching* or an *emotion-dismissing* approach (Gottman, 2011). The distinction between these approaches is most evident in the way the parent deals with the child's negative emotions (anger, frustration, sadness, and so on). *Emotion-coaching parents* monitor their children's emotions, view their children's negative emotions as opportunities for teaching, assist them in labeling emotions, and coach them in how to deal effectively with emotions. In contrast, *emotion-dismissing parents* view their role as to deny, ignore, or change negative emotions. Researchers have observed that emotion-coaching parents interact with their children in a less rejecting manner, use more scaffolding and praise, and are more nurturant than are emotion-dismissing parents (Gottman & DeClaire, 1997). Moreover, the children of emotion-coaching parents are better at soothing themselves when they got upset, more effective in regulating their negative affect, focus their attention better, and have fewer behavior problems than the children of emotion-dismissing parents (Gottman, 2011). A recent study found that fathers' emotion coaching was related to children's social competence (Baker, Fenning, & Crnic, 2011).

An emotion-coaching parent. *What are some differences in emotion-coaching and emotion-dismissing parents?*

Parents' knowledge of their children's emotional world can help them guide their children's emotional development and teach them how to cope effectively with problems. A recent study found that mothers' knowledge about what distresses and comforts their children predicts the children's coping, empathy, and prosocial behavior (Vinik, Almas, & Grusec, 2011).

Regulation of Emotion and Peer Relations Emotions play a strong role in determining the success of a child's peer relationships (Denham & others, 2011). Moody and emotionally negative children are more likely to experience rejection by their peers, whereas emotionally positive children are more popular. A recent study revealed that 4-year-olds recognized and generated strategies for controlling their anger more than did 3-year-olds (Cole & others, 2009).

MORAL DEVELOPMENT

Moral development involves the development of thoughts, feelings, and behaviors regarding rules and conventions about what people should do in their interactions with other people. Major developmental theories have focused on different aspects of moral development.

> What is moral is what you feel good after and what is immoral is what you feel bad after.
>
> —ERNEST HEMINGWAY
> *American Author, 20th Century*

Moral Feelings Feelings of anxiety and guilt are central to the account of moral development provided by Sigmund Freud's psychoanalytic theory (initially described in Chapter 1). According to Freud, to reduce anxiety, avoid punishment, and maintain parental affection, children identify with parents, internalizing their standards of right and wrong, and thus form the *superego*, the moral element of personality.

Freud's ideas are not backed by research, but guilt certainly can motivate moral behavior. Other emotions, however, also contribute to the child's moral development, including positive feelings. One important example is *empathy*, which is responding to another person's feelings with an emotion that echoes the other's feelings (Denham & others, 2011).

Infants have the capacity for some purely empathic responses, but empathy often requires the ability to discern another's inner psychological states, or what is called *perspective taking*, which we discussed earlier in our coverage of self-development. Learning how to identify a wide range of emotional states in others and to anticipate what kinds of action will improve another person's emotional state help to advance children's moral development (Thompson & Newton, 2010).

developmental **connection**

Theories. Freud theorized that individuals go through five psychosexual stages. Chapter 1, p. 22

moral development Development that involves thoughts, feelings, and behaviors regarding rules and conventions about what people should do in their interactions with other people.

How is this child's moral thinking likely to be different about stealing a cookie depending on whether he is in Piaget's heteronomous or autonomous stage?

Moral Reasoning Interest in how children think about moral issues was stimulated by Jean Piaget (1932), who extensively observed and interviewed children from the ages of 4 through 12. Piaget watched children play marbles to learn how they thought about and used the game's rules. He also asked children about ethical issues—theft, lies, punishment, and justice, for example. Piaget concluded that children go through two distinct stages in how they think about morality.

- From 4 to 7 years of age, children display **heteronomous morality,** the first stage of moral development in Piaget's theory. Children think of justice and rules as unchangeable properties of the world, removed from the control of people.

- From 7 to 10 years of age, children are in a transition, showing some features of the first stage of moral reasoning and some features of the second stage, autonomous morality.

- From about 10 years of age and older, children show **autonomous morality.** They become aware that rules and laws are created by people, and, in judging an action, they consider the actor's intentions as well as the consequences.

Because young children are heteronomous moralists, they judge the rightness or goodness of behavior by considering its consequences, not the intentions of the actor. For example, to the heteronomous moralist, breaking twelve cups accidentally is worse than breaking one cup intentionally. As children develop into moral autonomists, intentions become more important than consequences.

The heteronomous thinker also believes that rules are unchangeable and are handed down by all-powerful authorities. When Piaget suggested to young children that they use new rules in a game of marbles, they resisted. By contrast, older children—moral autonomists—accept change and recognize that rules are merely convenient conventions, subject to change.

The heteronomous thinker also believes in **immanent justice,** the concept that if a rule is broken, punishment will be meted out immediately. The young child believes that a violation is connected automatically to its punishment. Thus, young children often look around worriedly after doing something wrong, expecting inevitable punishment. Immanent justice also implies that if something unfortunate happens to someone, the person must have transgressed earlier. Older children are moral autonomists—that is, they recognize that punishment occurs only if someone witnesses the wrongdoing and that, even then, punishment is not inevitable.

How do these changes in moral reasoning occur? Piaget argued that as children develop, they become more sophisticated in thinking about social matters, especially about the possibilities and conditions of cooperation. Piaget emphasized that this social understanding comes about through the mutual give-and-take of peer relations. In the peer group, where others have power and status similar to the child's, plans are negotiated and coordinated, and disagreements are reasoned about and eventually settled. Parent-child relations, in which parents have the power and children do not, are less likely to advance moral reasoning, because rules are often handed down in an authoritarian way.

developmental **connection**

Cognitive Theory. Lawrence Kohlberg's theory, like Piaget's, emphasizes that peers play a much stronger role in the development of moral thinking than parents do. Chapter 13, p. 397

heteronomous morality The first stage of moral development in Piaget's theory, occurring from approximately 4 to 7 years of age. Justice and rules are conceived of as unchangeable properties of the world, removed from the control of people.

autonomous morality The second stage of moral development in Piaget's theory, displayed by older children (about 10 years of age and older). The child becomes aware that rules and laws are created by people and that, in judging an action, one should consider the actor's intentions as well as the consequences.

immanent justice The expectation that, if a rule is broken, punishment will be meted out immediately.

Moral Behavior The behavioral and social cognitive theory of child development, initially described in Chapter 1, focuses on moral behavior rather than on moral reasoning. It holds that the processes of reinforcement, punishment, and imitation explain the development of moral behavior. When children are rewarded for behavior that is consistent with laws and social conventions, they are likely to repeat that behavior. When models who behave morally are provided, children are likely to adopt their actions. And, when children are punished for immoral behavior, those behaviors are likely to be reduced or eliminated. However, because punishment may have adverse side effects, as we discuss later in this chapter, it needs to be used judiciously and cautiously.

If a 4-year-old boy has been rewarded by his mother for telling the truth when he breaks a glass at home, does that mean that he is likely to tell the truth to his preschool teacher when he knocks over a vase and breaks it? Not necessarily; the situation influences behavior. More than half a century ago, a comprehensive study of thousands of children in many situations—at home, at school, and at church, for example—found that the totally honest child was virtually nonexistent; so was the child who cheated in all situations (Hartshorne & May, 1928–1930). Behavioral and social cognitive researchers emphasize that what children do in one situation is often only weakly related to what they do in other situations. A child might cheat in class but not in a game; a child might steal a piece of candy when alone but not steal it when others are present.

Social cognitive theorists also believe that the ability to resist temptation is closely tied to the development of self-control (Mischel, 2004). To achieve this self-control, children must learn to delay gratification. According to social cognitive theorists, cognitive factors are important in the child's development of self-control (Bandura, 2010a, b).

Conscience   **Conscience** refers to an internal regulation of standards of right and wrong that involves an integration of all three components of moral development we have described so far—moral thought, feeling, and behavior (Kochanska & others, 2010). Reflecting the presence of a conscience in young children, researchers have found that young children are aware of right and wrong, have the capacity to show empathy toward others, experience guilt, indicate discomfort following a transgression, and are sensitive to violating rules (Kochanska & Aksan, 2007).

Parenting and Young Children's Moral Development   Young children's relationship with their parents is an important aspect of moral development (Thompson & Newton, 2010). Especially important in this regard is the emergence of the young children's willingness to embrace the values of their parents, which flows from a positive, close relationship. For example, children who are securely attached are more likely to internalize their parents' values and rules (Thompson & Newton, 2010).

In Ross Thompson's (2006) view, young children are moral apprentices, striving to understand what is moral. They can be assisted in this quest by the "sensitive guidance of adult mentors in the home who provide lessons about morality in everyday experiences" (Thompson, Meyer, & McGinley, 2006, p. 290). An important parenting strategy is to proactively avert potential misbehavior by children before it takes place (Thompson, Meyer, & McGinley, 2006). With younger children, being proactive means using diversion, such as distracting their attention or moving them to alternative activities. With older children, being proactive may involve talking with them about values that the parents deem important. Transmitting these values can help older children and adolescents to resist the temptations that inevitably emerge in such contexts as peer relations and the media that can be outside the scope of direct parental monitoring.

developmental **connection**

Social Cognitive Theory. What are the main themes of Bandura's social cognitive theory? Chapter 1, p. 28

What are some aspects of relationships between parents and children that contribute to children's moral development?

GENDER

Recall from Chapter 1 that gender refers to the characteristics of people as males and females. **Gender identity** involves a sense of one's own gender, including knowledge, understanding, and acceptance of being male or female (Egan & Perry, 2001).

conscience An internal regulation of standards of right and wrong that involves an integration of moral thought, feeling, and behavior.

gender identity The sense of one's own gender, including knowledge, understanding, and acceptance of being male or female.

One aspect of gender identity involves knowing whether you are a girl or boy, which most children can do by about 2½ years of age (Blakemore, Berenbaum, & Liben, 2009). **Gender roles** are sets of expectations that prescribe how females or males should think, act, and feel. During the preschool years, most children increasingly act in ways that match their culture's gender roles. **Gender typing** refers to acquisition of a traditional masculine or feminine role. For example, fighting is more characteristic of a traditional masculine role and crying is more characteristic of a traditional feminine role. One study revealed that sex-typed behavior (boys playing with cars and girls with jewelry, for example) increased during the preschool years, and children engaging in the most sex-typed behavior during the preschool years were still doing so at 8 years of age (Golombok & others, 2008).

How is gender influenced by biology? By children's social experiences? By cognitive factors?

Biological Influences   Biology clearly plays a role in gender development. Among the possible biological influences are chromosomes, hormones, and evolution.

Chromosomes and Hormones   Biologists have learned a great deal about how sex differences develop. Recall that humans normally have 46 chromosomes arranged in pairs (see Chapter 2, "Biological Beginnings"). The 23rd pair consists of a combination of X and Y chromosomes, usually two X chromosomes in a female and an X and a Y in a male. In the first few weeks of gestation, however, female and male embryos look alike.

Males start to differ from females when genes on the Y chromosome in the male embryo trigger the development of testes rather than ovaries; the testes secrete copious amounts of the class of hormones known as androgens, which lead to the development of male sex organs. Low levels of androgens in the female embryo allow the normal development of female sex organs.

Thus, hormones play a key role in the development of sex differences (Hines, 2011). The two main classes of sex hormones are estrogens and androgens, which are secreted by the *gonads* (ovaries in females, testes in males). *Estrogens,* such as estradiol, influence the development of female physical sex characteristics. *Androgens,* such as testosterone, promote the development of male physical sex characteristics. Sex hormones also can influence children's socioemotional development. A recent study revealed that higher fetal testosterone level measured from amniotic fluid was linked to increased male-typical play in 6- to 10-year-old boys and girls (Auyeung & others, 2009).

The Evolutionary Psychology View   How might physical differences between the sexes give rise to psychological differences between males and females? Evolutionary psychology (introduced in Chapter 2, "Biological Beginnings") offers one answer. According to evolutionary psychology, adaptation during human evolution produced psychological differences between males and females (Buss, 2012). Because of their differing roles in reproduction, males and females faced differing pressures when the human species was evolving. In particular, because having multiple sexual liaisons improves the likelihood that males will pass on their genes, natural selection favored males who adopted short-term mating strategies. These are strategies that allow a male to win the competition with other males for sexual access to females. Therefore, say evolutionary psychologists, males evolved dispositions that favor violence, competition, and risk taking.

In contrast, according to evolutionary psychologists, females' contributions to the gene pool were improved when they secured resources that ensured that their offspring would survive; this outcome was promoted by obtaining long-term mates who could provide their offspring with resources and protections (Buss, 2012). As a consequence, natural selection favored females who devoted effort to parenting and chose successful, ambitious mates who could provide their offspring with resources and protection.

gender role A set of expectations that prescribes how females or males should think, act, and feel.

gender typing Acquisition of a traditional masculine or feminine role.

social role theory A theory that gender differences result from the contrasting roles of men and women.

psychoanalytic theory of gender A theory deriving from Freud's view that the preschool child develops a sexual attraction to the opposite-sex parent, by approximately 5 or 6 years of age renounces this attraction because of anxious feelings, and subsequently identifies with the same-sex parent, unconsciously adopting the same-sex parent's characteristics.

Critics of evolutionary psychology argue that its hypotheses are backed by speculations about prehistory, not evidence, and that in any event people are not locked into behavior that was adaptive in the evolutionary past. Critics also claim that the evolutionary view pays little attention to cultural and individual variations in gender differences (Matlin, 2012).

Social Influences   Many social scientists do not locate the cause of psychological gender differences in biological dispositions. Rather, they argue that these differences are due to social experiences. Explanations for how gender differences come about through experience include both social and cognitive theories.

Social Theories of Gender   Three main social theories of gender have been proposed—social role theory, psychoanalytic theory, and social cognitive theory. Alice Eagly (2001, 2010) proposed **social role theory,** which states that gender differences result from the contrasting roles of women and men. In most cultures around the world, women have less power and status than men, and they control fewer resources (UNICEF, 2011). Compared with men, women perform more domestic work, spend fewer hours in paid employment, receive lower pay, and are more thinly represented in the highest levels of organizations. In Eagly's view, as women adapted to roles with less power and less status in society, they showed more cooperative, less dominant profiles than men. Thus, the social hierarchy and division of labor are important causes of gender differences in power, assertiveness, and nurture.

The **psychoanalytic theory of gender** stems from Freud's view that the preschool child develops a sexual attraction to the opposite-sex parent. This is the process known as the Oedipus complex (for boys) or Electra complex (for girls). At 5 or 6 years of age, the child renounces this attraction because of anxious feelings. Subsequently, the child identifies with the same-sex parent, unconsciously adopting the same-sex parent's characteristics. However, developmentalists have observed that gender development does not proceed as Freud proposed (Blakemore, Berenbaum, & Liben, 2009). Children become gender-typed much earlier than 5 or 6 years of age, and they become masculine or feminine even when the same-sex parent is not present in the family.

The social cognitive approach discussed in Chapter 2, "Biological Beginnings," provides an alternative explanation of how children develop gender-typed behavior. According to the **social cognitive theory of gender,** children's gender development occurs through observing and imitating what other people say and do, and through being rewarded and punished for gender-appropriate and gender-inappropriate behavior (Bussey & Bandura, 1999). From birth onward, males and females are treated differently. When infants and toddlers show gender differences, adults tend to reward them. Parents often use rewards and punishments to teach their daughters to be feminine ("Karen, you are being a good girl when you play gently with your doll") and their sons to be masculine ("Keith, a boy as big as you is not supposed to cry"). Parents, however, are only one of many sources through which children learn gender roles (Leaper & Bigler, 2011). Culture, schools, peers, the media, and other family members also provide gender-role models. For example, children also learn about gender from observing other adults in the neighborhood and on television. As children get older, peers become increasingly important. Let's take a closer look at the influence of parents and peers.

Parental Influences   Parents, by action and by example, influence their children's gender development. Both mothers and fathers are psychologically important to their children's gender development (Grusec & Davidov, 2007). Cultures around the world, however, tend to give mothers and fathers different roles (Chen & others, 2011). A research review provided these conclusions (Bronstein, 2006):

- *Mothers' socialization strategies.* In many cultures mothers socialize their daughters to be more obedient and responsible than their sons. They also place more restrictions on daughters' autonomy.

First imagine that this is a photograph of a baby girl. *What expectations would you have of her?* Then imagine that this is a photograph of a baby boy. *What expectations would you have of him?*

"How is it gendered?"
© Edward Koren/The New Yorker Collection/
www.cartoonbank.com

social cognitive theory of gender A theory that emphasizes that children's gender development occurs through the observation and imitation of gender behavior and through the rewards and punishments children experience for gender-appropriate and gender-inappropriate behavior.

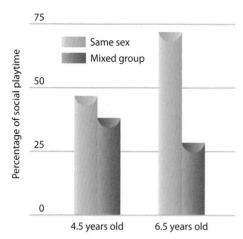

FIGURE **10.1**

DEVELOPMENTAL CHANGES IN PERCENTAGE OF TIME SPENT IN SAME-SEX AND MIXED-GROUP SETTINGS. Observations of children show that they are more likely to play in same-sex than mixed-sex groups. This tendency increases between 4 and 6 years of age.

How Would You...?
If you were a **human development and family studies professional,** how would you describe the ways in which parents influence their children's notions of gender roles?

gender schema theory The theory that gender typing emerges as children gradually develop gender schemas of what is considered gender-appropriate and gender-inappropriate in their culture.

• *Fathers' socialization strategies.* Fathers show more attention to sons than to daughters, engage in more activities with sons, and put forth more effort to promote sons' intellectual development.

Thus, despite increased awareness in the United States and other Western nations of the negative outcomes of gender stereotyping, many parents continue to foster behaviors and perceptions that reflect traditional gender-role norms (Bronstein, 2006).

Peer Influences   Parents provide the earliest discrimination of gender roles, but before long, peers join the process of responding to and modeling masculine and feminine behavior. In fact, peers become so important to gender development that the playground has been called "gender school" (Luria & Herzog, 1985).

Peers extensively reward and punish gender behavior (Leaper & Bigler, 2011). For example, when children play in ways that the culture says are sex-appropriate, their peers tend to reward them. But peers often reject children who act in a manner that is considered more characteristic of the other gender (Matlin, 2012). A little girl who brings a doll to the park may find herself surrounded by new friends; a little boy might be jeered at. However, there is greater pressure for boys to conform to a traditional male role than for girls to conform to a traditional female role (Fagot, Rodgers, & Leinbach, 2000). For example, a preschool girl who wants to wear boys' clothing receives considerably more approval than a boy who wants to wear a dress. The very term "tomboy" implies broad social acceptance of girls' adopting traditional male behaviors.

Gender molds important aspects of peer relations. It influences the composition of children's groups, the size of groups, and interactions within a group (Maccoby, 1998, 2002):

• *Gender composition of children's groups.* Around the age of 3, children already show a preference to spend time with same-sex playmates. From 4 to 12 years of age, this preference for playing in same-sex groups increases, and during the elementary school years children spend a large majority of their free time with children of their own sex (see Figure 10.1).

• *Group size.* From about 5 years of age onward, boys are more likely to associate together in larger clusters than girls are. Boys are also more likely to participate in organized group games than girls are.

• *Interaction in same-sex groups.* Boys are more likely than girls to engage in rough-and-tumble play, competition, conflict, ego displays, risk taking, and dominance seeking. By contrast, girls are more likely to engage in "collaborative discourse," in which they talk and act in a more reciprocal manner.

Cognitive Influences   One influential cognitive theory is **gender schema theory,** which states that gender typing emerges as children gradually develop gender schemas of what is gender-appropriate and gender-inappropriate in their culture (Blakemore, Berenbaum, & Liben, 2009). A *schema* is a cognitive structure, a network of associations that guide an individual's perceptions. A *gender schema* organizes the world in terms of female and male. Children are internally motivated to perceive the world

What role does gender play in children's peer relations?

and to act in accordance with their developing schemas. Bit by bit, children pick up what is gender-appropriate and gender-inappropriate in their culture, and develop gender schemas that shape how they perceive the world and what they remember. Children are motivated to act in ways that conform with these gender schemas. Thus, gender schemas fuel gender typing.

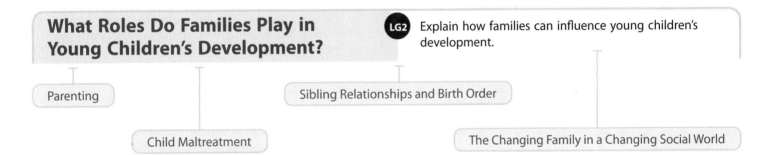

Review Connect Reflect

LG1 Discuss emotional and personality development in early childhood.

Review

- What changes in the self occur during early childhood?
- What changes take place in emotional development in early childhood?
- What are some key aspects of moral development in young children?
- How does gender develop in young children?

Connect

- In the previous section, you read about the influence of parents on children's gender development. How does this compare with what you learned about parents' influence on temperament that you read about in Chapter 7?

Reflect *Your Own Personal Journey of Life*

- Imagine you are the parent of a 4-year-old. What strategies would you use to increase your child's understanding of others?

What Roles Do Families Play in Young Children's Development?

LG2 Explain how families can influence young children's development.

```
Parenting

Child Maltreatment

Sibling Relationships and Birth Order

The Changing Family in a Changing Social World
```

Attachment to a caregiver is a key social relationship during infancy. Social and emotional development is also shaped by other relationships and by temperament, contexts, and social experiences in the early childhood years and later. In this section, we discuss social relationships of early childhood beyond attachment.

PARENTING

Good parenting takes time and effort (Grusec, 2011). You can't do it with a minute here and a minute there, such as playing Mozart CDs and reading

> Parenting is a very important profession, but no test of fitness for it is ever imposed in the interest of children.
>
> —GEORGE BERNARD SHAW
> *Irish Playwright, 20th Century*

Calvin and Hobbes

	Accepting, responsive	Rejecting, unresponsive
Demanding, controlling	Authoritative	Authoritarian
Undemanding, uncontrolling	Indulgent	Neglectful

FIGURE **10.2**

CLASSIFICATION OF PARENTING STYLES. The four types of parenting styles (authoritative, authoritarian, indulgent, and neglectful) involve the dimensions of acceptance and responsiveness, on the one hand, and demand and control on the other. For example, authoritative parenting involves being both accepting/responsive and demanding/controlling.

authoritarian parenting A restrictive punitive style in which parents exhort the child to follow their directions and to respect work and effort. The authoritarian parent places firm limits and controls on the child and allows little verbal exchange. Authoritarian parenting is associated with children's social incompetence.

authoritative parenting A parenting style in which parents encourage their children to be independent but still place limits and controls on their actions. Extensive verbal give-and-take is allowed, and parents are warm and nurturant toward the child. Authoritative parenting is associated with children's social competence.

neglectful parenting A style of parenting in which the parent is very uninvolved in the child's life; it is associated with children's social incompetence, especially a lack of self-control.

one-minute bedtime stories to children. Of course, it's not just the quantity of time parents spend with children that is important for children's development—the quality of the parenting is clearly influential as well (Russell, 2011).

Baumrind's Parenting Styles   Diana Baumrind (1971) holds that parents should be neither punitive nor aloof. Rather, they should develop rules for their children and be affectionate with them. She has described four types of parenting styles:

- **Authoritarian parenting** is a restrictive, punitive style in which parents exhort the child to follow their directions and respect their work and effort. The authoritarian parent places firm limits and controls on the child and allows little verbal exchange. For example, an authoritarian parent might say, "You do it my way or else." Authoritarian parents also might spank the child frequently, enforce rules rigidly but not explain them, and show rage toward the child. Children of authoritarian parents are often unhappy, fearful, and anxious about comparing themselves with others; fail to initiate activity; and have weak communication skills.

- **Authoritative parenting** encourages children to be independent but still places limits and controls on their actions. Extensive verbal give-and-take is allowed, and parents are warm and nurturant toward the child. An authoritative parent might put his arm around the child in a comforting way and say, "You know you should not have done that. Let's talk about how you can handle the situation better next time." Authoritative parents show pleasure and support in response to children's constructive behavior. They also expect mature, independent, and age-appropriate behavior by children. Children whose parents are authoritative are often cheerful, self-controlled and self-reliant, and achievement-oriented; they tend to maintain friendly relations with peers, cooperate with adults, and cope well with stress.

- **Neglectful parenting** is a style in which the parent is very uninvolved in the child's life. Children whose parents are neglectful develop the sense that other aspects of the parents' lives are more important than they are. These children tend to be socially incompetent. Many have poor self-control and don't handle independence well. They frequently have low self-esteem, are immature, and may be alienated from the family. In adolescence, they may show patterns of truancy and delinquency.

- **Indulgent parenting** is a style in which parents are highly involved with their children but place few demands or controls on them. Such parents let their children do what they want. The result is that the children never learn to control their own behavior and always expect to get their way. Some parents deliberately rear their children in this way because they believe the combination of warm involvement and few restraints will produce a creative, confident child. However, children whose parents are indulgent rarely learn respect for others and tend to have difficulty controlling their behavior. They might be domineering, egocentric, noncompliant, and have difficulties in peer relations.

These four classifications of parenting involve combinations of acceptance and responsiveness on the one hand and demand and control on the other (Maccoby & Martin, 1983). How these dimensions combine to produce authoritarian, authoritative, neglectful, and indulgent parenting is shown in Figure 10.2. Especially for non-Latino White children, authoritative parenting is linked with more positive child outcomes than the other three parenting styles (Bornstein & Zlotnik, 2008).

How Would You...?
If you were a **human development and family studies professional,** how would you characterize the parenting style that prevails within your own family?

Parenting Styles in Context   Do the benefits of authoritative parenting transcend the boundaries of ethnicity, socioeconomic status (SES), and household composition? Although occasional exceptions have been found, evidence linking authoritative parenting with competence on the part of the child occurs in research across a wide range of ethnic groups, social strata, cultures, and family structures (Steinberg, Blatt-Eisengart, & Cauffman, 2006).

Other research with ethnic groups suggests that some aspects of the authoritarian style may be associated with positive child outcomes (Parke & Clarke-Stewart, 2011). For example, Asian American parents exert considerable control over their children's lives. However, Ruth Chao (2005, 2007) argues that the style of parenting used by many Asian American parents, which she calls *training parents*, is distinct from the domineering control of the authoritarian style. In recent research on Chinese American adolescents and their parents, parental control was endorsed, as were the Confucian parental goals of perseverance, working hard in school, obedience, and being sensitive to parents' wishes (Russell, Crockett, & Chao, 2010).

An emphasis on requiring respect and obedience is also associated with the authoritarian style, but in Latino child rearing this focus may be positive rather than punitive. Rather than suppressing the child's development, it may encourage the development of a self and an identity that are embedded in the family and require respect and obedience (Dixon, Graber, & Brooks-Gunn, 2008).

Even physical punishment, another characteristic of the authoritarian style, may have varying effects in different contexts. African American parents are more likely than non-Latino White parents to use physical punishment (Deater-Deckard & Dodge, 1997). However, the use of physical punishment has been linked with increased externalized child problems (such as acting out and high levels of aggression) in non-Latino White families but not in African American families. One explanation of this finding points to the need for African American parents to enforce rules in the dangerous environments in which they are more likely to live (Harrison-Hale, McLoyd, & Smedley, 2004). As we see next, though, overall, the use of physical punishment in disciplining children raises many concerns.

According to Ruth Chao, what type of parenting style do many Asian American parents use?

Further Thoughts on Parenting Styles   Several caveats about parenting styles are in order. First, the parenting styles do not capture the important themes of reciprocal socialization and synchrony. Keep in mind that children socialize parents, just as parents socialize children (Parke & Clarke-Stewart, 2011). Second, many parents use a combination of techniques rather than a single technique, although one technique may be dominant. Although consistent parenting is usually recommended, the wise parent may sense the importance of being more permissive in certain situations, more authoritarian in others, and yet more authoritative in others. In addition, parenting styles often are talked about as if both parents have the same style, although this may not be the case. Finally, some critics argue that the concept of parenting style is too broad and that more research needs to be conducted to "unpack" parenting styles by studying various components that compose the styles (Maccoby, 2007). For example, is parental monitoring more important than warmth in predicting child and adolescent outcomes?

How Would You...?
If you were a **psychologist,** how would you use the research on parenting styles to design a parent education class that teaches effective skills for interacting with young children?

Punishment   Use of corporal (physical) punishment is legal in every state in the United States. A national survey of U.S. parents with 3- and 4-year-old children found that 26 percent of parents reported spanking their children frequently, and 67 percent reported yelling at their children frequently (Regalado & others, 2004). A cross-cultural comparison found that individuals in the United States and Canada were among those with the most favorable attitudes toward corporal punishment and were most likely to remember it being used by their parents (see Figure 10.3) (Curran & others, 2001).

indulgent parenting A style of parenting in which parents are highly involved with their children but place few demands or controls on them. Indulgent parenting is associated with children's social incompetence, especially a lack of self-control.

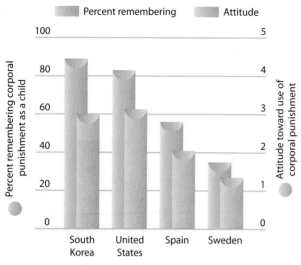

FIGURE **10.3**

CORPORAL PUNISHMENT IN DIFFERENT COUNTRIES.
A 5-point scale was used to assess attitudes toward corporal punishment with scores closer to 1 indicating an attitude against its use and scores closer to 5 suggesting an attitude favoring its use. *Why are studies of corporal punishment correlational studies, and how does that affect their usefulness?*

How Would You...?
If you were a **human development and family studies professional,** how would you advise parents about why they should not spank their children, and what alternatives to spanking would you recommend?

A research review concluded that corporal punishment by parents is associated with higher levels of immediate compliance and aggression by the children (Gershoff, 2002). The review also found that corporal punishment is linked to lower levels of moral internalization and mental health (Gershoff, 2002). A recent study in six countries revealed that mothers' use of physical punishment was linked to high rates of aggression in their children (Gershoff & others, 2010).

What are some reasons for avoiding spanking or similar punishments? They include the following considerations:

- When adults punish a child by yelling, screaming, or spanking, they are presenting children with out-of-control models for handling stressful situations. Children may imitate this behavior.

- Punishment can instill fear, rage, or avoidance. For example, spanking the child may cause the child to avoid being near the parent and to fear the parent.

- Punishment tells children what not to do rather than what to do. Children should be given feedback, such as "Why don't you try this?"

- Parents might unintentionally become so aroused when they are punishing the child that they become abusive (Durrant, 2008).

Debate about the effects of punishment on children's development continues (Grusec, 2011; Knox, 2010). A research review of 26 studies concluded that only severe or predominant use of spanking, not mild spanking, compared unfavorably with alternative discipline practices (Larzelere & Kuhn, 2005). There are few longitudinal studies of punishment and few studies that distinguish adequately between moderate and heavy use of punishment. Thus, in the view of some experts, it is still difficult to determine whether the effects of physical punishment are harmful to children's development, although such a view might be distasteful to some individuals (Grusec, 2011). It is nonetheless clear that when physical punishment involves abuse, it can be very harmful to children's development, as discussed later in this chapter (Cicchetti & others, 2011, 2012).

Most child psychologists recommend handling misbehavior by reasoning with the child, especially explaining the consequences of the child's actions for others. *Time out,* in which the child is removed from a setting that offers positive reinforcement for bad behavior, can also be effective. For example, when the child has misbehaved, a parent might take away TV viewing for a specified time.

In Chapter 7, "Socioemotional Development in Infancy," we described the family as a system and discussed possible links between marital relationships and parenting practices. See the *Connecting with Research* interlude to read about a study that reflects the family systems perspective.

Coparenting   The relationship between marital conflict and the use of punishment highlights the importance of *coparenting,* which is the support that parents provide one another in jointly raising a child. Poor coordination between parents, undermining of the other parent, lack of cooperation and warmth, and disconnection by one parent are conditions that place children at risk for problems (McHale & Sullivan, 2008; Solmeyer & others, 2011). One study revealed that coparenting predicted young children's effortful control above and beyond maternal and paternal parenting (Karreman & others, 2008). A recent study indicated that greater father involvement in a child's play was linked to an increase in coparenting one year later (Jia & Schoppe-Sullivan, 2011).

Parents who do not spend enough time with their children or who have problems in child rearing can benefit from counseling and therapy. To read about the work of marriage and family counselor Darla Botkin, see the *Connecting with Careers* profile.

Are Marital Conflict, Individual Hostility, and the Use of Physical Punishment Related?

A longitudinal study assessed couples as they made the transition to parenthood, investigating possible links between marital conflict, individual adult hostility, and the use of physical punishment with young children (Kanoy & others, 2003). Before the birth of the first child, the level of marital conflict was observed in a marital problem-solving discussion; answers to questionnaires regarding individual characteristics were also obtained. Thus, these characteristics of the couples were not influenced by characteristics of the child. When the children were 2 and 5 years old, the couples were interviewed about the frequency and intensity of their physical punishment of the children. At both ages, the parents' level of marital conflict was again observed in a marital problem-solving discussion.

The researchers found that both hostility and marital conflict were linked with the use of physical punishment. Individuals with high rates of hostility on the prenatal measures used more frequent and more severe physical punishment with their children. The same was evident for marital conflict—when marital conflict was high, both mothers and fathers were more likely to use physical punishment in disciplining their young children.

If parents who have a greater likelihood of using physical punishment can be identified in prenatal classes, these families could be encouraged to use other forms of discipline before they get into a pattern of physically punishing their children.

How might parents who are inclined to use physical punishment of children be identified by health professionals? What other methods of discipline would you recommend to these parents, and how would you make your case?

Darla Botkin, Marriage and Family Therapist

Darla Botkin is a marriage and family therapist who teaches, conducts research, and engages in marriage and family therapy. She is on the faculty of the University of Kentucky. Botkin obtained a bachelor's degree in elementary education with a concentration in special education and then went on to receive a master's degree in early childhood education. She spent the next six years working with children and their families in a variety of settings, including child care, elementary school, and Head Start. These experiences led Botkin to recognize the interdependence of the developmental settings that children and their parents experience (such as home, school, and work). She returned to graduate school and obtained a Ph.D. in family studies from the University of Tennessee. She then became a faculty member in the Family Studies program at the University of Kentucky. Completing further coursework and clinical training in marriage and family therapy, she became certified as a marriage and family therapist.

Botkin's current interests include working with young children in family therapy, exploring gender and ethnic issues in family therapy, and understanding the role of spirituality in family wellness.

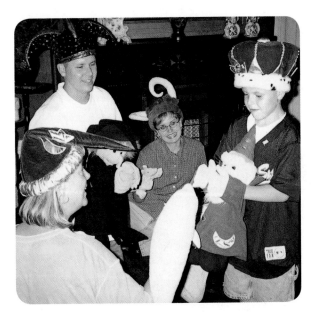

Darla Botkin (*left*), conducting a family therapy session.

For more information about what marriage and family therapists do, see the Careers in Children's Development appendix, p. 50.

CHILD MALTREATMENT

Unfortunately, punishment sometimes leads to the abuse of infants and children (Cicchetti, 2011a, b, 2012). In 2009, approximately 702,000 U.S. children were found to be victims of child abuse at least once during that year (U.S. Department of Health and Human Services, 2010). Eighty-one percent of these children were abused by a parent or parents. Laws in many states now require physicians and teachers to report suspected cases of child abuse, yet many cases go unreported, especially those involving battered infants.

Whereas the public and many professionals use the term *child abuse* to refer to both abuse and neglect, developmentalists increasingly use the term *child maltreatment* (Cicchetti & others, 2011). This term does not have quite the emotional impact of the term *abuse* and acknowledges that maltreatment includes diverse conditions.

Types of Child Maltreatment   The four main types of child maltreatment are physical abuse, child neglect, sexual abuse, and emotional abuse (National Clearinghouse on Child Abuse and Neglect, 2004):

- *Physical abuse* is characterized by the infliction of physical injury as a result of punching, beating, kicking, biting, burning, shaking, or otherwise physically harming a child. The parent or other person may not have intended to hurt the child; the injury may have resulted from excessive physical punishment (Milot & others, 2010).

> Child maltreatment involves grossly inadequate and destructive aspects of parenting.
>
> —Dante Cicchetti
> *Contemporary Developmental Psychologist, University of Minnesota*

- *Child neglect* is characterized by failure to provide for the child's basic needs. Neglect can be physical (abandonment, for example), educational (allowing chronic truancy, for example), or emotional (marked inattention to the child's needs, for example). Child neglect is by far the most common form of child maltreatment. In every country where relevant data have been collected, neglect occurs up to three times more often than abuse (U.S. Department of Health and Human Services, 2010).

- *Sexual abuse* includes fondling a child's genitals, intercourse, incest, rape, sodomy, exhibitionism, and commercial exploitation through prostitution or the production of pornographic materials (Bahali & others, 2010).

- *Emotional abuse (psychological/verbal abuse/mental injury)* includes acts or omissions by parents or other caregivers that have caused, or could cause, serious behavioral, cognitive, or emotional problems (van Harmelen & others, 2010).

Although any of these forms of child maltreatment may be found separately, they often occur in combination. Emotional abuse is almost always present when other forms are identified.

Eight-year-old Donnique Hein lovingly holds her younger sister, 6-month-old Maria Paschel, after a meal at Laura's Home, a crisis shelter in Westpark run by the City Mission, in March 2010.

The Context of Abuse   No single factor causes child maltreatment (Cicchetti, 2011a, b, 2012). A combination of factors, including the culture, family, and developmental characteristics of the child, likely contributes to child maltreatment (Prinz & others, 2009).

The extensive violence that takes place in American culture is reflected in the occurrence of violence in the family (Durrant, 2008). A regular diet of violence appears on television screens, and parents often resort to power assertion as a disciplinary technique. In China, where physical punishment is rarely used to discipline children, the incidence of child abuse is reported to be very low.

The family itself is obviously a key part of the context of abuse (Cicchetti, 2011,a, b, 2012; Trickett & Negriff, 2011). The interactions of all family members need to be considered, regardless of who performs the violent acts against the child. For example, even though the father may be the one who physically abuses the child, the behavior of the mother, the child, and siblings also should be evaluated. A mother who conveniently goes shopping whenever the father is angry with the child, or siblings who tease the child for "deserving" a beating, may contribute to the abuse.

Were parents who abuse children abused by their own parents? About one-third of parents who were abused themselves when they were young go on to abuse their own children (Cicchetti & others, 2011). Thus, some, but not a majority, of parents are involved in an intergenerational transmission of abuse. Mothers who break out of the intergenerational transmission of abuse often report having had at least one warm, caring adult in their background; have a close, positive marital relationship; and have received therapy (Egeland, Jacobvitz, & Sroufe, 1988).

How Would You...?

If you were a **health-care professional,** how would you work with parents during infant and child checkups to prevent child maltreatment?

Developmental Consequences of Abuse Among the consequences of child maltreatment in childhood and adolescence are poor emotion regulation, attachment problems, problems in peer relations, difficulty in adapting to school, and other psychological problems such as depression and delinquency (Cicchetti, 2011a, b). As shown in Figure 10.4, maltreated young children in foster care were more likely to show abnormal stress hormone levels than were middle-SES young children living with their birth family (Gunnar & others, 2006). In this study, the abnormal stress hormone levels were mainly present in the foster children who experienced neglect, best described as "institutional neglect" (Fisher, 2005). Adolescents who experienced abuse or neglect as children are more likely than adolescents who were not mal-treated as children to engage in violent romantic relationships, delinquency, sexual risk taking, and substance abuse (Trickett & others, 2011; Wekerle & others, 2009).

Later, during the adult years, individuals who were maltreated as children often have difficulty in establishing and maintaining healthy intimate relationships (Dozier, Stovall-McClough, & Albus, 2009). As adults, maltreated children are also at higher risk for violent behavior toward other adults—especially dating partners and marital partners—as well as for substance abuse, anxiety, and depression (Kennedy, 2009).

A recent study revealed that adults who experienced child maltreatment were at increased risk for financial and employment-related difficulties (Zielinski, 2009). An important strategy is to prevent child maltreatment (Cicchetti, 2011a, b, 2012). In one study of maltreating mothers and their 1-year-olds, two treatments were effective in reducing child maltreatment: (1) home visitation that emphasized improved parenting, coping with stress, and increasing support for the mother; and (2) psychotherapy that focused on improving maternal-infant attachment (Cicchetti, Toth, & Rogosch, 2005).

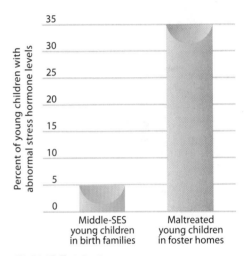

FIGURE 10.4

ABNORMAL STRESS HORMONE LEVELS IN YOUNG CHILDREN IN DIFFERENT TYPES OF REARING CONDITIONS

SIBLING RELATIONSHIPS AND BIRTH ORDER

How do developmentalists characterize sibling relationships? How extensively does birth order influence behavior?

Sibling Relationships Approximately 80 percent of American children have one or more siblings—that is, sisters and brothers (Dunn, 2007). If you grew up with siblings, you probably have a rich memory of aggressive, hostile interchanges. Sib-lings in the presence of each other when they are 2 to 4 years of age, on average, have a conflict once every 10 minutes and then the conflicts go down somewhat from 5 to 7 years of age (Kramer, 2006).

What do parents do when they encounter siblings having a verbal or physical confrontation? One study revealed that they do one of three things: (1) intervene and try to help them resolve the conflict, (2) admonish or threaten them, or (3) do noth-ing at all (Kramer & Perozynski, 1999). Of interest is that in families with two siblings 2 to 5 years of age, the most frequent parental reaction is to do nothing at all.

Laurie Kramer (2006), who had conducted a number of research studies on siblings, says that not intervening and letting sibling conflict escalate are not good strategies. She developed a program titled "More Fun with Sisters and Brothers," which teaches 4- to 8-year-old siblings social skills for developing positive interactions

(Kramer & Radey, 1997). Among the social skills taught in the program are how to appropriately initiate play, how to accept and refuse invitations to play, how to take another's perspective, how to deal with angry feelings, and how to manage conflict. A study of 5- to 10-year-old siblings and their parents found that training parents to mediate sibling disputes increased children's understanding of conflicts and reduced sibling conflict (Smith & Ross, 2007).

However, conflict is only one of the many dimensions of sibling relations (Howe, Ross, & Recchia, 2011). Sibling relations include helping, sharing, teaching, fighting, and playing—and siblings can act as emotional supports, rivals, and communication partners.

Judy Dunn (2007), a leading expert on sibling relationships, described three important characteristics of sibling relationships:

- *Emotional quality of the relationship.* Both intensive positive and negative emotions are often expressed by siblings toward each other. Many children have mixed feelings toward their siblings.

  - *Familiarity and intimacy of the relationship.* Siblings typically know each other very well and this intimacy suggests that they can either provide support or tease and undermine each other, depending on the situation.

    - *Variation in sibling relationships.* Some siblings describe their relationships more positively than others. Thus, there is considerable variation in sibling relationships. Above we saw that many siblings have mixed feelings about each other, but some children mainly describe their sibling in warm, affectionate ways, whereas others primarily talk about how irritating and mean a sibling is.

Birth Order   Whether a child has older or younger siblings has been linked to development of certain personality characteristics. For example, a recent review concluded that "firstborns are the most intelligent, achieving, and conscientious, while later-borns are the most rebellious, liberal, and agreeable" (Paulhus, 2008, p. 210). Compared with later-born children, firstborn children have also been described as more adult-oriented, helpful, conforming, and self-controlled. However, when such birth order differences are reported, they often are small.

What characterizes children's sibling relationships?

The one-child family is becoming much more common in China because of the strong motivation to limit the population growth in the People's Republic of China. The policy is still relatively new, and its effects on children have not been fully examined. *In general, though, what have researchers found the only child to be like?*

What might account for even small differences related to birth order? Proposed explanations usually point to variations in interactions with parents and siblings associated with being in a particular position in the family. This is especially true in the case of the firstborn child (Teti, 2001). The oldest child is the only one who does not have to share parental love and affection with other siblings—until another sibling comes along. An infant requires more attention than an older child; thus, the firstborn sibling receives less attention after the newborn arrives. Does this result in conflict between parents and the firstborn? In one research study, mothers became more negative, coercive, and restraining and played less with the firstborn following the birth of a second child (Dunn & Kendrick, 1982).

What is the only child like? The popular conception is that the only child is a "spoiled brat," with such undesirable characteristics as dependency, lack of self-control, and self-centered behavior. But researchers present a more positive portrayal of the only child. Only children often are achievement-oriented and display a desirable personality, especially in comparison with later-borns and children from large families (Falbo & Poston, 1993).

So far, our discussion suggests that birth order might be a strong predictor of behavior. However, an increasing number of family researchers stress that when all of the factors that influence behavior are considered, birth order itself shows limited ability to predict behavior. Think about some of the other important factors in children's lives that influence their behavior beyond birth order. They include heredity, models of competency or incompetency that parents present to children on a daily

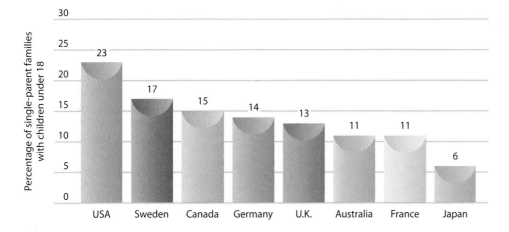

FIGURE **10.5**

SINGLE-PARENT FAMILIES IN DIFFERENT COUNTRIES

basis, peer influences, school influences, socioeconomic factors, sociohistorical factors, and cultural variations. When someone says firstborns are always like this but last-borns are always like that, the person is making overly simplistic statements that do not adequately take into account the complexity of influences on a child's development.

THE CHANGING FAMILY IN A CHANGING SOCIAL WORLD

Beyond variations in the number of siblings, the families that children experience differ in many important ways. The number of children growing up in single-parent families is staggering. As shown in Figure 10.5, the United States has one of the highest percentages of single-parent families in the world. Among two-parent families, there are those in which both parents work, those in which divorced parents have remarried, or those with gay or lesbian parents. Differences in culture and SES also influence families. How do these variations in families affect children?

Working Parents   More than one of every two U.S. mothers with a child under the age of 5 is in the labor force; more than two of every three with a child from 6 to 17 years of age is. Maternal employment is a part of modern life, but its effects are still being debated.

Most research on parental work has focused on young children and the mother's employment (Brooks-Gunn, Han, & Waldfogel, 2010). However, the effects of working parents involve the father as well as the mother when such matters as work schedules and work-family stress are considered (Parke & Clarke-Stewart, 2011). Recent research indicates that what matters for children's development is the nature of parents' work rather than whether one parent works outside the home (Han, 2009; Parke & Clarke-Stewart, 2011). Work can produce positive and negative effects on parenting (Crouter & McHale, 2005). Ann Crouter (2006) described how parents bring their experiences at work into their homes. She concluded that parents who have poor working conditions, such as long hours, overtime work, stressful work, and lack of autonomy at work, are likely to be more irritable at home and engage in less effective parenting than their counterparts who have better work conditions in their jobs. A consistent finding is that children (especially girls) of working mothers engage in less gender stereotyping and have more egalitarian views of gender (Goldberg & Lucas-Thompson, 2008).

How does work affect parenting?

developmental **connection**

Social Contexts. Research consistently shows that family factors are considerably better at predicting children's developmental outcomes than are child-care experiences. Chapter 7, p. 228

> As marriage has become a more optional, less permanent institution in contemporary America, children and adolescents are encountering stresses and adaptive challenges associated with their parents' marital transitions.
>
> —E. Mavis Hetherington
> *Contemporary Psychologist,*
> *University of Virginia*

Children in Divorced Families Divorce rates changed dramatically in the United States and many countries around the world in the late twentieth century (Amato & Dorius, 2010). The U.S. divorce rate increased enormously in the 1960s and 1970s but has declined since the 1980s. However, the divorce rate in the United States is still much higher than that of most other countries.

It is estimated that 40 percent of children born to married parents in the United States will experience their parents' divorce (Hetherington & Stanley-Hagan, 2002). Let's examine some important questions about children in divorced families:

- *Are children better adjusted in intact, never-divorced families than in divorced families?* Most researchers agree that children from divorced families show poorer adjustment than their counterparts in nondivorced families (Hetherington, 2006; Lansford, 2009; Wallerstein, 2008) (see Figure 10.6). Those who have experienced multiple divorces are at greater risk. Children in divorced families are more likely than children in nondivorced families to have academic problems, to show externalized problems (such as acting out and delinquency) and internalized problems (such as anxiety and depression), to be less socially responsible, to have less competent intimate relationships, to drop out of school, to become sexually active at an early age, to take drugs, to associate with antisocial peers, to have low self-esteem, and to be less securely attached as young adults (Conger & Chao, 1996). Nonetheless, keep in mind that a majority of children in divorced families do not have significant adjustment problems (Lansford, 2009). One study found that 20 years after their parents had divorced when they were children, approximately 80 percent of adults concluded that their parents' decision to divorce was a wise one (Ahrons, 2004).

- *Should parents stay together for the sake of the children?* Whether parents should stay in an unhappy or conflicted marriage for the sake of their children is one of the most commonly asked questions about divorce (Deutsch & Pruett, 2009; Hetherington, 2006; Ziol-Guest, 2009). If the stresses and disruptions in family relationships associated with an unhappy, conflictual marriage that erode the well-being of children are reduced by the move to a divorced, single-parent family, divorce can be advantageous. However, if the diminished resources and increased risks associated with divorce also are accompanied by inept parenting and sustained or increased conflict, not only between the divorced couple but also among the parents, children, and siblings, the best choice for the children would be for an unhappy marriage to be retained (Hetherington & Stanley-Hagan, 2002). It is difficult to determine how these "ifs" will play out when parents either remain together in an acrimonious marriage or become divorced.

Note that marital conflict may have negative consequences for children in the context of marriage or divorce (Cummings & Davies, 2010). A longitudinal study revealed that conflict in nondivorced families was associated with emotional problems in children (Amato, 2006). Indeed, many of the problems that children from divorced homes experience begin during the predivorce period, a time when parents are often in active conflict with each other. Thus, when children from divorced homes show problems, the problems may be due not only to the divorce, but also to the marital conflict that led to it.

E. Mark Cummings and his colleagues (Cummings & Davies, 2010; Cummings, El-Sheikh, & Kouros, 2009; Cummings & Merrilees, 2009; Koss & others, 2011) have proposed *emotion security theory,* which has its roots in attachment theory and states that children appraise marital conflict in terms of their sense of security and safety in the family. These researchers make a distinction between marital conflict that is negative for children (such as hostile emotional displays and destructive conflict tactics) and marital conflict that can be positive for children (such as marital disagreement that involves a calm discussion of each person's perspective and working together to reach a solution).

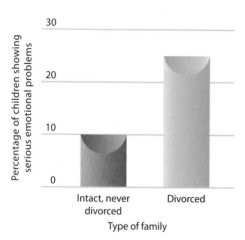

FIGURE 10.6

DIVORCE AND CHILDREN'S EMOTIONAL PROBLEMS. In Hetherington's research, 25 percent of children from divorced families showed serious emotional problems compared with only 10 percent of children from intact, never-divorced families. However, keep in mind that a substantial majority (75 percent) of the children from divorced families did not show serious emotional problems.

- *How much do family processes matter in divorced families?* In divorced families, family processes matter a great deal (Hetherington, 2006; Lansford, 2009; Parke & Clarke-Stewart, 2011). When the divorced parents have a harmonious relationship and use authoritative parenting, the adjustment of adolescents is improved (Hetherington, 2006). When the divorced parents can agree on child-rearing strategies and can maintain a cordial relationship with each other, frequent visits by the noncustodial parent usually benefit the child (Fabricius & others, 2010). Following a divorce, father involvement with children drops off more than mother involvement, especially for fathers of girls. Also, a recent study involving divorced families revealed that an intervention focused on improving the mother-child relationship was linked to improvements in relationship quality that increased children's coping skills over the short term (6 months) and long term (6 years) (Velez & others, 2011).

- *What factors influence an individual child's vulnerability to negative consequences from living in a divorced family?* Among the factors involved in the child's risk and vulnerability are the child's adjustment prior to the divorce, as well as the child's personality, temperament, and custody situation (Hetherington, 2006). Children whose parents later divorce show poorer adjustment before the breakup (Amato & Booth, 1996). Children who are socially mature and responsible, who show few behavioral problems, and who have an easy temperament are better able to cope with their parents' divorce. Children with a difficult temperament often have problems coping with their parents' divorce (Hetherington, 2006). Joint custody works best for children when the parents can get along with each other (Parke & Clarke-Stewart, 2011).

What concerns are involved in whether parents should stay together for the sake of the children or become divorced?

Earlier studies reported gender differences in response to divorce, with divorce being more negative for girls than for boys in mother-custody families. However, more recent studies have shown that gender differences are less pronounced and consistent than was previously believed. Some of the inconsistency may be due to the increase in father custody, joint custody, and involvement of noncustodial fathers, especially in their sons' lives.

- *What role does socioeconomic status play in the lives of children in divorced families?* Custodial mothers experience the loss of about one-fourth to one-half of their predivorce income, in comparison with a loss of only one-tenth by custodial fathers (Emery, 1994). This income loss for divorced mothers is accompanied by increased workloads, high rates of job instability, and residential moves to less desirable neighborhoods with inferior schools (Sayer, 2006).

In sum, many factors are involved in determining how divorce influences a child's development. To read about some strategies for helping children cope with their parents' divorce, see the *Caring Connections* interlude.

Gay and Lesbian Parents   An important aspect of gay and lesbian families with children is the sexual identity of parents at the time of a child's birth or adoption (Patterson, 2009). The largest group of children with gay and lesbian parents are likely those who were born in the context of heterosexual relationships, with one or both parents only later identifying themselves as gay or lesbian. Gay and lesbian parents may be single or have same-gender partners. In addition, gays and lesbians are increasingly choosing parenthood through donor insemination or adoption. Researchers have found that the children conceived through new reproductive technologies—such as in vitro fertilization—are as well adjusted as their counterparts conceived by natural means (Golombok, 2011a, b; Golombok & Tasker, 2010).

Another issue focuses on custody arrangements for adolescents. Many gays and lesbians have lost custody of their adolescents to heterosexual spouses following divorce. For this reason, many gay fathers and lesbian mothers are noncustodial parents.

How Would You...?
If you were a **human development and family studies professional,** how would you apply the guidelines on communicating about divorce to help parents discuss the death of a family member with their children?

caring connections

Communicating with Children About Divorce

Ellen Galinsky and Judy David (1988) developed a number of guidelines for communicating with children about divorce:

- ***Explain the separation.*** As soon as daily activities in the home make it obvious that one parent is leaving, tell the children. If possible, both parents should be present when children are told about the separation to come. The reasons for the separation are very difficult for young children to understand. No matter what parents tell children, children can find reasons to argue against the separation. It is extremely important for parents to tell the children who will take care of them and to describe the specific arrangements for seeing the other parent.

- ***Explain that the separation is not the child's fault.*** Young children often believe their parents' separation or divorce is their own fault. Therefore, it is important to tell children that they are not the cause of the separation. Parents need to repeat this message a number of times.

- ***Explain that it may take time to feel better.*** Tell young children that it's normal not to feel good about what is happening and that many other children feel this way when their parents become separated. It is also okay for divorced parents to share some of their emotions with children by saying something like "I'm having a hard time since the separation just like you, but I know it's going to get better after a

while." Such statements are best kept brief and should not criticize the other parent.

- ***Keep the door open for further discussion.*** Tell your children to come to you any time they want to talk about the separation. It is healthy for children to express their pent-up emotions in discussions with their parents and to learn that the parents are willing to listen to their feelings and fears.

- ***Provide as much continuity as possible.*** The less children's worlds are disrupted by the separation, the easier their transition to a single-parent family will be. This means maintaining the rules already in place as much as possible. Children need parents who care enough not only to give them warmth and nurturance but also to set reasonable limits.

- ***Provide support for your children and yourself.*** Parents are as important to children after a divorce or separation as they were before the divorce or separation. Divorced parents need to provide children with as much support as possible. Parents function best when other people are available to give them support as adults and as parents. Divorced parents can find people who provide practical help and with whom they can talk about their problems. For example, many individuals going through a divorce report that they benefit enormously from having a support system of friends to whom they can turn to discuss their situation.

What are the research findings regarding the development and psychological well-being of children raised by gay and lesbian couples?

Researchers have found few differences in children growing up with gay fathers or lesbian mothers and in children and adolescents growing up with heterosexual parents (Patterson & Wainright, 2011). For example, children growing up in gay or lesbian families are just as popular with their peers, and there are no differences in the adjustment and mental health of children living in these families as compared with children in heterosexual families (Hyde & DeLamater, 2011). Also, the overwhelming majority of children growing up in a gay or lesbian family have a heterosexual orientation (Golombok & Tasker, 2010).

Cultural, Ethnic, and Socioeconomic Variations
Parenting can be influenced by culture, ethnicity, and socioeconomic status. Recall from Bronfenbrenner's ecological theory (discussed in Chapter 1) that a number of social contexts influence the child's development. In Bronfenbrenner's theory, culture, ethnicity, and socioeconomic status are classified as part of the macrosystem because they represent broader, societal contexts.

Cross-Cultural Studies Different cultures often give different answers to such basic questions as what the father's role in the family should be, what support systems are available to families, and how children should be disciplined (Chen & others, 2011). There are important cross-cultural variations in parenting (Kagitcibasi, 2007). In some cultures (such as Arab countries), authoritarian parenting is widespread.

Cultural change, brought about by such factors as increasingly frequent international travel, the Internet and electronic communications, and economic globalization, is coming to families in many countries around the world. There are trends toward greater family mobility, migration to urban areas, separation as some family members work in cities or countries far from their homes, smaller families, fewer extended-family households, and increases in maternal employment (Brown & Larson, 2002). These trends can change the resources that are available to children. For example, when several generations no longer live near each other, children may lose support and guidance from grandparents, aunts, and uncles. On the positive side, smaller families may produce more openness and communication between parents and children.

Ethnicity   Families within different ethnic groups in the United States differ in their typical size, structure, composition, reliance on kinship networks, and levels of income and education (Cheah & Leung, 2011; Conger & others, 2012; Quintana, 2011). Large and extended families are more common among minority groups than among the non-Latino White majority. For example, 19 percent of Latino families have three or more children, compared with 14 percent of African American and 10 percent of non-Latino White families. African American and Latino children interact more with grandparents, aunts, uncles, cousins, and more-distant relatives than do non-Latino White children.

Single-parent families are more common among African Americans and Latinos than among non-Latino White Americans (McLoyd, 2011; Zeiders, Roosa, & Tein, 2011). In comparison with two-parent households, single parents often have more limited resources of time, money, and energy (Barajas, Phillipsen, & Brooks-Gunn, 2008). Ethnic minority parents also tend to be less educated and are more likely to live in low-income circumstances than their non-Latino White counterparts. Still, many impoverished ethnic minority families manage to find ways to raise competent children (Hattery & Smith, 2007).

Of course, individual families vary, and how ethnic minority families deal with stress depends on many factors (Landale, Thomas, & Van Hook, 2011; Nieto & Bode, 2012). Whether the parents are native-born or immigrants, how long the family has been in this country, and their socioeconomic status and national origin all make a difference (Parke & Clarke-Stewart, 2011). The characteristics of the family's social context also influence its adaptation. What are the attitudes toward the family's ethnic group within its neighborhood or city? Can the family's children attend good schools? Are there community groups that welcome people from the family's ethnic group? Do members of the family's ethnic group form community groups of their own? To read further about ethnic minority parenting, see the *Connecting with Diversity* interlude.

What are some characteristics of families within different ethnic groups?

Socioeconomic Status   Low-income families have less access to resources than higher-income families (Cooper, 2011; McLoyd, 2011). The differential in access to resources includes nutrition, health care, protection from danger, and enriching educational and socialization opportunities, such as tutoring and lessons in various activities. These differences are compounded in low-income families characterized by long-term poverty (Santiago & others, 2011; Williams & Hanzell, 2011). A recent study found that persistent economic hardship as well as very early poverty was linked to lower cognitive functioning in children at 5 years of age (Schoon & others, 2011). In the United States and most Western cultures, differences have been found in child rearing among different SES groups (Hoff, Laursen, & Tardif, 2002, p. 246):

- "Lower-SES parents (1) are more concerned that their children conform to society's expectations, (2) create a home atmosphere in which it is clear that parents have authority over children," (3) use physical punishment more in disciplining their children, and (4) are more directive and less conversational with their children.

- "Higher-SES parents (1) are more concerned with developing children's initiative" and delay of gratification, "(2) create a home atmosphere in which children are

connecting with diversity

Immigration and Ethnic Minority Parenting

Recent research indicates that many members of families that have recently immigrated to the United States adopt a bicultural orientation, selecting characteristics of the U.S. culture that help them to survive and advance, while still retaining aspects of their culture of origin (Cheah & Leung, 2011; Wright & others, 2012). Immigration also involves cultural brokering, which has increasingly occurred in the United States as children and adolescents serve as mediators (cultural and linguistic) for their immigrant parents (Buriel, 2011; Villanueva & Buriel, 2010).

In adopting characteristics of the U.S. culture, Latino families are increasingly embracing the importance of education (Cooper, 2011). Although their school

How is acculturation involved in ethnic minority parenting?

dropout rates have remained higher than for other ethnic groups, toward the end of the first decade of the 21st century they declined considerably (National Center for Education Statistics, 2010). In addition to adopting aspects of American culture, immigrants often retain positive aspects of their culture of origin. Research by Ross Parke and his colleagues (2011) indicates that Latino families are retaining a strong commitment to family when they immigrate to the United States even in the face of often holding low-paying jobs that make it difficult for them to advance economically. For example, divorce rates for Latino families are lower than those for non-Latino White families of similar socioeconomic status.

more nearly equal participants and in which rules are discussed as opposed to being laid down" in an authoritarian manner, (3) are less likely to use physical punishment, and (4) "are less directive and more conversational" with their children.

Parents in different socioeconomic groups also tend to think differently about education (Huston & Ripke, 2006). Middle- and upper-income parents more often think of education as something that should be mutually encouraged by parents and teachers. By contrast, low-income parents are more likely to view education as the teacher's job. Thus, increased school-family linkages can especially benefit students from low-income families.

How Would You...?

If you were an **educator,** how would you work with low-socioeconomic-status families to increase parental involvement in their children's educational activities?

Review *Connect* Reflect

LG2 Explain how families can influence young children's development.

Review

- What aspects of parenting are linked with young children's development?
- What are the types and consequences of child maltreatment?
- How are sibling relationships and birth order related to young children's development?
- How is children's development affected by having two wage-earning parents, having divorced parents, or being part of a particular cultural, ethnic, and socioeconomic group?

Connect

- In Chapter 5, you learned that fathers were most often the perpetrators of

shaken baby syndrome. Given what you learned in this section, which family interactions would a researcher or marriage and family therapist likely explore in the case of child maltreatment?

Reflect *Your Own Personal Journey of Life*

- Which style or styles of parenting did your mother and father use in rearing you? What effects do you think their parenting styles have had on your development?

Describe the roles of peers, play, and television in young children's development.

Peer Relations   Play   Television

The family is an important social context for children's development. However, children's development also is strongly influenced by what goes on in other social contexts, such as in peer groups, at play, or while watching television.

PEER RELATIONS

As children grow older, they spend an increasing amount of time with their peers—children of about the same age or maturity level.

What are the functions of a child's peer group? One of its most important functions is to provide a source of information and comparison about the world outside the family. Children receive feedback about their abilities from their peer group. Children evaluate what they do in terms of whether it is better than, as good as, or worse than what other children do. It is hard to make these judgments at home because siblings are usually older or younger.

Good peer relations can be necessary for normal socioemotional development (Ladd, Kochenderfer-Ladd, & Rydell, 2011). Special concerns focus on children who are withdrawn or aggressive (Rubin & others, 2011; Underwood, 2011). Withdrawn children who are rejected by peers or are victimized and feel lonely are at risk for depression. Children who are aggressive with their peers are at risk of developing a number of problems, including delinquency and dropping out of school (Bukowski, Buhrmester, & Underwood, 2011).

What are some characteristics of peer relations in early childhood?

Developmental Changes   Recall from our discussion of gender that by about the age of 3, children already prefer to spend time with same-sex rather than opposite-sex playmates, and this preference increases in early childhood. During these same years, the frequency of peer interaction, both positive and negative, picks up considerably (Cillessen & Bellmore, 2011). Many preschool children spend considerable time in peer interaction conversing with playmates about such matters as "negotiating roles and rules in play, arguing, and agreeing" (Rubin, Bukowski, & Parker, 2006). And during early childhood, children's interactions with peers become more coordinated and involve longer turns and sequences (Coplan & Arbeau, 2009).

Friends   In early childhood, children distinguish between friends and nonfriends (Howes, 2009). For most young children, a friend is someone to play with. Young preschool children are more likely than older children to have friends who are of different gender and ethnicity (Howes, 2009).

The Connected Worlds of Parent-Child and Peer Relations   Parents may influence their children's peer relations in many ways, both direct and indirect (Reich & Vandell, 2011). Parents affect their children's peer relations through their interactions with their children, how they manage their children's lives, and the opportunities they provide their children (Brown & Bakken, 2011).

Basic lifestyle decisions by parents—their choices of neighborhoods, churches, schools, and their own friends—largely determine the pool from which their children select possible friends. These choices in turn affect which children their children meet, their purpose in interacting, and eventually which children become their friends.

Researchers also have found that children's peer relations are linked to attachment security and parents' marital quality (Booth-Laforce & Kerns, 2009). Early attachments to caregivers provide a connection to children's peer relations not only

How are parent-child and peer relationships connected?

by creating a secure base from which children can explore social relationships beyond the family but also by conveying a working model of relationships (Hartup, 2009).

Do these results indicate that children's peer relations always are wedded to parent-child relationships? Although parent-child relationships influence children's subsequent peer relations, children also learn other modes of relating through their relationships with peers. For example, rough-and-tumble play occurs mainly with other children, not in parent-child interaction. In times of stress, children often turn to parents rather than peers for support. In parent-child relationships, children learn how to relate to authority figures. With their peers, children are likely to interact on a much more equal basis and to learn a mode of relating based on mutual influence. We will have much more to say about peer relations in Chapter 13, "Socioemotional Development in Middle and Late Childhood."

developmental connection

Peers. Children's peer relations have been classified in terms of five peer statuses. Chapter 13, p. 408

PLAY

An extensive amount of peer interaction during childhood involves play, but social play is only one type of play. *Play* is a pleasurable activity that is engaged in for its own sake, and its functions and forms vary.

Play's Functions   Play is essential to the young child's health. Theorists have focused on different aspects of play and highlighted a long list of functions (Coplan & Arbeau, 2009).

According to Freud and Erikson, play helps the child master anxieties and conflicts. Because tensions are relieved in play, the child can cope with life's problems. Play permits the child to work off excess physical energy and to release pent-up tensions. Therapists use *play therapy* both to allow the child to work off frustrations and to analyze the child's conflicts and ways of coping with them (Sanders, 2008). Children may feel less threatened and be more likely to express their true feelings in the context of play.

Play also is an important context for cognitive development (Power, 2011). Piaget (1962) maintained that play advances children's cognitive development. At the same time, he said that children's cognitive development constrains the way they play. Play permits children to practice their competencies and acquired skills in a relaxed, pleasurable way. Piaget thought that cognitive structures need to be exercised, and play provides the perfect setting for this exercise. For example, children who have just learned to add or multiply begin to play with numbers in different ways as they perfect these operations, laughing as they do so.

Lev Vygotsky (1962) also considered play to be an excellent setting for cognitive development. He was especially interested in the symbolic and make-believe aspects of play, as when a child substitutes a stick for a horse and rides the stick as if it were a horse. For young children, the imaginary situation is real. Parents should encourage such imaginary play, because it advances the child's cognitive development, especially creative thought.

Daniel Berlyne (1960) described play as exciting and pleasurable in itself because it satisfies our exploratory drive. This drive involves curiosity and a desire for information about something new or unusual. Play is a means whereby children can safely explore and seek out new information. Play encourages exploratory behavior by offering children the possibilities of novelty, complexity, uncertainty, surprise, and incongruity.

Let us play, for it is yet day
And we cannot go to sleep;
Besides, in the sky the little birds fly
And the hills are all covered with sheep.

—**WILLIAM BLAKE**
English Poet, 19th Century

developmental connection

Cognitive Theory. Vygotsky emphasized the importance of culture and social interaction in children's cognitive development. Chapter 9, p. 263

More recently, play has been described as an important context for the development of language and communication skills (Coplan & Arbeau, 2009). Language and communication skills may be enhanced through discussions and negotiations regarding roles and rules in play as young children practice various words and phrases. These types of social interactions during play can benefit young children's literacy skills (Coplan & Arbeau, 2009). And, as we saw in Chapter 9, "Cognitive Development in Early Childhood," play is a central focus of the child-centered kindergarten and thought to be an essential aspect of early childhood education (Morrison, 2011).

Types of Play   The contemporary perspective on play emphasizes both the cognitive and the social aspects of play. Among the most widely studied types of children's play today are sensorimotor and practice play, pretense/symbolic play, social play, constructive play, and games (Bergen, 1988).

A preschool "superhero" at play.

Sensorimotor and Practice Play   **Sensorimotor play** is behavior by infants to derive pleasure from exercising their sensorimotor schemes. The development of sensorimotor play follows Piaget's description of sensorimotor thought, which we discussed in Chapter 6, "Cognitive Development in Infancy." Infants initially engage in exploratory and playful visual and motor transactions in the second quarter of the first year of life. For example, at 9 months of age, infants begin to select novel objects for exploration and play, especially responsive objects, such as toys that make noise or bounce. At 12 months of age, infants enjoy making things work and exploring cause and effect.

Practice play involves the repetition of behavior when new skills are being learned or when physical or mental mastery and coordination of skills are required for games or sports. Sensorimotor play, which often involves practice play, is primarily confined to infancy, whereas practice play can be engaged in throughout life. During the preschool years, children often engage in practice play. Although practice play declines in the elementary school years, practice play activities such as running, jumping, sliding, twirling, and throwing balls or other objects are frequently observed on the playgrounds at elementary schools.

Pretense/Symbolic Play   **Pretense/symbolic play** occurs when the child transforms aspects of the physical environment into symbols. Between 9 and 30 months of age, children increase their use of objects in symbolic play. They learn to transform objects—substituting them for other objects and acting toward them as if they were these other objects (Kavanaugh, 2006). For example, a preschool child treats a table as if it were a car and says, "I'm fixing the car," as he grabs a leg of the table.

Many experts on play consider the preschool years the "golden age" of symbolic/pretense play that is dramatic or sociodramatic in nature (Fein, 1986). This type of make-believe play often appears at about 18 months of age and reaches a peak at 4 to 5 years of age, then gradually declines.

Some child psychologists conclude that pretend play is an important aspect of young children's development and often reflects advances in their cognitive development, especially as an indication of symbolic understanding. For example, Catherine Garvey (2000) and Angeline Lillard (2006) emphasize that hidden in young children's pretend play narratives are remarkable capacities for role-taking, balancing of social roles, metacognition (thinking about thinking), testing of the reality-pretense distinction, and numerous nonegocentric capacities that reveal the remarkable cognitive skills of young children. In a recent analysis, the development of children's ability to share their pretend play with peers was proposed as a major accomplishment in early childhood (Coplan & Arbeau, 2009).

Social Play   **Social play** involves interaction with peers. Social play increases dramatically during the preschool years. For many children, social play is the main context for social interactions with peers (Power, 2011).

Constructive Play   **Constructive play** combines sensorimotor/practice play with symbolic representation. Constructive play occurs when children engage in the self-regulated creation of a product or a solution. Constructive play increases in the

And that park
grew up with me; that
small world widened as
I learned its secrets and
boundaries, as I discovered new
refuges in its woods and jungles:
hidden homes and lairs for the
multitudes of imagination, for cowboys
and Indians. . . . I used to dawdle on half
holidays along the bent and Devon-
facing seashore, hoping for gold
watches or the skull of a sheep or a
message in a bottle to be washed
up with the tide.

—**DYLAN THOMAS**
Welsh Poet, 20th Century

sensorimotor play Behavior engaged in by infants to derive pleasure from exercising their existing sensorimotor schemas.

practice play Play that involves repetition of behavior when new skills are being learned or when physical or mental mastery and coordination of skills are required for games or sports.

pretense/symbolic play Play in which the child transforms the physical environment into a symbol.

social play Play that involves social interactions with peers.

constructive play Play that combines sensorimotor/practice play with symbolic representation. Constructive play occurs when children engage in self-regulated creation or construction of a product or a solution.

How Would You...?

If you were an **educator,** how would you integrate play in the learning process?

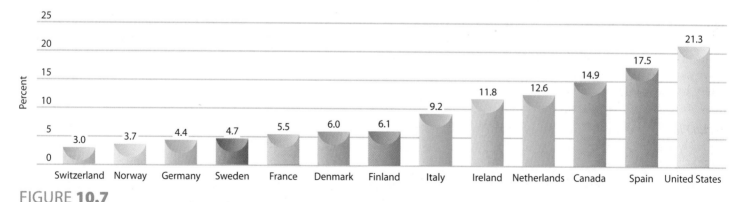

"Mrs. Horton, could you stop by school today?"
Copyright © Martha F. Campbell. Reprinted with permission.

preschool years as symbolic play increases and sensorimotor play decreases. Constructive play is also a frequent form of play in the elementary school years, both in and out of the classroom.

Games   **Games** are activities that are engaged in for pleasure and that have rules. Often they involve competition. Preschool children may begin to participate in social games that involve simple rules of reciprocity and turn-taking. However, games take on a much stronger role in the lives of elementary school children. After age 12, playground and neighborhood games decline in popularity (Bergen, 1988).

TELEVISION

Few developments in society in the second half of the twentieth century had a greater impact on children than television (Brown & Bobkowski, 2011). Although it is only one of the many types of mass media that affect children's behavior, television is the most influential. The persuasive capabilities of television are staggering (Scharrer & Demers, 2009).

Many children spend more time in front of the television set than they do with their parents. Just how much television do young children watch? Surveys vary, with the figures ranging from an average of two to four hours a day (Kaiser Family Foundation, 2006). Compared with their counterparts in other developed countries, children in the United States watch television for considerably longer periods (see Figure 10.7). Television can have a negative influence on children by making them

FIGURE **10.7**

PERCENTAGE OF 9-YEAR-OLD CHILDREN WHO REPORT WATCHING MORE THAN FIVE HOURS OF TELEVISION PER WEEKDAY

passive learners, distracting them from doing homework, teaching them stereotypes, providing them with violent models of aggression, presenting them with unrealistic views of the world, and increasing sleep problems (Dubow, Huesmann, & Greenwood, 2007; Murray, 2007). In a recent study, sleep problems were more common in 3- to 5-year-old children who (1) watched TV after 7 p.m. and (2) watched TV shows with violence (Garrison, Liekweg, & Christakis, 2011). However, television also can have a positive influence on children's development by presenting motivating educational programs, increasing their information about the world beyond their immediate environment, and providing models of prosocial behavior (Wilson, 2008).

How is watching television linked to children's aggression?

Effects of Television on Children's Aggression

The extent to which children are exposed to violence and aggression on television raises special concern (Gentile, Mathieson, & Crick, 2011). For example, Saturday morning cartoon shows average more than 25 violent acts per hour. Researchers have found links between watching television violence as a child and acting aggressively years later (Parke & others, 2008).

In addition to television violence, there is increased concern about children who play violent video games, especially those that are highly realistic (Escobar-Chaves & Anderson, 2008). Children can become so deeply immersed in some electronic games that they experience an altered state of consciousness in which rational thought is suspended and arousing aggressive scripts are learned (Roberts, Henriksen, & Foehr, 2004). Recent research reviews have concluded that playing violent video games is linked to aggression in both males and females (Gentile, 2011; Holtz & Appel, 2011).

Effects of Television on Children's Prosocial Behavior

Television also can teach children that it is better to behave in positive, prosocial ways than in negative, antisocial ways (Bryant, 2007). In an early study, Aimee Leifer (1973) selected episodes from the television show *Sesame Street* that reflected positive social interchanges in which children were taught how to use their social skills. For example, in one interchange, two men were fighting over the amount of space available to them; they gradually began to cooperate and to share the space. Children who watched these episodes copied these behaviors, and in later social situations they applied the prosocial lessons they had learned.

Television and Achievement

Watching television is also linked with lower school achievement (Comstock & Scharrer, 2006). However, some types of television—such as educational programming for young children—may enhance achievement. For example, in one longitudinal study, viewing educational programs such as *Sesame Street* and *Mr. Rogers' Neighborhood* as preschoolers was associated with a host of desirable characteristics in adolescence: getting higher grades, reading more books, placing a higher value on achievement, being more creative, and acting less aggressively (Anderson & others, 2001) (see Figure 10.8). These associations were more consistent for boys than girls.

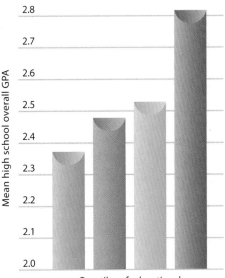

FIGURE 10.8

EDUCATIONAL TV VIEWING AND HIGH SCHOOL GRADE-POINT AVERAGE FOR BOYS. When boys watched more educational television (especially *Sesame Street*) as preschoolers, they had higher grade-point averages in high school (Anderson & others, 2001). The graph displays the boys' early TV-viewing patterns in quartiles and the means of their grade-point averages. The bar on the left is for the lowest 25 percent of boys who viewed educational TV programs, the next bar the next 25 percent, and so on, with the bar on the right for the 25 percent of the boys who watched the most educational TV shows as preschoolers.

How Would You...? If you were a **human development and family studies professional,** how would you talk with parents about strategies for improving television viewing by their children?

games Activities engaged in for pleasure that include rules and often competition with one or more individuals.

Review *Connect* Reflect

LG3 Describe the roles of peers, play, and television in young children's development.

Review

- How do peers affect young children's development?
- What are some theories and types of play?
- How does television influence children's development?

Connect

- Earlier in the chapter, you read about Laurie Kramer's program for teaching siblings social skills to reduce sibling conflict. Would her recommendations also apply to reducing conflict in peer relations? Explain.

Reflect *Your Own Personal Journey of Life*

- What guidelines would you adopt for your own children's television viewing?

topical **connections**

This chapter brings your exploration of early childhood to a close. In the next chapter you will begin to study middle and late childhood, especially the physical, brain, and motor skill changes that occur in this period of development. The middle and late childhood years also produce further changes in children's socioemotional development, which you will study in Chapter 13. Development of self-understanding and understanding others becomes more sophisticated, emotional understanding improves, and moral reasoning advances. Children now spend less time with parents, but parents still play very important roles in children's lives, especially in guiding their academic achievement and managing their opportunities. Peer status and friendship become more important in children's peer relations, and school takes on a stronger academic focus.

looking **forward**

reach your **learning goals**

What Characterizes Young Children's Emotional and Personality Development?

 LG1 Discuss emotional and personality development in early childhood.

The Self

- In Erikson's theory, early childhood is a period when development involves resolving the conflict of initiative versus guilt. The toddler's rudimentary self-understanding develops into the preschooler's representation of the self in terms of body attributes, material possessions, and physical activities. At about 4 to 5 years of age, children also begin to use traitlike self-descriptions. Young children display more sophisticated self-understanding and understanding of others than was previously thought.

Emotional Development

- Young children's range of emotions expands during early childhood as they increasingly experience self-conscious emotions such as pride, shame, and guilt. Between 2 and 4 years of age, children use an increasing number of terms to describe emotion and learn more about the causes and consequences of feelings. At 4 to 5 years of age, children show an increased ability to reflect on emotions and to understand that a single event can elicit different emotions in different people. They also show a growing awareness of the need to manage emotions to meet social standards. Emotion-coaching parents have children who engage in more effective self-regulation of their emotions than do emotion-dismissing parents. Emotional regulation plays an important role in successful peer relations.

Moral Development

• Moral development involves thoughts, feelings, and behaviors regarding rules and regulations about what people should do in their interactions with others. Freud's psychoanalytic theory emphasizes the importance of feelings in the development of the superego, the moral branch of personality. Positive emotions, such as empathy, also contribute to the child's moral development. Piaget analyzed moral reasoning and concluded that children from 4 to 7 years of age display heteronomous morality, judging behavior by its consequences. According to behavioral and social cognitive theorists, moral behavior develops as a result of reinforcement, punishment, and imitation, and there is considerable situational variability in moral behavior. Conscience refers to an internal regulation of standards of right and wrong that involves an integration of moral thought, feeling, and behavior. Young children's conscience emerges out of relationships with parents. Parents influence young children's moral development by developing quality parent-child relationships, by being proactive in helping children avert misbehavior, and by engaging children in conversational dialogue about moral issues.

Gender

• Gender refers to the characteristics of people as males or females. Gender identity involves a sense of one's own gender, including knowledge, understanding, and acceptance of being male or female. A gender role is a set of expectations that prescribes how females or males should think, act, and feel. Gender typing refers to the acquisition of a traditional masculine or feminine role. Biological influences on gender development include chromosomes and hormones. However, biology is not the complete destiny in gender development; children's socialization experiences matter a great deal. Social role theory, psychoanalytic theory, and social cognitive theory emphasize various aspects of social experiences in the development of gender characteristics. Parents influence children's gender development, and peers are especially adept at rewarding gender-appropriate behavior. Gender schema theory emphasizes that gender typing emerges as children develop schemas of their culture's gender-appropriate and gender-inappropriate behaviors.

What Roles Do Families Play in Young Children's Development?

 LG2 Explain how families can influence young children's development.

Parenting

• Authoritarian, authoritative, neglectful, and indulgent are four main parenting styles. Authoritative parenting is the most widely used style around the world and is the style most often associated with children's social competence. However, ethnic variations in parenting styles suggest that in Asian American families, some aspects of control may benefit children. Some criticisms of parenting styles have been made such as their failure to capture the themes of reciprocal socialization and synchrony. Physical punishment is widely used by U.S. parents, but there are a number of reasons why it is not a good choice. Coparenting has positive effects on children's development.

Child Maltreatment

• Child maltreatment may take the form of physical abuse, child neglect, sexual abuse, and emotional abuse. Child maltreatment places the child at risk for academic, emotional, and social problems. Adults who suffered child maltreatment are also vulnerable to a range of problems.

Sibling Relationships and Birth Order

• Siblings interact with each other in positive and negative ways. Birth order is related in certain ways to child characteristics, but by itself it is not a good predictor of behavior.

The Changing Family in a Changing Social World

• In general, having both parents employed full-time outside the home has not been shown to have negative effects on children. However, the nature of parents' work can affect their parenting quality. Divorce can have negative effects on children's adjustment, but so can an acrimonious relationship between parents who stay together for their children's sake. If divorced parents develop a harmonious relationship and practice authoritative parenting, children's adjustment improves. Researchers have found few differences between children growing up in gay or lesbian families and children growing up in heterosexual families. Cultures vary on a number of issues regarding families. African American and Latino children are more likely than White American children to live in single-parent families and larger families and to have extended-family connections. Low-income families have less access to resources than higher-income families. Lower-SES parents create a home atmosphere that involves more authority and physical punishment with children than higher-SES parents. Higher-SES parents are more concerned about developing children's initiative and delay of gratification.

How Are Peer Relations, Play, and Television Involved in Young Children's Development?

 LG3 Describe the roles of peers, play, and television in young children's development.

- Peer Relations

- Play

- Television

- Peers are powerful socialization agents. Peers provide a source of information and comparison about the world outside the family.

- Play's functions include affiliation with peers, tension release, advances in cognitive development, exploration, and provision of a safe haven. The contemporary perspective on play emphasizes both the cognitive and the social aspects of play. Among the most widely studied types of children's play are sensorimotor play, practice play, pretense/symbolic play, social play, constructive play, and games.

- Television can have both negative influences (such as turning children into passive learners and presenting them with aggressive models) and positive influences (such as providing models of prosocial behavior) on children's development. TV violence is not the only cause of children's aggression, but it can induce aggression. Prosocial behavior on TV can teach children positive behavior. Watching TV is linked to lower achievement in school.

key terms

self-understanding 290
perspective taking 291
moral development 293
heteronomous
    morality 294
autonomous morality 294
immanent justice 294

conscience 295
gender identity 295
gender role 296
gender typing 296
social role theory 297
psychoanalytic theory
    of gender 297

social cognitive theory
    of gender 297
gender schema theory 298
authoritarian parenting 300
authoritative parenting 300
neglectful parenting 300
indulgent parenting 300

sensorimotor play 315
practice play 315
pretense/symbolic play 315
social play 315
constructive play 315
games 316

key people

Erik Erikson 290
Sigmund Freud 293
Jean Piaget 294
Lawrence Kohlberg 294

Ross Thompson 295
Diana Baumrind 300
Ruth Chao 301
Laurie Kramer 305

Judy Dunn 306
Ann Crouter 307
E. Mark Cummings 308
Lev Vygotsky 314

Daniel Berlyne 314
Catherine Garvey 315
Angeline Lillard 315

connecting with improving the lives of children

MAKING A DIFFERENCE

Guiding Young Children's Socioemotional Development

How can young children's socioemotional skills be nourished? These strategies can help:

- *Look for opportunities to help children with their emotions.* Parents, teachers, and other adults can help children understand and handle their emotions in socially acceptable ways.
- *Present positive moral models for the child and use emotional situations to promote moral development.* Children benefit when they are around people who engage in prosocial rather than antisocial behavior. Encourage children to show empathy and learn to deal with their emotions.
- *Be an authoritative parent.* Children's self-control and social competence benefit when both parents are authoritative—that is, when they are neither punitive and overcontrolling nor permissive. Authoritative parents are nurturant, engage the child in verbal give-and-take, monitor the child, and use nonpunitive control.
- *Adapt to the child's developmental changes.* Parents should use less physical manipulation and more reasoning or withholding of special privileges in disciplining a 5-year-old, as opposed to disciplining a 2-year-old.
- *Communicate effectively with children in a divorced family.* Good strategies are to explain the separation and say it is not the child's fault, assure the child that it may take time to feel better, keep the door open for further discussion, provide as much continuity as possible, and supply a support system for the child.
- *Provide the child with opportunities for peer interaction.* Children learn a great deal from the mutual give-and-take of peer rela-

tions. Make sure the child gets considerable time to play with peers rather than watching TV or attending an academic early childhood program for the entire day.
- *Provide the child with many opportunities for play.* Positive play experiences can greatly support the young child's socioemotional development.
- *Monitor the child's TV viewing.* Keep exposure to TV violence to a minimum. Develop a set of guidelines for the child's TV viewing.

RESOURCES

The Emotional Development of Young Children
by Marylou Hyson (2004)
New York: Teachers College Press

An excellent book by a leading expert on early childhood that provides a good overview of young children's emotional development and offers many applications to children's emotional development in preschool and kindergarten.

For Better or For Worse: Divorce Reconsidered
by E. Mavis Hetherington and John Kelly (2002)
New York: W. W. Norton

E. Mavis Hetherington, a leading researcher, provides excellent descriptions of how divorce affects children and parents.

Gender Development
by Judith Blakemore, Sheri Berenbaum, and Lynn Liben (2009)
Clifton, NJ: Psychology Press

Coverage of many facets of children's gender development is provided by leading experts.

Every forward step we take we leave some phantom of ourselves behind.

—JOHN LANCASTER SPALDING
American Educator, 19th Century

Middle and Late Childhood

In middle and late childhood, children are on a different plane, belonging to a generation and feeling all their own. It is the wisdom of the human life span that at no time are children more ready to learn than during the period of expansive imagination at the end of early childhood. Children develop a sense of wanting to make things—and not just to make them, but to make them well and even perfectly. They seek to know and to understand. They are remarkable for their intelligence and for their curiosity. Their parents continue to be important influences in their lives, but their growth also is shaped by peers and friends. They don't think much about the future or about the past, but they enjoy the present moment. Section 5 consists of three chapters. "Physical Development in Middle and Late Childhood" (Chapter 11), "Cognitive Development in Middle and Late Childhood" (Chapter 12), and "Socioemotional Development in Middle and Late Childhood" (Chapter 13).

chapter 11

PHYSICAL DEVELOPMENT IN MIDDLE AND LATE CHILDHOOD

The following comments are by Angie, an elementary-school-age girl:

When I was eight years old, I weighed 125 pounds. My clothes were the size that large teenage girls wear. I hated my body and my classmates teased me all the time. I was so overweight and out of shape that when I took a P.E. class my face would get red and I had trouble breathing. I was jealous of the kids who played sports and weren't overweight like I was.

I'm nine years old now and I've lost 30 pounds. I'm much happier and proud of myself. How did I lose the weight? My mom said she had finally decided enough was enough. She took me to a pediatrician who specializes in helping children lose weight and keep it off. The pediatrician counseled my mom about my eating and exercise habits, then had us join a group that he had created for overweight children and their parents. My mom and I go to the group once a week and we've now been participating in the program for six months. I no longer eat fast-food meals and my mom is cooking more healthy meals. Now that I've lost weight, exercise is not as hard for me and I don't get teased by the kids at school. My mom's pretty happy too because she's lost 15 pounds herself since we've been in the counseling program.

Not all overweight children are as successful as Angie at reducing their weight. Indeed, being overweight in childhood has become a major national concern in the United States. Later in the chapter, we explore in detail being overweight in childhood, including its causes and outcomes.

topical **connections**

In the last chapter you concluded your study of early childhood by looking at socioemotional development in young children, the accompanying moral development that takes place, and children's growing sense of self and gender. You became familiar with the role of family, siblings, peers, play, and the media in early childhood. In Chapter 8, you learned that children grow more slowly in early childhood than in infancy, but they still grow an average of 2½ inches and 5 to 7 pounds a year. In early childhood, the most rapid growth in the brain occurs in the prefrontal cortex.

looking back

preview

Considerable progress in children's physical development continues to take place in the middle and late childhood years. Children grow taller, heavier, and stronger. They become more adept at using their physical skills. We begin the chapter by exploring the changes that characterize body growth and motor skills, then examine the central issues in children's health, and conclude by discussing children with disabilities and their education.

What Changes Take Place in Body Growth, the Brain, and Motor Development?

LG1 Discuss changes in body growth, the brain, and motor development in middle and late childhood.

Skeletal and Muscular Systems

The Brain

Motor Development

The period of middle and late childhood involves slow, consistent growth. This is a period of calm before the rapid growth spurt of adolescence. Among the important aspects of body growth and proportion in this developmental period are those involving skeletal and muscular systems, the brain, and motor development.

SKELETAL AND MUSCULAR SYSTEMS

During the elementary school years, children grow an average of 2 to 3 inches a year until, at the age of 11, the average girl is 4 feet, 9 inches tall, and the average boy is 4 feet, 7¾ inches tall. During the middle and late childhood years, children gain about 5 to 7 pounds a year. The weight increase is due mainly to increases in the size of the skeletal and muscular systems, as well as the size of some body organs. Muscle mass and strength gradually increase as "baby fat" decreases. The loose movements and knock-knees of early childhood give way to improved muscle tone. The increase in muscular strength is due both to heredity and to exercise. Children also double their strength capabilities during these years. Because of their greater number of muscle cells, boys are usually stronger than girls. A summary of the changes in height and weight in middle and late childhood appears in Figure 11.1.

Proportional changes are among the most pronounced physical changes in middle and late childhood (Kliegman & others, 2011). Head circumference, waist circumference, and leg length decrease in relation to body height. A less noticeable physical change is that bones continue to ossify (harden) during middle and late childhood.

THE BRAIN

The development of brain-imaging techniques, such as magnetic resonance imaging (MRI), has led to an increase in research on changes in the brain during middle and late childhood, and on how these brain changes are linked to improvements in cognitive development (Diamond, Casey, & Munakata, 2011). One such change involves increased myelination, which improves the speed of processing information and communication in the higher regions of the brain, such as the cerebral cortex. The increase in myelination during middle and late childhood is linked to more effective processing of information

What characterizes physical growth during middle and late childhood?

FIGURE **11.1**

	HEIGHT (INCHES)					
Age	Female Percentiles			Male Percentiles		
	25th	50th	75th	25th	50th	75th
6	43.75	45.00	46.50	44.25	45.75	47.00
7	46.00	47.50	49.00	46.25	48.00	49.25
8	48.00	49.75	51.50	48.50	50.00	51.50
9	50.25	53.00	53.75	50.50	52.00	53.50
10	52.50	54.50	56.25	52.50	54.25	55.75
11	55.00	57.00	58.75	54.50	55.75	57.25

	WEIGHT (POUNDS)					
6	39.25	43.00	47.25	42.00	45.50	49.50
7	43.50	48.50	53.25	46.25	50.25	55.00
8	49.00	54.75	61.50	51.00	55.75	61.50
9	55.75	62.75	71.50	56.00	62.00	69.25
10	63.25	71.75	82.75	62.00	69.25	78.50
11	71.75	81.25	94.25	69.00	77.75	89.00

CHANGES IN HEIGHT AND WEIGHT IN MIDDLE AND LATE CHILDHOOD. *Note:* The percentile tells how the child compares with other children of the same age. The 50th percentile tells us that half of the children of a particular age are taller (heavier) or shorter (lighter). The 25th percentile tells us that 25 percent of the children of that age are shorter (lighter) and 75 percent are taller (heavier).

on cognitive tasks (Thomason & Thompson, 2011). Recall from our discussion in Chapter 8, "Physical Development in Early Childhood," that myelination is the process of encasing axons with fat cells.

Total brain volume stabilizes by the end of middle and late childhood, but significant changes in various structures and regions of the brain continue to occur. In particular, the brain pathways and circuitry involving the prefrontal cortex, the highest level in the brain, continue to increase (Johnson & de Haan, 2011). These advances in the prefrontal cortex are linked to children's improved attention, reasoning, and cognitive control (Crone & others, 2009). (See Figure 8.4, p. 239, for the location of the prefrontal cortex in the brain.)

Leading developmental cognitive neuroscientist Mark Johnson and his colleagues (2009) recently proposed that the prefrontal cortex likely orchestrates the functions of many other brain regions during development. As part of this neural leadership and organizational role, the prefrontal cortex may provide an advantage to neural networks and connections that include the prefrontal cortex. According to these researchers, the prefrontal cortex coordinates the best neural connections for solving a problem at hand.

Changes also occur in the thickness of the cerebral cortex (cortical thickness) in middle and late childhood (Thomason & Thompson, 2011). One study used brain scans to assess cortical thickness in 5- to 11-year-old children (Sowell & others, 2004). Cortical thickening across a two-year time period was observed in the temporal and frontal lobe areas that function in language, which may account for improvements in language abilities such as reading.

As children develop, activation of some brain areas increases, while that of others decreases (Diamond, Casey, & Munakata, 2011; Nelson, 2011). One shift in activation that occurs as children develop is from diffuse, larger areas to more focal, smaller areas. This shift is characterized by synaptic pruning, in which areas of the brain not being used lose synaptic connections and those being used show an increase in connections. In one study, researchers found less diffusion and more focal activation in the prefrontal cortex from 7 to 30 years of age (Durston & others, 2006). The activation change was linked to advances in executive functioning, especially in cognitive control, which involves flexible and effective control in a number of areas. These areas include controlling attention, reducing

developmental connection

Brain Development. Synaptic pruning is an important aspect of the brain's development, and the pruning varies by region across children's development. Chapter 5, p. 139

Age	Motor skills
6	Children can skip.
	Children can throw with proper weight shift and step.
	Girls and boys can vertically jump 7 inches.
	Girls can do a standing long jump of 33 inches, boys 36 inches.
	Children can cut and paste.
	Children enjoy making simple figures in clay.
7	Children can balance on one foot without looking.
	Children can walk 2-inch-wide balance beams.
	Children can hop and jump accurately into small squares.
	Children can participate in jumping jack exercise.
	Girls can throw a ball 25 feet, boys 45 feet.
	Girls can vertically jump 8 inches, boys 9 inches.
	Girls can do a standing long jump of 41 inches, boys 43 inches.
8	Children can engage in alternate rhythmic hopping in different patterns.
	Girls can throw a ball 34 feet, boys 59 feet.
	Girls can vertically jump 9 inches, boys 10 inches.
	Girls can perform a standing long jump of 50 inches, boys 55 inches.
	Children's grip strength increases.
	Children can use common tools, such as a hammer.
9	Girls can throw a ball 41 feet, boys 71 feet.
	Girls can vertically jump 10 inches, boys 11 inches.
	Girls can perform a standing long jump of 53 inches, boys 57 inches.
	Children's perceptual-motor coordination becomes smoother.
10	Children can judge and intercept pathways of small balls thrown from a distance.
	Girls can throw a small ball 49 feet, boys 94 feet.
	Girls can vertically jump 10 inches, boys 11 inches.

FIGURE 11.2

CHANGES IN MOTOR SKILLS DURING MIDDLE AND LATE CHILDHOOD

interfering thoughts, inhibiting motor actions, and being flexible in switching between competing choices (Diamond, Casey, & Munakata, 2011).

MOTOR DEVELOPMENT

During middle and late childhood, children's motor development becomes much smoother and more coordinated than it was in early childhood. For example, only one child in a thousand can hit a tennis ball over the net at the age of 3, yet by the age of 10 or 11 most children can learn to play the sport. Running, climbing, skipping rope, swimming, bicycle riding, and skating are just a few of the many physical skills elementary school children can master. And, when mastered, these skills are a source of great pleasure and accomplishment for children. In gross motor skills involving large muscle activity, boys usually outperform girls.

As children move through the elementary school years, they gain greater control over their bodies and can sit for longer periods of time. However, elementary school children are far from being physically mature, and they need to be active. Elementary school children become more fatigued by long periods of sitting than by running, jumping, or bicycling. Physical action is essential for children to refine their developing skills, such as batting a ball, skipping rope, or balancing on a beam. An important principle of practice for elementary school children, therefore, is that they should be physically active whenever possible.

Increased myelination of the nervous system is reflected in the improvement of fine motor skills during middle and late childhood. Children use their hands more adroitly as tools. Six-year-olds can hammer, paste, tie shoes, and fasten clothes. By 7 years of age, children's hands have become steadier. At this age, children prefer a pencil to a crayon for printing, reversal of letters is less common, and printing becomes smaller. At 8 to 10 years of age, children can use their hands independently with more ease and precision. Fine motor coordination develops to the point at which children use cursive writing rather than printing. Letter size becomes smaller and more even. At 10 to 12 years of age, children begin to show manipulative skills similar to the abilities of adults. They can now master the complex, intricate, and rapid movements needed to produce fine-quality crafts or to play a difficult piece on a musical instrument. Girls usually outperform boys in fine motor skills. A summary of changes in motor skills in middle and late childhood appears in Figure 11.2. Note that some children perform these skills earlier or later than other children.

Review Connect Reflect

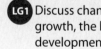 Discuss changes in body growth, the brain, and motor development in middle and late childhood.

Review

- How do skeletal and muscular systems change in middle and late childhood?
- What characterizes changes in the brain during middle and late childhood?
- How do children's gross and fine motor skills change in middle and late childhood?

Connect

- In this section, you learned about advances in the prefrontal cortex. In Chapter 9, "Cognitive Development in Early Childhood," you read about the prefrontal cortex's role in executive functioning. What executive functioning skills were described in Chapter 9 as important in early childhood cognitive development?

Reflect *Your Own Personal Journey of Life*

- Look at Figure 11.2. On which of the motor skills were you especially competent? Not competent? Do you think your motor skills as a child were primarily influenced by your heredity or your environment? Explain.

What Are the Central Issues in Children's Health?

LG2 Characterize children's health in middle and late childhood.

Nutrition   Exercise and Sports   Overweight Children   Diseases   Accidents and Injuries

Although we have become a health-conscious nation, many children as well as adults do not practice good health habits. Too much junk food and too much couch-potato behavior describe the habits of far too many children. We begin our exploration of children's health with nutrition and exercise, then turn to a number of health problems that can emerge.

NUTRITION

In the middle and late childhood years, children's average body weight doubles. Children exert considerable energy as they engage in many different motor activities. To support their growth and active lives, children need to consume more food than they did in early childhood. From 1 to 3 years of age, infants and toddlers should consume about 1,300 calories per day. At 4 to 6 years of age, young children should take in around 1,700 calories per day. From 7 to 10 years of age, children should consume about 2,400 calories per day; however, depending on the child's size, the range of recommended calories for 7- to 10-year-olds is 1,650 to 3,300 per day.

Within these calorie ranges, it is important to impress on children the value of a balanced diet to promote their growth (Schiff, 2011). Children usually eat as their families eat, so the quality of their diet often depends largely on their family's pattern of eating. Most children acquire a taste for an increasing variety of food in middle and late childhood. However, with the increased availability of fast-food restaurants and media inducements, too many children fill up on food that has "empty calories" that do not promote effective growth. Many of these empty-calorie foods have a high content of sugar, starch, and excess fat.

Both parents and teachers can help children learn to eat better. In this vein, they can help children learn about the Food Guide Pyramid and what a healthy diet entails (Wardlaw & Smith, 2011).

Children should begin their day by eating a healthy breakfast. According to nutritionists, breakfast should make up about one-fourth of the day's calories. A nutritious breakfast helps children have more energy and be more alert in the morning hours of school.

EXERCISE AND SPORTS

How much exercise do children get? What are children's sports like? These topics and more are explored in the following section of this chapter.

Exercise American children and adolescents are not getting enough exercise (Fahey, Insel, & Roth, 2011; Graham, Holt/Hale, & Parker, 2010; Lumpkin, 2011). Educators and policy makers in the United States and numerous countries around the world, including China, Finland, and Great Britain, have become very concerned about the sedentary lifestyles of many children and adolescents in their countries (Dowda & others, 2009).

Television watching is linked with low activity levels and obesity in children (Gable, Chang, & Krull, 2007). A related concern is the dramatic increase in computer use by children. A longitudinal study found that a higher incidence of watching TV in childhood and adolescence was linked with being overweight, being less physically fit, and having higher cholesterol levels at 26 years of age (Hancox, Milne, & Poulton, 2004).

We are underexercised as a nation. We look instead of play. We ride instead of walk. Our existence deprives us of the minimum of physical activity essential for healthy living.

—**JOHN F. KENNEDY**
American President, 20th Century

What are some good strategies for increasing children's exercise?

An increasing number of studies document the importance of exercise in children's physical development (Thivel & others, 2011; Tomporowski, Lambourne, & Okumura, 2011). One study revealed that a high-intensity resistance training program decreased children's body fat and increased their muscle strength (Benson, Torode, & Fiatarone Singh, 2008). Another study found that 45 minutes of moderate physical activity and 15 minutes of vigorous physical activity daily were related to decreased odds that the children were overweight (Wittmeier, Mollard, & Kriellaars, 2008). And a recent study of 9-year-olds revealed that a higher level of physical activity was linked to a lower level of metabolic disease risk based on measures such as cholesterol, waist circumference, and insulin (Parrett & others, 2011).

A recent research review concluded that aerobic exercise also increasingly is linked to children's cognitive skills (Best, 2010). Researchers have found that aerobic exercise benefits children's attention, memory, effortful and goal-directed thinking and behavior, and creativity (Budde & others, 2008; Davis & Cooper, 2011; Davis & others, 2007, 2011; Ellenberg & St. Louis-Deschenes, 2010; Hillman & others, 2009; Hinkle, Tuckman, & Sampson, 1993; Pesce & others, 2009).

developmental connection

Exercise. Guidelines recommend that preschool children engage in two hours of physical activity per day. Chapter 8, p. 249

Parents play important roles in children's exercise (Cottrell & others, 2011; Wuest & Fisette, 2012). Growing up with parents who regularly exercise provides positive models of exercise for children. A recent study revealed that mothers were more likely than fathers to limit boys' and girls' sedentary behavior (Edwardson & Gorely, 2010).

Some of the blame also falls on the nation's schools, many of which fail to provide daily physical education classes (Rink, 2009). Many children's school weeks do not include adequate physical education classes, and the majority of children do not exercise vigorously even when they are in such classes (Kovar & others, 2007). A recent study found that school-based physical activity was successful in improving children's fitness and lowering their levels of body fat (Kriemler & others, 2010).

Sports Despite the growing concern about lack of exercise, more and more children become involved in sports every year. Both in public schools and in community agencies, children's sports programs have changed the shape of many children's lives.

Participation in sports can have both positive and negative consequences for children (Myer & others, 2011). Participation can provide exercise, opportunities to learn how to compete, enhanced self-esteem, persistence, and a setting for developing peer relations and friendships (Theokas, 2009). Further, participating in sports reduces the likelihood that children will become obese (Sturm, 2005). A recent study revealed that 10- to 12-year-old girls who participated in more than 3 hours a week of extracurricular sports activities were 59 percent less likely to be overweight or obese than their nonparticipating counterparts (Antonogeorgos & others, 2011). However, sports also can bring pressure to achieve and win, physical injuries, a distraction from academic work, and unrealistic expectations for success as an athlete (Lerch, Cordes, & Baumeister, 2011; Seto, Statuta, & Solari, 2011).

In the *Caring Connections* interlude on page 331, you can read about some positive strategies for parents to follow regarding their children's sports participation.

Now let's turn our attention to additional children's health issues. For most children, middle and late childhood is a time of excellent health. Disease and death are less prevalent in this period than in other periods of childhood and adolescence. However, some children do have health problems, such as obesity, cancer, diabetes, cardiovascular disease, asthma, and injuries due to accidents.

How Would You...?
If you were a **human development and family studies professional,** how would you advise parents on making their children's participation in sports enjoyable?

Parents, Coaches, and Children's Sports

Most sports psychologists stress that it is important for parents to show an interest in their children's sports participation. Most children want their parents to watch them perform in sports. Many children whose parents do not come to watch them play in sporting events feel that their parents do not adequately support them. However, some children be-

What are some of the possible positive and negative aspects of children's participation in sports? What are some guidelines that can benefit parents and coaches of children in sports?

come extremely nervous when their parents watch them perform, or they get embarrassed when their parents cheer too loudly or make a fuss. If children request that their parents not watch them perform, parents should respect their children's wishes (Schreiber, 1990).

Parents should compliment their children for their sports performance, and if they don't become overinvolved, they can help their children build their physical skills and emotional maturity—discussing with them how to deal with a difficult coach, how to cope with a tough loss, and how to put in perspective a poorly played game. The following guidelines provided by the Women's Sports Foundation (2001) in its booklet *Parents' Guide to Girls' Sports* can benefit both parents and coaches of all children in sports:

The Do's

- Make sports fun; the more children enjoy sports, the more they will want to play.
- Remember that it is okay for children to make mistakes; it means they are trying.
- Allow children to ask questions about the sport and discuss the sport in a calm, supportive manner.
- Show respect for the child's sports participation.
- Be positive and convince the child that he or she is making a good effort.
- Be a positive role model for the child in sports.

The Don'ts

- Yell or scream at the child.
- Condemn the child for poor play or continue to bring up failures long after they happen.
- Point out the child's errors in front of others.
- Expect the child to learn something immediately.
- Expect the child to become a pro.
- Ridicule or make fun of the child.
- Compare the child to siblings or to more talented children.
- Make sports all work and no fun.

OVERWEIGHT CHILDREN

Being overweight is an increasingly prevalent health problem in the United States and elsewhere (Blake, 2011). Recall from Chapter 8, "Physical Development in Early Childhood," that being overweight is defined in terms of body mass index (BMI), which is computed by a formula that takes into account height and weight. Also, children at or above the 95th percentile of BMI are included in the overweight category, whereas children at or above the 85th percentile are described as at risk for being overweight (Centers for Disease Control and Prevention, 2011). Over the last four decades, the percentage of U.S. children who are at risk for being overweight has doubled from 15 percent in the 1970s to almost 30 percent today, and the percentage of children who are overweight has tripled during this time frame (Orsi, Hale, & Lynch, 2011). As we discussed in Chapter 8, recently, however, the increase in child obesity in the United States has begun to level off (Ogden, Carroll, & Flegal, 2008).

developmental **connection**

Nutrition and Weight. In one international comparison of 34 countries, the United States had the second highest rate of childhood obesity. Chapter 8, p. 248

Still, the levels of child obesity, overweight, and risk for being overweight are far too high (Wardlaw & Smith, 2011). Note that girls are more likely than boys to be overweight, and this gender difference occurs in many countries (Sweeting, 2008). In a recent large-scale U.S. study, African American and Latino children were more likely to be overweight or obese than non-Latino White children (Benson, Baer, & Kaelber, 2009).

Researchers have found that being overweight as a child is a risk factor for being obese as an adult (Janssen & others, 2005). For example, a longitudinal study revealed that girls who were overweight in childhood were 11 to 30 times more likely to be obese in adulthood than girls who were not overweight in childhood (Thompson & others, 2007). And a study found that children with high body mass index and waist circumference are at risk for metabolic syndrome (a constellation of factors including obesity, high blood pressure, and type 2 diabetes that places individuals at risk for developing cardiovascular disease) in adulthood (Sun & others, 2008).

What Factors Are Linked with Being Overweight in Childhood? Heredity and environmental contexts are related to being overweight in childhood. Recent genetic analysis indicates that heredity is an important factor in children becoming overweight (Jiao & others, 2011). Overweight parents tend to have overweight children (Vergara-Castaneda & others, 2010). For example, one study found that the greatest risk factor for being overweight at 9 years of age was having a parent who is overweight (Agras & others, 2004). And a recent study revealed that having two overweight/obese parents significantly increased the likelihood of a child being overweight/obese (Xu & others, 2011). Characteristics such as body type, height, body fat composition, and metabolism are inherited from parents (Walley, Blakemore, & Froguel, 2006). Environmental factors that influence whether children become overweight or not include the greater availability of food (especially food high in fat content), energy-saving devices, declining physical activity, parents' eating habits and monitoring of children's eating habits, the context in which a child eats, and heavy TV watching (Andreyeva, Kelly, & Harris, 2011; Zocca & others, 2011). A recent behavior modification study of overweight and obese children made watching TV contingent on their engagement in exercise (Goldfield, 2011). The intervention markedly increased their exercise and reduced their TV viewing time.

Consequences of Being Overweight in Childhood The increase in overweight children in recent decades is cause for great concern because being overweight raises the risk for many medical and psychological problems (Fahey, Insel, & Roth, 2011). Diabetes, hypertension (high blood pressure), and elevated blood cholesterol levels are common in children who are overweight (Hearst & others, 2011; Lipman & others, 2011). Once considered rare, hypertension in children has become increasingly common in overweight children (Gomes & others, 2011). Social and psychological consequences of being overweight in childhood include low self-esteem, depression, and some exclusion of obese children from peer groups (Puder & Munsch, 2010). In one study, obese children were perceived as less attractive, more tired, and more socially withdrawn than non-obese peers (Zeller, Reiter-Purtill, &

What are some concerns about overweight children?

Ramey, 2008). And in a recent study, overweight children reported being teased more by their peers and family members than did normal-weight children (McCormack & others, 2011).

Treatment of Children Who Are Overweight   Many experts recommend a program that involves a combination of diet, exercise, and behavior modification to help children lose weight (Cronk & others, 2011). Exercise is an extremely important component of a successful weight-loss program for overweight children (Wuest & Fisette, 2012). Exercise increases the child's lean body mass, which increases the child's resting metabolic rate. These changes result in more calories being burned in the resting state.

Children's activity levels are influenced by their motivation to engage in energetic activities, as well as by caregivers who model an active lifestyle and are motivated to provide children with opportunities to be active (Gunnarsdotter & others, 2011). In a typical behavior modification program, children are taught to monitor their own behavior, keeping a food diary while attempting to lose weight. The diary should record not only the type and amount of food eaten but also when, with whom, and where it was eaten. That is, do children eat in front of the TV, by themselves, or because they are angry or depressed? A diary identifies behaviors that need to be changed.

How Would You…?
If you were a **health-care professional,** how would you use your knowledge of risk factors for being overweight to design a workshop for parents and children about healthy lifestyle choices?

Parents play an important role in preventing children from becoming overweight (Cameron & others, 2011). They can encourage healthy eating habits in children by "increasing the number of family meals eaten together, making healthful foods available, and reducing the availability of sugar-sweetened beverages and sodas" (Lindsay & others, 2006, p. 173). They also can help reduce the likelihood their children will become overweight by reducing children's TV time, getting children involved in sports and other physical activities, and being healthy, physically active models themselves (Salmon, Campbell, & Crawford, 2006). As we learned in Angie's story at the beginning of the chapter, a combination of behavior modification techniques, parental involvement, and a structured program can effectively help overweight children. Recent research studies indicate intervention programs that emphasize getting parents to engage in healthier life styles themselves, as well as feeding their children healthier food and getting them to exercise more, can produce weight reduction in overweight and obese children (Magarey & others, 2011; Robertson & others, 2011). For example, a recent study found that a combination of a child-centered activity program and a parent-centered dietary modification program were successful in helping overweight children lose pounds over a two-year period (Collins & others, 2011).

What can parents do to prevent their children from being overweight or obese?

Some intervention programs with overweight children are conducted through schools and often focus on teaching children and parents about selecting a healthy diet, exercising more, and reducing screen activity (time spent watching TV, playing video games, texting, and so on) (Hendy, Williams, & Camise, 2011; Miller, 2011). A promising strategy is to provide students with more nutritious foods to eat at school (de Silva-Sanigorski & others, 2011). Several states now have laws that require more healthful foods to be sold in vending machines at schools. In one intervention, reducing soft drink consumption at schools was linked with a subsequent reduction in the number of 7- to 11-year-old children who were overweight (James & others, 2004).

DISEASES

Four childhood diseases can especially be harmful to children's development: cancer, diabetes, cardiovascular disease, and asthma.

Cancer   Cancer is the second leading cause of death in U.S. children 5 to 14 years of age. One in every 330 children in the United States develops cancer before the age of 19. The incidence of cancer in children has risen slightly in recent years (National Cancer Institute, 2011).

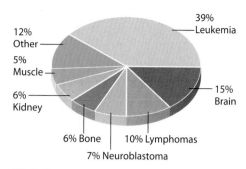

FIGURE 11.3

TYPES OF CANCER IN CHILDREN. Cancers in children have a different profile from adult cancers, which attack mainly the lungs, colon, breast, prostate, and pancreas.

Cancers in children mainly attack the white blood cells (leukemia), brain, bone, lymph system, muscles, kidneys, and nervous system. All are characterized by an uncontrolled proliferation of abnormal cells (de Vasconcellos & others, 2011; Ozono & others, 2011). As indicated in Figure 11.3, the most common cancer in children is leukemia, a cancer in which bone marrow manufactures an abundance of abnormal white blood cells, which crowd out normal cells, making the child susceptible to bruising and infection (Lund & others, 2011).

When cancer strikes children, it behaves differently from the way it attacks adults. Children frequently have a more advanced stage of cancer when they are first diagnosed. When cancer is first diagnosed in adults, it has spread to distant parts of the body in only about 20 percent of the cases; however, that figure rises to 80 percent in children. Most cancers in adults result from lifestyle factors, such as smoking, diet, occupation, and exposure to other cancer-causing agents. By contrast, little is known about the causes of childhood cancers. Researchers are searching for possible genetic links to childhood cancers (Crespi, 2011; Parsons & others, 2011).

Because of advancements in cancer treatment, children with cancer are surviving longer (National Cancer Institute, 2011). Approximately 80 percent of children with acute lymphoblastic leukemia are cured with current chemotherapy treatment (Wayne, 2011).

Diabetes   Diabetes is one of the most common chronic diseases in children and adolescents. Rates of diabetes in children have increased in the United States and other countries (Harron & others, 2011; National Center for Health Statistics, 2011). In type 1 diabetes, the body produces little or no insulin (the hormone that regulates the body's blood sugar level). **Type 1 diabetes** is an autoimmune disease in which the body's immune system destroys insulin-producing cells. In **type 2 diabetes,** the most common type of diabetes, the body is able to produce insulin, but it may be insufficient or the body's cells may be unable to use it. Risk factors for type 2 diabetes include being overweight and/or physically inactive, having relatives with this disease, or belonging to certain ethnic groups (Ahmed & others, 2011; Dean & others, 2011). Native Americans, African Americans, Latinos, and Asian Americans are at greater risk for developing diabetes.

Cardiovascular Disease   Cardiovascular disease is uncommon in children. Nonetheless, environmental experiences and behavior in the childhood years can sow the seeds for cardiovascular disease in adulthood. Many elementary-school-aged children already possess one or more of the risk factors for cardiovascular disease, such as hypertension and obesity (Durrani & Fatima, 2011; Hayes & others, 2011). A recent national study found that an increasing percentage of U.S. children and adolescents had elevated blood pressure from 1988 to 2006 (Ostchega & others, 2009). In this study, children who were obese were more likely to have elevated blood pressure. One study also revealed that high blood pressure goes undiagnosed in 75 percent of children with the disease (Hansen, Gunn, & Kaelber, 2007). Another study found that high blood pressure was most likely to be present in Latino children (25 percent) and least characteristic of Asian American children (14 percent) (Sorof & others, 2004). How might such research help us improve children's cardiovascular health? The Bogalusa Heart Study discussed in the *Connecting with Research* interlude seeks to answer this question.

What are some concerns about children's cardiovascular health and obesity?

type 1 diabetes An autoimmune disease in which the body's immune system destroys insulin-producing cells.

type 2 diabetes The most common type of diabetes, in which the body is able to produce insulin, but it may be insufficient or the body's cells may be unable to use it.

asthma A chronic lung disease that involves episodes of airflow obstruction.

Asthma   **Asthma** is a chronic lung disease that involves episodes of airflow obstruction. Symptoms of an asthma attack include shortness of breath, wheezing, or tightness in the chest (Castro-Rodriquez, 2011). The incidence of asthma has risen steadily in recent decades, possibly because of increased air pollution (Brown & others, 2011). Asthma is the most common chronic disease in U.S. children, being present in approximately 9 percent of them (National Center for Health Statistics,

Heart Smart

The Bogalusa Heart Study, also called Heart Smart, is a large-scale investigation designed to improve children's cardiovascular health. It involves an ongoing evaluation of 8,000 boys and girls in Bogalusa, Louisiana (Berenson, 2005; Camhi & others, 2010; Freedman & others, 2008, 2010a, b; Mokha & others, 2010). Heart Smart intervention takes place in schools. Since 95 percent of children and adolescents aged 5 to 18 are in school, school is an efficient context in which to educate individuals about health. Special attention is given to teachers, who serve as role models. Teachers who value the role of health in life and who engage in health-enhancing behavior present children and adolescents with positive models for health. Teacher in-service education is conducted by an interdisciplinary team of specialists, including physicians, psychologists, nutritionists, physical educators, and exercise physiologists. The school's staff is introduced to information about heart health, the nature of cardiovascular disease, and risk factors for heart disease. Coping behavior, exercise behavior, and eating behavior are discussed with the staff, and a Heart Smart curriculum is explained.

The Heart Smart curriculum for grade 5 includes strategies for improving cardiovascular health, eating behavior, and exercise. The physical education component of Heart Smart involves two to four class periods each week to incorporate a "Superkids-Superfit" exercise program. The physical education instructor teaches skills required by the school system plus aerobic activities aimed at cardiovascular conditioning, including jogging, racewalking, interval workouts, rope skipping, circuit training, aerobic dance, and games. Classes begin and end with five minutes of walking and stretching.

The school lunch program serves as an intervention site, where sodium, fat, and sugar levels are decreased. Children and adolescents are given reasons why they should eat healthy foods, such as a tuna sandwich, and why they should not eat unhealthy foods, such as a hot dog with chili. The school lunch program includes a salad bar, where children and adolescents can serve themselves. The amount and type of snack foods sold on the school premises are monitored.

High-risk children—those with elevated blood pressure, cholesterol, and high weight—are identified as part of Heart Smart (Freedman & others, 2008, 2010a, b). A multidisciplinary team of physicians, nutritionists, nurses, and behavioral counselors works with the high-risk boys and girls and their parents through group-oriented activities and individual-based family counseling. High-risk boys and girls and their parents receive diet, exercise, and relaxation prescriptions in an intensive 12-session program, followed by long-term monthly evaluations.

Extensive assessment is a part of this ongoing program. Short-term and long-term changes in children's knowledge about cardiovascular disease and changes in their behavior are assessed.

Following are some results from the Bogalusa Heart Study:

- More than half of the children exceeded the recommended intake of salt, fat, cholesterol, and sugar (Nicklas & others, 1995).
- Consumption of sweetened beverages, sweets (desserts, candy), and total consumption of low-quality food were associated with being overweight in childhood (Nicklas & others, 2003).
- Adiposity (having excess body weight) beginning in childhood was related to cardiovascular problems in adulthood (Freedman & others, 2008).
- Higher body mass index (BMI) in childhood was linked to the likelihood of developing metabolic syndrome (a cluster of characteristics that include excessive fat around the abdomen, high blood pressure, and diabetes) in adulthood (Freedman & others, 2005).

How do you think parents, siblings, and peers might influence children's health behavior such as exercise habits and food choices?

2009). Asthma is the primary reason for absences from school, and it is responsible for a number of pediatric admissions to emergency rooms and hospitals (Horner & Bacharier, 2009; Stepney, Kane, & Bruzzese, 2011).

The exact causes of asthma are not known, but it is believed that the disease results from hypersensitivity to environmental substances that triggers an allergic reaction (Ahluwalia & Matsui, 2011). A research review concluded that the following are asthma risk factors: being male, having one or both parents with asthma, and/or having allergy sensitivity, stress early in life, infections, obesity, and exposure to environmental tobacco smoke, indoor allergens, and outdoor pollutants (Feleszko & others, 2006).

Corticosteroids, which generally are inhaled, are the most effective anti-inflammatory drugs for treating asthmatic children (Vuillermin, Robertson, & South, 2011). Often, parents have kept asthmatic children from exercising because they fear exercise will provoke an asthma attack. However, today it is believed that children

connecting with careers

Sharon McLeod, Child Life Specialist

Sharon McLeod is a child life specialist who is clinical director of the Child Life and Recreational Therapy Department at the Children's Hospital Medical Center in Cincinnati.

Under McLeod's direction, the goals of the Child Life Department are to promote children's optimal growth and development, reduce the stress of health-care experiences, and provide support to child patients and their families. These goals are accomplished through therapeutic play and developmentally appropriate activities, educating and psychologically preparing children for medical procedures, and serving as a resource for parents and other professionals regarding children's development and health-care issues.

McLeod says that knowledge of human growth and development provides the foundation for her profession of child life specialist. She says her best times as a student were when she conducted fieldwork, had an internship, and received hands-on experience applying theories and concepts she learned in her courses.

Sharon McLeod, child life specialist, working with a child at Children's Hospital Medical Center in Cincinnati.

For more information about what child life specialists do, see the Careers in Children's Development appendix, p. 50.

with asthma should be encouraged to exercise, provided their asthma is under control, and participation should be evaluated on an individual basis (Basaran & others, 2006). Some asthmatic children lose their symptoms in adolescence and adulthood (Vonk & others, 2004).

One individual who helps children cope with their health-care experiences is child life specialist Sharon McLeod. To read about her work, see the *Connecting with Careers* profile.

> Blessed be childhood,
> which brings
> something of heaven
> into the midst of our
> rough earthliness.
>
> —HENRI FRÉDÉRIC AMIEL
> *Swiss Poet, Philosopher, 19th Century*

ACCIDENTS AND INJURIES

Injuries are the leading cause of death during middle and late childhood. The most common cause of severe injury and death during this period is motor vehicle accidents, either as a pedestrian or as a passenger (Committee on Injury, Violence, and Poison Prevention, 2011). The use of safety-belt restraint greatly reduces the severity of motor vehicle injuries. Other serious injuries involve bicycles, skateboards, roller skates, and other sports equipment.

Most accidents occur in or near the child's home or school. The most effective prevention strategy is to educate the child about proper use of equipment and the hazards of risk taking (Turner & others, 2011). Safety helmets, protective eye and mouth shields, and protective padding are recommended for children who engage in active sports.

As we saw in Chapter 8, "Physical Development in Early Childhood," caregivers play a key role in preventing childhood injuries. A study in four developing countries (Ethiopia, Peru, Vietnam, and India) revealed that depression in caregivers was consistently linked to children's risk of injury for all types of injury assessed (burns, serious falls, broken bones, and near-fatal injury) (Howe, Huttly, & Abramsky, 2006).

How Would You...?
If you were a **health-care professional,** how would you work with school-age children to reduce their chances of injury due to accidents?

336   CHAPTER 11   *Physical Development in Middle and Late Childhood*

Review

- What are key aspects of children's nutrition in middle and late childhood?
- What roles do exercise and sports play in children's development?
- What are the consequences of being overweight in childhood?
- What four diseases are especially harmful to children?
- What is the most common cause of severe injury and death in childhood?

Connect

- What are some positive and negative parental feeding patterns that were described in Chapter 8, "Physical Development in Early Childhood," that also likely play a role in children's eating patterns in middle and late childhood?

Reflect *Your Own Personal Journey of Life*

- How good were your eating habits as a child? How much did you exercise in middle and late childhood? Are your eating and exercise habits today similar to or different from your eating and exercise habits as a child? Why are they similar or different?

What Are the Prevalent Disabilities in Children?

LG3 Summarize information about children with disabilities.

Who Are Children with Disabilities? | The Range of Disabilities | Educational Issues

Our discussion of children's health has focused on nutrition and exercise. In addition, we have discussed some of the most common health problems, such as obesity, cancer, diabetes, cardiovascular disease, and asthma. In this section, we turn our attention to children with disabilities and the issues involved in their education.

WHO ARE CHILDREN WITH DISABILITIES?

Of all children from 3 to 21 years of age in the United States, 13.4 percent receive special education or related services (National Center for Education Statistics, 2010). Figure 11.4 shows the four largest groups of students with a disability who were served by federal programs in the 2007–2008 school year (National Center for Education Statistics, 2010). As indicated in Figure 11.4, students with a learning disability were by far the largest group of students with a disability to be given special education, followed by children with speech or language impairments, mental retardation, and emotional disturbance.

Educators now prefer to speak of "children with disabilities" rather than "handicapped children" to focus on the person rather than the disability (Hallahan, Kauffman, & Pullen, 2012). The term "handicapping conditions" is still used to describe impediments to the learning and functioning of individuals with a disability that have been imposed by society. For example, in the case of children who use a wheelchair and do not have access to a bathroom, transportation, and so on, this is referred to as a handicap situation.

THE RANGE OF DISABILITIES

In this section, we examine learning disabilities, attention deficit hyperactivity disorder, speech disorders, sensory disorders, physical disorders, emotional and behavioral disorders, and autism. In Chapter 12, "Cognitive Development in Middle and Late Childhood," we will study mental retardation.

Disability	Percentage of All Children in Public Schools
Learning disabilities	5.2
Speech and language impairments	3.0
Mental retardation	1.0
Emotional disturbance	0.9

FIGURE 11.4

U.S. CHILDREN WITH A DISABILITY WHO RECEIVE SPECIAL EDUCATION SERVICES. Figures are for the 2007–2008 school year and represent the four categories with the highest numbers and percentages of children. Both learning disability and attention deficit hyperactivity disorder are combined in the learning disabilities category (National Center for Education Statistics, 2010).

Learning Disabilities   Bobby's second-grade teacher complains that his spelling is awful. Eight-year-old Tim says reading is really hard for him, and often the words don't make much sense. Alisha has good oral language skills but has considerable difficulty in computing correct answers to arithmetic problems. Each of these students has a learning disability.

Characteristics and Identification   The U.S. government created a definition of learning disabilities in 1997 and then reauthorized the definition with a few minor changes in 2004. Following is a description of the government's definition of what determines whether a child should be classified as having a learning disability. A child with a **learning disability** has difficulty in learning that involves understanding or using spoken or written language, and the difficulty can appear in listening, thinking, reading, writing, or spelling. A learning disability also may involve difficulty in doing mathematics. To be classified as a learning disability, the learning problem is not primarily the result of visual, hearing, or motor disabilities; mental retardation; emotional disorders; or environmental, cultural, or economic disadvantage.

From the mid-1970s through the early 1990s, there was a dramatic increase in the percentage of U.S. students receiving special education services (from 1.8 percent in 1976–1977 to 12.2 percent in 1994–1995), although in the twenty-first century this percentage has decreased (from 6.1 percent in 2000 to 5.2 percent in 2007–2008) (National Center for Education Statistics, 2010). Some experts say that the dramatic increase reflected poor diagnostic practices and overidentification. They argue that teachers sometimes are too quick to label children with the slightest learning problem as having a learning disability, instead of recognizing that the problem may rest in their ineffective teaching. Other experts say the increase in the number of children being labeled with a "learning disability" is justified (Lerner & Johns, 2012; Rosenberg, Westling, & McLeskey, 2011).

About three times as many boys as girls are classified as having a learning disability. Among the explanations for this gender difference are a greater biological vulnerability among boys and referral bias (that is, boys are more likely to be referred by teachers for treatment because of their behavior) (Liederman, Kantrowitz, & Flannery, 2005).

Most learning disabilities are lifelong. Compared with children without a learning disability, children with a learning disability are more likely to show poor academic performance, high dropout rates, and poor employment and postsecondary education records (Berninger & O'Malley, 2011). Children with a learning disability who are taught in the regular classroom without extensive support rarely achieve even the level of competence attained by children who are low-achieving and do not have a disability (Hocutt, 1996). Still, despite the problems they encounter, many children with a learning disability grow up to lead normal lives and engage in productive work. For example, actress Whoopi Goldberg and investment company owner Charles Schwab have learning disabilities.

Diagnosing whether a child has a learning disability is often a difficult task (Friend, 2011; Lerner & Johns, 2012). Because federal guidelines are just that—guidelines—it is up to each state, or in some cases school systems within a state, to determine how to define and implement diagnosis of learning disabilities. The same child might be diagnosed as having a learning disability in one school system and receive services but not be diagnosed and not receive services in another school system. In such cases, parents sometimes will move to a new location to obtain or to avoid the diagnosis.

Initial identification of a possible learning disability usually is made by the classroom teacher. If a learning disability is suspected, the teacher calls on specialists. An interdisciplinary team of professionals is best suited to verify whether a student has a learning disability. Individual psychological evaluations (of intelligence) and educational assessments (such as current level of achievement) are required (Hallahan, Kauffman, & Pullen, 2012). In addition, tests of visual-motor skills, language, and memory may be used.

How Would You...?

If you were an **educator,** how would you explain the nature of learning disabilities to a parent whose child had recently been diagnosed with a learning disability?

learning disability Disability in which a child has difficulty in learning that involves understanding or using spoken or written language, and the difficulty can appear in listening, thinking, reading, writing, or spelling. A learning disability also may involve difficulty in doing mathematics. To be classified as a learning disability, the learning problem is not primarily the result of visual, hearing, or motor disabilities; mental retardation; emotional disorders; or environmental, cultural, or economic disadvantage.

Reading, Writing, and Math Difficulties The most common academic areas in which children with a learning disability have problems are reading, writing, and math (Kirk & others, 2012). A problem with reading affects approximately 80 percent of children with a learning disability (Shaywitz, Gruen, & Shaywitz, 2007). Such children have difficulty with phonological skills, which involve being able to understand how sounds and letters match up to make words, and also can have problems in comprehension. **Dyslexia** is a category reserved for individuals with a severe impairment in their ability to read and spell (Lipowska, Czaplewska, & Wysocka, 2011).

Dysgraphia is a learning disability that involves difficulty in handwriting (Overvelde & Hulstijn, 2011). Children with dysgraphia may write very slowly, their writing products may be virtually illegible, and they may make numerous spelling errors because of their inability to match up sounds and letters.

Dyscalculia, also known as developmental arithmetic disorder, is a learning disability that involves difficulty in math computation (Kucian & others, 2011). It is estimated to characterize 2 to 6 percent of U.S. elementary school children (National Center for Learning Disabilities, 2006). A child may have both a reading and a math disability, and there are cognitive deficits that characterize both types of disabilities, such as poor working memory (Siegel, 2003).

Causes and Intervention Strategies The precise causes of learning disabilities have not yet been determined. However, some possible causes have been proposed. Learning disabilities tend to run in families, with higher rates among children having one parent with a disability such as dyslexia or dyscalculia.

Researchers currently are exploring the role of genetics in learning disabilities (Elbert & others, 2011; Konig & others, 2011). Also, some learning disabilities are likely to be caused by problems during prenatal development or delivery. For example, a number of studies have found that learning disabilities are more prevalent in low birth weight infants (Litt & others, 2005).

Researchers also use brain-imaging techniques, such as magnetic resonance imaging, to reveal any regions of the brain that might be involved in learning disabilities (Shaywitz, Morris, & Shaywitz, 2008) (see Figure 11.5). This research indicates that it is unlikely learning disabilities stem from disorders in a single, specific brain location. More likely, learning disabilities are due to problems in integrating information from multiple brain regions or to subtle defects in brain structure and function.

Many interventions have focused on improving the child's reading ability (Lerner & Johns, 2012). Intensive instruction over a period of time by a competent teacher can help many children (Berninger & O'Malley, 2011). For example, a recent brain-imaging study involved 15 children with severe reading difficulties who had not shown adequate progress in response to reading instruction in the first grade and were given eight weeks of intensive instruction in phonological decoding skills followed by another intensive eight weeks of word recognition skills (Simos & others, 2007). Significant improvement in a majority of the children's reading skills and changes in brain regions involved in reading occurred as a result of the intensive instruction.

Attention Deficit Hyperactivity Disorder

Matthew has attention deficit hyperactivity disorder, and the outward signs are fairly typical. He has trouble attending to the teacher's instructions and is easily distracted. He can't sit still for more than a few minutes at a time, and his handwriting is messy. His mother describes him as very fidgety.

Characteristics **Attention deficit hyperactivity disorder (ADHD)** is a disability in which children consistently show one or more of the following characteristics

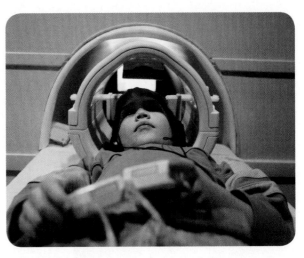

FIGURE **11.5**

BRAIN SCANS AND LEARNING DISABILITIES. An increasing number of studies are using MRI brain scans to examine the brain pathways involved in learning disabilities. Shown here is 9-year-old Patrick Price, who has dyslexia. Patrick is going through an MRI scanner disguised by drapes to look like a child-friendly castle. Inside the scanner, children must lie virtually motionless as words and symbols flash on a screen, and they are asked to identify them by clicking different buttons.

dyslexia A category of learning disabilities involving a severe impairment in the ability to read and spell.

dysgraphia A learning disability that involves difficulty in handwriting.

dyscalculia Also known as developmental arithmetic disorder; a learning disability that involves difficulty in math computation.

attention deficit hyperactivity disorder (ADHD) A disability in which children consistently show one or more of the following characteristics: (1) inattention, (2) hyperactivity, and (3) impulsivity.

over a period of time: (1) inattention, (2) hyperactivity, and (3) impulsivity. For an ADHD diagnosis, onset of these characteristics early in childhood is required, and the characteristics must be debilitating for the child.

Inattentive children have difficulty focusing on any one thing and may get bored with a task after only a few minutes. One study found that problems in sustaining attention were the most common type of attention problem in children with ADHD (Tsal, Shalev, & Mevorach, 2005). Hyperactive children show high levels of physical activity, almost always seeming to be in motion. Impulsive children have difficulty curbing their reactions and don't do a good job of thinking before they act. Depending on the characteristics that children with ADHD display, they can be diagnosed as (1) ADHD with predominantly inattention, (2) ADHD with predominantly hyperactivity/impulsivity, or (3) ADHD with both inattention and hyperactivity/impulsivity.

Diagnosis and Developmental Status   The number of children diagnosed and treated for ADHD has increased substantially, by some estimates doubling in the 1990s (Stein, 2004). A national survey found that 7 percent of U.S. children 3 to 17 years of age had ADHD (Bloom & Dey, 2006). The disorder occurs as much as four to nine times more in boys than in girls. There is controversy about the increased diagnosis of ADHD, however (Friend, 2011). Some experts attribute the increase mainly to heightened awareness of the disorder. Others are concerned that many children are being diagnosed without undergoing extensive professional evaluation based on input from multiple sources.

Many children and adolescents show impulsive behavior, such as this boy who is jumping out of his seat and throwing a paper airplane at classmates. *What is the best way for teachers to handle such situations?*

Unlike learning disabilities, ADHD is not supposed to be diagnosed by school teams because it is a disorder that appears, with specific diagnostic criteria, in the American Psychiatric Association's DSM-IV classification of psychiatric disorders (U. C. Muller & others, 2011). Although some school teams may diagnose a child as having ADHD, this is incorrectly done and can lead to legal problems for schools and teachers. One reason that is given as to why a school team should not do the diagnosis is that ADHD is difficult to differentiate from other childhood disorders, and accurate diagnosis requires the evaluation by a specialist in the disorder, such as a child psychiatrist.

Although signs of ADHD are often present during the preschool years, children with ADHD are not usually classified until the elementary school years (Zentall, 2006). The increased academic and social demands of formal schooling, as well as stricter standards for behavioral control, often illuminate the problems of the child with ADHD. Elementary school teachers typically report that this type of child has difficulty in working independently, completing seatwork, and organizing work. Restlessness and distractibility also are often noted. These problems are more likely to be observed in repetitive or difficult tasks, or tasks the child perceives to be boring (such as completing worksheets or doing homework).

It used to be thought that children with ADHD showed improvement during adolescence, but now it appears this often is not the case. Estimates suggest symptoms of ADHD decrease in only about one-third of adolescents. Increasingly, it is being recognized that these problems may continue into adulthood (Newcorn, 2011; Taurines & others, 2010).

Causes and Treatment   Definitive causes of ADHD have not been found. However, a number of causes have been proposed (American Academy of Pediatrics & Reiff, 2011; Purper-Ouakil & others, 2011). Some children likely inherit a tendency to develop ADHD from their parents (Bergman & others, 2011; Gainetdinov, 2010). Other children likely develop ADHD because of damage to their brain during prenatal or postnatal development (Waldie & Hausmann, 2010). Among early possible contributors to ADHD are cigarette and alcohol exposure during prenatal development and low birth weight (Knopik, 2009). For example, a recent study revealed cigarette smoking during pregnancy was linked to ADHD in 6- to 7-year-old children (Sciberras, Ukoumunne, & Efron, 2011).

As with learning disabilities, the development of brain-imaging techniques is leading to a better understanding of the brain's role in ADHD (Qui & others, 2011).

How Would You...?

If you were a **health-care professional,** how would you respond to the following remarks by a parent? "I do not believe that ADHD is a real disorder. Children are supposed to be active."

A study revealed that peak thickness of the cerebral cortex occurred three years later (10.5 years) in children with ADHD than in children without ADHD (peak at 7.5 years) (Shaw & others, 2007). The delay was more prominent in the prefrontal regions of the brain that are especially important in attention and planning (see Figure 11.6). A study also found delayed development in the brain's frontal lobes of children with ADHD, linked to delayed or decreased myelination (Nagel & others, 2011). Researchers also are exploring the roles that various neurotransmitters, such as serotonin and dopamine, might play in ADHD (Beaulieu & Gainetdinov, 2011; Mahmoudi-Gharaei & others, 2011).

The delays in brain development just described are in areas linked to executive functioning. An increasing interest in the study of children with ADHD is their difficulty on executive functioning tasks, such as inhibiting behavior when necessary, working memory, and effective planning (Jacobson & others, 2011; Rinsky & Hinshaw, 2011; Van De Voorde & others, 2011). Researchers also have found deficits in theory of mind in children with ADHD (Buhler & others, 2011; Shuai, Chan, & Wang, 2011).

Stimulant medication such as Ritalin (methylphenidate) or Adderall (amphetamine and dextroamphetamine) is effective in improving the attention of many children with ADHD, but it usually does not improve their attention to the same level as children who do not have ADHD (Brams, Mao, & Doyle, 2009). A recent meta-analysis concluded that behavior management treatments are effective in reducing the effects of ADHD (Fabiano & others, 2009). Researchers have often found that a combination of medication (such as Ritalin) and behavior management improves the behavior of children with ADHD better than medication alone or behavior management alone, although not in all cases (Parens & Johnston, 2009).

Critics argue that many physicians are too quick to prescribe stimulants for children with milder forms of ADHD (Marcovitch, 2004). Also, in 2006, the U.S. government issued a warning about the cardiovascular risks of stimulant medication used to treat ADHD.

Speech Disorders   Speech disorders include articulation disorders, voice disorders, and fluency disorders (Hulit, Howard, & Fahey, 2011). **Articulation disorders** are problems in pronouncing sounds correctly. A child's articulation at 6 to 7 years is still not always error-free, but it should be by age 8. A child with an articulation problem may find communication with peers and the teacher difficult or embarrassing. As a result, the child may avoid asking questions, participating in discussions, or communicating with peers. Articulation problems can usually be improved or resolved with speech therapy, though it may take months or years (Hale & Evans, 2011).

Voice disorders are reflected in speech that is hoarse, harsh, too loud, too high-pitched, or too low-pitched. Children with a cleft palate often have a voice disorder that makes their speech difficult to understand. If a student speaks in a way that is consistently difficult to understand, the child should be referred to a speech therapist (Kempster, 2011).

Fluency disorders often involve what is commonly called "stuttering." Stuttering occurs when a child's speech has a spasmodic hesitation, prolongation, or repetition. The anxiety many children feel because they stutter can make their stuttering worse. Speech therapy is recommended (Andrews, Trajkovski, & Onslow, 2011; Pelczarski & Yaruss, 2011).

One individual who helps children with their speech problems is Sharla Peltier. To read about her work, see the *Connecting with Careers* profile.

Sensory Disorders   Sensory disorders include visual and hearing impairments. Sometimes these impairments are described as part of a larger category called "communication disorders," along with speech and language disorders.

developmental **connection**

Cognitive Processes. Working memory is a "mental workbench" that includes a central executive function whereby individuals monitor and control information. Chapter 12, p. 357

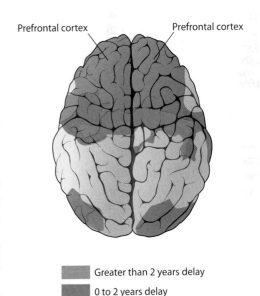

Prefrontal cortex · Prefrontal cortex

Greater than 2 years delay
0 to 2 years delay

FIGURE **11.6**

REGIONS OF THE BRAIN IN WHICH CHILDREN WITH ADHD HAD A DELAYED PEAK IN THE THICKNESS OF THE CEREBRAL CORTEX.
Note: The greatest delays occurred in the prefrontal cortex.

articulation disorders Problems in pronouncing sounds correctly.

voice disorders Disorders reflected in speech that is hoarse, harsh, too loud, too high-pitched, or too low-pitched.

fluency disorders Various disorders that involve what is commonly called "stuttering."

Sharla Peltier, Speech Pathologist

A speech pathologist is a health professional who works with individuals who have a communication disorder. Sharla Peltier is a speech patholo-gist in Manitoulin, Ontario, Canada. Peltier works with Native American children in the First Nations Schools. She conducts screening for speech/language and hearing problems and assesses infants as young as 6 months of age as well as school-age children. She works closely with community health nurses to identify hearing problems.

Diagnosing problems is only about half of what Peltier does in her work. She especially enjoys treating speech/language and hearing prob-lems. She conducts parent training sessions to help parents understand and help with their children's language problem. As part of this training, she guides parents in improving their communication skills with their children. To read more about what speech therapists do, see page 49 in the *Careers in Children's Development* appendix.

Speech therapist Sharla Peltier, helping a young child improve her language and communication skills.

---

low vision Visual acuity between 20/70 and 20/2000.

educationally blind Unable to use one's vision in learning and needing to use hearing and touch to learn.

oral approaches Educational approaches to help hearing-impaired children, including lip reading, speech reading, and use of whatever hearing the child has.

manual approaches Educational approaches to help hearing-impaired children, including sign language and finger spelling.

orthopedic impairments Restrictions in movement abilities due to muscle, bone, or joint problems.

Visual Impairments   Some children may have mild vision problems that have not been corrected (Pedigo, 2011). If children frequently squint, hold books close to their face when they read, rub their eyes often, say that things look blurred, or mention that words move about on the page, they should be referred to appropri-ate professionals to have their vision checked. In many cases, they need only cor-rective lenses. However, a small portion of children (about 1 in 1,000) have more serious visual problems and are classified as visually impaired. This includes children with low vision and blind children.

Children with **low vision** have visual acuity of between 20/70 and 20/2000 (on the Snellen scale, in which 20/20 is normal) with corrective lens. Children with low vision can read with the aid of large-print books or a magnifying glass. Children who are **educationally blind** cannot use their vision in learning and must use their hearing and touch to learn. Approximately 1 in every 3,000 children is edu-cationally blind. Almost half of these children were born blind, and another one-third lost their vision in the first year of life. Many children who are educationally blind have normal intelligence and function very well academically with appropriate supports and learning aids.

An important task when working with a visually impaired child is to determine the modality (such as touch or hearing) through which the child learns best. Pref-erential seating in the front of the class is also helpful.

Hearing Impairments   A hearing impairment can make learning difficult for chil-dren (Brueggeman, 2011). Children who are born deaf or experience a significant hearing loss in the first several years of life may not develop normal speech and language (Friend, 2011). Some children in middle and late childhood have hearing impairments that have not yet been detected. If children turn one ear toward the speaker, frequently ask to have something repeated, don't follow directions, or fre-quently complain of earaches, colds, and allergies, their hearing needs to be evalu-ated by a specialist, such as an audiologist (Patterson & Wright, 1990).

Many hearing-impaired children receive supplementary instruction beyond that of the regular classroom. Educational approaches to help children with hearing impairments learn fall into two categories: oral and manual (Hoskin & Herman, 2001).

- **Oral approaches** include using lip reading, speech reading (relies on visual cues to teach reading), and whatever hearing the child has.

- **Manual approaches** involve sign language and finger spelling. Sign language is a system of hand movements that symbolize words. Finger spelling consists of "spelling out" each word by placing the hand in different positions.

A total communication approach that includes both oral and manual approaches is increasingly being used with children who are hearing impaired (Hallahan, Kauffman, & Pullen, 2012).

Today many hearing-impaired children are educated in the regular classroom. With appropriate accommodations such as preferential seating and the assistance of hearing aids, cochlear implants, and other amplification devices, hearing-impaired children can be educated effectively (Asp, Eskilsson, & Berninger, 2011; Vandam, Ide-Helvie, & Moeller, 2011).

Many students with physical disabilities such as cerebral palsy cannot use a conventional keyboard and mouse. Many can use alternative keyboards effectively.

Physical Disorders   Physical disorders in middle and late childhood include orthopedic impairments such as cerebral palsy. Many children with physical disorders require special education as well as related services. The related services may include transportation, physical therapy, school health services, and psychological services.

Orthopedic impairments involve restricted movement or lack of control over movement due to muscle, bone, or joint problems. The severity of problems ranges widely. Orthopedic impairments can be caused by prenatal or perinatal problems, or they can be due to diseases or accidents during the childhood years. With the help of adaptive devices and medical technology, many children with orthopedic impairments function well in the classroom (Hallahan, Kauffman, & Pullen, 2012).

Cerebral palsy is a disorder that involves a lack of muscular coordination, shaking, and unclear speech. The most common cause of cerebral palsy is lack of oxygen at birth. In the most common type of cerebral palsy, which is called spastic, children's muscles are stiff and difficult to move. The rigid muscles often pull the limbs into contorted positions. In a less common type, ataxia, children's muscles are rigid one moment and floppy the next moment, making movements clumsy and jerky.

What are some characteristics of children with an emotional or behavioral disorder?

Computers especially help children with cerebral palsy learn. If they have the coordination to use the keyboard, they can do their written work on the computer. A pen with a light can be added to a computer and used by the child as a pointer. Children with cerebral palsy sometimes have unclear speech. For these children, speech and voice synthesizers, communication boards, and page turners can improve their communication (Best, Heller, & Bigge, 2010).

Emotional and Behavioral Disorders   Most children have minor emotional difficulties at some point during their school years. A small percentage have problems so serious and persistent that they are classified as having an emotional or a behavioral disorder (Flick, 2011). **Emotional and behavioral disorders** consist of serious, persistent problems that involve relationships, aggression, depression, fears associated with personal or school matters, as well as other inappropriate socioemotional characteristics. Approximately 8 percent of children who have a disability and require an individualized education plan fall into this classification. Boys are three times as likely as girls to have these disorders. We further discuss aggression in Chapter 13, "Socioemotional Development in Middle

cerebral palsy A disorder that involves a lack of muscular coordination, shaking, and unclear speech.

emotional and behavioral disorders Serious, persistent problems that involve relationships, aggression, depression, fears associated with personal or school matters, as well as other inappropriate socioemotional characteristics.

and Late Childhood," and depression in Chapter 16, "Socioemotional Development in Adolescence."

developmental **connection**

Disabilities. Autistic children have difficulty in developing a theory of mind, especially in understanding others' beliefs and emotions. Chapter 9, p. 274

Autism Spectrum Disorders Autism spectrum disorders (ASDs), also called pervasive developmental disorders, range from the severe disorder labeled autistic disorder to the milder disorder called *Asperger syndrome*. Autism spectrum disorders are characterized by problems in social interaction, problems in verbal and nonverbal communication, and repetitive behaviors (Hall, 2009; Hardman, Drew, & Egan, 2011). Children with these disorders may also show atypical responses to sensory experiences (National Institute of Mental Health, 2011). Autism spectrum disorders can often be detected in children as early as 1 to 3 years of age.

Recent estimates of autism spectrum disorders indicate that they are increasing in occurrence or are increasingly being detected and labeled (Neal, 2009). They were once thought to affect only 1 in 2,500 individuals, but today's estimates suggest that they occur in about 1 in 150 individuals (Centers for Disease Control and Prevention, 2007).

Autistic disorder is a severe developmental autism spectrum disorder that has its onset in the first three years of life and includes deficiencies in social relationships, abnormalities in communication, and restricted, repetitive, and stereotyped patterns of behavior. Estimates indicate that approximately 2 to 5 of every 10,000 young children in the United States have autistic disorder. Boys are about four times more likely to have an autistic disorder than girls.

Asperger syndrome is a relatively mild autism spectrum disorder in which the child has relatively good verbal language skills, milder nonverbal language problems, and a restricted range of interests and relationships (Sofronoff, Dark, & Stone, 2011). Children with Asperger syndrome often engage in obsessive, repetitive routines and are preoccupied with a particular subject (Chen, Rodgers, & McConachie, 2009). For example, a child may be obsessed with baseball scores or railroad timetables.

What characterizes autism spectrum disorders?

What causes the autism spectrum disorders? The current consensus is that autism is a brain dysfunction involving abnormalities in brain structure and neurotransmitters (Bosl & others, 2011; Nazeer, 2011; Shukla & others, 2011). Recently, interest has focused on a lack of connectivity between brain regions as a key factor in autism (Mostofsky & Ewen, 2011; R. A. Muller & others, 2011).

Genetic factors likely play a role in the development of the autism spectrum disorders (Ronald & Hoekstra, 2011). A recent study revealed that mutations—missing or duplicated pieces of DNA on chromosome 16—can raise a child's risk of developing autism 100-fold (Weiss & others, 2008). Estimates are that approximately 1 million U.S. children have an autistic disorder, so about 10,000 of them have this genetic mutation. There is no evidence that family socialization causes autism (Rutter & Schopler, 1987). Mental retardation is present in some children with autism; others show average or above-average intelligence (Boutot & Myles, 2011).

FIGURE 11.7

A SCENE FROM THE DVD ANIMATIONS USED IN A STUDY BY BARON-COHEN AND OTHERS (2007). *What did they do to improve autistic children's ability to read facial expressions?* © Crown copyright MMVI, www.thetransporters.com, courtesy of Changing Media Development.

Boys are four times as likely to have autism spectrum disorders as girls are (Gong & others, 2009). Expanding on autism's male-linkage, Simon Baron-Cohen (2008, 2011) recently argued that autism reflects an extreme male brain, especially indicative of males' less effective ability to show empathy and read facial expressions and gestures in comparison with girls. In an attempt to improve these skills in 4- to 8-year-old autistic boys, Baron-Cohen and his colleagues (2007) produced a number of animations on a DVD that place faces with different emotions on toy train and tractor characters in a boy's bedroom (see Figure 11.7). After watching the animations 15 minutes every weekday for one month, the autistic children's ability to recognize real faces in a different context equaled that of children without autism. A recent research review concluded that when these behavior modifications are intensely provided and used early in the autistic child's life, they are more effective (Howlin, Magiati, & Charman, 2009).

Many children with autism benefit from a well-structured classroom, individualized teaching, and small-group instruction. As with children who are mentally retarded, behavior modification techniques are sometimes effective in helping autistic children learn (Hall, 2009).

Increasingly, children with disabilities are being taught in the regular classroom, as is this child with mild mental retardation.

EDUCATIONAL ISSUES

The legal requirement that schools serve all children with a disability is fairly recent. Beginning in the mid-1960s and into the mid-1970s, legislators, the federal courts, and the U.S. Congress laid down special educational rights for children with disabilities. Prior to that time, most children with a disability were either refused enrollment or inadequately served by schools. In 1975, **Public Law 94-142,** the Education for All Handicapped Children Act, required that all students with disabilities be given a free, appropriate public education and be provided the funding to help implement this education.

In 1990, Public Law 94-142 was recast as the **Individuals with Disabilities Education Act (IDEA).** IDEA was amended in 1997 and then reauthorized in 2004 and renamed the Individuals with Disabilities Education Improvement Act. IDEA spells out broad mandates for providing services to all children with disabilities (Friend, 2011). These include evaluation and eligibility determination, appropriate education and an individualized education plan (IEP), and education in the least restrictive environment (LRE) (Yudof & others, 2012).

A major aspect of the 2004 reauthorization of IDEA involved aligning it with the government's No Child Left Behind (NCLB) legislation, which was designed to improve the educational achievement of all students, including those with disabilities. Both IDEA and NCLB mandate that most students with disabilities be included in general assessments of educational progress. This alignment includes requiring most students with disabilities "to take standard tests of academic achievement and to achieve at a level equal to that of students without disabilities. Whether this expectation is reasonable is an open question" (Hallahan & Kauffman, 2006, pp. 28–29). Alternate assessments for students with disabilities and funding to help states improve instruction, assessment, and accountability for educating students with disabilities are included in the 2004 reauthorization of IDEA.

Evaluation and Eligibility Determination Children who are thought to have a disability are evaluated to determine their eligibility for services under IDEA. Schools are prohibited from planning special education programs in advance and offering them on a space-available basis.

Children must be evaluated before a school can begin providing special services (Hardman, Drew, & Egan, 2011). Parents should be involved in the evaluation process. Reevaluation is required at least every three years (sometimes every year), when requested by parents, or when conditions suggest that a reevaluation is needed. A parent who disagrees with the school's evaluation can obtain an independent evaluation, which the school is required to consider in providing special education services. If the evaluation finds that the child has a disability and requires special services, the school must provide them to the child.

The IDEA has many specific provisions involving the parents of a child with a disability. These include requirements that schools send notices to parents of proposed actions, of attendance at meetings regarding the child's placement or

autism spectrum disorders (ASDs) Also called pervasive developmental disorders, this category ranges from the severe disorder labeled autistic disorder to the milder disorder called Asperger syndrome. Children with these disorders are characterized by problems with social interaction, verbal and nonverbal communication, and repetitive behaviors.

autistic disorder A severe autism spectrum disorder that has its onset in the first three years of life and includes deficiencies in social relationships, abnormalities in communication, and restricted, repetitive, and stereotyped patterns of behavior.

Asperger syndrome A relatively mild autism spectrum disorder in which the child has relatively good verbal language skills, milder nonverbal language problems, and a restricted range of interests and relationships.

Public Law 94-142 The Education for All Handicapped Children Act, created in 1975, which requires that all children with disabilities be given a free, appropriate public education and which provides the funding to help with the costs of implementing this education.

Individuals with Disabilities Education Act (IDEA) The IDEA spells out broad mandates for providing services to all children with disabilities (IDEA is a renaming of Public Law 94-142); these include evaluation and eligibility determination, appropriate education and an individualized education plan (IEP), and education in the least restrictive environment (LRE).

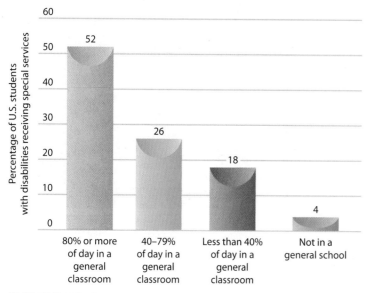

FIGURE 11.8

PERCENTAGE OF U.S. STUDENTS WITH DISABILITIES 6 TO 21 YEARS OF AGE RECEIVING SPECIAL SERVICES IN THE GENERAL CLASSROOM. *Note:* Data for 2004–2005 school year; National Center for Education Statistics (2007).

individualized education plan (IEP) A written statement that spells out a program tailored to a child with a disability. The plan should be (1) related to the child's learning capacity, (2) specially constructed to meet the child's individual needs and not merely a copy of what is offered to other children, and (3) designed to provide educational benefits.

least restrictive environment (LRE) The concept that a child with a disability must be educated in a setting that is as similar as possible to the one in which children who do not have a disability are educated.

inclusion Educating a child with special educational needs full-time in the regular classroom.

individualized education plan, and of the right to appeal school decisions to an impartial evaluator.

Appropriate Education and the Individualized Education Plan (IEP)
The IDEA requires that students with disabilities have an **individualized education plan (IEP),** a written statement that spells out a program tailored specifically for the student with a disability. In general, the IEP should be (1) related to the child's learning capacity, (2) specially constructed to meet the child's individual needs and not merely a copy of what is offered to other children, and (3) designed to provide educational benefits.

Amendments were made to the IDEA in 1997. Two of these involve positive behavioral support and functional behavioral assessment (U.S. Office of Education, 2000). *Positive behavioral support* focuses on culturally appropriate interventions to attain important behavioral changes in children. *Functional behavioral assessment* involves determining the consequences (what purpose the behavior serves), antecedents (what triggers the behavior), and setting events (in which contexts the behavior occurs).

Under IDEA, the child with a disability must be educated in the **least restrictive environment (LRE),** a setting as similar as possible to the one in which children who do not have a disability are educated. And schools must make an effort to educate children with a disability in the regular classroom. The term **inclusion** means educating a child with special educational needs full-time in the regular classroom (Boyle & Provost, 2012; Friend & Bursuck, 2012). Figure 11.8 indicates that for the 2004–2005 school year, slightly more than 50 percent of U.S. students with a disability spent more than 80 percent of their school day in a general classroom.

Not long ago, it was considered appropriate to educate children with disabilities outside the regular classroom. However, today, schools must make every effort to provide inclusion for children with disabilities (Smith & others, 2012). These efforts can be very costly financially and very time consuming in terms of faculty effort.

The principle of least restrictive environment compels schools to examine possible modifications of the regular classroom before moving the child with a disability to a more restrictive placement. Also, regular classroom teachers often need specialized training to help some children with a disability, and state educational agencies are required to provide such training.

Many of the legal changes regarding children with disabilities have been extremely positive. Compared with several decades ago, far more children today are receiving competent, specialized services. For many children, inclusion in the regular classroom, with modifications or supplemental services, is appropriate (Friend & Bursuck, 2012). However, some leading experts on special education argue that the effort to use inclusion to educate children with disabilities has become too extreme in some cases. For example, James Kauffman and his colleagues (Kauffman & Hallahan, 2005; Kauffman, McGee, & Brigham, 2004) state that inclusion too often has meant making accommodations in the regular classroom that do not always benefit children with disabilities. They advocate a more individualized approach that does not always involve full inclusion but provides options such as special education outside the regular classroom. Kauffman and his colleagues (2004, p. 620) acknowledge that children with disabilities "*do* need the services of specially trained professionals to achieve their full potential. They *do* sometimes need altered curricula or adaptations to make their learning possible." However, "we sell students with disabilities short when we pretend that they are not different from typical students. We make the same error when we pretend that they must not be expected to put forth extra effort if they are to learn to do

Disproportionate Representation of Minority Students in Special Education

The U.S. Office of Education (2000) has three concerns about the over-representation of minority students in special education programs and classes:

- Students may be unserved or receive services that do not meet their needs.
- Students may be misclassified or inappropriately labeled.
- Placement in special education classes may be a form of discrimination.

African American students are overrepresented in special education—15 percent of the U.S. student population is African American, but 20 percent of special education students are African American. In some disabilities, the discrepancies are even greater. For example, African American students represent 32 percent of the students in programs for mild mental retardation, 29 percent in programs for moderate mental retardation, and 24 percent in programs for serious emotional disturbance.

However, it is not just a simple matter of overrepresentation of certain minority groups in special education. Latino children may be underidentified in the categories of mental retardation and emotional disturbance.

More appropriate inclusion of minority students in special education is a complex problem and requires the creation of a successful school experience for all students. Recommendations for reducing disproportionate representation in special education include the following (Burnette, 1998):

- Reviewing school practices to identify and address factors that might contribute to having school difficulties
- Forming policy-making groups that include community members and promote partnerships with service agencies and cultural organizations
- Helping families get social, medical, mental health, and other support services
- Training more teachers from minority backgrounds and providing all teachers with more extensive course work and training in educating children with disabilities and in understanding diversity issues

some things—or learn to do something in a different way." Like general education, an important aspect of special education should be to challenge students with disabilities "to become all they can be."

One concern about special education involves disproportionate representation of students from minority backgrounds in special education programs and classes (Jarquin & others, 2011). The *Connecting with Diversity* interlude addresses this issue.

Review *Connect* Reflect

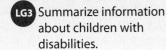 Summarize information about children with disabilities.

Review

- Who are children with disabilities?
- What are some characteristics of the range of children's disabilities?
- What are some important issues in the education of children with disabilities?

Connect

- In Chapters 6 and 9, you learned about the development of attention in infancy and early childhood. How might ADHD be linked to earlier attention difficulties during infancy and early childhood?

Reflect *Your Own Personal Journey of Life*

- Think back to your own schooling and how students with learning disabilities were or were not diagnosed. Were you aware of such individuals in your classes? Were they given special attention by teachers and/or specialists? You may know one or more individuals with a learning disability. Interview them about their school experiences. Ask them what they think could have been done better to help them with their disability.

This chapter introduced you to the physical and brain changes of middle and late childhood. In Chapter 14, you will read about how the slow physical growth of middle and late childhood gives way to the dramatic changes of puberty in early adolescence. Significant changes also occur in the adolescent's brain, and such changes may be linked to an increase in risk taking and sensation seeking. In Chapter 12, you will explore cognitive development in middle and late childhood, including Piaget's theory and a number of changes in children's information processing. You'll also read about some important processes that influence children's achievement and changes in language development in older children, including reading skills.

looking **forward**

reach your **learning goals**

What Changes Take Place in Body Growth, the Brain, and Motor Development?

 Discuss changes in body growth, the brain, and motor development in middle and late childhood.

Skeletal and Muscular Systems

The Brain

Motor Development

- The period of middle and late childhood involves slow, consistent growth. During this period, children grow an average of 2 to 3 inches a year. Muscle mass and strength gradually increase. Among the most pronounced changes are decreases in head circumference, waist circumference, and leg length in relation to body height.

- Changes in the brain continue to occur in middle and late childhood, and these changes, such as increased myelination, are linked to improvements in cognitive functioning. In particular, there is an increase in pathways involving the prefrontal cortex—changes that are related to improved attention, reasoning, and cognitive control. During middle and late childhood, less diffusion and more focal activation occur in the prefrontal cortex, changes that are associated with an increase in cognitive control.

- During the middle and late childhood years, motor development becomes much smoother and more coordinated. Children gain greater control over their bodies and can sit and attend for longer periods of time. However, their lives should be filled with physical activity. Gross motor skills are expanded, and children refine such skills as hitting a tennis ball, skipping rope, or balancing on a beam. Increased myelination of the nervous system is reflected in improved fine motor skills, such as developing improved handwriting and playing a difficult piece on a musical instrument. Boys are usually better at gross motor skills, girls at fine motor skills.

What Are the Central Issues in Children's Health?

 Characterize children's health in middle and late childhood.

Nutrition

- During the middle and late childhood years, weight doubles and considerable energy is expended in motor activities. To support their growth, children need to consume more calories than they did when they were younger. A balanced diet is important. A special concern is that too many children fill up on "empty-calorie" foods that are high in sugar, starch, and excess fat. A nutritious breakfast promotes higher energy and better alertness in school.

Exercise and Sports

- Every indication suggests that children in the United States are not getting enough exercise. Television viewing, parents who are poor role models for exercise, and inadequate physical education classes in schools are among the culprits. Children's participation in sports can have positive or negative consequences, however.

Overweight Children

- Although the increase of child obesity in the United States has begun to level off, over the last four decades the percentage of U.S. children who are overweight has tripled. An increasing number of children in many countries, such as mainland China and Australia, are overweight. Being overweight in middle and late childhood substantially increases the risk of being overweight in adolescence and adulthood. Factors linked with being overweight in childhood include heredity and environmental contexts. Being overweight in childhood is related to a number of problems. Diet, exercise, and behavior modification are recommended in helping children to lose weight.

Diseases

- Cancer is the second leading cause of death in children (after accidents). Childhood cancers have a different profile from that of adult cancers. Diabetes is also a common disease in childhood. Cardiovascular disease is uncommon in children, but the precursors to adult cardiovascular disease are often already apparent in children. Asthma is the most common chronic disease in U.S. children.

Accidents and Injuries

- The most common cause of severe injury and death in childhood is motor vehicle accidents.

What Are the Prevalent Disabilities in Children? Summarize information about children with disabilities.

Who Are Children with Disabilities?

- Approximately 14 percent of children from 3 to 21 years of age in the United States receive special education or related services. Students with a learning disability are by far the largest group of students with a disability who receive special education. Substantial percentages also include children with speech or language impairments, mental retardation, and emotional disturbance. The term "children with disabilities" is now recommended rather than "handicapped children." This terminology is intended to focus more on the child than on the disability.

The Range of Disabilities

- Children's disabilities cover a wide range and include learning disabilities, ADHD, speech disorders, sensory disorders, physical disorders, emotional and behavioral disorders, and autism spectrum disorders. A child with a learning disability has difficulty in learning that involves understanding or using spoken or written language, and the difficulty can appear in listening, thinking, reading, writing, and spelling. A learning disability also may involve difficulty in doing mathematics. To be classified as a learning disability, the learning problem is not primarily the result of visual, hearing, or motor disabilities; mental retardation; emotional disorders; or due to environmental, cultural, or economic disadvantage.

  Diagnosing whether a child has a learning disability is difficult. About three times as many boys as girls have a learning disability. The most common academic problem for children with a learning disability is difficulty reading. Dyslexia is a severe impairment in the ability to read and spell. Dysgraphia is a learning disability that involves having difficulty in handwriting. Dyscalculia is a learning disability that involves difficulties in math computation. Controversy surrounds the "learning disability" category. Many interventions targeted for learning disabilities focus on improving the child's reading ability and include such strategies as improving decoding skills.

Attention deficit hyperactivity disorder (ADHD) is a disability in which children consistently show problems in one or more of the following areas: inattention, hyperactivity, and impulsivity. For an ADHD diagnosis, the characteristics must appear early in childhood and be debilitating for the child. Although signs of ADHD may be present in early childhood, diagnosis of ADHD often doesn't occur until the elementary school years. Many experts recommend a combination of academic, behavioral, and medical interventions to help students with ADHD learn and adapt.

Speech disorders include articulation disorders, voice disorders, and fluency disorders. Sensory disorders include visual and hearing impairments. Physical disorders that children may have include orthopedic impairments and cerebral palsy. Emotional and behavioral disorders consist of serious, persistent problems that involve relationships, aggression, depression, fears associated with personal or school matters, as well as other inappropriate socioemotional characteristics.

Autistic disorder is a severe developmental autism spectrum disorder with an onset in the first three years of life, and it involves abnormalities in social relationships and communication. It also is characterized by repetitive behaviors. The current consensus is that autism spectrum disorders involve an organic brain dysfunction. Autism spectrum disorders (ASDs) range from autistic disorder to the milder Asperger syndrome.

Educational Issues

- Beginning in the 1960s and 1970s, the educational rights of children with disabilities were laid down. In 1975, Public Law 94-142 required all children to be given a free, appropriate public education. In 1990, Public Law 94-142 was renamed and called the Individuals with Disabilities Education Act (IDEA). Children who are thought to have a disability are evaluated to determine their eligibility for services. An individualized education plan (IEP) is a written plan that spells out a program tailored to the needs of a child with a disability. The concept of a least restrictive environment (LRE) is contained in the IDEA. The term *inclusion* means educating children with disabilities full-time in the general classroom. The trend is toward greater use of inclusion.

key terms

type 1 diabetes 334	articulation disorders 341	emotional and behavioral disorders 343	individualized education plan (IEP) 346
type 2 diabetes 334	voice disorders 341	autism spectrum disorders (ASDs) 344	least restrictive environment (LRE) 346
asthma 334	fluency disorders 341		
learning disability 338	low vision 342	autistic disorder 344	inclusion 346
dyslexia 339	educationally blind 342	Asperger syndrome 344	
dysgraphia 339	oral approaches 343	Public Law 94-142 345	
dyscalculia 339	manual approaches 343	Individuals with Disabilities Education Act (IDEA) 345	
attention deficit hyperactivity disorder (ADHD) 339	orthopedic impairments 343		
	cerebral palsy 343		

key people

Mark Johnson 327	Simon Baron-Cohen 344	James Kauffman 346

connecting with improving the lives of children

MAKING A DIFFERENCE

Nurturing Children's Physical Development and Health

What are some good strategies for supporting children's physical development and health in the middle and late childhood years?

- *Elementary school children should be physically active whenever possible.* Goals should especially include reducing TV watching and increasing participation in such activities as swimming, skating, and bicycling.
- *Parents should monitor children's eating behavior.* Children need more calories now than they did when they were younger. However, a special concern is the increasing number of obese children. Children who are overweight need to have a medical checkup, to revise their diet, and to participate in a regular exercise program.
- *Elementary schools need to develop more and better physical education programs.* Only about one of every three elementary school children participates in a physical education program daily. Many of those who do aren't exercising much during the program.
- *Parents need to engage in physical activities that they can enjoy together with their children.* Suggested activities include running, bicycling, hiking, and swimming.
- *Parents should try to make their children's experiences in sports positive ones.* They should stress the benefits of sports rather than displaying a win-at-all-costs philosophy.

- *Parents should help children avoid accidents and injuries.* They should educate their children about the hazards of risk taking and the improper use of equipment.

RESOURCES

Children's HeartLink
www.childrensheartlink.org

This organization provides treatment for needy children with heart disease and support for rheumatic fever prevention programs. It also supports the education of foreign medical professionals and provides technical advice and medical equipment and supplies.

The Council for Exceptional Children (CEC)
www.cec.sped.org

The CEC maintains an information center on the education of children and adolescents with disabilities and publishes materials on a wide variety of topics.

Learning Disabilities Association of America (LDA)
www.ldaamerica.org

The LDA provides education and support for parents of children with learning disabilities, interested professionals, and others. More than 500 chapters are in operation nationwide, offering information services, pamphlets, and book recommendations.

chapter 12 COGNITIVE DEVELOPMENT IN MIDDLE AND LATE CHILDHOOD

On the first day of school, Chicago teacher Marva Collins tells her students, many of whom are repeating the second grade,

"I know most of you can't spell your name. You don't know the alphabet, you don't know how to read. . . . I promise you that you will. None of you has ever failed. School may have failed you. Well, goodbye to failure, children. Welcome to success. You will read hard books in here and understand what you read. You will write every day. . . . But you must help me to help you. If you don't give anything, don't expect anything. Success is not coming to you, you must come to it." (Dweck, 2006, pp. 188–189)

Her second-grade students usually have to start off with the lowest level of reader available, but by the end of the school year most of the students are reading at the fifth-grade level.

Collins takes inner-city children living in low-income, often poverty-level, circumstances, and challenges them to be all they can be. She won't accept failure by her students and teaches students to be responsible for their behavior every day of their lives. Collins tells students that being excellent at something is not a one-time thing but a habit, that determination and persistence are what move the world, and that thinking others will make you successful is a sure way to fail.

Marva Collins, challenging a child to achieve.

topical connections

In the last chapter, you studied the physical changes that characterize development in middle and late childhood, including the substantial advances in the development of the brain. In Chapter 9, you read that early childhood is a period in which young children increasingly engage in symbolic thought. Young children's information-processing skills also improve considerably—executive and sustained attention advance, short-term memory gets better, and their understanding of the human mind makes considerable progress. Young children also increase their knowledge of language's rule systems and their literacy benefits from active participation in a wide range of language experiences. Most young children attend an early childhood education program, and there are many variations in these programs. In this chapter, you will study a number of advances in children's cognitive development during the elementary school years.

◀ – *looking back*

preview

We just saw that challenging children to succeed who had been taught to fail is an important theme of Marva Collins' teaching. Later in the chapter, we explore many aspects of achievement. First, we will examine three main aspects of cognitive changes—the concrete operational stage of Piaget's cognitive developmental theory, information processing, and intelligence—that characterize middle and late childhood. Then, we will look at language changes and explore children's achievement.

What Is Piaget's Theory of Cognitive Development in Middle and Late Childhood?

LG1 Discuss Piaget's stage of concrete operational thought and apply Piaget's theory to education.

Concrete Operational Thought

Evaluating Piaget's Concrete Operational Stage

Applications to Education

According to Piaget (1952), the preschool child's thought is preoperational. Preschool children can form stable concepts, and they have begun to reason, but their thinking is flawed by egocentrism and magical belief systems. As we discussed in Chapter 9, "Cognitive Development in Early Childhood," however, Piaget may have underestimated the cognitive skills of preschool children. Some researchers argue that under the right conditions, young children may display abilities that are characteristic of Piaget's next stage of cognitive development, the stage of concrete operational thought (Gelman, 1969). Here we cover the characteristics of concrete operational thought, an evaluation of Piaget's portrait of this stage, and applications of Piaget's ideas to education.

CONCRETE OPERATIONAL THOUGHT

developmental **connection**

Cognitive Processes. Centration, a centering of attention on one characteristic to the exclusion of others, is present in young children's lack of conservation. Chapter 9, p. 262

Piaget proposed that the *concrete operational stage* lasts from approximately 7 to 11 years of age. In this stage, children can perform concrete operations, and they can reason logically as long as they can apply their reasoning to specific or concrete examples. Remember that *operations* are mental actions that are reversible, and *concrete operations* are operations that are applied to real, concrete objects.

The conservation tasks described in Chapter 9, "Cognitive Development in Early Childhood," indicate whether children are capable of concrete operations. For example, recall that in one task involving conservation of matter, the child is presented with two identical balls of clay. The experimenter rolls one ball into a long, thin shape; the other remains in its original ball shape. The child is then asked if there is more clay in the ball or in the long, thin piece of clay. By the time children reach the age of 7 or 8, most answer that the amount of clay is the same. To answer this problem correctly, children have to imagine rolling the elongated clay back into a ball. This type of imagination involves a reversible mental action applied to a real, concrete object. Concrete operations allow the child to consider several characteristics rather than to focus on a single property of an object. In the clay example, the preoperational child is likely to focus on height or width. The concrete operational child coordinates information about both dimensions.

seriation The concrete operation that involves ordering stimuli along a quantitative dimension (such as length).

transitivity The ability to logically combine relations to understand certain conclusions.

neo-Piagetians Developmentalists who have elaborated on Piaget's theory, giving more emphasis to information processing, strategies, and precise cognitive steps.

What other abilities are characteristic of children who have reached the concrete operational stage? One important skill is the ability to classify or divide things into different sets or subsets and to consider their interrelationships. Consider the family tree of four generations that is shown in Figure 12.1 (Furth & Wachs, 1975). This family tree suggests that the grandfather (A) has three children (B, C, and D), each of whom has two children (E through J), and that one of these children (J) has three children (K, L, and M). A child who comprehends the classification system can move up and down a level, across a level, and up and down and across within the system. The concrete operational child understands that person J can at the same time be father, brother, and grandson, for example.

Children who have reached the concrete operational stage are also capable of **seriation,** which is the ability to order stimuli along a quantitative dimension (such as length). To see if students can serialize, a teacher might haphazardly place eight sticks of different lengths on a table. The teacher then asks the students to order the sticks by length. Many young children end up with two or three small groups of "big" sticks or "little" sticks, rather than a correct ordering of all eight sticks. Another mistaken strategy they use is to evenly line up the tops of the sticks but ignore the bottoms. The concrete operational thinker simultaneously understands that each stick must be longer than the one that precedes it and shorter than the one that follows it.

Another aspect of reasoning about the relations between classes is **transitivity,** which is the ability to logically combine relations to understand certain conclusions. In this case, consider three sticks (A, B, and C) of differing lengths. A is the longest, B is intermediate in length, and C is the shortest. Does the child understand that if A is longer than B and B is longer than C, then A is longer than C? In Piaget's theory, concrete operational thinkers do; preoperational thinkers do not.

EVALUATING PIAGET'S CONCRETE OPERATIONAL STAGE

Has Piaget's portrait of the concrete operational child stood the test of research? According to Piaget, various aspects of a stage should emerge at the same time. In fact, however, some concrete operational abilities do not appear in synchrony. For example, children do not learn to conserve at the same time they learn to cross-classify.

Furthermore, education and culture exert stronger influences on children's development than Piaget maintained (Cole & Packer, 2011). Some preoperational children can be trained to reason at a concrete operational stage. And the age at which children acquire conservation skills is related to how much practice their culture provides in these skills. Among Wolof children in the West African nation of Senegal, for example, only 50 percent of the 10- to 13-year-olds understood the principle of conservation (Greenfield, 1966). Comparable studies among cultures in central Australia, New Guinea (an island north of Australia), the Amazon jungle region of Brazil, and rural Sardinia (an island off the coast of Italy) yielded similar results (Dasen, 1977).

Thus, although Piaget was a giant in the field of developmental psychology, his conclusions about the concrete operational stage have been challenged. In Chapter 15, "Cognitive Development in Adolescence," after examining the final stage in his theory of cognitive development, we evaluate Piaget's contributions and discuss the criticisms of his theory.

Neo-Piagetians argue that Piaget got some things right but that his theory needs considerable revision. They place greater emphasis on how children use attention, memory, and strategies to process information (Case & Mueller, 2001; Morra & others, 2007). According to neo-Piagetians, a more accurate portrayal of children's thinking requires

FIGURE **12.1**

CLASSIFICATION: AN IMPORTANT ABILITY IN CONCRETE OPERATIONAL THOUGHT. A family tree of four generations (*I to IV*): The preoperational child has trouble classifying the members of the four generations; the concrete operational child can classify the members vertically, horizontally, and obliquely (up and down and across). For example, the concrete operational child understands that a family member can be a son, a brother, and a father, all at the same time.

An outstanding teacher and education in the logic of science and mathematics are important cultural experiences that promote the development of operational thought. *Might Piaget have underestimated the roles of culture and schooling in children's cognitive development?*

attention to children's strategies, the speed at which children process information, the particular task involved, and the division of problems into smaller, more precise steps. These are issues addressed by the information-processing approach, and we discuss some of them later in this chapter.

Another alternative to concrete operational thought comes from Vygotsky. As we discussed in Chapter 9, "Cognitive Development in Early Childhood," Vygotsky, like Piaget, held that children construct their knowledge of the world. But Vygotsky did not propose stages of cognitive development, and he emphasized the importance of social interaction, the social contexts of learning, and the young child's use of language to plan, guide, and monitor behavior (Daniels, 2011).

APPLICATIONS TO EDUCATION

Although Piaget was not an educator, he provided a sound conceptual framework for viewing learning and education. Following are some ideas in Piaget's theory that can be applied to teaching children (Elkind, 1976; Heuwinkel, 1996):

The thirst to know and
understand . . .
These are the goods in life's rich hand.

—Sir William Watson
British Poet, 20th Century

1. *Take a constructivist approach.* Piaget emphasized that children learn best when they are active and seek solutions for themselves. Piaget opposed teaching methods that treat children as passive receptacles. The educational implication of Piaget's view is that, in all subjects, students learn best by making discoveries, reflecting on them, and discussing them, rather than by blindly imitating the teacher or doing things by rote.

2. *Facilitate rather than direct learning.* Effective teachers design situations that allow students to learn by doing. These situations promote students' thinking and discovery. Teachers listen, watch, and question students, to help them gain better understanding.

3. *Consider the child's knowledge and level of thinking.* Students do not come to class with empty minds. They have concepts of space, time, quantity, and causality. These ideas differ from the ideas of adults. Teachers need to interpret what a student is saying and respond in a way that is not too far from the student's level. Also, Piaget suggested that it is important to examine children's mistakes in thinking, not just what they get correct, to help guide them to a higher level of understanding.

4. *Promote the student's intellectual health.* When Piaget came to lecture in the United States, he was asked, "What can I do to get my child to a higher cognitive stage sooner?" He was asked this question so often here compared with other countries that he called it the American question. For Piaget, children's learning should occur naturally. Children should not be pushed and pressured into achieving too much too early in their development, before they are maturationally ready. Some parents spend long hours every day holding up large flash cards with words on them to improve their baby's vocabulary. In the Piagetian view, this is not the best way for infants to learn. It places too much emphasis on speeding up intellectual development, involves passive learning, and will not lead to positive outcomes.

What are some educational strategies that can be derived from Piaget's theory?

long-term memory A relatively permanent type of memory that holds huge amounts of information for a long period of time.

working memory A mental "workbench" where individuals manipulate and assemble information when making decisions, solving problems, and comprehending written and spoken language.

5. *Turn the classroom into a setting of exploration and discovery.* What do actual classrooms look like when the teachers adopt Piaget's views? Several first- and second-grade math classrooms provide some good examples (Kamii, 1985, 1989). The teachers emphasize students' own exploration and discovery. The classrooms are less structured than what we think of as a typical classroom. Workbooks and predetermined assignments are not used. Rather, the teachers observe the students' interests and natural participation in activities to determine what the course of learning will be. For example, a math lesson might be constructed around counting the day's lunch money or dividing supplies among students. Games are often used in the classroom to stimulate mathematical thinking.

Review Connect Reflect

 Discuss Piaget's stage of concrete operational thought, and apply Piaget's theory to education.

Review

- How can concrete operational thought be characterized?
- How can Piaget's concrete operational stage be evaluated?
- How can Piaget's theory be applied to education?

Connect

- How is the application of Piaget's theory to children's education similar to or different from the application of Vygotsky's theory to their education (see Chapter 9)?

Reflect *Your Own Personal Journey of Life*

- Imagine that you are an elementary school teacher. Based on Piaget's theory, in what important ways is your thinking likely to differ from that of the children in your classroom? What adjustments in thinking might you need to make when you communicate with the children?

What Is the Nature of Children's Information Processing?

 Describe changes in information processing in middle and late childhood.

Memory   Thinking   Metacognition

During middle and late childhood, most children dramatically improve their ability to sustain and control attention. As we discussed in Chapter 9, "Cognitive Development in Early Childhood," they pay more attention to task-relevant stimuli such as teacher instructions than to salient stimuli such as the colors in the teacher's attire. Other changes in information processing during middle and late childhood involve memory, thinking, and metacognition. In the following pages, we examine each of these areas.

MEMORY

In Chapter 9, "Cognitive Development in Early Childhood," we concluded that short-term memory increases considerably during early childhood but after the age of 7 does not show as great an increase. **Long-term memory,** a relatively permanent and unlimited type of memory, increases with age during middle and late childhood. In part, improvements in memory reflect children's increased knowledge and their increased use of strategies to retain information (Bjorklund, 2012).

Working Memory   Short-term memory is like a passive storehouse with shelves to store information until it is moved to long-term memory. Alan Baddeley (2007, 2010a, b, 2012) defines **working memory** as a kind of mental "workbench" where individuals manipulate and assemble information when they make decisions, solve problems, and comprehend written and spoken language (see Figure 12.2). Working memory is described as more active and powerful in modifying information than short-term memory.

Note in Figure 12.2 that a key component of working memory is the *central executive*, which supervises and controls the flow of information. The central executive focuses on selective attention and inhibition, planning and decision making, and trouble shooting.

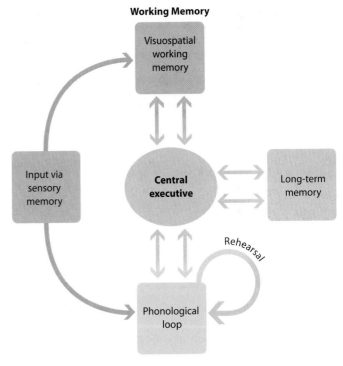

FIGURE **12.2**

WORKING MEMORY. In Baddeley's working memory model, working memory is like a mental workbench where a great deal of information processing is carried out. Working memory consists of three main components: the phonological loop and visuospatial working memory serve as assistants, helping the central executive do its work. Input from sensory memory goes to the phonological loop, where information about speech is stored and rehearsal takes place, and visuospatial working memory, where visual and spatial information, including imagery, are stored. Working memory is a limited-capacity system, and information is stored there for only a brief time. Working memory interacts with long-term memory, using information from long-term memory in its work and transmitting information to long-term memory for longer storage.

Recall from Chapter 9 our description of *executive functioning* as an umbrella-like concept that comprises a number of higher-level cognitive processes. One of those cognitive processes is working memory, especially its central executive dimension.

Working memory is linked to many aspects of children's development (Baddeley, 2010a, b, 2012; Towse & others, 2010). The following three recent studies illustrate the importance of working memory in children's cognitive and language development:

developmental **connection**

Cognitive Processes. In early childhood, executive functioning especially involves advances in cognitive inhibition, cognitive flexibility, and goal setting. Chapter 9, p. 271

- Working memory and attention control predicted growth in emergent literacy and number skills in young children in low-income families (Welsh & others, 2010).
- Working memory capacity at 9 to 10 years of age predicted foreign-language comprehension two years later at 11 to 12 years of age (Andersson, 2010).
- Working memory capacity predicted how many items on a to-be-remembered list that fourth-grade children forgot (Asian, Zellner, & Bauml, 2010).

Knowledge and Expertise Much of the research on the role of knowledge in memory has compared experts and novices (Ericsson & others, 2006). *Experts* have acquired extensive knowledge about a particular content area; this knowledge influences what they notice and how they organize, represent, and interpret information. These skills in turn affect their ability to remember, reason, and solve problems. When individuals have expertise about a particular subject, their memory also tends to be good regarding material related to that subject.

For example, one study found that 10- and 11-year-olds who were experienced chess players ("experts") were able to remember more information about the location of chess pieces than college students who were not chess players ("novices") (Chi, 1978) (see Figure 12.3). In contrast, when the college students were presented with other stimuli, they were able to remember them better than the children were. Thus, the children's expertise in chess gave them superior memories, but only for items involving chess.

There are developmental changes in expertise. Older children usually have more expertise about a subject than younger children do, which can contribute to their better memory for the subject.

Strategies If we know anything at all about long-term memory, it is that long-term memory depends on the learning activities individuals engage in when learning and remembering information (Block & Pressley, 2007). A key learning activity involves the use of **strategies,** which consist of deliberate mental activities to improve the processing of information. For example, organizing is a strategy that older children, adolescents, and adults use to remember information more effectively. Strategies do not occur automatically; they require effort and work. Strategies, which are also called *control processes,* are under the learner's conscious control and can be used to improve memory. Two important strategies are creating mental images and elaborating on information (Murray, 2007).

Elaboration is an important strategy that involves engaging in more extensive processing of information. When individuals engage in elaboration, their memory benefits (Schneider, 2011). Thinking of examples and referencing one's self are good ways to elaborate information. Thinking about personal associations with information makes the information more meaningful and helps children to remember it. For example, if the word *win* is on a list of words a child is asked to remember, the child might think of the last time he won a bicycle race with a friend.

Fuzzy Trace Theory Might something other than knowledge and strategies be responsible for improvement in memory during the elementary school years?

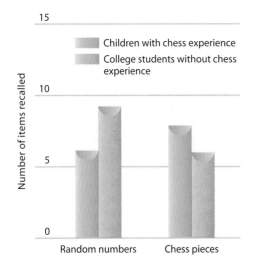

FIGURE 12.3

THE ROLE OF EXPERTISE IN MEMORY. Notice that when 10- to 11-year-old children and college students were asked to remember a string of random numbers that had been presented to them, the college students fared better. However, the 10- to 11-year-olds who had experience playing chess ("experts") had better memory for the location of chess pieces on a chess board than college students with no chess experience ("novices") (Chi, 1978).

strategies Deliberate mental activities designed to improve the processing of information.

elaboration An important strategy that involves engaging in more extensive processing of information.

Charles Brainerd and Valerie Reyna (1993; Reyna, 2004; Reyna & Brainerd, 1995) argue that *fuzzy traces* account for much of this improvement. Their **fuzzy trace theory** states that memory is best understood by considering two types of memory representations: (1) verbatim memory trace and (2) gist. The *verbatim memory trace* consists of the precise details of the information, whereas *gist* refers to the central idea of the information. When gist is used, fuzzy traces are built up. Although individuals of all ages extract gist, young children tend to store and retrieve verbatim traces. At some point during the early elementary school years, children begin to use gist more and, according to the theory, its use contributes to the improved memory and reasoning of older children because fuzzy traces are more enduring and less likely to be forgotten than verbatim traces.

Improving Children's Memory   Some strategies adults can adopt when guiding children to remember information more effectively over the long term include assisting them to organize information, elaborate the information, and develop images of the information. Another good strategy is to encourage children to understand the material that needs to be remembered rather than rotely memorizing it. Two additional strategies adults can use to guide children's retention of memory were recently proposed:

- *Repeat with variation on the instructional information and link early and often.* These are memory development research expert Patricia Bauer's (2009) recommendations to improve children's consolidation and reconsolidation of the information they are learning. Variations on a lesson theme increase the number of associations in memory storage, and linking expands the network of associations in memory storage; both strategies expand the routes for retrieving information from storage.

- *Embed memory-relevant language when instructing children.* Teachers vary considerably in how much they use memory-relevant language that encourages students to remember information. In recent research that involved extensive observations of a number of first-grade teachers in the classroom, Peter Ornstein and his colleagues (Ornstein, Grammer, & Coffman, 2010; Ornstein, Coffman, & Grammer, 2007; Ornstein & others, 2010) found that in the time segments observed, the teachers rarely used strategy suggestions or metacognitive (thinking about thinking) questions. In this research, when lower-achieving students were placed in classrooms in which teachers were categorized as "high-mnemonic teachers" who frequently embedded memory-relevant information in their teaching, their achievement increased (Ornstein & others, 2007).

THINKING

Three important aspects of thinking are being able to think critically, creatively, and scientifically.

Critical Thinking   Currently, there is considerable interest in critical thinking among psychologists and educators (Bonney & Sternberg, 2011; Fairweather & Cramond, 2011; Magno, 2010). **Critical thinking** involves thinking reflectively and productively, as well as evaluating evidence. In this book, the second and third parts of the Connect and Reflect questions at the end of each section challenge you to think critically about a topic or an issue related to the discussion.

According to Ellen Langer (2005), **mindfulness**—being alert, mentally present, and cognitively flexible while going through life's everyday activities and tasks—is an important aspect of thinking critically. Mindful children and adults maintain an active awareness of the circumstances in their life and are motivated to find the best solutions to tasks. Mindful individuals create new ideas, are open to new information, and operate from a single perspective. By contrast, mindless individuals are

> I think, therefore I am.
>
> —RENÉ DESCARTES
> *French Philosopher and Mathematician, 17th Century*

fuzzy trace theory A theory stating that memory is best understood by considering two types of memory representations: (1) verbatim memory trace and (2) gist. In this theory, older children's better memory is attributed to the fuzzy traces created by extracting the gist of information.

critical thinking The ability to think reflectively and productively, as well as to evaluate the evidence.

mindfulness Being alert, mentally present, and cognitively flexible while going through life's everyday activities and tasks.

"For God's sake, think! Why is he being so nice to you?"
© Sam Gross/The New Yorker Collection/www.cartoonbank.
com

developmental **connection**

Education. A criticism of the No Child Left Behind legislation is that it does not give adequate attention to critical thinking skills. Chapter 13, p. 414

How Would You...?

If you were a **psychologist,** how would you talk with teachers and parents about ways to improve children's creative thinking?

creative thinking The ability to think in novel and unusual ways and to come up with unique solutions to problems.

convergent thinking Thinking that produces one correct answer and is characteristic of the kind of thinking tested by standardized intelligence tests.

divergent thinking Thinking that produces many different answers to the same question and is characteristic of creativity.

entrapped in old ideas, engage in automatic behavior, and operate from a single perspective.

Jacqueline and Martin Brooks (2001) lament that few schools really teach students to think critically and develop a deep understanding of concepts. Deep understanding occurs when students are stimulated to rethink previously held ideas. In Brooks and Brooks' view, schools spend too much time getting students to give a single correct answer in an imitative way, rather than encouraging them to expand their thinking by coming up with new ideas and rethinking earlier conclusions. They observe that too often teachers ask students to recite, define, describe, state, and list, rather than to analyze, infer, connect, synthesize, criticize, create, evaluate, think, and rethink. Many successful students complete their assignments, do well on tests, and get good grades, yet they don't ever learn to think critically and deeply. They think superficially, staying on the surface of problems rather than stretching their minds and becoming deeply engaged in meaningful thinking.

Creative Thinking Cognitively competent children think not only critically, but also creatively (Runco & Spritzker, 2011). **Creative thinking** is the ability to think in novel and unusual ways and to come up with unique solutions to problems. Thus, intelligence and creativity are not the same thing. This difference was recognized by J. P. Guilford (1967), who distinguished between **convergent thinking,** which produces one correct answer and characterizes the kind of thinking that is required on conventional tests of intelligence, and **divergent thinking,** which produces many different answers to the same question and characterizes creativity. For example, a typical item on a conventional intelligence test is "How many quarters will you get in return for 60 dimes?" In contrast, the following question has many possible answers: "What image comes to mind when you hear the phrase 'sitting alone in a dark room' or 'some unique uses for a paper clip'?"

A special concern is that children's creative thinking appears to be declining. A study of approximately 300,000 U.S. children and adults found that creativity scores rose until 1990, but since then have been steadily declining (Kim, 2010). Among the likely causes of the creativity decline are the number of hours U.S. children watch TV and play video games instead of engaging in creative activities, as well as the lack of emphasis on creative thinking skills in schools (Beghetto & Kaufman, 2011; Runco, 2011; Sternberg, 2011d). Some countries, though, are placing increasing emphasis on creative thinking in schools. For example, historically, creative thinking has typically been discouraged in Chinese schools. However, Chinese educators are now encouraging teachers to spend more classroom time on creative activities (Plucker, 2010).

An important goal is to help children become more creative (Hennessey & Amabile, 2010). The *Caring Connections* interlude recommends some ways to accomplish this goal.

Scientific Thinking Like scientists, children ask fundamental questions about reality and seek answers to problems that seem utterly trivial or unanswerable to other people (such as "Why is the sky blue?"). Do children generate hypotheses, perform experiments, and reach conclusions about their data in ways resembling those of scientists?

What do you mean, "What is it?" It's the spontaneous, unfettered expression of a young mind not yet bound by the restraints of narrative or pictorial representation. ScienceCartoonsPlus.com. Used with permission.

Strategies for Increasing Children's Creative Thinking

Some strategies for increasing children's creative thinking include:

- **Encourage brainstorming. Brainstorming** is a technique in which people are encouraged to come up with creative ideas in a group, play off each other's ideas, and say practically whatever comes to mind that seems relevant to a particular issue. Participants are usually told to hold off from criticizing others' ideas at least until the end of the brainstorming session.

- **Provide environments that stimulate creativity.** Some environments nourish creativity, while others inhibit it. Parents and teachers who encourage creativity often rely on children's natural curiosity. They provide exercises and activities that stimulate children to find insightful solutions to problems, rather than ask a lot of questions that require rote answers. Teachers also encourage creativity by taking students on field trips to locations where creativity is valued. Howard Gardner (1993) emphasizes that science, discovery, and children's museums offer rich opportunities to stimulate creativity.

- **Don't overcontrol students.** Teresa Amabile (1993) says that telling children exactly how to do things leaves them feeling that originality is a mistake and exploration is a waste of time. If, instead of dictating which activities they should engage in, you let children select activities that match their interests and you support their inclinations, you will be less likely to destroy their natural curiosity (Hennessey, 2011).

- **Encourage internal motivation.** Excessive use of prizes, such as gold stars, money, or toys, can stifle creativity by undermining the intrinsic pleasure students derive from creative activities. Creative children's motivation is the satisfaction generated by the work itself. Competition for prizes and formal evaluations often undermine intrinsic motivation and creativity (Hennessey & Amabile, 2010). However, this strategy should not rule out material rewards altogether.

- **Build children's confidence.** To expand children's creativity, encourage children to believe in their own ability to create something innovative and worthwhile. Building children's confidence in their creative skills aligns with Bandura's (2010a) concept of *self-efficacy,* the belief that one can master a situation and produce positive outcomes.

What are some good strategies for guiding children in thinking more creatively?

- **Guide children to be persistent and delay gratification.** Most highly successful creative products take years to develop, and creative individuals often work on ideas and projects for months and years without being rewarded for their efforts (Sternberg & Williams, 1996). Children don't become experts at sports, music, or art overnight. It usually takes many years of working at something to become an expert at it; and it takes time for a creative thinker to produce a unique, worthwhile product (Sternberg, 2011d).

- **Encourage children to take intellectual risks.** Creative individuals take intellectual risks and seek to discover or invent something never before discovered or invented (Sternberg & Williams, 1996). They risk spending extensive time on an idea or project that may not work. Creative people are not afraid of failing or getting something wrong.

- **Introduce children to creative people.** Teachers can invite creative people to their classrooms and ask them to describe what helps them become creative or to demonstrate their creative skills. A writer, poet, musician, scientist, or another creative individual can bring their props and productions to the class, turning it into a theater for stimulating students' creativity.

Scientific reasoning often is aimed at identifying causal relations. Like scientists, children place a great deal of emphasis on causal mechanisms. Their understanding of how events are caused weighs more heavily in their causal inferences than even such strong influences as whether the cause happened immediately before the effect.

There also are important differences between the reasoning of children and the reasoning of scientists (Kuhn, 2011). Children are more influenced by happenstance events than by an overall pattern (Kuhn, 2011). Often, children maintain

brainstorming A technique in which individuals are encouraged to come up with creative ideas in a group, play off each other's ideas, and say practically whatever comes to mind.

Luis Recalde holds up a seaweed specimen in one of the hands-on, high-interest learning contexts he creates for students. Recalde, a fourth- and fifth-grade science teacher in New Haven, Connecticut, uses every opportunity to make science fascinating for students to learn. To help students get a better sense of what it is like to be a scientist, he brings lab coats to the classroom for students to wear. He often gives up his vacation time to help students with science projects.

Cognitive developmentalist John Flavell is a pioneer in providing insights about children's thinking. Among his many contributions are establishing the field of metacognition and conducting numerous studies in this area, including metamemory and theory of mind studies.

developmental **connection**

Cognitive Processes. Theory of mind— awareness of one's own mind and the mental processes of others—involves metacognition. Chapter 9, p. 271

metacognition Cognition about cognition, or knowing about knowing.

their old theories regardless of the evidence (Kuhn, Schauble, & Garcia-Mila, 1992).

Children might go through mental gymnastics trying to reconcile seemingly contradictory new information with their existing beliefs. For example, after learning about the solar system, children sometimes conclude that there are two earths, the seemingly flat world in which they live and the round ball floating in space that their teacher described.

Children also have difficulty designing experiments that can distinguish among alternative causes. Instead, they tend to bias the experiments in favor of whatever hypothesis they began with. Sometimes they see the results as supporting their original hypothesis even when the results directly contradict it. Thus, although there are important similarities between children and scientists in their basic curiosity and in the kinds of questions they ask, there are also important differences in the degree to which they can separate theory and evidence and in their ability to design conclusive experiments (Lehrer & Schauble, 2006).

Too often, the skills scientists use, such as careful observation, graphing, self-regulatory thinking, and knowing when and how to apply one's knowledge to solve problems, are not routinely taught in schools (Duschi & Hamilton, 2011; Peters & Stout, 2011). Children have many concepts that are incompatible with science and reality. Good teachers perceive and understand a child's underlying scientific concepts, then use the concepts as a scaffold for learning. Effective science teaching helps children distinguish between fruitful errors and misconceptions, and detect plainly wrong ideas that need to be replaced by more accurate conceptions (Fraser-Abder, 2011).

It is important for teachers to at a minimum initially scaffold students' science learning, extensively monitor their progress, and ensure that they are learning science content (Duschi & Hamilton, 2011). Thus, in pursuing science investigations, students need to learn inquiry skills and science content (Lehrer & Schauble, 2006).

METACOGNITION

One expert in children's thinking, Deanna Kuhn (1999), argues that to help students become better thinkers, schools should pay more attention to helping students develop skills that entail knowing about their own (and others') knowing. In other words, schools should do more to develop **metacognition,** which is cognition about cognition, or knowing about knowing (Flavell, 2004).

A number of early developmental studies classified as "metacognitive" focused on *metamemory,* or knowledge about memory. This includes general knowledge about memory, such as knowing that recognition tests are easier than recall tests. It also encompasses knowledge about one's own memory, such as a student's ability to monitor whether she has studied enough for a test that is coming up next week.

Young children do have some general knowledge about memory. By 5 or 6 years of age, children usually already know that familiar items are easier to learn than unfamiliar ones, that short lists are easier than long ones, that recognition is easier than recall, and that forgetting is more likely to occur over time (Lyon & Flavell, 1993). However, in other ways young children's metamemory is limited. They don't understand that related items are easier to remember than unrelated ones and that remembering the gist of a story is easier than remembering information verbatim (Kreutzer, Leonard, & Flavell, 1975). By the fifth grade, however, students understand that gist recall is easier than verbatim recall.

Young children also have only limited knowledge about their own memory. They have an inflated opinion of their memory abilities. For example, in one study a majority of young children predicted that they would be able to recall all 10 items on a list of 10 items. When tested for this, none of the young children managed this feat (Flavell, Friedrichs, & Hoyt, 1970). As they move through the elementary school years, children give more realistic evaluations of their memory skills (Bjorklund, 2012; Schneider, 2011).

In addition to metamemory, metacognition includes knowledge about strategies. In the view of Michael Pressley (2003), the key to education is helping students learn a rich repertoire of strategies that result in solutions to problems. Good thinkers routinely use strategies and effective planning to solve problems. Good thinkers also know when and where to use strategies. Understanding when and where to use strategies often results from monitoring the learning situation (Pressley & McCormick, 2007).

Pressley and his colleagues (Pressley & others, 2001, 2003, 2004; Pressley, Mohan, Fingeret, & others, 2007; Pressley, Mohan, Raphael, & Fingeret, 2007) have spent considerable time in recent years observing strategy instruction by teachers and strategy use by students in elementary and secondary school classrooms. They conclude that strategy instruction tends to be far less complete and intense than what students need in order to learn how to use strategies effectively. They argue that education ought to be restructured so that students are provided with more opportunities to become competent strategic learners.

What are some developmental changes in metacognition?

How Would You...?

If you were an **educator,** how would you advise teachers and parents about ways to improve their child's metacognitive skills?

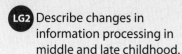

Review *Connect* **Reflect**

LG2 Describe changes in information processing in middle and late childhood.

Review

- What characterizes children's memory in middle and late childhood?
- What is involved in thinking critically, thinking creatively, and thinking scientifically?
- What is metacognition?

Connect

- In discussing memory, thinking, and metacognition, the topic of recommended education strategies came up. Compare

these recommendations in this main section with those you learned about in the Early Childhood Education section of Chapter 9.

Reflect *Your Own Personal Journey of Life*

- When you were in elementary school, did classroom instruction prepare you adequately for critical thinking tasks? If you were a parent of an 8-year-old, what would you do to guide your child to think more critically and creatively?

How Can Children's Intelligence Be Described?   **LG3** Characterize children's intelligence.

Intelligence and Its Assessment

Types of Intelligence

Interpreting Differences in IQ Scores

Extremes of Intelligence

Twentieth-century English novelist Aldous Huxley said that children are remarkable for their curiosity and intelligence. What did Huxley mean when he used the word *intelligence*? How can intelligence be assessed?

FIGURE **12.4**

THE NORMAL CURVE AND STANFORD-BINET IQ SCORES. The distribution of IQ scores approximates a normal curve. Most of the population falls in the middle range of scores. Notice that extremely high and extremely low scores are very rare. Slightly more than two-thirds of the scores fall between 85 and 115. Only about 1 in 50 individuals has an IQ of more than 130, and only about 1 in 50 individuals has an IQ of less than 70.

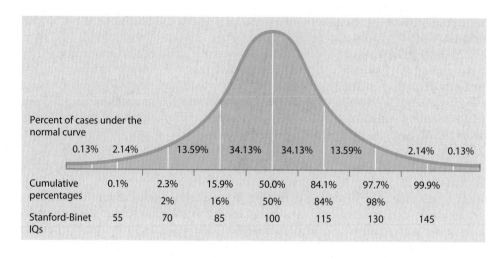

Percent of cases under the normal curve									
0.13%	2.14%		13.59%	34.13%	34.13%	13.59%		2.14%	0.13%
Cumulative percentages	0.1%	2.3%	15.9%	50.0%	84.1%	97.7%	99.9%		
		2%	16%	50%	84%	98%			
Stanford-Binet IQs	55	70	85	100	115	130	145		

INTELLIGENCE AND ITS ASSESSMENT

Just what is meant by the concept of "intelligence"? Some experts describe intelligence as problem-solving skills. Others describe it as the ability to adapt to and learn from life's everyday experiences. Combining these ideas, we can arrive at a definition of **intelligence** as problem-solving skills and the ability to learn from and adapt to life's everyday experiences.

Interest in intelligence has often focused on individual differences and assessment (Deary, 2012). **Individual differences** are the stable, consistent ways in which people are different from each other. We can talk about individual differences in personality or any other domain, but it is in the domain of intelligence that the most attention has been directed at individual differences. For example, an intelligence test purports to inform us about whether a student can reason better than others who have taken the test. Let's go back in history and see what the first intelligence test was like.

The Binet Tests In 1904, the French Ministry of Education asked psychologist Alfred Binet to devise a method of identifying children who were unable to learn in school. School officials wanted to reduce crowding by placing students who did not benefit from regular classroom teaching in special schools. Binet and his student Theophile Simon developed an intelligence test to meet this request. The test, called the 1905 Scale, consisted of 30 questions on topics ranging from the ability to touch one's ear to the ability to draw designs from memory and define abstract concepts.

Binet developed the concept of **mental age (MA),** an individual's level of mental development relative to that of others. Not much later, in 1912, William Stern created the concept of **intelligence quotient (IQ),** a person's mental age divided by chronological age (CA), multiplied by 100. That is: IQ = MA/CA × 100. If mental age is the same as chronological age, then the person's IQ is 100. If mental age is above chronological age, then IQ is more than 100. If mental age is below chronological age, then IQ is less than 100.

The Binet test has been revised many times to incorporate advances in the understanding of intelligence and intelligence tests. These revisions are called the *Stanford-Binet tests* (the revisions have been done at Stanford University). By administering the test to large numbers of people of different ages (from preschool through late adulthood) from different backgrounds, researchers have found that scores on the Stanford-Binet approximate a normal distribution (see Figure 12.4). A **normal distribution** is symmetrical, with a majority of the scores falling in the middle of the possible range of scores and few scores appearing toward the extremes of the range.

The Wechsler Scales Another set of tests widely used to assess students' intelligence is called the Wechsler scales. Developed by psychologist David Wechsler, they

---

intelligence Problem-solving skills and the ability to learn from and adapt to the experiences of everyday life.

individual differences The stable, consistent ways in which people differ from each other.

mental age (MA) Binet's measure of an individual's level of mental development, compared with that of others.

intelligence quotient (IQ) A person's mental age divided by chronological age, multiplied by 100.

normal distribution A symmetrical distribution with most scores falling in the middle of the possible range of scores and few scores appearing toward the extremes of the range.

triarchic theory of intelligence Sternberg's theory that intelligence consists of analytical intelligence, creative intelligence, and practical intelligence.

include the Wechsler Preschool and Primary Scale of Intelligence—Third Edition (WPPSI-III) to test children from the ages of 2 years 6 months to 7 years 3 months of age; the Wechsler Intelligence Scale for Children—Fourth Edition (WISC-IV) for children and adolescents 6 to 16 years of age; and the Wechsler Adult Intelligence Scale—Third Edition (WAIS-III).

The Wechsler scales not only provide an overall IQ score and scores on a number of subtests but also yield several composite indexes (for example, the Verbal Comprehension Index, the Working Memory Index, and the Processing Speed Index). The subtest and composite scores allow the examiner to quickly determine the areas in which a child is strong or weak. Three of the Wechsler subscales are shown in Figure 12.5.

TYPES OF INTELLIGENCE

Is it more appropriate to think of a child's intelligence as a general ability or as a number of specific abilities? Robert Sternberg and Howard Gardner have proposed influential theories oriented to this second viewpoint.

Sternberg's Triarchic Theory   Robert J. Sternberg (1986, 2004, 2010, 2011a, b) developed the **triarchic theory of intelligence,** which states that intelligence comes in three forms:

- *Analytical intelligence*, referring to the ability to analyze, judge, evaluate, compare, and contrast
- *Creative intelligence*, consisting of the ability to create, design, invent, originate, and imagine
- *Practical intelligence*, involving the ability to use, apply, implement, and put ideas into practice

Sternberg (2011a, b) says that children with different triarchic patterns "look different" in school. Students with high analytic intelligence tend to be favored in conventional schooling. They often do well under direct instruction, in which the teacher lectures and gives students objective tests. They often are considered to be "smart" students who get good grades, show up in high-level tracks, do well on traditional tests of intelligence and the SAT, and later get admitted to competitive colleges.

In contrast, children who are high in creative intelligence often are not on the top rung of their class. Many teachers have specific expectations about how assignments should be done, and creatively intelligent students may not conform to those expectations. Instead of giving conformist answers, they give unique answers, for which they might get reprimanded or marked down. No teacher wants to discourage creativity, but Sternberg stresses that too often a teacher's desire to improve students' knowledge suppresses creative thinking.

Like children high in creative intelligence, children who are high in practical intelligence often do not relate well to the demands of school. However, many of these children do well outside the classroom's walls. They may have excellent social skills and good common sense. As adults, some become successful managers, entrepreneurs, or politicians in spite of having undistinguished school records.

Recently, Sternberg (2011e; Karelitz, Jarvin, & Sternberg, 2010) has applied his triarchic theory of intelligence to the concept of *wisdom*. In his view, academic intelligence is a necessary but in many cases insufficient requirement for wisdom. Practical knowledge about the realities of life also is needed for wisdom. For Sternberg, balance between self-interest, the interests of others, and contexts produces a common good. Thus, wise individuals don't just look out for themselves—they also need to consider others' needs and perspectives, as well as the particular context involved. Sternberg assesses people's wisdom by presenting problems requiring solutions that highlight various intrapersonal, interpersonal, and contextual interests. He also

Verbal Subscales

Similarities

A child must think logically and abstractly to answer a number of questions about how things might be similar.

Example: "In what way are a lion and a tiger alike?"

Comprehension

This subscale is designed to measure an individual's judgment and common sense.

Example: "What is the advantage of keeping money in a bank?"

Nonverbal Subscales

Block Design

A child must assemble a set of multicolored blocks to match designs that the examiner shows.
Visual-motor coordination, perceptual organization, and the ability to visualize spatially are assessed.

Example: "Use the four blocks on the left to make the pattern on the right."

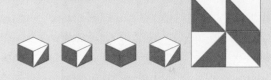

FIGURE **12.5**

SAMPLE SUBSCALES OF THE WECHSLER INTELLIGENCE SCALE FOR CHILDREN—FOURTH EDITION (WISC-IV). The Wechsler includes 11 subscales, 6 verbal and 5 nonverbal. Three of the subscales are shown here. Simulated items similar to those found in the *Wechsler Intelligence Scale for Children,* Fourth Edition. Copyright © 2003 NCS Pearson, Inc. Reproduced with permission. All rights reserved. "Wechsler Intelligence Scale for Children" and "WISC" are trademarks of Harcourt Assessment, Inc. registered in the United States of America and/or other jurisdictions.

Robert J. Sternberg, who developed the triarchic theory of intelligence.

"You're wise, but you lack tree smarts."
© Donald Reilly/The New Yorker Collection/
www.cartoonbank.com

Howard Gardner, here working with a young child, developed the view that intelligence comes in the forms of these eight kinds of skills: verbal, mathematical, spatial, bodily-kinesthetic, musical, intrapersonal, interpersonal, and naturalist.

How Would You...?

If you were a **psychologist,** how would you use Gardner's theory of multiple intelligences to respond to a child who is distressed to receive a below-average score on a traditional intelligence test?

emphasizes that such aspects of wisdom should be taught in schools (Sternberg, 2011e).

Gardner's Eight Frames of Mind   Howard Gardner (1983, 1993, 2002) suggests that there are eight types of intelligence, or "frames of mind." These are described here, with examples of the types of occupations in which they function as strengths (Campbell, Campbell, & Dickinson, 2004):

- *Verbal:* the ability to think in words and use language to express meaning (occupations: authors, journalists, speakers)
- *Mathematical:* the ability to carry out mathematical operations (occupations: scientists, engineers, accountants)
- *Spatial:* the ability to think three-dimensionally (occupations: architects, artists, sailors)
- *Bodily-kinesthetic:* the ability to manipulate objects and be physically adept (occupations: surgeons, craftspeople, dancers, athletes)
- *Musical:* a sensitivity to pitch, melody, rhythm, and tone (occupations: composers, musicians, sensitive listeners)
- *Interpersonal:* the ability to understand and interact effectively with others (occupations: successful teachers, mental health professionals)
- *Intrapersonal:* the ability to understand oneself (occupations: theologians, psychologists)
- *Naturalist:* the ability to observe patterns in nature and understand natural and human-made systems (occupations: farmers, botanists, ecologists, landscapers)

According to Gardner, everyone has all of these intelligences to varying degrees. As a result, we prefer to learn and process information in different ways. People learn best when they can do so in a way that uses their stronger intelligences.

Evaluating the Multiple-Intelligence Approaches   Sternberg's and Gardner's approaches have much to offer. They have stimulated teachers to think more broadly about what makes up children's competencies. And they have motivated educators to develop programs that instruct students in multiple domains. These approaches have also contributed to interest in assessing intelligence and classroom learning in innovative ways, such as by evaluating student portfolios.

Still, doubts about multiple-intelligence approaches persist. A number of psychologists think that the multiple-intelligence views have taken the concept of specific intelligences too far (Jensen, 2008). Some argue that a research base to support the three intelligences of Sternberg or the eight intelligences of Gardner has not yet emerged. One expert on intelligence, Nathan Brody (2007), observes that people who excel at one type of intellectual task are likely to excel in others. Thus, individuals who do well at memorizing lists of digits are also likely to be good at solving verbal problems and spatial layout problems. If musical skill reflects a distinct type of intelligence, ask other critics, why not label the skills of outstanding chess players, prizefighters, painters, and poets as types of intelligence?

The argument between those who support the concept of general intelligence and those who advocate the multiple-intelligences view is ongoing. Sternberg (2011a, b) actually accepts that there is a general intelligence for the kinds of analytical tasks that traditional IQ tests assess but thinks that the range of tasks those tests measure is far too narrow.

INTERPRETING DIFFERENCES IN IQ SCORES

The IQ scores that result from tests such as the Stanford-Binet and Wechsler scales provide information about children's mental abilities. However, the significance of performance on an intelligence test is debated (Deary, 2012; Sternberg, 2011a, b).

The Influence of Genetics   Have scientists been able to pinpoint specific genes that are linked to intelligence? A recent research review concluded that there may be more than 1,000 genes that affect intelligence, each possibly having a small influence on an individual's intelligence (Davies & others, 2011). However, researchers have not been able to identify the specific genes that contribute to intelligence (Deary, 2012).

How strong is the effect of genetics on intelligence? The concept of heritability attempts to tease apart the effects of heredity and environment in a population. **Heritability** is the fraction of the variance in a population that is attributed to genetics. The heritability index is computed using correlational techniques, which we first discussed in Chapter 1. Thus, 1.00 is the highest degree of heritability that is hypothetically possible, and correlations of .70 and above suggest a strong genetic influence. A committee of respected researchers convened by the American Psychological Association concluded that by late adolescence, the heritability of intelligence is about .75, which reflects a strong genetic influence (Neisser & others, 1996).

Most research on heredity and environment does not include environments that differ radically. Thus, it is not surprising that many genetic studies show environment to be a fairly weak influence on intelligence (Fraser, 1995).

The heritability index has several flaws. It is only as good as the data entered into its analysis and the interpretations made from it. The data are virtually all from traditional IQ tests, which some experts think are not always the best indicator of intelligence (Sternberg, 2011a, b, c). Also, the heritability index assumes that we can treat genetic and environmental influences as factors that can be separated, with each part contributing a distinct amount of influence. As we discussed in Chapter 2, "Biological Beginnings," genes and the environment interact: Genes always exist in an environment, and the environment shapes their activity.

One strategy for examining the role of heredity in intelligence is to compare the IQs of identical and fraternal twins, which we initially discussed in Chapter 2. Recall that identical twins have exactly the same genetic makeup but fraternal twins do not. If intelligence is genetically determined, say some investigators, the IQs of identical twins should be more similar than the intelligence of fraternal twins. A research review of many studies found that the difference in the average correlation of intelligence between identical and fraternal twins was .15, a relatively low correlation (Grigorenko, 2000) (see Figure 12.6).

Today, most researchers agree that genetics and environment interact to influence intelligence. For most people, this means that modifications in environment can change their IQ scores considerably. Although genetic endowment may always influence a person's intellectual ability, the environmental influences and opportunities we provide children and adults do make a difference (Birney & Sternberg, 2011).

Environmental Influences   In one study, researchers went into homes and observed how extensively parents from welfare and middle-income professional families talked and communicated with their young children (Hart & Risley, 1995). They found that the middle-income professional parents were much more likely to communicate with their young children than the welfare parents were. How much the parents communicated with their children in the first three years of their lives was correlated with the children's Stanford-Binet IQ scores at age 3. The more parents communicated with their children, the higher the children's IQs were.

Schooling also influences intelligence (Gustafsson, 2007). The biggest effects have been found when large groups of children have been deprived of formal education for an extended period, resulting in lower intelligence (Ceci & Gilstrap, 2000). Another possible effect of education can be seen in rapidly increasing IQ test scores around the world (Flynn, 1999, 2007). IQ scores have been increasing so quickly

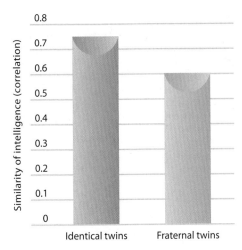

FIGURE 12.6

CORRELATION BETWEEN INTELLIGENCE TEST SCORES AND TWIN STATUS. The graph represents a summary of research findings that have compared the intelligence test scores of identical and fraternal twins. An approximate .15 difference has been found, with a higher correlation for identical twins (.75) and a lower correlation for fraternal twins.

developmental **connection**

Nature and Nurture. The epigenetic view emphasizes that development is an ongoing, bidirectional interchange between heredity and environment. Chapter 2, p. 77

heritability The fraction of variance in a population that is attributed to genetics and is computed using correlational techniques.

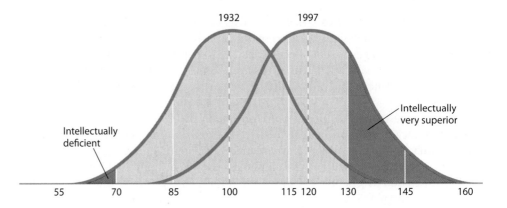

FIGURE **12.7**

INCREASING IQ SCORES FROM 1932 TO 1997.
As measured by the Stanford-Binet intelligence test, American children seem to be getting smarter. Scores of a group tested in 1932 fell along a bell-shaped curve with half below 100 and half above. Studies show that if children took that same test today, half would score above 120 on the 1932 scale. Very few of them would score in the "intellectually deficient" end, on the left side, and about one-fourth would rank in the "very superior" range.

that a high percentage of people regarded as having average intelligence at the turn of the century would be considered below average in intelligence today (see Figure 12.7). If a representative sample of people today took the Stanford-Binet test version used in 1932, about 25 percent would be defined as having very superior intelligence, a label usually accorded to less than 3 percent of the population. Because the increase has taken place within a relatively short time, it can't be due to heredity, but rather may be due to increasing levels of education attained by a much greater percentage of the world's population, or to other environmental factors such as the explosion of information to which people are exposed. And another recent study revealed that children with more educated (especially college-educated) mothers and/or children born into higher-income families showed higher scores on math achievement tests than children who had less-educated mothers and came from lower-income families (Ang, Rodgers, & Wanstrom, 2010). This worldwide increase in intelligence test scores over a short time frame is called the *Flynn effect* after the researcher who discovered it—James Flynn (1999, 2007).

Researchers are increasingly concerned about improving the early environment of children who are at risk for impoverished intelligence (Phillips & Lowenstein, 2011). For various reasons, many low-income parents have difficulty providing an intellectually stimulating environment for their children. Programs that educate parents to be more sensitive caregivers and better teachers, as well as support services such as quality child-care programs, can make a difference in a child's intellectual development (Bredekamp, 2011). Thus, the efforts to counteract a deprived early environment's effect on intelligence emphasize prevention rather than remediation.

A review of the research on early interventions concluded that (1) high-quality-child-care center-based interventions are associated with increases in children's intelligence and school achievement; (2) the interventions are most successful with poor children and children whose parents have little education; (3) the positive benefits continue through adolescence, but are not as strong as in early childhood or the beginning of elementary school; and (4) the programs that continue into middle and late childhood have the best long-term results (Brooks-Gunn, 2003).

Revisiting the Nature-Nurture Issue In sum, there is a consensus among psychologists that both heredity and environment influence intelligence. This consensus reflects the nature-nurture issue that was highlighted in Chapter 1. Recall that the nature-nurture issue focuses on the extent to which development is influenced by nature (heredity) and nurture (environment). Although psychologists agree that intelligence is the product of both nature and nurture, there is still disagreement about how strongly each influences intelligence.

Culture and Intelligence Do cultures define intelligence differently? Are there ethnic variations in children's intelligence? What are some cautions in interpreting IQ scores?

Culture and Culture-Fair Tests   Cultures vary in the way they describe what it means to be intelligent (Sternberg, 2011f; Zhang & Sternberg, 2011). People in Western cultures tend to view intelligence in terms of reasoning and thinking skills, whereas people in Eastern cultures see intelligence as a way for members of a community to successfully engage in social roles (Nisbett, 2003).

Culture-fair tests are tests of intelligence that are intended to be free of cultural bias. Two types of culture-fair tests have been devised. The first includes items that are familiar to children from all socioeconomic and ethnic backgrounds, or items that at least are familiar to the children taking the test. For example, a child might be asked how a bird and a dog are different, on the assumption that all children have been exposed to birds and dogs. The second type of culture-fair test has no verbal questions.

Why is it so hard to create culture-fair tests? Most tests tend to reflect what the dominant culture thinks is important (Greenfield, Suzuki, & Rothstein-Fisch, 2006). Time limits on tests will bias the test against groups not concerned with time. If languages differ, the same words might have different meanings for different language groups. Even pictures can produce bias because some cultures have less experience with drawings and photographs than others (Anastasi & Urbina, 1997). Within the same culture, different subgroups could have different attitudes, values, and motivation, and these could affect their performance on intelligence tests. Items that ask why buildings should be made of brick are biased against children who have little or no experience with brick houses. Questions about railroads, furnaces, snow, distances between cities, and so on can be biased against groups who have less experience than others with these contexts. Recall, too, that cultures define intelligence differently. Because of such difficulties in creating culture-fair tests, Robert Sternberg (2011f) concludes that there are no culture-fair tests, only *culture-reduced tests.*

"You can't build a hut, you don't know how to find edible roots and you know nothing about predicting the weather. In other words, you do terribly on our I.Q. test." ScienceCartoonsPlus.com. Used with permission.

Ethnic Variations   On average, African American schoolchildren in the United States score 10 to 15 points lower on standardized intelligence tests than White American schoolchildren do (Brody, 2000). Children from Latino families also score lower than White children. These are average scores, however, and there is significant overlap in the distribution of scores. About 15 to 25 percent of African American schoolchildren score higher than half of White schoolchildren do, and many White schoolchildren score lower than most African American schoolchildren.

As African Americans have gained better access to social, economic, and educational opportunities, the gap between African Americans and Whites on standardized intelligence tests has begun to narrow (Ogbu & Stern, 2001). This gap especially narrows in college, where African American and White students often experience more similar environments than in the elementary and high school years (Myerson & others, 1998). Also, when children from disadvantaged African American families are adopted into more advantaged middle-socioeconomic-status families, their scores on intelligence tests more closely resemble national averages for middle-socioeconomic-status children than for lower-socioeconomic-status children (Scarr & Weinberg, 1983).

Using Intelligence Tests   Psychological tests are tools. Like all tools, their effectiveness depends on the knowledge, skill, and integrity of the user. A hammer can be used to build a beautiful kitchen cabinet, or it can be used as a weapon of assault. Like a hammer, psychological tests can be used for positive purposes, or they can be badly abused. Here are some cautions about IQ that can help you avoid the pitfalls of using information about a child's intelligence in negative ways:

- *Avoid stereotyping and preconceived expectations.* A special concern is that the scores on an IQ test easily can lead to stereotypes and preconceived expectations about students. Sweeping generalizations are too often made on the basis of an IQ score. An IQ test should always be considered a measure of current performance. It is not a measure of fixed potential. Maturational

culture-fair tests Tests of intelligence that are designed to be free of cultural bias.

How Would You...?

If you were a **social worker**, how would you explain the role and purpose of intelligence test scores to a parent whose child is preparing to take a standardized intelligence test?

changes and enriched environmental experiences can advance a student's intelligence.

- *Know that IQ is not a sole indicator of competence.* Another concern about IQ tests occurs when they are used as the main or sole assessment of competence. A high IQ is not the ultimate human value. As we have seen in this chapter, it is important to consider students' intellectual competence not only in such areas as verbal skills but also in their creative and practical skills.

- *Use caution in interpreting an overall IQ score.* In evaluating a child's intelligence, it is wiser to think of intelligence as consisting of a number of domains. Keep in mind the different types of intelligence described by Sternberg and Gardner. By considering the different domains of intelligence, you will find that every child has areas of strength.

EXTREMES OF INTELLIGENCE

Intelligence tests have been used to discover indications of mental retardation or intellectual giftedness, the extremes of intelligence. At times, intelligence tests have been misused for this purpose. Keeping in mind the theme that an intelligence test should not be used as the sole indicator of mental retardation or giftedness, we will explore the nature of these intellectual extremes.

A child with Down syndrome. *What causes a child to develop Down syndrome? In which major classification of mental retardation does the condition fall?*

Mental Retardation   **Mental retardation** is a condition of limited mental ability in which an individual has a low IQ, usually below 70 on a traditional intelligence test, and has difficulty adapting to everyday life. About 5 million Americans fit this definition of mental retardation.

There are several classifications of mental retardation. About 89 percent of the mentally retarded fall into the mild category, with IQs of 55 to 70; most of them are able to live independently as adults and work at a variety of jobs. About 6 percent are classified as moderately retarded, with IQs of 40 to 54; these people can attain a second-grade level of skills and may be able to support themselves as adults through some types of labor. About 3.5 percent of the mentally retarded are in the severe category, with IQs of 25 to 39; these individuals learn to talk and accomplish very simple tasks but require extensive supervision. Less than 1 percent have IQs below 25; they fall into the profoundly mentally retarded classification and need constant supervision.

Mental retardation can have an organic cause, or it can be social and cultural in origin:

- **Organic retardation** is mental retardation that is caused by a genetic disorder or by brain damage; the word *organic* refers to the tissues or organs of the body and indicates physical damage. Most people who suffer from organic retardation have IQs that range between 0 and 50. However, children with Down syndrome have an average IQ of approximately 50. As discussed in Chapter 2, "Biological Beginnings," Down syndrome is caused by an extra copy of chromosome 21.

mental retardation A condition of limited mental ability in which an individual has a low IQ, usually below 70 on a traditional test of intelligence, and has difficulty adapting to everyday life.

organic retardation Mental retardation that involves physical causes such as a genetic disorder or brain damage.

cultural-familial retardation Retardation in which there is no evidence of organic brain damage but the individual's IQ generally is between 50 and 70.

gifted Having above-average intelligence (an IQ of 130 or higher) and/or superior talent for something.

- **Cultural-familial retardation** is a mental deficit in which no evidence of organic brain damage can be found; individuals' IQs generally range from 50 to 70. Psychologists suspect that such mental deficits result from the normal variation that distributes people along the range of intelligence scores combined with growing up in a below-average intellectual environment.

Giftedness   There have always been people whose abilities and accomplishments outshine those of others—the whiz kid in class, the star athlete, the natural musician. People who are **gifted** have above-average intelligence (an IQ of 130 or higher) and/or superior talent for something. When it comes to programs for the gifted, most school systems select children who have intellectual superiority and academic aptitude, whereas children who are talented in the visual and performing arts (arts, drama, dance), athletics, or have other special aptitudes tend to be overlooked (Clark, 2008; Karnes & Stephens, 2008).

Characteristics   What are the characteristics of children who are gifted? Despite speculation that giftedness is linked with having a mental disorder, no relation between giftedness and mental disorder has been found. Similarly, the idea that gifted children are maladjusted is a myth, as Lewis Terman (1925) found when he conducted an extensive study of 1,500 children whose Stanford-Binet IQs averaged 150. The children in Terman's study were socially well adjusted, and many went on to become successful doctors, lawyers, professors, and scientists. Studies support the conclusion that gifted people tend to be more mature than others, have fewer emotional problems, and grow up in a positive family climate (Davidson, 2000).

Ellen Winner (1996) described three criteria that characterize gifted children, whether in art, music, or academic domains:

1. *Precocity.* Gifted children are precocious. They begin to master an area earlier than their peers. Learning in their domain is more effortless for them than for ordinary children. In most instances, these gifted children are precocious because they have an inborn high ability in a particular domain or domains.

2. *Marching to their own drummer.* Gifted children learn in qualitatively different ways from ordinary children. One way that they march to a different drummer is that they need minimal help, or scaffolding, from adults to learn. In many instances, they resist any kind of explicit instruction. They often make discoveries on their own and solve problems in unique ways.

3. *A passion to master.* Gifted children are driven to understand the domain in which they have high ability. They display an intense, obsessive interest and an ability to focus. They motivate themselves, says Winner, and do not need to be "pushed" by their parents.

To read about one individual who is making a difference in programs for children who are gifted, see the *Connecting with Careers* profile.

At 2 years of age, art prodigy Alexandra Nechita colored in coloring books for hours and also took up pen and ink. She had no interest in dolls or friends. By age 5 she was using watercolors. Once she started school, she would start painting as soon as she got home. At the age of 8, in 1994, she saw the first public exhibit of her work. In succeeding years, working quickly and impulsively on canvases as large as 5 feet by 9 feet, she has completed hundreds of paintings, some of which sell for close to $100,000 apiece. As a teenager, she continues to paint—relentlessly and passionately. It is, she says, what she loves to do. *What are some characteristics of children who are gifted?*

connecting with careers

Sterling Jones, Supervisor of Gifted and Talented Education

Sterling Jones is program supervisor for gifted and talented children in the Detroit Public School System. Jones has been working for more than three decades with children who are gifted. He believes that students' mastery of skills mainly depends on the amount of time devoted to instruction and the length of time allowed for learning. Thus, he believes that many basic strategies for challenging children who are gifted to develop their skills can be applied to a wider range of students than was once believed. He has rewritten several pamphlets for use by teachers and parents, including *How to Help Your Child Succeed* and *Gifted and Talented Education for Everyone.*

Jones has undergraduate and graduate degrees from Wayne State University and taught English for a number of years before becoming

Sterling Jones with some of the children in the gifted program in the Detroit Public School System.

involved in the program for gifted children. He also has written materials on African Americans, such as *Voices from the Black Experience,* that are used in the Detroit schools.

To read more about what teachers of exceptional children do, see page 47 in the Careers in Children's Development appendix.

A young Bill Gates, founder of Microsoft and now one of the world's richest persons. Like many highly gifted students, Gates was not especially fond of school. He hacked a computer security system when he was 13, and as a high school student, he was allowed to take some college math classes. He dropped out of Harvard University and began developing a plan for what was to become Microsoft Corporation. *What are some ways that schools can enrich the education of such highly talented students as Gates to make it a more challenging, interesting, and meaningful experience?*

Nature-Nurture Issue Is giftedness a product of heredity or environment? Likely both (Sternberg, 2011g). Individuals who are gifted recall that they had signs of high ability in a particular area at a very young age, prior to or at the beginning of formal training (Howe & others, 1995). This suggests the importance of innate ability in giftedness. However, researchers have also found that individuals with world-class status in the arts, mathematics, science, and sports all report strong family support and years of training and practice (Bloom, 1985). Deliberate practice is an important characteristic of individuals who become experts in a particular domain.

Developmental Changes and Domain-Specific Giftedness Can we predict from infancy who will be gifted as children, adolescents, and adults? John Colombo and his colleagues (2004, 2009) have found that measures of infant attention and habituation are not good predictors of high cognitive ability later in development. However, they have discovered a link between assessment with the Home Observation for Measure of the Environment at 18 months of age and high cognitive ability in the preschool years. The best predictor at 18 months of high cognitive ability in the preschool years was the provision of materials and a variety of experiences in the home. These findings illustrate the importance of the cognitive environment provided by parents in the development of children's giftedness.

Individuals who are highly gifted are typically not gifted in many domains, and research on giftedness is increasingly focused on domain-specific developmental trajectories (Matthews, 2009; Winner, 2009). During the childhood years, the domain(s) in which individuals are gifted usually emerges. Thus, at some point in the childhood years, the child who is to become a gifted artist or the child who is to become a gifted mathematician begins to show expertise in that domain. Regarding domain-specific giftedness, software genius Bill Gates (1998), the founder of Microsoft and one of the world's richest persons, commented that sometimes you have to be careful when you are good at something and resist the urge to think that you will be good at everything. Gates says that because he has been so successful at software development, people expect him to be brilliant about other domains about which he is far from being a genius.

Identifying an individual's domain-specific talent and providing the person with individually appropriate and optional educational opportunities should be accomplished at the very latest by adolescence (Keating, 2009). During adolescence, individuals who are talented become less reliant on parental support and increasingly pursue their own interests.

Some children who are gifted become gifted adults, but many gifted children do not become gifted and highly creative adults. In Terman's research on children with superior IQs, the children typically became experts in a well-established domain, such as medicine, law, or business. However, they did not become major creators (Winner, 2000). That is, they did not create a new domain or revolutionize an old domain.

One reason that some gifted children do not become gifted adults is that they often have been pushed too hard by overzealous parents and teachers. As a result, they lose their intrinsic (internal) motivation (Winner, 2006). Another reason that gifted children may not become gifted adults is because the criteria for giftedness change—as an adult, an individual has to actually do something special to be labeled gifted.

Education An increasing number of experts argue that the education of children who are gifted in the United States requires a significant overhaul (Ambrose, Sternberg, & Sriraman, 2011; Sternberg, 2011g). Some educators also conclude that the inadequate education of children who are gifted has been compounded by the federal government's No Child Left Behind policy that seeks to raise the achievement level of students who are not doing well in school at the expense of enriching the education of children who are gifted (Clark, 2008; Cloud, 2007).

Ellen Winner (1996, 2006) argues that too often children who are gifted are socially isolated and underchallenged in the classroom. It is not unusual for them to be ostracized and labeled "nerds" or "geeks." A child who is truly gifted often is the only such child in the room and thus lacks the opportunity to learn with students of like ability. Many eminent adults report that school was a negative experience for them, that they were bored and sometimes knew more than their teachers (Bloom, 1985). Winner believes that American education will benefit when standards are raised for all children. When some children are still underchallenged, she recommends that they be allowed to attend advanced classes in their domain of exceptional ability—for example, that some especially precocious middle school students take college classes in their area of expertise. Bill Gates, founder of Microsoft, took college math classes and hacked a computer security system at 13; Yo-Yo Ma, famous cellist, graduated from high school at 15 and attended Juilliard School of Music in New York City.

How Would You...?

If you were an **educator,** how would you structure educational programs for children who are gifted that would challenge and expand their unique cognitive abilities?

Review *Connect* Reflect

LG3 Characterize children's intelligence.

Review

- What is intelligence? How can the Binet tests and the Wechsler scales be characterized?
- What are some different views of multiple intelligences? How can the multiple-intelligences approach be evaluated?
- What are some issues in interpreting differences in IQ scores? Explain them.
- What is the nature of children's mental retardation? How can children's giftedness be described?

Connect

- In this section, you learned how mental retardation is assessed and classified. What did you learn in Chapter 2 about the prevalence of Down syndrome in the population and the factors that might cause a child to be born with Down syndrome?

Reflect *Your Own Personal Journey of Life*

- A CD-ROM, *Children's IQ and Achievement Test,* is being sold to parents so they can test their child's IQ. Several parents tell you that they purchased the CD and assessed their children's IQ. Why might you be skeptical about giving your children an IQ test and interpreting the results yourself?

What Changes in Language Development Occur in Middle and Late Childhood?

LG4 Summarize language development in middle and late childhood.

Vocabulary, Grammar, and Metalinguistic Awareness

Reading

Bilingualism and Second-Language Learning

Knowledge of vocabulary words is a part of virtually all intelligence tests, and this as well as other aspects of language development are important aspects of children's intelligence. As they enter school, children gain new skills that make it possible for them to learn to read and write—these include increasingly using language to talk about things that are not physically present, learning what a word is, and learning how to recognize and talk about sounds (Berko Gleason, 2003). They have to learn the alphabetic principle—that the letters of the alphabet represent sounds of the language. As children develop during middle and late childhood, changes in their vocabulary and grammar also take place.

VOCABULARY, GRAMMAR, AND METALINGUISTIC AWARENESS

During middle and late childhood, changes occur in the way children organize their mental vocabulary. When asked to say the first word that comes to mind when they hear a word, young children typically provide a word that often follows the word in a sentence. For example, when asked to respond to "dog" the young child may say "barks," or to the word "eat" say "lunch." At about 7 years of age, children begin to respond with a word that is the same part of speech as the stimulus word. For example, children may now respond to the word "dog" with "cat" or "horse." To "eat," they now might say "drink." These responses are evidence that children now have begun to categorize their vocabulary by parts of speech (Berko Gleason, 2003).

The process of categorizing becomes easier as children increase their vocabulary. Children's vocabulary grows from an average of about 14,000 words at 6 years of age to an average of about 40,000 words by 11 years of age.

Children make similar advances in grammar (Lidz, 2010). During the elementary school years, children's improvement in logical reasoning and analytical skills helps them understand such constructions as the appropriate use of comparatives (*shorter, deeper*) and subjunctives ("If you were president . . ."). During the elementary school years, children become increasingly able to understand and use complex grammar, such as the following sentence: *The boy who kissed his mother wore a hat.* They also learn to use language in a more connected way, producing connected discourse. They become able to relate sentences to one another to produce descriptions, definitions, and narratives that make sense. Children must be able to do these things orally before they can be expected to deal with them in written assignments.

These advances in vocabulary and grammar during the elementary school years are accompanied by the development of **metalinguistic awareness,** which is knowledge about language, such as knowing what a preposition is or being able to discuss the sounds of a language. Metalinguistic awareness allows children "to think about their language, understand what words are, and even define them" (Berko Gleason, 2009, p. 4). It improves considerably during the elementary school years (Pan & Uccelli, 2009). Defining words becomes a regular part of classroom discourse, and children increase their knowledge of syntax as they study and talk about the components of sentences such as subjects and verbs (Meltzi & Ely, 2009).

Children also make progress in understanding how to use language in culturally appropriate ways—*pragmatics*. By the time they enter adolescence, most children know the rules for the use of language in everyday contexts—that is, what is appropriate to say and what is inappropriate to say.

READING

Before learning to read, children learn to use language to talk about things that are not present; they learn what a word is; and they learn how to recognize sounds and talk about them (Berko Gleason, 2003). If they develop a large vocabulary, their path to reading is eased. Children who begin elementary school with a small vocabulary are at risk when it comes to learning to read (Cunningham & Allington, 2011).

How should children be taught to read? Currently, debate focuses on the whole-language approach versus the phonics approach (Vacca & others, 2012; Tompkins, 2011).

The **whole-language approach** stresses that reading instruction should parallel children's natural language learning. In some whole-language classes, beginning readers are taught to recognize whole words or even entire sentences, and to use the context of what they are reading to guess at the meaning of words. Reading materials that support the whole-language approach are whole and meaningful—that is, children are given material in its complete form, such as stories and poems, so that they learn to understand language's communicative function. Reading is connected with listening and writing skills. Although there are variations in whole-language

metalinguistic awareness Knowledge about language, such as knowing what a preposition is or being able to discuss the sounds of a language.

whole-language approach An approach to reading instruction based on the idea that instruction should parallel children's natural language learning. Reading materials should be whole and meaningful.

programs, most share the premise that reading should be integrated with other skills and subjects, such as science and social studies, and that it should focus on real-world material. Thus, a class might read newspapers, magazines, or books, and then write about and discuss them.

In contrast, the **phonics approach** emphasizes that reading instruction should teach basic rules for translating written symbols into sounds. Early phonics-centered reading instruction should involve simplified materials. Only after children have learned correspondence rules that relate spoken phonemes to the alphabet letters that are used to represent them should they be given complex reading materials, such as books and poems (Fox, 2012). A recent study revealed that a computer-based phonics program improved first-grade students' reading skills (Savage & others, 2009).

Which approach is better? Research suggests that children can benefit from both approaches, but instruction in phonics needs to be emphasized (Fox & Alexander, 2011; Reutzel & Cooper, 2012). An increasing number of experts in the field of reading now conclude that direct instruction in phonics is a key aspect of learning to read (Cunningham & Allington, 2011).

This teacher is helping a student sound out words. Researchers have found that phonics instruction is a key aspect of teaching students to read, especially beginning readers and students with weak reading skills.

Beyond the phonics/whole-language issue in learning to read, becoming a good reader includes learning to read fluently (Christie, Enz, & Vukelich, 2011; Snowling & Gobel, 2011). Many beginning or poor readers do not recognize words automatically. Their processing capacity is consumed by the demands of word recognition, so they have less capacity to devote to comprehension of groupings of words as phrases or sentences. As their processing of words and passages becomes more automatic, it is said that their reading becomes more *fluent* (Fox & Alexander, 2011). Metacognitive strategies, such as learning to monitor one's reading progress, getting the gist of what is being read, and summarizing also are important in becoming a good reader (Nash-Ditzel, 2010).

BILINGUALISM AND SECOND-LANGUAGE LEARNING

Are there sensitive periods in learning a second language? That is, if individuals want to learn a second language, how important is the age at which they begin to learn it? For many years, it was claimed that if individuals did not learn a second language before puberty, they would never reach native-language speakers' proficiency in the second language (Johnson & Newport, 1991). However, recent research indicates a more complex conclusion: Sensitive periods likely vary across different language systems (Thomas & Johnson, 2008). Thus, for late language learners, such as adolescents and adults, new vocabulary is easier to learn than new sounds or new grammar (Neville, 2006; Werker & Tees, 2005). For example, children's ability to pronounce words with a native-like accent in a second language typically decreases with age, with an especially sharp drop occurring after the age of about 10 to 12. Also, adults tend to learn a second language faster than children, but their final level of second-language attainment is not as high as children's.

Some aspects of children's ability to learn a second language are transferred more easily to the second language than others (Pena & Bedore, 2009). Children who are fluent in two languages perform better than their single-language counterparts on tests of control of attention, concept formation, analytical reasoning, cognitive flexibility, and cognitive complexity (Bialystok, 2001, 2007, 2011; Bialystok & Craik, 2010). They also are more conscious of the structure of spoken and written language and better at noticing errors of grammar and meaning, skills that benefit their reading ability (Bialystok, 1997). However, recent research indicates that bilingual children have a smaller vocabulary in each language than monolingual children do (Bialystok, 2011).

Students in the United States are far behind their counterparts in many developed countries in learning a second language. For example, in Russia, schools have 10 grades,

phonics approach The idea that reading instruction should teach basic rules for translating written symbols into sounds.

connecting with diversity

Bilingual Education

For the last two decades, the preferred strategy for teaching children for whom English is not their primary language has been *bilingual education,* which teaches academic subjects to immigrant children in their native language while slowly teaching English (Diaz-Rico, 2012; Reiss, 2012). Advocates of bilingual education programs argue that if children who do not know English are taught only in English, they will fall behind in academic subjects. How, they ask, can 7-year-olds learn arithmetic or history taught only in English when they do not speak the language?

Some critics of bilingual programs argue that too often it is thought that immigrant children need only one year of bilingual education. However, in general it takes immigrant children approximately three to five years to develop speaking proficiency and seven years to develop reading proficiency in English (Hakuta, Butler, & Witt, 2001). Also, immigrant children vary in their ability to learn English (Echevarria & Graves, 2011; Herrera & Murry, 2011). Children who come from lower socioeconomic backgrounds have more difficulty than those from higher socioeconomic backgrounds (Hakuta, 2001). Thus, especially for immigrant children from low socioeconomic backgrounds, more years of bilingual education may be needed than they currently are receiving.

Critics who oppose bilingual education argue that as a result of these programs, the children of immigrants are not learning English, which puts them at a permanent disadvantage in U.S. society. What have researchers found regarding outcomes of bilingual education programs? Drawing conclusions about the effectiveness of bilingual education programs is difficult because of variations across programs in the number

A first- and second-grade bilingual English-Cantonese teacher instructing students in Chinese in Oakland, California. *What have researchers found about the effectiveness of bilingual education?*

of years they are in effect, type of instruction, qualities of schooling other than bilingual education, teachers, children, and other factors. Further, no experiments effectively comparing bilingual education with English-only education in the United States have been conducted (Snow & Kang, 2006). Some experts have concluded that the quality of instruction is more important in determining outcomes than the language in which it is delivered (Lesaux & Siegel, 2003).

Nonetheless, research supports bilingual education in that (1) children have difficulty learning a subject when it is taught in a language they do not understand; and (2) when both languages are integrated in the classroom, children learn the second language more readily and participate more actively (Hakuta, 2001, 2005).

---

called *forms,* which roughly correspond to the 12 grades in American schools. Russian children begin school at age 7 and begin learning English in the third form. Because of this emphasis on teaching English, most Russian citizens under the age of 40 today are able to speak at least some English. The United States is the only technologically advanced Western nation that does not have a national foreign language requirement at the high school level, even for students in rigorous academic programs.

American students who do not learn a second language may be missing more than the chance to acquire a skill (Combs, 2010; Tompkins, 2010). *Bilingualism*—the ability to speak two languages—has a positive effect on children's cognitive development (Gibbons & Ng, 2004). Children who are fluent in two languages perform better than their single-language counterparts on tests of control of attention, concept formation, analytical reasoning, cognitive flexibility, and cognitive complexity (Bialystok, 2001, 2011). They also are more conscious of the structure of spoken and written language and better at noticing errors of grammar and meaning, skills that benefit their reading ability (Bialystok, 1993, 1997).

In the United States, many immigrant children go from being monolingual in their home language to being bilingual in that language and in English, only to end up monolingual speakers of English. This *subtractive bilingualism* can have negative effects on children, who often become ashamed of their home language.

A current controversy related to bilingualism involves bilingual education. To read about this controversy, see the *Connecting with Diversity* interlude.

extrinsic motivation Involves external incentives such as rewards and punishments.

intrinsic motivation Involves internal factors such as self-determination, curiosity, challenge, and effort.

Review *Connect* Reflect

LG4 Summarize language development in middle and late childhood.

Review

- What are some changes in vocabulary, grammar, and metalinguistic awareness in the middle and late childhood years?
- What controversy surrounds teaching children to read?
- What is bilingual education? What issues are involved in bilingual education?

Connect

- In an earlier main section in this chapter, you read about metacognition. Compare that concept with the concept of metalinguistic awareness discussed in this section.

Reflect *Your Own Personal Journey of Life*

- Did you learn a second language as a child? If so, do you think it was beneficial to you? Why or why not? If you did not learn a second language as a child, do you wish you had? Why or why not?

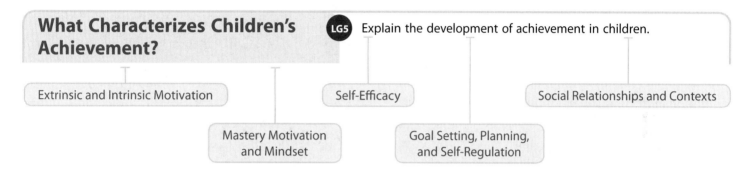

What Characterizes Children's Achievement?

LG5 Explain the development of achievement in children.

- Extrinsic and Intrinsic Motivation
- Mastery Motivation and Mindset
- Self-Efficacy
- Goal Setting, Planning, and Self-Regulation
- Social Relationships and Contexts

We are a species motivated to do well at what we attempt, to gain mastery over the world in which we live, to explore unknown environments with enthusiasm and curiosity, and to achieve the heights of success. In this section, we explore some of the many different ways children effectively achieve their potential during middle and late childhood.

EXTRINSIC AND INTRINSIC MOTIVATION

Extrinsic motivation involves external incentives such as rewards and punishments. The cognitive approaches stress the importance of intrinsic motivation in achievement. **Intrinsic motivation** is based on internal factors such as self-determination, curiosity, challenge, and effort. Some individuals study hard because they want to make good grades or avoid parental disapproval (extrinsic motivation). Others study hard because they are internally motivated to achieve high standards in their work (intrinsic motivation).

One view of intrinsic motivation emphasizes self-determination (Ryan & Deci, 2001). In this view, children want to believe that they are doing something because of their own will, not because of external success or rewards.

An overwhelming conclusion of motivation research is that teachers should encourage students to become intrinsically motivated. Similarly, teachers should create learning environments that promote students' cognitive engagement and self-responsibility for learning (Meece & Eccles, 2010; Patall, Cooper, & Robinson, 2008). That said, the real world includes both intrinsic and extrinsic motivation, and too often intrinsic and extrinsic motivation have been pitted against each other as polar opposites. In many aspects of students' lives, both intrinsic and extrinsic motivation are at work (Cameron & Pierce, 2008). Further, both intrinsic and extrinsic motivation can operate simultaneously. Thus, a student may work hard in a course because she enjoys the content and likes learning about it (intrinsic) and because she wants to earn a good grade (extrinsic) (Schunk, 2012). Keep in mind, though, that many psychologists recommend that extrinsic motivation by itself is not a good strategy.

Life is a gift . . . Accept it.
Life is a puzzle . . . Solve it.
Life is an adventure . . . Dare it.
Life is an opportunity . . . Take it.
Life is a mystery . . . Unfold it.
Life is a mission . . . Fulfill it.
Life is a struggle . . . Face it.
Life is a goal . . . Achieve it.

—AUTHOR UNKNOWN

These students were given an opportunity to write and perform their own play. These kinds of self-determining opportunities can enhance students' motivation to achieve.

Calvin and Hobbes   by Bill Watterson

MASTERY MOTIVATION AND MINDSET

Becoming cognitively engaged and self-motivated to improve are reflected in children with a mastery motivation. These children also have a growth mindset—a belief that they can produce positive outcomes if they put forth the effort.

Mastery Motivation   Developmental psychologists Valanne Henderson and Carol Dweck (1990) have found that children often show two distinct responses to difficult or challenging circumstances. Individuals who display **mastery motivation** are task-oriented; instead of focusing on their ability, they concentrate on learning strategies and the process of achievement rather than the outcome. Those with a **helpless orientation** seem trapped by the experience of difficulty, and they attribute their difficulty to lack of ability. They frequently make comments such as "I'm not very good at this," even though they might earlier have demonstrated their ability through many successes. And, once they view their behavior as failure, they often feel anxious, and their performance worsens even further.

In contrast, mastery-oriented children often instruct themselves to pay attention, to think carefully, and to remember strategies that have worked for them in previous situations. They frequently report feeling challenged and excited by difficult tasks, rather than being threatened by them (Anderman & Mueller, 2010).

Another issue in motivation involves whether to adopt a mastery or a performance orientation. Children with a **performance orientation** are focused on achievement outcomes, believing that winning is what matters most and that happiness results from winning. Does this mean that mastery-oriented individuals do not like to win and that performance-oriented individuals are not motivated to experience the self-efficacy that comes from being able to take credit for one's accomplishments? No. A matter of emphasis or degree is involved, though. For mastery-oriented individuals, winning isn't everything; for performance-oriented individuals, skill development and self-efficacy take a backseat to winning.

A final point needs to be made about mastery and performance goals: They are not always mutually exclusive. Students can be both mastery- and performance-oriented, and researchers have found that mastery goals combined with performance goals often benefit students' success (Anderman & Mueller, 2010).

Mindset   Carol Dweck's (2006, 2007, 2011) most recent analysis of motivation for achievement stresses the importance of developing a **mindset,** which she defines as the cognitive view individuals develop for themselves. She concludes that individuals have one of two mindsets: (1) a *fixed mindset,* in which they believe that their qualities are carved in stone and cannot change; or (2) a *growth mindset,* in

---

mastery motivation An orientation that focuses on tasks, learning strategies, and the achievement process rather than innate ability.

helpless orientation An orientation in which one seems trapped by the experience of difficulty and attributes one's difficulty to a lack of ability.

performance orientation An orientation in which one focuses on achievement outcomes; winning is what matters most, and happiness is thought to result from winning.

mindset The cognitive view, either fixed or growth, that individuals develop for themselves.

which they believe their qualities can change and improve through their effort. A fixed mindset is similar to a helpless orientation; a growth mindset is much like having mastery motivation.

In *Mindset*, Dweck (2006) argued that individuals' mindsets influence whether they will be optimistic or pessimistic, shape their goals and how hard they will strive to reach those goals, and affect many aspects of their lives, including achievement and success in school and sports. Dweck says that mindsets begin to be shaped as children and adolescents interact with parents, teachers, and coaches, who themselves have either a fixed mindset or a growth mindset.

Dweck and her colleagues (Blackwell & Dweck, 2008; Blackwell & others, 2007; Dweck, 2011; Dweck & Master, 2009) recently incorporated information about the brain's plasticity into their effort to improve students' motivation to achieve and succeed. In one study, they assigned two groups of students to eight sessions of either (1) study skills instruction or (2) study skills instruction plus information about the importance of developing a growth mindset (called *incremental theory* in the research) (Blackwell & others, 2007). One of the exercises in the growth mindset group, titled "You Can Grow Your Brain," emphasized that the brain is like a muscle that can change and grow as it is exercised and develops new connections. Students were informed that the more you challenge your brain to learn, the more your brain cells grow. Both groups had a pattern of declining math scores prior to the intervention. Following the intervention, the group who received only the study skills instruction continued to decline but the group who received a combination of study skills instruction and the growth mindset emphasis on exercising the brain reversed the downward trend and improved their math achievement.

In other work, Dweck has been creating a computer-based workshop, "Brainology," to teach students that their intelligence can change (Blackwell & Dweck, 2008). Students experience six modules about how the brain works and how they can make their brain improve. After the workshop was tested in 20 New York City schools recently, students strongly endorsed the value of the computer-based brain modules. Said one student, "I will try harder because I know that the more you try the more your brain knows" (Dweck & Master, 2009, p. 137).

SELF-EFFICACY

Like having a growth mindset, **self-efficacy**—the belief that one can master a situation and produce favorable outcomes—is an important cognitive view for children to develop (Walsh, 2008). Albert Bandura (2004, 2010a), whose social cognitive theory we discussed in Chapter 1, emphasizes that self-efficacy is a critical factor in

> Keep the growth mindset in your thoughts. Then, when you bump up against obstacles, you can turn to it . . . showing you a path into the future.
>
> —**Carol Dweck**
> *Contemporary Psychologist, Stanford University*

> They can because they think they can.
>
> —**Virgil**
> *Roman Poet, 1st Century B.C.*

A screen from Carol Dweck's Brainology program, which is designed to cultivate children's growth mindset.

self-efficacy The belief that one can master a situation and produce favorable outcomes.

What characterizes students with high self-efficacy?

How Would You...?

If you were an **educator,** how would you encourage enhanced self-efficacy in a student who says, "I can't do this work!"?

whether or not students achieve. Self-efficacy has much in common with mastery motivation and intrinsic motivation. Self-efficacy is the belief that "I can"; helplessness is the belief that "I cannot" (Stipek, 2002). Students with high self-efficacy endorse such statements as "I know that I will be able to learn the material in this class" and "I expect to be able to do well at this activity."

Dale Schunk (2012) has applied the concept of self-efficacy to many aspects of students' achievement. In his view, self-efficacy influences a student's choice of activities. Students with low self-efficacy for learning may avoid many learning tasks, especially those that are challenging. By contrast, their high-self-efficacy counterparts eagerly work at learning tasks. High-self-efficacy students are more likely to expend effort and persist longer at a learning task than low-self-efficacy students.

Children's achievement is influenced by their parents' self-efficacy. A recent study revealed a number of positive developmental outcomes, including more daily opportunities for optimal functioning, better peer relations, and fewer problems, for children and adolescents whose parents had high self-efficacy (Steca & others, 2011).

GOAL SETTING, PLANNING, AND SELF-REGULATION

Goal setting, planning, and self-monitoring are important aspects of achievement (Anderman & Mueller, 2010). Researchers have found that self-efficacy and achievement improve when individuals set goals that are specific, proximal, and challenging (Bandura, 2001). A nonspecific, fuzzy goal is "I want to be successful." A more concrete, specific goal is "I want to do well on my spelling test this week."

Individuals can set both long-term (distal) and short-term (proximal) goals. It is okay for individuals to set some long-term goals, such as "I want to graduate from high school" or "I want to go to college," but they also need to create short-term goals, which are steps along the way. "Getting an A on the next math test" is an example of a short-term, proximal goal. So is "Doing all of my homework by 4 p.m. Sunday."

Another good strategy is for individuals to set challenging goals. A challenging goal is a commitment to self-improvement. Strong interest and involvement in activities are sparked by challenges. Goals that are easy to reach generate little interest or effort. However, goals should be optimally matched to the individual's skill level. If goals are unrealistically high, the result will be repeated failures that lower the individual's self-efficacy.

It is not enough just to get individuals to set goals. It also is important to encourage them to plan how they will reach their goals. Being a good planner means managing time effectively, setting priorities, and being organized. Younger children will likely need help from parents or teachers to develop goal setting, planning, and organizational skills.

Individuals not only should plan their next week's activities but also should monitor how well they are sticking to their plan. Once engaged in a task, they need to monitor their progress, judge how well they are doing on the task, and evaluate the outcomes to regulate what they do in the future (Schunk, 2012).

SOCIAL RELATIONSHIPS AND CONTEXTS

Children's relationships with parents, peers, friends, teachers, mentors, and others can profoundly affect their achievement. So can the social contexts of ethnicity and culture.

Parents Parents' child-rearing practices are linked to children's achievement (Eccles, 2007). Here are some positive parenting practices that result in improved motivation and achievement: knowing enough about the child to provide the right amount of challenge and the right amount of support; providing a positive emotional climate that motivates children to internalize their parents' values and goals; and modeling motivated achievement behavior, such as working hard and persisting with effort at challenging tasks.

In addition to general child-rearing practices, parents provide various activities or resources at home that may influence students' interest and motivation to pursue various activities over time (Meece & Eccles, 2010). For example, reading to one's preschool children and providing reading materials in the home are positively related to students' later reading achievement and motivation (Wigfield & Asher, 1994).

How Would You...?

If you were an **educator,** how would you describe the importance of teachers in children's achievement?

Teachers   Teachers play an important role in students' achievement. When researchers have observed classrooms, they have found that effective, engaging teachers provide support for students to make good progress but also encourage them to become self-regulated achievers (Pressley, Mohan, Fingeret, & others, 2007). The encouragement takes place in a very positive environment, one in which students are constantly being motivated to try hard and to develop self-efficacy.

Teachers' expectations influence students' motivation and performance (Rubie-Davies, 2011). One study revealed that teachers' high expectations can help to buffer the negative effect of parents' low expectations for students' achievement (Wood, Kaplan, & McLoyd, 2007).

Ethnicity   The diversity that exists among ethnic minority children is evident in their achievement (Nieto & Bode, 2012). In addition to recognizing diversity of achievement within every cultural group, it also is important to distinguish between difference and deficiency (Banks, 2010; Bennett, 2012). Too often, the achievement levels of ethnic minority students—especially African Americans, Latinos, and Native Americans—have been interpreted as *deficits* by middle-socioeconomic-status White standards, when they simply are *culturally different and distinct* (Jones, 1994). An especially important factor in the lower achievement of students from low-income families is lack of adequate resources, such as an up-to-date computer in the home or even any computer at all, to support students' learning (Schunk, Pintrich, & Meece, 2008).

Sandra Graham (1986, 1990) has conducted a number of studies that reveal not only the stronger influence of socioeconomic status than ethnic differences in achievement but also the importance of studying ethnic minority student motivation in the context of general motivational theory. Her inquiries fall within the framework of attribution theory and focus on the causes that African American students give for their achievement orientation, such as why they succeed or fail. She is struck by how consistently middle-income African American students do not fit the stereotype of being unmotivated. Like their White middle-income counterparts, they have high achievement expectations and understand that failure is usually due to a lack of effort, rather than bad luck. A recent longitudinal study revealed that African American children or children from low-income families benefited more than children from higher-income families when they did homework more frequently, had Internet access at home, and had a community library card (Xia, 2010).

UCLA educational psychologist Sandra Graham is shown talking with adolescent boys about motivation. She has conducted a number of studies which reveal that middle-socioeconomic-status African American students—like their White counterparts—have high achievement expectations and attribute success to internal factors such as effort rather than external factors such as luck.

Cross-Cultural Comparisons   In the past three decades, the poor performance of American children in math and science has become well publicized. In a large-scale comparison of math and science achievement in fourth-grade students in 2007, the average U.S. fourth-grade math score was higher than 23 of the 35 countries and lower than 8 countries (all in Asia and Europe) (TIMMS, 2008). Fourth-graders from Hong Kong had the highest average math score. The average fourth-grade U.S. math score had improved slightly (11 points) from the same assessment in 1995, but some countries had improved their scores considerably more—the Hong Kong score was 50 points higher and the Slovenia score 40 points higher in 2007 than in 1995, for example.

In 2007, the fourth-grade U.S. science score was higher than those in 25 countries and lower than those in 4 countries (all in Asia). However, the average U.S. fourth-grade science score had decreased 3 points from 1995 to 2007, while the science scores for some countries had increased dramatically—63 points in Singapore, 56 points in Latvia, and 55 points in Iran, for example. Why do American students fare so poorly in mathematics? In the *Connecting with Research* interlude, you can read about Harold Stevenson's efforts to find out.

Why Does Children's Math Achievement Differ in the United States, China, Taiwan, and Japan?

Harold Stevenson's (1995, 2000; Stevenson, Hofer, & Randel, 1999; Stevenson & others, 1990) research explores reasons for the poor performance of American students. Stevenson and his colleagues have completed five cross-cultural comparisons of students in the United States, China, Taiwan, and Japan. In these studies, Asian students consistently outperform American students. And, the longer the students are in school, the wider the gap becomes between Asian and American students—the lowest difference is in the first grade, the highest in the eleventh grade (the highest grade studied).

To learn more about the reasons for these large cross-cultural differences, Stevenson and his colleagues spent thousands of hours observing in classrooms as well as interviewing and surveying teachers, students, and parents.

They found that the Asian teachers spent more of their time teaching math than did the American teachers. For example, more than one-fourth of total classroom time in the first grade was spent on math instruction in Japan, compared with only one-tenth of the time in the U.S. first-grade classrooms. Also, the Asian students were in school an average of 240 days a year, compared with 178 days in the United States.

In addition to the substantially greater time spent on math instruction in the Asian schools than the American schools, differences were found between the Asian and American parents. The American parents had much lower expectations for their children's education and achievement than did the Asian parents. Also, the American parents were more likely to believe that their children's math achievement was due to innate ability; the

Asian parents were more likely to say that their children's math achievement was the consequence of effort and training (see Figure 12.8). The Asian students were more likely to do math homework than were the American students, and the Asian parents were far more likely to help their children with their math homework than were the American parents (Chen & Stevenson, 1989).

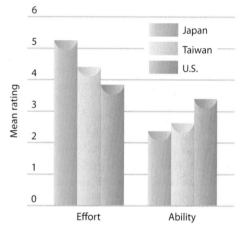

FIGURE **12.8**

MOTHERS' BELIEFS ABOUT THE FACTORS RESPONSIBLE FOR CHILDREN'S MATH ACHIEVEMENT IN THREE COUNTRIES.

In one study, mothers in Japan and Taiwan were more likely to believe that their children's math achievement was due to effort rather than innate ability, whereas U.S. mothers were more likely to believe their children's math achievement was due to innate ability (Stevenson, Lee, & Stigler, 1986). If parents believe that their children's math achievement is due to innate ability and their children are not doing well in math, the implication is that they are less likely to think their children will benefit from putting forth more effort. (From Stevenson et al., 1986, Figure 6, "Mathematics Achievement of Chinese, Japanese, and American Children," *Science*, vol. 231, pp. 693–699. Reprinted with permission from AAAS.)

Asian grade schools intersperse studying with frequent periods of activities. This approach helps children maintain their attention and likely makes learning more enjoyable. Shown here are Japanese fourth-graders making wearable masks. *What are some differences in the way children in many Asian countries are taught compared with children in the United States?*

How might the results from this research be applied to American children's education? Specifically, do you think child development professionals should try to change the roles and attitudes of American parents toward their children's math achievement?

Review Connect Reflect

LG5 Explain the development of achievement in children.

Review

- How does extrinsic motivation differ from intrinsic motivation?
- How does mastery motivation differ from helpless and performance orientations? What is mindset, and how does it influence children's achievement?
- What is self-efficacy, and how is it involved in achievement?
- What functions do goal setting, planning, and self-monitoring play in achievement?
- How are social relationships and contexts involved in children's achievement?

Connect

- In this section, you read about extrinsic and intrinsic motivation. Which theory discussed in Chapter 1 places the most emphasis on the importance of extrinsic motivation in children's development?

Reflect *Your Own Personal Journey of Life*

- Think about several of your own past schoolmates who showed low motivation in school. Why do you think they behaved that way? What teaching strategies might have helped them?

topical connections

In the next chapter you will study many aspects of children's socioemotional development in the elementary school years, including changes in the self, emotional development, moral development, and gender. You'll also explore changes in parent-child relationships, peer relations, and schooling in middle and late childhood.

In Chapter 15, you will read about how adolescent thought is more abstract, idealistic, and logical than children's. The transition to middle school or junior high is difficult for many individuals because it coincides with so many physical, cognitive, and socioemotional changes in development.

looking **forward**

reach your **learning goals**

What Is Piaget's Theory of Cognitive Development in Middle and Late Childhood?

 LG1 Discuss Piaget's stage of concrete operational thought and apply Piaget's theory to education.

Concrete Operational Thought

Evaluating Piaget's Concrete Operational Stage

Applications to Education

- Concrete operational thought involves operations, conservation, classification, seriation, and transitivity. Thought is not as abstract as it is later in development.

- Critics argue that elements of a stage do not appear at the same time, and that education and culture have more influence on development than Piaget predicted. Neo-Piagetians place more emphasis on how children process information, strategies, speed of information processing, and the division of cognitive problems into more precise steps.

- Application of Piaget's ideas to education especially involves a constructivist approach that focuses on the teacher as a guide rather than a director and turns the classroom into a setting of exploration and discovery.

What Is the Nature of Children's Information Processing?

 LG2 Describe changes in information processing in middle and late childhood.

Memory

- Long-term memory increases in middle and late childhood. Working memory is an important memory process that involves manipulating and assembling information. Knowledge and expertise influence memory. Strategies such as organization, imagery, and elaboration can be used by children to improve their memory. Fuzzy trace theory has been proposed to explain developmental changes in memory.

Thinking

- Critical thinking involves thinking reflectively and productively, as well as evaluating evidence. Mindfulness is an important aspect of critical thinking. A special concern is the lack of emphasis on critical thinking in many schools. Creative thinking is the ability to think in novel and unusual ways and to come up with unique solutions to problems. Guilford distinguished between convergent and divergent thinking. A number of strategies, including brainstorming, can be used to encourage children's creative thinking. Children think like scientists in some ways, but in other ways they don't.

Metacognition

- Metacognition is knowing about knowing, or cognition about cognition. Most metacognitive studies have focused on metamemory. Pressley views the key to education as helping students learn a rich repertoire of strategies.

How Can Children's Intelligence Be Described?

 LG3 Characterize children's intelligence.

Intelligence and Its Assessment

- Intelligence consists of problem-solving skills and the ability to adapt to and learn from life's everyday experiences. Interest in intelligence often focuses on individual differences and assessment. Widely used intelligence tests today include the Stanford-Binet tests and Wechsler scales. Results on these tests may be reported in terms of an overall IQ or in terms of performance on specific areas of the tests.

Types of Intelligence

- Sternberg proposed that intelligence comes in three main forms: analytical, creative, and practical. Gardner proposes that there are eight types of intelligence: verbal, math, spatial, bodily-kinesthetic, interpersonal skills, intrapersonal skills, musical skills, and naturalist skills. The multiple-intelligence approaches have expanded our conception of intelligence, but critics argue that the research base for these approaches is not well established.

Interpreting Differences in IQ Scores

- IQ scores are influenced both by genetics and by characteristics of the environment. Studies of heritability indicate that genetics has a strong influence on the variance in IQ scores within a population, but environmental changes can alter the IQ scores of most people considerably. Parenting, home environments, schools, and intervention programs can influence these scores. Intelligence test scores have risen considerably around the world in recent decades—called the Flynn effect—and this rise supports the role of environment in intelligence. Group differences in IQ scores may reflect many influences, including cultural bias. Tests may be biased against certain groups because they are not familiar with a standard form of English, with the content that is being tested, or with the testing situation.

Extremes of Intelligence

- Mental retardation involves low IQ and problems in adapting to everyday life. One classification of mental retardation distinguishes organic and cultural-familial retardation. A child who is gifted has above-average intelligence and/or superior talent for something. Terman contributed to our understanding that gifted children are not more maladjusted than non-gifted children. Three characteristics of gifted children are precocity, individuality, and a passion to master a domain. Critics argue that gifted children have been miseducated.

What Changes in Language Development Occur in Middle and Late Childhood?

 LG4 Summarize language development in middle and late childhood.

Vocabulary, Grammar, and Metalinguistic Awareness

- In middle and late childhood, children become more analytical and logical in their approach to words and grammar. In terms of grammar, children now better understand comparatives and subjunctives. They become increasingly able to use complex grammar and produce narratives that make sense. Improvements in metalinguistic awareness—knowledge about language—are evident during the elementary school years as children increasingly define words, expand their knowledge of syntax, and understand better how to use language in culturally appropriate ways.

Reading

- A current debate in reading focuses on the phonics approach versus the whole-language approach. The phonics approach advocates phonetics instruction and giving children simplified materials. The whole-language approach stresses that reading instruction should parallel children's natural language learning and recommends giving children whole-language materials, such as books and newspapers. An increasing number of experts now conclude that although both approaches can benefit children, direct instruction in phonics is a key aspect of learning to read.

Bilingualism and Second-Language Learning

- Bilingual education aims to teach academic subjects to immigrant children in their native language while gradually adding English instruction. Researchers have found that bilingualism does not interfere with performance in either language. Success in learning a second language is greater in childhood than in adolescence.

What Characterizes Children's Achievement?

 LG5 Explain the development of achievement in children.

Extrinsic and Intrinsic Motivation

- Extrinsic motivation involves external incentives such as rewards and punishments. Intrinsic motivation is based on internal factors such as self-determination, curiosity, challenge, and effort. Giving children some choice and providing opportunities for personal responsibility increase intrinsic motivation.

Mastery Motivation and Mindset

- Individuals with a mastery motivation focus on the task rather than ability and use solution-oriented strategies. Mastery motivation is preferred over a helpless orientation (in which individuals seem trapped by the experience of difficulty and attribute their difficulty to lack of ability) or a performance orientation (being concerned with achievement outcomes—winning is what matters). Mindset is the cognitive view, either fixed or growth, that individuals develop for themselves. Dweck argues that a key aspect of children's development is to guide them in developing a growth mindset.

Self-Efficacy

- Self-efficacy is the belief that one can master a situation and produce positive outcomes. Bandura stresses that self-efficacy is a critical factor in whether children will achieve.

Goal Setting, Planning, and Self-Regulation

- Setting specific, proximal (short-term), and challenging goals benefits children's self-efficacy and achievement. Being a good planner means managing time effectively, setting priorities, and being organized. Self-monitoring is a key aspect of self-regulation that benefits children's learning.

Social Relationships and Contexts

- Among the social relationships and contexts that are linked to children's achievement are those that involve parenting, teachers, ethnicity, and culture. American children are more achievement-oriented than children in many countries but are less achievement-oriented than many children in Asian countries such as China, Taiwan, and Japan.

key terms

seriation 355	creative thinking 360	triarchic theory of	whole-language
transitivity 355	convergent thinking 360	intelligence 365	approach 374
neo-Piagetians 355	divergent thinking 360	heritability 367	phonics approach 375
long-term memory 357	brainstorming 361	culture-fair tests 369	extrinsic motivation 377
working memory 357	metacognition 362	mental retardation 370	intrinsic motivation 377
strategies 358	intelligence 364	organic retardation 370	mastery motivation 378
elaboration 358	individual differences 364	cultural-familial	helpless orientation 378
fuzzy trace theory 359	mental age (MA) 364	retardation 370	performance orientation 378
critical thinking 359	intelligence quotient (IQ) 364	gifted 370	mindset 378
mindfulness 359	normal distribution 364	metalinguistic awareness 374	self-efficacy 379

key people

Jean Piaget 354	Martin Brooks 360	David Wechsler 364	Carol Dweck 378
Alan Baddeley 357	J. P. Guilford 360	Robert J. Sternberg 365	Albert Bandura 379
Charles Brainerd 359	Teresa Amabile 361	Howard Gardner 366	Dale Schunk 380
Valerie Reyna 359	Deanna Kuhn 362	Nathan Brody 366	Sandra Graham 381
Patricia Bauer 359	Michael Pressley 363	Lewis Terman 371	Harold Stevenson 382
Peter Ornstein 359	Alfred Binet 364	Ellen Winner 371	
Ellen Langer 359	Theophile Simon 364	John Colombo 372	
Jacqueline Brooks 360	William Stern 364	Valanne Henderson 378	

connecting with improving the lives of children

MAKING A DIFFERENCE

Supporting Children's Cognitive Development

What are some effective ways to help elementary school children develop their cognitive skills?

- *Facilitate rather than direct children's learning.* Design situations that let children learn by doing and that actively promote their thinking and discovery. Listen, watch, and question children to help them attain a better understanding of concepts.
- *Provide opportunities for children to think critically.* Encourage children to think reflectively, rather than automatically accepting everything as correct. Ask children questions about similarities and differences in things. Ask them questions of clarification, such as "What is the main point?" and "Why?" Ask children to justify their opinion. Ask them "what if" questions.
- *Be a good cognitive role model.* Model thinking and self-reflection for the child to see and hear. When children are around people who think critically and reflectively, they incorporate these cognitive styles into their own thinking repertoire.
- *Encourage collaboration with other children.* Children learn not only from adults but from other children as well. Cross-age teaching, in which older children who are competent thinkers interact with younger children, can be especially helpful. Collaborative problem solving teaches children how to work cooperatively with others.

- *Stimulate children's creative thinking.* Encourage children to take risks in their thinking. Don't overcontrol by telling children precisely what to do; let their originality come through. Don't set up grandiose expectations; it can hurt creativity. Encourage the child to think freely and come up with as many different ways of doing something as possible.

RESOURCES

ERIC Database
www.eric.ed.gov
ERIC provides wide-ranging references to many educational topics, including educational practices, parent-school relations, and community programs.

National Association for Gifted Children (NAGC)
www.nagc.org
The NAGC is an association of academics, educators, and librarians. Its goal is to improve the education of gifted children. It publishes periodic reports on the education of gifted children and the journal *Gifted Children Quarterly*.

Mindset
by Carol Dweck (2006)
New York: Random House
An outstanding book that emphasizes how critical it is for parents, teachers, and other adults to guide children in developing a growth rather than a fixed mindset.

chapter 13

SOCIOEMOTIONAL DEVELOPMENT IN MIDDLE AND LATE CHILDHOOD

chapter outline

What Is the Nature of Emotional and Personality Development in Middle and Late Childhood?

Learning Goal 1 Discuss emotional and personality development in middle and late childhood.

The Self
Emotional Development
Moral Development
Gender

What Are Some Changes in Parenting and Families in Middle and Late Childhood?

Learning Goal 2 Describe changes in parenting and families in middle and late childhood.

Developmental Changes in Parent-Child Relationships
Parents as Managers
Stepfamilies

What Changes Characterize Peer Relationships in Middle and Late Childhood?

Learning Goal 3 Identify changes in peer relationships in middle and late childhood.

Developmental Changes
Peer Status
Social Cognition
Bullying
Friends

What Are Some Important Aspects of Schools?

Learning Goal 4 Characterize contemporary approaches to student learning and sociocultural diversity in schools.

Contemporary Approaches to Student Learning
Socioeconomic Status and Ethnicity

At P.S. 30 in the South Bronx, Mr. Bedrock teaches fifth grade. One student in his class, Serafina, recently lost her mother to AIDS. When author Jonathan Kozol visited the class, he was told that two other children had taken the role of "allies in the child's struggle for emotional survival" (Kozol, 2005, p. 291).

Textbooks are in short supply for the class, and the social studies text is so out of date it claims that Ronald Reagan is the country's president. But Mr. Bedrock told Kozol that it's a "wonderful" class this year. About their teacher, 56-year-old Mr. Bedrock, one student said, "'He's getting old, . . . but we love him anyway'" (p. 292). Kozol found the students orderly, interested, and engaged.

By late childhood, most children, like these students at P.S. 30, have developed friendships, learned to interact with adults other than their parents, and developed ideas about fairness and other moral concepts.

Can children understand such concepts as discrimination, economic inequality, affirmative action, and comparable worth? Probably not, if you ask them about those terms. But Phyllis Katz (1987) found that children can understand situations that involve those concepts. Katz (1987) asked elementary-school-age children to pretend that they had taken a long ride on a spaceship to a make-believe planet called Pax. Once there, the children find problematic situations. For example, citizens of Pax who had dotted noses couldn't get jobs. Instead, the jobs went to the people with striped noses. "What would you do in this situation?" Katz asked the children.

She asked them for their opinions about various situations on this faraway planet. For example, what should a teacher do when two students were tied for a prize or when they had been fighting? The elementary school children often came up with

What are some of the challenges faced by children growing up in the South Bronx?

topical **connections** – – – – – – – – –

In Chapter 10, you learned that young children are in Erikson's stage of initiative versus guilt, parents continue to play an important role in their development, and a style of authoritative parenting is most likely to have positive outcomes for children. In early childhood, peer relations take on a more significant role as children's social worlds widen. Play has a special place in young children's lives and is an important context for both cognitive and socioemotional development. In the preceding chapter you studied children's cognitive development in middle and late childhood, including Piaget's view of children's thinking, their intelligence, achievement, and language skills. In this chapter, you will explore continuing advances in many aspects of children's socioemotional development.

◀ – *looking back* – – – – – – – – – – – –

interesting solutions to problems. For example, all but two children believed that teachers should earn as much as janitors—the holdouts said teachers should make less because they stay in one room or because cleaning toilets is more disgusting and therefore deserves higher wages. All but one thought that not giving a job to a qualified applicant who had different physical characteristics (a dotted rather than a striped nose) was unfair. War was mentioned as the biggest problem on Earth, although children were not certain whether it was currently occurring. Overall, the types of rules the children believed a society should abide by were quite sensible—almost all included the need for equitable sharing of resources and work and prohibitions against aggression.

preview

The years of middle and late childhood bring many changes to children's social and emotional lives. The development of their self-concepts, emotions, moral reasoning, and gendered behavior is significant. Transformations in their relationships with parents and peers also occur, and schooling takes on a more academic flavor.

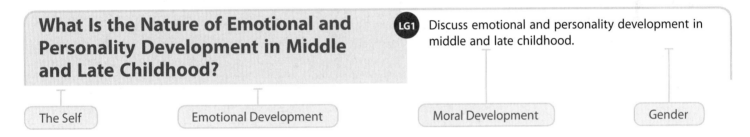

What Is the Nature of Emotional and Personality Development in Middle and Late Childhood?

LG1 Discuss emotional and personality development in middle and late childhood.

The Self   Emotional Development   Moral Development   Gender

In this section, we explore how the self continues to develop during middle and late childhood and the emotional changes that take place during these years. We also discuss children's moral development and many aspects of the role that gender plays in their development in middle and late childhood.

THE SELF

What is the nature of the child's self-understanding, understanding of others, and self-esteem during the elementary school years? What role does self-regulation play in children's achievement?

The Development of Self-Understanding In middle and late childhood, especially from 8 to 11 years of age, children increasingly describe themselves with psychological characteristics and traits in contrast to the more concrete self-descriptions of younger children. Older children are more likely to describe themselves as "popular, nice, helpful, mean, smart, and dumb" (Harter, 2006, p. 526).

In addition, during the elementary school years, children become more likely to recognize social aspects of the self (Harter, 2006). These include references to social groups in their self-descriptions, such as referring to themselves as Girl Scouts, as Catholics, or as someone who has two close friends (Livesly & Bromley, 1973).

Children's self-understanding in the elementary school years also includes increasing reference to social comparison (Harter, 2006). At this point in development,

Children are busy becoming something they have not quite grasped yet, something which keeps changing.

—**Alastair Reid**
American Poet, 20th Century

How Would You...?

If you were a **psychologist,** how would you explain the role of social comparison for the development of a child's sense of self?

children are more likely to distinguish themselves from others in comparative rather than in absolute terms. That is, elementary-school-aged children are no longer as likely to think about what they do or do not do, but are more likely to think about what they can do in comparison with others.

Consider a series of studies in which Diane Ruble (1983) investigated children's use of social comparison in their self-evaluations. Children were given a difficult task and then offered feedback on their performance, as well as information about the performances of other children their age. The children were then asked for self-evaluations. Children younger than 7 made virtually no reference to the information about other children's performances. However, many children older than 7 included socially comparative information in their self-descriptions.

In sum, in middle and late childhood, self-description increasingly involves psychological and social characteristics, including social comparison.

What are some changes in children's understanding of others in middle and late childhood?

Understanding Others   In Chapter 10, "Socioemotional Development in Early Childhood," we described the advances and limitations of young children's understanding of others. In middle and late childhood, children show an increase in *perspective taking,* the ability to assume other people's perspectives and understand their thoughts and feelings. In Robert Selman's (1980) view, at about 6 to 8 years of age, children begin to understand that others may have a different perspective because some people have more access to information. Then, he says, in the next several years, children become aware that each individual is aware of the other's perspective and that putting oneself in the other's place is a way of judging the other person's intentions, purposes, and actions.

Perspective taking is especially thought to be important in whether children develop prosocial or antisocial attitudes and behavior. In terms of prosocial behavior, taking another's perspective improves children's likelihood of understanding and sympathizing with others when they are distressed or in need. A recent study revealed that in children characterized as being emotionally reactive, good perspective-taking skills were linked to being able to regain a neutral emotional state after being emotionally aroused (Bengtsson & Arvidsson, 2011). In this study, children who made gains in perspective-taking skills reduced their emotional reactivity over a two-year period.

In middle and late childhood, children also become more skeptical of others' claims. In Chapter 10, "Socioemotional Development in Early Childhood," we indicated that even 4-year-old children show some skepticism of others' claims. In middle and late childhood, children become increasingly skeptical of some sources of information about psychological traits. For example, in one study, 10- to 11-year-olds were more likely to reject other children's self-reports that they were smart and honest than were 6- to 7-year-olds (Heyman & Legare, 2005). The more psychologically sophisticated 10- to 11-year-olds also showed a better understanding that others' self-reports may involve socially desirable tendencies than did the 6- to 7-year-olds.

How Would You...?

If you were an **educator,** how would you work with children to help them develop a healthy self-concept concerning their academic ability?

self-esteem The global evaluative dimension of the self. Self-esteem is also referred to as self-worth or self-image.

self-concept Domain-specific evaluations of the self.

Self-Esteem and Self-Concept   High self-esteem and a positive self-concept are important characteristics of children's well-being (Harter, 2006). Investigators sometimes use the terms *self-esteem* and *self-concept* interchangeably or do not precisely define them, but there is a meaningful difference between them. **Self-esteem** refers to global evaluations of the self; it is also called self-worth or self-image. For example, a child may perceive that she is not merely a person but a good person. **Self-concept** refers to domain-specific evaluations of the self. Children can make self-evaluations in many domains of their lives—academic, athletic, appearance, and so on. In sum, self-esteem refers to global self-evaluations, self-concept to domain-specific evaluations.

For most children, high self-esteem and a positive self-concept are important aspects of their well-being (Kaplan, 2009). However, for some children, self-esteem reflects perceptions that do not always match reality (Krueger, Vohs, & Baumeister, 2008). A child's self-esteem might reflect a belief about whether he or she is intelligent and attractive, for example, but that belief is not necessarily accurate. Thus, high self-esteem may refer to accurate, justified perceptions of one's worth as a person and one's successes and accomplishments, but it can also refer to an arrogant, grandiose, unwarranted sense of superiority over others. In the same manner, low self-esteem may reflect either an accurate perception of one's shortcomings or a distorted, even pathological insecurity and inferiority.

What are some issues involved in understanding children's self-esteem in school?

Variations in self-esteem have been linked with many aspects of children's development. However, much of the research is *correlational* rather than *experimental*. Recall from Chapter 1 that correlation does not equal causation. Thus, if a correlational study finds an association between children's low self-esteem and low academic achievement, low academic achievement could cause the low self-esteem as much as low self-esteem causes low academic achievement.

In fact, there are only moderate correlations between school performance and self-esteem, and these correlations do not suggest that high self-esteem produces better school performance (Baumeister & others, 2003). Efforts to increase students' self-esteem have not always led to improved school performance (Davies & Brember, 1999).

Children with high self-esteem have greater initiative, but this can produce positive or negative outcomes (Baumeister & others, 2003). High-self-esteem children are prone to both prosocial and antisocial actions. A study revealed that over time aggressive children with high self-esteem increasingly valued the rewards that aggression can bring and belittled their victims (Menon & others, 2007).

In addition, a current concern is that too many of today's children grow up receiving praise for mediocre or even poor performance and as a consequence have inflated self-esteem (Stipek, 2005). They may have difficulty handling competition and criticism. This theme is vividly captured by the title of a book, *Dumbing Down Our Kids: Why American Children Feel Good About Themselves But Can't Read, Write, or Add* (Sykes, 1995).

What are some good strategies for effectively increasing children's self-esteem? See the *Caring Connections* interlude for some answers to this question.

Self-Regulation   One of the most important aspects of the self in middle and late childhood is the increased capacity for self-regulation (Thompson, 2011a; Thompson & Waters, 2011). This increased capacity is characterized by deliberate efforts to manage one's behavior, emotions, and thoughts that lead to increased social competence and achievement (Eisenberg, 2010). For example, a recent study revealed that children from low-income families who had a higher level of self-regulation made better grades in school than their counterparts who had a lower level of self-regulation (Buckner, Mezzacappa, & Beardslee, 2009). Another recent study found that self-control increased from 4 to 10 years of age and that high self-control was linked to lower levels of deviant behavior (Vazsonyi & Huang, 2010).

The increased capacity for self-regulation is linked to developmental advances in the brain's prefrontal cortex, which was discussed in Chapter 3 (Diamond, Casey, & Munakata, 2011). In that discussion, increased focal activation in the prefrontal cortex was linked to improved cognitive control. Such cognitive control includes self-regulation.

Increasing Children's Self-Esteem

Four ways children's self-esteem can be improved include identifying the causes of low self-esteem, providing emotional support and social approval, helping children achieve, and helping children cope (Bednar, Wells, & Peterson, 1995; Harter, 2006):

- ***Identify the causes of low self-esteem.*** Intervention should target the causes of low self-esteem. Children have the highest self-esteem when they perform competently in domains that are important to them. Therefore, children should be encouraged to identify and value areas of competence. These areas might include academic skills, athletic skills, physical attractiveness, and social acceptance.

- ***Provide emotional support and social approval.*** Some children with low self-esteem come from conflicted families or conditions in which they experienced abuse or neglect—situations in which support was not available. In some cases, alternative sources of support can be arranged either informally through the encouragement of a teacher, a coach, or another significant adult, or more formally, through programs such as Big Brothers and Big Sisters.

- ***Help children achieve.*** Achievement also can improve children's self-esteem. For example, the straightforward teaching of real skills to children often results in increased achievement and, thus, in enhanced

How can parents help children develop higher self-esteem?

self-esteem. Children develop higher self-esteem because they know the important tasks that will achieve their goals, and they have performed them or similar behaviors in the past.

- ***Help children cope.*** Self-esteem is often increased when children face a problem and try to cope with it, rather than avoid it. If coping rather than avoidance prevails, children often face problems realistically, honestly, and nondefensively. This produces favorable self-evaluative thoughts, which lead to the self-generated approval that raises self-esteem.

What characterizes Erikson's stage of industry versus inferiority?

developmental connection

Erikson's Theory. Initiative versus guilt is Erikson's early childhood stage and identity versus identify confusion is his adolescence stage. Chapter 10, p. 290, and Chapter 16, p. 485

Industry Versus Inferiority   In Chapter 1, we discussed Erik Erikson's (1968) eight stages of human development. His fourth stage, industry versus inferiority, appears during middle and late childhood. The term *industry* expresses a dominant theme of this period: Children become interested in how things are made and how they work. When children are encouraged in their efforts to make, build, and work—whether building a model airplane, constructing a tree house, fixing a bicycle, solving an addition problem, or cooking—their sense of industry increases. However, parents who see their children's efforts at making things as "mischief" or "making a mess" encourage children's development of a sense of inferiority.

Children's social worlds beyond their families also contribute to a sense of industry. School becomes especially important in this regard. Consider children who are slightly below average in intelligence. They are too bright to be in special classes but not bright enough to be in gifted classes. Failing frequently in their academic efforts, they develop a sense of inferiority. By contrast, consider children whose sense of industry is disparaged at home. A series of sensitive and committed teachers may revitalize their sense of industry (Elkind, 1970).

EMOTIONAL DEVELOPMENT

In Chapter 10, "Socioemotional Development in Early Childhood," we saw that preschoolers become more adept at talking about their own and others' emotions. They also show a growing awareness of the need to control and manage their emotions to meet social standards. In middle and late childhood, children further develop their understanding and self-regulation of emotion (Thompson, 2011b).

Developmental Changes　Developmental changes in emotions during the middle and late childhood years include the following (Denham, Bassett, & Wyatt, 2007; Denham & others, 2011; Kuebli, 1994; Thompson, 2011b):

- *Improved emotional understanding.* For example, children in elementary school develop an increased ability to understand such complex emotions as pride and shame. These emotions become less tied to the reactions of other people; they become more self-generated and integrated with a sense of personal responsibility.

- *Increased understanding that more than one emotion can be experienced in a particular situation.* A third-grader, for example, may realize that achieving something might involve both anxiety and joy.

- *Increased tendency to be aware of the events leading to emotional reactions.* A fourth-grader may become aware that her sadness today is influenced by her friend's moving to another town last week.

- *Ability to suppress or conceal negative emotional reactions.* When one of his classmates irritates him, a fifth-grader has learned to tone down his anger better than he used to.

- *The use of self-initiated strategies for redirecting feelings.* In the elementary school years, children become more reflective about their emotional lives and increasingly use strategies to control their emotions. They become more effective at cognitively managing their emotions, such as soothing themselves after an upset.

- *A capacity for genuine empathy.* For example, a fourth-grader feels sympathy for a distressed person and experiences vicariously the sadness the distressed person is feeling.

What are some developmental changes in emotion during the middle and late childhood years?

Coping with Stress　An important aspect of children's lives is learning how to cope with stress (Bonnano, Mancini, & Westphal, 2011; Masten, 2012). As children get older, they are able to more accurately appraise a stressful situation and determine how much control they have over it. Older children generate more coping alternatives to stressful conditions and use more cognitive coping strategies (Saarni & others, 2006). For example, older children are better than younger children at intentionally shifting their thoughts to something that is less stressful. Older children are also better at reframing, or changing their perception of a stressful situation. For example, younger children may be very disappointed that their teacher did not say hello to them when they arrived at school. Older children may reframe this type of situation and think, "She may have been busy with other things and just forgot to say hello."

By 10 years of age, most children are able to use these cognitive strategies to cope with stress (Saarni & others, 2006). However, in families that have not been supportive and are characterized by turmoil or trauma, children may be so overwhelmed by stress that they do not use such strategies (Thabet & others, 2009).

Disasters can especially harm children's development and produce adjustment problems. Among the outcomes for children who experience disasters are acute stress reactions, depression, panic disorder, and post-traumatic stress disorder (Bonnano, Mancini, & Westphal, 2011). Proportions of children developing these

How Would You...?

If you were a **social worker,** how would you counsel a child who had been exposed to a traumatic event?

problems following a disaster depend on factors such as the nature and severity of the disaster, as well as the support available to the children.

Following are descriptions of recent studies of how various aspects of traumatic events and disasters affect children:

- In a study of mothers and their children aged 5 years and younger who were directly exposed to the 9/11 attacks in New York City, the mothers who developed post-traumatic stress disorder (PTSD) and depression were less likely to help their children regulate their emotions and behavior than mothers who were only depressed or only had PTSD (Chemtob & others, 2010). This outcome was linked to their children having anxiety, depression, aggression, and sleep problems.

- A study of the effects of the 2004 tsunami in Sri Lanka found that severe exposure to the tsunami combined with more exposure to other adversities, such as an ongoing war and family violence, was linked to poorer adjustment after the tsunami disaster (Catani & others, 2010).

- A research review revealed that children with disabilities are more likely than children without disabilities to live in poverty conditions, which increases their exposure to hazards and disasters (Peek & Stough, 2010). When a disaster occurs, children with disabilities have more difficulty escaping from the disaster.

In research on disasters and trauma, the term *dose-response effects* is often used. A widely supported finding in this research area is that the more severe the disaster or trauma (dose) is, the worse the adaptation and adjustment (response) following the event (Masten, 2012; Masten & Osofsky, 2010; Obradovic, Shaffer, & Masten, 2011).

Children who have a number of coping techniques have the best chance of adapting and functioning competently in the face of disasters and traumas. Following are some recommendations for helping children cope with the stress of especially devastating events (Gurwitch & others, 2001, pp. 4–11):

- *Reassure children of their safety and security.* This step may need to be taken numerous times.

- *Allow children to retell events and be patient in listening to them.*

What are some effective strategies to help children cope with traumatic events, such as the terrorist attacks on the United States on 9/11/2001, and hurricane Katrina in September 2005?

- *Encourage children to talk about any disturbing or confusing feelings.* Tell them that these are normal feelings after a stressful event.

- *Help children make sense of what happened.* Children may misunderstand what took place. For example, young children "may blame themselves, believe things happened that did not happen, believe that terrorists are in the school, etc. Gently help children develop a realistic understanding of the event" (p. 10).

- *Protect children from reexposure to frightening situations and reminders of the trauma.* This strategy includes limiting conversations about the event in front of the children.

MORAL DEVELOPMENT

Remember from Chapter 10, "Socioemotional Development in Early Childhood," our description of Piaget's view of moral development. Piaget proposed that younger children are characterized by *heteronomous morality* but that, by 10 years of age, they have moved into a higher stage called *autonomous morality*. According to Piaget, older children consider the intentions of the individual, believe that rules are subject to change, and are aware that punishment does not always follow wrongdoing.

Kohlberg's Theory A second major perspective on moral development was proposed by Lawrence Kohlberg (1958, 1986). Piaget's cognitive stages of development serve as the underpinnings for Kohlberg's theory, but Kohlberg suggested that there are six stages of moral development. These stages, he argued, are universal. Development from one stage to another, said Kohlberg, is fostered by opportunities to take the perspective of others and to experience conflict between one's current stage of moral thinking and the reasoning of someone at a higher stage.

Kohlberg arrived at his view after 20 years of using a unique interview with children. In the interview, children are presented with a series of stories in which characters face moral dilemmas. The following is the most popular Kohlberg dilemma:

Lawrence Kohlberg, the architect of a provocative cognitive developmental theory of moral development. *What is the nature of his theory?*

> In Europe a woman was near death from a special kind of cancer. There was one drug that the doctors thought might save her. It was a form of radium that a druggist in the same town had recently discovered. The drug was expensive to make, but the druggist was charging ten times what the drug cost him to make. He paid $200 for the radium and charged $2,000 for a small dose of the drug. The sick woman's husband, Heinz, went to everyone he knew to borrow the money, but he could only get together $1,000, which is half of what it cost. He told the druggist that his wife was dying and asked him to sell it cheaper or let him pay later. But the druggist said, "No, I discovered the drug, and I am going to make money from it." So Heinz got desperate and broke into the man's store to steal the drug for his wife. (Kohlberg, 1969, p. 379)

This story is one of eleven that Kohlberg devised to investigate the nature of moral thought. After reading the story, the interviewee answers a series of questions about the moral dilemma. Should Heinz have stolen the drug? Was stealing it right or wrong? Why? Is it a husband's duty to steal the drug for his wife if he can get it no other way? Would a good husband steal? Did the druggist have the right to charge that much when there was no law setting a limit on the price? Why or why not?

The Kohlberg Stages Based on the answers interviewees gave for this and other moral dilemmas, Kohlberg described three levels of moral thinking, each of which is characterized by two stages (see Figure 13.1). A key concept in understanding progression through the levels and stages is that their morality becomes more internal or mature. That is, their reasons for their moral decisions or values begin to go beyond the external or superficial reasons they gave when they were younger. Let's further examine Kohlberg's stages.

LEVEL 1 **Preconventional Level** **No Internalization**	LEVEL 2 **Conventional Level** **Intermediate Internalization**	LEVEL 3 **Postconventional Level** **Full Internalization**
Stage 1 Heteronomous Morality *Individuals pursue their own interests but let others do the same. What is right involves equal exchange.*	**Stage 3** Mutual Interpersonal Expectations, Relationships, and Interpersonal Conformity *Individuals value trust, caring, and loyalty to others as a basis for moral judgments.*	**Stage 5** Social Contract or Utility and Individual Rights *Individuals reason that values, rights, and principles undergird or transcend the law.*
Stage 2 Individualism, Purpose, and Exchange *Children obey because adults tell them to obey. People base their moral decisions on fear of punishment.*	**Stage 4** Social System Morality *Moral judgments are based on understanding and the social order, law, justice, and duty.*	**Stage 6** Universal Ethical Principles *The person has developed moral judgments that are based on universal human rights. When faced with a dilemma between law and conscience, a personal, individualized conscience is followed.*

FIGURE **13.1**

KOHLBERG'S THREE LEVELS AND SIX STAGES OF MORAL DEVELOPMENT. Kohlberg argued that people everywhere develop their moral reasoning by passing through these age-based stages. *Where does Kohlberg's theory stand on the nature-nurture and continuity-discontinuity issues discussed in Chapter 1?*

preconventional reasoning The lowest level in Kohlberg's theory of moral development. The individual's concept of good and bad is interpreted primarily in terms of external rewards and punishment.

heteronomous morality Kohlberg's first stage in preconventional reasoning in which moral thinking is tied to punishment.

individualism, instrumental purpose, and exchange The second Kohlberg stage in preconventional reasoning. At this stage, individuals pursue their own interests but also let others do the same.

conventional reasoning The second, or intermediate, level in Kohlberg's theory of moral development. At this level, individuals abide by certain standards, but they are the standards of others such as parents or the government.

mutual interpersonal expectations, relationships, and interpersonal conformity Kohlberg's third stage of moral development. At this stage, individuals value trust, caring, and loyalty to others as a basis of moral judgments.

social systems morality The fourth stage in Kohlberg's theory of moral development. Moral judgments are based on understanding the social order, law, justice, and duty.

postconventional reasoning The highest level in Kohlberg's theory of moral development. At this level, the individual recognizes alternative moral courses, explores the options, and then decides on a personal moral code.

social contract or utility and individual rights The fifth Kohlberg stage. At this stage, individuals reason that values, rights, and principles undergird or transcend the law.

Preconventional reasoning is the lowest level of moral reasoning, said Kohlberg. At this level, good and bad are interpreted in terms of external rewards and punishments.

- *Stage 1.* **Heteronomous morality** is the first stage in preconventional reasoning. At this stage, moral thinking is tied to punishment. For example, children think that they must obey because they fear punishment for disobedience.

- *Stage 2.* **Individualism, instrumental purpose, and exchange** is the second stage of preconventional reasoning. At this stage, individuals reason that pursuing their own interests is the right thing to do, but they let others do the same. Thus, they think that what is right involves an equal exchange. They reason that if they are nice to others, others will be nice to them in return.

Conventional reasoning is the second, or intermediate, level in Kohlberg's theory of moral development. At this level, individuals apply certain standards, but they are the standards set by others, such as parents or the government.

- *Stage 3.* **Mutual interpersonal expectations, relationships, and interpersonal conformity** is Kohlberg's third stage of moral development. At this stage, individuals value trust, caring, and loyalty to others as a basis of moral judgments. Children and adolescents often adopt their parents' moral standards at this stage, seeking to be thought of by their parents as a "good girl" or a "good boy."

- *Stage 4.* **Social systems morality** is the fourth stage in Kohlberg's theory of moral development. At this stage, moral judgments are based on understanding the social order, law, justice, and duty. For example, adolescents may reason that in order for a community to work effectively, it needs to be protected by laws that are adhered to by its members.

Postconventional reasoning is the highest level in Kohlberg's theory of moral development. At this level, the individual recognizes alternative moral courses, explores the options, and then decides on a personal moral code.

- *Stage 5.* **Social contract or utility and individual rights** is the fifth Kohlberg stage. At this stage, individuals reason that values, rights, and principles undergird or transcend the law. A person evaluates the validity of actual laws and realizes that social systems can be examined in terms of the degree to which they preserve and protect fundamental human rights and values.

- *Stage 6.* **Universal ethical principles** is the sixth and highest stage in Kohlberg's theory of moral development. At this stage, the person has developed a moral standard based on universal human rights. When faced with a conflict between law and conscience, the person reasons that conscience should be followed, even though the decision might bring risk.

Kohlberg held that these levels and stages occur in a sequence and are age-related. Before age 9, most children use level 1, preconventional reasoning based on external rewards and punishments, when they consider moral choices. By early adolescence, their moral reasoning is increasingly based on the application of standards set by others. Most adolescents reason at stage 3, with some signs of stages 2 and 4. By early adulthood, a small number of individuals reason in postconventional ways.

What evidence supports this description of development? A 20-year longitudinal investigation found that use of stages 1 and 2 decreased with age (Colby & others, 1983) (see Figure 13.2). Stage 4, which did not appear at all in the moral reasoning of 10-year-olds, was reflected in the moral thinking of 62 percent of the 36-year-olds. Stage 5 did not appear until age 20 to 22 and never characterized more than 10 percent of the individuals.

Thus, the moral stages appeared somewhat later than Kohlberg initially envisioned, and reasoning at the higher stages, especially stage 6, was rare. Although stage 6 has been removed from the Kohlberg moral judgment scoring manual, it still is considered to be theoretically important in the Kohlberg scheme of moral development.

Influences on the Kohlberg Stages What factors influence movement through Kohlberg's stages? Although moral reasoning at each stage presupposes a certain level of cognitive development, Kohlberg argued that advances in children's cognitive development did not ensure development of moral reasoning. Instead, moral reasoning also reflects children's experiences in dealing with moral questions and moral conflict.

Several investigators have tried to advance individuals' levels of moral development by having a model present arguments that reflect moral thinking one stage above the individuals' established levels. This approach applies the concepts of equilibrium and conflict that Piaget used to explain cognitive development. By presenting arguments slightly beyond the children's level of moral reasoning, the researchers created a disequilibrium that motivated the children to restructure their moral thought. The upshot of studies using this approach is that virtually any plus-stage discussion, for any length of time, seems to promote more advanced moral reasoning (Walker, 1982).

Kohlberg emphasized that peer interaction and perspective taking are critical aspects of the social stimulation that challenges children to change their moral reasoning. Whereas adults characteristically impose rules and regulations on children, the give-and-take among peers gives children an opportunity to take the perspective of another person and to generate rules democratically. Kohlberg stressed that in principle, encounters with any peers can produce perspective-taking opportunities that may advance a child's moral reasoning. A research review of cross-cultural studies involving Kohlberg's theory revealed strong support for a link between perspective-taking skills and more advanced moral judgments (Gibbs & others, 2007).

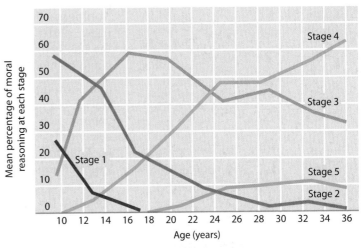

FIGURE **13.2**

AGE AND THE PERCENTAGE OF INDIVIDUALS AT EACH KOHLBERG STAGE. In one longitudinal study of males from 10 to 36 years of age, at age 10 most moral reasoning was at stage 2 (Colby & others, 1983). At 16 to 18 years of age, stage 3 became the most frequent type of moral reasoning, and it was not until the mid-twenties that stage 4 became the most frequent. Stage 5 did not appear until 20 to 22 years of age, and it never characterized more than 10 percent of the individuals. In this study, the moral stages appeared somewhat later than Kohlberg envisioned, and stage 6 was absent. *Do you think it matters that all of the participants in this study were males? Why or why not?*

How Would You...?
If you were a **human development and family studies professional,** how would you explain the progression of moral reasoning skills that develop during the elementary school years?

developmental **connection**

Peers. Piaget argued that the mutual give-and-take of peer relations is more important than parenting in enhancing children's moral reasoning. Chapter 10, p. 294

universal ethical principles The sixth and highest stage in Kohlberg's theory of moral development. Individuals develop a moral standard based on universal principles of human rights.

Kohlberg's Critics   Kohlberg's theory has provoked debate, research, and criticism (Gibbs, 2010; Smetana, 2011a, b; Walker & Frimer, 2011). Key criticisms involve the link between moral thought and moral behavior, the roles of culture and the family in moral development, and the significance of concern for others.

Moral Thought and Moral Behavior   Kohlberg's theory has been criticized for placing too much emphasis on moral thought and not enough emphasis on moral behavior (Walker, 2004). Moral reasons can sometimes be a shelter for immoral behavior. Corrupt CEOs and politicians endorse the loftiest of moral virtues in public before their own behavior is exposed. Whatever the latest public scandal, you will probably find that the culprits displayed virtuous thoughts but engaged in immoral behavior. No one wants a nation of cheaters and thieves who can reason at the postconventional level. The cheaters and thieves may know what is right yet still do what is wrong. Heinous actions can be cloaked in a mantle of moral virtue.

Culture and Moral Reasoning   Kohlberg emphasized that his stages of moral reasoning are universal, but some critics claim his theory is culturally biased (Miller, 2007). Both Kohlberg and his critics may be partially correct. One review of 45 studies in 27 cultures around the world, mostly non-European, provided support for the universality of Kohlberg's first four stages (Snarey, 1987). Individuals in diverse cultures developed through these four stages in sequence as Kohlberg predicted. More recent research revealed support for the qualitative shift from stage 2 to stage 3 across cultures (Gibbs & others, 2007). Stages 5 and 6, however, have not been found in all cultures (Gibbs & others, 2007; Snarey, 1987). Furthermore, critics assert that Kohlberg's scoring system does not recognize the higher-level moral reasoning of certain cultures and thus does not acknowledge that moral reasoning is more culture-specific than Kohlberg envisioned (Snarey, 1987).

In sum, although Kohlberg's approach does capture much of the moral reasoning voiced in various cultures around the world, his approach misses or misconstrues some important moral concepts in particular cultures (Gibbs, 2010).

A recent study explored links between culture, mindset, and moral judgment (Narváez & Hill, 2010). In this study, a higher level of multicultural experience was linked to being more open minded (more cognitively flexible), having a growth mindset (perceiving that one's qualities can change and improve through effort), and showing a higher level of moral judgment.

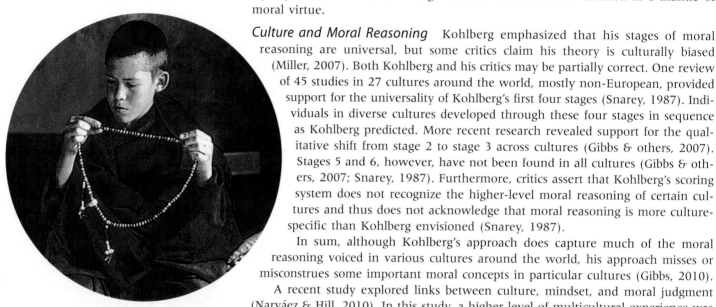

This 14-year-old boy in Nepal is thought to be the sixth holiest Buddhist in the world. In one study of 20 adolescent male Buddhist monks in Nepal, the issue of justice, a basic theme in Kohlberg's theory, was not a central focus in the monks' moral views (Huebner & Garrod, 1993). Also, the monks' concerns about prevention of suffering and the importance of compassion are not captured in Kohlberg's theory.

Families and Moral Development   Kohlberg argued that family processes are essentially unimportant in children's moral development. As noted earlier, he argued that parent-child relationships usually provide children with little opportunity for give-and-take or perspective taking. Rather, Kohlberg said that such opportunities are more likely to be provided by children's peer relations.

Did Kohlberg underestimate the contribution of family relationships to moral development? A number of developmentalists emphasize that *inductive discipline*, which uses reasoning and focuses children's attention on the consequences of their actions for others, positively influences moral development (Hoffman, 1970). They also stress that parents' moral values influence children's developing moral thoughts (Laible & Thompson, 2007). Nonetheless, most developmentalists agree with Kohlberg, and Piaget, that peers play an important role in the development of moral reasoning.

Gender and the Care Perspective   The most publicized criticism of Kohlberg's theory has come from Carol Gilligan (1982, 1992, 1996), who argues that Kohlberg's theory reflects a gender bias. According to Gilligan, Kohlberg's theory is based on a male norm that puts abstract principles above relationships and concern for others and sees the individual as standing alone and independently making moral decisions. It puts justice at the heart of morality. In contrast to Kohlberg's **justice perspective,** which focuses on the rights of the individual, Gilligan argues for a **care perspective,**

justice perspective A moral perspective that focuses on the rights of the individual; individuals independently make moral decisions.

care perspective The moral perspective of Carol Gilligan, which views people in terms of their connectedness with others and emphasizes interpersonal communication, relationships with others, and concern for others.

which is a moral perspective that views people in terms of their connectedness with others and emphasizes interpersonal communication, relationships with others, and concern for others. According to Gilligan, Kohlberg greatly underplayed the care perspective, perhaps because he was a male, because most of his research was with males rather than females, and because he used male responses as a model for his theory.

In extensive interviews with girls from 6 to 18 years of age, Gilligan and her colleagues found that girls consistently interpret moral dilemmas in terms of human relationships and base these interpretations on listening and watching other people (Gilligan, 1992; Gilligan & others, 2003). However, a meta-analysis (a statistical analysis that combines the results of many different studies) casts doubt on Gilligan's claim of substantial gender differences in moral judgment (Jaffee & Hyde, 2000). A recent review concluded that girls' moral orientations are "somewhat more likely to focus on care for others than on abstract principles of justice, but they can use both moral orientations when needed (as can boys . . .)" (Blakemore, Berenbaum, & Liben, 2009, p. 132).

Carol Gilligan. *What is Gilligan's view of moral development?*

Domain Theory: Moral, Social Conventional, and Personal Reasoning

The **domain theory of moral development** states that there are different domains of social knowledge and reasoning, including moral, social conventional, and personal domains. In domain theory, children's and adolescents' moral, social conventional, and personal knowledge and reasoning emerge from their attempts to understand and deal with different forms of social experience (Helwig & Turiel, 2011; Nucci & Gingo, 2011; Smetana, 2011a, b).

Some theorists and researchers argue that Kohlberg did not adequately distinguish between moral reasoning and social conventional reasoning (Helwig & Turiel, 2011; Nucci & Gingo, 2011; Smetana, 2011a, b). **Social conventional reasoning** focuses on conventional rules that have been established by social consensus in order to control behavior and maintain the social system. The rules themselves are arbitrary, such as raising your hand in class before speaking, using one staircase at school to go up, the other to go down, not cutting in front of someone standing in line to buy movie tickets, and stopping at a stop sign when driving. There are sanctions if we violate these conventions, although they can be changed by consensus.

In contrast, moral reasoning focuses on ethical issues and rules of morality. Unlike conventional rules, moral rules are not arbitrary. They are obligatory, widely accepted, and somewhat impersonal (Helwig & Turiel, 2011). Rules pertaining to lying, cheating, stealing, and physically harming another person are moral rules because violation of these rules affronts ethical standards that exist apart from social consensus and convention. Moral judgments involve concepts of justice, whereas social conventional judgments are concepts of social organization. Violating moral rules is usually more serious than violating conventional rules.

The social conventional approach is a serious challenge to Kohlberg's approach because Kohlberg argued that social conventions are a stop-over on the road to higher moral sophistication. For social conventional reasoning advocates, social conventional reasoning is not lower than postconventional reasoning but rather something that needs to be disentangled from the moral thread (Helwig & Turiel, 2011; Smetana, 2011a, b).

Recently, a distinction also has been made between moral and conventional issues, which are viewed as legitimately subject to adult social regulation, and personal issues, which are more likely subject to the child's or adolescent's independent decision making and personal discretion (Helwig & Turiel, 2011; Nucci & Gingo, 2011; Smetana, 2011a, b). Personal issues include control over one's body, privacy, and choice of friends and activities. Thus, some actions belong to a *personal* domain, not governed by moral strictures or social norms.

Moral, conventional, and personal domains of reasoning arise in families. Moral issues include actions such as lying to parents about engaging in a deviant behavior

domain theory of moral development Theory that traces social knowledge and reasoning to moral, social conventional, and personal domains. These domains arise from children's and adolescents' attempts to understand and deal with different forms of social experience.

social conventional reasoning Thoughts about social consensus and convention established in order to control behavior and maintain the social system.

or stealing money from a sibling. Conventional issues involve matters such as curfews and who takes out the garbage. Personal issues involve such things as what kinds of music to like, what styles of clothing to wear, what to put on the walls of one's bedroom, and which friends to choose.

In domain theory, boundaries are developed regarding adult authority, which can produce parent-adolescent conflict. Adolescents have a large personal domain and most parents can live with that; however, parents have a larger moral domain than adolescents think is reasonable (Smetana, 2011a, b).

> It is one of the beautiful compensations of this life that no one can sincerely try to help another without helping himself.
>
> —CHARLES DUDLEY WARNER
> *American Essayist, 19th Century*

Prosocial Behavior   Whereas Kohlberg's and Gilligan's theories have focused primarily on the development of moral reasoning, the study of prosocial moral behavior has placed more emphasis on the behavioral aspects of moral development (Grusec, Hastings, & Almas, 2011). Children engage in both immoral antisocial acts such as lying and cheating and prosocial moral behavior such as showing empathy or acting altruistically (Carlo, 2006). Even during the preschool years children may care for others or comfort others in distress, but prosocial behavior occurs more often in adolescence than in childhood (Eisenberg & Morris, 2004).

William Damon (1988) described how sharing develops. During their first years, when children share, it is usually not for reasons of empathy but for the fun of the social play ritual or out of imitation. Then, at about 4 years of age, a combination of empathic awareness and adult encouragement produces a sense of obligation on the part of the child to share with others. Most 4-year-olds are not selfless saints, however. Children believe they have an obligation to share but do not necessarily think they should be as generous to others as they are to themselves.

Children's sharing comes to reflect a more complex sense of what is just and right during middle and late childhood. By the start of the elementary school years, children begin to express objective ideas about fairness (Eisenberg, Fabes, & Spinrad, 2006). It is common to hear 6-year-old children use the word *fair* as synonymous with *equal* or *same*. By the mid to late elementary school years, children believe that equity instead sometimes means that people with special merit or special needs deserve special treatment.

How does children's sharing change from the preschool to the elementary school years?

Moral Personality   Beyond the development of moral reasoning and specific moral feelings and prosocial behaviors, do children also develop a pattern of moral characteristics that is distinctively their own? In other words, do children develop a *moral personality,* and if so, what are its components? Researchers have focused attention on three possible components: (1) moral identity, (2) moral character, and (3) moral exemplars:

- *Moral identity.* Individuals have a moral identity when moral notions and moral commitments are central to their lives. They construct the self with reference to moral categories. Violating their moral commitment would place the integrity of their self at risk (Narváez & Lapsley, 2009).

- *Moral character.* A person with moral character has the willpower, desires, and integrity to stand up to pressure, overcome distractions and disappointments, and behave morally (Walker & Frimer, 2011). A person of good moral character displays moral virtues such as "honesty, truthfulness, and trustworthiness, as well as those of care, compassion, thoughtfulness, and considerateness. Other salient traits revolve around virtues of dependability, loyalty, and conscientiousness" (Walker, 2002, p. 74).

- *Moral exemplars.* Moral exemplars are people who have lived exemplary moral live (Walker, Frimer, & Dunlop, 2011). Their moral personality, identity, character, and set of virtues reflect moral excellence and commitment.

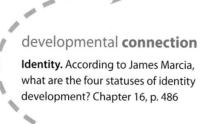

developmental **connection**

Identity. According to James Marcia, what are the four statuses of identity development? Chapter 16, p. 486

In sum, moral development is a multifaceted, complex concept. Included in this complexity are thoughts, feelings, behaviors, and personality.

GENDER

Gilligan's claim that Kohlberg's theory of moral development reflects gender bias reminds us of the pervasive influence of gender on development. Long before elementary school, boys and girls show preferences for different toys and activities. As we discussed in Chapter 10, "Socioemotional Development in Early Childhood," preschool children display a gender identity and gender-typed behavior that reflects biological, cognitive, and social influences. Here we will examine gender stereotypes, gender similarities and differences, and gender-role classification.

Gender Stereotypes   According to the old ditty, boys are made of "frogs and snails" and girls are made of "sugar and spice and all that's nice." In the past, a well-adjusted boy was supposed to be independent, aggressive, and powerful. A well-adjusted girl was supposed to be dependent, nurturing, and uninterested in power. The masculine characteristics were considered to be healthy and good by society; the feminine characteristics were considered undesirable. These notions reflect **gender stereotypes,** which are broad categories that reflect general impressions and beliefs about females and males.

Recent research has found that gender stereotypes are, to a great extent, still present in today's world, in the lives of both children and adults (Leaper & Bigler, 2011; Matlin, 2012). One study revealed that children's gender stereotyping increased from preschool through the fifth grade (Miller & others, 2008). In this study, preschoolers tended to stereotype dolls and appearance as characteristic of girls' interests and toys and behaviors (such as action heroes and hitting) as the province of boys. During middle and late childhood, children expanded the range and extent of their gender stereotyping in such areas as occupations, sports, and school tasks. Researchers also have found that boys' gender stereotypes are more rigid than girls' (Ruble, Martin, & Berenbaum, 2006).

A recent study of 3- to 10-year-old U.S. children revealed that girls and older children used a higher percentage of gender stereotypes (Miller & others, 2009). In this study, appearance stereotypes were more prevalent on the part of girls, whereas activity (sports, for example) and trait (aggressive, for example) stereotyping was more commonly engaged in by boys. Another recent study of 6- to 10-year-olds found that both boys and girls indicated that math is for boys (Cvencek, Meltzoff, & Greenwald, 2011).

Gender Similarities and Differences   What is the reality behind gender stereotypes? Let's examine some of the similarities and differences between the sexes, keeping in mind that (1) the differences are averages—not all females versus all males; (2) even when differences are reported, there is considerable overlap between the sexes; and (3) the differences may be due primarily to biological factors, sociocultural factors, or both. First, we examine physical similarities and differences, and then we will turn to cognitive and socioemotional similarities and differences.

Physical Development   Women have about twice the body fat of men, most of it concentrated around breasts and hips. In males, fat is more likely to go to the abdomen. On the average, males grow to be 10 percent taller than females. Other physical differences are less obvious. From conception on, females have a longer life expectancy than males, and females are less likely than males to develop physical or mental disorders. The risk of coronary disease is twice as high in males as in females.

Does gender matter when it comes to brain structure and function? Human brains are much alike, whether the brain belongs to a male or a female (Halpern, 2006;

What are little boys made of?
Frogs and snails
And puppy dogs' tails.
What are little girls made of?
Sugar and spice
And all that's nice.

—J. O. HALLIWELL
English Author, 19th Century

gender stereotypes Broad categories that reflect our impressions and beliefs about females and males.

Halpern & others, 2007). However, researchers have found some differences in the brains of males and females (Hofer & others, 2007). Among the differences that have been discovered are the following:

- Female brains are smaller than male brains, but female brains have more folds; the larger folds (called convolutions) allow more surface brain tissue within the skulls of females than males (Luders & others, 2004).

- One part of the hypothalamus responsible for sexual behavior is larger in men than women (Swaab & others, 2001).

- An area of the parietal lobe that functions in visuospatial skills is larger in males than females (Frederikse & others, 2000).

- The areas of the brain involved in emotional expression show more metabolic activity in females than males (Gur & others, 1995).

Although some differences in brain structure and function have been found, either many of these differences are small or research is inconsistent regarding the differences. Also, when sex differences in the brain have been revealed, in many cases they have not been directly linked to psychological differences (Blakemore, Berenbaum, & Liben, 2009). Although research on sex differences in the brain is still in its infancy, it is likely that there are far more similarities than differences in the brains of females and males.

Cognitive Development No gender differences in general intelligence have been revealed, but some gender differences have been found in some cognitive areas (Galambos, Berenbaum, & McHale, 2009). Research has shown that girls and women generally have slightly better verbal skills than boys and men, although in some verbal skills areas the differences are substantial (Blakemore, Berenbaum, & Liben, 2009). For example, in national assessments, girls were significantly better than boys in reading and writing (National Assessment of Educational Progress, 2005, 2007).

Are there gender differences in math aptitude? In the National Assessment of Educational Progress in the United States, fourth- and eighth-grade males continued to slightly outperform females in math through 2007 (National Assessment of Educational Progress, 2005, 2007). However, not all recent studies have shown differences. A very large-scale study of more than 7 million U.S. students in grades 2 through 11 revealed no differences in math scores for boys and girls (Hyde & others, 2008). And a recent meta-analysis found no gender differences in math for adolescents (Lindberg & others, 2010). A recent research review also concluded that girls have more negative math attitudes and that parents' and teachers' expectations for children's math competence are often gender-biased in favor of boys (Gunderson & others, 2011).

One area of math that has been examined for possible gender differences is visuospatial skills, which include being able to rotate objects mentally and determine what they would look like when rotated. These types of skills are important in courses such as plane and solid geometry and geography. A research review revealed that boys have better visuospatial skills than girls (Halpern & others, 2007). For example, despite equal participation in the National Geography Bee, in most years all 10 finalists were boys (Liben, 1995). However, some experts argue that the gender difference in visuospatial skills is small (Hyde, 2007a, b) (see Figure 13.3).

Socioemotional Development Four areas of socioemotional development in which gender similarities and differences have been studied extensively are aggression, communication in relationships, emotion, and prosocial behavior.

One of the most consistent gender differences is that boys are more physically aggressive than girls are (Coyne, Nelson, & Underwood, 2011). The difference occurs in all cultures and appears very early in children's development (White,

"So according to the stereotype, you can put two and two together, but I can read the handwriting on the wall." Copyright © 1994 Joel Pett. All rights reserved. Reprinted by permission.

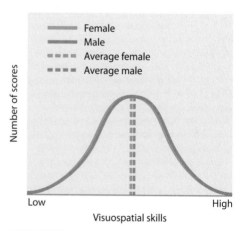

FIGURE 13.3

VISUOSPATIAL SKILLS OF MALES AND FEMALES. Notice that, although an average male's visuospatial skills are higher than an average female's, scores for the two sexes almost entirely overlap. Not all males have better visuospatial skills than all females—the overlap indicates that although the average male score is higher, many females outperform most males on such tasks.

2001). The physical aggression difference is especially pronounced when children are provoked. Both biological and environmental factors have been proposed to account for gender differences in aggression. Biological factors include heredity and hormones. Environmental factors include cultural expectations, adult and peer models, and social agents that reward aggression in boys and punish aggression in girls.

Although boys are consistently more physically aggressive than girls, might girls show at least as much verbal aggression, such as yelling, as boys do? When verbal aggression is examined, gender differences often disappear; sometimes, though, verbal aggression is more pronounced in girls (Eagly & Steffen, 1986).

Recently, increased interest has been directed toward *relational aggression*, which involves harming someone by manipulating a relationship (Coyne, Nelson, & Underwood, 2011; Underwood, 2011). Relational aggression includes behaviors such as trying to make others dislike a certain individual by spreading malicious rumors about the person. Mixed findings have characterized research on whether girls show more relational aggression than boys, but one consistency in findings is that relational aggression comprises a greater percentage of girls' overall aggression than is the case for boys (Putallaz & others, 2007). And a recent research review revealed that girls engage in more relational aggression than boys in adolescence but not in childhood (Smith, Rose, & Schwartz-Mette, 2010).

Gender differences occur in some aspects of emotion (Hertenstein & Keltner, 2011; Leaper & Bigler, 2011). Females express emotion more openly than males, are better than males at decoding emotion, smile more, cry more, and are happier (Brody & Hall, 2008; Gross, Frederickson, & Levenson, 1994; LaFrance, Hecht, & Paluck, 2003). Males report experiencing and expressing more anger than females (Kring, 2000). Girls also are better at reading others' emotions and more likely to show empathy than are boys (Blakemore, Berenbaum, & Liben, 2009).

An important skill is to be able to regulate and control one's emotions and behavior (Eisenberg, Spinrad, & Eggum, 2010; Thompson & Goodman, 2011). Boys usually show less self-regulation than girls (Blakemore, Berenbaum, & Liben, 2009). This low self-control can translate into behavior problems.

Are there gender differences in communication in relationships? Sociolinguist Deborah Tannen (1990) distinguishes between rapport talk and report talk:

- **Rapport talk** is the language of conversation and a way of establishing connections and negotiating relationships. Females enjoy rapport talk and conversation that is relationship-oriented more than males do.

- **Report talk** is talk that gives information. Public speaking is an example of report talk. Males hold center stage through report talk with verbal performances such as storytelling, joking, and lecturing with information.

How extensive are the gender differences in communication? Research has yielded somewhat mixed results. Recent studies do reveal some gender differences (Anderson, 2006; Matlin, 2012). Researchers have found that adolescent girls engage in more self-disclosure (communication of intimate details about themselves) in close relationships and are better at actively listening in a conversation than boys (Leaper & Friedman, 2007). One study of a sampling of students' e-mails found that people could guess the writer's gender two-thirds of the time (Thompson & Murachver, 2001). Another study revealed that women make 63 percent of phone calls and when talking to another woman stay on the phone longer (7.2 minutes) than men do when talking with other men (4.6 minutes) (Smoreda & Licoppe, 2000). However, meta-analyses suggest that overall gender differences in communication are small in both children and adults (Hyde, 2009; Leaper & Smith, 2004).

What gender differences characterize aggression?

How Would You...?

If you were a **psychologist,** how would you discuss gender similarities and differences with a parent or teacher who is concerned about a child's academic progress and social skills?

rapport talk The language of conversation and a way of establishing connections and negotiating relationships; more characteristic of females than of males.

report talk Talk that conveys information; more characteristic of males than females.

What gender differences characterize children's prosocial behavior?

Are there gender differences in emotion? Girls are more likely to express their emotions openly and intensely than are boys, especially in displaying sadness and fear (Blakemore, Berenbaum, & Liben, 2009). Girls also are better at reading others' emotions and more likely to show empathy than are boys (Blakemore, Berenbaum, & Liben, 2009). Males usually show less self-regulation of emotion than females, and this low self-control can translate into behavioral problems (Eisenberg, Spinrad, & Smith, 2004).

Are there gender differences in prosocial behavior? Across childhood and adolescence, females engage in more prosocial behavior (Eisenberg & others, 2009). The biggest gender difference occurs for kind and considerate behavior, with a smaller difference in sharing.

Gender in Context   The nature and extent of gender differences may depend on the context. The importance of considering gender in context is nowhere more apparent than when we examine what is culturally prescribed behavior for females and males in different countries around the world (Chuang & Tamis-Lemonda, 2009; Matlin, 2012). Although there has been greater acceptance of androgyny and similarities in male and female behavior in the United States, in many countries gender roles have remained gender-specific. For example, in many Middle Eastern countries, the division of labor between males and females is dramatic. Males are socialized and schooled to work in the public sphere, females in the private world of home and child rearing. For example, in many Middle Eastern countries, the dominant view is that the man's duty is to provide for his family and the woman's is to care for her family and household. China and India also have been male-dominant cultures. Although women have made some strides in China and India, especially in urban areas, the male role is still dominant. Most males in China and India do not accept androgynous behavior or gender equity.

developmental **connection**

Community and Culture.
Bronfenbrenner's ecological theory emphasizes the importance of contexts; in his theory, the macrosystem includes cross-cultural comparisons. Chapter 1, p. 30

In China, females and males are usually socialized to behave, feel, and think differently. The old patriarchal traditions of male supremacy have not been completely uprooted. Chinese women still make considerably less money than Chinese men do, and, in rural China (such as here in the Lixian Village of Sichuan) male supremacy still governs many women's lives.

Review Connect Reflect

LG1 Discuss emotional and personality development in middle and late childhood.

Review

- What changes take place in the self during the middle and late childhood years?
- How does emotion change during middle and late childhood?
- What is Kohlberg's theory of moral development, and how has it been criticized? How does prosocial behavior develop?

Connect

- What are gender stereotypes, and what are some important gender differences?
- In Chapter 6, you learned about the concept of joint attention. How is that concept similar to or different from the concept of perspective taking you learned about in this section?

Reflect *Your Own Personal Journey of Life*

- A young man who had been sentenced to serve 10 years for selling a small amount of marijuana walked away from a prison camp six months after he was sent there. He is now in his fifties and has been a model citizen. Should he be sent back to prison? Why or why not? At which Kohlberg stage should your response be placed? Do you think the stage at which you placed your response accurately captures the level of your moral thinking? Explain.

What Are Some Changes in Parenting and Families in Middle and Late Childhood?

 LG2 Describe changes in parenting and families in middle and late childhood.

Developmental Changes in Parent-Child Relationships — Parents as Managers — Stepfamilies

Our discussion of parenting and families in this section focuses on how parent-child interactions typically change in middle and late childhood, the importance of parents being effective managers of children's lives, and how elementary school children are affected by living with stepparents.

DEVELOPMENTAL CHANGES IN PARENT-CHILD RELATIONSHIPS

As children move into the middle and late childhood years, parents spend considerably less time with them. In one study, parents spent less than half as much time with their children aged 5 to 12 in caregiving, instruction, reading, talking, and playing as when the children were younger (Hill & Stafford, 1980). Although parents spend less time with their children in middle and late childhood than in early childhood, parents continue to be extremely important in their children's lives. In an analysis of the contributions of parents in middle and late childhood, the following conclusion was reached: "Parents serve as gatekeepers and provide scaffolding as children assume more responsibility for themselves and . . . regulate their own lives" (Huston & Ripke, 2006, p. 422).

Parents especially play an important role in supporting and stimulating children's academic achievement in middle and late childhood (Gupta, Thornton, & Huston, 2008; Huston & Ripke, 2006). The value parents place on education can determine whether children do well in school. Parents not only influence children's in-school achievement, but they also make decisions about children's out-of-school activities. Whether children participate in sports, music, and other activities is heavily influenced by the extent to which parents sign up children for such activities or encourage their participation (Simpkins & others, 2006).

Elementary school children tend to receive less physical discipline than they did as preschoolers. Instead of spanking or coercive holding, their parents are more

What are some changes in the focus of parent-child relationships in middle and late childhood?

likely to use deprivation of privileges, appeals to the child's self-esteem, comments designed to increase the child's sense of guilt, and statements that the child is responsible for his or her actions.

During middle and late childhood, some control is transferred from parent to child. The process is gradual, and it produces coregulation rather than control by either the child or the parent alone. Parents continue to exercise general supervision and control, while children are allowed to engage in moment-to-moment self-regulation. The major shift to autonomy does not occur until about the age of 12 or later. A key developmental task as children move toward autonomy is learning to relate to adults outside the family on a regular basis—adults such as teachers, who interact with the child much differently from parents.

PARENTS AS MANAGERS

Parents can play important roles as managers of children's opportunities, as monitors of their behavior, and as social initiators and arrangers (Parke & Clarke-Stewart, 2011). Mothers are more likely than fathers to take a managerial role in parenting.

Researchers have found that family management practices are positively related to students' grades and self-responsibility, and negatively to school-related problems (Eccles, 2007; Taylor & Lopez, 2005). Among the most important family management practices in this regard are maintaining a structured and organized family environment, such as establishing routines for homework, chores, meals, bedtime, and so on, and effectively monitoring the child's behavior. A research review of family functioning in African American students' academic achievement found that when African American parents monitored their sons' academic achievement by ensuring that homework was completed, restricted time spent on nonproductive distractions (such as video games and TV), and participated in a consistent, positive dialogue with teachers and school officials, their sons' academic achievement benefited (Mandara, 2006).

STEPFAMILIES

Not only has divorce become commonplace in the United States, so has getting remarried. It takes time for parents to marry, have children, get divorced, and then remarry. Consequently, there are far more elementary and secondary school children than infant or preschool children living in stepfamilies.

The number of remarriages involving children has grown steadily in recent years. Also, divorces occur at a 10 percent higher rate in remarriages than in first marriages (Cherlin & Furstenberg, 1994). About half of all children whose parents divorce will have a stepparent within four years of the separation.

Remarried parents face some unique tasks. The couple must define and strengthen their marriage and at the same time renegotiate the biological parent-child relationships and establish stepparent-stepchild and stepsibling relationships (Coleman, Ganong, & Fine, 2004). The complex histories and multiple relationships make adjustment in a stepfamily difficult (Hakvoort & others, 2011). Only one-third of stepfamily couples stay remarried.

In some cases, the stepfamily may have been preceded by the death of a spouse. However, by far the largest number of stepfamilies are preceded by divorce rather than death (Pasley & Moorefield, 2004). Three common types of stepfamily structure are (1) stepfather, (2) stepmother, and (3) blended or complex. In stepfather families, the mother typically had custody of the children and remarried, introducing a stepfather into her children's lives. In stepmother families, the father usually had custody and remarried, introducing a stepmother into his children's lives. In a blended or complex

How does living in a stepfamily influence a child's development?

stepfamily, both parents bring children from previous marriages to live in the newly formed stepfamily.

In E. Mavis Hetherington's (2006) longitudinal analyses, children and adolescents who had been in a simple stepfamily (stepfather or stepmother) for a number of years were adjusting better than in the early years of the remarried family and were functioning well in comparison with children and adolescents in conflicted nondivorced families and children and adolescents in complex (blended) stepfamilies. More than 75 percent of the adolescents in long-established simple stepfamilies described their relationships with their stepparents as "close" or "very close." Hetherington (2006) concluded that in long-established simple stepfamilies adolescents seem to eventually benefit from the presence of a stepparent and the resources provided by the stepparent.

Children often have better relationships with their custodial parents (mothers in stepfather families, fathers in stepmother families) than with simple stepparents (Santrock, Sitterle, & Warshak, 1988). Also, children in simple families (stepmother, stepfather) often show better adjustment than their counterparts in complex (blended) families (Hetherington & Kelly, 2002).

As in divorced families, children in stepfamilies show more adjustment problems than children in nondivorced families (Hetherington & Kelly, 2002). The adjustment problems are similar to those found among children of divorced parents—academic problems and lower self-esteem, for example (Anderson & others, 1999). However, it is important to recognize that a majority of children in stepfamilies do not have problems. In one analysis, 25 percent of children from stepfamilies showed adjustment problems compared with 10 percent in intact, never-divorced families (Hetherington & Kelly, 2002).

Adolescence is an especially difficult time for the formation of a stepfamily (Anderson & others, 1999; Gosselin, 2010). Problems may occur because becoming part of a stepfamily exacerbates normal adolescent concerns about identity, sexuality, and autonomy.

How Would You...?
If you were a **human development and family studies professional,** how would you advise divorced parents on strategies to ease their children's adjustment to remarriage?

Review *Connect* Reflect

 LG2 Describe changes in parenting and families in middle and late childhood.

Review

- What changes characterize parent-child relationships in middle and late childhood?
- How can parents be effective managers of their children's lives?

Connect

- In this section, you learned about how living in a stepfamily can influence children's development. What did you learn in Chapter 10 about how living in a divorced family can influence children's development?

Reflect *Your Own Personal Journey of Life*

- What was your relationship with your parents like when you were in elementary school? How do you think it influenced your development?

What Changes Characterize Peer Relationships in Middle and Late Childhood?

 LG3 Identify changes in peer relationships in middle and late childhood.

| Developmental Changes | Peer Status | Social Cognition | Bullying | Friends |

Having positive relationships with peers is especially important in middle and late childhood. Engaging in positive interactions with peers, resolving conflicts with peers in nonaggressive ways, and having quality friendships in middle and late childhood not only create positive outcomes at this time in children's lives, but also are linked to more positive relationship outcomes in adolescence and adulthood (Huston & Ripke, 2006). For example, in one longitudinal study, being popular with peers and engaging in low levels of aggression at 8 years of age were related to higher levels of occupational status at 48 years of age (Huesmann & others, 2006). Another study found that peer competence (a composite measure that included social contact with peers, popularity with peers, friendship, and social skills) in middle and late childhood was linked to having better relationships with co-workers in early adulthood (Collins & van Dulmen, 2006).

DEVELOPMENTAL CHANGES

As children enter the elementary school years, reciprocity becomes especially important in peer interchanges. Researchers estimate that the percentage of time spent in social interaction with peers increases from approximately 10 percent at 2 years of age to more than 30 percent in middle and late childhood (Rubin, Bukowski, & Parker, 2006). In one early study, a typical day in elementary school included approximately 300 episodes with peers (Barker & Wright, 1951). As children move through middle and late childhood, the size of their peer group increases, and peer interaction is less closely supervised by adults (Rubin, Bukowski, & Parker, 2006). Until about 12 years of age, children's preference for same-sex peer groups increases.

What are some statuses that children have with their peers?

PEER STATUS

Which children are likely to be popular with their peers and which ones tend to be disliked? Developmentalists address these and similar questions by examining sociometric status, a term that describes the extent to which children are liked or disliked by their peer group (Cillessen & Bellmore, 2011; Hymel & others, 2011). Sociometric status is typically assessed by asking children to rate how much they like or dislike each of their classmates. Or it may be assessed by asking children to nominate the children they like the most and those they like the least.

Developmentalists have distinguished five peer statuses (Wentzel & Asher, 1995):

- **Popular children** are frequently nominated as a best friend and are rarely disliked by their peers.

- **Average children** receive an average number of both positive and negative nominations from their peers.

- **Neglected children** are infrequently nominated as a best friend but are not disliked by their peers.

- **Rejected children** are infrequently nominated as someone's best friend and are actively disliked by their peers.

- **Controversial children** are frequently nominated both as someone's best friend and as being disliked.

Popular children have a number of social skills that contribute to their being well liked (Hymel & others, 2011). They give out reinforcements, listen carefully, maintain open lines of communication with peers, are happy, control their negative emotions, act like themselves, show enthusiasm and concern for others, and are self-confident without being conceited (Hartup, 1983; Rubin, Bukowski, & Parker, 1998).

Neglected children engage in low rates of interaction with their peers and are often described as shy by peers. The goal of many training programs for neglected children is to help them attract attention from their peers in positive ways and to hold that attention by asking questions, by listening in a warm and friendly way,

popular children Children who are frequently nominated as a best friend and are rarely disliked by their peers.

average children Children who receive an average number of both positive and negative nominations from peers.

neglected children Children who are infrequently nominated as a best friend but are not disliked by their peers.

rejected children Children who are infrequently nominated as a best friend and are actively disliked by their peers.

controversial children Children who are frequently nominated both as someone's best friend and as being disliked.

and by saying things about themselves that relate to the peers' interests. They also are taught to enter groups more effectively.

Rejected children often have more serious adjustment problems than those who are neglected (Dishion & Piehler, 2009; Prinstein & others, 2009). One study found that in kindergarten, children who were rejected by their peers were less likely to engage in classroom participation, more likely to express a desire to avoid school, and more likely to report being lonely than children who were accepted by their peers (Buhs & Ladd, 2001). The combination of being rejected by peers and being aggressive forecasts problems (Dishion & Piehler, 2009; Hymel & others, 2011). Another study evaluated 112 fifth-grade boys over a period of seven years until the end of high school (Kupersmidt & Coie, 1990). The best predictor of whether rejected children would engage in delinquent behavior or drop out of school later during adolescence was aggression toward peers in elementary school.

John Coie (2004, pp. 252–253) provided three reasons why aggressive peer-rejected boys have problems in social relationships:

- "First, the rejected, aggressive boys are more impulsive and have problems sustaining attention. As a result, they are more likely to be disruptive of ongoing activities in the classroom and in focused group play.

- Second, rejected, aggressive boys are more emotionally reactive. They are aroused to anger more easily and probably have more difficulty calming down once aroused. Because of this they are more prone to become angry at peers and attack them verbally and physically. . . .

- Third, rejected children have fewer social skills in making friends and maintaining positive relationships with peers."

Not all rejected children are aggressive (Rubin & others, 2011). Although aggression and its related characteristics of impulsiveness and disruptiveness underlie rejection about half the time, approximately 10 to 20 percent of rejected children are shy.

How can rejected children be trained to interact more effectively with their peers? Rejected children may be taught to more accurately assess whether the intentions of their peers are negative (Fontaine & others, 2010). They may be asked to engage in role playing or to discuss hypothetical situations involving negative encounters with peers, such as when a peer cuts into a line ahead of them. In some programs, children are shown videotapes of appropriate peer interaction and asked to draw lessons from what they have seen (Ladd, Buhs, & Troop, 2004).

SOCIAL COGNITION

A boy accidentally trips and knocks another boy's soft drink out of his hand. The second boy misconstrues the encounter as hostile, and his interpretation leads him to retaliate aggressively against the boy who tripped. Through repeated encounters of this kind, the aggressive boy's classmates come to perceive him as habitually acting in inappropriate ways.

This example demonstrates the importance of *social cognition*—thoughts about social matters, such as the aggressive boy's interpretation of an encounter as hostile and his classmates' perception of his behavior as inappropriate (Dodge, 2011a, b; Peets, Hodges, & Salmivalli, 2011). Children's social cognition about their peers becomes increasingly important for understanding peer relationships in middle and late childhood. Of special interest are the ways in which children process information about peer relations and their social knowledge (Dodge 2011a, b; White & Kistner, 2011).

Kenneth Dodge (1983) argues that children go through five steps in processing information about their social world. They decode social cues, interpret, search for a response, select an optimal response, and enact. Dodge has found that aggressive boys are more likely to perceive another child's actions as hostile when the child's intention is ambiguous. And, when aggressive boys search for cues to determine a

How Would You…?
If you were a **social worker,** how would you help a neglected child become more involved in peer activities?

How Would You…?
If you were a **psychologist,** how would you characterize differences in the social cognition of aggressive children compared with children who behave in less hostile ways?

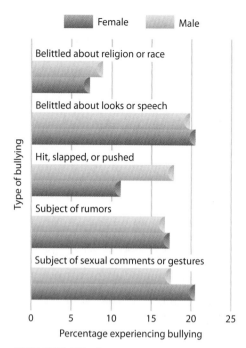

Female   Male

Type of bullying

Belittled about religion or race

Belittled about looks or speech

Hit, slapped, or pushed

Subject of rumors

Subject of sexual comments or gestures

0   5   10   15   20   25
Percentage experiencing bullying

FIGURE **13.4**

BULLYING BEHAVIORS AMONG U.S. YOUTH.
This graph shows the types of bullying most often experienced by U.S. youth. The percentages reflect the extent to which bullied students said that they had experienced a particular type of bullying. In terms of gender, note that when they were bullied, boys were more likely to be hit, slapped, or pushed than girls were.

peer's intention, they respond more rapidly, less efficiently, and less reflectively than do nonaggressive children. These are among the social cognitive factors believed to be involved in children's conflicts.

Social knowledge also is involved in children's ability to get along with peers (Lewis & Carpendale, 2011). They need to know what goals to pursue in poorly defined or ambiguous situations, how to initiate and maintain a social bond, and what scripts to follow to get other children to be their friends. For example, as part of the script for getting friends, it helps to know that saying nice things, regardless of what the peer does or says, will make the peer like the child more.

BULLYING

Significant numbers of students are victimized by bullies (Salmivalli, Peets, & Hodges, 2011). In a national survey of more than 15,000 students in grades 6 through 10, nearly one of every three students said that they had experienced occasional or frequent involvement as a victim or perpetrator in bullying (Nansel & others, 2001). In this study, bullying was defined as verbal or physical behavior intended to disturb someone less powerful (see Figure 13.4). Boys are more likely to be bullies than girls, but gender differences regarding victims of boys are less clear (Salmivalli & Peets, 2009).

Who is likely to be bullied? In the study just described, boys and younger middle school students were most likely to be affected (Nansel & others, 2001). Children who said they were bullied reported more loneliness and difficulty in making friends, while those who did the bullying were more likely to have low grades and to smoke and drink alcohol. Researchers have found that anxious, socially withdrawn, and aggressive children are often the victims of bullying (Hanish & Guerra, 2004). Anxious and socially withdrawn children may be victimized because they are nonthreatening and unlikely to retaliate if bullied, whereas aggressive children may be the targets of bullying because their behavior is irritating to bullies (Rubin & others, 2011).

Social contexts also influence bullying (Salmivalli, Peets, & Hodges, 2011). Recent research indicates that 70 to 80 percent of victims and their bullies are in the same school classroom (Salmivalli & Peets, 2009). Classmates are often aware of bullying incidents and in many cases witness bullying. The larger social context of the peer group plays an important role in bullying (Salmivalli, Peets, & Hodges, 2011). In many cases, bullies torment victims to gain higher status in the peer group and bullies need others to witness their power displays. Many bullies are not rejected by the peer group. In one study, bullies were only rejected by peers for whom they were a potential threat (Veenstra & others, 2010). In another study, bullies often affiliated with each other or in some cases maintained their position in the popular peer group (Witvliet & others, 2010).

What are the outcomes of bullying? One study indicated that bullies and their victims in adolescence were more likely to experience depression and engage in suicide ideation and attempt suicide than their counterparts who were not involved in bullying (Brunstein Klomek & others, 2007). Another study revealed that bullies, victims, or those who were both bullies and victims had more health problems (such as headaches, dizziness, sleep problems, and anxiety) than their counterparts who were not involved in bullying (Srabstein & others, 2006). Recently, bullying has been linked to these suicides: an 8-year-old jumped out of a two-story building in Houston; a 13-year-old girl hanged himself in Houston; and teenagers harassed a girl so mercilessly that she killed herself in Massachusetts (Meyers, 2010).

Who is likely to be bullied? What are some outcomes of bullying?

How Are Perspective Taking and Moral Motivation Linked to Bullying?

A recent study explored the roles that perspective taking and moral motivation play in the lives of bullies, bully-victims, victims, and prosocial children (Gasser & Keller, 2009):

- *Bullies* are highly aggressive toward other children but are not victims of bullying.
- *Bully-victims* are not only highly aggressive toward other children but also are the recipients of other children's bullying.
- *Victims* are passive, non-aggressive respondents to bullying.
- *Prosocial children* engage in such positive behaviors as sharing, helping, comforting, and empathizing.

Teacher and peer ratings in 34 classrooms were used to classify 212 7- to 8-year-old boys and girls into the aforementioned four categories. On a 5-point scale (from never to several times a week), teachers rated (1) how often the child bullied others and (2) how often the child was bullied. The ratings focused on three types of bullying and being victimized: physical aggression, verbal aggression, and excluding others. On a 4-point scale (from not applicable to very clearly applicable), teachers also rated children's prosocial behavior on three items: "willingly shares with others," "comforts others if necessary," and "empathizes with others." Peer ratings assessed children's nominations of which children in the classroom acted as bullies, were victimized by bullies, and engaged in prosocial behavior. Combining the teacher and peer ratings after eliminating those that did not agree on which children were bullies, victims, or prosocial children, the final sample consisted of 49 bullies, 80 bully-victims, 33 victims, and 50 prosocial children.

Children's perspective-taking skills were assessed using theory of mind tasks, and moral motivation was examined by interviewing children about aspects of right and wrong in stories about children's transgressions. In one theory of mind task, children were tested to see whether they understood that people may have false beliefs about another individual. In another theory of mind task, children were assessed to determine whether they understood that people sometimes hide their emotions by showing an emotion different from what they really feel. A moral interview also was conducted in which children were told four moral transgression stories (with content about being unwilling to share with a classmate, stealing sweets from a classmate, hiding a victim's shoes, and verbally bullying a victim) and then asked to judge whether the acts were right or wrong and how the participants in the stories likely felt.

The results of the study indicated that only bully-victims—but not bullies—were deficient in perspective taking. Further analysis revealed that both aggressive groups of children—bullies and bully-victims—had a deficiency in moral motivation. The analyses were consistent with a portrait of bullies as socially competent and knowledgeable in terms of perspective-taking skills and being able to effectively interact with peers. However, bullies use this social knowledge for their own manipulative purposes. The analysis also confirmed the picture of the bully as being morally insensitive. Another recent study also found that bullying was linked to moral disengagement (Obermann, 2011).

What possible solutions to the problem of bullying do these research results suggest? What else would you want to know about the relationship between bullies and their victims before you proposed possible remedies?

What leads some children to become bullies and others to fall victim to bullying? To read further about bullying, see the *Connecting with Research* interlude.

Extensive interest is being directed toward preventing and treating bullying and victimization (Salmivalli, Peets, & Hodges, 2011). A research review revealed mixed results for school-based intervention (Vreeman & Carroll, 2007). School-based interventions vary greatly, ranging from involving the whole school in an antibullying campaign to individualized social skills training. One of the most promising bullying intervention programs has been created by Dan Olweus. This program focuses on 6- to 15-year-olds with the goal of decreasing opportunities and rewards for bullying. School staff are instructed in ways to improve peer relations and make schools safer. When properly implemented, the program reduces bullying by 30 to 70 percent (Olweus, 2003). Information on how to implement the program can be obtained from the Center for the Prevention of Violence at the University of Colorado: www.colorado.edu/cspv/blueprints.

How Would You...?

If you were an **educator,** how would you design and implement a bullying-reduction program at your school?

Another concern is peer bullying and harassment on the Internet (called *cyberbullying*) (O'Keefe & others, 2011; Valkenburg & Peter, 2011). A recent survey found that peer bullying offline and online were the most frequent threats that children and adolescents encountered (Palfrey & others, 2009). And a recent study of third- to sixth-graders revealed that engaging in cyber aggression was related to loneliness, lower self-esteem, fewer mutual friendships, and lower peer popularity (Schoffstall & Cohen, 2011). Information about preventing cyberbullying can be found at www.stopcyberbullying.org/.

FRIENDS

Like adult friendships, children's friendships are typically characterized by similarity (Brechwald & Prinstein, 2011). Throughout childhood, friends are more similar than dissimilar in terms of age, sex, race, and many other factors. Friends often have similar attitudes toward school, similar educational aspirations, and closely aligned achievement orientations.

Why are children's friendships important? Willard Hartup (1983, 1996, 2008; Hartup & Abecassis, 2004) has studied peer relations and friendship for more than three decades. He recently concluded that friends can be cognitive and emotional resources from childhood through old age. Friends can foster self-esteem and a sense of well-being.

More specifically, children's friendships can serve six functions (Gottman & Parker, 1987):

- *Companionship.* Friendship provides children with a familiar partner and play-mate, someone who is willing to spend time with them and join in collaborative activities.

- *Stimulation.* Friendship provides children with interesting information, excitement, and amusement.

- *Physical support.* Friendship provides time, resources, and assistance.

- *Ego support.* Friendship provides the expectation of support, encouragement, and feedback, which helps children maintain an impression of themselves as competent, attractive, and worthwhile individuals.

- *Social comparison.* Friendship provides information about where the child stands vis-à-vis others and whether the child is doing okay.

- *Affection and intimacy.* Friendship provides children with a warm, close, trusting relationship with another individual. **Intimacy in friendships** is characterized by self-disclosure and the sharing of private thoughts. Research reveals that intimate friendships may not appear until early adolescence (Berndt & Perry, 1990).

What are some characteristics of children's friendships?

developmental **connection**

Peers. Beginning in early adolescence, teenagers typically prefer to have a smaller number of friendships that are more intense and intimate. Chapter 16, p. 493

Although having friends can be a developmental advantage, not all friendships are alike. People differ in the company they keep—that is, who their friends are. Developmental advantages occur when children have friends who are socially skilled and supportive. However, it is not developmentally advantageous to have coercive and conflict-ridden friendships (Rubin, Bukowski, & Parker, 2006).

The importance of friendship was underscored in a two-year longitudinal study (Wentzel, Barry, & Caldwell, 2004). Sixth-grade students who did not have a friend engaged in less prosocial behavior (cooperation, sharing, helping others), had lower grades, and were more emotionally distressed (displaying depression, low well-being) than their counterparts who had one or more friends. Two years later, in the eighth grade, the students who did not have a friend in the sixth grade continued to be more emotionally distressed.

intimacy in friendships Self-disclosure and the sharing of private thoughts.

Review

- What developmental changes characterize peer relations in middle and late childhood?
- How does children's peer status influence their development?
- How is social cognition involved in children's peer relations?
- What is the nature of bullying?
- What are children's friendships like?

Connect

- Earlier in the chapter you read that most developmentalists agree that peers play an important role in the development of moral reasoning. Of the five peer statuses that you read about in this section, in which group do you think children would have the least opportunity to fulfill their moral reasoning questions and why?

Reflect *Your Own Personal Journey of Life*

- Which of the five peer statuses characterized you as a child? Did your peer status change in adolescence? How do you think your peer status as a child influenced your development?

What Are Some Important Aspects of Schools?

LG4 Characterize contemporary approaches to student learning and sociocultural diversity in schools.

Contemporary Approaches to Student Learning

Socioeconomic Status and Ethnicity

For most children, entering the first grade signals new obligations. They form new relationships and develop new standards by which to judge themselves. School provides children with a rich source of new ideas to shape their sense of self. They will spend many years in schools as members of small societies in which there are tasks to be accomplished, people to be socialized and socialized by, and rules that define and limit behavior, feelings, and attitudes. By the time students graduate from high school, they will have spent 12,000 hours in the classroom.

> The whole art of teaching is the art of awakening the natural curiosity of young minds.
>
> **—ANATOLE FRANCE**
> *French Novelist, 20th Century*

CONTEMPORARY APPROACHES TO STUDENT LEARNING

Because there are so many approaches for teaching children, controversy swirls about the best way to teach children (Eby, Herrell, & Jordan, 2011). There also is considerable interest in education about the best way to hold schools and teachers accountable for whether children are learning (Witte, 2012).

Constructivist and Direct Instruction Approaches The **constructivist approach** is learner centered and it emphasizes the importance of individuals actively constructing their knowledge and understanding with guidance from the teacher. In the constructivist view, teachers should not attempt to simply pour information into children's minds. Rather, children should be encouraged to explore their world, discover knowledge, reflect, and think critically with careful monitoring and meaningful guidance from the teacher (Eby, Herrell, & Jordan, 2011). The constructivist belief is that for too long in American education children have been required to sit still, be passive learners, and rotely memorize irrelevant as well as relevant information. Today,

Is this classroom more likely constructivist or direct instruction? Explain.

constructivist approach A learner-centered approach that emphasizes the importance of individuals actively constructing their knowledge and understanding with guidance from the teacher.

What are some issues involved in the No Child Left Behind legislation?

constructivism may include an emphasis on collaboration—children working with each other in their efforts to know and understand (O'Donnell, 2012; Slavin, 2012).

By contrast, the **direct instruction approach** is structured and teacher centered. It is characterized by teacher direction and control, high teacher expectations for students' progress, maximum time spent by students on academic tasks, and efforts by the teacher to keep negative affect to a minimum. An important goal in the direct instruction approach is maximizing student learning time (Borich, 2011).

Advocates of the constructivist approach argue that the direct instruction approach turns children into passive learners and does not adequately challenge them to think in critical and creative ways (O'Donnell, 2012). The direct instruction enthusiasts say that the constructivist approaches do not give enough attention to the content of a discipline, such as history or science. They also believe that the constructivist approaches are too relativistic and vague.

Some experts in educational psychology believe that many effective teachers use both a constructivist *and* a direct instruction approach rather than relying on either exclusively (Bransford & others, 2006). Further, some circumstances may call more for a constructivist approach, others for a direction instruction approach. For example, experts increasingly recommend an explicit, intellectually engaging direct instruction approach when teaching students with a reading or a writing disability (Berninger & O'Malley, 2011).

Accountability   Since the 1990s, the U.S. public and governments at every level have demanded increased accountability from schools. One result has been the spread of state-mandated tests to measure just what students had or had not learned (Popham, 2011). Many states identified objectives for students in their state and created tests to measure whether students were meeting those objectives. This approach became national policy in 2002 when the No Child Left Behind (NCLB) legislation was signed into law.

Advocates argue that statewide standardized testing will have a number of positive effects. These include improved student performance; more time teaching the subjects that are tested; high expectations for all students; identification of poorly performing schools, teachers, and administrators; and improved confidence in schools as test scores rise.

Critics argue that the NCLB legislation is doing more harm than good (Yell & Drasgow, 2009). One criticism stresses that using a single test as the sole indicator of students' progress and competence presents a very narrow view of students' skills (Lewis, 2007). This criticism is similar to the one leveled at IQ tests, which we described in Chapter 12. To assess student progress and achievement, many psychologists and educators emphasize that a number of measures should be used, including tests, quizzes, projects, portfolios, classroom observations, and so on. Also, the tests used as part of NCLB don't measure creativity, motivation, persistence, flexible thinking, or social skills (Stiggins, 2008). Critics point out that teachers end up spending far too much class time "teaching to the test" by drilling students and having them memorize isolated facts at the expense of teaching that focuses on thinking skills, which students need for success in life (Pressley, 2007). Also, some individuals are concerned that in the era of No Child Left Behind policy there is a neglect of students who are gifted in the effort to raise the achievement level of students who are not doing well (Clark, 2008).

Consider also the following: Each state is allowed to have different criteria for what constitutes passing or failing grades on tests designated for NCLB inclusion. An analysis of NCLB data indicated that almost every fourth-grade student in Mississippi knows how to read but only half of Massachusetts' students do (Birman & others,

direct instruction approach A structured, teacher-centered approach that is characterized by teacher direction and control, mastery of academic skills, high expectations for students' progress, maximum time spent on learning tasks, and efforts to keep negative affect to a minimum.

2007). Clearly, Mississippi's standards for passing the reading test are far below those of Massachusetts. In the recent analysis of state-by-state comparisons, many states have taken the safe route and kept the standard for passing low. Thus, while one of NCLB's goals was to raise standards for achievement in U.S. schools, apparently allowing states to set their own standards has lowered achievement standards.

Despite such criticisms, the U.S. Department of Education is committed to implementing No Child Left Behind, and schools are making accommodations to meet the requirements of this law. Indeed, most educators support the importance of high expectations and high standards of excellence for students and teachers. At issue, however, is whether the tests and procedures mandated by NCLB are the best ones for achieving these high standards (Darling-Hammond, 2010; 2011; Nieto & Brookhart, 2011).

SOCIOECONOMIC STATUS AND ETHNICITY

Children from low-income, ethnic minority backgrounds often have more difficulties in school than do their middle-socioeconomic-status, non-Latino White counterparts. Why? Critics argue that schools have not done a good job of educating low-income, ethnic minority students to overcome the barriers to their achievement (Bennett, 2011). Let's further explore the roles of socioeconomic status and ethnicity in schools.

Jill Nakamura, teaching in her first-grade classroom. Jill Nakamura teaches at a school located in a high-poverty area. She visits students at home early in the school year in an effort to connect with them and develop a partnership with their parents. "She holds a daily after school club for students reading below grade level . . . ; those who don't want to attend must call parents to tell them." In one school year (2004), she raised the percentage of students reading at or above grade level from 29 percent to 76 percent (Wong Briggs, 2004, p. 6D).

The Education of Students from Low-Income Backgrounds Many children in poverty face problems that present barriers to their learning (McLoyd & others, 2011). They might have parents who don't set high educational standards for them, who are incapable of reading to them, or who don't have enough money to pay for educational materials and experiences, such as books and trips to zoos and museums. They might be malnourished or live in areas where crime and violence are a way of life. A recent study revealed that neighborhood disadvantage (involving such characteristics as low neighborhood income and high unemployment) was linked to less consistent, less stimulating, and more punitive parenting, and ultimately to negative child outcomes such as behavioral problems and low verbal ability (Kohen & others, 2008). Another recent study revealed that the longer children experienced poverty the more detrimental the poverty was to their cognitive development (Najman & others, 2009).

Compared with schools in higher-income areas, schools in low-income areas are more likely to have more students with low achievement test scores, low graduation rates, and small percentages of students going to college; they are more likely to have young teachers with less experience; and they are more likely to encourage rote learning (Koppelman & Goodhart, 2011). Too few schools in low-income neighborhoods provide students with environments that are conducive to learning (Nelson & Lee, 2009). Many of the schools' buildings and classrooms are old and crumbling. These are the types of undesirable conditions Jonathan Kozol (2005) observed in many inner-city schools, including the South Bronx in New York City, as described at the beginning of the chapter. To read about ways to improve the schools and families of children living in poverty, see the *Connecting with Diversity* interlude.

Ethnicity in Schools More than one-third of all African American and almost one-third of all Latino students attend schools in the 47 largest city school districts in the United States, compared with only 5 percent of all non-Latino White and 22 percent of all Asian American students. Many of these inner-city schools are still informally segregated, are grossly underfunded, and do not provide adequate opportunities for children to learn effectively. Thus, the effects of SES and the effects of ethnic minority status are often intertwined (Hill & Witherspoon, 2011; Koppelman & Goodhart, 2011).

The New Hope Intervention Program

In sum, as we have just discussed, far too many schools in low-income neighborhoods provide students with environments that are not conducive to effective learning (Chen & Brooks-Gunn, 2012; Chen, Howard, & Brooks-Gunn, 2011).

Might intervention with families of children living in poverty improve children's school performance? In a recent experimental study, Aletha Huston and her colleagues (2006; Gupta, Thornton, & Huston, 2007) evaluated the effects of New Hope, a program designed to increase parental employment and reduce family poverty, on adolescent development. They randomly assigned families with 6- to 10-year-old children living in poverty to the New Hope program and a control group. New Hope offered adults living in poverty who were employed 30 or more hours a week benefits that were designed to increase family income (a wage supplement that ensured that net income increased as parents earned more) and to provide work supports through subsidized child care (for any child under age 13) and health insurance. Management services were provided to New Hope participants to assist them in job searches and other needs. The New Hope program was available to the experimental group families for three years (until the children were 9 to 13 years old).

Five years after the program began and two years after it had ended, the program's effects on the children were examined when they were 11 to 16 years old. Compared with adolescents in the control group, New Hope adolescents were more competent at reading, had better school performance, were less likely to be in special education classes, had more positive social skills, and were more likely to be in formal after-school arrangements. New Hope parents reported better psychological well-being and a greater sense of self-efficacy in managing their adolescents than control parents did. In further assessment, the influence of the New Hope program on 9- to 19-year-olds after they left the program was evaluated (McLoyd & others, 2011). Positive outcomes especially occurred for African American boys, who became more optimistic about their future employment and career prospects after experiencing the New Hope program.

Even outside inner-city schools, school segregation remains a factor in U.S. education (Nieto & Bode, 2012). Almost one-third of all African American and Latino students attend schools in which 90 percent or more of the students are from minority groups (Banks, 2008).

The school experiences of students from different ethnic groups vary considerably (McLoyd & others, 2011; Rowley, Kurtz-Costas, & Cooper, 2010). African American and Latino students are much less likely than non-Latino White or Asian American students to be enrolled in academic, college preparatory programs and are much more likely to be enrolled in remedial and special education programs. Asian American students are far more likely than other ethnic minority groups to take advanced math and science courses in high school. African American students are twice as likely as Latinos, Native Americans, or Whites to be suspended from school.

Following are some effective strategies for improving relationships among ethnically diverse students:

In *The Shame of the Nation*, Jonathan Kozol (2005) criticized the inadequate quality and lack of resources in many U.S. schools, especially those in the poverty areas of inner cities that have high concentrations of ethnic minority children. Kozol praises teachers like Angela Lively (*above*), who keeps a box of shoes in her Indianapolis classroom for students in need.

- *Turn the class into a jigsaw classroom.* When Elliot Aronson was a professor at the University of Texas at Austin, the school system contacted him for ideas on how to reduce the increasing racial tension in classrooms. Aronson (1986) developed the concept of a "jigsaw classroom," in which students from different cultural backgrounds are placed in a cooperative group in which they have to construct different parts of a project to reach a common goal. Aronson used the term *jigsaw* because he saw the technique to be like a group of students cooperating to put different pieces together to complete a jigsaw puzzle.

James Comer, Child Psychiatrist

James Comer grew up in a low-income neighborhood in East Chicago, Indiana, and credits his parents with leaving no doubt about the importance of education. He obtained a BA degree from Indiana University. He went on to obtain a medical degree from Howard University College of Medicine, a Master of Public Health degree from the University of Michigan School of Public Health, and psychiatry training at the Yale University School of Medicine's Child Study Center. He currently is the Maurice Falk Professor of Child Psychiatry at the Yale University Child Study Center and an associate dean at the Yale University Medical School. During his years at Yale, Comer has concentrated his career on promoting a focus on child development as a way of improving schools. His efforts in support of healthy development of young people are known internationally.

Comer is, perhaps, best known for the founding of the School Development Program in 1968, which promotes the collaboration of parents, educators, and community to improve social, emotional, and academic outcomes for children.

James Comer is shown with some of the inner-city children who attend a school that became a better learning environment because of Comer's intervention.

For more about what child psychiatrists do, see page 48 in the Careers in Children's Development appendix.

How might this work? Team sports, drama productions, and music performances are examples of contexts in which students participate cooperatively to reach a common goal; however, the jigsaw technique also lends itself to group science projects, history reports, and other learning experiences with a variety of subject matter.

- *Encourage students to have positive personal contact with diverse other students.* Mere contact does not do the job of improving relationships with diverse others. For example, busing ethnic minority students to predominantly non-Latino White schools, or vice versa, has not reduced prejudice or improved interethnic relations. What matters is what happens after children get to school. Especially beneficial in improving interethnic relations is sharing one's worries, successes, failures, coping strategies, interests, and other personal information with people of other ethnicities. When this happens, people tend to look at others as individuals rather than as members of a homogeneous group.

- *Reduce bias.* Teachers can reduce bias by displaying images of children from diverse ethnic and cultural groups, selecting play materials and classroom activities that encourage cultural understanding, helping students resist stereotyping, and working with parents to reduce children's exposure to bias and prejudice at home.

- *View the school and community as a team.* James Comer (1988, 2004, 2006) advocates a community, team approach as the best way to educate children. Three important aspects of the Comer Project for Change are (1) a governance and management team that develops a comprehensive school plan, assessment strategy, and staff development plan; (2) a mental health or school support team; and (3) a parents' program. Comer believes that the entire school community should have a cooperative rather than an adversarial attitude. The Comer program is currently operating in more than 600 schools in 26 states. Read further about James Comer's work in the *Connecting with Careers* profile.

How Would You...?

If you were an **educator,** how would you attempt to improve the quality of schools with high concentrations of ethnic minority children?

- *Be a competent cultural mediator.* Teachers can play a powerful role as cultural mediators by being sensitive to biased content in materials and classroom interactions, learning more about different ethnic groups, being sensitive to children's ethnic attitudes, viewing students of color positively, and thinking of positive ways to get parents of color more involved as partners with teachers in educating children.

Review *Connect* Reflect

LG4 Characterize contemporary approaches to student learning and sociocultural diversity in schools.

Review

- What are two major contemporary issues in educating children?
- How do socioeconomic status and ethnicity influence schooling?

Connect

- In Chapter 12, you read about Carol Dweck's concept of mindset. How could the concept of mindset be applied to improving the education of elementary school children?

Reflect *Your Own Personal Journey of Life*

- How would you rate the quality of teachers in your elementary school? Were their expectations for achievement too high or too low? Describe the best elementary school teacher you had and the worst.

⌐ ·topical **connections**· ‒ ‒ ‒ ‒ ‒ ‒ ‒

This chapter concludes the discussion of children's development in middle and late childhood. In Chapter 14, you will read about the dramatic changes of puberty, how the brain changes in adolescence, sexuality, and various aspects of adolescents' health. In Chapter 15, you will examine impressive advances in adolescents' thinking and the challenges of educating adolescents effectively. In Chapter 16, you will learn about how adolescents spend far more time thinking about their identity—who they are, what they are all about, and where they are going in life—than when they were children. Transformations in relationships with parents and peers also characterize adolescents.

‒ ‒ ‒ ‒ ‒ ‒ ‒ ‒ ‒ ‒ ‒ ‒ ‒ ‒ ‒ *looking* forward ‒ ‒ ➤

reach your **learning goals**

What Is the Nature of Emotional and Personality Development in Middle and Late Childhood?

LG1 Discuss emotional and personality development in middle and late childhood.

> The Self

- In middle and late childhood, self-understanding increasingly involves social and psychological characteristics, including social comparison. Children increase their perspective taking in middle and late childhood, and their social understanding shows increasing psychological sophistication as well. Self-concept refers to domain-specific evaluations of the self. Self-esteem refers to global evaluations of the self and is also referred to as self-worth or self-image. Self-esteem is only moderately related to school performance but is more strongly linked to initiative. Four ways to increase self-esteem are to (1) identify the causes of low self-esteem, (2) provide emotional support and social approval, (3) help children achieve, and (4) help children cope. Erikson's fourth stage of development, industry versus inferiority, characterizes the middle and late childhood years.

Emotional Development

- Developmental changes in emotion include increasing one's understanding of complex emotions such as pride and shame, detecting that more than one emotion can be experienced in a particular situation, taking into account the circumstances that led up to an emotional reaction, improving the ability to suppress or conceal negative emotions, and using self-initiated strategies to redirect feelings. As children get older, they use a greater variety of coping strategies and more cognitive strategies.

Moral Development

- Kohlberg argued that moral development consists of three levels—preconventional, conventional, and postconventional—and six stages (two at each level). Kohlberg maintained that these stages were age-related. Influences on movement through the stages include cognitive development, imitation and cognitive conflict, peer relations, and perspective taking. Criticisms of Kohlberg's theory have been made, especially by Gilligan, who advocates a stronger care perspective. Other criticisms focus on the inadequacy of moral reasoning to predict moral behavior, and the influences of culture and family. The domain theory of moral development states that there are different domains of social knowledge and reasoning, including moral, social conventional, and personal. Prosocial behavior involves positive moral behaviors such as sharing. Most sharing in the first three years is not done for empathy, but at about 4 years of age empathy contributes to sharing. By the start of the elementary school years, children express objective ideas about fairness. Recently, there has been a surge of interest in moral personality.

Gender

- Gender stereotypes are broad categories that reflect impressions and beliefs about males and females. A number of physical differences exist between males and females. In terms of cognitive skills, girls have better reading and writing skills than do boys. Some experts argue that cognitive differences between males and females have been exaggerated. In terms of socioemotional differences, males are more physically aggressive than females. Females regulate their emotions better and engage in more prosocial behavior than males. Tannen argues that females prefer rapport talk and males prefer report talk, but recent research indicates that gender differences in communication are small. It is important to think about gender in terms of context.

What Are Some Changes in Parenting and Families in Middle and Late Childhood?

 Describe changes in parenting and families in middle and late childhood.

Developmental Changes in Parent-Child Relationships

- Parents spend less time with children during middle and late childhood than in early childhood. Parents especially play an important role in supporting and stimulating children's academic achievement. Discipline changes and control are more coregulatory.

Parents as Managers

- Parents have important roles as managers of children's opportunities, as monitors of their behavior, and as social initiators and arrangers. Mothers are more likely to function in these parental management roles than fathers.

Stepfamilies

- As in divorced families, children living in stepparent families have more adjustment problems than their counterparts in nondivorced families. However, a majority of children in stepfamilies do not have adjustment problems. Children in complex (blended) stepfamilies have more problems than children in simple stepfamilies or nondivorced families.

What Changes Characterize Peer Relationships in Middle and Late Childhood?

 Identify changes in peer relationships in middle and late childhood.

Developmental Changes

- Among the developmental changes in peer relations in middle and late childhood are increased preference for same-sex groups, an increase in time spent in peer interaction and the size of the peer group, and less supervision of the peer group by adults.

Peer Status

- Popular children are frequently nominated as a best friend and are rarely disliked by their peers. Average children receive an average number of both positive and negative nominations from their peers. Neglected children are infrequently nominated as a best friend but are not disliked by their peers. Rejected children are infrequently nominated as a best friend and are actively disliked by their peers. Controversial children are frequently nominated both as a best friend and as being disliked by peers. Rejected children are especially at risk for a number of problems.

Social Cognition

- Social information-processing skills and social knowledge are two important dimensions of social cognition in peer relations.

Bullying

- Significant numbers of children are bullied, and this can result in short-term and long-term negative effects for both the victims and the bullies.

Friends

- Like adult friends, children who are friends tend to be similar to each other. Children's friendships serve six functions: companionship, stimulation, physical support, ego support, social comparison, and intimacy/affection.

What Are Some Important Aspects of Schools?

 Characterize contemporary approaches to student learning and sociocultural diversity in schools.

Contemporary Approaches to Student Learning

- Contemporary approaches to student learning include the constructivist approach (a learner-centered approach) and the direct instruction approach (a teacher-centered approach). In the United States, standardized testing of elementary school students was mandated nationally in 2002 by the No Child Left Behind federal legislation. Numerous criticisms of NCLB have been made.

Socioeconomic Status and Ethnicity

- Children in poverty face many barriers to learning at school as well as at home. The effects of SES and ethnicity on schools are intertwined, as many U.S. schools are segregated. Low expectations for ethnic minority children represent one of the barriers to their learning.

key terms

self-esteem 390
self-concept 390
preconventional
  reasoning 396
heteronomous morality 396
individualism,
  instrumental purpose,
  and exchange 396
conventional reasoning 396
mutual interpersonal
  expectations,

relationships, and
  interpersonal
  conformity 396
social systems
  morality 396
postconventional
  reasoning 396
social contract or utility
  and individual rights 396
universal ethical
  principles 397

justice perspective 398
care perspective 398
domain theory of moral
  development 399
social conventional
  reasoning 399
gender stereotypes 401
rapport talk 403
report talk 403
popular children 408
average children 408

neglected children 408
rejected children 408
controversial children 408
intimacy in friendships 412
constructivist approach 413
direct instruction
  approach 414

key people

connecting with improving the lives of children

MAKING A DIFFERENCE

Guiding Children's Socioemotional Development

What are some good strategies for nourishing children's socioemotional skills?

- *Improve children's self-esteem.* This can be accomplished by identifying the causes of the child's low self-esteem, providing emotional support and social approval, and helping the child achieve.

- *Help children understand their emotions and cope with stress.* When children are experiencing considerable stress, try to remove at least one stressor from their lives. Also help the child learn effective coping strategies.

- *Nurture children's moral development.* Parents can improve their children's morality by being warm and supportive rather than punitive, using reasoning when disciplining, providing opportunities for children to learn about others' perspectives and feelings, involving children in family decision making, and modeling prosocial moral behavior.

- *Adapt to developmental changes in children.* Because parents typically spend less time with children in middle and late childhood, it is important to strengthen children's self-control. As in early childhood, authoritative parenting should continue to be the choice, rather than authoritarian or permissive parenting.

- *Improve children's peer and friendship skills.* Peer and friendship relations become increasingly important to elementary school children. Adults can talk with children about the importance of being nice, engaging in prosocial behavior, and providing support in getting peers and friends to like them. Parents also can communicate to children that being aggressive, self-centered, and inconsiderate of others harms peer and friendship relations.

- *Create schools that support children's socioemotional development.* Not only do good teachers know how to challenge and stimulate children's cognitive development, but they also know how to make children feel good about themselves. Too much of elementary school education involves negative feedback. We need more classrooms in which children are excited about learning. This learning should be designed to increase children's self-esteem, not wreck their emotional well-being. Parents need to encourage and support their children's educational accomplishments but not set unrealistic achievement expectations.

RESOURCES

Raising Black Children
by James P. Comer and Alvin E. Poussaint (1992)
New York: Plume

Raising Black Children is an excellent book for African American parents. It includes wise suggestions that are not in most child-rearing books (almost all others are written for middle-class White parents and do not deal with special problems faced by ethnic minority parents or parents from low-income backgrounds).

National Stepfamily Resource Center
www.stepfamilies.info

This center provides a clearinghouse and support network for stepparents, remarried parents, and their children.

In no order of things is adolescence the simple time of life.

—**JEAN ERSKINE STEWART**
American Writer, 20th Century

Adolescence

Adolescents try on one face after another, seeking to find a face of their own.

Their generation of young people is the fragile cable by which the best and the

worst of their parents' generation is transmitted to the present. In the end, there

are only two lasting bequests parents can leave youth—one is roots, the other

wings. Section 6 contains three chapters: "Physical Development in Adolescence"

(Chapter 14), "Cognitive Development in Adolescence" (Chapter 15), and "Socio-

emotional Development in Adolescence" (Chapter 16).

chapter 14 PHYSICAL DEVELOPMENT IN ADOLESCENCE

Fifteen-year-old Latisha developed a drinking problem, and recently she was kicked off the cheerleading squad for missing practice too often—but that didn't stop her drinking. She and her friends began skipping school regularly so they could drink.

Fourteen-year-old Arnie is a juvenile delinquent. Last week he stole a TV set, struck his mother and bloodied her face, broke out some streetlights in the neighborhood, and threatened a boy with a wrench and hammer.

Twelve-year-old Katie Bell, more than just about anything else, wanted a playground in her town. She knew that the other kids also wanted one, so she put together a group that generated funding ideas for the playground. They presented their ideas to the town council. Her group got more youth involved, and they raised money by selling candy and sandwiches door-to-door. The playground became a reality—a place where, as Katie says, "People have picnics and make friends." Katie's advice: "You won't get anywhere if you don't try."

Adolescents like Latisha and Arnie are the ones we hear about the most. But there are many adolescents like Katie who contribute in positive ways to their communities and competently make the transition through adolescence. Indeed, for most adolescents, adolescence is not a time of rebellion, crisis, pathology, and deviance. A far more accurate vision of adolescence is that it is a time of evaluation, decision making, commitment, and carving out a place in the world. Most of the problems of today's youth are not with the youth themselves. What adolescents need is access to a range of legitimate opportunities and to long-term support from adults who care deeply about them. In a recent survey, only 20 percent of U.S. 15-year-olds reported that they have had meaningful relationships outside of their family that help them to succeed in life (Search Institute, 2010).

Katie Bell (*front*) and some of her volunteers.

topical connections

In the previous three chapters that focused on middle and late childhood, you explored the physical, cognitive, and socioemotional development that characterizes children in the elementary school years. In regard to physical development, you learned that growth continues but at a slower pace than in infancy and early childhood. In middle and late childhood, gross motor skills become much smoother and more coordinated, and fine motor skills also improve. Significant advances in the development of the brain's prefrontal cortex also occur in middle and late childhood. In this chapter, you will study how the slower physical growth in middle and late childhood is replaced by the dramatic changes of puberty and continued transformations in the brain.

◀ *looking back*

preview

Adolescence is an important juncture in the lives of many individuals, a time when many health habits—good or bad—are formed and ingrained. In this chapter, we explore what adolescence is, examine its physical and psychological changes, discuss adolescent sexuality, and then describe several adolescent problems and health issues.

What Is the Nature of Adolescence?

 LG1 Discuss views and developmental transitions that involve adolescence.

Positive and Negative Views of Adolescence

Developmental Transitions

As in development during childhood, a number of genetic, biological, environmental, and social factors interact in adolescent development. During their first decade of life, adolescents experienced thousands of hours of interactions with parents, peers, and teachers, but now they face dramatic biological changes, new experiences, and new developmental tasks. Relationships with parents take a different form, moments with peers become more intimate, and dating occurs for the first time, as do sexual exploration and possibly intercourse. The adolescent's thoughts are more abstract and idealistic. Biological changes trigger a heightened interest in body image. Adolescence has both continuity and discontinuity with childhood.

> In youth, we clothe ourselves with rainbows and go brave as the zodiac.
>
> —RALPH WALDO EMERSON
> *American Poet and Essayist, 19th Century*

POSITIVE AND NEGATIVE VIEWS OF ADOLESCENCE

There is a long history of worrying about how adolescents will turn out. In 1904, G. Stanley Hall proposed the "storm-and-stress" view that adolescence is a turbulent time charged with conflict and mood swings. However, when Daniel Offer and his colleagues (1988) studied the self-images of adolescents in the United States, Australia, Bangladesh, Hungary, Israel, Italy, Japan, Taiwan, Turkey, and West Germany, at least 73 percent of the adolescents displayed a healthy self-image. Although there were differences among them, the adolescents were happy most of the time, they enjoyed life, they perceived themselves as able to exercise self-control, they valued work and school, they expressed confidence about their sexual selves, they expressed positive feelings toward their families, and they felt they had the capability to cope with life's stresses—not exactly a storm-and-stress portrayal of adolescence.

However, in matters of taste and manners, the young people of every generation have seemed radical, unnerving, and different from adults—different in how they look, in how they behave, in the music they enjoy, in their hairstyles, and in the clothing they choose. It would be an enormous error, though, to confuse adolescents' enthusiasm for trying on new identities and enjoying moderate amounts of outrageous behavior with hostility toward parental and societal standards. Acting out and boundary testing are time-honored ways in which adolescents move toward accepting, rather than rejecting, parental values.

Recall from Chapter 1 that *social policy* is the course of action designed by the national government to influence the welfare

Growing up has never been easy. However, adolescence is not best viewed as a time of rebellion, crisis, pathology, and deviance. A far more accurate vision of adolescence describes it as a time of evaluation, of decision making, of commitment, and of carving out a place in the world. Most of the problems of today's youth are not with the youth themselves. What adolescents need is access to a range of legitimate opportunities and to long-term support from adults who deeply care about them. *What might be some examples of such support and caring?*

of its citizens. Currently, many researchers in adolescent development are designing studies that ideally will facilitate wise and effective social policy decision making (Larson, 2011).

Peter Benson and his colleagues (Benson, 2010; Benson & Scales, 2009, 2011; Scales, Benson, & Roehlkepartain, 2011) argue that the United States has a fragmented social policy for youth that too often has focused only on the negative developmental deficits of adolescents, especially health-compromising behaviors such as drug use and delinquency, and not enough on positive strength-based approaches. According to Benson and his colleagues (2004), a strength-based approach, also referred to as *positive youth development (PYD)*, to social policy for youth

> adopts more of a wellness perspective, places particular emphasis on the existence of healthy conditions, and expands the concept of health to include the skills and competencies needed to succeed in employment, education, and life. It moves beyond the eradication of risk and deliberately argues for the promotion of well-being (Benson, 2004, p. 783).

Research indicates that youth benefit enormously when they have caring adults in their lives in addition to parents or guardians. Caring adults—such as coaches, neighbors, teachers, mentors, and after-school leaders—can serve as role models, confidants, advocates, and resources. Relationships with caring adults are powerful when youth know they are respected, that they matter to the adult, and that the adult wants to be a resource in their lives. However, in a recent survey, only 20 percent of U.S. 15-year-olds reported having had meaningful relationships outside of their family that help them to succeed in life (Search Institute, 2010).

Most adolescents negotiate the lengthy path to adult maturity successfully, but too large a group does not. Ethnic, cultural, gender, socioeconomic, age, and lifestyle differences influence the actual life trajectory of every adolescent (Cheah & Yeung, 2011; McLoyd & others, 2011; Schlegel & Hewlett, 2011). Different portrayals of adolescence emerge, depending on the particular group of adolescents being described. Today's adolescents are exposed to a complex menu of lifestyle options through technology, and many face the temptations of drug use and sexual activity at increasingly young ages. Too many adolescents are not provided with adequate opportunities and support to become competent adults (Larson, 2011).

DEVELOPMENTAL TRANSITIONS

Developmental transitions are often important junctures in people's lives. Such transitions include moving from the prenatal period to birth and infancy, from infancy to early childhood, and from early childhood to middle and late childhood. For adolescents, two important transitions are from childhood to adolescence and from adolescence to adulthood. Let's explore these transitions.

Childhood to Adolescence The transition from childhood to adolescence involves a number of biological, cognitive, and socioemotional changes. Among the biological changes are the growth spurt, hormonal changes, and sexual maturation that come with puberty. In early adolescence, changes take place in the brain that allow for more advanced thinking. Also at this time, adolescents begin to stay up later and sleep later in the morning.

Among the cognitive changes that occur during the transition from childhood to adolescence are increases in abstract, idealistic, and logical thinking. As they make this transition, adolescents begin to think in more egocentric ways, often sensing that they are onstage, unique, and invulnerable. In response to these changes, parents place more responsibility for decision making on the young adolescents' shoulders.

Among the socioemotional changes adolescents undergo are a quest for independence, conflict with parents, and a desire to spend more time with peers.

What are some physical, cognitive, and socioemotional changes involved in the transition from childhood to adolescence? What characterizes emerging adulthood?

Conversations with friends become more intimate and include more self-disclosure. As children enter adolescence, they attend schools that are larger and more impersonal than their neighborhood grade schools. Achievement becomes a more serious business, and academic challenges increase. At this time, increased sexual maturation produces a much greater interest in romantic relationships. Young adolescents also experience greater mood swings than they did when they were children.

In sum, the transition from childhood to adolescence is complex and multidimensional, involving change in many different aspects of an individual's life. Negotiating this transition successfully requires considerable adaptation and thoughtful, sensitive support from caring adults.

Adolescence to Adulthood: Emerging Adulthood   Another important transition occurs from adolescence to adulthood (Arnett, 2007). It has been said that adolescence begins in biology and ends in culture. That is, the transition from childhood to adolescence begins with the onset of pubertal maturation, whereas the transition from adolescence to adulthood is determined by cultural standards and experiences. Around the world, youth are increasingly expected to delay their entry into adulthood, in large part because the information society in which we now live requires that they obtain more education than their parents' generation. Thus, the transition between adolescence and adulthood can be a long one as adolescents develop more effective skills to become full members of society.

Recently, the transition from adolescence to adulthood has been referred to as emerging adulthood (Arnett, 2000, 2006, 2007). The age range for **emerging adulthood** is approximately 18 to 25 years of age. Experimentation and exploration characterize the emerging adult. At this point in their development, many individuals are still exploring which career path they want to follow, what they want their identity to be, and which lifestyle they want to adopt (for example, single, cohabiting, or married).

Jeffrey Arnett (2006) concluded that five key features characterize emerging adulthood:

- *Exploring identity, especially in love and work.* Emerging adulthood is the time during which key changes in identity take place for many individuals.

- *Experiencing instability.* Residential changes peak during early adulthood, a time during which there also is often instability in love, work, and education.

- *Being self-focused.* According to Arnett (2006, p. 10), emerging adults "are self-focused in the sense that they have little in the way of social obligations, little in the way of duties and commitments to others, which leaves them with a great deal of autonomy in running their own lives."

- *Feeling in-between.* Many emerging adults don't consider themselves adolescents or full-fledged adults.

- *Experiencing the age of possibilities, a time when individuals have an opportunity to transform their lives.* Arnett (2006) describes two ways in which emerging adulthood is the age of possibilities. First, many emerging adults are optimistic about their future. Second, for emerging adults who have experienced difficult times while growing up, emerging adulthood presents an opportunity to steer their lives in a more positive direction (Masten, 2011, 2012).

emerging adulthood Occurring from approximately 18 to 25 years of age, this transitional period between adolescence and adulthood is characterized by experimentation and exploration.

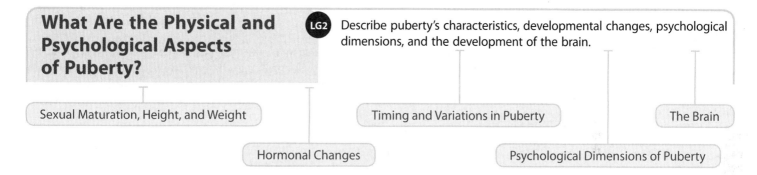

What Are the Physical and Psychological Aspects of Puberty?

LG2 Describe puberty's characteristics, developmental changes, psychological dimensions, and the development of the brain.

Sexual Maturation, Height, and Weight

Hormonal Changes

Timing and Variations in Puberty

Psychological Dimensions of Puberty

The Brain

One father remarked that the problem with his teenage son was not that he grew, but that he did not know when to stop growing. As we will see, there is considerable variation in the timing of the adolescent growth spurt. In addition to pubertal changes, other physical changes we explore involve sexuality and brain development.

Puberty is not the same as adolescence. For most of us, puberty ends long before adolescence does, although puberty is the most important marker of the beginning of adolescence. **Puberty** is a period of rapid physical maturation involving hormonal and bodily changes that occur primarily during early adolescence. Rather than a specific event, puberty is a process that unfolds through a series of coordinated neuroendocrine changes (Dorn & Biro, 2011). Among the most noticeable changes are signs of sexual maturation and increases in height and weight.

SEXUAL MATURATION, HEIGHT, AND WEIGHT

Male pubertal characteristics typically develop in the following order: increase in penis and testicle size, appearance of straight pubic hair, minor voice change, first ejaculation (which usually occurs through masturbation or a wet dream), appearance of curly pubic hair, onset of maximum growth in height and weight, growth of hair in armpits, more detectable voice changes, and, finally, growth of facial hair. A recent longitudinal study revealed that on average, boys' genital development preceded their pubic development by about 4 months (Susman & others, 2010).

What is the order of appearance of physical changes in females? First, either the breasts enlarge or pubic hair appears. Later, hair appears in the armpits. As these changes occur, the female grows in height and her hips become wider than her shoulders. **Menarche**—a girl's first menstruation—comes rather late in the pubertal cycle. Initially, her menstrual cycles may be highly irregular. For the first several years, she may not ovulate every menstrual cycle; some girls do not ovulate at all until a year or two after menstruation begins. No voice changes comparable to those in pubertal males occur in pubertal females. By the end of puberty, the female's breasts have become more fully rounded.

puberty A period of rapid physical maturation involving hormonal and bodily changes that occur primarily in early adolescence.

menarche A girl's first menstrual period.

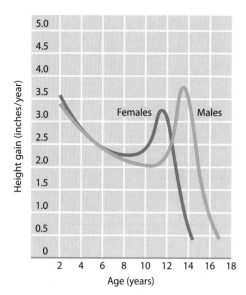

FIGURE **14.1**

PUBERTAL GROWTH SPURT. On the average, the peak of the growth spurt during puberty occurs two years earlier for girls (11½) than for boys (13½). *How are hormones related to the growth spurt and to the difference between the average height of adolescent boys and girls?*

ZITS **By Jerry Scott and Jim Borgman**

ZITS © ZITS Partnership, King Features Syndicate.

hormones Powerful chemical substances secreted by the endocrine glands and carried through the body by the bloodstream.

hypothalamus A structure in the brain that monitors eating and sex.

pituitary gland An important endocrine gland that controls growth and regulates other glands.

gonads The sex glands—the testes in males, the ovaries in females.

gonadotropins Hormones that stimulate the testes or ovaries.

testosterone A hormone associated in boys with the development of genitals, an increase in height, and a change in voice.

Marked weight gains coincide with the onset of puberty. During early adolescence, girls tend to outweigh boys, but by about age 14 boys begin to surpass girls. Similarly, at the beginning of the adolescent period, girls tend to be as tall as or taller than boys of their age, but by the end of the middle school years most boys have caught up or, in many cases, surpassed girls in height.

As indicated in Figure 14.1, the growth spurt occurs approximately two years earlier for girls than for boys. The mean age at the beginning of the growth spurt in girls is 9; for boys, it is 11. The peak rate of pubertal change occurs at 11½ years for girls and 13½ years for boys. During their growth spurt, girls increase in height about 3½ inches per year, boys about 4 inches. Boys and girls who are shorter or taller than their peers before adolescence are likely to remain so during adolescence; however, as much as 30 percent of an individual's height in late adolescence is unexplained by his or her height in the elementary school years.

HORMONAL CHANGES

Behind the first whisker in boys and the widening of hips in girls is a flood of **hormones,** powerful chemical substances secreted by the endocrine glands and carried through the body by the bloodstream. The endocrine system's role in puberty involves the interaction of the hypothalamus, the pituitary gland, and the gonads (see Figure 14.2). The **hypothalamus** is a structure in the brain that is involved with eating and sex. The **pituitary gland** is an important endocrine gland that controls growth and regulates other glands; among these, the **gonads**—the testes in males, the ovaries in females—are particularly important in giving rise to pubertal changes in the body.

How do the gonads, or sex glands, work? The pituitary sends a signal via **gonadotropins**—hormones that stimulate the testes or ovaries—to the appropriate gland to manufacture hormones. These hormones give rise to such changes as the production of sperm in males and menstruation and the release of eggs from the ovaries in females. The pituitary gland, through interaction with the hypothalamus, detects when the optimal level of hormones is reached and responds and maintains it with additional gonadotropin secretion.

Not only does the pituitary gland release gonadotropins that stimulate the testes and ovaries, but through interaction with the hypothalamus the pituitary gland also secretes hormones that either directly lead to growth and skeletal maturation or produce growth effects through interaction with the thyroid gland, located at the base of the throat.

The concentrations of certain hormones increase dramatically during adolescence (Dorn & Biro, 2011). **Testosterone** is a hormone associated in boys with

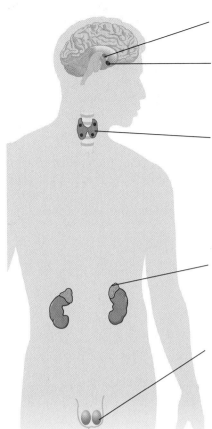

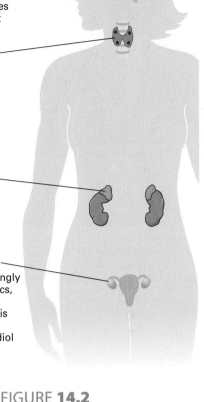

Hypothalamus: A structure in the brain that interacts with the pituitary gland to monitor the bodily regulation of hormones.

Pituitary: This master gland produces hormones that stimulate other glands. It also influences growth by producing growth hormones; it sends gonadotropins to the testes and ovaries and a thyroid-stimulating hormone to the thyroid gland. It sends a hormone to the adrenal gland as well.

Thyroid gland: It interacts with the pituitary gland to influence growth.

Adrenal gland: It interacts with the pituitary gland and likely plays a role in pubertal development, but less is known about its function than about sex glands. Recent research, however, suggests it may be involved in adolescent behavior, particularly for boys.

The gonads, or sex glands: These consist of the testes in males and the ovaries in females. The sex glands are strongly involved in the appearance of secondary sex characteristics, such as facial hair in males and breast development in females. The general class of hormones called estrogens is dominant in females, while androgens are dominant in males. More specifically, testosterone in males and estradiol in females are key hormones in pubertal development.

FIGURE **14.2**

THE MAJOR ENDOCRINE GLANDS INVOLVED IN PUBERTAL CHANGE

genital maturation, an increase in height, and a change in voice. **Estradiol** is a type of estrogen; in girls it is associated with breast, uterine, and skeletal development. In one study, testosterone levels increased eighteenfold in boys but only twofold in girls during puberty; estradiol increased eightfold in girls but only twofold in boys (Nottelmann & others, 1987). Thus, both testosterone and estradiol are present in the hormonal makeup of both boys and girls, but testosterone dominates in male pubertal development and estradiol in female pubertal development.

The same influx of hormones that grows hair on a male's chest and increases the fatty tissue in a female's breasts may also contribute to psychological development in adolescence. In one study of boys and girls ranging in age from 9 to 14, a higher concentration of testosterone was present in boys who rated themselves as more socially competent (Nottelmann & others, 1987). However, hormonal effects by themselves do not account for adolescent development (Graber, 2008). For example, in one study, social factors were much better predictors of young adolescent girls' depression and anger than hormonal factors (Brooks-Gunn & Warren, 1989). Behavior and moods also can affect hormones. Stress, eating patterns, exercise, sexual activity, tension, and depression can activate or suppress various aspects of the hormonal system (Sontag & others, 2008). In sum, the hormone-behavior link is complex (Dorn & Biro, 2011).

TIMING AND VARIATIONS IN PUBERTY

In the United States—where children mature up to a year earlier than children in European countries—the average age of menarche has declined significantly since the mid-nineteenth century. Fortunately, however, we are unlikely to see pubescent toddlers, since what has happened in the past century is likely the result of improved nutrition and health.

estradiol A hormone associated in girls with breast, uterine, and skeletal development.

Adolescents show a strong preoccupation with their changing bodies and develop images of what their bodies are like. *Why might adolescent males have more positive body images than adolescent females?*

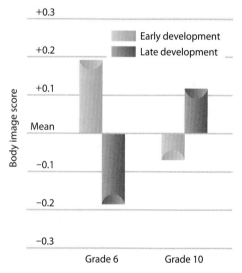

FIGURE 14.3

EARLY- AND LATE-MATURING ADOLESCENT GIRLS' PERCEPTIONS OF BODY IMAGE IN EARLY AND LATE ADOLESCENCE. The sixth-grade girls in this study had positive body image scores if they were early-maturers but negative body image scores if they were late-maturers (Simmons & Blyth, 1987). Positive body image scores indicated satisfaction with their figures. By the 10th grade, however, it was the late-maturers who had positive body image scores.

corpus callosum The location where fibers connect the brain's left and right hemispheres.

amygdala The seat of emotions, such as anger.

Why do the changes of puberty occur when they do, and how can variations in their timing be explained? Puberty is not an environmental accident. Programmed into the genes of every human being is the timing for the emergence of puberty (Elks & others, 2010). Puberty does not take place at 2 or 3 years of age and it does not occur in the twenties. Recently, scientists have begun to conduct molecular genetic studies in an attempt to identify specific genes that are linked to the onset and progression of puberty (He & others, 2010; Paris & others, 2010). Environmental factors can also influence its onset and duration (Belsky & others, 2010).

For most boys, the pubertal sequence may begin as early as age 10 or as late as 13½, and may end as early as age 13 or as late as 17. Thus, the normal range is wide enough that, given two boys of the same chronological age, one might complete the pubertal sequence before the other one has begun it. For girls, menarche is considered within the normal range if it appears between the ages of 9 and 15.

PSYCHOLOGICAL DIMENSIONS OF PUBERTY

A host of psychological changes accompanies pubertal development. These changes involve body image and early and late maturation.

Body Image   Preoccupation with body image is strong throughout adolescence, but it is especially acute during early adolescence, a time when adolescents are more dissatisfied with their bodies than in late adolescence (Graber & Brooks-Gunn, 2002).

Gender differences characterize adolescents' perceptions of their bodies (Natusaki & others, 2010). In general, throughout puberty girls are less happy with their bodies and have more negative body images than boys (Crespo & others, 2010). As pubertal change proceeds, girls often become more dissatisfied with their bodies, probably because their body fat increases (Yuan, 2010). In contrast, boys become more satisfied as they move through puberty, probably because their muscle mass increases.

The following two studies shed further light on gender differences in body image during adolescence:

- Adolescent girls placed a higher aesthetic value on body image but had a lower aesthetic satisfaction with their bodies than did adolescent boys (Abbott & Barber, 2010).

- The profile of adolescents with the most positive body images was characterized by health-enhancing behaviors, especially regular exercise (Frisen & Holmqvist, 2010).

Early and Late Maturation   Some people enter puberty early, others late, and still others on time. Adolescents who mature earlier or later than their peers perceive themselves differently (de Rose & others, 2011; Negriff, Susman, & Trickett, 2011). In the Berkeley Longitudinal Study conducted some years ago, early-maturing boys perceived themselves more positively and had more successful peer relations than did their late-maturing counterparts (Jones, 1965). When the late-maturing boys were in their thirties, however, they had developed a stronger sense of identity than the early-maturing boys had (Peskin, 1967). This may have occurred because the late-maturing boys had more time to explore life's options, or because the early-maturing boys continued to focus on their advantageous physical status instead of on career development and achievement. More recent research confirms, though, that at least during adolescence it is advantageous to be an early-maturing rather than a late-maturing boy (Graber, Brooks-Gunn, & Warren, 2006).

For girls, early and late maturation have been linked with body image. In the sixth grade, early-maturing girls show greater satisfaction with their figures than do late-maturing girls, but by the tenth grade late-maturing girls are more satisfied (Simmons & Blyth, 1987) (see Figure 14.3). One possible reason for this developmental change is that in late adolescence early-maturing girls are shorter and stockier, whereas late-maturing girls are taller and thinner. Thus, late-maturing girls in late adolescence have bodies that more closely approximate the current American ideal of feminine beauty—tall and thin.

An increasing number of researchers have found that early maturation increases girls' vulnerability to a number of problems (de Rose & others, 2011; Graber, Nichols, & Brooks-Gunn, 2010; Negriff, Susman, & Trickett, 2011). Early-maturing girls are more likely to smoke, drink, be depressed, have an eating disorder, engage in delinquency, struggle for earlier independence from their parents, and have older friends; and their bodies are likely to elicit responses from males that lead to earlier dating and earlier sexual experiences (Copeland & others, 2010; de Rose & others, 2011; Negriff, Susman, & Trickett, 2011). And early-maturing girls are less likely to graduate from high school and more likely to cohabit and marry earlier (Cavanagh, 2009). Apparently as a result of their social and cognitive immaturity, combined with early physical development, early-maturing girls are easily lured into problem behaviors, not recognizing the possible long-term effects of these on their development. The following two recent studies document the negative outcomes of early pubertal timing in girls:

How does early and late maturation influence adolescent development?

- Early-maturing girls were more likely to engage in substance abuse and early sexual intercourse (Gaudineau & others, 2010).

- A study of 9- to 13-year-old girls found that early pubertal timing at time 1 was linked to a higher level of sexual activity at time 2, which in turn was related to higher delinquency at time 3 (Negriff, Susman, & Trickett, 2011).

THE BRAIN

Along with the rest of the body, the brain is changing during adolescence, but the study of adolescent brain development is in its infancy. As advances in technology take place, significant strides will also likely be made in charting developmental changes in the adolescent brain (Casey, Jones, & Somerville, 2011; Lenroot & Giedd, 2011). What do we know now?

Using fMRI brain scans, scientists have recently discovered that adolescents' brains undergo significant structural changes (Shaw & others, 2011). The **corpus callosum,** where fibers connect the brain's left and right hemispheres, thickens in adolescence, and this change improves adolescents' ability to process information (Gilliam & others, 2011). We discussed advances in the development of the *prefrontal cortex*—the highest level of the frontal lobes involved in reasoning, decision making, and self-control—in Chapter 8, "Physical Development in Early Childhood," and Chapter 11, "Physical Development in Middle and Late Childhood." However, the prefrontal cortex does not finish maturing until the emerging adult years, approximately 18 to 25 years of age, or later (Gogtay & Thompson, 2010). However, the **amygdala**—the seat of emotions such as anger—matures earlier than the prefrontal cortex (Casey, Duhoux, & Malter Cohen, 2010; Raznahan & others, 2011). Figure 14.4 shows the locations of the corpus callosum, prefrontal cortex, and amygdala.

Many of the changes in the adolescent brain that we have described involve the rapidly emerging field of *social*

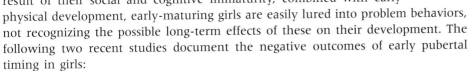

Prefrontal cortex
This "judgment" region reins in intense emotions but doesn't finish developing until at least emerging adulthood.

Corpus callosum
These nerve fibers connect the brain's two hemispheres; they thicken in adolescence to process information more effectively.

Amygdala
The seat of emotions such as anger; this area develops quickly before other regions that help to control it.

FIGURE 14.4
CHANGES IN THE ADOLESCENT BRAIN

developmental neuroscience, which involves connections between development, the brain, and socioemotional processes (Nelson & Guyer, 2011). For example, consider leading researcher Charles Nelson's (2003) view that although adolescents are capable of very strong emotions their prefrontal cortex has not adequately developed to the point at which they can control these passions. It is as if their brain does not have the brakes to slow down their emotions. Or consider this interpretation of the development of emotion and cognition in adolescents: "early activation of strong 'turbo-charged' feelings with a relatively un-skilled set of 'driving skills' or cognitive abilities to modulate strong emotions and motivations" (Dahl, 2004, p. 18).

Of course, a major issue is which comes first, biological changes in the brain or experiences that stimulate these changes (Lerner, Boyd, & Du, 2008). Consider a recent study in which the prefrontal cortex thickened and more brain connections formed when adolescents resisted peer pressure (Paus & others, 2008). Scientists have yet to determine whether the brain changes come first or whether the brain changes are the result of experiences with peers, parents, and others. Once again, we encounter the nature-nurture issue that is so prominent in examining development through the life span.

Review Connect Reflect

LG2 Describe puberty's characteristics, developmental changes, psychological dimensions, and the development of the brain.

Review

- What is puberty? What characterizes sexual maturation and the pubertal growth spurt?
- What are some hormonal changes in puberty?
- How has the timing of puberty changed, and what are some variations in puberty?
- What are some psychological dimensions of pubertal change?
- What developmental changes occur in the brain during adolescence?

Connect

- What developmental changes in the brain occur in middle and late childhood? (See Chapter 11, "Physical Development in Middle and Late Childhood.")

Reflect *Your Own Personal Journey of Life*

- Did you experience puberty early, late, or on time? How do you think the timing of your puberty influenced your development?

What Are the Dimensions of Adolescent Sexuality?   **LG3** Characterize adolescent sexuality.

Developing a Sexual Identity

Timing and Trends in Adolescent Sexual Behavior

Sexual Risk Taking in Adolescence

> Sexual arousal emerges as a new phenomenon in adolescence and it is important to view sexuality as a normal aspect of adolescent development.
>
> —SHIRLEY FELDMAN
> *Contemporary Psychologist, Stanford University*

Not only are adolescents characterized by substantial changes in physical growth and the development of the brain, but adolescence also is a bridge between the asexual child and the sexual adult (Tolman & McClelland, 2011). Adolescence is a time of sexual exploration and experimentation, of sexual fantasies and realities, of incorporating sexuality into one's identity. Adolescents have an almost insatiable curiosity about sexuality. They are concerned about whether they are sexually attractive, how to do sex, and what the future holds for their sexual lives. Although most adolescents experience times of vulnerability and confusion, the majority will eventually develop a mature sexual identity.

Every society gives some attention to adolescent sexuality. In some societies, adults resolutely protect adolescent females from males by chaperoning them, while other societies promote very early marriage. Then there are societies that allow some sexual experimentation.

In the United States, the sexual culture is widely available to adolescents. In addition to any advice adolescents get from parents, they learn a great deal about sex from television, videos, magazines, the lyrics of popular music, and the Internet (Welch, 2011).

DEVELOPING A SEXUAL IDENTITY

Mastering emerging sexual feelings and forming a sense of sexual identity are multifaceted and lengthy processes (Diamond & Savin-Williams, 2011). They involve learning to manage sexual feelings (such as sexual arousal and attraction), developing new forms of intimacy, and learning the skills to regulate sexual behavior to avoid undesirable consequences. Developing a sexual identity also involves more than just sexual behavior. Sexual identities emerge in the context of physical factors, social factors, and cultural factors, with most societies placing constraints on the sexual behavior of adolescents.

An adolescent's sexual identity involves activities, interests, styles of behavior, and an indication of sexual orientation (whether an individual has same-sex or other-sex attractions). For example, some adolescents have a high anxiety level about sex, others a low level. Some adolescents are strongly aroused sexually, others less so. Some adolescents are very active sexually, others not at all. Some adolescents are sexually inactive in response to their strong religious upbringing; others go to church regularly, yet their religious training does not inhibit their sexual activity.

It is commonly believed that most gays and lesbians quietly struggle with same-sex attractions in childhood, do not engage in heterosexual dating, and gradually recognize that they are a gay male or a lesbian in mid to late adolescence. Many youth do follow this developmental pathway, but others do not (Diamond & Savin-Williams, 2011). Gay and lesbian youth have diverse patterns of initial attraction, often have bisexual attractions, and may have physical or emotional attraction to same-sex individuals but do not always fall in love with them (Diamond, 2011).

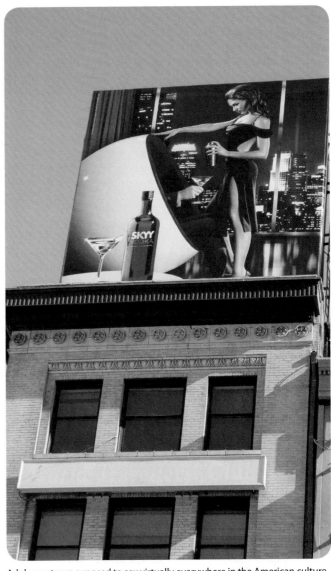

Adolescents are exposed to sex virtually everywhere in the American culture, and sex is used to sell just about everything.

TIMING AND TRENDS IN ADOLESCENT SEXUAL BEHAVIOR

The timing of sexual initiation varies by country as well as by gender and other socioeconomic characteristics (Tolman & McClelland, 2011). In one cross-cultural study, among females, the proportion having first intercourse by age 17 ranged from 72 percent in Mali to 47 percent in the United States and 45 percent in Tanzania (Singh & others, 2000). The percentage of males who had their first intercourse by age 17 ranged from 76 percent in Jamaica to 64 percent in the United States and 63 percent in Brazil.

What is the current profile of sexual activity of adolescents? In a recent U.S. national survey conducted in 2009, 62 percent of twelfth-graders reported that they had experienced sexual intercourse, compared with 32 percent of ninth-graders (Eaton & others, 2010). By age 20, 77 percent of U.S. youth have engaged in sexual intercourse (Dworkin & Santelli, 2007). Nationally, 49 percent of twelfth-graders, 40 percent of eleventh-graders, 29 percent of tenth-graders, and 21 percent of ninth-graders recently reported that they are currently sexually active (Eaton & others, 2010).

How Would You...?
If you were a **psychologist,** how would you describe the ethnic differences in the timing of an adolescent's first sexual experience?

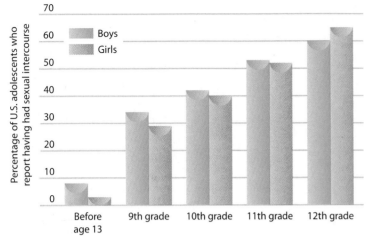

FIGURE **14.5**

TIMING OF SEXUAL INTERCOURSE IN U.S. ADOLESCENTS

What are some risks for early initiation of sexual intercourse?

What trends in adolescent sexual activity have occurred in the last two decades? From 1991 to 2009, fewer adolescents reported ever having had sexual intercourse, currently being sexually active, having had sexual intercourse before the age of 13, and having had sexual intercourse with four or more persons during their lifetime (Eaton & others, 2010). See Figure 14.5.

Until very recently, at all grade levels, adolescent males were more likely than adolescent females to say that they had had sexual intercourse and were sexually active (MMWR, 2006). However, in the 2009 national survey, a higher percentage of twelfth-grade females (65 percent) reported that they had experienced sexual intercourse than twelfth-grade males (60 percent); a higher percentage of ninth-grade males (34 percent) still reported that they had experienced sexual intercourse than ninth-grade females (29 percent) (Eaton & others, 2010). Adolescent males are more likely than their female counterparts to describe sexual intercourse as an enjoyable experience.

Sexual initiation varies by ethnic group in the United States (Tolman & McClelland, 2011). In a recent national U.S. survey of ninth- to twelfth-graders, 67 percent of African Americans, 51 percent of Latinos, and 43 percent of non-Latino Whites said they had ever experienced sexual intercourse (Eaton & others, 2010). In this study, 15 percent of African Americans (compared with 7 percent of Latinos and 3 percent of non-Latino Whites) said they had their first sexual experience before 13 years of age. Other research indicates that Asian American adolescents engage in sexual intercourse later than non-Latino Whites and adolescents from other ethnic groups (Feldman, Turner, & Araujo, 1999).

Recent research indicates that oral sex is now a common occurrence among U.S. adolescents (Song & Halpern-Felsher, 2011). In a national survey, 55 percent of U.S. 15- to 19-year-old boys and 54 percent of girls said they had engaged in oral sex (National Center for Health Statistics, 2002).

SEXUAL RISK TAKING IN ADOLESCENCE

Many adolescents are not emotionally prepared to handle sexual experiences, especially in early adolescence. Early sexual activity is linked with risky behaviors such as drug use, delinquency, and school-related problems (Yi & others, 2010). In a longitudinal study from 10 to 12 years of age to 25 years of age, early sexual intercourse and affiliation with deviant peers were linked to substance use disorders in emerging adulthood (Cornelius & others, 2007). A recent study of adolescents in five countries, including the United States, found that substance use was related to early sexual intercourse (Madkour & others, 2010).

In addition to having sex in early adolescence, other risk factors for sexual problems in adolescence include contextual factors such as socioeconomic status (SES) and poverty, family/parenting and peer factors, and school-related influences (Van Ryzin & others, 2011). The percentage of sexually active young adolescents is higher in low-income areas of inner cities (Silver & Bauman, 2006). A recent study revealed that neighborhood poverty concentrations predicted 15- to 17-year-old girls' and boys' sexual initiation (Cubbin & others, 2010).

A number of family factors are linked to sexuality outcomes for adolescents. A recent research review indicated that the following aspects of connectedness predicted sexual and reproductive health outcomes for youth: family connectedness, parent-adolescent communication about sexuality, parental monitoring, and partner connectedness (Markham & others, 2010). Also, having older sexually active

developmental **connection**

Self and Identity. One of the most important aspects of the self in middle and late childhood is the increased capacity for self-regulation. Chapter 13, p. 391

siblings or pregnant/parenting teenage sisters places adolescent girls at risk for pregnancy (Miller, Benson, & Galbraith, 2001). Further, recent research indicated that associating with more deviant peers in early adolescence was related to having more sexual partners at age 16 (Lansford & others, 2010). And a recent research review found that school connectedness was linked to positive sexuality outcomes (Markham & others, 2010).

Cognitive factors are increasingly implicated in sexual risk taking in adolescence (Fantasia, 2008). Two such factors are attention problems and self-regulation (the ability to control one's emotions and behavior). A longitudinal study revealed that attention problems and high rates of aggressive disruptive behavior at school entry increased the risk of multiple problem behaviors (school maladjustment, antisocial behavior, and substance use) in middle school, which in turn was linked to early initiation of sexual activity (Schofield & others, 2008). Another longitudinal study found that weak self-regulation at 8 to 9 years of age and risk proneness (tendency to seek sensation and make poor decisions) at 12 to 13 years of age set the stage for sexual risk taking at 16 to 17 years of age (Crockett, Raffaelli, & Shen, 2006).

Psychologists are exploring ways to encourage adolescents to make less risky sexual decisions. Here an adolescent participates in an interactive video session developed by Julie Downs and her colleagues at the Department of Social and Decision Making Sciences at Carnegie Mellon University. The videos help adolescents evaluate their responses and decisions in high-risk sexual contexts.

Contraceptive Use   Are adolescents increasingly using condoms? A recent national study revealed a substantial increase in the use of a contraceptive (61 percent in 2009 compared with 46 percent in 1991) by U.S. high school students the last time they had sexual intercourse (Eaton & others, 2010). However, in this study, rates of condom use by U.S. adolescents did not significantly change from 2003 through 2009.

Many sexually active adolescents still do not use contraceptives, or they use them inconsistently (Tschann & others, 2010). In 2009, 34 percent of sexually active adolescents did not use a condom the last time they had sexual intercourse (Eaton & others, 2010). Younger adolescents are less likely than older adolescents to take contraceptive precautions.

Sexually Transmitted Infections   Some forms of contraception, such as birth control pills or implants, do not protect against sexually transmitted infections, or STIs. **Sexually transmitted infections (STIs)** are diseases that are contracted primarily through sexual contact. This contact is not limited to vaginal intercourse but includes oral-genital and anal-genital contact as well. STIs are an increasing health problem. Approximately 25 percent of sexually active adolescents are estimated to become infected with an STI each year. Among the main STIs adolescents can get are bacterial infections (such as gonorrhea, syphilis, and chlamydia), and STIs caused by viruses—genital herpes, genital warts, and **AIDS** (acquired immune deficiency syndrome). Figure 14.6 describes these sexually transmitted infections.

No single STI has had a greater impact on sexual behavior, or created more fear, in the last two decades than AIDS. AIDS is caused by the human immunodeficiency virus (HIV), which destroys the body's immune system. Following exposure to HIV, an individual is vulnerable to germs that a normal immune system could destroy.

In 2006, 15 percent of all individuals who had been diagnosed with HIV/AIDS in the United States were 13 to 24 years of age (Centers for Disease Control and Prevention, 2008). Worldwide, the greatest concern about AIDS is in sub-Saharan Africa, where it has reached epidemic proportions (Burnett & others, 2011; UNICEF, 2011). Adolescent girls in many African countries are especially vulnerable to infection with the HIV virus by adult men. Approximately six times as many adolescent girls as boys have AIDS in these countries. In Kenya, 25 percent of the 15- to 19-year-old girls are HIV-positive, compared with only 4 percent of this age group of boys. In Botswana, more than 30 percent of the adolescent girls who are pregnant are infected with the HIV virus. In some sub-Saharan countries, less than 20 percent

How Would You...?

If you were a **social worker**, how would you design an educational campaign to increase adolescents' effective use of contraception?

A 13-year-old boy pushes his friends around in his barrow during a break from his work as a barrow boy in a community in sub-Saharan Africa. He became the breadwinner in the family because both of his parents died of AIDS.

sexually transmitted infections (STIs) Diseases that are contracted primarily through sexual contact. This contact is not limited to vaginal intercourse but includes oral-genital contact and anal-genital contact as well.

AIDS AIDS, or acquired immune deficiency syndrome, is caused by a virus, the human immunodeficiency virus (HIV), which destroys the body's immune system.

STI	Description/cause	Incidence	Treatment
Gonorrhea	Commonly called the "drip" or "clap." Caused by the bacterium *Neisseria gonorrhoeae*. Spread by contact between infected moist membranes (genital, oral-genital, or anal-genital) of two individuals. Characterized by discharge from penis or vagina and painful urination. Can lead to infertility.	500,000 cases annually in U.S.	Penicillin, other antibiotics
Syphilis	Caused by the bacterium *Treponema pallidum*. Characterized by the appearance of a sore where syphilis entered the body. The sore can be on the external genitals, vagina, or anus. Later, a skin rash breaks out on palms of hands and bottom of feet. If not treated, can eventually lead to paralysis or even death.	100,000 cases annually in U.S.	Penicillin
Chlamydia	A common STI named for the bacterium *Chlamydia trachomatis*, an organism that spreads by sexual contact and infects the genital organs of both sexes. A special concern is that females with chlamydia may become infertile. It is recommended that adolescent and young adult females have an annual screening for this STI.	About 3 million people in U.S. annually	Antibiotics
Genital herpes	Caused by a family of viruses with different strains. Involves an eruption of sores and blisters. Spread by sexual contact.	One of five U.S. adults	No known cure but antiviral medications can shorten outbreaks
AIDS	Caused by the human immunodeficiency virus (HIV), which destroys the body's immune system. Semen and blood are the main vehicles of transmission. Common symptoms include fevers, night sweats, weight loss, chronic fatigue, and swollen lymph nodes.	More than 300,000 cumulative cases of HIV virus in U.S. 25–34-year-olds; epidemic incidence in sub-Saharan countries	New treatments have slowed the progression from HIV to AIDS; no cure
Genital warts	Caused by the human papillomavirus, which does not always produce symptoms. Usually appear as small, hard painless bumps in the vaginal area, or around the anus. Very contagious. Certain high-risk types of this virus cause cervical cancer and other genital cancers. May recur despite treatment. A new HPV preventive vaccine, Gardasil, has been approved for girls and women 9–26 years of age.	About 5.5 million new cases annually; considered the most common STI in the U.S.	A topical drug, freezing, or surgery

FIGURE **14.6**

SEXUALLY TRANSMITTED INFECTIONS

of women and 40 percent of 15- to 19-year-olds reported having used a condom the last time they had sexual intercourse (Singh & others, 2004).

There continues to be great concern about AIDS in many parts of the world, not just sub-Saharan Africa. In the United States, prevention is especially targeted at groups that show the highest incidence of AIDS. These include drug users, individuals with other STIs, young gay males, individuals living in low-income circumstances, Latinos, and African Americans (Centers for Disease Control and Prevention, 2011).

Adolescent Pregnancy In cross-cultural comparisons, the United States continues to have one of the highest adolescent pregnancy and childbearing rates in the industrialized world, despite a considerable decline during the 1990s. The U.S. adolescent pregnancy rate is eight times as high as that in the Netherlands. Although U.S. adolescents are no more sexually active than their counterparts in the Netherlands, their adolescent pregnancy rate is dramatically higher.

Despite the negative comparisons of the United States with many other developed countries, there have been some encouraging trends in U.S. adolescent pregnancy rates. In 2009, births to adolescent girls fell to a record low (Ventura & Hamilton, 2011). The U.S. adolescent birth rate decreased 8 percent from 2007 to 2009 (Ventura & Hamilton, 2011). Fear of sexually transmitted infections, especially AIDS; school/community health classes; and a greater hope for the future are the likely reasons for the decrease in U.S. adolescent pregnancy rates in recent decades.

Ethnic variations characterize adolescent pregnancy (Casares & others, 2010) (see Figure 14.7). Latina adolescents are more likely than African American and non-Latina White adolescents to become pregnant (Ventura & Hamilton, 2011). Latina and African American adolescent girls who have a child are also more likely

connecting with diversity

Cross-Cultural Comparisons of Adolescent Pregnancy

Three reasons U.S. adolescent pregnancy rates are so high can be found in cross-cultural studies (Boonstra, 2002, pp. 9–10):

- *"Childbearing regarded as adult activity."* European countries, as well as Canada, give a strong consensus that childbearing belongs in adulthood "when young people have completed their education, have become employed and independent from their parents and are living in stable relationships. . . . In the United States, this attitude is much less strong and much more variable across groups and areas of the country."

- *"Clear messages about sexual behavior.* While adults in other countries strongly encourage teens to wait until they have established themselves before having children, they are generally more accepting than American adults of teens having sex. In France and Sweden, in particular, teen sexual expression is seen as normal and positive, but there is also widespread expectation that sexual intercourse will take place within committed relationships. In fact, relationships among U.S. teens tend to be more sporadic and of shorter duration. Equally strong is the expectation that young people who are having sex will take actions to protect themselves and their

partners from pregnancy and sexually transmitted infections," an expectation that is much stronger in Europe than in the United States. "In keeping with this view, . . . schools in Great Britain, France, Sweden, and most of Canada" have sex education programs that provide more comprehensive information about prevention than U.S. schools. In addition, these countries use the media more often in "government-sponsored campaigns for promoting responsible sexual behavior."

- *"Access to family-planning services.* In countries that are more accepting of teenage sexual relationships, teenagers also have easier access to reproductive health services. In Canada, France, Great Britain, and Sweden, contraceptive services are integrated into other types of primary health care and are available free or at low cost for all teenagers. Generally, teens [in these countries] know where to obtain information and services and receive confidential and nonjudgmental care. . . . In the United States, where attitudes about teenage sexual relationships are more conflicted, teens have a harder time obtaining contraceptive services. Many do not have health insurance or cannot get birth control as part of their basic health care."

to have a second child than are non-Latina White adolescent girls (Rosengard, 2009). And daughters of teenage mothers are at risk for teenage childbearing, thus perpetuating an intergenerational cycle (Meade, Kershaw, & Ickovics, 2008).

Why are U.S. adolescent pregnancy rates so high? We discuss possible answers to this question in the following *Connecting with Diversity* interlude.

Adolescent pregnancy creates health risks for both the baby and the mother. Infants born to adolescent mothers are more likely to have low birth weights—a prominent factor in infant mortality—as well as neurological problems and childhood illness

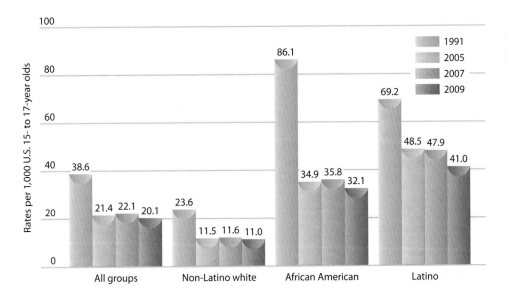

FIGURE 14.7

BIRTH RATES FOR U.S. 15- TO 17-YEAR-OLDS FROM 1991 TO 2009. Source: Ventura & Hamilton, 2011, Fig. 3.

What are some consequences of adolescent pregnancy?

How Would You...?

If you were an **educator,** how would you incorporate sex education throughout the curriculum to encourage adolescents' healthy, responsible sexual development?

(Khashan, Baker, & Kenny, 2010). Adolescent mothers often drop out of school. Although many adolescent mothers resume their education later in life, they generally never catch up economically with women who postpone childbearing until their twenties. One longitudinal study found that the children of women who had their first birth during their teens had lower achievement test scores and more behavioral problems than did children whose mothers had their first birth as adults (Hofferth & Reid, 2002).

Though the consequences of America's high adolescent pregnancy rate are cause for great concern, it often is not pregnancy alone that leads to negative consequences for an adolescent mother and her offspring. Adolescent mothers are more likely to come from low-SES backgrounds (Molina & others, 2010). Many adolescent mothers also were not good students before they became pregnant. However, not every adolescent female who bears a child lives a life of poverty and low achievement. Thus, although adolescent pregnancy is a high-risk circumstance, and adolescents who do not become pregnant generally fare better than those who do, some adolescent mothers do well in school and have positive outcomes (Leadbeater & Way, 2001).

Serious, extensive efforts are needed to help pregnant adolescents and young mothers enhance their educational and occupational opportunities. Adolescent mothers also need help in obtaining competent child care and in planning for the future.

All adolescents can benefit from age-appropriate family-life education (Graves & others, 2010). Family and consumer science educators teach life skills, such as effective decision making, to adolescents. To read about the work of one family and consumer science educator, see the *Connecting with Careers* profile. And to learn more about ways to reduce adolescent pregnancy, see the *Caring Connections* interlude.

connecting with careers

Lynn Blankenship, Family and Consumer Science Educator

Lynn Blankenship is a family and consumer science educator. She has an undergraduate degree in this field from University of Arizona. She has taught for more than 20 years, the last 14 at Tucson High Magnet School.

Blankenship was awarded the Tucson Federation of Teachers Educator of the Year Award for 1999–2000 and the Arizona Teacher of the Year in 1999.

Blankenship especially enjoys teaching life skills to adolescents. One of her favorite activities is having students care for an automated baby that imitates the needs of real babies. She says that this program has a profound impact on students because the baby must be cared for around the clock for the duration of the assignment. Blankenship also coordinates real-world work experiences and training for students in several child-care facilities in the Tucson area.

Lynn Blankenship (*center*) teaching life skills to students.

For more about what family and consumer science educators do, see p. 47 in the Careers in Children's Development appendix.

Reducing Adolescent Pregnancy

One strategy for reducing adolescent pregnancy, called the Teen Outreach Program (TOP), focuses on engaging adolescents in volunteer community service and stimulates discussions that help adolescents appreciate the lessons they learn through volunteerism. In one study, 695 adolescents in grades 9 to 12 were randomly assigned to either a Teen Outreach group or a control group (Allen & others, 1997). They were assessed both at program entry and at program exit nine months later. The rate of pregnancy was substantially lower for the Teen Outreach adolescents. These adolescents also had lower rates of school failure and academic suspension.

Girls, Inc. has four programs that are intended to increase adolescent girls' motivation to avoid pregnancy until they are mature enough to make responsible decisions about motherhood (Roth & others, 1998). "Growing Together," a series of five two-hour workshops for mothers and adolescents, and "Will Power/ Won't Power," a series of six two-hour sessions that focus on assertiveness training, are for 12- to 14-year-old girls. For older adolescent girls, "Taking Care of Business" provides nine sessions that emphasize career planning as well as information about sexuality, reproduction, and contraception. "Health Bridge" coordinates health and education services—girls can participate in this program as one of their club activities. Girls who participated in these programs were less likely to get pregnant than girls who did not participate (Girls, Inc., 1991).

Currently, a major controversy in sex education is whether schools should have an abstinence-only program or a program that

These are not adolescent mothers, but rather adolescents who are participating in the Teen Outreach Program (TOP), which engages adolescents in volunteer community service. These adolescent girls are serving as volunteers in a child-care center for crack babies. Researchers have found that such volunteer experiences can reduce the rate of adolescent pregnancy.

emphasizes contraceptive knowledge. A number of leading experts on adolescent sexuality now conclude that sex education programs that emphasize contraceptive knowledge do not increase the incidence of sexual intercourse and are more likely to reduce the risk of adolescent pregnancy and sexually transmitted infections than abstinence-only programs (Eisenberg & others, 2008; Hyde & DeLamater, 2011). Some sex education programs are starting to include abstinence-plus sexuality that promote abstinence as well as contraceptive use (Realini & others, 2010).

Review *Connect* Reflect

 LG3 Characterize adolescent sexuality.

Review

- How do adolescents develop a sexual identity?
- What characterizes timing and trends in adolescent sexual behavior?
- What is the nature of sexual risk taking in adolescence?

Connect

- How might the development of self-regulation that was discussed in Chapter 13

benefit adolescents when sexual decision making is involved?

Reflect *Your Own Personal Journey of Life*

- How would you describe your sexual identity an adolescent? What contributed to this identity?

How Can Adolescents' Health and Health-Enhancing Assets Be Characterized?

LG4 Summarize adolescents' health and eating disorders.

Adolescent Health

Leading Causes of Death in Adolescence

Substance Use and Abuse

Eating Problems and Disorders

To improve adolescent health, adults should aim (1) to increase adolescents' *health-enhancing behaviors*, such as eating nutritiously, exercising, wearing seat belts, and getting adequate sleep; and (2) to reduce adolescents' *health-compromising behaviors*, such as drug abuse, violence, unprotected sexual intercourse, and dangerous driving.

ADOLESCENT HEALTH

Adolescence is a critical juncture in the adoption of behaviors that are relevant to health (Spruijt-Metz, 2011). Many of the behaviors that are linked to poor health habits and early death in adults begin during adolescence. Conversely, the early formation of healthy behavior patterns, such as regular exercise and a preference for foods low in fat and cholesterol, not only has immediate health benefits but also helps in adulthood to delay or prevent disability and mortality from heart disease, stroke, diabetes, and cancer (Insel & Roth, 2012).

Nutrition Poor nutrition and being overweight are also key problems among adolescents (Spruijt-Metz, 2011). A comparison of adolescents in 28 countries found that U.S. adolescents ate more junk food than teenagers in most other countries (World Health Organization, 2000). The National Youth Risk Survey found that U.S. high school students decreased their intake of fruits and vegetables from 1999 through 2007 (Eaton & others, 2008).

The percentage of overweight adolescents and emerging adults increased dramatically in the 1980s, 1990s, and into the early part of the first decade of the twenty-first century. For example, being overweight increased from 11 to 17 percent for U.S. 12- to 19-year-olds from the early 1990s through 2004 (Eaton & others, 2006). However, research indicates that a leveling off began occurring about midway through the first decade of the twenty-first century (Ogden, Carroll, & Flegal, 2008). A recent analysis concluded that the leveling off in adolescents being overweight is occurring not only in the United States but also in Europe, Japan, and Australia (Rokholm, Baker, & Sorensen, 2010). In this analysis, the leveling off was less likely to occur in adolescents living in low-income conditions. Despite the recent leveling off in being overweight for some adolescents, overweight and obesity in adolescents remains at epidemic levels.

Being obese in adolescence predicts obesity in emerging adulthood. For example, a recent study of more than 8,000 12- to 21-year-olds found that obese adolescents were more likely to develop severe obesity in emerging adulthood than were overweight or normal-weight adolescents (The & others, 2010). And more emerging adults are overweight or obese than are adolescents. A recent longitudinal study tracked more than 1,500 adolescents for 10 years who were classified not overweight, overweight, or obese when they were 14 years of age (Patton & others, 2011). Across the 10-year period, the percentage of overweight individuals increased from 20 percent at 14 years of age to 33 percent at 24 years of age. Obesity increased from 4 percent to 7 percent across the 10 years.

developmental **connection**

Nutrition and Weight. Being overweight at age 3 is a risk factor for subsequently being overweight at age 12. Chapter 8, p. 248

Are there ethnic variations in being overweight during adolescence? A survey by the National Center for Health Statistics (2002) found that African American girls and Latino boys have especially high risks of being overweight during adolescence. Another study revealed that the higher obesity rate for African American girls is linked with a diet higher in calories and fat, as well as with sedentary behavior (Sanchez-Johnsen & others, 2004).

What types of interventions have been successful in reducing overweight in adolescents? One review indicated that a combination of calorie restriction, exercise (walking or biking to school, participating in a regular exercise program), reduction of sedentary activity (watching TV, playing video games), and behavioral therapy (such as keeping weight-loss diaries and receiving rewards for meeting goals) have been moderately effective in helping overweight adolescents lose weight (Fowler-Brown & Kahwati, 2004).

Exercise   There also is major concern about the low level of exercise by U.S. adolescents. In a cross-cultural study, just two-thirds of U.S. adolescents exercised at least twice a week, compared with 80 percent or more of adolescents in Ireland, Austria, Germany, and the Slovak Republic (World Health Organization, 2000).

Individuals tend to become less active as they reach and progress through adolescence (Pate & others, 2009). A recent national study of U.S. 9- to 15-year-olds revealed that almost all 9- and 11-year-olds met the federal government's moderate to vigorous exercise recommendations per day (a minimum of 60 minutes a day), but only 31 percent of 15-year-olds met the recommendations on weekdays, and on weekends only 17 percent met the recommendations (Nader & others, 2008). The same study also found that adolescent boys were more likely to engage in moderate to vigorous exercise than girls. Figure 14.8 shows the average amount of exercise among U.S. boys and girls from 9 to 15 years of age on weekdays and weekends. Another recent national study of U.S. adolescents revealed that physical activity increased until 13 years of age in boys and girls but then declined through 18 years of age (Kahn & others, 2008). In this study, adolescents were more likely to engage in regular exercise when they perceived it was important to present a positive body image to their friends and when exercise was important to their parents.

Ethnic differences in exercise participation rates of U.S. adolescents also occur, and these rates vary by gender. As indicated in Figure 14.9, in the National Youth Risk Survey, non-Latino White boys exercised the most, African American girls the least (Eaton & others, 2008).

Exercise is linked to a number of positive physical outcomes in adolescence. One outcome of regular exercise is a positive effect on adolescents' weight status (van der Heijden & others, 2010). Other positive outcomes of exercise in adolescence are reduced triglyceride levels, lower blood pressure, and a lower incidence of type II diabetes (Lobelo & others, 2010). A recent study revealed that low levels of exercise were related to depressive symptoms in young adolescents (Sund, Larsson, & Wichstrom, 2010). Another recent study found that eighth-, tenth-, and twelfth-grade students who engaged in higher levels of exercise had lower levels

What are some characteristics of adolescents' exercise patterns?

developmental **connection**

Exercise. Researchers have found that children who participate in sports are less likely to be overweight or obese than those who don't. Chapter 11, p. 330

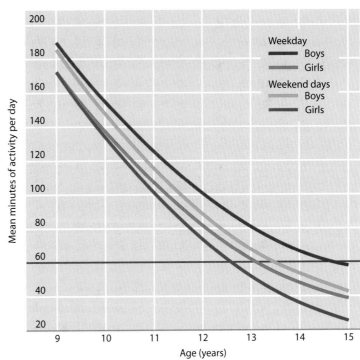

FIGURE **14.8**

AVERAGE AMOUNT OF MODERATE TO VIGOROUS EXERCISE ENGAGED IN BY U.S. 9- TO 15-YEAR-OLDS ON WEEKDAYS AND WEEKENDS. *Note:* The federal government recommends 60 minutes of moderate to vigorous physical activity per day.

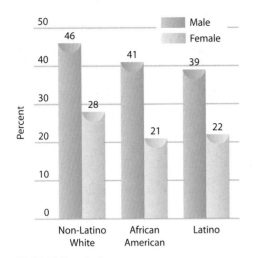

FIGURE **14.9**

EXERCISE RATES OF U.S. HIGH SCHOOL STUDENTS: GENDER AND ETHNICITY. *Note:* Data are for high school students who were physically active doing any kind of physical activity that increased their heart rate and made them breathe hard some of the time for a total of at least 60 minutes a day on five or more of the seven days preceding the survey.

How Would You...?

If you were a **health-care professional,** how would you explain the benefits of physical fitness in adolescence to adolescents, parents, and teachers?

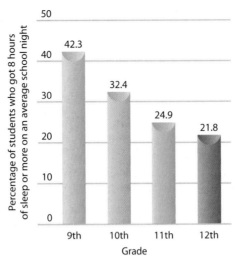

FIGURE **14.10**

DEVELOPMENTAL CHANGES IN U.S. ADOLESCENTS' SLEEP PATTERNS ON AN AVERAGE SCHOOL NIGHT

developmental connection

Sleep. Experts recommend that young children get 11 to 13 hours of sleep each night. Chapter 8, p. 244

of alcohol, cigarette, and marijuana use (Teery-McElrath, O'Malley, & Johnston, 2011).

Screen-based activity (watching television, using computers, talking on the phone, texting, and instant messaging for long hours) may be involved in lower levels of physical fitness in adolescence (Leatherdale, 2010). A recent study revealed that children and adolescents who engaged in the highest amount of daily screen-based activity (TV or video viewing and video game playing, in this study) were less likely to exercise daily (Sisson & others, 2010). In this study, children and adolescents who engaged in low physical activity and high screen-based activity were almost twice as likely to be overweight as their more active, less sedentary counterparts (Sisson & others, 2010).

Sleep Patterns   Might changing sleep patterns in adolescence contribute to adolescents' health-compromising behaviors? Recently there has been a surge of interest in adolescent sleep patterns (Beebe, 2011; Colrain & Baker, 2011).

In a recent national survey of youth, only 31 percent of U.S. adolescents got eight or more hours of sleep on an average school night (Eaton & others, 2008). In this study, the percentage of adolescents getting this much sleep on an average school night decreased as they got older (see Figure 14.10).

Another recent study also found that adolescents are not getting adequate sleep. The National Sleep Foundation (2006) conducted a U.S. survey of 1,602 caregivers and their 11- to 17-year-olds. Forty-five percent of the adolescents got inadequate sleep on school nights (less than eight hours). Older adolescents (ninth- to twelfth-graders) got markedly less sleep on school nights than younger adolescents (sixth- to eighth-graders)—62 percent of the older adolescents got inadequate sleep compared with 21 percent of the younger adolescents. Adolescents who got inadequate sleep (eight hours or less) on school nights were more likely to feel more tired or sleepy, be more cranky and irritable, fall asleep in school, be in a depressed mood, and drink caffeinated beverages than their counterparts who got optimal sleep (nine or more hours). In a recent study of more than 600 13- to 18-year-old boys and girls, 54 percent said they regularly got less than six to eight hours of sleep a night on school nights (Chen, Wang, & Jeng, 2006). In this study, getting less than six to eight hours of sleep per night during adolescence was linked to lower levels of exercise, less effective stress management, and adopting an unhealthy diet. In another recent study of 750 14- to 15-year-olds, getting less sleep at night was linked to higher levels of anxiety, depression, and fatigue the next day (Fuligni & Hardway, 2006).

Mary Carskadon and her colleagues (2002, 2004, 2006, 2011a, b; Crowley & Carskadon, 2010; Kurth & others, 2010; Tarokh, Carskadon, & Achermann, 2010) have conducted a number of research studies on adolescent sleep patterns. They found that when given the opportunity, adolescents will sleep an average of nine hours and 25 minutes a night. Most get considerably less than nine hours of sleep, especially during the week. This shortfall creates a sleep deficit, which adolescents often attempt to make up on the weekend. The researchers also found that older adolescents tend to be more sleepy during the day than younger adolescents. They theorized that this sleepiness was not due to academic work or social pressures. Rather, their research suggests that adolescents' biological clocks undergo a shift as they get older, delaying their period of wakefulness by about one hour. A delay in the nightly release of the sleep-inducing hormone **melatonin,** which is produced in the brain's pineal gland, seems to underlie this shift. Melatonin is secreted at about 9:30 p.m. in younger adolescents and approximately an hour later in older adolescents.

Carskadon has suggested that early school starting times may cause grogginess, inattention in class, and poor performance on tests. Based on her research, school officials in Edina, Minnesota, decided to start classes at 8:30 a.m. rather than the usual 7:25 a.m. Since then there have been fewer referrals for discipline problems, and the number of students who report being ill or depressed has decreased. The school system reports that test scores have improved for high school students, but not for middle school students. This finding supports Carskadon's suspicion that early start times are likely to be more stressful for older than for younger adolescents. Also, a recent study found that just a 30-minute delay in school start time was linked to improvements in adolescents' sleep, alertness, mood, and health (Owens, Belon, & Moss, 2010). And a recent research review found that Asian adolescents' bedtimes were even later than those of their peers in North America and Europe, resulting in less total sleep and more daytime sleepiness for the Asian adolescents (Gradisar, Gardner, & Dohnt, 2011).

Do sleep patterns change in emerging adulthood? Research indicates that they do (Galambos, Howard, & Maggs, 2011). A recent study revealed that more than 60 percent of college students were categorized as poor-quality sleepers (Lund & others, 2010). In this study, the weekday bedtimes and rise times of first-year college students were approximately 1 hour and 15 minutes later than those of seniors in high school (Lund & others, 2010). However, the first-year college students had later bedtimes and rise times than third- and fourth-year college students, indicating that at about 20 to 22 years of age, a reverse in the timing of bedtimes and rise times occurs.

In Mary Carskadon's sleep laboratory at Brown University, an adolescent girl's brain activity is being monitored. Carskadon (2005) says that in the morning, sleep-deprived adolescents'"brains are telling them it's night time . . . and the rest of the world is saying it's time to go to school" (p. 19).

How Would You...?

If you were an **educator,** how would you use developmental research to convince your school board to change the starting time of high school?

LEADING CAUSES OF DEATH IN ADOLESCENCE

The three leading causes of death in adolescence and emerging adulthood are accidents, homicide, and suicide (National Vital Statistics Reports, 2008). Almost half of all deaths from 15 to 24 years of age are due to unintentional injuries, approximately three-fourths of them involving motor vehicle accidents. Risky driving habits, such as speeding, tailgating, and driving under the influence of alcohol or other drugs, may be more important contributors to these accidents than lack of driving experience. In about 50 percent of motor vehicle fatalities involving adolescents, the driver has a blood alcohol level of 0.10 percent—twice the level needed to be designated as "under the influence" in some states. A high rate of intoxication is also found in adolescents who die as pedestrians or while using recreational vehicles.

Homicide is another leading cause of death in adolescence and emerging adulthood, especially among African American males, who are three times more likely to be killed by guns than by natural causes. Suicide is the third leading cause of death in adolescence and emerging adulthood. Since the 1950s, the adolescent and emerging adult suicide rate has tripled, although it has declined in recent years (Ash, 2008). We discuss suicide further in Chapter 16, "Socioemotional Development in Adolescence."

developmental **connection**

Problems, Diseases, and Disorders.
Both earlier and later experiences may be involved in adolescent suicide attempts. Chapter 16, p. 506

melatonin A sleep-inducing hormone that is produced in the brain's pineal gland.

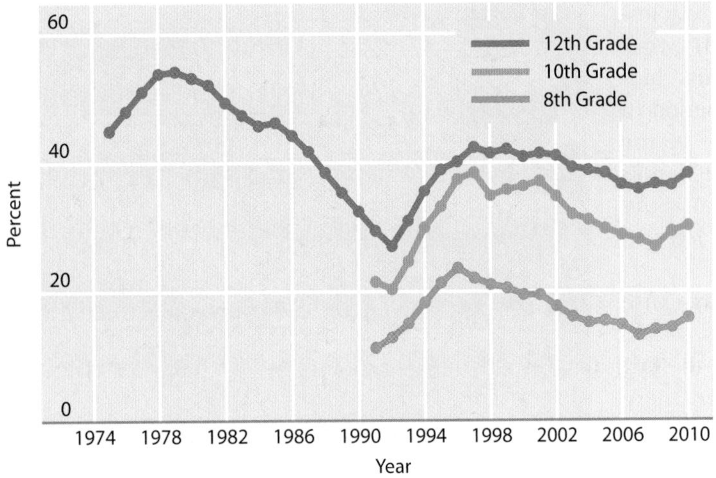

FIGURE **14.11**

TRENDS IN DRUG USE BY U.S. EIGHTH-, TENTH-, AND TWELFTH-GRADE STUDENTS. This graph shows the percentage of U.S. eighth-, tenth-, and twelfth-grade students who reported having taken an illicit drug in the last 12 months from 1991 to 2010, for eighth- and tenth graders, and from 1975 to 2010 for twelfth-graders (Johnston & others, 2011).

What are some trends in alcohol use by U.S. adolescents?

SUBSTANCE USE AND ABUSE

Among the significant problems that can develop in adolescence are substance use and abuse (Hart, Ksir, & Ray, 2011). We will discuss these problems here, and then in Chapter 16, "Socioemotional Development in Adolescence," we will explore the adolescent problems of juvenile delinquency, depression, and suicide.

Trends in Substance Use and Abuse   Each year since 1975, Lloyd Johnston and his colleagues at the Institute of Social Research at the University of Michigan have monitored the drug use of America's high school seniors in a wide range of public and private high schools. Since 1991, they also have surveyed drug use by eighth- and tenth-graders. In 2010, the study surveyed more than 46,000 secondary school students in more than 400 public and private schools (Johnston & others, 2011).

According to this study, the proportions of eighth-, tenth-, and twelfth-grade U.S. students who used any illicit drug declined during the late 1990s and the first years of the twenty-first century (Johnston & others, 2011) (see Figure 14.11). The use of drugs among U.S. secondary school students declined in the 1980s but began to increase in the early 1990s (Johnston & others, 2011). In the late 1990s and the early part of the twenty-first century, the proportion of secondary school students reporting the use of any illicit drug has been declining. The overall decline in the use of illicit drugs by adolescents during this time frame is approximately one-third for eighth-graders, one-fourth for tenth-graders, and one-eighth for twelfth-graders. The most notable declines in drug use by U.S. adolescents in the twenty-first century have occurred for LSD, cocaine, cigarettes, sedatives, tranquilizers, and Ecstasy. Marijuana is the illicit drug most widely used in the United States and Europe (Hibell & others, 2004; Johnston & others, 2011). Even with the recent decline in use, the United States still has one of the highest rates of adolescent drug use of any industrialized nation.

As shown in Figure 14.11, in which marijuana is included, an increase in illicit drug use by U.S. adolescents occurred in 2009 and 2010. However, when marijuana use is subtracted from the illicit drug index, no increase in U.S. adolescent drug use occurred in 2009 and 2010 (Johnston & others, 2011).

How extensive is alcohol use by U.S. adolescents? Sizable declines in adolescent alcohol use have occurred in recent years (Johnston & others, 2011). The percentage of U.S. eighth-graders reporting having had any alcohol to drink in the past 30 days fell from a 1996 high of 26 percent to 14 percent in 2010. The 30-day prevalence fell among tenth-graders from 39 percent in 2001 to 29 percent in 2010 and among high school seniors from 72 percent in 1980 to 41 percent in 2010. Binge drinking (defined in the University of Michigan surveys as having five or more drinks in a row in the last two weeks) by high school seniors declined from 41 percent in 1980 to 27 percent in 2010. Binge drinking by eighth- and tenth-graders also has dropped in recent years. A consistent sex difference occurs in binge drinking, with males engaging in this behavior more than females.

Cigarette smoking among U.S. adolescents peaked in 1996 and 1997 and has gradually declined since then (Johnston &

others, 2011). Following peak use in 1996, smoking rates for U.S. eighth-graders have fallen by 50 percent. In 2010, the percentages of adolescents who said they had smoked cigarettes in the last 30 days were 19 percent (twelfth grade), 14 percent (tenth grade), and 7 percent (eighth grade).

Cigarette smoking (in which the active drug is nicotine) is one of the most serious yet preventable health problems. Smoking is likely to begin in grades 7 through 9, although sizable proportions of youth are still establishing regular smoking habits during high school and college. Risk factors for becoming a regular smoker in adolescence include having a friend who smokes, a weak academic orientation, and low parental support (Tucker, Ellickson, & Klein, 2003).

The Roles of Development, Parents, Peers, and Educational Success

A special concern involves adolescents who begin to use drugs early in adolescence or even in childhood (Kinney, 2012). A longitudinal study of individuals from 8 to 42 years of age also found that early onset of drinking was linked to increased risk of heavy drinking in middle age (Pitkanen, Lyyra, & Pulkkinen, 2005).

Parents play an important role in preventing adolescent drug abuse (Kinney, 2012; Miller & Plant, 2010). Positive relationships with parents and others can reduce adolescents' drug use (Harakeh & others, 2010). Researchers have found that parental monitoring is linked with a lower incidence of drug use (Tobler & Komro, 2010). A recent research review concluded that the more frequently adolescents ate dinner with their family, the less likely they were to have substance abuse problems (Sen, 2010). And a recent study revealed that negative interactions with parents were linked to increased adolescent drinking and smoking, while positive identification with parents was related to declines in use of these substances (Gutman & others, 2011). Another study revealed that having friends in their school's social network and having fewer friends who use substances were related to a lower level of substance use by middle school students (Ennett & others, 2006).

Educational success is also a strong buffer for the emergence of drug problems in adolescence. An analysis by Jerald Bachman and his colleagues (2008) revealed that early educational achievement considerably reduced the likelihood that adolescents would develop drug problems, including those involving alcohol abuse, smoking, and abuse of various illicit drugs.

Can special programs effectively reduce adolescent drinking and smoking? See the *Connecting with Research* interlude for a description of one study that addressed this question.

EATING PROBLEMS AND DISORDERS

Eating disorders have become increasingly common among adolescents (Schiff, 2011; Wardlaw & Smith, 2011). Here are some research findings involving adolescent eating disorders:

- *Body image*. Body dissatisfaction and distorted body image play important roles in adolescent eating disorders (Espeset & others, 2011). One study revealed that in general, adolescents were dissatisfied with their bodies, with males desiring to increase their upper body and females wanting to decrease the overall size of their body (Ata, Ludden, & Lally, 2007). In this study, low self-esteem and social support, weight-related teasing, and pressure to lose weight were linked to adolescents' negative body images. In another study, girls who felt negatively about their bodies in early adolescence were more likely to develop eating disorders two years later than their counterparts who did not feel negatively about their bodies (Attie & Brooks-Gunn, 1989). And a recent study found that the key link for explaining depression in overweight adolescents involved body dissatisfaction (Mond & others, 2011).

What are ways that parents have been found to influence whether their adolescents take drugs?

How Would You...?
If you were a **human development and family studies professional,** how would you explain to parents the importance of parental monitoring in preventing adolescent substance abuse?

Evaluation of a Family Program Designed to Reduce Drinking and Smoking in Young Adolescents

Few experimental studies have been conducted to determine whether family programs can reduce drinking and smoking in young adolescents. In one experimental study, 1,326 families with 12- to 14-year-old adolescents living throughout the United States were interviewed (Bauman & others, 2002). After the baseline interviews, participants were randomly assigned either to go through the Family Matters program (experimental group) or not to experience the program (control group) (Bauman & others, 2002).

The families assigned to the Family Matters program received four mailings of booklets. Each mailing was followed by a telephone call from a health educator to "encourage participation by all family members, answer any questions, and record information" (Bauman & others, 2002, pp. 36–37). The first booklet focused on the negative consequences of adolescent substance abuse to the family. The second booklet emphasized "supervision, support, communication skills, attachment, time spent together, educational achievement, conflict reduction, and how well adolescence is understood." The third booklet asked parents to "list things that they do that might inadvertently encourage their child's use of tobacco or alcohol, identify rules that might influence the child's use, and consider ways to monitor use. Then adult family members and the child meet to agree upon rules and sanctions related to adolescent use." Booklet four deals with what "the child can do to resist peer and media pressures for use."

Two follow-up interviews with the parents and adolescents were conducted three months and one year after the experimental group completed the program. Adolescents in the Family Matters program reported

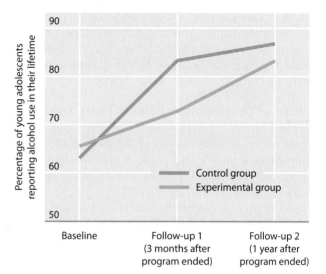

FIGURE 14.12

YOUNG ADOLESCENTS' REPORTS OF ALCOHOL USE IN THE FAMILY MATTERS PROGRAM. Note that at baseline (before the program started) the young adolescents in the Family Matters program (experimental group) and their counterparts who did not go through the program (control group) reported approximately the same lifetime use of alcohol (slightly higher use by the experimental group). However, three months after the program ended, the experimental group reported lower alcohol use, and this reduction was still present one year after the program ended, although at a reduced level.

lower alcohol and cigarette use both at three months and again one year after the program had been completed. Figure 14.12 shows the results for alcohol.

What other types of research efforts might help identify or design programs that are effective in reducing adolescent drinking and smoking?

- *Parenting.* Adolescents who reported observing more healthy eating patterns and exercise by their parents had more healthy eating patterns and exercised more themselves (Pakpreo & others, 2005). Negative parent-adolescent relationships were linked with increased dieting by girls over a one-year period (Archibald, Graber, & Brooks-Gunn, 1999).

- *Sexual activity.* Girls who were both sexually active with their boyfriends and in pubertal transition were the most likely to be dieting or engaging in disordered eating patterns (Cauffman, 1994).

- *Role models and the media.* Girls who were highly motivated to look like same-sex figures in the media were more likely than their peers to become very concerned about their weight (Field & others, 2001). Watching commercials with idealized thin female images increased adolescent girls' dissatisfaction with their bodies (Hargreaves & Tiggemann, 2004).

What types of interventions have been successful in reducing overweight in adolescents? Research indicates that regular exercise is a key component of weight reduction in adolescence (Ingul & others, 2010; Spruijt-Metz, 2011). One research review indicated that clinical approaches that focus on the individual adolescent and include a combination of caloric restriction, exercise (walking or biking to school, participating in a regular exercise program), reduction of sedentary activity (watching TV, playing video games), and behavioral therapy (such as keeping weight-loss diaries and receiving rewards for meeting goals) have been moderately effective in helping overweight adolescents lose weight (Fowler-Brown & Kahwati, 2004). A recent research review concluded that interventions targeted at changing family lifestyle were the most effective in helping children and adolescents lose weight (Oude Luttikhuis & others, 2009). In general, school-based approaches (such as instituting a school-wide program to improve eating habits) have been less effective than clinically based individual approaches (Lytle, 2009). A research review concluded that school-based approaches for reducing adolescents' weight have modest results, with TV watching the easiest behavior to change, followed by physical activity and then nutrition (Sharma, 2006).

These adolescent girls are attending a weight-management camp. *What types of interventions have been most successful in helping overweight adolescents lose weight?*

Let's now examine two other eating problems—anorexia nervosa and bulimia nervosa. Researchers consistently have discovered that the onset of anorexia nervosa and bulimia nervosa occurs in adolescence and that adult onset of these conditions is rare (Hebebrand & Bulik, 2011; Knoll, Bulik, & Hebebrand, 2011). They also have found that eating disorders, including anorexia nervosa and bulimia nervosa, are far more likely to characterize females than males.

Anorexia Nervosa   **Anorexia nervosa** is an eating disorder that involves the relentless pursuit of thinness through starvation. It is a serious disorder that can lead to death. Anorexia nervosa is about 10 times more likely to occur in females than males. Although most U.S. girls have been on a diet at some point, slightly less than 1 percent ever develop anorexia nervosa.

Three main characteristics of anorexia nervosa are (1) weighing less than 85 percent of what is considered normal for a person's age and height, (2) having an intense fear of gaining weight—a fear that does not decrease with weight loss, and (3) having a distorted image of body shape. Even when they are extremely thin, anorexics see themselves as too fat. They never think they are thin enough, especially in the abdomen, buttocks, and thighs. They usually weigh themselves frequently, often take their body measurements, and gaze critically at themselves in mirrors.

Anorexia nervosa typically begins in the early to middle teenage years, often following an episode of dieting and some type of life stress. When anorexia nervosa does occur in males, the symptoms and other characteristics (such as a distorted body image and family conflict) are usually similar to those reported by females who have the disorder (Ariceli & others, 2005).

Most anorexics are non-Latino White adolescent or emerging adult females from well-educated, middle- and upper-income families, and they are competitive and high-achieving (Schmidt, 2003). They become stressed about not being able to reach their high expectations and shift their focus to something they can control: their

Anorexia nervosa has become an increasing problem for adolescent girls and young adult women. *What are some possible causes of anorexia nervosa?*

anorexia nervosa An eating disorder that involves the relentless pursuit of thinness through starvation.

weight. Offspring of mothers with anorexia nervosa are at risk for becoming anorexic themselves (Striegel-Moore & Bulik, 2007). Problems in family functioning are increasingly being found to be linked to the appearance of anorexia nervosa in adolescent girls (Benninghoven & others, 2007), and a research review indicated that family therapy is often the most effective treatment (Bulik & others, 2007).

The fashion image in U.S. culture contributes to the incidence of anorexia nervosa (Striegel-Moore & Bulik, 2007). The media portray thin as beautiful in their choice of fashion models, and many adolescent girls strive to emulate them. And many adolescent girls who want to be thin hang out together. A study of adolescent girls revealed that friends often share similar body image and eating problems (Hutchinson & Rapee, 2007). In this study, an individual girl's dieting and extreme weight-loss behavior could be predicted from her friends' dieting and extreme weight-loss behavior.

Bulimia Nervosa Whereas anorexics control their eating by restricting it, most bulimics do not. **Bulimia nervosa** is an eating disorder in which the individual consistently follows a binge-and-purge pattern. The bulimic goes on an eating binge and then purges by self-inducing vomiting or using a laxative. Many people binge and purge occasionally and some experiment with it, but a person is considered to have a serious bulimic disorder if the episodes occur at least twice a week for three months.

About 90 percent of bulimics are females, and approximately 1 to 2 percent of U.S. females are estimated to develop bulimia nervosa. Bulimia nervosa typically begins in late adolescence or early adulthood. Many women who develop bulimia nervosa were somewhat overweight before the onset of the disorder, and the binge eating often began during an episode of dieting. Unlike anorexics, people who binge-and-purge typically fall within a normal weight range, which makes bulimia more difficult to detect.

As with anorexics, most bulimics are preoccupied with food, have a strong fear of becoming overweight, are depressed or anxious, and have a distorted body image. A study revealed that bulimics overvalued their body weight and shape, and this overvaluation was linked to higher depression and lower self-esteem (Hrabosky & others, 2007). A recent study of individuals with anorexia nervosa or bulimia nervosa revealed that attachment insecurity was linked with body dissatisfaction, which was a key aspect of predicting and perpetuating these eating disorders (Abbate-Daga & others, 2010). In this study, need for approval was an important predictor of bulimia nervosa. As with anorexia nervosa, about 70 percent of individuals who develop bulimia nervosa eventually recover from the disorder (Agras & others, 2004).

How Would You…?

If you were a **health-care professional,** how would you educate parents to identify the signs and symptoms that may signal an eating disorder?

bulimia nervosa An eating disorder in which the individual consistently follows a binge-and-purge eating pattern.

Review Connect Reflect

LG4 Summarize adolescents' health and eating disorders.

Review

- What are key concerns about the health of adolescents?
- What are the leading causes of death in adolescence and emerging adulthood?
- What are some characteristics of adolescents' substance use and abuse?
- What are the characteristics of the major eating disorders?

Connect

- How might eating patterns in childhood that were described in Chapters 8 and 11 possibly contribute to eating problems in adolescence?

Reflect *Your Own Personal Journey of Life*

- What were your health habits like from the time you entered puberty to the time you completed high school? Describe your health-compromising and health-enhancing behaviors during this time. Since high school, have you reduced your health-compromising behaviors? Explain.

topical connections ─ ─ ─ ─ ─ ─ ─ ─ ─ ─

In this chapter, you examined some significant changes that occur in the adolescent's brain—the early development of the amygdala and the delayed development of the prefrontal cortex—that may contribute to risk taking and sensation seeking. In the next chapter, you will read about how adolescent thinking becomes more abstract, idealistic, and logical—which Piaget described as the key aspects of formal operational thought. Other topics you will explore in the next chapter include adolescents' decision making and the influence of schools in their lives.

─ ─ ─ ─ ─ ─ ─ ─ ─ *looking forward* ─ ─ →

reach your learning goals

What Is the Nature of Adolescence?

 LG1 Discuss views and developmental transitions that involve adolescence.

Positive and Negative Views of Adolescence

- Many stereotypes about adolescents are negative. Today, however, the majority of adolescents successfully negotiate the path from childhood to adulthood, although too many are not provided with adequate support and opportunities. It is important to view adolescents as a heterogeneous group. Acting out and boundary testing by adolescents move them toward accepting, rather than rejecting, parental values. Recent interest has focused on a strength-based approach that focuses on positive youth development.

Developmental Transitions

- Two important transitions in development are those from childhood to adolescence and from adolescence to adulthood. In the transition from childhood to adolescence, pubertal change is prominent, although cognitive and socioemotional changes occur as well. Emerging adulthood recently has been proposed to describe the transition from adolescence to adulthood. Five key characteristics of emerging adulthood are identity exploration (especially in love and work), instability, being self-focused, feeling in-between, and experiencing possibilities to transform one's life.

What Are the Physical and Psychological Aspects of Puberty?

 LG2 Describe puberty's characteristics, developmental changes, psychological dimensions, and the development of the brain.

Sexual Maturation, Height, and Weight

- Puberty is a rapid physical maturation involving hormonal and bodily changes that take place primarily in early adolescence. A number of changes occur in sexual maturation including increased size of the penis and testicles in boys and breast growth and menarche in girls. The growth spurt involves height and weight and occurs about two years earlier for girls than for boys.

Hormonal Changes

- Extensive hormonal changes characterize puberty. The pituitary gland plays an important role in these hormonal changes. During puberty, testosterone concentrations increase considerably in boys, and estradiol increases considerably in girls.

Timing and Variations in Puberty

- In the United States, the age of menarche (a girl's first menstrual period) has declined since the mid-1800s. The basic genetic program for puberty is wired into the species, but nutrition, health, and other environmental factors affect puberty's timing and makeup. Menarche typically appears between 9 and 15 years of age. Boys can start the pubertal sequence as early as 10 years of age or as late as 17.

Psychological Dimensions of Puberty	

- Adolescents show heightened interest in their bodies and body images. Younger adolescents are more preoccupied with these images than are older adolescents. Adolescent girls often have a more negative body image than do adolescent boys. Early maturation often favors boys, at least during early adolescence, but as adults, late-maturing boys have a more positive identity than early-maturing boys. Early-maturing girls are at risk for a number of developmental problems. They are more likely to smoke and drink and have an eating disorder and are likely to have earlier sexual experiences than later-maturing girls.

The Brain	

- The thickening of the corpus callosum in adolescence is linked to improved processing of information. The amygdala, which is involved in emotions such as anger, matures earlier than the prefrontal cortex, which functions in reasoning and self-regulation. This gap in development may help to explain the increase in risk-taking behavior that often characterizes adolescence.

What Are the Dimensions of Adolescent Sexuality?

 LG3 Characterize adolescent sexuality.

Developing a Sexual Identity	

- Adolescence is a time of sexual exploration and sexual experimentation. Mastering emerging sexual feelings and forming a sense of sexual identity are multifaceted. An adolescent's sexual identity includes sexual orientation, activities, interests, and styles of behavior.

Timing and Trends in Adolescent Sexual Behavior	

- The timing of sexual initiation in adolescence varies by country, gender, and socioeconomic characteristics. In a 2009 study, 62 percent of twelfth-graders reported that they had experienced sexual intercourse. Also, recently there has been a decline in the number of adolescents who say they have experienced various aspects of sexuality. However, a dramatic increase in oral sex has occurred recently in adolescence.

Sexual Risk Taking in Adolescence	

- Having sexual intercourse in early adolescence, as well as various contextual and family factors, is associated with sexual problems and negative developmental outcomes. Adolescents are increasing their use of contraceptives, but large numbers still do not use them. Sexually transmitted infections (STIs) are contracted primarily through sexual contact. Approximately one in four sexually active adolescents have an STI. Among the STIs are bacterial infections such as gonorrhea, syphilis, and chlamydia, and viral infections such as genital herpes, genital warts, and AIDS. Although the U.S. adolescent pregnancy rate is still among the highest in the developed world, the rate declined considerably in the 1990s; however, the U.S. adolescent birth rate increased in 2006. Adolescent pregnancy often increases health risks for the mother and the offspring, although it often is not pregnancy alone that places adolescents at risk. Easy access to family-planning services and sex education programs in schools can help reduce the U.S. adolescent pregnancy rate.

How Can Adolescents' Health and Health-Enhancing Assets Be Characterized?

LG4 Summarize adolescents' health and eating disorders.

Adolescent Health	

- Adolescence is a critical juncture in health because many of the factors related to poor health habits and early death in the adult years begin during adolescence. Poor nutrition, lack of exercise, and inadequate sleep are concerns.

Leading Causes of Death in Adolescence	

- The three leading causes of death in adolescence and emerging adulthood are accidents, homicide, and suicide.

Substance Use and Abuse	

- Despite recent declines in use, the United States has one of the highest rates of adolescent drug use of any industrialized nation. Alcohol abuse is a major adolescent problem, although its rate has been dropping in recent years, as has the rate of cigarette smoking. A recent concern is the increased use of prescription painkillers by adolescents. Drug use in childhood or early adolescence has more negative outcomes than drug use that begins in late adolescence. Parents and peers play important roles in whether adolescents take drugs.

- Eating disorders have increased in adolescence, with a substantial increase in the percentage of adolescents who are overweight. Three eating disorders that may occur in adolescence are obesity, anorexia nervosa, and bulimia nervosa. A combination of behavioral therapy, calorie restriction, exercise, and reduction of sedentary activities such as TV watching has been more effective for overweight adolescents than school-based approaches. Anorexia nervosa is an eating disorder that involves the relentless pursuit of thinness through starvation. Anorexics are intensely afraid of weight gain, have a distorted body image, and weigh less than 85 percent of what would be considered normal for their height. Bulimia nervosa is an eating disorder in which a binge-and-purge pattern is consistently followed. Most bulimics are depressed or anxious and fearful of becoming overweight, and their weight typically falls within a normal range. About 70 percent of bulimics and anorexics eventually recover.

key terms

emerging adulthood 428
puberty 429
menarche 429
hormones 430
hypothalamus 430

pituitary gland 430
gonads 430
gonadotropins 430
testosterone 430
estradiol 431

corpus callosum 433
amygdala 433
sexually transmitted
  infections (STIs) 437
AIDS 437

melatonin 445
anorexia nervosa 449
bulimia nervosa 450

key people

G. Stanley Hall 426
Daniel Offer 426

Peter Benson 427
Jeffrey Arnett 428

Charles Nelson 434
Mary Carskadon 444

Lloyd Johnston 446

connecting with improving the lives of children

MAKING A DIFFERENCE

Supporting Adolescent Physical Development and Health

What are some strategies for supporting and guiding adolescent physical development and health?

- *Develop positive expectations for adolescents.* Adolescents often are negatively stereotyped. These negative expectations have a way of becoming self-fulfilling prophecies and harming adult-adolescent communication. Don't view adolescence as a time of crisis and rebellion. View it instead as a time of evaluation, decision making, commitment, and the carving out of a place in the world.
- *Understand the many physical changes adolescents are going through.* The physical changes adolescents go through can be very perplexing to them. They are not quite sure what they are going to change into, and this can create considerable uncertainty for them.
- *Be a good health role model for adolescents.* Adolescents benefit from being around adults who are good health role models: individuals who exercise regularly, eat healthily, and don't take drugs or smoke.
- *Communicate effectively with adolescents about sexuality.* Emphasize that young adolescents should abstain from sex. If adolescents are going to be sexually active, they need to take contraceptive precautions. Adolescents also need to learn about sexuality and human reproduction before they become sexually active.

RESOURCES

Search Institute
www.search-institute.org
The Search Institute has available a large number of resources for improving the lives of adolescents. In 1995, the Institute began distributing the excellent publications of the Center for Early Adolescence, University of North Carolina, which had recently closed. The brochures and books include resource lists and address topics such as school improvement, adolescent literacy, parent education, program planning, and adolescent health. A free quarterly newsletter is also available.

The Society for Adolescent Medicine (SAM)
www.adolescenthealth.org
SAM is a valuable source of information about competent physicians who specialize in treating adolescents. It maintains a list of recommended adolescence specialists across the United States.

The Path to Purpose
by William Damon (2008)
New York: Free Press
A provocative new book by leading expert William Damon on helping adolescents find their calling in life.

chapter 15

COGNITIVE DEVELOPMENT IN ADOLESCENCE

Kim-Chi Trinh was only 9 years old in Vietnam when her father used his savings to buy passage for her on a fishing boat. It was a costly and risky sacrifice for the family, who placed Kim-Chi on the small boat, among strangers, in the hope that she eventually would reach the United States, where she would get a good education and enjoy a better life.

Kim-Chi made it to the United States and coped with a succession of three foster families. When she graduated from high school in San Diego in 1988, she had a straight-A average and a number of college scholarship offers. When asked why she excels in school, Kim-Chi says that she has to do well because she owes it to her parents, who are still in Vietnam.

Kim-Chi is one of a wave of bright, highly motivated Asians who are immigrating to America. Percentage-wise, Asian Americans are the fastest-growing ethnic minority group in the United States—two out of five immigrants are now Asian. Although Asian Americans make up only 4 percent of the U.S. population, they constituted 18.5 percent of the 2008 freshman class at Harvard and a staggering 49 percent at the University of California at Irvine.

Not all Asian American youth do this well, however. Poorly educated Vietnamese, Cambodian, and Hmong refugee youth are especially at risk for school-related problems. Many refugee children's histories are replete with losses and trauma. Thuy, a 12-year-old Vietnamese girl, has been in the United States for two years and resides with her father in a small apartment with a cousin's family of five in the inner city of a West Coast metropolitan area (Huang, 1989). While trying to escape from Saigon, "the family became separated, and the wife and two younger children remained in Vietnam. . . . Thuy's father has had an especially difficult time adjusting to the United States. He struggles with English classes and has been unable to maintain several jobs as a waiter" (Huang, 1989, p. 307). When Thuy received a letter from her mother

topical connections

In the last chapter, you explored how early adolescence is a time of dramatic physical change as puberty unfolds. Pubertal change also brings considerable interest in one's body image. And pubertal change ushers in an intense interest in sexuality. Adolescence also is a critical time in the development of behaviors related to health, such as good nutrition and regular exercise, which are health enhancing, and drug abuse, which is health compromising. Significant changes occur in the adolescent's brain—the early development of the amygdala and the delayed development of the prefrontal cortex—that may contribute to risk taking and decision making. In Chapter 12, you read about cognitive advances in middle childhood, including improved thinking strategies and reading skills. This chapter examines continued advances in thinking skills, moral development and values, schools, and career development.

◀ — looking back

saying that her 5-year-old brother had died, Thuy's schoolwork began to deteriorate, and she showed marked signs of depression—lack of energy, loss of appetite, withdrawal from peer relations, and a general feeling of hopelessness. At the insistence of the school, she and her father went to the child and adolescent unit of a community mental health center. It took the therapist a long time to establish credibility with Thuy and her father, but eventually they began to trust the therapist, who was a good listener and gave them competent advice about how to handle different experiences in the new country. The therapist also contacted Thuy's teacher, who said that Thuy had been involved in several interethnic skirmishes at school. With the assistance of the mental health clinic, the school initiated interethnic student panels to address cultural differences and discuss reasons for ethnic hostility. Thuy was selected to participate in these panels. Her father became involved in the community mutual assistance association, and Thuy's academic performance began to improve.

preview

When people think of the changes that characterize adolescents, they often focus on puberty and adolescent problems. However, some impressive cognitive changes occur during adolescence. We begin this chapter by focusing on these cognitive changes and then turn our attention to adolescents' values, moral education, and religion. Next, we study the characteristics of schools for adolescents and conclude the chapter by examining career development in adolescence.

How Do Adolescents Think and Process Information?   **LG1** Discuss different approaches to adolescent cognition.

Piaget's Theory   Adolescent Egocentrism   Information Processing

Adolescents' developing power of thought opens up new cognitive and social horizons. Let's examine the characteristics of this developing power of thought, beginning with Piaget's theory (1952).

PIAGET'S THEORY

developmental **connection**

Cognitive Development. Piaget's first three stages are sensorimotor, preoperational, and concrete operational. Chapter 6, p. 174, Chapter 9, p. 260, and Chapter 12, p. 354

As we discussed in Chapter 12, "Cognitive Development in Middle and Late Childhood," Jean Piaget proposed that at about 7 years of age children enter the *concrete operational stage* of cognitive development. They can reason logically about concrete events and objects, and they make gains in their ability to classify objects and to reason about the relationships between classes of objects. According to Piaget, the concrete operational stage lasts until the child is about 11 years old, when the fourth and final stage of cognitive development begins—the formal operational stage.

The Formal Operational Stage What are the characteristics of the formal operational stage? Formal operational thought is more abstract than concrete operational thought. Adolescents are no longer limited to actual experiences as anchors for thought. They can conjure up make-believe situations—events that are purely hypothetical possibilities or abstract propositions—and can try to reason logically about them.

The abstract quality of thinking during the formal operational stage is evident in the adolescent's verbal problem-solving ability. Whereas the concrete operational thinker needs to see the concrete elements A, B, and C to be able to make the logical inference that, if A = B and B = C, then A = C, the formal operational thinker can solve this problem merely through verbal presentation.

Another indication of the abstract quality of adolescents' thought is their increased tendency to think about thought itself. One adolescent commented, "I began thinking about why I was thinking what I was. Then I began thinking about why I was thinking about what I was thinking about what I was." If this sounds abstract, it is, and it characterizes the adolescent's enhanced focus on thought and its abstract qualities.

Accompanying the abstract nature of formal operational thought is thought full of idealism and possibilities, especially during the beginning of the formal operational stage, when assimilation dominates. Adolescents engage in extended speculation about ideal characteristics—qualities they desire in themselves and in others. Such thoughts often lead adolescents to compare themselves with others in regard to such ideal standards. And their thoughts are often fantasy flights into future possibilities. It is not unusual for the adolescent to become impatient with these newfound ideal standards and to become perplexed over which of many ideal standards to adopt.

At the same time that adolescents think more abstractly and idealistically, they also think more logically about abstract concepts. Children are likely to solve problems through trial-and-error; adolescents begin to think more as a scientist thinks, devising plans to solve problems and systematically testing solutions. This type of problem solving requires **hypothetical-deductive reasoning.** Such reasoning involves creating a hypothesis and deducing its implications, which provide ways to test the hypothesis. Thus, formal operational thinkers develop hypotheses about ways to solve problems and then systematically deduce the best path to follow to solve the problem.

Evaluating Piaget's Theory Some of Piaget's ideas on the formal operational stage have been challenged (Diamond, Casey, & Munakata, 2011; Kuhn, 2011). The stage includes much more individual variation than Piaget envisioned. Only about one in three young adolescents is a formal operational thinker. Many American adults never become formal operational thinkers, and neither do many adults in other cultures.

Furthermore, education in the logic of science and mathematics promotes the development of formal operational thinking. This point recalls a criticism of Piaget's theory that we discussed in Chapter 12, "Cognitive Development in Middle and Late Childhood": Culture and education exert stronger influences on cognitive development than Piaget maintained (Daniels, 2011).

Piaget's theory of cognitive development has been challenged on other points as well (Bauer, Larkina, & Deocampo, 2011; Miller, 2011). As we noted in Chapter 9, "Cognitive Development in Early Childhood," Piaget conceived of stages as unitary structures of thought, with various aspects of a stage emerging at the same time. However, most contemporary developmentalists agree that cognitive development is not as stage-like as Piaget envisioned (Kuhn, 2011). Furthermore, children can be trained to reason at a higher cognitive stage, and some cognitive abilities emerge earlier than Piaget predicted (Aslin, 2009). For example, even 2-year-olds are nonegocentric in some contexts. When they realize that another

> The thoughts of youth are long, long thoughts.
>
> —Henry Wadsworth Longfellow
> *American Poet, 19th Century*

Might adolescents' ability to reason hypothetically and to evaluate what is ideal versus what is real lead them to engage in demonstrations, such as this protest related to better ethnic relations? What other causes might be attractive to adolescents' newfound cognitive abilities of hypothetical-deductive reasoning and idealistic thinking?

"and give me good abstract-reasoning ability, interpersonal skills, cultural perspective, linguistic comprehension, and a high sociodynamic potential."
© Ed Fisher/The New Yorker Collection/www.cartoonbank .com.

hypothetical-deductive reasoning Piaget's formal operational concept that adolescents have the cognitive ability to develop hypotheses, or best guesses, about ways to solve problems.

developmental **connection**

Cognitive Development. Neo-Piagetians are developmentalists who have elaborated on Piaget's theory, arguing that cognitive development is more specific than Piaget envisioned and that it gives more emphasis to information processing. Chapter 12, p. 355

person will not see an object, they investigate whether the person is blindfolded or looking in a different direction. Some understanding of the conservation of number has been demonstrated as early as age 3, although Piaget did not think it emerged until 7. Other cognitive abilities can emerge later than Piaget expected (Kuhn, 2011). As we have discussed, many adolescents still think in concrete operational ways or are just beginning to master formal operations. Even many adults are not formal operational thinkers.

Despite these challenges to Piaget's ideas, we owe him a tremendous debt. Piaget was the founder of the present field of cognitive development, and he established a long list of masterful concepts of enduring power and fascination: assimilation, accommodation, object permanence, egocentrism, conservation, and others. Psychologists also owe him the current vision of children as active, constructive thinkers. And they have a debt to him for creating a theory that generated a huge volume of research on children's cognitive development (Miller, 2011).

Piaget was a genius when it came to observing children. His careful observations demonstrated inventive ways to discover how children act on and adapt to their world. He also showed us how children need to make their experiences fit their schemes yet simultaneously adapt their schemes to reflect their experiences. Piaget revealed how cognitive change is likely to occur if the context is structured to allow gradual movement to the next higher level. Concepts do not emerge suddenly, full-blown, but instead develop through a series of partial accomplishments that lead to increasingly comprehensive understanding (Quinn, 2011).

ADOLESCENT EGOCENTRISM

In addition to thinking more logically, abstractly, and idealistically—characteristics of Piaget's formal operational thought stage—in what other ways do adolescents change cognitively? David Elkind (1978) described how adolescent egocentrism governs the way that adolescents think about social matters. **Adolescent egocentrism** is the heightened self-consciousness of adolescents, which is reflected in their belief that others are as interested in them as they are themselves, as well as in their sense of personal uniqueness and invincibility. Elkind argued that adolescent egocentrism can be dissected into two types of social thinking—imaginary audience and personal fable.

The **imaginary audience** refers to the aspect of adolescent egocentrism that involves feeling one is the center of everyone's attention and sensing that one is on stage. An adolescent boy might think that others are as aware of a few hairs that are out of place as he is. An adolescent girl walks into her classroom and thinks that all eyes are riveted on her complexion. Adolescents especially sense that they are "on stage" in early adolescence, believing they are the main actors and all others are the audience.

According to Elkind, the **personal fable** is the part of adolescent egocentrism that involves an adolescent's sense of personal uniqueness and invincibility. Adolescents' sense of personal uniqueness makes them believe that no one can understand how they really feel. For example, an adolescent girl thinks that her mother cannot possibly sense the hurt she feels because her boyfriend has broken up with her. As part of their effort to retain a sense of personal uniqueness, adolescents might craft stories about themselves that are filled with fantasy, immersing themselves in a world that is far removed from reality. Personal fables frequently show up in adolescent diaries.

Recent research studies, however, suggest that rather than perceiving themselves to be invulnerable, many adolescents portray themselves as vulnerable (Reyna & Rivers, 2008). For example, in a recent study, 12- to 18-year olds were

Many adolescent girls spend long hours in front of the mirror, depleting cans of hairspray, tubes of lipstick, and jars of cosmetics. *How might this behavior be related to changes in adolescent cognitive and physical development?*

adolescent egocentrism The heightened self-consciousness of adolescents that is reflected in their belief that others are as interested in them as they are in themselves, and in their sense of personal uniqueness and invincibility.

imaginary audience Refers to adolescents' belief that others are as interested in them as they themselves are, as well as their attention-getting behavior motivated by a desire to be noticed, visible, and "on stage."

personal fable The part of adolescent egocentrism that involves an adolescent's sense of uniqueness and invincibility.

asked about their chance of dying in the next year and prior to age 20 (Fischhoff & others, 2010). The adolescents greatly overestimated their chance of dying.

Some researchers have questioned the view that invulnerability is a unitary concept and argued rather that it consists of two dimensions (Duggan, Lapsley, & Norman, 2000; Lapsley & Hill, 2010):

- *Danger invulnerability,* which involves adolescents' sense of indestructibility and tendency to take on physical risks (driving recklessly at high speeds, for example)

- *Psychological invulnerability,* which captures an adolescent's felt invulnerability related to personal or psychological distress (getting one's feelings hurt, for example)

A recent study revealed that adolescents who scored high on a danger invulnerability scale were more likely to engage in juvenile delinquency or substance abuse, or to be depressed (Lapsley & Hill, 2010). In this study, adolescents who scored high on psychological invulnerability were less likely to be depressed, had higher self-esteem, and engaged in better interpersonal relationships. In terms of psychological invulnerability, adolescents often benefit from the normal developmental challenges of exploring identity options, making new friends, asking someone to go out on a date, and learning a new skill. All of these important adolescent tasks involve a risk of failure as well as a potential for enhanced self-image following a successful outcome.

INFORMATION PROCESSING

Deanna Kuhn (2009) recently discussed some important characteristics of adolescents' information processing and thinking. In her view, in the later years of childhood and continuing in adolescence, individuals approach cognitive levels that may or may not be achieved, in contrast with the largely universal cognitive levels that young children attain. By adolescence, considerable variation in cognitive functioning is present across individuals. This variability supports the argument that adolescents are producers of their own development to a greater extent than are children.

Kuhn (2009) further argues that the most important cognitive change in adolescence is improvement in *executive functioning,* which we discussed in Chapters 9, 11, and 12. Recall from Chapter 9 our description of *executive functioning* as an umbrella-like concept that consists of a number of higher-level cognitive processes linked to the development of the prefrontal cortex. Executive functioning involves managing one's thoughts to engage in goal-directed behavior and self-control. In Chapter 9, we indicated that executive functioning in early childhood especially involves developmental advances in cognitive inhibition, cognitive flexibility, and goal setting (Beck & others, 2011; Carlson & White, 2011). In Chapters 11 and 12, we described executive functioning advances in cognitive inhibition, as well as progress in working memory (Diamond, Casey, & Munakata, 2011). Our further coverage of executive functioning in adolescence focuses on monitoring and managing cognitive resources, controlling attention and reducing interfering thoughts, and then turns to a discussion of working memory, decision making, critical thinking, and metacognition.

Monitoring and Managing Cognitive Resources It is increasingly thought that executive functioning strengthens during adolescence (Kuhn, 2009). This executive functioning "assumes a role of monitoring and managing the deployment of cognitive resources as a function of a task demands. As a result, cognitive

I check my look in the mirror. I wanna change my clothes, my hair, my face.

—Bruce Springsteen
Contemporary American Rock Star

The error of youth is to believe that intelligence is a substitute for experience, while the error of age is to believe that experience is a substitute for intelligence.

—Lyman Bryson
American Author, 20th Century

developmental **connection**

The Brain. The prefrontal cortex is the location in the brain where much of executive functioning occurs. Chapter 9, p. 270, Chapter 11, p. 327, and Chapter 14, p. 433

	TASK			
	VERBAL		VISUOSPATIAL	
Age	Semantic Association	Digit/ Sentence	Mapping/ Directions	Visual Matrix
8	1.33	1.75	3.13	1.67
10	1.70	2.34	3.60	2.06
13	1.86	2.94	4.09	2.51
16	2.24	2.98	3.92	2.68
24	2.60	3.71	4.64	3.47

Highest Working Memory Performance

3.02 (age 45)	3.97 (age 35)	4.90 (age 35)	3.47 (age 24)

FIGURE 15.1

DEVELOPMENTAL CHANGES IN WORKING MEMORY. *Note:* The scores shown here are the means for each age group and the age also represents a mean age. Higher scores reflect superior working memory performance.

How Would You...?

If you were an **educator,** how would you incorporate decision-making exercises into the school curriculum for adolescents?

development and learning itself become more effective. . . . Emergence and strengthening of this executive (functioning) is arguably the single most important and consequential intellectual development to occur in the second decade of life" (Kuhn & Franklin, 2006, p. 987).

Attention An example of how executive functioning increases in adolescence is its role in determining how attention will be allocated. Controlling attention and reducing interfering thoughts are key aspects of learning and thinking in adolescence and emerging adulthood (Bjorklund, 2012). Distractions that can interfere with attention in adolescence and emerging adulthood come from the external environment (other students talking while the student is trying to listen to a lecture, or receiving a friend request when the student visits Facebook during a lecture, for example) or intrusive distractions from competing thoughts in the individual's mind. Self-oriented thinking, such as worrying, self-doubt, and intense emotionally laden thoughts, may especially interfere with focusing attention on thinking tasks (Gillig & Sanders, 2011; Walsh, 2011).

Working Memory Recall from Chapter 12 the discussion of *working memory,* which is a kind of "mental workbench" where people manipulate and assemble information to help make decisions, solve problems, and comprehend written and spoken language (Baddeley, 2010a, b, 2012). In one study, the performances of individuals from 6 to 57 years of age were examined on both verbal and visuospatial working memory tasks (Swanson, 1999). The two verbal tasks were auditory digit sequence (the ability to remember numerical information embedded in a short sentence, such as "Now suppose somebody wanted to go to the supermarket at 8651 Elm Street") and semantic association (the ability to organize words into abstract categories) (Swanson, 1999, p. 988).

In the semantic association task, the participant was presented with a series of words (such as shirt, saw, pants, hammer, shoes, and nails) and then asked to remember how they go together. The two visuospatial tasks involved mapping/ directions and a visual matrix. In the mapping/directions task, the participant was shown a street map indicating the route a bicycle (child/young adolescent) or car (adult) would take through a city. After briefly looking at the map, participants were asked to redraw the route on a blank map. In the visual matrix task, participants were asked to study a matrix showing a series of dots. After looking at the matrix for five seconds, they were asked to answer questions about the location of the dots. As shown in Figure 15.1, working memory increased substantially from 8 through 24 years of age—that is, through the transition to adulthood and beyond—no matter what the task. Thus, the adolescent years are likely to be an important developmental period for improvement in working memory (Swanson, 1999).

Decision Making Adolescence is a time of increased decision making—which friends to choose, which person to date, whether to have sex, buy a car, go to college, and so on (Steinberg, 2011). How competent are adolescents at making decisions? In some reviews, older adolescents are described as more competent than younger adolescents, who in turn are more competent than children (Keating, 2004). Compared with children, young adolescents are more likely to generate different options, examine a situation from a variety of perspectives, anticipate the consequences of decisions, and consider the credibility of sources.

However, older adolescents' (as well as adults') decision-making skills are far from perfect, and having the capacity to make competent decisions does not guarantee they will be made in everyday life, where breadth of experience often comes into play (Kuhn, 2009). As an example, driver-training courses improve adolescents' cognitive and motor skills to levels equal to, or sometimes superior to, those of adults. However, driver training has not been effective in reducing adolescents' high rate of traffic accidents, although recently researchers have found that implementing a graduated driver licensing (GDR) program can reduce crash and fatality rates for adolescent drivers (Keating, 2007). GDR components include a learner's holding period, practice-driving certification, night-driving restriction, and passenger restriction.

What are some of the decisions adolescents have to make? What characterizes their decision making?

Most people make better decisions when they are calm than when they are emotionally aroused, which often is the case for adolescents (Steinberg, 2011). Recall from our discussion of brain development in Chapter 14 that adolescents have a tendency to be emotionally intense. Thus, the same adolescent who makes a wise decision when calm may make an unwise decision when emotionally aroused. In the heat of the moment, then, adolescents' emotions may especially overwhelm their decision-making ability.

The social context plays a key role in adolescent decision making (Reyna & others, 2011; Steinberg, 2011). For example, adolescents' willingness to make risky decisions is more likely to occur in contexts where alcohol, drugs, and other temptations are readily available (Reyna & Rivers, 2008). Recent research reveals that the presence of peers in risk-taking situations increases the likelihood that adolescents will make risky decisions (Albert & Steinberg, 2011a, b). In one study of risk taking involving a simulated driving task, the presence of peers increased an adolescent's decision to engage in risky driving by 50 percent but had no effect on adults (Gardner & Steinberg, 2005). One view is that the presence of peers activates the brain's reward system, especially its dopamine pathways (Albert & Steinberg, 2011a, b).

Adolescents need more opportunities to practice and discuss realistic decision making. Many real-world decisions on matters such as sex, drugs, and daredevil driving occur in an atmosphere

How do emotions and social contexts influence adolescents' decision making?

of stress that includes time constraints and emotional involvement. One strategy for improving adolescent decision making in such circumstances is to provide more opportunities for them to engage in role playing and group problem solving. Another strategy is for parents to involve adolescents in appropriate decision-making activities.

One proposal to explain effective adolescent decision making is the **dual-process model,** which states that decision making is influenced by two cognitive systems—one analytical and one experiential—which compete with each other (Klaczynski, 2001; Reyna & Farley, 2006; Reyna & others, 2011). The dual-process model emphasizes that it is the experiential system—monitoring and managing actual experiences—that benefits adolescents' decision making, not the analytical system. In this view, adolescents don't benefit from engaging in reflective, detailed, higher-level cognitive analysis about a decision, especially in high-risk, real-world contexts. In such contexts, adolescents just need to know that there are some circumstances that are so dangerous that they need to be avoided at all costs (Mills, Reyna, & Estrada, 2008). However, some experts on adolescent cognition argue that in many cases adolescents benefit from both analytical and experiential systems (Kuhn, 2009).

developmental **connection**

Cognitive Processes. Mindfulness is an important aspect of critical thinking. Chapter 12, p. 359

Critical Thinking In Chapter 12, "Cognitive Development in Middle and Late Childhood," we defined *critical thinking* as thinking reflectively and productively and evaluating evidence. Here we discuss how critical thinking changes in adolescence. In one study of fifth-, eighth-, and eleventh-graders, critical thinking increased with age but still occurred only in 43 percent of eleventh-graders (Klaczynski & Narasimham, 1998). Among the factors that provide a basis for improvement in critical thinking during adolescence are (Keating, 1990):

- Increased speed, automaticity, and capacity of information processing, which free cognitive resources for other purposes
- Greater breadth of content knowledge in a variety of domains
- Increased ability to construct new combinations of knowledge
- A greater range and more spontaneous use of strategies and procedures for obtaining and applying knowledge, such as planning, considering the alternatives, and cognitive monitoring

Although adolescence is an important period in the development of critical-thinking skills, if an individual has not developed a solid basis of fundamental skills (such as literacy and math skills) during childhood, critical-thinking skills are unlikely to mature in adolescence. For the subset of adolescents who lack such fundamental skills, potential gains in adolescent thinking are not likely. Laura Bickford is a secondary school teacher who encourages her students to think critically. To read about her work, see the *Connecting with Careers* profile.

developmental **connection**

Cognitive Processes. Developing effective strategies is a key aspect of metacognition. Chapter 12, p. 363

Metacognition Recall from Chapter 12, "Cognitive Development in Middle and Late Childhood," that *metacognition* involves cognition about cognition, or "knowing about knowing." Metacognition is increasingly recognized as a very important cognitive skill not only in adolescence but also in emerging adulthood. In comparison with children, adolescents have a greater capacity to monitor and manage cognitive resources to effectively meet the demands of a learning task (Kuhn, 2009). This increased metacognitive ability results in improved cognitive functioning and learning. A recent longitudinal study revealed that from 12 to 14 years of age, young adolescents

dual-process model States that decision making is influenced by two systems—one analytical and one experiential, which compete with each other; in this model, it is the experiential system—monitoring and managing actual experiences—that benefits adolescent decision making.

Laura Bickford, Secondary School Teacher

Laura Bickford teaches English and journalism in grades 9 to 12, and she is chair of the English Department at Nordhoff High School in Ojai, California.

Bickford especially believes it is important to encourage students to think. Indeed, she says that "the call to teach is the call to teach students how to think." She believes teachers need to show students the value of asking their own questions, having discussions, and engaging in stimulating intellectual conversations. Bickford says that she also encourages students to engage in metacognitive strategies (knowing about knowing). For example, she asks students to comment on their learning after particular pieces of projects have been completed. She requires students to keep logs so they can observe their own thinking as it happens.

Laura Bickford, working with students writing papers.

increasingly used metacognitive skills and used them more effectively in math and history classes (van der Stel & Veenman, 2010). For example, 14-year-olds monitored their own text comprehension more frequently and did so more effectively than their younger counterparts. Another recent study documented the importance of metacognitive skills, such as planning, strategizing, and monitoring, in college students' ability to think critically (Magno, 2010).

Review Connect Reflect

LG1 Discuss different approaches to adolescent cognition.

Review

- What is Piaget's view of adolescent cognitive development?
- What is adolescent egocentrism?
- How does information processing change during adolescence?

Connect

- Egocentrism was also mentioned in Chapter 9 in the context of early childhood cognitive development. How

is egocentrism in adolescence similar to or different from egocentrism in early childhood?

Reflect *Your Own Personal Journey of Life*

- Think back to your early adolescent years. How would you describe the level of your thinking at that point in your development? Has your cognitive development changed since you were a young adolescent? Explain.

What Characterizes Adolescents' Values, Moral Education, and Religion?

LG2 Describe adolescents' values, moral education, and religion.

Values | Moral Education | Religion

What are the values of adolescents today? How can moral education be characterized? How powerful is the influence of religion in adolescents' lives?

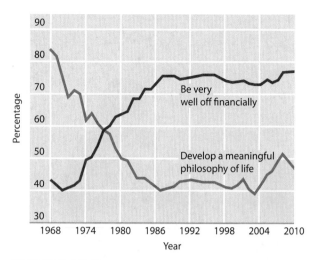

FIGURE **15.2**

CHANGING FRESHMAN LIFE GOALS, 1968 TO 2008. In the last four decades, a significant change has occurred in freshman students' life goals. A far greater percentage of today's college freshmen state that an "essential" or "very important" life goal is to be well off financially, and far fewer state that developing a meaningful philosophy of life is an "essential" or "very important" life goal.

What are some of the positive effects of service learning?

values Beliefs and attitudes about the way things should be.

service learning A form of education that promotes social responsibility and service to the community.

VALUES

Values are beliefs and attitudes about the way things should be. They involve what is important to us. We attach values to all sorts of things: politics, religion, money, sex, education, helping others, family, friends, career, cheating, self-respect, and so on.

Changing Values   One way of measuring what people value is to ask them what their goals are. Over the past four decades, traditional-aged college students have shown an increased concern for personal well-being and a decreased concern for the well-being of others, especially for the disadvantaged (Pryor & others, 2010). As shown in Figure 15.2, today's college freshmen are more strongly motivated to be well-off financially and less motivated to develop a meaningful philosophy of life than were their counterparts of 20 or even 10 years ago. In 2010, 77 percent of students viewed becoming well-off financially as an "essential" or a "very important" objective compared with only 42 percent in 1971.

There are, however, some signs that U.S. college students are shifting toward a stronger interest in the welfare of society. In the survey just described, interest in developing a meaningful philosophy of life increased from 39 percent to 47 percent of U.S. freshmen from 2001 through 2010 (Pryor & others, 2010) (see Figure 15.2). Also in this survey, the percentage of college freshmen who said the chances are very good that they will participate in volunteer or community service programs increased from 18 percent in 1990 to 32 percent in 2010 (Pryor & others, 2010).

Service Learning   **Service learning** is a form of education that promotes social responsibility and service to the community. In service learning, adolescents engage in activities such as tutoring, helping older adults, working in a hospital, assisting at a child-care center, or cleaning up a vacant lot to make a play area. An important goal of service learning is for adolescents to become less self-centered and more strongly motivated to help others (Davidson & others, 2010). Service learning is often more effective when two conditions are met (Nucci, 2006): (1) giving students some degree of choice in the service activities in which they participate, and (2) providing students with opportunities to reflect about their participation.

Service learning takes education out into the community (Zaff & others, 2010). Adolescent volunteers tend to be extraverted and committed to others, and to have a high level of self-understanding (Eisenberg & others, 2009). Also, one study revealed that adolescent girls participated in service learning more than adolescent boys (Webster & Worrell, 2008).

Researchers have found that service learning benefits adolescents in a number of ways (Hart, Matsuba, & Atkins, 2008). These improvements in adolescent development include higher grades in school, increased goal setting, higher self-esteem, a greater sense of being able to make a difference for others, and an increased likelihood that they will serve as volunteers in the future. A recent study of more than 4,000 high school students revealed that those who worked directly with individuals in need were better adjusted academically, whereas those who worked for organizations had better civic outcomes (Schmidt, Shumow, & Kackar, 2007).

One analysis revealed that 26 percent of U.S. public high schools require students to participate in service learning (Metz & Youniss, 2005). The benefits of service learning, for both the volunteer and the recipient, suggest that more adolescents should be required to participate in such programs (Enfield & Collins, 2008). What

Evaluating a Service-Learning Program Designed to Increase Civic Engagement

In one study, the possible benefits of a service-learning requirement for high school students were explored (Metz & Youniss, 2005). One group of students had a service-learning requirement, while the other group did not. Each group of students was also divided according to whether or not they were motivated to serve voluntarily. The participants in the study were 174 students (class of 2000) who were not required to engage in service learning, and 312 students (classes of 2001 and 2002) who were required to accumulate 40 hours of community service. The school was located in a middle- to upper-middle-SES suburban community outside Boston, Massachusetts. The focus of the study was to compare the 2001 and 2002 classes, which were the first ones to have a 40-hour community service requirement, with the class of 2000, the last year in which the school did not have this requirement. For purposes of comparison, the 2001 and 2002 classes were combined into one group to be compared with the 2000 class.

The service-learning requirement for the 2001 and 2002 classes was designed to give students a sense of participating in the community in positive ways. Among the most common service-learning activities that students engaged in were "tutoring, coaching, assisting at shelters or nursing homes, organizing food or clothing drives, and assisting value-centered service organizations or churches" (p. 420). To obtain credit for the activities, students were required to write reflectively about the activities and describe how the activities benefited both the recipients and themselves. Students also had to obtain an adult's or supervisor's signature to document their participation.

Detailed self-reported records of students' service in grades 10 through 12 were obtained. In addition to describing the number of service hours they accumulated toward their requirement, they also were asked to indicate any voluntary services they provided in addition to the required 40 hours. Since students in the 2000 class had no required service participation, all of their service was voluntary.

The students rated themselves on four 5-point scales of civic engagement: (1) their likelihood of voting when reaching 18; (2) the likelihood they would "volunteer" or "join a civic organization" after graduating from high school; (3) their future unconventional civic involvement (such as boycotting a product, demonstrating for a cause, or participating in a political campaign); and (4) their political interest and understanding (how much they discuss politics with parents and friends, read about politics in magazines and newspapers, or watch the news on TV).

The results indicated that students who were already inclined to engage in service learning scored high on the four scales of civic engagement throughout high school and showed no increase in service after it was required. However, students who were less motivated to engage in service learning increased their civic engagement on three of the four scales (future voting, joining a civic organization after graduating from high school, and interest and understanding) after they were required to participate. In sum, this research documented that a required service-learning program can especially benefit the civic engagement of students who are inclined not to engage in service learning.

How might you design a study to identify positive outcomes of service learning that did not rely on self-reports?

---

are some of these positive outcomes? See the *Connecting with Research* interlude for the results of one study that asked this question.

MORAL EDUCATION

Moral education is hotly debated in educational circles (Nucci & Narváez, 2008). We study one of the earliest analyses of moral education and then turn to some contemporary views.

The Hidden Curriculum   More than 70 years ago, educator John Dewey (1933) recognized that, even when schools do not offer specific programs in moral education, they provide moral education through a "hidden curriculum." The **hidden curriculum** is conveyed by the moral atmosphere that is a part of every school. The moral atmosphere is created by school and classroom rules, the moral orientation of teachers and school administrators, and text materials. Teachers serve as models of ethical or unethical behavior. Classroom rules and peer relations at school transmit attitudes about cheating, lying, stealing, and consideration of others. And, through its rules and regulations, the school administration infuses the school with a value system.

How Would You...?

If you were an **educator,** how would you devise a program to increase adolescents' motivation to participate in service learning?

hidden curriculum Dewey's concept that every school has a pervasive moral atmosphere, even if it doesn't have a program of moral education.

Recently, increasing interest has been directed toward the role of classroom and school climates as part of the hidden curriculum. Darcia Narváez (2010a) argues that attention should be given to the concept of "sustaining climates." In her view, a sustaining classroom climate is more than a positive learning environment and more than a caring context. Sustaining climates involve focusing on students' sense of purpose, social engagement, community connections, and ethics. In sustaining classroom and school climates, students learn skills for flourishing and reaching their potential and help others to do so as well.

Character Education

Currently 40 of 50 states have mandates regarding **character education,** a direct education approach that involves teaching students a basic moral literacy to prevent them from engaging in immoral behavior and doing harm to themselves or others (Nucci & Narváez, 2008). The argument is that behaviors such as lying, stealing, and cheating are wrong, and students should be taught this throughout their education (Berkowitz, Battistich, & Bier, 2008).

In the character education approach, every school is expected to have an explicit moral code that is clearly communicated to students. Any violations of the code will be met with sanctions. Instruction in specified moral concepts, such as cheating, can take the form of example and definition, class discussions and role playing, or rewarding students for proper behavior. More recently, an emphasis on the importance of encouraging students to develop a care perspective has been accepted as a relevant aspect of character education (Noddings, 2008). Rather than just instructing adolescents to refrain from engaging in morally deviant behavior, a care perspective emphasizes educating students about the importance of engaging in prosocial behaviors such as considering others' feelings, being sensitive to others, and helping others (Carlo & others, 2011).

Cognitive Moral Education

Cognitive moral education is based on the belief that students should learn to value aspects of life such as democracy and justice as their moral reasoning develops. Lawrence Kohlberg's theory, which we discussed in Chapter 13, "Socioemotional Development in Middle and Late Childhood," has been the basis for some cognitive moral education programs. In a typical program, high school students meet in a semester-long course to discuss a number of moral issues. The instructor acts as a facilitator, rather than as a director, of the class. The hope is that students will develop more advanced notions of concepts such as cooperation, trust, responsibility, and community (Enright & others, 2008). Toward the end of his career, Kohlberg (1986) recognized that the moral atmosphere of the school is more important than he initially envisioned. For example, in one study, a semester-long moral education class based on Kohlberg's theory was successful in advancing moral thinking in three democratic schools, but not in three authoritarian schools (Higgins, Power, & Kohlberg, 1983).

Recall from Chapter 13 that Carol Gilligan (1982, 1996), more than Kohlberg, argues that moral development should focus on social relationships. Thus, if we apply Gilligan's view to moral education, emphasis should be placed on topics such as caring, sensitivity to others' feelings, and relationships. In her view, schools should better recognize the importance of relationships in the development of adolescent girls.

Cheating

A concern involving moral education is whether students cheat and how to handle cheating if it is discovered (Anderman & Anderman, 2010). Academic cheating can take many forms, including plagiarism, using "cheat sheets" during an exam, copying from a neighbor during a test, purchasing papers, and falsifying lab results. A 2006 survey revealed that 60 percent of secondary school students said they had cheated on a test in school during the past year, and one-third of the students reported that they had plagiarized information from the Internet in the past year (Josephson Institute of Ethics, 2006).

character education A direct education approach that involves teaching students a basic moral literacy to prevent them from engaging in immoral behavior and doing harm to themselves and others.

cognitive moral education A concept based on the belief that students should develop such values as democracy and justice as their moral reasoning develops; Kohlberg's theory has been the basis of a number of cognitive moral education programs.

Why do students cheat? Among the reasons students give for cheating include pressure to get high grades, time pressures, poor teaching, and lack of interest (Stephens, 2008). In terms of poor teaching, "students are more likely to cheat when they perceive their teacher to be incompetent, unfair, and uncaring" (Stephens, 2008, p. 140).

A long history of research also implicates the power of the situation in determining whether students will cheat (Hartshorne & May, 1928–1930; Murdock, Miller, & Kohlhardt, 2004; Vandehey, Diekhoff, & LaBeff, 2007). For example, students are more likely to cheat when they are not being closely monitored during a test, when they know their peers are cheating, when they know whether another student has been caught cheating, and when student scores are made public (Anderman & Murdock, 2007; Carrell, Malmstrom, & West, 2008; Harmon, Lambrinos, & Kennedy, 2008).

Certain personality traits also are linked to cheating. For example, a recent study revealed that college students who engaged in academic cheating were characterized by the personality traits of low conscientiousness and low agreeableness (Williams, Nathanson, & Paulhus, 2010).

Among the strategies for decreasing academic cheating are preventive measures such as making sure students are aware of what constitutes cheating and what the consequences will be if they cheat, closely monitoring students' behavior while they are taking tests, and emphasizing the importance of being a moral, responsible individual who practices academic integrity. In promoting academic integrity, many colleges have instituted an honor code policy that emphasizes self-responsibility, fairness, trust, and scholarship. However, few secondary schools have developed honor code policies. The Center for Academic Integrity (www.academicintegrity. org/) offers an extensive selection of materials to help schools develop academic integrity policies.

Why do students cheat? What are some strategies teachers can adopt to prevent cheating?

How Would You...?

If you were an **educator,** how would you try to reduce the incidence of cheating in your school?

An Integrative Approach   Darcia Narváez (2006, 2008, 2010a, b) emphasizes an *integrative approach* to moral education that encompasses the reflective moral thinking and commitment to justice advocated in Kohlberg's approach along with an emphasis on developing a particular moral character as advocated in the character education approach. She highlights the Child Development Project as an excellent example of an integrative moral education approach. In the Child Development Project, students are given multiple opportunities to discuss other students' experiences, which encourages empathy and perspective taking, and they participate in exercises that encourage them to reflect on their own behaviors in terms of values such as fairness and social responsibility (Battistich, 2008). Adults coach students in ethical decision making and guide them in becoming more caring individuals. Students experience a caring community, not only in the classroom, but also in after-school activities and through parental involvement in the program. Research evaluations of the Child Development Project indicate that it is related to an improved sense of community, an increase in prosocial behavior, better interpersonal understanding, and an increase in social problem solving (Battistich, 2008; Solomon & others, 1990).

RELIGION

Can religion, religiousness, and spirituality be distinguished? A recent analysis by Pamela King and her colleagues (2011) makes the following distinctions:

- **Religion** is an organized set of beliefs, practices, rituals, and symbols that increases an individual's connection to a sacred or transcendent other (God, higher power, or ultimate truth).

religion An organized set of beliefs, practices, rituals, and symbols that increases an individual's connection to a sacred or transcendent other (God, higher power, or higher truth).

> Religion enlightens, terrifies, subdues; it gives faith, inflicts remorse, inspires resolutions, and inflames devotion.
>
> —HENRY NEWMAN
> *English Churchman and Writer, 19th Century*

- **Religiousness** refers to the degree of affiliation with an organized religion, participation in its prescribed rituals and practices, connection with its beliefs, and involvement in a community of believers.

- **Spirituality** involves experiencing something beyond oneself in a transcendent manner and living in a way that benefits others and society.

Religious issues are important to adolescents. In one survey, 95 percent of 13- to 18-year-olds said that they believe in God or a universal spirit (Gallup & Bezilla, 1992). Almost three-fourths of adolescents said that they pray, and about one-half indicated that they had attended religious services within the past week. Almost half of the youth said that it is very important for a young person to learn religious faith.

A recent developmental study revealed that religiousness declined in U.S. adolescents between age 14 and age 20 (Koenig, McGue, & Iacono, 2008) (see Figure 15.3). In this study, religiousness was assessed on the basis of criteria such as frequency of prayer, frequency of discussing religious teachings, frequency of deciding moral actions for religious reasons, and the overall importance of religion in everyday life. As indicated in Figure 15.3, more change in religiousness occurred from 14 to 18 years of age than from 20 to 25 years of age. Also, attending religious services was highest at 14 years of age, declined from 14 to 18 years of age, and increased at 20 years of age.

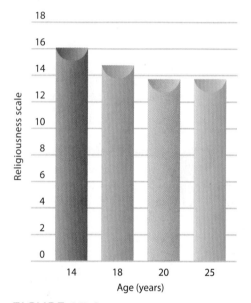

FIGURE 15.3

DEVELOPMENTAL CHANGES IN RELIGIOUSNESS FROM 14 TO 25 YEARS OF AGE. *Note:* The religiousness scale ranged from 0 to 32, with higher scores indicating stronger religiousness.

The Positive Role of Religion in Adolescents' Lives   Researchers have found that various aspects of religion are linked with positive outcomes for adolescents (Day, 2010; King, Ramos, & Clardy, 2012; Warren, Lerner, & Phelps, 2011). A recent study revealed that a higher level of church engagement (based on years of attendance, choice in attending, and participation in activities) was related to higher grades for male adolescents (Kang & Romo, 2011). Churchgoing may benefit students because religious communities encourage socially acceptable behavior, which includes doing well in school. Churchgoing also may benefit students because churches often offer positive role models for students.

Religion also plays a role in adolescents' health and whether they engage in problem behaviors (King, Ramos, & Clardy, 2012; King & Roeser, 2009). In a national random sample of more than 2,000 11- to 18-year-olds, those who were higher in religiosity were less likely to smoke, drink alcohol, use marijuana, be truant from school, engage in delinquent activities, and be depressed than their low-religiosity counterparts (Sinha, Cnaan, & Gelles, 2007). A recent study of ninth- to twelfth-graders revealed that more frequent religious attendance in one grade predicted lower levels of substance abuse in the next grade (Good & Willoughby, 2010).

Many religious adolescents also internalize their religion's message about caring and concern for people. For example, in one survey, religious youth were almost three times as likely to engage in community service as nonreligious youth (Youniss, McLellan, & Yates, 1999).

Developmental Changes   Adolescence can be an important juncture in religious development (Scarlett & Warren, 2010). Even if children have been indoctrinated into a religion by their parents, because of advances in their cognitive development they may begin to question what their own religious beliefs truly are.

Cognitive Changes   Many of the cognitive changes thought to influence religious development involve Piaget's cognitive developmental theory, which we discussed earlier in this chapter. In comparison with children, adolescents think more abstractly, idealistically, and logically. The increase in abstract thinking lets adolescents consider various ideas about religious and spiritual concepts. For example, an adolescent might ask how a loving God can possibly exist given the extensive suffering of many people in the world (Good & Willoughby, 2008). Adolescents' increased idealistic thinking provides a foundation for thinking about whether religion provides the best route to a better, more ideal world than the present. And adolescents' increased

religiousness The degree of affiliation with an organized religion, participation in prescribed rituals and practices, connection with its beliefs, and involvement in a community of believers.

spirituality Experiencing something beyond oneself in a transcendent manner and living in a way that benefits others and society.

logical reasoning gives them the ability to develop hypotheses and systematically sort through different answers to spiritual questions (Good & Willoughby, 2008).

Erikson's Theory and Identity   During adolescence, especially in late adolescence and the college years, identity development becomes a central focus. In Erik Erikson's (1968) theory, adolescents seek answers to questions like "Who am I?" "What am I all about as a person?" and "What kind of life do I want to lead?" As part of their search for identity, adolescents begin to grapple in more sophisticated, logical ways with such questions as "Why am I on this planet?" "Is there really a God or higher spiritual being, or have I just been believing what my parents and the church imprinted in my mind?" "What really are my religious views?" An analysis of the link between identity and spirituality concluded that adolescence and emerging adulthood can serve as gateways to a spiritual identity that "transcends, but not necessarily excludes, the assigned religious identity in childhood" (Templeton & Eccles, 2005, p. 261).

Adolescents participating in church choir. *What are some positive aspects of religion in adolescents' lives? What are some developmental changes in religious development during adolescence?*

Religious Beliefs and Parenting   Religious institutions created by adults are designed to introduce certain beliefs to children and thereby ensure that they will carry on a religious tradition. Various societies utilize Sunday schools, parochial education, tribal transmission of religious traditions, and parental teaching of children at home to further this aim.

Does this socialization work? In many cases it does (Paloutzian, 2000). In general, adults tend to adopt the religious teachings of their upbringing. However, when examining religious beliefs and adolescence, it is important to consider the quality of the parent-adolescent relationship (Brelsford & Mahoney, 2008). Adolescents who have a positive relationship with their parents or are securely attached to them are likely to adopt their parents' religious affiliation. But when conflict or insecure attachment characterizes parent-adolescent relationships, adolescents may seek a religious affiliation that is different from their parents' (Streib, 1999).

developmental **connection**

Self and Identity. In addition to religious/spiritual identity, what are some other identity components? Chapter 16, p. 484

Religiousness and Sexuality in Adolescence and Emerging Adulthood   One area of religion's influence on adolescent and emerging adult development involves sexual activity. Although variability and change in church teachings make it difficult to generalize about religious doctrines, most churches discourage premarital sex. Thus, the degree of adolescent and emerging adult participation in religious organizations may be more important than affiliation with a specific religion as a determinant of premarital sexual attitudes and behavior. Adolescents and emerging adults who frequently attend religious services are likely to hear messages about abstaining from sex. Involvement of adolescents and emerging adults in religious organizations also enhances the probability that they will become friends with adolescents who have restrictive attitudes toward premarital sex. A recent study revealed that adolescents with high religiosity were less likely to have had sexual intercourse (Gold & others, 2010).

A recent study found that parents' religiosity was linked to a lower level of risky sexual behavior among adolescents, in part because of friendships with less sexually permissive peers (Landor & others, 2010). Also, a recent research review concluded that *spirituality* (being spiritual, religious, or believing in a higher power, for example) was linked to the following positive adolescent outcomes: reduced likelihood of intending to have sex, refraining from early sex, having sex less frequently, and not becoming pregnant (House & others, 2010).

Review

- What characterizes adolescents' values? What is service learning?
- What are some variations in moral education?
- What are adolescents' religious views and experiences?

Connect

- In the first part of Chapter 14, we described five characteristics of emerging adults.

Might some of those characteristics be linked to an individual's religiousness and spirituality? Explain.

Reflect *Your Own Personal Journey of Life*

- What were your values, religious beliefs, and spiritual interests in middle school and high school? Have they changed since then? If so, how?

What Is the Nature of Schools for Adolescents?

LG3 Characterize schools for adolescents.

| The American Middle School | The American High School | High School Dropouts |

The impressive changes in adolescents' cognition lead us to examine the nature of schools for adolescents. In Chapter 13, "Socioemotional Development in Middle and Late Childhood," we discussed various ideas about the effects of schools on children's development. Here, we focus more exclusively on the nature of secondary schools.

THE AMERICAN MIDDLE SCHOOL

One worry expressed by educators and psychologists is that middle schools (most often consisting of grades 6 through 8) tend to be watered-down versions of high schools, mimicking their curricular and extracurricular schedules. The critics argue that unique curricular and extracurricular activities reflecting a wide range of individual differences in biological and psychological development in early adolescence should be incorporated into junior high and middle schools. The critics also stress that many high schools foster passivity rather than autonomy, and they urge schools to create a variety of pathways on which students can achieve an identity.

The Transition to Middle or Junior High School The transition to middle school from elementary school interests developmentalists because, even though it is a normative experience for virtually all children, the transition can be stressful (Anderman & Dawson, 2011; Howe & Richards, 2011). Why? The transition takes place at a time when many changes—in the individual, in the family, and in school—are occurring simultaneously. These changes include puberty and related concerns about body image; the emergence of at least some aspects of formal operational thought, including accompanying changes in social cognition; increased responsibility and independence in association with decreased dependence on parents; moving from a small, contained classroom structure to a larger, more impersonal school structure; switching from one teacher to many teachers and from a small, homogeneous set of peers to a larger, more heterogeneous set of peers; and adjusting to an increased focus on achievement and performance.

This list includes a number of negative, stressful features, but there can be positive aspects to the transition from elementary school to middle school or junior high. Students are more likely to feel grown up, to have more subjects from which to select, to have more opportunities to spend time with peers and to locate compatible friends, and to enjoy increased independence from direct parental monitoring—and they may be more challenged intellectually by academic work.

When students make the transition from elementary school to middle or junior high school, they experience the **top-dog phenomenon,** the circumstance of moving from the top position (in elementary school, being the oldest, biggest, and most powerful students in the school) to the lowest position (in middle or junior high school, being the youngest, smallest, and least powerful students in the school). Researchers who have charted the transition from elementary to middle school find that the first year of middle school can be difficult for many students (Hawkins & Berndt, 1985). A recent study in North Carolina schools revealed that sixth-grade students attending middle schools were far more likely to be cited for discipline problems than their counterparts who were attending elementary schools (Cook & others, 2008).

The transition from elementary to middle or junior high school occurs at the same time as a number of other developmental changes. *What are some of these other developmental changes?*

Effective Middle Schools How effective are the middle schools U.S. students attend? The Carnegie Council on Adolescent Development (1989) issued an extremely negative evaluation of U.S. middle schools. In the report—*Turning Points: Preparing American Youth for the Twenty-First Century*—the conclusion was reached that most young adolescents attend massive, impersonal schools; learn from seemingly irrelevant curricula; trust few adults in school; and lack access to health care and counseling. The Carnegie report recommended:

How Would You...?

If you were an **educator,** how would you improve middle schools?

- Developing smaller "communities" or "houses" to lessen the impersonal nature of large middle schools

- Lowering student-to-counselor ratios from several-hundred-to-1 to 10-to-1

- Involving parents and community leaders in schools

- Developing curricula that produce students who are literate, understand the sciences, and have a sense of health, ethics, and citizenship

- Having teachers team-teach in more flexibly designed curriculum blocks that integrate several disciplines, instead of presenting students with disconnected, rigidly separated 50-minute segments

- Boosting students' health and fitness with more in-school programs and helping students who need public health care to get it

Turning Points 2000 (Jackson & Davis, 2000) continued to endorse the recommendations set forth in *Turning Points 1989.* One new recommendation in the 2000 report stated that it is important to teach a curriculum grounded in rigorous academic standards for what students should know and should be able to learn. A second new recommendation was to engage in instruction that encourages students to achieve higher standards and become lifelong learners. These new recommendations reflect the increasing emphasis on challenging students to meet higher standards (Manzo, 2008).

Extracurricular Activities Adolescents in U.S. schools usually have a wide array of extracurricular activities they can participate in beyond their academic courses. These activities include such diverse activities as sports, academic clubs, band, drama, and math clubs. Researchers have found that participation in extracurricular activities is linked to higher grades, increased school engagement, a reduced likelihood of dropping out of school, improved probability of going to college, higher self-esteem, and lower rates of depression, delinquency, and substance abuse (Barber, Stone, & Eccles, 2010; Mahoney, Parente, & Zigler, 2010). Adolescents benefit from a breadth of extracurricular activities more than focusing on a single extracurricular activity.

top-dog phenomenon The circumstance of moving from the top position (in elementary school, the oldest, biggest, and most powerful students) to the lowest position (in middle or junior high school, the youngest, smallest, and least powerful students).

THE AMERICAN HIGH SCHOOL

Many high school graduates not only are poorly prepared for college but also are poorly prepared to meet the demands of the modern, high-performance workplace (Smith, 2009). In a review of hiring practices at major companies, it was concluded that many companies now want their employees to possess certain basic skills. These include the ability to read at relatively high levels, do at least elementary algebra, use personal computers for straightforward tasks such as word processing, solve semistructured problems in which hypotheses must be formed and tested, communicate effectively (orally and in writing), and work effectively in groups with persons of various backgrounds (Murnane & Levy, 1996).

The National Research Council (2004) made a number of recommendations for improving U.S. high schools. They especially emphasized the importance of finding ways to get students more engaged in learning. The council concluded that the best way to do this is to address the psychological factors involved in motivation. To increase students' engagement in learning, schools should promote a sense of belonging "by personalizing instruction, showing an interest in students' lives, and creating a supportive, caring social environment" (National Research Council, 2004, p. 3). The council said that this description of engaging students applies to very few urban high schools, which often are characterized by low expectations, alienation, and low achievement. A recent study examined school transition of multiethnic urban adolescents from the seventh to tenth grade (Benner & Graham, 2009). The transition to high school was especially challenging for African American and Latino youth when the number of students in their own ethnic groups declined from middle to high school.

A special concern regarding secondary schools—middle and high schools—involves adolescents who are growing up in economically disadvantaged contexts (McLoyd, & others, 2011). Although relevant studies are few, those that have been conducted indicate that living in economically disadvantaged families during adolescence may have more negative achievement outcomes than corresponding circumstances in childhood (McLoyd & others, 2009). The possible timing difference in poverty effects might be due to adolescents' awareness of barriers to their success and the difficulties they will encounter in becoming successful.

developmental **connection**

Schools. The New Hope intervention program is designed to enhance the development of children and adolescents growing up in poverty. Chapter 13, p. 416

Some innovative programs indicate that improving certain characteristics of schools raises achievement levels for adolescents from economically disadvantaged backgrounds (McLoyd & others, 2009). For example, a study of pilot schools in Boston revealed that the following changes were linked with higher levels of achievement in high school: having smaller class sizes and longer class periods, creating more advisory sessions, and allotting more time for teachers to explore teaching methods (Tung & Ouimette, 2007).

Are American secondary schools different from those in other countries? To explore this question, see the *Connecting with Diversity* interlude.

HIGH SCHOOL DROPOUTS

Dropping out of high school has been viewed as a serious educational and societal problem for many decades (White, 2010). When adolescents leave high school before graduating, they approach adult life with educational deficiencies that severely curtail their economic and social well-being (Vaughn & others, 2010). In this section, we study the scope of the problem, the causes of dropping out, and ways to reduce dropout rates.

High School Dropout Rates In the last half of the twentieth century and the first several years of the twenty-first century, U.S. high school dropout rates declined (National Center for Education Statistics, 2010). In the 1940s, more than half of

connecting with diversity

Cross-Cultural Comparisons of Secondary Schools

Secondary schools in different countries share a number of features but differ in many ways. Let's explore the similarities and differences in secondary schools in seven countries: Australia, Brazil, Germany, Japan, China, Russia, and the United States.

Most countries mandate that children begin school at 6 to 7 years of age and stay in school until they are 14 to 17 years of age. Brazil requires students to go to school only until they are 14 years old, whereas Russia mandates that students stay in school until they are 17. Germany, Japan, Australia, and the United States require school attendance until at least 15 to 16 years of age, with some states, such as California, recently raising the mandatory age to 18.

Most secondary schools around the world are divided into two or more levels, such as middle school (or junior high school) and high school. However, Germany's schools are divided according to three educational ability tracks: (1) the main school provides a basic level of education, (2) the middle school gives students a more advanced education, and (3) the academic school prepares students for entrance to a university. German schools, like most European schools, offer a classical education, which includes courses in Latin and Greek. Japanese secondary schools have an entrance exam, but secondary schools in the other five countries do not. Only Australia and Germany have comprehensive exit exams.

The United States and Australia are among the few countries in the world in which sports are an integral part of the public school system. Only a few private schools in other countries have their own sports teams, sports facilities, and highly organized sports events.

In Brazil, students are required to take Portuguese (the native language) and four foreign languages (Latin, French, English, and Spanish). Brazil requires these languages because of the country's international character and emphasis on trade and commerce. Seventh-grade students in Australia take courses in sheep husbandry and weaving, two areas of economic and cultural interest in the country. In Japan, students take a number of Western courses in addition to their basic Japanese courses; these courses include Western literature and languages (in addition to Japanese literature and language), Western physical education (in addition to Japanese martial arts classes), and Western sculpture and handicrafts (in addition to Japanese calligraphy). The Japanese school year is also much longer than that of other countries (225 days versus 180 days in the United States, for example).

The juku, or "cramming school," is available to Japanese children and adolescents in the summertime and after school. It provides coaching to help them improve their grades and their entrance exam scores for high schools and universities. The Japanese practice of requiring an entrance exam for high school is a rarity among the nations of the world.

I recently visited China and interviewed parents about their adolescents' education. Several aspects of education in China are noteworthy, especially in comparison with the United States. Parents' comments reflected motivation to provide adolescents with the best possible education and to ensure that they work extremely hard in school and on homework. Also, when I asked parents if there are disciplinary problems in Chinese schools, they responded that if an adolescent acts up in school, the school immediately sends the adolescent home. In China, it is considered the parents' responsibility to orient their adolescents to behave in school and focus on schoolwork. These observations coincide with the description in Chapter 10, "Socioemotional Development in Early Childhood," of Asian American parents as training parents. When Chinese adolescents are sent home because of discipline problems, they are not allowed to return until parents work with the adolescent to ensure that the discipline problems will not recur. In China, classroom sizes are often large, sometimes having as many as 50 to 70 students, yet observers describe such classes as orderly and disciplined (Cavanagh, 2007).

U.S. 16- to 24-year-olds had dropped out of school; by 2008, this figure had decreased to 8 percent. The dropout rates of Latino adolescents remains high, although it has been decreasing in the twenty-first century (from 28 percent in 2000 to 18 percent in 2008). The lowest dropout rate in 2008 occurred for Asian American adolescents (3.2 percent), followed by non-Latino White adolescents (6.2 percent), African American adolescents (10.4 percent), and Latino adolescents (19 percent). Native

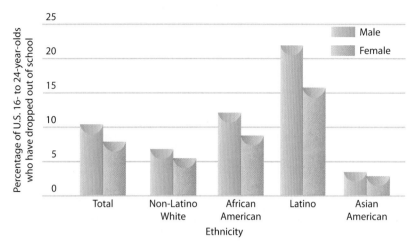

FIGURE **15.4**

SCHOOL DROPOUT RATES OF U.S. 16- TO 24-YEAR-OLDS BY GENDER AND ETHNICITY.
Source: National Center for Education Statistics (2010). *The condition of education 2010*. Washington, DC: U.S. Department of Education.

How Would You...?

If you were an **educator,** how would you reduce the school dropout rate of high-risk adolescents?

Students in the technology training center at Wellpoint Elementary/High School located on the Spokane Indian Reservation in Washington State. An important educational goal is to increase the high school graduation rate of Native American adolescents.

American adolescents also have a high dropout rate, although government statistics for this ethnic group have not been adequately compiled.

Gender differences characterize U.S. dropout rates, with males more likely to drop out than females (10.4 percent versus 7.9 percent) (data for 2008) (National Center for Education Statistics, 2010). The gender gap in dropout rates is especially large for Latino adolescents (21.9 versus 15 percent). Figure 15.4 shows the dropout rates of 16- to 24-year-olds by ethnicity and gender in 2008.

The average U.S. high school dropout rates just described mask some very high dropout rates in low-income areas of inner cities. For example, in cities such as Detroit, Cleveland, and Chicago, dropout rates are higher than 50 percent. Also, the percentages cited in Figure 15.4 are for 16- to 24-year-olds. When dropout rates are calculated in terms of students who do not graduate from high school in four years, the percentage of students is also much higher than in Figure 15.4. Thus, in considering high school dropout rates, it is important to examine age, the number of years it takes to complete high school, and various contexts including ethnicity, gender, and school location.

The Causes of Dropping Out of School   Students drop out of school for school-related, economic, family-related, peer-related, and personal reasons. School-related problems are consistently associated with dropping out of school (White, 2010). In one investigation, almost 50 percent of the dropouts cited school-related reasons for leaving school, such as not liking school, being suspended, or being expelled (Rumberger, 1995). Twenty percent of the dropouts (but 40 percent of the Latino students) cited economic reasons for dropping out. Many of these students quit school and go to work to help support their families. A recent study revealed that when children's parents were involved in their school in middle and late childhood, and when parents and adolescents had good relationships in early adolescence, a positive trajectory toward academic success was the likely outcome (Englund, Egeland, & Collins, 2008). By contrast, those who had poor relationships with their parents were more likely to drop out of high school despite doing well academically and behaviorally. Many school dropouts have friends who also are school dropouts. Approximately one-third of the girls who drop out of school do so for personal reasons, such as pregnancy or marriage.

Reducing the Dropout Rate   A review of school-based dropout programs found that the most effective programs provided early reading programs, tutoring, counseling, and mentoring (Lehr & others, 2003). They also emphasized the importance of creating caring environments and relationships and offered community-service opportunities.

Clearly, then, early detection of children's school-related difficulties, and getting children engaged with school in positive ways, are important strategies for reducing the dropout rate (Jimerson, 2009). Also, recently the Bill and Melinda Gates Foundation (2008) funded efforts to reduce the dropout rate in schools where dropout rates are high. One strategy that is being emphasized in the Gates' funding is keeping students who are at risk for dropping out of school with the same teachers through their high school years. The hope is that the teachers will get to know these students much better, their relationship with the students will improve, and they will be able to monitor and guide the students toward graduating from high school. One program that has been very effective in reducing school dropout rates is described in the following *Caring Connections* interlude.

The "I Have a Dream" Program

"I Have a Dream" (IHAD) is an innovative, comprehensive, long-term dropout prevention program administered by the National "I Have a Dream" Foundation in New York. Since the National IHAD Foundation was created in 1986, it has grown to encompass more than 180 projects in 64 cities and 27 states serving more than 15,000 children ("I Have a Dream" Foundation, 2011). Local IHAD projects around the country "adopt" entire grades (usually the third or fourth) from public elementary schools, or corresponding age cohorts from public housing developments. These children—"Dreamers"—are then provided with a program of academic, social, cultural, and recreational activities throughout their elementary, middle school, and high school years. An important part of this program is that it is personal rather than institutional: IHAD sponsors and staff develop close, long-term relationships with the children. When participants complete high school, IHAD provides the tuition assistance necessary for them to attend a state or local college or vocational school.

The IHAD program was created in 1981 when philanthropist Eugene Lang made an impromptu offer of college tuition to a class of graduating sixth-graders at P.S. 121 in East Harlem. Statistically, 75 percent of the students should have dropped out of school; instead, 90 percent graduated and 60 percent went on to college. Other evaluations of IHAD

These adolescents are participating in the "I Have a Dream" (IHAD) Program, a comprehensive, long-term dropout prevention program that has been very successful. *What are some other strategies for reducing high school dropout rates?*

programs have found dramatic improvements in grades, test scores, and school attendance, as well as a reduction of behavioral problems of Dreamers. For example, in Portland, Oregon, twice as many Dreamers as control-group students had reached a math standard, and the Dreamers were less likely to be referred to the juvenile justice system (Davis, Hyatt, & Arrasmith, 1998). And in a recent analysis of the "I Have a Dream" Program in Houston, 91 percent of the participants received passing grades in reading/English, 83 percent said they liked school, 98 percent said getting good grades is important to them, 100 percent said they plan to graduate from high school, and 94 percent reported they plan to go to college ("I Have a Dream" Foundation, 2011).

Review Connect Reflect

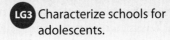 **LG3** Characterize schools for adolescents.

Review

- What is the transition from elementary to middle school like? What are some criticisms of, and recommendations for improving, U.S. middle schools?
- How can the American high school be improved so that students are better prepared for the demands of the modern workplace?
- What are some of the reasons why adolescents drop out of school?

Connect

- What impact might the concept of parents as "managers" (discussed in Chapter 13) have on reducing the high school dropout rate?

Reflect *Your Own Personal Journey of Life*

- What was your own middle or junior high school like? How did it measure up to the recommendations made by the Carnegie Foundation?

How Do Adolescents Experience Career Development?

LG4 Summarize career development in adolescence.

| Developmental Changes | Exploration, Decision Making, and Planning | Sociocultural Influences |

What are some developmental changes involved in career development? What cognitive processes are important to career development? How do sociocultural contexts influence career development?

"Your son has made a career choice, Mildred. He's going to win the lottery and travel a lot."
Copyright © 1985. Reprinted courtesy of Bunny Hoest.

DEVELOPMENTAL CHANGES

Many children have idealistic fantasies about what they want to be when they grow up. For example, many young children want to be superheroes, sports stars, or movie stars. In the high school years, they often begin to think about careers on a somewhat less idealistic basis. In their late teens and early twenties, their career decision making has usually turned more serious as they explore different career possibilities and zero in on the career they want to enter. In college, this often means choosing a major or specialization that is designed to lead to work in a particular field. By their early and mid-twenties, many individuals have completed their education or training and entered a full-time occupation.

William Damon (2008) recently described how it is not only children who have idealistic fantasies about careers but that too many of today's adolescents also dream about fantasy careers that may have no connection to reality. Too often the adolescents have no idea what it takes to become a star, and usually there is no one in their lives who can help them to reach this pinnacle in a career. Consider adolescents playing basketball who dream of becoming the next Kobe Bryant and adolescents participating in theater who want to become the next Angelina Jolie, for example.

EXPLORATION, DECISION MAKING, AND PLANNING

Exploration, decision making, and planning play important roles in adolescents' career choices (Hirschi, Niles, & Akos, 2011). In countries where equal employment opportunities have emerged—such as the United States, Canada, Great Britain, and France—the exploration of various career paths is critical in the adolescent's career development. Adolescents often approach career exploration and decision making with considerable ambiguity, uncertainty, and stress. Their career decisions often involve floundering and unplanned changes. Many adolescents not only do not know *what* information to seek about careers but also do not know *how* to seek it.

SOCIOCULTURAL INFLUENCES

Not every individual born into the world can grow up to become a nuclear physicist or a doctor—genetic limitations keep some adolescents from performing at the high intellectual levels necessary to enter such careers. Similarly, genetic limitations restrict some adolescents from becoming professional football players or professional golfers. But usually many careers are available to each of us, careers that provide a reasonable match with our abilities. Our sociocultural experiences exert strong influences on our career choices from among a wide range of possibilities (Bennett, 2008). Among the important sociocultural factors that influence career development are parents and peers, schools, and socioeconomic status.

Parents can play an important role in the adolescent's achievement and career development. It is important for parents to neither pressure the adolescent too much nor challenge the adolescent too little.

Parents and Peers   Parents and peers strongly influence adolescents' career choices. From an early age, children see and hear about their parents' jobs. Many factors influence the parent's role in the adolescent's career development (Messersmith & others, 2008). For one, mothers who work regularly outside the home and show effort and pride in their work probably exert strong influences on their adolescents' career development. It would be reasonable to conclude that when both parents work and enjoy what they do for a living, adolescents learn work values from both parents. Peers also can influence the adolescent's career development. A recent study of Vietnamese adolescents in the Washington, D.C., area revealed that peer support and English-language acculturation were the most important factors in career decision-making self-efficacy (Patel, Salahuddin, & O'Brien, 2008).

Armando Ronquillo, High School Counselor/College Advisor

Armando Ronquillo is a high school counselor and college advisor at Pueblo High School, which is in a low-socioeconomic-status area in Tucson, Arizona. More than 85 percent of the students have a Latino background. Ronquillo was named top high school counselor in the state of Arizona for the year 2000. He has especially helped to increase the number of Pueblo High School students who go to college.

Ronquillo has an undergraduate degree in elementary and special education and a master's degree in counseling. He counsels students on the merits of staying in school and on the lifelong opportunities provided by a college education. Ronquillo guides students in obtaining the academic preparation that will enable them to go to college, including how to apply for financial aid and scholarships. He also works with parents to help them understand that "their child going to college is not only doable but also affordable."

Armando Ronquillo, counseling a Latina high school student about college.

Ronquillo works with students on setting goals and planning. He has students plan for the future in terms of 1-year (short-term), 5-year (midrange), and 10-plus-year (long-term) time periods. Ronquillo says he does this "to help students visualize how the educational plans and decisions they make today will affect them in the future." He also organizes a number of college campus visitations for students from Pueblo High School each year.

To read more about what school counselors do, see p. 48 in the Careers in Children's Development appendix.

School Influences Schools, teachers, and counselors can exert a powerful influence on adolescents' career development (Diemer & Hsieh, 2008). School is the primary setting where individuals first encounter the world of work. School provides an atmosphere for continuing self-development in relation to achievement and work. And school is the only institution in society that is capable of providing the delivery systems necessary for career education—instruction, guidance, placement, and community connections.

Counselors' consultation with students about careers may change from middle school to high school (Baggerly, 2008). In middle schools, counselors often focus on students' career exploration, guiding students to examine work options in terms of their own strengths, weaknesses, interests, and skills. Middle school students are often taught how to use career exploration computer programs to assess their career talents and engage in occupational searches. High school counselors link students' interests and skills with occupational and educational options. They also advise students to engage in career planning and be realistic about their career possibilities. High school counselors may guide students to attend career fairs, visit college campuses, and participate in career internships.

However, too many adolescents receive little direction from school guidance counselors and do not adequately explore careers on their own. On the average, high school students spend less than three hours per year with guidance counselors, and in some schools the average is even less. School counseling has been criticized both inside and outside the educational establishment. Insiders complain about the large number of students per school counselor and the weight of noncounseling administrative duties. Outsiders complain that school counseling is ineffective, biased, and a waste of money. Clearly, major improvements can be made in the area of school counseling.

Armando Ronquillo is one high school counselor who has made a difference in the lives of many students. To read about his work helping youth to plot their course to college, see the *Connecting with Careers* profile.

How Would You...?
If you were a **psychologist,** how would you discuss career development with adolescents?

Socioeconomic Status   The channels of upward mobility open to lower-SES youth are largely educational in nature. The school hierarchy from grade school through high school, as well as through college and graduate school, is programmed to orient individuals toward some type of career. Less than 100 years ago, it was believed that only eight years of education were necessary for vocational competence, and anything beyond that qualified the individual for advanced placement in higher-status occupations. By the middle of the twentieth century, the high school diploma had already lost ground as a ticket to career success, and in today's workplace college is a prerequisite for entering a higher-status occupation.

Many of the ideas that have guided career development theory were based on experiences in middle-income and well-educated contexts. Underlying this theory is the concept that individuals have a wide range of career choices from which to select. However, youth in low-income circumstances may have more limited career choices. Barriers such as low-quality schools, violence, and lack of access to jobs can restrict low-income inner-city youths' access to desirable careers (Foskett, Dyke, & Maringe, 2008).

Review Connect Reflect

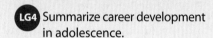 Summarize career development in adolescence.

Review

- What developmental changes characterize career development?
- What are some key cognitive processes in career development in adolescence?
- How do sociocultural contexts influence career development?

Connect

- Are there aspects of executive functioning (discussed earlier in this chapter and in Chapters 9 and 12) that might be applied to understanding the cognitive factors involved in adolescents' career development?

Reflect Your Own Personal Journey of Life

- What careers interested you during adolescence? How have your career interests changed since high school? What have been some key influences on your career decision making?

topical connections

The next chapter concludes our exploration of the journey through childhood and adolescence. You will read about how adolescents spend more time thinking about their identity—who they are, what they are all about, and where they are going in life—than they did when they were children. Time spent with peers increases in adolescence, and friendships become more intense and intimate. Dating and romantic relationships also become more central to the lives of most adolescents. Parents continue to have an important influence on adolescent development. Having good relationships with parents provides support for adolescents as they seek greater autonomy and explore a widening social world. Problems that adolescents can develop include juvenile delinquency, depression, and suicide.

looking forward

How Do Adolescents Think and Process Information?

 LG1 Discuss different approaches to adolescent cognition.

Piaget's Theory

- During the formal operational stage, Piaget's fourth stage of cognitive development, thinking is more abstract, idealistic, and logical than during the concrete operational stage. Adolescents become capable of hypothetical-deductive reasoning. However, many adolescents are not formal operational thinkers but are consolidating their concrete operational thought. Piaget made a number of important contributions to understanding children's development, but his theory has undergone considerable criticism.

Adolescent Egocentrism

- Elkind proposed that adolescents, especially young adolescents, develop an egocentrism that includes both an imaginary audience (the belief that others are as interested in the adolescent as the adolescent is) and a personal fable (a sense of uniqueness and invincibility).

Information Processing

- Key changes in information processing especially involve executive functioning. These changes focus on monitoring and management of cognitive resources, control of attention and reduction of interfering thoughts, use of working memory, decision making, critical thinking, and metacognition. It is increasingly thought that executive functioning strengthens during adolescence. Adolescence is a time of increased decision making. Older adolescents make better decisions than younger adolescents, who in turn are better at this skill than children are. Being able to make competent decisions, however, does not mean they actually will make such decisions in everyday life, where breadth of experience comes into play. One proposal to explain effective adolescent decision making is the dual-process model. Adolescence is an important transitional period in critical thinking because of cognitive changes such as increased speed, automaticity, and capacity of information processing; greater breadth of content knowledge; increased ability to construct new combinations of knowledge; and increased use of spontaneous strategies.

What Characterizes Adolescents' Values, Moral Education, and Religion?

 LG2 Describe adolescents' values, moral education, and religion.

Values

- Values are beliefs and attitudes about the way things should be. Over the past four decades, traditional-aged college students have shown an increased concern for personal well-being and a decreased interest in the welfare of others. Recently, U.S. college freshmen have shown an increased interest in developing a meaningful philosophy of life. Service learning is a form of education that promotes social responsibility and service to the community. Service learning is increasingly required by schools and has positive effects on adolescent development.

Moral Education

- The hidden curriculum is a term used by Dewey to describe his belief that even when schools do not have specific moral education programs, every school does provide a moral education. Character education is a direct education approach that advocates teaching adolescents a basic moral literacy. Cognitive moral education (often based on Kohlberg's theory) states that students should develop such values as democracy and justice as their moral reasoning develops. Cheating is a moral education concern and can take many forms. Various aspects of the situation influence whether students will cheat or not. Recently, an integrative moral education approach has been advocated.

- Distinctions have been made between the concepts of religion, religiousness, and spirituality. Religious issues are important to adolescents. Adolescence may be a special juncture in religious development for many individuals. Various aspects of religion are linked with positive outcomes in adolescent development. Religious affiliation is linked to lower drug use and delinquency rates, less school truancy, and lower rates of depression. Erikson's ideas on identity can be applied to understanding the increased interest in religion during adolescence. Piaget's theory provides a theoretical foundation for understanding developmental changes in religion. When adolescents have a positive relationship with parents, and/or are securely attached to them, they often adopt their parents' religious beliefs. Links have been found between adolescent sexuality and religiousness.

What Is the Nature of Schools for Adolescents?

LG3 Characterize schools for adolescents.

The American Middle School

- The transition to middle or junior high school coincides with many physical, cognitive, and socioemotional changes. The transition involves moving from the top-dog position to the lowest position, and this transition is difficult for many children. U.S. middle schools have been criticized as too massive and impersonal, with curricula that are often irrelevant. Recommendations for improving U.S. middle schools include developing small communities of students within the schools, maintaining lower student-to-counselor ratios, and raising academic standards. Participation in extracurricular activities is associated with positive academic and psychological outcomes.

The American High School

- The American high school needs to prepare students for today's workplace by providing them with an education that gives them skills in computer use, effective written and oral communication, high-level reading comprehension, and working in groups with diverse others.

High School Dropouts

- Many school dropouts have educational deficiencies that limit their economic and social well-being for much of their adult lives. Progress has been made in lowering the dropout rate for African American youth, but the dropout rates for Native American and Latino youth remain very high. Native American youth have the highest dropout rate. Males are more likely to drop out of high school than females. Dropping out of school is associated with demographic, family-related, peer-related, school-related, economic, and personal factors.

How Do Adolescents Experience Career Development?

 Summarize career development in adolescence.

Developmental Changes

- Many children have fantasies about what careers they want to enter when they grow up. In high school, these fantasies have decreased for many individuals, although too many adolescents have a fantasy career they want to reach but don't have an adequate plan for how to reach their aspirations. In the late teens and early twenties, career decision making usually has turned more serious.

Exploration, Decision Making, and Planning

- Exploration, decision making, and planning of career options are important aspects of adolescents' career development. Too many youth flounder and make unplanned career choices.

Sociocultural Influences

- Sociocultural influences include parents and peers, schools, and socioeconomic status. The channels of opportunity for adolescents from low-income families are primarily educational.

key terms

hypothetical-deductive reasoning 457	personal fable 458	hidden curriculum 465	religion 467
adolescent egocentrism 458	dual-process model 462	character education 466	religiousness 468
imaginary audience 458	values 464	cognitive moral education 466	spirituality 468
	service learning 464		top-dog phenomenon 471

key people

Jean Piaget 456	John Dewey 465	Pamela King 467	William Damon 476
David Elkind 458	Lawrence Kohlberg 466	Erik Erikson 469	
Deanna Kuhn 459	Darcia Narváez 466		

connecting with improving the lives of children

MAKING A DIFFERENCE

Supporting Adolescents' Cognitive Development

What are some good strategies for nourishing adolescents' cognitive development?

- *Provide support for adolescents' information processing.* Provide opportunities and guide adolescents in making good decisions, especially in real-world settings; stimulate adolescents to think critically; and encourage them to engage in self-regulatory learning.
- *Give adolescents opportunities to discuss moral dilemmas.* Provide adolescents with group opportunities to discuss the importance of cooperation, trust, and caring.
- *Create better schools for adolescents.* Schools for adolescents need to emphasize socioemotional development as well as cognitive development.
- *Take individual variation in adolescents seriously.*
- *Develop curricula that involve high expectations for success and the support to attain that success.*
- *Develop smaller communities.*
- *Involve parents and community leaders more.*
- *Break down the barriers between school and work to reduce the high school dropout rate.*
- *Provide adolescents with information about careers.* Adolescents do not get adequate information about careers. Career decision making needs to be given a higher priority in schools.

RESOURCES

Adolescent Thinking
by Deanna Kuhn (2009)
In R. M. Lerner & L. Steinberg (Eds.), *Handbook of Adolescent Psychology* (3rd ed.)
New York: Wiley

An in-depth examination of the important changes in executive functioning and other aspects of cognitive development in adolescence.

National Dropout Prevention Center
www.dropoutprevention.org

Acts as a clearinghouse for information about dropout prevention and at-risk youth and publishes the *National Dropout Prevention Newsletter*.

Turning Points 2000
by Gayle Davis and Anthony Jackson (2000)
New York: Teachers College Press.

This follow-up to earlier Turning Points recommendations includes a number of strategies for meeting the educational needs of adolescents, especially young adolescents.

SOCIOEMOTIONAL DEVELOPMENT IN ADOLESCENCE

The mayor of the city says that she is "everywhere." She recently persuaded the city's school committee to consider ending the practice of locking tardy students out of their classrooms. She also swayed a neighborhood group to support her proposal for a winter jobs program. According to one city councilman, "People are just impressed with the power of her arguments and the sophistication of the argument" (Silva, 2005, pp. B1, B4). She is Jewel E. Cash, and she is just 16 years old.

A junior at the prestigious Boston Latin Academy, Jewel was raised in one of Boston's housing projects by her mother, a single parent. Today she is a member of the Boston Student Advisory Council, mentors children, volunteers at a women's shelter, manages and dances in two troupes, and is a member of a neighborhood watch group—among other activities. Jewel is far from typical, but her activities illustrate that cognitive and socioemotional development allows adolescents—including adolescents from disadvantaged backgrounds—to be capable, effective individuals.

Jewel Cash seated next to her mother participating in a crime watch meeting at a community center.

topical connections

In the two preceding chapters, you explored changes in the physical and cognitive development of adolescents. And in Chapter 13, you read about socioemotional development in middle and late childhood, including how self-understanding and understanding others becomes more sophisticated, emotional understanding improves, and moral reasoning advances. In Erikson's view, in middle and late childhood, children are in the industry versus inferiority stage. Children at this developmental stage spend more time with peers, but parents continue to play important roles in their development, especially in guiding their academic achievement and managing their opportunities. Peer status and friendship become more important in children's peer relations, and school takes on a stronger academic focus. In this chapter, we will examine a key feature of adolescent development—exploring an identity. We will also look at changing relationships with parents and peers, then consider some problems that can develop, such as delinquency.

◀ — *looking back*

preview

Significant changes characterize socioemotional development in adolescence. These changes include increased efforts to understand oneself, a search for identity, and emotional fluctuations. Changes also occur in the social contexts of adolescents' lives, with transformations occurring in relationships with families and peers. Adolescents are also at risk for developing socioemotional problems such as delinquency and depression.

What Characterizes Emotional and Personality Development in Adolescence?

 LG1 Discuss changes in identity and emotional development during adolescence.

Identity   Emotional Development

> "Who are you?" said the Caterpillar. Alice replied, rather shyly, "I—I hardly know, Sir, just at present—at least I know who I was when I got up this morning, but I must have changed several times since then."
>
> —**LEWIS CARROLL**
> *English Writer, 19th Century*

Jewel Cash told an interviewer from the *Boston Globe,* "I see a problem and I say, 'How can I make a difference?' . . . I can't take on the world, even though I can try. . . . I'm moving forward but I want to make sure I'm bringing people with me" (Silva, 2005, pp. B1, B4). Jewel's confidence, positive identity, and emotional maturity sound at least as impressive as her activities. In this section, we examine how adolescents develop characteristics like these.

IDENTITY

"Who am I? What am I all about? What am I going to do with my life? What is different about me? How can I make it on my own?" These questions reflect the search for an identity. By far the most comprehensive and provocative theory of identity development is Erik Erikson's. In this section, we examine his views on identity. We also discuss contemporary research on how identity develops and how social contexts influence that development.

What Is Identity?   Identity is a self-portrait composed of many pieces, including these:

- The career and work path the person wants to follow (vocational/career identity)
- Whether the person is conservative, liberal, or middle-of-the-road (political identity)
- The person's spiritual beliefs (religious identity)
- Whether the person is single, married, divorced, and so on (relationship identity)
- The extent to which the person is motivated to achieve and is intellectual (achievement, intellectual identity)
- Whether the person is heterosexual, homosexual, or bisexual (sexual identity)
- Which part of the world or country a person is from and how intensely the person identifies with his or her cultural heritage (cultural/ethnic identity)
- The kinds of things a person likes to do, which can include sports, music, hobbies, and so on (interests)
- The individual's personality characteristics (such as being introverted or extraverted, anxious or calm, friendly or hostile, and so on) (personality)
- The individual's body image (physical identity)

What are some important dimensions of identity?

identity versus identity confusion Erikson's fifth developmental stage, which occurs at about the time of adolescence. At this time, adolescents are faced with deciding who they are, what they are all about, and where they are going in life.

Synthesizing the identity components can be a long and drawn-out process, with many negations and affirmations of various roles and faces (Syed, 2011). Decisions are not made once and for all, but have to be made again and again. Identity development does not happen neatly, and it does not happen cataclysmically (Duriez & others, 2011; Schwartz & others, 2011).

Erikson's View   Questions about identity surface as common, virtually universal, concerns during adolescence. Some decisions made during adolescence might seem trivial: whether to study or play, whether to take a part-time job after school, whom to date, whether to break up with someone or stay in the relationship, whether or not to be politically active, and so on. Over the years of adolescence, however, such decisions begin to form the core of what the individual is all about as a human being—what is called his or her identity.

It was Erik Erikson (1950, 1968) who first understood the importance of questions about identity in understanding adolescent development. The fact that identity is now believed to be a key aspect of adolescent development is a result of Erikson's masterful thinking and analysis.

We discussed Erikson's theory in Chapter 1. Recall that his fifth developmental stage, which individuals experience during adolescence, is **identity versus identity confusion.** During this time, said Erikson, adolescents are faced with deciding who they are, what they are all about, and where they are going in life.

The search for an identity during adolescence is aided by a **psychosocial moratorium,** which is Erikson's term for the gap between childhood security and adult autonomy. During this period, society leaves adolescents relatively free of responsibilities and able to try out different identities. Adolescents in effect search their culture's identity files, experimenting with different roles and personalities. They may want to pursue one career one month (lawyer, for example) and another career the next month (doctor, actor, teacher, social worker, or astronaut, for example). They may dress neatly one day, sloppily the next. This experimentation is a deliberate effort on the part of adolescents to find out where they fit into the world. Most adolescents eventually discard undesirable roles.

Youth who successfully cope with conflicting identities emerge with a new sense of self that is both refreshing and acceptable. Adolescents who do not successfully resolve this identity crisis suffer what Erikson calls *identity confusion.* The confusion takes one of two courses: Individuals withdraw, isolating themselves from peers and family, or they immerse themselves in the world of peers and lose their identity in the crowd.

Developmental Changes   Although questions about identity may be especially important during adolescence, identity formation neither begins nor ends during these years. It begins with the appearance of attachment, the development of the sense of self, and the emergence of independence in infancy; the process reaches its final phase with a life review and integration in old age. What is important about identity development in adolescence, especially late adolescence, is that for the first time, physical development, cognitive development, and socioemotional development advance to the point at which the individual can sort through and synthesize childhood identities and identifications to construct a viable path toward adult maturity.

How do individual adolescents go about the process of forming an identity? Eriksonian researcher James Marcia (1980, 1994) argues that Erikson's theory of identity development contains four identity statuses, or ways of resolving the identity crisis: identity diffusion, identity foreclosure, identity moratorium, and identity achievement. What determines an individual's identity status? Marcia classifies individuals based on the existence or extent of their crisis or commitment (see Figure 16.1). **Crisis** is defined

> As long as one keeps searching, the answers come.
>
> —**JOAN BAEZ**
> *American Folk Singer, 20th Century*

developmental **connection**

Self and Identity. Erikson proposed that individuals go through eight stages in the course of human development. Chapter 1, p. 22

Erik Erikson.

> Once formed, an identity furnishes individuals with a historical sense of who they have been, a meaningful sense of who they are now, and a sense of who they might become in the future.
>
> —**JAMES MARCIA**
> *Contemporary Psychologist, Simon Fraser University*

psychosocial moratorium Erikson's term for the gap between childhood security and adult autonomy.

crisis Marcia's term for a period of identity development during which the individual is exploring alternatives.

	Has the person made a commitment?	
	Yes	**No**
Has the person explored meaningful alternatives regarding some identity question? **Yes**	Identity Achievement	Identity Moratorium
No	Identity Foreclosure	Identity Diffusion

FIGURE **16.1**

MARCIA'S FOUR STATUSES OF IDENTITY

How Would You...?

If you were a **psychologist,** how would you apply Marcia's theory of identity formation to describe your current identity status or the identity status of adolescents you know?

How does identity change in emerging adulthood?

commitment Marcia's term for the part of identity development in which individuals show a personal investment in identity.

identity diffusion Marcia's term for the status of individuals who have not yet experienced a crisis (explored alternatives) or made any commitments.

identity foreclosure Marcia's term for the status of individuals who have made a commitment but have not experienced a crisis.

as a period of identity development during which the individual is exploring alternatives. Most researchers use the term *exploration* rather than *crisis*. **Commitment** is personal investment in identity.

The four statuses of identity are as follows:

- **Identity diffusion,** the status of individuals who have not yet experienced a crisis or made any commitments. Not only are they undecided about occupational and ideological choices, but they are also likely to show little interest in such matters.

- **Identity foreclosure** is the status of individuals who have made a commitment but have not experienced a crisis. This occurs most often when parents hand down commitments to their adolescents, usually in an authoritarian way, before adolescents have had a chance to explore different approaches, ideologies, and vocations on their own.

- **Identity moratorium** is the status of individuals who are in the midst of a crisis but whose commitments are either absent or only vaguely defined.

- **Identity achievement** is the status of individuals who have undergone a crisis and have made a commitment.

Emerging Adulthood and Beyond   A recent study found that as individuals aged from early adolescence to emerging adulthood, they increasingly engaged in in-depth exploration of their identity (Klimstra & others, 2010). And a recent meta-analysis of 124 studies by Jane Kroger and her colleagues (2010) revealed that during adolescence and emerging adulthood, identity moratorium status rose steadily to age 19 and then declined; identity achievement rose across late adolescence and emerging adulthood; and foreclosure and diffusion statuses declined across the high school years but fluctuated in the late teens and emerging adulthood. The studies also found that a large proportion of individuals were not identity achieved by the time they reached their twenties.

Indeed, a consensus is developing that the key changes in identity are more likely to take place in emerging adulthood (18 to 25 years of age) or later than in adolescence (Moshman, 2011; Syed, 2011). For example, Alan Waterman (1985, 1999) has found that from the years preceding high school through the last few years of college, the number of individuals who are identity achieved increases, while the number who are identity diffused decreases. College upperclassmen are more likely to be identity achieved than college freshmen or high school students. Many young adolescents, on the other hand, are identity diffused. These developmental changes are especially true for vocational choice. In terms of religious beliefs and political ideology, fewer college students reach the identity-achieved status; a substantial number are characterized by foreclosure and diffusion. Thus, the timing of identity development may depend on the particular dimension.

Why might college produce some key changes in identity? Increased complexity in the reasoning skills of college students combined with a wide range of new experiences that highlight contrasts between home and college and between themselves and others stimulates them to reach a higher level of integrating various dimensions of their identity (Phinney, 2008).

Resolution of the identity issue during adolescence and emerging adulthood does not mean that a person's identity will be stable through the remainder of life.

Many individuals who develop positive identities follow what are called "MAMA" cycles—that is, their identity status changes from *m*oratorium to *a*chievement to *m*oratorium to *a*chievement (Marcia, 1994). These cycles may be repeated throughout life (Francis, Fraser, & Marcia, 1989). Marcia (2002) argues that the first identity is just that—it should not be viewed as the final product.

In short, questions about identity come up throughout life. An individual who develops a healthy identity is flexible and adaptive, open to changes in society, in relationships, and in careers. This openness ensures numerous reorganizations of identity throughout the individual's life.

Family Influences Parents are important figures in the adolescent's development of identity (Cooper, 2011). Researchers have found that a family atmosphere that promotes both individuality and connectedness is important in the adolescent's identity development (Cooper & Grotevant, 1989):

- **Individuality** consists of two dimensions: self-assertion (the ability to have and communicate a point of view) and separateness (the use of communication patterns to express how one is different from others).

- **Connectedness** also consists of two dimensions: mutuality, which involves sensitivity to and respect for others' views, and permeability, which involves openness to others' views.

In general, then, research indicates that identity formation is enhanced by family relationships that sustain both individuation, which encourages adolescents to develop their own point of view, and connectedness, which provides a secure base from which adolescents can explore their widening social worlds (Cooper, 2011). When connectedness is strong and individuation weak, adolescents often have an identity foreclosure status. When connectedness is weak, adolescents often reveal identity confusion.

Ethnic Identity Throughout the world, ethnic minority groups have struggled to maintain their ethnic identities while blending in with the dominant culture (Erikson, 1968). **Ethnic identity** is an enduring aspect of the self that includes a sense of membership in an ethnic group, along with the attitudes and feelings related to that membership. Thus, for adolescents from ethnic minority groups, the process of identity formation has an added dimension: the choice between two or more sources of identification—their own ethnic group and the mainstream or dominant culture (Phinney, 2008). Many adolescents resolve this choice by developing a *bicultural identity*. That is, they identify in some ways with their ethnic group and in other ways with the majority culture (Phinney, 2006).

For ethnic minority individuals, adolescence and emerging adulthood are often special junctures in their development (Syed, 2011). Although children are aware of some ethnic and cultural differences, individuals consciously confront their ethnicity for the first time in adolescence or emerging adulthood. Unlike children, adolescents and emerging adults are able to interpret ethnic and cultural information, to reflect on the past, and to speculate about the future.

The indicators of identity change often differ for each succeeding generation (Phinney & Ong, 2007). First-generation immigrants are likely to be secure in their identities and unlikely to change much; they may or may not develop a new identity. The degree to which they begin to feel "American" appears to be related to whether or not they learn English, develop social networks beyond their ethnic group, and become culturally competent in their new country. Second-generation immigrants are more likely to think of themselves as "American," possibly because citizenship is granted at birth. Their ethnic identity is likely to be linked to retention of their ethnic language and social networks. In the third and later generations, the issues become more complex. Historical, contextual, and political factors that are unrelated to acculturation may affect the extent to which members of this generation retain their ethnic identities.

How Would You...?
If you were a **human development and family studies professional,** how would you design a community program that assists ethnic minority adolescents to develop a healthy bicultural identity?

Michelle Chin, age 16: "Parents do not understand that teenagers need to find out who they are, which means a lot of experimenting, a lot of mood swings, a lot of emotions and awkwardness. Like any teenager, I am facing an identity crisis. I am still trying to figure out whether I am a Chinese American or an American with Asian eyes."

identity moratorium Marcia's term for the status of individuals who are in the midst of a crisis, but their commitments are either absent or vaguely defined.

identity achievement Marcia's term for the status of individuals who have undergone a crisis and have made a commitment.

individuality Characteristic consisting of two dimensions: self-assertion (the ability to have and communicate a point of view) and separateness (the use of communication patterns to express how one is different from others).

connectedness Characteristic consisting of two dimensions: mutuality (sensitivity to and respect for others' views) and permeability (openness to others' views).

ethnic identity An enduring, basic aspect of the self that includes a sense of membership in an ethnic group and the attitudes and feelings related to that membership.

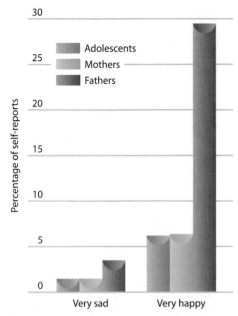

FIGURE 16.2

SELF-REPORTED EXTREMES OF EMOTION BY ADOLESCENTS, MOTHERS, AND FATHERS USING THE EXPERIENCE SAMPLING METHOD. In the study by Reed Larson and Maryse Richards (1994), adolescents and their mothers and fathers were beeped at random times by researchers using the experience sampling method. The researchers found that adolescents were more likely to report emotional extremes than their parents were.

Researchers are increasingly finding that a positive ethnic identity is linked to positive outcomes for ethnic minority adolescents (Umana-Taylor, Updegraff, & Gonzales-Bracken, 2011; Weisskirch & others, 2011). For example, in one study ethnic identity was related to higher school engagement and lower aggression (Van Buren & Graham, 2003). In another study, Navajo adolescents' affirmation and belonging to their ethnic heritage were linked to higher self-esteem, school connectedness, and social functioning (Jones & Galliher, 2007).

EMOTIONAL DEVELOPMENT

Adolescence has long been described as a time of emotional turmoil (Hall, 1904). In its extreme form, this view is too stereotypical because adolescents are not constantly in a state of "storm and stress." Nonetheless, early adolescence is a time when emotional highs and lows increase (Rosenblum & Lewis, 2003). Young adolescents can be on top of the world one moment and down in the dumps the next. In many instances, the intensity of their emotions seems out of proportion to the events that elicit them. Young adolescents might sulk a lot, not knowing how to adequately express their feelings. With little or no provocation, they might blow up at their parents or siblings or use defense mechanisms to displace their feelings onto another person.

Reed Larson and Maryse Richards (1994) found that adolescents reported more extreme emotions and more fleeting emotions than their parents did. For example, adolescents were five times more likely to report being "very happy" and three times more likely to report being "very sad" than their parents (see Figure 16.2). These findings lend support to the perception of adolescents as moody and changeable (Rosenblum & Lewis, 2003).

Researchers have also found that from the fifth through the ninth grades, both boys and girls experience a 50 percent decrease in being "very happy" (Larson & Lampman-Petraitis, 1989). In this same study, adolescents were more likely than preadolescents to report mildly negative mood states.

It is important for adults to recognize that moodiness is a *normal* aspect of early adolescence and that most adolescents make it through these moody times to become competent adults. Nonetheless, for some adolescents, such emotions can reflect serious problems. For example, rates of depressed moods become more elevated for girls during adolescence (Nolen-Hoeksema, 2011). Being able to control one's emotions is an important aspect of adolescent development (Steinberg & Collins, 2011).

Review *Connect* Reflect

LG1 Discuss changes in identity and emotional development during adolescence.

Review

- How does identity develop in adolescence?
- What factors affect emotional development in adolescence?

Connect

- What characterizes emotional development in middle adulthood? (See Chapter 13.) How do those changes compare with what you have just read about emotional development in adolescence?

Reflect *Your Own Personal Journey of Life*

- Where are you in your identity development? Get out a sheet of paper

and list each of the pieces of identity (vocational, political, religious, relationship, achievement/intellectual, sexual, cultural/ethnic, interests, personality, and physical) in a column on the left side of the paper. Then write the four identity statuses (diffused, foreclosed, moratorium, and achieved) across the top of the page. For each dimension of identity, place a check mark in the column that reflects your identity status. If you checked diffused or foreclosed for any of the dimensions, think about what you need to do to move on to a moratorium status in those areas.

What Is the Nature of Parent-Adolescent Relationships?

Parental Monitoring

Autonomy and Attachment

Parent-Adolescent Conflict

Adolescence typically alters the relationship between parents and their children. Among the most important aspects of family relationships that change during adolescence are those that involve parental monitoring, autonomy, attachment, and parent-adolescent conflict.

PARENTAL MONITORING

In Chapter 13, we discussed the important role that parents play as managers of their children's development. A key aspect of the managerial role of parenting is effective monitoring, which is especially important as children move into the adolescent years (Guilamo-Ramos, Jaccard, & Dittus, 2010; Smetana, 2011a, b). Monitoring includes supervising adolescents' choice of social settings, activities, and friends, as well as their academic efforts. Later in this chapter, we will describe lack of adequate parental monitoring as the parental factor most likely to be linked to juvenile delinquency.

A current interest involving parental monitoring focuses on adolescents' management of their parents' access to information, especially disclosing or concealing strategies about their activities (Amsel & Smetana, 2011; Hamza & Willoughby, 2010; Keijsers & Laird, 2010). Adolescents are more willing to disclose information when parents ask adolescents questions and when adolescents' relationship with parents is characterized by a high level of trust, acceptance, and quality (Daddis & Randolph, 2010; Keijsers & Laird, 2010). Researchers have found that adolescents' disclosure to parents about their whereabouts, activities, and friends is linked to positive adolescent adjustment (Laird & Marrero, 2010; Smetana, 2011a, b).

What role does parental monitoring play in adolescent development?

AUTONOMY AND ATTACHMENT

With most adolescents, parents are likely to find themselves engaged in a delicate balancing act, weighing competing needs for autonomy and control, for independence and connection.

The Push for Autonomy The typical adolescent's push for autonomy and responsibility puzzles and angers many parents. As parents see their teenager slipping from their grasp, they may have an urge to take stronger control. Heated emotional exchanges may ensue, with either side calling names, making threats, and doing whatever seems necessary to gain control. Parents may seem frustrated because they *expect* their teenager to heed their advice, to want to spend time with the family, and to grow up to do what is right. Most parents anticipate that their teenager will have some difficulty adjusting to the changes that adolescence brings, but few parents imagine and predict just how strong an adolescent's desires will be to spend time with peers or how intensely adolescents will want to show that it is they—not their parents—who are responsible for their successes and failures.

Adolescents' ability to attain autonomy and gain control over their behavior is acquired through appropriate adult reactions to their desire for control (Steinberg & Collins, 2011). At the onset of adolescence, the average individual does not have the knowledge to make appropriate or mature decisions in all areas

> In case you're worried about what's going to become of the younger generation, it's going to grow up and start worrying about the younger generation.
>
> —ROGER ALLEN
> *Contemporary American Writer*

> When I was a boy of 14, my father was so ignorant I could hardly stand to have the man around. But when I got to be 21, I was astonished at how much he had learnt in 7 years.
>
> —MARK TWAIN
> *American Writer and Humorist, 20th Century*

Stacey Christensen, age 16: "I am lucky enough to have open communication with my parents. Whenever I am in need or just need to talk, my parents are there for me. My advice to parents is to let your teens grow at their own pace, be open with them so that you can be there for them. We need guidance, our parents need to help but not be too overwhelming."

developmental **connection**

Attachment. In secure attachment, babies use the caregiver as a secure base from which to explore the environment. Chapter 7, p. 218

It is not enough for parents to understand children. They must accord children the privilege of understanding them.

—MILTON SAPIRSTEIN
American Psychiatrist, 20th Century

How Would You…?

If you were a **social worker,** how would you counsel parents who are experiencing stress about anticipated family conflicts as their child enters adolescence?

of life. As the adolescent pushes for autonomy, the wise adult relinquishes control in those areas where the adolescent can make reasonable decisions, but continues to guide the adolescent to make reasonable decisions in areas in which the adolescent's knowledge is more limited. Gradually, adolescents acquire the ability to make mature decisions on their own.

Gender differences characterize autonomy-granting in adolescence. Boys are given more independence than girls. In one study, this tendency was especially true in U.S. families with a traditional gender-role orientation (Bumpus, Crouter, & McHale, 2001). Also, Latino parents protect and monitor their daughters more closely than do non-Latino White parents (Allen & others, 2008).

The Role of Attachment   Recall from Chapter 7, "Socioemotional Development in Infancy," that one of the most widely discussed aspects of socioemotional development in infancy is secure attachment to caregivers (Sroufe, Coffino, & Carlson, 2010). In the past decade, researchers have explored whether secure attachment also might be an important concept in adolescents' relationships with their parents. For example, Joseph Allen and his colleagues (Allen, 2007, 2008; Allen & others, 2007, 2009) found that securely attached adolescents were less likely than those who were insecurely attached to engage in problem behaviors such as juvenile delinquency and drug abuse. In a recent longitudinal study, Allen and colleagues (2009) found that secure attachment at 14 years of age was linked to a number of positive outcomes at 21 years of age, including relationship competence, financial/career competence, and fewer problematic behaviors. In a recent analysis, it was concluded that the most consistent outcomes of secure attachment in adolescence involve positive peer relations and development of the adolescent's emotion regulation capacities (Allen & Miga, 2010).

A recent study using the Important People Interview (IPI) assessed the attachments of high school students (14 to 18 years old) and emerging adult college students (18 to 23 years old) to the four most important people in their lives, followed by their four most important peers (Rosenthal & Kobak, 2010). After identifying the important people in their lives, students rank-ordered the people in terms of the following contexts: attachment bond (closeness, separation distress, and an emergency situation), support seeking (comfort or support in daily contexts), and affiliative (enjoyable social contact). College students placed romantic partners in higher positions and fathers in lower positions than did high school students. Friends' placements in higher positions and fathers' exclusion from the most important people list or as the fourth most important person were linked to increased behavior problems (internalizing—depression, for example, and externalizing—rule-breaking, for example).

PARENT-ADOLESCENT CONFLICT

Although parent-adolescent conflict increases in early adolescence, it does not reach the tumultuous proportions G. Stanley Hall envisioned at the beginning of the twentieth century. Rather, much of the conflict involves the everyday events of family life, such as keeping a bedroom clean, dressing neatly, getting home by a certain time, and not talking for hours on the phone. The conflicts rarely involve major dilemmas such as drugs or delinquency.

Conflict with parents often escalates during early adolescence, remains somewhat stable during the high school years, and then lessens in emerging adulthood. Parent-adolescent relationships become more positive if adolescents go away to college than if they attend college while living at home (Sullivan & Sullivan, 1980).

The everyday conflicts that characterize parent-adolescent relationships may actually serve a positive developmental function. These minor disputes and negotiations

Strategies for Parenting Adolescents

Competent adolescent development is most likely when adolescents have parents who:

- *Show them warmth and respect, and avoid the tendency to be too controlling or too permissive.*
- *Serve as positive role models for adolescents.*
- *Demonstrate sustained interest in their lives.* Parents need to spend time with their adolescents and monitor their lives.
- *Understand and adapt to their cognitive and socioemotional development.*

- *Communicate expectations for high standards of conduct and achievement.*
- *Display constructive ways of dealing with problems and conflict.* Moderate conflict is a normal part of the adolescent's desire for independence and search for an identity.
- *Understand that adolescents don't become adults overnight.* Adolescence is a long journey.

facilitate the adolescent's transition from being dependent on parents to becoming an autonomous individual.

The old model of parent-adolescent relationships suggested that as adolescents mature they detach themselves from parents and move into a world of autonomy apart from parents. The old model also suggested that parent-adolescent conflict is intense and stressful throughout adolescence. The new model emphasizes that parents serve as important attachment figures and support systems while adolescents explore a wider, more complex social world. The new model also emphasizes that, in most families, parent-adolescent conflict is moderate rather than severe and that the everyday negotiations and minor disputes not only are normal but also can serve the positive developmental function of helping the adolescent make the transition from childhood dependency to adult independence (see Figure 16.3).

Still, a high degree of conflict characterizes some parent-adolescent relationships. One estimate of the proportion of parents and adolescents who engage in prolonged, intense, repeated, unhealthy conflict is about one in five families (Montemayor, 1982). This prolonged, intense conflict is associated with various adolescent problems: movement out of the home, juvenile delinquency, school dropout, pregnancy and early marriage, membership in religious cults, and drug abuse. To read about some effective strategies for parenting adolescents, see the *Caring Connections* interlude.

Conflict with parents increases in early adolescence. *What is the nature of this conflict in a majority of American families?*

Old Model		New Model
Autonomy, detachment from parents; parent and peer worlds are isolated		Attachment and autonomy; parents are important support systems and attachment figures; adolescent-parent and adolescent-peer worlds have some important connections
Intense, stressful conflict throughout adolescence; parent-adolescent relationships are filled with storm and stress on virtually a daily basis		Moderate parent-adolescent conflict is common and can serve a positive developmental function; conflict greater in early adolescence

FIGURE **16.3**

OLD AND NEW MODELS OF PARENT-ADOLESCENT RELATIONSHIPS

What Aspects of Peer Relationships Are Important in Adolescence?

LG3 Characterize the changes that occur in peer relations during adolescence.

Friendship | Peer Groups | Dating and Romantic Relationships

Peers play powerful roles in the lives of adolescents (Bukowski, Buhrmester, & Underwood, 2011). Peer relations undergo important changes in adolescence, including changes in friendships and in peer groups and the beginning of romantic relationships. In middle and late childhood, as we discussed in Chapter 13, "Socioemotional Development in Middle and Late Childhood," the focus of peer relations is on being liked by classmates and on being included in games or lunchroom conversations. Being overlooked or, worse yet, being rejected can have damaging effects on children's development that sometimes are carried forward to adolescence.

FRIENDSHIP

For most children, being popular with their peers is a strong motivator. In early adolescence, being popular with peers continues to be important but teenagers also typically begin to prefer to have a smaller number of friendships that are more intense and intimate than those of young children.

Harry Stack Sullivan (1953) was the most influential theorist to discuss the importance of adolescent friendships. In contrast with other psychoanalytic theorists who focused almost exclusively on parent-child relationships, Sullivan argued that friends are also important in shaping the development of children and adolescents. Everyone, said Sullivan, has basic social needs, such as the need for tenderness (secure attachment), playful companionship, social acceptance, intimacy, and sexual relations. Whether or not these needs are fulfilled largely determines our emotional well-being. For example, if the need for playful companionship goes unmet, then we become bored and depressed; if the need for social acceptance is not met, we suffer a lowered sense of self-worth.

During adolescence, said Sullivan, friends become increasingly important in meeting social needs. In particular, Sullivan argued, the need for intimacy intensifies during early adolescence and motivates teenagers to seek out close friends. If adolescents fail to forge such close friendships, they experience loneliness and a reduced sense of self-worth.

Many of Sullivan's ideas have withstood the test of time (Buhrmester & Chong, 2009). For example, adolescents report disclosing intimate and personal information

What changes take place in friendship during the adolescent years?

to their friends more often than do younger children (Buhrmester, 1998) (see Figure 16.4). Adolescents also say they depend more on friends than on parents to satisfy their needs for companionship, reassurance of worth, and intimacy. The ups and downs of experiences with friends shape adolescents' well-being (Vitaro, Boivin, & Bukowski, 2009).

Although having friends can be a developmental advantage, not all friendships are alike and the quality of friendship is also important to consider (Rubin & others, 2011). People differ in the company they keep—that is, who their friends are. It is a developmental disadvantage to have coercive, conflict-ridden, and poor-quality friendships (Ali & Dwyer, 2011; Poulin & others, 2011). Developmental advantages occur when adolescents have friends who are socially skilled, supportive, and oriented toward academic achievement (Crosnoe & others, 2008).

Researchers have found that interacting with delinquent peers and friends greatly increases the risk of becoming delinquent (Bukowski, Motzoi, & Meyer, 2009). Further, not having a close relationship with a best friend, having less contact with friends, having friends who are depressed, and experiencing peer rejection all increase depressive tendencies in adolescents (Brendgen & others, 2010).

Although most adolescents develop friendships with individuals who are close to their own age, some adolescents become best friends with younger or older individuals. Do older friends encourage adolescents to engage in delinquent behavior or early sexual behavior? Adolescents who interact with older youth engage in these behaviors more frequently (Billy, Rodgers, & Udry, 1984).

PEER GROUPS

How extensive is peer pressure in adolescence? What roles do cliques and crowds play in adolescents' lives? As we see next, researchers have found that the standards of peer groups and the influence of crowds and cliques become increasingly important during adolescence.

Peer Pressure   Young adolescents conform more to peer standards than children do. Around the eighth and ninth grades, conformity to peers—especially to their antisocial standards—peaks (Brown & Larson, 2009). At this point, adolescents are most likely to go along with a peer to steal hubcaps off a car, draw graffiti on a wall, or steal cosmetics from a store counter.

Which adolescents are most likely to conform to peers? Mitchell Prinstein and his colleagues (Cohen & Prinstein, 2006; Prinstein, 2007; Prinstein & others, 2009) have recently conducted research and analysis addressing this question. They conclude that adolescents who are uncertain about their social identity, which can appear in the form of low self-esteem and high social anxiety, are most likely to conform to peers. This uncertainty often increases during times of change, such as school and family transitions. Also, adolescents are more likely to conform when they are in the presence of someone they perceive to have higher status than themselves.

Cliques and Crowds   Cliques and crowds assume more important roles in the lives of adolescents than the lives of children (Brown, 2011; Daddis, 2010). **Cliques** are small groups that range from 2 to about 12 individuals and average about 5 or 6 individuals. The clique members are usually of the same sex and about the same age.

Cliques can form because adolescents engage in similar activities, such as being in a club or on a sports team (Brown, 2011; Brown & Dietz, 2009). Several adolescents may form a clique because they have spent time with each other, share mutual interests, and enjoy each other's company. Not necessarily friends, they often develop a friendship if they stay in the clique. What do adolescents do in cliques? They share ideas and hang out together. Often they develop an in-group identity in which they believe that their clique is better than other cliques.

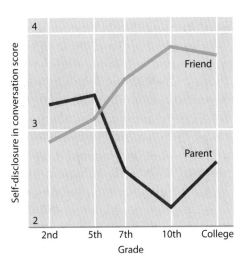

FIGURE **16.4**

DEVELOPMENTAL CHANGES IN SELF-DISCLOSING CONVERSATIONS: Self-disclosing conversations with friends increased dramatically in adolescence while declining in an equally dramatic fashion with parents. However, self-disclosing conversations with parents began to pick up somewhat during the college years. The measure of self-disclosure involved a 5-point rating scale completed by the children and youth, with a higher score representing greater self-disclosure. The data shown represent the means for each age group.

What characterizes peer pressure in adolescence?

clique A small group that ranges from 2 to about 12 individuals, averaging about 5 or 6 individuals, and one that can form because adolescents engage in similar activities.

What characterizes adolescents' cliques and crowds?

Crowds are larger than cliques and less personal. Adolescents are usually members of a crowd based on reputation, and they may or may not spend much time together. Many crowds are defined by the activities adolescents engage in (such as "jocks" who are good at sports or "druggies" who take drugs) (Brown, 2011). Reputation-based crowds often appear for the first time in early adolescence and usually become less prominent in late adolescence (Collins & Steinberg, 2006).

In one study, crowd membership was associated with adolescent self-esteem (Brown & Lohr, 1987). The crowds included jocks (athletically oriented), populars (well-known students who led social activities), normals (middle-of-the-road students who made up the masses), druggies or toughs (known for illicit drug use or other delinquent activities), and nobodies (low in social skills or intellectual abilities). The self-esteem of the jocks and the populars was highest, whereas that of the nobodies was lowest. One group of adolescents not in a crowd had self-esteem equivalent to that of the jocks and the populars; this group was the independents, who indicated that crowd membership was not important to them. Keep in mind that these data are correlational; self-esteem could increase an adolescent's probability of becoming a crowd member, just as crowd membership could increase the adolescent's self-esteem.

DATING AND ROMANTIC RELATIONSHIPS

Adolescents spend considerable time either dating or thinking about dating (Connolly & McIsaac, 2009). Dating can be a form of recreation, a source of status, and a setting for learning about close relationships, as well as a way of finding a mate.

Types of Dating and Developmental Changes   A number of dating variations and developmental changes characterize dating and romantic relationships. First, we examine heterosexual romantic relationships, and then we turn to romantic relationships among sexual minority youth (gay and lesbian adolescents).

Heterosexual Romantic Relationships   Three stages characterize the development of romantic relationships in adolescence (Connolly & McIsaac, 2009):

What are some developmental changes in romantic relationships in adolescence?

- *Entering into romantic attractions and affiliations at about 11 to 13 years of age.* This initial stage is triggered by puberty. From 11 to 13, adolescents become intensely interested in romance, and it dominates many conversations with same-sex friends. Developing a crush on someone is common, and the crush often is shared with a same-sex friend. Young adolescents may or may not interact with the individual who is the object of their infatuation. When dating occurs, it usually occurs in a group setting.

- *Exploring romantic relationships at approximately 14 to 16 years of age.* At this point in adolescence, two types of romantic involvement occur: casual dating and group dating. *Casual dating* emerges between individuals who are mutually attracted. These dating experiences are often short-lived, last a few months at best, and usually endure for only a few weeks. Dating in groups is common and reflects embeddedness in the peer context. Friends often act as a third-party facilitator of a potential dating relationship by communicating their friend's romantic interest and confirming whether this attraction is reciprocated.

crowd A larger group than a clique, one that is usually formed based on reputation; members may or may not spend much time together.

- *Consolidating dyadic romantic bonds at about 17 to 19 years of age.* At the end of the high school years, more serious romantic relationships develop. This is characterized by strong emotional bonds more closely resembling those in adult romantic relationships. These bonds often are more stable and enduring than earlier bonds, typically lasting one year or more.

Two variations on these stages in the development of romantic relationships in adolescence involve early and late bloomers (Connolly & McIsaac, 2009). *Early bloomers* include 15 to 20 percent of 11- to 13-year-olds who say that they currently are in a romantic relationship and 35 percent who indicate that they have had some prior experience in romantic relationships. *Late bloomers* comprise approximately 10 percent of 17- to 19-years-olds who say that they have had no experience with romantic relationships and another 15 percent who report that they have not engaged in any romantic relationships that lasted more than four months.

Romantic Relationships in Sexual Minority Youth   Recently, researchers have begun to study romantic relationships in gay and lesbian youth (Diamond, 2011; Savin-Williams, 2011). Many sexual minority youth date other-sex peers, a practice that can help them to clarify their sexual orientation or disguise it from others. Most gay and lesbian youth have had some same-sex sexual experience, often with peers who are "experimenting" and then go on to a primarily heterosexual orientation (Diamond, 2011; Savin-Williams, 2011); however, relatively few gay and lesbian youth have had same-sex romantic relationships.

Sociocultural Contexts and Dating   The sociocultural context exerts a powerful influence on adolescents' dating patterns. This influence may be seen in differences in dating patterns among ethnic groups within the United States.

Values, religious beliefs, and traditions often dictate at what age dating begins, how much freedom in dating is allowed, whether dates must be chaperoned by adults or parents, and the roles of males and females in dating. For example, Latino and Asian American cultures have more conservative standards regarding adolescent dating than does the Anglo-American culture. Dating may become a source of conflict within a family if the parents have immigrated from cultures in which dating begins at a late age, little freedom in dating is allowed, dates are chaperoned, and dating by adolescent girls is especially restricted. When immigrant adolescents choose to adopt the ways of the dominant U.S. culture (such as unchaperoned dating), they often clash with parents and extended-family members who have more traditional values.

In one study, Latina young adults in the midwestern United States reflected on their experiences in dating during adolescence (Raffaelli & Ontai, 2004). They said that their parents placed strict boundaries on their romantic involvement. As a result, the young women said that their adolescent dating experiences were filled with tension and conflict. Over half of the Latinas engaged in "sneak dating" without their parents' knowledge.

Dating and Adjustment   Researchers have linked dating and romantic relationships with how well adjusted adolescents are (Crissey, 2009). For example, a recent study of 200 tenth-graders revealed that the more romantic experiences they had, the higher were their reported levels of social acceptance, friendship competence, and romantic competence—however, having more romantic experience also was linked to a higher level of substance use, delinquency, and sexual behavior (Furman, Low, & Ho, 2009). In another study, for adolescent girls but not adolescent boys, having an older romantic partner was linked to an increase in depressive symptoms, largely influenced by an increase in substance use (Haydon & Halpern, 2010).

What characterizes romantic relationships in sexual minority youth?

How Would You...?
If you were a **human development and family studies professional,** how would you explain to parents the developmental challenges faced by a gay or lesbian adolescent?

How are romantic relationships linked to adolescent adjustment?

Dating and romantic relationships at an unusually early age also have been linked with several problems (Connolly & McIsaac, 2009). For example, early dating and "going with" someone are associated with adolescent pregnancy and problems at home and school (Furman & Collins, 2009). In one study, girls' early romantic involvement was linked with lower grades, less active participation in class discussion, and other school-related problems (Buhrmester, 2001).

Review Connect Reflect

LG3 Characterize the changes that occur in peer relations during adolescence.

Review

- What changes take place in friendship during adolescence?
- What are adolescents' peer groups like?
- What is the nature of adolescent dating and romantic relationships?

Connect

- Piece together the information discussed in Chapter 14 about sexual development in adolescence with the coverage of dating and romantic relationships in this chapter to construct a profile of positive adolescent development.

Reflect *Your Own Personal Journey of Life*

- What were your peer relationships like during adolescence? What peer groups were you involved in? How did they influence your development? What were your dating and romantic relationships like in adolescence? If you could change anything about the way you experienced peer relations in adolescence, what would it be?

Why Is Culture an Important Context for Adolescent Development?

LG4 Explain how culture influences adolescent development.

Cross-Cultural Comparisons   Ethnicity   Media and Technology

We live in an increasingly diverse world, one in which there is increasing contact between adolescents from different cultures and ethnic groups. In this section, we explore these differences as they relate to adolescents, and turn to media influences on adolescents.

CROSS-CULTURAL COMPARISONS

What traditions remain for adolescents around the globe? What circumstances are changing adolescents' lives?

Traditions and Changes in Adolescence Around the Globe Consider some of the variations of adolescence around the world (Brown & Larson, 2002):

- Two-thirds of Asian Indian adolescents accept their parents' choice of a marital partner for them.
- In the Philippines, many female adolescents sacrifice their own futures by migrating to the city to earn money that they send home to their families.
- In the Middle East, many adolescents are not allowed to interact with the other sex, even in school.
- Street youth in Kenya and other parts of the world learn to survive under highly stressful circumstances. In some cases abandoned by their parents, they may engage in delinquency or prostitution to provide for their economic needs.
- Whereas individuals in the United States are marrying later than in past generations, youth in Russia are marrying earlier to legitimize sexual activity.

(a) (b) (c)

(*a*) Asian Indian adolescents in a marriage ceremony. (*b*) Muslim school in Middle East with boys only. (*c*) Street youth in Rio de Janeiro.

Thus, depending on the culture being observed, adolescence may involve many different experiences (Larson & Wilson, 2004).

Some cultures have retained their traditions regarding adolescence, but rapid global change is altering the experience of adolescence in many places, presenting new opportunities and challenges to young people's health and well-being. Around the world, adolescents' experiences may differ.

Gender The experiences of male and female adolescents in many cultures continue to be quite different (Brown & Larson, 2002). Except in a few regions, such as Japan, the Philippines, and Western countries, males have far greater access to educational opportunities than females (UNICEF, 2011). In many countries, adolescent females have less freedom than males to pursue a variety of careers and engage in various leisure activities. Gender differences in sexual expression are widespread, especially in India, Southeast Asia, Latin America, and Arab countries, where there are far more restrictions on the sexual activity of adolescent females than on that of males. These gender differences do appear to be narrowing over time, however. In some countries, educational and career opportunities for women are expanding, and control over adolescent girls' romantic and sexual relationships is weakening.

Family In some countries, adolescents grow up in closely knit families with extensive extended-kin networks that retain a traditional way of life. For example, in Arab countries, adolescents are taught strict codes of conduct and loyalty (Brown & Larson, 2002). However, in Western countries such as the United States, parenting is less authoritarian than in the past, and much larger numbers of adolescents are growing up in divorced families and stepfamilies.

In many countries around the world, current trends "include greater family mobility, migration to urban areas, family members working in distant cities or countries, smaller families, fewer extended-family households, and increases in mothers' employment" (Brown & Larson, 2002, p. 7). Unfortunately, many of these changes may reduce the ability of families to spend time with their adolescents.

Peers Some cultures give peers a stronger role in adolescence than others (Brown & Larson, 2002). In most Western nations, peers figure prominently in adolescents' lives, in some cases taking on roles that would otherwise be assumed by parents.

connecting with diversity

How Adolescents Around the World Spend Their Time

Reed Larson and Suman Verma (Larson, 2001; Larson & Verma, 1999) have examined how adolescents spend their time in work, play, and developmental activities such as school. U.S. adolescents spend about 60 percent as much time on schoolwork as East Asian adolescents do, mainly because U.S. adolescents do less homework than East Asians do (Larson & Verma, 1999).

What U.S. adolescents have in greater quantities than do adolescents in other industrialized countries is discretionary time (Larson & Wilson, 2004). About 40 to 50 percent of U.S. adolescents' waking hours (not counting summer vacations) is spent in discretionary activities, compared with 25 to 35 percent in East Asia and 35 to 45 percent in Europe. Whether this additional discretionary time is a liability or an asset for U.S. adolescents, of course, depends on how they use it.

According to Larson (2001), U.S. adolescents may have more unstructured time than is beneficial for their development. Indeed, when adolescents are allowed to choose what to do with their time, they typically engage in unchallenging activities such as hanging out and watching TV. Although relaxation and social interaction are important aspects of adolescence, it seems unlikely that spending large numbers of hours per week in unchallenging activities fosters development. Structured voluntary activities may provide more promise for adolescent development

How do East Asian and U.S. adolescents spend their time differently?

than unstructured time, especially if adults give responsibility to adolescents, challenge them, and provide competent guidance in these activities (Larson & Walker, 2010; Larson & others, 2011).

These Congolese Kota boys painted their faces as part of the rite of passage to adulthood. *What rites of passage do American adolescents have?*

Among street youth in South America, the peer network serves as a surrogate family that supports survival in dangerous and stressful settings. In other regions of the world, such as in Arab countries, peer relations are restricted, especially for girls (Booth, 2002).

To read about how adolescents around the world spend their time, see the *Connecting with Diversity* interlude.

Rites of Passage Another variation in the experiences of adolescents in different cultures is whether the adolescents go through a rite of passage. Some societies have elaborate ceremonies that signal the adolescent's move to maturity and achievement of adult status (Kottak, 2004). A **rite of passage** is a ceremony or ritual that marks an individual's transition from one status to another. Most rites of passage focus on the transition to adult status. In some traditional cultures, rites of passage are the avenue through which adolescents gain access to sacred adult practices, to knowledge, and to sexuality. These rites often involve dramatic practices intended to facilitate the adolescent's separation from the immediate family, especially the mother. The transformation is usually characterized by some form of ritual death and rebirth, or by means of contact with the spiritual world. Bonds are forged between the adolescent and the adult instructors through shared rituals, hazards, and secrets to allow the adolescent to enter the adult world. This kind of ritual provides a forceful and discontinuous entry into the adult world at a time when the adolescent is perceived to be ready for the change.

An especially rich tradition of rites of passage for adolescents has prevailed in African cultures, especially sub-Saharan Africa. Under the influence of Western industrialized culture, many of these rites are disappearing today, although they are still prevalent in locations where formal education is not readily available.

Do we have such rites of passage for American adolescents? We certainly do not have universal formal ceremonies that mark the passage from adolescence to adulthood. Certain religious and social groups do, however, have initiation ceremonies that indicate that an advance in maturity has been reached: the Jewish bar and bat mitzvah, the Catholic confirmation, and social debuts, for example. School graduation ceremonies come the closest to being culture-wide rites of passage in the United States. The high school graduation ceremony has become nearly universal for middle-class adolescents and increasing numbers of adolescents from low-income backgrounds.

ETHNICITY

Earlier in this chapter, we explored the identity development of ethnic minority adolescents. Here we further examine immigration and the relationship between ethnicity and socioeconomic status.

Immigration   Relatively high rates of immigration are contributing to the growth of ethnic minorities in the United States (Grigorenko & Takanishi, 2010). Immigrants often experience stressors uncommon to or less prominent among longtime residents, such as language barriers, dislocations and separations from support networks, changes in SES status, and the dual struggle to preserve identity and to acculturate (Chao & Otsuki-Clutter, 2011; Ko & Perreira, 2010).

Many of the families that have immigrated in recent decades to the United States, such as Mexican Americans and Asian Americans, come from collective cultures in which family obligations are strong (Parke, Coltrane, & Schofield, 2011). Family obligations may take the form of assisting parents in their occupations and contributing to the family's welfare (Parke & Buriel, 2006; van Geel & Vedder, 2011). This often occurs in service and manual labor jobs, such as those in construction, gardening, cleaning, and restaurants.

Recent research indicates that many members of families that have recently immigrated to the United States adopt a bicultural orientation, selecting characteristics of the U.S. culture that help them to survive and advance, while still retaining aspects of their culture of origin (Cheah & Young, 2011; Marks, Patton, & Garcia Coll, 2011). Immigration also involves cultural brokering, which has increasingly occurred in the United States as children and adolescents serve as mediators (cultural and linguistic) for their immigrant parents (Villanueva & Buriel, 2010).

In adopting characteristics of the U.S. culture, Latino families are increasingly embracing the importance of education. Although their school dropout rates have remained higher than for other ethnic groups, toward the end of the first decade of the twenty-first century they declined considerably (National Center for Education Statistics, 2010). In regard to retaining positive aspects of their culture of origin, research by Ross Parke and his colleagues (2011) indicates that Latino families maintain a strong commitment to family when they immigrate to the United States, even in the face of often having low-paying jobs and struggling to advance economically. For example, divorce rates for Latino families are lower than for non-Latino White families of similar socioeconomic status.

Ethnicity and Socioeconomic Status   Much of the research on ethnic minority adolescents has failed to tease apart the influences of ethnicity and socioeconomic

How Would You...?

If you were an **educator,** how would you modify high school graduation to be a more meaningful rite of passage for adolescents in the United States?

Consider the flowers of a garden: Though differing in kind, color, form, and shape, yet, inasmuch as they are refreshed by the waters of one spring, revived by the breath of one wind, invigorated by the rays of one sun, this diversity increases their charm and adds to their beauty.... How unpleasing to the eye if all the flowers and plants, the leaves and blossoms, the fruits, the branches, and the trees of that garden were all of the same shape and color! Diversity of hues, form, and shape enriches and adorns the garden and heightens its effect.

—ABDU'L BAHA

Persian Baha'i Religious Leader, 19th/20th Century

What are some cultural adaptations these Mexican American girls likely have made as immigrants to the United States?

rite of passage A ceremony or ritual that marks an individual's transition from one status to another. Most rites of passage focus on the transition to adult status.

Jason Leonard, age 15: "I want America to know that most of us black teens are not troubled people from broken homes and headed to jail.... In my relationships with my parents, we show respect for each other and we have values in our house. We have traditions we celebrate together, including Christmas and Kwanzaa."

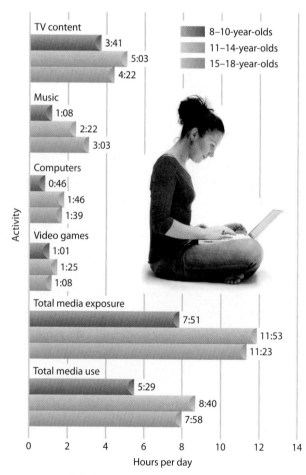

FIGURE 16.5

DEVELOPMENTAL CHANGES IN THE AMOUNT OF TIME U.S. 8- TO 18-YEAR-OLDS SPEND WITH DIFFERENT TYPES OF MEDIA

status. These two factors can interact in ways that exaggerate the influence of ethnicity because ethnic minority individuals are overrepresented in the lower socioeconomic levels of American society (Healey, 2009). Consequently, researchers too often have given ethnic explanations for aspects of adolescent development that were largely due instead to socioeconomic status.

Not all ethnic minority families are poor. However, poverty contributes to the stressful life experiences of many ethnic minority adolescents (Leon-Guerrero, 2009; Rivas-Drake, 2011). Thus, many ethnic minority adolescents experience a double disadvantage: (1) prejudice, discrimination, and bias because of their ethnic minority status; and (2) the stressful effects of poverty.

MEDIA AND TECHNOLOGY

In Chapter 10, "Socioemotional Development in Early Childhood," we discussed the role of television in children's development. Here we examine changes in TV watching from childhood to adolescence and the dramatically increasing influence of a number of other media in adolescence.

Media Use   If the amount of time spent in an activity is any indication of its importance, there is no doubt that media play important roles in adolescents' lives (Brown & Bobkowski, 2011). To better understand various aspects of U.S. adolescents' media use, the Kaiser Family Foundation funded national surveys in 1999, 2004, and 2009. The 2009 survey included more than 2,000 young people 8 to 18 years old and documented that adolescent media use has increased dramatically in the last decade (Rideout, Foehr, & Roberts, 2010). Today's youth live in a world in which they are encapsulated by media. In this survey, in 2009, 8- to 10-year-olds used media 5 hours and 29 minutes a day, but 11- to 14-year-olds used media an average of 8 hours and 40 minutes a day, and 15- to 18-year-olds an average of 7 hours and 58 minutes a day (see Figure 16.5). Thus, media use jumps more than 3 hours per day in early adolescence! The largest increase in media use in early adolescence comprises TV and video game use. TV use by youth increasingly has involved watching TV on the Internet, on an iPod/MP3 player, and on a cell phone. As indicated in Figure 16.5, listening to music and using computers also increase considerably in 11- to 14-year-old adolescents. And the 2009 survey, adding up the daily media use figures to obtain weekly media use leads to the staggering levels of more than 60 hours a week of media use by 11- to 14-year-olds and almost 56 hours a week by 15- to 18-year-olds!

A major trend in the use of technology is the dramatic increase in media multitasking (Brown & Bobkowski, 2011). In the 2009 survey, when the amount of time spent multitasking was included in computing media use, 11- to 14-year-olds spent nearly 12 hours a day (compared with almost 9 hours a day when multitasking was not included) exposed to media (Rideout, Foehr, & Roberts, 2010)! In this survey, 39 percent of seventh- to twelfth-graders said "most of the time" they use two or more media concurrently, such as surfing the Web while listening to music. In some cases, media multitasking—such as text messaging, listening to an iPod, and updating a YouTube site—is engaged in at the same time as doing homework. It is hard to imagine that this allows a student to do homework efficiently, although there has been little research on media multitasking. One study that compared heavy and light media multitaskers revealed that heavy media multitaskers were more susceptible to interference from irrelevant information (Ophir, Nass, & Wagner, 2009).

Mobile media, such as cell phones and iPods, are mainly driving the increased media use by adolescents. For example, in the 2004 survey, only 18 percent of youth owned an iPod or MP3 player; but in 2009, 76 percent owned them. Similarly, 39 percent owned a cell phone in 2004, as compared with 66 percent in 2009 (Rideout, Foehr, & Roberts, 2010).

Technology and Digitally Mediated Communication

Culture involves change, and nowhere is that change more apparent than in the technological revolution individuals are experiencing with increased use of computers and the Internet (Maloy & others, 2011). Society still relies on some basic nontechnological competencies—for example, good communication skills, positive attitudes, and the ability to solve problems and to think deeply and creatively. But how people pursue these competencies is changing in ways and at a speed

How much time do adolescents spend using different types of media?

that few people had to cope with in previous eras. For youth to be adequately prepared for tomorrow's jobs, technology needs to become an integral part of their lives (Lever-Duffy & McDonald, 2011).

The digitally mediated social environment of adolescents and emerging adults includes e-mail, instant messaging, social networking sites such as Facebook, chat rooms, videosharing and photosharing, multiplayer online computer games, and virtual worlds. The remarkable increase in the popularity of Facebook was reflected in its recent replacement of Google in 2010 as the most frequently visited Internet site. Most of these digitally mediated social interactions began on computers but more recently have also shifted to cell phones, especially smartphones (Blair & Fletcher, 2011; Valkenburg & Peter, 2011).

A national survey revealed dramatic increases in adolescents' use of social media and text messaging (Lenhart & others, 2010). In 2009, nearly three-fourths of U.S. 12- to 17-year-olds reported using social networking sites. Eighty-one percent of 18- to 24-year-olds had created a profile on a social networking site, and 31 percent of them were visiting a social networking site at least several times a day. More emerging adult women visited a social networking site several times a day (33 percent) than did their male counterparts (24 percent).

What characterizes the online social environment of adolescents and emerging adults?

Text messaging has become the main way that adolescents connect with their friends, surpassing face-to-face contact, e-mail, instant messaging, and voice calling (Lenhart & others, 2010). However, voice mailing is the primary way that most adolescents prefer to connect with parents.

Clearly, parents need to monitor and regulate adolescents' use of the Internet (Padilla-Walker & Coyne, 2011). Consider Bonita Williams, who began to worry about how obsessed her 15-year-old daughter, Jade, had become with MySpace (Kornblum, 2006). She became even more concerned when she discovered that Jade was posting suggestive photos of herself and had given her cell phone number out to people in different parts of the United States. Bonita grounded her daughter, blocked MySpace at home, and moved Jade's computer from her bedroom to the family room.

The following recent studies explored the role of parents in guiding adolescents' use of the Internet and other media:

- Parents' high estimates of online dangers were not matched by their low rates of setting limits and monitoring their adolescents' online activities (Rosen, Cheever, & Carrier, 2008). Also in this study, adolescents who perceived that their parents had an indulgent parenting style (high warmth and involvement but low levels of strictness and supervision) reported engaging in the most risky online behavior, such as meeting someone in person whom they had initially contacted on the Internet.

- Both maternal and paternal authoritative parenting predicted proactive monitoring of adolescent media use, including restriction of certain media from adolescent use and parent-adolescent discussion of exposure to questionable media content (Padilla-Walker & Coyne, 2011).
- Problematic mother-adolescent (age 13) relationships that involved undermining attachment and autonomy predicted emerging adults' preference for online communication and greater probability of forming a poor-quality relationship with someone met online (Szwedo, Mikami, & Allen, 2011).

Review Connect Reflect

 LG4 Explain how culture influences adolescent development.

Review

- What are some differences in the lives of adolescents in different cultures? How do adolescents around the world spend their time? What are some examples of rites of passage?
- How does ethnicity influence adolescent development?
- What characterizes adolescents' use of media and technology?

Connect

- How do ethnicity and poverty influence children's development? (See Chapter 13.)

Reflect *Your Own Personal Journey of Life*

- What is your ethnicity? Have you ever been stereotyped because of your ethnicity? In what ways is your ethnic identity similar to or different from the mainstream culture?

What Are Some Socioemotional Problems in Adolescence?

 LG5 Identify adolescent problems in socioemotional development and strategies for helping adolescents with problems.

Juvenile Delinquency

The Interrelation of Problems and Successful Prevention/Intervention Programs

Depression and Suicide

In Chapter 14, "Physical Development in Adolescence," we described several adolescent problems: substance abuse, sexually transmitted infections, and eating disorders. In this chapter, we examine the problems of juvenile delinquency, depression, and suicide. We also explore interrelationships among adolescent problems and describe how such problems can be prevented or remedied.

JUVENILE DELINQUENCY

The label **juvenile delinquent** is applied to an adolescent who breaks the law or engages in behavior that is considered illegal. Like other categories of disorders, juvenile delinquency is a broad concept; legal infractions range from littering to murder. Because the adolescent technically becomes a juvenile delinquent only after being judged guilty of a crime by a court of law, official records do not accurately reflect the number of illegal acts juvenile delinquents commit. Estimates of the number of juvenile delinquents in the United States are sketchy, but FBI statistics indicate that at least 2 percent of all youth are involved in juvenile court cases.

U.S. government statistics reveal that juvenile court caseloads for males were three times higher than for females in 2002 (National Center for Juvenile Justice, 2006). In the last two decades, however, there has been a greater increase in female delinquency than in male delinquency (National Center for Juvenile Justice, 2006). For both male and female delinquents, rates for property offenses are higher than rates for other offenses (such as offenses against persons, drug offenses, and public

juvenile delinquent An adolescent who breaks the law or engages in behavior that is considered illegal.

order offenses). Arrest rates of adolescent males for delinquency continue to be much higher than arrest rates among adolescent females.

A controversial issue in juvenile justice is whether an adolescent who commits a crime should be tried as an adult. In one study, trying adolescent offenders as adults increased rather than reduced their crime rate (Myers, 1999). The study evaluated more than 500 violent youth in Pennsylvania, which has adopted a "get tough" policy. Although these 500 offenders had been given harsher punishment than a comparison group retained in juvenile court, they were more likely to be rearrested—and rearrested more quickly—for new offenses once they were returned to the community. This pattern suggests that the price of short-term public safety attained by prosecuting juveniles as adults might be an increased number of criminal offenses over the long run.

A distinction is made between early-onset—before age 11—and late-onset—after 11—antisocial behavior of minors. Early-onset antisocial behavior is associated with more negative developmental outcomes than late-onset antisocial behavior (Schulenberg & Zarrett, 2006). Early-onset antisocial behavior is more likely to persist into emerging adulthood and is more frequently associated with mental health and relationship problems than is late-onset antisocial behavior (Burke, 2011; Loeber & Burke, 2011).

Causes of Delinquency What causes delinquency? Although delinquency is less exclusively a phenomenon of lower socioeconomic status (SES) than it was in the past, some characteristics of lower-SES culture might promote delinquency. The norms of many lower-SES peer groups and gangs are antisocial, or counterproductive, to the goals and norms of society at large (Thio, 2010). Getting into and staying out of trouble are prominent features of life for some adolescents in low-income neighborhoods. Also, adolescents in communities with high crime rates observe many models who engage in criminal activities (Loeber & Burke, 2011). These communities may be characterized by poverty, unemployment, and feelings of alienation toward the middle class (Farrington, Ttofi, & Coid, 2009). Quality schooling, educational funding, and organized neighborhood activities may be lacking in these communities. A recent study revealed that engaged parenting and mothers' social network support were linked to a lower level of delinquency in low-income families (Ghazarian & Roche, 2010). And another recent study found that youth whose families had experienced repeated poverty were more than twice as likely to be delinquent at 14 and 21 years of age (Najman & others, 2010).

Certain characteristics of family support systems are also associated with delinquency. Parental monitoring of adolescents is especially important in determining whether an adolescent becomes a delinquent (Laird & others, 2008). A recent study found that early parental monitoring in adolescence and ongoing parental support were linked to a lower incidence of criminal behavior in emerging adulthood (Johnson & others, 2011). A study of families living in high-risk neighborhoods revealed that parents' lack of knowledge of their young adolescents' whereabouts was linked to whether the adolescents engaged in delinquency later in adolescence (Lahey & others, 2008). Family discord and inconsistent and inappropriate discipline are also associated with delinquency (Bor, McGee, & Fagan, 2004).

An increasing number of studies have found that siblings can have a strong influence on delinquency (Bank, Burraston, & Snyder, 2004). In one study, high levels of hostile sibling relationships and older sibling delinquency were linked with younger sibling delinquency in both brother and sister pairs (Slomkowski & others, 2001).

Having delinquent peers greatly increases the risk of becoming delinquent (Loeber & Burke, 2011). For example, a recent study found that being rejected by peers and having deviant friends at 7 to 13 years of age were linked with increased delinquency at 14 to 15 years of age (Vitaro, Pedersen, & Brendgen, 2007).

Cognitive factors, such as low self-control, low intelligence, and lack of sustained attention, are also implicated in delinquency. For example, one study

What are some factors that are linked to whether adolescents engage in delinquent acts?

Rodney Hammond, Health Psychologist

In describing his college experiences, Rodney Hammond said, "When I started as an undergraduate at the University of Illinois, Champaign-Urbana, I hadn't decided on my major. But to help finance my education, I took a part-time job in a child development research program sponsored by the psychology department. There, I observed inner-city children in settings designed to enhance their learning. I saw firsthand the contribution psychology can make, and I knew I wanted to be a psychologist" (American Psychological Association, 2003, p. 26).

Rodney Hammond went on to obtain a doctorate in school and community psychology with a focus on children's development. For a number of years, he trained clinical psychologists at Wright State University in Ohio and directed a program to reduce violence in ethnic minority youth. Hammond and his associates taught at-risk youth how to use social skills to effectively manage conflict and how to recognize situations that could lead to violence. Today, Hammond is director of Violence Prevention at the Centers for Disease Control and Prevention in Atlanta. Hammond says that if you are interested in people and problem solving, psychology is a wonderful way to put these together. (Source: American Psychological Association, 2003, pp. 26–27)

Rodney Hammond counseling an adolescent girl about the risks of adolescence and how to effectively cope with them.

How Would You...?
If you were a **psychologist,** how would you seek to lower the risk of juvenile delinquency?

revealed that low-IQ serious-offense delinquents were characterized by low self-control (Koolhof & others, 2007). Another study found that at age 16 nondelinquents were more likely to have a higher verbal IQ and engage in sustained attention than delinquents (Loeber & others, 2007). And in a longitudinal study, one of the strongest predictors of reduced likelihood of engaging in serious theft was high school academic achievement (Loeber & others, 2008).

One individual whose goal is to help at-risk adolescents, such as juvenile delinquents, cope more effectively with their lives is Rodney Hammond. Read about his work in the *Connecting with Careers* profile.

DEPRESSION AND SUICIDE

What is the nature of depression in adolescence? What causes an adolescent to commit suicide?

Depression Depression is more likely to occur in adolescence than in childhood and more likely to occur in adulthood than adolescence. Researchers have found a linear increase in major depressive disorder from 15 to 22 years of age (Kessler & Waters, 1988). However, an early onset of a mood disorder, such as major depressive disorder in adolescence, is linked with more negative outcomes than late onset of a mood disorder (Schulenberg & Zarrett, 2006). For example, the early onset is associated with further recurrences of depression and with an increased risk of being diagnosed with an anxiety disorder, substance abuse, eating disorder, suicide attempt, and unemployment at a future point in development (Graber, 2004).

How serious a problem is depression in adolescence? Rates of ever experiencing a major depressive disorder range from 1.5 to 2.5 percent in school-age children and 15 to 20 percent for adolescents (Graber & Sontag, 2009). By about age 15, adolescent females have a rate of depression that is twice that of adolescent males. Among the reasons for this gender difference are that females tend to ruminate in their depressed mood and amplify it; females' self-images, especially their body images, are more negative than males'; females face more discrimination than males do; and puberty occurs earlier for girls than for boys. As a result, girls experience a confluence of changes and life experiences in the middle school years that can increase depression (Nolen-Hoeksema, 2011).

Do gender differences in adolescent depression hold for other cultures? In many cultures the gender difference of females experiencing more depression does hold, but a recent study of more than 17,000 Chinese 11- to 22-year-olds revealed that the male adolescents and emerging adults experienced more depression than their female counterparts did (Sun & others, 2010). Explanations of the higher rates of depression among males in China focused on stressful life events and a less positive coping style.

What are some characteristics of adolescents who become depressed? What are some factors that are linked with suicide attempts by adolescents?

Certain family factors place adolescents at risk for developing depression. These include having a depressed parent, emotionally unavailable parents, parents with high marital conflict, and parents with financial problems. A recent study revealed that mother-daughter co-rumination (extensively discussing, rehashing, and speculating about problems) was linked to an increase in anxiety and depression in adolescent daughters (Waller & Rose, 2010). Another study found that exposure to maternal depression by age 12 predicted risk processes during development (higher stress and difficulties in family relationships), which set the course for the development of the adolescent's depression (Garber & Cole, 2010).

Poor peer relationships also are associated with adolescent depression. Not having a close relationship with a best friend, having less contact with friends, and being rejected by peers increase depressive tendencies in adolescents (Vernberg, 1990). A recent study revealed that adolescent bullies, victims, and bully-victims, as well as victims of cyberbullying, had higher rates of depression than adolescents not involved in bullying (Wang, Nansel, & Iannotti, 2011). Problems in adolescent romantic relationships also can trigger depression (Steinberg & Davila, 2008).

Friendship often provides social support. A recent study found that friendship prevented an increase in depressive symptoms in adolescents who had avoided peer relations or been excluded from them as children (Bukowski, Laursen, & Hoza, 2010). However, a recent study of third- through ninth-graders revealed that one aspect of social support in friendship may have costs as well as benefits (Rose, Carlson, & Waller, 2007). In the study, girls' co-rumination predicted not only an increase in positive friendship quality but also an increase in further co-rumination as well as an increase in depressive and anxiety symptoms. However, for boys, co-rumination predicted only an increase in positive friendship quality and no increase in depressive and anxiety symptoms. One implication of the research is that some girls who are vulnerable to developing internalized problems may go undetected because they have supportive friendships.

Stress involving weight-related concerns is increasingly thought to contribute to the greater incidence of depression in adolescent girls than in adolescent boys. A recent study revealed that one explanation for adolescent girls' higher level of depressive symptoms is a heightened tendency to perceive oneself as overweight and to diet (Vaughan & Halpern, 2010).

What type of treatment is most likely to reduce depression in adolescence? According to the Treatment for Adolescents with Depression Study (TADS), depressed adolescents recovered faster when they took an antidepressant and received cognitive behavior therapy that involved improving their coping skills than when they took an antidepressant without receiving or received cognitive behavior therapy without medication (TADS, 2007). However, a safety concern has emerged with regard to the use of antidepressants such as Prozac (fluoxetine) by adolescents, and in 2004 the U.S. Food and Drug Administration assigned warnings to such drugs stating that they slightly increase the risk of suicidal behavior in adolescents.

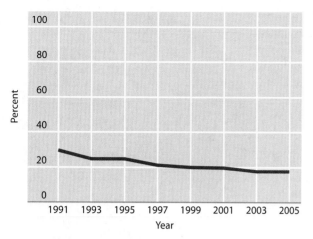

FIGURE **16.6**

PERCENTAGE OF U.S. NINTH- TO TWELFTH-GRADE STUDENTS WHO SERIOUSLY CONSIDERED ATTEMPTING SUICIDE IN THE PREVIOUS 12 MONTHS FROM 1991 TO 2005

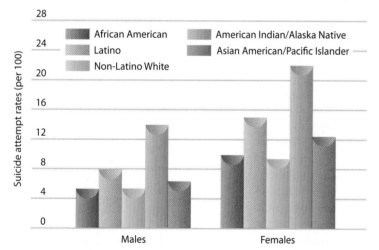

FIGURE **16.7**

SUICIDE ATTEMPTS BY U.S. ADOLESCENTS FROM DIFFERENT ETHNIC GROUPS. *Note:* Data shown are for one-year rates of self-reported suicide attempts.

Suicide Suicidal behavior is rare in childhood but escalates in adolescence and then increases further in emerging adulthood (Park & others, 2006). Suicide is the third leading cause of death in 10- to 19-year-olds today in the United States (National Center for Health Statistics, 2007). After increasing to high levels in the 1990s, suicide rates in adolescents have declined in recent years (Gould & others, 2003). In 2004, 4,214 U.S. individuals from 15 to 24 years of age committed suicide (Minino, Heron, & Smith, 2006). Emerging adults have triple the rate of suicide of adolescents (Park & others, 2006).

Although a suicide threat should always be taken seriously, far more adolescents contemplate or attempt it unsuccessfully than actually commit it (Miranda & others, 2008). In a national study conducted in 2005, 17 percent of U.S. high school students said that they had seriously considered or attempted suicide in the last 12 months (Eaton & others, 2006). As shown in Figure 16.6, this percentage had declined since 1991. In the 2005 survey, 2.3 percent reported a suicide attempt that had resulted in an injury, poisoning, or drug overdose that was treated by a doctor. Females were more likely to attempt suicide than males, but males were more likely to succeed in committing suicide. Males use more lethal means, such as guns, in their suicide attempts, whereas adolescent females are more likely to cut their wrists or take an overdose of sleeping pills—methods less likely to result in death.

Distal, or earlier, experiences often are involved in suicide attempts as well. The adolescent may have a long-standing history of family instability and unhappiness. Just as inadequate affection and emotional support, high control, and pressure for achievement by parents during childhood are related to adolescent depression, such combinations of family experiences also are likely to show up as distal factors in adolescents' suicide attempts.

Adolescents' peer relations also are linked to suicide attempts. A research review revealed that prior suicide attempts by members of an adolescent's social groups increased the probability the adolescent also would attempt suicide (de Leo & Heller, 2008). Adolescents who attempt suicide may lack supportive friendships. One study found that social isolation was linked with suicide attempts in adolescent girls (Bearman & Moody, 2004). Another study revealed that peer victimization was linked to suicide thoughts and attempts (Klomek & others, 2008).

Cultural contexts also are linked to suicide attempts, and adolescent suicide attempts vary across ethnic groups in the United States. As indicated in Figure 16.7, more than 20 percent of Native American/Alaska Native (NA/AN) female adolescents reported that they had attempted suicide in the previous year, and suicide accounts for almost 20 percent of NA/AN deaths in 15- to 19-year-olds (Goldston & others, 2008). African American and non-Latino White males reported the lowest incidence of suicide attempts. A major risk factor in the high rate of suicide attempts by NA/AN adolescents is their elevated rate of alcohol abuse.

Just as genetic factors are associated with depression, they also are associated with suicide (Kapornai & Vetro, 2008). The closer a person's genetic relationship is to someone who has committed suicide, the more likely is that person to commit suicide.

What is the psychological profile of the suicidal adolescent? Suicidal adolescents often have depressive symptoms. Although not all depressed adolescents are suicidal, depression is the most frequently cited factor associated with adolescent suicide (Thompson & Light, 2011; Verona & Javdani, 2011). A sense of hopelessness, low self-esteem, and high self-blame also are associated with adolescent suicide (O'Donnell & others, 2004). The following studies document a number of factors linked with adolescent suicide attempts:

- Overweight middle school students were more likely to think about, plan, and attempt suicide than their counterparts who were not overweight (Whetstone, Morrisey, & Cummings, 2007).

- Adolescents who used alcohol while they were sad or depressed were at risk for making a suicide attempt (Schilling & others, 2009).

- Data from the National Longitudinal Study of Adolescent Health indicated that the following were indicators of suicide risk: depressive symptoms, a sense of hopelessness, engaging in suicidal ideation, having a family background of suicidal behavior, and having friends with a history of suicidal behavior (Thompson, Kuruwita, & Foster, 2009).

- Another analysis based on the National Longitudinal Study of Adolescent Health found that parental loss predicted an increase in suicide attempts one year later but not seven years later (Thompson & Light, 2011).

- Frequent, escalating stress, especially at home, was linked with suicide attempts in young Latinas (Zayas & others, 2010).

- Sexual victimization was linked to a risk for suicide attempts in adolescence (Plener, Singer, & Goldbeck, 2011).

How Would You...?
If you were a **psychologist,** how would you talk with someone who has just threatened suicide?

THE INTERRELATION OF PROBLEMS AND SUCCESSFUL PREVENTION/INTERVENTION PROGRAMS

We have discussed adolescent problems in this chapter and in Chapters 14 and 15: substance abuse; juvenile delinquency; school-related problems, such as dropping out of high school; adolescent pregnancy and sexually transmitted infections; eating disorders; depression; and suicide.

The four problems that affect the most adolescents are (1) drug abuse, (2) juvenile delinquency, (3) sexual problems, and (4) school-related problems (Dryfoos, 1990; Dryfoos & Barkin, 2006). The adolescents most at risk have more than one of these problems. Researchers are increasingly finding that problem behaviors in adolescence are interrelated (Elkington, Bauermeister, & Zimmerman, 2011). For example, heavy substance abuse is related to early sexual activity, lower grades, dropping out of school, and delinquency (Brady & others, 2008; Marti, Stice, & Springer, 2010). Early initiation of sexual activity is associated with the use of cigarettes and alcohol, use of marijuana and other illicit drugs, lower grades, dropping out of school, and delinquency (Harden & Mendle, 2011). Delinquency is related to early sexual activity, early pregnancy, substance abuse, and dropping out of school (Pedersen & Mastekaasa, 2011). As much as 10 percent of the adolescent population in the United States have serious multiple-problem behaviors (adolescents who have dropped out of school, or are behind in their grade level, are users of heavy drugs, regularly use cigarettes and marijuana, and are sexually active but do not use contraception). Many, but not all, of these very high-risk youth "do it all." In 1990, it was estimated that another 15 percent of adolescents participate in many of these same behaviors but with slightly lower frequency and less deleterious consequences (Dryfoos, 1990). These high-risk youth often engage in two or three problem behaviors (Dryfoos, 1990). It was estimated that in 2005 the figure for high-risk youth had increased to 20 percent of all U.S. adolescents (Dryfoos & Barkin, 2006).

A review of the programs that have been successful in preventing or reducing adolescent problems, found the following common components (Dryfoos, 1990; Dryfoos & Barkin, 2006):

1. *Intensive individualized attention.* In successful programs, high-risk adolescents are attached to a responsible adult who gives the adolescent attention and deals with the adolescent's specific needs. This theme occurs in a number of

Fast Track

A program that attempts to lower the risk of juvenile delinquency and other problems is *Fast Track* (Conduct Problems Prevention Research Group, 2007, 2010a, b, 2011; Dodge & McCourt, 2010; Jones & others, 2010; Miller & others, 2011). Schools in four areas (Durham, North Carolina; Nashville, Tennessee; Seattle, Washington; and rural central Pennsylvania) were identified as high-risk based on neighborhood crime and poverty data. Researchers screened more than 9,000 kindergarten children in the four schools and randomly assigned 891 of the highest-risk and moderate-risk children to intervention or control conditions. The average age of the children when the intervention began was 6.5 years of age. The 10-year intervention consisted of behavior management training of parents, social cognitive skills training of children, reading tutoring, home visitations, mentoring, and a revised classroom curriculum that was designed to increase socioemotional competence and decrease aggression.

The extensive intervention was most successful for children and adolescents who were identified as the highest risk in kindergarten, lowering their incidence of conduct disorder, attention deficit hyperactivity disorder, any externalized disorder, and antisocial behavior. Positive outcomes for the intervention occurred as early as the third grade and continued through the ninth grade. For example, in the ninth grade the intervention reduced the likelihood that the highest-risk kindergarten children would develop conduct disorder by 75 percent, attention deficit hyperactivity disorder by 53 percent, and any externalized disorder by 43 percent. Recently, data have been reported through age 19 (Miller & others, 2011). Findings indicate that the comprehensive Fast Track intervention was successful in reducing youth arrest rates (Conduct Problems Prevention Research Group, 2010a).

How might educators apply the results of this research to their daily work with adolescents in school settings?

programs. In a successful substance-abuse program, a student assistance counselor is available full-time for individual counseling and referral for treatment.

2. *Community-wide multiagency collaborative approaches.* The basic philosophy of community-wide programs is that a number of different programs and services have to be in place. In one successful substance-abuse program, a community-wide health promotion campaign has been implemented that uses local media and community education, in concert with a substance-abuse curriculum in the schools.

3. *Early identification and intervention.* Reaching younger children and their families before children develop problems, or at the beginning of their problems, is a successful strategy (Aber & others, 2006). One preschool program serves as an excellent model for the prevention of delinquency, pregnancy, substance abuse, and dropping out of school. Operated by the High/Scope Foundation in Ypsilanti, Michigan, the Perry Preschool has had a long-term positive impact on its students. This enrichment program, directed by David Weikart, serves disadvantaged African American children. They attend a high-quality two-year preschool program and receive weekly home visits from program personnel. Based on official police records, by age 19, individuals who had attended the Perry Preschool program were less likely to have been arrested and reported fewer adult offenses than a control group did. The Perry Preschool students also were less likely to drop out of school, and teachers rated their social behavior as more competent than that of a control group who had not received the enriched preschool experience (Schweinhart & others, 2005). What other effects can intervention programs achieve? For a description of one successful program, see the *Connecting with Research* interlude.

What are some strategies for preventing and intervening in adolescent problems?

Review *Connect* Reflect

LG5 Identify adolescent problems in socioemotional development and strategies for helping adolescents with problems.

Review

- What is juvenile delinquency? What causes it?
- What is the nature of depression and suicide in adolescence?
- How are adolescent problems inter-related? What are some components of successful prevention/intervention programs for adolescents?

Connect

- In Chapter 13, what did you learn about the connection between bullying and problems and the development of problems?

Reflect *Your Own Personal Journey of Life*

- Did you have any of the problems during adolescence discussed in this chapter or Chapters 14 and 15? If you had one or more of the problems, why do you think you developed the problem(s)? If you did not have any of the problems, why do you think you didn't develop one or more of them?

reach your **learning goals**

What Characterizes Emotional and Personality Development in Adolescence?

 LG1 Discuss changes in identity and emotional development during adolescence.

Identity

- Identity development is a complex process that happens in bits and pieces. Erikson argues that identity versus identity confusion is the fifth stage of the human life span, which individuals experience during adolescence. A psychosocial moratorium during adolescence allows the personality and role experimentation that are important aspects of identity development. James Marcia proposed four identity statuses—identity diffusion, foreclosure, moratorium, and achievement—that are based on crisis (exploration) and commitment. Increasingly, experts argue that the main changes in identity occur in emerging adulthood rather than adolescence. Individuals often follow *m*oratorium-*a*chievement-*m*oratorium-*a*chievement ("MAMA") cycles in their lives. Parents are important figures in adolescents' identity development. Identity development is facilitated by family relations that promote both individuality and connectedness. Throughout the world ethnic minority groups have struggled to maintain their identities while blending into the majority culture.

Emotional Development

- Adolescents report more extreme and fleeting emotions than their parents, and as individuals go through early adolescence they are less likely to report being very happy. However, it is important to view moodiness as a normal aspect of early adolescence. Although pubertal change is associated with an increase in negative emotions, hormonal influences are often small, and environmental experiences may contribute more to the emotions of adolescence than hormonal changes.

What Is the Nature of Parent-Adolescent Relationships?

 LG2 Describe changes that take place in adolescents' relationships with their parents.

Parental Monitoring

- A key aspect of the managerial role in parent-adolescent relationships involves parental monitoring. A current focus of interest is adolescents' willingness to disclose information about their activities to parents.

| Autonomy and Attachment |
| Parent-Adolescent Conflict |

- Many parents have a difficult time handling the adolescent's push for autonomy, even though the push is one of the hallmarks of adolescence. Adolescents do not simply move into a world isolated from parents; attachment to parents increases the probability that an adolescent will be socially competent.

- Parent-adolescent conflict increases in early adolescence. The conflict is usually moderate rather than severe, and the increased conflict may serve the positive developmental function of promoting autonomy and identity. A subset of adolescents experiences high parent-adolescent conflict, which is linked with negative outcomes.

What Aspects of Peer Relationships Are Important in Adolescence?

 LG3 Characterize the changes that occur in peer relations during adolescence.

| Friendship |
| Peer Groups |
| Dating and Romantic Relationships |

- Harry Stack Sullivan was the most influential theorist to discuss the importance of adolescent friendships. He argued that there is a dramatic increase in the psychological importance and intimacy of close friends in early adolescence.

- Groups of children are less formal and less heterogeneous than groups of adolescents. The pressure to conform to peers is strong during adolescence, especially during the eighth and ninth grades. Cliques and crowds assume more importance in the lives of adolescents than in the lives of children. Membership in certain crowds—especially jocks and populars—is associated with increased self-esteem. Independents also show high self-esteem.

- Three stages characterize the development of romantic relationships in adolescence: (1) entry into romantic attractions and affiliations at about 11 to 13 years of age, (2) exploring romantic relationships at approximately 14 to 16 years of age, and (3) consolidating dyadic romantic bonds at about 17 to 19 years of age. A special concern is early dating, which is associated with a number of problems. Most sexual minority youth (gays and lesbians) have had some same-sex sexual experience, but relatively few have had same-sex romantic relationships. Many sexual minority youth date other-sex peers, which can help them to clarify their sexual orientation or disguise it from others. Adolescents who date have more problems, such as substance abuse, than those who do not date, but they also have more acceptance with peers. Culture can exert a powerful influence on dating. Many adolescents from immigrant families face conflicts with their parents about dating.

Why Is Culture an Important Context for Adolescent Development?

 LG4 Explain how culture influences adolescent development.

| Cross-Cultural Comparisons |

- There are similarities and differences in adolescents across different countries. In some countries, traditions are being continued in the socialization of adolescents, whereas in others, substantial changes in the experiences of adolescents are taking place. The ways in which adolescents fill their time vary, depending on the culture in which they live. Rites of passage are ceremonies that mark an individual's transition from one status to another, especially into adulthood. In primitive cultures, rites of passage are often well defined. In contemporary America, universal, formal rites of passage to adulthood are ill-defined, but certain religious groups have initiation ceremonies, such as the Jewish bat and bar mitzvah and the Catholic confirmation. The high school graduation ceremony has become a nearly universal rite of passage for U.S. adolescents.

| Ethnicity |

- Many of the families that have immigrated to the United States in recent decades come from collectivist cultures in which there is a strong sense of family obligation.

Much of the research on ethnic minority adolescents has not teased apart the influences of ethnicity and socioeconomic status. Because of this failure, too often researchers have given ethnic explanations for characteristics that were largely due to socioeconomic factors. Although not all ethnic minority families are poor, poverty contributes to the stress of many ethnic minority adolescents.

Media and Technology

- In terms of exposure, a significant increase in media use occurs in 11- to 14-year-olds. Adolescents are spending more time in media multitasking. The social environment of adolescents has increasingly become digitally mediated. The Internet continues to serve as the main focus of digitally mediated social interaction for adolescents but now encompasses a variety of digital devices, including cell phones (especially smartphones). Adolescents' online time can have positive or negative outcomes. Large numbers of adolescents and college students engage in social networking on Facebook. A special concern is the difficulty parents face in monitoring the information their children are accessing.

What Are Some Socioemotional Problems in Adolescence?

 LG5 Identify adolescent problems in socioemotional development and strategies for helping adolescents with problems.

Juvenile Delinquency

Depression and Suicide

The Interrelation of Problems and Successful Prevention/Intervention Programs

- A juvenile delinquent is an adolescent who breaks the law or engages in conduct that is considered illegal. Heredity, identity problems, community influences, and family experiences have been proposed as causes of juvenile delinquency.

- Adolescents and emerging adults have a rate of depression higher than that among children. Female adolescents and emerging adult women are more likely to have mood and depressive disorders than their male counterparts. Adolescent suicide is the third leading cause of death in U.S. 10- to 19-year-olds. Both proximal (recent) and distal (earlier) factors are likely involved in suicide's causes.

- Researchers are increasingly finding that problem behaviors in adolescence are interrelated. A number of common components are found in programs that successfully prevent or reduce adolescent problems: providing individual attention to high-risk adolescents, developing community-wide intervention, and providing early identification and intervention.

key terms

identity versus identity confusion 485
psychosocial moratorium 485
crisis 485

commitment 486
identity diffusion 486
identity foreclosure 486
identity moratorium 486
identity achievement 486

individuality 487
connectedness 487
ethnic identity 487
clique 493
crowd 494

rite of passage 498
juvenile delinquent 502

key people

Erik Erikson 484
James Marcia 485

Alan Waterman 486
Reed Larson 488

Maryse Richards 488
G. Stanley Hall 490

Harry Stack Sullivan 492
Ross Parke 499

connecting with improving the lives of children

MAKING A DIFFERENCE

Supporting Adolescents' Socioemotional Development

What are some good strategies for helping adolescents improve their socioemotional competencies?

- *Let adolescents explore their identity.* Adolescence is a time of identity exploration. Adults should encourage adolescents to try out different options as they seek to identify what type of life they want to pursue.

- *Engage in effective monitoring of adolescents' activities.* Especially important is using strategies for getting adolescents to disclose information about their activities.

- *Understand the importance of autonomy and attachment.* A common stereotype is that parents are less important in adolescent development than in child development. However, parents continue to play a crucial role in adolescents' development. They need their parents as a resource and support system, especially in stressful times. Value the adolescent's motivation for independence. However, continue to monitor the adolescent's whereabouts, although less intrusively and directly than in childhood.

- *Keep parent-adolescent conflict from being turbulent, and use good communication skills with the adolescent.* Adolescents' socioemotional development benefits when conflict with parents is either low or moderate. Keep communication channels open with the adolescent. Be an active listener and show respect for the adolescent's advancing developmental status. As with childhood, authoritative parenting is the best choice in most situations. Communicate expectations for high standards of achievement and conduct.

- *Recognize the importance of peers, youth organizations, and mentors.* Respected peers need to be used more frequently in programs that promote health and education. Adolescents need greater access to youth organizations staffed by caring peers and adults. Mentors can play a strong role in supporting adolescents' socioemotional development.

- *Help adolescents better understand the nature of differences, diversity, and value conflicts.* Adolescents need to be encouraged to take the perspective of adolescents from diverse ethnic backgrounds.

- *Give adolescents individualized attention.* One of the reasons adolescents develop problems is that they have not been given adequate attention.

- *Provide better community-wide collaboration for helping youth.* In successful programs, a number of different services and programs cooperate to help adolescents.

- *Prevent adolescent problems through early identification and intervention.* The seeds of many adolescent problems are already in place in childhood.

RESOURCES

Adolescence: Growing Up in America Today
by Joy Dryfoos and Carol Barkin (2006)
New York: Oxford University Press

Dryfoos' recent update of her 1990 book on at-risk adolescents contains extensive information about programs and strategies for improving adolescents' lives.

101 Insights and Strategies for Parenting Teenagers
by Sheryl Feinstein (2010)
Monterey, CA: Healthy Learning

An excellent, easy-to-read book for parents that provides valuable strategies for guiding adolescents through the transition from childhood to emerging adulthood.

You and Your Adolescent
by Laurence Steinberg (2011)
New York: HarperCollins

You and Your Adolescent provides a broad, developmental overview of adolescence, with parental advice mixed in along the way.

National Adolescent Suicide Hotline
800–621–4000

This hotline can be used 24 hours a day by teenagers contemplating suicide, as well as by their parents.

National Clearinghouse for Alcohol Information
www.health.org

This clearinghouse provides information about a wide variety of issues related to drinking problems, including adolescent drinking.

glossary

A

accommodation Piagetian concept of adjusting schemes to fit new information and experiences.

active (niche-picking) genotype-environment correlations Correlations that exist when children seek out environments they find compatible and stimulating.

adolescence The developmental period of transition from childhood to early adulthood, entered at approximately 10 to 12 years of age and ending at 18 to 22 years of age.

adolescent egocentrism The heightened self-consciousness of adolescents that is reflected in their belief that others are as interested in them as they are in themselves, and in their sense of personal uniqueness and invincibility.

adoption study A study in which investigators seek to discover whether, in behavior and psychological characteristics, adopted children are more like their adoptive parents, who provided a home environment, or more like their biological parents, who contributed their heredity. Another form of the adoption study compares adopted and biological siblings.

affordances Opportunities for interaction offered by objects that fit within our capabilities to perform functional activities.

afterbirth The third stage of birth, when the placenta, umbilical cord, and other membranes are detached and expelled.

AIDS AIDS, or acquired immune deficiency syndrome, is caused by a virus, the human immunodeficiency virus (HIV), which destroys the body's immune system.

amnion The life-support system that is a thin bag or envelope that contains a clear fluid in which the developing embryo floats.

amygdala The seat of emotions, such as anger.

analgesics Drugs used to alleviate pain, such as tranquilizers, barbiturates, and narcotics.

anesthesia Drugs used in late first-stage labor and during expulsion of the baby to block sensation in an area of the body or to block consciousness.

anger cry A cry similar to the basic cry, with more excess air forced through the vocal cords.

animism The belief that inanimate objects have lifelike qualities and are capable of action.

anorexia nervosa An eating disorder that involves the relentless pursuit of thinness through starvation.

A-not-B error This occurs when infants make the mistake of selecting the familiar hiding place (A) rather than the new hiding place (B) as they progress into substage 4 in Piaget's sensorimotor stage.

Apgar Scale A widely used method to assess the health of newborns at one and five minutes after birth. The Apgar Scale evaluates infants' heart rate, respiratory effort, muscle tone, body color, and reflex irritability.

aphasia A loss or impairment of language processing caused by brain damage in Broca's area or Wernicke's area.

articulation disorders Problems in pronouncing sounds correctly.

Asperger syndrome A relatively mild autism spectrum disorder in which the child has relatively good verbal language skills, milder nonverbal language problems, and a restricted range of interests and relationships.

assimilation Piagetian concept involving incorporation of new information into existing schemes.

asthma A chronic lung disease that involves episodes of airflow obstruction.

attachment A close emotional bond between two people.

attention The focusing of mental resources on select information.

attention deficit hyperactivity disorder (ADHD) A disability in which children consistently show one or more of the following characteristics: (1) inattention, (2) hyperactivity, and (3) impulsivity.

authoritarian parenting A restrictive punitive style in which parents exhort the child to follow their directions and to respect work and effort. The authoritarian parent places firm limits and controls on the child and allows little verbal exchange. Authoritarian parenting is associated with children's social incompetence.

authoritative parenting A parenting style in which parents encourage their children to be independent but still place limits and controls on their actions. Extensive verbal give-and-take is allowed, and parents are warm and

nurturant toward the child. Authoritative parenting is associated with children's social competence.

autism spectrum disorders (ASDs) Also called pervasive developmental disorders, this category ranges from the severe disorder labeled autistic disorder to the milder disorder called Asperger syndrome. Children with these disorders are characterized by problems with social interaction, verbal and nonverbal communication, and repetitive behaviors.

autistic disorder A severe autism spectrum disorder that has its onset in the first three years of life and includes deficiencies in social relationships, abnormalities in communication, and restricted, repetitive, and stereotyped patterns of behavior.

autonomous morality The second stage of moral development in Piaget's theory, displayed by older children (about 10 years of age and older). The child becomes aware that rules and laws are created by people and that, in judging an action, one should consider the actor's intentions as well as the consequences.

average children Children who receive an average number of both positive and negative nominations from peers.

B

basic cry A rhythmic pattern usually consisting of a cry, a briefer silence, a shorter inspiratory whistle that is higher pitched than the main cry, and then a brief rest before the next cry.

Bayley Scales of Infant Development Scales developed by Nancy Bayley that are widely used in assessing infant development. The current version, the Bayley Scales of Infant and Toddler Development—Third Edition (Bayley-III), has five components: a cognitive scale, a language scale, a motor scale, a socio-emotional scale, and an adaptive scale.

behavior genetics The field that seeks to discover the influence of heredity and environment on individual differences in human traits and development.

biological processes Changes in an individual's body.

blastocyst The inner mass of cells that develops during the germinal period. These cells later develop into the embryo.

bonding A close connection, especially a physical bond between parents and their newborn in the period shortly after birth.

brainstorming A technique in which individuals are encouraged to come up with creative ideas in a group, play off each other's ideas, and say practically whatever comes to mind.

Brazelton Neonatal Behavioral Assessment Scale (NBAS) A test performed within 24 to 36 hours after birth to assess newborns' neurological development, reflexes, and reactions to people.

breech position Position of the baby within the uterus that causes the buttocks to be the first part to emerge from the vagina.

Broca's area An area in the brain's left frontal lobe involved in speech production.

Bronfenbrenner's ecological theory An environmental systems theory that focuses on five environmental systems: microsystem, mesosystem, exosystem, macrosystem, and chronosystem.

bulimia nervosa An eating disorder in which the individual consistently follows a binge-and-purge eating pattern.

C

care perspective The moral perspective of Carol Gilligan, which views people in terms of their connectedness with others and emphasizes interpersonal communication, relationships with others, and concern for others.

case study An in-depth look at a single individual.

centration The focusing of attention on one characteristic to the exclusion of all others.

cephalocaudal pattern The sequence in which the earliest growth always occurs at the top—the head—with physical growth and feature differentiation gradually working from top to bottom.

cerebral cortex Tissue that covers the forebrain like a wrinkled cap and includes two halves, or hemispheres.

cerebral palsy A disorder that involves a lack of muscular coordination, shaking, and unclear speech.

cesarean delivery Delivery in which the baby is removed from the mother's uterus through an incision made in her abdomen. This also is sometimes referred to as a cesarean section.

character education A direct education approach that involves teaching students a basic moral literacy to prevent them from engaging in immoral behavior and doing harm to themselves and others.

child-centered kindergarten Education that involves the whole child by considering the child's physical, cognitive, and socioemotional development and addressing the child's needs, interests, and learning styles.

child-directed speech Language spoken in a higher pitch than normal, with simple words and sentences.

chromosomes Threadlike structures made up of deoxyribonucleic acid, or DNA.

clique A small group that ranges from 2 to about 12 individuals, averaging about 5 or 6 individuals, and one that can form because adolescents engage in similar activities.

cognitive moral education A concept based on the belief that students should develop such values as democracy and justice as their moral reasoning develops; Kohlberg's theory has been the basis of a number of cognitive moral education programs.

cognitive processes Changes in an individual's thought, intelligence, and language.

cohort effects Effects due to a person's time of birth, era, or generation but not to actual age.

commitment Marcia's term for the part of identity development in which individuals show a personal investment in identity.

concepts Cognitive groupings of similar objects, events, people, or ideas.

connectedness Characteristic consisting of two dimensions: mutuality (sensitivity to and respect for others' views) and permeability (openness to others' views).

conscience An internal regulation of standards of right and wrong that involves an integration of moral thought, feeling, and behavior.

conservation The concept that an object's or substance's basic properties stay the same even though its appearance has been altered.

constructive play Play that combines sensorimotor/practice play with symbolic representation. Constructive play occurs when children engage in self-regulated creation or construction of a product or a solution.

constructivist approach A learner-centered approach that emphasizes the importance of individuals actively constructing their knowledge and understanding with guidance from the teacher.

context The settings, influenced by historical, economic, social, and cultural factors, in which development occurs.

continuity-discontinuity issue The issue regarding whether development involves gradual, cumulative change (continuity) or distinct stages (discontinuity).

controversial children Children who are frequently nominated both as someone's best friend and as being disliked.

conventional reasoning The second, or intermediate, level in Kohlberg's theory of moral development. At this level, individuals abide by certain standards, but they are the standards of others such as parents or the government.

convergent thinking Thinking that produces one correct answer and is characteristic of the kind of thinking tested by standardized intelligence tests.

coordination of secondary circular reactions Piaget's fourth sensorimotor substage, which develops between 8 and 12 months of age. Actions become more outwardly directed, and infants coordinate schemes and act with intentionality.

core knowledge approach View that infants are born with domain-specific innate knowledge systems.

corpus callosum The location where fibers connect the brain's left and right hemispheres.

correlational research A research design whose goal is to describe the strength of the relationship between two or more events or characteristics.

correlation coefficient A number based on statistical analysis that is used to describe the degree of association between two variables.

creative thinking The ability to think in novel and unusual ways and to come up with unique solutions to problems.

crisis Marcia's term for a period of identity development during which the individual is exploring alternatives.

critical thinking The ability to think reflectively and productively, as well as to evaluate the evidence.

cross-cultural studies Comparisons of one culture with one or more other cultures. These comparisons provide information about the degree to which children's development is similar, or universal, across cultures, and the degree to which it is culture-specific.

cross-sectional approach A research strategy in which individuals of different ages are compared at one time.

crowd A larger group than a clique, one that is usually formed based on reputation; members may or may not spend much time together.

cultural-familial retardation Retardation in which there is no evidence of organic brain damage but the individual's IQ generally is between 50 and 70.

culture The behavior patterns, beliefs, and all other products of a group that are passed on from generation to generation.

culture-fair tests Tests of intelligence that are designed to be free of cultural bias.

D

deferred imitation Imitation that occurs after a delay of hours or days.

Denver Development Screening Test II A test used to diagnose developmental delay in children from birth to 6 years of age; includes separate assessments of gross and fine motor skills, language, and personal-social ability.

descriptive research A research design that has the purpose of observing and recording behavior.

design stage Kellogg's term for 3- to 4-year-olds' drawings that mix two basic shapes into more complex designs.

development The pattern of movement or change that begins at conception and continues through the human life span.

developmental quotient (DQ) An overall score that combines subscores in motor, language, adaptive, and personal-social domains in the Gesell assessment of infants.

developmentally appropriate practice (DAP) Education that focuses on the typical developmental patterns of children (age appropriateness) as well as the uniqueness of each child (individual appropriateness). Such practice contrasts with *developmentally inappropriate practice*, which ignores the concrete, hands-on approach to learning. For example, direct teaching largely through abstract paper-and-pencil activities presented to large groups of young children is believed to be developmentally inappropriate.

difficult child A child who tends to react negatively and cry frequently, who engages in irregular daily routines, and who is slow to accept new experiences.

direct instruction approach A structured, teacher-centered approach that is characterized by teacher direction and control, mastery of academic skills, high expectations for students' progress, maximum time spent on learning tasks, and efforts to keep negative affect to a minimum.

dishabituation Recovery of a habituated response after a change in stimulation.

divergent thinking Thinking that produces many different answers to the same question and is characteristic of creativity.

DNA A complex molecule with a double helix shape; contains genetic information.

domain theory of moral development Theory that traces social knowledge and reasoning to moral, social conventional, and personal domains. These domains arise from children's and adolescents' attempts to understand and deal with different forms of social experience.

doula A caregiver who provides continuous physical, emotional, and educational support to the mother before, during, and after childbirth.

Down syndrome A chromosomally transmitted form of mental retardation, caused by the presence of an extra copy of chromosome 21.

dual-process model States that decision making is influenced by two systems—one analytical and one experiential, which compete with each other; in this model, it is the experiential system—monitoring and managing actual experiences—that benefits adolescent decision making.

dynamic systems theory The perspective on motor development that seeks to explain how motor skills are assembled for perceiving and acting.

dyscalculia Also known as developmental arithmetic disorder; a learning disability that involves difficulty in math computation.

dysgraphia A learning disability that involves difficulty in handwriting.

dyslexia A category of learning disabilities involving a severe impairment in the ability to read and spell.

E

early childhood The developmental period that extends from the end of infancy to about 5 to 6 years of age; sometimes called the preschool years.

early-later experience issue The issue of the degree to which early experiences (especially infancy) or later experiences are the key determinants of the child's development.

easy child A child who is generally in a positive mood, who quickly establishes regular routines in infancy, and who adapts easily to new experiences.

eclectic theoretical orientation An orientation that does not follow any one theoretical approach but rather selects from each theory whatever is considered the best in it.

ecological view The view that perception functions to bring organisms in contact with the environment and to increase adaptation.

ectoderm The outermost layer of cells, which becomes the nervous system and brain, sensory receptors (ears, nose, and eyes, for example), and skin parts (hair and nails, for example).

educationally blind Unable to use one's vision in learning and needing to use hearing and touch to learn.

egocentrism Piaget's concept that describes the inability to distinguish between one's own perspective and someone else's perspective.

elaboration An important strategy that involves engaging in more extensive processing of information.

embryonic period The period of prenatal development that occurs two to eight weeks after conception. During the embryonic period, the rate of cell differentiation intensifies, support systems for the cells form, and organs appear.

emerging adulthood Occurring from approximately 18 to 25 years of age, this transitional period between adolescence and adulthood is characterized by experimentation and exploration.

emotion Feeling, or affect, that occurs when a person is in a state or interaction that is important to him or her. Emotion can be characterized as positive (enthusiasm, joy, love, for example) or negative (anxiety, guilt, or sadness, for example).

emotional and behavioral disorders Serious, persistent problems that involve relationships, aggression, depression, fears associated with personal or school matters, as well as other inappropriate socioemotional characteristics.

endoderm The inner layer of cells, which develops into digestive and respiratory systems.

epigenetic view Emphasizes that development is the result of an ongoing, bidirectional interchange between heredity and environment.

equilibration A mechanism that Piaget proposed to explain how children shift from one stage of thought to the next.

Erikson's theory Includes eight stages of human development. Each stage consists of a unique developmental task that confronts individuals with a crisis that must be resolved.

estradiol A hormone associated in girls with breast, uterine, and skeletal development.

ethnic gloss The use of an ethnic label such as African American or Latino in a superficial way that portrays an ethnic group as being more homogeneous than it really is.

ethnic identity An enduring, basic aspect of the self that includes a sense of membership in an ethnic group and the attitudes and feelings related to that membership.

ethnicity A characteristic based on cultural heritage, nationality, race, religion, and language.

ethology Stresses that behavior is strongly influenced by biology, is tied to evolution, and is characterized by critical or sensitive periods.

evocative genotype-environment correlations Correlations that exist when the child's characteristics elicit certain types of physical and social environments.

evolutionary psychology Branch of psychology that emphasizes the importance of adaptation, reproduction, and "survival of the fittest" in shaping behavior.

executive attention Involves action planning, allocating attention to goals, error detection and compensation, monitoring progress on tasks, and dealing with novel or difficult circumstances.

executive functioning An umbrella-like concept that consists of a number of higher-level cognitive processes linked to the development of the brain's prefrontal cortex. Executive functioning involves managing one's thoughts to engage in goal-directed behavior and self-control.

experiment A carefully regulated procedure in which one or more of the factors believed to influence the behavior being studied are manipulated, while all other factors are held constant.

explicit memory Conscious memory of facts and experiences.

extrinsic motivation Involves external incentives such as rewards and punishments.

F

fertilization A stage in reproduction whereby an egg and a sperm fuse to create a single cell, called a zygote.

fetal alcohol spectrum disorders (FASD) A cluster of abnormalities and problems that appears in the offspring of mothers who drink alcohol heavily during pregnancy.

fetal period The prenatal period of development that begins two months after conception and lasts for seven months on average.

fine motor skills Motor skills that involve finely tuned movements, such as finger dexterity.

first habits and primary circular reactions Piaget's second sensorimotor substage, which develops between 1 and 4 months of age. In this substage, the infant coordinates sensation and two types of schemes: habits and primary circular reactions.

fluency disorders Various disorders that involve what is commonly called "stuttering."

forebrain The region of the brain that is farthest from the spinal cord and includes the cerebral cortex and several structures beneath it.

fragile X syndrome A genetic disorder involving an abnormality in the X chromosome, which becomes constricted and often breaks.

fuzzy trace theory A theory stating that memory is best understood by considering two types of memory representations: (1) verbatim memory trace and (2) gist. In this theory, older children's better memory is attributed to the fuzzy traces created by extracting the gist of information.

G

games Activities engaged in for pleasure that include rules and often competition with one or more individuals.

gender The characteristics of people as females or males.

gender identity The sense of one's own gender, including knowledge, understanding, and acceptance of being male or female.

gender role A set of expectations that prescribes how females or males should think, act, and feel.

gender schema theory The theory that gender typing emerges as children gradually develop gender schemas of what is considered gender-appropriate and gender-inappropriate in their culture.

gender stereotypes Broad categories that reflect our impressions and beliefs about females and males.

gender typing Acquisition of a traditional masculine or feminine role.

gene × environment (G × E) interaction The interaction of a specific measured variation in the DNA and a specific measured aspect of the environment.

genes Units of hereditary information composed of DNA. Genes direct cells to reproduce themselves and manufacture the proteins that maintain life.

genotype A person's genetic heritage; the actual genetic material.

germinal period The period of prenatal development that takes place in the first two weeks after conception. It includes the creation of the zygote, continued cell division, and the attachment of the zygote to the uterine wall.

gifted Having above-average intelligence (an IQ of 130 or higher) and/or superior talent for something.

gonadotropins Hormones that stimulate the testes or ovaries.

gonads The sex glands—the testes in males, the ovaries in females.

goodness of fit Refers to the match between a child's temperament and the environmental demands with which the child must cope.

grasping reflex A neonatal reflex that occurs when something touches the infant's palms. The infant responds by grasping tightly.

gross motor skills Motor skills that involve large-muscle activities, such as walking.

growth hormone deficiency The absence or deficiency of growth hormone produced by the pituitary gland to stimulate the body to grow.

H

habituation Decreased responsiveness to a stimulus after repeated presentations of the stimulus.

helpless orientation An orientation in which one seems trapped by the experience of difficulty and attributes one's difficulty to a lack of ability.

heritability The fraction of variance in a population that is attributed to genetics and is computed using correlational techniques.

heteronomous morality (1) Kohlberg's first stage in preconventional reasoning in which moral thinking is tied to punishment. (2) The first stage of moral development in Piaget's theory, occurring from approximately 4 to 7 years of age. Justice and rules are conceived of as unchangeable properties of the world, removed from the control of people.

hidden curriculum Dewey's concept that every school has a pervasive moral atmosphere, even if it doesn't have a program of moral education.

hormones Powerful chemical substances secreted by the endocrine glands and carried through the body by the bloodstream.

hypothalamus A structure in the brain that monitors eating and sex.

hypothesis A specific assumption or prediction that can be tested to determine its accuracy.

hypothetical-deductive reasoning Piaget's formal operational concept that adolescents have the cognitive ability to develop hypotheses, or best guesses, about ways to solve problems.

I

identity achievement Marcia's term for the status of individuals who have undergone a crisis and have made a commitment.

identity diffusion Marcia's term for the status of individuals who have not yet experienced a crisis (explored alternatives) or made any commitments.

identity foreclosure   Marcia's term for the status of individuals who have made a commitment but have not experienced a crisis.

identity moratorium   Marcia's term for the status of individuals who are in the midst of a crisis, but their commitments are either absent or vaguely defined.

identity versus identity confusion   Erikson's fifth developmental stage, which occurs at about the time of adolescence. At this time, adolescents are faced with deciding who they are, what they are all about, and where they are going in life.

imaginary audience   Refers to adolescents' belief that others are as interested in them as they themselves are, as well as their attention-getting behavior motivated by a desire to be noticed, visible, and "on stage."

immanent justice   The expectation that, if a rule is broken, punishment will be meted out immediately.

implicit memory   Memory without conscious recollection; involves skills and routine procedures that are automatically performed.

inclusion   Educating a child with special educational needs full-time in the regular classroom.

individual differences   The stable, consistent ways in which people differ from each other.

individualism, instrumental purpose, and exchange   The second Kohlberg stage in preconventional reasoning. At this stage, individuals pursue their own interests but also let others do the same.

individuality   Characteristic consisting of two dimensions: self-assertion (the ability to have and communicate a point of view) and separateness (the use of communication patterns to express how one is different from others).

individualized education plan (IEP)   A written statement that spells out a program tailored to a child with a disability. The plan should be (1) related to the child's learning capacity, (2) specially constructed to meet the child's individual needs and not merely a copy of what is offered to other children, and (3) designed to provide educational benefits.

Individuals with Disabilities Education Act (IDEA)   The IDEA spells out broad mandates for providing services to all children with disabilities (IDEA is a renaming of Public Law 94-142); these include evaluation and eligibility determination, appropriate education and an individualized education plan (IEP), and education in the least restrictive environment (LRE).

indulgent parenting   A style of parenting in which parents are highly involved with their

children but place few demands or controls on them. Indulgent parenting is associated with children's social incompetence, especially a lack of self-control.

infancy   The developmental period that extends from birth to 18 to 24 months of age.

infinite generativity   The ability to produce an endless number of meaningful sentences using a finite set of words and rules.

information-processing theory   Emphasizes that individuals manipulate information, monitor it, and strategize about it. Central to this theory are the processes of memory and thinking.

insecure avoidant babies   Babies that show insecurity by avoiding the caregiver.

insecure disorganized babies   Babies that show insecurity by being disorganized and disoriented.

insecure resistant babies   Babies that often cling to the caregiver, then resist her by fighting against the closeness, perhaps by kicking or pushing away.

intelligence   Problem-solving skills and the ability to learn from and adapt to the experiences of everyday life.

intelligence quotient (IQ)   A person's mental age divided by chronological age, multiplied by 100.

intermodal perception   The ability to relate and integrate information from two or more sensory modalities, such as vision and hearing.

internalization of schemes   Piaget's sixth and final sensorimotor substage, which develops between 18 and 24 months of age. In this substage, the infant develops the ability to use primitive symbols.

intimacy in friendships   Self-disclosure and the sharing of private thoughts.

intrinsic motivation   Involves internal factors such as self-determination, curiosity, challenge, and effort.

intuitive thought substage   Piaget's second substage of preoperational thought, in which children begin to use primitive reasoning and want to know the answers to all sorts of questions (occurs between about 4 and 7 years of age).

involution   The process by which the uterus returns to its prepregnant size.

J

joint attention   Occurs when individuals focus on the same object or event and are able to track each other's behavior; one individual directs another's attention, and reciprocal interaction is present.

justice perspective   A moral perspective that focuses on the rights of the individual; individuals independently make moral decisions.

juvenile delinquent   An adolescent who breaks the law or engages in behavior that is considered illegal.

K

kangaroo care   A way of holding a preterm infant so that there is skin-to-skin contact.

Klinefelter syndrome   A genetic disorder in which males have an extra X chromosome, making them XXY instead of XY.

kwashiorkor   A condition caused by a severe deficiency in protein in which the child's abdomen and feet become swollen with water; usually appears between 1 and 3 years of age.

L

laboratory   A controlled setting in which many of the complex factors of the "real world" are removed.

language   A form of communication, whether spoken, written, or signed, that is based on a system of symbols.

language acquisition device (LAD)   Chomsky's term that describes a biological endowment that enables the child to detect the features and rules of language, including phonology, syntax, and semantics.

lateralization   Specialization of function in one hemisphere of the cerebral cortex or the other.

learning disability   Disability in which a child has difficulty in learning that involves understanding or using spoken or written language, and the difficulty can appear in listening, thinking, reading, writing, or spelling. A learning disability also may involve difficulty in doing mathematics. To be classified as a learning disability, the learning problem is not primarily the result of visual, hearing, or motor disabilities; mental retardation; emotional disorders; or environmental, cultural, or economic disadvantage.

least restrictive environment (LRE)   The concept that a child with a disability must be educated in a setting that is as similar as possible to the one in which children who do not have a disability are educated.

longitudinal approach   A research strategy in which the same individuals are studied over a period of time, usually several years or more.

long-term memory   A relatively permanent type of memory that holds huge amounts of information for a long period of time.

low birth weight infants Babies that weigh less than 5½ pounds at birth.

low vision Visual acuity between 20/70 and 20/2000.

M

manual approaches Educational approaches to help hearing-impaired children, including sign language and finger spelling.

marasmus A wasting away of body tissues in the infant's first year, caused by severe protein-calorie deficiency.

mastery motivation An orientation that focuses on tasks, learning strategies, and the achievement process rather than innate ability.

meiosis A specialized form of cell division that occurs to form eggs and sperm (or gametes).

melatonin A sleep-inducing hormone that is produced in the brain's pineal gland.

memory A central feature of cognitive development, involving the retention of information over time.

menarche A girl's first menstrual period.

mental age (MA) Binet's measure of an individual's level of mental development, compared with that of others.

mental retardation A condition of limited mental ability in which an individual has a low IQ, usually below 70 on a traditional test of intelligence, and has difficulty adapting to everyday life.

mesoderm The middle layer of cells, which becomes the circulatory system, bones, muscles, excretory system, and reproductive system.

metacognition Cognition about cognition, or knowing about knowing.

metalinguistic awareness Knowledge about language, such as knowing what a preposition is or being able to discuss the sounds of a language.

middle and late childhood The developmental period that extends from about 6 to 11 years of age; sometimes called the elementary school years.

Millennials The generation born after 1980, which is the first generation to come of age and enter emerging adulthood in the new millennium; members of this generation are characterized by their ethnic diversity and their connection to technology.

mindfulness Being alert, mentally present, and cognitively flexible while going through life's everyday activities and tasks.

mindset The cognitive view, either fixed or growth, that individuals develop for themselves.

mitosis Cellular reproduction in which the cell's nucleus duplicates itself with two new cells being formed, each containing the same DNA as the parent cell, arranged in the same 23 pairs of chromosomes.

Montessori approach An educational philosophy in which children are given considerable freedom and spontaneity in choosing activities and specially designed curriculum materials.

moral development Development that involves thoughts, feelings, and behaviors regarding rules and conventions about what people should do in their interactions with other people.

Moro reflex A neonatal startle response that occurs in reaction to a sudden, intense noise or movement. When startled, newborns arch their back, throw their head back, and fling out their arms and legs. Then they rapidly close their arms and legs, bringing them close to the center of the body.

morphology Units of meaning involved in word formation.

mutual interpersonal expectations, relationships, and interpersonal conformity Kohlberg's third stage of moral development. At this stage, individuals value trust, caring, and loyalty to others as a basis of moral judgments.

myelination The process in which the nerve cells are covered and insulated with a layer of fat cells, which increases the speed at which information travels through the nervous system.

N

natural childbirth Method developed in 1914 by English obstetrician Grantly Dick-Read that attempts to reduce the mother's pain by decreasing her fear through education about childbirth and breathing methods and relaxation techniques during delivery.

naturalistic observation Observing behavior in real-world settings.

nature-nurture issue The issue regarding whether development is primarily influenced by nature or nurture. The "nature" proponents claim that biological inheritance is the more important influence on development; the "nurture" proponents assert that environmental experiences are more important.

neglected children Children who are infrequently nominated as a best friend but are not disliked by their peers.

neglectful parenting A style of parenting in which the parent is very uninvolved in the child's life; it is associated with children's

social incompetence, especially a lack of self-control.

Neonatal Intensive Care Unit Network Neurobehavioral Scale (NNNS) An "offspring" of the NBAS, the NNNS provides a more comprehensive analysis of the newborn's behavior, neurological and stress responses, and regulatory capacities.

neo-Piagetians Developmentalists who have elaborated on Piaget's theory, giving more emphasis to information processing, strategies, and precise cognitive steps.

neuroconstructivist view In this view, biological processes and environmental conditions influence the brain's development; the brain has plasticity and is context dependent; and brain development is closely linked with cognitive development.

neurogenesis The formation of new neurons.

neurons The term for nerve cells, which handle information processing at the cellular level.

nightmares Frightening dreams that awaken the sleeper.

night terrors Incidents characterized by sudden arousal from sleep, intense fear, and usually physiological reactions such as rapid heart rate and breathing, loud screams, heavy perspiration, and physical movement.

nonshared environmental experiences The child's own unique experiences, both within the family and outside the family, that are not shared by another sibling. Thus, experiences occurring within the family can be part of the "nonshared environment."

normal distribution A symmetrical distribution with most scores falling in the middle of the possible range of scores and few scores appearing toward the extremes of the range.

O

object permanence Piagetian term for understanding that objects continue to exist, even when they cannot directly be seen, heard, or touched.

operations In Piaget's theory, reversible mental actions that allow children to do mentally what they formerly did physically.

oral approaches Educational approaches to help hearing-impaired children, including lip reading, speech reading, and use of whatever hearing the child has.

organic retardation Mental retardation that involves physical causes such as a genetic disorder or brain damage.

organization Piaget's concept of grouping isolated behaviors and thoughts into a higher-order system, a more smoothly functioning cognitive system.

organogenesis Process of organ formation that takes place during the first two months of prenatal development.

orthopedic impairments Restrictions in movement abilities due to muscle, bone, or joint problems.

oxytocin A synthetic hormone that is used to stimulate contractions.

P

pain cry A sudden appearance of a long, initial loud cry without preliminary moaning, followed by breath holding.

passive genotype-environment correlations Correlations that exist when the biological parents, who are genetically related to the child, provide a rearing environment for the child.

perception The interpretation of what is sensed.

performance orientation An orientation in which one focuses on achievement outcomes; winning is what matters most, and happiness is thought to result from winning.

personal fable The part of adolescent egocentrism that involves an adolescent's sense of uniqueness and invincibility.

perspective taking The social cognitive process involved in assuming the perspective of others and understanding their thoughts and feelings.

phenotype The way an individual's genotype is expressed in observed and measurable characteristics.

phenylketonuria (PKU) A genetic disorder in which the individual cannot properly metabolize phenylalanine, an amino acid. PKU is now easily detected—but if left untreated, results in mental retardation and hyperactivity.

phonics approach The idea that reading instruction should teach basic rules for translating written symbols into sounds.

phonology The sound system of the language, including the sounds that are used and how they may be combined.

Piaget's theory States that children actively construct their understanding of the world and go through four stages of cognitive development.

pictorial stage Kellogg's term for 4- to 5-year-olds' drawings depicting objects that adults can recognize.

pituitary gland An important endocrine gland that controls growth and regulates other glands.

placement stage Kellogg's term for 2- to 3-year-olds' drawings that are drawn on a page in placement patterns.

placenta A disk-shaped group of tissues in which small blood vessels from the mother and the offspring intertwine but don't join.

popular children Children who are frequently nominated as a best friend and are rarely disliked by their peers.

postconventional reasoning The highest level in Kohlberg's theory of moral development. At this level, the individual recognizes alternative moral courses, explores the options, and then decides on a personal moral code.

postpartum depression Involves a major depressive episode characterized by strong feelings of sadness, anxiety, or despair in new mothers, making it difficult for them to carry out daily tasks.

postpartum period The period after childbirth when the mother adjusts, both physically and psychologically, to the process of childbearing. This period lasts for about six weeks, or until her body has completed its adjustment and has returned to a near-prepregnant state.

practice play Play that involves repetition of behavior when new skills are being learned or when physical or mental mastery and coordination of skills are required for games or sports.

pragmatics The appropriate use of language in different contexts.

preconventional reasoning The lowest level in Kohlberg's theory of moral development. The individual's concept of good and bad is interpreted primarily in terms of external rewards and punishment.

prenatal period The time from conception to birth.

preoperational stage Piaget's second stage, lasting from 2 to 7 years of age, during which time children begin to represent the world with words, images, and drawings. In this stage, they also form stable concepts and begin to reason. At the same time, their cognitive world is dominated by egocentrism and magical beliefs.

prepared childbirth Developed by French obstetrician Ferdinand Lamaze; this childbirth method is similar to natural childbirth but teaches a special breathing technique to control pushing in the final stages of labor and also provides a more detailed anatomy and physiology course.

pretense/symbolic play Play in which the child transforms the physical environment into a symbol.

preterm infants Babies born three weeks or more before the pregnancy has reached its full term.

primary circular reaction A scheme based on the attempt to reproduce an event that initially occurred by chance.

primary emotions Emotions that are present in humans and other animals, and emerge early in life; examples are joy, anger, sadness, fear, and disgust.

Project Head Start Compensatory education designed to provide children from low-income families the opportunity to acquire skills and experiences that are important for school success.

proximodistal pattern The sequence in which growth starts at the center of the body and moves toward the extremities.

psychoanalytic theories Describe development as primarily unconscious and heavily colored by emotion. Behavior is merely a surface characteristic, and the symbolic workings of the mind have to be analyzed to understand behavior. Early experiences with parents are emphasized.

psychoanalytic theory of gender A theory deriving from Freud's view that the preschool child develops a sexual attraction to the opposite-sex parent, by approximately 5 or 6 years of age renounces this attraction because of anxious feelings, and subsequently identifies with the same-sex parent, unconsciously adopting the same-sex parent's characteristics.

psychosocial moratorium Erikson's term for the gap between childhood security and adult autonomy.

puberty A period of rapid physical maturation involving hormonal and bodily changes that occur primarily in early adolescence.

Public Law 94-142 The Education for All Handicapped Children Act, created in 1975, which requires that all children with disabilities be given a free, appropriate public education and which provides the funding to help with the costs of implementing this education.

R

rapport talk The language of conversation and a way of establishing connections and negotiating relationships; more characteristic of females than of males.

reciprocal socialization Socialization that is bidirectional; children socialize parents, just as parents socialize children.

reflexes Built-in reactions to stimuli that govern the newborn's movements, which are automatic and beyond the newborn's control.

reflexive smile A smile that does not occur in response to external stimuli. It happens during the month after birth, usually during sleep.

rejected children Children who are infrequently nominated as a best friend and are actively disliked by their peers.

religion An organized set of beliefs, practices, rituals, and symbols that increases an individual's connection to a sacred or transcendent other (God, higher power, or higher truth).

religiousness The degree of affiliation with an organized religion, participation in prescribed rituals and practices, connection with its beliefs, and involvement in a community of believers.

report talk Talk that conveys information; more characteristic of males than females.

rite of passage A ceremony or ritual that marks an individual's transition from one status to another. Most rites of passage focus on the transition to adult status.

rooting reflex A newborn's built-in reaction that occurs when the infant's cheek is stroked or the side of the mouth is touched. In response, the infant turns its head toward the side that was touched in an apparent effort to find something to suck.

S

scaffolding (caregiver-infant interaction) Adjusting the level of guidance to fit the child's performance.

scaffolding (Vygotsky) In regard to cognitive development, Vygotsky used this term to describe the changing level of support over the course of a teaching session, with the more-skilled person adjusting guidance to fit the child's current performance level.

schemes In Piaget's theory, actions or mental representations that organize knowledge.

scientific method An approach that can be used to obtain accurate information. It includes these steps: (1) conceptualize the problem, (2) collect data, (3) draw conclusions, and (4) revise research conclusions and theory.

secondary circular reactions Piaget's third sensorimotor substage, which develops between 4 and 8 months of age. In this substage, the infant becomes more object-oriented, moving beyond preoccupation with the self.

securely attached babies Babies that use the caregiver as a secure base from which to explore their environment.

self-concept Domain-specific evaluations of the self.

self-conscious emotions Emotions that require self-awareness, especially consciousness and a sense of "me"; examples include jealousy, empathy, and embarrassment.

self-efficacy The belief that one can master a situation and produce favorable outcomes.

self-esteem The global evaluative dimension of the self. Self-esteem is also referred to as self-worth or self-image.

self-understanding The child's cognitive representation of self, the substance and content of the child's self-conceptions.

semantics The meaning of words and sentences.

sensation The product of the interaction between information and the sensory receptors—the eyes, ears, tongue, nostrils, and skin.

sensorimotor play Behavior engaged in by infants to derive pleasure from exercising their existing sensorimotor schemas.

sensorimotor stage The first of Piaget's stages, which lasts from birth to about 2 years of age, in which infants construct an understanding of the world by coordinating sensory experiences with motoric actions.

separation protest An infant's distressed reaction when the caregiver leaves.

seriation The concrete operation that involves ordering stimuli along a quantitative dimension (such as length).

service learning A form of education that promotes social responsibility and service to the community.

sexually transmitted infections (STIs) Diseases that are contracted primarily through sexual contact. This contact is not limited to vaginal intercourse but includes oral-genital contact and anal-genital contact as well.

shape constancy The recognition that an object's shape remains the same even though its orientation to us changes.

shape stage Kellogg's term for 3-year-olds' drawings consisting of diagrams in different shapes.

shared environmental experiences Siblings' common experiences, such as their parents' personalities and intellectual orientation, the family's socioeconomic status, and the neighborhood in which they live.

short-term memory The memory component in which individuals retain information for up to 30 seconds, assuming there is no rehearsal.

sickle-cell anemia A genetic disorder that affects the red blood cells and occurs most often in people of African descent.

simple reflexes Piaget's first sensorimotor substage, which corresponds to the first month after birth. In this substage, sensation and action are coordinated primarily through reflexive behaviors.

size constancy The recognition that an object remains the same even though the retinal image of the object changes as you move toward or away from the object.

slow-to-warm-up child A child who has a low activity level, is somewhat negative, and displays a low intensity of mood.

small for date (small for gestational age) infants Babies whose birth weight is below normal when the length of pregnancy is considered.

social cognitive theory The view of psychologists who emphasize behavior, environment, and cognition as the key factors in development.

social cognitive theory of gender A theory that emphasizes that children's gender development occurs through the observation and imitation of gender behavior and through the rewards and punishments children experience for gender-appropriate and gender-inappropriate behavior.

social constructivist approach An approach that emphasizes the social contexts of learning and the fact that knowledge is mutually built and constructed; Vygotsky's theory is a social constructivist approach.

social contract or utility and individual rights The fifth Kohlberg stage. At this stage, individuals reason that values, rights, and principles undergird or transcend the law.

social conventional reasoning Thoughts about social consensus and convention established in order to control behavior and maintain the social system.

social play Play that involves social interactions with peers.

social policy A government's course of action designed to promote the welfare of its citizens.

social referencing "Reading" emotional cues in others to help determine how to act in a particular situation.

social role theory A theory that gender differences result from the contrasting roles of men and women.

social smile A smile in response to an external stimulus, which, early in development, typically is a face.

social systems morality The fourth stage in Kohlberg's theory of moral development. Moral judgments are based on understanding the social order, law, justice, and duty.

socioeconomic status (SES)   An individual's position within society based on occupational, educational, and economic characteristics.

socioemotional processes   Changes in an individual's relationships with other people, changes in emotions, and changes in personality.

somnambulism   Sleep walking; occurs in the deepest stage of sleep.

spirituality   Experiencing something beyond oneself in a transcendent manner and living in a way that benefits others and society.

standardized test   A test with uniform procedures for administration and scoring. Many standardized tests allow a person's performance to be compared with the performance of other individuals.

stranger anxiety   An infant's fear and wariness of strangers; it tends to appear in the second half of the first year of life.

Strange Situation   An observational measure of infant attachment that requires the infant to move through a series of introductions, separations, and reunions with the caregiver and an adult stranger in a prescribed order.

strategies   Deliberate mental activities designed to improve the processing of information.

sucking reflex   A newborn's built-in reaction to automatically suck an object placed in the mouth. The sucking reflex enables the infant to get nourishment before he or she has associated a nipple with food and also serves as a self-soothing or self-regulating mechanism.

sudden infant death syndrome (SIDS)   A condition that occurs when an infant stops breathing, usually during the night, and suddenly dies without an apparent cause.

sustained attention   Focused and extended engagement with an object, task, event, or other aspect of the environment.

symbolic function substage   Piaget's first substage of preoperational thought, in which the child gains the ability to mentally represent an object that is not present (occurs roughly between 2 and 4 years of age).

syntax   The ways words are combined to form acceptable phrases and sentences.

T

telegraphic speech   The use of content words without grammatical markers such as articles, auxiliary verbs, and other connectives.

temperament   An individual's behavioral style and characteristic way of emotionally responding.

teratogen   Any agent that can potentially cause a physical birth defect. The field of study that investigates the causes of birth defects is called *teratology*.

tertiary circular reactions, novelty, and curiosity   Piaget's fifth sensorimotor substage, which develops between 12 and 18 months of age. In this substage, infants become intrigued by the many properties of objects and by the many things that they can make happen to objects.

testosterone   A hormone associated in boys with the development of genitals, an increase in height, and a change in voice.

theory   An interrelated, coherent set of ideas that helps to explain and make predictions.

theory of mind   A concept that refers to awareness of one's own mental processes and the mental processes of others.

top-dog phenomenon   The circumstance of moving from the top position (in elementary school, the oldest, biggest, and most powerful students) to the lowest position (in middle or junior high school, the youngest, smallest, and least powerful students).

transitivity   The ability to logically combine relations to understand certain conclusions.

triarchic theory of intelligence   Sternberg's theory that intelligence consists of analytical intelligence, creative intelligence, and practical intelligence.

trophoblast   The outer layer of cells that develops in the germinal period. These cells later provide nutrition and support for the embryo.

Turner syndrome   A chromosomal disorder in females in which either an X chromosome is missing, making the person XO instead of XX, or the second X chromosome is partially deleted.

twin study   A study in which the behavioral similarity of identical twins is compared with the behavioral similarity of fraternal twins.

type 1 diabetes   An autoimmune disease in which the body's immune system destroys insulin-producing cells.

type 2 diabetes   The most common type of diabetes, in which the body is able to produce insulin, but it may be insufficient or the body's cells may be unable to use it.

U

umbilical cord   Contains two arteries and one vein, and connects the baby to the placenta.

universal ethical principles   The sixth and highest stage in Kohlberg's theory of moral development. Individuals develop a moral standard based on universal principles of human rights.

V

values   Beliefs and attitudes about the way things should be.

visual preference method   A method used to determine whether infants can distinguish one stimulus from another by measuring the length of time they attend to different stimuli.

voice disorders   Disorders reflected in speech that is hoarse, harsh, too loud, too high-pitched, or too low-pitched.

Vygotsky's theory   A sociocultural cognitive theory that emphasizes how culture and social interaction guide cognitive development.

W

Wernicke's area   An area of the brain's left hemisphere that is involved in language comprehension.

whole-language approach   An approach to reading instruction based on the idea that instruction should parallel children's natural language learning. Reading materials should be whole and meaningful.

working memory   A mental "workbench" where individuals manipulate and assemble information when making decisions, solving problems, and comprehending written and spoken language.

X

XYY syndrome   A chromosomal disorder in which males have an extra Y chromosome.

Z

zone of proximal development (ZPD)   Vygotsky's term for the range of tasks that are too difficult for children to achieve alone but can be achieved with the guidance and assistance of adults or more-skilled children.

zygote   A single cell formed through fertilization.

references

A

Abbasi, M., & others. (2010). The effect of hypnosis on pain relief during labor and childbirth in Iranian pregnant women. *International Journal of Clinical and Experimental Hypnosis, 57,* 174–183.

Abbate-Daga, G., Gramaglia, C., Amianto, F., Marzola, E., & Fassino, S. (2010). Attachment insecurity, personality, and body dissatisfaction in eating disorders. *Journal of Nervous and Mental Disease, 198,* 520–524.

Abbott, B. D., & Barber, B. L. (2010). Embodied image: Gender differences in functional and aesthetic body image among Australian adolescents. *Body Image, 7,* 22–31.

ABC News. (2005, December 12). Larry Page and Sergey Brin. Retrieved June 24, 2006, from www.Montessori.org/enews/barbara_Walters.html

Abelsohn, A. R., & Sanborn, M. (2010). Lead and children: Clinical management for family physicians. *Canadian Family Physician, 56,* 531–535.

Aber, J. L., Bishop-Josef, S. J., Jones, S. M., McLern, T., & Phillips, D. A. (2006). *Child development and social policy.* Washington, DC: American Psychological Association.

Accornero, V. H., Amado, A. J., Morrow, C. E., Xue, L., Anthony, J. C., & Bandstra, E. S. (2007). Impact of prenatal cocaine exposure on attention and response inhibition as assessed by continuous performance tests. *Journal of Developmental and Behavioral Pediatrics, 28,* 195–205.

Ackerman, J. P., Riggins, T., & Black, M. M. (2010). A review of the effects of prenatal cocaine exposure among school-aged children. *Pediatrics, 125,* 554–565.

Adamson, L., & Frick, J. (2003). The still face: A history of a shared experimental paradigm. *Infancy, 4,* 451–473.

Adler, N., Nadler, B., Eviater, Z., & Shamay-Tsoory, S. G. (2010). The relationship between theory of mind and autobiographical memory in high-functioning autism and Asperger syndrome. *Psychiatry Research, 178,* 214–216.

Administration for Children & Families. (2008). Statistical fact sheet fiscal year 2008. Washington, DC: Author.

Adolph, K. E. (1997). Learning in the development of infant locomotion. *Monographs of the Society for Research in Child Development, 62*(3, Serial No. 251).

Adolph, K. E., & Berger, S. E. (2005). Physical and motor development. In M. H. Bornstein & M. E. Lamb (Eds.), *Developmental psychology* (5th ed.). Mahwah, NJ: Erlbaum.

Adolph, K. E., & Berger, S. E. (2011). Development of the motor system. In H. Pashler & others (Eds.), *Encyclopedia of the mind.* Thousand Oaks, CA: Sage.

Adolph, K. E., & Joh, A. S. (2009). Multiple learning mechanisms in the development of action. In A. Needham & A. Woodward (Eds.), *Learning and the infant mind.* New York: Oxford University Press.

Adolph, K. E., Karasik, L. B., & Tamis-LeMonda, C. S. (2010). Motor skills. In M. Bornstein (Ed.), *Handbook of cultural developmental science.* New York: Psychology Press.

Adolph, K. E., & Robinson, S. R. R. (2012, in press). The road to walking: What learning to walk tells us about development. In P. Zelazo (Ed.), *Oxford handbook of developmental psychology.* New York: Oxford University Press.

Agency for Healthcare Research and Quality. (2007). Evidence report/Technology assessment Number 153: Breastfeeding and maternal and health outcomes in developed countries. Rockville, MD: U.S. Department of Health and Human Services.

Agras, W. S., Hammer, L. D., McNicholas, F., & Kraemer, H. C. (2004). Risk factors for childhood overweight: A prospective study from birth to 9.5 years. *Journal of Pediatrics, 145,* 20–25.

Agras, W. S., & others. (2004). Report of the National Institutes of Health workshop on overcoming barriers to treatment research in anorexia nervosa. *International Journal of Eating Disorders, 35,* 509–521.

Ahamed, M., Verma, S., Kumar, A., & Siddiqui, M. K. (2005). Environmental exposure to lead and its correlation with biochemical indices in children. *Science of the Total Environment, 346,* 48–55.

Ahluwalia, I. B., Tessaro, I., Grumer-Strawn, L. M., MacGowan, C., & Benton-Davis, S. (2000). Georgia's breastfeeding promotion program for low-income women. *Pediatrics, 105,* E85–E87.

Ahluwalia, S. K., & Matsui, E. C. (2011). The indoor environment and its effect on childhood asthma. *Current Opinion in Allergy and Clinical Immunology, 11,* 137–143.

Ahmed, S., & others. (2011). Community kangaroo mother care: Implementation and potential for neonatal survival and health in very low-income settings. *Journal of Perinatology, 31*(5), 361–367.

Ahrens, B., Beyer, K., Wahn, U., & Niggemann, B. (2008). Differential diagnosis of food-induced symptoms. *Pediatric Allergy & Immunology, 19,* 92–96.

Ahrons, C. (2004). *We're still family.* New York: HarperCollins.

Ainsworth, M. D. S. (1979). Infant-mother attachment. *American Psychologist, 34,* 932–937.

Akbari, A., & others. (2011). Parity and breastfeeding are preventive measures against breast cancer in Iranian women. *Breast Cancer, 18,* 51–55.

Akhaven, S., & Lundgren, I. (2011, in press). Midwives' experiences of doula support for immigrant women in Sweden—A qualitative study. *Midwifery.*

Akolekar, R., Brown, S., Flack, N., Bilardo, C. M., & Nicolaides, K. H. (2011). Prediction of miscarriage and stillbirth at 11–13 weeks and the contribution of chorionic villus sampling. *Prenatal Diagnosis, 31,* 38–45.

Aksglaede, L., Skakkebaek, N. E., Almstrup, K., & Juul, A. (2011). Clinical and biological parameters in 166 boys, adolescents, and adults with non-mosaic Klinefelter syndrome. A Copenhagen experience. *Acta Paediatrica, 100*(6), 793–806.

Aktar, N., & Herold, K. (2008). Pragmatic development. In M. M. Haith & J. B. Benson (Eds.), *Encyclopedia of infant and early childhood development.* Oxford, UK: Elsevier.

Albert, D., & Steinberg, L. (2011a). Judgment and decision making in adolescence. *Journal of Research on Adolescence, 21,* 211–224.

Albert, D., & Steinberg, L. (2011b). Peer influences on adolescent risk behavior. In M. Bardo, D. Fishbein, & R. Milich (Eds.), *Inhibitory control and drug abuse prevention: From research to translation.* New York: Springer.

Albertsson-Wikland, K. (2011, in press). Growth hormone in children with idiopathic short stature. *British Medical Journal.*

Ali, M. M., & Dwyer, D. S. (2011). Estimating peer effects in sexual behavior among adolescents. *Journal of Adolescence, 34*(1), 183–190.

Allen, J. P. (2007, March). *A transformational perspective on the attachment system in adolescence.* Paper presented at the meeting of the Society for Research in Child Development, Boston.

Allen, J. P. (2008). The attachment system in adolescence. In J. Cassidy & P. R. Shaver (Eds.), *Handbook of attachment* (2nd ed.). New York: Guilford.

Allen, J. P., & Miga, E. M. (2010). Attachment in adolescence: A move to the level of emotion regulation. *Journal of Social and Personal Relationships, 27,* 181–190.

Allen, J. P., Philliber, S., Herring, S., & Kuperminc, G. P. (1997). Preventing teen pregnancy and academic failure: Experimental evaluation of a developmentally-based approach. *Child Development, 68,* 729–742.

Allen, J. P., Porter, M., McFarland, C., Boykin McElhaney, K., & Marsh, P. (2007). The relation of attachment security to adolescents' paternal and peer relationships, depression, and externalizing behavior. *Child Development, 78.* 1222–1239.

Allen, J. P., & others. (2009, April). *Portrait of the secure teen as an adult.* Paper presented at the meeting of the Society for Research in Child Development, Denver.

Allen, M., Svetaz, M. V., Hardeman, R., & Resnick, M. D. (2008, February). What research tells us about parenting practices and their relationship to youth sexual behavior. Campaign to Prevent Teen and Unplanned Pregnancy. Retrieved December 2, 2008, from http://www.TheNationalCampaign.org

Amabile, T. (1993). Commentary. In D. Goleman, P. Kafman, & M. Ray (Eds.), *The creative spirit.* New York: Plume.

Amato, P. R. (2006). Marital discord, divorce, and children's well-being: Results from a 20-year longitudinal study of two generations. In A. Clarke-Stewart & J. Dunn (Eds.), *Families count.* New York: Cambridge University Press.

Amato, P. R., & Booth, A. (1996). A prospective study of divorce and parent-child relationships. *Journal of Marriage and the Family, 58,* 356–365.

Amato, P. R., & Dorius, C. R. (2010). Fathers, children, and divorce. In M. E. Lamb (Ed.), *The role of the father in child development* (5th ed.). New York: Wiley.

Ambrose, D., Sternberg, R. J., & Sriraman, B. (2011). Considering the effects of dogmatism on giftedness and talent development. In D. Ambrose, R. J. Sternberg, & B. Sriraman (Eds.), *Confronting dogmatism in gifted education.* New York: Taylor & Francis.

Amed, S., & others. (2011). Risk factors for medication-induced diabetes and Type 2 diabetes. *Journal of Pediatrics, 159*(2), 291–296.

American Academy of Pediatrics. (2001). Falls from heights: Windows, roofs, and balconies. *Pediatrics, 107,* 1188–1191.

American Academy of Pediatrics & Reiff, M. I. (2011). *ADHD: What every parent needs to know* (2nd ed.). Washington, DC: Author.

American Academy of Pediatrics Task Force on Infant Positioning and SIDS (AAPTFIPS). (2000). Changing concepts of sudden infant death syndrome. *Pediatrics, 105,* 650–656.

American Academy of Pediatrics Work Group on Breastfeeding (AAPWGB). (1997). Breastfeeding and the use of human milk. *Pediatrics, 100,* 1035–1039.

American College of Obstetricians and Gynecologists. (2008). *Exercise during pregnancy.* Retrieved October 13, 2008, from http://www.acog.org/publications/patient_education/bp119.cfm

American Pregnancy Association. (2011). *Mercury levels in fish.* Retrieved March 6, 2011, from http://www.americanpregnancy.org/pregnancyhealth/fishmercury.htm

American Psychological Association (2003). *Psychology: Scientific problem solvers.* Washington, DC: Author.

American Public Health Association. (2006). *Understanding the health culture of recent immigrants to the United States.* Retrieved July 28, 2006, from http://www.apha.org/ppp/red/Intro.htm

Amsel, E., & Smetana, J. G. (Eds.). (2011). *Adolescent vulnerabilities and opportunities: Constructivist and developmental perspectives.* New York: Cambridge University Press.

Amsterdam, R. K. (1968). *Mirror behavior in children under two years of age.* Unpublished doctoral dissertation. University of North Carolina, Chapel Hill.

Amuna, P., & Zotor, F. B. (2008). Epidemiological and nutrition transition in developing countries: Impact on human health and development. *Proceedings of the Nutrition Society, 67,* 82–90.

Anastasi, A., & Urbina, S. (1997). *Psychological testing* (11th ed.). Upper Saddle River, NJ: Prentice Hall.

Anderman, E. M., & Anderman, L. H. (2010). *Classroom motivation.* Upper Saddle River, NJ: Pearson.

Anderman, E. M., & Dawson, H. (2011). Learning and motivation. In P. Alexander & R. Mayer (Eds.), *Handbook of learning and instruction.* New York: Routledge.

Anderman, E. M., & Mueller, C. E. (2010). Middle school transitions and adolescent development: Disentangling psychological, social, and biological effects. In J. Meece & J. Eccles (Eds.). *Handbook of research on schools, schooling, and human development.* Clifton, NJ: Psychology Press.

Anderman, E. M., & Murdock, T. B. (Eds.). (2007). *Psychology of academic cheating.* San Diego: Academic Press.

Anderson, B. L., & Cu-Uvin, S. (2009). Pregnancy and optimal care of HIV-infected patients. *Clinical Infectious Diseases, 48,* 449–435.

Anderson, D. R., Huston, A. C., Schmitt, K., Linebarger, D. L., & Wright, J. C. (2001). Early childhood viewing and adolescent behavior: The recontact study. *Monographs of the Society for Research in Child Development, 66*(1, Serial No. 264).

Anderson, D. R., Torch, E. P., Held, D. E, Collins, P. A., & Nathan, J. G. (1985, April). *Television viewing at home: Age trends in visual attention and time with TV.* Paper presented at the biennial meeting of the Society for Research in Child Development, Toronto.

Anderson, E., Greene, S. M., Hetherington, E. M., & Clingempeel, W. G. (1999). The dynamics of parental remarriage. In E. M. Hetherington (Ed.), *Coping with divorce, single parenting, and remarriage.* Mahwah, NJ: Erlbaum.

Anderson, J. L., Waller, D. K., Canfield, M. A., Shaw, G. M., Watkins, M. L., & Werler, M. M. (2005). Maternal obesity, gestational diabetes, and central nervous system birth defects. *Epidemiology, 16,* 87–92.

Anderson, P. A. (2006). The evolution of biological sex differences in communication. In K. Dindia & D. J. Canary (Eds.), *Sex differences and similarities in communication.* Mahwah, NJ: Erlbaum.

Anderson, P. J., & others. (2011). Attention problems in a representative sample of extremely preterm/extremely low birth weight children. *Developmental Neuropsychology, 36,* 57–73.

Andersson, U. (2010). The contribution of working memory capacity to foreign language comprehension in children. *Memory, 18,* 458–472.

Andrews, C., Trajkovski, N., & Onslow, M. (2011). Fluency: Syllable timed speech to treat stuttering in a school-aged child. In S. S. Chabon & E. R. Cohn (Eds.), *Communication disorders casebook.* Upper Saddle River, NJ: Pearson.

Andreyeva, T., Kelly, I. R., & Harris, J. L. (2011, in press). Exposure to food advertising on television: Associations with children's fast food and soft drink consumption and obesity. *Economics and Human Biology.*

Ang, S., Rodgers, J. L., & Wanstrom, L. (2010). The Flynn effect within subgroups in the U.S.: Gender, race, income, education, and urbanization differences in the NYLS-children data. *Intelligence, 38,* 367–384.

Antonarakis, S. E. (2009). Whole genome association studies. What have we learned and where do we go from here? *Annual Review of Genomes and Human Genetics* (Vol. 10). Palo Alto, CA: Annual Reviews.

Antonogeorgos, G., & others. (2011). Association of extracurricular sports participation with obesity in Greek children. *Journal of Sports Medicine and Physical Fitness, 51,* 121–127.

Antonopoulos, C., & others. (2011). Maternal smoking during pregnancy and childhood lymphoma: A meta-analysis. *International Journal of Cancer, 129*(11), 2694–2703.

Archibald, A. B., Graeber, J. A., & Brooks-Gunn, J. (1999). Associations among parent-adolescent relationships, pubertal growth, dieting, and body image in young adolescent girls: A short-term longitudinal study. *Journal of Research on Adolescence, 9,* 395–415.

Ariceli, G., Castro, J., Cesena, J., & Toro, J. (2005). Anorexia nervosa in male adolescents: Body image, eating attitudes, and psychological traits. *Journal of Adolescent Health, 36,* 221–226.

Arnett, J. J. (2000). Emerging adulthood. *American Psychologist, 55,* 469–480.

Arnett, J. J. (2006). Emerging adulthood: Understanding the new way of coming of age. In J. J. Arnett & J. L. Tanner (Eds.), *Emerging adults in America.* Washington, DC: American Psychological Association.

Arnett, J. J. (2007). Socialization in emerging adulthood. In J. E. Grusec & P. D. Hastings (Eds.), *Handbook of socialization.* New York: Guilford.

Aronson, E. (1986, August). *Teaching students things they think they already know about: The case of prejudice and desegregation.* Paper presented at the meeting of the American Psychological Association, Washington, DC.

Arora, S. (2009). Kangaroo mother care. *Nursing Journal of India, 99,* 248–250.

Arria, A. M., & others. (2006). Methamphetamine and other substance use during pregnancy: Preliminary estimates from the Infant Development, Environment, and Lifestyle (IDEAL) Study. *Maternal and Child Health Journal, 5,* 1–10.

Arterberry, M. E. (2008). Perceptual development. In M. M. Haith & J. B. Benson (Eds.), *Encyclopedia of infant and early childhood development.* Oxford, UK: Elsevier.

Asendorph, J. B. (2008). Shyness. In M. M. Haith & J. B. Benson (Eds.), *Encyclopedia of infant and early childhood development.* Oxford, UK: Elsevier.

Ash, P. (2008). Suicidal behavior in children and adolescents. *Journal of Psychosocial Nursing and Mental Health Services, 46,* 26–30.

Asian, A., Zellner, M., & Bauml, K. H. (2010). Working memory capacity predicts listwise directed forgetting in adults and children. *Memory, 18,* 442–450.

Aslin, R. N. (2009). The role of learning in cognitive development. In A. Woodward & A. Needham (Eds.), *Learning and the infant mind.* New York: Oxford University Press.

Aslin, R. N., Jusczyk, P. W., & Pisoni, D. B. (1998). Speech and auditory processing during infancy: Constraints on and precursors to language. In W. Damon (Ed.), *Handbook of child psychology* (5th ed., Vol. 2). New York: Wiley.

Aslin, R. N., & Lathrop, A. L. (2008). Visual perception. In M. M. Haith & J. B. Benson (Eds.), *Encyclopedia of infant and early childhood development.* Oxford, UK: Elsevier.

Asp, F., Eskilsson, G., & Berninger, E. (2011). Horizontal sound localization in children with bilateral cochlear implants: Effects of auditory experience and age at implantation. *Otology and Neurology, 32*(4), 558–564.

Assanand, S., Dias, M., Richardson, E., & Waxier-Morrison, N. (1990). The South Asians. In N. Waxier-Morrison, J. M. Anderson, & E. Richardson (Eds.), *Cross-cultural caring.* Vancouver, BC: UBC Press.

Ata, R. N., Ludden, A. B., & Lally, M. M. (2007). The effect of gender and family, friend, and media influences on eating behaviors and body image during adolescence. *Journal of Youth and Adolescence, 36,* 1024–1037.

Athanasiadis, A. P., & others. (2011). Correlation of 2nd trimester amniotic fluid amino acid profile with gestational age and estimated fetal weight. *Journal of Maternal-Fetal and Neonatal Medicine, 24*(8), 1033–1038.

Attie, I., & Brooks-Gunn, J. (1989). Development of eating problems in adolescent girls: A longitudinal study. *Developmental Psychology, 25,* 70–79.

Auyeung, B., & others. (2009). Fetal testosterone predicts sexually differentiated childhood behavior in girls and in boys. *Psychological Science, 20,* 144–148.

Axelrad, D. A., Bellinger, D. C., Ryan, L. M., & Woodruff, T. J. (2007). Dose-response relationship of prenatal mercury exposure and IQ: An integrative analysis of epidemiologic data. *Environmental Health Perspectives, 115,* 609–615.

Ayoub, C., Vallotton, C. D., & Mastergeorge, A. M. (2011). Developmental pathways to integrated social skills: The role of parenting and early intervention. *Child Development, 82,* 583–600.

B

Babble, E. R. (2011). *The basics of social research* (5th ed.). Boston: Cengage.

Bachman, J. G., O'Malley, P. M., Schulenberg, J. E., Johnston, L. D., Freedman-Doan, P., & Messersmith, E. E. (2008). *The education–drug use connection.* Clifton, NJ: Psychology Press.

Baddeley, A. D. (2007). *Working memory, thought, and action.* New York: Oxford University Press.

Baddeley, A. D. (2010a). Working memory. *Current Biology, 20,* 136–140.

Baddeley, A. D. (2010b). Long-term and working memory: How do they interact? In L. Backman & L. Nyberg (Eds.), *Memory, aging, and the brain.* New York: Psychology Press.

Baddeley, A. D. (2012). Prefatory. *Annual Review of Psychology* (Vol. 63). Palo Alto, CA: Annual Reviews.

Baggerly, J. (2008). School counseling. In N. J. Salkind (Ed.), *Encyclopedia of educational psychology.* Thousand Oaks, CA: Sage.

Bahali, K., Akcan, R., Tahiroglu, A. Y., & Avci, A. (2010). Child sexual abuse: Seven years into practice. *Journal of Forensic Science, 55,* 633–636.

Bahrick, L. E. (2010). Intermodal perception and selective attention to intersensory redundancy: Implications for social development and autism. In J. G. Bremner & T. D. Wachs (Eds.), *Wiley-Blackwell handbook of infant development* (2nd ed.). New York: Wiley.

Bahrick, L. E., & Hollich, G. (2008). Intermodal perception. In M. M. Haith & J. B. Benson (Eds.), *Encyclopedia of infant and early childhood development.* Oxford, UK: Elsevier.

Baillargeon, R. (1995). The object concept revisited: New directions in the investigation of infants' physical knowledge. In C. E. Granrud (Ed.), *Visual perception and cognition in infancy.* Hillsdale, NJ: Erlbaum.

Baillargeon, R. (2004). The acquisition of physical knowledge in infancy: A summary in eight lessons. In U. Goswami (Ed.), *Blackwell handbook of childhood cognitive development.* Malden, MA: Blackwell.

Baillargeon, R. (2008). Innate ideas revisited: For a principle of persistence in infants' physical reasoning. *Perspectives on Psychological Science, 3,* 2–13.

Baillargeon, R., & DeVos, J. (1991). Object permanence in young children: Further evidence. *Child Development, 62,* 1227–1246.

Baillargeon, R., Li, J., Gertner, Y., & Wu, D. (2011). How do infants reason about physical events? In U. Goswami (Ed.), *Wiley-Blackwell handbook of childhood cognitive development* (2nd ed.). New York: Wiley.

Bajaj, K., & Gross, S. (2011). Genetic aspects of perinatology. In R. J. Martin, A. A. Fanaroff, & M. C. Walsh, *Fanaroff and Martin's neonatal-perinatal medicine* (9th ed.). New York: Elsevier.

Bajanowski, T., & others. (2007). Nicotine and cotinine in infants dying from sudden infant death syndrome. *International Journal of Legal Medicine, 122,* 23–28.

Bakeman, R., & Brown, J. V. (1980). Early interaction: Consequences for social and mental development at three years. *Child Development, 51,* 437–447.

Baker, J. K., Fenning, R. M., & Crnic, K. A. (2011). Emotion socialization by mothers and fathers: Coherence among behaviors and associations with parent attitudes and children's competence. *Social Development, 20,* 412–430.

Bakermans-Kranenburg, M. J., Breddels-Van Bardewijk, F., Juffer, M. K., Velderman, M. H., & van IJzenddorn, M. H. (2007). Insecure mothers with temperamentally reactive infants. In F. Juffer, M. J. Bakermans-Kranenburg, & M. H. van IJzendoorn (Eds.), *Promoting positive parenting.* Mahwah, NJ: Erlbaum.

Bakermans-Kranenburg, M. J., & van IJzendoorn, M. H. (2011). Differential susceptibility to rearing environment depending on dopamine-related genes: New evidence and a meta-analysis. *Development and Psychopathology, 23,* 39–52.

Bales, K. L., & Carter, C. S. (2009). Neuroendocrine mechanisms of social bonds and child-parent attachment, from the child's perspective. In M. De Haan & M. R. Gunnar (Eds.), *Handbook of developmental social neuroscience.* New York: Guilford.

Ballard, S. (2011). Blood tests for investigating maternal wellbeing. 4. When nausea and vomiting in pregnancy becomes pathological: Hyperemesis gravidarum. *Practicing Midwife, 14,* 37–41.

Bandura, A. (1998, August). *Swimming against the mainstream: Accentuating the positive aspects of humanity.* Paper presented at the meeting of the American Psychological Association, San Francisco.

Bandura, A. (2001). Social cognitive theory. *Annual Review of Psychology* (Vol. 52). Palo Alto, CA: Annual Reviews.

Bandura, A. (2004, May). *Toward a psychology of human agency.* Paper presented at the meeting of the American Psychological Society, Chicago.

Bandura, A. (2007). Self-efficacy in health functioning. In S. Ayers & others (Eds.), *Cambridge handbook of psychology, health & medicine* (2nd ed.). New York: Cambridge University Press.

Bandura, A. (2010a). Self-efficacy. In D. Matsumoto (Ed.), *Cambridge dictionary of psychology.* New York: Cambridge University Press.

Bandura, A. (2010b). Self-reinforcement. In D. Matsumoto (Ed.), *Cambridge dictionary of psychology.* New York: Cambridge University Press.

Bandura, A. (2010c). Vicarious learning. In D. Matsumoto (Ed.), *Cambridge dictionary of psychology.* New York: Cambridge University Press.

Bangdiwala, S. I., & others. (2010). NIH consensus development conference draft statement on vaginal birth after cesarean: New insights. *NIH Consensus Statements and Scientific Statements, 34,* 351–365.

Bank, L., Burraston, B., & Snyder, J. (2004). Sibling conflict and ineffective parenting as predictors of adolescent boys' antisocial behavior and peer difficulties: Additive and interactive effects. *Journal of Research on Adolescence, 14,* 99–125.

Banks, J. A. (2008). *Introduction to multicultural education* (4th ed.). Boston: Allyn & Bacon.

Banks, J. A. (Ed.). (2010). *The Routledge international companion to multicultural education.* New York: Routledge.

Barajas, R. G., Phillipsen, N., & Brooks-Gunn, J. (2008). Cognitive and emotional outcomes for children in poverty. In D. R. Crane & T. B. Heaton (Eds.), *Handbook of families and poverty.* Thousand Oaks, CA: Sage.

Barakat, R., & others. (2011). Exercise during pregnancy improves maternal health perception: A randomized controlled trial. *American Journal of Obstetrics and Gynecology, 204*(5), 402.

Barbarin, O. A., & Aikens, N. (2009). Supporting parental practices in the language and literacy development of young children. In O. A. Barbarin & H. Wasik (Eds.), *Handbook of child development and early education.* New York: Guilford.

Barbarin, O. A., & Miller, K. M. (2009). Developmental science and early education: An introduction. In O. A. Barbarin & B. H. Wasik (Eds.), *Handbook of child development and early education.* New York: Oxford University.

Barber, B., Stone, M., & Eccles, J. (2010). Protect, prepare, support, and engage: The roles of school-based extracurricular activities in students' development. In J. Meece & J. Eccles (Eds.), *Handbook of research on schools, schooling, and human development.* New York: Routledge.

Barber, T. D., Derinkuyu, B. E., Wickiser, J., Joglar, J., Koral, K., & Baker, L. A. (2011). Wilms tumor: Preoperative risk factors identified for intraoperative tumor spill. *Journal of Urology, 185*(4), 1414–1418.

Barger, M. K. (2010). Maternal nutrition and perinatal outcomes. *Journal of Midwifery and Women's Health, 55,* 502–511.

Barker, R., & Wright, H. F. (1951). *One boy's day.* New York: Harper & Row.

Barnett, J. H., Xu, K., Heron, J., Goldman, D., & Jones, P. B. (2011). Cognitive effects of genetic variation in monoamine neurotransmitter systems: A population-based study of COMT, MAOA, and 5HTTLPR. *American Journal of Medical Genetics B: Neuropsychiatric Genetics, 156,* 158–167.

Baron, I. S., Erickson, K., Ahronovich, M. D., Baker, R., & Litman, F. R. (2011). Neuropsychological and behavioral outcomes of extremely low birth weight at age three. *Developmental Neuropsychology, 36,* 5–21.

Baron, N. S. (1992). *Growing up with language.* Reading, MA: Addison-Wesley.

Baron-Cohen, S. (2008). Autism, hyper-systemizing, and truth. *Quarterly Journal of Experimental Psychology, 61,* 64–75.

Baron-Cohen, S. (2009). Autism: The empathizing-systemizing (E-S) theory. *Annals of the New York Academy of Sciences, 1156,* 68–80.

Baron-Cohen, S. (2011). The empathizing-systemizing (E-S) theory of autism: A cognitive developmental account. In U. Goswami (Ed.), *Wiley-Blackwell handbook of childhood cognitive development* (2nd ed.). New York: Wiley-Blackwell.

Baron-Cohen, S., Golan, O., Chapman, E., & Granader, Y. (2007). Transported to a world of emotion. *The Psychologist, 20,* 76–77.

Barrett, D. E., Radke-Yarrow, M., & Klein, R. E. (1982). Chronic malnutrition and child behavior: Effects of calorie supplementation on social and emotional functioning at school age. *Developmental Psychology, 18,* 541–556.

Bartle, C. (2007). Developing a service for children with iron deficiency anemia. *Nursing Standard, 21,* 44–49.

Bartsch, K., & Wellman, H. M. (1995). *Children talk about the mind.* New York: Oxford University Press.

Basaran, A., Basaran, M., & Topatan, B. (2011). Chorionic villus sampling and the risk of preeclampsia: A systematic review and meta-analysis. *Archives of Gynecology and Obstetrics, 283*(6), 1175–1181.

Basaran, S., Guler-Uysal, F., Ergen, N., Seydaoglu, G., Bingol-Karakoe, G., & Ufuk Altintas, D. (2006). Effects of physical exercise on quality of life, exercise capacity, and pulmonary function in children with asthma. *Journal of Rehabilitation Medicine and Science, 38,* 130–135.

Basatemur, E., & Sutcliffe, A. (2008). Follow-up of children born after ART. *Placenta, 29* (Suppl. B), 135–140.

Bateman, B. T., & Simpson, L. L. (2006). Higher rate of stillbirth at the extremes of reproductive age: A large nationwide sample of deliveries in the United States. *American Journal of Obstetrics and Gynecology, 194,* 840–845.

Bates, J. E. (2008). Unpublished review of J. W. Santrock's *Children,* 11th ed. New York: McGraw-Hill.

Bates, J. E., Schermerhorn, A. C., & Goodnight, J. A. (2010). Temperament and personality through the life span. In A. Freund, M. Lamb, & R. M. Lerner (Eds.), *Handbook of life-span development.* New York: Wiley.

Battistich, V. A. (2008). The Child Development Project: Creating caring school communities. In L. Nucci & D. Narváez (Eds.), *Handbook of moral and character education.* Clifton, NJ: Psychology Press.

Bauer, P. J. (2009a). Learning and memory: Like a horse and carriage. In A. Needham & A. Woodward (Eds.), *Learning and the infant mind.* New York: Oxford University Press.

Bauer, P. J. (2009b). Neurodevelopmental changes in infancy and beyond: Implications for learning and memory. In O. A. Barbarin & B. H. Wasik (Eds.), *Handbook of child development and early education.* New York: Oxford University Press.

Bauer, P. J., Larkina, M., & Deocampo, J. (2011). Early memory development. In U. Goswami (Ed.), *Wiley-Blackwell handbook of childhood cognitive development* (2nd ed.). New York: Wiley-Blackwell.

Bauer, P. J., Wenner, J. A., Dropik, P. I., & Wewerka, S. S. (2000). Parameters of remembering and forgetting in the transition from infancy to early childhood. *Monographs of the Society for Research in Child Development, 65*(4, Serial No. 263).

Bauer, P. J., & others. (2003). Developments in long-term explicit memory late in the first year of life: Behavioral and electrophysiological indices. *Psychological Science, 14,* 629–635.

Bauman, K. E., Ennett, S. T., Foshee, V. A., Pemberton, M., King, T. S., & Koch, G. G. (2002). Influence of a family program on adolescent smoking and drinking prevalence. *Prevention Science, 3,* 35–42.

Baumeister, R. F., Campbell, J. D., Krueger, J. I., & Vohs, K. D. (2003). Does high self-esteem cause better performance, interpersonal success, happiness, or healthier lifestyles? *Psychological Science in the Public Interest, 4*(1), 1–44.

Baumrind, D. (1971). Current patterns of parental authority. *Developmental Psychology Monographs, 4*(1, Pt. 2).

Baxley, F., & Miller, M. (2006). Parental misperceptions about children and firearms. *Archives of Pediatric and Adolescent Medicine, 160,* 542–547.

Baye, T. M., & others. (2011). Differences in candidate gene association between European ancestry and African American asthmatic children. *PLoS One, 6,* e16522.

Bayley, N. (1969). *Manual for the Bayley Scales of Infant Development.* New York: Psychological Corporation.

Bayley, N. (2005). *Bayley Scales of Infant and Toddler Development* (3rd ed.). San Antonio: Harcourt Assessment.

Bearman, P. S., & Moody, J. (2004). Suicide and friendships among American adolescents. *American Journal of Public Health, 94,* 89–95.

Beatty, J. J., & Pratt, L. (2011). Early literacy in preschool and kindergarten (3rd ed.). Boston: Allyn & Bacon.

Beauchamp, G., & Mennella, J. A. (2009). Early flavor learning and its impact on later feeding behavior. *Journal of Pediatric Gastroenterology and Nutrition, 48* (Suppl. 1), S25–S30.

Beauchamp, M. H., & Anderson, V. (2010). SOCIAL: An integrative framework for the development of social skills. *Psychological Bulletin, 136,* 39–64.

Beaulieu, J. M., & Gainetdinov, R. R. (2011). The physiology, signaling, and pharmacology of dopamine receptors. *Pharmacology Review, 63,* 182–217.

Bechtold, A. G., Bushnell, E. W., & Salapatek, P. (1979, April). *Infants' visual localization of visual and auditory targets.* Paper presented at the meeting of the Society for Research in Child Development, San Francisco.

Beck, D. M., Schaefer, C., & Pang, K., & Carlson, S. M. (2011). Executive function in preschool children: Test-retest reliability. *Journal of Cognition and Development, 12*(2), 169–193.

Bednar, R. L., Wells, M. G., & Peterson, S. R. (1995). *Self-esteem* (2nd ed.). Washington, DC: American Psychological Association.

Beebe, D. W. (2011). Cognitive, behavioral, and functional consequences of inadequate sleep in children and adolescents. *Pediatric Clinics of North America, 58,* 649–665.

Beeghly, M., & others. (2006). Prenatal cocaine exposure and children's language functioning at 6 and 9.5 years: Moderating effects of child age, birthweight, and gender. *Journal of Pediatric Psychology, 31,* 98–115.

Beets, M. W., & Foley, J. T. (2008). Association of father involvement and neighborhood quality with kindergarteners' physical activity: A multilevel structural equation model. *American Journal of Health Promotion, 22,* 195–203.

Beghetto, R. A., & Kaufman, J. C. (Eds.). (2011). *Nurturing creativity in the classroom.* New York: Cambridge University Press.

Bell, C. J., & others. (2011, in press). Carrier testing for severe childhood recessive diseases by next-generation sequencing. *Science Translational Medicine.*

Bell, M. A. (2011, in press). A psychobiological perspective on working memory performance at 8 months of age. *Child Development.*

Bell, M. A., & Diaz, A. (2011, in press). EEG/ERP measures of emotion-cognition integration during development. In T. A Gennis, K. A. Buss, & P. D. Hastings (Eds.), Physiological measures of emotion from a developmental perspective: State of the science. *Monographs of the Society for Research in Child Development.*

Bell, M. A., & Fox, N. A. (1992). The relations between frontal brain electrical activity and cognitive development during infancy. *Child Development, 63,* 1142–1163.

Bell, M. A., Greene, D. R., & Wolfe, C. D. (2010). Psychobiological mechanisms of cognition-emotion integration in early development. In S. D. Calkins & M. A. Bell (Eds.), *Child development at the intersection of emotion and cognition.* Washington, DC: American Psychological Association.

Bell, S. M., & Ainsworth, M. D. S. (1972). Infant crying and maternal responsiveness. *Child Development, 43,* 1171–1190.

Bellinger, D. C. (2008). Very low lead exposures and children's neurodevelopment. *Current Opinion in Pediatrics, 20,* 172–177.

Belsky, J. (1981). Early human experience: A family perspective. *Developmental Psychology, 17,* 3–23.

Belsky, J. (2009). Classroom composition, childcare history, and social development: Are childcare effects disappearing or spreading? *Social Development, 18,* 230–238.

Belsky, J., Steinberg, L., Houts, R. M., Halpern-Felsher, B. L., & the NICHD Child Care Research Network. (2010). The development of reproductive strategy in females: Early maternal harshness n earlier menarche n increased sexual risk. *Developmental Psychology, 46,* 120–128.

Bendersky, M., & Sullivan, M. W. (2007). Basic methods in infant research. In A. Slater & M. Lewis (Eds.), *Introduction to infant development* (2nd ed.). New York: Oxford University Press.

Bengtsson, H., & Arvidsson, A. (2011). The impact of developing social perspective-taking skills on emotionality in middle and late childhood. *Social Development, 20,* 353–375.

Benn, P. A., & Chapman, A. R. (2010). Ethical challenges in providing noninvasive prenatal diagnosis. *Current Opinion in Obstetrics and Gynecology, 22,* 128–134.

Benner, A. D., & Graham, S. (2009). The transition to high school as a developmental process among multiethnic urban youth. *Child Development, 80,* 356–376.

Bennett, C. I. (2011a). *Comprehensive multicultural education.* Boston: Allyn & Bacon.

Bennett, C. I. (2011b). *Perspectives on human differences.* Boston: Allyn & Bacon.

Bennett, C. I. (2012). *Comprehensive multicultural education* (7th ed.). Boston: Allyn & Bacon.

Bennett, S. L. R. (2008). Contextual affordances of rural Appalachian individuals. *Journal of Career Development, 34,* 241–262.

Benninghoven, D., Tetsch, N., Kunzendorf, S., & Jantschek, G. (2007). Body image in patients with eating disorders and their mothers, and the role of family functioning. *Comprehensive Psychiatry, 48,* 118–123.

Benson, A. C., Torode, M. E., & Fiatarone Singh, M. A. (2008). The effects of high-intensity progressive resistance training on adiposity in children: A randomized controlled trial. *International Journal of Obesity, 32,* 1016–1027.

Benson, L., Baer, H. J., & Kaelber, D. C. (2009). Trends in the diagnosis of overweight and obesity in children and adolescents: 1999–2007. *Pediatrics, 123,* e153–e158.

Benson, P. L. (2010). *Parent, teacher, mentor, friend: How every adult can change kids' lives.* Minneapolis: Search Institute Press.

Benson, P. L., Mannes, M., Pittman, K., & Ferber, T. (2004). Youth development, developmental assets, and public policy. In R. Lerner & L. Steinberg (Eds.), *Handbook of adolescent psychology* (2nd ed.). New York: Wiley.

Benson, P. L., & Scales, P. C. (2009). The definition and preliminary measurement of thriving in adolescence. *Journal of Positive Psychology, 4,* 85–104.

Benson, P. L., & Scales, P. C. (2011a, in press). Positive youth development and the prevention of youth aggression and violence. *European Journal of Developmental Science.*

Benson, P. L., & Scales, P. C. (2011b). Thriving and sparks: Development and emergence of new core concepts in positive youth development. In R. J. R. Levesque (Ed.), *Encyclopedia of adolescence.* Berlin: Springer.

Bentley, M. E., Wasser, H. M., & Creed-Kanashiro, H. M. (2011). Responsive feeding and child undernutrition in low- and middle-income countries. *Journal of Nutrition, 141,* 502–507.

Berenson, G. S. (2005). Obesity—A critical issue in preventive cardiology: The Bogalusa Heart Study. *Preventive Cardiology, 8,* 234–241.

Bergen, D. (1988). Stages of play development. In D. Bergen (Ed.), *Play as medium for learning and development.* Portsmouth, NH: Heinemann.

Bergman, O., Westberg, L., Lichtenstein, P., Eriksson, E., & Larsson, H. (2011). Study on the possible association of brain-deprived neurotrophic factor polymorphism with the developmental course of symptoms of attention deficit and hyperactivity. *International Journal of Neuropsychopharmacology, 14*(10), 1367–1376.

Berk, L. E. (1994). Why children talk to themselves. *Scientific American, 271*(5), 78–83.

Berk, L. E., & Spuhl, S. T. (1995). Maternal interaction, private speech, and task performance in preschool children. *Early Childhood Research Quarterly, 10,* 145–169.

Berko, J. (1958). The child's learning of English morphology. *Word, 14,* 150–177.

Berko Gleason, J. (2003). Unpublished review of J. W. Santrock's *Life-span development,* 9th ed. (New York: McGraw-Hill).

Berko Gleason, J. (2009). The development of language. An overview. In J. Berko Gleason & N. B. Ratner (Eds.), *The development of language* (7th ed.). Boston: Allyn & Bacon.

Berkowitz, M. W., Battistich, V. A., & Bier, M. (2008). What works in character education: What is known and what needs to be known. In L. Nucci & D. Narváez (Eds.), *Handbook of moral and character education.* Clifton, NJ: Psychology Press.

Berlin, L.J., Cassidy, J., & Appleyard, K. (2009). The influence of early attachment on other relationships. In J. Cassidy & P. R. Shaver (Eds.), *Handbook of attachment* (2nd ed.). New York: Guilford.

Berlyne, D. E. (1960). *Conflict, arousal, and curiosity.* New York: McGraw-Hill.

Bermejo-Alvarez, P., Rizos, D., Lonergan, P., & Adan, A. G. (2011). 181 transcriptional sexual dimorphism in autosomal genes on bovine day 14 embryos. *Reproduction, Fertility, and Development, 23*(1).

Bernard, K., & Dozier, M. (2008). Adoption and foster placement. In M. M. Haith & J. B. Benson (Eds.), *Encyclopedia of infant and early childhood development.* Oxford, UK: Elsevier.

Berndt, T. J., & Perry, T. B. (1990). Distinctive features and effects of early adolescent friendships. In R. Montemayor (Ed.), *Advances in adolescent research.* Greenwich, CT: JAI Press.

Berninger, V. W., & O'Malley, M. M. (2011). Evidence-based diagnosis and treatment for specific learning disabilities involving impairments in written and/or oral language. *Journal of Learning Disabilities, 44*, 167–183.

Bertenthal, B. I. (2008). Perception and action. In M. M. Haith & J. B. Benson (Eds.), *Encyclopedia of infant and early childhood development*. Oxford, UK: Elsevier.

Bertenthal, B. I., Longo, M. R., & Kenny, S. (2007). Phenomenal permanence and the development of predictive tracking in infancy. *Child Development, 78*, 350–363.

Best, D. L. (2010). Gender. In M. H. Bornstein (Ed.), *Handbook of cultural developmental science*. New York: Psychology Press.

Best, J. R. (2010). Effects of physical activity on children's executive function: Contributions of experimental research on aerobic exercise. *Developmental Review, 30*, 331–351.

Best, S. J., Heller, K. W., & Bigge, J. L. (2010). *Teaching individuals with physical or multiple disabilities* (6th ed.). Upper Saddle River, NJ: Pearson.

Beyerlein, A., Ruckinger, S., Toschke, A. M., Schaffrath Rosario, A., & von Kries, R. (2011). Is low birth weight in the causal pathway of the association between maternal smoking in pregnancy and higher BMI in the offspring? *European Journal of Epidemiology, 26*(5), 413–420.

Bhatt, J. M., & Smyth, A. R. (2011). The management of pre-school wheeze. *Pediatric Respiratory Review, 12*, 70–77.

Bhutta, Z. A., & others. (2011). Improvement of perinatal and newborn care in rural Pakistan through community-based strategies: A cluster-randomized effectiveness trial. *Lancet, 377*, 403–412.

Bialystok, E. (1993). Metalinguistic awareness: The development of children's representations in language. In C. Pratt & A. Garton (Eds.), *Systems of representation in children*. London: Wiley.

Bialystok, E. (1997). Effects of bilingualism and biliteracy on children's emerging concepts of print. *Developmental Psychology, 33*, 429–440.

Bialystok, E. (2001). *Bilingualism in development: Language, literacy, and cognition*. New York: Cambridge University Press.

Bialystok, E. (2007). Acquisition of literacy in preschool children: A framework for research. *Language Learning, 57*, 45–77.

Bialystok, E. (2011, April). *Becoming bilingual: Emergence of cognitive outcomes of bilingualism in immersion education*. Paper presented at the meeting of the Society for Research in Child Development, Montreal.

Bialystok, E., & Craik, F. I. M. (2010). Cognitive and linguistic processing in the bilingual mind. *Current Directions in Psychological Science, 19*, 19–23.

Bibok, M. B., Carpendale, J. I. M., & Muller, U. (2009). Parental scaffolding and the development of executive function. In C. Lewis & J. I. M. Carpendale (Eds.), *Social interaction and the development of executive function. New*

Directions in Child and Adolescent Development, *123*, 17–34.

Bierman, K. L., Nix, R. L., Greenberg, M. T., Domitrovich, C. E., & Blair, C. (2008). Executive functions and school readiness intervention: Impact, moderation, and mediation in the Head Start-REDI Program. *Development and Psychopathology, 20*, 821–843.

Bigelow, A. E., & others. (2010). Maternal sensitivity throughout infancy: Continuity and relation to attachment security. *Infant Behavior and Development, 33*, 50–60.

Bill and Melinda Gates Foundation. (2008). Report gives voice to dropouts. Retrieved July 5, 2008, from http://www.gatesfoundation.org/UnitedStates/Education/TransformingHighSchools/Related...

Billy, J. O. G., Rodgers, J. L., & Udry, J. R. (1984). Adolescent sexual behavior and friendship choice. *Social Forces, 62*, 653–678.

Birch, S., & Bloom, P. (2003). Children are cursed: An asymmetric bias in mental state attribution. *Psychological Science, 14*, 283–286.

Birman, B. F., & others. (2007). *State and local implementation of the "No Child Left Behind Act." Volume II—Teacher quality under "NCLB": Interim report*. Jessup, MD: U.S. Department of Education.

Birnbach, D. J., & Ranasinghe, J. S. (2008). Anesthesia complications in the birthplace: Is the neuraxial block always to blame? *Clinical Perinatology, 35*, 35–52.

Birney, D. P., & Sternberg, R. J. (2011). The development of cognitive abilities. In M. H. Bornstein & M. E. Lamb (Eds.), *Cognitive development*. New York: Psychology Press.

Bishop, D. V., & others. (2011, in press). Autism, language, and communication in children with sex chromosome trisomies. *Archives of Disease in Childhood*.

Bjorklund, D. F. (2007). *Why youth is not wasted on the young*. Malden, MA: Blackwell.

Bjorklund, D. F. (2012). *Children's thinking* (5th ed.). Boston: Cengage.

Bjorklund, D. F., & Pellegrini, A. D. (2002). *The origins of human nature*. New York: Oxford University Press.

Bjorklund, D. F., & Pellegrini, A. D. (2011). Evolutionary perspectives on social development. In P. K. Smith & C. H. Hart (Eds.), *Wiley-Blackwell handbook of childhood social development* (2nd ed.). New York: Wiley.

Black, M. M., & Hurley, K. M. (2007). Helping children develop healthy eating habits. In R. E. Tremblay, R. G. Barr, R. Peters, & M. Boivin (Eds.), *Encyclopedia of early childhood development* (Rev. Ed.). Retrieved March 11, 2008, from http://www.child-encyclopedia.com/documents/Black-Hurley ANGxp_rev-Eating.pdf

Black, M. M., & Lozoff, B. (2008). Nutrition and diet. In M. M. Haith & J. B. Benson (Eds.), *Encyclopedia of infant and early childhood development*. Oxford, UK: Elsevier.

Black, M. M., & others. (2009). Participants' comments on changes in the revised special

supplemental nutrition program for women, infants, and children food packages: The Maryland food preference study. *Journal of the American Dietetic Association, 109*, 116–123.

Black, R. E., & others. (2008). Maternal and child undernutrition: Global and regional exposures and health consequences. *Lancet, 371*, 243–260.

Blackwell, L. S., & Dweck, C. S. (2008). *The motivational impact of a computer-based program that teaches how the brain changes with learning*. Unpublished manuscript, Department of Psychology, Stanford University, Palo Alto, CA.

Blackwell, L. S., Trzesniewski, K. H., & Dweck, C. S. (2007). Implicit theories of intelligence predict achievement across an adolescent tradition: A longitudinal study and an intervention. *Child Development, 78*, 246–263.

Blaga, O. M., Shaddy, D. J., Anderson, C. J., Kannass, K. N., Little, T. D., & Colombo, J. (2009). Structure and continuity of intellectual development in early childhood. *Intelligence, 37*, 106–113.

Blair, B. L., & Fletcher, A. C. (2011). "The only 13-year-old on planet Earth without a cell phone": Meanings of cell phones in early adolescents' everyday lives. *Journal of Adolescent Research, 26*(2), 155.

Blake, J. S. (2011). *Nutrition and you*. Upper Saddle River, NJ: Pearson.

Blakemore, J. E. O., Berenbaum, S. A., & Liben, L. S. (2009). *Gender development*. New York: Psychology Press.

Blakemore, S. J., Dahl, R. E., Frith, U., & Pine, D. S. (2011, in press). Developmental cognitive neuroscience. *Developmental Cognitive Neuroscience*.

Blakey, J. (2011). Normal births or spontaneous vertex delivery? *Practicing Midwife, 14*, 12–13.

Blandthorn, J., Forster, D. A., & Love, V. (2011). Neonatal and maternal outcomes following maternal use of buprenorphine or methadone during pregnancy: Findings of a retrospective audit. *Women and Birth, 24*, 32–39.

Blass, E. (2008). Suckling. In M. M. Haith & J. B. Benson (Eds.), *Encyclopedia of infant and early childhood development*. Oxford, UK: Elsevier.

Block, C. C., & Pressley, M. (2007). Best practices in teaching comprehension. In L. B. Gambrell, L. M. Morrow, & M. Pressley (Eds.), *Best practices in literacy instruction*. New York: Guilford.

Bloom, B. (1985). *Developing talent in young people*. New York: Ballantine.

Bloom, B., & Dey, A. N. (2006). Summary health statistics for U.S. children: National Health Interview Survey, 2004. *Vital Health Statistics, 227*, 1–85.

Bloom, L., Lifter, K., & Broughton, J. (1985). The convergence of early cognition and language in the second year of life: Problems in conceptualization and measurement. In M. Barrett (Ed.), *Single word speech*. London: Wiley.

Bloom, P., & German, T. P. (2000). Two reasons to abandon the false belief task as a test of theory of mind. *Cognition, 77*, B25–B31.

Blum, J. W., Beaudoin, C. M., & Caton-Lemos, L. (2005). Physical activity patterns and maternal well-being in postpartum women. *Maternal and Child Health Journal, 8,* 163–169.

Bodrova, E., & Leong, D. J. (2007). *Tools of the mind* (2nd ed.). Geneva, Switzerland: International Bureau of Education, UNESCO.

Boeving, C. A., & Forsyth, B. (2008). AIDS and HIV. In M. M. Haith & J. B. Benson (Eds.), *Encyclopedia of infant and early childhood development.* Oxford, UK: Elsevier.

Bohannon, J. N., & Bonvillian, J. D. (2009). Theoretical approaches to language acquisition. In J. Berko Gleason & N. B. Ratner (Eds.), *The development of language* (7th ed.). Boston: Allyn & Bacon.

Bohlin, G., & Hagekull, B. (2009). Socio-emotional development: From infancy to young adulthood. *Scandinavian Journal of Psychology, 50,* 592–601.

Bonnano, G. A., Mancini, A. D., & Westphal, M. (2011). Resilience to extreme adversity. *Annual Review of Clinical Psychology* (Vol. 7). Palo Alto, CA: Annual Reviews.

Bonney, C., & Sternberg, R. J. (2011). Learning to think critically. In P. A. Alexander & R. E. Mayer (Eds.), *Handbook of research on learning and instruction.* New York: Routledge.

Boonstra, H. (2002, February). Teen pregnancy: Trends and lessons learned. *The Guttmacher Report on Public Policy,* pp. 7–10.

Booth, A. (2006). Object function and categorization in infancy: Two mechanisms of facilitation. *Infancy, 10,* 145–169.

Booth, M. (2002). Arab adolescents facing the future: Enduring ideals and pressures to change. In B. B. Brown, R. W. Larson, & T. S. Saraswathi (Eds.), *The world's youth.* New York: Cambridge University Press.

Booth-Laforce, C., & Kerns, K. A. (2009). Child-parent attachment relationships, peer relationships, and peer-group functioning. In K. H. Rubin, W. M. Bukowski, & B. Laursen (Eds.), *Handbook of peer interactions, relationships, and groups.* New York: Guilford.

Bor, W., McGee, T. R., & Fagan, A. A. (2004). Early risk factors for adolescent antisocial behavior: An Australian longitudinal study. *Australian and New Zealand Journal of Psychiatry, 38,* 365–372.

Borich, G. D. (2011). Effective teaching methods (7th ed.). Boston: Allyn & Bacon.

Borjas, L., & others. (2010). Intragenic polymorphisms of factor VIII and IX genes and their utility in the indirect diagnosis of carriers of Haemophilias A and B. *Investigacion Clinica, 57,* 391–401.

Bornstein, M. H. (1975). Qualities of color vision in infancy. *Journal of Experimental Child Psychology, 19,* 401–409.

Bornstein, M. H., & Zlotnik, D. (2008). Parenting styles and their effects. In M. M. Haith & J. B. Benson (Eds.), *Encyclopedia of infant and early childhood development.* Oxford, UK: Elsevier.

Borup, L., Wurlitzer, W., Hedegaard, M., Kesmodel, U.S., & Hvidman, L. (2009). Acupuncture as pain relief during delivery: A randomized controlled trial. *Birth, 36,* 5–12.

Bose-O'Reilly, S., McCarty, K. M., Steckling, N., & Lettmeier, B. (2010). Mercury exposure and children's health. *Current Problems in Pediatric and Adolescent Health Care, 40,* 186–215.

Bosl, W., Tierney, A., Tager-Flusberg, H., & Nelson, C. (2011). EEG complexity as a biomarker for autism spectrum disorder risk. *BMC Medicine, 9,* 18.

Bouchard, T. J. (1995, August). *Heritability of intelligence.* Paper presented at the meeting of the American Psychological Association, New York.

Bouchard, T. J. (2008). Genes and human psychological traits. In P. Carruthers, S. Laurence, & S. Stich (Eds.), *The innate mind: Foundations for the future* (Vol. 3). Oxford: Oxford University Press.

Boutot, E. A., & Myles, B. S. (2011). *Autism spectrum disorders.* Upper Saddle River, NJ: Pearson.

Bower, J. K., Hales, D. P., Tate, D. F., Rubin, D. A., Benjamin, S. E., & Ward, D. S. (2008). The childcare environment and children's physical activity. *American Journal of Preventive Medicine, 34,* 23–29.

Bower, T. G. R. (1966). Slant perception and shape constancy in infants. *Science, 151,* 832–834.

Bowlby, J. (1969). *Attachment and loss* (Vol. 1). London: Hogarth Press.

Bowlby, J. (1989). *Secure and insecure attachment.* New York: Basic Books.

Boyd, P. A., Loane, M., Ganrne, E., Khoshnood, B., Dolk, H., & The EUROCAT Working Group. (2011). Sex chromosome trisomies in Europe: Prevalence, prenatal detection, and outcome of pregnancy. *European Journal of Human Genetics, 19,* 231–234.

Boyer, K., & Diamond, A. (1992). Development of memory for temporal order in infants and young children. In A. Diamond (Ed.), *Development and neural bases of higher cognitive function.* New York: Academy of Sciences.

Boyle, J., & Cropley, M. (2004). Children's sleep: Problems and solutions. *Journal of Family Health Care, 14,* 61–63.

Boyle, J. R., & Provost, M. C. (2012). *Strategies for teaching students with disabilities in inclusive classrooms.* Upper Saddle River, NJ: Pearson.

Bracken, M. B., Eskenazi, B., Sachse, K., McSharry, J., Hellenbrand, K., & Leo-Summers, L. (1990). Association of cocaine use with sperm concentration, motility, and morphology. *Fertility and Sterility, 53,* 315–322.

Brady, S. S., Tschann, J. M., Pasch, L. A., Flores, E., & Ozer, E. J. (2008). Violence involvement, substance use, and sexual activity among Mexican-American and European-American adolescents. *Journal of Adolescent Health, 43,* 285–295.

Brady-Smith, C., & others. (2011, in press). Parenting in context, parenting as context: Examining patterns of parenting and their relations to infant development among Mexican, African, and European low-income mothers. *Parenting: Science and Practice.*

Brainerd, C. J., & Reyna, V. E. (1993). Domains of fuzzy-trace theory. In M. L. Howe & R. Pasnak (Eds.), *Emerging themes in cognitive development.* New York: Springer.

Brams, H., Mao, A. R., & Doyle, R. L. (2009). Onset of efficacy of long-lasting psychostimulants in pediatric attention-deficit/hyperactivity disorder. *Postgraduate Medicine, 120,* 69–88.

Bransford, J., & others. (2006). Learning theories in education. In P. A. Alexander & P. H. Winne (Eds.), *Handbook of educational psychology* (2nd ed.). Mahwah, NJ: Erlbaum.

Brazelton, T. B. (2004). Preface: The Neonatal Intensive Care Unit Network Neurobehavioral Scale. *Pediatrics, 113*(Suppl.), S632–S633.

Brechwald, W. A., & Prinstein, M. J. (2011). Beyond homophily: A decade of advances in understanding peer influence processes. *Journal of Research on Adolescence, 21,* 166–179.

Bredekamp, S. (2011). *Effective practices in early childhood education.* Upper Saddle River, NJ: Merrill.

Breedlove, G., & Fryzelka, D. (2011). Depression screening in pregnancy. *Journal of Midwifery and Women's Health, 56,* 18–25.

Brelsford, G. M., & Mahoney, A. (2008). Spiritual disclosure between older adolescents and their mothers. *Journal of Family Psychology, 22,* 62–70.

Bremner, J. G. (2010). Cognitive development: Knowledge of the physical world. In J. G. Bremner & T. D. Wachs (Eds.), *Wiley-Blackwell handbook of childhood cognitive development* (2nd ed.). New York: Wiley.

Bremner, J. G., Slater, A. M., Johnson, S. P., Mason, U. C., Spring, J., & Bremner, M. E. (2011). Two- to 8-month-old infants' cross-modal perception of dynamic auditory-visual spatial co-location. *Child Development, 82*(4), 1210–1223.

Brendgen, M., Lamarche, V., Wanner, B., & Vitaro, F. (2010). Links between friendship relations and early adolescents' trajectories of depressed mood. *Developmental Psychology, 46,* 491–501.

Brent, R. L. (2009). Saving lives and changing family histories: Appropriate counseling of pregnant women and men and women of reproductive age concerning the risk of diagnostic radiation exposure during and before pregnancy. *American Journal of Obstetrics and Gynecology, 200,* 4–24.

Brent, R. L. (2011). The pulmonologist's role in caring for pregnant women with regard to the reproductive risks of diagnostic radiological studies or radiation therapy. *Clinics in Chest Medicine, 32*(1), 33–42.

Brent, R. L., Christian, M. S., & Diener, R. M. (2011, in press). Evaluation of the reproductive and developmental risks of caffeine. *Birth Defects Research B: Developmental and Reproductive Toxicology.*

Breslau, N., Paneth, N. S., & Lucia, V. C. (2004). The lingering academic deficits of low birth weight children. *Pediatrics, 114,* 1035–1040.

Brocardo, P. S., Gil-Mohapel, J., & Christie, B. R. (2011). The role of oxidative stress in fetal alcohol spectrum disorders. *Brain Research Reviews, 67*(1–2), 209–225.

Brodsky, J. L., Viner-Brown, S., & Handler, A. S. (2009). Changes in maternal cigarette smoking among pregnant WIC participants in Rhode Island. *Maternal and Child Health Journal, 13*, 822–831.

Brody, L. R., & Hall, J. A. (2008). Gender, emotion, and expression. In M. Lewis & J. M. Haviland-Jones (Eds.), *Handbook of emotions* (3rd ed.). New York: Guilford.

Brody, N. (2000). Intelligence. In A. Kazdin (Ed.), *Encyclopedia of psychology.* New York: Oxford University Press.

Brody, N. (2007). Does education influence intelligence? In P. C. Kyllonen, R. D. Roberts, & L. Stankov (Eds.), *Extending intelligence.* Mahwah, NJ: Erlbaum.

Brodzinsky, D. M., & Pinderhughes, E. (2002). Parenting and child development in adoptive families. In M. H. Bornstein (Ed.), *Handbook of parenting* (Vol. I). Mahwah, NJ: Erlbaum.

Bronfenbrenner, U. (1986). Ecology of the family as a context for human development: Research perspectives. *Developmental Psychology, 22*, 723–742.

Bronfenbrenner, U. (2000). Ecological theory. In A. Kazdin (Ed.), *Encyclopedia of psychology.* New York: Oxford University Press.

Bronfenbrenner, U., & Morris, P. A. (2006). The ecology of developmental processes. In W. Damon & R. Lerner (Eds.), *Handbook of child psychology* (6th ed.). New York: Wiley.

Bronstein, P. (2006). The family environment: Where gender role socialization begins. In J. Worell & C. D. Goodheart (Eds.), *Handbook of girls' and women's psychological health.* New York: Oxford University Press.

Brooker, R. (2011). *Biology* (2nd ed.). New York: McGraw-Hill.

Brooks, J. G., & Brooks, M. G. (2001). *The case for constructivist classrooms* (2nd ed.). Upper Saddle River, NJ: Erlbaum.

Brooks, R., & Meltzoff, A. N. (2005). The development of gaze in relation to language. *Developmental Science, 8*, 535–543.

Brooks, R., & Meltzoff, A. N. (2008). Infant gaze following and pointing predict accelerated vocabulary growth through two years of age: A longitudinal, growth curve modeling study. *Journal of Child Language, 35*, 207–220.

Brooks-Gunn, J. (2003). Do you believe in magic?: What we can expect from early childhood programs. *Social Policy Report, Society for Research in Child Development, XVII*(1), 1–13.

Brooks-Gunn, J., & Warren, M. P. (1989). The psychological significance of secondary sexual characteristics in 9- to 11-year-old girls. *Child Development, 59*, 161–169.

Brooks-Gunn, J., Han, W-J., & Waldfogel, J. (2010). First-year maternal employment and child development in the first seven years.

Monographs of the Society for Research in Child Development (SRCD), 75(2), 1–147.

Brown, A. S., & others. (2011). Family and home asthma services across the Controlling Asthma in American Cities Project. *Journal of Urban Health, 88*(Suppl. 1), S100–S112.

Brown, B. B. (2011). Popularity in peer group perspective: The role of status in adolescent peer systems. In A. H. N. Cillessen, D. Schwartz, & L. Mayeux (Eds.), *Popularity in the peer system.* New York: Guilford.

Brown, B. B., & Bakken, J. P. (2011). Parenting and peer relationships: Reinvigorating research on family-peer linkages in adolescence. *Journal of Research on Adolescence, 21*, 153–165.

Brown, B. B., & Dietz, E. L. (2009). Informal peer groups in middle childhood and adolescence. In K. H. Rubin, W. M. Bukowski, & B. Laursen (Eds.), *Handbook of peer interaction, relationships, and groups.* New York: Guilford.

Brown, B. B., & Larson, J. (2009). Peer relationships in adolescence. In R. M. Lerner & L. Steinberg (Eds.), *Handbook of adolescent development* (3rd ed.). New York: Wiley.

Brown, B. B., & Larson, R. W. (2002). The kaleidoscope of adolescence: Experiences of the world's youth at the beginning of the 21st century. In B. B. Brown, R. W. Larson, & T. S. Saraswathi (Eds.), *The world's youth.* New York: Cambridge University Press.

Brown, B. B., & Lohr, M. J. (1987). Peer-group affiliation and adolescent self-esteem: An integration of ego-identity and symbolic-interaction theories. *Journal of Personality and Social Psychology, 52*, 47–55.

Brown, J. D., & Bobkowski, P. S. (2011). Older and newer media: Patterns of use and effects on adolescents' health and well-being. *Journal of Research on Adolescence, 21*, 95–113.

Brown, R. (1958). *Words and things.* Glencoe, IL: Free Press.

Brown, R. (1973). *A first language: The early stages.* Cambridge, MA: Harvard University Press.

Brown, W. H., Pfeiffer, K. A., McIver, K. L., Dowda, M., Addy, C. L., & Pate, R. R. (2009). Social and environmental factors associated with preschoolers' nonsedentary physical activity. *Child Development, 80*, 45–58.

Brownell, C. (2011). Brownell–Early social development lab. Retrieved March 24, 2011, from http://www.pitt.edu/~toddlers/ESDL/brownell.html

Brownell, C., Nichols, S., Svetlova, M., Zerwas, S. & Ramani, G. (2009). The head bone's connected to the neck bone: When do toddlers represent their own body topography? *Child Development, 81*(3), 797–810.

Brownell, C. A., Ramani, G. B., & Zerwas, S. (2006). Becoming a social partner with peers: Cooperation and social understanding in one- and two-year-olds. *Child Development, 77*, 803–821.

Bruck, M., & Ceci, S. J. (1999). The suggestibility of children's memory. *Annual Review of Psychology, 50*, 419–439.

Bruck, M., & Ceci, S. J. (2011). Forensic developmental psychology in the courtroom. In D. Faust & M. Ziskin (Eds.), *Coping with psychiatric and psychological testimony.* New York: Cambridge University Press.

Bruck, M., & Melnyk, L. (2004). Individual differences in children's suggestibility: A review and a synthesis. *Applied Cognitive Psychology, 18*, 947–996.

Brueggeman, P. (2011). Hearing: Late-identification of hearing loss. In S. S. Chabon & E. R. Cohn (Eds.), *Communication disorders casebook.* Upper Saddle River, NJ: Pearson.

Bruni, O., Ferri, R., Novelli, L., Finotti, E., Miano, S., & Guilleminault, C. (2008). NREM sleep instability in children with sleep terrors: The role of slow wave activity interruptions. *Clinical Neurophysiology, 119*, 985–992.

Brunstein Klomek, A., Marrocco, F., Kleinman, M., Schofeld, I. S., & Gould, M. S. (2007). Bullying, depression, and suicidality in adolescents. *Journal of the American Academy of Child and Adolescent Psychiatry, 46*, 40–49.

Brunton, P. J., & Russell, J. A. (2011). Neuroendocrine control of maternal stress responses and fetal programming by stress in pregnancy. *Progress in Neuro-Pharmacology and Biological Psychiatry, 35*(5), 1178–1191.

Bryant, J. B. (Ed.). (2007). *The children's television community.* Mahwah, NJ: Erlbaum.

Bryant, J. B. (2009). Language in social contexts: Communication competence in the preschool years. In J. Berko Gleason & N. Ratner (Eds.), *The development of language* (7th ed.). Boston: Allyn & Bacon.

Buckner, J. C., Mezzacappa, E., & Beardslee, W. R. (2009). Self-regulation and its relations to adaptive functioning in low-income youths. *American Journal of Orthopsychiatry, 79*, 19–30.

Budde, H., Voelcker-Rehage, C., Pietrabyk-Kendziorra, P., Ribeiro, P., & Tidow, G. (2008). Acute aerobic exercise improves attentional performance in adolescence. *Neuroscience Letters, 441*, 219–223.

Buhler, E., & others. (2011, in press). Differential diagnosis of autism spectrum disorder and attention deficit hyperactivity disorder by means of inhibitory control and "theory of mind." *Journal of Autism and Developmental Disorders.*

Buhrmester, D. (1998). Need fulfillment, interpersonal competence, and the developmental contexts of early adolescent friendship. In W. M. Bukowski & A. F. Newcomb (Eds.), *The company they keep: Friendship in childhood and adolescence.* New York: Cambridge University Press.

Buhrmester, D. (2001, April). *Does age at which romantic involvement starts matter?* Paper presented at the meeting of the Society for Research in Child Development, Minneapolis.

Buhrmester, D., & Chong, C. M. (2009). Friendship in adolescence. In H. Reis & S. Sprecher (Eds.), *Encyclopedia of human relationships.* Thousand Oaks, CA: Sage.

Buhs, E. S., & Ladd, G. W. (2001). Peer rejection as an antecedent of young children's school adjustment: An examination of mediating processes. *Developmental Psychology, 37,* 550–560.

Bukowski, R., & others. (2008, January). *Folic acid and preterm birth.* Paper presented at the meeting of the Society for Maternal-Fetal Medicine, Dallas.

Bukowski, W. M., Buhrmester, D., & Underwood, M. K. (2011). Peer relations as a developmental context. In M. K. Underwood & L. H. Rosen (Eds.), *Social development.* New York: Guilford.

Bukowski, W. M., Laursen, B., & Hoza, B. (2010). The snowball effect: Friendship moderates escalations in depressed affect among avoidant and excluded children. *Development and Psychopathology, 22,* 749–757.

Bukowski, W. M., Motzoi, C., & Meyer, F. (2009). Friendship process, function, and outcome. In K. H. Rubin, W. M. Bukowksi, & B. Laursen (Eds.), *Handbook of peer interaction, relationships, and groups.* New York: Guilford.

Bulik, C. M., Berkman, N. D., Brownley, K. A., Sedway, J. A., & Lohr, K. N. (2007). Anorexia nervosa treatment: A systematic review of randomized controlled trials. *International Journal of Eating Disorders, 40,* 310–320.

Bullock, M., & Lutkenhaus, P. (1990). Who am I? Self-understanding in toddlers. *Merrill-Palmer Quarterly, 36,* 217–238.

Bumpus, M. F., Crouter, A. C., & McHale, M. (2001). Parental autonomy granting during adolescence: Exploring gender differences in context. *Developmental Psychology, 37,* 163–173.

Burger, S. (2010). A cost consequence analysis of outreach strategies for high risk pregnant women. *Journal of Community Health Nursing, 27,* 137–145.

Buriel, R. (2011). Historical origins of the immigrant paradox in the Mexican-origin population. In C. Garcia Coll & A. K. Marks (Eds.), *The immigrant paradox in children and adolescents: Is becoming an American a risk?* Washington, DC: American Psychological Association.

Burke, J. D. (2011). The relationship between conduct disorder and oppositional defiant disorder and their continuity with antisocial behaviors. In D. Shaffer, E. Leibenluft, & L. A. Rohde (Eds.), *Externalizing disorders of childhood: Refining the research agenda for DSM-V.* Arlington, VA: American Psychiatric Association.

Burke, M. G., & Miller, M. D. (2011). Practical guidelines for evaluating lead exposure in children with mental health conditions: Molecular effects and clinical implications. *Postgraduate Medicine, 123,* 160–168.

Burnett, S. M., Weaver, M. R., Mody-Pan, P. N., Reynolds Thomas, L. A., & Mar, C. M. (2011, in press). Evaluation of an intervention to increase human immunodeficiency virus testing among youth in Manzini, Swaziland: A randomized control trial. *Journal of Adolescent Health.*

Burnette, J. (1998). Reducing the disproportionate representation of minority students in special education. *ERIC/OSEP Digest,* No. E566.

Burnham, D., & Mattock, K. (2010). Auditory development. In J. G. Bremner & T. D. Wachs (Eds.), *Wiley-Blackwell handbook of infant development* (2nd ed.). New York: Wiley.

Burns, C., Dunn, A., Brady, M., Starr, N. B., & Blosser, C. (2009). *Pediatric primary care.* Oxford, UK: Elsevier.

Burns, L., Mattick, R. P., Lim, K., & Wallace, C. (2007). Methadone in pregnancy: Treatment retention and neonatal outcomes. *Addiction, 102,* 264–270.

Burt, S. A., Klahr, A. M., Rueter, M. A., McGue, M., & Iacono, W. G. (2011). Confirming the etiology of adolescent acting-out behaviors: An examination of observer ratings in a sample of adoptive and biological siblings. *Journal of Child Psychology and Psychiatry, 52,* 519–526.

Burt, S. A., McGue, M., & Iacono, W. G. (2010). Environmental contributions to the stability of antisocial behavior over time: Are they shared or non-shared? *Journal of Abnormal Child Psychology, 38,* 327–337.

Bushnell, I. W. R. (2003). Newborn face recognition. In O. Pascalis & A. Slater (Eds.), *The development of face processing in infancy and early childhood.* New York: NOVA Science.

Buss, D. M. (1995): Psychological sex differences: Origins through sexual selection. *American Psychologist, 50,* 164–168.

Buss, D. M. (2008). *Evolutionary psychology* (3rd ed.). Boston: Allyn & Bacon.

Buss, D. M. (2012). *Evolutionary psychology* (4th ed.). Boston: Allyn & Bacon.

Buss, K. A., & Goldsmith, H. H. (2007). Biobehavioral approaches to early socioemotional development. In C. A. Brownell & C. B. Kopp (Eds.), *Socioemotional development in the toddler years.* New York: Guilford.

Bussey, K., & Bandura, A. (1999). Social cognitive theory of gender development and differentiation. *Psychological Review, 106,* 676–713.

Butcher, K., Sallis, J. F., Mayer, J. A., & Woodruff, S. (2008). Correlates of physical activity guideline compliance for adolescents in 100 cities. *Journal of Adolescent Health, 42,* 360–368.

Butte, N. F. (2006). Energy requirements of infants and children. *Nestle Nutrition Workshop Series: Pediatric Program, 58,* 19–32.

Butterworth, G. (2004). Joint visual attention in infancy. In G. Bremner & A. Slater (Eds.), *Theories of infant development.* Malden, MA: Blackwell.

Byrnes, J. P. (2008). Piaget's cognitive developmental theory. In M. M. Haith & J. B. Benson (Eds.), *Encyclopedia of infant and early childhood development.* Oxford, UK: Elsevier.

Byrom, S., & Symon, A. (2011). Developing the midwife's role in public health. *Practicing Midwife, 14,* 16–17.

C

Caddy, S. C., & others. (2011). Pregnancy and neonatal outcomes of women with reactive syphilis serology in Alberta, 2002–2006. *Journal of Obstetrics and Gynecology Canada, 33,* 453–459.

Calkins, S. D., & Marcovitch, S. (2010). Emotion regulation and executive functioning in early development: Integrated mechanisms of control supporting adaptive functioning. In S. D. Calkins & M. A. Bell (Eds.), *Child development at the intersection of emotion and cognition.* Washington, DC: American Psychological Association.

Callaway, L. K., Lust, K., & McIntyre, H. D. (2005). Pregnancy outcomes in women of very advanced maternal age. *Obstetrics and Gynecology Survey, 60,* 562–563.

Cameron, A. J., & others. (2011). Clustering of obesity-related risk behaviors in children and their mothers. *Annals of Epidemiology, 21,* 95–102.

Cameron, J., & Pierce, D. (2008). Intrinsic versus extrinsic motivation. In N. J. Salkind (Ed.), *Encyclopedia of educational psychology.* Thousand Oaks, CA: Sage.

Camhi, S. M., & others. (2010). Predicting adult body mass index-specific metabolic risk from childhood. *Metabolic Syndrome and Related Disorders, 8,* 165–172.

Campbell, A. (2010). Oxytocin and human social behavior. *Personality and Social Psychology Review, 14*(3), 281–295.

Campbell, D. A., Lake, M. F., Falk, M., & Backstrand, J. R. (2006). A randomized controlled trial of continuous support by a lay doula. *Journal of Obstetrics and Gynecology: Neonatal Nursing, 35,* 456–464.

Campbell, G. R., & Mahad, D. J. (2011, in press). Mitochondria as crucial players in demyelinated axons: Lessons from neuropathology and experimental demyelination. *Autoimmune Diseases.*

Campbell, L., Campbell, B., & Dickinson, D. (2004). *Teaching and learning through multiple intelligence* (3rd ed.). Boston: Allyn & Bacon.

Campbell, M. K., & Mottols, M. F. (2001). Recreational exercise and occupational safety during pregnancy and birth weight: A case control study. *American Journal of Obstetrics and Gynecology, 184,* 403–408.

Campos, J. J. (2005). Unpublished review of J. W. Santrock's *Life-span development* (10th ed.). New York: McGraw-Hill.

Campos, J. J. (2009). Unpublished review of J. W. Santrock's *Life-span development* (13th ed.). New York: McGraw-Hill.

Campos, J. J., Langer, A., & Krowitz, A. (1970). Cardiac responses on the visual cliff in prelocomotor human infants. *Science, 170,* 196–197.

Canfield, R. L., & Jusko, T. A. (2008). Lead poisoning. In M. M. Haith & J. B. Benson (Eds.), *Encyclopedia of infancy and early childhood.* Oxford, UK: Elsevier.

Canfield, R. L., Gendle, M. H., & Cory-Slechta, D. A. (2004). Impaired neuropsychological functioning in lead-exposed children. *Developmental Neuropsychology, 26,* 513–540.

Canterino, J. C, Ananth, C. V., Smulian, J., Harrigan, J. T., & Vintzileos, A. M. (2004). Maternal age and risk of fetal death in singleton gestation, United States, 1995–2000. *Obstetrics and Gynecology Survey, 59*, 649–650.

Carlo, G. (2006). Care-based and altruistically-based morality. In M. Killen & J. Smetana (Eds.), *Handbook of moral development.* Mahwah, NJ: Erlbaum.

Carlo, G., Crockett, L. J., Carranza, M. A., & Martinez, M. M. (2011). Understanding ethnic/racial health disparities in youth and families in the U.S. *Nebraska Symposium on Motivation, 57,* 1–11.

Carlo, G., Mestre, M. V., Samper, P., Tur, A., & McGinley, M. (2011, March). *Emotional instability and empathy as mediators of the links between coping and prosocial and aggressive behaviors.* Paper presented at the meeting of the Society for Research in Child Development, Montreal, Canada.

Carlson, S., & White, R. (2011). Unpublished research, Minneapolis: Institute of Child Development, University of Minnesota.

Carlson, S. M. (2010). Development of conscious control and imagination. In R. F. Baumeister, A. R. Mele, & K. D. Vohs (Eds.), *Free will and consciousness: How might they work?* New York: Oxford.

Carlson, S. M., Davis, A. C., & Leach, J. G. (2005). Executive function and symbolic representation in preschool children. *Psychological Science, 16,* 609–616.

Carlson, S. M., & White, R. (2011). Unpublished manuscript. Minneapolis: Institute of Child Development, University of Minnesota.

Carlson, S. M., & Zelazo, P. D. (2008). Symbolic thought. In M. M. Haith & J. B. Benson (Eds.), *Encyclopedia of infant and early childhood development.* Oxford, UK: Elsevier.

Carnegie Council on Adolescent Development. (1989). *Turning points: Preparing American youth for the twenty-first century.* New York: Carnegie Foundation.

Carpendale, J. I., & Chandler, M. J. (1996). On the distinction between false belief understanding and subscribing to an interpretive theory of mind. *Child Development, 67,* 1686–1706.

Carpenter, J., Nagell, K., & Tomasello, M. (1998). Social cognition, joint attention, and communicative competence from 9 to 15 months of age. *Monographs of the Society for Research in Child Development, 70*(1, Serial No. 279).

Carpenter, M. (2011). Social cognition and social motivations in infancy. In U. Goswami (Ed.), *Wiley-Blackwell handbook of childhood cognitive development* (2nd ed.). New York: Wiley.

Carrell, S. E., Malmstrom, F. V., & West, J. E. (2008). Peer effects in academic cheating. *Journal of Human Resources, 43,* 173–207.

Carskadon, M. A. (Ed.). (2002). *Adolescent sleep patterns.* New York: Cambridge University Press.

Carskadon, M. A. (2004). Sleep difficulties in young people. *Archives of Pediatric and Adolescent Health, 158,* 597–598.

Carskadon, M. A. (2005). Sleep and circadian rhythms in children and adolescents: Relevance for athletic performance of young people. *Clinical Sports Medicine, 24,* 319–328.

Carskadon, M. A. (2006, April). *Adolescent sleep: The perfect storm.* Paper presented at the meeting of the Society for Research on Adolescence, San Francisco.

Carskadon, M. A. (2011a). Sleep in adolescents: The perfect storm. *Pediatric Clinics of North America, 58,* 637–647.

Carskadon, M. A. (2011b). Sleep's effects on cognition and learning in adolescence. *Progress in Brain Research, 190,* 137–143.

Cartwright, R., Agargun, M. Y., Kirkby, J., & Friedman, J. K. (2006). Relation of dreams to waking concerns. *Psychiatry Research, 141,* 261–270.

Carvalho Bos, S., & others. (2009). Sleep and behavioral/emotional problems in children: A population-based study. *Sleep Medicine, 10,* 66–74.

Carver, L. J., & Bauer, P. J. (2001). The dawning of the past: The emergence of long-term explicit memory in infancy. *Journal of Experimental Psychology: General, 130,* 726–745.

Casares, W. N., Lahiff, M., Eskensazi, B., & Halpern-Felsher, B. L. (2010). Unpredicted trajectories: The relationship between race/ethnicity, pregnancy during adolescence, and young women's outcomes. *Journal of Adolescent Health, 47,* 143–160.

Case, R., & Mueller, M. P. (2001). Differentiation, integration, and covariance mapping as fundamental processes in cognitive and neurological growth. In J. L. McClelland & R. S. Siegler (Eds.), *Mechanisms of cognitive development.* Mahwah, NJ: Erlbaum.

Casey, B. J., Duhoux, S., & Malter Cohen, M. (2010). Adolescence: What do transmission, transition, and translation have to do with it? *Neuron, 67,* 749–760.

Casey, B. J., Jones, R. M., & Somerville, L. H. (2011). Braking and accelerating of the adolescent brain. *Journal of Research on Adolescence, 21,* 21–33.

Caspers, K. M., Paraiso, S., Yucuis, R., Troutman, B., Arndt, S., & Philibert, R. (2009). Association between the serotonin transporter polymorphism (5-HTTLPR) and adult unresolved attachment. *Developmental Psychology, 45,* 64–76.

Caspi, A., Hariri, A. R., Holmes, A., Uher, R., & Moffitt, T. E. (2011). Genetic sensitivity to the environment: The case of the serotonin transporter gene and its implications for studying complex diseases and traits. In K. A. Dodge & M. Rutter (Eds.), *Gene-environment interaction and developmental psychopathology.* New York: Guilford.

Caspi, A., Sugden, K., Moffitt, T. E., Taylor, A., Craig, I., Harrington, H., & others. (2003). Influence of life stress on depression: Moderation by a polymorphism in the 5-HTT gene. *Science, 301,* 386–389.

Cassidy, J., & others. (2011). Enhancing infant attachment security: An examination of treatment efficacy and differential susceptibility. *Development and Psychopathology, 23,* 131–148.

Castle, J., & others. (2010). Parents' evaluation of adoption success: A follow-up study of intercountry and domestic adoptions. *American Journal of Orthopsychiatry, 79,* 522–531.

Castro-Rodriquez, J. A. (2011). The asthma predictive index: Early diagnosis of asthma. *Current Opinion in Allergy and Clinical Immunology, 11*(3), 157–161.

Catani, C., Gewirtz, A. H., Wieling, E., Schauer, E., Elbert, T., & Neuner, F. (2010). Tsunami, war, and cumulative risk in the lives of Sri Lankan school children. *Child Development, 81,* 1176–1191.

Cauffinan, B. E. (1994, February). *The effects of puberty, dating, and sexual involvement on dieting and disordered eating in young adolescent girls.* Paper presented at the meeting of the Society for Research on Adolescence, San Diego.

Caughey, A. B., Hopkins, L. M., & Norton, M. E. (2006). Chorionic villus sampling compared with amniocentesis and the difference in the rate of pregnancy loss. *Obstetrics and Gynecology, 108,* 612–616.

Cavalcante, S. R., Cecatti, J. G., Pereira, R. I., Baciuk, E. P., Bernardo, A. L., & Silveira, C. (2009). Water aerobics II: Maternal body composition and perinatal outcomes after a program for low risk pregnant women. *Reproductive Health, 6,* 1.

Cavanagh, S. (2007, October 3). U.S.-Chinese exchanges nurture ties between principals. *Education Week.* Retrieved July 15, 2008, from http://www.edweek.org

Cavanagh, S. E. (2009). Puberty. In D. Carr (Ed.), *Encyclopedia of the life course and human development.* Boston: Gale Cengage.

Cease, A. T., King, W. D., & Monroe, K. W. (2011). Analysis of child passenger safety restraint use at a pediatric emergency department. *Pediatric Emergency Care, 27,* 102–105.

Ceci, S. J., Fitneva, S., Aydin, C., & Chernyak, N. L. (2010). The legal context of memory development. In A. Slater & G. Bremner (Eds.), *An introduction to developmental psychology* (2nd ed.). London: Blackwell.

Ceci, S. J., & Gilstrap, L. L. (2000). Determinants of intelligence: Schooling and intelligence. In A. Kazdin (Ed.), *Encyclopedia of psychology.* New York: Oxford University Press.

Ceci, S. J., Kulkofsky, S., Klemfuss, J. Z., Sweeney, C. D., & Bruck, M. (2007). Unwarranted assumptions about children's testimonial accuracy. *Annual Review of Clinical Psychology, 3,* 311–328.

Ceci, S. J., Papierno, P. B., & Kulkovsky, S. (2007). Representational constraints on children's suggestibility. *Psychological Science, 18,* 503–509.

Center for Science in the Public Interest. (2008). Obesity on the kids' menu at top chains. Retrieved October 24, 2008, from http://www.cspinet.org/new/200808041.html

Centers for Disease Control and Prevention. (2000). *CDC growth charts: United States.* Atlanta: Author.

Centers for Disease Control and Prevention. (2004). *Fertility*. Retrieved June 6, 2006, from www.cdc.gov/ART/ART2004/sect2_fig5–15. htm#12

Centers for Disease Control and Prevention. (2007). *Autism and developmental disabilities monitoring (ADDM) network*. Atlanta: Author.

Centers for Disease Control and Prevention. (2008). *Sexually transmitted disease surveillance*. Atlanta: U.S. Department of Health and Human Services.

Centers for Disease Control and Prevention. (2011a). *Body mass index for children and teens*. Atlanta: Author.

Centers for Disease Control and Prevention. (2011b). CDCC grand rounds: Childhood obesity in the United States. *MMWR, 60*, 42–46.

Centers for Disease Control and Prevention. (2011c). *HIV/AIDS statistics and surveillance*. Atlanta: Author.

Centers for Disease Control and Prevention. (2011d). *SIDS*. Retrieved January 10, 2011, from http://www.cdc.gov/SIDS/index.htm

Chang, J. S. (2009). Parental smoking and childhood leukemia. *Methods in Molecular Biology, 472*, 103–137.

Chang, M. Y., Chen, C. H., & Huang, K. F. (2006). A comparison of massage effects on labor pain using the McGill Pain Questionnaire. *Journal of Nursing Research, 14*, 190–197.

Chao, R. K. (2005, April). *The importance of Guan in describing control of immigrant Chinese*. Paper presented at the meeting of the Society for Research in Child Development, Atlanta.

Chao, R. K. (2007, March). *Research with Asian Americans. Looking back and moving forward*. Paper presented at the meeting of the Society for Research in Child Development, Boston.

Chao, R. K., & Otsuki-Clutter, M. (2011). Racial and ethnic differences: Sociocultural and contextual explanations. *Journal of Research on Adolescence, 21*, 47–60.

Chaplin, J. E., & others. (2011). Improvements in behavior and self-esteem following growth hormone treatment in short prepubertal children. *Hormone Research in Pediatrics, 75*(4), 291–303.

Chattin-McNichols, J. (1992). *The Montessori controversy*. Albany, NY: Delmar.

Cheah, C. S. L., & Leung, C. Y. Y. (2011). The social development of immigrant children: A focus on Asian and Hispanic children in the United States. In P. K. Smith & C. H. Hart (Eds.), *Wiley-Blackwell handbook of childhood social development* (2nd ed.). New York: Wiley.

Chemtob, C. M., Nomura, Y., Rajendran, K., Yehuda, R., Schwartz, D., & Abramovitz, R. (2010). Impact of maternal posttraumatic stress disorder and depression following exposure to the September 11 attacks on preschool children's behavior. *Child Development, 81*, 1129–1141.

Chen, C., & Stevenson, H. W. (1989). Homework: A cross-cultural examination. *Child Development, 60*, 551–561.

Chen, J. J., & Brooks-Gunn, J. (2012). Neighborhoods, schools, and achievement. In K. R. Harris, S. Graham, & T. Urdan (Eds.), *APA handbook of educational psychology*. Washington, DC: American Psychological Association.

Chen, J. J., Howard, K. S., & Brooks-Gunn, J. (2011). Neighborhoods matter: How neighborhood context influences individual development. In K. Fingerman, C. Berg, T. Antonucci, & J. Smith (Eds.), *Handbook of lifespan psychology*. New York: Springer.

Chen, M. Y., Wang, E. K., & Jeng, Y. J. (2006). Adequate sleep among adolescents is positively associated with health status and health-related behaviors. *BMC Public Health, 6*, 59.

Chen, X., Chung, J., Lechcier-Kimel, R., & French, D. (2011). Culture and social development. In P. K. Smith & C. H. Hart (Eds.), *Wiley-Blackwell perspectives on social development* (2nd ed.). New York: Wiley.

Chen, X., Hastings, P. D., Rubin, K. H., Chen, H., Cen, G., & Stewart, S. L. (1998). Childrearing attitudes and behavioral inhibition in Chinese and Canadian toddlers: A cross-cultural study. *Developmental Psychology, 34*, 677–686.

Chen, X. K., Wen, S. W., Yang, Q., & Walker, M. C. (2007). Adequacy of prenatal care and neonatal mortality in infants born to mothers with and without antenatal high-risk conditions. *Australian and New Zealand Journal of Obstetrics and Gynecology, 47*, 122–127.

Chen, Y. H., Rodgers, J., & McConachie, H. (2009). Restricted and repetitive behaviors, sensory processing, and cognitive style in children with autism spectrum disorders. *Journal of Autism and Developmental Disorders, 39*, 635–642.

Cheng, D., Kettinger, L., Uduhiri, K., & Hurt, L. (2011). Alcohol consumption during pregnancy: Prevalence and provider assessment. *Obstetrics and Gynecology, 117*(2, Pt. 2), 212–217.

Cherlin, A. J., & Furstenberg, F. F. (1994). Stepfamilies in the United States: A reconsideration. In J. Blake & J. Hagen (Eds.), *Annual review of sociology*. Palo Alto, CA: Annual Reviews.

Chess, S., & Thomas, A. (1977). Temperamental individuality from childhood to adolescence. *Journal of Child Psychiatry, 16*, 218–226.

Cheung, A. P. (2006). Assisted reproductive technology: Both sides now. *Journal of Reproductive Medicine, 51*, 283–292.

Chi, M. T. (1978). Knowledge structures and memory development. In R. S. Siegler (Ed.), *Children's thinking: What develops?* Hillsdale, NJ: Erlbaum.

Childstats.gov. (2010). Retrieved October 21, 2010, from http://www.childstats.gov/americaschildren/eco.asp

Chomsky, N. (1957). *Syntactic structures*. The Hague: Mouton.

Choufani, S., Shuman, C., & Weksberg, R. (2010). Beckwith-Wiedemann syndrome. *American Journal of Medical Genetics: Part C, Seminars in Medical Genetics, 154C*, 343–354.

Christian, P. (2009). Prenatal origins of undernutrition. *Nestlé Nutrition Workshop Series: Pediatric Program, 63*, 59–73.

Christie, J., Enz, B. J., & Vukelich, C. (2011). *Teaching language and literacy* (4th ed.). Boston: Allyn & Bacon.

Chuang, S. S., & Tamis-Lemonda, C. (2009). Gender roles in immigrant families: Parenting views, practices, and child development. *Sex Roles, 60*, 451–455.

Cicchetti, D. (2010). Developmental psychopathology. In A. Freund, M. Lamb, & R. M. Lerner (Eds.), *Handbook of life-span development*. New York: Wiley.

Cicchetti, D. (2011a). Developmental psychopathology. In P. Zelazo (Ed.), *Oxford handbook of developmental psychology*. New York: Oxford University Press.

Cicchetti, D. (2011b). Pathways to resilient functioning in maltreated children: From single level to multilevel investigations. In D. Cicchetti & G. I. Roisman (Eds.), *The origins and organization of adaptation and maladaptation: Minnesota Symposia on Child Psychology* (Vol. 36). New York: Wiley.

Cicchetti, D. (2012). Developmental psychopathology. In P. Zelazo (Ed.), *Oxford handbook of developmental psychology*. New York: Oxford University Press.

Cicchetti, D., & Toth, S. L. (2011). Child maltreatment: The research imperative and the exploration of results to clinical contexts. In B. Lester & J. D. Sparrow (Eds.), *Nurturing children and families*. New York: Wiley.

Cicchetti, D., Toth, S. L., Nilsen, W. J., & Manly, J. T. (2011). What do we know and why does it matter? The dissemination of evidence-based interventions for child maltreatment. In H. R. Schaffer & K. Durkin (Eds.), *Blackwell handbook of developmental psychology in action*. Oxford: Blackwell.

Cicchetti, D., Toth, S. L., & Rogosch, F. A. (2005). *A prevention program for child maltreatment*. Unpublished manuscript. Rochester, NY: University of Rochester.

Cillessen, A. H. N., & Bellmore, A. D. (2011). Social skills and social competence in interactions with peers. In P. K. Smith & C. H. Hart (Eds.), *Wiley-Blackwell handbook of childhood social development* (2nd ed.). New York: Wiley.

Cisneros-Cohernour, E. J., Moreno, R. P., & Cisneros, A. A. (2000). Curriculum reform in Mexico: Kindergarten teachers' challenges and dilemmas. Proceedings of the Lilian Katz Symposium. In D. Rothenberg (Ed.), *Issues in early childhood education: Curriculum reform, teacher education, and dissemination of information*. Urbana-Champaign, IL: University of Illinois.

Citkovitz, C., Klimenko, E., Bolyai, M., Applewhite, L., Julliard, K., & Weiner, Z. (2009). Effects of acupuncture during labor and delivery in a U.S. hospital setting: A case-control panel. *Journal of Alternative and Complementary Medicine, 15*, 501–505.

Citkovitz, C., Schnyer, R. N., & Hoskins, I. A. (2011). Acupuncture during labour: Data are more promising than a recent review suggests. *British Journal of Obstetrics and Gynaecology, 118*, 101.

Civelek, E., & others. (2011). Risk factors for current wheezing and its phenotypes among elementary school children. *Pediatric Pulmonology, 46,* 166–174.

Clark, B. (2008). *Growing up gifted* (7th ed.). Upper Saddle River, NJ: Prentice Hall.

Clark, E. (1993). *The lexicon in acquisition.* New York: Cambridge University Press.

Clark, E. V. (2009). What shapes children's language? Child-directed speech and the process of acquisition. In V. C. M. Gathercole (Ed.), *Routes to language: Essays in honor of Melissa Bowerman.* New York: Psychology Press.

Clarke, A., & Thirlaway, K. (2011, in press). "Genomic counseling"? Genetic counseling in the genomic era. *Genome Medicine.*

Clarke-Stewart, A. K., & Miner, J. L. (2008). Effects of child and day care. In M. M. Haith & J. B. Benson (Eds.), *Encyclopedia of infant and early childhood development.* Oxford, UK: Elsevier.

Class, Q. A., Lichtenstein, P., Langstrom, N., & D'Onofrio, B. M. (2011). Timing of prenatal maternal exposure to severe life events and adverse pregnancy outcomes: A population study of 2.6 million pregnancies. *Psychosomatic Medicine, 73*(3), 234–241.

Clay, R. (2001, February). Fulfilling an unmet need. Copy edition. *Monitor on Psychology,* No. 2 (no page number available).

Clearfield, M. W., Diedrich, F. J., Smith, L. B., & Thelen, E. (2006). Young infants reach correctly in A-not-B tasks: On the development of stability and perseveration. *Infant Behavior and Development, 29,* 435–444.

Clifton, R. K., Morrongiello, B. A., Kulig, J. W., & Dowd, J. M. (1981). Developmental changes in auditory localization in infancy. In R. N. Aslin, J. R. Alberts, & M. R. Petersen (Eds.), *Development of perception* (Vol. 1). Orlando, FL: Academic Press.

Clifton, R. K., Muir, D. W., Ashmead, D. H., & Clarkson, M. G. (1993). Is visually guided reaching in early infancy a myth? *Child Development, 64,* 1099–1110.

Cloud, J. (2007, August 27). Failing our geniuses. *Time,* 40–47.

Cluett, E. R., & Burns, E. (2009). Immersion in water in labor and birth. *Cochrane Database of Systematic Reviews, 2,* CD000111.

Cohen, D. (2009). *What every man should know about being a dad.* New York: Psychology Press.

Cohen, G. L., & Prinstein, M. J. (2006). Peer contagion of aggression and health-risk behavior among adolescent males: An experimental investigation of effects of public conduct and private attitudes. *Child Development, 77,* 967–983.

Cohn, B. A., Cirillo, P. M., Sholtz, R. I., Ferrara, A., Park, J. S., & Schwingl, P. J. (2011). Polychlorinated biphenyl (PCB) exposure in mothers and time to pregnancy in daughters. *Reproductive Toxicology, 31*(3), 290–296.

Coie, J. (2004). The impact of negative social experiences on the development of antisocial behavior. In J. B. Kupersmidt & K. A. Dodge (Eds.), *Children's peer relations: From development to intervention.* Washington, DC: American Psychological Association.

Colby, A., Kohlberg, L., Gibbs, J., & Lieberman, M. (1983). A longitudinal study of moral judgment. *Monographs of the Society for Research in Child Development* (Serial No. 201).

Cole, M., & Packer, M. (2011). Culture in development. In M. H. Bornstein & M. E. Lamb (Eds.), *Cognitive development.* New York: Psychology Press.

Cole, P. M., Dennis, T. A., Smith-Simon, K. E., & Cohen, L. H. (2009). Preschoolers' emotion regulation strategy understanding: Relations with emotion socialization and child self-regulation. *Social Development, 18*(2), 324–352.

Cole, P. M., & Tan, P. Z. (2007). Emotion socialization from a cultural perspective. In J. E. Grusec & P. D. Hastings (Eds.), *Handbook of socialization.* New York: Guilford.

Coleman, M., Ganong, L., & Fine, M. (2004). Communication in stepfamilies. In A. L. Vangelisti (Ed.), *Handbook of family communication.* Mahwah, NJ: Erlbaum.

Coleman-Phox, K., Odouli, R., & Li, D-K. (2008). Use of a fan during sleep and the risk of sudden infant death syndrome. *Archives of Pediatric and Adolescent Medicine, 162,* 963–968.

Collett-Solberg, P. F. (2011). Update in growth hormone therapy of children. *Journal of Clinical Endocrinology and Metabolism, 96,* 573–579.

Collins, C. E., & others. (2011). Parent diet modification, child activity, or both in obese children: An RCT. *Pediatrics, 127,* 619–627.

Collins, J. S., Atkinson, K. K., Dean, J. H., Best, R. G., & Stevenson, R. E. (2011). Long-term maintenance of neural tube defects prevention in a high prevalence state. *Journal of Pediatrics, 159*(1), 143–149.

Collins, W. A., & Steinberg, L. (2006). Adolescent development in interpersonal context. In W. Damon & R. Lerner (Eds.), *Handbook of child psychology* (6th ed.). New York: Wiley.

Collins, W. A., & van Dulmen, M. (2006). The significance of middle childhood peer competence for work and relationships in early childhood. In A. C. Huston & M. N. Ripke (Eds.), *Developmental contexts in middle childhood.* New York: Cambridge University Press.

Colombo, J., Kapa, L., & Curtendale, L. (2011). Varieties of attention in infancy. In L. Oakes, C. Cashon, M. Casasola, & D. Rakison (Eds.), *Infant perception and cognition.* New York: Oxford University Press.

Colombo, J., & Mitchell, D. W. (2009). Infant visual habituation. *Neurobiology of Learning and Memory, 92,* 225–234.

Colombo, J., Shaddy, D. J., Blaga, O. M., Anderson, C. J., & Kannass, K. N. (2009). High cognitive ability in infancy and early childhood. In F. D. Horowitz, R. F. Subotnik, & D. J. Matthews (Eds.), *The development of giftedness and talent across the life span.* Washington, DC: American Psychological Association.

Colombo, J., Shaddy, D. J., Richman, W. A., Maikranz, J. M., & Blaga, O. M. (2004). The developmental course of attention in infancy and preschool cognitive outcome. *Infancy, 4,* 1–38.

Colonnesi, C., Stams, G. J., Koster, I., & Noom, M. J. (2011). The relation between pointing and language development: A meta-analysis. *Developmental Review, 30,* 352–366.

Colrain, I. M., & Baker, F. C. (2011). Changes in sleep as a function of adolescent development. *Neuropsychology Review, 21,* 5–21.

Combs, M. (2010). *Readers and writers in the primary grades.* Boston: Allyn & Bacon.

Comer, J. (2004). *Leave no child behind.* New Haven, CT: Yale University Press.

Comer, J. (2006). Child development: The under-weighted aspect of intelligence. In P. C. Kyllonen, R. D. Roberts, & L. Stankov (Eds.), *Extending intelligence.* Mahwah, NJ: Erlbaum.

Comer, J. P. (1988). Educating poor minority children. *Scientific American, 259,* 42–48.

Committee on Injury, Violence, and Poison Prevention. (2010). Prevention of choking among children. *Pediatrics, 125,* 601–607.

Committee on Injury, Violence, and Poison Prevention. (2011). Child passenger safety. *Pediatrics, 127,* e1050–e1066.

Commoner, B. (2002). Unraveling the DNA myth: The spurious foundation of genetic engineering. *Harper's Magazine, 304,* 39–47.

Comstock, G., & Scharrer., E. (2006). Media and popular culture. In W. Damon & R. Lerner (Eds.), *Handbook of child psychology* (6th ed.). New York: Wiley.

Conde-Agudelo, A., Belizan, J. M., & Diaz-Rossello, J. (2011, March 16). Kangaroo care to reduce morbidity and mortality in low birthweight infants. *Cochrane Database of Systematic Reviews,* (3) CD002771.

Conduct Problems Prevention Research Group. (2007). The Fast Track randomized controlled trial to prevent externalizing psychiatric disorders: Findings from grades 3 to 9. *Journal of the American Academy of Child and Adolescent Psychiatry, 46,* 1250–1262.

Conduct Problems Prevention Research Group. (2010a). The effects of the Fast Track preventive intervention on the development of conduct disorder across childhood. *Child Development, 82*(1), 331–345.

Conduct Problems Prevention Research Group. (2010b). The difficulty of maintaining positive intervention effects: A look at disruptive behavior, deviant peer relations, and social skills during the middle school years. *Journal of Early Adolescence, 30*(4), 593–624.

Cong, X., Ludington-Hoe, S. M., & Walsh, S. (2011). Randomized crossover trial of kangaroo care to reduce biobehavioral pain responses in preterm infants: A pilot study. *Biological Research for Nursing, 13*(2), 204–216.

Conger, R. D., & Chao, W. (1996). Adolescent depressed mood. In R. L. Simons (Ed.), *Understanding differences between divorced and intact families: Stress, interaction, and child outcome.* Thousand Oaks, CA: Sage.

Conger, R. D., & others. (2012). Resilience and vulnerability of Mexican origin youth and their families: A test of a culturally-informed model of family economic stress. In P. K. Kerig, M. S. Schulz, & S. T. Hauser (Eds.), *Adolescence and beyond.* New York: Oxford University Press.

Connell-Carrick, K. (2011). Child abuse and neglect. In J. G. Bremner & T. Wachs (Eds.), *Wiley-Blackwell handbook of infant development* (2nd ed.). New York: Wiley.

Connolly, J. A., & Mclsaac, C. (2009). Romantic relationships in adolescence. In R. M. Lerner & L. Steinberg (Eds.), *Handbook of adolescent psychology* (3rd ed.). New York: Wiley.

Conradt, E., & Ablow, J. (2010). Infant physiological response to the still-face paradigm: Contributions of maternal sensitivity and infants' early regulatory behavior. *Infant Behavior and Development, 33,* 251–265.

Constant, C., & others. (2011). Environmental tobacco smoke (ETS) exposure and respiratory morbidity in school age children. *Portuguese Journal of Pulmonology, 17,* 20–26.

Cook, M., & Birch, R. (1984). Infant perception of the shapes of tilted plane forms. *Infant Behavior and Development, 7,* 389–402.

Cook, P. J., MacCoun, R., Muschkin, C., & Vigdoi, J. (2008). The negative impacts of starting middle school in the sixth grade. *Journal of Policy Analysis and Management, 27,* 104–121.

Cooper, C. R. (2011). *Bridging multiple worlds: Cultures, identities, and pathways to college.* New York: Oxford University Press.

Cooper, C. R., & Grotevant, H. D. (1989, April). *Individuality and connectedness in the family and adolescent's self and relational competence.* Paper presented at the meeting of the Society for Research in Child Development, Kansas City.

Copeland, W., Shanahan, L., Miller, S., Costello, E. J., Angold, A., & Maughan, B. (2010). Outcomes of early pubertal timing in young women: A prospective. *American Journal of Psychiatry, 167,* 1218–1225.

Coplan, R. J., & Arbeau, K. A. (2009). Peer interactions and play in early childhood. In K. H. Rubin, W. M. Bukowski, & B. Laursen (Eds.), *Handbook of peer interactions, relationships, and groups.* New York: Guilford.

Corbetta, D. (2009). Brain, body, and mind: Lessons from infant development. In J. P. Spencer, M. Thomas, & J. McClelland (Eds.), *Connectionism and dynamic systems theory reconsidered.* New York: Oxford University Press.

Cordier, S. (2008). Evidence for a role of paternal exposure in developmental toxicity. *Basic and Clinical Pharmacology and Toxicology, 102,* 176–181.

Cornelius, J. R., Clark, D. B., Reynolds, M., Kirisci, L., & Tarter, R. (2007). Early age of first sexual intercourse and affiliation with deviant peers predict development of SUD: A prospective longitudinal study. *Addictive Behavior, 32,* 850–854.

Cortes, E., Basra, R., & Kelleher, C. J. (2011). Waterbirth and pelvic floor injury: A retrospective study and postal survey using ICIQ modular long form questionnaires. *European Journal of Obstetrics, Gynecology, and Reproductive Biology, 155,* 27–30.

Costa, R., & Figueiredo, B. (2011). Infants' psychophysiological profile and temperament at 3 and 12 months. *Infant Behavior and Development, 34*(2), 270–279.

Cottrell, L., & others. (2011, in press). Identifying the people and factors that influence children's intentions to make lifestyle changes. *Health Promotion Practice.*

Cotugno, G., & others. (2011). Adherence to diet and quality of life in patients with phenylketonuria. *Acta Paediatrica, 100*(8), 1144–1149.

Courage, M. L., & Richards, J. E. (2008). Attention. In M. M. Haith & J. B. Benson (Eds.), *Encyclopedia of infant and early childhood development.* Oxford, UK: Elsevier.

Cousineau, M. R., Stevens, G. D., & Farias, A. (2011). Measuring the impact of outreach and enrollment strategies for public health insurance in California. *Health Services Research, 46,* 319–335.

Cowan, C. P., & Cowan, P. A. (2000). *When partners become parents.* Mahwah, NJ: Erlbaum.

Cowan, P., Cowan, C., Ablow, J., Johnson, V. K., & Measelle, J. (2005) *The family context of parenting in children's adaptation to elementary school.* Mahwah, NJ: Erlbaum.

Coyne, S. M., Nelson, D. A., & Underwood, M. K. (2011). Aggression in children. In P. K. Smith & C. H. Hart (Eds.), *Wiley-Blackwell handbook of childhood social development* (2nd ed.). New York: Wiley.

Craik, F. I. M. (2006). Brain-behavior relations across the lifespan: A commentary. *Neuroscience and Biobehavioral Reviews, 30,* 885–892.

Crespi, B. (2011). The evolutionary biology of child health. Proceedings. *Biological Sciences, 278,* 1441–1449.

Crespo, C., Kielpikowski, M., Jose, P. E., & Pryor, J. (2010). Relationships between family connectedness and body satisfaction: A longitudinal study of adolescent girls and boys. *Journal of Youth and Adolescence, 39,* 1392–1401.

Crissey, S. R. (2009). Dating and romantic relationships, childhood and adolescence. In D. Carr (Ed.), *Encyclopedia of the life course and human development.* Boston: Gale Cengage.

Crockett, L. J., Raffaeli, M., & Shen, Y-L. (2006). Linking self-regulation and risk proneness to risky sexual behavior: Pathways through peer pressure and early substance use. *Journal of Research on Adolescence, 16,* 503–525.

Crone, E. A., Windelken, C., van Leijenhorst, L., Honomichi, R. D., Christoff, K., & Bunge, S. A. (2009). Neurocognitive development of relational reasoning. *Developmental Science, 12,* 55–66.

Cronk, C. E., & others. (2011). Effects of a culturally tailored intervention on changes in body mass index and health-related quality of life of Latino children and their parents. *American Journal of Health Promotion, 25,* el–e11.

Crosnoe, R., Riegle-Crumb, C., Field, S., Frank, K., & Muller, C. (2008). Peer group contexts of girls' and boys' academic experiences. *Child Development, 79,* 139–155.

Crouter, A. C. (2006). Mothers and fathers at work. In A. Clarke-Stewart & J. Dunn (Eds.), *Families count.* New York: Cambridge University Press.

Crouter, A. C., & McHale, S. (2005). The long arm of the job revisited: Parenting in dual-earner families. In T. Luster & L. Okagaki (Eds.), *Parenting.* Mahwah, NJ: Erlbaum.

Crowley, K., Callahan, M. A., Tenenbaum, H. R., & Allen, E. (2001). Parents explain more to boys than to girls during shared scientific thinking. *Psychological Science, 12,* 258–261.

Crowley, S. J., & Carskadon, M. A. (2010). Modifications to weekend recovery sleep delay circadian phase in older adolescents. *Chronobiology International, 27,* 1469–1492.

Cubbin, C., Brindis, C. D., Jain, S., Santelli, J., & Braveman, P. (2010). Neighborhood poverty, aspirations and expectations, and initiation of sex. *Journal of Adolescent Health, 47,* 399–406.

Cuevas, K., & Bell, M. A. (2010). Developmental progression of looking and reaching performance on the A-not-B task. *Developmental Psychology, 46,* 1363–1371.

Cuevas, K., & Bell, M. A. (2011). EEG and ECG from 5 to 10 months of age: Developmental changes in baseline activation and cognitive processing during a working memory task. *International Journal of Psychophysiology, 80,* 119–128.

Cummings, E. M., & Davies, P. T. (2010). *Marital conflict and children: An emotional security perspective.* New York: Guilford.

Cummings, E. M., El-Sheikh, M., & Kouros, C. D. (2009). Children and violence: The role of children's regulation in the marital aggression–child adjustment link. *Clinical Child and Family Psychology Review, 12*(1), 3–15.

Cummings, E. M., & Merrilees, C. E. (2009). Identifying the dynamic processes underlying links between marital conflict and child adjustment. In M. S. Schulz, P. K. Kerig, M. K. Pruett, & R. D. Parke (Eds.), *Feathering the nest.* Washington, DC: American Psychological Association.

Cunningham, P. M., & Allington, R. L. (2011). *Classrooms that work: They can all read and write* (5th ed.). Boston: Allyn & Bacon.

Curran, K., DuCette, J., Eisenstein, J., & Hyman, I. A. (2001, August). *Statistical analysis of the cross-cultural data: The third year.* Paper presented at the meeting of the American Psychological Association, San Francisco.

Cvencek, D., Meltzoff, A. N., & Greenwald, A. G. (2011). Math-gender stereotypes in elementary school children. *Child Development, 82,* 766–779.

D

da Fonseca, E. B., Bittar, R. E., Damiao, R., & Zugiab, M. (2009). Prematurity prevention: The role of progesterone. *Current Opinion in Obstetrics and Gynecology, 21,* 142–147.

Daddis, C. (2010). Adolescent peer crowds and patterns of belief in the boundaries of personal authority. *Journal of Adolescence, 33,* 699–708.

Daddis, C., & Randolph, D. (2010). Dating and disclosure: Adolescent management of information regarding romantic involvement. *Journal of Adolescence, 33,* 309–320.

Dahl, R. E. (2004). Adolescent brain development: A period of vulnerabilities and opportunities. *Annals of the New York Academy of Sciences, 1021,* 1–22.

Dahlen, H. G., Jackson, M., & Stevens, J. (2011). Homebirth, freebirth, and doulas: Casualty and consequences of a broken maternity system. *Women and Birth, 24,* 47–50.

Dalen, K., Bruaroy, S., Wentzel-Larsen, T., & Laegreid, L. M. (2009). Cognitive functioning in children prenatally exposed to alcohol and psychotropic drugs. *Neuropediatrics, 40,* 162–167.

Daley, A. J., Macarthur, C., & Winter, H. (2007). The role of exercise in treating postpartum depression: A review of the literature. *Journal of Midwifery and Women's Health, 52,* 56–62.

Damon, W. (1988). *The moral child.* New York: Free Press.

Damon, W. (2008). *The path to purpose: Helping our children find their calling in life.* New York: Free Press.

Daniels, H. (2011). Vygotsky and psychology. In U. Goswami (Ed.), *Wiley-Blackwell handbook of childhood cognitive development* (2nd ed.). New York: Wiley-Blackwell.

Darling-Hammond, L. (2010). The flat world and education. Washington, DC, and New York: Economic Policy Institute and Teachers College.

Darling-Hammond, L. (2011, March). *The flat world and education.* Paper presented at the ASCD conference, San Francisco.

Darwin, C. (1859). *On the origin of species.* London: John Murray.

Dasen, P. R. (1977). Are cognitive processes universal? A contribution to cross-cultural Piagetian psychology. In N. Warran (Ed.), *Studies in cross-cultural psychology* (Vol. 1). London: Academic Press.

Davidson, J. (2000). Giftedness. In A. Kazdin (Ed.), *Encyclopedia of psychology.* Washington, DC, & New York: American Psychological Association and Oxford University Press.

Davidson, M. R., Davidson, M., London, M. L., & Ladewig, P. W. (2012). *Olds' maternal-newborn nursing and women's health across the lifespan: International edition* (9th ed.). Upper Saddle River, NJ: Pearson.

Davidson, W. S., Jimenez, T. R., Onifade, E., & Hankins, S. S. (2010). Student experiences of the adolescent diversion project: A community-based exemplar in the pedagogy of service-learning. *American Journal of Community Psychology, 46,* 442–458.

Davies, G., & others (2011, in press). Genome-wide association studies establish that human intelligence is highly heritable and polygenic. *Molecular Psychiatry.*

Davies, J., & Brember, I. (1999). Reading and mathematics attainments and self-esteem in years 2 and 6—an eight-year cross-sectional study. *Educational Studies, 25,* 145–157.

Davies, W. (2010). Genomic imprinting on the X chromosome: Implications for brain and behavioral phenotypes. *Annals of the New York Academy of Sciences, 1204* (Suppl. E), S14–S19.

Davis, A. E., Hyatt, G., & Arrasmith, D. (1998, February). *"I Have a Dream" program. Class One Evaluation Report.* Portland, OR: Northwest Regional Education Laboratory.

Davis, B. E., Moon, R. Y., Sachs, M. C., & Ottolini, M. C. (1998). Effects of sleep position on infant motor development. *Pediatrics, 102,* 1135–1140.

Davis, C. F., Lazariu, V., & Sekhobo, J. P. (2010). Smoking cessation in the WIC program. *Maternal and Child Health Journal, 14,* 474–477.

Davis, C. L., & Cooper, S. (2011, in press). Fitness, fatness, cognition, behavior, and academic achievement in overweight children: Do cross-sectional associations correspond to exercise trial outcomes? *Preventive Medicine.*

Davis, C. L., & others. (2007). Effects of aerobic exercise on overweight children's cognitive functioning: A randomized controlled trial. *Research Quarterly for Exercise and Sport, 78,* 510–519.

Davis, C. L., & others. (2011, in press). Exercise improves executive function and alters neural activation in overweight children. *Health Psychology.*

Davis, D. K. (2005). Leading the midwifery renaissance. *RCM Midwives, 8,* 264–268.

Davison, K. K., & Birth, L. L. (2001). Weight status, parent reaction, and self-concept in five-year-old girls. *Pediatrics, 107,* 46–53.

Day, J. M. (2010). Religion, spirituality, and positive psychology in adulthood: A developmental view. *Journal of Adult Development, 17,* 215–229.

Day, N. X., Goldschmidt, L., & Thomas, C. A. (2006). Prenatal marijuana exposure contributes to the prediction of marijuana use at age 14. *Addiction, 101,* 1313–1322.

Day, R. H., & McKenzie, B. E. (1973). Perceptual shape constancy in early infancy. *Perception, 2,* 315–320.

de Haan, M., & Gunnar, M. R. (Eds.). (2009). *Handbook of developmental social neuroscience.* New York: Guilford.

de la Rocheborchard, E., & Thonneau, F. (2002). Paternal age and maternal age are risk factors for miscarriage: Results of a multicentre European study. *Human Reproduction, 17,* 1649–1656.

de Leo, D., & Heller, T. (2008). Social modeling in the transmission of suicidality. *Crisis, 29,* 11–19.

de Rose, L. M., Shiyko, M. P., Foster, H., & Brooks-Gunn, J. (2011, in press). Associations between menarcheal timing and behavioral developmental trajectories for girls from age 6 to age 15. *Journal of Youth and Adolescence.*

de Silva-Sanigorski, A., & others. (2011). Government food service policies and guidelines do not create healthy school canteens. *Australian and New Zealand Journal of Public Health, 35,* 117–121.

de Vasconcellos, J. F., & others. (2011). Increased CCL2 and IL-8 in the bone marrow microenvironment in acute lymphoblastic leukemia. *Pediatric Blood Cancer, 56,* 568–577.

Dean, H., & others. (2011, in press). Obesity and type 2 diabetes mellitus in a birth cohort of First Nation children born to mothers with pediatric-onset type 2 diabetes. *Pediatric Diabetes.*

Deary, I. (2012). Intelligence. *Annual Review of Psychology* (Vol. 63). Palo Alto, CA: Annual Reviews.

Deater-Deckard, K., & Dodge, K. (1997). Externalizing behavior problems and discipline revisited: Non-linear effects and variation by culture, context and gender. *Psychological Inquiry, 8,* 161–175.

DeCasper, A. J., & Spence, M. J. (1986). Prenatal maternal speech influences newborn's perception of speech sounds. *Infant Behavior and Development, 9,* 133–150.

DeLoache, J. S. (2011). Early development of the understanding and use of symbolic artifacts. In U. Goswami (Ed.), *Wiley-Blackwell handbook of childhood cognitive development* (2nd ed.). New York: Wiley.

DeLoache, J. S., & Ganea, P. A. (2009). Symbol-based learning in infancy. In A. Woodward & A. Needham (Eds.), *Learning and the infant mind.* New York: Oxford University Press.

Deloache, J. S., Simcock, G., & Macari, S. (2007). Planes, trains, automobiles and tea-sets: Extremely intense interests in very young children. *Developmental Psychology, 43,* 1579–1586.

Dempster, F. N. (1981). Memory span: Sources of individual and developmental differences. *Psychological Bulletin, 80,* 63–100.

Deng, Y. H., & others. (2011, in press). Non-invasive prenatal diagnosis of trisomy 21 by reverse transcriptase multiplex ligation-dependent probe amplification. *Clinical Chemistry and Laboratory Medicine.*

Denham, S. A., Bassett, H. H., & Wyatt, T. (2007). The socialization of emotional competence. In J. E. Grusec & P. D. Hastings (Eds.), *Handbook of socialization.* New York: Guilford.

Denham, S., Warren, H., von Salisch, M., Benga, O., Chin, J-C., & Geangu, E. (2011). Emotions and social development in childhood. In P. K. Smith & C. H. Hart (Eds.), *Wiley-Blackwell handbook of childhood social development* (2nd ed.). New York: Wiley.

Denham, S., & others. (2011). Emotions and social development in childhood. In P. K. Smith

& C. H. Hart (Eds.), *Wiley-Blackwell handbook of childhood social development* (2nd ed.). New York: Wiley.

Denmark, F. L., Russo, N. F., Frieze, I. H., & Eschuzur, J. (1988). Guidelines for avoiding sexism in psychological research: A report of the ad hoc committee on nonsexist research. *American Psychologist, 43,* 582–585.

Deodati, A., & Cianfarani, S. (2011, in press). Impact of growth hormone therapy on adult height of children with idiopathic short stature: Systematic review. *British Medical Journal.*

DeSantis, L. (1998). Building healthy communities with immigrants and refugees. *Journal of Transcultural Nursing, 9,* 20–31.

Deutsch, R., & Pruett, M. K. (2009). Child adjustment and high conflict divorce. In R. M. Galatzer-Levy & L. Kraus (Eds.), *The scientific basis of custody decisions* (2nd ed.). New York: Wiley.

Devaney, S. A., Palomaki, G. E., Scott, J. A., & Bianchi, D. W. (2011). Noninvasive fetal sex determination using cell-free fetal DNA: A systematic review and meta-analysis. *Journal of the American Medical Association, 306,* 627–636.

Dewey, J. (1933). *How we think.* Lexington. MA: D. C. Heath.

Diamond, A. (2001). A model system for studying the role of dopamine in the prefrontal cortex during early development in humans: Early and continuously treated phenylketonuria. In C. Nelson & M. Luciana (Eds.), *Handbook of developmental cognitive neuroscience.* Cambridge, MA: MIT Press.

Diamond, A. D. (1985). Development of the ability to use recall to guide action, as indicated by infants' performance on AB. *Child Development, 56,* 868–883.

Diamond, A. D., Casey, B. J., & Munakata, Y. (2011). *Developmental cognitive neuroscience.* New York: Oxford University Press.

Diamond, L. M. (2011). Sexuality. In B. Brown & M. Prinstein (Eds.), *Encyclopedia of adolescence.* New York: Academic Press.

Diamond, L. M., & Savin-Williams, R. C. (2011). Same-sex activity in adolescence: Multiple meanings and implications. In R. F. Fassinger & S. L. Morrow (Eds.), *Sex in the margins: Erotic experiences and behaviors of sexual minorities.* Washington, DC: American Psychological Association.

Diaz, M. T., Barrett, K. T., & Hogstrom, L. J. (2011). The influence of sentence novelty and figurativeness on brain activity. *Neuropsychologia, 49,* 320–330.

Diaz, M. T., & Hogstrom, L. J. (2011, in press). The influence of context on hemispheric recruitment during metaphor processing. *Journal of Cognitive Neuroscience.*

Diaz-Rico, L. T. (2012). *Course for teaching English language learners* (2nd ed.). Boston: Allyn & Bacon.

Diego, M. A., Field, T., & Hernandez-Reif, M. (2008). Temperature increases in preterm infants during massage therapy. *Infant Behavior and Development, 31,* 149–152.

Diemer, M. A., & Hsieh, C. (2008). Sociopolitical development and vocational expectations among lower socioeconomic status adolescents of color. *Career Development Quarterly, 56,* 257–267.

Dietz, L. J., Jennings, K. D., Kelley, S. A., & Marshal, M. (2009). Maternal depression, paternal psychopathology, and toddlers' behavior problems. *Journal of Clinical Child and Adolescent Psychology, 38,* 48–61.

Dietz, P. M., & others. (2010). Infant morbidity and mortality attributable to prenatal smoking in the U.S. *American Journal of Preventive Medicine, 39,* 45–62.

DiPietro, J. (2008). Unpublished review of J. W. Santrock's *Children,* 11th ed. (New York: McGraw-Hill).

Dishion, T. J., & Piehler, T. F. (2009). Deviant by design: Peer contagion in development, interventions, and schools. In K. H. Rubin, W. M. Bukowski, & B. Laursen (Eds.), *Handbook of peer interactions, relationships, and groups.* New York: Guilford.

Dixon, S. V., Graber, J. A., & Brooks-Gunn, J. (2008). The roles of respect for parental authority and parenting practices in parent-child conflict among African American, Latino, and European American families. *Journal of Family Psychology, 22,* 1–10.

Dodge, K. A. (1983). Behavioral antecedents of peer social status. *Child Development, 54,* 1386–1399.

Dodge, K. A. (2011a). Context matters in child and family policy. *Child Development, 82,* 433–442.

Dodge, K. A. (2011b). Social information processing models of aggressive behavior. In M. Mikulincer & P. R. Shaver (Eds.), *Understanding and reducing aggression, violence, and their consequences.* Washington, DC: American Psychological Association.

Dodge, K. A., & McCourt, S. N. (2010). Translating models of antisocial behavioral development into efficacious intervention policy to prevent adolescence violence. *Developmental Psychobiology, 52,* 277–285.

Dodge, K. A., & Rutter, M. (Eds.). (2011). *Gene-environment interaction and developmental psychopathology.* New York: Guilford.

Doherty, M. (2008). *Theory of mind.* Philadelphia: Psychology Press.

Domsch, H., Lohaus, A., & Thomas, H. (2009). Influences of information processing and disengagement on infants' looking behavior. *Infant and Child Development, 19,* 161–174.

Dondi, M., Simion, F., & Caltran, G. (1999). Can newborns discriminate between their own cry and the cry of another newborn infant? *Developmental Psychology, 35*(2), 418–426.

Donnegan,, S., Maluccio, J. A., Myers, C. K., Menon, P., Ruel, M. T., & Habicht, J. P. (2010). Two food-assisted maternal and child health nutrition programs helped mitigate the impact of economic hardship on child stunting in Haiti. *Journal of Nutrition, 140,* 1139–1145.

Dorn, C. M., Madeja, S. S., & Sabol, F. R. (2004). *Assessing expressive learning.* Mahwah, NJ: Erlbaum.

Dorn, L. H., & Biro, F. M. (2011). Puberty and its measurement: A decade in review. *Journal of Research on Adolescence, 21,* 180–195.

Doty, R. L., & Shah, M. (2008). Taste and smell. In M. M. Haith & J. B. Benson (Eds.), *Encyclopedia of infant and early childhood development.* Oxford, UK: Elsevier.

Dovey, T. M., Staples, P. A., Gibson, E. L., & Halford, J. C. (2008). Food neophobia and "picky/fussy" eating in children: A review. *Appetite, 50,* 181–193.

Dowda, M., & others. (2009). Policies and characteristics of the preschool environment and physical activity of young children. *Pediatrics, 123,* e261–e266.

Dozier, M., Stovall-McClough, K. C., & Albus, K. E. (2009). Attachment and psychopathology in adulthood. In J. Cassidy & P. R. Shaver (Eds.), *Handbook of attachment* (2nd ed.). New York: Guilford.

Draghi-Lorenz, R. (2007, July). *Self-conscious emotions in young infants and the direct perception of self and others in interaction.* Paper presented at the meeting of the International Society for Research on Emotions, Sunshine Coast, Australia.

Drummond, R. J., & Jones, K. D. (2010). *Assessment procedures* (7th ed.). Upper Saddle River, NJ: Pearson.

Dryfoos, J. G. (1990). *Adolescents at risk: Prevalence and prevention.* New York: Oxford University Press.

Dryfoos, J. G., & Barkin, C. (2006). *Adolescence.* New York: Oxford University Press.

Du, Y., & others. (2011). Hypomethylated DSCR4 is a placenta-derived epigenetic marker for trisomy 21. *Prenatal Diagnostics, 31,* 207–214.

Dubow, E. F., Huesmann, L. R., & Greenwood, D. (2007). Media and youth socialization. In J. E. Grusec & P. D. Hastings (Eds.), *Handbook of socialization.* New York: Guilford.

Dufour-Rainfray, D., & others. (2011, in press). Fetal exposure to teratogens: Evidence of genes involved in autism. *Neuroscience and Biobehavioral Reviews.*

Duggan, P. M., Lapsley, D. K., & Norman, K. (2000, April). *Adolescent invulnerability and personal uniqueness: Scale development and initial contact validation.* Paper presented at the biennial meeting of the Society for Research in Child Development, Chicago.

Duke, J., & others. (2011, in press). A study of burn hospitalizations for children younger than 5 years of age: 1983–2008. *Pediatrics.*

Duncan, A. F., & others. (2011, in press). Elevated systolic blood pressure in preterm very-low-birthweight infants ≤ 3 years of life. *Pediatric Nephrology.*

Duncan, G. J., & others. (2007). School readiness and later achievement. *Developmental Psychology, 43,* 1428–1446.

Duncan, J. R., & others. (2010). Brainstem serotonergic deficiency in sudden infant death. *Journal of the American Medical Association, 303,* 430–437.

Dundek, L. H. (2006). Establishment of a Somali doula program at a large metropolitan hospital. *Journal of Perinatal and Neonatal Nursing, 20,* 128–137.

Dunkel Schetter, C. (2011). Psychological science in the study of pregnancy and birth. *Annual Review of Psychology* (Vol. 62). Palo Alto, CA: Annual Reviews.

Dunn, J. (2007). Siblings and socialization. In J. E. Grusec & P. D. Hastings (Eds.), *Handbook of socialization.* New York: Guilford.

Dunn, J., & Kendrick, C. (1982). *Siblings.* Cambridge, MA: Harvard University Press.

Dunson, D. B., Baird, D. D., & Columbo, B. (2004). Increased fertility with age in men and women. *Obstetrics and Gynecology, 103,* 51–56.

Durbin, D. R. (2011, in press). Technical report—child passenger safety. *Pediatrics.*

Duriez, B., Luyckx, K., Soenens, B., & Berzonsky, M. (2011, in press). A process-content approach to adolescent identity formation: Examining longitudinal associations between identity styles and goal pursuits. *Journal of Personality.*

Durrani, A. M., & Fatima, W. (2011, in press). Determinants of blood pressure distribution in school children. *European Journal of Public Health.*

Durrant, J. E. (2008). Physical punishment, culture, and rights: Current issues for professionals. *Journal of Developmental and Behavioral Pediatrics, 29,* 55–66.

Durston, S., & others. (2006). A shift from diffuse to focal cortical activity with development. *Developmental Science, 9,* 1–8.

Duschi, R., & Hamilton, R. (2011). Learning science. In P. A. Alexander & R. E. Mayer (Eds.), *Handbook of research on learning and instruction.* New York: Routledge.

Dweck, C. (2006). *Mindset.* New York: Random House.

Dweck, C. S. (2007). Boosting achievement with messages that motivate. *Education Canada, 47,* 6–10.

Dweck, C. S. (2011, in press). Social development. In P. Zelazo (Ed.), *Oxford handbook of developmental psychology.* New York: Oxford University Press.

Dweck, C. S., & Master, A. (2009). Self-theories and motivation: Students' beliefs about intelligence. In K. R. Wentzel & A. Wigfield (Eds.), *Handbook of motivation at school.* New York: Routledge.

Dworkin, S. L., & Santelli, J. (2007). Do abstinence-plus interventions reduce sexual risk behavior among youth? *PLoS Medicine, 4,* 1437–1439.

Dworkis, D. A., & others. (2011). Severe sickle-cell anemia is associated with increased plasma levels of TNF-R1 and VCAM-1. *American Journal of Hematology, 86,* 220–223.

Dykes, F. (2011). Twenty-five years of breast-feeding research in midwifery. *Midwifery, 27,* 8–14.

E

Eagly, A. H. (2001). Social role theory of sex differences and similarities. In J. Worrell (Ed.), *Encyclopedia of women and gender.* San Diego: Academic Press.

Eagly, A. H. (2010) Gender roles. In J. Levine & M. Hogg (Eds.), *Encyclopedia of group process and intergroup relations.* Thousand Oaks, CA: Sage.

Eagly, A. H., & Steffen, V. J. (1986). Gender and aggressive behavior: A meta-analytic review of the social psychological literature. *Psychological Bulletin, 100,* 309–330.

Eagly, A. H., & Wood, W. (2011). Gender roles in a biosocial world. In P. van Lange, A. Kruglanski, & E. T. Higgins (Eds.), *Handbook of theories in social psychology.* Thousand Oaks, CA: Sage.

Eaton, D. K., & others. (2006, June 9). Youth risk behavior surveillance—United States, 2005. *MMWR, 55,* 1–108.

Eaton, D. K., & others. (2008). Youth risk behavior surveillance—United States, 2007. *MMWR, 57,* 1–131.

Eaton, D. K., & others. (2010). Youth risk behavior surveillance—United States, 2009. *MMWR Surveillance Summary, 59*(5), 1–142.

Eaton, W. O. (2008). Milestones: Physical. In M. M. Haith & J. B. Benson (Eds.), *Encyclopedia of infant and early childhood development.* Oxford, UK: Elsevier.

Eby, J. W., Herrell, A. L., & Jordan, M. L. (2011). *Teaching in elementary school: A reflective approach* (6th ed.). Boston: Allyn & Bacon.

Eccles, J. S. (2007). Families, schools, and developing achievement-related motivations and engagement. In J. E. Grusec & P. D. Hastings (Eds.), *Handbook of socialization.* New York: Guilford.

Echevarria, J. L., & Graves, A. (2011). *Sheltered content instruction: Teaching English Language Learners with diverse abilities* (4th ed.). Boston: Allyn & Bacon.

Eckman, J. R., & Embury, S. H. (2011). Sickle cell anemia pathophysiology: Back to the data. *American Journal of Hematology, 86,* 121–122.

Eckstein, K. C., & others. (2006). Parents' perceptions of their child's weight and health. *Pediatrics, 117,* 681–690.

Ednick, M., & others. (2010). Sleep-related respiratory abnormalities and arousal pattern in achondroplasia during early infancy. *Journal of Pediatrics, 155,* 510–515.

Edwardson, C. L., & Gorely, T. (2010). Activity-related parenting practices and children's objectively measured physical activity. *Pediatric Exercise Science, 22,* 105–113.

Egan, S. K., & Perry, D. G. (2001). Gender identity: A multidimensional analysis with implications for psychosocial adjustment. *Developmental Psychology, 37,* 451–463.

Egeland, B., Jacobvitz, D., & Sroufe, L. A. (1988). Breaking the cycle of abuse. *New Directions for Child Development, 11,* 77–92.

Eisenberg, M. E., Bernat, D. H., Bearinger, L. H., & Resnick, M. D. (2008). Support for comprehensive sexuality education: Perspectives from parents of school-aged youth. *Journal of Adolescent Research, 42,* 352–359.

Eisenberg, N. (2010). Emotion regulation in children. *Annual Review of Clinical Psychology* (Vol. 6). Palo Alto, CA: Annual Reviews.

Eisenberg, N., Fabes, R. A., & Spinrad, T. L. (2006). Prosocial development. In W. Damon & R. Lerner (Eds.), *Handbook of child psychology* (6th ed.). New York: Wiley.

Eisenberg, N., & Morris, A. S. (2004). Moral cognitions and social responding in adolescence. In R. Lerner & L. Steinberg (Eds.), *Handbook of adolescent psychology.* New York: Wiley.

Eisenberg, N., Morris, A. S., McDaniel, B., & Spinrad, T. L. (2009). Moral cognitions and prosocial responding in adolescence. In R. M. Lerner & L. Steinberg (Eds.), *Handbook of adolescent psychology* (3rd ed.). New York: Wiley.

Eisenberg, N., Spinrad, T. L., & Eggum, N. D. (2010). Emotion-focused self-regulation and its relation to children's maladjustment. *Annual Review of Clinical Psychology* (Vol. 6). Palo Alto, CA: Annual Reviews.

Eisenberg, N., Spinrad, T. L., & Smith, C. L. (2004). Emotion-related regulation: Its conceptualization, relations to social functioning, and socialization. In P. Philippot & R. S. Feldman (Eds.), *The regulation of emotion.* Mahwah, NJ: Erlbaum.

Elbert, A., & others. (2011). Genetic variation in the KIAAoe19 5' region as a possible contributor to dyslexia. *Behavior Genetics.*

Elkind, D. (1970, April 5). Erik Erikson's eight ages of man. *New York Times Magazine.*

Elkind, D. (1976). *Child development and education: A Piagetian perspective.* New York: Oxford University Press.

Elkind, D. (1978). Understanding the young adolescent. *Adolescence, 13,* 127–134.

Elkington, K. S., Bauermeister, J. A., & Zimmerman, M. A. (2011, in press). Do parents and peers matter? A prospective socio-ecological examination of substance use and sexual risk among African American youth. *Journal of Adolescence.*

Elks, C. E., & others. (2010). Thirty new loci for age at menarche identified by a meta-analysis of genome-wide association studies. *Nature Genetics, 42,* 1077–1085.

Ellenberg, D., & St. Louis-Deschenes, M. (2010). The effect of acute physical activity on cognitive function during development. *Psychology of Sport and Exercise, 11,* 122–126.

Elliott, V. S. (2004). Methamphetamine use increasing. Retrieved January 16, 2005, from http://www.amaasson.org/amednews/2004/07/26/hlsc0726.htm

Emery, R. E. (1994). *Renegotiating family relationships.* New York: Guilford.

Enfield, A., & Collins, D. (2008). The relationship of service-learning, social justice, multicultural competence, and civic engagement. *Journal of College Student Development, 49,* 95–109.

Engler, C., & Marillonnet, S. (2011). Generation of families of construct variants using golden gate shuffling. *Methods in Molecular Biology, 729*, 167–181.

Englund, M. M., Egeland, B., & Collins, W. A. (2008). Exceptions to high school dropout predictions in a low-income sample: Do adults make a difference? *Journal of Social Issues, 64*, 1, 77–93.

Ennett, S. T., Bauman, K. E., Hussong, A., Faris, R., Foshee, V. A., & Cai, L. (2006). The peer context of adolescent substance use: Findings from social network analysis. *Journal of Research on Adolescence, 16*, 159–186.

Enright, M. S., Schaefer, L. V., Schaefer, P., & Schaefer, K. A. (2008). Building a just adolescent community. *Montessori Life, 20*, 36–42.

Ensembl Human. (2008). *Explore the Homo sapiens genome.* Retrieved October 10, 2008, from http://www.ensembl.org/Homo_sapiens/index.html

Ensor, R., Spencer, D., & Hughes, C. (2010). "You feel sad?" Emotional understanding mediates effects of verbal ability and mother-child mutuality on prosocial behaviors: Findings from 2 to 4 years. *Social Development, 20*, 93–110.

Erickson, R. P. (2010). Genes, environment, and orofacial clefting: N-acetyltransferase and folic acid. *Journal of Craniofacial Surgery, 21*, 1384–1387.

Ericsson, K. A., Charness, N., Feltovich, P. J., & Hoffman, R. R. (Eds.). (2006). *The Cambridge handbook of expertise and expert performance.* New York: Cambridge University Press.

Erikson, E. H. (1950). *Childhood and society.* New York: W. W. Norton.

Erikson, E. H. (1968). *Identity: Youth and crisis.* New York: W. W. Norton.

Eriksson, U. J. (2009). Congenital malformations in diabetic pregnancy. *Seminar in Fetal and Neonatal Medicine, 14*, 85–93.

Erkal, S. (2010). Identification of the number of home accidents per year involving children in the 0–6 age group and the measures taken by mothers to prevent home accidents. *Turkish Journal of Pediatrics, 52*, 150–157.

Escobar-Chaves, S. L., & Anderson, C. A. (2008). Media and risky behavior. *Future of Children, 18*(1), 147–180.

Eshkoli, T., Sheiner, E., Ben-Zvi, Z., & Holcberg, G. (2011, in press). Drug transport across the placenta. *Current Pharmaceutical Biotechnology.*

Espeset, E. M., & others. (2011). The concept of body image disturbance in anorexia nervosa: An empirical inquiry utilizing patients' subjective experiences. *Eating Disorders, 19*, 175–193.

Etzel, R. (1988, October). *Children of smokers.* Paper presented at the American Academy of Pediatrics meeting, New Orleans.

Evans, G. W., & English, G. W. (2002). The environment of poverty. *Child Development, 73*, 1238–1248.

Evans, G. W., & Kim, P. (2007). Childhood poverty and health: Cumulative risk exposure and stress dysregulation. *Psychological Science, 18*, 953–957.

F

Fabiano, G. A., Pelham, W. E., Coles, E. K., Gnagy, E. M., Chronis-Tuscano, A., & O'Connor, B. C. (2009). A meta-analysis of behavioral treatments for attention deficit/hyperactivity disorder. *Clinical Psychology Review, 29*(2), 129–140.

Fabricius, W. V., Braver, S. L., Diaz, P., & Schenck, C. (2010). Custody and parenting time: Links to family relationships and well-being after divorce. In M. E. Lamb (Ed.), *The role of the father in child development* (5th ed.). New York: Wiley.

Fagan, J. F. (1992). Intelligence: A theoretical viewpoint. *Current Directions in Psychological Science, 1*, 82–86.

Fagan, J. F., Holland, C. R., & Wheeler, K. (2007). The prediction, from infancy, of adult IQ and achievement. *Intelligence, 35*, 225–231.

Fagot, B. I., Rodgers, C. S., & Leinbach, M. D. (2000). Theories of gender socialization. In T. Eckes & H. M. Trautner (Eds.), *The developmental social psychology of gender.* Mahwah, NJ: Erlbaum.

Fahey, T. D., Insel, P. M., & Roth, W. T. (2011). *Fit and well* (9th ed.). New York: McGraw-Hill.

Fairweather, E., & Cramond, B. (2011). Infusing creative and critical thinking into the classroom. In R. A. Beghetto & J. C. Kaufman (Eds.), *Nurturing creativity in the classroom.* New York: Cambridge University Press.

Falbo, T., & Poston, D. L. (1993). The academic, personality, and physical outcomes of only children in China. *Child Development, 64*, 18–35.

Fantasia, H. C. (2008). Concept analysis: Sexual decision-making in adolescence. *Nursing Forum, 43*, 80–90.

Fantz, R. L. (1963). Pattern vision in newborn infants. *Science, 140*, 286–297.

Farrington, D. P., Ttofi, M. M., & Coid, J. W. (2009). Development of adolescence-limited, late-onset, and persistent offenders from 8 to age 48. *Aggressive Behavior, 35*, 150–163.

Fasig, L. (2000). Toddlers' understanding of ownership: Implications for self-concept development. *Social Development, 9*, 370–382.

Fear, N. T., Hey, K., Vincent, T., & Murphy, M. (2007). Paternal occupation and neural tube defects: A case-control study based on the Oxford Record Linkage Study register. *Pediatric and Perinatal Epidemiology, 21*, 163–168.

Fearon, R. P., & others. (2010). The significance of insecure attachment and disorganization in the development of children's externalizing behavior: A meta-analytic study. *Child Development, 81*, 435–456.

Fein, G. G. (1986). Pretend play. In D. Görlitz & J. E. Wohlwill (Eds.), *Curiosity, imagination, and play.* Hillsdale, NJ: Erlbaum.

Feldman, S. S., Turner, R., & Araujo, K. (1999). Interpersonal context as an influence on sexual timetables of youths: Gender and ethnic effects. *Journal of Research on Adolescence, 9*, 25–52.

Feleszko, W., & others. (2006). Parental tobacco smoking is associated with IL-13 secretion in children with allergic asthma. *Journal of Allergy and Clinical Immunology, 117*, 97–102.

Fenson, L., Marchman, V. A., Thal, D., Dale, P. S., Bates, E., & Reznick, J. S. (2007). *The MacArthur-Bates communicative development inventories user's guide and technical manual* (2nd ed.). Baltimore: Brookes.

Ferber, S. G., & Makhoul, I. R. (2008). Neurobehavioral assessment of skin-to-skin effects on reaction to pain in preterm infants: A randomized, controlled within-subject trial. *Acta Paediatrica, 97*, 171–176.

Ferguson, D. M., Harwood, L. J., & Shannon, F. T. (1987). Breastfeeding and subsequent social adjustment in 6- to 8-year-old children. *Journal of Child Psychology and Psychiatry, 28*, 378–386.

Fernandez, O., Sabharwal, M., Smiley, T., Pastuszak, A., Koren, G., & Einarson, T. (1998). Moderate to heavy caffeine consumption during pregnancy and relationship to spontaneous abortion and abnormal fetal growth: A meta-analysis. *Reproductive Toxicology, 12*, 435–444.

Fertig, A. R. (2010). Selection and the effect of prenatal smoking. *Health Economics, 19*, 209–226.

Field, A. E., Cambargo, C. A., Taylor, C. B., Berkey, C. S., Roberts, S. B., & Colditz, G. A. (2001). Peer, parent, and media influences on the development of weight concerns and frequent dieting among preadolescent and adolescent girls and boys. *Pediatrics, 107*, 54–60.

Field, T. (2001). Massage therapy facilitates weight gain in preterm infants. *Current Directions in Psychological Science, 10*, 51–55.

Field, T. (2007). *The amazing infant.* Malden, MA: Blackwell.

Field, T. (2010). Postpartum depression effects on early interactions, parenting, and safety practices: A review. *Infant Behavior and Development, 33*, 1–6.

Field, T., Diego, M., & Hernandez-Reif, M. (2008). Prematurity and potential predictors. *International Journal of Neuroscience, 118*, 277–289.

Field, T., Diego, M., & Hernandez-Reif, M. (2010). Preterm infant massage therapy research: A review. *Infant Behavior and Development, 33*, 115–124.

Field, T., Diego, M., Hernandez-Reif, M., Deeds, O., Holder, V., Schanberg, S., & Kuhn, C. (2009). Depressed pregnant black women have a greater incidence of prematurity and low birthweight outcomes. *Infant Behavior and Development, 32*, 10–16.

Field, T., Figueiredo, B., Hernandez-Reif, M., Diego, M., Deeds, O., & Ascencio, A. (2008). Massage therapy reduces pain in pregnant women, alleviates prenatal depression in both parents and improves their relationships. *Journal of Bodywork and Movement Therapies, 12*, 146–150.

Field, T., Grizzle, N., Scafidi, F., & Schanberg, S. (1996). Massage and relaxation therapies' effects on depressed adolescent mothers. *Adolescence, 31*, 903–911.

Field, T., & Hernandez-Reif, M. (2008). Touch and pain. In M. M. Haith & J. B. Benson (Eds.), *Encyclopedia of infant and early childhood development*. Oxford, UK: Elsevier.

Field, T., Hernandez-Reif, M., & Freedman, J. (2004, Fall). Stimulation programs for preterm infants. *SRCD Social Policy Reports, XVIII* (No. 1), 1–20.

Field, T. M., Diego, M., & Hernandez-Reif, M. (2011). Preterm infant massage therapy research: A review. *Infant Behavior and Development, 34,* 383–389.

Finger, B., Hans, S. L., Bernstein, V. J., & Cox, S. M. (2009). Parent relationship quality and infant-mother attachment. *Attachment and Human Development, 11,* 285–306.

Fingerman, K. L., & Birditt, K. S. (2011). Intergenerational communication practices. In K. W. Schaie & S. L. Willis (Eds.), *Handbook of the psychology of aging* (7th ed.). New York: Elsevier.

Fischhoff, B., Bruine de Bruin, W., Parker, A. M., Millstein, S. G., & Halpern-Felsher, B. L. (2010). Adolescents' perceived risk of dying. *Journal of Adolescent Health, 46,* 265–269.

Fisher, P. A. (2005, April). *Translational research on underlying mechanisms of risk among foster children: Implications for prevention science*. Paper presented at the meeting of the Society for Research in Child Development, Washington, DC.

Flavell, J. H. (2004). Theory-of-mind development: Retrospect and prospect. *Merrill-Palmer Quarterly, 50,* 274–290.

Flavell, J. H., Friedrichs, A., & Hoyt, J. (1970). Developmental changes in memorization processes. *Cognitive Psychology, 1,* 324–340.

Flavell, J. H., Green, F. L., & Flavell, E. R. (1993). Children's understanding of the stream of consciousness. *Child Development, 64,* 95–120.

Flavell, J. H., Green, F. L., & Flavell, E. R. (1995). The development of children's knowledge about attentional focus. *Developmental Psychology, 31,* 706–712.

Flavell, J. H., Green, F. L., & Flavell, E. R. (1998). The mind has a mind of its own: Developing knowledge about mental uncontrollability. *Cognitive Development, 13,* 127–138.

Flavell, J. H., Green, F. L., & Flavell, E. R. (2000). Development of children's awareness of their own thoughts. *Journal of Cognition and Development, 1,* 97–112.

Flavell, J., Mumme, D., Green, F., & Flavell E. (1992). Young children's understanding of different types of beliefs. *Child Development, 63,* 960–977.

Flick, G. L. (2011). *Understanding and managing emotional and behavioral disorders in the classroom.* Upper Saddle River, NJ: Pearson.

Flint, M. S., Baum, A., Chambers, W. H., & Jenkins, F. J. (2007). Induction of DNA damage, alteration of DNA repair, and transcriptional activation by stress hormones. *Psychoneuroendocrinolgy, 32,* 470–479.

Flom, R., & Pick, A. D. (2003). Verbal encouragement and joint attention in 18-month-old infants. *Infant Behavior and Development, 26,* 121–134.

Flores, G., Abreu, M., & Tomany-Korman, S. C. (2005). Limited English proficiency, primary language at home, and disparities in children's health care: How language barriers are measured matters. *Public Health Reports, 120,* 418–420.

Florin, T., & Ludwig, S. (2011). *Netter's Pediatrics.* New York: Elsevier.

Flynn, J. R. (1999). Searching for justice: The discovery of IQ gains over time. *American Psychologist, 54,* 5–20.

Flynn, J. R. (2007). The history of the American mind in the 20th century: A scenario to explain IQ gains over time and a case for the relevance of g. In P. C. Kyllonen, R. D. Roberts, & L. Stankov (Eds.), *Extending intelligence.* Mahwah, NJ: Erlbaum.

Follari, L. (2011). *Foundations and best practices in early childhood education* (2nd ed.). Upper Saddle River, NJ: Merrill.

Fontaine, R. G., Tanha, M., Yang, C., Dodge, K. A., Bates, J. E., & Pettit, G. S. (2010). Does response evaluation and decision (RED) mediate the relation between hostile attributional style and antisocial behavior in adolescence? *Journal of Abnormal Child Psychology, 38,* 615–626.

Fontenot, H. B. (2007). Transition and adaptation to adoptive motherhood. *Journal of Obstetric, Gynecologic, and Neonatal Nursing, 36,* 175–182.

Food & Nutrition Service. (2009). The new look of the women, infants, and children (WIC) program. Retrieved January 21, 2009, from http://www.health.state.ny.us/prevention/nutrition/wic/the_new_look_of_wic.htm

Forrester, M. B., & Merz, R. D. (2007). Risk of selected birth defects with prenatal illicit drug use, Hawaii, 1986–2002. *Journal of Toxicology and Environmental Health A, 70,* 7–18.

Foskett, N., Dyke, M., & Maringe, F. (2008). The influence of the school in the decision to participate in learning post-16. *British Educational Research Journal, 34,* 37–61.

Fowler-Brown, A., & Kahwati, L. C. (2004). Prevention and treatment of overweight in children and adolescents. *American Family Physician, 69,* 2591–2598.

Fox, B. J. (2012). *Word identification strategies* (5th ed.). Boston: Allyn & Bacon.

Fox, E., & Alexander, P. A. (2011). Learning to read. In P. A. Alexander & R. E. Mayer (Eds.), *Handbook of research on learning and instruction.* New York: Routledge.

Fox, M. K., Condon, E., Briefel, R. R., Reidy, K. C., & Deming, D. M. (2010). Food consumption patterns of young preschoolers: Are they starting off on the right path? *Journal of the American Dietetic Association, 110* (Suppl. 12), S52–S59.

Fox, M. K., Pac, S., Devaney, B., & Jankowski, L. (2004). Feeding infants and toddlers study: What foods are infants and toddlers eating? *American Dietetic Association Journal, 104* (Suppl.), S22–S30.

Fox, S. E., Levitt, P., & Nelson, C. A. (2010). How the timing and quality of early experiences influence the development of brain architecture. *Child Development, 81,* 28–40.

Fraga, A. M., Fraga, G. P., Stanley, C., Costantini, T. W., & Coimbra, R. (2010). Children at danger: Injury fatalities among children in San Diego County. *European Journal of Epidemiology, 25,* 211–217.

Fraga, C. G., Motchnik, P. A., Shigenaga, M. K., Helbock, H. J., Jacob, R. A., & Ames, B. N. (1991). Ascorbic acid protects against endogenous oxidative DNA damage in human sperm. *Proceedings of the National Academy of Sciences USA, 88,* 11003–11006.

Franchak, J. M., Kretch, K. S., Soska, K. C., & Adolph, K. E. (2011, in press). Head-mounted eye-tracking: A new method to describe the visual ecology of infants. *Child Development.*

Francis, J., Fraser, G., & Marcia, J. E. (1989). *Cognitive and experimental factors in moratorium-achievement (MAMA) cycles.* Unpublished manuscript, Department of Psychology, Simon Fraser University, Burnaby, British Columbia.

Franco, P., Kato, I., Richardson, H. L., Yang, J. S., Montemitro, E., & Horne, R. S. (2010). Arousal from sleep mechanisms in infants. *Sleep Medicine, 11,* 603–614.

Franklin, A., Vevis, L., Ling, Y., & Hurlbert, A. (2010). Biological components of color preference in infancy. *Developmental Science, 13,* 346–354.

Fraser, S. (Ed.). (1995). *The bell curve wars: Race, intelligence, and the future of America.* New York: Basic Books.

Fraser-Abder, P. (2011). *Teaching budding scientists.* Boston: Allyn & Bacon.

Frederick, I. O., Williams, M. A., Sales, A. E., Martin, D. P., & Killien, M. (2008). Pre-pregnancy body mass index, gestational weight gain, and other maternal characteristics in relation to infant birth weight. *Maternal Child Health Journal, 12*(5), 557–567.

Frederikse, M., Lu, A., Aylward, E., Barta, P., Sharma, T., & Pearlson, G. (2000). Sex differences in inferior lobule volume in schizophrenia. *American Journal of Psychiatry, 157,* 422–427.

Freedman, D. S., Khan, L. K., Serdula, M. K., Dietz, W. H., Srinivasan, S. R., & Berensen, G. S. (2005). The relation of childhood BMI to adult adiposity: The Bogalusa Heart Study. *Pediatrics, 115,* 22–27.

Freedman, D. S., Patel, D. A., & others. (2008). The contribution of childhood obesity to adult carotid intima-media thickness: The Bogalusa Heart Study. *International Journal of Obesity, 32,* 749–756.

Freedman, D. S., & others. (2010a). Changes in variability in high levels of low-density lipoprotein cholesterol among children. *Pediatrics, 126,* 266–273.

Freedman, D. S., & others. (2010b). The identification of children with adverse risk factor levels by body mass index cutoffs from

2 classification systems: The Bogalusa Heart Study. *American Journal of Clinical Nutrition, 92,* 1298–1305.

Fretts, R. C., Zera, C., & Heffner, C. Z. (2008). Maternal age and pregnancy. In M. M. Haith & J. B. Benson (Eds.), *Encyclopedia of infancy and early childhood.* London, UK: Elsevier.

Freud, S. (1917). *A general introduction to psychoanalysis .* New York: Washington Square Press.

Friedman, S. L., Melhuish, E., & Hill, C. (2010). Childcare research at the dawn of a new millennium: Update. In J. G. Bremner & T. D. Wachs (Eds.), *Wiley-Blackwell handbook of infant development* (2nd ed.). New York: Wiley.

Friend, M. (2011). *Special education* (3rd ed.). Upper Saddle River, NJ: Pearson.

Friend, M., & Bursuck, W. D. (2012). *Including parents with special needs* (6th ed.). Upper Saddle River, NJ: Pearson.

Frisen, A., & Holmqvist, K. (2010). What characterizes early adolescents with a positive body image? A qualitative investigation of Swedish boys and girls. *Body Image, 7,* 205–212.

Frost, E. A., Gist, R. S., & Adriano, E. (2011). Drugs, alcohol, pregnancy, and fetal alcohol syndrome. *International Anesthesiology Clinics, 49,* 119–133.

Fuligni, A. J., & Hardway, C. (2006). Daily variation in adolescents' sleep, activities, and psychological well-being. *Journal of Research on Adolescence, 16,* 353–378.

Fung, H. (2011). Cultural psychological perspectives on social development in childhood. In P. K. Smith & C. H. Hart (Eds.), *Wiley-Blackwell handbook of childhood social development* (2nd ed.). New York: Wiley.

Furman, W., & Collins, W. A. (2009). Adolescent romantic relationships and experiences. In K. H. Rubin, W. M. Bukowksi, & B. Laursen (Eds.), *Handbook of peer interactions, relationships, and groups.* New York: Wiley.

Furman, W., Low, S., & Ho, M. J. (2009). Romantic experience and psychosocial adjustment in middle adolescence. *Journal of Clinical Child and Adolescent Psychology, 38,* 75–90.

Furth, H. G., & Wachs, H. (1975). *Thinking goes to school.* New York: Oxford University Press.

G

Gable, S., Chang, Y., & Krull, J. L. (2007). Television watching and frequency of family meals are predictive of overweight onset and persistence in a national sample of preschool children. *Journal of the American Dietetic Association, 107,* 53–61.

Gainetdinov, R. R. (2010). Strengths and limitations of genetic models of ADHD. *Attention Deficit and Hyperactivity Disorder, 2,* 21–30.

Galambos, N. L., Berenbaum, S. A., & McHale, S. M. (2009). Gender development in adolescence. In R. M. Lerner & L. Steinberg (Eds.), *Handbook of adolescent psychology.* New York: Wiley.

Galambos, N. L., Howard, A. L., & Maggs, J. L. (2011, in press). Rise and fall of sleep quality with student experiences across the first year of the university. *Journal of Research on Adolescence.*

Galinksy, E. (2010). *Mind in the making.* New York: HarperCollins.

Galinsky, E., & David, J. (1988). *The preschool years: Family strategies that work—from experts and parents.* New York: Times Books.

Galland, B. C., Taylor, B. J., Edler, D. E., & Herbison, P. (2011, in press). Normal sleep patterns in infants and children: A systematic review of observational studies. *Sleep Medicine Review.*

Galloway, J. C., & Thelen, E. (2004). Feet first: Object exploration in young infants. *Infant Behavior & Development, 27,* 107–112.

Gallup, G. W., & Bezilla, R. (1992). *The religious life of young Americans.* Princeton, NJ: Gallup Institute.

Garber, J., & Cole, D. A. (2010). Intergenerational transmission of depression: A launch and grow model of change across adolescence. *Development and Psychopathology, 22*(4), 819–830.

Gardner, H. (1983). *Frames of mind.* New York: Basic Books.

Gardner, H. (1993). *Multiple intelligences.* New York: Basic Books.

Gardner, H. (2002). The pursuit of excellence through education. In M. Ferrari (Ed.), *Learning from extraordinary minds.* Mahwah, NJ: Erlbaum.

Gardner, M., & Steinberg, L. (2005). Peer influence on risk taking, risk preference, and risky decision making in adolescence and adulthood: An experimental study. *Developmental Psychology, 41,* 625–635.

Garofalo, R. (2010). Cytokines in human milk. *Journal of Pediatrics, 156* (Suppl. 2), S36–S40.

Garrison, M. M., Liekweg, K., & Christakis, D. A. (2011, in press). Media use and child sleep: The impact of content, timing, and environment. *Pediatrics.*

Garvey, C. (2000). *Play* (Enlarged Ed.). Cambridge, MA: Harvard University Press.

Gasser, L., & Keller, M. (2009). Are the competent morally good? Perspective taking and moral motivation of children involved in bullying. *Social Development, 18*(4), 798–816.

Gates, W. (1998, July 20). Charity begins when I'm ready (interview). *Fortune Magazine.*

Gathwala, G., Singh, B., & Singh, J. (2011). Effect of kangaroo care on physical growth, breastfeeding, and its acceptability. *Tropical Doctor, 40,* 199–202.

Gaudineau, A., Ehlinger, V., Vayssiere, C., Jouret, B., Arnaud, C., & Godeau, E. (2010). Factors associated with early menarche: Results from the French Health Behavior in School-Aged Children (HBSC) Study. *BMC Public Health, 10,* 175.

Gauvain, M. (2008). Vygotsky's sociocultural theory. In M. M. Haith & J. B. Benson (Eds.), *Encyclopedia of infant and early childhood development.* Oxford, UK: Elsevier.

Gauvain, M., & Parke, R. D. (2010a). Parenting. In M. H. Bornstein (Ed.), *Handbook of cultural developmental science.* New York: Psychology Press.

Gauvain, M., & Parke, R. D. (2010b). Socialization. In M. H. Bornstein (Ed.), *Handbook of cultural developmental science.* New York: Psychology Press.

Geborek. A., & Hjelte, L. (2011, in press). Association between genotype and pulmonary phenotype in cystic fibrosis patients with severe mutations. *Journal of Cystic Fibrosis.*

Gee, C. L., & Heyman, G. D. (2007). Children's evaluations of other people's self-descriptions. *Social Development, 16,* 800–818.

Gelman, R. (1969). Conservation acquisition: A problem of learning to attend to relevant attributes. *Journal of Experimental Child Psychology, 7,* 67–87.

Gelman, S. A. (2009). Learning from others: Children's construction of concepts. *Annual Review of Psychology* (Vol. 60). Palo Alto, CA: Annual Reviews.

Gelman, S. A., & Kalish, C. W. (2006). Conceptual development. In W. Damon & R. Lerner (Eds.), *Handbook of child psychology* (6th ed.). New York: Wiley.

Gennetian, L. A., & Miller, C. (2002). Children and welfare reform: A view from an experimental welfare reform program in Minnesota. *Child Development, 73,* 601–620.

Gentile, D. A. (2011). The multiple dimensions of video game effects. *Child Development Perspectives, 5,* 75–81.

Gentile, D. A., Mathieson, L. C., & Crick, N. R. (2010). Media violence associations with the form and function of aggression among elementary school children. *Social Development, 20,* 213–230.

Georgakilas, A. G. (2011, in press). From chemistry of DNA damage to repair and biological significance. Comprehending the future. *Mutation Research.*

Gershoff, E. T. (2002). Corporal punishment by parents and associated child behaviors and experiences: A meta-analysis and theoretical review. *Psychological Bulletin, 128,* 539–579.

Gershoff, E. T., & others. (2010). Parent discipline practices in an international sample: Associations with child behaviors and moderation by perceived normativeness. *Child Development, 81,* 487–502.

Gesell, A. (1934a). *An atlas of infant behavior.* New Haven, CT: Yale University Press.

Gesell, A. L. (1934b). *Infancy and human growth.* New York: Macmillan.

Gewirtz, J. (1977). Maternal responding and the conditioning of infant crying: Directions of influence within the attachment-acquisition process. In B. C. Etzel, J. M. LeBlanc, & D. M. Baer (Eds.), *New developments in behavioral research.* Hillsdale, NJ: Erlbaum.

Ghazarian, S. R., & Roche, K. M. (2010). Social support and low-income, urban mothers: Longitudinal associations with delinquency. *Journal of Youth and Adolescence, 39,* 1097–1108.

Ghetti, S., & Alexander, K. W. (2004). "If it happened, I would remember it": Strategic use of event memorability in the rejection of false autobiographical events. *Child Development, 75,* 542–561.

Ghosh, S., Feingold, E., Chakraborty, S., & Dey, S. K. (2010). Telomere length is associated with types of chromosome 21 nondisjunction: A new insight into the maternal age effect on Down syndrome birth. *Human Genetics, 127,* 403.

Gibbons, J., & Ng, S. H. (2004). Acting bilingual and thinking bilingual. *Journal of Language & Social Psychology, 23,* 4–6.

Gibbons, R. D., Hedeker, D., & DuToit, S. (2010). Advances in analysis of longitudinal data. *Annual Review of Clinical Psychology* (Vol. 6). Palo Alto, CA: Annual Reviews.

Gibbs, J. C. (2010). *Moral development and reality: Beyond the theories of Kohlberg and Hoffman* (2nd ed.). Boston: Allyn & Bacon.

Gibbs, J. C., Basinger, K. S., Grime, R. L., & Snarey, J. R. (2007). Moral judgment development across cultures: Revisiting Kohlberg's universality claims. *Developmental Review, 27,* 443–500.

Gibson, E. J. (1969). *Principles of perceptual learning and development.* New York: Appleton-Century-Crofts.

Gibson, E. J. (1989). Exploratory behavior in the development of perceiving, acting, and the acquiring of knowledge. *Annual Review of Psychology* (Vol. 39). Palo Alto, CA: Annual Reviews.

Gibson, E. J. (2001). *Perceiving the affordances.* Mahwah, NJ: Erlbaum.

Gibson, E. J., Riccio, G., Schmuckler, M. A., Stoffregen, T. A., Rosenberg, D., & Taormina, J. (1987). Detection of the traversability of surfaces by crawling and walking infants. *Journal of Experimental Psychology: Human Perception and Performance, 13,* 533–544.

Gibson, E. J., & Walk, R. D. (1960). The "visual cliff." *Scientific American, 202,* 64–71.

Gibson, J. J. (1966). *The senses considered as perceptual systems.* Boston: Houghton Mifflin.

Gibson, J. J. (1979). *The ecological approach to visual perception.* Boston: Houghton Mifflin.

Gilliam, M., & others. (2011). Developmental trajectories of the corpus callosum in attention-deficit/hyperactivity disorder. *Biological Psychiatry, 69,* 839–846.

Gillig, P. M., & Sanders, R. D. (2011). Higher cortical functions: Attention and vigilance. *Innovations in Clinical Neuroscience, 8,* 43–46.

Gilligan, C. (1982). *In a different voice.* Cambridge, MA: Harvard University Press.

Gilligan, C. (1992, May). *Joining the resistance: Girls' development in adolescence.* Paper presented at the symposium on development and vulnerability in close relationships, Montreal, Quebec.

Gilligan, C. (1996). The centrality of relationships in psychological development: A puzzle, some evidence, and a theory. In G. G. Noam & K. W. Fischer (Eds.), *Development and vulnerability in close relationships.* Hillsdale, NJ: Erlbaum.

Gilligan, C., Spencer, R., Weinberg, M. K., & Bertsch, T. (2003). On the listening guide: A voice-centered relational model. In P. M. Carnic & J. E. Rhodes (Eds.), *Qualitative research in psychology.* Washington, DC: American Psychological Association.

Girling, A. (2006). The benefits of using the Neonatal Behavioral Assessment Scale in health visiting practice. *Community Practice, 79,* 118–120.

Girls, Inc. (1991). *Truth, trusting and technology: New research on preventing adolescent pregnancy.* Indianapolis: Author.

Glover, M. B., Mullineaux, P. Y., Deater-Deckard, K., & Petrill, S. A. (2010). Parents' feelings toward their adoptive and non-adoptive children. *Infant and Child Development, 19*(3), 238–251.

Gluck, M. E., Venti, C. A., Lindsay, R. S., Knowler, W. C. Salbe, A. D., & Krakoff, J. (2009). Maternal influence, not diabetic intrauterine environment, predicts children's energy intake. *Obesity, 17,* 772–777.

Godding, V., & others. (2004). Does in utero exposure to heavy maternal smoking induce nicotine withdrawal symptoms in neonates? *Pediatric Research, S5,* 645–651.

Goffin, S. G., & Wilson, C. S. (2001). *Curriculum models and early childhood education: Appraising the relationship* (2nd ed.). Upper Saddle River, NJ: Prentice Hall.

Gogtay, N., & Thompson, P. M. (2010). Mapping gray matter development: Implications for typical development and vulnerability to psychopathology. *Brain and Cognition, 72,* 6–15.

Gold, M. A., & others. (2010). Associations between religiosity and sexual and contraceptive behaviors. *Journal of Pediatric and Adolescent Gynecology, 23,* 290–297.

Goldberg, W. A., & Lucas-Thompson, R. (2008). Maternal and paternal employment, effects of. In M. M. Haith & J. B. Benson (Eds.), *Encyclopedia of infant and early childhood development.* Oxford, UK: Elsevier.

Goldenberg, R. L., & Culhane, J. F. (2007). Low birth weight in the United States. *American Journal of Clinical Nutrition, 85* (Suppl.), S584–S590.

Goldfield, B. A., & Snow, C. A. (2009). Individual differences in language development. In J. Berko Gleason & N. Ratner (Eds.), *The development of language* (7th ed.). Boston: Allyn & Bacon.

Goldfield, G. S. (2011, in press). Making access to TV contingent on physical activity: Effects on liking and relative reinforcing value of TV and physical activity in overweight and obese children. *Journal of Behavioral Medicine.*

Goldin-Meadow, S., & Iverson, J. (2010). Gesturing across the lifespan. In R. M. Lerner (Ed.), *Handbook of life-span development.* New York: Wiley.

Goldman, N., Giel, D. A., Lin, Y. H., & Weinstein, M. (2010). The serotonin transporter polymorphism (5-HTTLPR): Allelic variation and its link with depressive symptoms. *Depression and Anxiety, 27,* 260–269.

Goldschmidt, L., Richardson, G. A., Willford, J., & Day, N. N. (2008). Prenatal marijuana exposure and intelligence test performance at age 6. *Journal of the American Academy of Child and Adolescent Psychiatry, 47,* 254–263.

Goldstein, M. H., King, A. P., & West, M. J. (2003). Social interaction shapes babbling: Testing parallels between birdsong and speech. *Proceedings of the National Academy of Sciences, 100*(13), 8030–8035.

Goldstein, M. H., & Schwade, J. A. (2008). Social feedback to infants' babbling facilitates rapid phonological learning. *Psychological Science, 19,* 515–523.

Goldston, D. B., Molock, S. D., Whitbeck, L. B., Murakami, J. L., Zayas, L. H., & Hall, G. C. (2008). Cultural considerations in adolescent suicide prevention and psychosocial treatment. *American Psychologist, 63,* 14–31.

Goleman, D., Kaufman, P., & Ray, M. (1993). *The creative spirit.* New York: Plume.

Golomb, C. (2002). *Child art in context.* Washington, DC: American Psychological Association.

Golomb, C. (2008). Artistic development. In M. M. Haith & J. B. Benson (Eds.), *Encyclopedia of infant and early childhood development.* Oxford, UK: Elsevier.

Golombok, S. (2011a). Why I study lesbian families. In S. Ellis, V. Clarke, E. Peel, & D. Riggs (Eds.), *LGBTQ Psychologies.* New York: Cambridge University Press.

Golombok, S. (2011b). Children in new family formations. In R. Gross (Ed.), *Psychology* (6th ed.). London: Holder Education.

Golombok, S., MacCallum, F., & Goodman, E. (2001). The "test-tube" generation: Parent-child relationships and the psychological well-being of in vitro fertilization children at adolescence. *Child Development, 72,* 599–608.

Golombok, S., Rust, J., Zervoulis, K., Croudace, T., Golding, J., & Hines, M. (2008). Developmental trajectories of sex-typed behavior in boys and girls: A longitudinal general population study of children aged 2.5–8 years. *Child Development, 79,* 1583–1593.

Golombok, S., & Tasker, F. (2010). Gay fathers. In M. E. Lamb (Ed.), *The role of the father in child development* (5th ed.). New York: Wiley.

Gomes, R. S., & others. (2011). Primary versus secondary hypertension in children followed up at an outpatient tertiary unit. *Pediatric Nephrology, 26,* 441–447.

Goncu, A., & Gauvain, M. (2011). Sociocultural approaches to educational psychology: Theory, research, and application. In K. R. Harris, S. Graham, & T. Urdan (Eds.), *APA educational psychology handbook.* Washington, DC: American Psychological Association.

Gong, X., & others. (2009). An investigation of ribosomal protein L10 gene in autism spectrum disorders. *BMC Medical Genetics, 10,* 7.

Gonzalez, A., Atkinson, L., & Fleming, A. S. (2009). Attachment and the comparative psychobiology of mothering. In M. De Haan &

M. R. Gunnar (Eds.), *Handbook of developmental social neuroscience*. New York: Guilford.

Good, M., & Willoughby, T. (2008). Adolescence as a sensitive period for spiritual development. *Child Development Perspectives, 2*, 32–37.

Good, M., & Willoughby, T. (2010). Evaluating the direction of effects in the relationship between religious versus non-religious activities, academic success, and substance use. *Journal of Youth and Adolescence, 40*(6), 680–693.

Goodenough, J., & McGuire, B. A. (2012). *Biology of humans* (4th ed.). Upper Saddle River, NJ: Pearson.

Goodman, G. S., Batterman-Faunce, J. M., & Kenney, R. (1992). Optimizing children's testimony: Research and social policy issues concerning allegations of child sexual abuse. In D. Cicchetti & S. Toth (Eds.), *Child abuse, child development and social policy*. Norwood, NJ: Ablex.

Goodnough, L. T., Daniels, K., Wong, A. E., Viele, M., Fontaine, M. F., & Butwick, A. J. (2011, in press). How we treat: Transfusion medicine support of obstetric services. *Tranfusion.*

Gopnik, A. (2010). Commentary. In R. E. Gitlivsky, *Mind in the making*. New York: HarperCollins.

Gosselin, J. (2010). Individual and family factors related to psychosocial adjustment in stepmother families with adolescents. *Journal of Divorce and Remarriage, 51*, 108–123.

Gottlieb, G. (2007). Probabilistic epigenesis. *Developmental Science, 10*, 1–11.

Gottlieb, G., Wahlsten, D., & Lickliter, R. (2006). The significance of biology for human development: A developmental psychobiological systems view. In W. Damon & R. Lerner (Eds.), *Handbook of child psychology* (6th ed.). New York: Wiley.

Gottman, J. M. (2011). Research on parenting. Retrieved March 25, 2011, from http://www.gottman.com/parenting/research

Gottman, J. M., & DeClaire, J. (1997). *The heart of parenting: Raising an emotionally intelligent child*. New York: Simon & Schuster.

Gottman, J. M., & Parker, J. G. (Eds.). (1987). *Conversations of friends*. New York: Cambridge University Press.

Gottman, J. M., Shapiro, A. F., & Parthemer, J. (2004). Bringing baby home: A preventative intervention program for expectant couples. *International Journal of Childbirth Education, 19*, 28–30.

Gouin, K., & others. (2011, in press). Effects of cocaine use during pregnancy on low birthweight and preterm birth: Systematic and metaanalyses. *American Journal of Obstetrics and Gynecology.*

Gould, M. S., Greenberg, T., Velting, D. M., & Shaffer, D. (2003). Youth suicide risk and preventive interventions: A review of the past 10 years. *Journal of the American Academy of Child and Adolescent Psychiatry, 42*, 386–405.

Gould, S. J. (1981). *The mismeasure of man*. New York: W. W. Norton.

Graber, J. A. (2004). Internalizing problems during adolescence. In R. Lerner & L. Steinberg (Eds.), *Handbook of adolescent psychology*. New York: Wiley.

Graber, J. A. (2008). Pubertal and neuroendocrine development and risk for depressive disorders. In N. B. Allen & L. Sheeber (Eds.), *Adolescent emotional development and the emergence of depressive disorders*. New York: Cambridge University Press.

Graber, J. A., & Brooks-Gunn, J. (2002). Adolescent girls' sexual development. In G. M. Wingood & R. J. DiClemente (Eds.), *Handbook of women's sexual and reproductive health*. New York: Kluwer Academic/Plenum Publishers.

Graber, J. A., Brooks-Gunn, J., & Warren, M. P. (2006). Pubertal effects on adjustment in girls: Moving from demonstrating effects to identifying pathways. *Journal of Youth and Adolescence, 35*, 391–401.

Graber, J. A., Nichols, T. R., & Brooks-Gunn, J. (2010). Putting pubertal timing in developmental context: Implications for prevention. *Developmental Psychobiology, 52*, 254–262.

Graber, J. A., & Sontag, L. (2009). Internalizing problems during adolescence. In R. M. Lerner & L. Steinberg (Eds.), *Handbook of adolescent psychology* (3rd ed.). New York: Wiley.

Gradisar, M., Gardner, G., & Dohnt, H. (2011). Recent worldwide sleep patterns and problems during adolescence: A review and meta-analysis of age, region, and sleep. *Sleep Medicine, 12*, 110–118.

Grafenhain, M., Behne, T., Carpenter, M., & Tomasello. M. (2009). Young children's understanding of joint commitments. *Developmental Psychology, 45*(5), 1430–1443.

Graham, G. M., Holt/Hale, S. A., & Parker, M. A. (2010). *Children moving* (8th ed.). New York: McGraw-Hill.

Graham, S. (1986, August). *Can attribution theory tell us something about motivation in blacks?* Paper presented at the meeting of the American Psychological Association, Washington, DC.

Graham, S. (1990). Motivation in Afro-Americans. In G. L. Berry & J. K. Asamen (Eds.), *Black students: Psychosocial issues and academic achievement*. Newbury Park, CA: Sage.

Graven, S. (2006). Sleep and brain development. *Clinical Perinatology, 33*, 693–706.

Graves, K. N., Sentner, A., Workman, J., & Mackey, W. (2010). Building positive life skills the Smart Girls Way: Evaluation of a school-based sexual responsibility program for adolescent girls. *Health Promotion Practice, 12*(3), 463–471.

Gravetter, R. J., & Forzano, L. B. (2012). *Research methods for the behavioral sciences* (4th ed.). Boston: Cengage.

Gray, K. A., Day, N. X., Leech, S., & Richardson, G. A. (2005). Prenatal marijuana exposure: Effect on child depressive symptoms at ten years of age. *Neurotoxicology and Teratology, 27*, 439–448.

Gredeback, G., Johnson, S., & von Hofsten, C. (2010). Eye tracking in infancy research. *Developmental Neuropsychology, 35*, 1–19.

Greene, M. F. (2009). Making small risks even smaller. *New England Journal of Medicine, 360*, 183–184.

Greenfield, P. M. (1966). On culture and conservation. In J. S. Bruner, R. P. Oliver, & P. M. Greenfield (Eds.), *Studies in cognitive growth*. New York: Wiley.

Greenfield, P. M., Suzuki, L. K., & Rothstein-Fisch, C. (2006). Cultural pathways through human development. In W. Damon & R. Lerner (Eds.), *Handbook of child psychology* (6th ed.). New York: Wiley.

Greer, F. R., Sicherer, S. H., Burks, A. W., & The Committee on Nutrition and Section on Allergy and Immunology. (2008). Effects of early nutritional interventions on the development of atopic disease in infants and children: The role of maternal dietary restriction, breast feeding, timing of introduction of complementary foods, and hydrolyzed formulas. *Pediatrics, 121*, 183–191.

Gregory, A. M., Ball, H. A., & Button, T. M. M. (2011). Behavioral genetics. In P. K. Smith & C. H. Hart (Eds.), *Wiley-Blackwell handbook of childhood social development* (2nd ed.). New York: Wiley.

Gregory, R. J. (2011). *Psychological testing* (6th ed.). Upper Saddle River, NJ: Pearson.

Grigorenko, E. (2000). Heritability and intelligence. In R. J. Sternberg (Ed.), *Handbook of intelligence*. New York: Cambridge University Press.

Grigorenko, E. L., & Takanishi, R. (2010). *Handbook of U.S. immigration and education*. New York: Springer.

Gross, J. J., Frederickson, B. L., & Levenson, R. W. (1994). The psychology of crying. *Psychophysiology, 31*, 460–468.

Grossmann, K., Grossmann, K. E., Spangler, G., Suess, G., & Unzner, L. (1985). Maternal sensitivity and newborns' orientation responses as related to quality of attachment in northern Germany. In I. Bretherton & E. Waters (Eds.), Growing points of attachment theory and research. *Monographs of the Society for Research in Child Development, 50*(1–2, Serial No. 209).

Grossmann, T., & Johnson, M. H. (2010). Selective prefrontal cortex responses to joint attention in early infancy. *Biological Letters, 6*, 540–543.

Grusec, J. E. (2011a). Human development: Development in the family. *Annual Review of Psychology* (Vol. 62). Palo Alto, CA: Annual Reviews.

Grusec, J. E. (2011b). Socialization processes in the family: Social and emotional development. *Annual Review of Psychology* (Vol. 62). Palo Alto, CA: Annual Reviews.

Grusec, J. E., & Davidov, M. (2007). Socialization in the family: The role of parents. In J. E. Grusec & P. D. Hastings (Eds.), *Handbook of socialization*. New York: Guilford.

Grusec, J. E., Hastings, P., & Almas, A. (2011). Children's understanding of society. In P. K. Smith & C. H. Hart (Eds.), *Wiley-Blackwell handbook of childhood social development* (2nd ed.). New York: Wiley.

Gu, M. L., & Zhao, J. (2011). Mapping and localization of susceptible genes in asthma. *China Medicine, 124,* 132–143.

Guidozzi, F., & Black, V. (2009). The obstetric face and challenge of HIV/AIDS. *Clinical Obstetrics and Gynecology, 52,* 270–284.

Guilamo-Ramos, V., Jaccard, J., & Dittus, P. (Eds.). (2010). *Parental monitoring of adolescents: Current perspectives for researchers and practitioners.* New York: Columbia University Press.

Guilford, J. P. (1967). *The structure of intellect.* New York: McGraw-Hill.

Gunderson, E. A., Ramirez, G., Beilock, S. L., & Levine, S. C. (2011, in press). The role of parents and teachers in the development of gender-related attitudes. *Sex Roles.*

Gunnar, M. R., Fisher, P. A., & The Early Experience, Stress, and Prevention Science Network. (2006). Bringing basic research on early experience and stress neurobiology to bear on preventive interventions for neglected and maltreated children. *Development and Psychopathology, 18,* 651–677.

Gunnar, M. R., Malone, S., & Fisch, R. O. (1987). The psychobiology of stress and coping in the human neonate: Studies of the adreno-cortical activity in response to stress in the first week of life. In T. Field, P. McCabe, & N. Schneiderman (Eds.), *Stress and coping.* Hillsdale, NJ: Erlbaum.

Gunnarsdotter, T., & others. (2011, in press). The role of parental motivation in family-based treatment for childhood obesity. *Obesity.*

Gupta, A., Thornton, J. W., & Huston, A. C. (2008). Working families should not be poor—the New Hope project. In D. R. Crane & T. B. Heaton (Eds.), *Handbook of families and poverty.* Thousand Oaks, CA: Sage.

Gur, R. C., & others. (1995). Sex differences in regional cerebral glucose metabolism during a resting state. *Science, 267,* 528–531.

Gurgan, T., & Demirol, A. (2007). Unresolved issues regarding assisted reproduction technology. *Reproductive Biomedicine Online, 14* (Suppl. 1), S40–S43.

Gurwitch, R. H., Silovksy, J. F., Schultz, S., Kees, M., & Burlingame, S. (2001). *Reactions and guidelines for children following trauma/disaster.* Norman, OK: Department of Pediatrics, University of Oklahoma Health Science Center.

Gustafsson, J-E. (2007). Schooling and intelligence: Effects of track of study on level and profile of cognitive abilities. In P. C. Kyllonen, R. D. Roberts, & L. Stankov (Eds.), *Extending intelligence.* Mahwah, NJ: Erlbaum.

Gutman, L. M., Eccles, J. S., Peck, S., & Malanchuk, O. (2011, in press). The influence of early family relations on trajectories of cigarette and alcohol use from early to late adolescence. *Journal of Adolescence.*

H

Hack, M., Taylor, H. G., Schulchter, M., Andreias, L., Drotar, D., & Klein, N. (2009). Behavioral outcomes of extremely low birth weight children at age 8 years. *Journal of Developmental and Behavioral Pediatrics, 30,* 122–130.

Hahn, D. B., Payne, W. A., & Lucas, E. B. (2011). *Focus on health* (10th ed.). New York: McGraw-Hill.

Hahn, W. K. (1987). Cerebral lateralization of function: From infancy through childhood. *Psychological Bulletin, 101,* 376–392.

Hakuta, K. (2001, April 5). *Key policy milestones and directions in the education of English language learners.* Paper prepared for the Rockefeller Foundation Symposium, "Leveraging change: An emerging framework for educational equity," Washington, DC.

Hakuta, K. (2005, April). *Bilingualism at the intersection of research and public policy.* Paper presented at the meeting of the Society for Research in Child Development, Atlanta.

Hakuta, K., Butler, Y. G., & Witt, D. (2001). *How long does it take English learners to attain proficiency?* Berkeley, CA: The University of California Linguistic Minority Research Institute Policy Report 2000–1.

Hakvoort, E. M., Bos, H. M. W., Van Balen, F., & Hermanns, J. M. A. (2011). Postdivorce relationships in families and children's psycho-social adjustment. *Journal of Divorce and Remarriage, 52,* 125–146.

Hale, S., & Evans, L. (2011). Articulation/phonology: Of mouth and mind. In S. S. Chabon & E. R. Cohn (Eds.), *Communication disorders casebook.* Upper Saddle River, NJ: Pearson.

Halford, G. S. (2008). Cognitive developmental theories. In M. M. Haith & J. B. Benson (Eds.), *Encyclopedia of infant and early childhood development.* Oxford, UK: Elsevier.

Halford, G. S., & Andrews, G. (2011). Information-processing models of cognitive development. In U. Goswami (Ed.), *Wiley-Blackwell handbook of childhood cognitive development.* New York: Wiley.

Hall, G. S. (1904). *Adolescence* (Vols. 1 & 2). Englewood Cliffs, NJ: Prentice Hall.

Hall, L. (2009). *Autism spectrum disorders: From therapy to practice.* Boston: Allyn & Bacon.

Hallahan, D. P., & Kauffman, J. M. (2006). *Exceptional learners* (10th ed.). Boston: Allyn & Bacon.

Hallahan, D. P., Kauffman, J. M., & Pullen, P. C. (2012). *Exceptional learners* (12th ed.). Upper Saddle River, NJ: Pearson.

Halpern, D. (2006). Assessing gender gaps in learning and academic achievement. In P. A. Alexander & P. H. Wynne (Eds.), *Handbook of educational psychology* (2nd ed.). Mahwah, NJ: Erlbaum.

Halpern, D. F., Benbow, C. P., Geary, D. C., Gur, R. C., Hyde, J. S., & Gernsbacher, M. A. (2007). The science of sex differences in science and mathematics. *Psychological Science in the Public Interest, 8,* 1–51.

Hamilton, B. E., Martin, J. A., & Ventura, S. J. (2009, March 18). Births: Preliminary data for 2007. *National Vital Statistics Reports, 57*(12), 1–23.

Hammer, L. D., & others. (2010). Increasing immunization coverage. *Pediatrics, 125,* 1295–1304.

Hamza, C. A., & Willoughby, T. (2010). Perceived parental monitoring, adolescent disclosure, and adolescent depressive symptoms: A longitudinal examination. *Journal of Youth and Adolescence, 40*(7), 902–915.

Han, W-J. (2009). Maternal employment. In D. Carr (Ed.), *Encyclopedia of the life course and human development.* Boston: Gale Cengage.

Hancox, R. J., Milne, B. J., & Poulton, R. (2004). Association between child and adolescent television viewing and adult health: A longitudinal birth cohort study. *Lancet, 364,* 257–262.

Handler, A., Rankin, K., Rosenberg, D., & Sinha, K. (2011, in press). Extent of documented adherence to recommended prenatal care content: Provider site differences and effect on outcomes among low-income women. *Maternal and Child Health.*

Hanish, L. D., & Guerra, N. G. (2004). Aggressive victims, passive victims, and bullies: Developmental continuity or developmental change? *Merrill-Palmer Quarterly, 50,* 17–38.

Hansen, M. L., Gunn, P. W., & Kaelber, D. C. (2007). Underdiagnosis of hypertension in children and adolescents. *Journal of the American Medical Association, 298,* 874–879.

Harakeh, Z., Scholte, R. H. J., Vermulst, A. A., de Vries, H., & Engels, R. C. (2010). The relations between parents' smoking, general parenting, parental smoking communication, and adolescents' smoking. *Journal of Research on Adolescence, 20,* 140–165.

Harden, K. P., & Mendle, J. (2011, in press). Adolescent sexual activity and the development of delinquent behavior: The role of relationship context. *Journal of Youth and Adolescence.*

Hardman, M. L., Drew, C. J., & Egan, M. W. (2011). *Human exceptionality* (10th ed.). Boston: Cengage.

Hargreaves, D. A., & Tiggemann, M. (2004). Idealized body images and adolescent body image: "Comparing" boys and girls. *Body Image, 1,* 351–361.

Harkness, S., & Super, E. M. (1995). Culture and parenting. In M. H. Bornstein (Ed.), *Handbook of parenting* (Vol. 3). Hillsdale, NJ: Erlbaum.

Harlow, H. R. (1958). The nature of love. *American Psychologist, 13,* 673–685.

Harmon, O. R., Lambrinos, J., & Kennedy, P. (2008). Are online exams an invitation to cheat? *Journal of Economic Education, 39,* 116–125.

Harris, J. R. (1998). *The nurture assumption: Why children turn out the way they do: Parents matter less than you think and peers matter more.* New York: Free Press.

Harris, J. R. (2009). *The nurture assumption* (revised and updated edition). New York: Free Press.

Harris, J. L., & others. (2011). Effects of serving high-sugar cereals on children's breakfast-eating behavior. *Pediatrics, 127,* 71–76.

Harris, P. L. (2000). *The work of the imagination.* New York: Oxford University Press.

Harris, P. L. (2006). Social cognition. In W. Damon & R. Lerner (Eds.), *Handbook of child psychology* (6th ed.). New York: Wiley.

Harrison-Hale, A. O., McLoyd, V. C., & Smedley, B. (2004). Racial and ethnic status: Risk and protective processes among African-American families. In K. L. Maton, C. J. Schellenbach, B. J. Leadbetter, & A. L. Solarz (Eds.), *Investing in children, families, and communities.* Washington, DC: American Psychological Association.

Harrist, A. W. (1993, March). *Family interaction styles as predictors of children's competence: The role of synchrony and nonsynchrony.* Paper presented at the biennial meeting of the Society for Research in Child Development, New Orleans.

Harron, K. L., & others. (2011). Rising rates of all types of diabetes in south Asian and non-south Asian children and young people aged 0–29 years in West Yorkshire, U.K., 1991–2006. *Diabetes Care, 34,* 652–654.

Hart, B., & Risley, T. R. (1995). *Meaningful differences in the everyday experience of young Americans.* Baltimore: Paul H. Brookes.

Hart, C. H., Yang, C., Charlesworth, R., & Burts, D. C. (2003, April). *Early childhood teachers' curriculum beliefs, classroom practices, and children's outcomes: What are the connections?* Paper presented at the biennial meeting of the Society for Research in Child Development, Tampa, FL.

Hart, C. L., Ksir, C. J., & Ray, O. S. (2011). *Drugs, society, and behavior* (14th ed.). New York: McGraw-Hill.

Hart, C. N., Cairns, A., & Jelalian, E. (2011). Sleep and obesity in children and adolescents. *Pediatric Clinics of North America, 58,* 715–733.

Hart, D., & Karmel, M. P. (1996). Self-awareness and self-knowledge in humans, great apes, and monkeys. In A. Russon, K. Bard, & S. Parker (Eds.), *Reaching into thought.* New York: Cambridge University Press.

Hart, D., Matsuba, M. K., & Atkins, R. (2008). The moral and civic effects of learning to serve. In L. Nucci & D. Narváez (Eds.), *Handbook of moral and character education.* Clifton, NJ: Psychology Press.

Hart, S., & Carrington, H. (2002). Jealousy in 6-month-old infants. *Infancy, 3,* 395–402.

Hart, S., Carrington, H., Tronick, E. Z., & Carroll, S. R. (2004). When infants lose exclusive maternal attention: Is it jealousy? *Infancy, 6,* 57–78.

Harter, S. (2006). The self. In W. Damon & R. Lerner (Eds.), *Handbook of child psychology* (6th ed.). New York: Wiley.

Hartshorne, H., & May, M. S. (1928–1930). *Moral studies in the nature of character: Studies in deceit (Vol. 1); Studies in self-control (Vol. 2); Studies in the organization of character (Vol. 3).* New York: Macmillan.

Hartup, W. W. (1983). The peer system. In P. H. Mussen (Ed.), *Handbook of child psychology* (4th ed., Vol. 4). New York: Wiley.

Hartup, W. W. (1996). The company they keep: Friendships and their development significance. *Child Development, 67,* 1–13.

Hartup, W. W. (2009). Critical issues and theoretical viewpoints. In K. H. Rubin, W. M. Bukowski, & B. Laursen (Eds.), *Handbook of peer interactions, relationships, and groups.* New York: Guilford.

Hartup, W. W., & Abecassis, M. (2004). Friends and enemies. In P. K. Smith & C. H. Hart (Eds.), *Blackwell handbook of childhood social development.* Malden, MA: Blackwell.

Hashimoto-Toril, Kawasawa, Y. I., Kuhn, A., & Rakic, P. (2011, in press). Combined transcriptome analysis of fetal human and mouse cerebral cortex exposed to alcohol. *Proceedings of the National Academy of Sciences U.S.A.*

Hattery, A. J., & Smith, E. (2007). *African American families.* Thousand Oaks, CA: Sage.

Hauck, F. R., & others. (2011). Breastfeeding and reduced risk of sudden infant death syndrome: A meta-analysis. *Pediatrics, 128,* 103–110.

Hausman, B. L. (2005). Risky business: Framing childbirth in hospital settings. *Journal of Medical Ethics, 26,* 23–38.

Hawkins, J. A., & Berndt, T. J. (1985, April). *Adjustment following the transition to junior high school.* Paper presented at the biennial meeting of the Society for Research in Child Development, Toronto.

Haydon, A., & Halpern, G. T. (2010). Older romantic partners and depressive symptoms during adolescence. *Journal of Youth and Adolescence, 39,* 1240–1251.

Hayes, H. M., & others. (2011). Joint association of fatness and physical activity on resting blood pressure in 5- to 9-year-old children. *Pediatric Exercise Science, 23,* 97–105.

He, C., & others. (2010). A large-scale candidate gene association study of age at menarche and age at natural menopause. *Human Genetics, 128,* 515–527.

Healey, J. F. (2009). *Race, ethnicity, and class* (5th ed.). Thousand Oaks, CA: Sage.

Hearst, M. O., & others. (2011, in press). The co-occurrence of obesity, elevated blood pressure, and acanthosis nigricans among American Indian school children: Identifying individual heritage and environmental-level correlates. *American Journal of Human Biology.*

Hebebrand, J., & Bulik, C. M. (2011, in press). Critical appraisal of provisional DSM-5 Criteria for anorexia nervosa and an alternative proposal. *International Journal of Eating Disorders.*

Hegaard, H. K., Hedegaard, M., Damm, P. Ottesen, B., Petersson, K., & Heruriksen, T. B. (2008). Leisure time physical activity is associated with a reduced risk of preterm delivery. *American Journal of Obstetrics and Gynecology, 198,* e1–e5.

Heiman, G. W. (2012). *Basic statistics for the behavioral sciences* (6th ed.). Boston: Cengage.

Heimann, M., Strid, K., Smith, L., Tjus, T., Ulvund, S. E., & Meltzoff, A. N. (2006). Exploring the relation between memory, gestural communication, and the emergence of language in infancy: A longitudinal study. *Infant and Child Development, 15,* 233–249.

Helwig, C. C., & Turiel, E. (2011). Children's social and moral reasoning. In P. K. Smith & C. H. Hart (Eds.), *Wiley-Blackwell handbook of childhood social development* (2nd ed.). New York: Wiley.

Henderson, V. L., & Dweck, C. S. (1990). Motivation and achievement. In S. S. Feldman & G. R. Elliott (Eds.), *At the threshold: The developing adolescent.* Cambridge, MA: Harvard University Press.

Hendrick, J., & Weissman, P. (2010). *The whole child: Developmental education for the early years* (9th ed.). Upper Saddle River, NJ: Prentice Hall.

Hendry, J. (1995). *Understanding Japanese society.* London: Routledge.

Hendy, H. M., Williams, K. E., & Camise, T. S. (2011). Kids' Choice Program improves weight management behaviors and weight status in school children. *Appetite, 56,* 484–494.

Hennessey, B. A. (2011). Intrinsic motivation and creativity: Have we come full circle? In R. A. Beghetto & J. C. Kaufman (Eds.), *Nurturing creativity in the classroom.* New York: Cambridge University Press.

Hennessey, B. A., & Amabile, T. M. (2010). Creativity. *Annual Review of Psychology* (Vol. 61). Palo Alto, CA: Annual Reviews.

Henriksen, T. B., & others. (2004). Alcohol consumption at the time of conception and spontaneous abortion. *American Journal of Epidemiology, 160,* 661–667.

Hensen, E. F., & others. (2011, in press). High prevalence of founder mutations of the succinate dehydrogenase genes in the Netherlands. *Clinical Genetics.*

Herbst, M. A., Mercer, B. M., Beasley, D., Meyer, R., & Carr, T. (2003). Relationship of prenatal care and perinatal morbidity in low-birth-weight infants. *American Journal of Obstetrics and Gynecology, 189,* 930–933.

Hernandez, V. R., Montana, S., & Clarke, K. (2010). Child health inequality: Framing a social work response. *Health and Social Work, 35,* 291–301.

Hernandez-Martinez, C., & others. (2011). Effects of iron deficiency on neonatal behavior at different stages of pregnancy. *Early Human Development, 87,* 165–169.

Hernandez-Reif, M., Diego, M., & Field, T. (2007). Preterm infants show reduced stress behaviors and activity after 5 days of massage therapy. *Infant Behavior and Development, 30,* 557–561.

Herrera, S. G., & Murry, K. G. (2011). *Mastering ESL and bilingual methods* (2nd ed.). Boston: Allyn & Bacon.

Hertenstein, M. J., & Keltner, D. (2011). Gender and the communication of emotion via touch. *Sex Roles, 64,* 70–80.

Hesmet, S., & Lo, K. C. (2006). Evaluation and treatment of ejaculatory duct obstruction in infertile men. *Canadian Journal of Urology, 13* (Suppl. 1), 18–21.

Hetherington, E. M. (2006). The influence of conflict, marital problem solving, and parenting on children's adjustment in nondivorced, divorced, and remarried families. In A. Clarke-Stewart & J. Dunn (Eds.), *Families count.* New York: Cambridge University Press.

Hetherington, E. M., & Kelly, J. (2002). *For better or for worse: Divorce reconsidered.* New York: Norton.

Hetherington, E. M., Reiss, D., & Plomin, R. (Eds.). (1994). *Separate social worlds of siblings: The impact of nonshared environment on development.* Hillsdale, NJ: Erlbaum.

Hetherington, E. M., & Stanley-Hagan, M. (2002). Parenting in divorced and remarried families. In M. H. Bornstein (Ed.), *Handbook of parenting* (2nd ed., Vol. 3). Mahwah, NJ: Erlbaum.

Heude, B., & others. (2011, in press). Pre-pregnancy body mass index and weight gain during pregnancy: Relations with gestational diabetes, hypertension, and birth outcomes. *Maternal and Child Health Journal.*

Heulins, I., & Kooy, F. (2011). Fragile X syndrome: From gene discovery to therapy. *Frontiers in Bioscience, 16,* 1211–1232.

Heuwinkel, M. K. (1996). New ways of learning = new ways of teaching. *Childhood Education, 72,* 27–31.

Hewlett, B. S. (2000). Culture, history and sex: Anthropological perspectives on father involvement. *Marriage and Family Review, 29,* 324–340.

Hewlett, B. S., & MacFarlan, S. J. (2010). Fathers' roles in hunter-gatherer and other small-scale cultures. In M. E. Lamb (Ed.), *The role of the father in child development* (5th ed.). New York: Wiley.

Heyman, G. D., & Legare, C. H. (2005). Children's evaluation of sources of information about traits. *Developmental Psychology, 41,* 636–647.

Hibell, B., & others. (2004). *The ESPAD report 2003: Alcohol and other drug use among students in 35 European countries.* The Swedish Council for Information on Alcohol and Other Drugs (CAN) and Council of Europe Pompidou Group.

Hickson, G. B., & Clayton, E. W. (2002). Parents and children's doctors. In M. H. Bornstein (Ed.), *Handbook of parenting* (Vol. 5). Mahwah, NJ: Erlbaum.

Higginbotham, H., Yokota, Y., & Anton, E. S. (2011, in press). Strategies for analyzing neuronal progenitor development and neuronal migration in the developing cerebral cortex. *Cerebral Cortex.*

Higgins, A., Power, C., & Kohlberg, L. (1983, April). *Moral atmosphere and moral judgment.* Paper presented at the biennial meeting of the Society for Research in Child Development, Detroit.

Highfield, R. (2008, April 30). Harvard's baby brain research lab. Retrieved January 24, 2009, from http://www.telegraph.co.uk/scienceandtechnology/science/sciencenews/3341166/Harvards

Hill, C. R., & Stafford, F. P. (1980). Parental care of children: Time diary estimate of quantity, predictability, and variety. *Journal of Human Resources, 15,* 219–239.

Hill, M., & others. (2011). Non-invasive prenatal determination of fetal sex: Translating research into clinical practice. *Clinical Genetics, 80,* 68–75.

Hill, N. E., & Witherspoon, D. P. (2011). Race, ethnicity, and social class. In M. K. Underwood & L. H. Rosen (Eds.), *Social development.* New York: Guilford.

Hillman, C. H., & others. (2009). The effect of acute treadmill walking on cognitive control and academic achievement in preadolescent children. *Neuroscience, 3,* 1044–1054.

Hindman, A. H., Skibbek, L. E., Miller, A., & Zimmerman, M. (2010). Ecological contexts and early learning: Contributions of child, family, and classroom factors during Head Start to literacy and mathematics growth through first grade. *Early Childhood Research Quarterly, 25,* 235–250.

Hines, M. (2011). Gender development and the human brain. *Annual Review of Neuroscience* (Vol. 34). Palo Alto, CA: Annual Reviews.

Hinkle, J. S., Tuckman, B. W., & Sampson, J. P. (1993). The psychology, physiology, and the creativity of middle school aerobic exercisers. *Elementary School Guidance & Counseling, 28,* 133–145.

Hirotani, M., Stets, T., Striano, T., & Friederici, A. D. (2009). Joint attention helps infants learn new words: Event-related potential evidence. *NeuroReport, 20,* 600–605.

Hirschi, A., Niles, S. G., & Akos, P. (2011, in press). Engagement in adolescent career preparation: Social support, personality, and the development of choice decidedness and congruence. *Journal of Adolescence.*

Hoban, T. F. (2004). Sleep and its disorders in children. *Seminars in Neurology, 24,* 327–340.

Hockenberry, M., & Wilson, D. (2011). Wong's essentials of pediatric nursing (9th ed.). Oxford, UK: Elsevier.

Hocutt, A. M. (1996). Effectiveness of special education: Is placement the critical factor? *Future of Children, 6*(1), 77–102.

Hofer, A., & others. (2007). Sex differences in brain activation patterns during processing of positively and negatively balanced emotional stimuli. *Psychological Medicine, 37,* 109–119.

Hoff, E., Laursen, B., & Tardif, T. (2002). Socioeconomic status and parenting. In M. H. Bornstein (Ed.), *Handbook of parenting* (2nd ed.). Mahwah, NJ: Erlbaum.

Hofferth, S. L., & Reid, L. (2002). Early child-bearing and children's achievement behavior over time. *Perspectives on Sexual and Reproductive Health, 34,* 41–49.

Hoffman, E., & Ewen, D. (2007). Supporting families, nurturing young children. *CLASP Policy Brief,* No. 9, 1–11.

Hoffman, M. L. (1970). Moral development. In P. H. Mussen (Ed.), *Manual of child psychology* (3rd ed., Vol. 2). New York: Wiley.

Hogan, M. A., Glazebrook, R., Brancato, V., & Rogers, J. (2007). *Maternal-newborn nursing: Review and rationales* (2nd ed.). Upper Saddle River, NJ: Prentice Hall.

Holden, G. W., Vittrup, B., & Rosen, L. H. (2011). Families, parenting, and discipline. In M. K. Underwood & L. H. Rosen (Eds.), *Social development.* New York: Guilford.

Hollich, G., Newman, R. S., & Jusczyk, P. W. (2005). Infants' use of synchronized visual information to separate streams of speech. *Child Development, 76,* 598–613.

Holmes, L. B. (2011, in press). Human teratogens: Update 2010. *Birth Defects Research A: Clinical and Molecular Teratology.*

Holmes, L. B., & Westgate, M. N. (2011, in press). Inclusion and exclusion criteria for malformations in newborn infants exposed to potential teratogens. *Birth Defects Research. Part A. Clinical and Molecular Teratology.*

Holtz, P., & Appel, M. (2011, in press). Internet use and video gaming predict problem behavior in early adolescence. *Journal of Adolescence.*

Hooper, S. R., & others. (2008). Executive functions in young males with fragile X syndrome in comparison to mental age-matched controls: Baseline findings from a longitudinal study. *Neuropsychology, 22,* 36–47.

Hopkins, B. (1991). Facilitating early motor development: An intracultural study of West Indian mothers and their infants living in Britain. In J. K. Nugent, B. M. Lester, & T. B. Brazelton (Eds.), *The cultural contexts of infancy, Vol. 2: Multicultural and interdisciplinary approaches to parent-infant relations.* Norwood, NJ: Ablex.

Hopkins, B., & Westra, T. (1990). Motor development, maternal expectations, and the role of handling. *Infant Behavior and Development, 13,* 117–122.

Horne, R. S., Franco, P., Adamson, T. M., Groswasser, J., & Kahn, A. (2002). Effects of body position on sleep and arousal characteristics in infants. *Early Human Development, 69,* 25–33.

Horner, C. C., & Bacharier, L. B. (2009). Diagnosis and management of asthma in preschool and school age children: Focus on the 2007 NAEPP guidelines. *Current Opinion in Pulmonary Medicine, 15,* 52–56.

Hoskin, J., & Herman, R. (2001). The communication, speech, and gestures of a group of hearing impaired children. *International Journal of Language and Communication Disorders, 36* (Suppl.), 206–209.

Hotelling, B. A. (2009). Teaching normal birth, normally. *Journal of Perinatal Education, 18,* 51–55.

Houde, O., & others. (2011, in press). Functional magnetic resonance imaging study of Piaget's conservation-of-number task in preschool and school-age children: A neo-Piagetian approach. *Journal of Experimental Child Psychology.*

House, L. D., Mueller, T., Reininger, B., Brown, K., & Markham, C. M. (2010). Character as a predictor of reproductive health outcomes for youth: A systematic review. *Journal of Adolescent Health, 46* (Suppl. 1), S59–S74.

Howard, K., & others. (2011, in press). Biological and environmental factors as predictors of language skills in very preterm children at 5 years of age. *Journal of Developmental and Behavioral Pediatrics.*

Howe, A., & Richards, V. (2011). *Bridging the transition from primary to secondary school.* New York: Routledge.

Howe, L. D., Huttly, S. R., & Abramsky, T. (2006). Risk factors for injuries in young children in four developing countries: The Young Lives Study. *Tropic Medicine and International Health, 11,* 1557–1566.

Howe, M. J. A., Davidson, J. W., Moore, D. G., & Sloboda, J. A. (1995). Are there early childhood signs of musical ability? *Psychology of Music, 23,* 162–176.

Howe, N., Ross, H. S., & Recchia, H. (2011). Sibling relations in early and middle childhood. In P. K. Smith & C. H. Hart (Eds.), *Wiley-Blackwell handbook of childhood social development* (2nd ed.). New York: Wiley.

Howes, C. (2009). Friendship in early childhood. In K. H. Rubin, W. M. Bukowski, & B. Laursen (Eds.), *Handbook of peer interactions, relationships, and groups.* New York: Guilford.

Howlin, P., Magiati, I., & Charman, T. (2009). Systematic review of early intensive behavioral interventions with autism. *American Journal on Intellectual and Developmental Disabilities, 114,* 23–41.

Hrabosky, J. I., Masheb, R. M., White, M. A., & Grilo, C. M. (2007). Overvaluation of shape and weight in binge eating disorder. *Journal of Consulting and Clinical Psychology, 75,* 175–180.

Hsu, H-C. (2004). Antecedents and consequences of separation anxiety in first-time mothers: Infant, mother, and social-contextual characteristics. *Infant Behavior & Development, 27,* 113–133.

Hu, H., & others. (2007). Fetal lead exposure at each stage of pregnancy as a predictor of infant mental development. *Environmental Health Perspectives, 114,* 1730–1735.

Huang, L. N. (1989). Southeast Asian refugee children and adolescents. In J. T. Gibbs & L. N. Huang (Eds.), *Children of color.* San Francisco: Jossey-Bass.

Huesmann, L. R., Dubow, E. F., Eron, L. D., & Boxer, P. (2006). Middle childhood family-contextual and personal factors as predictors of adult outcomes. In A. C. Huston & M. N. Ripke (Eds.), *Developmental contexts in middle childhood: Bridges to adolescence and adulthood.* New York: Cambridge University Press.

Huizink, A. C., & Mulder, E. J. (2006). Maternal smoking, drinking, or cannabis use during pregnancy and neurobehavioral and cognitive functioning in human offspring. *Neuroscience and Biobehavioral Research, 30,* 24–41.

Hulit, L. M., Howard, M. R., & Fahey, K. R. (2011). *Born to talk: An introduction to speech and language development* (5th ed.). Boston: Allyn & Bacon.

Hunter, L. P. (2009). A descriptive study of "being with woman" during labor and birth. *Journal of Midwifery and Women's Health, 54,* 111–118.

Hunter, L. P., Rychnovsky, J. D., & Yount, S. M. (2009). A selective review of maternal sleep characteristics in the postpartum period. *Journal of Obstetric, Gynecologic, and Neonatal Nursing, 38*(1), 60–68.

Hurt, H., Brodsky, N. L., Roth, H., Malmud, F., & Giannetta, J. M. (2005). School performance of children with gestational cocaine exposure. *Neurotoxicology and Teratology, 27,* 203–211.

Huston, A. C., Epps, S. R., Shim, M. S., Duncan, G. J., Crosby, D. A., & Ripke, M. N. (2006). Effects of a poverty intervention program last from middle childhood to adolescence. In A. C. Huston & M. N. Ripke (Eds.), *Developmental contexts of middle childhood: Bridges to adolescence and adulthood.* New York: Cambridge University Press.

Huston, A. C., & Ripke, M. N. (2006). Experiences in middle childhood and children's development: A summary and integration of research. In A. C. Huston & M. N. Ripke (Eds.), *Developmental contexts in middle childhood.* New York: Cambridge University Press.

Hutchinson, D. M., & Rapee, R. M. (2007). Do friends share similar body image and eating problems? The role of social networks and peer influences in early adolescence. *Behavior Research and Therapy, 45,* 1557–1577.

Huttenlocher, J., Haight, W., Bruk, A., Seltzer, M., & Lyons, T. (1991). Early vocabulary growth: Relation to language input and gender. *Developmental Psychology, 27,* 236–248.

Huttenlocher, P. R., & Dabholkar, A. S. (1997). Regional differences in synaptogenesis in human cerebral cortex. *Journal of Comparative Neurology, 37*(2), 167–178.

Hyde, D. C., & Spelke, E. S. (2011). Neural signatures of number processing in human infants: Evidence for two core systems underlying numerical cognition. *Developmental Science, 14,* 360–371.

Hyde, J. S. (2007a). *Half the human experience* (7th ed.). Boston: Houghton Mifflin.

Hyde, J. S. (2007b). New directions in the study of gender similarities and differences. *Current Directions in Psychological Science, 16,* 259–263.

Hyde, J. S. (2009). The gender similarities hypothesis. *American Psychologist, 60,* 581–592.

Hyde, J. S., & DeLamater, J. D. (2011). *Human sexuality* (11th ed.). New York: McGraw-Hill.

Hyde, J. S., Lindberg, S. M., Linn, M. C., Ellis, A. B., & Williams, C. C. (2008). Gender similarities characterize math performance. *Science, 321,* 494–495.

Hymel, S., Closson, L. M., Caravita, C. S., & Vaillancourt, T. (2011). Social status among peers: From sociometric attraction to peer acceptance to perceived popularity. In P. K. Smith & C. H. Hart (Eds.), *Wiley-Blackwell handbook of childhood social development* (2nd ed.). New York: Wiley.

Hyson, M. C., Copple, C., & Jones, J. (2006). Early childhood development and education. In W. Damon & R. Lerner (Eds.), *Handbook of child psychology* (6th ed.). New York: Wiley.

I

"I Have a Dream" Foundation. (2011). About us. Retrieved April 22, 2011, from http://www.ihad.org

Ickovics, J. R., & others. (2011). Effects of group prenatal care on psychosocial risk in pregnancy: Results from a randomized controlled trial. *Psychology and Health, 26,* 235–250.

Ige, F., & Shelton, D. (2004). Reducing the risk of sudden infant death syndrome (SIDS) in African-American communities. *Journal of Pediatric Nursing, 19,* 290–292.

Imdad, A., Sadig, K., & Bhutta, Z. A. (2011, in press). Evidence-based prevention of childhood malnutrition. *Current Opinion in Clinical Nutrition and Metabolic Care.*

Inan, M. Z., Trundle, H. Z., & Kantor, R. (2010). Understanding natural sciences education in a Reggio Emilia–inspired preschool. *Journal of Research in Science Teaching, 47,* 1186–1208.

Ingul, C. B., Tjonna, A. E., Stolen, T. O., Stoylen, A., & Wisloff, U. (2010). Impaired cardiac function among obese adolescents: Effect of aerobic interval training. *Archives of Pediatric and Adolescent Medicine, 164,* 852–859.

Innis, S. M. (2011). Metabolic programming of long-term outcomes due to fatty acid nutrition in early life. *Maternal and Child Nutrition, 7* (Suppl. 2), S112–S123.

Insel, P. N., & Roth, W. T. (2012). *Connect core concepts in health* (12th ed.). New York: McGraw-Hill.

International Montessori Council. (2006). Larry Page and Sergey Brin, founders of Google.com, credit their Montessori education for much of their success on prime-time television. Retrieved June 24, 2006, from http://www.Montessori.org/enews/Barbara_walters.html

Ip, S., Chung, M., Raman, G., Trikaliinos, T. A., & Lau, J. (2009). A summary of the Agency for Healthcare Research and Quality's evidence report on breastfeeding in developed countries. *Breastfeeding Medicine, 4* (Suppl. 1), S17–S30.

Isen, J. D., Bakeer, L. A., Raine, A., & Bezdjian, S. (2009). Genetic and environmental influences on the Junior Temperament and

Character Inventory in a preadolescent twin sample. *Behavior Genetics, 39,* 36–47.

Ishaque, S., & others. (2011). Effectiveness of interventions to screen and manage infections during pregnancy on reducing stillbirths: A review. *BMC Public Health, 11,* (Suppl. 3), S3.

Issel, L. M., & others. (2011, in press). A review of prenatal home-visiting effectiveness for improving birth outcomes. *Journal of Obstetric, Gynecologic, and Neonatal Nursing.*

Izard, C. E. (2009). Emotion theory and research: Highlights, unanswered questions, and emerging issues. *Annual Review of Psychology* (Vol. 60). Palo Alto, CA: Annual Reviews.

J

Jackson, A., & Davis, G. (2000). *Turning points 2000.* New York: Teachers College Press.

Jackson, L., & Pyeritz, R. E. (2011, in press). Molecular technologies open new clinical genetic vistas. *Science Translational Medicine.*

Jackson, S. L. (2011). *Research methods* (2nd ed.). Boston: Cengage.

Jacobson, J. L., & Jacobson, S. W. (2002). Association of prenatal exposure to an environmental contaminant with intellectual function in childhood. *Journal of Toxicology—Clinical Toxicology, 40,* 467–475.

Jacobson, J. L., & Jacobson, S. W. (2003). Prenatal exposure to polychlorinated biphenyls and attention at school age. *Journal of Pediatrics, 143,* 780–788.

Jacobson, J. L., Jacobson, S. W., Fein, G. G., Schwartz, P. M., & Dowler, J. (1984). Prenatal exposure to an environmental toxin: A test of the multiple-effects model. *Developmental Psychology, 20,* 523–532.

Jacobson, L. A., & others. (2011, in press). Working memory influences processing speed and reading fluency in ADHD. *Child Neuropsychology.*

Jaddoe, V. W., & others. (2008). Active and passive smoking during pregnancy and the risks of low birth weight and preterm birth: The Generation R Study. *Pediatric and Perinatal Epidemiology, 22,* 162–171.

Jaeggi, S. M., Berman, M. G., & Jonides, J. (2009). Training attentional processes. *Trends in Cognitive Science, 37,* 644–654.

Jaffee, S., & Hyde, J. S. (2000). Gender differences in moral orientation: A meta-analysis. *Psychological Bulletin, 126,* 703–726.

Jago, R., Frobert, K., Cooper, A. R., Eiberg, S., & Anderson, L. B. (2010). Three-year changes in fitness and adiposity are independently associated with cardiovascular risk factors among young Danish children. *Journal of Physical Activity and Health, 7,* 37–44.

Jalongo, M. R. (2011). *Early childhood language arts* (5th ed.). Boston: Allyn & Bacon.

James, A. H., Brancazio, L. R., & Price, T. (2008). Aspirin and reproductive outcomes. *Obstetrical and Gynecological Survey, 63,* 49–57.

James, D. C., & Dobson, B. (2005). Position of the American Dietetic Association: Promoting

and supporting breastfeeding. *Journal of the American Dietetic Association, 105,* 810–818.

James, J., Thomas, P., Cavan, D., & Kerr, D. (2004). Preventing childhood obesity by reducing consumption of carbonated drinks: Cluster randomized trial. *British Medical Journal, 328,* 1237.

James, W. (1890/1950). *The principles of psychology.* New York: Dover.

Jan, J. E., & others. (2010). Long-term sleep disturbances in children: A cause of neuronal loss. *European Journal of Pediatric Neurology, 14*(5), 380–390.

Janssen, I., & others. (2005). Comparison of overweight and obesity prevalence in school-aged youth from 34 countries and their relationships with physical activity and dietary patterns. *Obesity Reviews, 6,* 123–132.

Jarquin, V. G., & others. (2011). Racial disparities in community identification of autism spectrum disorders over time: Metropolitan Atlanta, Georgia, 2000–2006. *Journal of Developmental and Behavioral Pediatrics, 32,* 179–187.

Jaswal, V. K., & Fernald, A. (2007). Learning to communicate. In A. Slater & M. Lewis (Eds.), *Introduction to infant development* (2nd ed.). New York: Oxford University Press.

Jenik, A. G., & Vain, N. (2010). The pacifier debate. *Early Human Development, 85* (Suppl. 10), S89–S91.

Jenkins, J. M., & Astington, J. W. (1996). Cognitive factors and family structure associated with theory of mind development in young children. *Developmental Psychology, 32,* 70–78.

Jensen, A. R. (2008). Book review. *Intelligence, 36,* 96–97.

Jentarra, G. M., Rice, S. G., Olfers, S., Safen, D., & Narayanan, V. (2011, in press). Evidence for a population variation in TSC1 and TSC2 gene expression. *BMC Medical Genetics.*

Ji, B. T., & others. (1997). Paternal cigarette smoking and the risk of childhood cancer among offspring of nonsmoking mothers. *Journal of the National Cancer Institute, 89,* 235–244.

Jia, R., & Schoppe-Sullivan, S. J. (2011). Relations between coparenting and father involvement in families with preschool-age children. *Developmental Psychology, 47,* 106–118.

Jiao, H., & others. (2011, in press). Genetic association and gene expression analysis identify FGFR1 as a new susceptibility gene for human obesity. *Journal of Clinical Endocrinology and Metabolism.*

Jimerson, S. R. (2009). High school dropout. In D. Carr (Ed.), *Encyclopedia of the life course and human development.* Boston: Gale Cengage.

Johnson, J. S., & Newport, E. L. (1991). Critical period effects on universal properties of language: The status of subjacency in the acquisition of a second language. *Cognition, 39,* 215–258.

Johnson, L., Giordano, P. C., Manning, W. D., & Longmore, M. A. (2011, in press).

Parent-child relations and offending during young adulthood. *Journal of Youth and Adolescence.*

Johnson, M. D. (2012). *Human biology* (6th ed.). Upper Saddle River, NJ: Pearson.

Johnson, M. H. (2011). Developmental neuroscience, psychophysiology, and genetics. In M. H. Bornstein & M. E. Lamb (Eds.), *Developmental science* (6th ed.). New York: Psychology Press.

Johnson, M. H., & de Haan, M. (2011). *Developmental cognitive neuroscience* (3rd ed.). New York: Wiley-Blackwell.

Johnson, M. H., Grossmann, T., & Cohen-Kadosh, K. (2009). Mapping functional brain development: Building a social brain through interactive specialization. *Developmental Psychology, 45,* 151–159.

Johnson, S. (2007). Cognitive and behavioral outcomes following very preterm birth. *Seminars in Fetal and Neonatal Medicine, 12,* 363–373.

Johnson, S. P. (2010). Perceptual completion in infancy. In S. P. Johnson (Ed.), *Neoconstructivism: The new science of cognitive development* (pp. 45–60). New York: Oxford University Press.

Johnson, S. P. (2011). A constructivist view of object perception in infancy. In L. M. Oakes, C. H. Cashon, M. Casasola, & D. H. Rakison (Eds.), *Infant perception and cognition.* New York: Oxford University Press.

Johnson, S. P. (2012a). A constructivist view of object perception in infancy. In L. M. Oakes, C. H. Cashon, M. Casasola, & D. H. Rakison (Eds.), *Early perceptual and cognitive development.* New York: Oxford University Press.

Johnson, S. P. (2012b). *Development of the visual system.* In P. Rakic & J. Rubenstein (Eds.), *Developmental neuroscience—Basic and clinical mechanisms.* New York: Elsevier.

Johnson, S. P. (2012c). Object perception. In P. D. Zelazo (Ed.), *Handbook of developmental psychology.* New York: Oxford University Press.

Johnson, W., & others. (2007). Genetic and environmental influences on the Verbal-Perceptual-Image Rotation (VPR) Model of the Structure of Mental Abilities in the Minnesota Study of Twins Reared Apart. *Intelligence, 35,* 542–562.

John-Steiner, V. (2007). Vygotsky on thinking and speaking. In H. Daniels, J. Wertsch, & M. Cole (Eds.), *The Cambridge companion to Vygotsky.* New York: Cambridge University Press.

Johnston, L. D., O'Malley, P. M., Bachman, J. G., & Schulenberg, J. E. (2011). *Monitoring the Future national results on adolescent drug use: Overview of key findings.* Ann Arbor: Institute for Social Research, University of Michigan.

Johnston, M. (2008, April 30). Commentary in R. Highfield, Harvard's baby brain research lab. Retrieved January 24, 2008, from http://www.telegraph.co.uk/science/science-news/3341166/Harvards-baby-brain-research-lab.html

Jones, D., & others. (2010). The impact of the Fast Track prevention trial on health services utilization by youth at risk for conduct problems. *Pediatrics, 125,* 130–136.

Jones, H. W. (2007). Iatrogenic multiple births: A 2003 checkup. *Fertility and Sterility, 87,* 453–455.

Jones, J. M. (1994). The African American: A duality dilemma? In W. J. Lonner & R. Malpass (Eds.), *Psychology and culture.* Needham Heights, MA: Allyn & Bacon.

Jones, M. C. (1965). Psychological correlates of somatic development. *Child Development, 36,* 899–911.

Jones, M. D., & Galliher, R. V. (2007). Ethnic identity and psychosocial functioning in Navajo adolescents. *Journal of Research on Adolescence, 17,* 683–696.

Joseph, J. (2006). *The missing gene.* New York: Algora.

Josephson Institute of Ethics. (2006). *2006 Josephson Institute report card on the ethics of American youth. Part one—integrity.* Los Angeles: Josephson Institute.

Juffer, F., & van IJzendoorn, M. H. (2005). Behavior problems and mental health referrals of international adoptees: A meta-analysis. *Journal of the American Medical Association, 293,* 2501–2513.

Juffer, F., & van IJzendoorn, M. H. (2007). Adoptees do not lack self-esteem: A meta-analysis of studies on self-esteem of transracial, international, and domestic adoptees. *Psychological Bulletin, 133,* 1067–1083.

Juhl, M., & others. (2008). Physical exercise during pregnancy and the risk of preterm birth: A study within the Danish National Birth Cohort. *American Journal of Epidemiology, 167*(7), 859–866.

Jylhava, J., & others. (2009). Genetics of C-reactive protein and complement factor H have an epistatic effect on carotid artery compliance: The Cardiovascular Risk in Young Finns Study. *Clinical and Experimental Immunology, 155,* 53–58.

K

Kagan, J. (1992). Yesterday's promises, tomorrow's promises. *Developmental Psychology. 28,* 990–997.

Kagan, J. (2000). Temperament. In A. Kazdin (Ed.), *Encyclopedia of psychology.* New York: Oxford University Press.

Kagan, J. (2002). Behavioral inhibition as a temperamental category. In R. J. Davidson, K. R. Scherer, & H. H. Goldsmith (Eds.), *Handbook of affective sciences.* New York: Oxford University Press.

Kagan, J. (2008). Fear and wariness. In M. M. Haith & J. B. Benson (Eds.), *Encyclopedia of infant and early childhood development.* Oxford, UK: Elsevier.

Kagan, J. (2010). Emotions and temperament. In M. H. Bornstein (Ed.), *Handbook of cultural developmental science.* New York: Psychology Press.

Kagan, J., & Snidman, N. (1991). Infant predictors of inhibited and uninhibited behavioral profiles. *Psychological Science, 2,* 40–44.

Kagan, J. J., Kearsley, R. B., & Zelazo, P. R. (1978). *Infancy: Its place in human development.* Cambridge, MA: Harvard University Press.

Kagitcibasi, C. (2007). *Family, self, and human development across cultures.* Mahwah, NJ: Erlbaum.

Kahn, J. A., & others. (2008). Patterns and determinants of physical activity in U.S. adolescents. *Journal of Adolescent Health, 42,* 369–377.

Kail, R. V. (2007). Longitudinal evidence that increases in processing speed and working memory enhance children's reasoning. *Psychological Science, 18,* 312–313.

Kaiser Family Foundation. (2006). *The media family: Electronic media in the lives of infants, toddlers, preschoolers, and their parents.* Menlo Park, CA: Kaiser Family Foundation.

Kalant, H. (2004). Adverse effects of cannabis on health: An update of the literature since 1996. *Progress in Neuropsychopharmacology and Biological Psychiatry, 28,* 849–863.

Kalder, M., Knoblauch, K., Hrgovic, I., & Munstedt, K. (2011). Use of complementary and alternative medicine during pregnancy and delivery. *Archives of Gynecology and Obstetrics, 283,* 475–482.

Kamii, C. (1985). *Young children reinvent arithmetic: Implications of Piaget's theory.* New York: Teachers College Press.

Kamii, C. (1989). *Young children continue to reinvent arithmetic.* New York: Teachers College Press.

Kang, P. P., & Romo, L. F. (2011, in press). The role of religious involvement on depression, risky behavior, and academic performance among Korean American adolescents. *Journal of Adolescence.*

Kanoy, K., Ulku-Steiner, B., Cox, M., & Burchinal, M. (2003). Marital relationship and individual psychological characteristics that predict physical punishment of children. *Journal of Family Psychology, 17,* 20–28.

Kaplan, H. B. (2009). Self-esteem. In D. Carr (Ed.), *Encyclopedia of the life course and human development.* Boston: Gale Cengage.

Kapornai, K., & Vetro, A. (2008). Depression in children. *Current Opinion in Psychiatry, 21,* 1–7.

Karelitz, T. M., Jarvin, L., & Sternberg, R. J. (2010). The meaning of wisdom and its development throughout life. In W. Overton (Ed.), *Handbook of lifespan human development.* New York: Wiley.

Karnes, F. A., & Stephens, K. R. (2008). *Achieving excellence: Educating the gifted and talented.* Upper Saddle River, NJ: Prentice Hall.

Karoly, L. A., & Bigelow, J. H. (2005). *The economics of investing in universal preschool education in California.* Santa Monica, CA: RAND Corporation.

Karpov, Y. V. (2006). *The neo-Vygotskian approach to child development.* New York: Cambridge University Press.

Karreman, A., van Tuijl, C., van Aken, M. A. G., & Dekovic, M. (2008). Parenting, coparenting, and effortful control in preschoolers. *Journal of Family Psychology, 22,* 30–40.

Katz, L. (1999). *Curriculum disputes in early childhood education.* ERIC Clearinghouse on Elementary and Early Childhood Education, Document EDO-PS-99-13.

Katz, P. A. (1987, August). *Children and social issues.* Paper presented at the meeting of the American Psychological Association, New York.

Kauffman Early Education Exchange. (2002). *Set for success: Building a strong foundation for school readiness based on the social-emotional development of young children* (Vol. 1, No. 1). Kansas City: The Ewing Marion Kauffman Foundation.

Kauffman, J. M., & Hallahan, D. P. (2005). *Special education.* Boston: Allyn & Bacon.

Kauffman, J. M., McGee, K,. & Brigham, M. (2004). Enabling or disabling? Observations on changes in special education. *Phi Delta Kappan, 85,* 613–620.

Kavanaugh, R. D. (2006). Pretend play. In B. Spodek & O. N. Saracho (Eds.), *Handbook of research on the education of young children* (2nd ed.). Mahwah, NJ: Erlbaum.

Kavsek, M. (2004). Predicting IQ from infant visual habituation and dishabituation: A meta-analysis. *Journal of Applied Developmental Psychology, 25,* 369–393.

Keating, D. P. (1990). Adolescent thinking. In S. S. Feldman & G. R. Elliott (Eds.), *At the threshold: The developing adolescent.* Cambridge, MA: Harvard University Press.

Keating, D. P. (2004). Cognitive and brain development. In R. Lerner & L. Steinberg (Eds.), *Handbook of adolescent psychology.* New York: Wiley.

Keating, D. P. (2007). Understanding adolescent development: Implications for driving safety. *Journal of Safety Research, 38,* 147–157.

Keating, D. P. (2009). Developmental science and giftedness: An integrated life-span framework. In F. D. Horowitz, R. F. Subotnik, & D. J. Matthews (Eds.), *The development of giftedness and talent across the life span.* Washington, DC: American Psychological Association.

Keen, R. (2005). Unpublished review of J. W. Santrock's *A topical approach to life-span development,* 3rd ed. (New York: McGraw-Hill).

Keen, R. (2011). The development of problem solving in young children: A critical cognitive skill. *Annual Review of Psychology* (Vol. 63). Palo Alto, CA: Annual Reviews.

Keijsers, L., & Laird, R. D. (2010). Introduction to special issue: Careful conversations: Adolescents managing their parents' access to information. *Journal of Adolescence, 33,* 255–259.

Keller, A., Ford, L., & Meacham, J. (1978). Dimensions of self-concept in preschool children. *Developmental Psychology, 14,* 483–489.

Kellman, P. J., & Banks, M. S. (1998). Infant visual perception. In W. Damon (Ed.), *Handbook of child psychology* (5th ed., Vol. 2). New York: Wiley.

Kellogg, R. (1970). *Understanding children's art: Readings in developmental psychology today.* Del Mar, CA: CRM.

Kelly, D. J., & others. (2007). Cross-race preferences for same-race faces extend beyond the African versus Caucasian contrast in 3-month-old infants. *Infancy, 11*, 87–95.

Kelly, D. J., & others. (2009). Development of the other-race effect in infancy: Evidence towards universality? *Journal of Experimental Child Psychology, 104*, 105–114.

Kelly, J. P., Borchert, J., & Teller, D. Y. (1997). The development of chromatic and achromatic sensitivity in infancy as tested with the sweep VEP. *Vision Research, 37*, 2057–2072.

Kelmanson, I. A. (2010). Sleep disturbances in two-month-old infants sharing the bed with parent(s). *Minerva Pediatrica, 62*, 162–169.

Kempster, G. (2011). VOICE: Vocal cord dysfunction in a teenaged athlete. In S. S. Chabon & E. R. Cohn (Eds.), *Communication disorders casebook.* Upper Saddle River, NJ: Pearson.

Kennedy, M. A. (2009). Child abuse. In D. Carr (Ed.), *Encyclopedia of the life course and human development.* Boston: Gale Cengage.

Kennell, J. H. (2006). Randomized controlled trial of skin-to-skin contact from birth versus conventional incubator for physiological stabilization in 1200 g to 2199 g newborns. *Acta Paediatrica, 95*, 15–16.

Kenner, C., Sugrue, N. M., & Finkelman, A. (2007). How nurses around the world can make a difference. *Nursing for women's health, 11*, 468–473.

Kersey, M., Chi, M., & Cutts, D. (2011, in press). Anemia, lead poisoning, and vitamin D deficiency in low-income children: Do current screening recommendations match the burden of the illness? *Public Health Nutrition.*

Kessler, R. C., & Waters, E. E. (1988). Epidemiology of DSM-III-R major depression and minor depression among adolescents and young adults in the National Comorbidity Survey. *Depression and Anxiety, 7*, 3–14.

Khandekar, A. A., Augustyn, M., Sanders, L., & Zuckerman, B. (2011, in press). Improving early literacy promotion: A quality-improvement project for Reach Out and Read. *Pediatrics.*

Khashan, A. S., Baker, P. N., & Kenny, L. C. (2010). Preterm birth and reduced birthweight in first and second teenage pregnancies: A register-based cohort study. *BMC Pregnancy and Childbirth, 10*, 36.

Kim, G., Walden, T. A., & Knieps, L. J. (2010). Impact and characteristics of positive and fearful emotional messages during infant social referencing. *Infant Behavior and Development, 33*, 189–195.

Kim, H. K., & others. (2011). Cardiovascular anomalies in Turner syndrome: Spectrum, prevalence, and cardiac MRI findings in a pediatric and young adult population. *American Journal of Roentgenology, 196*, 454–460.

Kim, J., & others. (2006). Trends in overweight from 1980 through 2001 among preschool-aged children enrolled in a health maintenance organization. *Obesity, 14*, 1107–1112.

Kim, K. H. (2010, May). Unpublished data. School of Education, College of William & Mary, Williamsburg, VA.

King, L., & Kepner, A. (2008). States getting serious about pre-K programs. Retrieved October 24, 2008, from http://www.delawareonline.com/apps/pbcs.dll/article?Date=20080103&Category=NEWS...

King, P. E., Carr, A., & Boiter, C. (2011, in press). Spirituality, religiosity, and youth thriving. In R. M. Lerner, J. V. Lerner, & J. B. Benson (Eds.), *Advances in child development and behavior: Positive youth development.* New York: Elsevier.

King, P. E., Ramos, J. S., & Clardy, C. E. (2012, in press). Searching for the sacred: Religious and spiritual development among adolescents. In K. I. Pargament, J. Exline, & J. Jones (Eds.), *APA handbook of psychology, religion, and spirituality.* Washington, DC: American Psychological Association.

King, P. E., & Roeser, R. W. (2009). Religion and spirituality in adolescent development. In R. M. Lerner & L. Steinberg (Eds.), *Handbook of adolescent psychology* (3rd ed.). New York: Wiley.

Kinney, J. (2012). *Loosening the grip: A handbook of alcohol information* (10th ed.). New York: McGraw-Hill.

Kinzler, K. D., Dupoux, E., & Spelke, E. S. (2011, in press). "Native" objects and collaborators: Infants' object choices and acts of giving reflect favor for native over foreign speakers. *Journal of Cognition and Development.*

Kirk, S. A., Gallagher, J. J., Coleman, M. R., & Anastaslow, N. J. (2012). *Educating exceptional children* (13th ed.). Boston: Cengage.

Kisilevsky, B. S., & others. (2009). Fetal sensitivity to properties of maternal speech and language. *Infant Behavior and Development, 32*, 59–71.

Kitayama, S. (2011). Psychology and culture: Cross-country or regional comparisons. *Annual Review of Psychology* (Vol. 62). Palo Alto, CA: Annual Reviews.

Kitsantas, P., & Gaffney, K. F. (2010). Racial/ethnic disparities in infant mortality. *Journal of Perinatal Medicine, 38*, 87–94.

Kitzinger, S. (2011). Human rights and midwifery. *Birth, 38*, 86–87.

Klaczynski, P. (2001). The influence of analytic and heuristic processing on adolescent reasoning and decision making. *Child Development, 72*, 844–861.

Klaczynski, P. A., & Narasimham, G. (1998). Development of scientific reasoning biases: Cognitive versus ego-protective explanations. *Developmental Psychology, 34*, 175–187.

Klahr, A. M., & others. (2011). The relationship between parent-child conflict and adolescent antisocial development: Confirming shared environment mediation. *Journal of Abnormal Psychology, 120*, 46–56.

Klaus, M., & Kennell, H. H. (1976). *Maternal-infant bonding.* St. Louis: Mosby.

Kliegman, R., Stanton, B., St. Geme, J., Schor, N., & Behrman, R. (2011). *Nelson textbook of pediatrics* (20th ed.). New York: Elsevier.

Klima, C., Norr, K., Conderheld, S., & Handler, A. (2009) Introduction of Centering Pregnancy in a public health clinic. *Journal of Midwifery and Women's Health, 54*, 27–34.

Klimstra, T. A., Hale, W. W., Raaijmakers, Q. A. W., Branje, S. J. T., & Meeus, W. H. H. (2010). Identity formation in adolescence: Change or stability? *Journal of Youth and Adolescence, 39*, 150–162.

Klingenberg, C. P., & others. (2010). Prenatal alcohol exposure alters the patterns of facial asymmetry. *Alcohol, 44*, 649–657.

Klomek, A. B., Marrocco, F., Kleinman, M., Schonfeld, I. S., & Gould, M. S. (2008). Peer victimization, depression, and suicidality in adolescents. *Suicide and Life Threatening Behavior, 38*, 166–180.

Knafo, A., Israel, S., & Ebstein, R. P. (2011). Heritability of children's prosocial behavior and differential susceptibility to parenting by variation in the dopamine receptor D4 gene. *Development and Psychopathology, 23*, 53–67.

Knoll, S., Bulik, C. M., & Hebebrand, J. (2011, in press). Do the currently proposed DSM-5 criteria for anorexia nervosa adequately consider developmental aspects of children and adolescents? *European Child and Adolescent Psychiatry.*

Knopik, V. S. (2009). Maternal smoking during pregnancy and child outcomes: Real or spurious effect? *Developmental Neuropsychology, 34*, 1–36.

Knox, M. (2010). On hitting children: A review of corporal punishment in the United States. *Journal of Pediatric Health Care, 24*, 103–107.

Ko, L. K., & Perreira, K. M. (2010). "It turned my world upside down": Latino youths' perspectives on immigration. *Journal of Adolescent Research, 25*, 465–493.

Kobayashi, K., Tajima, M., Toishi, S., Fujimori, K., Suzuki, Y., & Udagama, H. (2005). Fetal growth restriction associated with measles virus infection during pregnancy. *Journal of Perinatal Medicine, 31*, 67–68.

Kochanska, G., & Aksan, N. (2007). Conscience in childhood: Past, present, and future. *Merrill-Palmer Quarterly, 50*, 299–310.

Kochanska, G., Barry, R. A., Stellern, S. A., & O'Bleness, J. J. (2010). Early attachment organization moderates the parent-child mutually coercive pathway to children's antisocial conduct. *Child Development, 80*, 1288–1300.

Koenig, L. B., McGue, M., & Iacono, W. G. (2008). Stability and change in religiousness during emerging adulthood. *Developmental Psychology, 44*, 523–543.

Kohen, D. E., Leventhal, T., Dahinten, V. S., & McIntosh, C. N. (2008). Neighborhood disadvantage: Pathways of effects for young children. *Child Development, 79*, 156–169.

Kohlberg, L. (1958). *The development of modes of moral thinking and choice in the years 10 to 16.* Unpublished doctoral dissertation, University of Chicago.

Kohlberg, L. (1969). Stage and sequence: The cognitive-developmental approach to socialization. In D. A. Goslin (Ed.), *Handbook of socialization theory and research.* Chicago: Rand McNally.

Kohlberg, L. (1986). A current statement of some theoretical issues. In S. Modgil & C. Modgil (Eds.), *Lawrence Kohlberg*. Philadelphia: Falmer.

Konig, I. R., & others. (2011, in press). Mapping for dyslexia and related cognitive trait loci provides strong evidence for further risk genes on chromosome 6p21. *American Journal of Medical Genetics B: Neuropsychiatric Genetics.*

Koolhof, R., Loeber, R., Wei, E. H., Pardini, D., & D'Escury, A. C. (2007). Inhibition deficits of serious delinquent boys of low intelligence. *Criminal Behavior and Mental Health, 17,* 274–292.

Kopp, C. B. (2008). Self-regulatory processes. In M. M. Haith & J. B. Benson (Eds.), *Encyclopedia of infant and early childhood development*. Oxford, UK: Elsevier.

Kopp, F., & Lindenberger, U. (2011, in press). Effects of joint attention on long-term memory in 9-month-old infants: An event-related potentials study. *Developmental Science.*

Koppelman, K., & Goodhart, L. (2011). *Understanding human differences* (3rd ed.). Boston: Allyn & Bacon.

Korat, O. (2009). The effect of maternal teaching talk on children's emergent literacy as a function of type of activity and maternal education level. *Journal of Applied Developmental Psychology, 30,* 34–42.

Kornblum, J. (2006, March 9). How to monitor the kids? *USA Today,* 1D, p.1.

Koss, K. J., & others. (2011). Understanding children's emotional processes and behavioral strategies in the context of marital conflict. *Journal of Experimental Child Psychology, 109,* 336–352.

Kostelnik, M. J., Soderman, A. K., & Whiren, A. P. (2011). *Developmentally appropriate curricula* (5th ed.). Upper Saddle River, NJ: Merrill.

Kostovic, I., Judas, M., & Sedmark, G. (2011). Developmental history of the subplate zone, subplate neurons, and interstitial white matter neurons: Relevance for schizophrenia. *International Journal of Developmental Neuroscience.*

Kotovsky, L., & Baillargeon, R. (1994). Calibration-based reasoning about collision events in 11-month-old infants. *Cognition, 51,* 107–129.

Kottak, C. P. (2004). *Cultural anthropology* (10th ed.). New York: McGraw-Hill.

Kottak, C. P., & Kozaitis, K. A. (2012). *On being different* (4th ed.) New York: McGraw-Hill.

Koulouglioti, C., Cole, R., & Kitzman, H. (2008). Inadequate sleep and unintentional injuries in young children. *Public Health Nursing, 25,* 106–114.

Kovar, S. K., Combs, C. A., Campbell, K., Napper-Owen, G., & Worrell, V. J. (2007). *Elementary classroom teachers as movement educators* (2nd ed.). New York: McGraw-Hill.

Kozol, J. (2005). *The shame of the nation.* New York: Crown.

Kraft, J., & Freiman, A. (2011). Management of acne. *Canadian Medical Association Journal, 183,* E430–E435.

Kramer, L. (2006, July 10). Commentary in "How your siblings make you who you are" by J. Kluger. *Time,* pp. 46–55.

Kramer, L., & Perozynski, L. (1999). Parental beliefs about managing sibling conflict. *Developmental Psychology, 35,* 489–499.

Kramer, L., & Radey, C. (1997). Improving sibling relationships among young children: A social skills training model. *Family Relations, 46,* 237–246.

Kranz, S., & Siega-Riz, A. M. (2002). Sociodemographic determinants of added sugar intake in preschoolers 2 to 5 years old. *Journal of Pediatrics, 140,* 667–672.

Kranz, S., Lin, P. J., & Wagstaff, D. A. (2007). Children's dairy intake in the United States: Too little, too fat? *Journal of Pediatrics, 151,* 642–646.

Kreutzer, M., Leonard, C., & Flavell, J. H. (1975). An interview study of children's knowledge about memory. *Monographs of the Society for Research in Child Development, 40* (1, Serial No. 159).

Kriemler, S., & others. (2010). Effect of school-based physical activity programme (KISS) on fitness and adiposity in primary schoolchildren: Cluster randomised controlled trial. *British Medical Journal, 340.*

Krimer, L. S., & Goldman-Rakic, P. S. (2001). Prefrontal microcircuits. *Journal of Neuroscience, 21,* 3788–3796.

Kring, A. M. (2000). Gender and anger. In A. H. Fischer (Ed.), *Gender and emotion*. New York: Cambridge University Press.

Kroger, J., Martinussen, M., & Marcia, J. E. (2010). Identity change during adolescence and young adulthood: A meta-analysis. *Journal of Adolescence, 33,* 683–698.

Krueger, J. I., Vohs, K. D., & Baumeister, R. F. (2008). Is the allure of self-esteem a mirage after all? *American Psychologist, 63,* 64.

Kucian, K., & others. (2011, in press). Mental number line training in children with developmental dyscalculia. *NeuroImage.*

Kuebli, J. (1994, March). Young children's understanding of everyday emotions. *Young Children,* pp. 36–48.

Kuehn, B. M. (2011). Scientists find promising therapies for fragile X and Down syndromes. *Journal of the American Medical Association, 305,* 344–346.

Kuhl, P. K. (1993). Infant speech perception: A window on psycholinguistic development. *International Journal of Psycholinguistics, 9,* 33–56.

Kuhl, P. K. (2000). A new view of language acquisition. *Proceedings of the National Academy of Science, 97*(22), 11850–11857.

Kuhl, P. K. (2007). Is speech learning "gated" by the social brain? *Developmental Science, 10,* 110–120.

Kuhl, P. K. (2009). Linking infant speech perception to language acquisition: Phonetic learning predicts language growth. In J. Colombo, P. McCardle, & L. Freund (Eds.), *Infant pathways to language*. Clifton, NJ: Psychology Press.

Kuhl, P. K. (2011, in press). Social mechanisms in early language acquisition: Understanding integrated brain systems and supporting language. In J. Decety & J. Cacioppo (Eds.), *Handbook of social neuroscience*. New York: Oxford University Press.

Kuhl, P. K., & Damasio, A. (2011, in press). Language. In E. R. Kandel, J. H. Schwartz, T. M. Jessell, S. Siegelbaum, & J. Hudspeth (Eds.), *Principles of neural science* (5th ed.). New York: McGraw-Hill.

Kuhn, D. (1998). Afterword to Volume 2: Cognition, perception, and language. In W. Damon (Ed.), *Handbook of child psychology* (5th ed., Vol. 2). New York: Wiley.

Kuhn, D. (1999). Metacognitive development. In L. Balter & S. Tamis-Lemonda (Eds.), *Child psychology: A handbook of contemporary issues*. Philadelphia: Psychology Press.

Kuhn, D. (2009). Adolescent thinking. In R. M. Lerner & L. Steinberg (Eds.), *Handbook of adolescent psychology* (3rd ed.). New York: Wiley.

Kuhn, D. (2011). What is scientific thinking and how does it develop? In U. Goswami (Ed.), *Wiley-Blackwell handbook of childhood cognitive development* (2nd ed.). New York: Wiley.

Kuhn, D., Cheney, R., & Weinstock, M. (2000). The development of epistemological understanding. *Cognitive Development, 15,* 309–328.

Kuhn, D., & Franklin, S. (2006). The second decade: What develops (and how)? In W. Damon & R. Lerner (Eds.), *Handbook of child psychology* (6th ed.). New York: Wiley.

Kuhn, D., Schauble, L., & Garcia-Mila, M. (1992). Cross-domain development of scientific reasoning. *Cognition and Instruction, 9,* 285–327.

Kupersmidt, J. B., & Coie, J. D. (1990). Preadolescent peer status, aggression, and school adjustment as predictors of externalizing problems in adolescence. *Child Development, 61,* 1350–1363.

Kurth, S., Jenni, O. G., Riedner, B. A., Tononi, G., Carskadon, M. A., & Huber, R. (2010). Characteristics of sleep slow waves in children and adolescents. *Sleep, 33,* 475–480.

L

Ladd, G., Buhs, E., & Troop, W. (2004). School adjustment and social skills training. In P. K. Smith & C. H. Hart (Eds.), *Blackwell handbook of childhood social development*. Malden, MA: Blackwell.

Ladd, G. W., Kochenderfer-Ladd, B., & Rydell, A-M. (2011). Children's interpersonal skills and school-based relationships. In P. K. Smith & C. H. Hart (Eds.), *Wiley-Blackwell handbook of social development* (2nd ed.). New York: Wiley.

LaFrance, M., Hecht, M. A., & Paluck, E. L. (2003). The contingent smile: A meta-analysis of sex differences in smiling. *Psychological Bulletin, 129,* 305–334.

Lahey, B. B., & others. (2011). Interactions between early parenting and a polymorphism of the child's dopamine transporter genes in predicting future child conduct disorder symptoms. *Journal of Abnormal Psychology, 120,* 33–45.

Lahey, B. B., Van Hulle, C. A., D'Onofrio, B. M., Rodgers, J. L., & Waldman, I. D. (2008). Is parental knowledge of their offspring's whereabouts and peer associations spuriously associated with offspring delinquency? *Journal of Abnormal Child Psychology, 36,* 807–823.

Laible, D. J., & Thompson, R. A. (2007). Early socialization: A relationship perspective. In J. E. Grusec & P. D. Hastings (Eds.), *Handbook of socialization.* New York: Guilford.

Laird, R. D., Criss, M. M., Pettit, G. S., Dodge, K. A., & Bates, J. E. (2008). Parents' monitoring knowledge attenuates the link between antisocial friends and adolescent delinquent behavior. *Journal of Abnormal Child Psychology, 36,* 299–310.

Laird, R. D., & Marrero, M. D. (2010). Information management and behavior problems: Is concealing misbehavior necessarily a sign of trouble? *Journal of Adolescence, 33,* 297–308.

Lamb, M. E. (1994). Infant care practices and the application of knowledge. In C. B. Fisher & R. M. Lerner (Eds.), *Applied developmental psychology.* New York: McGraw-Hill.

Lamb, M. E. (2010). How do fathers influence children's development? In M. E. Lamb (Ed.), *The role of the father in child development* (5th ed.). New York: Wiley.

Lamb, M. E., Bornstein, M. H., & Teti, D. M. (2002). *Development in infancy* (4th ed.). Mahwah, NJ: Erlbaum.

Lamb, M. E., & Sternberg, K. J. (1992). Sociocultural perspectives in nonparental childcare. In M. E. Lamb, K. J. Sternberg, C. Hwang, & A. G. Broberg (Eds.), *Child care in context.* Hillsdale, NJ: Erlbaum.

Landale, N. S., Thomas, K. J., & Van Hook, J. (2011). The living arrangements of children of immigrants. *Future of Children, 21,* 43–70.

Landau, B., Smith, L., & Jones, S. (1998). Object perception and object naming in early development. *Trends in Cognitive Science, 2,* 19–24.

Landor, A., Simons, L. G., Simons, R. L., Brody, G. H., & Gibbons, F. X. (2010, in press). The role of religiosity in the relationship between parents, peers, and adolescent risky sexual behavior. *Journal of Youth and Adolescence, 40*(3), 296–309.

Lane, H. (1976). *The wild boy of Aveyron.* Cambridge, MA: Harvard University Press.

Langer, E. J. (2005). *On becoming an artist.* New York: Ballantine.

Langston, W. (2011). *Research methods laboratory manual for psychology* (3rd ed.). Boston: Cengage.

Lansford, J. E. (2009). Parental divorce and children's adjustment. *Perspectives on Psychological Science, 4,* 140–152.

Lansford, J. E., Yu, T., Erath, S. A., Pettit, G. S., Bates, J. E., & Dodge, K. A. (2010). Developmental precursors of number of sexual partners from ages 16 to 22. *Journal of Research on Adolescence, 20,* 651–677.

Lapsley, D. K., & Hill, P. L. (2010). Subjective invulnerability, optimism bias, and adjustment in emerging adulthood. *Journal of Youth and Adolescence, 39,* 847–857.

Larson, R., & Angus, R. (2011, in press). Pursuing paradox: The role of adults in creating empowering settings for youth. Prepared for M. Aber, K. Maton, & E. Seidman (Eds.), *Empowerment settings and voices for social change.* New York: Oxford.

Larson, R., & Richards, M. H. (1994). *Divergent realities.* New York: Basic Books.

Larson, R. W. (2001). How U.S. children and adolescents spend their time: What it does (and doesn't) tell us about their development. *Current Directions in Psychological Science, 10,* 160–164.

Larson, R. W. (2011). Positive development in a disorderly world. *Journal of Research on Adolescence, 21,* 317–334.

Larson, R. W., & Angus, R. M. (2011, in press). Adolescents' development of skills for agency in youth programs: Learning to think strategically. *Child Development.*

Larson, R. W., & Lampman-Petraitis, C. (1989). Daily emotional states as reported by children and adolescents. *Child Development, 60,* 1250–1260.

Larson, R. W., Rickman, A. N., Gibbons, C. M. & Walker, K. C. (2011, in press). Practitioner expertise: Creating quality within the daily tumble of events in youth settings. *New Directions in Youth Development.*

Larson, R. W., & Verma, S. (1999). How children and adolescents spend time across the world: Work, play, and developmental opportunities. *Psychological Bulletin, 125,* 701–736.

Larson, R. W., & Walker, K. C. (2010). Dilemmas of practice: Challenges to program quality encountered by youth program leaders. *American Journal of Community Psychology, 45,* 338–349.

Larson, R. W., & Wilson, S. (2004). Adolescence across place and time: Globalization and the changing pathways to adulthood. In R. Lerner & L. Steinberg (Eds.), *Handbook of Adolescent Psychology.* New York: Wiley.

Larzelere, R. E., & Kuhn, B. R. (2005). Comparing child outcomes of physical punishment and alternative disciplinary tactics: A meta-analysis. *Clinical Child and Family Psychology Review, 8,* 1–37.

Laubjerg, M., & Petersson, B. (2011). Juvenile delinquency and psychiatric contact among adoptees compared to non-adoptees in Denmark: A nationwide register-based comparative study. *Nordic Journal of Psychiatry, 65*(5), 365–372.

Laus, M. F., Vales, L. D., Costa, T. M., & Almeida, S. S. (2011). Early postnatal protein-calorie malnutrition and cognition: A review of human and animal studies. *International Journal of Environmental Research and Public Health, 8,* 590–612.

Leadbeater, B. J., & Way, N. (2001). *Growing up fast.* Mahwah, NJ: Erlbaum.

Leaper, C., & Bigler, R. S. (2011). Gender. In M. H. Underwood & L. H. Rosen (Eds.), *Social development.* New York: Guilford.

Leaper, C., & Friedman, C. K. (2007). The socialization of gender. In J. E. Grusec & P. D. Hastings (Eds.), *Handbook of socialization.* New York: Guilford.

Leaper, C., & Smith, T. E. (2004). A meta-analytic review of gender variations in children's language use: Talkativeness, affiliative speech, and assertive speech. *Developmental Psychology, 40,* 993–1027.

Leatherdale, S. T. (2010). Factors associated with communication-based sedentary behaviors among youth: Are talking on the phone, texting, and instant messaging new sedentary behaviors to be concerned about? *Journal of Adolescent Health, 47,* 315–318.

Lee, E., Mitchell-Herzfeld, S. D., Lowenfels, A. A., Greene, R., Dorabawila, V., & DuMont, K. A. (2009). Reducing low birth weight through home visitation: A randomized controlled trial. *American Journal of Preventive Medicine, 36,* 154–160.

Lee, J. M., & Howell, J. D. (2006). Tall girls: The social shaping of a medical therapy. *Archives of Pediatric and Adolescent Medicine, 160,* 1035–1059.

Lee, K., Cameron, C. A., Doucette, J., & Talwar, V. (2002). Phantoms and fabrications: Young children's detection of implausible lies. *Child Development, 73,* 1688–1702.

Lee, K., Quinn, P. C., Pascalis, O., & Slater, A. (2011, in press). Development of face processing ability in childhood. In P. D. Zelazo (Ed.), *Oxford handbook of developmental psychology.* Oxford, UK: Oxford University Press.

Lee, K. Y., & others. (2011). Effects of combined radiofrequency radiation exposure on the cell cycle and its regulatory proteins. *Bioelectromagnetics, 32,* 169–178.

Leedy, P. D., & Ormrod, J. E. (2010). *Practical research* (9th ed.). Upper Saddle River, NJ: Prentice Hall.

Leerkes, E. M., Parade, S. H., & Gudmundson, J. A. (2011, in press). Mothers' emotional reactions to crying pose risk for subsequent attachment insecurity. *Journal of Family Psychology.*

Legerstee, M. (1997). Contingency effects of people and objects on subsequent cognitive functioning in 3-month-old infants. *Social Development, 6,* 307–321.

Lehr, C. A., Hanson, A., Sinclair, M. F., & Christensen, S. I. (2003). Moving beyond dropout prevention towards school completion. *School Psychology Review, 32,* 342–364.

Lehrer, R., & Schauble, L. (2006). Scientific thinking and scientific literacy. In W. Damon & R. Lerner (Eds.), *Handbook of child psychology* (6th ed.). New York: Wiley.

Leifer, A. D. (1973). *Television and the development of social behavior.* Paper presented at the meeting of the International Society for the

Study of Behavioral Development, Ann Arbor, Michigan.

Lempers, J. D., Flavell, E. R., & Flavell, J. H. (1977). The development in very young children of tacit knowledge concerning visual perception. *Genetic Psychology Monographs, 95,* 3–53.

Lenhart, A., Purcel, K., Smith, A., & Zickuhr, K. (2010, February 3). *Social media and mobile Internet use among teens and young adults.* Washington, DC: Pew Research Center.

Lennon, E. M., Gardner, J. M., Karmel, B. Z., & Flory, M. J. (2008). Bayley Scales of Infant Development. In M. M. Haith & J. B. Benson (Eds.), *Encyclopedia of infant and early childhood development.* Oxford, UK: Elsevier.

Lenoir, C. P., Mallet, E, & Calenda, E. (2000). Siblings of sudden infant death syndrome and near miss in about 30 families: Is there a genetic link? *Medical Hypotheses, 54,* 408–411.

Lenroot, R. K., & Giedd, J. N. (2006). Brain development in children and adolescents: Insights from anatomical magnetic resonance imaging. *Neuroscience and Biobehavioral Reviews, 30,* 718–729.

Lenroot, R. K., & Giedd, J. N. (2011). Annual research review: Developmental considerations of gene by environment interactions. *Journal of Child Psychology and Psychiatry, 52,* 429–441.

Leonardi-Bee, J. A., Smyth, A. R., Britton, J., & Coleman, T. (2008). Environmental tobacco smoke and fetal health: Systematic review and analysis. *Archives of Disease in Childhood: Fetal and Neonatal Edition, 93,* F351–F361.

Leon-Guerrero, A. (2009). *Social problems* (2nd ed.). Thousand Oaks, CA: Sage.

Leppanen, J. M., Moulson, M., Vogel-Farley, V. K., & Nelson, C. A. (2007). An ERP study of emotional face processing in the adult and infant brain. *Child Development, 78,* 232–245.

Lerch, C., Cordes, M., & Baumeister, J. (2011). Effectiveness of prevention programs in female youth soccer: A systematic review. *British Journal of Sports Medicine, 45,* 359.

Lerner, J. W., & Johns, B. (2012). *Learning disabilities and related mild disabilities* (12th ed.). Boston: Cengage.

Lerner, R. M., Boyd, M., & Du, D. (2008). Adolescent development. In I. B. Weiner & C. B. Craighead (Eds.), *Encyclopedia of psychology* (4th ed.). New York: Wiley.

Lesaux, N. K., & Siegel, L. S. (2003). The development of reading in children who speak English as a second language. *Developmental Psychology, 39,* 1005–1019.

Lesley, C. (2005). *Burning fence: A Western memoir of fatherhood.* New York: St. Martin's Press.

Lester, B. M., Tronick, E. Z., & Brazelton, T. B. (2004). The Neonatal Intensive Care Unit Network Neurobehavioral Scale procedures. *Pediatrics, 113* (Suppl.), S641–S667.

Lester, B. M., & others. (2002). The maternal lifestyle study: Effects of substance exposure during pregnancy on neurodevelopmental outcome in 1-month-old infants. *Pediatrics, 110,* 1182–1192.

Lester, B. M., & others. (2011). Infant neurobehavioral development. *Seminars in Perinatology, 35,* 8–19.

Leung, E., Tasker, S. L., Atkinson, L., Vaillancourt, T., Schulkin, J., & Schmidt, L. A. (2010). Perceived maternal stress during pregnancy and its relation to infant stress reactivity at 2 days and 10 months of postnatal life. *Clinical Pediatrics, 49,* 158–165.

Lever-Duffy, J., & McDonald, J. B. (2011). *Teaching and learning with technology* (4th ed.). Boston: Allyn & Bacon.

Levine, T. P., & others. (2008). Effects of prenatal cocaine exposure on special education in school-aged children. *Pediatrics, 122,* e83–e91.

Lewis, A. C. (2007). Looking beyond NCLB. *Phi Delta Kappan, 88,* 483–484.

Lewis, B. A., & others. (2007). Prenatal cocaine and tobacco effects on children's language trajectories. *Pediatrics, 120,* e78–e85.

Lewis, C., & Carpendale, J. (2011). Social cognition. In P. K. Smith & C. H. Hart (Eds.), *Wiley-Blackwell handbook of childhood social development.* New York: Wiley.

Lewis, M. (1997). *Altering fate: Why the past does not predict the future.* New York: Guilford.

Lewis, M. (2005). Selfhood. In B. Hopkins (Ed.), *The Cambridge encyclopedia of child development.* Cambridge, UK: Cambridge University Press.

Lewis, M. (2007). Early emotional development. In A. Slater & M. Lewis (Eds.), *Introduction to infant development.* Malden, MA: Blackwell.

Lewis, M. (2008). The emergence of human emotions. In M. Lewis, J. M. Haviland Jones, & L. Feldman Barrett (Eds.), *Handbook of emotions* (3rd ed.). New York: Guilford.

Lewis, M. (2010). The emergence of consciousness and its role in human development. In W. F. Overton & R. M. Lerner (Eds.), *Handbook of life-span development* (2nd ed.). New York: Wiley.

Lewis, M., & Brooks-Gunn, J. (1979). *Social cognition and the acquisition of the self.* New York: Plenum.

Lewis, R. (2010). *Human genetics* (8th ed.). New York: McGraw-Hill.

Lhila, A., & Long, S. (2011, in press). What is driving the black-white difference in low birthweight in the U.S.? *Health Economics.*

Li, J., Olsen, J., Vestergaard, M., & Obel, C. (2011, in press). Low Apgar scores and risk of childhood attention deficit hyperactivity disorder. *Journal of Pediatrics.*

Li, J. M., Chen, Y. R., Li, X. T., & Xu, W. C. (2011). Screening of Herpes simplex virus 2 infection among pregnant women in southern China. *Journal of Dermatology, 38,* 120–124.

Li, P. (2009). What's in a lexical system? Discovering meaning through an interactive eye. In V. C. M. Gathercole (Ed.), *Routes to language: Essays in honor of Melissa Bowerman.* New York: Psychology Press.

Li, Y. (2011). Controlling sugar consumption still has a role to play in the prevention of dental caries. *Journal of Evidence-Based Dental Practice, 11,* 24–26.

Liben, L. S. (1995). Psychology meets geography: Exploring the gender gap on the national geography bee. *Psychological Science Agenda, 8,* 8–9.

Libertus, K., & Needham, A. (2010). Teach to reach: The effects of active vs. passive reaching experiences on action and perception. *Vision Research, 50,* 2750–2757.

Lidz, J. (2010). The abstract nature of syntactic representations: Consequences for a theory of learning. In E. Hoff & M. Shatz (Eds.), *Blackwell handbook of language development* (2nd ed.). New York: Wiley.

Lie, E., & Newcombe, N. (1999). Elementary school children's explicit and implicit memory for faces of preschool classmates. *Developmental Psychology, 35,* 102–112.

Liederman, J., Kantrowitz, L., & Flannery, K. (2005). Male vulnerability to reading disability is not likely to be a myth: A call for new data. *Journal of Learning Disabilities, 38,* 109–129.

Lieven, E. (2008). Language development: Overview. In M. M. Haith & J. B. Benson (Eds.), *Encyclopedia of infant and early childhood development.* Oxford, UK: Elsevier.

Lieven, E., & Stoll, S. (2010). Language development. In M. Bornstein (Ed.), *The handbook of cross-cultural developmental science.* New York: Psychology Press.

Lillard, A. (2006). Pretend play in toddlers. In C. A. Brownell & C. B. Kopp (Eds.), *Socioemotional development in the toddler years.* New York: Oxford University Press.

Lin, M., Johnson, J. E., & Johnson, K. M. (2003). *Dramatic play in Montessori kindergartens in Taiwan and Mainland China.* Unpublished manuscript, Department of Curriculum and Instruction, Pennsylvania State University, University Park, PA.

Lindberg, S. M., Hyde, J. S., Petersen, J. L., & Linn, M. C. (2010). New trends in gender and mathematics performance: A meta-analysis. *Psychological Bulletin, 136,* 1123–1136.

Linder, S. M. (2010). A lesson-planning model. *Teaching children mathematics, 17,* 249–254.

Lindsay, A. C., Sussner, K. M., Kim, J., & Gortmaker, S. (2006). The role of parents in preventing childhood obesity. *The Future of Children, 16*(1), 169–186.

Lipman, T. H., & others. (2011). Diabetes risk factors in children: A partnership between nurse practitioner and high school students. *MCN American Journal of Maternal and Child Nursing, 36,* 56–62.

Lipowska, M., Czaplewska, E., & Wysocka, A. (2011). Visuospatial deficits of dyslexic children. *Medical Science Monitor, 17,* CR216–CR221.

Litt, J., Taylor, H. G., Klein, N., & Hack, M. (2005). Learning disabilities in children with very low birthweight: Prevalence, neuropsychological correlates, and educational interventions. *Journal of Learning Disabilities, 38,* 130–141.

Liu, C., Ackerman, H. H., & Carulli, J. P. (2011). A genome-wide screen of gene-gene interactions for rheumatoid arthritis. *Human Genetics, 129,* 473–485.

Liu, D., Wellman, H. M., Tardif, T., & Sabbagh, M. A. (2008). Theory of mind development in Chinese children: A meta-analysis of false-belief understanding across cultures and languages. *Developmental Psychology, 44,* 523–531.

Liu, J., Raine, A., Venables, P. H., Dalais, C., & Mednick, S. A. (2003). Malnutrition at age 3 years and lower cognitive ability at age 11 years: Independence from psychosocial adversity. *Archives of Pediatric and Adolescent Medicine, 157,* 593–600.

Liu, J., Raine, A., Venables, P. H., & Mednick, S. A. (2004). Malnutrition at 3 years and externalizing behavior problems at age 8, 11, and 17 years. *American Journal of Psychiatry, 161,* 2005–2013.

Liu, J. S. (2011). Molecular genetics of neuronal migration disorders. *Current Neurology and Neuroscience Reports, 11,* 171–178.

Liu, S., Quinn, P. C., Wheeler, A., Xiao, N., Ge, L., & Lee, K. (2011, in press). Similarity and difference in the processing of same- and other-race faces as revealed by eye-tracking in 4- to 9-month-old infants. *Journal of Experimental Child Psychology.*

Liu, Y. H., Chang, M. Y., & Chen, C. H. (2010). Effects of music therapy on labor pain and anxiety in Taiwanese first-time mothers. *Journal of Clinical Nursing, 19,* 1065–1072.

Lively, W., & Bromley, D. (1973). *Person perception in childhood and adolescence.* New York: Wiley.

Lobelo, F., Pate, R. R., Dowda, M., Liese, A. D., & Daniels, S. R. (2010). Cardiorespiratory fitness and clustered cardiovascular disease risk in U.S. adolescents. *Journal of Adolescent Health, 47,* 352–359.

Lock, A., & Zukow-Goldring, P. (2010). Preverbal communication. In J. G. Bremner & T. D. Wachs (Eds.), *Wiley-Blackwell handbook of infant development* (2nd ed.). New York: Wiley.

Lockl, K., & Schneider, W. (2007). Knowledge about the mind: Links between theory of mind and later metamemory. *Child Development, 78,* 147–167.

Loebel, M., & Yali, A. M. (1999, August). *Effects of positive expectancies on adjustments to pregnancy.* Paper presented at the meeting of the American Psychological Association, Boston.

Loeber, R., & Burke, J. D. (2011). Developmental pathways in juvenile externalizing and internalizing problems. *Journal of Research on Adolescence, 21,* 34–46.

Loeber, R., Farrington, D. P., Stouthamer-Loeber, M., & White, H. R. (2008). *Violence and serious theft: Development and prediction from childhood to adulthood.* New York: Routledge.

Loeber, R., Pardini, D. A., Stouthamer-Loeber, M., & Raine, A. (2007). Do cognitive, physiological, and psychosocial risk and promotive factors predict desistance from delinquency in males? *Development and Psychopathology, 19,* 867–887.

Loehlin, J. C. (2010). Is there an active gene-environment correlation in adolescent drinking behavior? *Behavior Genetics, 40,* 447–451.

Logsdon, M. C., Wisner, K., & Hanusa, B. H. (2009). Does maternal role functioning improve with antidepressant treatment in women with postpartum depression? *Journal of Women's Health, 18,* 85–90.

London, M. L., & others. (2011). *Maternal and child nursing care* (3rd ed.). Upper Saddle River, NJ: Pearson.

Lonnerdal, B., & Kelleher, S. L. (2007). Iron metabolism in infants and children. *Food and Nutrition Bulletin, 28* (Suppl. 4), S491–S499.

Lorenz, K. Z. (1965). *Evolution and the modification of behavior.* Chicago: University of Chicago Press.

Lovelady, C. (2011, in press). Balancing exercise and food intake with lactation to promote post-partum weight loss. *Proceedings of the Nutrition Society.*

Lowdermilk, D. L., & Perry (2012). *Maternity and women's health care* (10th ed.). New York: Elsevier.

Lowdermilk, D. L., Perry, S. E., & Cashion, M. C. (2011). *Maternity nursing* (8th ed.). New York: Elsevier.

Lucovnik, M., & others (2011, in press). Progestin treatment for the prevention of preterm births. *Acta Obstetricia et Gynecologica Scandinavica.*

Luders, E., & others. (2004). Gender differences in cortical complexity. *Nature Neuroscience, 1,* 799–800.

Lumpkin, A. (2011). *Introduction to physical education, exercise science, and sport studies* (8th ed.). New York: McGraw-Hill.

Lund, B., & others. (2011). Risk factors for treatment-related mortality in childhood acute lymphoblastic leukemia. *Pediatric Blood Cancer, 56,* 551–559.

Lund, H. G., Reider, B. D., Whiting, A. B., & Prichard, J. R. (2010). Sleep patterns and predictors of disturbed sleep in a large population of college students. *Journal of Adolescent Health, 46,* 124–132.

Luo, Y., & Baillargeon, R. (2011, in press). Toward a mentalistic account of early psychological reasoning. *Current Directions in Psychological Science.*

Luria, A., & Herzog, E. (1985, April). *Gender segregation across and within settings.* Paper presented at the biennial meeting of the Society for Research in Child Development, Toronto.

Lyon, T. D., & Flavell, J. H. (1993). Young children's understanding of forgetting over time. *Child Development, 64,* 789–800.

Lytle, L.A. (2009). School-based interventions: Where do we go from here? *Archives of Pediatric and Adolescent Medicine, 163,* 388–389.

M

Maas, J. (2008, March 4). Commentary in L. Szabo, "Parents with babies need time to reset inner clock." *USA Today,* p. 4D.

Maccoby, E. E. (1998). *The two sexes: Growing up apart, coming together.* Cambridge, MA: Harvard University Press.

Maccoby, E. E. (2002). Gender and group processes. *Current Directions in Psychological Science, 11,* 54–58.

Maccoby, E. E. (2007). Historical overview of socialization theory and research. In J. E. Grusec & P. D. Hastings (Eds.), *Handbook of socialization.* New York: Guilford.

Maccoby, E. E., & Martin, J. A. (1983). Socialization in the context of the family: Parent-child interaction. In P. H. Mussen (Ed.), *Handbook of child psychology* (4th ed., Vol. 4). New York: Wiley.

MacDorman, M. F., Declercq, E., & Menacker, F. (2011). Trends and characteristics of home births in the United States by race and ethnicity, 1990–2006. *Birth, 38,* 17–23.

MacFarlane, J. A. (1975). Olfaction in the development of social preferences in the human neonate. In *Parent-infant interaction.* Ciba Foundation Symposium No. 33. Amsterdam: Elsevier.

Maconochie N., Doyle, P., Prior, S., & Simmons, R. (2007). Risk factors for first trimester miscarriage—results from a UK-population-based case control study. *British Journal of Obstetrics and Gynaecology, 114,* 170–176.

Macpherson, A. K., Jones, J., Rothman, L., Macarthur, C., & Howard, A. W. (2010). Safety standards and socioeconomic disparities in school playground injuries: A retrospective cohort study. *BMC Public Health, 10,* 542.

MacWhinney, B. (2010). Language development. In W. F. Overton & R. M. Lerner (Eds.), *Handbook of life-span development.* New York: Wiley.

Mader, S. S. (2012). *Biology* (11th ed.). New York: McGraw-Hill.

Madkour, A. S., Farhat, T., Halpern, C. T., Godeu, E., & Gabhainn, S. N. (2010). Early adolescent sexual initiation as a problem behavior: A comparative study of five nations. *Journal of Adolescent Health, 47(4),* 389–398.

Magarey, A. M., & others. (2011). A parent-led family-focused treatment program for overweight children aged 5 to 9 years: The PEACH RCT. *Pediatrics, 127,* 214–222.

Magno, C. (2010). The role of metacognitive skills in developing critical thinking. *Metacognition and Learning, 5,* 137–156.

Magriples, U., Kershaw, T. S., Rising, S. S., Massey, Z., & Ickovics, J. R. (2008). Prenatal health care beyond the obstetrics service: Utilization and predictors of unscheduled care. *American Journal of Obstetrics and Gynecology, 198,* el–e7.

Mahler, M. (1979). *Separation-individuation* (Vol. 2). London: Jason Aronson.

Mahmoudi-Gharaei, J., Dodangi, N., Tehrani-Doost, M., & Faghihi, T. (2011, in press). Duloxetine in the treatment of adolescents with attention deficit/hyperactivity disorder: An open-label study. *Human Psychopharmacology.*

Mahoney, J., Parente, M. E., & Zigler, E. (2010). After-school program engagement and in-school competence: Program quality, content, and staffing. In J. Meece & J. Eccles (Eds.), *Handbook of research on schools, schooling, and human development*. New York: Routledge.

Malamitsi-Puchner, A., & Boutsikou, T. (2006). Adolescent pregnancy and perinatal outcome. *Pediatric Endocrinology Reviews, 3* (Suppl. 1), 170–171.

Malizia, B. A., Hacker, M. R., & Penzias, A. S. (2009). Cumulative live-birth rates after in vitro fertilization. *New England Journal of Medicine, 360,* 236–243.

Maloy, R. W., Verock-O'Loughlin, R-E., Edwards, S. A., & Woolf, B. P. (2011). *Transforming learning with new technologies.* Boston: Allyn & Bacon.

Mandara, J. (2006). The impact of family functioning on African American males' academic achievement: A review and clarification of the empirical literature. *Teachers College Record, 108,* 206–233.

Mandler, J. M. (2004). *The foundations of the mind: Origins of conceptual thought.* New York: Oxford University Press.

Mandler, J. M. (2009). Jean Mandler. Retrieved March 22, 2009, from http://cogsici.ucsd.edu/-jean/

Mandler, J. M., & McDonough, L. (1993). Concept formation in infancy. *Cognitive Development, 8,* 291–318.

Mangelsdorf, S. C., & Wong, M. S. (2008). Independence/dependence. In M. M. Haith & J. B. Benson (Eds.), *Encyclopedia of infant and early childhood development.* Oxford, UK: Elsevier.

Mangione, R., & others. (2011). Neuro-developmental outcome following prenatal diagnosis of an isolated anomaly of the corpus callosum. *Ultrasound in Obstetrics and Gynecology, 37,* 290–295.

Manzo, K. K. (2008). Motivating students in the middle years. *Education Week, 27,* 22–25.

Marcdante, K., Kliegman, R., & Behrman, R. (2011). *Nelson essentials of pediatrics* (6th ed.). New York: Elsevier.

Marcia, J. E. (1980). Ego identity development. In J. Adelson (Ed.), *Handbook of adolescent psychology.* New York: Wiley.

Marcia, J. E. (1994). The empirical study of ego identity. In H. A. Bosma, T. L. G. Graafsma, H. D. Grotevant, & D. J. De Levita (Eds.), *Identity and development.* Newbury Park, CA: Sage.

Marcia, J. E. (2002). Identity and psychosocial development in adulthood. *Identity: An International Journal of Theory and Research, 2,* 7–28.

Marcon, R. A. (2003). The physical side of development. *Young Children, 58,* 80–87.

Marcovitch, H. (2004). Use of stimulants for attention deficit hyperactivity disorder: AGAINST. *British Medical Journal, 329,* 908–909.

Marinucci, L., & others. (2009). Patterns of some extracellular matrix gene expression are similar in cells from cleft lip-palate patients and in human palatal fibroblasts to diazepam in culture. *Toxicology, 257,* 10–16.

Marion, M. C. (2010). *Introduction to early childhood education.* Upper Saddle River, NJ: Prentice Hall.

Markham, C. M., & others. (2010). Connectedness as a predictor of sexual and reproductive health outcomes for youth. *Journal of Adolescent Health* (Suppl. 1), S23–S41.

Marks, A. K., Patton, F., & Garcia Coll, C. (2011). Being bicultural: A mixed-methods study of adolescents' implicitly and explicitly measured multiethnic identities. *Developmental Psychology, 47,* 270–288.

Marret, S., & others. (2010). Prenatal low-dose aspirin and neurobehavioral outcomes of children born very preterm. *Pediatrics, 125,* e29–e34.

Marti, C. N., Stice, E., & Springer, D. W. (2010). Substance use and abuse trajectories across adolescence: A latent trajectory analysis of a community-recruited sample of girls. *Journal of Adolescence, 33,* 449–461.

Martin, J. A., Hamilton, B. E., Sutton, P. D., Ventura, S. J., Menacker, F., & Munson, M. L. (2005, September). Births: Final data for 2003. *National Vital Statistics Reports, 54*(2), 1–116.

Martin, J. A., Kochanek, K. D., Strobino, D. M., Guyer, B., & MacDorman, M. F. (2005). Annual summary of vital statistics—2003. *Pediatrics, 115,* 619–634.

Mashburn, A. J., Justice, L. M., Downer, J. T., & Pianta, R. C. (2009). Peer effects on children's language achievement during pre-kindergarten. *Child Development, 80,* 686–702.

Maslova, E., Bhattacharya, S., Lin, S. W., & Michels, K. B. (2010). Caffeine consumption during pregnancy and risk of preterm birth: A meta-analysis. *American Journal of Clinical Nutrition, 92,* 1120–1132.

Massaro, A. N., Hammad, T. A., Jazzo, B., & Aly, H. (2009). Massage with kinesthetic stimulation improves weight gain in preterm infants. *Journal of Perinatology, 29,* 352–357.

Masselli, G., & others. (2011). MR imaging in the evaluation of placental abruption: Correlation with sonographic findings. *Radiology.*

Massey, Z., Rising, S. S., & Ickovics, J. (2006). Centering Pregnancy group prenatal care: Promoting relationship-centered care. *Journal of Obstetric, Gynecologic, and Neonatal Nursing, 35,* 286–294.

Masten, A. S. (2001). Ordinary magic: Resilience processes in development. *American Psychologist, 56,* 227–238.

Masten, A. S. (2006). Developmental psychopathology: Pathways to the future. *International Journal of Behavioral Development, 31,* 46–53.

Masten, A. S. (2007). Resilience in developing systems: Progress and promise as the fourth wave rises. *Development and Psychopathology, 19,* 921–930.

Masten, A. S. (2009). Ordinary magic: Lessons from research on resilience in human development. Retrieved October 15, 2009, from http://www.cea-ace.ca/media/en/Ordinary_Magic_Summer09.pdf

Masten, A. S. (2011a). Resilience in children threatened by extreme adversity: Frameworks for research, practice, and translational synergy. *Development and Psychopathology, 23,* 493–506.

Masten, A. S. (2011b, in press). Understanding and promoting resilience in children. *Current Opinion in Psychiatry.*

Masten, A. S. (2012, in press). Risk and resilience in development. In P. D. Zelazo (Ed.), *Oxford handbook of developmental psychology.* New York: Oxford University Press.

Masten, A. S., & Osofsky, J. D. (2010). Disasters and their impact on child development: Introduction to the special section. *Child Development, 81,* 1029–1039.

Matlin, M. W. (2012). *The psychology of women* (7th ed.). Belmont. CA: Wadsworth.

Matsumoto, D., & Juang, L. (2012, in press). *Culture and psychology* (5th ed.). Boston: Cengage.

Matthews, D. J. (2009). Developmental transitions in giftedness and talent: Childhood into adolescence. In F. D. Horowitz, R. F. Subotnik, & D. J. Matthews (Eds.), *The development of giftedness and talent across the life span.* Washington, DC: American Psychological Association.

Mattson, S., & Smith, J. E. (2011). *Core curriculum for maternal-newborn nursing* (4th ed.). New York: Elsevier.

Mayer, K. D., & Zhang, L. (2009). Short- and long-term effects of cocaine abuse during pregnancy on heart development. *Therapeutic Advances in Cardiovascular Disease, 3,* 7–16.

Mayo Clinic. (2011). Pregnancy and fish: What's safe to eat? Retrieved March 6, 2011, from http://www.mayoclinic.com/health/pregnancy-and-fish/PR00158

Mbonye, A. K., Neema, S., & Magnussen, P. (2006). Treatment-seeking practices for malaria in pregnancy among rural women in Mukono district, Uganda. *Journal of Biosocial Science, 38,* 221–237.

Mbugua Gitau, G., Liversedge, H., Goffey, D., Hawton, A., Liversedge, N., & Taylor, M. (2009). The influence of maternal age on the outcomes of pregnancy complicated by bleeding at less than 12 weeks. *Acta Obstetricia et Gynecologica Scandinavica, 88,* 116–118.

McAlister, A., & Peterson, C. (2007). A longitudinal study of child siblings and theory of mind development. *Cognitive Development, 22,* 258–270.

McBride-Chang, C. (2004). *Children's literacy development* (Texts in Developmental Psychology Series). London: Edward Arnold/Oxford Press.

McBride-Chang, C., & others. (2005). Changing models across cultures: Associations of phonological and morphological awareness to reading in Beijing, Hong Kong, Korea, and America. *Journal of Experimental Child Psychology, 92,* 140–160.

McBride-Chang, C., Lam, F., Lam, C., Doo, S., Wong, S. W., L., & Chow, Y. Y. Y. (2008). Word recognition and cognitive profiles of

Chinese preschool children at-risk for dyslexia through language delay or familial history of dyslexia. *Journal of Child Psychology and Psychiatry, 49,* 211–218.

McCartney, K. (2003, July 16). Interview with Kathleen McCartney in A. Bucuvalas, "Child care and behavior." *HGSE News,* pp. 1–4. Cambridge, MA: Harvard Graduate School of Education.

McCormack, L. A., & others. (2011). Weight-related teasing in a racially diverse sample of sixth-grade children. *Journal of the American Dietetic Association, 111,* 431–436.

McDermott, U., Downing, J. R., & Stratton, M. R. (2011). Genomics and the continuum of cancer care. *New England Journal of Medicine, 364,* 340–350.

McFarlin, B. L. (2009). Solving the puzzle of prematurity. *American Journal of Nursing, 109,* 60–63.

McGarry, J., Kim, H., Sheng, X., Egger, M., & Baksh, L. (2009). Postpartum depression and help-seeking behavior. *Journal of Midwifery and Women's Health, 54,* 50–56.

McGarvey, C., McDonnell, M., Hamilton, K., O'Regan, M., & Matthews, T. (2006). An 8-year study of risk factors for SIDS: Bed-sharing versus non-bed-sharing. *Archives of Disease in Childhood, 91,* 318–323.

McHale, J., & Sullivan, M. (2008). Family systems. In M. Hersen & A. Gross (Eds.), *Handbook of clinical psychology, Volume II: Children and adolescents.* New York: Wiley.

McIntosh, C. G., Tonkin, S. L., & Gunn, A. J. (2010). What is the mechanism of sudden infant deaths associated with co-sleeping? *New Zealand Medical Journal, 122,* 69–75.

McKnight, J. R., & others. (2011). Obesity in pregnancy: Problems and potential solutions. *Frontiers in Bioscience, 3,* 442–452.

McLoyd, V. C. (2011). How money matters for children's socioemotional adjustment: Family processes and parental investment. *Nebraska Symposium on Motivation, 57,* 33–72.

McLoyd, V. C., Kaplan, R., Purtell, K. M., Bagley, E., Hardaway, C. R., & Smalls, C. (2009). Poverty and social disadvantage in adolescence. In R. M. Lerner & L. Steinberg (Eds.), *Handbook of adolescent psychology* (3rd ed.). New York: Wiley.

McLoyd, V. C., Kaplan, R., Purtell, K. M., & Huston, A. C. (2011). Assessing the effects of a work-based antipoverty program for parents on youth's future orientation and employment experiences. *Child Development, 82,* 113–132.

McMahon, M., & Stryjewski, G. (2012). *Pediatrics.* New York: Elsevier.

McMillen, I. C., MacLaughlin, S. M., Muhlhausler, B. S., Gentili, S., Duffield, J. L., & Morrison, J. L. (2008). Developmental origins of adult health and disease: The role of periconceptional and fetal nutrition. *Basic and Clinical Pharmacology and Toxicology, 102,* 82–89.

McNamara, F., & Sullivan, C. E. (2000). Obstructive sleep apnea in infants. *Journal of Pediatrics, 136,* 318–323.

Meade, C. S., Kershaw, T. S., & Ickovics, J. R. (2008). The intergenerational cycle of teenage motherhood: An ecological approach. *Health Psychology, 27,* 419–429.

Meece, J., & Eccles, J. (Eds.). (2010). *Handbook of research on schools, schooling and human development.* Clifton, NJ: Psychology Press.

Meeker, J. D., & others. (2011, in press). Serum concentrations of polychlorinated biphenyls (PCBs) in relation to in vitro fertilization (IVF) outcomes. *Environmental Health Perspectives.*

Meerlo, P., Sgoifo, A., & Suchecki, D. (2008). Restricted and disrupted sleep: Effects on autonomic function, neuroendocrine stress systems, and stress responsivity. *Sleep Medicine Review, 12,* 197–210.

Meltzi, G., & Ely, R. (2009). Language development in the school years. In J. B. Gleason & N. Ratner (Eds.), *The development of language* (7th ed.). Boston: Allyn & Bacon.

Meltzoff, A. N. (1988). Infant imitation and memory: Nine-month-old infants in immediate and deferred tests. *Child Development, 59,* 217–225.

Meltzoff, A. N. (2004). Imitation as a mechanism of social cognition: Origins of empathy, theory of mind, and the representation of action. In U. Goswami (Ed.), *Blackwell handbook of childhood cognitive development.* Malden, MA: Blackwell.

Meltzoff, A. N. (2005). Imitation. In B. Hopkins (Ed.), *Cambridge encyclopedia of child development.* Cambridge, UK: Cambridge University Press.

Meltzoff, A. N. (2007). "Like me": A foundation for social cognition. *Developmental Science, 10,* 126–134.

Meltzoff, A. N. (2011). Social cognition and the origins of imitation, empathy, and theory of mind. In U. Goswami (Ed.), *Wiley-Blackwell handbook of childhood cognitive development* (2nd ed.). New York: Wiley.

Meltzoff, A. N., & Brooks, R. (2006). Eyes wide shut: The importance of eyes in infant gaze following and understanding of other minds. In R. Flom, K. Lee, & D. Muir (Eds.), *Gaze following: Its development and significance.* Mahwah, NJ: Erlbaum.

Meltzoff, A. N., & Moore, M. K. (1999). A new foundation for cognitive development in infancy: The birth of the representational infant. In E. K. Skolnick, K. Nelson, S. A. Gelman, & P. H. Miller (Eds.), *Conceptual development.* Mahwah, NJ: Erlbaum.

Meltzoff, A. N., & Williamson, R. A. (2010). The importance of imitation for theories of social-cognitive development. In J. G. Bremner & T. D. Wachs (Eds.), *Wiley-Blackwell handbook of infant development* (2nd ed.). New York: Wiley.

Mendelson, C. R. (2009). Minireview: Fetal-maternal hormonal signaling in pregnancy and labor. *Molecular Endocrinology, 23,* 947–954.

Menezes, V., Malek, A., & Keelan, J. A. (2011, in press). Nanoparticulate drug delivery during pregnancy: Placental passage and fetal exposure. *Current Pharmaceutical Biotechnology.*

Menias, C. O., Elsayes, K. M., Peterson, C. M., Huete, A., Gratz, B. I., & Bhalla, S. (2007). CT of pregnancy-related complications. *Emergency Radiology, 13,* 299–306.

Menn, L., & Stoel-Gammon, C. (2009). Phonological development: Learning sounds and sound patterns. In J. Berko Gleason (Ed.), *The development of language* (7th ed.). Boston: Allyn & Bacon.

Mennella, J. A. (2009). Taste and smell. In R. A. Shweder & others (Eds.), *The child: An encyclopedic companion.* Chicago: University of Chicago Press.

Menon, M., Tobin, D. D., Corby, B. C., Menon, M., Hodges, E. V. E., & Perry, D. G. (2007). The developmental costs of high self-esteem in aggressive children. *Child Development, 78,* 1627–1639.

Menon, R., & others. (2011, in press). Cigarette smoking induces oxidative stress and atopsis in normal fetal membranes. *Placenta.*

Menyuk, P., Liebergott, J., & Schultz, M. (1995). *Early language development in full-term and premature infants.* Hillsdale, NJ: Erlbaum.

Mepham, S., Zondi, Z., Mbuyszi, A., Mkhwanazi, N., & Newell, M. L. (2011, in press). Challenges in PTCCT antiretroviral adherence in northern KwaZulu-Natal, South Africa. *AIDS Care.*

Meredith, N. V. (1978). Research between 1960 and 1970 on the standing height of young children in different parts of the world. In H. W. Reece & L. P. Lipsitt (Eds.), *Advances in child development and behavior* (Vol. 12). New York: Academic Press.

Merewood, A., & others. (2007). Breastfeeding duration rates and factors affecting continued breastfeeding among infants born at an inner-city U.S. baby-friendly hospital. *Journal of Human Lactation, 23,* 157–164.

Meschia, G. (2011). Fetal oxygenation and maternal ventilation. *Clinics in Chest Medicine, 32,* 15–19.

Messermith, E. E., Garrett, J. L., Davis-Kean, P. E., Malanchuk, O., & Eccles, J. S. (2008). Career development from adolescence through emerging adulthood: Insights from information technology occupations. *Journal of Adolescent Research, 23,* 206–227.

Messiah, S. E., Miller, T. L., Lipshultz, S. E., & Bandstra, E. S. (2011). Potential latent effects of prenatal cocaine exposure on growth and the risk of cardiovascular and metabolic disease in childhood. *Progress in Pediatric Cardiology, 31,* 59–65.

Metz, E. C., & Youniss, J. (2005). Longitudinal gains in civic development through school based required service. *Political Psychology, 26,* 413–437.

Meyer, S. L., Weible, C. M., & Woeber, K. (2010). Perceptions and practice of waterbirth: A survey of Georgia midwives. *Journal of Midwifery and Women's Health, 55,* 55–59.

Meyers, J. (2010, April 1). Suicides open eyes to bullying. *Dallas Morning News,* pp. 1A–2A.

Miller, B. C., Benson, B., & Galbraith, K. A. (2001). Family relationships and adolescent pregnancy risk: A research synthesis. *Developmental Review, 21*, 1–38.

Miller, B. C., Fan, X., Christensen M., Grotevant, H. D., & von Dulmen, M. (2000). Comparisons of adopted and nonadopted adolescents in a large, nationally representative sample. *Child Development, 71*, 1458–1473.

Miller, C. F., Lurye, L. E., Zosuls, K. M., & Ruble, D. N. (2008). *Content and accessibility of children's gender stereotypes: Girls are what they look like and boys are what they do.* Unpublished manuscript, Department of Psychology, Princeton, NJ.

Miller, C. F., Lurye, L. E., Zosuls, K. M., & Ruble, D. N. (2009). Accessibility of gender stereotype domains: Developmental and gender differences in children. *Sex Roles, 60*, 870–881.

Miller, D. P. (2011). Associations between the home and school environments and child body mass index. *Social Science & Medicine, 72*, 677–684.

Miller, J. (2007). Cultural psychology of moral development. In S. Kitayama & D. Cohen (Eds.), *Handbook of cultural psychology.* New York: Guilford.

Miller, L. J., & Larusso, E. M. (2011). Preventing postpartum depression. *Psychiatric Clinics of North America, 34*, 53–65.

Miller, P., & Plant, M. (2010). Parental guidance about drinking: Relationship with teenage psychoactive substance use. *Journal of Adolescence, 33*, 55–68.

Miller, P. H. (2011). Piaget's theory: Past, present, and future. In U. Goswami (Ed.), *Wiley-Blackwell handbook of childhood cognitive development* (2nd ed.). New York: Wiley.

Miller, S., Malone, P., Dodge, K. A., & Conduct Problems Prevention Research Group. (2011, in press). Developmental trajectories of boys' and girls' delinquency: Sex differences and links to later adolescent outcomes. *Journal of Abnormal Child Psychology.*

Miller, W. D., SadeghNobari, T., & Lillie-Blanton, M. (2011). Healthy starts for all: Policy prescriptions. *American Journal of Preventive Medicine, 40* (Suppl. 1), S19–S37.

Mills, B., Reyna, V., & Estrada, S. (2008). Explaining contradictory relations between risk perception and risk taking. *Psychological Science, 19*, 429–433.

Mills, C. M., Elashi, F. B., & Archacki, M. A. (2011, March). *Evaluating sources of information and misinformation: Developmental and individual differences in the elementary school years.* Paper presented at the biennial meeting of the Society for Research in Child Development, Montreal.

Mills, D., & Mills, C. (2000). *Hungarian kindergarten curriculum translation.* London: Mills Production.

Milot, T., Ethier, L. S., St-Laurent, D., & Provost, M. A. (2010). The role of trauma symptoms in the development of behavioral problems in maltreated preschoolers. *Child Abuse and Neglect, 34*, 225–234.

Miltenberger, R. G. (2012). *Behavior modification* (5th ed.). Boston: Cengage.

Minguez-Milio, J. A., & others. (2011, in press). Perinatal outcome and long-term follow-up of extremely low birth weight infants depending on the mode of delivery. *Journal of Maternal-Fetal and Neonatal Medicine.*

Minino, A. M., Heron, M. P., & Smith, B. L. (2006). Deaths: Preliminary data 2004. *National Vital Statistics Report, 54*, 1–49.

Minnes, S., & others. (2010). The effects of prenatal cocaine exposure on problem behavior in children 4–10 years. *Neurotoxicology and Teratology, 32*, 443–451.

Minnesota Family Investment Program. (2011). *Longitudinal study of early MFIP recipients.* Retrieved March 3, 2011, from http://www.dhs.state.mn.us/main/idcplg?IdcService=GET_DYNAMIC_CONVERSION&RevisionSelectionMethod=LatestReleased&dDocName=id_005467

Miranda, R., Scott, M., Hicks, R., Wilcox, H. C., Harris Munfakh, J. L., & Shaffer, D. (2008). Suicide attempt characteristics, diagnoses, and future attempts: Comparing multiple attempters to single attempters and ideators. *Journal of the American Academy of Child and Adolescent Psychiatry, 47*, 32–40.

Mischel, W. (2004). Toward an integrative science of the person. *Annual Review of Psychology* (Vol. 55). Palo Alto, CA: Annual Reviews.

Mitchell, E. A. (2009). What is the mechanism of SIDS? Clues from epidemiology. *Developmental Psychobiology, 51*, 215–222.

Mitchell, E. A., Stewart, A. W., Crampton, P., & Salmond, C. (2000). Deprivation and sudden infant death syndrome. *Social Science and Medicine, 19*, 147–150.

Miura, M., & others. (2011, in press). Non-invasive tool for fetal sex determination at an early gestational age. *Hemophilia.*

Miyake, K., Chen, S., & Campos, J. (1985). Infants' temperament, mothers' mode of interaction and attachment in Japan: An interim report. In I. Bretherton & F. Waters (Eds.), Growing points of attachment theory and research, *Monographs of the Society for Research in Child Development, 50*(1–2, Serial No. 109), 276–297.

MMWR. (2006, June 9). *Youth risk behavior surveillance—United States 2005*, Vol. 255. Atlanta: Centers for Disease Control and Prevention

Mokha, J. S., & others. (2010). Utility of waist-to-height ratio in assessing the status of central obesity and related cardiometabolic risk profile among normal weight and overweight/obese children: The Bogalusa Heart Study. *BMC Pediatrics, 10*, 73.

Moleti, C. A. (2009). Trends and controversies in labor induction. *MCN: American Journal of Maternal Child Nursing, 34*, 40–47.

Molina, R. C., Roca, C. G., Zamorano, J. S., & Araya, E. G. (2010). Family planning and adolescent pregnancy. *Best Practices and Research: Clinical Obstetrics and Gynecology, 24*, 209–222.

Mond, J., & others. (2011). Obesity, body satisfaction, and emotional well-being in early and late adolescence: Findings from the Project EAT Study. *Journal of Adolescent Health, 48*, 373–378.

Monge, P., & others. (2007). Parental occupation exposure to pesticides and the risk of childhood leukemia in Costa Rica. *Scandinavian Journal of Work, Environment, and Health, 33*, 291–303.

Monica, K. C., & du Plessis, R. A. (2011). Discussion of health benefits of breastfeeding within small groups. *Community Practice, 84*, 31–34.

Monk, C., Fitelson, E. M., & Werner, E. (2011, in press). Mood disorders and their pharmacological treatment during pregnancy: Is the future child affected? *Pediatric Research.*

Montagna, P., & Chokroverty, S. (2011). *Sleep disorders.* New York: Elsevier.

Montan, S. (2007). Increased risk in the elderly parturient. *Current Opinion in Obstetrics and Gynecology, 19*, 110–112.

Montemayor, R. (1982). The relationship between patent-adolescent conflict and the amount of time adolescents spend with parents, peers, and alone. *Child Development, 53*, 1512–1519.

Montgomery-Downs, H. E., Insana, S. P., Clegg-Kraynok, M. M., & Mancini, L. M. (2010). Normative longitudinal maternal sleep: The first four postpartum months. *American Journal of Obstetrics and Gynecology, 203*, e1–e7.

Montoya Arizabaleta, A. V., Orozco Buitrago, L., Aqilar de Plata, A. C., Mosquera Escudero, M., & Ramirez-Velez, R. (2010). Aerobic exercise during pregnancy improves health-related quality of life: A randomised trial. *Journal of Physiotherapy, 56*(4), 253–258.

Moon, R. Y., & others. (2011, in press). Pacifier use and SIDS: Evidence for a consistently reduced risk. *Maternal and Child Health Journal.*

Moore, D. (2001). *The dependent gene.* New York: W. H. Freeman.

Morasch, K. C., & Bell, M. A. (2009). Patterns of frontal and temporal brain electrical activity during declarative memory performance in 10-month-old infants. *Brain and Cognition, 71*, 215–222.

Morra, S., Gobbo, C., Marini, Z., & Sheese, R. (2007). *Cognitive development: Neo-Piagetian perspectives.* Mahwah, NJ: Erlbaum.

Morrison, F. J., & Hindman, A. H. (2008). School readiness. In M. M. Haith & J. B. Benson (Eds.), *Encyclopedia of infant and early childhood development.* Oxford, UK: Elsevier.

Morrison, G. S. (2011). *Fundamentals of early childhood education* (6th ed.). Upper Saddle River, NJ: Merrill.

Morrissey, T. W. (2009). Multiple child-care arrangements and young children's behavioral outcomes. *Child Development, 80*, 59–76.

Morrissey-Ross, M. (2000). Lead poisoning and its elimination. *Public Health Nursing, 17*, 229–230.

Morrow, C. E., Culbertson, J. L., Accornero, V. H., Xue, L., Anthony, J. C., & Bandstra,

E. S. (2006). Learning disabilities and intellectual functioning in school-aged children with prenatal cocaine exposure. *Developmental Neuropsychology, 30*, 905–931.

Morse, S. B., Zheng, H., Tang, Y., & Roth, J. (2009). Early school-age outcomes of late preterm infants. *Pediatrics, 123*, e622–e629.

Mortensen, L. H., Diderichsen, F., Davery-Smith, G., & Andersen, A. M. (2009). Time is on whose side? Time trends in the association between social disadvantage and offspring fetal growth. A study of 1,409,339 births in Denmark 1981–2004. *Journal of Epidemiology and Community Health, 63*, 281–285.

Moshman, D. (2011). *Adolescent rationality and development: Cognition, morality, and identity* (3rd ed.). New York: Psychology Press.

Mostofsky, S. H., & Ewen, J. B. (2011, in press). Altered connectivity and action model formation in autism is autism. *Neuroscientist.*

Moulson, M. C., & Nelson, C. A. (2008). Neurological development. In M. M. Haith & J. B Benson (Eds.), *Encyclopedia of infant and early childhood development.* Oxford, UK: Elsevier.

Muller, R. A., & others. (2011, in press). Underconnected, but how? A survey of functional connectivity MRI studies in autism spectrum disorders. *Cerebral Cortex.*

Muller, U. C., & others. (2011, in press). The impact of study design and diagnostic approach in a large multi-center ADHD study. Part 1. ADHD symptom patterns. *BMC Psychiatry.*

Mundy, P., Block, J., Delgado, C., Pomares, Y., Van Hecke, A. V., & Parlade, M. V. (2007). Individual differences and the development of joint attention in infancy. *Child Development, 78*, 938–954.

Murdock, T. B., Miller, A., & Kohlhardt, J. (2004). Effects of classroom context variables on high school students' judgments of the acceptability and likelihood of cheating. *Journal of Educational Psychology, 96*, 765–777.

Murin, S., Rafii, R., & Bilello, K. (2011). Smoking and smoking cessation in pregnancy. *Clinics in Chest Medicine, 32*, 75–91.

Murnane, R. J., & Levy, F. (1996). *Teaching the new basic skills.* New York: Free Press.

Murphy, M. M., & Mazzocco, M. M. (2008). Mathematics learning disabilities in girls with fragile X or Turner syndrome during late elementary school. *Journal of Learning Disabilities, 41*, 29–46.

Murray, A. (2011). Montessori elementary philosophy reflects current motivation theories. *Montessori Life, 23*, 22–33.

Murray, E. A. (2007). Visual memory. *Annual Review of Neuroscience* (Vol. 29). Palo Alto, CA: Annual Reviews.

Murray, J. P. (2007). TV violence: Research and controversy. In N. Pecora, J. P. Murray, & E. A. Wartella (Eds.), *Children and television.* Mahwah, NJ: Erlbaum.

Murray, S. S., & McKinney, E. L. (2010). *Foundations of maternal-newborn and women's health* (5th ed.). New York: Elsevier.

Murry, V. B., Berkel, C., Gaylord-Harden, N. K., Copeland-Linder, N., & Nation, M. (2011). Neighborhood poverty and adolescent development. *Journal of Research on Adolescence, 21*, 114–128.

Mwiru, R. S., & others. (2011, in press). Relationship of exclusive breast-feeding to infections and growth of Tanzanian children born to HIV-infected women. *Public Health Nutrition.*

Myer, G. D., & others. (2011). Integrative training for children and adolescents: Techniques and practices for reducing sports-related injuries and enhancing athletic performance. *The Physician and Sports Medicine, 39*, 74–84.

Myers, D. G. (2010). *Psychology* (9th ed.). New York: Worth.

Myers, D. L. (1999). *Excluding violent youths from juvenile court: The effectiveness of legislative waiver.* Doctoral dissertation, University of Maryland, College Park.

Myerson, J., Rank, M. R., Raines, F. Q., & Schnitzler, M. A. (1998). Race and general cognitive ability: The myth of diminishing returns in education. *Psychological Science, 9*, 139–142.

N

Nader, P., & others. (2006). Identifying risk for obesity in early childhood. *Pediatrics, 118*, e594–e601.

Nader, P. R., Bradley, R. H., Houts, R. M., McRitchie, S. L., & O'Brian, M. (2008). Moderate-to-vigorous physical activity from 9 to 15 years. *Journal of the American Medical Association, 300*, 295–305.

NAEYC. (2002). *Early learning standards: Creating the conditions for success.* Washington, DC: Author.

NAEYC. (2009). *Developmentally appropriate practice in early childhood programs serving children from birth through age 8.* Washington, DC: Author.

Nagahawatte, N. T., & Goldenberg, R. (2008). Poverty, maternal health, and adverse pregnancy outcomes. *Annals of the New York Academy of Sciences, 1136*, 80–85.

Nagel, B. J., & others. (2011). Altered white matter microstructure in children with attention-deficit/hyperactivity disorder. *Journal of the American Academy of Child and Adolescent Psychiatry, 50*, 283–292.

Najman, J. M., Hayatbakhsh, M. R., Heron, M. A., Bor, W., O'Callaghan, M. J., & Williams, G. M. (2009). The impact of episodic and chronic poverty on child cognitive development. *Journal of Pediatrics, 154*, 284–289.

Najman, J. M., & others. (2010). Timing and chronicity of family poverty and development of unhealthy behaviors in children: A longitudinal study. *Journal of Adolescent Health, 46*, 538–544.

Nansel, T. R., Overpeck, M., Pilla, R., Ruan, W., Simons-Morton, B., & Scheidt, P. (2001). Bullying behaviors among U.S. youth. *Journal of the American Medical Association, 285*, 2094–2100.

Narváez, D. (2006). Integrative moral education. In M. Killen & J. Smetana (Eds.), *Handbook of moral development.* Mahwah, NJ: Erlbaum.

Narváez, D. (2008). Four component model. In F. C. Power, R. J. Nuzzi, D. Narváez, D. K. Lapsley, & T. C. Hunt (Eds.), *Moral education: A handbook.* Westport, CT: Greenwood Publishing.

Narváez, D. (2010a). Building a sustaining classroom climate for purposeful ethical citizenship. In T. Lovat, R. Toomey, & N. Clement (Eds.), *International research handbook of values education and student wellbeing.* New York: Springer.

Narváez, D. (2010b). The embodied dynamism of moral becoming. *Perspectives on Psychological Science, 5*(2), 185–186.

Narváez, D., & Hill, P. L. (2010). The relation of multicultural experiences to moral judgment and mindsets. *Journal of Diversity in Higher Education, 3*, 43–55.

Narváez, D., & Lapsley, D. (Eds.). (2009). *Moral personality, identity, and character: An interdisciplinary future.* New York: Cambridge University Press.

Nash-Ditzel, S. (2010). Metacognitive reading strategies can improve comprehension. *Journal of College Reading and Learning, 40*, 45–63.

National Assessment of Educational Progress. (2005). *The nation's report card.* Washington, DC: U.S. Department of Education.

National Assessment of Educational Progress. (2007). *The nation's report card.* Washington, DC: U.S. Department of Education.

National Association for Sport and Physical Education. (2002). *Active start: A statement of physical activity guidelines for children birth to five years.* Reston, VA: National Association for Sport and Physical Education.

National Autism Association. (2010). *All about autism.* Retrieved January 5, 2010, from http://www.nationalautismassociation.org/definitions.php

National Cancer Institute. (2011). *Report to nation finds continued declines in many cancer rates.* Rockville, MD: Author

National Center for Education Statistics. (2010a). *Digest of education statistics, 2009.* Washington, DC: U.S. Department of Education.

National Center for Education Statistics. (2010b). *School dropouts.* Washington, DC: U.S. Department of Education.

National Center for Education Statistics. (2010c). *The condition of education 2010.* Washington, DC: U.S. Department of Education.

National Center for Health Statistics. (2002a). Prevalence of overweight among children and adolescents: United States 1999–2000 (Table 71), *Health United States, 2002.* Atlanta: Centers for Disease Control and Prevention.

National Center for Health Statistics. (2002b). *Sexual behavior and selected health measures: Men and women 15–44 years of age, United States, 2002, PHS 2003–1250.* Atlanta: Centers for Disease Control and Prevention.

National Center for Health Statistics. (2007). *Death rates.* Atlanta: Centers for Disease Control and Prevention.

National Center for Health Statistics. (2009). *Summary health statistics for U.S. children: National Health Interview Study.* Atlanta: Centers for Disease Control and Prevention.

National Center for Health Statistics. (2009, January 7). *Public Release Statement: Preterm births rise 36 percent since early 1980s.* Atlanta: Centers for Disease Control and Prevention.

National Center for Health Statistics. (2011a). *Births.* Atlanta: Centers for Disease Control and Prevention.

National Center for Health Statistics. (2011b). *National diabetes fact sheet.* Atlanta: Centers for Disease Control and Prevention.

National Center for Juvenile Justice. (2006). *Juvenile offenders and victims: 2006 national report.* Pittsburgh: Author.

National Center for Learning Disabilities. (2006). *Learning disabilities.* Retrieved March 6, 2006, from http://www.ncld.org/

National Center on Shaken Baby Syndrome. (2011). *Shaken baby syndrome.* Retrieved January 10, 2011, from http://www.dontshake.org/

National Clearinghouse on Child Abuse and Neglect. (2004). *What is child abuse and neglect?* Washington, DC: U.S. Department of Health and Human Services.

National Institute of Mental Health. (2011). *Autism spectrum disorders (pervasive developmental disorders).* Retrieved August 19, 2011, from http://www.nimh.nih.gov/Publicat/autism.clm

National Institutes of Health. (2008). *Clinical trial.gov.* Retrieved April 22, 2008, from http://clinicaltrials.gov/ct2/show/NCT00059293?cond=%22Intracranial+Embolism%22&r...

National Research Council. (2004). *Engaging schools: Fostering high school students' motivation to learn.* Washington, DC: National Academies Press.

National Sleep Foundation. (2006). *Sleep in America poll 2006.* Washington, DC: National Sleep Foundation.

National Sleep Foundation. (2007). *Sleep in America poll 2007.* Washington, DC: Author.

National Sleep Foundation. (2011). *Children's sleep habits.* Retrieved March 26, 2011, from http://www.sleepfoundation.org

National Vital Statistics Reports. (2004, March 7). *Deaths: Leading causes for 2002.* Atlanta: Centers for Disease Control and Prevention.

National Vital Statistics Reports. (2008, June 11). Table 7. Deaths and death rates for the 10 leading causes of death in specified age groups: United States, preliminary 2006. *National Vital Statistics Reports, 56*(16), 30.

Natusaki, M. N., & others. (2010). Early pubertal maturation and internalizing problems in adolescence: Sex differences in the role of cortical reactivity to interpersonal stress. *Journal of Clinical Child and Adolescent Psychology, 38,* 513–524.

Nazeer, A. (2011). Psychopharmacology of autism spectrum disorders in children and adolescents. *Pediatric Clinics of North America, 58,* 85–97.

Neal, A. R. (2009). Autism. In D. Carr (Ed.), *Encyclopedia of the life course and human development.* Boston: Gale Cengage.

Nearing, G. B., & others. (2011, in press). Psychosocial parental support programs and short-term clinical outcomes in extremely low-birth-weight infants. *Journal of Maternal-Fetal and Neonatal Medicine.*

Needham, A. (2009). Learning in infants' object perception, object-directed action, and tool use. In A. Needham & A. Woodward (Eds.), *Learning and the infant mind.* New York: Oxford University Press.

Needham, A., Barrett, T., & Peterman, K. (2002). A pick-me-up for infants' exploratory skills: Early simulated experiences reaching for objects using "sticky mittens" enhances young infants' object exploration skills. *Infant Behavior and Development, 25,* 279–295.

Negriff, S., Susman, E. J., & Trickett, P. K. (2011, in press). The development pathway from pubertal timing to delinquency and sexual activity from early to late adolescence. *Journal of Youth and Adolescence.*

Neisser, U., & others. (1996). Intelligence: Knowns and unknowns. *American Psychologist, 51,* 77–101.

Nelson, C. A. (2003). Neural development and lifelong plasticity. In R. M. Lerner, F. Jacobs, & D. Wertlieb (Eds.), *Handbook of applied developmental science* (Vol. 1). Thousand Oaks, CA: Sage.

Nelson, C. A. (2007). A developmental cognitive neuroscience approach to the study of atypical development: A model system involving infants of diabetic mothers. In D. Coch, G. Dawson, & K. W. Fischer (Eds.), *Human behavior, learning, and the developing brain.* New York: Guilford.

Nelson, C. A. (2011). Brain development and behavior. In A. M. Rudolph, C. Rudolph, L. First, G. Lister, & A. A. Gershon (Eds.), *Rudolph's pediatrics* (22nd ed.). New York: McGraw-Hill.

Nelson, D. M., & Burton, G. J. (2011). A technical note to improve the reporting of studies of the human placenta. *Placenta, 32,* 195–196.

Nelson, E. E., & Guyer, A. E. (2011). The development of the ventral prefrontal cortex and social flexibility. *Developmental Cognitive Neuroscience, 1,* 233–245.

Nelson, K. (1999). Levels and modes of representation: Issues for the theory of conceptual change and development. In E. K. Skolnick, K. Nelson, S. A. Gelman, & P. H. Miller (Eds.), *Conceptual development.* Mahwah, NJ: Erlbaum.

Nelson, S. L., & Lee, J. C. (2009). Socioeconomic inequality in education. In D. Carr (Ed.), *Encyclopedia of the life course and human development.* Boston: Gale Cengage.

Nemec, S. F., & others. (2011, in press). Male sexual development in utero: Testicular descent on prenatal MRI. *Ultrasound in Obstetrics and Gynecology.*

Neumann, C. G., Gewa, C., & Bwibo, N. B. (2004). Child nutrition in developing countries. *Pediatric Annals, 33,* 658–674.

Nevarez, M. D., & others. (2010). Associations of early life risk factors with infant sleep duration. *Academic Pediatrics, 10,* 187–193.

Neville, H. J. (2006). Different profiles of plasticity within human cognition. In Y. Munakata & M. H. Johnson (Eds.), *Attention and Performance XXI: Processes of change in brain and cognitive development.* Oxford, UK: Oxford University Press.

Newcombe, N. (2008). The development of implicit and explicit memory. In N. Cowan & M. Courage (Eds.), *The development of memory in childhood.* Philadelphia: Psychology Press.

Newcorn, J. H. (2011, in press). Risks and benefits of available treatments for adult ADHD. *Journal of Clinical Psychiatry.*

Newell, K., Scully, D. M., McDonald, P. V., & Baillargeon, R. (1989). Task constraints and infant grip configurations. *Developmental Psychobiology, 22,* 817–832.

Ni, T. L., Huang, C. C., & Guo, N. W. (2011). Executive function deficit in preschool children born very low birth weight with normal early development. *Early Human Development, 87,* 137–141.

NICHD Early Child Care Research Network. (2001). Nonmaternal care and family factors in early development: An overview of the NICHD study of early child care. *Journal of Applied Developmental Psychology, 22,* 457–492.

NICHD Early Child Care Research Network. (2002). Structure→process→outcome: Direct and indirect effects of child care quality on young children's development. *Psychological Science, 13,* 199–206.

NICHD Early Child Care Research Network. (2003). Does amount of time spent in child care predict socioemotional adjustment during the transition to kindergarten? *Child Development, 74,* 976–1005.

NICHD Early Child Care Research Network. (2004). Type of child care and children's development at 54 months. *Early Childhood Research Quarterly, 19,* 203–230.

NICHD Early Child Care Research Network. (2005). *Child care and development.* New York: Guilford.

NICHD Early Child Care Research Network. (2005a). Duration and developmental timing of poverty and children's cognitive and social development from birth through third grade. *Child Development, 76,* 795–810.

NICHD Early Child Care Research Network. (2005b). Predicting individual differences in attention, memory, and planning in first graders from experiences at home, child care, and school. *Developmental Psychology, 41,* 99–114.

NICHD Early Child Care Research Network. (2006). Infant-mother attachment classification: Risk and protection in relation to changing maternal caregiving quality. *Developmental Psychology, 42,* 38–58.

NICHD Early Child Care Research Network. (2009). Family-peer linkages: The mediational role of attentional processes. *Social Development, 18*, 875–895.

Nicklas, T. A., Webber, L. S., Jonson, C. S., Srinivasan, S. R., & Berensen, G. G. (1995). Foundations for health promotion with youth: A review of observations from the Bogalusa Heart Study. *Journal of Health Education, 26,* S18–S26.

Nicklas, T. A., Yang, S. J., Baranowski, T., Zakeri, I., & Berensen, G. (2003). Eating patterns and obesity in children: The Bogalusa Heart Study. *American Journal of Preventive Medicine, 25,* 9–16.

Nielsen, S. J., Siega-Riz, A. M., & Popkin, B. M. (2002). Trends in energy intake in U.S. between 1977 and 1996: Similar shifts seen across age groups. *Obesity Research, 10,* 370–378.

Nieto, A. J., & Brookhart, S. M. (2011). *Educational assessment of students* (6th ed.). Boston: Allyn & Bacon.

Nieto, S., & Bode, P. (2012). *Affirming diversity: The sociopolitical context of multicultural education* (6th ed.). Boston: Allyn & Bacon.

Nigro, G., & others. (2011, in press). Role of the infections in recurrent spontaneous abortion. *Journal of Maternal-Fetal and Neonatal Medicine.*

Nisbett, R. (2003). *The geography of thought.* New York: Free Press.

Noddings, N. (2008). Caring and moral education. In L. Nucci & D. Narváez (Ed.), *Handbook of moral and character education.* Clifton, NJ: Psychology Press.

Nolen-Hoeksema, S. (2011). *Abnormal psychology* (5th ed.). New York: McGraw-Hill.

Nommsen-Rivers, L. A., Mastergeorge, A. M., Hansen, R. L., Cullum, A. S., & Dewey, K. G. (2009). Doula care, early breastfeeding outcomes, and breastfeeding status at 6 weeks post-partum among low-income primiparae. *Journal of Obstetric, Gynecologic, and Neonatal Nursing, 38,* 157–173.

Norton, P. J., & Grellner, K. W. (2011). A retrospective study on infant bed-sharing in a clinical population. *Maternal and Child Health Journal, 15,* 507–513.

Nottelmann, E. D., & others. (1987). Gonadal and adrenal hormone correlates of adjustment in early adolescence. In R. M. Leiner & T. T. Foch (Eds.), *Biological-psychological interactions in early adolescence.* Hillsdale, NJ: Erlbaum.

Nowicka, P., & Flodmark, C. E. (2008). Family in pediatric obesity management: A literature review. *International Journal of Pediatric Obesity, 3* (Suppl. 1), S44–S50.

Nucci, L. (2006). Education for moral development. In M. Killen & J. Smetana (Eds.), *Handbook of moral development.* Mahwah, NJ: Erlbaum.

Nucci, L., & Gingo, M. (2011). Moral reasoning. In U. Goswami (Ed.), *Wiley-Blackwell handbook of childhood cognitive development* (2nd ed.). New York: Wiley.

Nucci, L., & Narváez, D. (Eds.). (2008). *Handbook of moral and character education.* New York: Psychology Press.

Nyqvist, K. H., & others. (2010). Towards universal kangaroo mother care: Recommendations and report from the first European conference and seventh international workshop on kangaroo care. *Acta Paediatrica, 99,* 820–826.

O

O'Donnell, A. M. (2012). Constructivism. In K. R. Harris, S. Graham, & T. Urdan (Eds.), *APA educational psychology handbook.* Washington, DC: American Psychological Association.

O'Mara, T. A., & others. (2011, in press). CHEK2, MGMT, SULT1E1, and SULT1A1 polymorphisms and endometrial cancer risk. *Twin Research and Human Genetics.*

Oberg, M., & others. (2011). Worldwide burden of disease from exposure to second-hand smoke: A retrospective analysis of data from 192 countries. *Lancet, 377,* 139–146.

Obermann, M. L. (2011). Moral disengagement in self-reported and peer-nominated school bullying. *Aggressive Behavior, 37,* 133–144.

Obradovic, J., Shaffer, A., & Masten, A. S. (2011, in press). Risk in developmental psychopathology: Progress and future directions. In L. C. Mayes & M. Lewis (Eds.), *The environment of human development: A handbook of theory and measurement.* New York: Cambridge University Press.

O'Callaghan, F. V., & others. (2010). The link between sleep problems in infancy and early childhood and attention problems at 5 and 14 years: Evidence from a birth cohort study. *Early Human Development, 86,* 419–424.

Ochs, E., & Schieffelin, B. (2008). Language socialization and language acquisition. In P. A. Duff & N. H. Hornberger (Eds.), *Encyclopedia of language and education.* New York: Springer.

O'Donnell, L., O'Donnell, C., Wardlaw, D. M., & Stueve, A. (2004). Risk and resiliency factors influencing suicidality among urban African American and Latino youth. *American Journal of Community Psychology, 33,* 37–49.

Offer, D., Ostrov E., Howard, K. I., & Atkinson, R. (1988). *The teenage world: Adolescents' self-image in ten countries.* New York: Plenum.

Ogbu, J., & Stern, P. (2001). Caste status and intellectual development. In R. J. Sternberg & E. L. Grigorenko (Eds.), *Environmental effects on cognitive abilities.* Mahwah, NJ: Erlbaum.

Ogden, C. L., Carroll, M. D., & Flegal. K. M. (2008). High body mass index for age among U.S. children and adolescents, 2003–2006. *Journal of the American Medical Association, 299,* 2401–2405.

O'Keefe, G. S., & others. (2011). The impact of social media on children, adolescents, and families. *Pediatrics, 127,* 800–804.

Olds, D. L., & others. (2004). Effects of home visits by paraprofessionals and nurses: Age 4 follow-up of a randomized trial. *Pediatrics, 114,* 1560–1568.

Olds, D. L., & others. (2007). Effects of nurse home visiting on maternal and child functioning: Age 9 follow-up of a randomized trial. *Pediatrics, 120,* e832–e845.

Olson, B. H., Haider, S. J., Vangjel, L., Bolton, T. A., & Gold, J. G. (2010). A quasi-experimental evaluation of a breastfeeding support program for low income women in Michigan. *Maternal and Child Health Journal, 14,* 86–93.

Olson, D., Sikka, R. S., Hayman, J., Novak, M., & Stavig, C. (2009). Exercise in pregnancy. *Current Sports Medicine Reports, 8,* 147–153.

Olweus, D. (2003). Prevalence estimation of school bullying with the Olweus bully/victim questionnaire. *Aggressive Behavior, 29*(3), 239–269.

Opfer, J. E., & Gelman, S. A. (2011). Development of the animate-inanimate distinction. In U. Goswami (Ed.), *Wiley-Blackwell handbook of childhood cognitive development* (2nd ed.). New York: Wiley.

Ophir, E., Nass, C., & Wagner, A. D. (2009). Cognitive control in media multitaskers. *Proceedings of the National Academy of Sciences USA, 106,* 15583–15587.

Ornstein, P., Coffman, J. L., & Grammer, J. K., (2007, April). *Teachers' memory-relevant conversations and children's memory performance.* Paper presented at the biennial meeting of the Society for Research in Child Development, Boston.

Ornstein, P., Grammer, J., & Coffman, J. (2010). Teachers' "mnemonic style" and the development of skilled memory. In H. S. Waters & W. Schneider (Eds.), *Metacognition, strategy use, and instruction.* New York: Guilford.

Ornstein, P. A., Coffman, J. L., Grammer, J. K., San Souci, P. P., & McCall, L. E. (2010). Linking the classroom context and the development of children's memory skills. In J. Meece & J. Eccles (Eds.), *The handbook of research on schools, schooling, and human development.* New York: Routledge.

Orsi, C. M., Hale, D. E., & Lynch, J. L. (2011). Pediatric obesity epidemiology. *Current Opinion in Endocrinology, Diabetes, and Obesity, 18,* 14–22.

Ortigosa Gomez, S., & others. (2011, in press). Use of illicit drugs over gestation and their neonatal impact. Comparison between periods 1982–1988 and 2002–2008. *Medicina Clinica.*

Ostbye, T., & others. (2011, in press). Kids and Adults Now! Defeat Obesity (KAN-DO): Rationale, design, and baseline characteristics. *Contemporary Clinical Trials.*

Ostchega, Y., Carroll, M., Prineas, R. J., McDowell, M. A., Louis, T., & Tilert, T. (2009). Trends of elevated blood pressure among children and adolescents: Data from the National Health and Nutrition Examination Survey 1988–2006. *American Journal of Hypertension, 22,* 59–67.

Otto, B. W. (2010). *Language development in early childhood* (3rd ed.). Upper Saddle River, NJ: Merrill.

Oude Luttikhuis, L. H., & others. (2009). Interventions for treating obesity in children. *Cochrane Database of Systematic Reviews, 1,* CD001872.

Overvelde, A., & Hulstijn, W. (2011). Handwriting development in grade 2 and grade 3 primary school children with normal, at risk, or dysgraphic characteristics. *Research in Developmental Disabilities, 32,* 540–548.

Ovesen, P., Rasmussen, S., & Kesmodel, U. (2011). Effect of prepregnancy maternal overweight and obesity on pregnancy outcome. *Obstetrics and Gynecology, 118,* 305–312.

Owens, J. A., Belon, K., & Moss, P. (2010). Impact of delaying school start time on adolescent sleep, mood, and behavior. *Archives of Pediatric and Adolescent Medicine, 164,* 608–614.

Owens, J., & Mindell, J. (2011). *Sleep in children and adolescents.* New York: Elsevier.

Ozono, S., & others. (2011). Juvenile myelomonocytic leukemia characterized by cutaneous lesion containing Langerhans cell histiocytosis-like cells. *International Journal of Hematology, 93,* 389–393.

P

Padilla-Walker, L. M., & Coyne, S. M. (2011, in press). "Turn that thing off!" Parent and adolescent predictors of proactive media monitoring. *Journal of Youth and Adolescence.*

Pakpreo, P., Ryan, S., Auinger, P., & Aten, M. (2005). The association between parental lifestyle behaviors and adolescent knowledge, attitudes, intentions, and nutritional and physical activity behaviors. *Journal of Adolescent Health, 34,* 129–130.

Palfrey, J., Sacco, D., Boyd, D., & DeBonis, L. (2009). *Enhancing child safety and online technologies.* Cambridge, MA: Berkman Center for Internet & Society.

Paloutzian, R. F. (2000). *Invitation to the psychology of religion* (3rd ed.). Needham Heights, MA: Allyn & Bacon.

Pan, B. A. (2008). Unpublished review of J. W. Santrock's *Life-span development,* 12th ed. (New York: McGraw-Hill).

Pan, B. A., Rowe, M. L., Singer, J. D., & Snow, C. E. (2005). Maternal correlates of growth in toddler vocabulary production in low-income families. *Child Development, 76,* 763–782.

Pan, B. A., & Uccelli, P. (2009). Semantic development. In J. Berko Gleason & N. Rather (Eds.), *The development of language* (7th ed.). Boston: Allyn & Bacon.

Pang, E. W., Wang, F., Malone, M., Kadis, D. S., & Donner, E. J. (2011). Localization of Broca's area using verb generation tasks in the MEG: Validation against fMRI. *Neuroscience Letters, 490,* 215–219.

Parens, E., & Johnston, J. (2009). Fact, values, and attention-deficit hyperactivity disorder (ADHD): An update on the controversies. *Child and Adolescent Psychiatry and Mental Health, 3,* 1.

Paris, F., & others. (2010). Premature pubarche in Mediterranean girls: High prevalence of heterozygous CYP21 mutation carriers. *Gynecological Endocrinology, 26,* 319–324.

Park, D. C., & Bischof, G. N. (2011). Neuroplasticity, aging, and cognitive function. In K. W. Schaie & S. L. Willis (Eds.), *Handbook of the psychology of aging* (7th ed.). New York: Elsevier.

Park, H. Y., & others. (2010). Neurodevelopmental toxicity of prenatal polychlorinated biphenyls (PCBs) by chemical structure and activity: A birth cohort study. *Environmental Health, 23,* 51.

Park, M. J., Paul Mulye, T., Adams, S. H., Brindis, C. D., & Irwin, C. E., Jr. (2006). The health status of young adults in the United States. *Journal of Adolescent Health, 39,* 305–317.

Parke, R. D., & Buriel, R. (2006). Socialization in the family: Ethnic and ecological perspectives. In W. Damon & R. Lerner (Eds.), *Handbook of child psychology* (6th ed.). New York: Wiley.

Parke, R. D., & Clarke-Stewart, A. (2011). *Social development.* New York: Wiley.

Parke, R. D., Coltrane, S., & Schofield, T. (2011, in press). The bicultural advantage. In J. Marsh, R. Menoza-Denton, & J. A. Smith (Eds.), *Are we born racist?* Boston: Beacon Press.

Parke, R. D., Leidy, M. S., Schofield, T. J., Miller, M. A., & Morris, K. L. (2008). Socialization. In M. M. Haith & J. B. Benson (Eds.), *Encyclopedia of infant and early childhood development.* Oxford, UK: Elsevier.

Parrett, A. L., & others. (2011). Adiposity and aerobic fitness are associated with metabolic disease risk in children. *Applied Physiology, Nutrition, and Metabolism, 36,* 72–79.

Parsons, C. E., Young, K. S., Murray, L., Stein, A., & Kringelbach, M. L. (2010). The functional neuroanatomy of the evolving parent-infant relationship. *Progress in Neurobiology, 91*(3), 220–241.

Parsons, D. W., & others. (2011). The genetic landscape of the childhood cancer medulloblastoma. *Science, 331,* 435–439.

Pasley, K., & Moorefield, B. S. (2004). Stepfamilies. In M. Coleman & L. Ganong (Eds.), *Handbook of contemporary families.* Thousand Oaks, CA: Sage.

Pate, R. R., Pfeiffer, K. A., Trost, S. G., Ziegler, P., & Dowda, M. (2004). Physical activity among children attending preschools. *Pediatrics, 114,* 1258–1263.

Pate, R. R., & others. (2009). Age-related change in physical activity in adolescent girls. *Journal of Adolescent Health, 44,* 275–282.

Patel, B. N., Beste, J., & Blackwell, J. C. (2011). Antidepressant use during pregnancy: FPIN's clinical inquiries. *American Family Physician, 83,* 1211–1215.

Patel, R., & others. (2011). European guideline for the management of genital herpes, 2010. *International Journal of STD and AIDS, 22,* 1–10.

Patel, S. G., Salahuddin, N. M., & O'Brien, M. (2008). Career decision-making self-efficacy of Vietnamese adolescents: The role of acculturation, social support, socioeconomic status, and racism. *Journal of Career Development, 34,* 218–240.

Patell, E. A., Cooper, H., & Robinson, J. C. (2008). The effects of choice on intrinsic motivation and related outcomes: A meta-analysis of research findings. *Psychological Bulletin, 134*(2), 270–300.

Patterson, C. J. (2009). Lesbian and gay parents and their children: A social sciences perspective. *Nebraska Symposium on Motivation, 54,* 142–182.

Patterson, C. J., & Wainright, J. L. (2011, in press). Adolescents with same-sex parents: Findings from the National Longitudinal Study of Adolescent Health. In D. Brodzinsky, A. Pertman, & D. Kunz (Eds.), *Lesbian and gay adoption: A new American reality.* New York: Oxford University Press.

Patterson, K., & Wright, A. E. (1990, Winter). The speech language, or hearing-impaired child: At-risk academically. *Childhood Education,* pp. 91–95.

Patton, G. C., & others. (2011, in press). Overweight and obesity between adolescence and early adulthood: A 10-year prospective study. *Journal of Adolescent Health.*

Paulhus, D. L. (2008). Birth order. In M. M. Haith & J. B. Benson (Eds.), *Encyclopedia of infant and early childhood development.* Oxford, UK: Elsevier.

Paus, T., & others. (2008). Morphological properties of the action-observation cortical network in adolescents with low and high resistance to peer influence. *Social Neuroscience, 3*(3), 303–316.

Pavlov, I. P. (1927). In G. V. Anrep (Trans.), *Conditioned reflexes.* London: Oxford University Press.

Pearlstein, T., Howard, M., Salisbury, A., & Zlotnick, C. (2009). Postpartum depression. *American Journal of Obstetrics and Gynecology, 200,* 357–364.

Pedersen, W., & Mastekaasa, A. (2011). Conduct disorder symptoms and subsequent pregnancy, child-birth, and abortion: A population-based longitudinal study of adolescents. *Journal of Adolescence, 34*(5), 1025–1033.

Pederson, D. R., & Moran, G. (1996). Expressions of the attachment relationship outside of the Strange Situation. *Child Development, 67,* 915–927.

Pedigo, J. (2011). Visual impairment: Cognitive-linguistic intervention with a preschool child who has a visual impairment. In S. S. Chabon & E. R. Cohn (Eds.), *Communication disorders casebook.* Upper Saddle River, NJ: Pearson.

Pedroso, F. S. (2008). Reflexes. In M. H. Haith & J. B. Benson (Eds.), *Infant and early childhood development.* Oxford, UK: Elsevier.

Peek, L., & Stough, L. M. (2010). Children with disabilities in the context of disaster: A social vulnerability perspective. *Child Development, 81,* 1260–1270.

Peets, K., Hodges, E. V. E., & Salmivalli, C. (2011). Actualization of social cognition into aggressive behavior toward disliked targets. *Social Development, 20,* 233–250.

Pelayo, R., Owens, J., Mindell, J., & Sheldon, S. (2006). Bed sharing with unimpaired parents is not an important risk for sudden infant death syndrome [Letter to the editor]. *Pediatrics, 117,* 993–994.

Pelczarski, K., & Yaruss, S. (2011). Fluency: A preschool child who stutters. In S. S. Chabon & E .R. Cohn (Eds.), *Communication disorders casebook.* Upper Saddle River, NJ: Pearson.

Pelton, S. I, & Leibovitz, E. (2009). Recent advances in otitis media. *Pediatric and Infectious Disease Journal, 28*(10, Suppl.), S133–S137.

Pena, E., & Bedore, J. A. (2009). Bilingualism. In R. G. Schwartz (Ed.), *Handbook of child language disorders.* Clifton, NJ: Psychology Press.

Pennell, A., Salo-Coombs, V., Hering, A., Spielman, F., & Fecho, K. (2011). Anesthesia and analgesia-related preferences and outcomes of women who have birth plans. *Journal of Midwifery and Women's Health, 56,* 376–381.

Persson, K. E., Fridlund, B., Kvist, L. J., & Dykes, A. K. (2011). Mothers' sense of security in the first postnatal week: Interview study. *Journal of Advanced Nursing, 67,* 105–116.

Pesce, C., Crova, L., Cereatti, L., Casella, R., & Bellucci, M. (2009). Physical activity and mental performance in preadolescents: Effects of acute exercise on free-recall memory. *Mental Health and Physical Activity, 2,* 16–22.

Peskin, H. (1967). Pubertal onset and ego functioning. *Journal of Abnormal Psychology, 72,* 1–15.

Peters, J. M., & Stout, D. L. (2011). *Science in elementary education* (11th ed.). Boston: Allyn & Bacon.

Peters, K. F., & Petrill, S. A. (2011, in press). Comparison of background, needs, and expectations for genetic counseling of adults with experience with Down syndrome, Marfan syndrome, and neurofibromatosis. *American Journal of Medical Genetics A.*

Peterson, C. C. (2005). Mind and body: Concepts of human cognition, physiology and false belief in children with autism or typical development. *Journal of Autism and Developmental Disorders, 35,* 487–497.

Pew Research Center. (2010). *Millennials: Confident, connected, open to change.* Washington, DC: Pew Research Center.

Phelan, S., & others. (2011, in press). Randomized trial of a behavioral intervention to prevent excessive gestational weight gain: The Fit for Delivery Study. *American Journal of Clinical Nutrition.*

Phillips, D. A., & Lowenstein, A. (2011). Early care, education, and development. *Annual Review of Psychology* (Vol. 62). Palo Alto, CA: Annual Reviews.

Phinney, J. S. (2006). Ethnic identity exploration in emerging adulthood. In J. J. Arnett & J. L. Tanner (Eds.), *Emerging adults in America.* Washington, DC: American Psychological Association.

Phinney, J. S. (2008). Bridging identities and disciplines: Advances and challenges in understanding multiple identities. In M. Azmitia, M. Syed, & K. Radmacher (Eds.), The intersections of personal and social identities. *New Directions for Child and Adolescent Development, 120,* 81–95.

Phinney, J. S., & Ong, A. D. (2007). Conceptualization and measurement of ethnic identity: Current status and future directions. *Journal of Counseling Psychology, 54,* 271–281.

Piaget, J. (1932). *The moral judgment of the child.* New York: Harcourt Brace Jovanovich.

Piaget, J. (1952). *The origins of intelligence in children* (M. Cook, Trans.). New York: International Universities Press.

Piaget, J. (1954). *The construction of reality in the child.* New York: Basic Books.

Piaget, J. (1962). *Play, dreams, and imitation.* New York. W. W. Norton.

Piaget, J., & Inhelder, B. (1969). *The child's conception of space* (F. J. Langdon & J. L. Lunger, Trans.). New York: W. W. Norton.

Ping, H., & Hagopian, W. (2006). Environmental factors in the development of type 1 diabetes. *Reviews in Endocrine and Metabolic Disorders, 7,* 149–162.

Piper, B. J., & others. (2011, in press). Abnormalities in parentally rated executive function in methamphetamine/polysubstance exposed children. *Pharmacology, Biochemistry, and Behavior.*

Pitkanen, T., Lyyra, A. L., & Pulkkinen, L. (2005). Age of onset of drinking and the use of alcohol in adulthood: A follow-up study from age 8–42 for females and males. *Addiction, 100,* 652–661.

Plener, P. L., Singer, H., & Goldbeck, L. (2011). Traumatic events and suicidality in a German adolescent community sample. *Journal of Traumatic Stress, 24,* 121–124.

Plomin, R. (2004). Genetics and developmental psychology. *Merrill-Palmer Quarterly, 50,* 341–352.

Plomin, R. (2011). Commentary: Why are children in the same family so different? Nonshared environment three decades later. *International Journal of Epidemiology, 40,* 582–592.

Plomin, R., & Daniels, D. (2011). Why are children in the same family so different from one another? *International Journal of Epidemiology, 40,* 563–582.

Plucker, J. (2010, July 19). Commentary in P. Bronson & A. Merryman, The creativity crisis. *Newsweek,* 45–46.

Pluess, M., & Belsky, J. (2009). Differential susceptibility to rearing experience: The case of child care. *Journal of Child Psychology and Psychiatry, 50*(4), 396–404.

Pluess, M., & Belsky, J. (2011). Prenatal programming of postnatal plasticity? *Development and Psychopathology, 23,* 29–38.

Pluess, M., & others. (2011) Serotonin transporter polymorphism moderates effects of prenatal maternal anxiety on infant negative emotionality. *Biological Psychiatry, 69,* 520–525.

Pollitt, E. P., Gorman, K. S., Engle, P. L., Martorell, R., & Rivera, J. (1993). Early supplementary feeding and cognition. *Monographs of the Society for Research in Child Development, 58*(7, Serial No. 235).

Poole, D. A., & Lindsay, D. S. (1995). Interviewing preschoolers: Effects of nonsuggestive techniques, parental coaching, and leading questions on reports of nonexperienced events. *Journal of Experimental Child Psychology, 60,* 129–154.

Popham, W. J. (2011). *Classroom assessment* (6th ed.). Boston: Allyn & Bacon.

Porath, A. J., & Fried, P. A. (2005). Effects of prenatal cigarette and marijuana exposure on drug use among offspring. *Neurotoxicology and Teratology, 27,* 267–277.

Posada, G., & Kaloustian, G. (2010a). Attachment in infancy. In J. G. Bremmer & T. D. Wachs (Eds.), *Wiley-Blackwell handbook of infant development* (2nd ed.). New York: Wiley.

Posada, G., & Kaloustian, G. (2010b). Early social cognitive skills at play in toddlers' peer interactions. In J. G. Bremner & T. D. Wachs (Eds.), *Wiley-Blackwell handbook of infant development* (2nd ed.). New York: Wiley.

Posada, G., & others. (2002). Maternal caregiving and infant security in two cultures. *Developmental Psychology, 38,* 67–78.

Posner, M. I. (2003). Imaging a science of mind. *Trends in Cognitive Science, 7,* 450–453.

Posner, M. I., & Rothbart, M. K. (2007). *Educating the human brain.* Washington, DC: American Psychological Association.

Poston, L., & others. (2011). Obesity in pregnancy: Implications for the mother and lifelong health of the child. A consensus statement. *Pediatric Research, 69,* 175–180.

Poulin, F., Kiesner, J., Pedersen, S., & Dishion, T. J. (2011, in press). A short-term longitudinal analysis of friendship selection on early adolescent substance use. *Journal of Adolescence.*

Powell, S. D. (2012). *Your introduction to education* (2nd ed.). Upper Saddle River, NJ: Pearson.

Power, T. G. (2011). Social play. In P. K. Smith & C. H. Hart (Eds.), *Wiley-Blackwell handbook of childhood social development* (2nd ed.). New York: Wiley.

Pratt, C., & Bryant, P. E. (1990). Young children understand that looking leads to knowing (so long as they are looking in a single barrel). *Child Development, 61,* 973–982.

Pressley, M. (2003). Psychology of literacy and literacy instruction. In I. B. Weiner (Ed.), *Handbook of psychology* (Vol. 7). New York: Wiley.

Pressley, M. (2007). An interview with Michael Pressley by Terri Flowerday and Michael Shaughnessy. *Educational Psychology Review, 19,* 1–12.

Pressley, M., Allington, R., Wharton-McDonald, R., Block, C. C., & Morrow, L. M.

(2001). *Learning to read: Lessons from exemplary first grades.* New York: Guilford.

Pressley, M., Dolezal, S. E, Raphael, L. M., Welsh, L. M., Bogner, K., & Roehrig, A. D. (2003). *Motivating primary-grades teachers.* New York: Guilford.

Pressley, M., & McCormick, C. B. (2007). *Child and adolescent development for educators.* New York: Guilford.

Pressley, M., Mohan, L., Fingeret, L., Reffitt, K., & Raphael-Bogaert, L. R. (2007). Writing instruction in engaging and effective elementary settings. In S. Graham, C. A. MacArthur, & J. Fitzgerald (Eds.), *Best practices in writing instruction.* New York: Guilford.

Pressley, M., Mohan, L., Raphael, L. M., & Fingeret, L. (2007). How does Bennett Woods Elementary School produce such high reading and writing achievement? *Journal of Educational Psychology, 99,* 221–240.

Pressley, M., Raphael, L. Gallagher, D., & DiBella, J. (2004). Providence-St. Mel School: How a school that works for African-American students works. *Journal of Educational Psychology, 96,* 216–235.

Prinstein, M. J. (2007). Moderators of peer contagion: A longitudinal examination of depression socialization between adolescents and their best friends. *Journal of Clinical Child and Adolescent Psychology, 36,* 159–170.

Prinstein, M. J., Rancourt, D., Guerry, J. D., & Browne, C. B. (2009). Peer reputations and psychological adjustment. In K. H. Rubin, W. M. Bukowksi, & B. Laursen (Eds.), *Handbook of peer interactions, relationships, and groups.* New York: Guilford.

Prinz, R. J., Sanders, M. R., Shapiro, C. J., Witaker, D. J., & Lutzker, J. R. (2009). Population-based prevention of child maltreatment: The U.S. Triple P System Population Trial. *Prevention Science, 10,* 1–12.

Pryor, J. H., Hurtado, S., DeAngelo, L., Blake, L. P., & Tran, S. (2010). *The American freshman: National norms for fall 2010.* Los Angeles: Higher Education Institute, UCLA.

Puder, J. J., & Munsch, S. (2010). Psychological correlates of childhood obesity. *International Journal of Obesity, 34* (Suppl. 2), S37–S43.

Pujol, J., & others. (2004). Delayed myelination in children with developmental delay detected by volumetric MRI. *NeuroImage, 22,* 897–903.

Puma, M., & others. (2010). *Head Start impact study: Final report.* Washington, DC: Administration for Children & Families.

Pungello, E. P., Iruka, I. U., Dotterer, A. M., Mills-Koonce, R., & Reznick, J. S. (2009). The effects of socioeconomic status, race, and parenting on language development in early childhood. *Developmental Psychology, 45,* 544–557.

Purper-Ouakil, D., & others. (2011). Neurobiology of attention deficit/hyperactivity disorder. *Pediatric Research, 69,* 69R–76R.

Putallaz, M., Grimes, C. L., Foster, K. J., Kupersmidt, J. B., Clie, J. D., & Dearing, K. (2007). Overt and relational aggression and victimization: Multiple perspectives within the school setting. *Journal of School Psychology, 45,* 523–547.

Q

Qui, M. G., & others. (2011, in press). Changes of brain structure and function in ADHD children. *Brain Topography.*

Quinn, P. C. (2011). Born to categorize. In U. Goswami (Ed.), *Wiley-Blackwell handbook of childhood cognitive development* (2nd ed.). New York: Wiley-Blackwell.

Quintana, S. M. (2011). Ethnicity, race, and children's social development. In P. K. Smith & C. H. Hart (Eds.), *Wiley-Blackwell handbook of childhood social development* (2nd ed.). New York: Wiley.

R

Raabe, A., & Muller, W. U. (2008). Radiation exposure during pregnancy. *Neurosurgery Review, 31,* 351–362.

Raffaelli, M., & Ontai, L. L. (2004). Gender socialization in Latino/a families: Results from two retrospective studies. *Sex Roles, 50,* 287–299.

Rafla, N., Nair, M. S., & Kumar, S. (2008). Exercise in pregnancy. In J. Studd, S. L. Tan, & F. A. Cherenak (Eds.), *Progress in obstetrics and gynecology.* Oxford, UK: Elsevier.

Raikes, H. A., & Thompson, R. A. (2009). Attachment security and parenting quality predict children's problem-solving, attributions, and loneliness with peers. *Attachment and Human Development, 10,* 319–344.

Raikes, H., & others. (2006). Mother-child bookreading in low-income families: Correlates and outcomes during the first three years of life. *Child Development, 77,* 924–953.

Raizada, R. S., Richards, T. L., Meltzoff, A. N., & Kuhl, P. K. (2008). Socioeconomic status predicts hemispheric specialization of the left inferior frontal gyrus in young children. *NeuroImage, 40,* 1392–1401.

Rajaraman, P., & others. (2011, in press). Early life exposure to diagnostic radiation and ultrasound scans and risk of childhood cancer: Case-control study. *British Medical Journal.*

Rambusch, N. M. (2010). Freedom, order, and the child: Self-control and mastery of the world mark the dynamic Montessori method. *Montessori Life, 22,* 38–43.

Ramchandani, P. G., Sein, A., O'Connor, T. G., Heron, J., Murray, L., & Evans, J. (2008). Depression in men in the postnatal period and later psychopathology: A population cohort study. *Journal of the American Academy of Child and Adolescent Psychiatry, 47,* 390–398.

Ramey, C. T., & Ramey, S. L. (2004). Early learning and school readiness: Can early intervention make a difference? *Merrill-Palmer Quarterly, 50,* 471–491.

Ramey, S. L. (2005). Human developmental science serving children and families: Contributions of the NICHD study of early child care. In NICHD Early Child Care Network (Eds.), *Child care and development.* New York: Guilford.

Ramey, S. L., & Ramey, C. T. (1999). *Going to school: How to help your child succeed.* New York: Goddard Press.

Ramsey-Rennels, J. L., & Langlois, J. H. (2007). How infants perceive and process faces. In A. Slater & M. Lewis (Eds.), *Introduction to infant development* (2nd ed.). Malden, MA: Blackwell.

Ranke, M. B., & Lindberg, A. (2011, in press). Observed and predicted total pubertal growth during treatment with growth hormone in adolescents with idiopathic growth hormone deficiency, Turner syndrome, short stature, born small for gestational age, and idiopathic short stature: KIGS analysis and review. *Hormone Research in Pediatrics.*

Rasmussen, K., & others. (2010). Recommendations for weight gain during pregnancy in the context of the obesity epidemic. *Obstetrics and Gynecology, 116,* 1191–1195.

Rasmussen, M. M., & Clemmensen, D. (2010). Folic acid supplementation in pregnant women. *Danish Medical Bulletin, 57,* A4134.

Ratcliffe, S. D. (2008). *Family medicine obstetrics* (3rd ed.). Oxford, UK: Elsevier.

Raven, P. H. (2011). *Biology* (9th ed.). New York: McGraw-Hill.

Raznahan, A., & others. (2011). How does your cortex grow? *Journal of Neuroscience, 31,* 7174–7177.

Realini, J. P., Buzi, R. S. Smith, P. B., & Martinez, M. (2010). Evaluation of "big decisions": An abstinence-plus sexuality. *Journal of Sex and Marital Therapy, 36,* 313–326.

Reddy, U. M., Wapner, R. J., Rebar, R. W., & Tasca, R. J. (2007). Infertility, assisted reproductive technology, and adverse pregnancy outcomes: Executive summary of a National Institute of Child Health and Human Development workshop. *Obstetrics and Gynecology, 109,* 967–977.

Reef, S. E., & others. (2011). Progress toward control of rubella and prevention of congenital rubella syndrome—worldwide, 2009. *Journal of Infectious Diseases, 204* (Suppl. 1), S24–S27.

Regalado, M., Sareen, H., Inkelas, M., Wissow, L. S., & Halfon, N. (2004). Parents' discipline of young children: Results from the National Survey of Early Childhood Health. *Pediatrics, 113,* 1952–1958.

Regev, R. H., & others. (2003). Excess mortality and morbidity among small-for-gestational-age premature infants: A population-based study. *Journal of Pediatrics, 143,* 186–191.

Reich, S. M., & Vandell, D. L. (2011). The interplay between parents and peers as socializing influences on children's development. In P. K. Smith & C. H. Hart (Eds.), *Wiley-Blackwell handbook of childhood social development* (2nd ed.). New York: Wiley.

Reid, P. T., & Zalk, S. R. (2001). Academic environments: Gender and ethnicity in U. S. higher education. In J. Worell (Ed.), *Encyclopedia of women and gender*. San Diego: Academic Press.

Reijmerink, N. E., & others. (2011, in press). Toll-like receptors and microbial exposure: gene-gene and gene-environment interaction in the development of atopy. *European Respiratory Journal*.

Reiss, J. (2012). *120 content strategies for English language learners* (2nd ed.). Boston: Allyn & Bacon.

Repacholi, B. M., & Gopnik, A. (1997). Early reasoning about desires: Evidence from 14- and 18-month-olds. *Developmental Psychology, 33,* 12–21.

Reutzel, D. R., & Cooper, R. B. (2012). *Teaching children to read* (6th ed.). Boston: Allyn & Bacon.

Reyna, V., & Farley, F. (2006). Risk and rationality in adolescent decision-making: Implications for theory, practice, and public policy. *Psychological Science in the Public Interest, 7,* 1–44.

Reyna, V. F. (2004). How people make decisions that involve risk: A dual-process approach. *Current Directions in Psychological Science, 13,* 60–66.

Reyna, V. F., & Brainerd, C. J. (1995). Fuzzy-trace theory: An interim analysis. *Learning and Individual Differences, 7,* 1–75.

Reyna, V. F., Estrada, S. M., DeMarinis, J. A., Myers, R. M., Stanisz, J. M., & Mills, B. A. (2011, in press). Neurobiological and memory models of risky decision making in adolescents versus young adults. *Journal of Experimental Psychology: Learning, Memory, and Cognition*.

Reyna, V. F., & Rivers, S. E. (2008). Current theories of risk and rational decision making. *Developmental Review, 28,* 1–11.

Reynolds, F. (2010). The effects of maternal labour analgesia on the fetus. *Best Practices & Research. Clinical Obstetrics & Gynaecology, 24,* 289–302.

Richards, J. E. (2009). Attention to the brain in infancy. In S. Johnson (Ed.), *Neuroconstructivism: The new science of cognitive development*. New York: Oxford University Press.

Richards, J. E. (2010). Infant attention, arousal, and the brain. In L. M. Oakes, C. H. Cashon, M. Casasola, & D. H. Rakison (Eds.), *Infant perception and cognition*. New York: Oxford University Press.

Richards, J. E., Reynolds, G. D., & Courage, M. I. (2010). The neural bases of infant attention. *Current Directions in Psychological Science, 19,* 41–46.

Richardson, G. A., Goldschmidt, L., & Larkby, C. (2008). Effects of prenatal cocaine exposure on growth: A longitudinal analysis. *Pediatrics, 120,* e1017–e1027.

Richardson, G. A., Goldschmidt, L., Leech, S., & Willford, J. (2011). Prenatal cocaine exposure: Effects on mother- and teacher-rated behavior problems and growth in school-aged children. *Neurotoxicology and Teratology, 33,* 69–77.

Richardson, G. A., Ryan, C., Willford, J., Day, N. L., & Goldschmidt, L. (2002). Prenatal alcohol and marijuana exposure: Effects on neuropsychological outcomes at 10 years. *Neurotoxicology and Teratology, 24,* 309–320.

Riddle, D. B., & Prinz, R. (1984, August). *Sugar consumption in young children*. Paper presented at the meeting of the American Psychological Association, Toronto.

Rideout, V. J., Foehr, U. G., & Roberts, D. F. (2010). *Generation M^2: Media in the lives of 8- to 18-year-olds*. Menlo Park, CA: Kaiser Family Foundation.

Rink, J. E. (2009). *Designing the physical education curriculum*. New York: McGraw-Hill.

Rinsky, J. R., & Hinshaw, S. P. (2011, in press). Linkages between childhood executive functioning and adolescent social functioning and psychopathology in girls with ADHD. *Child Neuropsychology*.

Risch, N., & others. (2009). Interaction between the serotonin transporter gene (5-HTTLPR), stressful life events, and risk of depression: A meta-analysis. *Journal of the American Medical Association, 301,* 2462–2471.

Rivas-Drake, D. (2011, in press). Ethnic-racial socialization and adjustment among Latino college students: The mediating roles of ethnic centrality, public regard, and perceived barriers to opportunity. *Journal of Youth and Adolescence*.

Rizzo, M. S. (1999, May 8). Genetic counseling combines science with a human touch. *Kansas City Star*, p. 3.

Roberts, D. F., Henriksen, L., & Foehr, U. G. (2004). Adolescents and the media. In R. Lerner & L. Steinberg (Eds.), *Handbook of adolescent psychology* (2nd ed.). New York: Wiley.

Robertson, W., Thorogood, M., Inglis, N., Grainger, C., & Stewart-Brown, S. (2011, in press). Two-year follow-up of the "Families for Health" programme for the treatment of childhood obesity. *Child Care, Health, and Development*.

Rochlen, A. B., McKelley, R. A., Suizzo, M. A., & Scaringi, V. (2008). Predictors of relationship satisfaction, psychological well-being, and life-satisfaction among stay-at-home fathers. *Psychology of Men and Masculinity, 9,* 17–28.

Rode, S. S., Chang, P., Fisch, R. O., & Sroufe, L. A. (1981). Attachment patterns of infants separated at birth. *Developmental Psychology, 17,* 188–191.

Rodriguez, E. T., & others. (2009). The formative role of home literacy experiences across the first three years of life in children from low-income families. *Journal of Applied Developmental Psychology, 30,* 677–694.

Roisman, G. I., & Groh, A. M. (2011). Attachment theory and research in developmental psychology. In M. K. Underwood & L. H. Rosen (Eds.), *Social development*. New York: Guilford.

Rokholm, B., Baker, J. L., & Sorensen, T. I. (2010). The leveling off of the obesity epidemic since the year 1999—a review of evidence and perspectives. *Obesity Reviews, 11,* 835–846.

Roman, A. S., & others. (2011, in press). The effect of maternal obesity on pregnancy outcomes in women with gestational diabetes. *Journal of Maternal-Fetal and Neonatal Medicine*.

Romano, A. M., & Lothian, J. A. (2008). Promoting, protecting, and supporting normal birth: A look at the evidence. *Journal of Obstetric, Gynecological, and Neonatal Nursing, 37,* 94–104.

Romo, A., Carceller, R., & Tobajas, J. (2009). Intrauterine growth retardation (IGUR): Epidemiology and etiology. *Pediatric Endocrinology Reviews, 6* (Suppl. 3), S332–S336.

Ronald, A., & Hoekstra, R. A. (2011). Autism spectrum disorders and autistic traits: A decade of new twin studies. *American Journal of Medical Genetics B: Neuropsychiatric Genetics, 156,* 255–274.

Roopnarine, J. L., & Metindogan, A. (2006). Early childhood education research in cross-national perspective. In B. Spodek & O. N. Saracho (Eds.), *Handbook of research on the education of young children*. Mahwah, NJ: Erlbaum.

Rose, A. J., Carlson, W., & Waller, E. M. (2007). Prospective associations of co-rumination with friendship and emotional adjustment: Considering the socioemotional trade-offs of co-rumination. *Developmental Psychology, 43,* 1019–1031.

Rose, S. A., Feldman, J. F., & Wallace, I. F. (1992). Infant information processing in relation to six-year cognitive outcomes. *Child Development, 63,* 1126–1141.

Rosen, L. D., Cheever, N. A., & Carrier, L. M. (2008). The association of parenting style and child age with parental limit setting and adolescent MySpace behavior. *Journal of Applied Developmental Psychology, 29,* 459–471.

Rosenberg, M. S., Westling, D. L., & McLeskey, J. (2011). *Special education for today's teachers* (2nd ed.). Upper Saddle River, NJ: Pearson.

Rosenblith, J. F. (1992). *In the beginning* (2nd ed.). Newbury Park, CA: Sage.

Rosenblum, G. D., & Lewis, M. (2003). Emotional development in adolescence. In G. Adams & M. Berzonsky (Eds.), *Blackwell handbook of adolescence*. Malden, MA: Blackwell.

Rosenfeld, R. G., & Bakker, B. (2008). Compliance and persistence in pediatric and adult patients receiving growth hormone therapy. *Endocrine Practice, 14,* 143–154.

Rosengard, C. (2009). Confronting the intendedness of adolescent rapid repeat pregnancy. *Journal of Adolescent Health, 44,* 5–6.

Rosenstein, D., & Oster, H. (1988). Differential facial responses to four basic tastes in newborns. *Child Development, 59,* 1555–1568.

Rosenthal, N. L., & Kobak, R. (2010). Assessing adolescents' attachment hierarchies:

Differences across developmental periods and associations with individual adaptation. *Journal of Research on Adolescence, 20,* 678–706.

Ross, J. L., & others. (2008). Cognitive and motor development during childhood in boys with Klinefelter syndrome. *American Journal of Medical Genetics A, 146A,* 708–719.

Roth, J. L., Brooks-Gunn, J., Murray, L., & Foster, W. (1998). Promoting healthy adolescents: Synthesis of youth development program evaluations. *Journal of Research on Adolescence, 8,* 423–459.

Rothbart, M. K. (2004). Temperament and the pursuit of an integrated developmental psychology. *Merrill-Palmer Quarterly, 50,* 492–505.

Rothbart, M. K. (2011). *Becoming who we are.* New York: Guilford.

Rothbart, M. K., & Bates, J. E. (2006). Temperament. In W. Damon & R. Lerner (Eds.), *Handbook of child psychology* (6th ed.). New York: Wiley.

Rothbart, M. K., & Gartstein, M. A. (2008). Temperament. In M. M. Haith & J. B. Benson (Eds.), *Encyclopedia of infant and early childhood development.* Oxford, UK: Elsevier.

Rothbaum, F., & Trommsdorff, G. (2007). Do roots and wings complement or oppose one another?: The socialization of relatedness and autonomy in cultural context. In J. E. Grusec & P. D. Hastings (Eds.), *Handbook of socialization.* New York: Guilford.

Rothbaum, F., Weisz, J., Pott, M., Miyake, K., & Morelli, G. (2000). Attachment and culture: Security in the United States and Japan. *American Psychologist, 55,* 1093–1104.

Roussssotte, F. F. (2011). Abnormal brain activation during working memory in children with prenatal exposure to drugs of abuse: The effects of methamphetamine, alcohol, and polydrug exposure. *NeuroImage, 54,* 3067–3075.

Rovee-Collier, C. (1987). Learning and memory in children. In J. D. Osofsky (Ed.), *Handbook of infant development* (2nd ed.). New York: Wiley.

Rovee-Collier, C. (2004). Infant learning and memory. In U. Goswami (Ed.), *Blackwell handbook of childhood cognitive development.* Malden, MA: Blackwell.

Rovee-Collier, C. (2008). The development of infant memory. In N. Cowan & M. Courage (Eds.), *The development of memory in infancy and childhood.* Philadelphia: Psychology Press.

Rovee-Collier, C., & Barr, R. (2010). Infant learning and memory. In J. G. Bremner & T. D. Wachs (Eds.), *Wiley-Blackwell handbook of infant development* (2nd ed.). New York: Wiley.

Rovee-Collier, C., & Cuevas, K. (2009). The development of infant memory. In M. L. Courage & N. Cowan (Eds.), *The development of memory in infancy and childhood.* New York: Psychology Press.

Rowe, M. L., & Goldin-Meadow, S. (2009). Differences in early gesture explain SES disparities in child vocabulary size at school entry. *Science, 323,* 951–953.

Rowley, S. R., Kurtz-Costas, B., & Cooper, S. M. (2010). The role of schooling in ethnic minority achievement and attainment, In J. Meece & J. Eccles (Eds.), *Handbook of research on schools, schooling, and human development.* New York: Psychology Press.

Roza, S. J., & others. (2010). Maternal folic acid supplement use in early pregnancy and child behavioral problems: The Generation R Study. *British Journal of Nursing, 103,* 445–452.

Rubie-Davies, C. M. (Ed.). (2011). *Educational psychology.* New York: Routledge.

Rubin, D. H., Krasilnikoff, P. A., Leventhal, J. M., Weile, B., & Berget, A. (1986, August 23). Effect of passive smoking on birth weight. *The Lancet,* 415–417.

Rubin, K. H., Bukowski, W., & Parker, J. G. (1998). Peer interactions, relationships, and groups. In N. Eisenberg (Ed.), *Handbook of child psychology* (5th ed., Vol. 3). New York: Wiley.

Rubin, K. H., Bukowski, W., & Parker, J. G. (2006). Peer interactions, relationships, and groups. In W. Damon & R. Lerner (Eds.), *Handbook of child psychology* (6th ed.). New York: Wiley.

Rubin, K. H., Coplan, R. J., Bowker, J. C., & Menzer, M. (2011). Social withdrawal and shyness. In P. K. Smith & C. H. Hart (Eds.), *Wiley-Blackwell handbook of childhood social development* (2nd ed.). New York: Wiley.

Rubin, K. H., Coplan, R. J., Chen, X., Bowker, J. C., & McDonald, K. L. (2011). Peer relationships in childhood. In M. E. Lamb & M. H. Bornstein (Eds.), *Social and personality development.* New York: Psychology Press.

Ruble, D. (1983). The development of social comparison processes and their role in achievement-related self-socialization. In E. Higgins, D. Ruble, & W. Hartup (Eds.), *Social cognitive development: A social-cultural perspective.* New York: Cambridge University Press.

Ruble, D. N., Martin, C. L., & Berenbaum, S. (2006). Gender development. In W. Damon & R. Lerner (Eds.), *Handbook of child psychology* (6th ed.). New York: Wiley.

Rudang, R., Mellstrom, D., Clark, E., Ohlsson, C., & Lorentzon, M. (2011, in press). Advancing maternal age is associated with lower bone mineral density in young adult male offspring. *Osteoporosis International.*

Rueda, M. R., Posner, M. I., & Rothbart, M. K. (2005). The development of executive attention: Contributions to the emergence of self-regulation. *Developmental Neuropsychology, 28,* 573–594.

Ruff, H. A., & Capozzoli, M. C. (2003). Development of attention and distractibility in the first 4 years of life. *Developmental Psychology, 39,* 877–890.

Ruffman, T., Slade, L., & Crowe, E. (2002). The relation between children's and mothers' mental state language and theory-of-mind understanding. *Child Development, 73,* 734–751.

Rumberger, R. W. (1995). Dropping out of middle school: A multilevel analysis of students and schools. *American Education Research Journal, 3,* 583–625.

Runco, M. (Ed.). (2011, in press). *Encyclopedia of creativity.* New York: Elsevier.

Runco, M., & Spritzker, S. (Eds.). (2011). *Encyclopedia of creativity* (2nd ed.). New York: Elsevier.

Russell, A. (2011). Parent-child relationships and influences. In P. K. Smith & C. H. Hart (Eds.), *Wiley-Blackwell handbook of childhood social development* (2nd ed.). New York: Wiley.

Russell, S. T., Crockett, L. J., & Chao, R. K. (2010). *Asian American parenting and parent-adolescent relationships.* New York: Springer.

Rutter, M., & Dodge, K. A. (2011). Gene-environment interaction: State of the science. In K. A. Dodge & M. Rutter (Eds.), *Gene-environment interaction and developmental psychopathology.* New York: Guilford.

Rutter, M., & Schopler, E. (1987). Autism and pervasive developmental disorders: Concepts and diagnostic issues. *Journal of Autism and Pervasive Developmental Disorders, 17,* 159–186.

Ryan, R. M., & Deci, E. I. (2001). When rewards compete with nature. In C. Sansone & J. M. Harackiewicz (Eds.), *Intrinsic and extrinsic motivation.* San Diego: Academic Press.

Ryan, S. (2010). The adolescent and young adult with Klinefelter syndrome: Ensuring successful transitions to adulthood. *Pediatric Endocrinology Reviews, 8* (Suppl. 10), S169–S177.

S

Saarni, C., Campos, J., Camras, L. A., & Witherington, D. (2006). Emotional development. In W. Damon & R. Lerner (Eds.), *Handbook of child psychology* (6th ed.). New York: Wiley.

Sabbagh, M. A., Xu, F., Carlson, S. M., Moses, L. J., & Lee, K. (2006). The development of executive functioning and theory of mind: A comparison of Chinese and U.S. preschoolers. *Psychological Science, 17,* 74–81.

Sachs, J. (2009). Communication development in infancy. In J. Berko Gleason & N. B. Ratner (Eds.), *The development of language* (7th ed.). Boston: Allyn & Bacon.

Sadeh, A. (2008). Sleep. In M. M. Haith & J. B. Benson (Eds.), *Encyclopedia of infant and early childhood development.* Oxford, UK: Elsevier.

Salmivalli, C., & Peets, K. (2009). Bullies, victims, and bully-victim relationships in middle childhood and adolescence. In K. H. Rubin, W. M. Bukowski, & B. Laursen (Eds.), *Handbook of peer interactions, relationships, and groups.* New York: Guilford.

Salmivalli, C., Peets, K., & Hodges, E. V. E. (2011). Bullying. In P. K. Smith & C. H. Hart (Eds.), *Wiley-Blackwell handbook of childhood social development* (2nd ed.). New York: Wiley.

Salmon, J., Campbell, K. J., & Crawford, D. A. (2006). Television viewing habits associated with obesity risk factors: A survey of Melbourne schoolchildren. *Medical Journal of Australia, 184,* 64–67.

Sameroff, A. J. (2009). The transactional model. In A. J. Sameroff (Ed.), *The transactional model of development: How children and contexts shape each other.* Washington, DC: American Psychological Association.

Sanchez, C. E., Richards, J. E., & Almi, C. R. (2011, in press). Neurodevelopmental MRI brain templates for children 2 weeks to 4 years of age. *Developmental Psychobiology.*

Sanchez-Johnsen, L. A., Fitzgibbon, M. L., Martinovich, Z., Stolley, M. R., Dyer, A.R., & Van Horn, L. (2004). Ethnic differences in correlates of obesity between Latin-American and black women. *Obesity Research, 12,* 652–660.

Sanders, E. (2008). Medial art and play therapy with accident survivors. In C. A. Malchiodi (Ed.), *Creative interventions with traumatized children.* New York: Guilford.

Sankupellay, M., & others. (2011). Characteristics of sleep EEG power spectra in healthy infants in the first two years of life. *Clinical Neurophysiology, 122,* 236–243.

Sann, C., & Streri, A. (2007). Perception of object shape and texture in human newborns: Evidence from cross-modal tasks. *Developmental Science, 10,* 399–410.

Sanson, A., & Rothbart, M. K. (1995). Child temperament and parenting. In M. H. Bornstein (Ed.), *Handbook of parenting* (Vol. 4). Hillsdale, NJ: Erlbaum.

Santiago, C. D., Etter, E. M., Wadsworth, M. E., & Raviv, T. (2011, in press). Predictors of responses to stress among families coping with poverty-related stress. *Anxiety, Stress, and Coping.*

Santo, J. L., Portuguez, M. W., & Nunes, M. L. (2009). Cognitive and behavioral status of low birth weight preterm children raised in a developing country at preschool age. *Journal of Pediatrics, 85,* 35–41.

Santrock, J. W., Sitterle, K. A., & Warshak, R. A. (1988). Parent-child relationships in stepfather families. In P. Bronstein & C. P. Cowan (Eds.), *Fatherhood today: Men's changing roles in the family.* New York: Wiley.

Savage, R. S., Abrami, P., Hipps, G., & Dealut, L. (2009). A randomized controlled trial study of the ABRACADABRA reading intervention program in grade 1. *Journal of Educational Psychology, 101,* 590–604.

Savin-Williams, R. (2011, in press). Identity development in sexual-minority youth. In S. Schwartz, K. Luyckx, & V. Vignoles (Eds.), *Handbook of identity theory and research.* New York: Springer.

Sayer, L. C. (2006). Economic aspects of divorce and relationship dissolution. In M. A. Fine & J. H. Harvey (Eds.), *Handbook of divorce and relationship dissolution.* Mahwah, NJ: Erlbaum.

Scales, P. C., Benson, P. L., & Roehlkepartain, E. C. (2011, in press). Adolescent thriving: The role of sparks, relationships, and empowerment. *Journal of Youth and Adolescence.*

Scarlett, W. G., & Warren, A. E. A. (2010). Religious and spiritual development across the life span: A behavioral and social science perspective. In M. E. Lamb, A. M. Freund, & R. M. Lerner (Eds.), *Handbook of life-span development.* New York: Wiley.

Scarr, S. (1993). Biological and cultural diversity: The legacy of Darwin for development. *Child Development, 64,* 1333–1353.

Scarr, S., & Weinberg, R. A. (1983). The Minnesota adoption studies: Genetic differences and malleability. *Child Development, 54,* 182–259.

Schachter, A. D., & Kohane, I. S. (2011, in press). Drug target-gene signatures that predict teratogenicity are enrichers for developmentally related genes. *Reproductive Toxicology.*

Schaffer, H. R. (1996). *Social development.* Cambridge, MA: Blackwell.

Schaie, K. W. (2011, in press). *Developmental influences on adult intellectual development.* New York: Oxford University Press.

Schaie, K. W., & Willis, S. L. (2012). *Adult development and aging.* Upper Saddle River, NJ: Pearson.

Scharrer, E., & Demers, L. (2009). Media effects. In D. Carr (Ed.), *Encyclopedia of the life course and human development.* Boston: Gale Cengage.

Scher, A., & Harel, J. (2008). Separation and stranger anxiety. In M. M. Haith & J. B. Benson (Eds.), *Encyclopedia of infant and early childhood development.* Oxford, UK: Elsevier.

Schieffelin, B. (2005). *The give and take of everyday life.* Tucson, AZ: Fenestra.

Schiff, W. J. (2011). *Nutrition for healthy living* (2nd ed.). New York: McGraw-Hill.

Schilling, E. A., Aseltine, R. H., Glanovsky, J. L., James, A., & Jacobs, D. (2009). Adolescent alcohol use, suicidal ideation, and suicide attempts. *Journal of Adolescent Health, 44,* 335–341.

Schlegel, A., & Hewlett, B. L. (2011). Contributions of anthropology to the study of adolescence. *Journal of Research on Adolescence, 21,* 281–289.

Schlegel, M. (2000). All work and play. *Monitor on Psychology, 31*(11), 50–51.

Schmid, M., & others. (2011, in press). Maternal smoking and fetal lung volume: An in utero MRI investigation. *Prenatal Diagnosis.*

Schmidt, J., Shumow, L., & Kackar, H. (2007). Adolescents' participation in service activities and its impact on academic, behavioral, and civic outcomes. *Journal of Youth and Adolescence, 36,* 127–140.

Schmidt, U. (2003). Aetiology of eating disorders in the 21st century: New answers to old questions. *European Child and Adolescent Psychiatry, 12* (Suppl. 1), 1130–1137.

Schmitt, D. P., & Pilcher, J. J. (2004). Evaluating evidence of psychological adaptation: How do we know one when we see one? *Psychological Science, 15,* 643–649.

Schneider, B. H., & others. (2011). Cooperation and competition. In P. K. Smith & C. H. Hart (Eds.), *Wiley-Blackwell handbook of childhood social development* (2nd ed.). New York: Wiley.

Schneider, W. (2011). Memory development in childhood. In U. Goswami (Ed.), *Wiley-Blackwell handbook of childhood cognitive development.* New York: Wiley.

Schnitzer, P. G., Covington, T. M., & Kruse, R. L. (2011). Assessment of caregiver responsibility in unintentional child injury deaths: Challenges for injury prevention. *Injury Prevention, 17* (Suppl.), S45–S54.

Schoffstall, C. L., & Cohen, R. (2011). Cyber aggression: The relation between online offenders and offline social competence. *Social Development, 20*(3), 587–604.

Schofield, H. L., Bierman, K. L., Heinrichs, B., Nix, R. L., & Conduct Problems Prevention Research Group. (2008). Predicting early sexual activity with behavior problems exhibited at school entry and in early adolescence. *Journal of Abnormal Child Psychology, 36*(8), 1175–1188.

Schoon, I., Jones, E., Cheng, H., & Maughan, B. (2011, in press). Family hardship, family instability, and cognitive development. *Journal of Epidemiology and Community Health.*

Schrag, S. G., & Dixon, R. L. (1985). Occupational exposure associated with male reproductive dysfunction. *Annual Review of Pharmacology and Toxicology, 25,* 467–592.

Schreiber, L. R. (1990). *The parents' guide to kids' sports.* Boston: Little, Brown.

Schroeder-Yu, G. (2008). Documentation: Ideas and applications from the Reggio Emilia approach. *Teaching Artist Journal, 6,* 126–134.

Schulenberg, J. E., & Zarrett, N. R. (2006). Mental health during emerging adulthood: Continuity and discontinuity in courses, causes, and functions. In J. J. Arnett & J. L. Tanner (Eds.), *Emerging adults in America.* Washington, DC. American Psychological Association.

Schumacher, M., Zubaran, C., & White, G. (2008). Bringing birth-related paternal depression to the fore. *Women and Birth, 21,* 65–70.

Schunk, D. H. (2012). *Learning theories: An educational perspective* (6th ed.). Upper Saddle River, NJ: Prentice Hall.

Schunk, D. H., Pintrich, P. R., & Meece, J. (2008). *Motivation in education: Theory, research and applications* (3rd ed.). Upper Saddle River, NJ: Prentice Hall.

Schwartz, S. J., & others. (2011). Examining the light and dark sides of emerging adults' identity: A study of identity status differences in positive and negative psychosocial functioning. *Journal of Youth and Adolescence, 40,* 839–859.

Schweinhart, L. J., Montie, J., Xiang, Z., Barnett, W. S., Belfield, C. R., & Nores, M. (2005). *Lifetime effects: The High/Scope Petty Preschool study through age 40.* Ypsilanti, MI: High/Scope Press.

Sciberras, E., Ukoumunne, O. C., & Efron, D. (2011, in press). Predictors of parent-reported attention-deficit/hyperactivity disorder in children aged 6–7 years: A national longitudinal study. *Journal of Abnormal Child Psychology.*

Scott, K. A., Roberts, J. A., & Glennen, S. (2011, in press). How well do children who are internationally adopted acquire language? A meta-analysis. *Journal of Speech, Language, and Hearing Research.*

Scourfield, J., Van den Bree, M., Martin, N., & McGuffin, P. (2004). Conduct problems in children and adolescents: A twin study. *Archives of General Psychiatry, 61,* 489–496.

Search Institute. (2010a). *Teen voice.* Minneapolis: Search Institute.

Search Institute. (2010b). *Teens' relationships.* Minneapolis: Search Institute.

Sekhobo, J. P., Edmunds, L. S., Reynolds, D. K., Dalenius, K., & Sharma, A. (2010). Trends in the prevalence of obesity and overweight among children enrolled in the New York State WIC program, 2002–2007. *Public Health Reports, 125,* 218–224.

Selman, R. L. (1980). *The growth of interpersonal understanding.* New York: Academic Press.

Sen, B. (2010). The relationship between frequency of family dinner and adolescent problem behaviors after adjusting for other characteristics. *Journal of Adolescence, 33,* 187–196.

Senter, L., Sackoff, J., Landi, K., & Boyd, L. (2010). Studying sudden and unexpected deaths in a time of changing death certification and investigation practices: Evaluating sleep-related risk factors for infant death in New York City. *Maternal and Child Health, 15*(2), 242–248.

Seto, C. K., Statuta, S. M., & Solari, I. L. (2010). Pediatric running injuries. *Clinics in Sports Medicine, 29,* 499–511.

Shankaran, S., & others. (2010). Prenatal cocaine exposure and BMI and blood pressure at 9 years of age. *Journal of Hypertension, 28,* 1166–1175.

Shankaran, S., & others. (2011, in press). Risk for obesity in adolescence starts in childhood. *Journal of Perinatology.*

Shapiro, A. F., & Gottman, J. M. (2005). Effects on marriage of a psycho-education intervention with couples undergoing the transition to parenthood, evaluation at 1-year post-intervention. *Journal of Family Communication, 5,* 1–24.

Sharma, A. R., McGue, M. K., & Benson, P. L. (1996). The emotional and behavioral adjustment of adopted adolescents: Part I: Age at adoption. *Children and Youth Services Review, 18,* 101–114.

Sharma, M. (2006). School-based interventions for childhood and adolescent obesity. *Obesity Review, 7,* 261–269.

Shatz, M., & Gelman, R. (1973). The development of communication skills: Modifications in the speech of young children as a function of the listener. *Monographs of the Society for Research in Child Development, 38* (Serial No. 152).

Shaw, D. J., Grosbras, M. H., Leonard, G., Pike, G. B., & Paus, T. (2011, in press). Development of functional connectivity during adolescence: A longitudinal study using an action-observation paradigm. *Journal of Cognitive Neuroscience.*

Shaw, P., & others. (2007). Attention-deficit/hyperactivity disorder is characterized by a delay in cortical maturation. *Proceedings of the National Academy of Sciences USA, 104,* 19649–19654.

Shaywitz, S. E., Gruen, J. R., & Shaywitz, B. A. (2007). Management of dyslexia, its rationale, and underlying neurobiology. *Pediatric Clinics of North America, 54,* 609–623.

Shaywitz, S. E., Morris, R., & Shaywitz, B. A. (2008). The education of dyslexic children from childhood to young adulthood. *Annual Review of Psychology* (Vol. 59). Palo Alto, CA: Annual Reviews.

Shehata, F., & others. (2011, in press). Placenta/birthweight ratio and perinatal outcome: A retrospective cohort analysis. *British Journal of Obstetrics and Gynaecology.*

Shi, L., & Stevens, G. D. (2005). Disparities in access to care and satisfaction among U.S. children: The roles of race/ethnicity and poverty status. *Public Health Report, 120,* 431–441.

Shiraev, E. (2011). *A history of psychology: A global perspective.* Thousand Oaks, CA: Sage.

Shiraev, E., & Levy, D. (2010). *Cross-cultural psychology: Critical thinking and critical applications* (4th ed.). Boston: Allyn & Bacon.

Shiva, F., Nasiri, M., Sadeghi, B., & Padyab, M. (2004). Effects of passive smoking on common respiratory symptoms in young children. *Acta Paediatrica, 92,* 1394–1397.

Shuai, L., Chan, R. C., & Wang, Y. (2011). Executive function profile of Chinese boys with attention-deficit hyperactivity disorder: Different subtypes and comorbidity. *Archives of Clinical Neuropsychology, 26,* 120–132.

Shukla, D. K., Keehn, B., Smylie, D. M., & Muller, R. A. (2011, in press). Microstructural abnormalities of short-distance white matter tracts in autism spectrum disorders. *Neuropsychologia.*

Siegel, L. S. (2003). Learning disabilities In I. B. Weiner (Ed.), *Handbook of psychology* (Vol. VI). New York: Wiley.

Siegler, R. S. (2006). Microgenetic analysis of learning. In W. Damon & R. Lerner (Eds.), *Handbook of child psychology* (6th ed.). New York: Wiley.

Siegler, R. S. (2007). Cognitive variability. *Developmental Science, 10,* 104–109.

Siegler, R. S. (2011a, in press). How do people become experts? In J. Staszewski (Ed.), *Experience and skill acquisition.* New York: Taylor & Francis.

Siegler, R. S. (2011b, in press). From theory to application and back: Following in the giant footsteps of David Klahr. In J. Shrager (Ed.), *From child to scientist.* Thousand Oaks, CA: Sage.

Silberg, J. L., Maes, H., & Eaves, L. J. (2010). Genetic and environmental influences on the transmission of parental depression to children's

depression and conduct disturbance: An extended Children of Twins study. *Journal of Child Psychology and Psychiatry, 51,* 734–744.

Silfverdal, S. A. (2011). Important to overcome barriers in translating evidence based breast-feeding information into practice. *Acta Paediatrica, 100,* 482–483.

Silva, C. (2005, October 31). When teen dynamo talks, city listens. *Boston Globe,* pp. B1, B4.

Silver, E. J., & Bauman, L. J. (2006). The association of sexual experience with attitudes, beliefs, and risk behaviors of inner-city adolescents. *Journal of Research on Adolescence, 16,* 29–45.

Simkin, P., & Bolding, A. (2004). Update on nonpharmacological approaches to relieve labor pain and prevent suffering. *Journal of Midwifery and Women's Health, 49,* 489–504.

Simmons, D. (2011). Diabetes and obesity in pregnancy. *Best Practice and Research, Clinical Obstetrics and Gynecology, 25,* 25–36.

Simmons, L. E., Rubens, C. E., Darmstadt, G. L., & Gravett, M. G. (2010). Preventing preterm birth and neonatal mortality: Exploring the epidemiology, causes, and interventions. *Seminars in Perinatology, 34,* 408–415.

Simmons, R. G., & Blyth, D. A. (1987). *Moving into adolescence.* Hawthorne, NY: Aldine.

Simonetti, G. D., & others. (2011). Determinants of blood pressure in preschool children: The role of parental smoking. *Circulation, 123,* 292–298.

Simos, P. G., Fletcher, J. M., Sarkari, S., Billingsley, R. L., Denton, C., & Papanicolaou, A. C. (2007). Altering the brain circuits for reading through intervention: A magnetic source imaging study. *Neuropsychology, 21,* 485–496.

Simpkins, S. D., Fredricks, J. A., Davis-Kean, P. E., & Eccles, J. S. (2006). Healthy mind, healthy habits: The influence of activity involvement in middle childhood. In A. C. Huston & M. N. Ripke (Eds.), *Developmental contexts in middle childhood.* New York: Cambridge University Press.

Singh, S., Darroch, J. E., Vlasoff, M., & Nadeau, J. (2004). *Adding it up: The benefits of investing in sexual and reproductive health care.* New York: The Alan Guttmacher Institute.

Singh, S., Wulf, D., Samara, R., & Cuca, Y. P. (2000). Gender differences in the timing of first intercourse: Data from 14 countries. *International Family Planning Perspectives, 26,* 21–28, 43.

Sinha, J. W., Cnaan, R. A., & Gelles, R. J. (2007). Adolescent risk behaviors and religion: Findings from a national study. *Journal of Adolescence, 30,* 231–249.

Sisson, S. B., Broyles, S. T., Baker, B. L., & Katzmarzyk, P. T. (2010). Screen time, physical activity, and overweight in U.S. youth: National Survey of Children's Health 2003. *Journal of Adolescent Health, 47,* 309–311.

Sivell, S., & others. (2008). How risk is perceived, constructed, and interpreted by clients in clinical genetics, and the effects on decision making: A review. *Journal of Genetic Counseling, 17,* 30–63.

Skinner, B. F. (1938). *The behavior of organisms: An experimental analysis.* New York: Appleton-Century-Crofts.

Skinner, B. F. (1957). *Verbal behavior.* New York: Appleton-Century-Crofts.

Slater, A. M., Bremner, J. G., Johnson, S. P., & Hayes, R. (2011, in press). The role of perceptual processes in infant addition/subtraction events. In L. M. Oakes, C. H. Cashon, M. Casasola, & D. H. Rakison (Eds.), *Early perceptual and cognitive development.* New York: Oxford University Press.

Slater, A., Field, T., & Hernandez-Reif, M. (2007). The development of the senses. In A. Slater & M. Lewis (Eds.), *Introduction to infant development* (2nd ed.). New York: Oxford University Press.

Slater, A., Morison, V., & Somers, M. (1988). Orientation discrimination and cortical function in the human newborn. *Perception, 17,* 597–602.

Slater, A., Riddell, P., Quinn, P. C., Pascalis, O., Lee, K., & Kelly, D. J. (2010). Visual perception. In J. G. Bremner & T. D. Wachs (Eds.), *Wiley-Blackwell handbook of infant development* (2nd ed.). New York: Wiley.

Slavin, R. E. (2012). Classroom applications of cooperative learning. In K. R. Harris, S. Graham, & T. Urdan (Eds.), *APA educational psychology handbook.* Washington, DC: American Psychological Association.

Sleet, D. A., & Mercy, J. A. (2003). Promotion of safety, security, and well-being. In M. H. Bornstein, L. Davidson, C. L. M. Keyes, & K. A. Moore (Eds.), *Well-being.* Mahwah, NJ: Erlbaum.

Sliwinski, M. J. (2011). Approaches to modeling intraindividual and interindividual facets of change for developmental research. In K. L. Fingerman, C. A. Berg, J. Smith, & T. C. Antonucci (Eds.), *Handbook of life-span development.* New York: Springer.

Slobin, D. (1972, July). Children and language: They learn the same way around the world. *Psychology Today,* 71–76.

Slomkowski, C., Rende, R., Conger, K. J., Simons, R. L., & Conger, R. D. (2001). Sisters, brothers, and delinquency: Social influence during early and middle adolescence. *Child Development, 72,* 271–283.

Smetana, J. G. (2011a, in press). *Adolescents, families, and social development: How adolescents construct their worlds.* New York: Wiley-Blackwell.

Smetana, J. G. (2011b, in press). Adolescents' social reasoning and relationships with parents: Conflicts and coordinations within and across domains. In E. Amsel & J. Smetana (Eds.), *Adolescent vulnerabilities and opportunities: Constructivist and developmental perspectives.* New York: Cambridge University Press.

Smith, C. A., Collins, C. T., Crowther, C. A., & Levett, K. M. (2011, July 6). Acupuncture or acupressure for pain management of labor. *Cochrane Database of Systematic Reviews, 7,* CD009232.

Smith, J., & Ross, H. (2007). Training parents to mediate sibling disputes affects children's negotiation and conflict understanding. *Child Development, 78,* 790–805.

Smith, J. B. (2009). High school organization. In D. Carr (Ed.), *Encyclopedia of the life course and human development.* Boston: Gale Cengage.

Smith, L. B. (1999). Do infants possess innate knowledge structures? The con side. *Developmental Science, 2,* 133–144.

Smith, L. E., & Howard, K. S. (2008). Continuity of paternal social support and depressive symptoms among new mothers. *Journal of Family Psychology, 22,* 763–773.

Smith, L. M., & others. (2008). The infant development, environment, and lifestyle study: Effects of prenatal methamphetamine exposure, polydrug exposure, and poverty on intrauterine growth. *Pediatrics, 118,* 1149–1156.

Smith, R. L., Rose, A. J., & Schwartz-Mette, R. A. (2010). Relational and overt aggression in childhood and adolescence: Clarifying mean-level gender differences and associations with peer acceptance. *Social Development, 19,* 243–269.

Smith, T. E., Polloway, E. A., Patton, J. R., & Dowdy, C. A. (2012). *Teaching students with special needs in inclusive settings* (6th ed.). Upper Saddle River, NJ: Pearson.

Smithbattle, L. (2007). Legacies of advantage and disadvantage: The case of teen mothers. *Public Health Nursing, 24,* 409–420.

Smitsman, A. W., & Corbetta, D. (2010). Action in infancy—perspectives, concepts, and challenges. In J. G. Bremner & T. D. Wachs (Eds.), *Wiley-Blackwell handbook of infant development* (2nd ed.). New York: Wiley.

Smoreda, Z., & Licoppe, C. (2000). Gender-specific use of the domestic telephone. *Social Psychology Quarterly, 63,* 238–252.

Snapp-Childs, W., & Corbetta, D. (2009). Evidence of early strategies in learning to walk. *Infancy, 14,* 101–116.

Snarey, J. (1987, June). A question of morality. *Psychology Today,* pp. 6–8.

Snow, C. E., Burns, M. S., & Griffin, P. (1998). *Preventing reading difficulties in young children.* Washington, DC: National Academy Press.

Snow, C. E., & Kang, J. Y. (2006). Becoming bilingual, biliterate, and bicultural. In W. Damon & R. Lerner (Eds.), *Handbook of child psychology* (6th ed.). New York: Wiley.

Snowdon, A. W., Hussein, A., High, L., Millar-Polgar, J., Patrick, L., & Ahmed, E. (2008). The effectiveness of a multimedia intervention on parents' knowledge and use of vehicle safety systems for children. *Journal of Pediatric Nursing, 23,* 126–139.

Snowling, M. J., & Gobel, S. M. (2011). Reading development and dyslexia. In U. Goswami (Ed.), *Wiley-Blackwell handbook of childhood cognitive development.* New York: Wiley.

Snyder, K. A., & Torrence, C. M. (2008). Habituation and novelty. In M. M. Haith & J. B.

Benson (Eds.), *Encyclopedia of infant and early childhood development.* Oxford, UK: Elsevier.

Sofronoff, K., Dark, E., & Stone, V. (2011, in press). Social vulnerability and bullying in children with Asperger syndrome. *Autism.*

Sokol, B. W., Snjezana, H., & Muller, U. (2010). Social understanding and self-regulation: From perspective-taking to theory of mind. In B. Sokol, U. Muller, J. Carpendale, A. Young, & G. Iarocci (Eds.), *Self- and social regulation.* New York: Oxford University Press.

Solheim, K. N., & others. (2011, in press). The effect of cesarean delivery rates on the future incidence of placenta previa, placenta accreta, and maternal mortality. *Journal of Maternal-Fetal and Neonatal Medicine.*

Solmeyer, A. R., McHale, S. M., Killoren, S. E., & Updegraff, K. A. (2011). Coparenting around siblings' differential treatment in Mexican-origin families. *Developmental Psychology, 25,* 251–260.

Solomon, D., Watson, P., Schapes, E., Battistich, V., & Solomon, J. (1990). Cooperative learning as part of a comprehensive program designed to promote prosocial development. In S. Sharan (Ed.), *Cooperative learning.* New York: Praeger.

Song, A. V., & Halpern-Felsher, B. L. (2011). Predictive relationship between adolescent oral and vaginal sex: Results from a prospective, longitudinal study. *Archives of Pediatric and Adolescent Medicine, 165,* 243–249.

Sontag, L. M., Graber, J., Brooks-Gunn, J., & Warren, M. P. (2008). Coping with social stress: Implications for psychopathology in young adolescent girls. *Journal of Abnormal Child Psychology, 36,* 1159–1174.

Sophian, C. (1985). Perseveration and infants' search: A comparison of two- and three-location tasks. *Developmental Psychology, 21,* 187–194.

Sorof, J. M., Lai, D., Turner, J., Poffenberger, T., & Portman, R. J. (2004). Overweight, ethnicity, and the prevalence of hypertension in school-aged children. *Pediatrics, 113,* 475–482.

Sorte, J., Daeschel, I., & Amador, C. (2011). *Nutrition, health, and wellness.* Upper Saddle River, NJ: Prentice Hall.

Soto-Jimenez, M. F., & Flegal, A. R. (2011, in press). Childhood lead poisoning from the smelter in Torreon, Mexico. *Environmental Research.*

Sowell, E. R., Thompson, P. M., Leonard, C. M., Welcome, S. E., Kan, E., & Toga, A. W. (2004). Longitudinal mapping of cortical thickness and brain growth in children. *Journal of Neuroscience, 24,* 8223–8231.

Spangler, G., Johann, M., Ronai, Z., & Zimmermann, P. (2009). Genetic and environmental influence on attachment disorganization. *Journal of Child Psychology and Psychiatry, 50,* 952–961.

Spatz, C. (2012). *Basic statistics* (10th ed.). Boston: Cengage.

Spelke, E. S. (1979). Perceiving bimodally specified events in infancy. *Developmental Psychology, 5,* 626–636.

Spelke, E. S. (1991). Physical knowledge in infancy: Reflections on Piaget's theory. In S. Carey & R. Gelman (Eds.), *The epigenesis of mind: Essays on biology and cognition*. Hillsdale, NJ: Erlbaum.

Spelke, E. S. (2000). Core knowledge. *American Psychologist, 55,* 1233–1243.

Spelke, E. S., Breinlinger, K., Macomber, J., & Jacobson, K. (1992). Origins of knowledge. *Psychological Review, 99,* 605–632.

Spelke, E. S., & Hespos, S. J. (2001). Continuity, competence, and the object concept. In E. Dupoux (Ed.), *Language, brain, and behavior.* Cambridge, MA: Bradford/MIT Press.

Spelke, E. S., & Kinzler, K. D. (2007). Core knowledge. *Developmental Science, 10,* 89–96.

Spelke, E. S., & Owsley, C. J. (1979). Intermodal exploration and knowledge in infancy. *Infant Behavior and Development, 2,* 13–28.

Spencer, J. (2009). *Dynamic systems and connectionist approaches to development.* New York: Oxford University Press.

Spruijt-Metz, D. (2011). Etiology, treatment, and prevention of obesity in childhood and adolescence: A decade in review. *Journal of Research on Adolescence, 21,* 129–152.

Squier, W. (2011, in press). The shaken baby syndrome: Pathology and mechanisms. *Acta Neuropathology.*

Srabstein, J. C., McCarter, R. J., Shao, C., & Huang, Z. J. (2006). Morbidities associated with bullying behaviors in adolescents: School-based study of American adolescents. *International Journal of Adolescent Medicine and Health, 18,* 587–596.

Sroufe, L. A., Coffino, B., & Carlson, E. A. (2010). Conceptualizing the role of early experience: Lessons from the Minnesota longitudinal study. *Developmental Review, 30,* 36–51.

Sroufe, L. A., Egeland, B., Carlson, E., & Collins, W. A. (2005). The place of early attachment in developmental context. In K. E. Grossman, K. Krossman, & E. Waters (Eds.), *The power of longitudinal attachment research: From infancy and childhood to adulthood.* New York: Guilford.

Stager, L. (2009–2010). Supporting women during labor and birth. *Midwifery Today with International Midwife, 23,* 12–15.

Stanford University Medical Center. (2012). *Growth hormone deficiency.* Palo Alto, CA: Author.

Stangor, C. (2011). *Research methods for the behavioral sciences* (4th ed.). Boston: Cengage.

Starr, C. (2011). *Biology* (8th ed.). Boston: Cengage.

Steca, P., Bassi, M., Caprara, G. V., & Fave, A. D. (2011, in press). Parents' self-efficacy beliefs and their children's psychosocial adaptation during adolescence. *Journal of Youth and Adolescence.*

Stein, M. T. (2004). ADHD: The diagnostic process from different perspectives. *Journal of Developmental and Behavioral Pediatrics, 25* (Suppl. 5), S54–S58.

Steinberg, L. (2011). Adolescent risk-taking: A social neuroscience perspective. In E. Amsel & J. Smetana (Eds.), *Adolescent vulnerabilities and opportunities: Constructivist developmental perspectives.* New York: Cambridge University Press.

Steinberg, L., Blatt-Eisengart, I., & Cauffman, E. (2006). Patterns of competence and adjustment among adolescents from authoritative, authoritarian, indulgent, and neglectful homes: A replication in a sample of serious juvenile offenders. *Journal of Research on Adolescence, 16,* 47–58.

Steinberg, L., & Collins, W. A. (2011). Psychosocial development and behavior. In M. Fisher, E. Alderman, R. Kreipe, & W. Rosenfeld (Eds.), *Textbook of adolescent health care.* Elk Grove, IL: American Academy of Pediatrics.

Steiner, J. E. (1979). Human facial expressions in response to taste and smell stimulation. In H. Reese & L. Lipsitt (Eds.), *Advances in child development* (Vol. 13). New York: Academic Press.

Steiner, N. J., Sheldrick, R. C., Gotthelf, D., & Perrin, E. C. (2011, in press). Computer-based attention training in schools for children with attention deficit hyperactivity disorder: A preliminary trial. *Clinical Pediatrics.*

Stephens, J. M. (2008). Cheating. In N. J. Salkind (Ed.), *Encyclopedia of educational psychology.* Thousand Oaks, CA: Sage.

Stepney, C., Kane, K., & Bruzzese, J. M. (2011, in press). My child is diagnosed with asthma, now what? Motivating parents to help their children control asthma. *Journal of School Nursing.*

Stern, D. N., Beebe, B., Jaffe, J., & Bennett, S. L. (1977). The infant's stimulus world during social interaction: A study of caregiver behaviors with particular reference to repetition and timing. In H. R. Schaffer (Ed.), *Studies in mother-infant interaction.* London: Academic Press.

Sternberg, R. J. (1986). *Intelligence applied.* San Diego: Harcourt Brace Jovanovich.

Sternberg, R. J. (2004). Individual differences in cognitive development. In U. Goswami (Ed.), *Blackwell handbook of childhood cognitive development.* Malden, MA: Blackwell.

Sternberg, R. J. (2010). Intelligence. In B. McGaw, P. Peterson, & E. Baker (Eds.), *International encyclopedia of education* (3rd ed.). New York: Elsevier.

Sternberg, R. J. (2011a). Individual differences in cognitive development. In U. Goswami (Ed.), *Blackwell handbook of childhood cognitive development.* Malden, MA: Blackwell.

Sternberg, R. J. (2011b). Human intelligence. In V. S. Ramachandran (Ed.), *Encyclopedia of human behavior* (2nd ed.). New York: Elsevier.

Sternberg, R. J. (2011c). Intelligence. In I. Weiner (Series Editor) & D. Freedheim (Volume Editor), *Handbook of psychology* (2nd ed.). New York: Wiley.

Sternberg, R. J. (2011d). Componential models of creativity. In M. Runco & S. Spritzker (Eds.), *Encyclopedia of creativity* (2nd ed.). New York: Elsevier.

Sternberg, R. J. (2011e). Personal wisdom in the balance. In M. Ferrari & N. Weststrate (Eds.), *Personal wisdom.* Amsterdam: Springer.

Sternberg, R. J. (2011f). Intelligence in its cultural context. In M. Gelfand, C.-.Y Chiu, & Y.-Y. Hong (Eds.), *Advances in cultures and psychology* (Vol. 2). New York: Oxford University Press.

Sternberg, R. J. (2011g). Dogmatism and giftedness: Major themes. In D. Ambrose, R. J. Sternberg, & B. Sriraman (Eds.), *Confronting dogmatism in gifted education.* New York: Taylor & Francis.

Sternberg, R. J., & Sternberg, K. (2012). *Cognitive psychology* (6th ed.). Boston: Cengage.

Sternberg, R. J., & Williams, W. M. (1996). *How to develop student creativity.* Alexandria, VA: ASCD.

Sternberg, S. J., & Davila, J. (2008). Romantic functioning and depressive symptoms among early adolescent girls: The moderating role of parental emotional availability. *Journal of Clinical Child and Adolescent Psychology, 37,* 350–362.

Stevenson, H. W. (1995). Mathematics achievement of American students: First in the world by the year 2000? In C. A. Nelson (Ed.), *Basic and applied perspectives on learning, cognition, and development.* Minneapolis: University of Minnesota Press.

Stevenson, H. W. (2000). Middle childhood: Education and schooling. In A. Kazdin (Ed.), *Encyclopedia of psychology.* Washington, DC, & New York: American Psychological Association and Oxford University Press.

Stevenson, H. W., Hofer, B. K., & Randel, B. (1999). *Middle childhood: Education and schooling.* Unpublished manuscript, Department of Psychology, University of Michigan, Ann Arbor.

Stevenson, H. W., Lee, S., Chen, C., Stigler, J. W., Hsu, C., & Kitamura, S. (1990). Contexts of achievement. *Monographs of the Society for Research in Child Development, 55* (Serial No. 221).

Stevenson, H. W., Lee, S., & Stigler, J. W. (1986). Mathematics achievement of Chinese, Japanese, and American children. *Science, 231,* 693–699.

Stiggins, R. (2008). *Introduction to student-involved assessment for learning* (5th ed.). Upper Saddle River. NJ: Prentice Hall.

Stipek, D. (2005, February 16). Commentary in *USA Today,* p. 1D.

Stipek, D. J. (2002). *Motivation to learn* (4th ed.). Boston: Allyn & Bacon.

Stoel-Gammon, C., & Sosa, A. V. (2010). Phonological development. In E. Hoff &

M. Shatz (Eds.), *Blackwell handbook of language development* (2nd ed.). New York: Wiley.

Stoll, C., Dott, B., Alembik, Y., & Roth, M. P. (2011, in press). Associated malformations among infants with neural tube defects. *American Journal of Medical Genetics A.*

Strathearn, L. (2007). Exploring the neurobiology of attachment. In L. C. Mayes, P. Fonagy, & M. Target (Eds.), *Developmental science and psychoanalysis*. London: Karnac Press.

Streib, H. (1999). Off-road religion? A narrative approach to fundamentalist and occult orientations of adolescents. *Journal of Adolescence, 22,* 255–267.

Streuling, I., & others. (2011). Physical activity and gestational weight gain: A meta-analysis of intervention trials. *British Journal of Obstetrics and Gynaecology, 118,* 278–284.

Striegel-Moore, R. H., & Bulik, C. M. (2007). Risk factors for eating disorders. *American Psychologist, 62,* 181–198.

Stright, A. D., Herr, M. Y., & Neitzel, C. (2009). Maternal scaffolding of children's problem solving and children's adjustment in states. *Journal of Educational Psychology, 101,* 207–218.

Stringer, M., Ratcliffe, S. J., Evans, E. C., & Brown, L. P. (2005). The cost of prenatal care attendance and pregnancy outcomes in low-income working women. *Journal of Obstetrical, Gynecologic, and Neonatal Nursing, 34,* 551–560.

Stroobant, N., Buijus, D., & Vingerhoets, G. (2009). Variation in brain lateralization during various language tasks: A functional transcranial Doppler study. *Behavioral Brain Research, 199,* 190–196.

Stuebe, A. M., & Schwarz, E. G. (2010). The risks and benefits of infant feeding practices for women and their children. *Journal of Perinatology, 30,* 155–162.

Sturm, R. (2005). Childhood obesity—what we can learn from existing data and social trends. *Prevention of Chronic Diseases, 2,* A12.

Suarez, L., & others (2011). Maternal smoking, passive tobacco smoke, and neural tube defects. *Birth Defects Research A: Clinical and Molecular Teratology, 91,* 29–33.

Sugita, Y. (2004). Experience in early infancy is indispensable for color perception. *Current Biology, 14,* 1267–1271.

Sullivan, H. S. (1953). *The interpersonal theory of psychiatry.* New York: W. W. Norton.

Sullivan, K., & Sullivan, A. (1980). Adolescent-parent separation. *Developmental Psychology, 16,* 93–99.

Sun, S. S., & others. (2008). Childhood obesity predicts adult metabolic syndrome: The Fels Longitudinal Study. *Journal of Pediatrics, 152,* 191–200.

Sun, Y., Tao, F., Hao, J., & Wan, Y. (2010). The mediating effects of stress and coping on depression among adolescents in China. *Journal of Child and Adolescent Psychiatric Nursing, 23,* 173–180.

Sund, A. M., Larsson, B., & Wichstrom, L. (2011). Role of physical and sedentary activities in the development of depressive symptoms in early adolescence. *Social Psychiatry and Psychiatric Epidemiology, 46,* 431–441.

Super, C. M., & Harkness, S. (2010). Culture in infancy. In J. G. Bremner & T. D. Wachs (Eds.), *Wiley-Blackwell handbook of infant development* (2nd ed.). New York: Wiley.

Susman, E. J., & others. (2010). Longitudinal development of secondary sexual characteristics in girls and boys between 9½ and 15½ years. *Archives of Pediatric and Adolescent Medicine, 164,* 166–173.

Sutterby, J. A., & Frost, J. (2006). Creating play environments for early childhood: Indoors and out. In B. Spodek & O. N. Saracho (Eds.), *Handbook of research on the education of young children* (2nd ed.). Mahwah, NJ: Erlbaum.

Swaab, D. F., Chung, W. C., Kruijver, F. P., Hofman, M. A., & Ishunina, T. A. (2001). Structural and functional sex differences in the human hypothalamus. *Hormones and Behavior, 40,* 93–98.

Swamy, G. K., Ostbye, T., & Skjaerven, R. (2008). Association of preterm birth with long-term survival, reproduction, and next-generation preterm birth. *Journal of the American Medical Association, 299,* 1429–1436.

Swanson, H. L. (1999). What develops in working memory? A life-span perspective. *Developmental Psychology, 35,* 986–1000.

Sweeting, H. N. (2008). Gendered dimensions of obesity in childhood and adolescence. *Nutrition Journal, 7,* 1.

Swing, E. L., Gentile, D. A., Anderson, C. A., & Walsh, D. A. (2010). Television and video game exposure and the development of attention problems. *Pediatrics, 126,* 214–221.

Syed, M. (2011, in press). Developing an integrated self: Academic and ethnic identities among ethnically-diverse college students. *Developmental Psychology.*

Sykes, C. J. (1995). *Dumbing down our kids: Why America's children feel good about themselves but can't read, write, or add.* New York: St. Martin's Press.

Szwedo, D. E., Mikami, A. Y., & Allen, J. P. (2011, in press). Qualities of peer relations on social networking websites: Predictions from negative mother-teen interactions. *Journal of Research on Adolescence.*

T

Taddio, A. (2008). Circumcision. In M. M. Haith & J. B. Benson (Eds.), *Encyclopedia of infant and early childhood development.* Oxford, UK: Elsevier.

TADS. (2007). The Treatment for Adolescents with Depression Study: Long-term effectiveness and safety outcomes. *Archives of General Psychiatry, 64,* 1132–1143.

Tager-Flusberg, H., & Zukowski, A. (2009). Putting words together: Morphology and syntax in the preschool years. In J. Berko Gleason &

N. Ratner (Eds.), *The development of language* (7th ed.). Boston: Allyn & Bacon.

Taige, N. M., Neal, C., Glover, V., and the Early Stress, Translational Research and Prevention Science Network: Fetal and Neonatal Experience on Child and Adolescent Mental Health. (2007). Antenatal maternal stress and long-term effects on neurodevelopment: How and why? *Journal of Child Psychology and Psychiatry, 48,* 245–261.

Talaulikar, V. S., & Arulkumaran, S. (2011). Folic acid in obstetric practice: A review. *Obstetrical and Gynecological Survey, 66,* 240–247.

Tang, Y., & Posner, M. I. (2009). Attention training and attention state training. *Trends in Cognitive Science, 13,* 222–227.

Tannen, D. (1990). *You just don't understand!* New York: Ballantine.

Tarini, B. A. (2012, in press). Ethical issues in screening in the genomics era. *Annual Review of Genetics* (Vol. 13). Palo Alto, CA: Annual Reviews.

Tarokh, L., Carskadon, M. A., & Achermann, P. (2010). Developmental changes in brain connectivity assessed using the sleep EEG. *Neuroscience, 17*(2), 622–634.

Taurines, R., & others. (2010). Developmental comorbidity in attention-deficit hyperactivity disorder. *Attention Deficit and Hyperactivity Disorders, 2,* 267–289.

Taylor, F. M. A., Ko, R., & Pan, M. (1999). Prenatal and reproductive health care. In E. J. Kramer, S. L. Ivey, & Y. W. Ying (Eds.), *Immigrant women's health.* San Francisco: Jossey-Bass.

Taylor, L. M., & Fratto, J. M. (2012). *Transforming learning through 21st century skills.* Boston: Allyn & Bacon.

Taylor, R. D., & Lopez, E. I. (2005). Family management practice, school achievement, and problem behavior in African American adolescents: Mediating processes. *Applied Developmental Psychology, 26,* 39–49.

Teate, A., Leap, N., Rising, S. S., & Homer, C. S. (2009). Women's experiences of group antenatal care in Australia—the Centering Pregnancy pilot study. *Midwifery, 26,* 389–393.

Teenage Research Unlimited. (2004, November 10). *Diversity in word and deed: Most teens claim multicultural friends.* Northbrook, IL: Teenage Research Unlimited

Teery-McElrath, Y. M., O'Malley, P. M., & Johnston, L. D. (2011). Exercise and substance use among American youth, 1991–2009. *American Journal of Preventive Medicine, 40,* 530–540.

Templeton, J. L., & Eccles, J. S. (2005). The relation between spiritual development and identity processes. In E. Roehlkepartain, P. E. King, L. Wagener, & P. L. Benson (Eds.), *The handbook of spirituality in childhood and adolescence.* Thousand Oaks, CA: Sage.

Tenenbaum, H. R., Callahan, M., Alba-Speyer, C., & Sandoval, L. (2002). Parent-child science conversations in Mexican-descent families: Educational background, activity, and past experience as moderators. *Hispanic Journal of Behavioral Sciences, 24,* 225–248.

Terman, L. (1925). *Genetic studies of genius. Vol. 1: Mental and physical traits of a thousand gifted children.* Stanford, CA: Stanford University Press.

Teti, D. (2001). Retrospect and prospect in the psychological study of sibling relationships. In J. P. McHale & W. S. Grolnick (Eds.), *Retrospect and prospect in the psychological study of families.* Mahwah, NJ: Erlbaum.

Teti, D. M., Kim, B. R., Mayer G., & Countermine, M. (2010). Maternal emotional availability at bedtime predicts infant sleep quality. *Journal of Family Psychology, 24,* 307–315.

Thabet, A. A., Ibraheem, A. N., Shivram, R., Winter, E. A., & Vostanis, P. (2009). Parenting support and PTSD in children of a war zone. *International Journal of Social Psychiatry, 55,* 225–227.

Tharp, R. G. (1994). Intergroup differences among Native Americans in socialization and child cognition: An ethnogenetic analysis. In P. M. Greenfield & R. Cocking (Eds.), *Cross-cultural roots of minority child development.* Mahwah, NJ: Erlbaum.

Tharp, R. G., & Gallimore, R. (1988). *Rousing minds to life: Teaching, learning, and schooling in social context.* New York: Cambridge University Press.

The Hospital for Sick Children & others. (2010). *Infant sleep.* Toronto: Author.

The, N. S., & others. (2010). Association of adolescent obesity with risk of severe obesity in adulthood. *Journal of the American Psychological Association, 304,* 2042–2047.

Thelen, E. (2000). Perception and motor development. In A. Kazdin (Ed.), *Encyclopedia of psychology.* New York: Oxford University Press.

Thelen, E., Corbetta, D., Kamm, K., Spencer, J. P., Schneider, K., & Zernicke, R. F. (1993). The transition to reaching: Mapping intention and intrinsic dynamics. *Child Development, 64,* 1058–1098.

Thelen, E., & Smith, L. B. (1998). Dynamic systems theory. In W. Damon (Ed.), *Handbook of child psychology* (5th ed., Vol. 1.). New York: Wiley.

Thelen, E., & Smith, L. B. (2006). Dynamic development of action and thought. In W. Damon & R. Lerner (Eds.), *Handbook of child psychology* (6th ed.). New York: Wiley.

Theokas, C. (2009). Youth sports participation—A view of the issues: Introduction to the special section. *Developmental Psychology, 45,* 303–306.

Therrell, B. L., & others. (2010). Newborn Screening System Performance Evaluation Assessment (PEAS). *Seminars in Perinatology, 34,* 105–120.

Thio, A. (2010). *Deviant behavior* (10th ed.). Boston: Allyn & Bacon.

Thivel, D., & others. (2011, in press). Effects of a 6-month school-based physical activity program on body composition and physical fitness in lean and obese schoolchildren. *European Journal of Pediatrics.*

Thomas, A., & Chess, S. (1991). Temperament in adolescence and its functional significance. In R. M. Lerner, A. C. Petersen, & J. Brooks-Gunn (Eds.), *Encyclopedia of adolescence* (Vol. 2). New York: Garland.

Thomas, M. S. C., & Johnson, M. H. (2008). New advances in understanding sensitive periods in brain development. *Current Directions in Psychological Science, 17,* 1–5.

Thomason, M. E., & Thompson, P. M. (2011). Diffusion imaging, white matter, and psychopathology. *Annual Review of Clinical Psychology* (Vol. 7). Palo Alto, CA: Annual Reviews.

Thompson, C. M. (2006). Repositioning the visual arts in early childhood education: A decade of reconsideration. In B. Spodek & O. N. Saracho (Eds.), *Handbook of research on the education of young children* (2nd ed.). Mahwah, NJ: Erlbaum.

Thompson, D. R., & others. (2007). Childhood overweight and cardiovascular disease risk factors: The National Heart, Lung, and Blood Institute Growth and Health Study. *Journal of Pediatrics, 150,* 18–25.

Thompson, L. A., Tuli, S. Y., Saliba, H., DiPietro, M., & Nackashi, J. A. (2010). Improving developmental screening in pediatric resident education. *Clinical Pediatrics, 49,* 737–742.

Thompson, M., Kuruwita, C., & Foster, E. M. (2009). Transitions in suicide risk in a nationally representative sample of adolescents. *Journal of Adolescent Health, 44,* 458–463.

Thompson, M. P., & Light, L. S. (2011, in press). Examining gender differences in risk factors in suicide attempts made 1 and 7 years later in a nationally representative sample. *Journal of Adolescent Health.*

Thompson, P. M., Giedd, J. N., Woods, R. P., MacDonald, D., Evans, A. C., & Toga, A. W. (2000). Growth patterns in the developing brain detected by using continuum mechanical tensor maps. *Nature, 404,* 190–193.

Thompson, R. A. (2006). The development of the person. In W. Damon & R. Lerner (Eds.), *Handbook of child psychology* (6th ed.). New York: Wiley.

Thompson, R. A. (2010). Feeling and understanding through the prism of relationship. In S. D. Calkins & M. A. Bell (Eds.), *Child development at the intersection of emotion and cognition* Washington, DC: American Psychological Association.

Thompson, R. A. (2011a). Attachment and development: Precis and prospect. In P. Zelazo (Ed.), *Oxford handbook of developmental psychology.* New York: Oxford University Press.

Thompson, R. A. (2011b). Emotion and emotion regulation: Two sides of the developing coin. *Emotion Review, 3,* 53–61.

Thompson, R. A. (2011c). The emotionate child. In D. Cicchetti & G. I. Roissman (Eds.), *The origins and organization of adaptation and maladaptation. Minnesota Symposium on Child Psychology* (Vol. 36). New York: Wiley.

Thompson, R. A. (2012). Attachment and its development: Precis and prospect. In P. Zelazo (Ed.), *Oxford handbook of developmental psychology.* New York: Oxford University Press.

Thompson, R. A., & Goodman, M. (2011). The architecture of social developmental science: Theoretical and historical perspectives. In M. K. Underwood & L. H. Rosen (Eds.), *Social development.* New York: Guilford.

Thompson, R. A., Meyer, S., & McGinley, M. (2006). Understanding values in relationships: The development of conscience. In M. Killen & J. Smetana (Eds.), *Handbook of moral development.* Mahwah, NJ: Erlbaum.

Thompson, R. A., & Newton, E. K. (2010). Emotion in early conscience. In W. Arsenio & E. Lemerise (Eds.), *Emotions, aggression, and morality: Bridging development and psychopathology* (pp. 6–32), Washington, DC: American Psychological Association.

Thompson, R. A., & Virmani, E. A. (2011). Socioemotional development. In V. S. Ramachandran (Ed.), *Encyclopedia of human behavior* (2nd ed.). New York: Elsevier.

Thompson, R. A., & Waters, S. F. (2011). The development of emotion regulation: Parent and peer influences. In R. Sanchez-Aragon (Ed.), *Emotion regulation.* San Angelo, Del. Alvaro Obregon, Mexico: Miguel Angel Porrua.

Thompson, R. A., Winer, A. C., & Goodvin, R. (2011). The individual child: Temperament, emotion, self, and personality. In M. Bornstein & M. E. Lamb (Eds.), *Developmental science: An advanced textbook* (6th ed.). New York: Psychology Press.

Thomson, R., & Murachver, T. (2001). Predicting gender from electronic discourse. *British Journal of Social Psychology, 40,* 193–208.

Tikotzky, L., Sadeh, A., & Glickman-Gavrieli, T. (2010). Infant sleep and paternal involvement in infant caregiving during the first 6 months of life. *Journal of Pediatric Psychology, 36*(1), 36–46.

TIMMS. (2008). *Trends in International Mathematics and Science Study 2007.* Washington, DC: National Center for Education Statistics.

Tinsley, B. J. (2003). *How children learn to be healthy.* New York: Cambridge University Press.

Tobin, J. J., Wu, D. Y. H., & Davidson, D. H. (1989). *Preschool in three cultures.* New Haven, CT: Yale University Press.

Tobler, A. L., & Komro, K. A. (2010). Trajectories of parental monitoring and communication and effects on drug use among urban young adolescents. *Journal of Adolescent Health, 46*(6), 560–568.

Tolani, N., & Brooks-Gunn, J. (2008). Family support, international trends. In M. M. Haith &

J. B. Benson (Eds.), *Encyclopedia of infant and early childhood development*. Oxford, UK: Elsevier.

Tolman, D. L., & McClelland, S. I. (2011). Normative sexuality development in adolescence: A decade in review, 2000–2009. *Journal of Research on Adolescence, 21,* 242–255.

Tomasello, M. (2003). *Constructing a language: A usage-based theory of language acquisition.* Harvard University Press.

Tomasello, M. (2006). Acquiring linguistic constructions. In W. Damon & R. Lerner (Eds.), *Handbook of child psychology* (6th ed.). New York: Wiley.

Tomasello, M. (2011). Language development. In U. Goswami (Ed.), *Wiley-Blackwell handbook of childhood cognitive development* (2nd ed.). New York: Wiley.

Tompkins, G. E. (2010). *Literacy for the 21st century* (5th ed.). Boston: Allyn & Bacon.

Tompkins, G. E. (2011). *Literacy in the early grades* (3rd ed.). Boston: Allyn & Bacon.

Tomporowski, P. D., Lambourne, K., & Okumura, M. S. (2011, in press). Physical activity interventions and children's mental function: An introduction and overview. *Preventive Medicine.*

Tough, S. C., Newburn-Cook, C., Johnston, D. W., Svenson, L. W., Rose, S., & Belik, J. (2002). Delayed childbearing and its impact on population rate changes in lower birth weight, multiple birth, and preterm delivery. *Pediatrics, 109,* 399–403.

Towse, J. N., Hitch, G. J., Horton, N., & Harvey, K. (2010). Synergies between processing and memory in children's reading span. *Developmental Science, 13,* 779–789.

Trehub, S. E., Schneider, B. A., Thorpe, I. A., & Judge, P. (1991). Observational measures of auditory sensitivity in early infancy. *Developmental Psychology, 27,* 40–49.

Trickett, P. K., & Negriff, S. (2011). Child maltreatment and social relationships. In M. H. Underwood & L. H. Rosen (Eds.), *Social development.* New York: Guilford.

Trickett, P. K., Negriff, S., Ji, J., & Peckins, M. (2011). Child maltreatment and adolescent development. *Journal of Research on Adolescence, 21,* 3–20.

Trimble, J. E. (1988, August). *The enculturation of contemporary psychology.* Paper presented at the meeting of the American Psychological Association, New Orleans.

Triulzi, F., Manganaro, L., & Volpe, P. (2011, in press). Fetal magnetic resonance imaging: Indications, study protocols, and safety. *La Radiologia Medica.*

Tsal, Y., Shalev, L., & Mevorach, C. (2005). The diversity of attention deficits in ADHD. *Journal of Learning Disabilities, 38,* 142–157.

Tschann, J. M., Flores, E., de Groat, C. L., Deardorff, J., & Wibbelsman, C. J. (2010). Condom negotiation strategies and actual condom use among Latino youth. *Journal of Adolescent Health, 47,* 254–262.

Tsui, N. B., Chiu, M. M., & Lo, K. C. (2011, in press). Noninvasive prenatal diagnosis of hemophilia by microfluidics digital PCR analysis of maternal plasma DNA. *Blood.*

Tucker, J. S., Ellickson, P. L., & Klein, M. S. (2003). Predictors of the transition to regular smoking during adolescence and young adulthood. *Journal of Adolescent Health, 32,* 314–324.

Tung, R., & Ouimette, M. (2007). *Strong results, high demand: A four-year study of Boston's pilot high schools.* Boston: Center for Collaborative Education.

Turner, S., & others. (2011). Modification of the home environment for the reduction of injuries. *Cochrane Database of Systematic Reviews, 2,* CD003600.

Turrigiano, G. (2010). Synaptic homeostasis. *Annual Review of Neuroscience* (Vol. 33). Palo Alto, CA: Annual Reviews.

U

U.S. Census Bureau. (2012). *The 2012 statistical abstract.* Washington, DC: U.S. Department of Labor.

U.S. Department of Energy. (2001). *The human genome project.* Washington, DC: U.S. Department of Energy.

U.S. Department of Health and Human Services. (2010). *Child maltreatment 2009.* Washington, DC: Author.

U.S. Food and Drug Administration. (2004, March 19). *An important message for pregnant women and women of childbearing age who may become pregnant about the risk of mercury in fish.* Washington, DC: Author.

U. S. Office of Education. (2000). *To assure a free and appropriate public education of all children with disabilities.* Washington, DC: U.S. Office of Education.

Uba, L. (1992). Cultural barriers to health care for Southeast Asian refugees. *Public Health Reports, 107,* 544–549.

Umana-Taylor, A. J., Updegraff, K. A., & Gonzales-Bracken, M. A. (2011). Mexican-origin adolescent mothers' stressors and psychological functioning: Examining ethnic identity affirmation and familism as moderators. *Journal of Youth and Adolescence, 40,* 140–157.

Underwood, M. K. (2011). Aggression. In M. K. Underwood & L. H. Rosen (Eds.), *Social development.* New York: Wiley.

UNICEF. (2004). *The state of the world's children, 2004.* Geneva, Switzerland: Author.

UNICEF. (2007). *The state of the world's children, 2007.* Geneva, Switzerland: Author.

UNICEF. (2008). *The state of the world's children, 2008.* Geneva, Switzerland: Author.

UNICEF. (2009). *The state of the world's children, 2009.* Geneva, Switzerland: Author.

UNICEF. (2011). *The state of the world's children, 2011.* Geneva, Switzerland: Author.

UNICEF. (2012). *The state of the world's children, 2012.* Geneva, Switzerland: Author.

V

Vacca, J. A. L., & others. (2012). *Reading and learning to read* (8th ed.). Boston: Allyn & Bacon.

Vahratian, A., Siega-Riz, A. M., Savitz, D. A., & Thorp, J. M. (2004). Multivitamin use and risk of preterm birth. *American Journal Epidemiology, 160,* 886–892.

Valkenburg, P. M., & Peter, J. (2011). Online communication among adolescents: An integrated model of its attraction, opportunities, and risks. *Journal of Adolescent Health, 48,* 121–127.

Van Beveren, T. T. (2011, January). *Personal conversation.* Richardson, TX: Department of Psychology, University of Texas at Dallas.

Van Buren, E., & Graham, S. (2003). *Redefining ethnic identity: Its relationship to positive and negative school adjustment outcomes for minority youth.* Paper presented at the meeting of the Society for Research in Child Development, Tampa.

Van De Voorde, S., Roeyers, H., Verte, S., & Wiersema, J. R. (2011, in press). The influence of working memory load on response inhibition in children with attention-deficit/hyperactivity disorder or reading disorder. *Journal of Clinical Neuropsychology.*

van den Boom, D. C. (1989). Neonatal irritability and the development of attachment. In G. A. Kohnstamm, J. E. Bates, & M. K. Rothbart (Eds.), *Temperament in childhood.* New York: Wiley.

van den Dries, L., Juffer, F., van IJzendoorn, M. H., & Bakersman-Kranenburg, M. J. (2010). Infants' physical and cognitive development after international adoption from foster care or institutions in China. *Journal of Developmental and Behavioral Pediatrics, 31,* 144–150.

van der Heijden, G. J., & others. (2010). Strength exercise improves muscle mass and hepatic insulin sensitivity in obese youth. *Medicine and Science in Sports and Exercise, 42*(11), 1973–1980.

van der Stel, M., & Veenman, M. V. J. (2010). Development of metacognitive skillfulness: A longitudinal study. *Learning and Individual Differences, 20,* 220–224.

van Ettinger-Veenstra, H. M., & others. (2010). Right-hemispheric brain activation correlates to language performance. *NeuroImage, 49,* 3481–3488.

Van Geel, M., & Vedder, P. (2011, in press). The role of family obligations and school adjustment in explaining the immigrant paradox. *Journal of Youth and Adolescence.*

van Harmelen, A. L., & others. (2010). Child abuse and negative explicit and automatic self-associations: The cognitive scars of emotional maltreatment. *Behavior Research and Therapy, 48,* 486–494.

van IJzendoorn, M. H., & Kroonenberg, P. M. (1988). Cross-cultural patterns of attachment: A meta-analysis of the Strange Situation. *Child Development, 59,* 147–156.

van IJzendoorn, M. H., & Sagi-Schwartz, A. (2009). Cross-cultural patterns of attachment: Universal and contextual dimensions. In J. Cassidy & P. R. Shaver (Eds.), *Handbook of attachment* (2nd ed.). New York: Guilford.

Van Ryzin, M. J., Johnson, A. B., Leve, L. D., & Kim, H. K. (2011, in press). The number of sexual partners and health-risking sexual behavior: Prediction from high school entry to high school exit. *Archives of Sexual Behavior.*

Vandam, M., Ide-Helvie, D., & Moeller, M. P. (2011, in press). Point vowel duration in children with hearing aids and cochlear implants at 4 and 5 years of age. *Clinical Linguistics and Phonetics.*

Vandehey, M., Diekhoff, G., & LaBeff, E. (2007). College cheating: A 20-year follow-up and the addition of an honor code. *Journal of College Development, 48,* 468–480.

Vandell, D. L., & others. (2010). Do effects of early childcare extend to age 15 years? From the NICHD Study of Early Child Care and Youth Development. *Child Development, 81,* 737–756.

Vargas, L., & Koss-Chiono, J. (1999). *Working with Latino youth.* San Francisco: Jossey-Bass.

Vaughan, C. A., & Halpern, C. T. (2010). Gender differences in depressive symptoms during adolescence: The contributions of weight-related concerns and behaviors. *Journal of Research on Adolescence, 20,* 389–419.

Vaughn, M. G., Beaver, K. M., Wexler, J., DeLisi, M., & Roberts, G. J. (2010). The effect of school dropout on verbal ability in adulthood: A propensity score matching approach. *Journal of Youth and Adolescence, 40*(2), 197–206.

Vazsonyi, A. T., & Huang, L. (2010). Where self-control comes from: On the development of self-control and its relationship to deviance over time. *Developmental Psychology, 46,* 245–257.

Veenstra, A., Lindenberg, S., Munniksma, A., & Dijkstra, J. K. (2010). The complex relationship between bullying, victimization, acceptance, and rejection: Giving special attention to status, affection, and sex differences. *Social Development, 19,* 480–486.

Velez, C. E., Wolchik, S. A., Tein, J. Y., & Sandler, I. (2011). Protecting children from the consequences of divorce: A longitudinal study of the effects of parenting on children's coping responses. *Child Development, 82,* 244–257.

Venners, S. A., & others. (2004). Paternal smoking and pregnancy loss: A prospective study using a biomarker of pregnancy. *American Journal of Epidemiology, 159,* 993–1001.

Ventura, A. K., Gromis, J. C., & Lohse, B. (2010). Feeding practices and styles used by a diverse sample of low-income parents of preschool-age children. *Journal of Nutrition Education and Behavior, 42,* 242–249.

Ventura, S. J., Abma, C., Mosher, W. D., & Henshaw, S. K. (2008). Estimated pregnancy rates by outcome for the United States, 1990–2004. *National Vital Statistics Reports, 56,* 1–25, 28.

Ventura, S. J., & Hamilton, B. E. (2011, February). U.S. teenage birth rate resumes decline. *NCHS (National Center for Health Statistics) Data Brief, 58,* 1–3.

Vergara-Castaneda, A., & others. (2010). Overweight, obesity, high blood pressure, and lifestyle factors among Mexican children and their parents. *Environmental Health and Preventive Medicine, 15,* 358–366.

Vernberg, E. M. (1990). Psychological adjustment and experience with peers during early adolescence: Reciprocal, incidental, or unidirectional relationships? *Journal of Abnormal Child Psychology, 18,* 187–198.

Verona, E., & Javdani, S. (2011, in press). Dimensions of adolescent psychopathology and relationships to suicide risk indicators. *Journal of Youth and Adolescence.*

Villanueva, C. M., & Buriel, R. (2010). Speaking on behalf of others: A qualitative study of the perceptions and feelings of adolescent Latina language brokers. *Journal of Social Issues, 66,* 197–210.

Villegas, R., & others. (2008). Duration of breast-feeding and the incidence of type 2 diabetes mellitus in the Shanghai Women's Health Study. *Diabetologia, 51*(2), 258–266.

Vinik, J., Almas, A., & Grusec, J. (2011). Mothers' knowledge of what distresses and comforts their children predicts children's coping, empathy, and prosocial behavior. *Parenting:Science and Practice, 11,* 56–71.

Vitaro, F., Boivin, M., & Bukowski, W. M. (2009). The role of friendship in child and adolescent psychosocial development. In K. H. Rubin, W. M. Bukowski, & B. Laursen (Eds.), *Handbook of peer interaction, relationships, and groups.* New York: Guilford.

Vitaro, F., Pedersen, S., & Brendgen, M. (2007). Children's disruptiveness, peer rejection, friends' deviancy, and delinquent behaviors: A process-oriented approach. *Development and Psychopathology, 19,* 433–453.

Vittrup, B., Holden, G. W., & Buck, M. (2006). Attitudes predict the use of physical punishment: A prospective study of the emergence of disciplinary practices. *Pediatrics, 117,* 2055–2064.

Vladutiu, C. J., Evenson, K. R., & Marshall, S. W. (2010). Physical activity and injuries during pregnancy. *Journal of Physical Activity and Health, 7*(6), 761–769.

Volbrecht, M. M., & Goldsmith, H. H. (2010). Early temperamental and family predictors of shyness and anxiety. *Developmental Psychology, 46,* 1192–1205.

Von Hofsten, C. (2008). Motor and physical development manual. In M. M Haith & J. B. Benson (Eds.), *Encyclopedia of infant and early childhood development.* Oxford, UK: Elsevier.

Von Korff, L., & Grotevant, H. D. (2011, in press). Contact in adoption and adoptive family identity formation: The mediating role of family conversation. *Journal of Family Psychology.*

Vonk, J. M., & others. (2004). Childhood factors associated with asthma remission after year follow up. *Thorax, 59,* 925–929.

Vos, J., & others. (2011, in press). Family communication matters: The impact of telling relatives about unclassified variants and uninformative DNA-test results. *Genetics in Medicine.*

Vreeman, R. C., & Carroll, A. E. (2007). A systematic review of school-based interventions to prevent bullying. *Archives of Pediatric and Adolescent Medicine, 161,* 78–88.

Vuillermin, P. J., Robertson, C. F., & South, M. (2011, in press). The role of parent-initiated oral corticosteroids in preschool wheeze and school-aged asthma. *Current Opinion in Allergy and Clinical Immunology.*

Vurpillot, E. (1968). The development of scanning strategies and their relation to visual differentiation. *Journal of Experimental Child Psychology, 6,* 632–650.

Vygotsky, L. S. (1962). *Thought and language.* Cambridge, MA: MIT Press.

W

Wachs, T. D. (2000). *Necessary but not sufficient.* Washington, DC: American Psychological Association.

Wachs, T. D., & Bates, J. E. (2010). Temperament. In J. G. Bremner & T. D. Wachs (Eds.), *Wiley-Blackwell handbook of infant development* (2nd ed.). New York: Wiley.

Wagenaar, K., Ceelen, M., van Weissenbruch, M. M., Knol, D. L., Delemarre-van de Waal, H. A., & Huisman, J. (2008). School functioning in 8- to 18-year-old children born after in vitro fertilization. *European Journal of Pediatrics, 167,* 1289–1295.

Wakeling, E. L. (2011, in press). Silver-Russell syndrome. *Archives of Disease in Childhood.*

Waldie, K. E., & Hausmann, M. (2010). Right frontal-parietal dysfunction in children with ADHD and developmental dyslexia as determined by line bisection judgments. *Neuropsychologia.*

Walker, D. M., & Gore, A. C. (2011, in press). Transgenerational neuroendocrine disruption of reproduction. *Nature Review: Endocrinology.*

Walker, L. (1982). The sequentiality of Kohlberg's stages of moral development. *Child Development, 53,* 1130–1136.

Walker, L. J. (2002). In W. Damon (Ed.), *Bringing in a new era of character education.* Stanford, CA: Hoover Press.

Walker, L. J. (2004). Progress and prospects in the psychology of moral development. *Merrill-Palmer Quarterly, 50,* 546–557.

Walker, L. J., & Frimer, J. A. (2011). The science of moral development. In M. K. Underwood & L. H. Rosen (Eds.), *Social development.* New York: Guilford.

Walker, L. J., Frimer, J. A., & Dunlop, W. L. (2011, in press). Varieties of moral personality: Beyond the banality of heroism. *Journal of Personality.*

Waller, E. M., & Rose, A. J. (2010). Adjustment trade-offs of co-rumination in mother-adolescent relationships. *Journal of Adolescence, 33,* 487–497.

Wallerstein, J. S. (2008). Divorce. In M. M. Haith & J. B. Benson (Eds.), *Encyclopedia of infant and early childhood development.* Oxford, UK: Elsevier.

Walley, A. J., Blakemore, A. I., & Froguel, P. (2006). Genetics of obesity and the prediction of risk for health. *Human Molecular Genetics, 15,* (Suppl. 2), R124–R130.

Walsh, J. (2008). Self-efficacy. In N. J. Salkind (Ed.), *Encyclopedia of educational psychology.* Thousand Oaks, CA: Sage.

Walsh, L. V. (2006). Beliefs and rituals in traditional birth attendant practice in Guatemala. *Journal of Transcultural Nursing, 17,* 148–154.

Walsh, R. (2011, in press). Lifestyle and mental health. *American Psychologist.*

Walshaw, C. A., & Owens, J. M. (2006). Low breastfeeding rates and milk insufficiency. *British Journal of General Practice, 56,* 379.

Wang, J., Nansel, T. R., & Iannotti, R. J. (2011). Cyber and traditional bullying: Differential association with depression. *Journal of Adolescent Health, 48*(4), 415–417.

Wardlaw, G. M., & Smith, A. M. (2011). *Contemporary nutrition* (8th ed.). New York: McGraw-Hill.

Warren, A., Lerner, R. M., & Phelps, E. (2011). *Thriving and spirituality among youth.* New York: Wiley.

Warrick, P. (1992, March 1). The fantastic voyage of Tanner Roberts. *Los Angeles Times,* pp. E1, E11, E12.

Warshak, R. A. (2008, January). Personal communication. Department of Psychology, University of Texas at Dallas, Richardson.

Wasik, B. H., & Newman, B. A. (2009). Teaching and learning to read. In O. A. Barbarin & B. H. Wasik, *Handbook of child development and early education* (pp. 303–327). New York: Guilford.

Wasserman, M., Bender, D., & Lee, S. Y. (2007). Use of preventive maternal and child health services by Latina women: A review of published intervention studies. *Medical Care Research and Review, 64,* 4–45.

Watamura, S. E., Phillips, D. A., Morrissey, T. W., McCartney, K., & Bub, K. (2011). Double jeopardy: Poorer socio-emotional outcomes for children in the NICHD SECCYD experience home and child-care environments that confer risk. *Child Development, 82,* 48–65.

Waterman, A. S. (1985). Identity in the context of adolescent psychology. In A. S. Waterman (Ed.), *Identity in adolescence: Processes and contents.* San Francisco: Jossey-Bass.

Waterman, A. S. (1999). Identity, the identity statuses, and identity status development: A contemporary statement. *Developmental Review, 19,* 591–621.

Watson, J. B. (1928). *Psychological care of infant and child.* New York: W. W. Norton.

Watson, J. B., & Rayner, R. (1920). Conditioned emotional reactions. *Journal of Experimental Psychology, 3,* 1–14.

Wayne, A. (2011). Commentary in interview: Childhood cancers in transition. Retrieved April 12, 2011, from http://home.ccr.cancer.gov/connections/2010/Vol4_No2/clinic2.asp

Webster, N. S., & Worrell, F. C. (2008). Academically-talented adolescents' attitudes toward service in the community. *Gifted Child Quarterly, 52,* 170–179.

Wegman, M. E. (1987). Annual summary of vital statistics—1986. *Pediatrics, 80,* 817–827.

Weikart, D. P. (1993). [Long-term positive effects in the Perry Preschool Head Start Program.] Unpublished data. HighScope Foundation, Ypsilanti, MI.

Weiss, L. A., & others. (2008). Association between microdeletion and microduplication at 16p11.2 and autism. *New England Journal of Medicine, 358,* 667–675.

Weisskirch, R. S., Kim, S. Y., Zamboanga, B. L., Schwartz, S. J., Bersamin, M., & Umaña-Taylor, A. J. (2011, in press). Cultural influences for college student language brokers. *Cultural Diversity & Ethnic Minority Psychology.*

Wekerle, C., & others. (2009). The contribution of childhood emotional abuse to teen dating violence among child protective services–involved youth. *Child Abuse and Neglect, 33*(1), 45–58.

Welch, K. J. (2011). *THINK human sexuality.* Upper Saddle River, NJ: Pearson.

Wellman, H. M. (2011). Developing a theory of mind. In U. Goswami (Ed.), *Wiley-Blackwell handbook of childhood cognitive development* (2nd ed.). Wiley.

Wellman, H. M., Cross, D., & Watson, J. (2001). Meta-analysis of theory-of-mind development: The truth about false belief. *Child Development, 72,* 655–684.

Wellman, H. M., & Woolley, J. D. (1990). From simple desires to ordinary beliefs: The early development of everyday psychology. *Cognition, 35,* 245–275.

Wells, E. M., & others. (2011, in press). Body burdens of mercury, lead, selenium, and copper among Baltimore newborns. *Environmental Research.*

Welsh, J. A., Nix, R. L., Blair, C., Bierman, K. L., & Nelson, K. E. (2010). The development of cognitive skills and gains in academic school readiness for children from low-income families. *Journal of Educational Psychology, 102,* 43–53.

Weng, X., Odouli, R., & Li, D. K. (2008). Maternal caffeine consumption during pregnancy and the risk of miscarriage: A prospective cohort study. *American Journal of Obstetrics and Gynecology, 198,* e1–e8.

Wentzel, K. R., Barry, C. M., & Caldwell, K. A. (2004). Friendships in middle school: Influences on motivation and school adjustment. *Journal of Educational Psychology, 96,* 195–203.

Wentzel, K. R., & Asher, S. R. (1995). The academic lives of neglected, rejected, popular, and controversial children. *Child Development, 66,* 754–763.

Werker, J. F., & Tees, R. C. (2005). Speech perception as a window for understanding plasticity and commitment in language systems of the brain. *Developmental Psychobiology, 46,* 233–251.

Wertsch, J. (2008). From social interaction to higher psychological processes. *Human Development, 51,* 66–79.

Westerman, G., Thomas, M. S. C., & Karmiloff-Smith, A. (2011). Neuroconstructivism. In U. Goswami (Ed.), *Wiley-Blackwell handbook of childhood cognitive development* (2nd ed.). New York: Wiley.

Wheeden, A., Scafidi, F. A., Field, T., Ironson, G., Valdeon, C., & Bandstra, E. (1993). Massage effects on cocaine-exposed preterm neonates. *Journal of Developmental and Behavioral Pediatrics, 14,* 318–322.

Whetstone, L. M., Morrissey, S. L., & Cummings, D. M. (2007). Children at risk: The association between perceived weight status and suicidal thoughts and attempts in middle school youth. *Journal of School Health, 77,* 59–66.

White, B. A., & Kistner, J. A. (2011). Biased self-perceptions, peer rejection, and aggression in children. *Journal of Abnormal Child Psychology, 39,* 645–656.

White, J. W. (2001). Aggression and gender. In J. Worell (Ed.), *Encyclopedia of women and gender.* San Diego: Academic Press.

White, S. W. (2010). The school counselor's role in dropout prevention. *Journal of Counseling and Development, 88,* 227–235.

Whitescarver, K. (2006, April). *Montessori rising: Montessori education in the United States, 1955–present.* Paper presented at the meeting of the American Education Research Association, San Francisco.

WIC New York. (2011). *WIC program: Women, infants, and children.* Retrieved March 12, 2011, from http://www.health.state.ny.us/prevention/nutrition/wis/

Wiersman, W., & Jurs, S. G. (2009). *Research methods in education* (9th ed.). Upper Saddle River, NJ: Prentice Hall.

Wiesel, A., & others. (2011, in press). Maternal occupation exposure to ionizing radiation and birth defects. *Radiation and Environmental Biophysics.*

Wigfield, A., & Asher, S. R. (1994). Social and motivational influences on reading. In P. D. Pearson & others (Eds.), *Handbook of reading research.* New York: Longman.

Wikstrom, A. H., Ahlstrom, H., & Axelsson, O. (2011, in press). Second-trimester fetal magnetic resonance imaging improves diagnosis of non-CNS anomalies. *Acta Obstetricia et Gynecologica Scandinavica.*

Wilcox, J. (2010). The easiest birth yet. *Midwifery Today with International Midwife, 23,* 63–64.

Williams, D., & Happe, F. (2010). Representing intentions in self and others: Studies of autism and typical development. *Developmental Science, 13,* 307–319.

Williams, J. H., & Ross, L. (2007). Consequences of prenatal toxin exposure for mental health in children and adolescents: A systematic review. *European Child and Adolescent Psychiatry, 16,* 243–253.

Williams, K. M., Nathanson, C., & Paulhus, D. L. (2010). Identifying and profiling academic cheaters: Their personality, cognitive ability, and motivation. *Journal of Experimental Psychology: Applied, 16,* 293–307.

Williams, R., & Hanzell, P. (2011). Austerity, poverty, resilience, and the future of mental health services for children and adolescents. *Current Opinion in Psychiatry, 24,* 263–266.

Wilson, B. J. (2008). Media and children's aggression, fear, and altruism. *Future of Children, 18*(1), 87–118.

Winner, E. (1986, August). Where pelicans kiss seals. *Psychology Today,* pp. 24–35.

Winner, E. (1996). *Gifted children: Myths and realities.* New York: Basic Books.

Winner, E. (2000). The origins and ends of giftedness. *American Psychologist, 55,* 159–169.

Winner, E. (2006). Development in the arts. In W. Damon & R. Lerner (Eds.), *Handbook of child psychology* (6th ed.). New York: Wiley.

Winner, E. (2009). Toward broadening our understanding of giftedness: The spatial domain. In F. D. Horowitz, R. F. Subotnik, & D. J. Matthews (Eds.), *The development of giftedness and talent across the life span.* Washington, DC: American Psychological Association.

Winsler, A., Carlton, M. P., & Barry, M. J. (2000). Age-related changes in preschool children's systematic use of private speech in a natural setting. *Journal of Child Language, 27,* 665–687.

Wit, J. M., Kiess, W., & Mullis, P. (2011). Genetic evaluation of short stature. *Best Practices & Research: Clinical Endocrinology and Metabolism, 25,* 1–17.

Witherington, D. C., Campos, J. J., Harriger, J. A., Bryan, C., & Margett, T. E. (2010). Emotion and its development in infancy. In J. G. Bremner & T. D. Wachs (Eds.), *Wiley-Blackwell handbook of infant development* (2nd ed.). New York: Wiley.

Witte, R. (2012). *Classroom assessment for teachers.* New York: McGraw-Hill.

Wittmeier, K. D., Mollard, R. C., & Kriellaars, D. J. (2008). Physical activity intensity and risk of overweight and adiposity in children. *Obesity, 16,* 415–420.

Witvliet, M., & others. (2010). Peer group affiliation in children: The role of perceived popularity, likeability, and behavioral similarity in bullying. *Social Development, 19,* 285–303.

Wojtowicz, A., & others. (2011, in press). Aspirin resistance may be associated with adverse pregnancy outcomes. *Neuroendocrinology Letters.*

Women's Sports Foundation. (2001). *The 10 commandments for parents and coaches in youth sports.* Eisenhower Park, NY: Women's Sports Foundation.

Wong, M. M., Brower, K. J., Nigg, J. T., & Zucker, R. A. (2010). Childhood sleep problems, response inhibition, and alcohol and drug outcomes in adolescence and young adulthood. *Alcoholism, Clinical and Experimental Research, 34,* 1033–1044.

Wong Briggs, T. W. (2004, October 14). USA Today's 2004 all-USA teacher team. *USA Today,* p. 6D.

Wood, D., Kaplan, R., & McLoyd, V. C. (2007). Gender differences in educational expectations of urban, low-income African American youth: The role of parents and school. *Journal of Youth and Adolescence, 36,* 417–427.

Woodward, A. L., & Markman, E. M. (1998). Early word learning. In D. Kuhn & R. S. Siegler (Eds.), *Handbook of child psychology* (5th ed., Vol. 2). New York: Wiley.

Woolett, L. A. (2011). Review: Transport of maternal cholesterol to the fetal circulation. *Placenta, 32* (Suppl. 2), S18–S21.

World Health Organization. (2000, February 2). Adolescent health behavior in 28 countries. Geneva, Switzerland: World Health Organization.

Wright, R. H., Mindel, C. H., Tran, T. V., & Habenstein, R. W. (2012). *Ethnic families in America* (5th ed.). Upper Saddle River, NJ: Pearson.

Wuest, D. A., & Fisette, J. L. (2012). *Foundations of physical education, exercise science, and sport* (17th ed.). New York: McGraw-Hill.

X

Xia, N. (2010). *Family factors and student outcomes.* Unpublished doctoral dissertation, RAND Corporation, Pardee RAND Graduate School, Pittsburgh.

Xie, Q., & Young, M. E. (1999). Integrated child development in rural China. *Education: The World Bank.* Washington, DC: The World Bank.

Xu, L., & others. (2011, in press). Parental overweight/obesity, social factors, and child overweight/obesity at 7 years of age. *Pediatric International.*

Xue, F., Holzman, C., Rahbar, M. H., Trosko, K., & Fischer, L. (2007). Maternal fish consumption, mercury levels, and risk of preterm delivery. *Environmental Health Perspectives, 115,* 42–47.

Y

Yakoob, M. Y., Lawn, J. E., Darmstadt, G. L., & Bhutta, Z. A. (2010). Stillbirths: Epidemiology, evidence, and priorities for action. *Seminars in Perinatology, 34,* 387–394.

Yang, Q., Wen, S. W., Leader, A., Chen, X. K., Lipson, J. & Walker, M. (2007). Paternal age and birth defects: How strong is the association? *Human Reproduction, 22,* 696–701.

Yarrow, A. W. (2010). Children's art as dynamic storytelling. *The Early Childhood Leader's Magazine, 194,* 68–71.

Yazdy, M. M., Liu, S., Mitchell, A. A., & Werler, N. M. (2010). Maternal dietary glycemic intake and the risk of neural tube defects. *American Journal of Epidemiology, 171,* 407–414.

Yell, M. L., & Drasgow, E. (2009). *What every teacher should know about No Child Left Behind* (2nd ed.). Upper Saddle River, NJ: Prentice Hall.

Yi, S., & others. (2010). Role of risk and protective factors in risky sexual behavior among high school students in Cambodia. *BMC Public Health, 10,* 477.

Yiallourou, S. R., Sands, S. A., Walker, A. M., & Horne, R. S. (2011). Baroreflex sensitivity during sleep in infants: Impact of sleeping position and sleep state. *Sleep, 34,* 725–732.

Yolton, K., & others. (2010). Associations between secondhand smoke and exposure and sleep patterns in children. *Pediatrics, 125,* e261–e268.

Young, K. T. (1990). American conceptions of infant development from 1955 to 1984: What the experts are telling parents. *Child Development, 61,* 17–28.

Youniss, J., McLellan, J. A., & Yates, M. (1999). Religion, community service, and identity in American youth. *Journal of Adolescence, 22,* 243–253.

Yuan, A. S. V. (2010). Body perceptions, weight control behavior, and changes in adolescents' psychological well-being over time: A longitudinal examination of gender. *Journal of Youth and Adolescence, 39,* 927–939.

Yudof, M. G., Levin, B., Moran, R., & Ryan, J. M. (2012). *Educational policy and the law* (5th ed.). Boston: Cengage.

Z

Zaff, J. F., Hart, D., Flanagan, C., Youniss, J., & Levine, P. (2010). Developing civic engagement within a civic context. In M. E. Lamb, A. M. Freund, & R. M. Lerner (Eds.), *Handbook of life-span development* (Vol. 2). New York: Wiley.

Zayas, L., Guibas, L. E., Fedoravicius, N., & Cabassa, L. J. (2010). Patterns of distress, precipitating events, and reflections on suicide attempts by young Latinas. *Social Science & Medicine, 70,* 1773–1779.

Zeiders, K. H., Roosa, M. W., & Tein, J. Y. (2011). Family structure and family processes in Mexican-American families. *Family Process, 50,* 77–91.

Zeisel, S. H. (2011, in press). The supply of choline is important for fetal progenitor cells. *Seminars in Cell and Developmental Biology.*

Zelazo, P. D., & Lee, W. S. C. (2010). Brain development: An overview. In W. F. Overton

(Ed.), *Handbook of life-span development* (Vol.1). New York: Wiley.

Zelazo, P. D., & Muller, U. (2011). Executive function in typical and atypical children. In U. Goswami (Ed.), *Wiley-Blackwell handbook of childhood cognitive development* (2nd ed.). New York: Wiley.

Zelazo, P. D., Qu, L., & Kesek, A. C. (2010). Hot executive function: Emotion and the development of cognitive control. In S. D. Calkins & M. A. Bell (Eds.), *Child development at the intersection of emotion and cognition*. Washington, DC: American Psychological Association.

Zeller, M. H., Reiter-Purtill, J., & Ramey, C. (2008). Negative peer perceptions of obese children in the classroom environment. *Obesity, 16,* 755–762.

Zentall, S. S. (2006). *ADHD and education.* Upper Saddle River, NJ: Prentice Hall.

Zeskind, P. S. (2007). Impact of the cry of the infant at risk on psychosocial development.

In R. E. Tremblay, R. deV. Peters, M. Boivin, & R. G. Barr (Eds.), *Encyclopedia on early childhood development*. Montreal: Centre of Excellence for Early Childhood Development. Retrieved November 24, 2008, from http://www.child-encyclopedia.com/en-ca/list-of-topics.html

Zhang, L., Zhang, X. H., Liang, M. Y., & Ren, M. H. (2010). Prenatal cytogenetic diagnosis study of 2782 cases of high-risk pregnant women. *China Medicine (English), 123,* 423–430.

Zhang, L.-F., & Sternberg, R. J. (2011). Learning in cross-cultural perspective. In T. Husen & T. N. Postlethwaite (Eds.), *International encyclopedia of education* (3rd ed.). New York: Elsevier.

Zielinski, D. S. (2009). Child maltreatment and adult socioeconomic well-being. *Child Abuse and Neglect, 33,* 666–678.

Zielinski, D. S., Eckenrode, J., & Olds, D. L. (2009). Nurse home visitation and the prevention of child maltreatment: Impact on the timing of official reports. *Development and Psychopathology, 21,* 441–453.

Zigler, E., Gilliam, W. S., & Jones, S. M. (2006). *A vision for universal preschool education.* New York: Cambridge University Press.

Zigler, E. F., & Styfco, S. J. (1994). Head Start: Criticisms in a constructive context. *American Psychologist, 49,* 127–132.

Zigler, E. F., & Styfco, S. J. (2010). *The hidden history of Head Start.* New York: Oxford University Press.

Ziol-Guest, K. M. (2009). Child custody and support. In D. Carr (Ed.), *Encyclopedia of the life course and human development.* Boston: Cengage.

Zocca, J. M., & others. (2011). Links between mothers' and children's disinhibited eating and children's adiposity. *Appetite, 56,* 324–331.

credits

PHOTO CREDITS

Prologue: Ariel Skelley/Blend Images/Getty Images

Section Openers

pp. 4–5: © Ariel Skelley/Corbis; pp. 52–53: MedicalRF.com/Getty Images; pp. 132–133: Jose Luis Pelaez Inc./Blend Images/Getty Images; pp. 232–233: Image Source/Getty Images; pp. 322–323: Monkey Business Images/PhotoLibrary; pp. 422–423: © Rolf Bruderer/Corbis

Chapter 1

p. 6: © Ariel Skelley/Corbis; p. 7 (top to bottom): © Seanna O'Sullivan; WBBM-TV/AFP/Getty Images; © AP Wide World Photos; Photograph of Alice Walker, Alice Walker Papers, Manuscript, Archives and Rare Book Library, Emory University; p. 9 (top): Courtesy of Luis Vargas; p. 9 (bottom): National Association for the Education of Young Children, Robert Maust/Photo Agora; p. 11: © Nancy Agostini; p. 12: Naser Siddique/UNICEF Bangladesh; p. 13: Courtesy of Marian Wright Edelman and The Children's Defense Fund; p. 17, fig. 1.4 (left to right): © Brand X Pictures/PunchStock; Courtesy of John Santrock; Laurence Mouton/Photoalto/PictureQuest; McGraw-Hill Companies Inc./Ken Karp, photographer; Getty Images/SW Productions; p. 17 (bottom): © Jason Brindel Commercial/Alamy; p. 19: Rubberball/PictureQuest; p. 22 (top): Ingram Publishing; p. 22 (bottom): © Sarah Putman; p. 24 (left to right): Royalty-free/Corbis; Royalty-free/Corbis; © Veer; Royalty-free/Corbis; p. 25, fig. 1.8 (left to right): © Stockbyte/Getty Images; © BananaStock/PunchStock; image100/Corbis; © RF/Corbis; p. 26: © Yves de Braine/Black Star/Stock Photo; p. 27 (top): A.R. Lauria/Dr. Michael Cole, Laboratory of Human Cognition, University of California, San Diego; p. 27 (bottom): Creatas Images/Jupiter Images; p. 28 (top): Courtesy of Professor Benjamin Harris; p. 28 (bottom): © AP Wide World Photos; p. 29: Courtesy Albert Bandura, Stanford University; p. 30: Time & Life Pictures/Getty Images; p. 31: Courtesy of Urie Bronfenbrenner; p. 32, fig. 1.11: (Freud): © Bettmann/Corbis; (Pavlov): © Bettmann/Corbis; (Piaget): © Yves de Braine/Black Star/Stock Photo; (Vygotsky): A.R. Lauria/Dr. Michael Cole, Laboratory of Human Cognition, University of California, San Diego; (Skinner): Harvard University News Office; (Erikson): © Bettmann/Corbis; (Bandura): Courtesy Albert Bandura, Stanford University; (Bronfenbrenner): Courtesy of Urie Bronfenbrenner; p. 33: © AP Wide World Photos; p. 35, fig. 1.14: Courtesy of Susan F. Tapert, Ph.D., University of California, San Diego; p. 35 (bottom): © Bettmann/Corbis; p. 36: © Digital Vision/PunchStock; p. 39: © McGraw-Hill Companies, Inc., photographer John Thoeming; p. 41 (top): Courtesy of Dr. Pamela Reid; p. 41 (bottom left): © Kevin Fleming/Corbis; p. 41 (bottom right): Ed Honowitz/Stone/Getty Images

Chapter 2

p. 54: Image Source/Getty Images; p. 55: © Enrico Ferorelli Enterprises; p. 57: © Frans Lemmens/Corbis; p. 58, fig. 2.1: © 1996 PhotoDisc, Inc./Getty Images; p. 58 (bottom): © David Wilkie; p. 60: Rick Rickman; p. 61, fig. 2.3: © Science Source/Photo Researchers; p. 61, fig. 2.4: © Custom Medical Stock Photo; p. 64: © James Shaffer/Photo Edit; p. 65: From R. Simensen and

R. Curtis Rogers, "Fragile X Syndrome," *American Family Physician,* 39 (5): 186, May 1989. © American Academy of Family Physicians; p. 66: © Andrew Eccles/JBGPHOTO.COM; p. 67: Courtesy of Holly Ishmael; p. 68 (top): © Jacques Pavlosky/Sygma/Corbis; p. 68, fig. 2.8: © Larry Berman; p. 70: © Newscom; p. 72: © Newscom; p. 73: Photodisc/Getty Images; p. 74: © Myrleen Ferguson Cate/Photo Edit; p. 76: GREG WOOD/AFP/Getty Images; p. 78: istockphoto.com/© Francisco Romero

Chapter 3

p. 83: © Lennart Nilsson; p. 84: © John Santrock; p. 88, fig. 3.3 (all): © Lennart Nilsson; p. 89, fig. 3.4: © Lennart Nilsson; p. 89 (bottom): © AP Wide World Photos; p. 90: Tony Metaxas/Asia Images/Getty Images; p. 91: Photographer's Choice/Getty RF; p. 92 (top): © Tracy Frankel/The Image Bank/Getty Images; p. 92 (bottom): © Roger Tully/Stone/Getty Images; p. 93: Stockbyte/Getty RF; p. 94: Courtesy of Rachel Thompson; p. 95: © Stephen Maturen; p. 96: © Viviane Moos/Corbis; p. 99: Courtesy of Ann Streissguth; p. 100 (top): Monkey Business Images Ltd/Photolibrary; p. 100 (bottom): © John Chiasson; p. 102: © R.I.A. Novosti/Gamma/H.P.P./Eyedea; p. 104: © Betty Press/Woodfin Camp & Associates; p. 105 (top): © iStock Photos; p. 105 (bottom): Barbara Penoyar/Getty Images; p. 106: © Rafal Strzechowski/age fotostock; p. 107: © David Butow/Corbis

Chapter 4

p. 111: ERproductions Ltd/Blend Images/Getty Images; p. 114: Marjorie Shostak/Anthro-Photo; p. 115: © RF/Corbis; p. 116 (top): Courtesy of Linda Pugh and Paul Schreck, Photographer, Wellspan Health System; p. 116 (bottom): © Barros & Barros/Getty Images; p. 117 (top): Dr. Holly Beckwith; p. 117 (bottom): Nova Development RF; p. 118: ERproductions Ltd/Getty Images; p. 119: © Jonathan Nourok/Getty Images; p. 122: © AP Wide World Photos; p. 123: © Marc Asnin/Corbis SABA; p. 124: Courtesy of Dr. Tiffany Field; p. 127 (top): © Tony Schanuel; p. 127 (bottom); Howard Grey/Getty Images; p. 128: © Kaz Mori/The Image Bank/Getty Images

Chapter 5

p. 134: Image Source/Getty Images; p. 135 (top): © Wendy Stone/Corbis; p. 135 (bottom): © Dave Bartruff/Corbis; p. 137: Benjamin Benschneider/The Seattle Times; p. 138, fig. 5.3: © A. Glauberman/Photo Researchers; p. 138, fig. 5.4: ER Productions/Getty Images; p. 141, fig. 5.8 (left to right): Courtesy of Dr. Harry T. Chugani, Children's Hospital of Michigan; © David Grugin Productions, Inc. Reprinted by permission; p. 141, fig. 5.9: Image Courtesy of Dana Boatman, Ph.D., Department of Neurology, John Hopkins University, Reprinted with Permission from *The Secret Life of the Brain,* Joseph Henry Press; p. 143: © Tom Rosenthal/SuperStock; p. 144: Mark Steinmetz/The McGraw-Hill Companies, Inc.; p. 146: © Bob Daemmrich/The Image Works; p. 148 (top): © Syracuse Newspapers/D. Blume/The Image Works; p. 148 (bottom): Courtesy Dr. T. Berry Brazelton and Brazelton Touchpoints Center; p. 149: Courtesy of Esther Thelan; p. 150: Harry Bartlett/Taxi/Getty Images; p. 151, fig. 5.14 (left to right): © Elizabeth Crews/The Image Works; James G. White; © Petit Format/Photo Researchers; p. 152:

© Fabio Cardosa/zefa/Corbis; p. 153: Courtesy Dr. Karen Adolph, New York University; p. 154, fig. 5.16 (left to right): © Barbara Penoyar/Getty Images; Digital Vision/Getty Images; © Image Source/Alamy; Titus/Getty Images; © Digital Vision; BananaStock/PictureQuest; Corbis/PictureQuest; © BrandX/PunchStock; p. 155 (top left): © Michael Greenlar/The Image Works; p. 155 (top right): © Frank Baily Studios; p. 155 (bottom): © Newstockimages/SuperStock RF; p. 156: Courtesy Amy Needham, Duke University; p. 157: Trish Gant/Dorling Kindersley/Getty Images; p. 158: Adapted from "The Origin of Form and Perception" by R.L. Fantz © 1961 by *Scientific American*. Photo © by David Linton; p. 159: Photo from Karen Adolph's laboratory at New York University; p. 160: Kevin Peterson/Getty Images/Simulation by Vischeck; p. 162 (top): © Mark Richards/Photo Edit; p. 162 (bottom left): © Jill Braaten; p. 162 (bottom right): © Dr. Melanie Spence, University of Texas; p. 163: © Jean Guichard; p. 164, fig. 5.26: From D. Rosenstein and H. Oster, "Differential Facial Responses to Four Basic Tastes in Newborns," *Child Development,* Vol. 59, 1988. © Society for Research in Child Development, Inc.; p. 164 (bottom): © David Young-Wolff/Photo Edit; p. 165: altrendo images/Getty Images; p. 166: Anthony Cain/Flickr/Getty Images

Chapter 6

p. 170: © Marcus Mok/Asia Images/Corbis; p. 173 (top): © Digital Vision/PhotoLibrary; p. 173 (bottom): Plush Studios/Brand X Pictures/Jupiterimages; p. 175 (top): Johnny Valley/Cultura/Getty Images; p. 175 (bottom): © PunchStock; p. 176: © Doug Goodman/Photo Researchers; p. 178: © Joe McNally; p. 179: © baobao ou/Flickr/Getty Images; p. 180: Courtesy of Dr. Carolyn Rovee-Collier; p. 181 (top): © Myrleen Ferguson Cate/Photo Edit; p. 181 (bottom): © Tom Stewart/Corbis; p. 182: Photos from Meltzoff, A.N., & Brooks, R. (2007). Intersubjectivity before language: Three windows on preverbal sharing. In S. Braten (Ed.), *On being moved: From mirror neurons to empathy* (pp. 149–174). Philadelphia, PA: John Benjamins; p. 183: © Andrew Meltzoff; p. 184: From Jean Mandler, University of California, San Diego. Reprinted by permission of Oxford University Press, Inc.; p. 185: © John Santrock; p. 186: Courtesy of John Santrock; p. 187: Bayley Scales of Infant and Toddler Development—Third Edition (Bayley-III). Copyright © 2006 by NCS Pearson, Inc. Reproduced with permission. All rights reserved; p. 188: © Vanessa Davies/Dorling Kindersley/Getty Images; p. 190: © 2003 University of Washington, Institute for Learning and Brain Sciences (I-LABS); p. 191 (top): © Don Hammond/Design Pics/Corbis RF; p. 191 (bottom): © Niki Mareschal/Photographers Choice/Getty Images; p. 192: © ABPL Image Library/Animals Animals/Earth Scenes; p. 193: © Digital Vision/PunchStock; p. 194: Michael Goldstein, Cornell University; p. 196: Brand X Pictures/Jupiter Images; p. 197: © John Carter/Photo Researchers

Chapter 7

p. 202: © Vanessa Gavalya/Stockbyte/Getty Images; p. 203: © Rick Gomez/Corbis; p. 205 (top): © Zen Sekizawa/Getty; p. 205, fig. 7.1 (clockwise): © BananaStock/PictureQuest; The McGraw-Hill Companies, Inc./Jill Braaten, photographer; David Sacks/Getty Images; © Getty Images; p. 206, fig. 7.2: Photo by Kenny Braun and courtesy of Dr. Sybil L. Hart, Texas Tech University; p. 206 (bottom): Andy

Cox/Stone/Getty Images; p. 208 (top): Photodisc Collection/Getty Images; pp. 208–209: Tom Merton/Getty Images; p. 211: © Judith Oddie/Photo Edit Inc.; p. 212: © Ariel Skelley/Blend Images LLC; p. 213, fig. 7.4: Digital Vision/Getty Images; p. 213 (bottom): Jules Frazier/Getty Images; p. 215: © Britt Erlanson/Getty Images, p. 216, fig. 7.5: Courtesy Celia A. Brownell, University of Pittsburgh; p. 216 (bottom): Dan Lepp/Etsa/Corbis; p. 217, fig. 7.6: © Martin Rogers/Stock Boston; p. 217 (bottom): © Corbis RF; p. 219: © David Young-Wolff/Photo Edit, Inc.; p. 220: © Penny Tweedie/Stone/Getty Images; p. 223 (top): Frare/Davis Photography/Brand X/Corbis; p. 223 (bottom left): © Purestock/PunchStock; p. 223 (bottom right): Jessie Jean/Getty Images; p. 225 (top): Courtesy of Dr. Barry Hewlett; p. 225 (bottom): Polka Dot Images/PhotoLibrary; p. 226: © Lawrence Schwartzwald; p. 227: Courtesy of Wanda Mitchell; p. 228: © Lawrence Migdale/Stone/Getty Images

Chapter 8

p. 234: © Susanne Dittrich/Corbis; p. 236: DK Stock/Robert Glenn/Getty Images; p. 238: © Photo Researchers; p. 239, fig. 8.4: Sam Gilbert, Institute of Cognitive Neuroscience, UK; p. 240: © C Squared Studios/Getty Images; p. 241: © Nestor Bachmann/dpa/Corbis; p. 244: © Ocean/Corbis; p. 245: © Dennis Welsh/The Image Bank/Getty Images; p. 246: © Ariel Skelley/Corbis; p. 248: Lilian Perez/Corbis; p. 249: RubberBall Productions/Getty Images; p. 250: © Michael Newman/Photo Edit; p. 252: Image Source/Getty Images; p. 253: Courtesy of Barbara Deloin; p. 254: © AP Wide World Photos

Chapter 9

p. 258: Ariel Skelley/Blend Images/Getty Images; p. 259: From "Open Window" © 1994 Municipality of Reggio Emilia Infant-toddler Centers and Preschools Published by Reggio Children; p. 262: © Michael Newman/PhotoEdit; p. 264: Jose Luis Pelaez Inc./Blend Images/Getty Images; p. 265 (top): © James Wertsch/Washington University at St. Louis; p. 265 (bottom): © BananaStock/PunchStock; p. 267, fig. 9.7 (left to right): A.R. Lauria/Dr. Michael Cole, Laboratory of Human Cognition, University of California, San Diego; © Bettmann/Corbis; p. 267 (bottom): © Ariel Skelley/Corbis; p. 270: © 2005 JAMESKAMP.com; p. 271 (top): Photo by Dawn Villella, Courtesy of Stephanie Carlson; p. 271 (bottom): © Joe Baker, Images.com/Corbis; p. 272: Courtesy of Helen Hadani; p. 274: © Robin Nelson/Photo Edit; p. 276: Matsunaga Takuya/Aflo/Getty Images; p. 277: © JGI/Jamie Grill/Blend Images/Getty Images; p. 279 (top): © istockphoto.com/fatihhoca; p. 279 (bottom): Michael Grecco/Hulton Archive/Getty Images; p. 280: © BananaStock/PunchStock; p. 282 (top): Courtesy of Yolanda Garcia; p. 282 (bottom): © Ronnie Kaurman/The Stock Market/Corbis; p. 283: © image100/SuperStock RF; p. 284 (top): © Karen Kasmauski/Corbis; p. 284 (bottom): © SOS Children's Villages (www.sos-usa.org)

Chapter 10

p. 288: Fotosearch/PhotoLibrary; p. 291 (top): © Kevin Dodge/Corbis; p. 291 (bottom): © RF/Corbis; p. 292: James Woodson/Digital Vision/Getty Images; p. 293: © LWA-Dann Tardif/zefa/Corbis; p. 294: © Tom Grill/Corbis; p. 295: Tanya Constantine/Blend Images/Getty Images; p. 297: © Getty Images; p. 298 (left): altrendo images/Getty Images; p. 298 (right): © Cindy Charles/Photo Edit; p. 300: © Ariel Skelley/Corbis; p. 301: © Jose Luis Pelaez/Corbis; p. 303: D.Botkin (2000), Family play therapy: A creative approach to including young children in family therapy. *Journal of Systematic Therapies*, 19, 30–41; p. 304: Joshua Gunter/The Plain Dealer/Landov; p. 306 (top to bottom): RubberBall

Productions/Getty Images; Image Source/Getty Images; p. 307: Eric Audras/Photoalto/PictureQuest; p. 309: © Image Source/PunchStock; p. 310: © 2009 Jupiterimages Corporation; p. 311: © Karen Kasmauski/Woodfin Camp & Associates; p. 312: © Spencer Grant/Photo Edit; p. 313 (top to bottom): Ariel Skelley/Corbis; © istockphoto.com/Catherine Yeulet; © istockphoto.com/Daniela Andreea Spyropoulos; p. 314: © Big Stock Photos; p. 315: Jean-Pierre Pieuchot/Stockbyte/Getty Images; p. 316: Jose Luis Pelaez Inc./Blend Images/Getty Images; p. 317: © Newscom

Chapter 11

p. 324: © Christopher Futcher/The Agency Collection/Getty Images; p. 326: Chris Windsor/Digital Vision/Getty Images; p. 329: © Image Source/Corbis RF; p. 330 (top): © Ariel Skelley/Corbis; p. 330 (bottom): © PhotoDisc/Getty RF; p. 331: © Getty Images; p. 332 (top): Jules Frazier/Getty Images; p. 332 (bottom): © Image Source/PunchStock; p. 333: © Corbis RF; p. 334: © Felicia Martinez/PhotoEdit; p. 336: Courtesy of Sharon McLeod; p. 339: © AP Wide World Photos; p. 340: © David Young-Wolff/Photo Edit; p. 342: Courtesy of Sharla Peltier; p. 343 (top): Used by permission of Don Johnston Inc; p. 343 (bottom): © PunchStock RF; p. 344 (top): © Pixland/PunchStock; p. 344 (bottom): Crown copyright MMVI, www.thetransporters.com, courtesy Changing Media Development; p. 345: © Richard Hutchings/Photo Researchers

Chapter 12

p. 352: Peter Dazeley/Getty Images; p. 353: © Milwaukee Journal Sentinel, photographer Elizabeth Flores, © 2007 Journal Sentinel Inc., reproduced with permission; p. 355: © M&E Bernheim/Woodfin Camp & Associates; p. 356: Blend Images/John Lund/Mark Romanelli/Getty Images; p. 359: Anthony Harve/Getty RF; p. 361: © RF/Corbis; p. 362 (top): © Stan Godlewski Photography; p. 362 (bottom): © John Flavell; p. 363: © Ellen Senis/The Image Works; p. 365: Robert J. Sternberg, Tufts University; permission granted in previous edition for future editions; p. 366: © Jay Gardner, 1998; p. 370: © Stockbyte/Veer; p. 371 (top): © Koichi Kamoshida/Newsmakers/Getty Images; p. 371 (bottom): Courtesy of Sterling Jones; p. 372: © Doug Wilson/Corbis; p. 375: © Gideon Mendel/Corbis; p. 376: © Elizabeth Crews; p. 377: © Elizabeth Crews/The Image Works; p. 379: Courtesy of Carol Dweck; p. 380: © Ariel Skelley/Blend Images/Corbis RF; p. 381: Courtesy of Sandra Graham; p. 382: © Eiji Miyazawa/Stock Photo

Chapter 13

p. 387: © Edith Held/Corbis; p. 388: © Joseph Sohm/Visions of America/Corbis; p. 390: © Paul Edmondson/Corbis; p. 391: Inti St Clair/Getty Images; p. 392 (top): © Masterfile; p. 392 (bottom): © Jim Craigmyle/Corbis; p. 393: MacGregor & Gordon/Getty Images; p. 394 (left): © Sean Adair/Reuters/Corbis; p. 394 (right): Michael Rieger/FEMA; p. 398: © Raghu-Rai/Magnum Photos; p. 399: Photo by Joyce Ravid and Courtesy of Dr. Carol Gilligan; p. 400: © Norbert Schaefer/Corbis; p. 403: © RF/Corbis; p. 404 (top): Somos Images/Corbis; p. 404 (bottom): Copyright 1997 IMS Communications Ltd./Capstone Design. All Rights Reserved; p. 406 (top): © Ariel Skelley/Corbis; p. 406 (bottom): Todd Wright/Blend Images/Getty Images; p. 408: © BananaStock; p. 410: SW Productions/Getty Images; p. 412: © Purestock/PunchStock; p. 413: © Elizabeth Crews; p. 414 (top): Image Source/Alamy; p. 414 (bottom): © Martin Poole/Getty Images; p. 415: © 2004, USA Today. Reprinted with permission; p. 416: © AP Wide World Photos; p. 417: © Chris Volpe Photography

Chapter 14

p. 424: © Rob Melnychuk/Brand X/Corbis RF; p. 425: © Ronald Cortes; p. 426: © BananaStock/PunchStock; p. 428 (top): © IT Stock/PunchStock; p. 428 (bottom): © Chuck Savage/The Stock Market/Corbis; p. 432: © Jon Feingersh; p. 433 (top): © Value RF/Corbis RF; p. 433 (bottom): ER Productions/Getty Images; p. 435: © The McGraw-Hill Companies, Inc./John Flournoy, photographer; p. 436: © Stockbyte/PunchStock; p. 437 (top): © Michael Ray; p. 437 (bottom): © Louise Gubb/Corbis SABA; p. 440 (top): Geoff Manasse/Getty Images; p. 440 (bottom): Courtesy of Lynn Blankenship; p. 441: © 1998 Frank Fournier; p. 442: Image Source/PunchStock; p. 443: Tom Stewart/Corbis; p. 445: © Jim LoScalzo; p. 446: © PunchStock/Image Source; p. 447: © Charles Gullung/zefa/Corbis; p. 449 (top): © Mark Richards/Corbis; p. 449 (bottom): © Ian Thraves/Alamy

Chapter 15

p. 454: © Corbis/RF; p. 457: © David Young-Wolff/Photo Edit; p. 458: Image Source/JupiterImages; p. 461 (top): © Big Cheese Photo/SuperStock RF; p. 461 (bottom): Scott Houston/Corbis; p. 463: Courtesy of Laura Bickford; p. 464: © David Young-Wolff/Photo Edit; p. 467: Eric Audras/PhotoAlto Agency RF Collections/Getty Images; p. 469: Digital Vision/Getty Images; p. 471 (top to bottom): © Creatas/PunchStock; © Photo Spin/Getty RF; © D. Hurst/Alamy Images RF; p. 473: © Fujifotos/The Image Works; p. 474: © Ed Kashi/Corbis; p. 475: © Ray A. Llanos; p. 476: © SW Productions/Photodisc/Getty Images; p. 477: Courtesy of Dr. Armando Ronquillo

Chapter 16

p. 482: © Ariel Skelley/Blend Images/PhotoLibrary; p. 483: © Copyright 2005, Globe Newspaper Company, Matthew J. Lee photographer/Landov Images; p. 484: © Dominic Rouse/The Image Bank/Getty Images; p. 485: © Bettmann/Corbis; p. 486: Tom Grill/Corbis; p. 487: © USA Today Library, Photo by Robert Deutsch; p. 489: © BananaStock/PunchStock; p. 490: © Pat Vasquez-Cunningham 1999/ USA Today Library; p. 491 (top): © BananaStock/PunchStock; p. 491, fig. 16.3: © BananaStock/PunchStock; p. 492: Getty Images/SW Productions; p. 493: Jose Luis Pelaez Inc./Blend Images/Getty Images; p. 494 (top): © Rolf Bruderer/Corbis; p. 494 (bottom): © Digital Vision/Getty Images; p. 495 (top): Pinto/Zefa/Corbis; p. 495 (bottom): Jenny Acheson/Getty Images; p. 497 (left to right): PhotosIndia; © AFP/Getty Images; Tom Stoddart/Getty Images; p. 498 (top): © Image Source/Alamy; p. 498 (bottom): © D. Laine/ HOA-QUI/Imagestate; p. 499: Caroline Woodham/Photographer's Choice RF/Getty Images; p. 500 (top): © USA Today Library, photo by H. Darr Beiser; p. 500, fig. 16.5: © iStockphoto.com/Dan Wilton; p. 501 (top): © Blend Images/TIPS Images; p. 501 (bottom): Digital Vision/Alamy; p. 503 (top): Comstock Images/Alamy; p. 503 (bottom): © Chuck Savage/Corbis; p. 504: Courtesy of Rodney Hammond; p. 505: © BananaStock/PunchStock; p. 508: Image Source/Getty Images

TEXT/LINE ART CREDITS

Chapter 1

p. 1: From the book *100 Ways to Build Self-Esteem and Teach Values.* Copyright © 1994, 2003 by Diana Loomans. Reprinted with permission of H J Kramer/New World Library, Novato, CA www.newworldlibrary.com. **Fig. 1.2:** From John Santrock, *Life-Span Development,* 11th ed., Fig. 1.4. Copyright © 2008 The McGraw-Hill Companies, Inc. Reproduced by permission. **Figs. 1.3, 1.4, 1.5, 1.6, 1.7, 1.8, 1.9:** From John Santrock, *Child*

Development, 13th ed., Figs. 1.6–1.12. Copyright © 2011 The McGraw-Hill Companies, Inc. Reproduced by permission. **Fig. 1.10:** "Bronfenbrenner's Ecological Theory of Development," from Kopp, Claire B., Krakow, Joanne B., *The Child: Development in Social Context*, 1st ed. © 1982. Printed and Electronically reproduced by permission of Pearson Education, Inc., Upper Saddle River, New Jersey. Data from Bronfenbrenner, U. (1979). *The Ecology of Human Development: Experiments by Nature and Design*. Cambridge, MA: Harvard University Press. **Fig. 1.13:** From Crowley, et al., 2001, "Parents Explain More to Boys Than Girls During Shared Scientific Thinking," *Psychological Science*, 12, 258–261. Reprinted by permission of Wiley-Blackwell. **Fig. 1.15:** From John Santrock, *Adolescence*, 12th ed., Fig. 2.4. Copyright © 2008 The McGraw-Hill Companies, Inc. Reproduced by permission.

Chapter 2

Fig. 2.1: From Bonner, John T., *The Evolution of Culture in Animals*. © 1980 Princeton University Press. Reprinted by permission of Princeton University Press. **Figs. 2.2, 2.6:** From John Santrock, *Life-Span Development*, 11th ed., Figs. 3.3, 3.7. Copyright © 2008 The McGraw-Hill Companies, Inc. Reproduced by permission. **Figs. 2.7, 2.9:** From John Santrock, *Child Development*, 13th ed., Figs. 2.7, 2.9. Copyright © 2011 The McGraw-Hill Companies, Inc. Reproduced by permission. **Fig. 2.10:** From John Santrock, *Life-Span Development*, 13th ed., Fig. 2.10. Copyright © 2011 The McGraw-Hill Companies, Inc. Reproduced by permission. Data from Golombok et al., 2001, "The 'Test-Tube' Generation," *Child Development*, 72, 599–608. Reprinted with permission. **Fig. 2.12:** From John Santrock, *Life-Span Development*, 12th ed., Fig. 2.12. Copyright © 2009 The McGraw-Hill Companies, Inc. Reproduced by permission.

Chapter 3

Fig. 3.1: From Charles Carroll and Dean Miller, *Health: The Science of Human Adaptations*, 5th ed., Fig. 1.2. Copyright © 1991 The McGraw-Hill Companies, Inc. Reproduced by permission. **Fig. 3.2:** From John Santrock, *Child Development*, 13th ed., Fig. 3.2. Copyright © 2011 The McGraw-Hill Companies, Inc. Reproduced by permission. **Fig. 3.3:** © 2001 by Parent Trust for Washington Children. Printed in *Pregnancy, Childbirth and the Newborn* and used with permission from Meadowbrook Press. **Fig. 3.5:** Data from Food and Nutrition Board, "Recommended Nutrient Increases for Expectant Mothers," National Academy of Sciences, Washington, DC. **p. 93:** From *Olds, Maternal Newborn Nursing: A Family-Centered Approach*, 3rd ed., © 1988. Printed and Electronically reproduced by permission of Pearson Education, Inc., Upper Saddle River, NJ. **Fig. 3.6:** From data presented by MacDorman, et al., 2002, "Annual Summary of Vital Statistics-2001," *Pediatrics*, 10, 1037–1052. **Fig. 3.7:** This article was published in *The Developing Human: Clinically Oriented Embryology*, 4th ed., by K.L. Moore, p. 173, Copyright Elsevier 1988. Reprinted with permission from Elsevier.

Chapter 4

p. 112: Excerpt from P. Warrick, March 1, 1992, "The Fantastic Voyage of Tanner Roberts," *Los Angeles Times*, pp. E1, E12, E13. Reprinted by permission of the Los Angeles Times. **Fig. 4.2:** From Virginia A. Apgar, 1953, "A Proposal for a New Method of Evaluation of the Newborn Infant," in *Anesthesia and Analgesia*, Vol. 32, pp. 260–267. Reprinted by permission of Wolters Kluwer Health/Lippincott, Williams & Wilkins. **Fig. 4.4:** From John Santrock, *Child Development*, 12th ed., Fig. 3.9. Copyright © 2009 The McGraw-Hill Companies, Inc. Reproduced by permission. **Fig. 4.5:** Reprinted from *Infant Behavior and Development*, Vol. 30, issue 4, Maria

Hernandez-Reif, Miguel Diego, and Tiffany Field, "Preterm Infants Show Reduced Stress Behaviors and Activity After Five Days of Massage Therapy," pp. 557–561, Copyright 2007, with permission from Elsevier. **Fig. 4.6:** From John Santrock, *Child Development*, 13th ed., Fig. 3.10. Copyright © 2011 The McGraw-Hill Companies, Inc. Reproduced by permission. **Fig. 4.7:** American College of Obstetricians and Gynecologists, 2002, *Postpartum Depression*. Obtained from the World Wide Web Medem Medical Library: www.medem.com/medlib.

Chapter 5

Figs. 5.1, 5.4: From John Santrock, *Life-Span Development*, 12th ed., Figs. 4.1, 4.4. Copyright © 2009 The McGraw-Hill Companies, Inc. Reproduced by permission. **Fig. 5.5:** From John Santrock, *Child Development: An Introduction*, 9th ed. Copyright © 2001 The McGraw-Hill Companies, Inc. Reproduced by permission. **Fig. 5.7:** From Huttenlocher and Dabholkar, 1997, "Regional Differences in Synaptogenesis in Human Cerebral Cortex," *Journal of Comparative Neurology*, 387(2), 167–168, Fig. 2. Reprinted with permission of Wiley-Blackwell. **Fig. 5.11:** From John Santrock, *Life-Span Development*, 13th ed., Fig. 4.11. Copyright © 2011 The McGraw-Hill Companies, Inc. Reproduced by permission. Data from J. Kim (2006), "Trends in Overweight from 1980 through 2001 among Preschool-Aged Children Enrolled in a Health Maintenance Organization," *Obesity*, 14, 1107–1112. Macmillan Publishers, Ltd. **Fig. 5.12:** From John Santrock, *Child Development*, 10th ed., Fig. 5.11. Copyright © 2004 The McGraw-Hill Companies, Inc. Reproduced by permission. **Fig. 5.14:** From John Santrock, *Child Development*, 13th ed., Fig. 5.1. Copyright © 2011 The McGraw-Hill Companies, Inc. Reproduced by permission. **Fig. 5.18 (line art):** Fantz's Experiment on Infants' Visual Perception, adapted from "The Origin of Form Perception," by R.L. Fantz, *Scientific American*, 1961. Used with permission. **Fig. 5.19:** From Slater, A., Morison, V. & Somers, M., 1988, "Orientation Discrimination and Cortical Functions in the Human Newborn," *Perception*, Vol. 17, pp. 597–602, Fig. 1 and Table 1. Reprinted by permission of Pion, London. **Fig. 5.22:** From B.I Bertenthal, M.R. Longo, and S. Kenny (2007). "Phenomenal Permanence and the Development of Predictive Tracking in Infancy," *Child Development*, 78, p. 354. Copyright © 2007 by the Society for Research in Child Development, Inc. Reproduced with permission from John Wiley & Sons, Ltd.

Chapter 6

Fig. 6.1: From John Santrock, *Life-Span Development*, 10th ed., Fig. 5.1. Copyright © 2006 The McGraw-Hill Companies, Inc. Reproduced by permission. **Fig. 6.3:** Baillargeon, R., & DeVos, J., "Using the Violation of Expectations Method to Study Object Permanence in Infants," 1991, "Object Permanence in Young Infants: Further Evidence," *Child Development*, 62, pp. 1227–1246. Reprinted with permission from Wiley-Blackwell. **Figs. 6.7, 6.10:** From John Santrock, *Life-Span Development*, 12th ed., Figs. 5.6, 5.9. Copyright © 2009 The McGraw-Hill Companies, Inc. Reproduced by permission. **Fig. 6.11:** "The Rule Systems of Language," from Sherrel Lee Haight, *Language Overview*. Reprinted by permission. **Fig. 6.13:** From L. Bloom, "Language Acquisition in Development Context," in *Handbook of Child Psychology*, by W. Damon, ed. John Wiley & Sons, 1998. Reprinted by permission of John Wiley & Sons, Inc. **Fig. 6.14:** From John Santrock, *Life-Span Development*, 12th ed., Fig. 5.13. Copyright © 2009 The McGraw-Hill Companies, Inc. Reproduced by permission. **Fig. 6.15:** From Floyd Bloom, Charles A. Nelson & Arlyne Lazerson, *Brain, Mind, and Behavior*, 3rd ed. Educational Broadcasting Corporation—Worth Publishers, 1985. Used with permission.

Chapter 7

Fig. 7.4: From John Santrock, *Life-Span Development*, 12th ed., p. 189. Copyright © 2009 The McGraw-Hill Companies, Inc. Reproduced by permission. **Fig. 7.6:** From John Santrock, *Life-Span Development*, 11th ed., Fig. 7.5. Copyright © 2008 The McGraw-Hill Companies, Inc. Reproduced by permission. **Fig. 7.7:** From van IJzendoorn & Kroonenberg, 1988, "Cross cultural Patterns of Attachment," *Child Development*, 59, 147–156, Table 2. Used by permission of Wiley-Blackwell. **Fig. 7.9:** From Jay Belsky, "Early Human Experiences: A Family Perspective," *Developmental Psychology*, 59, 147–156, 1981, published by American Psychological Association. Reprinted with permission. **Fig. 7.11:** Data from U.S. Census Bureau, 2006. **Fig. 7.12:** From John Santrock, *Life-Span Development*, 13th ed., Fig. 6.11. Copyright © 2011 The McGraw-Hill Companies, Inc. Reproduced by permission.

Chapter 8

Fig. 8.1: *CDC Growth Charts*, 2000. Center for Disease Control and Prevention, Atlanta, GA. **Fig. 8.5:** Data from *Performance Objectives for Preschool Children*, C.J. Schiner, ed. Sioux Falls, SD: Adapt Press, 1974. **Fig. 8.7:** Based on "The Stages of Young Children's Artistic Drawings," from Rhoda Kellogg, 1970, "Understanding Children's Art," in *Readings in Developmental Psychology Today*, P. Cramer, ed. Del Mar, CA: CRM. **Fig. 8.8:** Data from the Food and Nutrition Board. **Fig. 8.9:** From John Santrock, *Life-Span Development*, 13e, Fig. 7.2. Copyright © 2011 The McGraw-Hill Companies, Inc. Reproduced by permission. **Fig. 8.10:** From "Contexts and Young Children's Safety" from Sleet & Mercy, "Promotion of Safety, Security, and Well-Being," in M.H. Bornstein, et al. (eds.), *Well-Being*, Table 7.2. Reprinted with permission of Taylor & Francis Group, LLP.

Chapter 9

Fig. 9.1: From John Santrock, *Psychology: Essentials*, 2nd ed. Copyright © 2005 The McGraw-Hill Companies, Inc. Reproduced by permission. **Fig. 9.2:** "The Symbolic Drawings of Young Children," reprinted courtesy of D. Wolf and J. Nove. Reprinted by permission of Dennie Palmer Wolf, Annenberg Institute, Brown University. **Figs. 9.3(b), 9.4:** From John Santrock, *Life-Span Development*, 13th ed., Figs. 7.6–7.7. Copyright © 2011 The McGraw-Hill Companies, Inc. Reproduced by permission. **Fig. 9.6:** From Deborah J. Leong and Elena Bodrova. (2001, 2007). *Tools of the Mind*. Geneva, Switzerland: International Bureau of Education, UNESCO. Reprinted with permission of the authors. **Fig. 9.7:** From John Santrock, *Life-Span Development*, 13th ed., Fig. 7.10. Copyright © 2011 The McGraw-Hill Companies, Inc. Reproduced by permission. **Fig. 9.9:** "Developmental Changes in Memory Span," from Dempster, 1981, "Memory Span," *Psychological Bulletin*, 80, 63–100. Copyright © 1981 by the American Psychological Association. Reprinted by permission. **Fig. 9.10:** From John Santrock, *Life-Span Development*, 13th ed., Fig. 7.13. Copyright © 2011 The McGraw-Hill Companies, Inc. Reproduced by permission. **Fig. 9.11:** From John Santrock, *Child Development*, 12th ed., Fig. 7.14. Copyright © 2009 The McGraw-Hill Companies, Inc. Reproduced by permission. Based on U. Frith, 1989. "The Sally-Anne Experiment." *Autism: Explaining the Enigma*, p. 83. Blackwell Publishing, 1989. **Fig. 9.13:** From Jean Berko, 1958, "The Child's Learning of English Morphology," in *Word*, Vol. 14, p. 154. Reprinted courtesy of Jean Berko Gleason. **Fig. 9.14:** NAEYC. 2009. "Developmentally Appropriate Practice in Early Childhood Programs Serving Children from Birth Through Age 8." Position statement. Washington, DC: NAEYC. www.naeyc.org/files/naeyc/file/positions/PSDAP.pdf. Reprinted with permission from the National Association for the Education of Young Children (NAEYC). Copyright © 2009 by

name index

Levy, F., 472
Lewis, B. A., 100
Lewis, C., 290, 291, 292, 410
Lewis, Jim, 55
Lewis, Michael, 62, 205, 213, 220, 414, 488
Lhila, A., 121
Li, D. K., 99, 102, 143
Li, J. M., 103, 119
Li, Y., 247
Liben, L. S., 296, 297, 298, 399, 402, 403, 404
Libertus, K., 156–157
Lickliter, R., 76
Licoppe, C., 403
Lidz, J., 374
Lie, E., 182
Liebergott, J., 191
Liederman, J., 338
Liekweg, K., 317
Lieven, E., 191, 192, 196, 276
Lifter, K., 191
Light, L. S., 506, 507
Lillard, Angeline, 315
Lillie-Blanton, M., 252
Lin, M., 284
Lin, P. J., 247
Lindberg, A., 65
Lindberg, S. M., 402
Lindenberger, U., 181
Linder, S. M., 259
Lindsay, A. C., 333
Lindsay, D. Stephen, 270
Lipman, T. H., 332
Lipowska, M., 339
Litt, J., 339
Liu, C., 63
Liu, D., 273
Liu, J., 248, 249
Liu, S., 160
Liu, Y. H., 117
Lively, Angela, 416
Livesly, W., 389
Lo, K. C., 69, 70
Lobelo, F., 443
Lock, A., 191
Lockl, K., 271
Loebel, M., 106
Loeber, R., 503, 504
Loehlin, J. C., 75
Logsdon, M. C., 126
Lohaus, A., 187
Lohose, B., 147
Lohr, M. J., 494
London, M. L., 92, 122
Long, S., 121
Longfellow, Henry Wadsworth, 14, 457
Longo, M. R., 161
Lonnerdal, B., 248
Lopez, E. I., 406
Lorenz, Konrad, 29–30, 32, 127
Lorenz, Lee, 262
Lothian, J. A., 116
Love, V., 102
Lovelady, C., 91
Low, S., 495
Lowdermilk, D. L., 92, 104, 115
Lowenstein, A., 14, 225, 281–282, 368
Lozoff, B., 246
Lucas, E. B., 9
Lucas-Thompson, R., 307
Lucia, V. C., 122
Lucovnik, M., 121
Ludden, A. B., 447

Luders, E., 402
Ludington-Hoe, S. M., 123
Ludwig, S., 236
Lumpkin, A., 249, 329
Lund, B., 334
Lund, H. G., 445
Lundgren, I., 115
Luo, Y., 177
Luria, A., 298
Lust, K., 106
Lutkenhaus, P., 213
Lynch, J. H., 332
Lyon, T. D., 362
Lytle, L. A., 449
Lyyra, A. L., 447

M

Ma, Yo-Yo, 373
Maas, J., 125
Macari, S., 184
Macarthur, C., 126
Maccoby, E. E., 298, 300, 301
MacCullum, F., 71
MacDorman, M. F., 114
MacFarlan, S. J., 225
Maconochie, N., 107
Macpherson, A. K., 251
MacWhinney, B., 188, 189
Madeja, S. S., 243
Mader, S. S., 18, 57, 59, 62
Madkour, A. S., 436
Maes, H., 74
Magarey, A. M., 333
Maggs, J. L., 445
Magiati, I., 345
Magno, C., 359, 463
Magnussen, P., 95
Magriples, U., 94
Mahad, D. J., 138
Mahler, Margaret, 213
Mahmoudi-Gharaei, J., 341
Mahoney, A., 469
Mahoney, J., 471
Makhoul, I. R., 123
Malamitsi-Puchner, A., 121
Malek, A., 86
Malizia, B. A., 105
Mallet, E., 143
Malmstrom, F. V., 467
Maloy, R. W., 501
Malter Cohen, M., 433
Mancini, A. D., 393
Mandara, J., 406
Mandler, Jean M., 182, 183, 184, 185, 269
Manganaro, L., 68
Mangelsdorf, S. C., 213
Mangione, R., 68
Manzo, K. K., 471
Mao, A. R., 341
Marcdante, K., 237, 247
Marcia, James E., 485–486, 487, 509
Marcon, R. A., 248
Marcovitch, H., 341
Marcovitch, S., 207
Marillounnet, S., 63
Maringe, F., 478
Marinucci, L., 97
Marion, M. C., 278
Markham, C. M., 436, 437
Markman, E. M., 192
Marks, A. K., 11, 42, 499
Marrero, M. D., 489
Marrett, S., 99

Marshall, S. W., 91
Marti, C. N., 507
Martin, C. L., 401
Martin, J. A., 94, 114, 300
Marx, Groucho, 247
Mashburn, A. J., 277
Maslova, E., 99
Massaro, A. N., 123
Masselli, G., 68
Massey, Z., 94
Mastekaasa, A., 507
Masten, Ann S., 12, 393, 394, 428
Master, A., 379
Mastergeorge, A. M., 281
Mathieson, L. C., 317
Matlin, M. W., 11, 40, 297, 298, 401, 403, 404
Matsuba, M. K., 464
Matsui, E. C., 335
Matsumoto, D., 10
Matthews, D. J., 372
Mattock, K., 163
Mattson, S., 92, 125
May, M. S., 295, 467
Mayer, K. D., 100
Mayo Clinic, 105
Mazzocco, M. M., 65
Mbonye, A. K., 95
Mbugua Gitau, G., 105
McAlister, A., 274
McBride-Chang, C., 277
McCartney, Kathleen, 226–227
McClelland, S. I., 434, 435, 436
McConachie, H., 344
McCormack, L. A., 333
McCormick, C. B., 363
McCourt, S. N., 508
McDermott, U., 66
McDonald, J. B., 501
McDonough, L., 182, 184
McFarlin, B. L., 92
McGarry, J., 126
McGarvey, C., 143
McGee, K., 346
McGee, T. R., 503
McGinley, M., 295
McGue, M. K., 71, 76, 468
McGuire, B. A., 62
McHale, J., 302
McHale, M., 490
McHale, S. M., 307, 402
McIntosh, C. G., 142
McIntyre, H. D., 106
McIsaac, C., 494–495, 496
McKenzie, B. E., 161
McKinney, E. L., 92
McKnight, J. R., 104
McLellan, J. A., 468
McLeod, Sharon, 336
McLeskey, J., 338
McLoyd, V. C., 11, 13, 14, 301, 311, 381, 415, 416, 427, 472
McMahon, M., 236
McMillen, I. C., 104
McNamara, F., 143
McNight, J. R., 90
Meacham, J., 291
Meade, C. S., 439
Meece, J., 377, 381
Meeker, J. D., 105
Meerlo, P., 125
Melhuish, E., 225, 228
Melnyk, L., 270
Meltzi, G., 374
Meltzoff, Andrew N., 179, 181, 183, 194, 215, 401

Menacker, F., 114
Mendelson, C. R., 115
Mendle, J., 507
Menezes, V., 86
Menias, C. O., 102
Menn, L., 159
Mennella, J. A., 163
Menon, M., 391
Menon, R., 86, 101
Menyuk, P., 191
Mepham, S., 135, 146, 147
Mercy, J. A., 251
Meredith, N. V., 236
Merewood, A., 146
Merrilees, C. E., 308
Merz, R. D., 100–101
Meschia, G., 86
Messersmith, E. E., 476
Messiah, S. E., 100
Metindogan, A., 284
Metz, E. C., 464, 465
Mevorach, C., 340
Meyer, F., 493
Meyer, S. L., 117, 295
Meyers, J., 410
Mezzacappa, E., 391
Miga, E. M., 490
Mikai, A. Y., 502
Miller, A., 467
Miller, B. C., 72, 437
Miller, C., 14
Miller, C. F., 401
Miller, D. P., 25
Miller, F., 251
Miller, J., 398
Miller, K. M., 280
Miller, L. J., 126
Miller, M. D., 253
Miller, P. H., 447, 457
Miller, S., 268
Miller, W. D., 252
Mills, B., 462
Mills, C., 268
Mills, C. M., 291
Mills, D., 268
Milne, B. J., 329
Miloler, P. H., 458
Milot, T., 304
Miltenberger, R. G., 27
Mindell, J., 245
Miner, J. L., 226
Minguez-Milio, J. A., 117
Minino, A. M., 506
Minnes, S., 100
Mischel, W., 295
Mitchell, D. W., 181
Mitchell, E. A., 143
Mitchell, Wanda, 227
Miura, M., 70
Miyake, K., 219
MMWR, 436
Moeller, M. P., 343
Mohan, L., 363, 381
Mokha, J. S., 335
Molina, R. C., 440
Mollard, R. C., 330
Mond, J., 447
Monge, P., 106
Monica, K. C., 145
Monk, C., 106
Monroe, K. W., 251
Montagna, P., 143
Montana, S., 106, 252
Montemayor, R., 491
Montessori, Maria, 279–280
Montgomery-Downs, H. E., 125

subject index

Baby blues, 126–127
Baby-friendly initiatives, 135
Bandura's theory, 28–29
Basic cry, 206
Baumrind's parenting styles, 300–301
Bayley Scales of Infant and Toddler Development—Third Edition (Bayley-III), 186–187
Bayley Scales of Infant Development, 186–187
Beckwith-Wiedemann syndrome, 63
Behavioral disorders, 343–344
Behavioral inhibition and temperament, 209
Behavioral teratology, 97
Behavioral theories, 27–29
    evaluation of, 29
Behavior genetics, 74–75
Behaviorism, 27
    and language learning, 193–194
Bias. See also Gender
    research, minimizing in, 40–41
    schools, reducing in, 417
Biculturalism, 42
Bicycle accidents, 336
Bicycling and pregnancy, 93
Bidirectional view, 58
Big picture idea of natural selection, 58
Bilingualism
    in education, 376
    in middle/late childhood, 375–376
Binge drinking, 446
Bioecological theory, 31
Biology, 15
    aggression and, 403
    attachment and, 217
    emotions, influences on, 204–205
    gender identity and, 296–297
    language, influences on, 192–193
    nature-nurture issue, 18–19
    temperament and, 210
Birth control, 437
Birthing teams, 115
Birth order, 306–307
Birth process, 112
    afterbirth, 114
    attendants to, 114–115
    Cesarean delivery, 116–118
    doulas, 115
    effective birth strategies, 131
    methods of, 115–118
    midwives in, 114
    music therapy, 118
    natural childbirth, 115–116
    prepared childbirth, 115–116
    settings for, 114–115
    stages of, 113–114
    waterbirth, 117
Blastocysts, 85
Blended families, 406
Blindness, 342
Blinking reflex, 151
Blood
    maternal blood screening, 69
    prenatal development and blood types, 102
BMI (body mass index)
    in early childhood, 247–248
    metabolic syndrome and, 335
Bodily-kinesthetic intelligence, 366

Body image
    depression and, 504
    eating disorders and, 447
    puberty and, 432
Body mass index (BMI). See BMI (body mass index)
Bogalusa Heart Study, 334, 335
Boldness, 209
Bonding
    postpartum depression and, 126
    in postpartum period, 127–128
Bones
    breast feeding and, 146
    cancer, 334
Books. See Reading
Bottle feeding vs. breast feeding, 144–145
Bradley method, 116
Brain. See also Adolescence; Amygdala; Cerebral cortex; Developmental social neuroscience; Hypothalamus; Neurons; Prefrontal cortex
    ADHD (attention deficit hyperactivity disorder) and, 340–341
    attachment and, 221
    autism spectrum disorders and, 344
    cancer of, 334
    corpus callosum, 432, 433
    early childhood, development in, 238–240
    early deprivation and, 141
    emotions and, 204–205
    explicit memory development and, 183
    infants, development in, 137–141
    language development and, 193–194
    mapping of, 138
    in middle/late childhood, 326–328
    neuroconstructivist view of, 140–141
    prenatal development of, 89
    preterm infants, damage in, 122
    of primates, 58
    SIDS (sudden infant death syndrome) and, 143
    Wernicke's area, 193–194
Brainology program, 379
Brainstorming, 361
Braxton Hicks contractions, 112
Brazelton Neonatal Behavioral Assessment Scale (NBAS), 119–120, 148
Breast feeding
    in African cultures, 135
    baby-friendly initiatives, 135
    benefits of, 145–146
    bottle feeding compared, 144–145
    HIV/AIDS and, 103
    involution and, 125
    mothers, benefits of, 146
    SIDS (sudden infant death syndrome) and, 143, 146
Breasts
    cancer and breast feeding, 146
    puberty, development in, 429
Breech position, 116–117
Bringing Home Baby project, 223
Broca's area, 193–194

Bronfenbrenner's ecological theory, 30–31
Brothers. See Siblings
Bulimia nervosa, 450
Bullying, 410–412
    cyberbullying, 412
    moral motivation and, 411
    perspective taking and, 411
Bully-victims, 411
Burning Fence: A Western Memoir of Fatherhood (Lesley), 289
Burns and infants, 147

C

Caffeine and prenatal development, 99
Cancer. See also specific types
    breast feeding and, 146
    gene-gene interaction and, 63
    in middle/late childhood, 333–334
Carbon monoxide and prenatal development, 102
Cardiovascular system
    breast feeding benefits, 146
    gene-gene interaction and, 63
    in middle/late childhood, 334
Career counselors, 48
Careers, 46–50
    adolescence, career development in, 475–478
    child care directors, 227
    child psychiatrists, 417
    clinical careers, 48
    clinical psychologists, 9, 127
    college advisors, 477
    counseling careers, 48
    director of children's services, 282
    educational and development psychologists, 41
    families and relationships careers, 50
    family and consumer science educators, 440
    genetic counselors, 67
    gynecologists, 94
    health psychologists, 504
    high school counselors, 477
    infant assessment specialists, 186
    marriage therapists, 50, 303
    medical careers, 48–50
    nursing careers, 48–50
    obstetricians, 94
    pediatric nurses, 253
    physical development careers, 48–50
    prenatal nurses, 116
    secondary school teachers, 463
    speech pathologists, 342
    teaching careers, 46–47
Caregiving
    attachment and, 219–221
    by fathers, 224–225
Care perspective, 398–399
The Carnegie Report, 471
Car seats, 147, 251
Case studies, 34–35
Categorization
    gender differences in, 184–185
    in infants, 184
The Cat in the Hat (Dr. Seuss), 162–163
Casual dating, 494
Causality, research on, 177
Cell phones, 501

Center for Academic Integrity, 467
CenteringPregnancy, 94–95
Centration, 262–263
Cephalocaudal pattern, 136
Cerebral cortex, 138, 139
    ADHD (attention deficit hyperactivity disorder) and, 341
    in middle/late childhood, 327
Cerebral palsy, 343
Cesarean delivery, 116–118
Character education, 466
Cheating, 466–467
Chewing, development of, 144
Child abuse and neglect, 408–409
    context of, 304–305
    developmental consequences of, 305
    disorganized babies and, 219
Childbirth. See Birth process; Postpartum period
Child care, 225–227
    for adolescent mothers, 440
    culture and, 226
    depression of caregiver and accidents, 336
    difficult children and, 209
    high-quality child care, 226
    NICHD Study of Early Child Care and Youth Development, 227–228
    safety issues, 252
    variations in, 225–226
Child care directors, 227
Child-centered kindergarten, 278–279
Child Development journal, 39
Child Development Project, 467
Child-directed speech, 194–195, 197
Childhood amnesia, 182–183
Child labor laws, 12–13
Child life specialists, 50
Child maltreatment. See Child abuse and neglect
Child psychiatrists, 417
Children's Defense Fund, 13, 45
Children with disabilities, 337. See also ADHD (attention deficit hyperactivity disorder); Down syndrome; Learning disabilities; Sensory disorders
    educational issues, 345–347
    emotional/behavioral disorders, 343–344
    evaluation of, 345–346
    IDEA (Individuals with Disabilities Education Act) and, 345–346
    IEPs (Individualized Education Plans) for, 345, 346
    inclusion education, 346
    least restrictive environment (LRE) for, 345, 346
    physical disorders, 343
    range of disabilities, 337–338
    speech disorders, 341, 342
    teachers of, 47
Child welfare workers, 50
Chlamydia, 437, 438
Cholesterol and overweight/obesity, 332
Chorionic villus sampling (CVS), 68–69

Identity confusion, 484, 485
Identity *vs.* identity confusion, 23, 484–485
IEPs (Individualized Education Plans), 345, 346
"I Have a Dream" Foundation, 475
"I Have a Dream" (IHAD) program, 475
Illnesses. *See* Diseases/illnesses
Imaginary audience, 458
Imitation, 28
  deferred imitation, 183
  in infants, 183
Immanent justice, 294
Immigration, 499
  parenting and, 312
Immune system and gene-gene interaction, 63
Immunization schedule for infants, 147
Implantation, 85
Implicit memory, 182
  in early childhood, 269
Implosion, 161
Important People Interview (IPI), 490
Imprinting, 29–30
  genetic imprinting, 63
Impulsivity and ADHD (attention deficit hyperactivity disorder), 340
Inclusion education, 346
Incremental theory, 379
Independence, development of, 213–214
Independent variables, 37
India, pregnancy in, 96
Individual differences in intelligence, 364
Individualism, instrumental purpose, and exchange, 396
Individuality, 487
Individuals with Disabilities Education Act (IDEA), 345–346
Individuation by infants, 213–214
Inductive discipline, 398
Indulgent parenting, 300, 301
Industry *vs.* inferiority, 23, 392
Infancy, 16–17, 132–169. *See also* Attachment; Breast feeding; Language; Low birth weight infants; Newborns; Preterm infants
  adoption in, 70–73
  A-not-B error, 176
  attention in, 180–181
  brain development, 137–141
  cognitive skills in, 140
  color vision in, 160
  concept formation in, 183–184
  conditioning in, 180
  cooperation, 215–216
  core-knowledge approach, 178–179
  depth perception in, 161–162
  dynamic systems theory, 149–150
  early-later experience issue and, 19
  ecological view of, 157
  Erikson's theory and, 24
  fear and, 205, 207
  gaze following, 181–182
  goal-directed behavior, 215–216
  growth patterns in, 136–137

  guiding behavior in, 224
  habituation/dishabituation in, 180–181
  hearing in, 162–163
  height in, 137
  imitation in, 183
  immunization schedule for, 147
  independence, development of, 213–214
  intention in, 215–216
  intermodal perception and, 164
  jealousy and, 205–206
  joint attention in, 181–182
  malnutrition in, 146–148
  managing behavior in, 224
  measures of development, 186–187
  memory and, 182–183
  nature-nurture issue and development, 178–179
  nighttime waking problems, 141–142
  nourishing cognitive development, 201
  nurturing socioemotional development, 231
  nutrition in, 144–148
  occluded objects, perception of, 161
  perceptual constancy in, 160–161
  personality development, 211–213
  Piaget's theory of development, 171–177
  posture, development of, 152
  reflexes in, 150–152
  REM sleep in infants, 142
  sense of self, developing, 212–213
  shared sleeping, 142–143
  SIDS (sudden infant death syndrome), 143
  sleep in, 141–143
  social orientation/understanding, development of, 214–218
  social referencing, 216
  social sophistication and insight in, 216
  sounds in, 191
  supporting physical development, 169
  temperament and, 208–211
  visual acuity, 160
  visual perception in, 157–162
  visual self-recognition, 212–213
  weight in, 137
Infant assessment specialists, 186
Infant Behavior and Development journal, 39
Infantile amnesia, 182–183
Infant mortality. *See also* SIDS (sudden infant death syndrome)
  kangaroo care and, 123
  maternal age and, 105
  prenatal care and, 93–94
Inferiority, industry *vs.*, 23, 392
Infertility, 70
  cocaine-related infertility, 106
Infinite generativity, 188
Influenza immunization, 147
Information processing, 27
  in adolescence, 459–463
  in early childhood, 267–275
Informed consent, 40
Inhibition to the unfamiliar, 209

Initiative *vs.* guilt, 23, 290
Injuries. *See* Accidents and injuries
Inner speech, 264
Insecure avoidant babies, 218
Insecure disorganized babies, 218
Insecure resistant babies, 218
Insight of infants, 216
Integrative approach to moral education, 467
Integrity *vs.* despair stage, 23
Intellectual health, 356
Intellectual risk-taking, 361
Intelligence, 363–373. *See also* Giftedness; IQ (intelligence quotient); Mental retardation
  assessment of, 364–366
  Binet tests of, 364
  culture and, 368–369
  culture-fair tests, 369
  defined, 364
  environmental factors and, 367–368
  ethnicity and, 369
  Flynn effect, 368
  frames of mind and, 366
  genetics and heredity and, 367
  juvenile delinquency and, 503–504
  multiple-intelligence approaches, 365–366
  nature-nurture issue and, 368
  predicting intelligence in infants, 187
  triarchic theory of intelligence, 364, 365
  types of, 365–366
  using intelligence tests, 369–370
  Wechsler scales, 364–365
Intelligence quotient (IQ). *See* IQ (intelligence quotient)
Intensive individualized attention programs, 507–508
Intention in infants, 215–216
Interactionist view of language development, 196
Intermodal perception, 164
Internalization of schemes, 174–175
Internal working model of attachment, 218
International Association of Infant Formula Manufacturers, 135
Internet
  adolescence and, 501–502
  cyberbullying, 412
  parents regulating use of, 501–502
Interpersonal intelligence, 366
Interview research, 34
Intimacy
  friends for, 412
  vs. isolation stage, 23
Intrapersonal intelligence, 366
Intrinsic motivation, 376, 377
  self-efficacy and, 380
Introductions in journals, 39
Intuitive thought substage, 261–262
In vitro fertilization (IVF), 70
  adolescents, assessment of, 71
Involution, 125
Invulnerability in adolescence, 459
IPods, 500–501

IQ (intelligence quotient)
  Binet tests of, 3643
  differences in scores, interpreting, 366–370
  of preterm infants, 122
Iron deficiency anemia, 248

J

Japan, early childhood education in, 284
Jealousy, infants displaying, 205–206
Jigsaw classrooms, 416–417
Jocks crowd, 494
Jogging in pregnancy, 91
Joint attention, 181–182
  intention and, 215–216
Journal of Consulting and Clinical Psychology, 39
Journal of Cross-Cultural Research, 39
Journal of Educational Psychology, 39
Journal of Marriage and the Family, 39
Journal of Research on Adolescence, 39
Journals and research, 39
Joy, infants displaying, 205
Junior high schools. *See* Middle schools
Junk food and infants, 144
Justice perspective, 398–399
Juvenile delinquency, 502–504
  causes of, 503–504
  prevention/intervention for, 507–508
  rejected children and, 409

K

Kamehameha Elementary Education Program (KEEP), 265
Kangaroo care, 123
Kidney cancer, 334
Kindergarten
  child-centered kindergarten, 278–279
  teachers, 47
The King, the Mice, and the Cheese, 162–163
Klinefelter syndrome, 64
Knowledge and expertise, 358
Kohlberg's theory, 395–397
  critics of, 398–399
  culture and moral reasoning, 398
  gender bias in, 398–399
  influences on, 397
  social conventional reasoning and, 399
  stages in, 395–397
!Kung culture, childbirth in, 114
Kwashiorkor, 146–147

L

Labeling
  difficult children, 212
  and language, 196
  by toddlers, 213
Laboratory research. *See* Research
Lamaze method, 116
LANGO, 272
Language. *See also* Grammar; Vocabulary
  babbling, 190–191
  biological influences on, 192–193

SIDS (sudden infant death syndrome), 143
  smoking and, 100
Sign language, 343
Simple reflexes, 174
Single-parent families, 311
Sisters. *See* Siblings
Size constancy in infants, 161
Skateboard accidents, 336
Skeletal system in middle/late childhood, 326
Skepticism, development of, 390
Slapping infants, 224
Sleep and sleep problems
  in adolescence, 444–445
  in early childhood, 244–245
  in infants, 141–143
  in postpartum period, 125, 126
Sleep apnea, SIDS (sudden infant death syndrome) and, 143
Sleep in America Survey, 125
Sleepwalking in early childhood, 245
Slow-to-warm-up children, 208–209
Small for date infants, 120–121
Smartphones, 501
Smell and newborns, 163
Smiles by infants, 206–207
Smoking. *See also* Adolescence
  early childhood, environmental smoke and, 252–253
  Family Matters program and, 448
  neural tube defects and, 89
  paternal smoking and prenatal development, 106–107
  placenta and, 86
  pregnancy and, 100
  SIDS (sudden infant death syndrome) and, 143
Social anxiety. *See* Anxiety
Social cognitive theory, 27–29
  Bandura's theory, 28–29
  evaluation of, 29
  of gender, 297
Social comparison, friends for, 412
Social constructivist approach, 265–267
Social contract or utility and individual rights, 396–397
Social conventional reasoning, 399–400
Social development
  in early childhood, 292
  malnutrition and, 147
  in middle/late childhood, 409–410
  reciprocal socialization, 222–223
Social developmental neuroscience, 433–434
Social factors. *See also* Friends; Peers
  and dating, 495
  decision making in adolescence and, 461
  emotional expression and, 205–206
  gender identity and, 297–298
  in middle/late childhood, 380–381
  self-esteem and, 392
Social media, 501
Social orientation/understanding, 214–218
Social play, 315
Social policy, 11, 12–13
  adolescence and, 426–427

Social referencing, 216
Social role theory, 297
Social smiles, 206–207
Social sophistication of infants, 216
Social systems morality, 396
Social workers, 48
Society for Research in Child Development, 148
Sociocultural cognitive theory, 26–27
Socioeconomic status (SES). *See* SES (socioeconomic status)
Socioemotional development, 15
  in adolescence, 427–428
  gender and, 402–403
  in vitro fertilization (IVF), outcomes from, 71
Somnambulism in early childhood, 245
Soothing crying infants, 207–208
Spanking. *See* Discipline and punishment
Spastic cerebral palsy, 343
Spatial intelligence, 366
Special education teachers, 47
Special Olympics, 64
Speech. *See* Language
Speech pathologists, 342
Speech reading, 343
Speech therapists, 49–50, 341
Speed-of-processing and memory, 269
Sperm
  cocaine use and, 106
  Down syndrome and health of, 64
  fertilization and, 61
  infertility and, 70
  meiosis and, 62
Spina bifida, 66, 89
  maternal blood screening detecting, 69
Spirituality, 468
  sexual behavior and, 469
Spoiling infants, 207–208
Spokane Indian Reservation, 474
Spoken vocabulary, 191
Sports in middle/late childhood, 330–331
Standardized tests, 34
Stanford-Binet IQ scores, 364
Stanford-Binet tests, 34, 364
Startle reflex, 150–151
Statistical procedures, 21
Stepfamilies, 406–407
  adjustments in, 407
Stepping reflex, 151
Stereotypes
  gender stereotypes, 401
  intelligence tests and, 369–370
Sternberg's triarchic theory of intelligence, 365–366
Sticky mittens for infants, 155–156
Still-face paradigm, 215
Stimulation, friends for, 412
STIs (sexually transmitted infections), 437–438. *See also* HIV/AIDS
Stoicism and pregnancy, 96
Stranger anxiety, 207
Strange Situation, 218–219
Strategies, 358
  metacognition and, 363
Stress
  attachment and, 220
  of birth, 118

coping with, 393–395
  depression and, 505
  gene expression and, 60
  prenatal development and, 106
  PTSD (posttraumatic stress disorder), 394
  suicide and, 506
Stressors, exposure to, 13
Stuttering, 341
Substance abuse. *See also* Alcohol use; Drug use
  in adolescents, 446–447
  early maturation and, 433
  parents, role of, 447
  preterm infants and, 121
Subtractive bilingualism, 376
Sucking
  high-amplitude sucking, 158–159
  reflex, 150–151, 152
Sudden infant death syndrome (SIDS). *See* SIDS (sudden infant death syndrome)
Suffocation in infants, 147
Sugar consumption, 247
Suggestion susceptibility in early childhood, 269–270
Suicide
  in adolescence, 445, 506–507
  bullying in, 410
Superego, 22, 293
Surprise, infants displaying, 205
Survey research, 34
Survival of the fittest, 57
Sustained attention
  in early childhood, 268
  in infants, 180
Sustaining climates, 466
Swaddling, 155
Sweden, child care in, 226
Swimming
  and pregnancy, 93
  reflex, 151
Symbolic function substage, 260–261
Symbolism
  in early childhood, 260–261
  pretense/symbolic play, 315
Synapses, 138–139
  density of, 140
  middle/late childhood, pruning in, 327
Synaptic density, 140
Syntax, 189, 190
  early childhood, understanding in, 276
Syphilis, 437, 438
  prenatal development and, 103

T

Taste, newborns and, 163–164
Tay-Sachs disease, 66
Teachers
  adolescents and, 427
  careers in teaching, 46–47
  hidden curriculum and, 465
  middle/late childhood and, 381
  secondary school teachers, 463
Technology
  adolescence and, 500–501
  Millennials and, 16–17
Teen Outreach Program (TOP), 441
Telegraphic speech, 192
Television
  achievement and, 317
  adolescence and, 500–501

and aggression, 317
  and early childhood development, 315–317
  eating disorders and, 448–449
  middle/late childhood and, 329
  overweight/obesity and, 333
  prosocial behavior and, 317
Temperament. *See also* Personality
  behavioral inhibition and, 209–210
  Chess and Thomas' classification of, 208–209
  culture and, 211
  developmental links and, 210–211
  goodness of fit and, 211
  of infants, 208–211
  parenting and, 211, 212
  sense of self, developing, 212–213
Temperature and gene expression, 60
Temporal lobes, 138
Temptation, resisting, 295
Teratogens, 97–98
  time of exposure to, 97–98
Teratology, 97–98
Tertiary circular reactions, novelty, and curiosity, 174–175
Testes, 296
  in puberty, 429, 430–431
Testosterone, 296, 430–431
Tests. *See also* Prenatal tests
  standardized tests, 34
Tetanus immunization, 147
Text messaging, 501
Thalidomide, effect of, 98–99
Theories of development, 21. *See also* specific theories
  comparison of, 32
  timeline for, 32
Theory of mind
  and autism, 274
  in early childhood, 271–274
  false beliefs and, 273
Thinking
  convergent thinking, 360
  creative thinking, 360, 361
  critical thinking, 359–360
  divergent thinking, 360
  early childhood, understanding in, 273
  in middle/late childhood, 359–362
  scientific thinking, 360–362
Three mountains task, 261
Time outs, 302
Timidity, 209
Tobacco use. *See* Smoking
Toddlers. *See* Early childhood
Tonic neck reflex, 151
Tools of the Mind, 266
Top-dog phenomenon, 471
Touch, newborns and, 163
Tracking, 159
Training parents, 301
Tranquilizers, 446
Transactional processes, 223
Transitivity, 354–355
Trauma, coping with, 393–395
Treatment for Adolescents with Depression Study (TADS), 505
Triarchic theory of intelligence, 364, 365
Trimesters of prenatal development, 88–89